ANNUAL REVIEW OF PSYCHOLOGY

VOLUME 57, 2006

SUSAN T. FISKE, *Editor*
Princeton University

ALAN E. KAZDIN, *Associate Editor*
Yale University School of Medicine

DANIEL L. SCHACTER, *Associate Editor*
Harvard University

www.annualreviews.org   science@annualreviews.org   650-493-4400

ANNUAL REVIEWS
4139 El Camino Way • P.O. Box 10139 • Palo Alto, California 94303-0139

ANNUAL REVIEWS
Palo Alto, California, USA

International Standard Serial Number: 0066-4308
International Standard Book Number: 0-8243-0256-7
Library of Congress Catalog Card Number: 50-13143

TYPESET BY TECHBOOKS, FAIRFAX, VA
PRINTED AND BOUND BY MALLOY INCORPORATED, ANN ARBOR, MI

PREFACE

Psychology is building in all directions at once. Partly, this results from sheer numbers of people in the field and our collective productivity. Partly, this also results from the multiplication of specialties and sub-specialties. Each has its theories, paradigms, and literatures that psychological scientists must track. The *Annual Review of Psychology* series, of course, aims to help all of us keep up in precisely these ways. A measure of the field's collective success and the *Annual Review's* role in the enterprise is its high usage: electronic access, subscriptions, citations, all placing the *Annual Review of Psychology* consistently among the top 1 to 3 psychology journals. With such success comes proliferation.

The *Annual Review of Neuroscience* spun off many years ago, becoming an established top-ranked outlet. Just a year ago, the *Annual Review of Clinical Psychology* commenced, and although its record is too young to gauge, its initial indicators all bode well for taking its place alongside its siblings. It's said that psychological science is uniquely a life science *and* a social science. In fact, the *Annual Review of Psychology* is listed both as a social science and a science journal by the Institute for Scientific Information. The two sibling series span the breadth of psychology, from biopsychology and neuroscience to clinical and applicable ("translational") research, and the marriage of the two ends.

The *Annual Review of Psychology* continues to publish chapters on both neuroscience and clinical psychology topics (as well as chapters on topics that overlap, for example, in clinical neuropsychology). The divisions thus are not "either. . .or" but "both. . .and." The expansion of our family of psychological science reviews increases the number of possible outlets for our rapidly expanding but simultaneously interrelated field. The Annual Review series reflects the disciplinary glue that links our research, regardless of the specific Annual Review title. With all this fortuitous overlap, how do readers know where to look? Every Annual Review volume lists, next to its own table of contents, related articles from other series. The search engine of the Web site pulls relevant chapters from all databases.

In virtual bookstores, as in physical ones, locating all the shops in the same neighborhood increases traffic to all of them, so we invite *Annual Review of Psychology* readers to browse our neighbors' wares when they visit our own. Proximity serves everyone.

SUSAN T. FISKE, Princeton
DANIEL L. SCHACTER, Cambridge
ALAN E. KAZDIN, New Haven

 *Annual Review of Psychology*
Volume 57, 2006

CONTENTS

ERRATA

An online log of corrections to *Annual Review of Psychology* chapters
may be found at http://psych.annualreviews.org/errata.shtml

RELATED ARTICLES

Graduate Education, Richard M. McFall

Methodological and Conceptual Issues in Functional Magnetic Resonance Imaging Research Related to Schizophrenia and Its Treatments, Gregory G. Brown and Lisa T. Eyler

Obesity, Thomas A. Wadden and Anthony Fabricatore

Personality Characteristics as Risk Factors for Physical Illness, Timothy W. Smith and Justin MacKenzie

Posttraumatic Stress Disorder: Etiology and Treatment, Terence M. Keane

Recovered Memories, Elizabeth F. Loftus and Deborah Davis

Reinterpreting Comorbidity: A Model-Based Approach to Understanding and Classifying Psychopathology, Robert F. Krueger and Kristian E. Markon

Schizotypal Personality: Neurodevelopmental and Psychosocial Trajectories, Adrian Raine

The Impact of Psychoanalytic Concepts, Lester Luborsky and Marna S. Barrett

The Use of Structural Analysis of Social Behavior (SASB) as an Assessment Tool, Lorna Smith Benjamin, Jeffrey Conrad Rothweiler, and Kenneth L. Critchfield

Women's Mental Health Research, Mary C. Blehar

From the ***Annual Review of Law and Social Science***, Volume 1 (2005)

The Comparative Study of Criminal Punishment, James Q. Whitman

Economic Theories of Settlement Bargaining, Andrew F. Daughety and Jennifer F. Reinganum

Expert Evidence after Daubert, Michael J. Saks and David L. Faigman

Plea Bargaining and the Eclipse of the Jury, Bruce P. Smith

The Death Penalty Meets Social Science: Deterrence and Jury Behavior Under New Scrutiny, Robert Weisberg

Voice, Control, and Belonging: The Double-Edged Sword of Procedural Fairness, Robert J. MacCoun

Law, Race, and Education in the United States, Samuel R. Lucas and Marcel Paret

Real Juries, Shari Seidman Diamond and Mary R. Rose

Why Law, Economics, and Organization? Oliver E. Williamson

Reversal of Fortune: The Resurgence of Individual Risk Assessment in Criminal Justice, Jonathan Simon

From the ***Annual Review of Neuroscience***, Volume 28 (2005)

Genetics of Brain Structure and Intelligence, Arthur W. Toga and Paul M. Thompson

From the ***Annual Review of Political Science***, Volume 8 (2005)

Herbert C Kelman

Annu. Rev. Psychol. 2006. 57:1–26
doi: 10.1146/annurev.psych.57.102904.190156
First published online as a Review in Advance on September 30, 2005

INTERESTS, RELATIONSHIPS, IDENTITIES: Three Central Issues for Individuals and Groups in Negotiating Their Social Environment

Herbert C. Kelman

*Department of Psychology, Harvard University, Cambridge, Massachusetts 02138;
email: hck@wjh.harvard.edu*

Key Words   social influence, political orientation, legitimate authority, international conflict, reconciliation

■ **Abstract**   This chapter begins with a summary of a model, developed half a century ago, that distinguishes three qualitatively different processes of social influence: compliance, identification, and internalization. The model, originally geared to and experimentally tested in the context of persuasive communication, was subsequently applied to influence in the context of long-term relationships, including psychotherapy, international exchanges, and the socialization of national/ethnic identity. It has been extended to analysis of the relationship of individuals to social systems. Individuals' rule, role, and value orientations to a system—conceptually linked to compliance, identification, and internalization—predict different reactions to their own violations of societal standards, different patterns of personal involvement in the political system, and differences in attitude toward authorities and readiness to obey. In a further extension of the model, three approaches to peacemaking in international or intergroup conflicts are identified—conflict settlement, conflict resolution, and reconciliation—which, respectively, focus on the accommodation of interests, relationships, and identities, and are conducive to changes at the level of compliance, identification, and internalization.

CONTENTS

0066-4308/06/0110-0001$20.00

INTRODUCTION

Fifty years ago, I submitted a 192-page essay to the American Association for the Advancement of Science (AAAS), entitled *Compliance, Identification, and Internalization: A Theoretical and Experimental Approach to the Study of Social Influence* (Kelman 1956). The essay was awarded the AAAS Socio-Psychological Prize for 1956.

I had planned to publish the theory and research reported in that essay in book form. In fact, I signed a contract with a major publisher, whose psychology editor considered the manuscript virtually ready for publication, requiring only an introductory chapter and minor editorial changes. I felt, however, that the book required some additional experimental work and further theoretical elaboration. Over the next few years, I did in fact carry out and supervise several additional experiments; I revised and expanded several chapters; and I stayed on top of the rapidly growing experimental literature. But the task grew larger and I allowed myself to be sidetracked by numerous other projects. As a consequence, the book has remained unpublished (at least so far!).

I did publish an article summarizing the theoretical model (Kelman 1961) and an abbreviated report of the original experimental test of the model (Kelman 1958). Also, elaborations of the model were presented in later publications (Kelman 1974, Kelman & Hamilton 1989). The 1958 and 1961 articles have been reprinted many times and frequently cited in textbooks and research publications. *Processes of Opinion Change* (Kelman 1961) was in fact selected as a "citation classic" some years ago. The model continues to be used as a framework for research, particularly in applied contexts.

Though, happily, the model has not been ignored or forgotten in the field, it did not follow the conventional career that I had in mind for it in the late 1950s and early 1960s. I did not publish the full original manuscript or the edited version that I was working on for some time, nor did I pursue the systematic experimental program designed to test the propositions derived from the model. Nevertheless, the model has continued to play a central role in my professional work across the years. For one thing, I have used it extensively in my teaching. Beyond that, I have drawn on it, expanded on it, and applied it in my theoretical and empirical work in several different domains over the years. Again and again, it has influenced my thinking on a variety of issues and emerged as an organizing framework in my efforts to conceptualize them.

This prefatory chapter gives me the opportunity to summarize some of the uses to which I have put my three-process model of social influence and to trace its evolution into a broader social-psychological model of the core issues that social entities—individuals, groups, organizations, societies, collectivities—must address as they negotiate their social environment.

THE ORIGINAL MODEL OF SOCIAL INFLUENCE

A central focus of my work throughout the years—starting with my early research on the effects of persuasive communication on attitudes, continuing in my later work on the cognitive and affective impact of psychotherapy, socialization, and international educational and cultural exchange, and culminating in my more recent work on the effects of conflict resolution efforts on the relationship between former enemies—has been on the depth and durability of change produced by social influence.

In this vein, my doctoral dissertation (published in Kelman 1953) explored the relationship between public conformity to the position advocated in a persuasive communication and private acceptance of that position, as manifested by attitude change on a subsequent questionnaire. Seventh-grade students were exposed to a communication about comic books presenting a position that went counter to their initial attitudes and then asked to write essays presenting their own views. In the high restriction condition, they were strongly encouraged—via instructions and the offer of an attractive and assured reward—to support the communicator's position. In the low restriction condition, both the instructions and the reward structure allowed the participants much greater freedom of choice. The results showed that conformity with the communicator's position was highest in the high restriction group, but the amount of attitude change—as measured independently in before-and-after questionnaires—was highest in the low restriction group (even among those participants who wrote nonconforming essays).

Additional data from this study, along with research by other investigators, confirmed my view that public conformity to social influence and private acceptance of the opinions or positions advocated by the other represent qualitatively distinct processes, each with its own distinct set of determinants. As I explored a variety of real-life social influence situations, I became dissatisfied with this dichotomy. Close examination of some extreme cases, such as religious or ideological conversion of the "true believer" variety (cf. Hoffer 1951) and "brainwashing" or "thought reform" (cf. Lifton 1956), as well as of certain aspects of childhood and adult socialization and of psychotherapy, persuaded me that they could not be captured by the distinction between public conformity and private acceptance. They clearly go beyond overt conformity, producing changes in underlying beliefs, and yet these beliefs are not fully integrated into the person's own value system and remain highly dependent on external support. These explorations eventually led me to distinguish three processes of social influence—compliance, identification, and internalization—each defined by its own set of antecedent and consequent conditions.

Very briefly, compliance can be said to occur when an individual accepts influence from another person or a group in order to attain a favorable reaction from the other—either to gain a specific reward or avoid a specific punishment controlled by the other, or to gain approval or avoid disapproval from the other. Identification can be said to occur when an individual accepts influence from another person or a group in order to establish or maintain a satisfying self-defining relationship to the other. The relationship may be based on reciprocity, where the person seeks to meet the other's expectations for his or her own role, which stands in a reciprocal relationship to the other's role (or the expectations of a group whose members stand in a reciprocal relationship to each other). Alternatively, the relationship may be based on modeling, as in classical identification, where the person vicariously seeks to take on the role (or part of the role) of the other—to be like or actually to be the other person. Finally, internalization can be said to occur when an individual accepts influence from another in order to maintain the congruence of actions and beliefs with his or her own value system. Value congruence may take either the form of cognitive consistency, where the induced behavior is perceived as conducive to the maximization of the person's own values, or the form of affective appropriateness, where the induced behavior is perceived as continuous with the person's self-concept.

Note that, for each of the three processes, I distinguish between two possible underlying concerns that might motivate acceptance of influence: concerns about specific rewards and punishments, or about approval/disapproval in the case of compliance; concerns about meeting reciprocal-role expectations, or about enacting the role of the other in the case of identification; and concerns about the cognitive consistency or the affective appropriateness of one's behavior in the case of internalization. These distinctions were originally made on a strictly ad hoc basis to capture the range of motivations that underlie each process. On closer examination, however, they suggest a crosscutting dimension in the analysis of social influence: a distinction between two types of personal concerns that govern the person's reaction in the influence situation. On the one hand, reactions may be governed primarily by instrumental concerns, such as assuring one's attainment of rewards and avoidance of punishments, living up to the expectations of one's role in a reciprocal relationship, and maximizing one's values. On the other hand, reactions may be governed primarily by self-maintenance concerns, such as managing one's public image, living up to one's role models, and confirming one's self-concept. This distinction between two types of personal concerns prefigures a more systematic crosscutting distinction in some of the extensions of the model to be discussed below.

Each of the three processes of influence is characterized by a distinct set of antecedent and consequent conditions, which are summarized in Table 1. On the antecedent side, three qualitative features of the influence situation determine which process is likely to ensue. To the extent that the primary concern of the person exposed to influence (P) is with the social effect of her or his behavior, that the influencing agent's (O) power is based largely on means-control (i.e., ability to supply or withhold material or psychological resources on which P's goal achievement depends), and that the influence techniques are designed to limit P's choice behavior, influence is likely to take the form of compliance. To the extent that P's primary concern in the situation is with the social anchorage of her or his behavior, that O's power is based largely on attractiveness (i.e., possession of qualities that make a continued relationship to O particularly desirable), and that the influence techniques serve to delineate the requirements of a role relationship in which P's self-definition is anchored (such as the expectations of a relevant reference group), influence is likely to take the form of identification. Finally, influence is likely to take the form of internalization if P's primary concern in the situation is with the value congruence of her or his behavior, if O's power is based largely on credibility (i.e., expertness and trustworthiness), and if the influence techniques serve to reorganize P's means-ends framework (i.e., P's conception of the paths toward maximizing her or his values).

Each of the processes generated by its respective set of antecedents corresponds to a characteristic pattern of thoughts and feelings accompanying P's adoption of the induced behavior. As a result, the nature of the changes produced by each of the three processes tends to be different (see the lower half of Table 1). Most important, perhaps, are the differences in the conditions under which the newly acquired behavior is likely to manifest itself. Behavior accepted through compliance

TABLE 1   Summary of the distinctions between the three processes of social influence

	Compliance	**Identification**	**Internalization**
Antecedents			
1. Basis for the importance of the induction	Concern with social effect of behavior	Concern with social anchorage of behavior	Concern with value congruence of behavior
2. Source of power of the influencing agent	Means control	Attractiveness	Credibility
3. Manner of achieving prepotency of the induced response	Limitation of choice behavior	Delineation of role requirements	Reorganization of means-ends framework
Consequents			
1. Conditions of performance of induced response	Surveillance by influencing agent	Salience of relationship to agent	Relevance of values to issue
2. Conditions of change and extinction of induced response	Changed perception of conditions for social rewards	Changed perception of conditions for satisfying self-defining relationships	Changed perception of conditions for value maximization
3. Type of behavior system in which induced response is embedded	External demands of a specific setting	Expectations defining a specific role	Person's value system

Source: Kelman 1961, "Processes of Opinion Change," *Public Opin. Q.* 25(Spring):67. Reprinted by permission of Oxford Univ. Press.

depends on surveillance: It is likely to manifest itself only when P's actions are directly or indirectly observable by O. Behavior accepted through identification, though independent of observability by O, remains dependent on social support: It is likely to manifest itself only when P's relationship to O and the role associated with it are brought into salience. By contrast, internalized behavior becomes independent of the external source and integrated into P's own value system: It tends to manifest itself whenever the values on which it is based are relevant to the issues at hand (although, of course, it does not always prevail in the face of competing value considerations and situational demands). Because of its interplay with other parts of P's value system, internalized behavior tends to be more idiosyncratic, flexible, and complex.

The model can be tested experimentally by varying, in an influence situation, one or more of the antecedents postulated for the three processes and observing the effects on the consequents—in other words, by ascertaining whether the antecedents and consequents match up as predicted by the model. Thus, the original experimental test of the model (Kelman 1958) varied the source of the influencing agent's power and observed the effects on the conditions of performance of the induced response. Black college freshmen were exposed to one of four tape-recorded interviews dealing with an aspect of the 1954 Supreme Court decision on school segregation. The four interviewees were introduced and presented themselves as, respectively, high in means-control, high in attractiveness, high in credibility, and (for the control condition) low in all three sources of power. Postcommunication attitudes were measured on three separate questionnaires, filled out, respectively, under conditions of (*a*) communicator surveillance and salience, (*b*) salience without surveillance, and (*c*) nonsurveillance and nonsalience. As predicted by the three-process model, the manifestation of change depended on surveillance for the subjects in the means-control (compliance) condition, on salience for those in the attractiveness (identification) condition, and on neither surveillance nor salience for those in the credibility (internalization) condition.

In another experiment (Kelman 1960), participants listened to a tape-recorded communication promoting a novel program in science education. The two experimental communications augmented the basic message (used in the control condition) with information designed to vary the basis for the importance of the induction and the manner of achieving prepotency of the induced response, so as to create the antecedent conditions for identification and internalization, respectively (see Table 1). In the role-orientation condition, positive reference groups were associated with acceptance of the message and negative reference groups with opposition to it. In the value-orientation condition, additional information spelled out the implications of the proposed program for maximizing the important value of personal responsibility. Several measures of the nature of change supported the hypothesis that role orientation produces identification, whereas value orientation produces internalization: In the value-orientation group, the manifestation of change was less dependent on salience of the communicator, and the new attitudes tended to be more flexible, more complex, and more readily generalized to other issues.

Although the three processes are distinguished in terms of the types of motivations that underlie them (the three types of concerns identified in Table 1) and the model has generally been grouped with the functional theories of attitudes, they do not correspond readily to the distinctions of the functional models (Katz 1960, Smith et al. 1956). Nor do they match up clearly with the dual-process models (Chaiken 1980, Petty & Cacioppo 1981) of attitude change (see Hamilton 2004, Wood 2000). On the other hand, there seems to be a readier fit of compliance and internalization with the distinction between majority and minority influence (cf. Maass & Clark 1983) and between identification and social influence within the theoretical framework of social-identity and social-categorization theory (Turner 1991).

The way the three-process model matches up with these other models reflects the fact that, from the beginning, it has been based on a distinction between three social-psychological processes, referring to three distinctive ways in which P interacts with or relates to O as P accepts influence from O. Thus, we can speak of P's compliance to O's demands, P's identification with O's expectations, and P's internalization of O's ideas.

INFLUENCE IN A LONG-TERM RELATIONSHIP

The formulation of the original model was geared to the experimental paradigm in which I planned to test it: a one-time and one-way persuasive communication, intended to influence a specific attitude or behavior of individual members of the audience. The model could readily be applied to any dyadic interaction episode in which one party (O) was exerting influence (deliberately or otherwise) on the other (P) and one can observe the nature and amount of change manifested by P. I was well aware that influence flows in both directions in social interaction, even (at least over time) in the mass media. But, for purposes of systematic analysis (within an essentially linear approach), I felt it necessary to specify O and P—the agent and the target of influence—for any given episode of interaction.

From the beginning, however, my interest was in extending the model, beyond the study of O's influence on a specific behavior or attitude of P in the context of a particular interaction between P and O, to the study of O's influence on a broader set of P's behaviors and attitudes in the context of a longer-term relationship between P and O (or a set of Os). This interest was signaled in the conclusion of the report on my doctoral research, when I wrote that it has "some interesting implications for the study of reference groups and the process of internalization of group norms" (Kelman 1953, p. 212). In pursuit of this interest, I decided to study psychotherapy—and particularly group therapy—which I conceived as an influence situation extending over a period of time and designed to produce broad and deep changes in the attitudes and behavior patterns of the clients. Upon completion of my PhD in 1951, I received a postdoctoral fellowship for work in group therapy and accepted an invitation to spend the fellowship year at the Phipps Psychiatric

Clinic, Johns Hopkins Hospital, in Baltimore, where Jerome Frank and colleagues were conducting an extensive, systematic research program on group and individual psychotherapy. Frank's evolving view of psychotherapy as essentially a social influence situation, in which the nature of the patient-therapist relationship is the major determinant of therapeutic change [see his *Persuasion and Healing* (Frank 1961)], provided me with a congenial setting for developing my model of social influence and extending it from the context of persuasive communication to the context of longer-term relationships between P and O conducive to broader changes in attitude and behavior.

In the end, I spent a total of three years at Johns Hopkins, dividing my time between the hospital and the university's Homewood campus. It was during this period that I developed the three-process model of social influence and conducted the original—the defining, as it were—experimental test of the model. In the development of the model, I focused much of my reading and thinking on a variety of contexts that are socially defined as influence situations: social contexts that are explicitly designed to exert influence, over an extended period of time, on broad patterns of attitudes and behaviors of a selected set of individuals. Most socially defined influence situations fall into one of two categories. They may be situations of socialization—including childhood, adult (or life-span), occupational/ professional, and political socialization—that prepare individuals for roles within a society, group, or organization. Alternatively, they may be situations of resocialization—including, among others, psychotherapy, brainwashing or thought reform, religious or political conversion, assimilation or acculturation of immigrants, and international exchange—designed to move individuals, for one or another reason, from old to new roles with their accompanying beliefs and values. Reflection on what happens in these different influence settings contributed significantly to the development of the model—for example, as mentioned earlier, to my decision to add identification to the two processes with which I had started. By the same token, I subsequently applied the model to the analysis of changes in some of these real-life settings.

Thus, in an analysis of changes in group psychotherapy (Kelman 1963), I proposed that the three processes of influence "play a part in each of two phases of behavior change with which therapy is concerned . . . . and contribute to the achievement of a therapeutic effect" (p. 405). The two phases of behavior change that I differentiated here, drawing on an earlier analysis (Kelman 1952), refer to influence on the patient's behavior (*a*) within the therapy situation and (*b*) outside of the therapy situation (while the therapy is still in progress). The argument is summarized in Table 2. A key point in distinguishing the two phases of change is that they may represent competing demands: Features of the therapy situation and the therapist's techniques that are most conducive to change—to unfreezing old behavior and eliciting new behavior—within the therapy session may, at the same time, interfere with the generalization of this behavior to the patient's everyday life (Kelman 1963). Thus, a major challenge to therapeutic practice "is to find the proper balance between forces toward change in within-therapy

TABLE 2   Types of influence involved in the production of therapeutic change

Processes of influence	Type of patient behavior induced by this process	Therapist's role in the induction of this behavior	Group's role in the induction of this behavior
A. Directed to the patient's behavior within the therapy situation			
Compliance	Engagement in the therapeutic work (obeying the "basic rule")	Trainer	Sanctioning agents
Identification	Commitment to the therapeutic situation	Accepting, permissive, expert listener	Facilitating agents; comparison reference group
Internalization	Occurrence of corrective emotional experiences	Transference object	Interaction objects; role reciprocators
B. Directed to the patient's behavior outside of the therapy situation			
Compliance	Experimentation with new actions	Imaginary interlocutor	Anticipated audience
Identification	Adoption of the therapist's and/or group's standpoint for viewing the self and interpersonal relations	Role model; norm setter	Normative reference group
Internalization	Generalization of therapeutic insights to specific real-life situations	Auxiliary reality tester	Representatives of society

Source: Kelman 1963, "The Role of the Group in the Induction of Therapeutic Change," *Int. J. Group Psychother.* 13:406 and 422. Reprinted by permission of Guilford Press.

behavior and forces toward change in extratherapy behavior" (p. 405). This distinction prefigures a central concept in my later work with problem-solving workshops in international conflict resolution: I argue that workshops have a dual purpose—change in the individual workshop participants and transfer of these changes to the political process—and that these two purposes may create contradictory requirements that must be balanced in workshop practice (Kelman 1972a, 1979, 2000).

Another real-life influence situation that was the focus of some of my research in the late 1950s and the 1960s was the international exchange experience. In two projects, my colleagues and I explored the impact of a sojourn in the United States on the images and attitudes of foreign students and professionals. Although we were clearly concerned with the depth and durability of change—and in fact, both studies included follow-up interviews and questionnaires a year after the participants' return to their home countries—the research was not explicitly designed to test hypotheses derived from the three-process model. The model was of some use, however, in the formulation of questions and the analysis of findings.

Thus, in one analysis (Bailyn & Kelman 1962), we found it useful to distinguish two types of change in the professional self-images of exchange students and scholars whose experience in the host country was professionally involving and rewarding: a change in the internal structure of the self-image, which bore the characteristics of internalization, and a change in the social anchorage of the self-image, which met the criteria of identification. We also identified two parallel processes of maintenance of the original self-image—confirmation and resistance—among individuals whose exchange experience tended to be less involving and rewarding.

I have applied the three-process model more systematically to the development of national or ethnic identity—i.e., the process of socialization of individuals into membership in a national or ethnic (or indeed other identity) group. National identity is a collective product that is acquired by individual members of the collectivity in the course of their socialization and incorporated into their personal identities to different degrees and in different ways. A social-influence analysis of the acquisition of national identity can address two issues: (*a*) the adoption of the specific elements of the national identity, i.e., of the beliefs, values, assumptions, and expectations that make up the national identity as a collective product; and (*b*) the development of an orientation to the nation itself (Kelman 1997a, 1998). I propose that the specific elements can be adopted via the processes of compliance, identification, and internalization. The antecedents and consequents of adopting identity elements at each of these levels (postulated in Kelman 1998) can be readily derived from the original model, as summarized in Table 1. On the consequent side, I distinguished between authentic identity, which is largely based on internalization; vicarious identity, largely based on identification; and conferred identity, largely based on compliance (p. 12). I made it clear, however, that a person's identity is generally composed of all three types of elements, and that these build on and interact with each other in a variety of ways.

My analysis of the second issue in a person's acquisition of national identity—the development of an orientation to the group itself—also draws on the three-process model. It distinguishes between three types of orientation to the group (or bases of integration in it)—rule, role, and value orientation—which correspond to the processes of compliance, identification, and internalization, respectively (Kelman 1997a, 1998). This analysis essentially applies an earlier framework for conceptualizing patterns of personal involvement in the political system (Kelman 1969, Kelman & Hamilton 1989) to the involvement of individuals in a national, ethnic, or other identity group. I return to that framework below after I discuss a reconceptualization of the three processes of influence, moving from a focus on the relationship (short-term or long-term) between P and O in the influence situation to a focus on the relationship of the individual to the social system that provides the context of the influence. The reconceptualization—which yielded the distinction between rule, role, and value orientation—allows for extension of the model to the analysis of the involvement of individuals in larger social systems: societies, organizations, groups.

SOCIAL INFLUENCE AS LINKAGE BETWEEN
THE INDIVIDUAL AND THE SOCIAL SYSTEM

My original model of social influence conceptualized it at the level of social interaction, focusing on the relationship between P and O in the influence situation—or in the array of situations in which P interacts with a set of Os in a long-term relationship, such as socialization or resocialization in all their varieties. For many purposes, this level of analysis is entirely appropriate and can yield useful, empirically testable propositions. However, in my continuing effort to define what precisely distinguishes the three processes from each other and, in particular, in my increasing focus on legitimate influence in authority relationships, I became convinced of the importance of bringing the social context of the influence relationship explicitly into the analysis. "Social influence always occurs within a larger social context. Even interactions between strangers on a train or between friends and lovers are defined and at least minimally structured by the larger society. Participants enact prescribed roles and their interaction is governed by the expectations associated with those roles. Many social influence situations are more thoroughly embedded in the organizational or societal context than these informal relationships. They represent episodes in the functioning of social units—part of the process whereby the society or organization . . . socializes and controls its members and carries out its daily business, and whereby the members advocate policies, protest against existing practices, or seek to advance their personal or subgroup interests" (Kelman & Hamilton 1989, p. 87).

The three processes can thus be reconceptualized with reference to the social system—society, organization, or group—within which they are generated and to which a person's acceptance of influence is directed. When viewed in the context of a particular social system, each process represents a distinct way in which P meets the demands of the system and maintains personal integration in it (Kelman 1974, Kelman & Hamilton 1989). Compliance represents adherence to the rules or norms of the system (including its laws and customs)—i.e., the behavioral requirements it sets for its members. In accepting influence via this process, members assure themselves of continued access to rewards and approval (and avoidance of penalties and disapproval) contingent on adherence to system rules. Identification reflects an orientation to the role of system member and/or other roles within the system, not just as a set of behavioral requirements, but as an important part of P's self-definition. In accepting influence via this process, members are meeting the expectations of their system roles, thus maintaining their desired relationship to the system and their self-concept as fully embedded in these roles. Finally, internalization reflects an orientation to system values that the individual personally shares. In accepting influence via this process, members live up to the implications of these shared values, thus maintaining the integrity of their personal value framework.

In short, viewed in terms of linkage of the individual to the social system, the three processes suggest different ways in which people may be integrated in a society, organization, or group: via adherence to its rules, involvement in its roles, and sharing of its values. Rules, roles, and values are three components of any social system that are interrelated but analytically separable. Each of these components constitutes a set of standards for the behavior of individual members—criteria against which the quality of their performance as members can be evaluated. Compliance, identification, and internalization are, in effect, designed to meet each of these standards, respectively.

Conceptualizing social influence in terms of properties of the social system helps to bridge analyses of social influence, which proceed from the point of view of the individual (the target of influence), with analyses of social control, which usually proceed from the system point of view (Kelman 1974, Kelman & Hamilton 1989). The operation of rules, roles, and values in socialization and social control is illustrated in an analysis of people's emotional reactions when they find themselves deviating from societal standards in the domain of responsibility or of propriety (see Table 3). Deviations in the domain of responsibility typically involve actions that cause harm to others, while deviations in the domain of propriety involve behavior deemed inappropriate for someone in the actor's position or for any socialized member of the society. Deviations from standards in either of these two domains may take the form of violations of rules, role expectations, or values, depending on the level at which a given standard has been socialized (compliance, identification, or internalization) and is represented in the person's cognitive structure.

Each of the six types of deviation from societal standards distinguished in this analysis is hypothesized to arouse a distinct set of concerns and emotional reactions in the person (as summarized in Table 3 and discussed in detail in Kelman 1974 and 1980). Moreover, in each of these six situations, people can be expected to use distinct strategies for dealing with the emotion that has been aroused, for rectifying the situation, and for avoiding or minimizing the consequences of the violation of standards. Specific hypotheses about people's emotional reactions

TABLE 3   A classification of types of discrepant action in terms of the societal standards from which they depart[a]

Source of standards from which P's action has departed	Behavioral dimension on which P's departure from societal standards has occurred	
	Responsibility	**Propriety**
External rules or norms (compliance based)	Social fear	Embarrassment
Role expectations (identification based)	Guilt	Shame
Social values (internalized)	Regret	Self-disappointment

[a]Cell entries refer to the dominant emotional reactions that each type of discrepant action is hypothesized to arouse.
Source: Kelman 1974, "Social Influence and Linkages Between the Individual and the Social System." In *Perspectives on Social Power*, ed. J Tedeschi, p. 151. ©1974 by Aldine Publ. Reprinted by permission of Aldine Transaction, a division of Transaction Publ.

in each case and their ways of coping with them are derived from the three-process model. Several of these hypotheses were tested and largely confirmed in Nancy Adler's doctoral research, which explored the behavioral, cognitive, and emotional responses of women undergoing abortion (Adler 1974, 2004).

In further pursuit of a subplot of this chapter, let me point out that the dimension crosscutting the three sources of standards—the distinction between the domains of responsibility and propriety—seems to correspond to the crosscutting distinction that arose serendipitously in my definition of each of the three processes of influence. As noted earlier, a person's reaction in an influence situation may be governed primarily either by instrumental or by self-maintenance concerns. Such concerns are conducive to responsible and role-appropriate behavior, respectively—both of which are critical to the smooth and effective functioning of societies and organizations. Rules, roles, and values provide standards for motivating and evaluating behavior in both of these domains.

The differing reactions to violations of standards anchored in rules, roles, and values suggest how the three processes of influence might affect the exercise of social control. From the point of view of a society's or organization's interest in social control, identification—with its associated emotions of guilt and shame—would appear to be the most effective avenue of socialization. "Individuals operating at the level of compliance are 'insufficiently' socialized. Their adherence to social norms depends on surveillance, which makes them less reliable and more difficult to control. Individuals operating at the level of internalization are, in a sense, 'excessively' socialized from the point of view of agencies charged with social control. Since societal standards are integrated with their personal value systems, they tend to make their own judgments about the validity of authoritative demands. Their conformity to such demands is, thus, more conditional. Individuals operating at the level of identification are likely to conform to authoritative demands with less surveillance than those at the level of compliance and with less questioning than those at the level of internalization" (Kelman & Hamilton 1989, pp. 115–16).

Conceptualizing social influence in terms of the linkage between the individual and the social system is most useful for the analysis of influence in the context of legitimate authority. I turn next to the extension of the three-process model to this context—starting, specifically, with the relationship of individuals to the national political system.

PERSONAL INVOLVEMENT IN THE NATIONAL POLITICAL SYSTEM

In the 1960s, I collaborated with Daniel Katz and several of our students at the University of Michigan in a study of nationalism and the involvement of individuals in the national political system (DeLamater et al. 1969; Katz et al. 1964, 1970). The work focused on qualitative differences in the ways in which individuals adopt nationalist ideology and relate to the political system. As I continued to think

TABLE 4   Patterns of personal involvement in the national political system

Sources of attachment to the political system	Types of orientation to political processes		
	Rule orientation (compliance with societal rules)	Role orientation (identification with societal roles)	Value orientation (internalization of societal values)
Sentimental	Acceptance of rules that secure person's inclusion in society	Involvement in role of national citizen which enhances person's sense of status	Commitment to basic cultural values for which the society stands
Instrumental	Acceptance of rules that protect person's interests	Involvement in societal roles that contribute to person's status	Commitment to values underlying institutional arrangements

Source: Kelman & Hamilton 1989, *Crimes of Obedience*, p. 119. Reprinted by permission of Yale Univ. Press.

about the issue, I noted some parallels between the qualitative distinctions that our research had identified and the three processes of influence. Eventually, I came up with a typology that distinguished six patterns of personal involvement in the national system, yielded by a crosscutting of two qualitative dimensions (Kelman 1969). The formulation was later modified to conform to the terminology of rule, role, and value orientation, which we had found useful in other contexts (Kelman & Hamilton 1989). The scheme, summarized in Table 4, is based on the assumption that different individuals and groups within a population may relate themselves in different ways to the political system. The six patterns are not meant to be mutually exclusive; although different patterns may be predominant for a given individual or subgroup, various combinations of them are possible and likely.

The rows of Table 4 refer to two sources of an individual's attachment or loyalty to the political system: Individuals are sentimentally attached to the state to the extent that they see it as representing them and reflecting the population's (and their own) ethnic and cultural identity. Individuals are instrumentally attached to the state to the extent that they see it as meeting the population's (and their own) needs and interests. At the societal level, the distinction is reminiscent of Durkheim's (1947) distinction between the mechanical solidarity of more traditional societies and the organic solidarity of more industrialized societies. At the individual level, sentimental and instrumental attachment correspond to the two types of concern that may govern a person's reaction in an influence situation: self-maintenance and instrumental concerns, which, as noted earlier, cut across the three processes of influence.

The columns of Table 4 distinguish three types of political orientation, defined in terms of the three components of a social system through which members may be bound to it: rules, roles, and values, which are linked to the processes of compliance, identification, and internalization, respectively. They represent three different ways in which sentimental and instrumental attachments may be channeled to produce loyalty and support to the state. In *Crimes of Obedience* (Kelman & Hamilton 1989), we spell out how sentimental attachment and instrumental attachment to the political system play themselves out in each of the three ideal types of rule-oriented, role-oriented, and value-oriented citizens (pp. 120–22).

Central to this analysis of personal involvement in the political system is the concept of legitimacy, which, in essence, refers to the moral basis of the system's authority: its perceived right to make demands on its members and to expect their loyalty (Kelman 2001). Thus, when defined in terms of the legitimacy of the political system, the two types of attachment refer to the bases or the ultimate sources of its perceived legitimacy: To be sentimentally attached to the system means to perceive it as legitimate and entitled to the population's loyalty because it represents them and reflects their identity; to be instrumentally attached to the system means to accord legitimacy and loyalty to it because it meets the needs and interests of the population. The three orientations refer to the processes and criteria by which perceived legitimacy is generated, assessed, and maintained: For the three orientations, perceived legitimacy depends on the system's capacity, respectively, to uphold societal rules and preserve security and order; to sustain societal roles and assure the status of the nation and its citizens; and to advance societal values and pursue policies reflective of them.

Rule, role, and value orientations are not mutually exclusive. Like the three processes of influence to which they are linked, they are likely to manifest themselves at some level in all individuals, depending on the situation in which they find themselves, the particular relationship that is brought into play, and the circumstances of the moment. Nevertheless, they may help to highlight systematic differences in the way in which individuals define their roles as citizens and relate themselves to the political authorities. These differences can be clarified by treating the orientations as ideal types and postulating their implications for the citizen-authority relationship. Table 5 summarizes the defining characteristics of the three ideal types of political orientation and some of the social and psychological tendencies associated with each. In essence, the three orientations represent different conceptions of citizenship and civic responsibility, which are elaborated in *Crimes of Obedience* (Kelman & Hamilton 1989, pp. 267–76; see also Kelman 1993).

As already indicated, I have extended the framework for analyzing personal involvement in the political system to the analysis of personal involvement in a national or ethnic group—i.e., of the different manifestations of national or group identity (Kelman 1997a, 1998). I have also applied it to the analysis of several issues relating to the perceived legitimacy of the nation state: the obstacles to the development of loyalties to transnational institutions posed by the exclusive claim to legitimacy on the part of the national state and how these might be overcome (Kelman 1968); the potential effects—both positive and negative—of policies directed toward establishment of a common language on the development of perceived legitimacy and national identity in multilingual states (Kelman 1971); and the differences between black and white student protest movements in the 1960s

TABLE 5   Characteristics and correlates of three types of political orientation

	Rule orientation	**Role orientation**	**Value orientation**
Expectation from citizen	Follow rules; avoid trouble	Meet citizen obligation to obey and support the government	Take active part in formulating, evaluating, and questioning policies
Expectation from government	Uphold rules; assure security and order	Uphold roles; assure national and personal status	Uphold values; pursue policies reflecting national principles
Participation in duties	Passive: minimal compliance (as necessary to protect interests)	Supportive: active part in carrying out policies	Evaluative: active part in formulating and assessing policies
Participation in benefits	Minimal: subsidiary and service roles; tenuous integration; low level of education and occupation	Moderately high: active role in conducting society's affairs; comfortable integration; middle level of education and occupation	High: role in ownership and management of system; integration in establishment; high level of education and occupation
Socialization process	Compliance	Identification	Internalization
Role of morality in citizen action	Moral principles irrelevant	Moral obligation to government overrides personal morality	Personal moral principles must enter into consideration
Role of morality in state action	Moral principles irrelevant	Special set of moral principles applies	Moral principles fundamental
Level of moral reasoning	Preconventional	Conventional	Postconventional
Nature of support to government	Compliant	Reliable, enthusiastic	Firm but conditional
Conditions for protest	Threat to security	Threat to status	Threat to values
View of responsibility	Liability to sanctions for nonperformance	Reliable fulfillment of role obligations	Internalized standards for evaluating consequences of action

Source: Kelman & Hamilton 1989, *Crimes of Obedience*, p. 269. Reprinted by permission of Yale Univ. Press.

in terms of the nature of their challenge to the legitimacy of the political system (Kelman 1970). In subsequent analyses of social protest movements, I have distinguished between rule-oriented, role-oriented, and value-oriented movements. Social protest arises when a segment of the population perceives the authorities, their policies, or the system as a whole to be illegitimate. The distinction between the three types of movements is based on the extent to which their challenge to legitimacy is primarily at the level of the integrity of the rules, roles, or values, and their struggle focuses primarily on resources, status, or policy, respectively.

Although my own thinking has largely dwelled on the nature of personal involvement in the nation and the state, the framework should be equally applicable to any other social unit—society, community, organization, institution—or any other identity group or collectivity that has a defined membership, some continuity over time, and a set of shared norms and expectations. I have applied it, for example, to an analysis of the university as a community, focusing on the central importance of legitimacy and participation to creating the sense of community (Kelman 1972b).

SOCIAL INFLUENCE IN THE CONTEXT OF LEGITIMATE AUTHORITY

I have proposed that rule, role, and value orientation represent three ways in which an individual may be integrated in a social system and accept its legitimacy. Conceptually, they are linked to the three processes of influence in two ways. First, the orientations may differ in terms of the predominant process of influence whereby individuals are integrated in the system and socialized into their roles within it (see the fifth row in Table 5). Second, the orientations may differ in terms of the general way in which individuals relate themselves to the system's demands and expectations—the quality (not necessarily the degree) of their support for government policies (see the ninth row in Table 5).

However, the three-process model may also be extended more directly to the analysis of individuals' responses to specific influence attempts emanating from legitimate authorities. I differ from French & Raven (1959; see also Raven 1965) in viewing legitimacy not as a separate base of power, but as cutting across the three processes of influence, so that it might be associated with any of the three sources of power—means control, attractiveness, and credibility—differentiated in my original model. Accordingly, I hypothesized that rule, role, and value orientation should lead to different reactions to demands or requests from legitimate authorities, reminiscent of compliance, identification, and internalization, respectively.

Before elaborating on this point, I should note that legitimate influence differs in one important respect from the standard type of influence that my original model envisaged, as exemplified by persuasive communications. In the standard influence situation, people are presumed to react on the basis of their personal preferences. Even when an influencing agent uses coercive power, people can be presumed to comply because they prefer to avoid the consequences of noncompliance. In contrast, in situations of legitimate influence, P accepts O's right to make certain demands or present certain requests and feels an obligation to accede to them. Examples of legitimate influence would be situations in which O asks P to follow through on an earlier promise or to reciprocate an earlier favor. But "the most clearly structured cases of legitimate influence. . . occur in the context of an authority relationship. In modern bureaucratic settings, such a relationship means that the authority holder is entitled to make demands (within specified domains) and the subordinate is obligated to accede to them by virtue of their respective positions within the political or organizational hierarchy" (Kelman & Hamilton 1989, p. 89). Thus, in principle, legitimate authorities do not have to persuade subordinates that the behavior demanded of them is preferable for them, but merely that it is required. In practice, authorities usually buttress their demands with the capacity to coerce and the attempt to persuade and, moreover, choice and preference enter into people's reactions to authority in a variety of ways (discussed in detail in Kelman & Hamilton 1989, pp. 91–97).

When legitimate authorities issue demands, they have to communicate to their subordinates or their citizenry that these are indeed demands, which system members are obligated to obey, rather than requests or suggestions whose acceptance is left to the members' personal preference. One can distinguish three kinds of indicators that people may use to asses the obligatory character of the induced behavior, corresponding to the three processes of influence and the three types of political orientation: the existence of sanctions for disobedience; the invocation of national (or other group) symbols that bring the role of citizen (or group member) with its associated requirements to the fore; and the invocation of societal (or group) values that justify the demands. In "ordinary" influence situations, these different indicators would motivate compliance, identification, and internalization, respectively (see Table 1). In the context of legitimate authority, they serve primarily as cues to the obligatory character of the induced behavior. Nevertheless, we can distinguish reactions to demands from legitimate authorities that have the flavor of compliance, identification, and internalization, respectively. All three types of reactions take place within a framework of legitimacy, but the perception of requiredness takes a qualitatively different form in each case. Moreover, the nature of the obedient response is likely to be different in the three cases: more calculative in the compliance-tinged reaction, more enthusiastic in the identification-tinged reaction, and more conditional in the internalization-tinged reaction.

At the level of individual differences, rule-, role-, and value-oriented individuals—given the qualitatively different ways in which they relate to authority—are likely to use different criteria in assessing the obligatory character of demands from authority, i.e., to be especially responsive to sanctions, symbols, and values, respectively. The nature of their reaction is also likely to be different, bearing the earmarks, respectively, of compliance, identification, and internalization. Furthermore, political orientation should be related to people's readiness to challenge the legitimacy of authority demands and to the particular conditions under which such challenges are likely to be mounted. Legitimate rule implies that there are criteria for challenging the legitimacy of demands from authority, but there are also great obstacles to mounting such challenges (cf. Kelman & Hamilton 1989, Ch. 5). Value-oriented individuals are more likely to challenge authority, and to do so when they consider official policies to be in violation of fundamental societal values. Both rule- and role-oriented individuals are likely to go along with authority demands; if they do challenge authority, the rule-oriented may be responding to implied threats to the integrity of the rules on which their security depends, and the role-oriented to implied threats to the integrity of the roles on which their status depends.

Lee Hamilton and I had the opportunity to examine some of the attitudinal correlates of the three political orientations as part of our research on U.S. public reactions to the trial and conviction of Lt. William Calley for his role in the My Lai massacre during the Vietnam War (Kelman & Hamilton 1989). The research began with a national survey in 1971 (Kelman & Lawrence [Hamilton] 1972). Subsequently, in collaboration with Frederick D. Miller and later also with John D. Winkler, we developed scales for the three types of political orientation (as well as for sentimental and instrumental attachment), which we were able to include in a follow-up survey of the Boston population in 1976. The findings (Kelman & Hamilton 1989, Ch. 9) by and large supported our theoretical distinctions between the three types of political orientation. Value-oriented respondents stood out in their independent stance toward authority, their assertion of personal responsibility for actions taken under orders, their readiness to disobey illegitimate orders, and their support for resistance to the war and the draft. In contrast, both rule and role orientation were associated with a tendency to deny personal responsibility for actions taken under orders and a disposition to obey authoritative orders. The data suggest, however, that they represent two different paths to an obedient outcome, based on a view of obedience as a pragmatic necessity (with the flavor of compliance) for the rule-oriented and as a good citizen's moral obligation (with the flavor of identification) for the role-oriented.

RULE, ROLE, AND VALUE ORIENTATIONS FROM THE SYSTEM'S PERSPECTIVE

Rules, roles, and values are properties of both the social system and the individual—which, I might add, make them useful concepts for social-psychological analysis. So far, I have looked at them primarily from the perspective of individual members of a social system, for whom they represent standards for their own behavior and vehicles for integration in the society or organization. One can also look at them from the perspective of the social system, keeping in mind that societies and organizations are not persons, but function through the agency of their individual members—present and past—and the social norms and cultural products they create. The functioning of social systems can be analyzed systematically with the help of such concepts as rules, roles, and values (as well as interests, relationships, and identities, which I introduce below).

In the first exposition of my model of personal involvement in the political system (Kelman 1969), I proposed that the prevalence of one or another of the three types of political orientation (or integration, as I described it at the time) "in a given society depends on such system characteristics as its stage of development and the particular requirements that it must meet at a given point in time" (p. 287). Thus, if the primary system requirement is to assure the conformity of the population, crucial to the smooth operation of the system during periods of relative quiet, the authorities are likely to promote and draw on rule orientation. If the primary requirement is mobilization of the population, crucial during periods of national crisis or major social and political change, they are likely to promote and draw on role orientation. Finally, if the primary requirement is consolidation of the population, crucial during periods of nation building or—in established nation-states—periods of serious internal division, the authorities are likely to promote and draw on value orientation.

In an entirely different context, I applied this framework to an analysis of the ethical issues raised by social-science research from the perspective of the larger society (Kelman 1982). I distinguished three levels at which the potential impact of social research may become a matter of societal concern and hence of concern to the social-science community itself (see Table 6): its impact on the concrete interests of the individuals and communities who participate in the research, on the quality of the relationship between the investigators and the research participants, and on broader societal values.

TABLE 6   A classification of ethical issues in social science research

	Types of impact of the research		
Issue areas	Concrete interests of participants	Quality of interpersonal relationships	Wider social values
Harm and benefit	Injury (physical, psychological, material)	Stress and indignity (discomfort, embarrassment, feelings of inadequacy)	Diffuse harm (perversion of political process, inequity, manipulation, arbitrariness)
Privacy and confidentiality	Public exposure	Reduced control over self-presentation	Reduction of private space
Informed consent and deception	Impaired capacity for decision making	Deprivation of respect (lack of candor, choice, reciprocity)	Erosion of trust (cynicism, anomie)
Social control	Government regulation	Professional standards	Social policy

Source: Kelman 1982, "Ethical Issues in Different Social Science Methods." In *Ethical Issues in Social Science Research*, ed. TL Beauchamp, RR Faden, RJ Wallace Jr, L Walters, p. 46, Figure 2.1. ©1982 Johns Hopkins Univ. Press. Reprinted with permission of Johns Hopkins Univ. Press.

The conceptual link of these three types of potential impact of social research to the three processes of influence and the three types of system orientation becomes clear in the fourth row of Table 6, which refers to different forms of social control for insuring ethical conduct of social scientists. I propose that, insofar as our concern focuses on protecting the concrete interests of research participants, the most appropriate form of control is probably government regulation, establishing rules with which researchers and research organizations have to comply. Insofar as our concern focuses on the quality of the relationship between investigators and research participants, social control is exercised most effectively through the development and refinement of professional standards governing that relationship, which are incorporated as integral parts of the roles with which well-socialized professionals identify. Finally, insofar as our concern focuses on the impact of social research on wider social values, social control is most appropriately exercised through the processes by which social policy is formulated. Assessing the impact of social research on wider values is a legitimate part of the public debate—in which social scientists and their organizations themselves need to be active participants—about the amount and allocation of public support for social research and about the use of social-science data and findings in policy development and implementation.

PROCESSES OF PEACEMAKING

My work over many years has focused on international conflict and its resolution. Drawing, in particular, on the work of John Burton (1969), I have developed interactive problem solving, an unofficial approach to the resolution of international and intercommunal conflicts, based on social-psychological principles, and applied it to the Israeli-Palestinian conflict and other conflicts between identity groups (see, e.g., Kelman 1972a, 1979, 2000). There are obvious continuities between this work and my interest in processes of social influence. Interactive problem solving is in essence a process of mutual influence. At the macro level too, influence is a key component of my analysis of international conflict (Kelman 1997b) and negotiation (Kelman 1996).

In my work on international conflict, as in my work on social influence, "I have been concerned with the *quality* of change: its depth, durability, sustainability, and integration in the belief systems of individuals and societies" (Kelman 2004a, p. 267). In this spirit, I have proposed that an influence strategy based on threats and bribes is likely to induce changes only at the level of compliance, whereas a strategy based on responsiveness to the adversary's needs and on reciprocity is likely to enhance the value of the relationship between the parties and therefore induce changes at the level of identification. As the relationship is transformed, the parties become better able to engage in joint problem solving, generating agreements that meet their needs and elicit their commitment and are therefore conducive to relatively stable and enduring changes at the level of internalization (see Kelman 1996, 1997b).

Although I have used the concepts of compliance, identification, and internalization in my discussions of influence processes in international conflict, I have only recently attempted to link them systematically to different types of peacemaking (Kelman 2004b). I am indebted to Nadim Rouhana (2004) for postulating conflict settlement, conflict resolution, and reconciliation as three distinct processes, which are not designed to achieve the same endpoint (p. 174). My formulation of reconciliation, in particular, differs from Rouhana's in several important respects. But the idea of thinking of reconciliation as a distinct process, commensurate with conflict settlement and resolution, struck me as a very useful tool for analyzing different approaches to peacemaking. Not surprisingly, I was intrigued by the correspondence between these three processes of peacemaking and my three processes of influence. Establishing this link, of course (no matter how pleasing it may be to me), is useful only if it can provide conceptual handles for distinguishing settlement, resolution, and reconciliation as qualitatively different (though not necessarily always empirically separate) processes with distinct antecedent and consequent conditions.

Briefly, I propose that conflict settlement involves a mutual accommodation of the parties' interests, conflict resolution involves an accommodation in their relationship, and reconciliation an accommodation of their identities (Kelman 2004b).

Conflict settlement yields an agreement that meets the interests of both parties to the extent that their relative power positions enable them to prevail or that third parties intervene on their behalf. The agreement may have the support of conflict-weary publics, but it is not likely to change mutual attitudes or the quality of the relationship between the two societies. As is the case with compliance as a form of social influence, the stability of the settlement ultimately depends on surveillance by the parties, outside powers, and international organizations. Nevertheless, conflict settlement may be a significant achievement in a destructive conflict with escalatory potential and—depending on the fairness of the negotiating process and outcome—may help set the stage for conflict resolution.

Conflict resolution at its best moves beyond interest-based settlement and its dependence on the balance of power. It yields an agreement that is arrived at interactively, so that the parties feel committed to it; that addresses both parties' basic needs and fears so that it can sustain itself over time; and that builds a degree of working trust between the parties, so that it is less dependent on continuing surveillance. Conflict resolution represents a strategic change in the relationship between the parties, based on the recognition that stable peace and cooperation are in their mutual interest. They form a pragmatic partnership, in which each party is responsive to the other's needs and constraints and committed to reciprocity. Conflict resolution generates public support to the agreement and encourages the development of new images. The new relationship, however, remains vulnerable to changes in interests, circumstances, and leadership. As is the case with identification as a form of social influence, the new relationship and the associated attitudes are developed alongside of the old attitudes and not fully integrated into a new worldview. This makes for some instability in the new relationship, since changing circumstances may trigger the old attitudes—including fundamental distrust and negation of the other—in full force.

Reconciliation presupposes the transformation of the relationship between the parties produced by conflict resolution as I have described it. But it goes further in representing a change in each party's identity. The primary feature of that change in identity is removal of the negation of the other as a central component of each party's own identity. Such a change implies a degree of acceptance of the other's identity, at least in the sense of acknowledging the legitimacy of the other's narrative without necessarily agreeing with it. What is essential to reconciliation is that each party revise its own identity just enough to accommodate the identity of the other—not an easy assignment in deep-rooted conflicts, such as that between Israelis and Palestinians, in which negation of the other has been a central element of the identity of each party (Kelman 1999). Reconciliation goes beyond the level of pragmatic partnership and enables the parties to internalize the new relationship, integrating it into their own identities and gradually replacing old attitudes with new ones. Old fears and suspicions may reemerge at times, but the relationship is less vulnerable to situational changes.

The view of reconciliation as identity change linked to the process of internalization has important implications for the nature of the change involved. Just as internalization represents a change in a given attitude as a way of maintaining the integrity of one's own value system, reconciliation represents a change in more peripheral elements of identity as a way of strengthening the core of the identity. Indeed, I would argue that reconciliation, with its attendant change in the group's identity and revision of its narrative, becomes possible only if the core of each group's identity is confirmed in the process. A large part of the work of reconciliation is a process of negotiating identity, whereby each party is sufficiently reassured by the other's acknowledgment of its identity so that it in turn becomes free to remove negation of the other as a central element of its own identity.

In sum, I am suggesting that the three-process model of social influence can help us specify the concerns that underlie the peacemaking processes of conflict settlement, conflict resolution, and reconciliation, respectively, and the quality and durability of the changes that each of these processes is likely to produce. Thus, conflict settlement can be said to produce changes at the level of compliance through accommodation of the parties' interests, conflict resolution to produce changes at the level of identification through transformation of their relationship, and reconciliation to produce changes at the level of internalization through negotiation of their identities.

INTERESTS, RELATIONSHIPS, AND IDENTITIES

The distinction between the three processes of peacemaking suggests the three broad tasks that all social entities—individuals, groups, organizations, societies, collectivities—must perform as they negotiate their social environments and seek to balance the requirements of self-maintenance and social order: protecting and promoting their interests, establishing and maintaining their relationships, and affirming and expressing their identities (Kelman 2004a, p. 267). The distinction between these three tasks was foreshadowed in my discussion of ethical issues in social research (Kelman 1982), summarized earlier in this chapter.

In managing their interests, relationships, and identities, individuals and groups must attend to the requirements of both social order and self-maintenance, and of ensuring the proper balance between them. These two sets of requirements capture the crosscutting dichotomies that have repeatedly emerged in the evolution of my original model: instrumental and self-maintenance concerns in the acceptance of influence, instrumental and sentimental attachment to nation or state, responsibility and propriety as domains of socially prescribed behavior. For example, individuals must coordinate their actions with others in pursuing their interests, performing their roles, and maximizing their values; and, across time and situations, they must ensure that they live up to their public images, their role models, and their self-concepts.

Interests, relationships, and identities are distinctly social-psychological concepts "in the sense that they refer to the relationship between individuals and the social system, and also in the sense that they refer to properties of both individuals and social systems. Individuals have interests, relationships, and identities, which they pursue and express through the various groups and organizations with which they are affiliated. The groups and organizations—formed, essentially, to serve their members—in turn develop their own interests, relationships, and identities, which become personally important to the members and which the members are expected to support" (Kelman 2004a, pp. 267–68).

The concepts of interests, relationships, and identities broaden the original three-process model of influence to capture interactions of individuals or groups with each other and with larger social systems, and their integration within these larger systems. The microprocesses of social influence can be subsumed under this broader framework by distinguishing three foci for the interaction between P and O: a focus on individual and group interests, whose coordination is governed by a system of enforceable rules with which individuals are expected to comply; a focus on the relationships between individuals or groups, which are managed through a system of shared roles with which individuals identify; and a focus on personal and group identities, expressing a value system that individuals internalize.

The *Annual Review of Psychology* is online at http://psych.annualreviews.org

LITERATURE CITED

Adler N. 1974. *Reaction of women to therapeutic abortion: a social-psychological analysis.* PhD dissert. Harvard Univ.

Adler N. 2004. Rigor and vigor: spanning basic and applied research. See Eagly et al. 2004, pp. 83–96

Bailyn L, Kelman HC. 1962. The effects of a year's experience in America on the self-image of Scandinavians: a preliminary analysis of reactions to a new environment. *J. Soc. Issues* 18(1):30–40

Burton JW. 1969. *Conflict and Communication: The Use of Controlled Communication in International Relations.* London: Macmillan

Chaiken S. 1980. Heuristic versus systematic information processing and the use of source versus message cues in persuasion. *J. Personal. Soc. Psychol.* 39:752–66

DeLamater J, Katz D, Kelman HC. 1969. On the nature of national involvement: a preliminary study. *J. Confl. Resolut.* 13:320–57

Durkheim E. 1947. *The Division of Labor in Society.* New York: Free Press

Eagly AH, Baron RM, Hamilton VL, eds. 2004. *The Social Psychology of Group Identity and Social Conflict: Theory, Application, and Practice.* Washington, DC: Am. Psychol. Assoc.

Frank JD. 1961. *Persuasion and Healing: A Comparative Study of Psychotherapy.* Baltimore, MD: Johns Hopkins Press

French JRP Jr, Raven BH. 1959. The bases of social power. In *Studies in Social Power*, ed. D Cartwright, pp. 150–67. Ann Arbor, MI: Inst. Soc. Res.

Hamilton VL. 2004. Identification as a challenge to dual-process theories of persuasion. See Eagly et al. 2004, pp. 65–76

Hoffer E. 1951. *The True Believer.* New York: Harper

Katz D. 1960. The functional approach to the study of attitudes. *Public Opin. Q.* 24:163–204

Katz D, Kelman HC, Flacks R. 1964. The national role: some hypotheses about the relation of individuals to nation in America today. *Peace Res. Soc. (Intern.) Papers* 1:113–27

Katz D, Kelman HC, Vassiliou V. 1970. A comparative approach to the study of nationalism. *Peace Res. Soc. (Intern.) Papers* 14:1–13

Kelman HC. 1952. Two phases of behavior change. *J. Soc. Issues* 8(2):81–88

Kelman HC. 1953. Attitude change as a function of response restriction. *Human Relat.* 6:185–214

Kelman HC. 1956. *Compliance, Identification, and Internalization: A Theoretical and Experimental Approach to the Study of Social Influence.* Unpubl. manuscr.

Kelman HC. 1958. Compliance, identification, and internalization: three processes of attitude change. *J. Confl. Resolut.* 2:51–60

Kelman HC. 1960. *Effects of role-orientation and value-orientation on the nature of attitude change.* Paper presented at Meet. East. Psychol. Assoc., New York, NY

Kelman HC. 1961. Processes of opinion change. *Public Opin. Q.* 25:57–78

Kelman HC. 1963. The role of the group in the induction of therapeutic change. *Int. J. Group Psychother.* 13:399–432

Kelman HC. 1968. Education for the concept of a global society. *Soc. Educ.* 32:661–66

Kelman HC. 1969. Patterns of personal involvement in the national system: a social-psychological analysis of political legitimacy. In *International Politics and Foreign Policy: A Reader in Research and Theory*, ed. JN Rosenau, pp. 276–88. New York: Free Press. Rev. ed.

Kelman HC. 1970. A social-psychological model of political legitimacy and its relevance to black and white protest movements. *Psychiatry* 33:224–46

Kelman HC. 1971. Language as an aid and barrier to involvement in the national system. In *Can Language Be Planned? Sociolinguistic Theory and Practice for Developing Nations*, ed. J Rubin, BH Jernudd, pp. 21–51. Honolulu: Univ. Press Hawaii

Kelman HC. 1972a. The problem-solving workshop in conflict resolution. In *Communication in International Politics*, ed. RL Merritt, pp. 168–204. Urbana: Univ. Ill. Press

Kelman HC. 1972b. Legitimacy and participation: reflections on the university as a community. Address presented at Dedication Zool.-Psychol. Building, Univ. Maryland, College Park

Kelman HC. 1974. Social influence and linkages between the individual and the social system: further thoughts on the processes of compliance, identification, and internalization. In *Perspectives on Social Power*, ed. J Tedeschi, pp. 125–71. Chicago: Aldine

Kelman HC. 1979. An interactional approach to conflict resolution and its application to Israeli-Palestinian relations. *Int. Interact.* 6:99–122

Kelman HC. 1980. The role of action in attitude change. In *Nebraska Symposium on Motivation, 1979: Attitudes, Values, and Beliefs*, ed. HE Howe Jr, MM Page, pp. 117–94. Lincoln: Univ. Nebraska Press

Kelman HC. 1982. Ethical issues in different social science methods. In *Ethical Issues in Social Science Research*, ed. TL Beauchamp, RR Faden, RJ Wallace Jr, L Walters, pp. 40–98. Baltimore, MD: Johns Hopkins Univ. Press

Kelman HC. 1993. Conceptions of civic responsibility and the role of education in a multicultural world. *Swarthmore Papers* 1(1):33–49

Kelman HC. 1996. Negotiation as interactive problem solving. *Int. Negotiation* 1:99–123

Kelman HC. 1997a. Nationalism, patriotism, and national identity: social-psychological dimensions. In *Patriotism in the Lives of Individuals and Nations*, ed. D Bar-Tal, E Staub, pp. 165–89. Chicago: Nelson-Hall

Kelman HC. 1997b. Social-psychological dimensions of international conflict. In *Peacemaking in International Conflict: Methods and Techniques*, ed. IW Zartman, JL Rasmussen, pp. 191–237. Washington, DC: U.S. Inst. Peace

Kelman HC. 1998. The place of ethnic identity in the development of personal identity. In *Coping with Life and Death: Jewish Families in the Twentieth Century*, ed. PY Medding, pp. 3–26. New York: Oxford Univ. Press

Kelman HC. 1999. The interdependence of Israeli and Palestinian national identities: the role of the other in existential conflicts. *J. Soc. Issues* 55:581–600

Kelman HC. 2000. The role of the scholar-practitioner in international conflict resolution. *Int. Stud. Perspect.* 1:273–88

Kelman HC. 2001. Reflections on social and psychological processes of legitimization and delegitimization. In *The Psychology of Legitimacy: Emerging Perspectives on Ideology, Justice, and Intergroup Relations*, ed. JT Jost, B Major, pp. 54–73. Cambridge: Cambridge Univ. Press

Kelman HC. 2004a. Continuity and change: my life as a social psychologist. See Eagly et al. 2004, pp. 233–75

Kelman HC. 2004b. Reconciliation as identity change: a social-psychological perspective. In *From Conflict Resolution to Reconciliation*, ed. Y Bar-Siman-Tov, pp. 111–24. Oxford: Oxford Univ. Press

Kelman HC, Hamilton VL. 1989. *Crimes of Obedience: Toward a Social Psychology of Authority and Responsibility*. New Haven, CT: Yale Univ. Press

Kelman HC, Lawrence LH [Hamilton VL]. 1972. Assignment of responsibility in the case of Lt. Calley: preliminary report on a national survey. *J. Soc. Issues* 28(1):177–212

Lifton RJ. 1956. "Thought reform" of Western civilians in Chinese Communist prisons. *Psychiatry* 19:173–95

Maass A, Clark RD. 1983. Internalization versus compliance: differential responses underlying minority influence and conformity. *Eur. J. Soc. Psychol.* 13:197–215

Petty RE, Cacioppo JT. 1981. *Attitudes and Persuasion: Classic and Contemporary Approaches*. Dubuque, IA: Wm. C. Brown

Raven BH. 1965. Social influence and power. In *Current Studies in Social Psychology*, ed. ID Steiner, M Fishbein, pp. 371–82. New York: Holt, Rinehart & Winston

Rouhana NN. 2004. Identity and power in the reconciliation of international conflict. See Eagly et al. 2004, pp. 173–87

Smith MB, Bruner JS, White RW. 1956. *Opinions and Personality*. New York: Wiley

Turner JC. 1991. *Social Influence*. Milton Keynes, UK: Open Univ. Press

Wood W. 2000. Attitude change and social influence. *Annu. Rev. Psychol.* 50:539–70

Annu. Rev. Psychol. 2006. 57:27–53
doi: 10.1146/annurev.psych.56.091103.070234
First published online as a Review in Advance on September 30, 2005

EMOTION AND COGNITION: Insights from Studies of the Human Amygdala

Elizabeth A. Phelps

*Department of Psychology, New York University, New York, New York 10003;
email: liz.phelps@nyu.edu*

Key Words   emotion regulation, learning, memory, attention, hippocampus

■ **Abstract**   Traditional approaches to the study of cognition emphasize an inform-ation-processing view that has generally excluded emotion. In contrast, the recent emergence of cognitive neuroscience as an inspiration for understanding human cog-nition has highlighted its interaction with emotion. This review explores insights into the relations between emotion and cognition that have resulted from studies of the human amygdala. Five topics are explored: emotional learning, emotion and memory, emotion's influence on attention and perception, processing emotion in social stimuli, and changing emotional responses. Investigations into the neural systems underlying human behavior demonstrate that the mechanisms of emotion and cognition are in-tertwined from early perception to reasoning. These findings suggest that the classic division between the study of emotion and cognition may be unrealistic and that an understanding of human cognition requires the consideration of emotion.

CONTENTS

INTRODUCTION

The emergence of the study of cognition as a discipline within psychology began with the cognitive revolution, which is often characterized as a reaction to the dominance of behaviorism in the middle of the past century (Miller 2003). The cognitive revolution emphasized a view of human cognition as information pro-cessing. As a result, a primary goal of cognitive psychology was to explore "the way man collects, stores, modifies, and interprets environmental information or information already stored internally" (Lachman et al. 1979, p. 7). This approach, inspired in part by the computer metaphor, generally excluded emotion. Instead, emotion was considered a topic of investigation more appropriate for other disciplines of psychology, such as social, personality, or clinical psychology. Although there has been significant debate over the past 30 years about the appropriate role for emotion in the study of cognition (Lazarus 1984, Neisser 1976, Zajonc 1984), until recently these different approaches to the study of human behavior rarely overlapped.

The cognitive revolution provided an important model to aid in the exploration of the nature of mental representation. However, the computer metaphor is no longer the primary inspiration in studies of human cognition. There has been a new revolution inspired by advances in neuroscience and techniques for studying the human brain. Understanding how cognition is linked to neural function is increasingly driving the questions and means of investigation in cognitive psychology. The cognitive neuroscience approach has relied on animal models of neural function as a starting point for studying the representation of cognition in the human brain. Some of these animal models highlight the importance of emotion in understanding cognitive functions (e.g., see LeDoux 1996). These animal models have created a renewed interest in exploring the interaction of emotion and cognition in humans. This emphasis on linking mental processes to neural function has aided in breaking down barriers between traditional psychological disciplines in efforts to understand human behavior. As our understanding of the neural basis of human cognition grows, it has become increasingly apparent that the neural circuitry of emotion and cognition interact from early perception to decision making and reasoning.

In this review, I explore how the cognitive neuroscience approach has informed our understanding of the interaction of emotion and cognition. Animal models of the neural circuitry of emotion have emphasized specific brain structures that appear to be primarily linked to emotional processes, yet interact extensively with other brain systems underlying cognitive function. One of these structures is the amygdala, an almond-shaped structure on the medial temporal lobe that sits adjacent and anterior to the hippocampus (Figure 1, see color insert). The notion that the amygdala might play a role in emotion first emerged when Kluver & Bucy (1937) demonstrated that medial temporal lobe lesions in monkeys resulted in a range of odd behaviors, including approaching normally feared objects, orally exploring objects, and exhibiting unusual sexual behaviors. Approximately 20 years later, Weiskrantz (1956) demonstrated that it was the amygdala within the medial temporal lobe whose damage resulted in the range of behaviors that came to be known as Kluver-Bucy syndrome. Since that time, the amygdala has been a primary focus of researchers interested in the neural systems of emotion. The amygdala is a structure with extensive connections to brain areas thought to underlie cognitive functions, such as sensory cortices, the hippocampal complex, and the prefrontal cortex (Young et al. 1994). Because of its broad connectivity, the amygdala is ideally situated to influence cognitive functions in reaction to emotional stimuli.

Consistent with this, recent research has suggested that a primary function of the human amygdala is the modulation of neural systems underlying cognitive and social behaviors in response to emotional cues (Anderson & Phelps 2000, Whalen 1998).

This review examines insights into the interaction of emotion and cognition that have emerged from studies of the human amygdala. The amygdala is not the only brain structure that has been identified as important for emotional processes in humans[1], but it is the most thoroughly investigated to date. The cognitive neuroscience research on the human amygdala has drawn from neuroscience studies in nonhuman animals and behavioral paradigms derived from cognitive, social, personality, and clinical psychology. This review highlights five areas of research that demonstrate a role for the human amygdala in the interaction of emotion and cognition: emotional learning, emotion and memory, emotion's influence on attention and perception, processing emotion in social stimuli, and changing emotional responses.

EMOTIONAL LEARNING

Understanding how a stimulus acquires emotional properties is the primary goal in studies of emotional learning. Once a stimulus comes to elicit an emotional reaction, how it is processed may differ from neutral stimuli. Animal models of amygdala function have emphasized its role in emotional learning. This research has primarily examined classical fear conditioning. In a typical study, a neutral stimulus, such as a tone, is paired with an aversive event, such as a footshock. After a few pairings, the animal learns that the tone, the conditioned stimulus (CS), predicts the aversive event, the unconditioned stimulus (US), and the presentation of the tone alone begins to elicit a range of emotional reactions, such as freezing, changes in heart rate and blood pressure, increased startle responses, and stress hormone release. These acquired emotional reactions are conditioned fear responses. Using fear conditioning as a model paradigm, researchers studying nonhuman animals have mapped the pathways for fear learning from stimulus input to response output. These studies have demonstrated that the amygdala is critical for the acquisition, storage, and expression of a conditioned fear response (Davis 1992, Kapp et al. 1992, LeDoux 1996, Maren 2001, but see also Cahill et al. 1999).

---

[1]The current review is limited in that only the role of the amygdala is examined and the representation of emotion in the human brain involves a network of structures, including, but not limited to, the orbitofrontal cortex and the striatum. Limits in neuroscience techniques have generally encouraged the investigations of separate neural structures, but it is obvious that complex circuits of neural mechanisms are important for all aspects of human emotion and cognition. Recent Annual Review chapters that may provide additional information concerning topics discussed in this review include Fanselow & Poulos (2005), McGaugh (2004), Rolls (2000), Schultz (2006), Shors (2006), and Stuss & Levine (2002).

In humans, studies of fear conditioning are consistent with these animal models. Research using functional magnetic resonance imaging (fMRI) has reported increased blood oxygenation level-dependent (BOLD) signal in the amygdala in response to a neutral stimulus paired with an aversive event, called the CS+, compared to another neutral stimulus that did not predict an aversive event, called the CS- (Buchel et al. 1998, LaBar et al. 1998). The conditioned response, measured as a change in skin conductance (an indication of arousal) to the CS+, was correlated with the magnitude of this amygdala activation (LaBar et al. 1998). These results suggest the amygdala is involved in fear conditioning in humans. However, studies of brain imaging only show a correlation between brain activation and stimuli, processes, or behaviors (Cabeza & Kingstone 2001) and do not indicate a critical role for the amygdala. Consistent with animal models, patients with lesions including the right, left, or bilateral amygdala do not demonstrate a conditioned response as measured by skin conductance, even though the response to the US is intact (Bechara et al. 1995, LaBar et al. 1995). These results indicate that the human amygdala plays a critical role in fear conditioning.

The initial findings on fear conditioning in humans were predicted by animal models. However, these studies also demonstrated that the human amygdala's role in fear conditioning is limited to the physiological expression of conditioned fear. Studies in patients with amygdala damage demonstrate that even though they fail to show conditioned fear responses as measured by physiological responses to the CS+, they are able to acquire explicit knowledge about the contingencies between the CS+ and the aversive US. For example, Patient SP, who suffers from bilateral amygdala damage, and normal control subjects were shown a blue square (the CS+) that was paired with a mild shock to the wrist (the US). After a few pairings, normal control subjects showed an increased skin conductance response to the blue square, indicating a conditioned fear response. SP failed to acquire a conditioned response. She was then shown her skin conductance responses indicating a lack of conditioned fear and asked to comment:

"I knew that there was an anticipation that the blue square, at some particular point in time, would bring on one of the volt shocks. But even though I knew that, and I knew that from the very beginning, except for the very first one where I was surprised, that was my response—I knew it was going to happen. I expected that it was going to happen. So I learned from the very beginning that it was going to happen: blue and shock. And it happened. I turned out to be right, it happened!" (Gazzaniga et al. 2002, p. 559).

As her statement clearly indicates, SP had an explicit understanding of the parameters of the fear-conditioning procedure even though she did not show any physiological indication of conditioned fear. This type of explicit knowledge depends on the hippocampal complex for acquisition (Squire & Zola-Morgan 1991), and patients with damage to the hippocampus, whose amygdala are intact, show the opposite pattern; that is, a normal conditioned response as indicated by a physiological measures, but no explicit knowledge of the relation between the CS+ and the US (Bechara et al. 1995). These results highlight the notion that there are multiple forms of representation and expression for emotional learning and these different forms may rely on different neural substrates.

The normal acquisition of explicit knowledge of the parameters of fear conditioning following amygdala damage raises some questions as to how extensive the human amygdala's role in emotional learning is. Although learning that a stimulus predicts an aversive event through direct personal experience of this event—as in fear conditioning—is a powerful means of emotional learning, it is rather inefficient in that it requires an aversive experience. Humans have developed more efficient, symbolic means of communication, namely language, that allow for the acquisition of the emotional properties of a stimulus without aversive consequences. For instance, one could learn to fear and avoid a neighborhood dog by being bitten, an example of learning through direct aversive experience. However, one could also learn to fear and avoid a neighborhood dog by listening to a neighbor discuss how the dog is mean and dangerous. This type of instructed learning will result in a fear response when the dog is encountered, even though there is only explicit, symbolic knowledge of the dog's emotional properties.

A paradigm called instructed fear was used to determine if the human amygdala plays a role in the expression of symbolically acquired fear responses. In this paradigm, subjects are told that they might receive a mild shock to the wrist paired with one stimulus, such as a blue square (the threat stimulus), while the presentation of another stimulus, such as a yellow square (the safe stimulus), indicates that no shock will be presented. It has been demonstrated that instructed fear results in robust physiological fear responses to the threat stimulus that are similar to responses to a CS+ in fear conditioning (Hugdahl & Ohman 1977). With fMRI, it was found that presentations of the threat stimulus, relative to the safe stimulus, resulted in activation of the left amygdala that was correlated with the magnitude of the skin conductance response to threat versus safe, even though none of the subjects actually received a shock to the wrist (Phelps et al. 2001). A study in patients with right, left, and bilateral amygdala damage found that only those patients whose damage included the left amygdala showed an impairment in the physiological expression of instructed fear (Funayama et al. 2001). These results indicate that the left amygdala is critical for the expression of symbolically acquired fears—fears that are imagined and anticipated, but are never actually experienced.

The results with instructed fear suggest that the neural substrates underlying its expression are similar, but not identical, to those underlying fear conditioning. Although studies have demonstrated instructed fear and conditioned fear are similar in their physiological expression (Hugdahl & Ohman 1977), the slight differences in their neural circuitry suggest there may be subtle differences. In an effort to explore this possibility, the expression of acquired fear responses to subliminally presented stimuli was examined. Previous research has found that when representations of certain natural categories of stimuli, such as pictures of spiders, snakes, and angry faces (called biologically prepared stimuli), are used as a CS+ during fear conditioning, the conditioned response will be expressed through physiological measures, even if the CS+ is presented subliminally and the subject is unaware of its presentation (see Ohman & Mineka 2001 for a review). In these fear-conditioning paradigms, the CS+ is presented briefly (less than 30 msec) and is immediately followed by a masking stimulus preventing awareness of its presentation as assessed by explicit report (Esteves et al. 1994).

Olsson & Phelps (2004) exposed subjects to classical fear conditioning and instructed fear. In addition, they added a third emotional learning paradigm, observational fear. Learning through social observation is another indirect means for acquiring fear responses. Both humans and nonhuman primates have been shown to learn emotional properties of stimuli vicariously, through observing the emotional reactions of a conspecific (Ohman & Mineka 2001). The procedures for fear conditioning and instructed fear were similar to that described above. The subjects in the observational fear paradigm watched a video of a confederate receiving a mild shock to the wrist paired with some presentations of one stimulus (the observational CS+) and not another (the observational CS−). In all three of the learning groups, the CS+ and CS− were presented supraliminally (with awareness) on some trials, and subliminally (without awareness) on others. Consistent with previous results (Esteves et al. 1994), learning through fear conditioning resulted in expression of conditioned fear with supraliminal and subliminal presentation. In contrast, instructed learning required awareness for expression. This symbolically represented fear was not expressed when the threat stimulus was presented subliminally. Surprisingly, the results for observational fear mirrored those of fear conditioning. With vicarious learning through observation, subjects demonstrated a physiological arousal response to an observational CS+ presented either supraliminally or subliminally.

Instructed and observational fear learning are social means of learning that, unlike fear conditioning, do not require direct aversive experience. However, the similarity in the expression of fears acquired through fear conditioning and social observation suggests a greater degree of overlap in the amygdala's involvement. Research with nonhuman animals has shown that the amygdala is important for the acquisition, storage, and expression of fear conditioning (LeDoux 1996, but see also Cahill et al. 1999). Instructed fear, which depends on language and is unique to humans, most likely relies on the hippocampal complex for acquisition of the episodic knowledge of the link between the neutral and aversive event. It is unlikely the amygdala plays a role in the acquisition of this symbolic, abstract knowledge. In contrast, a recent fMRI study found that observational fear learning results in activation of the bilateral amygdala both during the observation of a confederate undergoing fear conditioning as well as the later test of this fear learning when subjects believed they might receive a shock themselves (Olsson et al. 2004). The magnitude of amygdala activation was similar in both stages, even though subjects knew that there was no possibility they would receive a shock during the observation/learning stage. These results suggest that, like fear conditioning, the bilateral amygdala is important for the acquisition and expression of fears acquired through the vicarious experience of social observation.

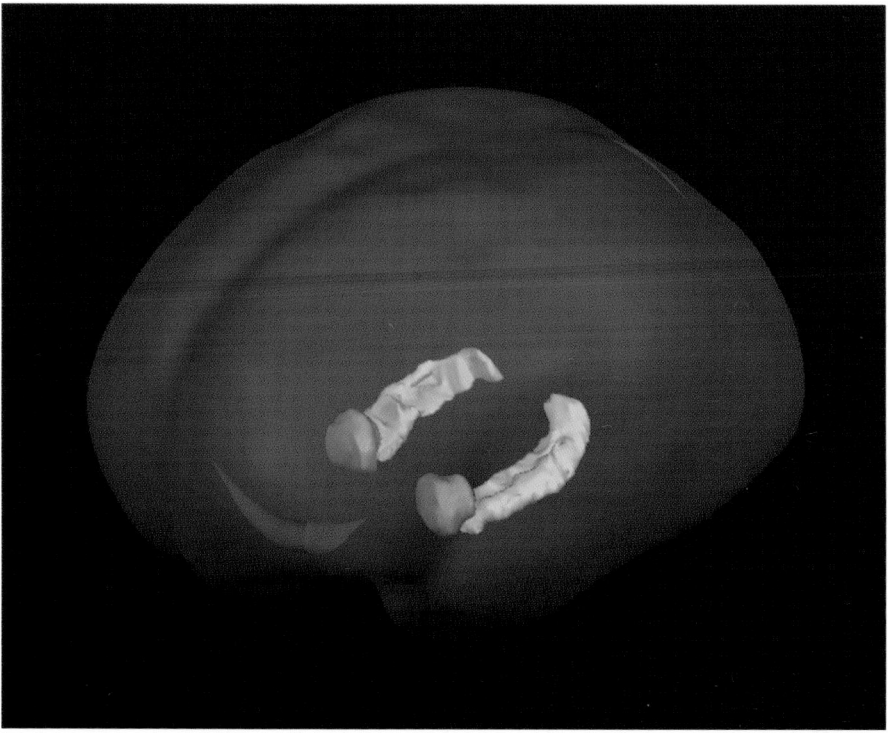

Figure 1 The amygdala (*blue*) and hippocampus (*green*). Reprinted from Phelps (2004).

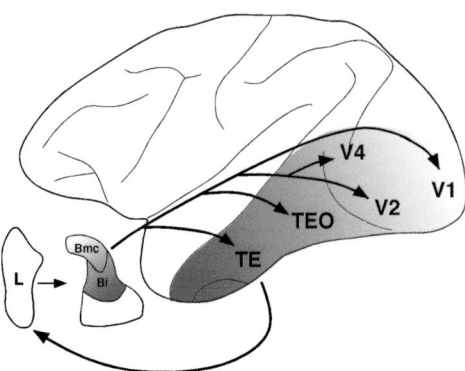

Figure 2 The connectivity of subregions of the amygdala (L, Bi, Bmc) and ventral visual cortical regions (V1, V2, V4, TEO, TE) in the macaque monkey. Reprinted from Freese & Amaral (2005).

Regardless of the means of emotional learning, the amygdala plays an important role in the physiological expression of fear learning and, in some cases, its acquisition as well. More recently, it has been suggested that the amygdala's involvement in the expression of fear learning through social means extends to cultural learning of social group stereotypes based on race and the indirect expression of race bias (Cunningham et al. 2004, Hart et al. 2000, Phelps et al. 2000). Although the current review has focused on fear learning, there is evidence from research with nonhuman animals that the amygdala may also play a role in appetitive conditioning and reward learning (Baxter & Murray 2002, Everitt et al. 2003, Holland & Gallagher 2004). There is some evidence in humans that the amygdala may be involved in learning to associate stimuli with positive outcomes (Johnsrude et al. 2000), but future research will need to explore the extent of the human amygdala's role in appetitive emotional learning.

EMOTION AND MEMORY

As William James wrote in *The Principles of Psychology*, "An impression may be so exciting emotionally as almost to leave a scar upon the cerebral tissues" (James 1890, p. 670). This phrase highlights the commonly held belief that emotion enhances episodic memory. Research on the cognitive neuroscience of emotion and memory has specified a range of means by which emotion can change the formation and recollection of episodic memory. It has been suggested that emotion, through the amygdala's influence, can alter three components of episodic memory: encoding, consolidation, and the subjective sense of remembering. Although episodic memory critically depends on other brain regions, most notably the hippocampal complex (Eichenbaum 2002, Squire & Zola-Morgan 1991), the amygdala may be important for modulating the neural circuitry of episodic memory.

The initial stage of episodic memory formation is encoding. Emotion can influence the encoding of to-be-remembered stimuli through its modulation of attention and perception (Easterbrook 1959). As will be discussed in the next section, emotion, via the amygdala, can influence attention and perception. Previous studies have shown that manipulations of attention will significantly impact memory encoding (e.g., Craik et al. 1996), and these changes in initial stimulus processing with emotion should lead to differences in memory performance. A recent study found that patients with amygdala damage only show an impairment in memory for details of emotional scenes that are central to the event, with intact memory for details that are more peripheral (Adolphs et al. 2005b). This study suggests that the amygdala may be involved in the narrowing of attention around the central emotional details leading to enhanced memory for these details in normal subjects (see also Easterbrook 1959). However, most studies to date have failed to differentiate the amygdala's influence on encoding and consolidation processes. Although a number of brain imaging studies have demonstrated that amygdala activation during encoding can predict later recognition or recall for emotional stimuli (Cahill et al. 1996, Canli et al. 2000, Hamann et al. 1999), these studies often attribute this effect to emotion's influence on the modulation of memory storage (e.g., Cahill et al. 1996) rather than attention.

The primary neural mechanism that has been explored in an effort to understand emotion's influence on episodic memory is the amygdala's modulation of hippocampal consolidation. Consolidation is a storage process by which memories become more stable over time, and evidence across species suggests that the consolidation of episodic memory critically depends on the hippocampus (Knowlton & Fanselow 1998, Squire & Zola-Morgan 1991). Emotion, specifically arousal, is proposed to enhance hippocampal-dependent consolidation. Using animal models, research by James McGaugh and colleagues has identified the neural systems underlying the effect of arousal on episodic memory consolidation (see McGaugh 2000, 2004 for a review). These studies have shown that physiological arousal results in activation of the beta-adrenergic receptors in the amygdala. The amygdala, in turn, modulates hippocampal processing, resulting in enhanced consolidation or storage for events that elicit an arousal response. Damage to the amygdala does not impair episodic memory for a stimulus, but rather it eliminates any enhancement observed with physiological arousal. Evidence that this effect is due to the modulation of consolidation, as opposed to encoding, comes from studies demonstrating that manipulations of amygdala function *after* stimulus encoding will alter arousal's influence on episodic memory (Packard & Teather 1998). It is suggested that one adaptive function of having a slow consolidation process is to allow for the emotional reaction to a stimulus, which follows its presentation, to influence the memory strength (McGaugh 2004). In this way, events that result in an emotional response, and are more likely to be important for future survival, are less likely to be forgotten.

In humans, a number of studies have reported that arousal enhances the retention of episodic memories (Berlyne 1969, Heuer & Reisberg 1992, Kleinsmith & Kaplan 1963), consistent with the modulation of hippocampal consolidation. Evidence that the human amygdala plays a role in this enhanced memory with arousal comes from studies using a range of cognitive neuroscience techniques. As mentioned above, brain-imaging studies have reported that activation of the amygdala at encoding can predict later retention for emotional stimuli. The amygdala has direct projections to the anterior portion of the hippocampus (Stefanacci et al. 1996). A recent study found that the activation of the amygdala and anterior hippocampus is correlated during the encoding of emotional scenes that were later remembered (Dolcos et al. 2004). In addition, patients with amygdala damage fail to show the normal enhancement of episodic memory with arousal (Cahill et al. 1995). Consistent with a role for the amygdala in modulating storage or consolidation, amygdala damage results in similar forgetting curves for arousing and neutral stimuli, in contrast to normal control subjects who show enhanced retention for arousing stimuli (LaBar & Phelps 1998). Finally, the administration of drugs that block beta-adrenergic receptors also block the impact of arousal on episodic memory (Cahill et al. 1994), consistent with animal models.

Although the effect of arousal on episodic memory is clearly documented, the magnitude of this effect varies depending on the paradigm. It can be quite subtle (e.g., LaBar & Phelps 1998) and is not always observed (e.g., Ochsner 2000). Furthermore, more extreme stress can have an opposite effect; that is, an impairment of hippocampal function and episodic memory (see McEwen & Sapolsky 1995 for a review). Nevertheless, there is robust evidence that the human amygdala, through its modulation of hippocampal consolidation, plays a critical role in situations where physiological arousal leads to enhanced episodic memory.

Until recently, most of the research examining the neural systems underlying the influence of emotion on episodic memory has focused on memory accuracy. However, studies of episodic memory for real life, public, emotional events have suggested that emotion may also influence the subjective experience of memory retrieval, irrespective of memory accuracy. These studies examining "flashbulb" memories have found that for highly emotional, public events the confidence that a memory is accurate and the sense that it is detailed and vivid may not reflect actual accuracy. In one of the first examples of this effect, Neisser & Harsh (1992) examined memory for the Challenger explosion. Within a few days of this tragedy, they asked subjects to record their memory for the circumstances in which they become aware of this event. Two and a half years later, the subjects were asked to report the same memory. Even though the subjects gave detailed recollections and were highly confident in their accuracy, most of these memories were inaccurate. More recently, a study examining memory for the terrorist attack of September 11, 2001 (Talarico & Rubin 2003) found that accuracy for memories of learning about this event did not differ from other, nonemotional events that occurred around the same time. However, memories of the terrorist attacks in comparison with more mundane events were rated as more confident, vivid, detailed, and recollected. Although a study of memory for the O.J. Simpson verdict found that reported emotional arousal at the time of the event is one of the few factors that can predict memory accuracy three years later (Schmolck et al. 2000), all of these studies of "flashbulb" memories suggest that emotion also has an independent effect enhancing the subjective sense of remembering.

One of the difficulties in exploring the neural systems underlying emotion's impact on the subjective sense of remembering is that most of these studies have examined memories for emotional, public events, which are challenging to investigate using cognitive neuroscience techniques. A recent laboratory study using the remember/know paradigm suggests a similar pattern. Recognition memory judgments are thought to rely on two independent processes: recollection, which includes the retrieval of contextual details, and familiarity, which is a sense that a stimulus is familiar in the absence of contextual details (see Yonelinas 2002 for a review). A subjective measure of these two processes is the remember/know procedure. During recognition judgments, subjects view old and new stimuli and are asked to judge if each stimulus is "new" (not presented before), "known" (familiar, but there is no specific recollection of details for the encoding context), or "remembered" (recollected with details of the encoding context). Using this procedure, Ochsner (2000) examined recognition for emotional and neutral scenes and found that emotion specifically enhances the proportion of "remember" judgments, even though there was no difference in memory accuracy for emotional and neutral scenes.

A similar paradigm was used to examine the neural mechanisms underlying emotion's impact on this subjective judgment of recollection (Sharot et al. 2004). As in the Ochsner (2000) study, emotion significantly enhanced the likelihood of "remember" judgments, even though there was no effect of emotion on accuracy. An examination of fMRI responses found that activation patterns in different medial temporal lobe regions were related to the subjective judgment of recollection for emotional and neutral stimuli. Consistent with previous studies (Henson et al. 1999, Wheeler & Buckner 2004), BOLD responses in the posterior parahippocampus differentiated "remember" and "know" judgments for neutral scenes. In contrast, BOLD signals on the amygdala differentiated "remember" and "know" judgments for emotional scenes. The posterior parahippocampus has previously been linked to memory for details of visual scenes (Kohler et al. 2002), which is the type of information that might be expected to result in a judgment of recollection versus familiarity. However, responses in this region were not similarly enhanced for "remembered" emotional stimuli. These results suggest that the neural mechanisms underlying the subjective judgment of recollection differ for emotional and neutral stimuli. The amygdala was specifically linked to judgments of recollection for emotional scenes. For emotional stimuli, judgments of the subjective sense of remembering may be influenced by the emotional qualities of the stimulus with less emphasis on mnemonic details. Consistent with studies of "flashbulb" memories suggesting emotion enhances the feeling of retrieval accuracy irrespective of actual accuracy, these brain-imaging results indicate emotion may alter the neural mechanisms underlying subjective judgments of remembering.

Although there is significant evidence that emotion interacts with episodic memory, and that the amygdala plays an important role in this interaction, an understanding of the complexity of this relationship is just beginning to emerge. Most studies in humans examining the neural systems underlying emotion's influence on episodic memory have emphasized arousal's impact on memory consolidation, perhaps inspired by the elegant animal models outlining this mechanism (McGaugh 2000). However, only a few studies have clearly documented arousal's specific influence on memory consolidation in humans, independent of its effect on encoding (Cahill & Alkire 2003, Cahill et al. 2003, Sharot & Phelps 2004).

Aside from the factors mentioned above, emotion might interact with episodic memory by other means. Emotional stimuli may differ from neutral stimuli in semantic similarity and distinctiveness, factors that have been shown to influence episodic memory (see, e.g., Phelps et al. 1998). Mood at retrieval has also been shown to influence episodic memory (Bower 1981). It is unlikely the amygdala has any role in these other effects of emotion on memory (Kensinger & Corkin 2004, Phelps et al. 1998). An exploration of the underlying neural mechanisms will aid in determining the complex components of the "scar upon the cerebral tissues" that characterizes emotion's impact on human episodic memory.

EMOTION'S INFLUENCE ON ATTENTION
AND PERCEPTION

Attention and perception are the first stages of stimulus processing, and factors that influence these early processes will also influence downstream cognitive functions, such as memory and reasoning. The importance of emotional salience in attention is well documented (e.g., Niendenthal & Kitayama 1994). An early example of this is the classic "cocktail party effect" described by Cherry (1953), in which an emotionally significant item, such as the subject's name, was noticed even when it was presented among a stream of unattended stimuli during an attentionally demanding dichotic listening task. This finding and others (e.g., Hansen & Hansen 1998, Ohman et al. 2001) suggests that emotion can facilitate awareness for emotionally salient stimuli in situations where attentional resources are limited.

Recent evidence indicates that the amygdala may mediate the facilitation of attention with emotion (Anderson & Phelps 2001, Morris et al. 1998a). This was investigated using a paradigm that tests the temporal limitations of attention, called the attentional blink (Raymond et al. 1992). In this paradigm, stimuli are presented in rapid succession (e.g., every 100 msec), so quickly it is difficult for subjects to identify any individual stimulus. However, if subjects are told that they can ignore most of the stimuli presented and selectively attend to a few target exemplars, such as those printed in a different color ink, subjects are able to selectively process the target stimuli and later identify them. This ability to selectively attend to specific stimuli in a rapidly presented visual stream is limited by the temporal relation between the different target stimuli. If a second target stimulus is presented a few items after the first target, in what is called the early lag period, subjects will often miss it. It is as if noticing and encoding the first target stimulus results in a temporary refractory period during which time it is difficult to notice and encode a second target. In other words, it is as if attention "blinked" (Chun & Potter 1995).

Using emotional and neutral words as stimuli, Anderson (2005) found that when the second target word is arousing, the attentional blink effect is attenuated. The ability to detect the arousing words was enhanced relative to neutral words when they were presented as the second target in the early lag period. Unlike normal control subjects, patients with left amygdala damage failed to show the normal attenuation of the attentional blink effect with emotion (Anderson & Phelps 2001). These findings indicate that in situations with limited attentional resources, emotional stimuli are more likely to reach awareness, and the amygdala plays a critical role in this facilitation of attention with emotion.

Two mechanisms have been proposed for the amygdala's facilitation of attentional processing. The first was suggested by Weinberger (1995). In studies with rats, Weinberger demonstrated that sensory cortices (specifically auditory cortex) may be tuned through fear conditioning to be especially sensitive to stimuli used as a CS+. This sensory tuning with emotional learning depends on the amygdala. This mechanism, which has not been clearly demonstrated in humans, suggests a long-lasting change in perceptual processing for stimuli that have acquired emotional properties through learning.

The second mechanism is a more transient change in attentional thresholds in the presence of emotional stimuli. As seen in Figure 2 (see color insert), anatomical studies have demonstrated that there are reciprocal connections between the amygdala and sensory cortical processing regions, such as the visual cortex (Amaral et al. 2003). The amygdala has been shown to receive input about the emotional significance of a stimulus quickly (Romanski & LeDoux 1992) and prior to awareness (Morris et al. 1998b, Whalen et al. 1998). For instance, robust amygdala activation has been observed in response to faces with fearful versus neutral expressions that are presented subliminally and supraliminally (Whalen et al. 1998). A number of studies indicate that attention and awareness have little impact on the amygdala's response to fearful stimuli (Anderson et al. 2003, Vuilleumier et al. 2001, but see also Pessoa et al. 2002). These results are consistent with previous psychological research indicating that the emotional qualities of stimuli are processed automatically (e.g., Zajonc 1984). It is suggested that this early, automatic amygdala response to fear or threat stimuli is an important factor in its ability to modulate attention and responses to potential danger (Davis & Whalen 2001).

The amygdala's transient facilitation of attention is thought to result from its modulation of sensory cortical regions in the presence of emotional stimuli (Morris et al. 1998a). It is proposed that early in stimulus processing the amygdala receives input about the emotional significance of a stimulus, and through projections to sensory cortical regions, modulates further attentional and perceptual processes (Anderson & Phelps 2001, Vuilleumier et al. 2004). In support of this model, brain imaging studies have demonstrated that visual cortical regions show enhanced activation in response to novel emotional stimuli (Kosslyn et al. 1996). The magnitude of this enhanced visual cortex activation is correlated with amygdala activation in response to these same stimuli (Morris et al. 1998a). Further support that the amygdala is mediating enhanced responses in visual cortical regions for emotional stimuli comes from an fMRI study conducted in patients with medial temporal lobe damage. Vuilleumier and colleagues (2004) presented faces with fear and neutral expressions to three groups of subjects: normal control subjects, patients with damage limited to the hippocampus, and patients with damage to the hippocampus and amygdala. Consistent with earlier studies (Morris et al. 1998a), enhanced activation was observed in visual cortical regions for fear versus neutral faces in normal control subjects. Patients with damage confined to the hippocampus also showed this pattern. However, patients with damage to the amygdala did not show any significant activation for fear versus neutral faces in the visual cortex. These results indicate that the amygdala plays a critical role in mediating the transient changes in visual cortical processing that occur for emotional stimuli.

The anatomical and brain imaging studies supporting a role for the amygdala in the transient modulation of visual cortex have identified regions thought to be important for perceptual functions, including early visual areas such as V1 (Amaral et al. 2003, Vuilleumier et al. 2004). However, the allocation of attention is more often linked to other brain regions, such as the parietal cortex (Corbetta & Shulman 2002). Given this, it is possible that the observed effects of emotion on attention are linked to its effect on perceptual regions. It has been suggested that at least some of the classic effects of attention are the result of the impact of attention on perception (Carrasco 2004), and brain imaging studies have shown that attention leads to enhanced activation in early visual processing regions (Gandhi et al. 1999). The anatomical connectivity between the amygdala and visual cortex suggests that stimuli that lead to amygdala activation, such as fear faces, should enhance perception as well as attention.

In order to examine whether emotion influences perceptual processes that are known to be coded by early visual regions, a psychophysical paradigm was used to examine the effect of fearful face cues on contrast sensitivity (Phelps et al. 2005). The ability to detect contrast is an early perceptual function that has been linked to primary visual cortex. A task that was previously used to demonstrate that covert attention enhances contrast sensitivity (Carrasco et al. 2000) was modified to include cues that were faces with fearful or neutral expressions. It was found that when a face cue directed covert attention, contrast sensitivity was enhanced, replicating the previous effect of covert attention on early perception. In addition, two effects for the emotional expression of the face cue were observed. First, irrespective of whether or not the face cue directed covert attention, a fear face cue enhanced contrast sensitivity. Second, if a fear face cue directed covert attention, contrast sensitivity was enhanced more than would have been predicted by the independent effects of a fear face cue and covert attention on perception. In other words, emotion enhances perception and potentiates the perceptual benefit of attention. These results are consistent with a model in which the emotion, via the amygdala, modulates processing in early visual regions.

The amygdala, through its extensive connectivity with sensory processing regions (Amaral et al. 1992, Freese & Amaral 2005), is ideally situated to influence perception with emotion. The evidence indicates that the amygdala's influence on perception may underlie emotion's facilitation of attention. However, emotion is also proposed to have another effect on attention, which is to capture attention. When attention is captured by emotion, there is impaired processing of nonemotional aspects of the stimulus or event. A number of studies have demonstrated the capture of attention with emotion (Pratto & John 1991), and it is suggested that this effect is due to difficulty disengaging attention from the emotional qualities of a stimulus (Fox et al. 2001). Little is known about the neural systems underlying the capture of attention with emotion, or how this effect may be related to the facilitation of attention and perception observed when processing emotional aspects of a cue or stimulus.

The studies examining emotion's facilitation or capture of attention have primarily used negative, fearful, or threatening stimuli. For some paradigms, it appears arousal is the key component for the facilitation of attention (Anderson 2005), and for others the effects appear to be specific for negative or threatening stimuli (Ohman et al. 2001). Discussions of the adaptive function of emotion's facilitation of attention emphasize the preferential detection of stimuli that signal potential importance or threat (Whalen 1998) and suggest a primary role for the amygdala is the modulation of vigilance in the presence of these stimuli. The current evidence of emotion's influence on attention and perception is largely consistent with this interpretation.

PROCESSING EMOTION IN SOCIAL STIMULI

There is some debate as to whether there are specialized neural mechanisms for processing social stimuli. For instance, some regions of the fusiform gyrus are proposed to be specialized for the recognition of facial identity (Kanwisher et al. 1997). Patients with damage to this region show deficits in recognizing individuals from their faces (Farah 1990). However, it also proposed that processing in this region may reflect a more general mechanism for the identification of individual exemplars from classes of stimuli for which subjects have developed some level of expertise (Tarr & Gauthier 2000).

Studies of the cognitive mechanisms underlying the recognition of facial identity indicate that faces are not processed like most other objects. Recognizing faces depends on holistic and configural processing to a greater extent (Farah et al. 1998). Although the debate remains open as to whether the neural systems underlying the processing of face stimuli are unique to faces, it is clear that we have developed complex cognitive mechanisms that allow us to quickly distinguish friends from strangers.

Studies on the recognition of facial expression suggest that identifying emotion from face stimuli relies on yet a different set of processes and different neural substrates. This is perhaps not surprising given that the consistent identification of expressions across individuals requires recognizing similarities among different exemplars of face stimuli, whereas the recognition of identity requires recognizing differences among exemplars. It has been proposed that depending on the particular facial expression, different neural mechanisms may be important. In general, these brain regions are not thought to be specialized for recognizing a specific facial expression, but rather are thought to have more general role in the processing of different emotions. For example, it is suggested that insular cortex is important for the recognition of disgust in social and nonsocial stimuli, whereas the basal ganglia play a role in the recognition of anger (Calder et al. 2001, Lawrence et al. 2002). Although brain imaging studies of the amygdala indicate it responds to a range of facial expressions (e.g., Anderson et al. 2003), it appears to play a critical role in perceiving fear. Patients with amygdala damage show impairments in identifying the intensity of fear in facial expressions (Adolphs et al. 1999). These patients are able to generate normal facial expressions of fear (Anderson & Phelps 2000), but consistently rate expressions of fear in others as less fearful than do normal control subjects. As mentioned earlier, brain-imaging studies show a preferential response to expressions of fear (Breiter et al. 1996), even when presented subliminally (Whalen et al. 1998).

Given that different neural mechanisms may underlie the recognition of facial identity and the recognition of different facial expressions, it would not be surprising that different types of information are necessary to make these judgments. Two recent studies examining the amygdala's role in the identification of fear expressions highlight this point. It is known that recognizing identity from face stimuli depends critically on the specific configuration of different facial features (see Farah et al. 1998 for a review). Subtle changes in this configuration, such altering the distance between the eyes and mouth, can significantly impair the recognition of facial identity. In contrast, recognizing fear from face stimuli seems to depend critically on a single facial feature—the eyes. A recent imaging study by Whalen and colleagues (2004) demonstrated that amygdala activation was more robust in response to subliminal presentation of the eyes alone for fearful than for happy facial expressions. The magnitude of amygdala activation in response to the eyes of fearful versus happy faces was similar to that observed when the entire face is presented.

Another recent study by Adolphs and colleagues (2005a) used a technique that helped identify which aspects of a face are most important when recognizing expressions. Consistent with the imaging results (Whalen et al. 2004), the identification of fear seemed to depend critically on the eyes. An examination of eye movements when subjects were presented fearful facial expressions showed that normal control subjects predominately fixated on the eyes. A patient with bilateral damage to the amygdala showed a different pattern of eye movements, which suggests she was relying on other facial features in her efforts to identify the emotion. Surprisingly, when this patient was cued to focus on the eyes, her ability to identify fear from facial expressions improved to normal levels; however, she failed to adopt this strategy in the absence of explicit instructions. These results indicate that the amygdala not only responds preferentially to the eyes in face stimuli, but also may be involved in generating behaviors that aid in the identification of facial expressions of fear. Although a unique pattern of facial movements are needed to generate a facial expression of fear (Ekman & Freisen 1976), it seems that not all of these characteristic facial movements have equal importance in communicating this emotion.

The studies identifying the perceptual cues necessary for the identification of fearful facial expressions, which differ for the recognition of identity and, perhaps, other facial expressions, emphasize the complexity in understanding the range of information conveyed in face stimuli and how it is used to communicate information about social interactions. In addition, it has recently been shown that the context of the presentation of a facial expression can significantly alter the amygdala response. Fear and surprise are the two facial expressions that are likely to be confused due to the similarity in the characteristic facial configurations for these expressions. A recent brain-imaging study found that if a surprise facial expression is preceded by a sentence consistent with a surprise reaction, such as "She just won $500 dollars," there is less of a BOLD response in the amygdala than if the sentence is consistent with a fear reaction, such as "He just lost $500 dollars." In other words, an emotional context conveyed verbally can alter the amygdala response to a facial expression. In addition, other cues, such as body movements consistent with fear, lead to amygdala activation (de Gelder et al. 2004). These studies suggest that although it is possible to identify the perceptual cues that are most important in evaluating facial expressions of fear, contextual and symbolic information can alter responses in brain regions that mediate the identification of facial expressions from face cues.

When interpreting emotion from facial expression, the amygdala appears to have a specialized role in processing fear. This role may also extend to other facial cues that signal potential threat. For example, two recent studies examined the role of the amygdala in the perception of trust from an individual's face. Although the facial characteristics that convey trust are not well understood, it was found that this type of judgment seems to depend on the amygdala. When viewing pictures of faces that are rated as more or less "trustworthy," greater amygdala activation was observed in response to pictures of individuals who were rated as untrustworthy based on their faces (Winston et al. 2002). Consistent with this result, patients with amygdala damage rated pictures of individuals whose faces were deemed untrustworthy by normal controls as both more trustworthy and more approachable (Adolphs et al. 1998).

Although the amygdala may be especially attuned to facial signals of threat or danger, it may also have a broader role in perceiving complex social and emotional signals from both social and nonsocial stimuli. A study by Adolphs and colleagues demonstrated the subtlety of the amygdala's role in the processing of social cues by showing that it extends to the perception of social and emotional information from nonsocial stimuli. Heberlein & Adolphs (2004) examined the ability to anthropomorphize. It is a natural human tendency to see social and emotional cues and interactions among ambiguous or nonsocial stimuli. This tendency to see human social motives and emotional reactions can extend to inanimate objects. In a classic study, Heider & Simmel (1944) showed subjects a film of different geometric shapes moving around a box. Although these were simple shapes, the nature of the movements resulted in subjects describing the shapes as characters with motives interacting in a complex social situation. Heberlein & Adolphs (2004) showed this video to patients with amygdala damage and found that, unlike normal control subjects, their description of the film emphasized the actual movements of the geometric shapes, devoid of any social or emotional context or motives. These results indicate that the amygdala may play a more general role in perceiving and interpreting emotion from a wide range of stimuli, and the precise perceptual features conveying this information may be less important than the social or emotional content that can be interpreted.

Cognitive psychology research on the processing of social stimuli has primarily focused on understanding the types of cues that are critical to recognize facial identity. The emerging cognitive neuroscience research on the processing of emotion in faces indicates that a different set of processes and cues are required to perceive social, emotional information. The notion that there are different neural substrates that may respond to different facial expressions (Calder et al. 2001) suggests that depending on emotional expression, different types of cues may be important. In addition, the context in which an expression is conveyed can alter the amygdala's response. These results indicate that understanding how faces communicate social or emotional information may depend on the confluence of a range of cues, including, but not limited to, those that signal facial identity, the social context, and the facial expression.

Although the amygdala seems to play a critical role in the processing of fear from facial expressions, it may also play a broader role in perceiving and processing emotion from social and nonsocial cues. As previously mentioned, the amygdala responds to a range of social information, including information about social groups defined by race (Hart et al. 2000, Phelps et al. 2000), bodily cues conveying emotion (de Gelder et al. 2004), other facial expressions (Anderson et al. 2003, Whalen et al. 2001), and interpreting social, emotional information from nonsocial stimuli (Heberlein & Adolphs 2004). It appears that the amygdala is not specialized for detecting fear from faces, even though it is especially attuned to process fearful expressions.

CHANGING EMOTIONAL RESPONSES

A few decades ago, there was debate among psychologists Robert Zajonc and Richard Lazarus concerning the relation between emotion and cognition. The debate, which was highlighted in adjoining articles in the *American Psychologist,* centered around the question of whether the detection of emotion preceded cognitive processing (Zajonc 1984), or whether cognitive functions were a necessary component in the detection and experience of emotion (Lazarus 1984).

Given that the early cognitive neuroscience research on the neural systems of emotion in humans was inspired by studies conducted with nonhuman animals, mostly rats, these studies tended to focus on the primacy of affective responses and not the influence of cognition. Indeed, there is significant evidence that signals of emotion are processed by the amygdala automatically, irrespective of attention (Anderson et al. 2003, Vuilleumier et al. 2001) and awareness (Morris et al. 1998b, Whalen et al. 1998), and that this early detection of emotion can influence a range of cognitive functions, including perception, attention, and memory. Research with nonhuman animals has found that there are specialized subcortical pathways that allow for the early detection of emotion so that the amygdala can perceive potential threat in the environment prior to the completion of standard perceptual functions (Romanski & LeDoux 1992), and there is some evidence that this pathway exists in humans (de Gelder et al. 1999, but see also Pessoa et al. 2002). These findings strongly support the position that the processing of emotion occurs prior to a complete cognitive analysis (Zajonc 1984).

However, an emerging body of research suggests that a range of cognitive functions can also affect the amygdala and the experience of emotion. These studies indicate that the results of cognitive interpretations are an important factor in the perception of emotion. A few examples of this were described above. For instance, the studies on instructed fear demonstrate that in some circumstances linguistic interpretation and episodic memory are critical for emotional learning. Abstract representations of the emotional properties of a stimulus will influence the amygdala (Phelps et al. 2001), which in turn mediates the physiological expression of fear (Funayama et al. 2001). An emotional context conveyed through language can also alter the amygdala's response to facial expressions, as was demonstrated in the study by Whalen and colleagues (2004) in which the amygdala's response to a surprise face was modulated by the sentence preceding its presentation. In addition, the amygdala's response to social groups defined by race can be modulated by task demands (Wheeler & Fiske 2004). These studies support the position that cognitive functions are a necessary component in understanding the neural systems and processing of emotion (Lazarus 1984).

More recently, there has been a renewed interest in the influence of cognition on emotion inspired by investigations of emotion regulation (see Gross 2002 for a review). The ability to regulate our emotional responses and states is a critical component of normal social function and adaptive interactions with the environment. Although certain stimuli may be prone to evoke an emotional reaction, how those stimuli are processed and interpreted can have a profound impact on both internal states and expressed behaviors and actions. Through conscious strategies and practice, individuals can change their interpretation of specific stimuli, and this can alter emotional reactions. Changing emotional responses through reasoning and strategies emphasizes the impact of cognition on emotion.

Recent studies exploring the neural mechanisms of regulating emotional responses to negative stimuli have suggested one consequence of these conscious regulation strategies is to alter the amygdala response. In a study by Ochsner and colleagues (2002), subjects viewed pictures of emotional and neutral scenes. For some scenes, the subjects were asked to simply attend to their natural emotional reactions. For other scenes, subjects were instructed to reappraise the emotional significance of the situation presented in the scene. For example, if a scene of women crying outside a church is presented, one interpretation is that it is a funeral and the women are crying in grief. However, if instructed to "reappraise" the emotional scene, subjects might instead imagine that the women crying in joy at the wedding of a loved one. Reappraisal is similar to viewing the cup as half full as opposed to half empty. Reappraising the scene can alter the experience of emotion (Gross 2002). Ochsner and colleagues (2002) found that it also diminishes amygdala activation (see Schaefer et al. 2002 for a similar result). A comparison of "reappraise" and "attend" trials for negative scenes showed decreased activation of the amygdala and increased activation in the middle frontal gyrus of the left, lateral prefrontal cortex (PFC). This lateral PFC region has previously been linked to executive processes of working memory (see, e.g., Smith & Jonides 1999), which suggests this region may be involved in the online processing of the interpretation of the scene. Activation in this left lateral PFC region was correlated with reappraisal success. Those subjects who showed greater activation in this region to "reappraise" versus "attend" trials showed a greater change in their reported emotional response to scenes with reappraisal. In addition, activation in this lateral PFC region was correlated with activation of the amygdala, which suggests a role for this region in inhibiting the amygdala response to these complex scenes.

The finding that brain regions linked to executive function and working memory are correlated with the amygdala response during the conscious reappraisal of scenes suggests one pathway by which complex cognitive manipulations of stimuli might influence the neural circuitry of emotion. However, anatomical connectivity studies of the amygdala and PFC suggest that communication between these regions is not direct. Within the PFC, more ventral and medial regions are thought to be more similar across species, and the amygdala's connectivity with the PFC is primarily through these regions (McDonald et al. 1996, Stefanacci & Amaral 2002). Studies that have explored the role of the PFC in the inhibition of affect and amygdala function in nonhuman animals have emphasized the involvement of more ventral, medial PFC (vmPFC) areas (Milad & Quirk 2002, Morgan & LeDoux 1995). These studies have primarily examined the extinction of conditioned fear. Once a conditioned fear is acquired, this fear response can be changed through extinction. During a typical extinction procedure, the CS is no longer paired with the US. The animal eventually learns that the CS does not predict the US and the expression of conditioned fear is diminished. A number of studies in nonhuman animals have demonstrated that the vmPFC plays an important role in the retention of extinction learning and inhibiting the amygdala response. This inhibition of the amygdala mediates the diminished expression of conditioned fear with extinction (see Milad & Quirk 2002 for a review). Results from a brain imaging study in humans examining the neural mechanisms of extinction learning were consistent with this animal model (Phelps et al. 2004).

A recent study investigated if the conscious regulation of emotion, which is unique to humans and depends on cognitive strategies, is linked to the mechanisms of extinction learning (Delgado et al. 2004). Both means of changing emotional responses involve interactions between the amygdala and PFC, but the precise region of the PFC seems to vary. In this study, subjects were asked to regulate a conditioned fear response in which the CS's were colored squares, one of which was paired with a mild shock to the wrist (the US). On the "regulation" trials, subjects were instructed to imagine a soothing scene from nature that incorporated the color of the CS. On the "attend" trials, subjects were instructed to simply attend to their natural feelings and reactions. Consistent with the findings of Ochsner and colleagues (2002), using an emotion regulation strategy diminished the conditioned fear response, resulted in decreased activation of the amygdala, and enhanced activation in the left lateral PFC. In addition, activation was also observed in the vmPFC region during emotion regulation. The pattern of this activation and its location within the medial PFC mirrored those observed when fear was diminished with extinction learning (Phelps et al. 2004). These results suggest that conscious, emotion regulation strategies, which depend on lateral PFC regions known to be important for executive processes and working memory (Smith & Jonides 1999), may act to diminish negative emotional responses by virtue of their influence on medial PFC regions that have been shown to inhibit the amygdala during extinction. In other words, emotion regulation strategies, which are unique to humans and seem to depend on regions of the PFC that differ in humans, may inhibit fear responses by co-opting the mechanisms of fear extinction that are similar across species.

As our understanding of the influence of higher cognitive functions on emotion processing grows, it has become increasingly apparent that even subcortical neural mechanisms that are preserved across a wide range of species, such as the amygdala, can be significantly influenced by neural systems and behaviors that are uniquely human, such as reasoning and strategies. These higher cognitive functions may influence the amygdala by taking advantage of neural mechanisms that evolved to accomplish more simple tasks across species. These findings highlight the complexity of the debate made famous by Lazarus (1984) and Zajonc (1984) more than 20 years ago. At that time, it seemed reasonable to debate whether emotion or cognition is primary when processing and interpreting stimuli. More recent research from cognitive neuroscience suggests that the answer could not be so simple. The mechanisms of emotion and cognition are intertwined from early perception to complex reasoning. It appears that understanding the separate contributions of emotion and cognition when processing stimuli becomes increasingly difficult as we learn more about the nature of the psychological and neural representations of behaviors typically categorized as either emotion or cognition.

CONCLUSION

As our understanding of the cognitive neuroscience of emotion and cognition grows, it is increasingly apparent that the division of human behavior into emotion and cognition is not as clear as previous philosophical and psychological investigations have suggested. The mechanisms of emotion and cognition appear to be intertwined at all stages of stimulus processing and their distinction can be difficult. It is also apparent that much like the study of cognition divided functions into different domains, such as memory, attention, and reasoning, the concept of emotion has a structural architecture that may be similarly diverse and complex (Russell & Barrett 1999, Scherer 2000). This review has focused on "emotion" overall, but for the different cognitive domains explored the precise characteristics of emotion that influence specific cognitive functions may differ.

As we move forward in the study of the representation of cognition, it is clear that a consideration of emotion is necessary. Examining cognitive functions without an appreciation for the social, emotional, and motivational context will result in an understanding that may be limited in its applicability outside of the research laboratory. The traditional research domains of psychology, such as cognitive, social, and clinical, may help create unified areas of research, but may also diminish our appreciation of the complexity of human behavior by discouraging discussion of their interactions. Adding the complexity of emotion to the study of cognition can be daunting, but investigations of the neural mechanisms underlying these behaviors can help clarify the structure and mechanisms.

ACKNOWLEDGMENTS

The author would like to acknowledge Meridith Carson and Joel Pearson for assistance with the preparation of this manuscript, and the James McKeen Catell Foundation.

The *Annual Review of Psychology* is online at http://psych.annualreviews.org

LITERATURE CITED

Adolphs R, Gosselin F, Buchanan TW, Tranel D, Schyns P, Damasio AR. 2005a. A mechanism for impaired fear recognition after amygdala damage. *Nature* 433:68–72

Adolphs R, Tranel D, Buchanan TW. 2005b. Amygdala damage impairs emotional memory for gist but not details of complex stimuli. *Nat. Neurosci.* 8(4):512–18

Adolphs R, Tranel D, Damasio AR. 1998. The human amygdala in social judgment. *Nature* 393:470–74

Adolphs R, Tranel D, Hamann S, Young AW, Calder AJ, et al. 1999. Recognition of facial emotion in nine individuals with bilateral amygdala damage. *Neuropsychologia* 37:1111–17

Amaral DG, Behniea H, Kelly JL. 2003. Topographic organization of projections from the amygdala to the visual cortex in the macaque monkey. *Neuroscience* 118:1099–120

Amaral DG, Price JL, Pitkanen A, Carmichael ST. 1992. Anatomical organization of the primate amygdaloid complex. In *The Amygdala: Neurobiological Aspects of Emotion, Memory, and Mental Dysfunction*, ed. JP Aggleton, pp. 1–65. New York: Wiley-Liss

Anderson AK. 2005. Affective influences on the attentional dynamics supporting awareness. *J. Exp. Psychol.: Gen.* 134(2):258–81

Anderson AK, Christoff K, Panitz D, DeRosa E, Gabrieli JD. 2003. Neural correlates of the automatic processing of threat facial signs. *J. Neurosci.* 23(13):5627–33

Anderson AK, Phelps EA. 2000a. Perceiving emotion: more than meets the eye. *Curr. Biol.* 10:551–54

Anderson AK, Phelps EA. 2000b. Expression without recognition: contributions of the human amygdala to emotional communication. *Psychol. Sci.* 11:106–11

Anderson AK, Phelps EA. 2001. Lesions of the human amygdala impair enhanced perception of emotionally salient events. *Nature* 411:305–9

Baxter MG, Murray EA. 2002. The amygdala and reward. *Nat. Rev. Neurosci.* 3:563–73

Bechara A, Tranel D, Damasio H, Adolphs R, Rockland C, Damasio AR. 1995. Double dissociation of conditioning and declarative knowledge relative to the amygdala and hippocampus in humans. *Science* 269:1115–18

Berlyne DE. 1969. Arousal, reward and learning. *Ann. NY Acad. Sci.* 159(3):1059–70

Bower GH. 1981. Mood and memory. *Am. Psychol.* 36:129–48

Breiter HC, Etcoff NL, Whalen PJ, Kennedy WA, Rauch SL, et al. 1996. Response and habituation of the human amygdala during visual processing of facial expression. *Neuron* 17(5):875–87

Buchel C, Morris J, Dolan RJ, Friston KJ. 1998. Brain systems mediating aversive conditioning: an event-related fMRI study. *Neuron* 20:947–57

Cabeza R, Kingstone A. 2001. *Handbook of Functional Neuroimaging of Cognition.* Cambridge, MA: MIT Press

Cahill L, Alkire MT. 2003. Epinephrine enhancement of human memory consolidation: interaction with arousal at encoding. *Neurobiol. Learn. Mem.* 79:194–98

Cahill L, Babinsky R, Markowitsch HJ, McGaugh JL. 1995. The amygdala and emotional memory. *Nature* 377:295–96

Cahill L, Gorski L, Le K. 2003. Enhanced human memory consolidation with post-learning stress: interaction with the degree of arousal at encoding. *Learn. Mem.* 10:270–74

Cahill L, Haier RJ, Fallon J, Alkire MT, Tang C, et al. 1996. Amygdala activity at encoding correlated with long-term, free recall of emotional information. *Proc. Natl. Acad. Sci. USA* 93:8016–21

Cahill L, Prins B, Weber M, McGaugh JL. 1994. Beta-adrenergic activation and memory for emotional events. *Nature* 371:702–4

Cahill L, Weinberger NM, Roozendaal B, McGaugh JL. 1999. Is the amygdala a locus of "conditioned fear"? Some questions and caveats. *Neuron* 23:227–28

Calder AJ, Lawrence AD, Young AW. 2001. Neuropsychology of fear and loathing. *Neuroscience* 2:352–63

Canli T, Zhao Z, Brewer J, Gabrieli JD, Cahill L. 2000. Event-related activation in the human amygdala associates with later memory for individual emotional experience. *J. Neurosci.* 20:RC99

Carrasco M. 2004. Covert transient attention increases contrast sensitivity and spatial resolution: support for signal enhancement. In *Neurobiology of Attention,* ed. L Itti, G Rees, J Tsotsos, pp. 442–47. San Diego, CA: Elsevier

Carrasco M, Penpeci-Talgar C, Eckstein M. 2000. Spatial covert attention increases contrast sensitivity across the CSF: support for signal enhancement. *Vis. Res.* 40:1203–15

Cherry EC. 1953. Some experiments on the recognition of speech, with one and two ears. *J. Acoust. Soc. Am.* 25:975–79

Chun MM, Potter MC. 1995. A two-stage model for multiple target detection in rapid serial visual presentation. *J. Exp. Psychol. Hum. Percept. Perform.* 21(1):109–27

Corbetta M, Shulman GL. 2002. Control of goal-directed and stimulus-driven attention in the brain. *Nat. Rev. Neurosci.* 3:201–15

Craik FIM, Govoni R, Naveh-Benjamin M, Anderson ND. 1996. The effects of divided attention on encoding and retrieval processes in human memory. *J. Exp. Psychol. Gen.* 125:159–80

Cunningham WA, Johnson MK, Raye CL, Chris Gatenby J, Gore JC, Banaji MR. 2004. Separable neural components in the processing of black and white faces. *Psychol. Sci.* 15(12):806–13

Davis M. 1992. The role of the amygdala in conditioned fear. In *The Amygdala: Neurobiological Aspects of Emotion, Memory and Mental Dysfunction,* ed. JP Aggleton, pp. 255–306. New York: Wiley-Liss

Davis M, Whalen PJ. 2001. The amygdala: vigilance and emotion. *Mol. Psychiatry* 6:13–34

de Gelder B, Snyder J, Greve D, Gerard G, Hadjikhani N. 2004. Fear fosters flight: a mechanism for fear contagion when perceiving emotion expressed by a whole body. *Proc. Natl. Acad. Sci. USA* 101:16701–6

de Gelder B, Vroomen J, Pourtois G, Weiskrantz L. 1999. Non-conscious recognition of affect in the absence of striate cortex. *Neuroreport* 10:3759–63

Delgado MR, Trujillo JL, Holmes B, Nearing KI, LeDoux JE, Phelps EA. 2004. *Emotion regulation of conditioned fear: the contributions of reappraisal.* Presented at Annu. Meet. Cogn. Neurosci. Soc., 11th, San Francisco

Dolcos F, LaBar KS, Cabeza R. 2004. Interaction between the amygdala and the medial temporal lobe memory system predicts better memory for emotional events. *Neuron* 42:855–63

Easterbrook JA. 1959. The effect of emotion on cue utilization and the organization of behavior. *Psychol. Rev.* 66(3):183–201

Eichenbaum H. 2002. *The Cognitive Neuroscience of Memory.* New York: Oxford Univ. Press

Ekman P, Friesen W. 1976. *Pictures of Facial Affect.* Palo Alto, CA: Consult. Psychol. Press

Esteves F, Dimberg U, Ohman A. 1994. Automatically elicited fear: conditioned skin conductance responses to masked facial stimuli. *Cogn. Emot.* 8:393–413

Everitt BJ, Cardinal RN, Parkinson JA, Robbins TW. 2003. Appetitive behavior: impact of amygdala-dependent mechanisms of emotional learning. *Ann. NY Acad. Sci.* 985:233–50

Fanselow MS, Poulos AM. 2005. The neuroscience of mammalian associative learning. *Annu. Rev. Psychol.* 56:207–34

Farah M. 1990. *Visual Agnosia: Disorders of Object Recognition and What They Tell Us About Normal Vision.* Cambridge, MA: MIT Press

Farah MJ, Wilson KD, Drain M, Tanaka JN. 1998. What is "special" about face perception? *Psychol. Rev.* 105(3):482–98

Fox E, Russo R, Bowles R, Dutton K. 2001. Do threatening stimuli draw or hold visual attention in subclinical anxiety? *J. Exp. Psychol. Gen.* 130(4):681–700

Freese JL, Amaral DG. 2005. The organization of projections from the amygdala to visual cortical areas TE and V1 in the Macaque monkey. *J. Comp. Neurol.* 486(4):295–317

Funayama ES, Grillon C, Davis M, Phelps EA.

2001. A double dissociation in the affective modulation of startle in humans: effects of unilateral temporal lobectomy. *J. Cogn. Neurosci.* 13:721–29

Gandhi SP, Heeger DJ, Boynton GM. 1999. Spatial attention affects brain activity in human primary visual cortex. *Proc. Natl. Acad. Sci. USA* 96:3314–19

Garcia R. 2002. Stress, synaptic plasticity, and psychopathology. *Rev. Neurosci.* 13:195–208

Gazzaniga MS, Irvy RB, Mangun GR. 2002. *Cognitive Neuroscience.* New York: Norton. 2nd ed.

Gross JJ. 2002. Emotion regulation: affective, cognitive, and social consequences. *Psychophysiology* 39:281–91

Hamann SB, Ely TD, Grafton ST, Kilts CD. 1999. Amygdala activity related to enhanced memory for pleasant and aversive stimuli. *Nat. Neurosci.* 2:289–93

Hansen CH, Hansen RD. 1988. Finding the face in the crowd: an anger superiority effect. *J. Personal. Soc. Psychol.* 54:917–24

Hart AJ, Whalen PJ, Shin LM, McInerney SC, Fischer H, Rauch SL. 2000. Differential response in the human amygdala to racial outgroup vs. ingroup face stimuli. *Neuroreport* 11(11):2351–55

Heberlein AS, Adolphs R. 2004. Impaired spontaneous anthropomorphizing despite intact perception and social knowledge. *Proc. Natl. Acad. Sci. USA* 101:7487–91

Heider F, Simmel M. 1944. An experimental study of apparent behavior. *Am. J. Psychol.* 57:243–59

Henson RN, Rugg MD, Shallice T, Josephs O, Dolan RA. 1999. Recollection and familiarity in recognition memory: an event-related functional magnetic resonance imaging study. *J. Neurosci.* 19:3962–72

Heuer F. Reisberg D. 1992. Emotion, arousal, and memory for detail. In *The Handbook of Emotion and Memory*, ed. S. Christianson, pp. 151–64. Hillsdale, NJ: Erlbaum

Holland PC, Gallagher M. 2004. Amygdalo-frontal interactions and reward expectancy. *Curr. Opin. Neurobiol.* 14:148–55

Hugdahl K, Ohman A. 1977. Effects of instruction acquisition and extinction of electrodermal responses to fear-relevant stimuli. *J. Exp. Psychol. Hum. Learn. Mem.* 3:608–18

James W. 1890. *The Principles of Psychology.* New York: Dover. 670 pp.

Johnsrude IS, Owen AM, White NM, Zhao WV, Bohbot V. 2000. Impaired preference conditioning after anterior temporal lobe resection in humans. *J. Neurosci.* 20:2649–56

Kanwisher N, McDermott J, Chun MM. 1997. The fusiform face area: a module in human extrastriate cortex specialized for face perception. *J. Neurosci.* 17(11):4302–11

Kapp BS, Whalen PJ, Supple WF, Pascoe JP. 1992. Amygdaloid contributions to conditioned arousal and sensory information processing. In *The Amygdala: Neurobiological Aspects of Emotion, Memory, and Mental Dysfunction*, ed. JP Aggleton, pp. 229–54. New York: Wiley-Liss

Kensinger EA, Corkin S. 2004. Two routes to emotional memory: distinct neural processes for valence and arousal. *Proc. Natl. Acad. Sci. USA* 101(9):3310–15

Kim H, Somerville LH, Johnstone T, Alexander AL, Whalen PJ. 2003. Inverse amygdala and medial prefrontal cortex responses to surprised faces. *Neuroreport* 14:2317–22

Kim H, Somerville LH, Johnstone T, Polis S, Alexander AL, et al. 2004. Contextual modulation of amygdala responsivity to surprised faces. *J. Cogn. Neurosci.* 16(10):1730–45

Kleinsmith LJ, Kaplan S. 1963. Paired-associate learning as a function of arousal and interpolated interval. *J. Exp. Psychol.* 65:190–93

Kluver H, Bucy PC. 1937. "Psychic blindness" and other symptoms following bilateral temporal lobectomy in rhesus monkeys. *Am. J. Physiol.* 119:352–53

Knowlton BJ, Fanselow MS. 1998. The hippocampus, consolidation and on-line memory. *Curr. Opin. Neurobiol.* 8(2):293–96

Kohler S, Crane J, Milner B. 2002. Differential contributions of the parahippocampal place area and the anterior hippocampus to human memory for scenes. *Hippocampus* 12:718–23

Kosslyn SM, Shin LM, Thompson WL, McNally PJ, Rauch SL, et al. 1996. Neural effects of visualizing and perceiving aversive stimuli: a PET investigation. *Neuroreport* 7:1569–76

LaBar KS, Gatenby JC, Gore JC, LeDoux JE, Phelps EA. 1998. Human amygdala activation during conditioned fear acquisition and extinction: a mixed-trial fMRI study. *Neuron* 20:937–45

LaBar KS, LeDoux JE, Spencer DD, Phelps EA. 1995. Impaired fear conditioning following unilateral temporal lobectomy in humans. *J. Neurosci.* 15:6846–55

LaBar KS, Phelps EA. 1998. Arousal-mediated memory consolidation: role of the medial temporal lobe in humans. *Psychol. Sci.* 9:490–93

Lachman R, Lachman JL, Butterfield EC. 1979. *Cognitive Psychology and Information Processing: An Introduction.* Hillsdale, NJ: Erlbaum

Lawrence AD, Calder AJ, McGowan SW, Grasby PM. 2002. Selective disruption of the recognition of facial expressions of anger. *Neuroreport* 13(6):881–84

Lazarus RS. 1984. On the primacy of cognition. *Am. Psychol.* 39(2):124–29

LeDoux JE. 1996. *The Emotional Brain.* New York: Simon & Schuster

Maren S. 2001. Neurobiology of Pavlovian fear conditioning. *Annu. Rev. Neurosci.* 24:897–931

McDonald AJ, Mascagni F, Guo L. 1996. Projections of the medial and lateral prefrontal cortices to the amygdala: a *Phaseolus vulgaris* leucoagglutinin study in the rat. *Neuroscience* 71:55–75

McEwen BS, Sapolsky RM. 1995. Stress and cognitive function. *Curr. Opin. Neurobiol.* 5(2):205–16

McGaugh JL. 2000. Memory—a century of consolidation. *Science* 287:248–51

McGaugh JL. 2002. Memory consolidation and the amygdala: a systems perspective. *Trends Neurosci.* 25:456

McGaugh JL. 2004. The amygdala modulates the consolidation of memories of emotionally arousing experiences. *Annu. Rev. Neurosci.* 27:1–28

Milad MR, Quirk GJ. 2002. Neurons in medial prefrontal cortex signal memory for fear extinction. *Nature* 420:70–74

Miller GA. 2003. The cognitive revolution: a historical perspective. *Trends Cogn. Sci.* 7:141–44

Morgan MA, LeDoux JE. 1995. Differential contribution of dorsal and ventral medial prefrontal cortex to the acquisition and extinction of conditioned fear in rats. *Behav. Neurosci.* 109:681–88

Morgan MA, Romanski LM, LeDoux JE. 1993. Extinction of emotional learning: contribution of medial prefrontal cortex. *Neurosci. Lett.* 163:109–13

Morris JS, Friston KJ, Buchel C, Frith CD, Young AW, et al. 1998a. A neuromodulatory role for the human amygdala in processing emotional facial expressions. *Brain* 121 (Pt. 1):47–57

Morris JS, Ohman A, Dolan RJ. 1998b. Conscious and unconscious emotional learning in the human amygdala. *Nature* 393:467–70

Myers KM, Davis M. 2002. Behavioral and neural analysis of extinction. *Neuron* 36:567–84

Neisser U. 1976. *Cognition and Reality: Principles and Implications of Cognitive Psychology.* New York: Freeman

Neisser U, Harsch N. 1992. Phantom flashbulbs: false recollections of hearing news about the Challenger. In *Affect and Accuracy in Recall: Studies of "Flashbulb" Memories,* ed. E Winograd, U Neisser, pp. 9–31. London: Cambridge Univ. Press

Niendenthal PM, Kitayama S. 1994. *The Heart's Eye: Emotional Influences in Perception and Attention.* San Diego, CA: Academic

Ochsner KN. 2000. Are affective events richly recollected or simply familiar? The experience and process of recognizing feelings past. *J. Exp. Psychol. Gen.* 129(2):242–61

Ochsner KN, Bunge SA, Gross JJ, Gabrieli JD. 2002. Rethinking feelings: an fMRI study of the cognitive regulation of emotion. *J. Cogn. Neurosci.* 14:1215–29

Ohman A, Flykt A, Esteves F. 2001. Emotion drives attention: detecting a snake in the grass. *J. Exp. Psychol.: Gen.* 127:69–82

Ohman A, Mineka S. 2001. Fears, phobias, and preparedness: toward an evolved module of fear and fear learning. *Psychol. Rev.* 108:483–522

Olsson A, Nearing K, Zheng J, Phelps EA. 2004. *Learning by observing: neural correlates of fear learning through social observation.* Presented at Annu. Meet. Cogn. Neurosci. Soc., 11th, San Francisco

Olsson A, Phelps EA. 2004. Learned fear of "unseen" faces after Pavlovian, observational, and instructed fear. *Psychol. Sci.* 15(12):822–28

Packard MG, Teather LA. 1998. Amygdala modulation of multiple memory systems: hippocampus and caudate-putamen. *Neurobiol. Learn. Mem.* 69:163–203

Pessoa L, McKenna M, Gutierrez E, Ungerleider LG. 2002. Neural processing of emotional faces requires attention. *Proc. Natl. Acad. Sci. USA* 99:11458–63

Phelps EA. 2004. The human amygdala and awareness: interaction of the amygdala and hippocampal complex. *Curr. Opin. Neurobiol.* 14:198–202

Phelps EA, Delgado MR, Nearing KI, LeDoux JE. 2004. Extinction learning in humans: role of the amygdala and vmPFC. *Neuron* 43:897–905

Phelps EA, LaBar KS, Anderson A, O'Connor KJ, Fulbright RK, Spencer DD. 1998. Specifying the contributions of the human amygdala to emotional memory: a case study. *Neurocase* 4:527–40

Phelps EA, Ling S, Carrasco M. 2005. Emotion facilitates perception and potentiates the perceptual benefit of attention. *Psychol. Sci.* In press

Phelps EA, O'Connor KJ, Cunningham WA, Funayama ES, Gatenby JC, et al. 2000.

Performance on indirect measures of race evaluation predicts amygdala activation. *J. Cogn. Neurosci.* 12:729–38

Phelps EA, O'Connor KJ, Gatenby JC, Gore JC, Grillon C, Davis M. 2001. Activation of the left amygdala to a cognitive representation of fear. *Nat. Neurosci.* 4:437–41

Pratto F, John OP. 1991. Automatic vigilance: the attention-grabbing power of negative social information. *J. Personal. Soc. Psychol.* 61(3):380–91

Quirk GJ, Russo GK, Barron JL, Lebron K. 2000. The role of ventromedial prefrontal cortex in the recovery of extinguished fear. *J. Neurosci.* 20:6225–31

Raymond JE, Shapiro KL, Arnell KM. 1992. Temporary suppression of visual processing in an RSVP task: an attentional blink? *J. Exp. Psychol.: Hum. Percept. Perform.* 18:849–60

Rolls ET. 2000. Memory systems in the brain. *Annu. Rev. Psychol.* 51:599–630

Romanski LM, LeDoux JE. 1992. Equipotentiality of thalamo-amygdala and thalamo-cortico-amygdala circuits in auditory fear conditioning. *J. Neurosci.* 12:4501–9

Russell JA, Barrett LF. 1999. Core affect, prototypical emotional episodes, and other things called emotion: dissecting the elephant. *J. Personal. Soc. Psychol.* 69:379–99

Schaefer SM, Jackson DC, Davidson RJ, Aguirre GK, Kimberg DY, Thompson-Schill SL. 2002. Modulation of amygdalar activity by the conscious regulation of negative emotion. *J. Cogn. Neurosci.* 14:913–21

Scherer KR. 2000. Psychological models of emotion. In *The Neuropsychology of Emotion.* ed. JC Borod, pp. 137–62. New York: Oxford Univ. Press

Schmolck H, Buffalo EA, Squire LR. 2000. Memory for distortions develop over time: recollections of the O.J. Simpson trial verdict after 15 and 32 months. *Psychol. Sci.* 11:39–45

Schultz W. 2006. Behavioral theories and the neurophysiology of reward. *Annu. Rev. Psychol.* 57:87–115

Sharot T, Delgado MR. Phelps EA. 2004. How emotion enhances the feeling of remembering. *Nat. Neurosci.* 7:1376–80

Sharot T, Phelps EA. 2004. How arousal modulates memory: disentangling the effects of attention and retention. *Cogn. Affect. Behav. Neurosci.* 4:294–306

Shors T. 2006. Stressful experience and learning across the lifespan. *Annu. Rev. Psychol.* 57:55–85

Smith EE, Jonides J. 1999. Storage and executive processes in the frontal lobes. *Science* 283:1657–61

Squire LR, Zola-Morgan S. 1991. The medial temporal lobe memory system. *Science* 253(5026):1380–86

Stefanacci L, Amaral DG. 2002. Some observations in cortical inputs to the macaque monkey amygdala: an anterograde tracing study. *J. Comp. Neurol.* 451:301–23

Stefanacci L, Suzuki WA, Amaral DG. 1996. Organization of connections between the amygdaloid complex and the perirhinal and parahippocampal cortices in macaque monkeys. *J. Comp. Neurol.* 375(4):552–82

Stuss DT, Levine B. 2002. Adult clinical neuropsychology: lessons from studies of the frontal lobes. *Annu. Rev. Psychol.* 53:401–33

Talarico JM, Rubin DC. 2003. Confidence, not consistency, characterizes flashbulb memories. *Psychol. Sci.* 14:455–61

Tarr MJ, Gauthier I. 2000. FFA: a flexible fusiform area for subordinate-level visual processing automatized by expertise. *Nat. Neurosci.* 3(8):764–69

Vuilleumier P, Armony JL, Driver J, Dolan RJ. 2001. Effects of attention and emotion on face processing in the human brain: an event-related fMRI study. *Neuron* 30:829–41

Vuilleumier P, Richardson MP, Armony JL, Driver J, Dolan RJ. 2004. Distant influences of amygdala lesion on visual cortical activation during emotional face processing. *Nat. Neurosci.* 7:1271–78

Weinberger NM. 1995. Retuning the brain by fear conditioning. In *The Cognitive Neurosciences,* ed. MS Gazzaniga, pp. 1071–90. Cambridge, MA: MIT Press

Weiskrantz L. 1956. Behavioral changes associated with ablation of the amygdaloid complex in monkeys. *J. Comp. Physiol. Psychol.* 49:381–91

Whalen PJ. 1998. Fear, vigilance, and ambiguity: initial neuroimaging studies of the human amygdala. *Curr. Dir. Psychol. Sci.* 7:177–88

Whalen PJ, Kagan J, Cook RG, Davis FC, Kim H, et al. 2004. Human amygdala responsivity to masked fearful eye whites. *Science* 306:2061

Whalen PJ, Rauch SL, Etcoff NL, McInerney SC, Lee MB, Jenike MA. 1998. Masked presentations of emotional facial expressions modulate amygdala activity without explicit knowledge. *J. Neurosci.* 18:411–18

Whalen PJ, Shin LM, McInerney SC, Fischer H, Wright CI, Rauch SL. 2001. A functional MRI study of human amygdala responses to facial expressions of fear versus anger. *Emotion* 1(1):70–83

Wheeler ME, Buckner RL. 2004. Functional-anatomic correlates of remembering and knowing. *Neuroimage* 21:1337–49

Wheeler ME, Fiske ST. 2004. Controlling racial prejudice: Social-cognitive goals affect amygdala and stereotype activation. *Psychol. Sci.* 16:56–63

Winston JS, Strange BA, O'Doherty J, Dolan RJ. 2002. Automatic and intentional brain responses during evaluation of trustworthiness of faces. *Nat. Neurosci.* 5:277–83

Yonelinas AP. 2002. The nature of recollection and familiarity: a review of 30 years of research. *J. Mem. Lang.* 46:441–517

Young MP, Scannell JW, Burns GA, Blakemore C. 1994. Analysis of connectivity: neural systems in the cerebral cortex. *Rev. Neurosci.* 5:227–50

Zajonc RB. 1984. On the primacy of affect. *Am. Psychol.* 39:117–23

Annu. Rev. Psychol. 2006. 57:55–85
doi: 10.1146/annurev.psych.57.102904.190205
Copyright © 2006 by Annual Reviews. All rights reserved
First published online as a Review in Advance on September 16, 2005

STRESSFUL EXPERIENCE AND LEARNING ACROSS THE LIFESPAN

Tracey J. Shors

Department of Psychology, Center for Collaborative Neuroscience, Rutgers University, Piscataway, New Jersey 08854; email: shors@rci.rutgers.edu

Key Words   memory, sex differences, neurogenesis, hippocampus, amygdala

■ **Abstract**   It is usually assumed that stressful life events interfere with our ability to acquire new information. However, many studies suggest that stressful experience can enhance processes involved in learning. The types of learning that are enhanced after stressful experiences include classical fear and eyeblink conditioning, as well as processes related to learning about threatening stimuli. Stressful life experiences do seem to interfere with processes involved in memory, often expressed as deficits in the retention or retrieval of information that was acquired prior to and was unrelated to the stressful experience. The trends are limited, as are their implications, because most studies examine adult males, yet the effects of stress on learning processes are influenced by age and sex differences. With respect to mechanisms and anatomical substrates, the effects of stress on learning are usually dependent on the action of stress hormones in combination with neuronal activities within the hippocampus, amygdala, the bed nucleus of the stria terminalis, and the prefrontal cortex.

CONTENTS

0066-4308/06/0110-0055$20.00

INTRODUCTION

The effects of acute stressful experience on subsequent learning are diverse and vary in their direction, strength, and occurrence. The variability in the types of responses is attributable, at least in part, to organismal properties, such as age, sex differences, and species. The responses are also dependent on the types of stressful events that occur, the length and intensity of those experiences, and finally, on the type of learning that is assessed. Because of this, there is no consistent or simple relationship between stress and learning. In this review, the effects of stressful experience on learning abilities in human and nonhuman animals are reviewed. Changes that occur across the lifespan are highlighted, as are effects that differ between males and females. Finally, the brain substrates and neuronal mechanisms that underlie the effects of stress on learning are assessed, with an emphasis on glucocorticoids and changes that occur within the hippocampus, amygdala, bed nucleus of the stria terminalis, and prefrontal cortex.

STRESS EFFECTS ON PROCESSES OF LEARNING AND MEMORY

The Effects of Acute Traumatic Stress on Learning and Memory in Humans

It is understandable that there would be numerous types of effects of stress on learning because there are so many types of stressful events that animals can experience in their lives. In humans, the effect of two types of stressful experience are most often studied—those that occur naturally during a severe trauma or those that are experimentally induced and often are not as stressful, such as public speaking or social interaction. The effects of traumatic experience on processes involved in learning abilities are discussed first. According to the *Diagnostic and Statistical Manual of Mental Disorders* (*DSM-IV-TR*; Am. Psychiatric Assoc. 2000), a traumatic stressor is an event that includes "actual or threatened death or serious injury, or other threat to one's physical integrity or others." Traumatic events include military combat, violent personal assault, being kidnapped, being taken hostage, terrorist attack, torture, incarceration as a prisoner of war or in a concentration camp, natural or manmade disasters, severe automobile accidents, or being diagnosed with a life-threatening illness. The ways in which traumatic stress can affect learning processes tend to fall into three categories: the learning abilities that exist before and during the traumatic experience (i.e., intelligence), memory processes that are affected during the experience itself (memory for the trauma and related stimuli), and the more incidental effects of the trauma on subsequent learning abilities.

There have been numerous reports that intelligence and general learning abilities at the time of trauma can predict whether a person will develop the pathological symptoms associated with posttraumatic stress disorder (PTSD) (Buckley 2000). In particular, several studies have reported a negative correlation between intelligence and the likelihood that a person will develop PTSD, such that war veterans with low IQ are more likely to develop symptoms of PTSD (Pitman et al. 1991). In one study, veterans from Operation Desert Storm were subjected to tests of attention, verbal memory, and visuospatial memory after returning home from the war (Vasterling et al. 1997). There was no relationship between PTSD and attention, but those that developed PTSD were more likely to have low scores on tests of verbal memory, which is thought to represent a more crystallized form of intelligence. This relationship between verbal memory and PTSD was apparently not affected by the amount or severity of the trauma but instead was a reflection of the degree of verbal memory skills prior to combat exposure. Thus, the data suggest that pretrauma abilities predict how the stressful event will affect future abilities, some of which include processes involved in learning and memory.

Several attempts have been made to directly assess associative learning in humans who have been exposed to a traumatic life event. One of the most common procedures involves classical eyeblink conditioning. In the standard paradigm, a human is presented with an airpuff to the eye, which elicits an eyeblink as an unconditioned response (UR). When the airpuff is immediately preceded by an auditory stimulus as the conditioned stimulus (CS), humans learn the association between the tone and the airpuff and blink in response to the tone, in anticipation of the airpuff. This blink is the conditioned response (CR) and is used as an indirect measure of learning. Performance of this task has been assessed in patients that have experienced trauma, and at least one study reports deficits in conditioning (Ayers et al. 2003). Interestingly, the deficits occurred in groups that experienced trauma associated with combat, irrespective of whether they suffered from PTSD, although medication may have contributed to the deficits. Aside from this effect, there are few demonstrations that learning per se is impaired by traumatic experience. Rather, it appears that processes involved in memory recall and retrieval are more vulnerable. For example, veterans with PTSD were able to acquire new information at the time of encoding; however, when asked to recall that information later, they expressed deficits (Yehuda et al. 1995). These effects of trauma on memory function are not limited to war stress but extend to other stressors such as childhood abuse (Bremner et al. 1995).

In the studies discussed thus far, the stimuli embedded in the learning tasks were unrelated or at least not directly associated with the trauma itself, yet humans react to stimuli that are related to stressful events differently than they react to stimuli that are unrelated to the stressful event. Some studies find that PTSD patients respond to threatening stimuli faster than to unthreatening stimuli (Bryant & Harvey 1995, 1997), although others suggest no bias exists (Trandel & McNally 1987). One of the more popular methods of assessing information processing after a stressful experience is a modified Stroop test, in which people are presented with words that are either threatening or neutral. The words are presented in colors, and the subject is asked to name the color of the word. In one study, rape victims with PTSD responded slower when naming the color of rape-related words than when naming neutral words; this bias did not occur in rape victims without PTSD or in women that had not been raped (Foa et al. 1991). This delayed recall of threat words has also been observed in patients that were victims of motor vehicle accidents and combat (Bryant & Harvey 1995). Thus, these studies suggest that humans respond to the cues related to trauma at a slower rate than to cues that are unrelated to trauma. These findings can be interpreted in at least one of two ways; one is that the victims are avoiding the threatening stimuli, which retards their response. The other is that the victims are paying more attention to the threat-related cues, which retards their response. Most studies seem to support the later explanation. In an implicit memory test, PTSD subjects showed a facilitated response for the threatening words, which suggests that the words had been encoded correctly and perhaps even in a facilitated manner at the time of training (Kaspi et al. 1995).

The Effects of Acute Social Stress on Learning and Memory in Humans

The relationship between stress and learning in humans that suffer from PTSD is complex and not easily summarized. It is also critical to note that most humans who experience severe trauma recover completely and do not suffer the consequences of PTSD (Bonanno 2004, McNally 2003). As such, an analysis of patients with mental disorders may not reveal the natural relationship between stress and learning. Minimally, the effects of stress on learning and memory in healthy humans must be considered. That said, it is difficult to study the effects of stress on learning in humans that are not victims of trauma. Some studies have used aversive stimuli such as shocks to induce stress in humans, but the practice is infrequent; more importantly, the degree of stress induced by mild shock is much different from that during trauma such as rape or combat. Often, anticipation of shock is used, as well as more benign experiences of public speaking, social interaction, and exposure to arousing pictures. A sample of findings from these types of manipulations is presented.

The effects of stressful experience on classical conditioning have been examined in humans. In one study, participants were exposed to emotionally arousing photographs that depicted pleasant, neutral, or unpleasant scenes. The participants were then classically conditioned using an eyeblink response as the measure of performance (Grillon & Hill 2003). In general, their responses were unaffected. However, about 50 years ago, Spence and colleagues conducted a series of studies in which they manipulated anxiety or took advantage of endogenous differences and measured performance during eyelid conditioning. In general, they found that greater degrees of anxiety were associated with increases in performance and that emotionally responsive subjects emitted more learned responses (Spence & Beecroft 1954, Spence & Goldstein 1961, Spence & Taylor 1951). Thus, if anything, arousing and stressful situations seem to enhance performance during classical conditioning.

A commonly used stressor in human studies is the Trier Social Stress Test, in which humans are asked to organize and perform a five-minute speech in front of observers while being videotaped. They are then asked to conduct several minutes of mental arithmetic. In one study, adult men were exposed to a list of words and then asked to perform the speech and the mental arithmetic tasks. After the stressful experience, the men were unable to recall as many emotionally arousing words as those who did not experience social stress (Kuhlmann et al. 2005). There was no effect of the stressful experience on cued recall, working memory, or attention. In another study, exposure to the stressful event was associated with poor recognition of pleasant, but not unpleasant, words; recall was unaffected (Domes et al. 2004). Studies using public speaking as a stressor have presented mixed results. In one study, there was no effect of public speaking on performance about 30 minutes later when using such measures as verbal learning, digit memory spans, and recall. Similarly, there was no effect on learning or recall of words presented either before or after a psychosocial stressor (Wolf et al. 2002). Others find enhanced performance after public speaking. For example, one study found that public speaking increased performance during a dichotic listening test, in which subjects were instructed to attend to the presentation of auditory stimuli delivered to one ear versus the other (Al'Absi et al. 2002). The effect size was not large, but most of the effects of public speaking stress are not. It would be surprising if the effects were large, since dramatic changes in learning abilities in response to minor fluctuations in the stress response would not be very adaptive.

The effects of stress on memory in nonpatient populations seem to depend on not only the quality and intensity of the stressful experience but also on what is asked to be remembered. Using a more intense stressor than public speaking, Cahill and colleagues have reported some interesting findings (Cahill et al. 2003). Participants first were exposed to slides that were emotionally arousing or neutral. Immediately afterward, they were asked to immerse their arm in a bucket of ice-cold water for several minutes. This type of stressor is perceived as very aversive and elicits robust increases in stress hormones, such as cortisol. One week after the stressful event, the participants were asked to recall the pictures that they had seen prior to the stressor. Those that experienced the stressor recalled more of the arousing pictures and in greater detail than did those that did not experience the stressor. The acute stressor did not affect the recall of neutral words. Thus, exposure to a relatively intense stressful experience in humans was associated with enhanced recall of information that was arousing in nature. These results are perhaps similar to those observed in humans with PTSD, who tend to express a bias toward remembering stimuli that are threatening and/or related to the traumatic event from which they suffered.

The Effects of Acute Stress on Learning and Memory in Nonhuman Animals

The effects of a stressful experience on learning processes in nonhuman animals are most often studied in one of two ways. The first is considered an acute stressful event and often consists of brief shocks or swimming for tens of minutes. The second is a more chronic stressful event, usually consisting of hours of restraint each day for several weeks. Other procedures include naturalistic stressors such as predator odors and social dominance manipulations, again under acute and chronic situations, respectively. The effects of stressful experience on learning in laboratory animals, as in humans, are assessed at different times, sometimes during the acquisition of new information but most often during the recall or retrieval of memories that were acquired prior to the stressful event.

The most well-known and investigated stress/learning phenomenon is that of learned helplessness (Overmier & Seligman 1967, Seligman & Maier 1967). In this manipulation, animals are exposed to a series of shocks, typically footshocks, from which they can learn to escape. A yoked control animal is exposed to the same amount and numbers of shocks but cannot escape. Thus, in this manipulation, two animals are exposed to shocks, but one animal learns to control the amount of stress that it receives and is therefore considered to have established control over the stressful events. With this type of stressor, it has been shown that animals that cannot establish control over the shock are impaired in their ability to learn to escape a shock in another task. For example, during the stressful event manipulation, one animal would learn to escape a shock by running once through a door to the other side of a shuttle box (Figure 1A). A yoked control animal would not be able

---

Figure 1   The effects of controllable versus uncontrollable stress on "learning" depend on what the animal can learn. (A) Adult male rats were trained each day for seven days (d1–d7) on an operant conditioning task in which they could learn to escape from a mild footshock. The graph to the left shows response times (mean latency in seconds ± SEM) for rats that could escape. These rats were yoked to animals that could not escape but were nonetheless exposed to the same amounts of shocks. One day after this manipulation, all animals were trained on a similar task except that they had to cross the shuttle box twice in order to terminate the shocks. The new task was also conducted in a new context. As shown, those that were exposed to the inescapable stress in the first phase did not learn to escape in the second phase of training, whereas those that were exposed to the escapable stress rapidly learned to escape (Shors et al. 2005). Rats that were not pretrained on the escape task (*No Stress*) performed moderately well, but not as well as those that learned to escape. Asterisk denotes a significant change in response relative to the response from the No Stress group. (B) As represented in Figure 1A, adult male rats were trained each day for seven days (d1–d7) on an operant conditioning task in which they could learn to escape from a mild footshock. The graph on the left shows response times (mean latency in seconds ± SEM) for rats that could escape. These rats were yoked to animals that could not escape but were nonetheless exposed to the same amounts of shocks. One day after this manipulation, all animals were trained with a classical eyeblink conditioning task using a trace paradigm in which the conditioned stimulus and the unconditioned stimulus are separated slightly in time (500 ms). The graph on the right shows the percentage of conditioned responses in all groups, including a group of animals that were not exposed to the escape training. Only the animals exposed to the uncontrollable stress responded differently, and they responded with a greater percentage of conditioned responses (Leuner et al. 2004b). Asterisk denotes a significant change in response relative to the response from the No Stress group.

A) Controllability and operant conditioning

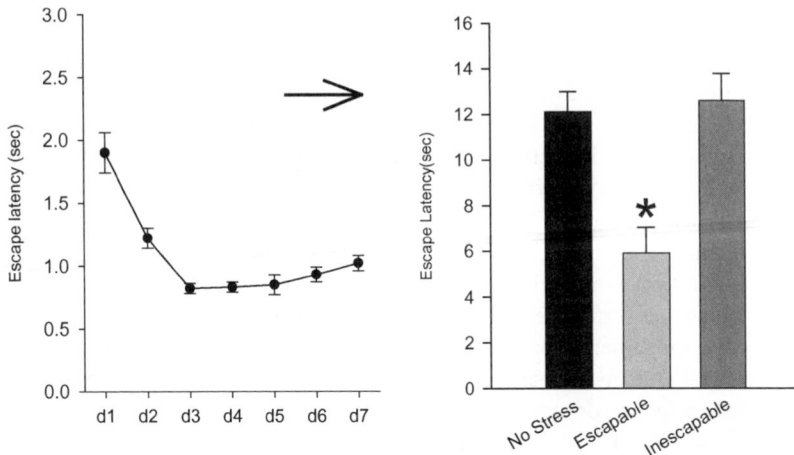

B) Controllability and classical conditioning

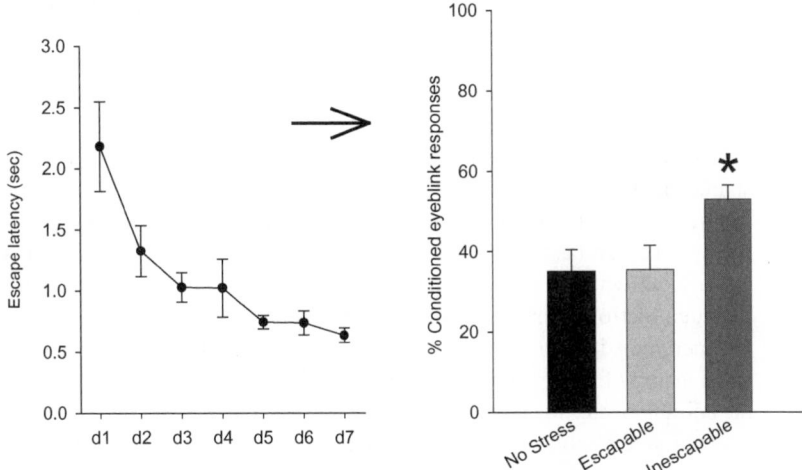

to escape but would be exposed to the same amount of stress as the escapable stress animal. Subsequently, both animals would be trained in a new context on a task in which they could learn to escape a shock by running back and forth across a shuttle box. The animal that had learned to escape by running through the door rapidly learns to run back through the door and escape the shock. The animal that learned that escape was not possible would not move as much upon exposure to the new learning situation and thus would not learn to escape (Figure 1A). This effect of not learning to escape after being exposed to inescapable stress is termed "learned helplessness" and has been associated with a number of negative symptoms in humans such as passivity, sleeping and eating disturbances, and depressive-like behavior. The important point is that the animals exposed to the uncontrollable stress learn that their responses are ineffectual.

There has been much discussion about learned helplessness and whether it represents a deficit in learning or performance (Maier & Jackson 1979, Minor et al. 1991). It is certainly the case that animals that cannot learn to escape are impaired later on a task in which escape is possible (Figure 1A). It is also the case that they do not move much when being trained because they learned that movement did not alleviate the shock. This is in part why the failure to learn is called "learned helplessness": Animals exposed to the inescapable shock have "learned" to be helpless. Interestingly, animals exposed to inescapable stress show enhanced learning (or at least performance) during training on other tasks that are not as dependent on overt movement. For example, male rats that are exposed to inescapable stressful events emit more learned responses during classical conditioning using either a fear response or eyeblinks as the dependent measure (Figure 1B) (Leuner et al. 2004b, Maier 1990). Neither of these types of conditioning is affected by exposure to the same amount of escapable stress. This combination of findings illustrates the futility of identifying one type of stress effect on learning. Clearly, exposure to the very same type of stressful experience, in this case inescapable footshocks, can either impair or enhance performance during various learning tasks. Minimally, the effects of stress on learning depend on what the animal is asked to learn and what it learned before.

The other type of learning that is studied frequently in laboratory animals is spatial navigation and memory for locations in space. This type of learning is frequently measured using two types of tasks, the Morris water maze task and the radial maze task. In the Morris water maze, an animal is placed in a pool of water from which it cannot escape. As it explores, the animal eventually locates a hidden platform just under the surface of the water. After reaching the platform and perching itself there, the animal learns its location by learning the spatial relationship of cues around the outside of the maze. Upon reentry into the maze, the animal locates the platform using those cues and the way in which the platform is positioned relative to its location. This task has been used extensively because it is dependent on the hippocampus, a brain structure involved in learning and one that possesses cells that are specialized to encode spatial location (Riedel et al. 1999). It is also a useful and relatively easy task for assessing performance and learning in rodents. The effects of stress on this type of learning are somewhat varied and depend on the type of stressor, but even more so on when the stressor is experienced. For example, animals that are exposed to a stressful event of brief intermittent tailshocks learn to navigate in the Morris water maze and do so at the same rate as animals that are unstressed (Kim et al. 2005). There are also examples of enhanced learning in the Morris water maze after a stressful experience. For example, male rats learn faster after having had a stressful aggressive encounter with another male (Buwalda et al. 2005). However, stressed animals can express deficits later in their ability to recall where the platform was located (Kim et al.

2005). Similarly, if animals are exposed to brief shocks after they are trained in the Morris water maze, they express a memory deficit for the platform location (de Quervain et al. 1998). Interestingly, this effect is time limited since the deficit occurred only in animals that were exposed to the stressor 30 minutes before the retention test and not in those that were stressed two minutes or four hours before. In the end, the effects of stress on performance in the Morris water maze are mixed: In general, exposure to a stressful event tends to impair retention and/or retrieval but not learning per se.

In addition to the Morris water maze, a land maze with arms radiating from the center is used. In this task, the rat is food deprived and is given the opportunity to locate food pellets in the arms of the maze. The most efficient strategy is to enter an arm once and not again after the food has been consumed. In the typical eight-arm radial maze, animals use spatial cues in the room to remember which arms they have already entered. In one study, animals were exposed to brief intermittent tailshocks and trained in the radial maze task 24 hours later (Shors & Dryver 1992). Although the stressed animals did accrue more errors (reentries into arms that had already been debaited), a closer analysis of the data revealed that the stressed animals did know the spatial locations of the food pellets; they were simply taking the pellets to a safe arm (their first arm entry) and consuming the food there instead of in a novel location. This type of strategy is consistent with how animals might behave in a naturalistic situation after confrontation with a predator or a potential threat. Eventually, they would need to venture out to obtain food, but would likely consume it in a location that that was not associated with that threat. Therefore, in this instance, what looks to be a learning deficit is likely not one, but rather an adaptive response to a threatening stimulus event. For other types of stressors, such as restraint, the results are mixed. After 7 days consisting of hours of restraint each day, the behavior of animals in the radial maze is unaffected, whereas after 13 days, they seem to perform better, and after 21 days, they accrue more errors (Luine et al. 1996). Finally, there are reports that stress can specifically alter learning that is dependent on the hippocampus but not learning that is independent of the structure. For example, exposure to a predator after training reduced performance in a working-memory version of the radial maze task (Woodson et al. 2003). Again, most studies find that a stressful experience is associated with deficits in the retrieval of information but not deficits in learning itself.

It is most often assumed that stress has a negative impact on learning processes. But as shown above, the negative effects tend to occur upon retrieval of information that has already been learned, with relatively few demonstrations that stress impairs learning itself. What about the effects that stress has on new learning? Some investigators report enhancements, at least in adult male animals. For example, two hours of restraint stress as well as the more chronic experience of hours each day for 21 days enhanced the amount of conditioned fear that animals expressed toward the context (Conrad 1999, Cordero et al. 2003). There are also reports that exposure to inescapable stressful events enhances the conditioning of fine motor responses such as the eyeblink response (Figure 2) (Shors et al. 1992).

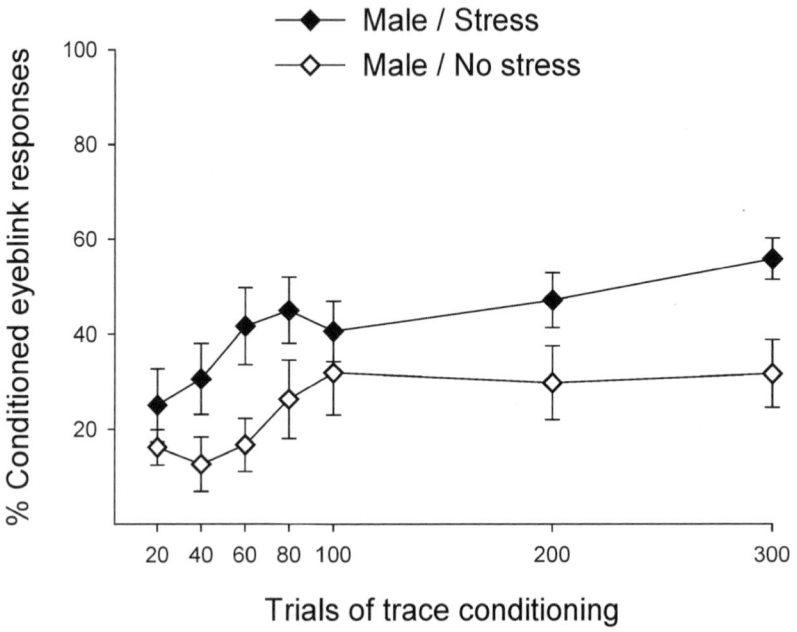

Figure 2   Exposure to an acute stressful event enhances subsequent responses to an associative learning task. Adult male rats were exposed to an acute stressor of brief, low-intensity tailshocks over 30 minutes and were trained 24 hours later on the classically conditioned eyeblink task. The trace paradigm was used, which consisted of a white-noise conditioned stimulus (CS) that predicted the occurrence of an eyelid stimulation unconditioned stimulus (US). The CS and US were separated by a 500-ms trace interval. Rats exposed to the stressor emitted a greater percentage of conditioned responses (eyeblink responses during the trace interval) to the CS than did animals that were not exposed to the stressful event (Hodes & Shors 2005a).

The enhanced effect of stress occurs under numerous conditions, stressors, and paradigms. For example, the enhancement occurs in response to brief intermittent tailshocks and swim stress (Shors 2001). It occurs during training on tasks that are dependent on the hippocampus, such as trace conditioning, as well as during training on tasks that are not dependent on the hippocampus. The effect has a protracted time course in that the increase in performance is evident immediately after exposure to the stressful event but also persists for days. To be specific, if an animal is exposed to the stressful event and then placed in its home cage for a day or two, it will emit more conditioned responses upon exposure to the new training situation (Shors & Servatius 1997). This effect appears to be related to the initial acquisition and not to the retention or performance of the conditioned response since exposure to the stressor during training does not alter the expression of the conditioned response (Shors 2001) or the magnitude of the unconditioned response (Servatius et al. 2001). In some studies, the rate of acquisition is increased, and in most, asymptotic performance is also enhanced. Thus, it cannot be stated with certainty that this phenomenon represents a learning effect, although the data are certainly suggestive. Finally, and as noted previously, the effect is dependent on the absence of control, because conditioning in animals that can learn to control the stress is unaffected, whereas conditioning in animals that cannot establish control is enhanced (Figure 1*B*) (Leuner et al. 2004b).

STRESS AND LEARNING AS A FUNCTION OF AGE AND SEX DIFFERENCES

Sex Differences in Stress Effects on Learning

The effects reported up to this point are primarily those of adult males and suggest that, if anything, stressful experience tends to enhance new learning but reduces performance at the time of memory retrieval. In other words, if the stressful event occurs before the acquisition of new information, the learning is either unaffected or enhanced. However, if the stressful experience occurs after the information has been acquired, the retrieval of that information can be disrupted, and performance is oftentimes impaired. These findings suggest that negative effects of stress may be confined to disrupting information that has already been encoded. However, some studies suggest that stress can impair learning and that memory can be enhanced by stress (Nielson et al. 2005). Many of these reports, interestingly enough, involve differences that arise either because of gender or because of age.

Some years ago now, we reported sex differences in how animals respond to stress. As described, males that are exposed to the uncontrollable stressors of either brief intermittent tailshocks or swim stress tend to outperform males that are unstressed. Females, on the other hand, show the opposite pattern (Wood & Shors 1998). Thus, upon exposure to the same uncontrollable stressful events, their ability to acquire the classically conditioned eyeblink response is compromised. This effect, like that in male animals, is dependent on the absence of control; conditioning in females that could learn to control the shock during escape training is unaffected (Leuner et al. 2004b). Also like the effect in males, the effect in females is evident during training on the hippocampal-dependent task of trace conditioning as well as the hippocampal-independent task of delay conditioning. In summary, the effects of a stressful experience on new learning are very different in males versus females, and in some cases, the effects are opposite.

How general is this phenomenon, and does it apply to other types of conditioning or learning situations? This question is difficult to address because many of the tasks that are used rely on exploratory behavior, which has different patterns in male animals than in females. Some studies find that females are more exploratory than are males after being exposed to shocks, are more likely to enter a compartment where they were previously shocked, and are less likely to freeze in a context previously associated with shock (Beatty 1979, Maren et al. 1994, Shors 1998). Thus, a stressful experience can alter behaviors differently in males than in females. In fact, it was reported decades ago that females did not express helplessness behavior (Kirk & Blampied 1985, Steenbergen et al. 1989). Females were trained to either escape a footshock or they could not escape. They were then trained on a task in which they could escape the shocks. As noted earlier, male rats that learn they cannot escape do not learn the new task very well. Females, on the other hand, move more than males do after they have been exposed to inescapable shocks. When they encounter the new learning situation involving escape, they move and consequently learn, or are not as impaired as males are. It is difficult in the end to know whether these findings represent learning effects or differences in performance that nonetheless affect the expression of learned responses.

Acute Stressful Experience and Learning from Gestation Through Puberty

Most humans experience stressful events throughout their lives, but those that occur during pregnancy are a concern not only for the mother but also for the offspring. Surprisingly, only a few studies have found that stress during pregnancy has consequences for learning in the offspring once they become adults. In one study, pregnant female rats were restrained daily for one week before giving birth. Apparently, the male offspring expressed more latent inhibition as adults (Bethus et al. 2005). Interestingly, the investigators found no effect of the stressful experience on latent inhibition in females. Another study found that prenatal stress increases fear conditioning in male rats as adults (Griffen et al. 2003). Many more studies have been directed at the period immediately after birth, usually by manipulating contact with the mother (Levine et al. 1956). Typically, the offspring are removed from their mothers, often for hours each day; a control group is not removed. Their responses to learning opportunities are assessed in adulthood. Overall, the data suggest that male rats are more vulnerable than are females to this manipulation. Male offspring that were separated from their mothers on gestational day nine showed enhanced learning during an active avoidance task and a spatial water maze task as adults (Lehmann et al. 1999). Females were unaffected. Others have found that stress during the juvenile period can alter learning abilities, at least in males. For example, animals that were stressed chronically for four weeks expressed a deficit in performance in the spatial water maze task as adults (Isgor et al. 2004). In another study, male rats that were isolated from other rats between 15–21 days after birth emitted more errors in a working memory task as adults (Sandstrom & Hart 2005). In yet another study, monkeys were socially isolated for brief periods during early development (postnatal weeks 17–27) and then tested as adults (Parker et al. 2005). The monkeys that had been isolated and therefore stressed during development made fewer errors using a response-inhibition testing paradigm. Most intriguing are the additive effects of multiple stressors on new learning. In one study, rats were exposed to a stressful event as juveniles and then again as adults. The ones that were exposed to both stressful events outperformed those that were exposed to just one stressful event in their lives. However, those that were exposed to two stressors as adults were not as affected as were those exposed to one stressor as juveniles and one as adults (Avital & Richter-Levin 2005). Thus, stressful experience was shown to have a positive influence on performance and new learning in the water maze, and the effect was dependent on the stage of life in which the stressor occurred.

We recently examined the effects of acute stressful experience on learning in males and females before, during, and after puberty (Figure 3) (Hodes & Shors 2005a). Animals were stressed with brief intermittent tailshocks and 24 hours later were trained with the classically conditioned eyeblink response using a trace paradigm. We found no effect of stress on conditioning before puberty. This was surprising in some ways since this period is well beyond the so-called stress hyporesponsive period, a time when the stress response is diminished. In fact, these prepubescent animals had robust stress responses as measured by the release of the stress hormones, the glucocorticoids. Nonetheless, there was no effect of the stressful event on new learning. During puberty, however, both males and females that were previously exposed to the stressful event emitted more learned response during training. In adulthood, the sex differences in response to stress emerged; adult males that were exposed to the stressful event emitted more learned responses, whereas females emitted fewer learned responses after exposure to the same stressor. These data indicate that the detrimental effect of stress on learning in females emerges in adulthood and is not evident before or during puberty. Thus, the way in which stress affects learning abilities is not only dependent on the sex of the animal but also on the stage of life during which it occurs.

Stress and Learning from Sexual Maturity Through Motherhood

It is clear that stress can affect learning differently in males than in females, and in some cases can even have opposite effects on learning in males and females. Moreover, the effects of stress on learning in females often depend on the stage of estrus during which the stress and/or training occur (Shors et al. 1998). For the effects of stress on classical eyeblink conditioning, it appears that females in proestrus are most affected. That is, females that are stressed and then trained in proestrus emit many fewer conditioned responses than do females that are unstressed. However, if they are in proestrus and not exposed to a stressful event, females emit more conditioned responses than do females in any other stage of estrus and than do males. Thus, females in proestrus learn best but are also most susceptible to the negative consequences of a stressful experience. Similar results have been reported in human studies. In fact, in 19 out of 20 separate experiments, women emitted more conditioned eyeblink responses than did men (Spence & Spence 1966). Stages of the menstrual cycle were not monitored. Nonetheless, a

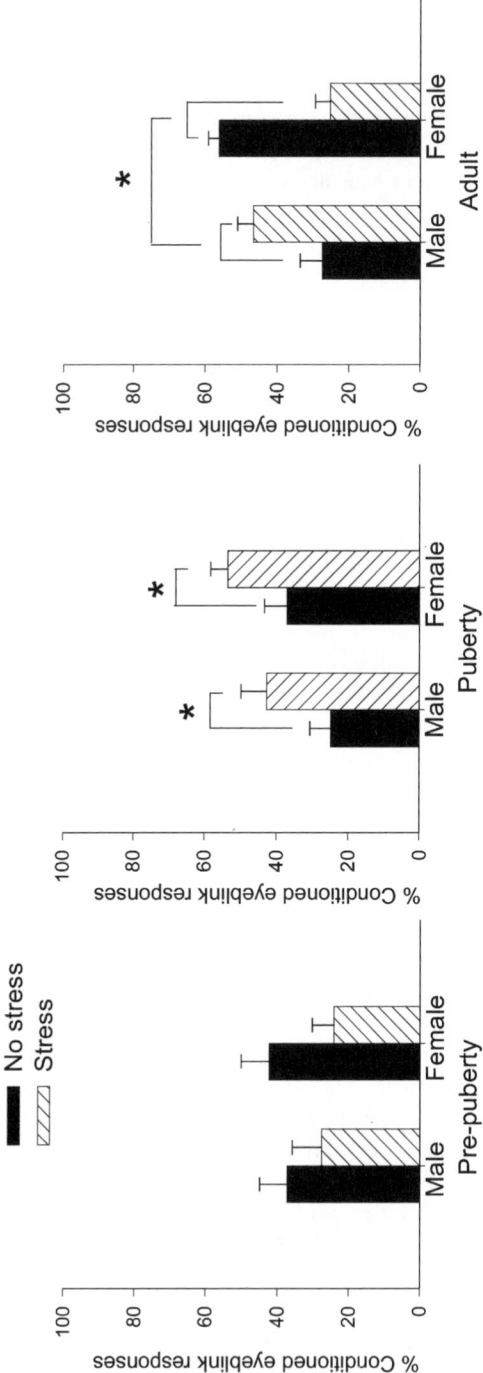

Figure 3 Stress during puberty and its effect on subsequent learning. Male and female rats of different ages were exposed to an acute stressor of brief intermittent tailshocks and were trained 24 hours later on a classical eyeblink conditioning task using a trace paradigm. Conditioning in males and females that were stressed and trained before puberty was unaffected by exposure to the stressful event. In contrast, conditioning in males and females that were stressed and trained during puberty was enhanced. As adults, however, sex differences in conditioning and the response to stress emerged. Specifically, females emitted fewer conditioned responses after exposure to the stressful event, especially if they were trained in proestrus (Hodes & Shors 2005a).

very consistent sex difference in classical conditioning was apparent, and it was one similar to that observed in male and female rats. Also, the effects of anxiety on conditioning seem to interact with sex differences in humans. During differential conditioning, anxious men expressed more excitatory conditioning for the positive cue, whereas anxious women expressed greater excitation for both negative and positive cues (Spence & Farber 1954). A more recent study found that a stressful experience of public speaking and mental arithmetic enhanced fear conditioning in males yet had no effect on acquisition in females (Jackson et al. 2005). Overall, the amount of data is insufficient at this time to draw strong conclusions about how stress affects learning differently in males and females, much less to answer why. This is in part because females are usually excluded from animal studies, whereas in human studies, they are included but often are not distinguished from males during data analysis. Fortunately, this practice is beginning to change (Cahill 2005).

Females respond differently to stressful experiences during specific stages of life. The period immediately after giving birth is one of those times. In general, postpartum females (including women) are less anxious while they are lactating and show blunted responses to stressful experience (Carter et al. 2001). Consistent with these effects, female rats that are lactating do not express a deficit in conditioning after stressor exposure, whereas those that are cycling or pregnant express a profound deficit (Figure 4) (Leuner & Shors 2005). This effect is dependent on the presence of the offspring, since the deficit will reemerge if the mothers are separated from their offspring. Also, the effect can be induced in virgins that behave maternally (Figure 5). This process, known as "maternal sensitization," occurs when virgin females are exposed to offspring of other females. After several days, the virgin females begin to take care of the offspring and express many of the behaviors associated with motherhood. Amazingly enough, in the absence of giving birth, these virgins become resistant to the negative consequences of stressful experience. Thus, learning in females that are induced to act like mothers becomes resistant to stress, as it does in the postpartum female. The way in which the expression of maternal behavior, induced either by birth or by exposure to offspring, alters the response to stress is unknown, and why learning abilities would be protected is probably unknowable. Obviously, new mothers must learn many new behaviors and associative responses, and must do so oftentimes under threatening conditions. The point here is that the effect of stress on learning changes across the lifespan, particularly across the life of a female.

One of the most significant changes in life is the cessation of reproductive potential, a process that occurs most overtly in women but is also experienced in the lives of men. It is often assumed that stress will have more of an impact on the aged than on the young, and that the everyday stressors that occur in life can interfere with cognitive processing in the elderly. However, very few studies have examined how stress affects learning in aged animals. We recently examined the effects of acute stressful experience using brief intermittent tailshocks on classical eyeblink conditioning (Hodes & Shors 2005b). As discussed above, exposure to this event enhances conditioning in males but interferes with performance in females. In

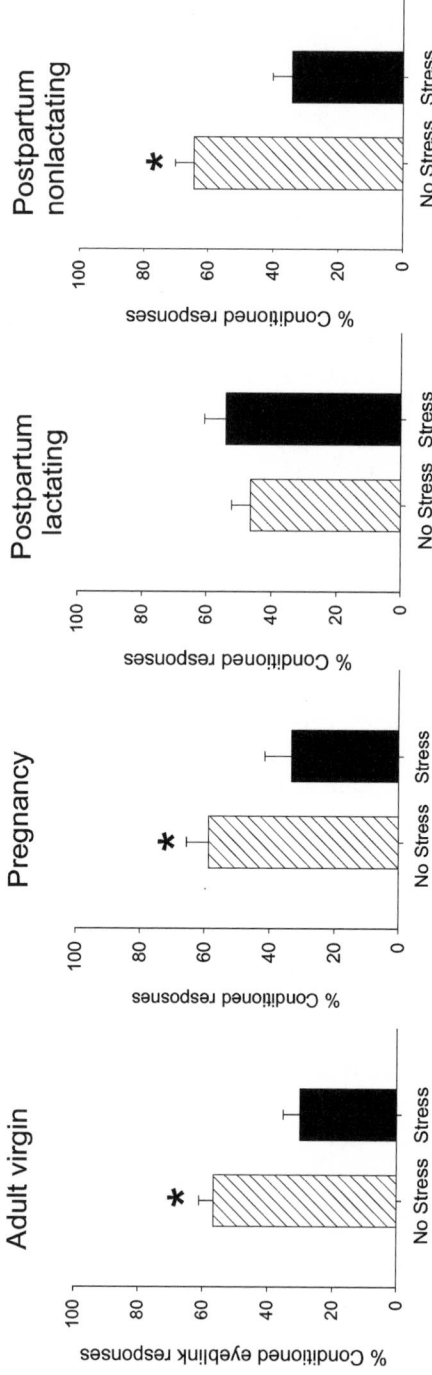

Figure 4 The female response changes from pregnancy to postpartum. Females were exposed to an acute stressful event and trained 24 hours later on the classically conditioned eyeblink response using a trace paradigm. As shown previously, stress reduced the percentage of conditioned responses in adult females that were cycling. Stress also reduced conditioning in females that were pregnant and therefore not cycling. However, stress did not alter conditioning in females that were lactating. Upon removal of their offspring, lactation ceased and these females emitted a smaller percentage of conditioned responses after exposure to the stressful event (Leuner & Shors 2005).

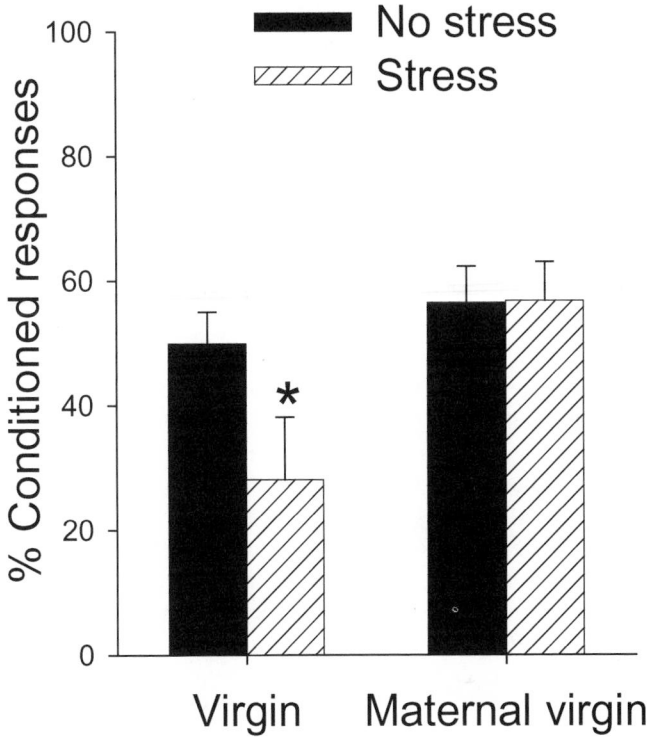

Figure 5   The female response to stress is absent in virgins that express maternal behavior. Virgin females were induced to behave maternally with repeated exposure to offspring. While behaving in this way, they were exposed to an acute stressful event and 24 hrs later trained on the classically conditioned eyeblink response using a trace paradigm. Conditioning in the maternal virgins was not affected by exposure to the stressful event and thus their response was similar to females that are postpartum and lactating (Leuner & Shors 2005). This response (or lack thereof) is contrasted with that of virgin females that were not exposed to offspring; they emitted many fewer conditioned responses after exposure to the stressor. Asterisk denotes a significant change in response relative to the response from the No Stress group.

aged rats, however, there was no effect of stress whatsoever on conditioning. Thus, the enhancing effect of stress on conditioned responding in males did not occur and the deficits in females did not occur. These findings suggest that the older animals become immune to the effects of stress on this type of conditioning, irrespective of whether the effect is positive or negative. It is perhaps worth noting that before puberty, there are also no observable effects of acute stress on this type of learning (Figure 3). Therefore, the effects of stress on new learning of this response seem to emerge with sexual maturity and diminish with the loss of reproductive potential.

HORMOMES, BRAIN MECHANISMS, AND ANATOMICAL SUBSTRATES

The Glucocorticoid Connection

Glucocorticoids are most often associated with stress and are important for their interaction with learning processes. These stress hormones are released in response to nearly every stressful event that a person encounters in life and their effects on the central nervous system are nothing short of profound. Mostly, they are anti-inflammatory and thus are critical for reestablishing and maintaining homeostasis after a stressful experience. Because glucocorticoids have direct effects on processes involved in learning and memory, they are studied in their own right. Readers are referred to current reviews and analyses of the glucocorticoid literature (Het et al. 2005, Lupien et al. 2004, McEwen & Wingfield 2003, Roozendaal 2002) that are not discussed here because of space limitations. Rather, the focus here is on studies that tested whether glucocorticoids are necessary for the effects of a stressful experience on learning and memory.

The methods available to address this issue are not feasible for use in humans; thus, these studies have been conducted in laboratory animals. Probably the most conclusive method is to remove the adrenal gland via an adrenalectomy. This surgical manipulation removes the sole source of glucocorticoids. However, it also removes a source of epinephrine since epinephrine is also released from the adrenal medulla within the glands. Thus, to be sure that the effects observed after adrenalectomy are due to the absence of glucocorticoids, adrenalectomy studies should be followed up by adrenal demedullations, in which the adrenal medulla is removed, leaving the adrenal cortex and the source of glucocorticoids intact. This approach has been used to determine whether the enhancing effect of acute stress on classical eyeblink conditioning is dependent on the presence of glucocorticoids (Beylin & Shors 2003). As shown in Figure 6A, adrenalectomy did not affect the overall level of conditioning, but did prevent the enhanced conditioning in response to an acute stressful experience of intermittent tailshocks. However, removal of the adrenal medulla did not prevent the enhanced responding after stress. Together, these data indicate that the effect of stress on classical eyeblink conditioning is dependent on the presence of stress hormones released from the adrenal cortex, i.e., glucocorticoids. Although necessary, these studies do not address whether the presence of stress levels of the hormones are sufficient to enhance learning. To address this issue, we conducted a subsequent study in which intact male rats were injected with a bolus of corticosterone at a concentration similar to that induced by stressful experience. Conditioning was increased while the glucocorticoid levels were elevated. However, once the hormone levels returned to baseline, the enhanced conditioning did not occur. In other words, conditioning in animals that were injected with the glucocorticoids and trained for the first time 24 hours later was unaffected. This is in contrast to the effects of an actual stressful event, where the enhanced learning occurs days after the stressful event has ceased and long

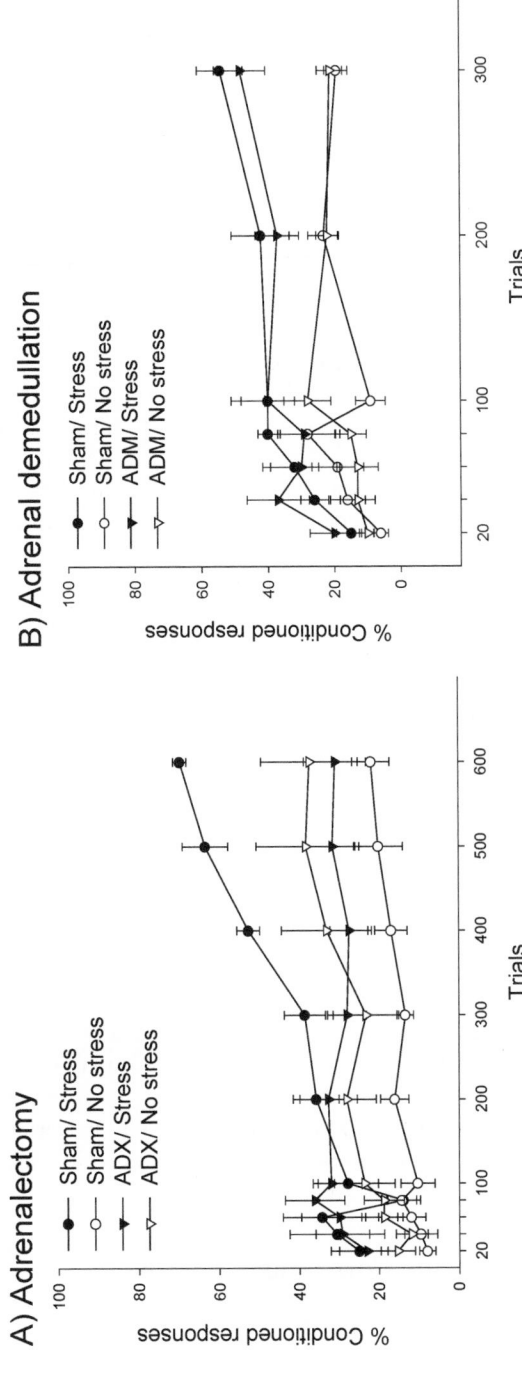

Figure 6 The presence of glucocorticoids is necessary but not sufficient for the persistent increase in learning after stressful experience. (A) The graph shows the percentage of conditioned responses in animals that were adrenalectomized (ADX) and provided basal levels of corticosterone through their drinking water. The other groups were exposed to a sham surgery. The group that was stressed and trained emitted a greater percentage of conditioned responses than did the unstressed groups, unless they were adrenalectomized. There was no effect of stress on trace conditioning in the ADX group (Beylin & Shors 2003). (B) The effects of stress on trace conditioning were examined in rats after their adrenal medulla was removed. In this experiment, adrenal demedullation did not prevent the enhancing effect of stress on conditioning, a finding that indicates the effect is mediated by the presence of glucocorticoids released from the adrenal cortex (Beylin & Shors 2003).

after glucocorticoid levels have returned to baseline. Together, these findings indicate that glucocorticoids are necessary but not sufficient for the persistent increase in eyeblink conditioning that occurs in males after an acute stressful experience.

Others have examined the contribution of glucocorticoids to the effects of stress on learning by using a classically conditioned preference for morphine. Exposure to uncontrollable, but not to controllable, stress enhances the rewarding effects of drugs of abuse. Specifically, a stressful experience enhances an animal's ability to learn and remember where the rewarding effects of morphine were experienced (Der-Avakian et al. 2005). This effect of stress on learning is also dependent on the presence of adrenal hormones, since adrenalectomy eliminated the enhanced preference for the morphine context. Like the effects of stress on eyeblink conditioning, these findings indicate that glucocorticoids are usually necessary for stress effects on learning, However, in their study, Der-Avakian et al. (2005) found the presence of glucocorticoids to be important during the morphine experience and not during the stressor. Thus, the release of glucocorticoids during the stressful event was not as important as the release during the training experience.

The previous two studies indicated that the enhancing effects of stress on learning are dependent on the presence of glucocorticoids. What about the more negative effects that stress has on memory? A stressful experience can impair retrieval of information that was acquired before the stressful event (de Quervain et al. 1998). The release of glucocorticoids also seems necessary for this effect, since rats that were administered a drug that inhibits the synthesis of glucocorticoids did not express the memory deficit. In this case, the effect could be mimicked with an injection of glucocorticoids; therefore, the hormones were necessary and sufficient.

These few examples illustrate the many ways that the hypothalamic-pituitary adrenal response to stress interacts with processes involved in learning and memory. In general, glucocorticoid levels correlate with stress effects on learning. The existence of this relationship is not surprising because more stressful experiences result in both the release of more glucocorticoids and the increased likelihood to induce changes in learned responses. Despite the existence of this correlation, it does not necessarily mean that glucocorticoids are playing a critical role, and in some cases, they are playing none. For example, female rats have very high levels of glucocorticoids, particularly after exposure to a stressful event, yet the detrimental effect of stress on subsequent learning does not depend on their presence (Wood et al. 2001). In summary, the role that glucocorticoids play in the effects of stress on learning is complicated. Their presence appears to be necessary for most effects, although the critical period varies depending on the learning situation. There are also significant differences in the hypothalamic-pituitary adrenal response to stress between species and even the sexes.

The Hippocampal Formation and Correlations Within

The hippocampus is the brain structure most often associated with stress and learning. This is in part because it possesses an abundance of glucocorticoid receptors

(McEwen & Wallach 1973). Two types reside there: type I or mineralocorticoid receptor, which is occupied at low basal levels of the hormone, and type II or glucocorticoid receptor, which is occupied during stressful times. Type I receptors are heavily concentrated in the hippocampus, whereas the stress-related type II receptors are especially prevalent in other brain regions, such as the hypothalamus and prefrontal cortex (Reul & De Kloet, Lupien & Lepage 2001). Nonetheless, the hippocampus remains a structure of interest because it is involved in and is even necessary for some types of learning. Moreover, it is extremely sensitive to stressful experiences.

Relatively few attempts have been made to show that the hippocampus is necessarily involved in stress effects on learning. This is in part because the structure is involved in some types of learning and therefore its disruption will affect learning, even in the absence of stress. For example, it has been proposed that the stress-induced increase in trace conditioning is dependent on the hippocampus, but this has not been shown because disrupting the hippocampus would disrupt learning itself. There are, however, numerous correlations between stress effects on learning and changes within the hippocampal formation. For example, exposure to 21 days of restraint reduces the branching of CA3 pyramidal cells in the hippocampus (Wantanabe et al. 1992). The reduction in synaptic connections correlates with performance deficits in the Y maze (Conrad 1999). In other studies, it has been shown that exposure to the acute stressful event that enhances classical eyeblink conditioning also increases the excitability of pyramidal cells in area CA1 of the hippocampus. The increase persists for at least 24 hours and thus would be evident during the time when animals are being trained. These results suggest a positive relationship between cell excitability and new learning after stressful experience. Similarly, it has been shown that exposure to the stressor that enhances trace conditioning increases the density of dendritic spines in the hippocampus (Figure 7*B*) (Shors et al. 2001a). Again, this effect suggests that an increase in spine density may relate to the increase in learning. The effect of stress on spine density is quite different in the female hippocampus, where exposure to the same stressor reduces spine density. Since acute stress enhances conditioning in males but impairs it in females, these data represent another positive correlation between the presence of dendritic spines and classical eyeblink conditioning. It would be interesting to know whether exposure to the stressor decreases cell excitability in the female hippocampus. If so, this would suggest a causal relationship between these various phenomena; however, the relationships would still be only correlational. It is nonetheless noted that this type of learning is associated with changes in both cell excitability and spine density. In males that are trained with eyeblink conditioning, neuronal activity increases as does the number of spines on dendrites in area CA1 (Figure 7*C*) (Berger et al. 1983, Leuner et al. 2003, McEchron & Disterhoft 1999). Thus, a stressful experience induces changes in neuronal function and structures that are affected by learning itself, indicating a convergence on common substrates.

There has been much discussion about how neurogenesis may contribute to the effects of stress on learning. It has been established that the adult brain continues

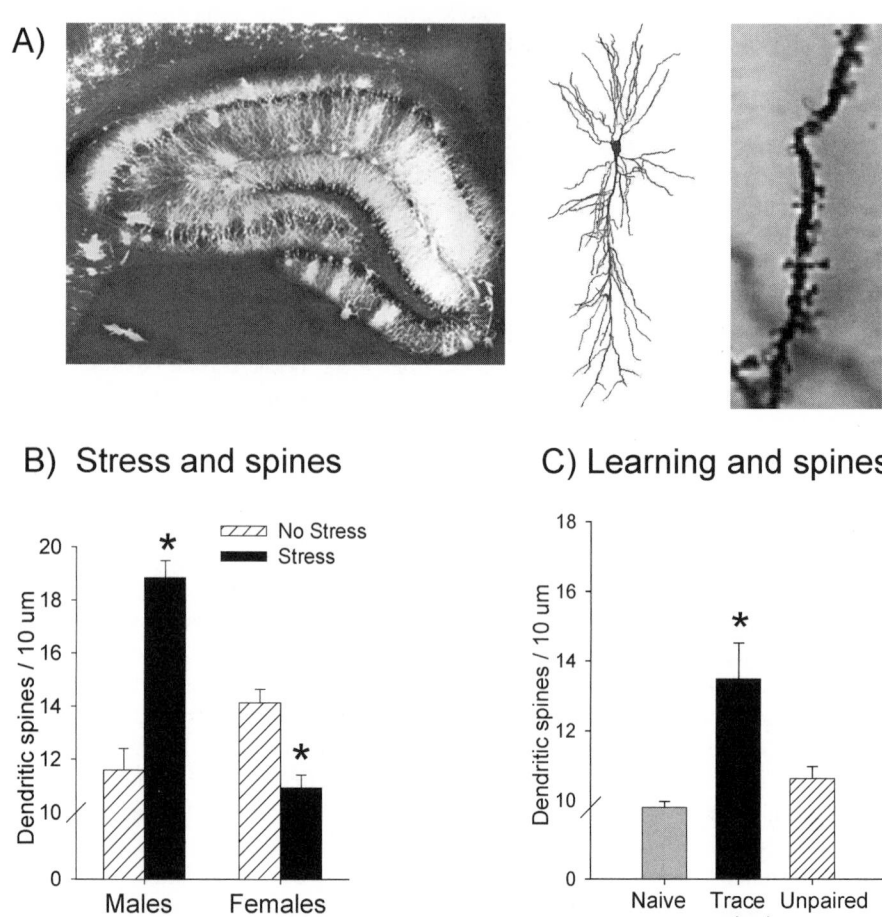

Figure 7   The presence of dendritic spines is affected by stressful experience and learning. (*A*) A photomicrograph illustrates the massive amount of dendritic branching that exists within the hippocampal formation. To the right is a CA1 pyramidal cell and dendritic spines on those cells. (*B*) It was determined, using Golgi staining techniques, that exposure to an acute stressful experience increases the presence of dendritic spines in the hippocampus of the male rat. Exposure to the same stressor reduces spine density in females. These responses to stress are represented in the graph as the mean number of spines along 10 um of a dendrite in area CA1 of the hippocampus, as well as in representative photomicrographs (Shors et al. 2001a, 2004). Asterisk denotes a significant change in response relative to the response from the No Stress group. (*C*) The presence of spines also increased in response to learning the classically conditioned eyeblink response, at least in males. Thus, spine density in the hippocampus correlates with learning after stress and is enhanced by learning.

to produce new neurons throughout life, and many of those are produced in the dentate gyrus of the hippocampus (Cameron et al. 1995, Gould et al. 1997, van Praag et al. 2002). The production of new cells is especially sensitive to stressful experience; stressors such as social dominance, maternal deprivation, and predator odors all reduce the production of new cells in this brain region (Kosorovitskiy & Gould 2004, Mirescu et al. 2004, Tanapat et al. 2001). These cells have also been associated with some types of learning and thus it is tempting to conclude that stress effects on learning are mediated by changes in neurogenesis. This is probably not a viable explanation, at least not for the effects of acute stress on new learning. Most studies indicate that the new cells do not become involved in learning for at least a week after they are born (Gould et al. 1999, Leuner et al. 2004a). Thus, a change in cell production in response to acute stress would most likely not affect cells that are involved in learning. Also, the data to date suggest that the new neurons respond to relatively few types of learning situations (Shors 2004). It is possible, however, that chronic stressful experiences over weeks or months could alter the production of cells to such an extent that changes in learned behaviors would emerge.

The Amygdala, Bed Nucleus, and Connections Between

The amygdala has been associated with stress and learning almost as much as the hippocampus. It is involved in aspects of emotional responses as well as learning about fearful events. In general, the amygdala allows emotional events to be remembered, and remembered well (McGaugh 2004). Many studies have focused on memory retrieval and its interactions with glucocorticoids in the amygdala, and as noted above, this literature is not reviewed here. There are also those that have examined whether the amygdala is necessary for the stress effects on learning and memory. For example, the enhancing effect of stress on classical eyeblink conditioning could be prevented by blocking N-methyl-D-asparate (NMDA) receptors in the amygdala (Figure 8) (Shors & Mathew 1998). This effect was locally specific because antagonism in the basolateral, but not the central, nucleus was effective. Also, the effect was temporally specific because antagonism during, but not after, the stress was effective. These data suggest that a stressful experience activates NMDA receptors in the amygdala during the experience itself, which then induces more long-term changes in processes involved in learning. Others have shown a similar dependence. Recall that acute stress can reduce retention for spatial location in the Morris water maze. This effect can be prevented by inactivating the amygdala during, but not after, the stressful event (Kim et al. 2005). Thus, it would appear that the amygdala is involved in stress effects on learning and memory, whether they are enhancements in learning or deficits in memory.

One of the major outputs of the amygdala is the stria terminalis. Some years ago, it was shown that lesions of this structure prevent the effects of glucocorticoids on memory processes, thereby suggesting that the "information" in the amygdala was

A) The amygdala

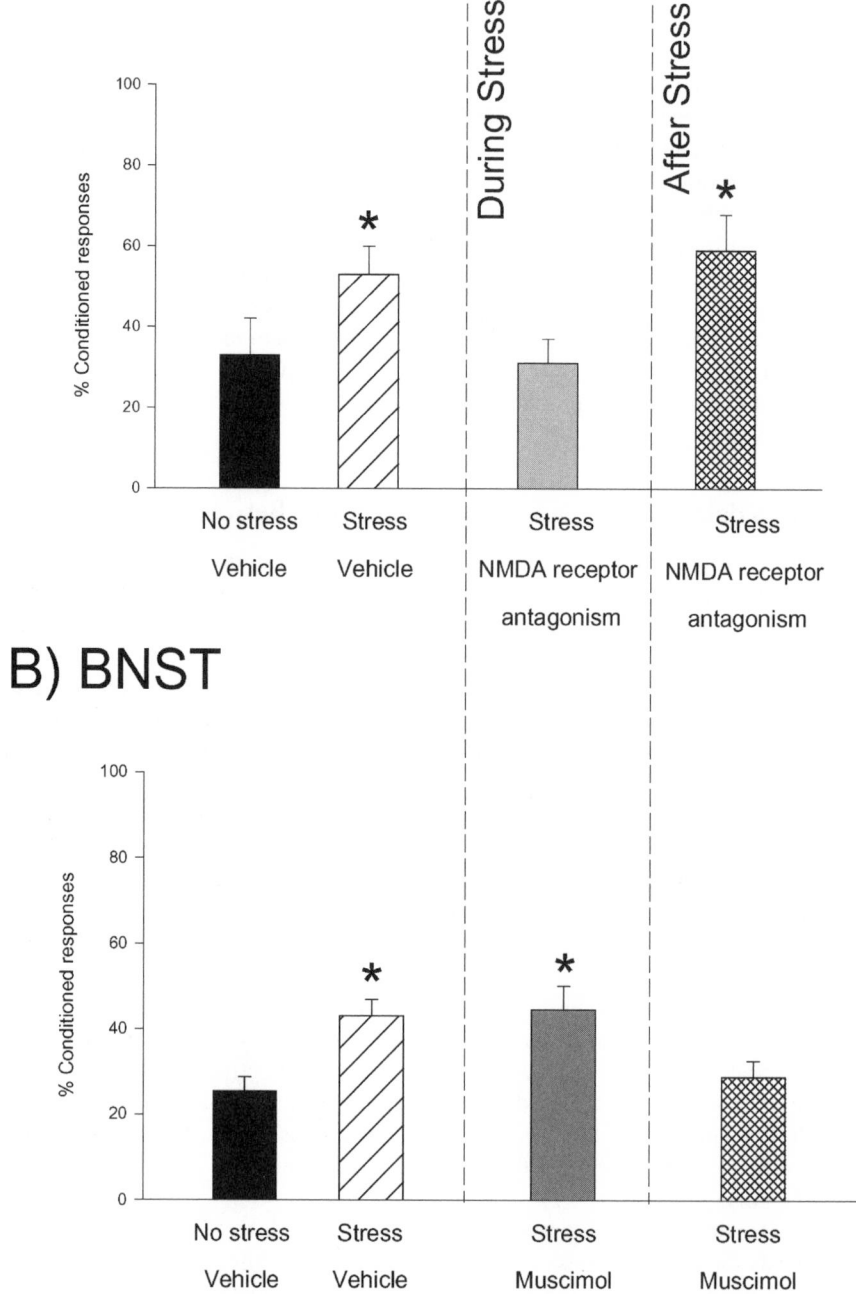

being relayed to afferent structures (McGaugh 2004, Roozendaal & McGaugh 1996). The primary target of the stria terminalis is the bed nucleus, which is a structure known to be involved in stress, anxiety, and sex differences. Recent studies have indicated its involvement in anxiety (Walker & Davis 1997). Thus, the bed nucleus is a structure that can maintain a state of anxiety in animals, a state that would likely alter an animal's ability to learn and remember. Consistent with this idea, the stress-induced increase in classical eyeblink conditioning is prevented by inactivating the bed nucleus (Bangasser et al. 2005). However, inactivation was only effective if it was done during the learning experience and not during the stressful event (Figure 8). The data suggest that the BNST is critical for maintaining the effects of stress for several days in case a new learning situation arises in which the increased responding can be used. It appears that the effect of stress on this type of learning is induced by activity within the amygdala, but that the response is maintained by changes in activity elsewhere, including within the bed nucleus of the stria terminalis.

Considering the Prefrontal Cortex

The prefrontal cortex is involved in cognitive processes that are generally referred to as executive functions. Recently, a number of studies have suggested that the prefrontal cortex may be involved in stress effects on learning (Birnbaum et al. 2004). One of the more persuasive studies involves the effects of uncontrollable versus controllable stress on subsequent fear conditioning and escape behaviors. As discussed above, exposure to uncontrollable, but not to the same amount of controllable, stress enhances fear conditioning and impairs escape performance in a shuttle box escape task. However, neither effect occurred if the prefrontal cortex was inactivated during the stressful experience (Amat et al. 2005). Others have

←————————————————————————————————————

Figure 8   The amygdala and bed nucleus of the stria terminalis (BNST) are involved, but at different times. (*A*) The percentage of conditioned responses in groups of male rats is shown. They were either unstressed or stressed in the presence of a vehicle or an N-methyl-D-aspartate (NMDA) receptor antagonist in the basolateral nucleus of the amygdala. Exposure to the stressor enhanced the percentage of conditioned responses in groups that were injected with a vehicle or if they were injected with the antagonist after the stressful event was over. The group that was injected with the NMDA receptor antagonist prior to the stressful event did not express an increase in conditioned responses (Shors & Mathew 1998). Asterisk denotes a significant change in response relative to the response from the No Stress group. (*B*) As described above, exposure to the stressor enhanced the percentage of conditioned eyeblink responses in males. However, inactivation of the BNST during the stressful event did not prevent the enhanced conditioning, whereas inactivation during training was effective (Bangasser et al. 2005). Asterisk denotes a significant change in response relative to the response from the No Stress group.

found correlations between stress effects on learning and changes in the prefrontal cortex. For example, exposure to a predator odor can disrupt memory for a spatial location, and the deficit correlates with the expression of a neural cell adhesion molecule in the prefrontal cortex (Sandi et al. 2005). Others report that retrieval of fearful memories increases activity in the prefrontal cortex (Bremner et al. 1999). This area of the brain is not as well delineated in the rat as it is in primates, making a direct comparison between species difficult. Nonetheless, given the involvement of the prefrontal cortex in executive function, its high concentration of stress hormone receptors, and its elaborate network of connections to most brain regions, a role in stress and learning is nearly assured.

CONCLUSION

In the end, is stress good or bad for learning? Intuitively, most would answer that it is bad. However, a slightly different view emerges from the literature. Overall, exposure to an acute stressful event tends to enhance learning of new information, if there is an effect at all, whereas exposure to a similar stressful event tends to impair the retrieval of information that has already been acquired. Although the implications are compelling, they are limited because most studies have been done exclusively in adult male animals. When age and sex differences are considered, these trends are nonexistent, and an even more diverse repertoire of responses emerges. This is especially so in females as they change their reproductive status. This should not be that surprising, since changes in learning abilities will have different consequences for survival during different phases of life, and oftentimes ones that cannot be anticipated. Nonetheless, a malleable stress response that interacts with learning is what one would expect from a complex biological system that must respond rapidly and appropriately to a changing environment. As such, it is unlikely that one mechanism or even a handful of mechanisms can account for the diversity of behavioral responses to stressful experience.

The *Annual Review of Psychology* is online at http://psych.annualreviews.org

LITERATURE CITED

Al'Absi M, Hugdahl K, Lovallo WR. 2002. Adrenalcortical stress responses and altered working memory performance. *Psychophysiology* 39:95–99

Amat J, Baratta MV, Paul E, Bland ST, Watkins LR, Maier SF. 2005. Medial prefrontal cortex determines how stressor controllability affects behavior and dorsal raphe nucleus. *Nat. Neurosci.* 8:365–71

Am. Psychiatric Assoc. 2000. *Diagnostic and Statistical Manual of Mental Disorders: DSM-IV-TR.* Washington, DC: Am. Psychiatric Assoc.

Avital A, Richter-Levin G. 2005. Exposure to juvenile stress exacerbates the behavioral consequences of exposure to stress in the adult rat. *Int. J. Neuropsychopharmacol.* 8:163–73

Ayers ED, White J, Powell DA. 2003. Pavlovian eyeblink conditioning in combat veterans with and without post-traumatic stress disorder. *Integr. Physiol. Behav. Sci.* 38:230–47

Bangasser DA, Santollo J, Shors TJ. 2005. The bed nucleus of the stria terminalis is involved in the persistent increase in associative learning after stress. *Behav. Neurosci.* In press

Beatty WW. 1979. Gonadal hormones and sex differences in nonreproductive behaviors in rodents: organizational and activational influences. *Horm. Behav.* 12:112–63

Berger TW, Rinaldi PC, Weisz DJ, Thompson RF. 1983. Neuronal substrate of classical conditioning in the hippocampus. *Science* 192:483–85

Bethus I, Lemaire V, Lhomme M, Goodall G. 2005. Does prenatal stress affect latent inhibition? It depends on gender. *Behav. Brain Res.* 158:331–38

Beylin AV, Shors TJ. 2003. Glucocorticoids are necessary for enhancing memory formation after stressful experience. *Horm. Behav.* 43:124–31

Birnbaum SG, Yuan PX, Wang M, Vijayraghavan S, Bloom AK, et al. 2004. Protein kinase C overactivity impairs prefrontal cortical regulation of working memory. *Science* 306:882–84

Bonanno GA. 2004. Loss, trauma, and human resilience: Have we underestimated the human capacity to thrive after extremely aversive events? *Am. Psychol.* 59:20–28

Bremner JD, Narayan M, Staib LH, Southwick SM, McGlashan T, Charney DS. 1999. Neural correlates of memories of childhood sexual abuse in women with and without posttraumatic stress disorder. *Am. J. Psychiatry* 156:1787–95

Bremner JD, Randall P, Scott TM, Capelli S, Delaney R, et al. 1995. Deficits in short-term memory in adult survivors of childhood abuse. *Psychiatry Res.* 59:97–107

Bryant RA, Harvey AG. 1995. Processing threatening information in posttraumatic stress disorder. *J. Traum. Stress* 10:635–44

Buckley TC. 2000. Information processing and PTSD: a review of the empirical literature. *Clin. Psychol. Rev.* 28:1041–65

Buwalda B, Kole MHP, Veenema AH, Huininga M, de Boer SF, et al. 2005. Long-term effects of social stress on brain and behavior: a focus on hippocampal functioning. *Neurosci. Biobehav. Rev.* 29:83–97

Cahill L. 2005. His brain, her brain. *Sci. Am.* 292:40–47

Cahill L, Gorski L, Le K. 2003. Enhanced human memory consolidation with post-learning stress: interaction with the degree of arousal at encoding. *Learn. Mem.* 10:270–74

Cameron HA, McEwen BS, Gould E. 1995. Regulations of adult neurogenesis by excitatory input and NMDA receptor activation in the dentate gyrus. *J. Neurosci.* 15:4687–92

Carter CS, Altemus M, Chrousos GP. 2001. Neuroendocrine and emotional changes in the post-partum period. *Prog. Brain Res.* 133:241–49

Conrad CD. 1999. Repeated restraint stress facilitates fear conditioning independently of causing hippocampal CA3 dendritic atrophy. *Behav. Neurosci.* 113:902–18

Cordero MI, Venero C, Kruyt ND, Sandi C. 2003. Prior exposure to a single stress session facilitates subsequent contextual fear conditioning in rats: evidence for a role of corticosterone. *Horm. Behav.* 44:338–45

de Quervain DJF, Roozendaal B, McGaugh JL. 1998. Stress and glucocorticoids impair retrieval of long-term spatial memory. *Nature* 394:787–90

Der-Avakian A, Will MJ, Bland ST, Deak T, Nguyen KT, et al. 2005. Surgical and pharmacological suppression of glucocorticoids prevents the enhancement of morphine conditioned place preference by uncontrollable stress in rats. *Psychopharmacology* 179:409–17

Domes G, Heinrichs M, Rimmele U, Reichwald U, Hautzinger M. 2004. Acute stress impairs recognition for positive words—association with stress-induced cortisol secretion. *Stress* 7:173–81

Foa EB, Feske U, Murdock TB, Kozak MJ, McCarthy PR. 1991. Processing of threat-related information in rape victims. *J. Abnorm. Psychol.* 100:156–62

Gould E, Beylin AV, Tanapat P, Reeves A, Shors TJ. 1999. Learning enhances adult neurogenesis in the adult hippocampal formation. *Nat. Neurosci.* 2(3):260–65

Gould E, McEwen BS, Tanapat P, Galea LAM, Fuchs E. 1997. Neurogenesis in the dentate gyrus of the adult tree shrew is regulated by psychosocial stress and NMDA receptor activation. *J. Neurosci.* 17(7):2492–98

Griffen WC, Skinner HD, Salm AK, Birkle DL. 2003. Mild prenatal stress in rats is associated with enhanced conditioned fear. *Physiol. Behav.* 79:209–15

Grillon C, Hill J. 2003. Emotional arousal does not affect delay eyeblink conditioning. *Cogn. Brain Res.* 17:400–5

Het S, Ramlow G, Wolf OT. 2005. A meta-analytic review of the effects of acute cortisol administration on human memory. *Psychoneuroendocrinology* 30:771–84

Hodes G, Shors TJ. 2005a. Distinctive stress effects on learning during puberty. *Horm. Behav.* 48:163–71

Hodes G, Shors TJ. 2005b. Stress does not affect learning in aged males or females. *Soc. Neurosci. Abstr.* In press

Isgor C, Kabbaj M, Akil H, Watson SJ. 2004. Delayed effects of chronic variable stress during peripubertal-juvenile period on hippocampal morphology and on cognitive and stress axis functions in rats. *Hippocampus* 14:636–48

Jackson ED, Payne JD, Nadel L, Jacobs WJ. 2005. Stress differentially modulates fear conditioning in healthy men and women. *Biol. Psychiatry.* In press

Kaspi SP, McNally RJ, Amir N. 1995. Cognitive processing of emotional information in posttraumatic stress disorder. *Cogn. Ther. Res.* 19:433–44

Kim JJ, Koo JW, Lee HJ, Han J. 2005. Amygdalar inactivation blocks stress-induced impairments in hippocampal long-term potentiation and spatial memory. *J. Neurosci.* 25:1532–39

Kirk RC, Blampied NM. 1985. Activity during inescapable shock and subsequent escape avoidance learning: female and male

rats compared. *N. Z. J. Psychol.* 14:9–14

Kosorovitskiy Y, Gould E. 2004. Dominance hierarchy influences adult neurogenesis in the dentate gyrus. *J. Neurosci.* 24:6755–59

Kuhlmann S, Piel M, Wolf OT. 2005. Impaired memory retrieval after psychosocial stress in healthy young men. *J. Neurosci.* 25:2977–82

Lehmann J, Pryce CR, Bettschen D, Feldon J. 1999. The maternal separation paradigm and adult emotionality and cognition in male and female Wistar rats. *Pharmacol. Biochem. Behav.* 64:705–15

Leuner B, Falduto J, Shors TJ. 2003. Associative memory formation increases the observation of dendritic spines in the hippocampus. *J. Neurosci.* 23:659–65

Leuner B, Mendolia-Loffredo S, Kozorovitskiy Y, Samburg D, Gould E, Shors TJ. 2004a. Learning enhances the survival of new neurons beyond the time when the hippocampus is required for memory. *J. Neurosci.* 24:7477–81

Leuner B, Mendolia-Loffredo S, Shors TJ. 2004b. Males and females respond differently to controllability and antidepressant treatment. *Biol. Psychiatry* 56:964–70

Leuner B, Shors TJ. 2005. Motherhood and memory: a resistance to stress. *Horm. Behav.* In press

Levine S, Chevalier JA, Korchin SJ. 1956. The effects of early shock and handling on later avoidance learning. *J. Personal.* 24:475–93

Luine VN, Martinez C, Villegas M, Margarinos AM, McEwen BS. 1996. Restraint stress reversibly enhances spatial memory performance. *Physiol. Behav.* 59:27–32

Lupien SJ, Fiocco A, Wan N, Maheu F, Lord C, et al. 2004. Stress hormones and human memory function across the lifespan. *Psychoneuroendocrinology* 30:225–42

Lupien SJ, Lepage M. 2001. Stress, memory, and the hippocampus: Can't live with it, can't live without it. *Behav. Brain Res.* 127:137–58

Maier SF. 1990. Role of fear in mediating shuttle escape learning deficit produced by inescapable shock. *J. Exp. Psychol. Anim. Behav. Process.* 16:137–49

Maier SF, Jackson RL. 1979. Learned helplessness: All of us were right (and wrong). Inescapable shock has multiple effects. In *Advances in Learning and Motivation*, ed. B Bower, 13:155–215. New York: Academic

Maren S, de Oca B, Fanselow MS. 1994. Sex differences in hippocampal long-term potentiation (LTP) and Pavlovian fear conditioning in rats: positive correlation between LTP and contextual learning. *Brain Res.* 661:25–34

McEchron MD, Disterhoft JF. 1999. Sequence of single neuron changes in CA1 hippocampus of rabbits during acquisition of trace eyeblink conditioned responses. *J. Neurophysiol.* 78(2):1030–44

McEwen BS, Wallach G. 1973. Corticosterone binding to the hippocampus: nuclear and cytosol binding in vitro. *Brain Res.* 57:373–86

McEwen BS, Wingfield JC. 2003. The concept of allostasis in biology and biomedicine. *Horm. Behav.* 43:2–15

McGaugh JL. 2004. The amygdala modulates the consolidation of memories of emotionally arousing experiences. *Annu. Rev. Neurosci.* 27:1–28

McNally RJ. 2003. Progress and controversy in the study of posttraumatic stress disorder. *Annu. Rev. Psychol.* 54:229–52

Minor TR, Dess NK, Overmier JB. 1991. Inverting the traditional view of "learned helplessness." In *Fear, Avoidance, and Phobias: A Fundamental Analysis*, ed. MR Denny, pp. 87–133. Hillsdale, NJ: Erlbaum

Mirescu C, Peters JD, Gould E. 2004. Early life experience alters response of adult neurogenesis to stress. *Nat. Neurosci.* 7:841–46

Nielson KA, Yee D, Erickson KI. 2005. Memory enhancement by a semantically unrelated emotional arousal source induced after learning. *Neurobiol. Learn. Mem.* 84:49–56

Overmier JB, Seligman MEP. 1967. Effects of inescapable shock on subsequent escape and avoidance learning. *J. Comp. Physiol. Psychol.* 63:23–33

Parker KJ, Buckmaster CL, Justus KR, Shatzberg AF, Lyons DM. 2005. Mild early life stress enhances prefrontal-dependent response inhibition in monkeys. *Biol. Psychiatry* 57:848–55

Pitman RK, Orr SP, Lowenhagen MJ, Macklin ML, Altman B. 1991. Pre-Vietnam contents of PTSD veteran's service medical and personnel records. *Compr. Psychiatry* 32:1–7

Reul JMHM, De Kloet ER. 1985. Two receptor systems for corticosterone in the rat brain: microdistribution and differential occupation. *Endocrinology* 117:2505–12

Riedel G, Micheau J, Lam AGM, Roloff EVL, Martin SJ, et al. 1999. Reversible neural activation reveals hippocampal participation in several memory processes. *Nat. Neurosci.* 2: 898–906

Roozendaal B. 2002. Stress and memory: opposing effects of glucocorticoids on memory consolidation and memory retrieval. *Neurobiol. Learn. Mem.* 78:578–95

Roozendaal B, McGaugh J. 1996. The memory-modulatory effects of glucocorticoids depend on an intact stria terminalis. *Brain Res.* 709:243–50

Sandi C, Woodson JC, Haynes VF, Park CR, Touyarot K, et al. 2005. Acute stress-induced impairment of spatial memory is associated with decreased expression of neural cell adhesion molecule in the hippocampus and prefrontal cortex. *Biol. Psychiatry* 57:856–64

Sandstrom NJ, Hart SR. 2005. Isolation stress during the third postnatal week alters radial arm maze performance and corticosterone levels in adulthood. *Behav. Brain Res.* 156:289–96

Seligman MEP, Maier SF. 1967. Failure to escape traumatic shock. *J. Comp. Physiol. Psychol.* 74:1–9

Servatius RJ, Brennan FX, Beck KD, Beldowicz D, Coyle-DiNorcia K. 2001. Stress facilitates acquisition of the classically conditioned eyeblink response at both long and short interstimulus intervals. *Learn. Motiv.* 32:178–92

Shors TJ. 1998. Stress and sex effects on associative learning: for better or for worse. *Neuroscientist* 4:353–64

Shors TJ. 2001. Acute stress rapidly and persistently enhances memory formation in the male rat. *Neurobiol. Learn. Mem.* 75:10–29

Shors TJ. 2004. Memory traces of trace memories: neurogenesis, synaptogenesis and awareness. *Trends Neurosci.* 27:250–56

Shors TJ, Chua C, Falduto J. 2001a. Sex differences and opposite effects of stress on dendritic spine density in the male versus female hippocampus. *J. Neurosci.* 21:6292–97

Shors TJ, Dryver E. 1992. Stress impedes exploration and the acquisition of spatial information in the eight-arm radial maze. *Psychobiology* 20:247–53

Shors TJ, Falduto J, Leuner B. 2004. The opposite effects of stress on dendritic spines in male vs. female rats are NMDA receptor-dependent. *Eur. J. Neurosci.* 19:145–50

Shors TJ, Lewczyk C, Paczynski M, Mathew PR, Pickett J. 1998. Stages of estrus mediate the stress-induced impairment of associative learning in the female rat. *Neuroreport* 9:419–23

Shors TJ, Mathew PR. 1998. NMDA receptor antagonism in the basolateral but not central nucleus of the amygdala prevents the induction of facilitated learning in response to stress. *J. Learn. Mem.* 5:220–30

Shors TJ, Mathew J, Edgecomb C, Sisti HM. 2005. Neurogenesis and depression: uncontrollable but not controllable stress reduces proliferation in the adult hippocampus. *Neurosci. Abstr.* In press

Shors TJ, Seib TB, Levine S, Thompson RF. 1989. Inescapable versus escapable shock modulates long-term potentiation (LTP) in rat hippocampus. *Science* 244:224–26

Shors TJ, Servatius RJ. 1997. The contribution of stressor intensity, duration, and context to the stress-induced facilitation of associative learning. *Neurobiol. Learn. Mem.* 67:92–96

Shors TJ, Weiss C, Thompson RF. 1992. Stress-induced facilitation of classical conditioning. *Science* 257:537–39

Spence KW, Beecroft RS. 1954. Differential conditioning and level of anxiety. *J. Exp. Psychol.* 48:399–403

Spence KW, Goldstein H. 1961. Eyelid conditioning performance as a function of emotion-producing instructions. *J. Exp. Psychol.* 62:291–94

Spence KW, Spence JT. 1966. Sex and anxiety differences in eyelid conditioning. *Psychol. Bull.* 65:137–42

Spence KW, Taylor J. 1951. Anxiety and strength of the UCS as determiners of the amount of eyelid conditioning. *J. Exp. Psychol.* 42:183–88

Steenbergen HL, Heinsbroek RPM, Van Haaren F, van de Poll NE. 1989. Sex-dependent effects of inescapable shock administration on behavior and subsequent escape performance in rats. *Physiol. Behav.* 45:781–87

Tanapat P, Hastings NB, Rydel TA, Galea LAM, Gould E. 2001. Exposure to fox odor inhibits cell proliferation in the hippocampus of adult rats via an adrenal hormone-dependent mechanism. *J. Comp. Neurol.* 437:496–504

Trandel DV, McNally RJ. 1987. Perception of threat cues in post-traumatic stress disorder: semantic processing without awareness? *Behav. Res. Ther.* 25:469–76

van Praag H, Schinder AF, Christie BR, Toni N, Palmer TD, Gage FH. 2002. Functional neurogenesis in the adult hippocampus. *Nature* 415:1030–34

Vasterling JJ, Brailey K, Constans JI, Borges A, Sutker PB. 1997. Assessment of intellectual resources in Gulf War veterans: relationship to PTSD. *Assessment* 4:51–59

Walker DL, Davis M. 1997. Double dissociation between the involvement of the bed nucleus of the stria terminalis and the central nucleus of the amygdala in startle increases produced by conditioned versus unconditioned fear. *J. Neurosci.* 17:9375–83

Wantanabe Y, Gould E, McEwen BS. 1992. Stress induces atrophy of apical dendrites of hippocampal pyramidal neurons. *Brain Res.* 588:341–45

Wolf OT, Schommer NC, Hellhammer DH, Reischies FM, Kirschbaum C. 2002. Moderate psychosocial stress appears not to impair recall of words learned 4 weeks prior to stressor exposure. *Stress* 5:59–64

Wood GE, Beylin A, Shors TJ. 2001. The contribution of adrenal and reproductive hormones to the opposing effects of stress on trace conditioning in males versus females. *Behav. Neurosci.* 115:175–87

Wood GE, Shors TJ. 1998. Stress facilitates classical conditioning in males but impairs conditioning in females through activational influences of ovarian hormones. *Proc. Natl. Acad. Sci. USA* 95:4066–71

Woodson JC, Macintosh D, Fleshner M, Diamond DM. 2003. Emotion-induced amnesia in rats: working memory–specific impairment, corticosterone-memory correlation, and fear versus arousal effects on memory. *Learn. Mem.* 10:326–36

Yehuda R, Keefe RSE, Harvey PD, Levengood RA, Gerber DK, et al. 1995. Learning and memory in combat veterans with post-traumatic stress disorder. *Am. J. Psychiatry* 152:137–39

Annu. Rev. Psychol. 2006. 57:87–115
doi: 10.1146/annurev.psych.56.091103.070229
Copyright © 2006 by Annual Reviews. All rights reserved
First published online as a Review in Advance on September 16, 2005

BEHAVIORAL THEORIES AND THE NEUROPHYSIOLOGY OF REWARD

Wolfram Schultz

*Department of Anatomy, University of Cambridge, CB2 3DY United Kingdom;
email: ws234@cam.ac.uk*

Key Words   learning theory, conditioning, microeconomics, utility theory, uncertainty

■ **Abstract**   The functions of rewards are based primarily on their effects on behavior and are less directly governed by the physics and chemistry of input events as in sensory systems. Therefore, the investigation of neural mechanisms underlying reward functions requires behavioral theories that can conceptualize the different effects of rewards on behavior. The scientific investigation of behavioral processes by animal learning theory and economic utility theory has produced a theoretical framework that can help to elucidate the neural correlates for reward functions in learning, goal-directed approach behavior, and decision making under uncertainty. Individual neurons can be studied in the reward systems of the brain, including dopamine neurons, orbitofrontal cortex, and striatum. The neural activity can be related to basic theoretical terms of reward and uncertainty, such as contiguity, contingency, prediction error, magnitude, probability, expected value, and variance.

CONTENTS

INTRODUCTION

How can we understand the common denominator of Pavlov's salivating dogs, an ale named Hobgoblin, a market in southern France, and the bargaining for lock access on the Mississippi River? Pavlov's dogs were presented with pieces of delicious sausage that undoubtedly made them salivate. We know that the same animal will salivate also when it hears a bell that has repeatedly sounded a few seconds before the sausage appears, as if the bell induced the well-known, pleasant anticipation of the desired sausage. Changing slightly the scenery, imagine you are in Cambridge, walk down Mill Lane, and unfailingly end up in the Mill pub by the river Cam. The known attraction inducing the pleasant anticipation is a pint of Hobgoblin. Hobgoblin's provocative ad reads something like "What's the matter Lager boy, afraid you might taste something?" and refers to a full-bodied, dark ale whose taste alone is a reward. Changing the scenery again, you are in the middle of a Saturday morning market in a small town in southern France and run into a nicely arranged stand of rosé and red wines. Knowing the presumably delicious contents of the differently priced bottles to varying degrees, you need to make a decision about what to get for lunch. You can do a numerical calculation and weigh the price of each bottle by the probability that its contents will please your taste, but chances are that a more automatic decision mechanism kicks in that is based on anticipation and will tell you quite quickly what to choose. However, you cannot use the same simple emotional judgment when you are in the shoes of an economist trying to optimize the access to the locks on the Mississippi River. The task is to find a pricing structure that assures the most efficient and uninterrupted use of the infrastructure over a 24-hour day, by avoiding long queues during prime daytime hours and inactive periods during the wee hours of the night. A proper pricing structure known in advance to the captains of the barges will shape their decisions to enter the locks at a moment that is economically most appropriate for the whole journey. The common denominator in these tasks appears to relate to the anticipation of outcomes of behavior in situations with varying degrees of uncertainty: the merely automatic salivation of a dog without much alternative, the choice of sophisticated but partly unknown liquids, or the well-calculated decision of a barge captain on how to get the most out of his money and time.

The performance in these tasks is managed by the brain, which assesses the values and uncertainties of predictable outcomes (sausage, ale, wine, lock pricing, and access to resources) and directs the individuals' decisions toward the current optimum. This review describes some of the knowledge on brain mechanisms related to rewarding outcomes, without attempting to provide a complete account of all the studies done. We focus on the activity of single neurons studied by neurophysiological techniques in behaving animals, in particular monkeys, and emphasize the formative role of behavioral theories, such as animal learning theory and microeconomic utility theory, on the understanding of these brain mechanisms. Given the space limits and the only just beginning neurophysiological studies based on game theory (Barraclough et al. 2004, Dorris & Glimcher 2004), the description of the neurophysiology of this promising field will have to wait until more data have been gathered. The review will not describe the neurobiology of artificial drug rewards, which constitutes a field of its own but does not require vastly different theoretical backgrounds of reward function for its understanding. Readers interested in the rapidly emerging and increasingly large field of human neuroimaging of reward and reward-directed decision making are referred to other reviews (O'Doherty 2004).

GENERAL IDEAS ON REWARD FUNCTION, AND A CALL FOR THEORY

Homer's Odysseus proclaims, "Whatever my distress may be, I would ask you now to let me eat. There is nothing more devoid of shame than the accursed belly; it thrusts itself upon a man's mind in spite of his afflictions. . .my heart is sad but my belly keeps urging me to have food and drink. . .it says imperiously: 'eat and be filled'." (*The Odyssey*, Book VII, 800 BC). Despite these suggestive words, Homer's description hardly fits the common-sensical perceptions of reward, which largely belong to one of two categories. People often consider a reward as a particular object or event that one receives for having done something well. You succeed in an endeavor, and you receive your reward. This reward function could be most easily accommodated within the framework of instrumental conditioning, according to which the reward serves as a positive reinforcer of a behavioral act. The second common perception of reward relates to subjective feelings of liking and pleasure. You do something again because it produced a pleasant outcome before. We refer to this as the hedonic function of rewards. The following descriptions will show that both of these perceptions of reward fall well short of providing a complete and coherent description of reward functions.

One of the earliest scientifically driven definitions of reward function comes from Pavlov (1927), who defined it as an object that produces a change in behavior, also called learning. The dog salivates to a bell only after the sound has been paired with a sausage, but not to a different, nonpaired sound, suggesting that its behavioral response (salivation) has changed after food conditioning. It is noteworthy that this definition bypasses both common-sensical reward notions, as the dog does not need to do anything in particular for the reward to occur (notion 1) nor is it relevant what the dog feels (notion 2). Yet we will see that this definition is a key to neurobiological studies.

Around this time, Thorndike's (1911) Law of Effect postulated that a reward increases the frequency and intensity of a specific behavioral act that has resulted in a reward before or, as a common interpretation has it, "rewards make you come back for more." This definition comes close to the idea of instrumental conditioning, in that you get a reward for having done something well, and not automatically as with Pavlovian conditioning. It resembles Pavlov's definition of learning function, as it suggests that you will do more of the same behavior that has led previously to the rewarding outcome (positive reinforcement). Skinner pushed the definition of instrumental, or operant, conditioning further by defining rewards as reinforcers of stimulus-response links that do not require mental processes such as intention, representation of goal, or consciousness. Although the explicit antimental stance reduced the impact of his concept, the purely behaviorist approach to studying reward function allowed scientists to acquire a huge body of knowledge by studying the behavior of animals, and it paved the way to neurobiological investigations without the confounds of subjective feelings.

Reward objects for animals are primarily vegetative in nature, such as different foodstuffs and liquids with various tastes. These rewards are necessary for survival, their motivational value can be determined by controlled access, and they can be delivered in quantifiable amounts in laboratory situations. The other main vegetative reward, sex, is impossible to deliver in neurophysiological laboratory situations requiring hundreds of daily trials. Animals are also sensitive to other, nonvegetative rewards, such as touch to the skin or fur and presentation of novel objects and situations eliciting exploratory responses, but these again are difficult to parameterize for laboratory situations. Humans use a wide range of nonvegetative rewards, such as money, challenge, acclaim, visual and acoustic beauty, power, security, and many others, but these are not considered as this review considers neural mechanisms in animals.

An issue with vegetative rewards is the precise definition of the rewarding effect. Is it the seeing of an apple, its taste on the tongue, the swallowing of a bite of it, the feeling of its going down the throat, or the rise in blood sugar subsequent to its digestion that makes it a reward and has one come back for more? Which of these events constitutes the primary rewarding effect, and do different objects draw their rewarding effects from different events (Wise 2002)? In some cases, the reward may be the taste experienced when an object activates the gustatory receptors, as with saccharin, which has no nutritional effects but increases behavioral reactions. The ultimate rewarding effect of many nutrient objects may be the specific influence on vegetative parameters, such as electrolyte, glucose, and amino acid concentrations in plasma and brain. This would explain why animals avoid foods that lack such nutrients as essential amino acids (Delaney & Gelperin 1986, Hrupka et al. 1997, Rogers & Harper 1970, Wang et al. 1996). The behavioral function of some reward objects may be determined by innate mechanisms, whereas a much larger variety might be learned through experience.

Although these theories provide important insights into reward function, they tend to neglect the fact that individuals usually operate in a world with limited nutritional and mating resources, and that most resources occur with different degrees of uncertainty. The animal in the wild is not certain whether it will encounter a particular fruit or prey object at a particular moment, nor is the restaurant goer certain that her preferred chef will cook that night. To make the uncertainty of outcomes tractable was the main motive that led Blaise Pascal to develop probability theory around 1650 (see Glimcher 2003 for details). He soon realized that humans make decisions by weighing the potential outcomes by their associated probabilities and then go for the largest result. Or, mathematically speaking, they sum the products of magnitude and probability of all potential outcomes of each option and then choose the option with the highest expected value. Nearly one hundred years later, Bernoulli (1738) discovered that the utility of outcomes for decision making does not increase linearly but frequently follows a concave function, which marks the beginning of microeconomic decision theory. The theory provides quantifiable assessments of outcomes under uncertainty and has gone a long way to explain human and animal decision making, even though more recent data cast doubt on the logic in some decision situations (Kahneman & Tversky 1984).

A Call for Behavioral Theory

Primary sensory systems have dedicated physical and chemical receptors that translate environmental energy and information into neural language. Thus, the functions of primary sensory systems are governed by the laws of mechanics, optics, acoustics, and receptor binding. By contrast, there are no dedicated receptors for reward, and the information enters the brain through mechanical, gustatory, visual, and auditory receptors of the sensory systems. The functions of rewards cannot be derived entirely from the physics and chemistry of input events but are based primarily on behavioral effects, and the investigation of reward functions requires behavioral theories that can conceptualize the different effects of rewards on behavior. Thus, the exploration of neural reward mechanisms should not be based primarily on the physics and chemistry of reward objects but on specific behavioral theories that define reward functions. Animal learning theory and microeconomics are two prominent examples of such behavioral theories and constitute the basis for this review.

REWARD FUNCTIONS DEFINED BY ANIMAL LEARNING THEORY

This section will combine some of the central tenets of animal learning theories in an attempt to define a coherent framework for the investigation of neural reward mechanisms. The framework is based on the description of observable behavior and superficially resembles the behaviorist approach, although mental states of representation and prediction are essential. Dropping the issues of subjective feelings of pleasure will allow us to do objective behavioral measurements in controlled neurophysiological experiments on animals. To induce subjective feelings of pleasure and positive emotion is a key function of rewards, although it is unclear whether the pleasure itself has a reinforcing, causal effect for behavior (i.e., I feel good because of the outcome I got and therefore will do again what produced the pleasant outcome) or is simply an epiphenomenon (i.e., my behavior gets reinforced and, in addition, I feel good because of the outcome).

Learning

Rewards induce changes in observable behavior and serve as positive reinforcers by increasing the frequency of the behavior that results in reward. In Pavlovian, or classical, conditioning, the outcome follows the conditioned stimulus (CS) irrespective of any behavioral reaction, and repeated pairing of stimuli with outcomes leads to a representation of the outcome that is evoked by the stimulus and elicits the behavioral reaction (Figure 1a). By contrast, instrumental, or operant, conditioning requires the subject to execute a behavioral response; without such response there will be no reward. Instrumental conditioning increases the frequency of those behaviors that are followed by reward by reinforcing stimulus-response links. Instrumental conditioning allows subjects to influence their environment and determine their rate of reward.

The behavioral reactions studied classically by Pavlov are vegetative responses governed by smooth muscle contraction and gland discharge, whereas more recent Pavlovian tasks also involve reactions of striated muscles. In the latter case, the final reward usually needs to be collected by an instrumental contraction of striated muscle, but the behavioral reaction to the CS itself, for example, anticipatory licking, is not required for the reward to occur and thus is classically conditioned. As a further emphasis on Pavlovian mechanisms, the individual stimuli in instrumental tasks that predict rewards are considered to be Pavlovian conditioned. These distinctions are helpful when trying to understand why the neural mechanisms of reward prediction reveal strong influences of Pavlovian conditioning.

Three factors govern conditioning, namely contiguity, contingency, and prediction error. Contiguity refers to the requirement of near simultaneity (Figure 1a). Specifically, a reward needs to follow a CS or response by an optimal interval of a few seconds, whereas rewards occurring before a stimulus or response do not contribute to learning (backward conditioning). The contingency requirement postulates that a reward needs to occur more frequently in the presence of a stimulus as compared with its absence in order to induce "excitatory" conditioning of the stimulus (Figure 1b); the occurrence of the CS predicts a higher incidence of reward compared with no stimulus, and the stimulus becomes a reward predictor. By contrast, if a reward occurs less frequently in the absence of a stimulus, compared with its presence, the occurrence of the stimulus predicts a lower incidence of reward, and the stimulus becomes a conditioned inhibitor, even though the contiguity

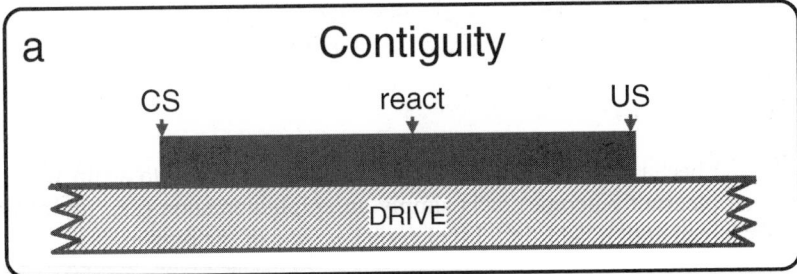

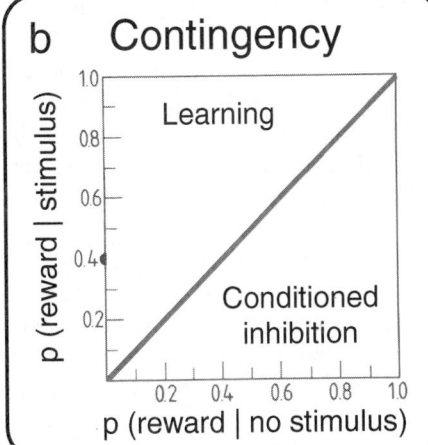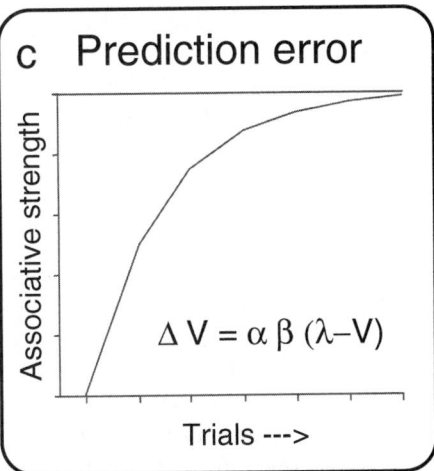

Figure 1 Basic assumptions of animal learning theory defining the behavioral functions of rewards. (*a*) Contiguity refers to the temporal proximity of a conditioned stimulus (CS), or action, and the reward. (*b*) Contingency refers to the conditional probability of reward occurring in the presence of a conditioned stimulus as opposed to its absence (modified from Dickinson 1980). (*c*) Prediction error denotes the discrepancy between an actually received reward and its prediction. Learning (ΔV, associative strength) is proportional to the prediction error ($\lambda-V$) and reaches its asymptote when the prediction error approaches zero after several learning trials. All three requirements need to be fulfilled for learning to occur. US, unconditioned stimulus.

requirement is fulfilled. The crucial role of prediction error is derived from Kamin's (1969) blocking effect, which postulates that a reward that is fully predicted does not contribute to learning, even when it occurs in a contiguous and contingent manner. This is conceptualized in the associative learning rules (Rescorla & Wagner 1972), according to which learning advances only to the extent to which a reinforcer is unpredicted and slows progressively as the reinforcer becomes more predicted (Figure 1*c*). The omission of a predicted reinforcer reduces the strength of the CS and produces extinction of behavior. So-called attentional learning rules in addition relate the capacity to learn (associability) in certain situations to the degree of attention evoked by the CS or reward (Mackintosh 1975, Pearce & Hall 1980).

Approach Behavior

Rewards elicit two forms of behavioral reactions, approach and consumption. This is because the objects are labeled with appetitive value through innate mechanisms (primary rewards) or, in most cases, classical or instrumental conditioning, after which these objects constitute, strictly speaking, conditioned reinforcers (Wise 2002). Nutritional rewards can derive their value from hunger and thirst states, and satiation of the animal reduces the reward value and consequently the behavioral reactions.

Conditioned, reward-predicting stimuli also induce preparatory or approach behavior toward the reward. In Pavlovian conditioning, subjects automatically show nonconsummatory behavioral reactions that would otherwise occur after the primary reward and that increase the chance of consuming the reward, as if a part of the behavioral response has been transferred from the primary reward to the CS (Pavlovian response transfer).

In instrumental conditioning, a reward can become a goal for instrumental behavior if two conditions are met. The goal needs to be represented at the time the behavior is being prepared and executed. This representation should contain a prediction of the future reward together with the contingency that associates the behavioral action to the reward (Dickinson & Balleine 1994). Behavioral tests for the role of "incentive" reward-predicting mechanisms include assessing behavioral performance in extinction following devaluation of the reward by satiation or aversive conditioning in the absence of the opportunity to perform the instrumental action (Balleine & Dickinson 1998). A reduction of behavior in this situation indicates that subjects have established an internal representation of the reward that is updated when the reward changes its value. (Performing the action together with the devalued outcome would result in reduced behavior due to partial extinction, as the reduced reward value would diminish the strength of the association.) To test the role of action-reward contingencies, the frequency of "free" rewards in the absence of the action can be varied to change the strength of association between the action and the reward and thereby modulate instrumental behavior (Balleine & Dickinson 1998).

Motivational Valence

Punishers have opposite valence to rewards, induce withdrawal behavior, and act as negative reinforcers by increasing the behavior that results in decreasing the aversive outcome. Avoidance can be passive when subjects increasingly refrain from doing something that is associated with a punisher (don't do it); active avoidance involves increasing an instrumental response that is likely to reduce the impact of a punisher (get away from it). Punishers induce negative emotional states of anger, fear, and panic.

NEUROPHYSIOLOGY OF REWARD BASED
ON ANIMAL LEARNING THEORY

Primary Reward

Neurons responding to liquid or food rewards are found in a number of brain structures, such as orbitofrontal, premotor and prefrontal cortex, striatum, amygdala, and dopamine neurons (Amador et al. 2000, Apicella et al. 1991, Bowman et al. 1996, Hikosaka et al. 1989, Ljungberg et al. 1992, Markowitsch & Pritzel 1976, Nakamura et al. 1992, Nishijo et al. 1988, Pratt & Mizumori 1998, Ravel et al. 1999, Shidara et al. 1998, Thorpe et al. 1983, Tremblay & Schultz 1999). Satiation of the animal reduces the reward responses in orbitofrontal cortex (Critchley & Rolls 1996) and in the secondary gustatory area of caudal orbitofrontal cortex (Rolls et al. 1989), a finding that suggests that the responses reflect the rewarding functions of the objects and not their taste. Taste responses are found in the primary gustatory area of the insula and frontal operculum and are insensitive to satiation (Rolls et al. 1988).

Contiguity

Procedures involving Pavlovian conditioning provide simple paradigms for learning and allow the experimenter to test the basic requirements of contiguity, contingency, and prediction error. Contiguity can be tested by presenting a reward 1.5–2.0 seconds after an untrained, arbitrary visual or auditory stimulus for several trials. A dopamine neuron that responds initially to a liquid or food reward acquires a response to the CS after some tens of paired CS-reward trials (Figure 2, see color insert) (Mirenowicz & Schultz 1994, Waelti 2000). Responses to conditioned, reward-predicting stimuli occur in all known reward structures of the brain, including the orbitofrontal cortex, striatum, and amygdala (e.g., Hassani et al. 2001, Liu & Richmond 2000, Nishijo et al. 1988, Rolls et al. 1996, Thorpe et al. 1983, Tremblay & Schultz 1999). (Figure 2 shows that the response to the reward itself disappears in dopamine neurons, but this is not a general phenomenon with other neurons.)

Contingency

The contingency requirement postulates that in order to be involved in reward prediction, neurons should discriminate between three kinds of stimuli, namely reward-predicting CSs (conditioned exciters), after which reward occurs more frequently compared with no CS (Figure 1b, top left); conditioned inhibitors, after which reward occurs less frequently compared with no CS (Figure 1b, bottom right); and neutral stimuli that are not associated with changes in reward frequency compared with no stimulus (diagonal line in Figure 1b). In agreement with these postulates, dopamine neurons are activated by reward-predicting CSs, show depressions of activity following conditioned inhibitors, which may be accompanied by small activations, and hardly respond to neutral stimuli when response generalization is excluded (Figure 3) (Tobler et al. 2003). The conditioned inhibitor in these experiments is set up by pairing the inhibitor with a reward-predicting CS while withholding the reward, which amounts to a lower probability of reward in the presence of the inhibitor compared with its absence (reward-predicting stimulus alone) and thus follows the scheme of Figure 1*b* (bottom right). Without conditioned inhibitors being tested, many studies find CS responses that distinguish between reward-predicting and neutral stimuli in all reward structures (e.g., Aosaki et al. 1994, Hollerman et al. 1998, Kawagoe et al. 1998, Kimura et al. 1984, Nishijo et al. 1988, Ravel et al. 1999, Shidara et al. 1998, Waelti et al. 2001).

Further tests assess the specificity of information contained in CS responses. In the typical behavioral tasks used in monkey experiments, the CS may contain several different stimulus components, namely spatial position; visual object features such as color, form, and spatial frequency; and motivational features such as reward prediction. It would be necessary to establish through behavioral testing which of these features is particularly effective in evoking a neural response. For example, neurons in the orbitofrontal cortex discriminate between different CSs on the basis of their prediction of different food and liquid rewards (Figure 4) (Critchley & Rolls 1996, Tremblay & Schultz 1999). By contrast, these neurons are less sensitive to the visual object features of the same CSs, and they rarely code their spatial position, although neurons in other parts of frontal cortex are particularly tuned to these nonreward parameters (Rao et al. 1997). CS responses that are primarily sensitive to the reward features are found also in the amygdala (Nishijo et al. 1988) and striatum (Hassani et al. 2001). These data suggest that individual neurons in these structures can extract the reward components from the multidimensional stimuli used in these experiments as well as in everyday life.

Reward neurons should distinguish rewards from punishers. Different neurons in orbitofrontal cortex respond to rewarding and aversive liquids (Thorpe et al. 1983). Dopamine neurons are activated preferentially by rewards and reward-predicting stimuli but are only rarely activated by aversive air puffs and saline (Mirenowicz & Schultz 1996). In anesthetized animals, dopamine neurons show depressions following painful stimuli (Schultz & Romo 1987, Ungless et al. 2004). Nucleus accumbens neurons in rats show differential activating or depressing responses to CSs predicting rewarding sucrose versus aversive quinine solutions in a Pavlovian task (Roitman et al. 2005). By contrast, the group of tonically active neurons of the striatum responds to both rewards and aversive air puffs, but not to neutral stimuli (Ravel et al. 1999). They seem to be sensitive to reinforcers in general, without specifying their valence. Alternatively, their responses might reflect the higher attention-inducing effects of reinforcers compared with neutral stimuli.

The omission of reward following a CS moves the contingency toward the diagonal line in Figure 1*b* and leads to extinction of learned behavior. By analogy, the withholding of reward reduces the activation of dopamine neurons by CSs within several tens of trials (Figure 5, see color insert) (Tobler at al. 2003).

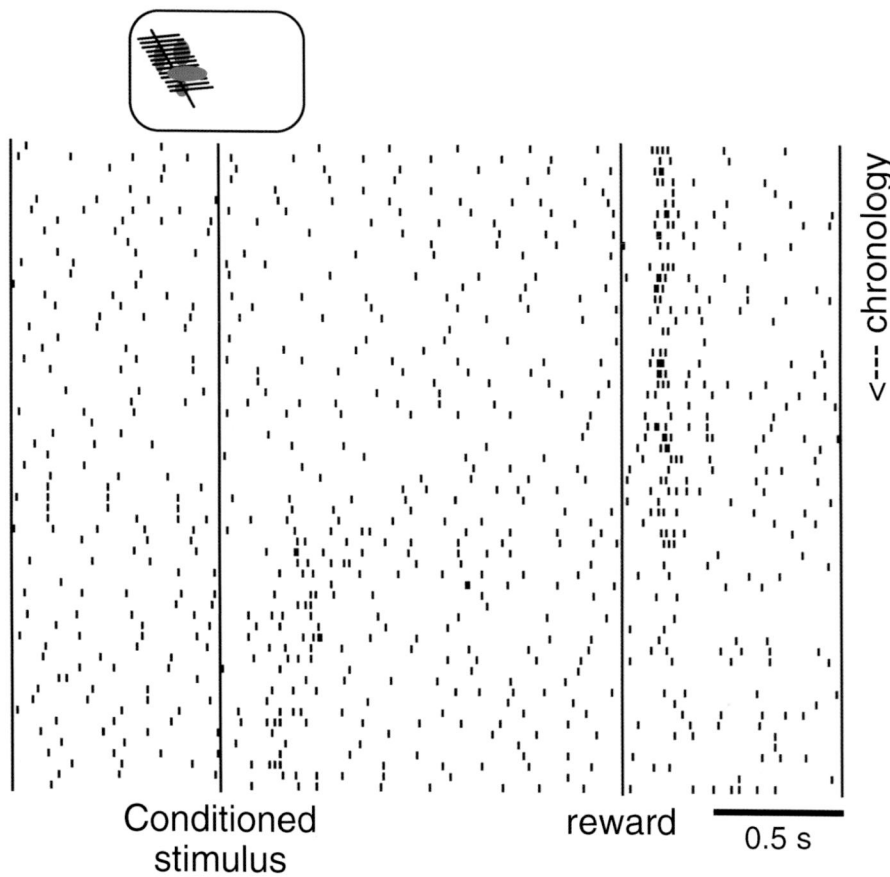

Figure 2 Testing the contiguity requirement for associative learning: acquisition of neural response in a single dopamine neuron during a full learning episode. Each line of dots represents a trial, each dot represents the time of the discharge of the dopamine neuron, the vertical lines indicate the time of the stimulus and juice reward, and the picture above the raster shows the visual conditioned stimulus presented to the monkey on a computer screen. Chronology of trials is from top to bottom. The top trial shows the activity of the neuron while the animal saw the stimulus for the first time in its life, whereas it had previous experience with the liquid reward. Data from Waelti (2000).

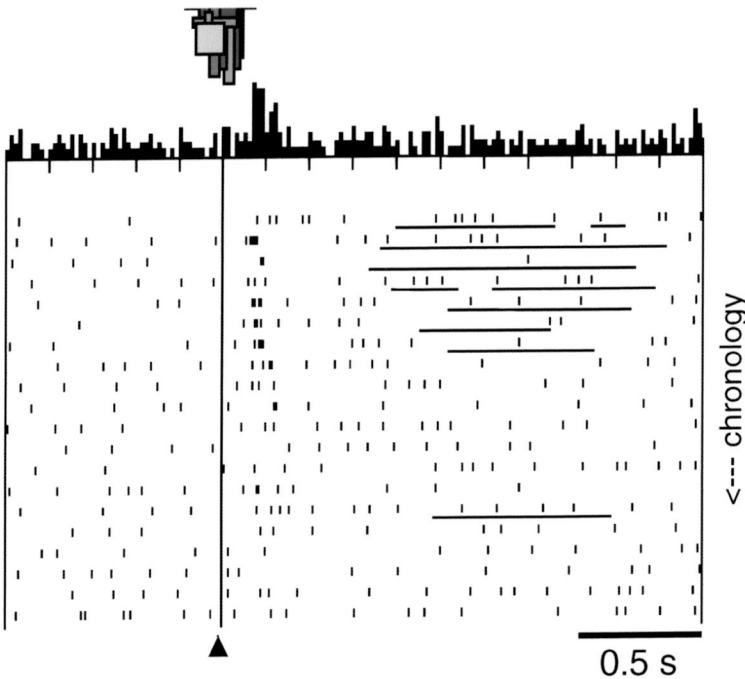

Figure 5 Loss of response in dopamine neuron to the conditioned stimulus following withholding of reward. This manipulation violates the contiguity requirement (co-occurrence of reward and stimulus) and produces a negative prediction error that brings down the associative strength of the stimulus. The contingency moves toward the neutral situation. Data from Tobler et al. (2003).

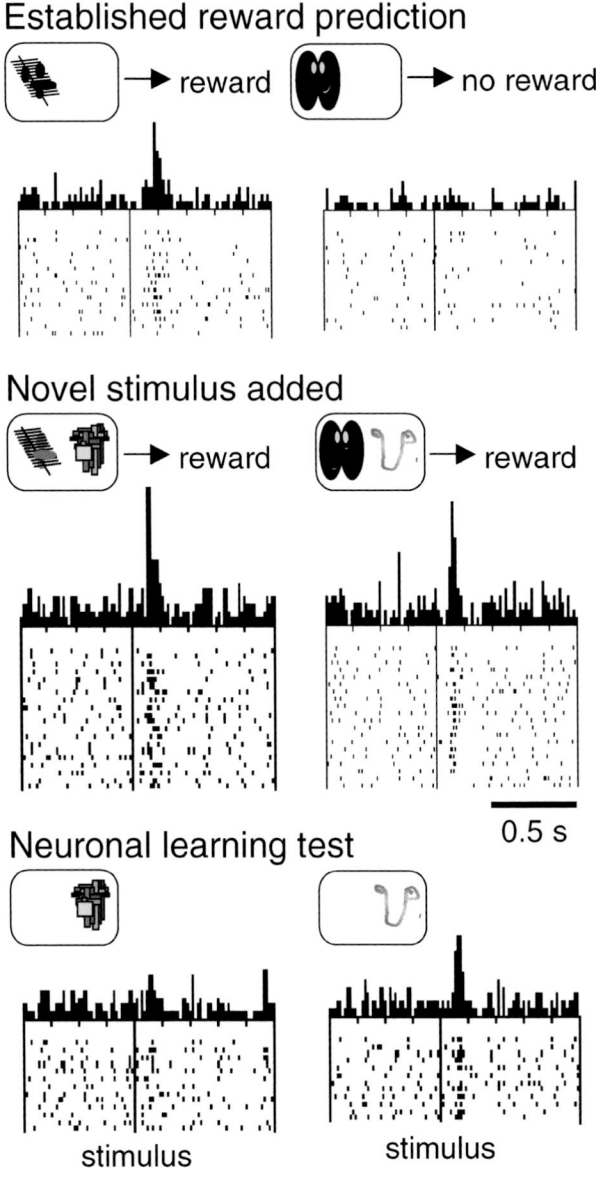

Established reward prediction

Novel stimulus added

0.5 s

Neuronal learning test

stimulus   stimulus

See legend on next page

Figure 6 Acquisition of dopamine response to reward-predicting stimulus is governed by prediction error. Neural learning is blocked when the reward is predicted by another stimulus (*left*) but is intact in the same neuron when reward is unpredicted in control trials with different stimuli (*right*). The neuron has the capacity to respond to reward-predicting stimuli (*top left*) and discriminates against unrewarded stimuli (*top right*). The addition of a second stimulus results in maintenance and acquisition of response, respectively (*middle*). Testing the added stimulus reveals absence of learning when the reward is already predicted by a previously conditioned stimulus (*bottom left*). Data from Waelti et al. (2001).

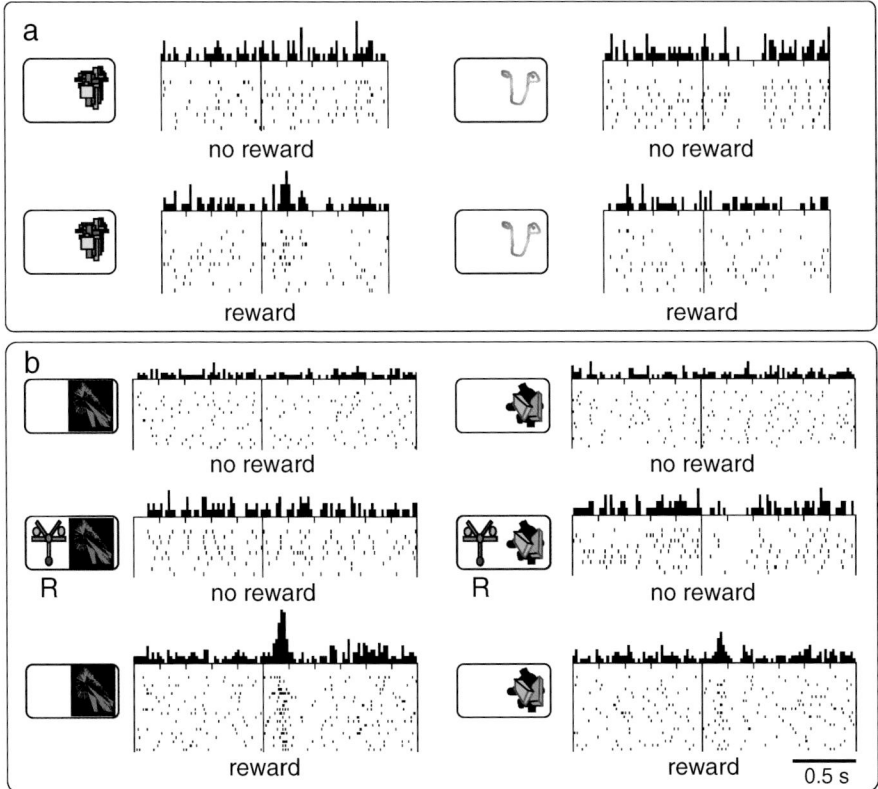

Figure 8   Coding of prediction errors by dopamine neurons in specific paradigms. (*a*) Blocking test. Lack of response to absence of reward following the blocked stimulus, but positive signal to delivery of reward (*left*), in contrast to control trials with a learned stimulus (*right*). Data from Waelti et al. 2001. (*b*) Conditioned inhibition task. Lack of response to absence of reward following the stimulus predicting no reward (*top*), even if the stimulus is paired with an otherwise reward-predicting stimulus (R, *middle*, summation test), but strong activation to reward following a stimulus predicting no reward (*bottom*). These responses contrast with those following the neutral control stimulus (*right*). Data from Tobler et al. (2003).

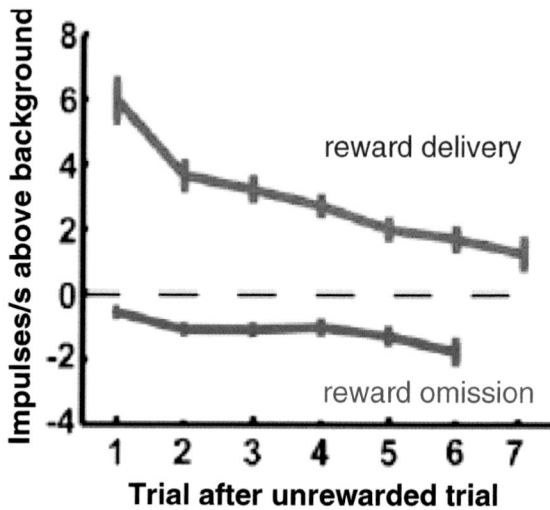

Figure 9 Time information contained in predictions acting on dopamine neurons. In the particular behavioral task, the probability of reward, and thus the reward prediction, increases with increasing numbers of trials after the last reward, reaching p = 1.0 after six unrewarded trials. Accordingly, the positive dopamine error response to a rewarding event decreases over consecutive trials (*upper curve*), and the negative response to a nonrewarding event becomes more prominent (*lower curve*). Data are averaged from 32 dopamine neurons studied by Nakahara et al. (2004), © Cell. Press.

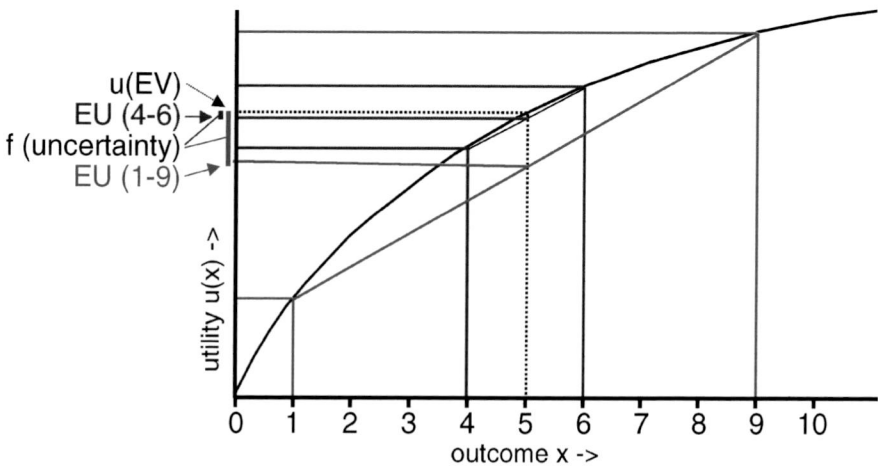

Figure 12 A hypothetical concave utility function. EV, expected value (5 in both gambles with outcomes of 1 and 9, and 4 and 6); EU, expected utility. See text for description.

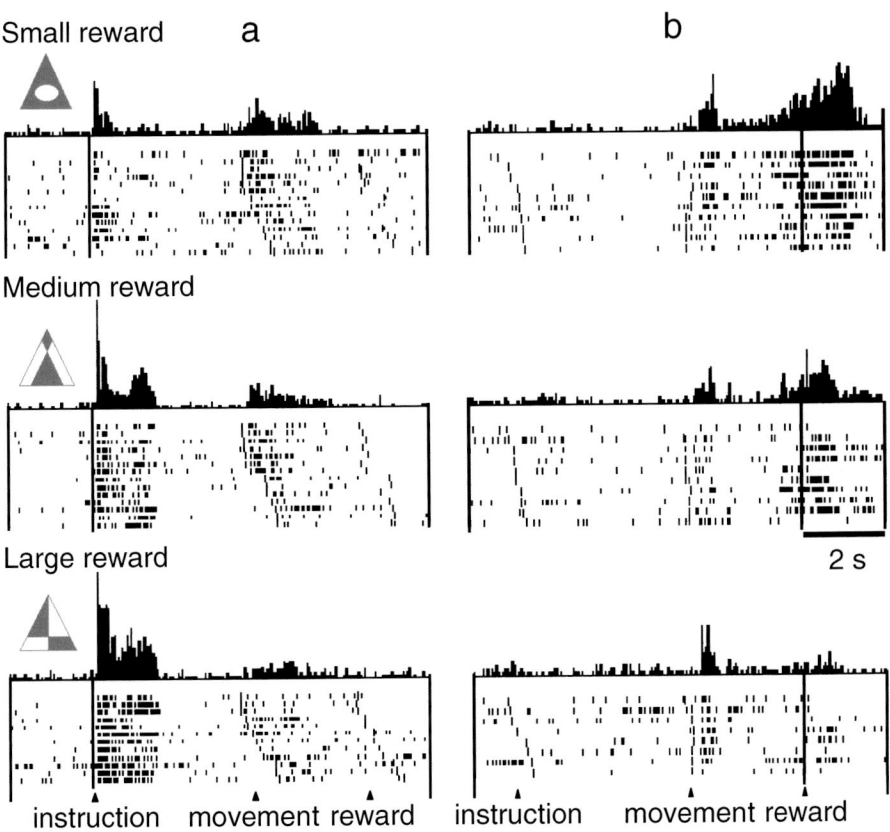

Figure 13   Discrimination of reward magnitude by striatal neurons. (*a*) Increasing response in a caudate neuron to instruction cues predicting increasing magnitudes of reward (0.12, 0.18, 0.24 ml). (*b*) Decreasing response in a ventral striatum neuron to rewards with increasing volumes. Data from Cromwell & Schultz 2003.

Conditioned stimulus predicting reward

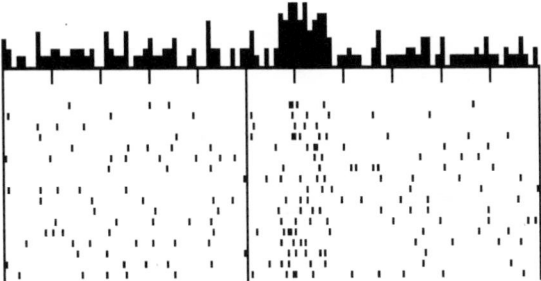

Conditioned stimulus predicting absence of reward

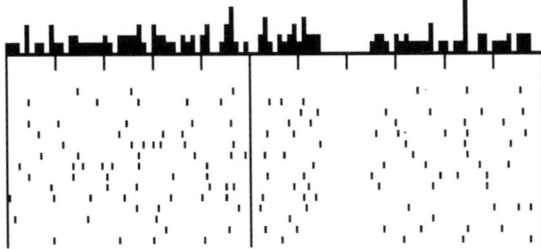

Known neutral stimulus

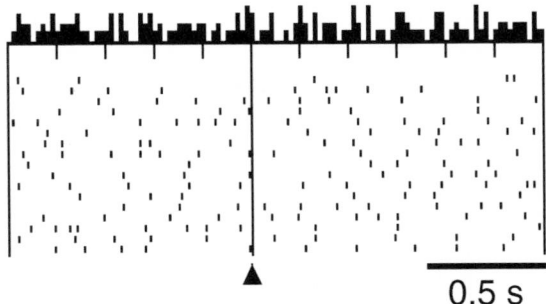

0.5 s

Figure 3   Testing the contingency requirement for associative learning: responses of a single dopamine neuron to three types of stimuli. (*Top*) Activating response to a reward-predicting stimulus (higher occurrence of reward in the presence as opposed to absence of stimulus). (*Middle*) Depressant response to a different stimulus predicting the absence of reward (lower occurrence of reward in the presence as opposed to absence of stimulus). (*Bottom*) Neutral stimulus (no change in reward occurrence after stimulus). Vertical line and arrow indicate time of stimulus.

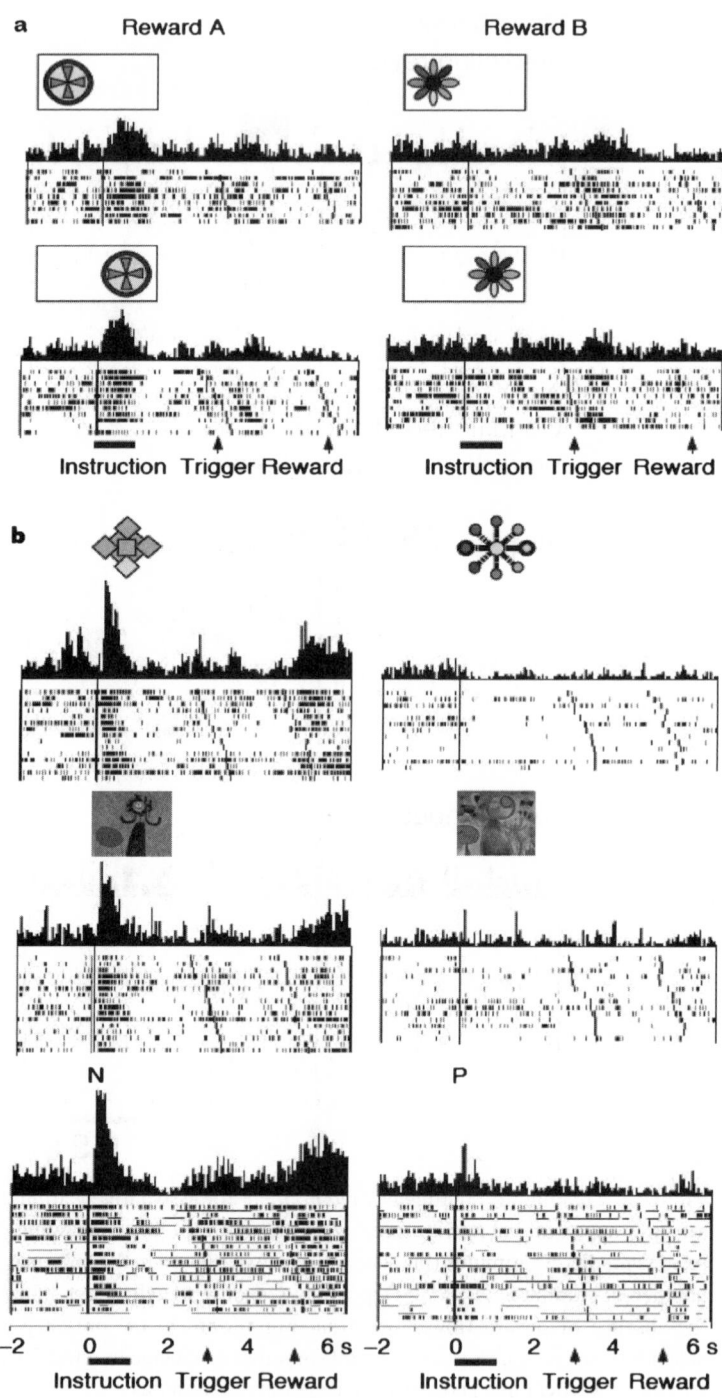

Prediction Error

Just as with behavioral learning, the acquisition of neuronal responses to reward-predicting CSs should depend on prediction errors. In the prediction error–defining blocking paradigm, dopamine neurons acquire a response to a CS only when the CS is associated with an unpredicted reward, but not when the CS is paired with a reward that is already predicted by another CS and the occurrence of the reward does not generate a prediction error (Figure 6, see color insert) (Waelti et al. 2001). The neurons fail to learn to respond to reward predictors despite the fact that contiguity and contingency requirements for excitatory learning are fulfilled. These data demonstrate the crucial importance of prediction errors for associative neural learning and suggest that learning at the single-neuron level may follow similar rules as those for behavioral learning. This suggests that some behavioral learning functions may be carried by populations of single neurons.

Neurons may not only be sensitive to prediction errors during learning, but they may also emit a prediction error signal. Dopamine neurons, and some neurons in orbitofrontal cortex, show reward activations only when the reward occurs unpredictably and fail to respond to well-predicted rewards, and their activity is depressed when the predicted reward fails to occur (Figure 7) (Mirenowicz & Schultz 1994, Tremblay & Schultz 2000a). This result has prompted the notion that dopamine neurons emit a positive signal (activation) when an appetitive event is better than predicted, no signal (no change in activity) when an appetitive event occurs as predicted, and a negative signal (decreased activity) when an appetitive event is worse than predicted (Schultz et al. 1997). In contrast to this bidirectional error signal, some neurons in the prefrontal, anterior, and posterior cingulate cortex show a unidirectional error signal upon activation when a reward fails to occur because of a behavioral error of the animal (Ito et al. 2003, McCoy et al. 2003, Watanabe 1989; for review of neural prediction errors, see Schultz & Dickinson 2000).

More stringent tests for the neural coding of prediction errors include formal paradigms of animal learning theory in which prediction errors occur in specific situations. In the blocking paradigm, the blocked CS does not predict a reward. Accordingly, the absence of a reward following that stimulus does not produce a prediction error nor a response in dopamine neurons, and the delivery of a reward does produce a positive prediction error and a dopamine response (Figure 8a, see color insert; left) (Waelti et al. 2001). By contrast, after a well-trained,

---

Figure 4   Reward discrimination in orbitofrontal cortex. (*a*) A neuron responding to the instruction cue predicting grenadine juice (*left*) but not apple juice (*right*), irrespective of the left or right position of the cue in front of the animal. (*b*) A different neuron responding to the cue predicting grape juice (*left*) but not orange juice (*right*), irrespective of the picture object predicting the juice. From Tremblay & Schultz 1999, © Nature MacMillan Publishers.

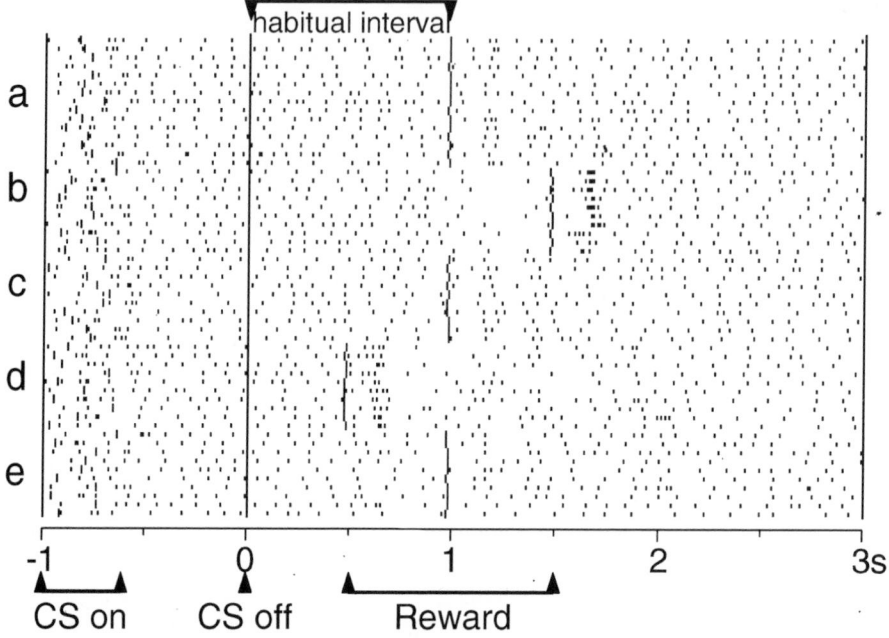

Figure 7   Dopamine response codes temporal reward prediction error. (*a, c, e*) No response to reward delivered at habitual time. (*b*) Delay in reward induces depression at previous time of reward, and activation at new reward time. (*d*) Precocious reward delivery induces activation at new reward time, but no depression at previous reward time. Trial sequence is from top to bottom. Data from Hollerman & Schultz (1998). CS, conditioned stimulus.

reward-predicting CS, reward omission produces a negative prediction error and a depressant neural response, and reward delivery does not lead to a prediction error or a response in the same dopamine neuron (Figure 8*a*; right). In a conditioned inhibition paradigm, the conditioned inhibitor predicts the absence of reward, and the absence of reward after this stimulus does not produce a prediction error or a response in dopamine neurons, even when another, otherwise reward-predicting stimulus is added (Figure 8*b*) (Tobler at al. 2003). By contrast, the occurrence of reward after an inhibitor produces an enhanced prediction error, as the prediction error represents the difference between the actual reward and the negative prediction from the inhibitor, and the dopamine neuron shows a strong response (Figure 8*b*; bottom). Taken together, these data suggest that dopamine neurons show bidirectional coding of reward prediction errors, following the equation

$$\text{Dopamine response} = \text{Reward occurred} - \text{Reward predicted.}$$

This equation may constitute a neural equivalent for the prediction error term of $(\lambda - V)$ of the Rescorla-Wagner learning rule. With these characteristics, the bidirectional dopamine error response would constitute an ideal teaching signal for neural plasticity.

The neural prediction error signal provides an additional means to investigate the kinds of information contained in the representations evoked by CSs. Time apparently plays a major role in behavioral learning, as demonstrated by the unblocking effects of temporal variations of reinforcement (Dickinson et al. 1976). Figure 7 shows that the prediction acting on dopamine neurons concerns the exact time of reward occurrence. Temporal deviations induce a depression when the reward fails to occur at the predicted time (time-sensitive reward omission response), and an activation when the reward occurs at a moment other than predicted (Hollerman & Schultz 1998). This time sensitivity also explains why neural prediction errors occur at all in the laboratory in which animals know that they will receive ample quantities of reward but without knowing when exactly the reward will occur. Another form of time representation is revealed by tests in which the probability of receiving a reward after the last reward increases over consecutive trials. Thus, the animal's reward prediction should increase after each unrewarded trial, the positive prediction error with reward should decrease, and the negative prediction error with reward omission should increase. In line with this reasoning, dopamine neurons show progressively decreasing activations to reward delivery as the number of trials since the last reward increases, and increasing depressions in unrewarded trials (Figure 9, see color insert) (Nakahara et al. 2004). The result suggests that, for the neurons, the reward prediction in the CS increases after every unrewarded trial, due to the temporal profile of the task evoked by the CS, and contradicts an assumption from temporal difference reinforcement modeling that the prediction error of the preceding unrewarded trial would reduce the current reward prediction in the CS, in which case the neural prediction error responses should increase, which is the opposite to what is actually observed (although the authors attribute the temporal conditioning to the context and have the CS conform to the temporal difference model). The results from the two experiments demonstrate that dopamine neurons are sensitive to different aspects of temporal information evoked by reward-predicting CSs and demonstrate how experiments based on specific behavioral concepts, namely prediction error, reveal important characteristics of neural coding.

The uncertainty of reward is a major factor for generating the attention that determines learning according to the associability learning rules (Mackintosh 1975, Pearce & Hall 1980). When varying the probability of reward in individual trials from 0 to 1, reward becomes most uncertain at $p = 0.5$, as it is most unclear whether or not a reward will occur. (Common perception might say that reward is even more uncertain at $p = 0.25$; however, at this low probability, it is nearly certain that reward will not occur.) Dopamine neurons show a slowly increasing activation between the CS and reward that is maximal at $p = 0.5$ (Fiorillo et al. 2003). This response may constitute an explicit uncertainty signal and is different in time and occurrence from the prediction error response. The response might contribute to a teaching signal in situations defined by the associability learning rules.

Approach Behavior and Goal Directedness

Many behavioral tasks in the laboratory involve more than a CS and a reward and comprise instrumental ocular or skeletal reactions, mnemonic delays between instruction cues and behavioral reactions, and delays between behavioral reactions and rewards during which animals can expect the reward.

Appropriately conditioned stimuli can evoke specific expectations of reward, and phasic neural responses to these CSs may reflect the process of evocation (see above). Once the representations have been evoked, their content can influence the behavior during some time. Neurons in a number of brain structures show sustained activations after an initial CS has occurred. The activations arise usually during specific epochs of well-differentiated instrumental tasks, such as during movement preparation (Figure 10a) and immediately preceding the reward (Figure 10b), whereas few activations last during the entire period between CS and reward. The activations differentiate between reward and no reward, between different kinds of liquid and food reward, and between different magnitudes of reward. They occur in all trial types in which reward is expected, irrespective of the type of behavioral action (Figure 10). Thus, the activations appear to represent reward expectations. They are found in the striatum (caudate, putamen, ventral

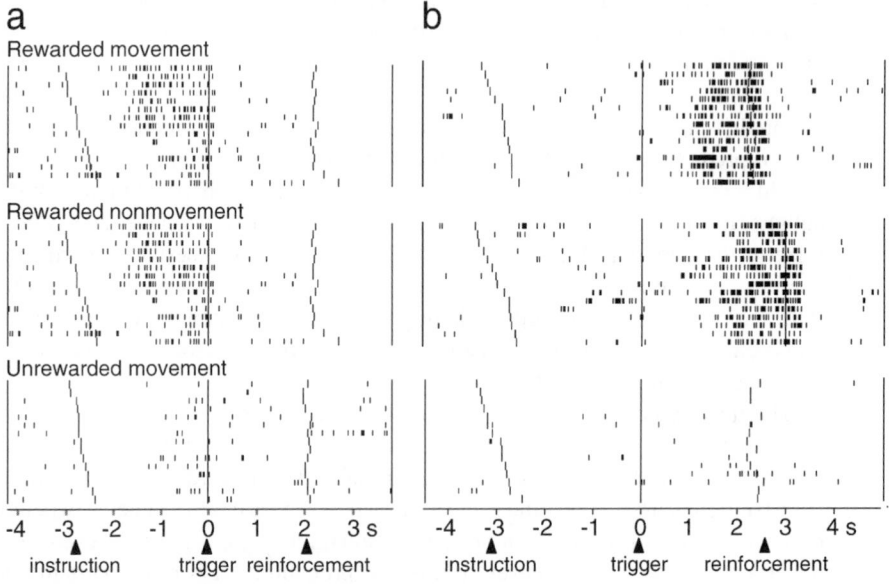

Figure 10   Reward expectation in the striatum. (*a*) Activation in a caudate neuron preceding the stimulus that triggers the movement or nonmovement reaction in both rewarded trial types irrespective of movement, but not in unrewarded movement trials. (*b*) Activation in a putamen neuron preceding the delivery of liquid reward in both rewarded trial types, but not before the reinforcing sound in unrewarded movement trials. Data from Hollerman et al. (1998).

striatum), amygdala, orbitofrontal cortex, dorsolateral prefrontal cortex, anterior cingulate, and supplementary eye field (Amador et al. 2000, Apicella et al. 1992, Cromwell & Schultz 2003, Hikosaka et al. 1989, Hollerman et al. 1998, Pratt & Mizumori 2001, Schoenbaum et al. 1998, Schultz et al. 1992, Shidara & Richmond 2002, Tremblay & Schultz 1999, 2000a, Watanabe 1996, Watanabe et al. 2002). Reward expectation-related activity in orbitofrontal cortex and amygdala develops as the reward becomes predictable during learning (Schoenbaum et al. 1999). In learning episodes with pre-existing reward expectations, orbitofrontal and striatal activations occur initially in all situations but adapt to the currently valid expectations, for example when novel stimuli come to indicate rewarded versus unrewarded trials. The neural changes occur in parallel with the animal's behavioral differentiation (Tremblay et al. 1998, Tremblay & Schultz 2000b).

In some neurons, the differential reward expectation-related activity discriminates in addition between different behavioral responses, such as eye and limb movements toward different spatial targets and movement versus nonmovement reactions (Figure 11). Such neurons are found in the dorsolateral prefrontal cortex (Kobayashi et al. 2002, Matsumoto et al. 2003, Watanabe 1996) and striatum

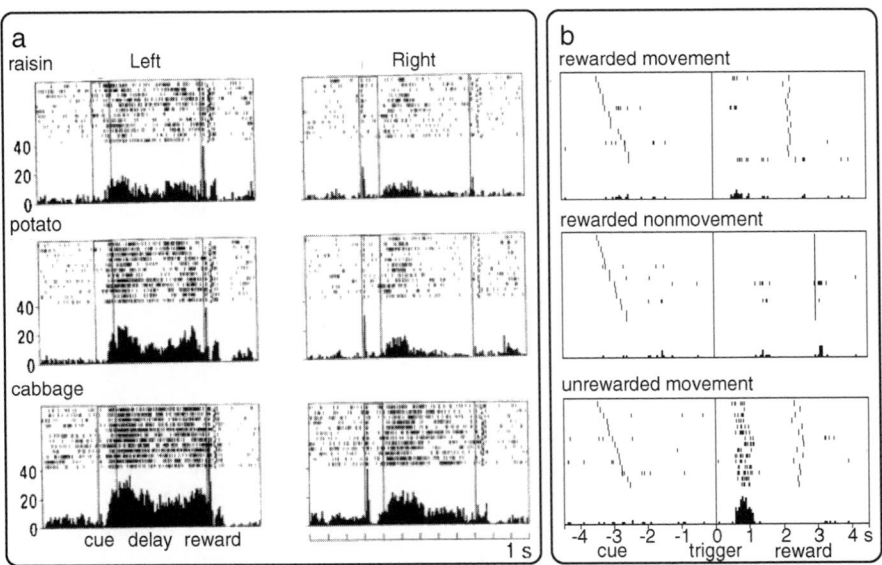

Figure 11   Potential neural mechanisms underlying goal-directed behavior. (*a*) Delay activity of a neuron in primate prefrontal cortex that encodes, while the movement is being prepared, both the behavioral reaction (left versus right targets) and the kind of outcome obtained for performing the action. From Watanabe (1996), © Nature MacMillan Publishers. (*b*) Response of a caudate neuron to the movement-triggering stimulus exclusively in unrewarded trials, thus coding both the behavioral reaction being executed and the anticipated outcome of the reaction. Data from Hollerman et al. (1998).

(Cromwell & Schultz 2003, Hassani et al. 2001, Hollerman et al. 1998, Kawagoe et al. 1998). The activations occur during task epochs related to the preparation and execution of the movement that is performed in order to obtain the reward. They do not simply represent outcome expectation, as they differentiate between different behavioral reactions despite the same outcome (Figure 11*a*, left versus right; Figure 11*b*, movement versus nonmovement), and they do not simply reflect different behavioral reactions, as they differentiate between the expected outcomes (Figure 11*a,b*, top versus bottom). Or, expressed in another way, the neurons show differential, behavior-related activations that depend on the outcome of the trial, namely reward or no reward and different kinds and magnitudes of reward. The differential nature of the activations develops during learning while the different reward expectations are being acquired, similar to simple reward expectation-related activity (Tremblay et al. 1998).

It is known that rewards have strong attention-inducing functions, and reward-related activity in parietal association cortex might simply reflect the known involvement of these areas in attention (Maunsell 2004). It is often tedious to disentangle attention from reward, but one viable solution would be to test neurons for specificity for reinforcers with opposing valence while keeping the levels of reinforcement strength similar for rewards and punishers. The results of such tests suggest that dopamine neurons and some neurons in orbitofrontal cortex discriminate between rewards and aversive events and thus report reward-related but not attention-related stimulus components (Mirenowicz & Schultz 1996, Thorpe et al. 1983). Also, neurons showing increasing activations with decreasing reward value or magnitude are unlikely to reflect the attention associated with stronger rewards. Such inversely related neurons exist in the striatum and orbitofrontal cortex (Hassani et al. 2001, Hollerman et al. 1998, Kawagoe et al. 1998, Watanabe 1996).

General learning theory suggests that Pavlovian associations of reward-predicting stimuli in instrumental tasks relate either to explicit CSs or to contexts. The neural correlates of behavioral associations with explicit stimuli may not only involve the phasic responses to CSs described above but also activations at other task epochs. Further neural correlates of Pavlovian conditioning may consist of the sustained activations that occur during the different task periods preceding movements or rewards (Figure 10), which are only sensitive to reward parameters and not to the types of behavioral reactions necessary to obtain the rewards.

Theories of goal-directed instrumental behavior postulate that in order to consider rewards as goals of behavior, there should be (*a*) an expectation of the outcome at the time of the behavior that leads to the reward, and (*b*) a representation of the contingency between the instrumental action and the outcome (Dickinson & Balleine 1994). The sustained, reward-discriminating activations may constitute a neural mechanism for simple reward expectation, as they reflect the expected reward without differentiating between behavioral reactions (Figure 10). However, these activations are not fully sufficient correlates for goal-directed behavior, as the reward expectation is not necessarily related to the specific action that results in the goal being attained; rather, it might refer to an unrelated reward that occurs in parallel and irrespective of the action. Such a reward would not constitute a goal of the action, and the reward-expecting activation might simply reflect the upcoming reward without being involved in any goal mechanism. By contrast, reward-expecting activations might fulfill the second, more stringent criterion if they are also specific for the action necessary to obtain the reward. These reward-expecting activations differentiate between different behavioral acts and arise only under the condition that the behavior leading to the reward is being prepared or executed (Figure 11). Mechanistically speaking, the observed neural activations may be the result of convergent neural coding of reward and behavior, but from a theoretical point, the activations could represent evidence for neural correlates of goal-directed mechanisms. To distinguish between the two possibilities, it would be helpful to test explicitly the contingency requirement by varying the probabilities of reward in the presence versus absence of behavioral reactions. Further tests could employ reward devaluations to distinguish between goal-directed and habit mechanisms, as the relatively more simple habits might also rely on combined neural mechanisms of expected reward and behavioral action but lack the more flexible representations of reward that are the hallmark of goal mechanisms.

REWARD FUNCTIONS DEFINED BY MICROECONOMIC UTILITY THEORY

How can we compare apples and pears? We need a numerical scale in order to assess the influence of different rewards on behavior. A good way to quantify the value of individual rewards is to compare them in choice behavior. Given two options, I would choose the one that at this moment has the higher value for me. Give me the choice between a one-dollar bill and an apple, and you will see which one I prefer and thus my action will tell you whether the value of the apple for me is higher or lower or similar compared with one dollar. To be able to put a quantifiable, numerical value onto every reward, even when the value is short-lived, has enormous advantages for getting reward-related behavior under experimental control.

To obtain a more complete picture, we need to take into account the uncertainty with which rewards frequently occur. One possibility would be to weigh the value of individual rewards with the probability with which they occur, an approach taken by Pascal ca. 1650. The sum of the products of each potential reward and its probability defines the expected value (EV) of the probability distribution and thus the theoretically expected payoff of an option, according to

$$EV = \sum_i (p_i \cdot x_i); \ i = 1, n; \ n = \text{number of rewards.}$$

With increasing numbers of trials, the measured mean of the actually occurring distribution will approach the expected value. Pascal conjectured that human choice behavior could be approximated by this procedure.

Despite its advantages, expected value theory has limits when comparing very small with very large rewards or when comparing values at different start positions. Rather than following physical sizes of reward value in a linear fashion, human choice behavior in many instances increases more slowly as the values get higher, and the term of utility, or in some cases prospect, replaces the term of value when the impact of rewards on choices is assessed (Bernoulli 1738, Kahneman & Tversky 1984, Savage 1954, von Neumann & Morgenstern 1944). The utility function can be modeled by various equations (for detailed descriptions, see Gintis 2000, Huang & Litzenberger 1988), such as

1. The logarithmic utility function, $u(x) = \ln(x)$, yields a concave curve similar to the Weber (1850) function of psychophysics.

2. The power utility function, $u(x) = x^a$. With a $\in$ (0,1), and often a $\in$ [0.66, 0.75], the function is concave and resembles the power law of psychophysics (Stevens 1957). By contrast, $a = 1.0$ produces a linear function in which utility (value) = value. With a > 1, the curve becomes convex and increases faster toward higher values.

3. The exponential utility function, $u(x) = 1 - e^{-bx}$, produces a concave function for b $\in$ (0,1).

4. With the weighted reward value being expressed as utility, the expected value of a gamble becomes the expected utility (EU) according to

$$EU = \sum_i (p_i \cdot u(x_i)); i = 1, n; n = \text{number of rewards.}$$

Assessing the expected utility allows comparisons between gambles that have several outcomes with different values occurring at different probabilities. Note that a gamble with a single reward occurring at a p < 1 actually has two outcomes, the reward occurring with p and the nonreward with (1 − p). A gamble with only one reward at p = 1.0 is called a safe option. Risk refers simply to known probabilities of < 1.0 and does not necessarily involve loss. Risky gambles have known probabilities; ambiguous gambles have probabilities·unknown to the agent.

The shape of the utility function allows us to deal with the influence of uncertainty on decision-making. Let us assume an agent whose decision making is characterized by a concave utility function, as shown in Figure 12 (see color insert), who performs in a gamble with two outcomes of values 1 and 9 at p = 0.5 each (either the lower or the higher outcome will occur, with equal probability). The EV of the gamble is 5 (vertical dotted line), and the utility u(EV) (horizontal dotted line) lies between u(1) and u(9) (horizontal lines). Interestingly, u(EV) lies closer to u(9) than to u(1), suggesting that the agent foregoes more utility when the gamble produces u(1) than she wins with u(9) over u(EV). Given that outcomes 1 and 9 occur with the same frequency, this agent would profit more from a safe reward at EV, with u(EV), over the gamble. She should be risk averse. Thus, a concave utility function suggests risk aversion, whereas a convex function, in which an agent foregoes less reward than she wins, suggests risk seeking. Different agents with different attitudes toward risk have differently shaped utility functions.

A direct measure of the influence of uncertainty is obtained by considering the difference between u(EV) and the EU of the gamble. The EU in the case of equal probabilities is the mean of u(1) and u(9), as marked by EU(1–9), which is considerably lower than u(EV) and thus indicates the loss in utility due to risk. By comparison, the gamble of 4 and 6 involves a smaller range of reward magnitudes and thus less risk and less loss due to uncertainty, as seen by comparing the vertical bars associated with EU(4–6) and EU(1–9). This graphical analysis suggests that value and uncertainty of outcome can be considered as separable measures.

A separation of value and uncertainty as components of utility can be achieved mathematically by using, for example, the negative exponential utility function often employed in financial mathematics. Using the exponential utility function for EU results in

$$EU = \sum_i (p_i \cdot -e^{-b x_i}),$$

which can be developed by the Laplace transform into

$$EU = -e^{-b(EV - b/2 \cdot var)},$$

where EV is expected value, var is variance, and the probability distribution pi is Gaussian. Thus, EU is expressed as f(EV, variance). This procedure uses variance as a measure of uncertainty. Another measure of uncertainty is the entropy of information theory, which might be appropriate to use when dealing with information processing in neural systems, but entropy is not commonly employed for describing decision making in microeconomics.

Taken together, microeconomic utility theory has defined basic reward parameters, such as magnitude, probability, expected value, expected utility, and variance, that can be used for neurobiological experiments searching for neural correlates of decision making under uncertainty.

NEUROPHYSIOLOGY OF REWARD BASED ON ECONOMIC THEORY

Magnitude

The easiest quantifiable measure of reward for animals is the volume of juice, which animals can discriminate in submilliliter quantities (Tobler et al. 2005). Neurons show increasing responses to reward-predicting CSs with higher volumes of reward in a number of reward structures, such as the striatum (Cromwell & Schultz 2003) (Figure 13a, see color insert), dorsolateral and orbital prefrontal cortex (Leon & Shadlen 1999, Roesch & Olson 2004, Wallis & Miller 2003), parietal and posterior cingulate cortex (McCoy et al. 2003, Musallam et al. 2004,

Platt & Glimcher 1999), and dopamine neurons (Satoh et al. 2003, Tobler et al. 2005). Similar reward magnitude–discriminating activations are found in these structures in relation to other task events, before and after reward delivery. Many of these studies also report decreasing responses with increasing reward magnitude (Figure 13*b*), although not with dopamine neurons. The decreasing responses are likely to reflect true magnitude discrimination rather than simply the attention induced by rewards, which should increase with increasing magnitude.

Recent considerations cast doubt on the nature of some of the reward magnitude–discriminating, behavior-related activations, in particular in structures involved in motor and attentional processes, such as the premotor cortex, frontal eye fields, supplementary eye fields, parietal association cortex, and striatum. Some reward-related differences in movement-related activations might reflect the differences in movements elicited by different reward magnitudes (Lauwereyns et al. 2002, Roesch & Olson 2004). A larger reward might make the animal move faster, and increased neural activity in premotor cortex with larger reward might reflect the higher movement speed. Although a useful explanation for motor structures, the issue might be more difficult to resolve for areas more remote from motor output, such as prefrontal cortex, parietal cortex, and caudate nucleus. It would be help-ful to correlate reward magnitude–discriminating activity in single neurons with movement parameters, such as reaction time and movement speed, and, separately, with reward parameters, and see where higher correlations are obtained. However, the usually measured movement parameters may not be sensitive enough to make these distinctions when neural activity varies relatively little with reward magni-tude. On the other hand, inverse relationships, such as higher neural activity for slower movements associated with smaller rewards, would argue against a pri-marily motor origin of reward-related differences, as relatively few neurons show higher activity with slower movements.

Probability

Simple tests for reward probability involve CSs that differentially predict the prob-ability with which a reward, as opposed to no reward, will be delivered for trial completion in Pavlovian or instrumental tasks. Dopamine neurons show increasing phasic responses to CSs that predict reward with increasing probability (Fiorillo et al. 2003, Morris et al. 2004). Similar increases in task-related activity occur in parietal cortex and globus pallidus during memory and movement-related task periods (Arkadir et al. 2004, Musallam et al. 2004, Platt & Glimcher 1999). How-ever, reward-responsive tonically active neurons in the striatum do not appear to be sensitive to reward probability (Morris et al. 2004), indicating that not all neurons sensitive to reward may code its value in terms of probability. In a decision-making situation with varying reward probabilities, parietal neurons track the recently ex-perienced reward value, indicating a memory process that would provide important input information for decision making (Sugrue et al. 2004).

Expected Value

Parietal neurons show increasing task-related activations with both the magnitude and probability of reward that do not seem to distinguish between the two components of expected value (Musallam et al. 2004). When the two value parameters are tested separately and in combination, dopamine neurons show monotonically increasing responses to CSs that predict increasing value (Tobler et al. 2005). The neurons fail to distinguish between magnitude and probability and seem to code their product (Figure 14a). However, the neural noise inherent in the stimulus-response relationships makes it difficult to determine exactly whether dopamine neurons encode expected value or expected utility. In either case, it appears as if neural responses show a good relationship to theoretical notions of outcome value that form a basis for decision making.

Uncertainty

Graphical analysis and application of the Laplace transform on the exponential utility function would permit experimenters to separate the components of expected value and utility from the uncertainty inherent in probabilistic gambles. Would the

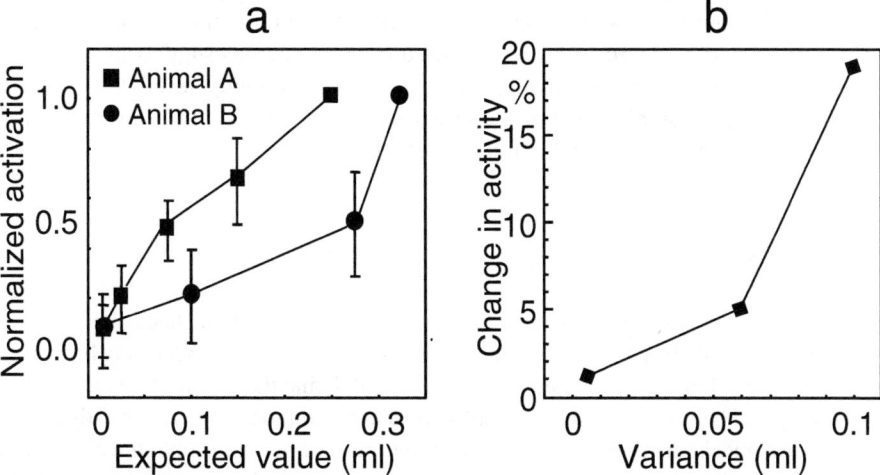

Figure 14   Separate coding of reward value and uncertainty in dopamine neurons. (*a*) Phasic response to conditioned, reward-predicting stimuli scales with increasing expected value (EV, summed magnitude × probability). Data points represent median responses normalized to response to highest EV (animal A, 57 neurons; animal B, 53 neurons). Data from Tobler et al. (2005). (*b*) Sustained activation during conditioned stimulus–reward interval scales with increasing uncertainty, as measured by variance. Two reward magnitudes are delivered at p = 0.5 each (0.05–0.15, 0.15–0.5 ml, 0.05–0.5 ml). Ordinate shows medians of changes above background activity from 53 neurons. Note that the entropy stays 1 bit for all three probability distributions. Data from Fiorillo et al. (2003).

brain be able to produce an explicit signal that reflects the level of uncertainty, similar to producing a reward signal? For both reward and uncertainty, there are no specialized sensory receptors. A proportion of dopamine neurons show a sustained activation during the CS-reward interval when tested with CSs that predict reward at increasing probabilities, as opposed to no reward. The activation is highest for reward at $p = 0.5$ and progressively lower for probabilities further away from $p = 0.5$ in either direction (Fiorillo et al. 2003). The activation does not occur when reward is substituted by a visual stimulus. The activations appear to follow common measures of uncertainty, such as statistical variance and entropy, both of which are maximal at $p = 0.5$. Most of the dopamine neurons signaling reward uncertainty also show phasic responses to reward-predicting CSs that encode expected value, and the two responses coding different reward terms are not correlated with each other. When in a refined experiment two different reward magnitudes alternate randomly (each at $p = 0.5$), dopamine neurons show the highest sustained activation when the reward range is largest, indicating a relationship to the statistical variance and thus to the uncertainty of the reward (Figure 14b). In a somewhat comparable experiment, neurons in posterior cingulate cortex show increased task-related activations as animals choose among rewards with larger variance compared with safe options (McCoy & Platt 2003). Although only a beginning, these data suggest that indeed the brain may produce an uncertainty signal about rewards that could provide essential information when making decisions under uncertainty. The data on dopamine neurons suggest that the brain may code the expected value separately from the uncertainty, just as the two terms constitute separable components of expected utility when applying the Laplace transform on the exponential utility function.

CONCLUSIONS

It is intuitively simple to understand that the use of well-established behavioral theories can only be beneficial when working with mechanisms underlying behavioral reactions. Indeed, these theories can very well define the different functions of rewards on behavior. It is then a small step on firm ground to base the investigation of neural mechanisms underlying the different reward functions onto the phenomena characterized by these theories. Although each theory has its own particular emphasis, they deal with the same kinds of outcome events of behavior, and it is more confirmation than surprise to see that many neural reward mechanisms can be commonly based on, and understood with, several theories. For the experimenter, the use of different theories provides good explanations for an interesting spectrum of reward functions that may not be so easily accessible by using only a single theory. For example, it seems that uncertainty plays a larger role in parts of microeconomic theory than in learning theory, and the investigation of neural mechanisms of uncertainty in outcomes of behavior can rely on several hundred years of thoughts about decision making (Pascal 1650 in Glimcher 2003, Bernoulli 1738).

ACKNOWLEDGMENTS

This article is based on lectures delivered at a Society for Neuroscience Meeting in October 2004 in San Diego and on a Max-Planck Symposium in January 2005 in Frankfurt, Germany. The author wishes to thank Drs. Anthony Dickinson and Peter Bossaerts for illuminating discussions on behavioral theories. Our work was supported by grants from the Wellcome Trust, Swiss National Science Foundation, Human Frontiers, and European Community.

The *Annual Review of Psychology* is online at http://psych.annualreviews.org

LITERATURE CITED

Amador N, Schlag-Rey M, Schlag J. 2000. Reward-predicting and reward-detecting neuronal activity in the primate supplementary eye field. *J. Neurophysiol.* 84:2166–70

Aosaki T, Tsubokawa H, Ishida A, Watanabe K, Graybiel AM, Kimura M. 1994. Responses of tonically active neurons in the primate's striatum undergo systematic changes during behavioral sensorimotor conditioning. *J. Neurosci.* 14:3969–84

Apicella P, Ljungberg T, Scarnati E, Schultz W. 1991. Responses to reward in monkey dorsal and ventral striatum. *Exp. Brain Res.* 85:491–500

Apicella P, Scarnati E, Ljungberg T, Schultz W. 1992. Neuronal activity in monkey striatum related to the expectation of predictable environmental events. *J. Neurophysiol.* 68:945–60

Arkadir D, Morris G, Vaadia E, Bergman H. 2004. Independent coding of movement direction and reward prediction by single pallidal neurons. *J. Neurosci.* 24:10047–56

Balleine B, Dickinson A. 1998. Goal-directed instrumental action: contingency and incentive learning and their cortical substrates. *Neuropharmacology* 37:407–19

Barraclough D, Conroy ML, Lee DJ. 2004. Prefrontal cortex and decision making in a mixed-strategy game. *Nat. Neurosci.* 7:405–10

Bernoulli J. (1738) 1954. Exposition of a new theory on the measurement of risk. *Econometrica* 22:23–36

Bowman EM, Aigner TG, Richmond BJ. 1996. Neural signals in the monkey ventral striatum related to motivation for juice and cocaine rewards. *J. Neurophysiol.* 75:1061–73

Critchley HG, Rolls ET. 1996. Hunger and satiety modify the responses of olfactory and visual neurons in the primate orbitofrontal cortex. *J. Neurophysiol.* 75:1673–86

Cromwell HC, Schultz W. 2003. Effects of expectations for different reward magnitudes on neuronal activity in primate striatum. *J. Neurophysiol.* 89:2823–38

Delaney K, Gelperin A. 1986. Post-ingestive food-aversion learning to amino acid deficient diets by the terrestrial slug *Limax maximus*. *J. Comp. Physiol. A* 159:281–95

Dickinson A. 1980. *Contemporary Animal Learning Theory*. Cambridge, UK: Cambridge Univ. Press

Dickinson A, Balleine B. 1994. Motivational control of goal-directed action. *Anim. Learn. Behav.* 22:1–18

Dickinson A, Hall G, Mackintosh NJ. 1976. Surprise and the attenuation of blocking. *J. Exp. Psychol. Anim. Behav. Process.* 2:313–22

Dorris MC, Glimcher PW. 2004. Activity in posterior parietal cortex is correlated with the relative subjective desirability of action. *Neuron* 44:365–78

Fiorillo CD, Tobler PN, Schultz W. 2003. Discrete coding of reward probability and uncertainty by dopamine neurons. *Science* 299:1898–902

Gintis H. 2000. *Game Theory Evolving*. Princeton, NJ: Princeton Univ. Press

Glimcher PW. 2003. *Decisions, Uncertainty and the Brain*. Cambridge, MA: MIT Press

Hassani OK, Cromwell HC, Schultz W. 2001. Influence of expectation of different rewards on behavior-related neuronal activity in the striatum. *J. Neurophysiol.* 85:2477–89

Hikosaka K, Watanabe M. 2000. Delay activity of orbital and lateral prefrontal neurons of the monkey varying with different rewards. *Cereb. Cortex* 10:263–71

Hikosaka O, Sakamoto M, Usui S. 1989. Functional properties of monkey caudate neurons. III. Activities related to expectation of target and reward. *J. Neurophysiol.* 61:814–32

Hollerman JR, Schultz W. 1998. Dopamine neurons report an error in the temporal prediction of reward during learning. *Nat. Neurosci.* 1:304–9

Hollerman JR, Tremblay L, Schultz W. 1998. Influence of reward expectation on behavior-related neuronal activity in primate striatum. *J. Neurophysiol.* 80:947–63

Hrupka BJ, Lin YM, Gietzen DW, Rogers QR. 1997. Small changes in essential amino acid concentrations alter diet selection in amino acid-deficient rats. *J. Nutr.* 127:777–84

Huang C-F, Litzenberger RH. 1988. *Foundations for Financial Economics*. Upper Saddle River, NJ: Prentice Hall

Ito S, Stuphorn V, Brown JW, Schall JD. 2003. Performance monitoring by the anterior cingulate cortex during saccade countermanding. *Science* 302:120–22

Kahneman D, Tversky A. 1984. Choices, values, and frames. *Am. Psychol.* 4:341–50

Kamin LJ. 1969. Selective association and conditioning. In *Fundamental Issues in Instrumental Learning*, ed. NJ Mackintosh, WK Honig, pp. 42–64. Halifax, NS: Dalhousie Univ. Press

Kawagoe R, Takikawa Y, Hikosaka O. 1998. Expectation of reward modulates cognitive signals in the basal ganglia. *Nat. Neurosci.* 1:411–16

Kimura M, Rajkowski J, Evarts E. 1984. Tonically discharging putamen neurons exhibit set-dependent responses. *Proc. Natl. Acad. Sci. USA* 81:4998–5001

Kobayashi S, Lauwereyns J, Koizumi M, Sakagami M, Hikosaka O. 2002. Influence of reward expectation on visuospatial processing in macaque lateral prefrontal cortex. *J. Neurophysiol.* 87:1488–98

Lauwereyns J, Watanabe K, Coe B, Hikosaka O. 2002. A neural correlate of response bias in monkey caudate nucleus. *Nature* 418:413–17

Leon MI, Shadlen MN. 1999. Effect of expected reward magnitude on the responses of neurons in the dorsolateral prefrontal cortex of the macaque. *Neuron* 24:415–25

Liu Z, Richmond BJ. 2000. Response differences in monkey TE and perirhinal cortex: stimulus association related to reward schedules. *J. Neurophysiol.* 83:1677–92

Ljungberg T, Apicella P, Schultz W. 1992. Responses of monkey dopamine neurons during learning of behavioral reactions. *J. Neurophysiol.* 67:145–63

Mackintosh NJ. 1975. A theory of attention: variations in the associability of stimulus with reinforcement. *Psychol. Rev.* 82:276–98

Markowitsch HJ, Pritzel M. 1976. Reward-related neurons in cat association cortex. *Brain Res.* 111:185–88

Matsumoto K, Suzuki W, Tanaka K. 2003. Neuronal correlates of goal-based motor selection in the prefrontal cortex. *Science* 301:229–32

Maunsell JHR. 2004. Neuronal representations of cognitive state: reward or attention? *Trends Cogn. Sci.* 8:261–65

McCoy AN, Crowley JC, Haghighian G, Dean HL, Platt ML. 2003. Saccade reward signals in posterior cingulate cortex. *Neuron* 40:1031–40

Mirenowicz J, Schultz W. 1994. Importance of unpredictability for reward responses in primate dopamine neurons. *J. Neurophysiol.* 72:1024–27

Mirenowicz J, Schultz W. 1996. Preferential activation of midbrain dopamine neurons by appetitive rather than aversive stimuli. *Nature* 379:449–51

Morris G, Arkadir D, Nevet A, Vaadia E, Bergman H. 2004. Coincident but distinct messages of midbrain dopamine and striatal tonically active neurons. *Neuron* 43:133–43

Musallam S, Corneil BD, Greger B, Scherberger H, Andersen RA. 2004. Cognitive control signals for neural prosthetics. *Science* 305:258–62

Nakahara H, Itoh H, Kawagoe R, Takikawa Y, Hikosaka O. 2004. Dopamine neurons can represent context-dependent prediction error. *Neuron* 41:269–80

Nakamura K, Mikami A, Kubota K. 1992. Activity of single neurons in the monkey amygdala during performance of a visual discrimination task. *J. Neurophysiol.* 67:1447–63

Nishijo H, Ono T, Nishino H. 1988. Single neuron responses in amygdala of alert monkey during complex sensory stimulation with affective significance. *J. Neurosci.* 8:3570–83

O'Doherty JP. 2004. Reward representations and reward-related learning in the human brain: insights from neuroimaging. *Curr. Opin. Neurobiol.* 14:769–76

Pavlov PI. 1927. *Conditioned Reflexes.* London: Oxford Univ. Press

Pearce JM, Hall G. 1980. A model for Pavlovian conditioning: variations in the effectiveness of conditioned but not of unconditioned stimuli. *Psychol. Rev.* 87:532–52

Platt ML, Glimcher PW. 1999. Neural correlates of decision variables in parietal cortex. *Nature* 400:233–38

Pratt WE, Mizumori SJY. 1998. Characteristics of basolateral amygdala neuronal firing on a spatial memory task involving differential reward. *Behav. Neurosci.* 112:554–70

Pratt WE, Mizumori SJY. 2001. Neurons in rat medial prefrontal cortex show anticipatory rate changes to predictable differential rewards in a spatial memory task. *Behav. Brain Res.* 123:165–83

Rao SC, Rainer G, Miller EK. 1997. Integration of what and where in the primate prefrontal cortex. *Science* 276:821–24

Ravel S, Legallet E, Apicella P. 1999. Tonically active neurons in the monkey striatum do not preferentially respond to appetitive stimuli. *Exp. Brain Res.* 128:531–34

Rescorla RA, Wagner AR. 1972. A theory of Pavlovian conditioning: variations in the effectiveness of reinforcement and nonreinforcement. In *Classical Conditioning II: Current Research and Theory*, ed. AH Black, WF Prokasy, pp. 64–99. New York: Appleton-Century-Crofts

Roesch MR, Olson CR. 2004. Neuronal activity related to reward value and motivation in primate frontal cortex. *Science* 304:307–10

Rogers QR, Harper AE. 1970. Selection of a solution containing histidine by rats fed a histidine-imbalanced diet. *J. Comp. Physiol. Psychol.* 72:66–71

Roitman MF, Wheeler RA, Carelli RM. 2005. Nucleus accumbens neurons are innately tuned for rewarding and aversive taste stimuli, encode their predictors, and are linked to motor output. *Neuron* 45:587–97

Rolls ET, Critchley HD, Mason R, Wakeman EA. 1996. Orbitofrontal cortex neurons: role in olfactory and visual association learning. *J. Neurophysiol.* 75:1970–81

Rolls ET, Scott TR, Sienkiewicz ZJ, Yaxley S. 1988. The responsiveness of neurones in the frontal opercular gustatory cortex of the macaque monkey is independent of hunger. *J. Physiol.* 397:1–12

Rolls ET, Sienkiewicz ZJ, Yaxley S. 1989. Hunger modulates the responses to gustatory stimuli of single neurons in the caudolateral orbitofrontal cortex of the macaque monkey. *Eur. J. Neurosci.* 1:53–60

Satoh T, Nakai S, Sato T, Kimura M. 2003. Correlated coding of motivation and outcome of decision by dopamine neurons. *J. Neurosci.* 23:9913–23

Savage LJ. 1954. *The Foundations of Statistics.* New York: Wiley

Schoenbaum G, Chiba AA, Gallagher M. 1998. Orbitofrontal cortex and basolateral amygdala encode expected outcomes during learning. *Nat. Neurosci.* 1:155–59

Schoenbaum G, Chiba AA, Gallagher M. 1999.

Neural encoding in orbitofrontal cortex and basolateral amygdala during olfactory discrimination learning. *J. Neurosci.* 19:1876–84

Schultz W, Apicella P, Scarnati E, Ljungberg T. 1992. Neuronal activity in monkey ventral striatum related to the expectation of reward. *J. Neurosci.* 12:4595–10

Schultz W, Dayan P, Montague RR. 1997. A neural substrate of prediction and reward. *Science* 275:1593–99

Schultz W, Dickinson A. 2000. Neuronal coding of prediction errors. *Annu. Rev. Neurosci.* 23:473–500

Schultz W, Romo R. 1987. Responses of nigrostriatal dopamine neurons to high intensity somatosensory stimulation in the anesthetized monkey. *J. Neurophysiol.* 57:201–17

Shidara M, Aigner TG, Richmond BJ. 1998. Neuronal signals in the monkey ventral striatum related to progress through a predictable series of trials. *J. Neurosci.* 18:2613–25

Shidara M, Richmond BJ. 2002. Anterior cingulate: single neuron signals related to degree of reward expectancy. *Science* 296:1709–11

Stevens SS. 1957. On the psychophysical law. *Psychol. Rev.* 64:153–81

Sugrue LP, Corrado GS, Newsome WT. 2004. Matching behavior and the representation of value in the parietal cortex. *Science* 304:1782–87

Thorndike EL. 1911. *Animal Intelligence: Experimental Studies.* New York: MacMillan

Thorpe SJ, Rolls ET, Maddison S. 1983. The orbitofrontal cortex: neuronal activity in the behaving monkey. *Exp. Brain Res.* 49:93–115

Tobler PN, Dickinson A, Schultz W. 2003. Coding of predicted reward omission by dopamine neurons in a conditioned inhibition paradigm. *J. Neurosci.* 23:10402–10

Tobler PN, Fiorillo CD, Schultz W. 2005. Adaptive coding of reward value by dopamine neurons. *Science* 307:1642–45

Tremblay L, Hollerman JR, Schultz W. 1998. Modifications of reward expectation-related neuronal activity during learning in primate striatum. *J. Neurophysiol.* 80:964–77

Tremblay L, Schultz W. 1999. Relative reward preference in primate orbitofrontal cortex. *Nature* 398:704–8

Tremblay L, Schultz W. 2000a. Reward-related neuronal activity during go-nogo task performance in primate orbitofrontal cortex. *J. Neurophysiol.* 83:1864–76

Tremblay L, Schultz W. 2000b. Modifications of reward expectation-related neuronal activity during learning in primate orbitofrontal cortex. *J. Neurophysiol.* 83:1877–85

Ungless MA, Magill PJ, Bolam JP. 2004. Uniform inhibition of dopamine neurons in the ventral tegmental area by aversive stimuli. *Science* 303:2040–42

von Neumann J, Morgenstern O. 1944. *The Theory of Games and Economic Behavior.* Princeton, NJ: Princeton Univ. Press

Waelti P. 2000. *Activité phasique des neurones dopaminergiques durant une tâche de discrimination et une tâche de blocage chez le primate vigile.* PhD thesis. Univ. de Fribourg, Switzerland

Waelti P, Dickinson A, Schultz W. 2001. Dopamine responses comply with basic assumptions of formal learning theory. *Nature* 412:43–48.

Wallis JD, Miller EK. 2003. Neuronal activity in primate dorsolateral and orbital prefrontal cortex during performance of a reward preference task. *Eur. J. Neurosci.* 18:2069–81

Wang Y, Cummings SL, Gietzen DW. 1996. Temporal-spatial pattern of c-fos expression in the rat brain in response to indispensable amino acid deficiency. I. The initial recognition phase. *Mol. Brain Res.* 40:27–34

Watanabe M. 1989. The appropriateness of behavioral responses coded in post-trial activity of primate prefrontal units. *Neurosci. Lett.* 101:113–17

Watanabe M. 1996. Reward expectancy in primate prefrontal neurons. *Nature* 382:629–32

Watanabe M, Hikosaka K, Sakagami M, Shirakawa SI. 2002. Coding and monitoring of behavioral context in the primate prefrontal cortex. *J. Neurosci.* 22:2391–400

Weber EH. 1850. Der Tastsinn und das Gemeingefuehl. In *Handwoerterbuch der Physiologie*, Vol. 3, Part 2, ed. R Wagner, pp. 481–588. Braunschweig, Germany: Vieweg

Wise RA. 2002. Brain reward circuitry: insights from unsensed incentives. *Neuron* 36:229–40

Annu. Rev. Psychol. 2006. 57:117–37
doi: 10.1146/annurev.psych.57.102904.190118
Copyright © 2006 by Annual Reviews. All rights reserved
First published online as a Review in Advance on September 7, 2005

GENETICS OF AFFECTIVE AND ANXIETY DISORDERS

E. D. Leonardo[1,2,4] and René Hen[1,3]

Center for Neurobiology and Behavior[1], Department of Psychiatry[2], and Department of Pharmacology[3] at Columbia University, and the New York State Psychiatric Institute[4], New York, New York 10032; email: el367@columbia.edu, rh95@columbia.edu

Key Words   depression, serotonin, endophenotype, critical period

■ **Abstract**   The study of the genetics of complex behaviors has evolved dramatically from the days of the nature versus nurture debates that dominated much of the past century. Here we discuss advances in our understanding of the genetics of affective and anxiety disorders. In particular, we highlight our growing understanding of specific gene-environment interactions that occur during critical periods in development, setting the stage for later behavioral phenotypes. We review the recent literature in the field, focusing on recent advances in our understanding of the role of the serotonin system in establishing normal anxiety levels during development. We emphasize the importance of understanding the effect of genetic variation at the level of functional circuits and provide examples from the literature of how such an approach has been exploited to study novel genetic endpoints, including genetically based variation in response to medication, a potentially valuable phenotype that has not received much attention to date.

CONTENTS

INTRODUCTION

Previous reviews in the *Annual Review of Psychology* addressing the genetics of behavior have tackled the subject by species (human versus nonhuman) (Rose 1995, Wimer & Wimer 1985) or by methodology (single gene versus biometrical) (Wahlsten 1999). In this review, we focus our discussion on a subset of behaviors, namely those related to affective and anxiety disorders. We do not limit our discussion to human studies or to animal studies. Instead, we focus on unifying concepts and themes that have been instrumental in the significant advances that this field has seen in the past few years. The first and perhaps most important realization is that behaviors related to anxiety and mood disorders are not caused by alterations in single genes, but rather are the result of more subtle alterations in multiple genes, each contributing partially to the expression of behavior. Second, it is clear that classical genetics alone is not sufficient to explain behavioral outcomes that are observed, but that the environment makes a significant contribution to the ultimate phenotype. Although these two ideas are far from new, we have only recently developed the technology and the conceptual framework to tackle the problems of behavioral genetics in ways that meaningfully incorporate these ideas and yield productive results.

In this chapter, we first introduce anxiety and affective disorders and review recent advances in genetic approaches to these disorders in both mice and men. We then turn to the advances in our understanding of gene-environment interactions, with particular attention to the role of development and critical periods. Finally, we illustrate these concepts using examples of specific genes that have emerged as a result of these approaches.

ANXIETY AND DEPRESSION

Interest in the genetics of anxiety and depression is driven by the fact that these disorders are highly prevalent within the population and are associated with high levels of morbidity and mortality as well as with great economic cost. It is estimated that anxiety disorders affect over 20% of the population at some point in their lifetime, with an annual estimated cost of $44 billion in the United States alone (Greenberg et al. 1999). The estimates for the cost of depression are nearly double that of anxiety, with a total cost of $83 billion (Greenberg et al. 2003). In addition, the World Health Organization estimates that major depression is the second leading cause of disease burden in established market economies and is the major cause of disability worldwide among people five years and older.

Wariness of threatening aspects of the environment is a protective, if at times uncomfortable, trait. In humans, the experience of such wariness is called anxiety, and it is typically accompanied by characteristic autonomic responses and defensive behaviors. Whereas anxiety in many settings is protective, excessive anxiety can prove disabling.

In its nonpathological form, anxiety can be divided into two categories: state anxiety, a measure of the immediate or acute level of anxiety, and trait anxiety, which reflects the long-term tendency of an individual to show an increased anxiety response. In its pathological form, anxiety can severely interfere with normal life and has been classified into six disorders described in the Diagnostic and Statistical Manual of the American Psychiatric Association: generalized anxiety disorder, social phobia, simple phobia, panic disorder, posttraumatic stress disorder (PTSD), and obsessive-compulsive disorder (Am. Psychiatric Assoc. 2000).

Like anxiety, depressed mood is a normal occurrence throughout life and is often experienced in the face of adverse environmental conditions such as the loss of a loved one, adverse events at work, or the loss of a relationship. What separates normal from depressed mood is the emergence over time of a consistent behavioral pattern that is distinct from baseline behavior. The pattern includes disruption of sleep (difficulty sleeping or excessive sleep), changes in appetite (weight gain or weight loss), fatigue, decreased energy, and withdrawal from usual activities. In addition to its behavioral manifestations, depression is characterized by a set of thoughts, including feelings of worthlessness, difficulty in concentration, and feelings of hopelessness and helplessness.

THE HERITABILITY OF ANXIETY AND DEPRESSION: HUMAN STUDIES

Individuals seem to have a rather consistent level of trait anxiety over their lifetime (Kagan & Snidman 1999, Schwartz et al. 1999, Van Ameringen et al. 1998), an indication that the degree of anxious behavior persists over long periods and reflects fundamental differences in brain composition or wiring. Such differences in the brains of highly anxious versus less anxious individuals are likely to have developed as a result of differences in both the genetic makeup of individuals and the environment they have experienced during their life. Twin studies confirm this hypothesis. An analysis of the incidence of anxiety and depressive disorders in monozygotic and dizygotic twins revealed that approximately 30%–40% of the variance in occurrence between individuals can be attributed to genetic variation (Hettema et al. 2001, Sullivan et al. 2000). Thus, the magnitude of the genetic contribution to anxiety and mood disorders is relatively moderate and is less than that for more heritable psychiatric disorders such as schizophrenia or neurological disorders such as Huntington's disease.

There is a high level of comorbidity between anxiety and depressive disorders, with co-occurrence rates of up to 60% (Gorman 1996). These figures suggest that comorbid anxiety and depression are the rule rather than the exception. In addition, anxiety and depression cosegregate in pedigrees of families with high incidences of these disorders, suggesting overlapping etiologies for anxiety and mood disorders (Ninan & Berger 2001). Some have suggested that individuals with generalized anxiety and depression share similar genetic vulnerabilities whose phenotypes are modified by environmental factors (Kendler et al. 1992, Roy et al. 1995). This hypothesis is further supported by the common neuropharmacology of these disorders. For example, the selective serotonin reuptake inhibitors (SSRIs) are effective treatments for both depression and a number of anxiety disorders.

Studying the genetic contribution of these disorders is further complicated by the possibility that genetic factors affect how individuals interact with their environment. For example, twin studies have consistently demonstrated a genetic predisposition that accounts for 30%–35% of the liability to develop PTSD following exposure to traumatic events (Goldberg et al. 1990, True et al. 1993). Intriguingly, there is also a genetic predisposition for exposure to certain types of trauma; thus, genetic factors account for 20%–35% of the liability to exposure to assault- and combat-related trauma, respectively (Lyons et al. 1993, Stein et al. 2002). With regard to civilian assaults, a high correlation between genetic effects on exposure to trauma and development of PTSD symptoms suggests the existence of common genetic factors that increase the likelihood of both exposure and pathological reaction to extreme trauma (Stein et al. 2002). Kendler (2001) has suggested that up to 20% of genetic influences in psychiatric disorders could be mediated by such indirect mechanisms.

The evidence is now overwhelming that anxiety and mood disorders carry significant genetic components whose ultimate phenotypic expression is highly dependent on environmental factors. Until recently, the combined challenge of dissecting diseases that were polygenic in nature, along with potentially complex environmental interactions seemed daunting. However, there has recently been significant progress in this area, both in direct human studies and in animal studies.

GENETIC APPROACHES IN RODENTS

While human estimates of heritability rely on epidemiological methods, analyses of complex behavioral traits in mice have generally relied on the use of genetic studies using inbred lines that differ in a behavior of interest. In particular, there has been significant work dissecting the genetics of a construct termed "emotionality" (Crawley 2000) that is thought to be related to anxiety in humans. The approach is conceptually straightforward. Specifically, two lines of inbred mice that exhibit distinct baseline emotionality are mated to each other. The resulting offspring (F1 generation) are in turn mated to each other to produce an F2 intercross. These animals can then be assessed behaviorally in paradigms thought to be reflective of anxiety or depression. Because the original parents are homozygous at each allele, it is possible from such a cross to trace the origin of specific chromosomal segments to a parental strain. By analyzing many offspring from such crosses, it is possible to generate a list of genetic loci that influence variation in a specific behavior. These loci are termed quantitative trait loci (QTL). Studies assessing a variety of anxiety-related behaviors have found that single genetic loci usually account for less than 5% of the genetic variance for any given behavioral measure

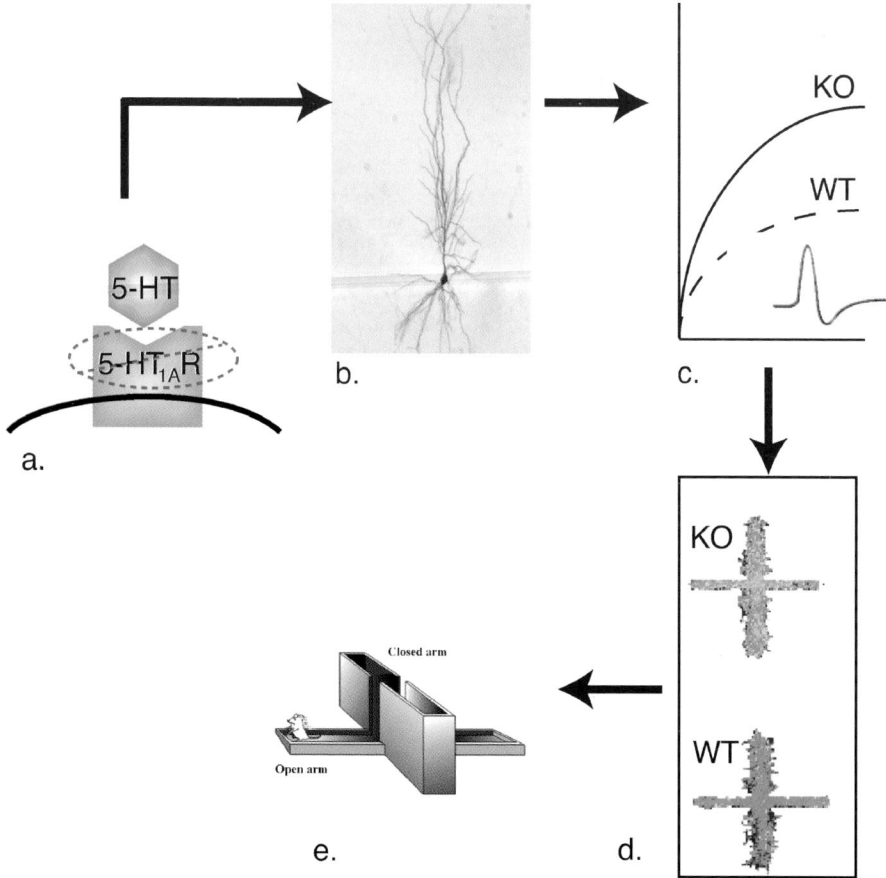

Figure 2   Schematic illustrating a possible path from deletion of the 5-HT1A receptor to anxiety-related behavioral changes. Deletion of the receptor at the membrane (*a*) results in changes at the level of cell structure, illustrated here as alterations in dendritic arborization (*b*) during development. Changes in cell structure may in turn lead to changes in physiological properties of neuronal populations, illustrated here as an increase in the input/output curve (*c*) of CA1 neurons in 5-HT1A-deficient mice. Altered hippocampal CA1 physiology can in turn affect circuit level function, illustrated here as increased theta oscillations (*d*) in 5-HT1A-deficient mice during exploration of an elevated plus maze. Ultimately, changes at the molecular-, cellular-, and circuit-level physiology result in altered behavioral outputs, in this case increased anxiety of 5-HT1A-deficient mice in an elevated plus maze (*e*). In principal, a similar schematic should be possible for all genes with behavioral phenotypes. Note the lack of a direct path from the receptor to the behavior.

(Flint 2003). Studies of this nature have reproducibly identified a number of loci, including loci on chromosomes 1 and 15 (Flint et al. 1995, Singer et al. 2005), with estimates of the number of loci affecting anxiety ranging from 6 to 14 (Turri et al. 2004). Less work has been done using this approach to measure correlates of depression (Yoshikawa et al. 2002).

Despite the ability to reproducibly detect in the genome the loci that modulate anxiety and depression-like behaviors, the limitations of the QTL approach are evident in the difficulty that has been encountered in moving from QTL to genes. This barrier has recently been broken by Yalcin et al. (2004), who identify RGS2, a regulator of G protein signaling, as a candidate gene in the well-replicated chromosome 1 QTL region. The investigators in this study used a combination of high-resolution mapping in an outbred population along with a quantitative complementation method. The availability of a null mutant RGS2 greatly aided this effort (Oliveira-Dos-Santos et al. 2000). Yalcin et al. (2004) also revealed the likely existence of two additional independent linkage peaks in the immediate vicinity that comprise the originally defined QTL, further illustrating the complexity of analyzing these loci. It will be interesting to see if this approach will be successful in identifying genes in other regions that have been identified through QTL studies.

THE IMPACT OF ANIMAL MODELS

One of the challenges that the field must come to terms with is how to integrate data that come from diverse experimental systems. Whereas human studies have established the genetic basis of anxiety and depression, investigators have turned to animal studies in an attempt to clarify further the genetic determinants of anxiety and depression. However, attempts to model the clinical constructs of anxiety and depression in animals by necessity have required a reductionist approach. It is not possible to model faithfully all aspects of a complex human behavioral disorder such as anxiety or depression. The difficulty exists at two levels. On one hand, these disorders involve emotions and experiences that may be uniquely human. On the other hand, the clinical entities are likely heterogeneous even in humans, and attempts to study their genetic basis or to model them directly in animals may be misguided (Chakravarti & Little 2003, Charney et al. 2002).

One construct that has been helpful in addressing these issues is the concept of the endophenotype (Gottesman & Gould 2003). Endophenotypes have been defined as measurable components, unseen by the aided eye along the pathway between disease and distal genotype (Gottesman & Gould 2003). Classically, endophenotypes have been anything from biochemical to self-report measures. In affective disorders, they have included such things as sensitivity to panic via CO_2 inhalation, failure to suppress cortisol in a dexamethasone challenge, and psychological constructs such as "neuroticism." These concepts have all been used in human studies as part of an effort to bridge the gap between heterogeneous disorders and their underlying genetic constructs (Hasler et al. 2004). They attempt to break down the disorders into phenomena that are coherent and simple to measure.

The endophenotype concept reminds us that genes do not encode behaviors. Genes encode proteins that in turn are the building blocks of cells. In the nervous system, during development, individual neurons become integrated into circuits that are a part of larger systems. Ultimately, behavior is the result of interactions of circuits and systems with environmental stimuli. It is at this level of resolution that animal models are likely to be most useful.

At the molecular, anatomical, and physiological level, mice are remarkably similar to humans (Chrousos 1998, Cooper et al. 2003). Brain circuitry is remarkably conserved, although interspecies differences do exist. Neurotransmitter and neuromodulatory systems are conserved. Glutamate, serotonin, gamma-aminobutryic acid, and dopamine signaling systems are highly homologous in their function. These systems process and integrate information from the environment to generate the context-dependent, species-relevant behavior that the organism requires.

Animal models of anxiety- and depression-related behaviors rely on the circuit- and physiology-level homology that exists between species. Like humans, animals respond to the potential presence of a threat with characteristic autonomic responses and defensive behaviors. These physiological and behavioral parameters can be measured with relative ease and have been validated with drugs known to be anxiolytic or anxiogenic in humans. This approach has been used to characterize numerous models of anxiety-like behavior in laboratory animals (Borsini et al. 2002). Paradigms such as fear-conditioned freezing and fear-potentiated startle rely on learned associations between innocuous and painful stimuli; pairing of, say, a particular sound with a mild shock causes the animal to display anxiety-like defensive behaviors such as freezing (periods of attentive stillness) or enhanced startle (heightened reactivity to a loud sudden noise) in response to later presentations of the sound (Davis et al. 2003, LeDoux 2000). Other animal models of anxiety depend on innate species-specific danger signals. The elevated plus maze and novelty-suppressed feeding tasks, for example, measure a rodent's avoidance of exposed or novel areas in which they might be more vulnerable to predation (Rodgers & Dalvi 1997, Santarelli et al. 2003). Anxiolytic drugs, such as benzodiazepines, reduce the expression of anxiety-like behaviors in each of these paradigms (Conti et al. 1990, Pellow & File 1986, Shephard & Broadhurst 1982). One of the simplest ways to validate models has been the use of pharmacological tools. Benzodiazepines, the archetypal anxiolytic drugs, reduce the level of anxiety in virtually every animal model of anxiety (Borsini et al. 2002).

Paradigms of depression-related behavior have relied primarily on the response of animals to a chronic or inescapable stressor. One such example is the forced swim test, in which animals are placed in a bucket of water from which they cannot escape. Escape behaviors (climbing or swimming) are compared to defeat behaviors (floating) and are used as a measure of depression-like behavior. Other approaches include resident/intruder paradigms where the behavior of an animal in the face of an unfamiliar or dominant animal is measured. One measure of validity of an animal model of depression is the ability of chronic antidepressant drug treatment to modify the behavior of interest. These models have been reviewed elsewhere (Crowley & Lucki 2005, Dulawa & Hen 2005, Dulawa et al. 2004, Mitchell & Redfern 2005).

Much of the genetic and pharmacological work to date in both the human and the animal literature has focused on the study of adults. The goal has been to isolate the genetic component of a behavioral paradigm or of a specific endophenotype. Attempts to account for environmental factors or to integrate them into any analysis until recently had been lacking in the genetics literature. Advances in this area are discussed below.

DEVELOPMENT, CRITICAL PERIODS, AND BEHAVIOR

A number of recent breakthroughs in understanding the genetic underpinnings of affective and anxiety disorders come from studies that take a developmental view of these disorders. The fields of psychology and psychiatry have long understood the importance of early environmental factors in mediating behavioral outcomes. Psychologists have long supposed that early-life trauma increases the risk of psychiatric disorders developing subsequently. This hypothesis is supported by studies in which the number of severe early traumas suffered by patients was correlated with increased risk for adult disease pathology, including mood disorders (Chapman et al. 2004, Felitti et al. 1998, Tweed et al. 1989). For example, adults who had experienced four out of a list of seven severe early traumatic events had a 4.6-fold increased risk of developing depressive symptoms and were 12.2-fold more likely to attempt suicide. No direct correlation between any specific childhood trauma and a specific adult anxiety disorder was evident, however, which indicates that other possibly genetic factors determine the precise pathology that is precipitated by childhood trauma. In such a model, outlined in Figure 1, genetic risk factors for specific psychiatric disorders would depend on environmental influences acting early during the life of the individual. However, until recently, genetic studies have not succeeded in incorporating this model into their approaches. This is due in part to the attempt of separate fields of inquiry to assess environmental or genetic influences on behavior. Recently, a few elegant studies have demonstrated the power of combining the study of genes and environment into a single, coordinated approach.

Fundamental to this approach is the idea that adult patterns of behavior are shaped by the complex aggregate of responses made by an organism to its environment during development. These responses are encoded by neural systems within the brain that in turn are built from simpler circuits. These circuits are established during the course of development, often during defined periods of time, and requiring interactions with the environment (Hensch 2004, Knudsen 2004). Put another way, the genetic program unfolds in a predictable time that samples the surrounding environment and in turn is shaped by it. A developmental approach

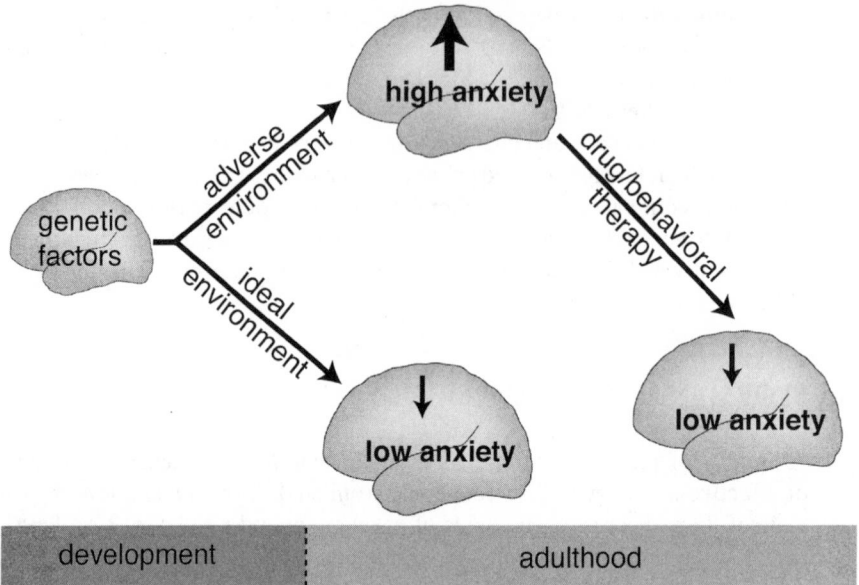

Figure 1 During development, genetic and environmental factors interact to set trait-level anxiety in the adult brain. Mature circuits in adulthood can be further modified using pharmacologic and psychotherapeutic approaches that can induce compensatory changes in the circuits underlying anxious behavior.

predicts that genes that are active in establishing the circuits that mediate the relevant behaviors in psychiatric illness may be susceptibility genes. It also predicts that environmental influences at the time of circuit formation are of critical importance. In this approach, one must develop an understanding of the functional circuits as well as the genes and environmental factors that contribute to their development. Identifying endophenotypes in a developmental approach means identifying behaviors or paradigms that are suited to probing specific circuits at specific points in time. Genetic approaches can then be devised that take into account the endophenotype and the environmental influences of the critical period. Such an approach has been used fruitfully to examine the genetics of the developing visual system (reviewed in Hensch 2004) and is already showing promise in the study of genetic influences on anxiety and depression.

BRAIN CIRCUITS AND ANXIETY

The study of molecular mechanisms by which early environmental influences alter circuits that may mediate anxiety and depression in the brain is in its infancy. There is significant evidence for a role of the amygdala and temporal and prefrontal cortices. In addition, we know that monoaminergic systems play a significant role because drugs that affect monoamines, such as serotonin and norepinephrine, are effective in treating anxiety and depression. Finally, there is ample evidence to suggest that the stress-hormone response system is involved in the pathophysiology of anxiety and affective disorders.

The current challenge in the field is to move from a general understanding that these systems are important, to a specific understanding of the mechanisms by which alterations in these systems result in pathology. Examples of such advances are discussed in the following section.

THE 5-HT1A RECEPTOR AND A CRITICAL PERIOD FOR ANXIETY   The 5-HT1A receptor has been implicated in mediating the effects of serotonergic agents in anxiety and depression. Selective desensitization of 5-HT1A autoreceptors has been postulated to be a key change that allows antidepressant action (Albert & Lemonde 2004). Mice that have been genetically engineered to be lacking the 5-HT1A receptor show increased anxiety in a number of tests, including hippocampal-dependent tasks (Klemenhagen et al. 2005, Parks et al. 1998, Ramboz et al. 1998). In order to test for the specific spatial and temporal requirements of the receptor in mediating anxious behaviors, investigators generated a conditional knockout mouse that allowed for the selective rescue of postsynaptic 1A receptors in a temporally regulatable manner. This strategy was used to show that, whereas repression of receptor expression in the adult is ineffective in modulating anxiety, repression of receptor expression until four weeks of age is sufficient to produce adult mice with increased anxiety-related behavior. This finding indicates that 5-HT is essential to the establishment of normal anxiety-modulating circuits in the brain during postnatal development.

Because expression of the receptor in the forebrain of rescued mice is detectable only after the second postnatal week, the critical period for establishment of the knockout phenotype is probably in the third and fourth postnatal weeks, a period of dramatic synaptogenesis and dendritic growth in the forebrain. These results are supported by behavioral data showing that the anxiety-related phenotype of the knockout mice first appears at three weeks of age (C. Gross, personal communication). Furthermore, dendritic branching and neuronal excitability are increased in the CA1 region of the hippocampus of mice that lack the 5-HT1A receptor (J. Monckton, J. Hornung, personal communication), and neural recordings from the CA1 region in these awake behaving mice have demonstrated changes in the magnitude of theta oscillations when the animals are in an anxiogenic, but not familiar, environment (Gordon et al. 2005). The hippocampus has previously been shown to be important for regulating innate anxiety-related behaviors that are abnormal in 5-HT1A-receptor knockout mice (Deacon et al. 2002, Kjelstrup et al. 2002). Maturation of dendritic branches in the CA1 region of the hippocampus occurs during the second, third, and fourth weeks after birth, and overlaps with the sensitive period of 5-HT1A function (Pokorny & Yamamoto 1981). The hypothesized progression from a molecular lesion in the 5-HT1AR, through cellular, physiological, circuit-level, and ultimately behavioral changes is illustrated in Figure 2 (see color insert). It is interesting to speculate that this period of active synaptic development is a particularly crucial time for the adjustment of anxiety circuits in response to experience-dependent signals.

Genetic data supporting a role for the 5-HT1A receptor in mediating anxiety is not limited to the rodent literature. Recent association studies in humans have found correlations between a single functional polymorphism in the promoter of the 5-HT1A receptor and both trait anxiety and depression (Lemonde et al. 2004, Strobel et al. 2003). Interestingly, this polymorphism appears to alter the transcriptional regulation of the 5-HT1A gene (Albert & Lemonde 2004, Lemonde et al. 2003). In light of the data in mice, one might speculate that altered transcription levels during development may be responsible for the altered trait anxiety (Lesch & Gutknecht 2004).

SEROTONIN TRANSPORTER AND DEVELOPMENT   The selective serotonin reuptake inhibitors (SSRIs) are effective in treating a wide variety of anxiety disorders as well as depression. Not surprisingly, the serotonin transporter (5-HTT), the primary target of SSRIs, has been the subject of intensive study in both animal and human models. The results of these studies, in particular their relevance to circuit development and critical periods, are described below.

Mice lacking the 5-HTT gene exhibit anxiety and depression-related behaviors (Holmes et al. 2003, Lira et al. 2003). These results initially appear paradoxical, as treatment with SSRIs during adulthood results in decreased anxiety. To address this paradox, Mark Ansorge and colleagues (Ansorge et al. 2004) hypothesized that the seemingly paradoxical effects of the 5-HTT knockout resulted from its effects on brain maturation. In an attempt to address this question, they treated young mice (from postnatal day 4–21) with fluoxetine, thereby mimicking the effect of the genetic deletion through pharmacologic means. Interestingly, mice treated during this period showed adult anxiety and depression-like phenotypes that were similar to that of lifelong deletion of the 5-HTT gene. The effect of the medication was dependent on the presence of the transporter, as no effect was seen in null mutant mice. Perhaps more interesting is that in at least some tests, a treatment-by-genotype interaction occurred: Mice that were heterozygous for the 5-HTT gene responded to fluoxetine with increased anxiety, whereas wild-type mice did not (see Figure 3) (Ansorge et al. 2004). Once again, as in the case of the 5-HT1A genetic rescue mouse described above, these experiments suggest that the serotonergic system is involved in modulating the development of neural circuits that are responsible for mediating anxiety and depression-like behaviors in the mouse. In an independent study, Ishiwata et al. (2005) examined the effect of SSRI treatment of mice that had been stressed prenatally. Prenatal stress has previously been shown to disrupt hypothalamic-pituitary-adrenal (HPA) axis regulations. Interestingly, treatment with an SSRI during weeks 1–3 but not during weeks 6–8 normalized the HPA axis response in these animals. Together, these experiments point to the first three weeks of life (in mice) as a critical period for setting serotonergic and possibly HPA reactivity.

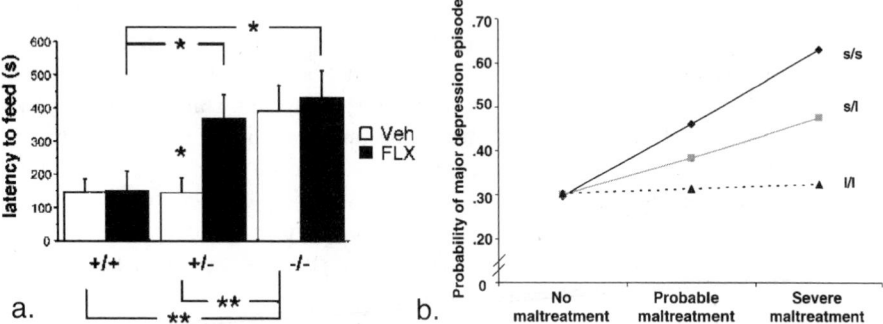

Figure 3 Gene-environment interactions show striking parallels in human and mouse studies of the serotonin transporter gene. (*a*) Results of the novelty suppressed feeding test performed on animals that vary in their serotonin transporter genotype. Note that wild-type (+/+) animals have short latencies (less anxiety) and appear unaffected by early-life treatment with fluoxetine (FLX). Mice heterozygous (±) for the serotonin transporter show short latencies (less anxiety) when treated with vehicle but show more anxiety as a result of early-life treatment with FLX. Serotonin transporter knockout mice (−/−) show high levels of anxiety regardless of FLX treatment status. (*b*) The probability of an episode of depression in human individuals carrying distinct alleles of the serotonin transporter gene as a function of early childhood maltreatment. Note that individuals carrying the l/l genotype are relatively insensitive to early childhood maltreatment, whereas individuals carrying the s/s allele are exquisitely sensitive to early childhood maltreatment. Reprinted with permission from Ansorge et al. (2004) and Caspi et al. (2003).

Fortunately, in the case of the serotonin transporter, the story does not end there. Models of early adverse experience in nonhuman primates suggest that the serotonin transporter may mediate the effects of early life stress on later anxiety and depression (Barr et al. 2003). More recently, in one of a series of landmark studies, Caspi et al. (2003) found that a functional polymorphism in the 5-HTT gene in humans moderated the effects of early life stress on the later development of depressive disorders, a finding that was recently replicated by an independent group (Kendler et al. 2005). Caspi and colleagues (2003) found that people who carried one or two versions of the short (s) allele of the 5-HTT-linked polymorphic region (5-HTTLPR) had more depressive symptoms, diagnosable depression, and suicidal behavior in relation to stressful life events than did people who carried two copies of the long allele (see Figure 3). In this study, carriers of an s allele who experienced more than four adverse life events constituted only 10% of the cohort but accounted for nearly 25% of all cases of diagnosed depression. In the case of suicidal ideation or attempt, the effect was even more pronounced. In individuals without stressful events, there was little difference in suicidal ideation or attempts between genotypes (1%–3%). However, when faced with four or more stressful life events, 15% of s homozygotes experienced an episode of suicide ideation or attempt, compared with less than 5% of the long (l) homozygotes. This study demonstrates the power of identifying specific environmental factors that may affect expression of underlying genetic differences. It is important to point out that in this study, if one does not account for stressful life events, no association between the 5-HTTLPR and depression would be detected. This fact fits nicely with experimental data from animal studies. For example, in rhesus macaques that have a similar functional polymorphism, animals that are raised under stressful conditions and have an s allele demonstrate decreased serotonergic function, whereas those animals with an s allele reared under normal conditions do not (Barr et al. 2003). From the studies cited above, it is clear that a stressful environment reveals an underlying genetic vulnerability to depression in these individuals. One question, then, is whether these genetic differences are reflected at the level of neuronal circuits; i.e., is the individual's vulnerability to environmental stress detectable as a difference in brain function?

Imaging studies in humans demonstrate that this is indeed the case. Healthy individuals with one or two copies of the s allele exhibit greater amygdala neuronal activity to fearful stimuli than do individuals who are homozygous for the l allele (Hariri et al. 2002, 2005; Hariri & Weinberger 2003). The effects are robust even though these individuals do not show signs of anxiety or depression. This suggests that allelic differences in the 5-HTT do affect circuitry in measurable ways (a true endophenotype) and that the effects on behavior are seen only under the appropriate environmental conditions. In addition to increased amygdala reactivity, investigators have now found an effect of the 5-HTTLPR on circuit-level processing. Specifically, investigators have found that individuals who carry the s form of the allele show uncoupling of a cingulate-amygdala feedback circuit that is present in individuals who carry the l allele (Pezawas et al. 2005). When and how this uncoupling occurs is unclear. However, it is reasonable to speculate that in humans, like in the mouse, there is a critical period during which environmental influences might moderate this circuit. Of interest in this regard is the recent controversy over the use of serotonergic agents in children and adolescents. This controversy is due to increasing concern over the possible long-term effects of administering these drugs during a time that may fall within the critical period for the development of circuits regulating affect and anxiety.

TRYPTOPHAN HYDROXYLASE   The examples discussed above nicely illustrate the effect of altered serotonergic signaling during development on anxiety and depression-like behaviors. If the developmental hypothesis is correct, then other genes that affect serotonin levels during development might also be candidates for regulating baseline anxiety and/or tendency toward depression. Of interest in this regard is the tryptophan hydroxylase 2 gene (TPH2). The enzyme produced from this gene is the rate-limiting step for serotonin synthesis in the brain (Walther et al. 2003, Zhang et al. 2004). Another gene, TPH1, is responsible for this function in the periphery. There have been several recent reports of an association between the TPH2 locus and depression. Zhang et al. (2004) describe a functional single nucleotide polymorphism (SNP) in mice that results in a 50% reduction in brain serotonin levels. Inbred mouse lines that carry the 1473G allele (Balb C, DBA) show decreased serotonin synthesis and brain serotonin content in comparison to strains that carry the 1473C allele (C57Bl6,129X1/SvJ). The results of their studies with mice spurred Zhang et al. to search for functional SNPs in humans, where they identified a novel functional polymorphism that results in the replacement of an arginine with a histidine at position 441. In vitro expression studies suggest that the mutant allele results in an 80% decrease in serotonin synthesis in comparison with the wild-type allele. Zhang et al. (2005) then searched for this SNP in a cohort of depressed individuals and controls. They found a significant increase of the histidine-encoding SNP in depressed individuals: 9 of 87 depressed subjects carried a histidine-encoding allele. In the control group, 3 of 219 subjects carried the histidine-encoding allele. The difference in allele frequency between groups was significant at $p < 0.001$ (Zhang et al. 2005). Independently, another group of investigators had previously shown an association between TPH2 SNPs and haplotypes in major depression in a group of 300 depressed patients and 265 healthy controls (Zill et al. 2004a). An association between TPH2 SNPs and completed suicide has also been reported (Zill et al. 2004b). However, unlike the Zhang et al. (2005) study, the Zill et al. studies do not provide any mechanistic insight beyond the linkage to a specific haplotype. Although the data suggest a role for TPH2 in depression, the specific link to the 441 SNP awaits replication.

Hypothalamic-Pituitary-Adrenal Axis in Anxiety and Depression

Like the serotonin system, the HPA axis has been implicated in the pathogenesis of anxiety and depression. Significant evidence suggests that early environmental factors establish an HPA axis reactivity that can be set for life and can be transmitted epigenetically to subsequent generations (Gorman et al. 2002, Weaver et al. 2004). Some of this evidence comes from studies in which nonhuman primates are raised under conditions that alter maternal stress levels through use of a variable foraging demand paradigm. In these studies, macaques that experience stress in early life manifest characteristics that are reminiscent of anxiety and depression in humans. Interestingly, the researchers found that exposure to the variable foraging paradigm at different times in infancy can result in opposite phenotypes. These findings are manifested at both behavioral and biochemical levels, including changes in the HPA axis (Mathew et al. 2002). Perhaps not unexpectedly, these changes are also correlated with changes in the serotonergic system of these animals.

Human data have also established a genetic contribution of the HPA axis in anxiety and depression. Altered physiology and function of the HPA axis have consistently been found in individuals with major depression and anxiety (Carroll et al. 1981, Nemeroff et al. 1984, Sachar et al. 1970, Strohle & Holsboer 2003). In addition, antidepressants of various classes suppress HPA activity in depressed and healthy humans (Strohle & Holsboer 2003). Components of the HPA axis have been proposed as possible endophenotypes for depression (Hasler et al. 2004).

Corticotrophin-releasing hormone (CRH) is the primary mediator of HPA activity. Stress induces the release of CRH from the hypothalamus, which causes the release of adrenocorticotropin from the pituitary and ultimately leads to the release of glucocorticoid stress hormones from the adrenal glands (Miller & O'Callaghan 2002). CRH also modulates anxiety when injected directly into the brain (Dunn & Swiergiel 1999, Eckart et al. 1999, Martins et al. 1997). Knockout studies in mice have examined the possible role of two CRH receptors in mediating anxiety (Holsboer 2000, Keck et al. 2004, Muller et al. 2003): CRH-R1 and CRH-R2 (Finn et al. 2003). Mice lacking the CRH-R1 gene have decreased anxiety-like behavior in the elevated plus maze and light-dark test, two commonly used models of conflict-based anxiety in rodents (Smith et al. 1998, Timpl et al. 1998). Anxiety measures in CRH-R2 knockout mice have been inconsistent across three different groups (Bale et al. 2000, 2002; Coste et al. 2000; Finn et al. 2003; Kishimoto et al. 2000). Although it is unclear why different groups have reported different results, the data do suggest that CRH or a related ligand acts on CRH-R1 to increase anxiety-related behavior. Further studies with a forebrain-specific knockout of CRH-R1 in the forebrain but not in the hypothalamus or pituitary demonstrate that the anxiety phenotype that had been previously observed is the result of direct CRH effects in the forebrain or limbic areas and not effects on the HPA axis (Muller et al. 2003).

In light of the above data, a number of groups have used a candidate approach to examine the involvement of HPA axis genes in anxiety and depression. In one approach, Licinio and colleagues (Licinio et al. 2004) assessed the possible association of CRH-R1 gene variants with a response to antidepressant drugs. They reasoned that stratifying their sample by both factors might be fruitful because of the association of the HPA axis with both anxiety and depression. Indeed, they found that a CRH-R1 variant was associated with a greater response to SSRI treatment in individuals who were homozygous for a GAG haplotype in the CRH-R1 locus. The association was found specifically for the subpopulation of individuals who were highly anxious and depressed. No association was seen in the subgroup of depressed patients that were not anxious. Although the Licinio et al. (2004) study did not directly address the contribution of CRH and the HPA axis in the pathophysiology of anxiety and depression, the demonstration that variants in the CRH-R1 gene can affect treatment response does bring us one step closer to understanding the mechanisms by which antidepressants exert their function. The study's limitations include its relatively small sample size in a single ethnic group (Mexican Americans in the Los Angeles area).

In a related approach, Binder and colleagues (Binder et al. 2004) sought to examine whether polymorphisms in genes related to the glucocorticoid receptor affected either the susceptibility for developing depression or the response to antidepressants. Specifically, they examined the SNPs in the glucocorticoid receptor, CRH, and arginine vasopressin as well as five cochaperones that are involved in regulating glucocorticoid activity. In their examination of 298 depressed individual and 340 matched controls, they were unable to find an association between any SNPs and a risk for being depressed. However, they did find an association between FKBP5—one of the cochaperones—and response to antidepressant treatment. Specifically, several SNPs showed faster response time to antidepressants. In addition, Binder and colleagues found that one of the alleles, the TT allele, was associated with a risk for having more prior episodes of major depression. They went one step further and genotyped an independent sample of depressed patients and again found the same relationship. To examine for a possible mechanism, Binder et al. (2004) examined the effect of one of the polymorphisms on levels of FKBP5 in the lymphocytes of patients. They found that individuals with the TT allele (the one with the faster response) have FKBP5 levels that are twice that of the other genotypes. This was of interest because several lines of evidence suggest that FKBP5 decreases glucocorticoid receptor-binding affinity. The authors then probed responsiveness of the HPA axis using a dexamethasone-CRH test. In this test, dexamethasone—a synthetic glucocorticoid—is administered to suppress the HPA axis. Individuals are then challenged with CRH to see how effectively the HPA axis is suppressed. The results suggest that although individuals carrying the TT polymorphism are as depressed as the other members of the cohort, their HPA axis regulation may be less impaired. This finding is interesting because resolution of depressive symptomatology has been linked to a normalization of HPA axis hyperactivity, providing a potential explanation for the more rapid response to antidepressants in these patients (Holsboer 2000). The results suggest that individuals with a TT allele may be both more sensitive to HPA axis hyperactivity after a stressor and more amenable to normalization after treatment.

Results of the Binder et al. (2004) study appear to confirm the potential usefulness of the dexamethasone-CRH suppression test as an endophenotype for depression. The Binder et al. (2004) and Licinio et al. (2004) findings also suggest that looking for genetic variation in the response to antidepressant treatment may be an additional way to break down the complexities of the anxiety and depression phenotypes into tractable endophenotypes.

CONCLUSIONS

After years of limited success, the study of complex behavioral traits appears poised for a period of rapid development. The field has conceptually evolved from trying to find genes that are partially responsible for a clinical construct like major depression or generalized anxiety to one in which the phenotypes are more limited and more rigorously defined. These proximal phenotypes or endophenotypes, combined with our increasing knowledge of the basic neurobiology of functional circuits, will increasingly provide productive synergy in the search for genes that affect anxiety and depression-like behaviors. For example, the finding of association between FKBP5 and rate of response to antidepressant medication was the result of such synergy. Although the rate of response to a medication is not itself clearly validated as an endophenotype, the authors of the Binder et al. (2004)

study were able to relate secondarily their observation to an altered dexamethasone suppression-CRH stimulation test.

Another area we expect will continue to yield valuable data is the study of circuit development and maturation in the brain. Already, the examples provided by the 5-HT1A receptor and the serotonin transporter demonstrate the importance of attending to effects of genes during critical periods. This concept of critical periods also highlights the need for greater integration of environmental contributions to the expression of underlying genetic traits. The finding that early stressors modulate the phenotypic expression of polymorphisms in the serotonin transporter heralds the beginning of an era in which the inclusion of environmental factors will be used to enhance the power of genetic analysis. In the Caspi et al. (2003) study, the impact of the serotonin polymorphism was seen only in the context of the environmental stressors. A mechanistic study of this nature is now possible by, for example, pairing mice heterozygous for the serotonin transporter with a specific stress paradigm, such as maternal separation. Finally, as we become better versed in environmental factors that affect phenotypes and as we refine relevant endophenotypes, we expect that we will find not only novel genes, but also new polymorphisms and novel forms of regulation in genes that are already under investigation as candidates for mediating genetic effects.

The *Annual Review of Psychology* is online at http://psych.annualreviews.org

LITERATURE CITED

Albert PR, Lemonde S. 2004. 5-HT1A receptors, gene repression, and depression: guilt by association. *Neuroscientist* 10:575–93

Am. Psychiatric Assoc. 2000. *Diagnostic and Statistical Manual of Mental Disorders: DSM-IV-TR*. Washington, DC: Am. Psychiatric Assoc. 943 pp.

Ansorge MS, Zhou M, Lira A, Hen R, Gingrich JA. 2004. Early-life blockade of the 5-HT transporter alters emotional behavior in adult mice. *Science* 306:879–81

Bale TL, Contarino A, Smith GW, Chan R, Gold LH, et al. 2000. Mice deficient for corticotropin-releasing hormone receptor-2 display anxiety-like behaviour and are hypersensitive to stress. *Nat. Genet.* 24:410–14

Bale TL, Picetti R, Contarino A, Koob GF, Vale WW, Lee KF. 2002. Mice deficient for both corticotropin-releasing factor receptor 1 (CRFR1) and CRFR2 have an impaired stress response and display sexually dichotomous anxiety-like behavior. *J. Neurosci.* 22:193–99

Barr CS, Newman TK, Becker ML, Parker CC, Champoux M, et al. 2003. The utility of the non-human primate; model for studying gene by environment interactions in behavioral research. *Genes Brain Behav.* 2:336–40

Binder EB, Salyakina D, Lichtner P, Wochnik GM, Ising M, et al. 2004. Polymorphisms in FKBP5 are associated with increased recurrence of depressive episodes and rapid response to antidepressant treatment. *Nat. Genet.* 36:1319–25

Borsini F, Podhorna J, Marazziti D. 2002. Do animal models of anxiety predict anxiolytic-like effects of antidepressants? *Psychopharmacology (Berl.)* 163:121–41

Carroll BJ, Feinberg M, Greden JF, Tarika J, Albala AA, et al. 1981. A specific laboratory test for the diagnosis of melancholia. Standardization, validation, and clinical utility. *Arch. Gen. Psychiatry* 38:15–22

Caspi A, Sugden K, Moffitt TE, Taylor A, Craig IW, et al. 2003. Influence of life stress on depression: moderation by a polymorphism in the 5-HTT gene. *Science* 301:386–89

Chakravarti A, Little P. 2003. Nature, nurture and human disease. *Nature* 421:412–14

Chapman DP, Whitfield CL, Felitti VJ, Dube SR, Edwards VJ, Anda RF. 2004. Adverse childhood experiences and the risk of depressive disorders in adulthood. *J. Affect. Disord.* 82:217–25

Charney DS, Barlow DH, Botteron KN, Conhen JD, Goldman D, et al. 2002. Neuroscience research agenda to guide development of a pathophysiologically based classification system. In *A Research Agenda for DSM-V*, ed. DJ Kupfer, MB First, DA Regier, pp. 31–83. Washington, DC: Am. Psychiatric Assoc.

Chrousos GP. 1998. Stressors, stress, and neuroendocrine integration of the adaptive response. The 1997 Hans Selye Memorial Lecture. *Ann. NY Acad. Sci.* 851:311–35

Conti LH, Maciver CR, Ferkany JW, Abreu ME. 1990. Footshock-induced freezing behavior in rats as a model for assessing anxiolytics. *Psychopharmacology (Berl.)* 102:492–97

Cooper JR, Bloom FE, Roth RH. 2003. *The Biochemical Basis of Neuropharmacology*. New York: Oxford Univ. Press. 405 pp.

Coste SC, Kesterson RA, Heldwein KA, Stevens SL, Heard AD, et al. 2000. Abnormal adaptations to stress and impaired cardiovascular function in mice lacking corticotropin-releasing hormone receptor-2. *Nat. Genet.* 24:403–9

Crawley JN. 2000. *What's Wrong with My Mouse? Behavioral Phenotyping of Transgenic and Knockout Mice*. New York: Wiley-Liss. 329 pp.

Crowley JJ, Lucki I. 2005. Opportunities to discover genes regulating depression and antidepressant response from rodent behavioral genetics. *Curr. Pharm. Des.* 11:157–69

Davis M, Walker DL, Myers KM. 2003. Role of the amygdala in fear extinction measured with potentiated startle. *Ann. NY Acad. Sci.* 985:218–32

Deacon RM, Bannerman DM, Rawlins JN. 2002. Anxiolytic effects of cytotoxic hippocampal lesions in rats. *Behav. Neurosci.* 116:494–97

Dulawa SC, Hen R. 2005. Recent advances in animal models of chronic antidepressant effects: the novelty-induced hypophagia test. *Neurosci. Biobehav. Rev.* 29:771–83

Dulawa SC, Holick KA, Gundersen B, Hen R. 2004. Effects of chronic fluoxetine in animal models of anxiety and depression. *Neuropsychopharmacology* 29:1321–30

Dunn AJ, Swiergiel AH. 1999. Behavioral responses to stress are intact in CRF-deficient mice. *Brain Res.* 845:14–20

Eckart K, Radulovic J, Radulovic M, Jahn O, Blank T, et al. 1999. Actions of CRF and its analogs. *Curr. Med. Chem.* 6:1035–53

Felitti VJ, Anda RF, Nordenberg D, Williamson DF, Spitz AM, et al. 1998. Relationship of childhood abuse and household dysfunction to many of the leading causes of death in adults. The Adverse Childhood Experiences (ACE) Study. *Am. J. Prev. Med.* 14:245–58

Finn DA, Rutledge-Gorman MT, Crabbe JC. 2003. Genetic animal models of anxiety. *Neurogenetics* 4:109–35

Flint J. 2003. Analysis of quantitative trait loci that influence animal behavior. *J. Neurobiol.* 54:46–77

Flint J, Corley R, DeFries JC, Fulker DW, Gray JA, et al. 1995. A simple genetic basis for a complex psychological trait in laboratory mice. *Science* 269:1432–35

Goldberg J, True WR, Eisen SA, Henderson WG. 1990. A twin study of the effects of the Vietnam War on posttraumatic stress disorder. *JAMA* 263:1227–32

Gordon JA, Lacefield CO, Kentros CG, Hen R. 2005. State-dependent alterations in hippocampal oscillations in serotonin 1a receptor-deficient mice. *J. Neurosci.* 25:6509–19

Gorman JM. 1996. Comorbid depression and

anxiety spectrum disorders. *Depress. Anxiety* 4:160–68

Gorman JM, Mathew S, Coplan J. 2002. Neurobiology of early life stress: nonhuman primate models. *Semin. Clin. Neuropsychiatry* 7:96–103

Gottesman II, Gould TD. 2003. The endophenotype concept in psychiatry: etymology and strategic intentions. *Am. J. Psychiatry* 160:636–45

Greenberg PE, Kessler RC, Birnbaum HG, Leong SA, Lowe SW, et al. 2003. The economic burden of depression in the United States: How did it change between 1990 and 2000? *J. Clin. Psychiatry* 64:1465–75

Greenberg PE, Sisitsky T, Kessler RC, Finkelstein SN, Berndt ER, et al. 1999. The economic burden of anxiety disorders in the 1990s. *J. Clin. Psychiatry* 60:427–35

Hariri AR, Drabant EM, Munoz KE, Kolachana BS, Mattay VS, et al. 2005. A susceptibility gene for affective disorders and the response of the human amygdala. *Arch. Gen. Psychiatry* 62:146–52

Hariri AR, Mattay VS, Tessitore A, Kolachana B, Fera F, et al. 2002. Serotonin transporter genetic variation and the response of the human amygdala. *Science* 297:400–3

Hariri AR, Weinberger DR. 2003. Functional neuroimaging of genetic variation in serotonergic neurotransmission. *Genes Brain Behav.* 2:341–49

Hasler G, Drevets WC, Manji HK, Charney DS. 2004. Discovering endophenotypes for major depression. *Neuropsychopharmacology* 29:1765–81

Hensch TK. 2004. Critical period regulation. *Annu. Rev. Neurosci.* 27:549–79

Hettema JM, Neale MC, Kendler KS. 2001. A review and meta-analysis of the genetic epidemiology of anxiety disorders. *Am. J. Psychiatry* 158:1568–78

Holmes A, Lit Q, Murphy DL, Gold E, Crawley JN. 2003. Abnormal anxiety-related behavior in serotonin transporter null mutant mice: the influence of genetic background. *Genes Brain Behav.* 2:365–80

Holsboer F. 2000. The corticosteroid receptor hypothesis of depression. *Neuropsychopharmacology* 23:477–501

Ishiwata H, Shiga T, Okado N. 2005. Selective serotonin reuptake inhibitor treatment of early postnatal mice reverses their prenatal stress-induced brain dysfunction. *Neuroscience* 133(4):893–901

Kagan J, Snidman N. 1999. Early childhood predictors of adult anxiety disorders. *Biol. Psychiatry* 46:1536–41

Keck ME, Holsboer F, Muller MB. 2004. Mouse mutants for the study of corticotropin-releasing hormone receptor function: development of novel treatment strategies for mood disorders. *Ann. NY Acad. Sci.* 1018:445–57

Kendler KS. 2001. Twin studies of psychiatric illness: an update. *Arch. Gen. Psychiatry* 58:1005–14

Kendler KS, Kuhn JW, Vittum J, Prescott CA, Riley B. 2005. The interaction of stressful life events and a serotonin transporter polymorphism in the prediction of episodes of major depression: a replication. *Arch. Gen. Psychiatry* 62:529–35

Kendler KS, Neale MC, Kessler RC, Heath AC, Eaves LJ. 1992. Major depression and generalized anxiety disorder. Same genes, (partly) different environments? *Arch. Gen. Psychiatry* 49:716–22

Kishimoto T, Radulovic J, Radulovic M, Lin CR, Schrick C, et al. 2000. Deletion of crhr2 reveals an anxiolytic role for corticotropin-releasing hormone receptor-2. *Nat. Genet.* 24:415–19

Kjelstrup KG, Tuvnes FA, Steffenach HA, Murison R, Moser EI, Moser MB. 2002. Reduced fear expression after lesions of the ventral hippocampus. *Proc. Natl. Acad. Sci. USA* 99:10825–30

Klemenhagen KC, Gordon JA, David DJ, Hen R, Gross CT. 2005. Increased fear response to contextual cues in mice lacking the 5-HT1A receptor. *Neuropsychopharmacology.* doi:10.1038/sj.npp.1300774 (epub. ahead of print)

Knudsen EI. 2004. Sensitive periods in the

development of the brain and behavior. *J. Cogn. Neurosci.* 16:1412–25

LeDoux JE. 2000. Emotion circuits in the brain. *Annu. Rev. Neurosci.* 23:155–84

Lemonde S, Du L, Bakish D, Hrdina P, Albert PR. 2004. Association of the C(-1019)G 5-HT1A functional promoter polymorphism with antidepressant response. *Int. J. Neuropsychopharmacol.* 7:501–6

Lemonde S, Turecki G, Bakish D, Du L, Hrdina PD, et al. 2003. Impaired repression at a 5-hydroxytryptamine 1A receptor gene polymorphism associated with major depression and suicide. *J. Neurosci.* 23:8788–99

Lesch KP, Gutknecht L. 2004. Focus on the 5-HT1A receptor: emerging role of a gene regulatory variant in psychopathology and pharmacogenetics. *Int. J. Neuropsychopharmacol.* 7:381–85

Licinio J, O'Kirwan F, Irizarry K, Merriman B, Thakur S, et al. 2004. Association of a corticotropin-releasing hormone receptor 1 haplotype and antidepressant treatment response in Mexican-Americans. *Mol. Psychiatry* 9:1075–82

Lira A, Zhou M, Castanon N, Ansorge MS, Gordon JA, et al. 2003. Altered depression-related behaviors and functional changes in the dorsal raphe nucleus of serotonin transporter-deficient mice. *Biol. Psychiatry* 54:960–71

Lyons MJ, Goldberg J, Eisen SA, True W, Tsuang MT, et al. 1993. Do genes influence exposure to trauma? A twin study of combat. *Am. J. Med. Genet.* 48:22–27

Martins AP, Marras RA, Guimaraes FS. 1997. Anxiogenic effect of corticotropin-releasing hormone in the dorsal periaqueductal grey. *Neuroreport* 8:3601–4

Mathew SJ, Coplan JD, Smith EL, Scharf BA, Owens MJ, et al. 2002. Cerebrospinal fluid concentrations of biogenic amines and corticotropin-releasing factor in adolescent non-human primates as a function of the timing of adverse early rearing. *Stress* 5:185–93

Miller DB, O'Callaghan JP. 2002. Neuroendocrine aspects of the response to stress. *Metabolism* 51:5–10

Mitchell PJ, Redfern PH. 2005. Animal models of depressive illness: the importance of chronic drug treatment. *Curr. Pharm. Des.* 11:171–203

Muller MB, Zimmermann S, Sillaber I, Hagemeyer TP, Deussing JM, et al. 2003. Limbic corticotropin-releasing hormone receptor 1 mediates anxiety-related behavior and hormonal adaptation to stress. *Nat. Neurosci.* 6:1100–7

Nemeroff CB, Widerlov E, Bissette G, Walleus H, Karlsson I, et al. 1984. Elevated concentrations of CSF corticotropin-releasing factor-like immunoreactivity in depressed patients. *Science* 226:1342–44

Ninan PT, Berger J. 2001. Symptomatic and syndromal anxiety and depression. *Depress. Anxiety* 14:79–85

Oliveira-Dos-Santos AJ, Matsumoto G, Snow BE, Bai D, Houston FP, et al. 2000. Regulation of T cell activation, anxiety, and male aggression by RGS2. *Proc. Natl. Acad. Sci. USA* 97:12272–77

Parks CL, Robinson PS, Sibille E, Shenk T, Toth M. 1998. Increased anxiety of mice lacking the serotonin1A receptor. *Proc. Natl. Acad. Sci. USA* 95:10734–39

Pellow S, File SE. 1986. Anxiolytic and anxiogenic drug effects on exploratory activity in an elevated plus-maze: a novel test of anxiety in the rat. *Pharmacol. Biochem. Behav.* 24:525–29

Pezawas L, Meyer-Lindenberg A, Drabant EM, Verchinski BA, Munoz KE, et al. 2005. 5-HTTLPR polymorphism impacts human cingulate-amygdala interactions: a genetic susceptibility mechanism for depression. *Nat. Neurosci.* 8:828–34

Pokorny J, Yamamoto T. 1981. Postnatal ontogenesis of hippocampal CA1 area in rats. II. Development of ultrastructure in stratum lacunosum and moleculare. *Brain Res. Bull.* 7:121–30

Ramboz S, Oosting R, Amara DA, Kung HF, Blier P, et al. 1998. Serotonin receptor 1A knockout: an animal model of anxiety-related disorder. *Proc. Natl. Acad. Sci. USA* 95:14476–81

Rodgers RJ, Dalvi A. 1997. Anxiety, defence and the elevated plus-maze. *Neurosci. Biobehav. Rev.* 21:801–10

Rose RJ. 1995. Genes and human behavior. *Annu. Rev. Psychol.* 46:625–54

Roy MA, Neale MC, Pedersen NL, Mathe AA, Kendler KS. 1995. A twin study of generalized anxiety disorder and major depression. *Psychol. Med.* 25:1037–49

Sachar EJ, Hellman L, Fukushima DK, Gallagher TF. 1970. Cortisol production in depressive illness. A clinical and biochemical clarification. *Arch. Gen. Psychiatry* 23:289–98

Santarelli L, Saxe M, Gross C, Surget A, Battaglia F, et al. 2003. Requirement of hippocampal neurogenesis for the behavioral effects of antidepressants. *Science* 301:805–9

Schwartz CE, Snidman N, Kagan J. 1999. Adolescent social anxiety as an outcome of inhibited temperament in childhood. *J. Am. Acad. Child Adolesc. Psychiatry* 38:1008–15

Shephard RA, Broadhurst PL. 1982. Hyponeophagia and arousal in rats: effects of diazepam, 5-methoxy-N, N-dimethyltryptamine, d-amphetamine and food deprivation. *Psychopharmacology (Berl.)* 78:368–72

Singer JB, Hill AE, Nadeau JH, Lander ES. 2005. Mapping quantitative trait loci for anxiety in chromosome substitution strains of mice. *Genetics* 169:855–62

Smith GW, Aubry JM, Dellu F, Contarino A, Bilezikjian LM, et al. 1998. Corticotropin releasing factor receptor 1-deficient mice display decreased anxiety, impaired stress response, and aberrant neuroendocrine development. *Neuron* 20:1093–102

Stein MB, Jang KL, Taylor S, Vernon PA, Livesley WJ. 2002. Genetic and environmental influences on trauma exposure and posttraumatic stress disorder symptoms: a twin study. *Am. J. Psychiatry* 159:1675–81

Strobel A, Gutknecht L, Rothe C, Reif A, Mossner R, et al. 2003. Allelic variation in 5-HT1A receptor expression is associated with anxiety- and depression-related personality traits. *J. Neural Transm.* 110:1445–53

Strohle A, Holsboer F. 2003. Stress responsive neurohormones in depression and anxiety. *Pharmacopsychiatry* 36(Suppl. 3):207–14

Sullivan PF, Neale MC, Kendler KS. 2000. Genetic epidemiology of major depression: review and meta-analysis. *Am. J. Psychiatry* 157:1552–62

Timpl P, Spanagel R, Sillaber I, Kresse A, Reul JM, et al. 1998. Impaired stress response and reduced anxiety in mice lacking a functional corticotropin-releasing hormone receptor 1. *Nat. Genet.* 19:162–66

True WR, Rice J, Eisen SA, Heath AC, Goldberg J, et al. 1993. A twin study of genetic and environmental contributions to liability for posttraumatic stress symptoms. *Arch. Gen. Psychiatry* 50:257–64

Turri MG, DeFries JC, Henderson ND, Flint J. 2004. Multivariate analysis of quantitative trait loci influencing variation in anxiety-related behavior in laboratory mice. *Mamm. Genome* 15:69–76

Tweed JL, Schoenbach VJ, George LK, Blazer DG. 1989. The effects of childhood parental death and divorce on six-month history of anxiety disorders. *Br. J. Psychiatry* 154:823–28

Van Ameringen M, Mancini C, Oakman JM. 1998. The relationship of behavioral inhibition and shyness to anxiety disorder. *J. Nerv. Ment. Dis.* 186:425–31

Wahlsten D. 1999. Single-gene influences on brain and behavior. *Annu. Rev. Psychol.* 50:599–624

Walther DJ, Peter JU, Bashammakh S, Hortnagl H, Voits M, et al. 2003. Synthesis of serotonin by a second tryptophan hydroxylase isoform. *Science* 299:76

Weaver IC, Cervoni N, Champagne FA, D'Alessio AC, Sharma S, et al. 2004. Epigenetic programming by maternal behavior. *Nat. Neurosci.* 7:847–54

Wimer RE, Wimer CC. 1985. Animal behavior genetics: a search for the biological foundations of behavior. *Annu. Rev. Psychol.* 36:171–218

Yalcin B, Willis-Owen SA, Fullerton J, Meesaq A, Deacon RM, et al. 2004. Genetic dissection of a behavioral quantitative trait locus shows that Rgs2 modulates anxiety in mice. *Nat. Genet.* 36:1197–202

Yoshikawa T, Watanabe A, Ishitsuka Y, Nakaya A, Nakatani N. 2002. Identification of multiple genetic loci linked to the propensity for "behavioral despair" in mice. *Genome Res.* 12:357–66

Zhang X, Beaulieu JM, Sotnikova TD, Gainetdinov RR, Caron MG. 2004. Tryptophan hydroxylase-2 controls brain serotonin synthesis. *Science* 305:217

Zhang X, Gainetdinov RR, Beaulieu JM, Sotnikova TD, Burch LH, et al. 2005. Loss-of-function mutation in tryptophan hydroxylase-2 identified in unipolar major depression. *Neuron* 45:11–16

Zill P, Baghai TC, Zwanzger P, Schule C, Eser D, et al. 2004a. SNP and haplotype analysis of a novel tryptophan hydroxylase isoform (TPH2) gene provide evidence for association with major depression. *Mol. Psychiatry* 9:1030–36

Zill P, Buttner A, Eisenmenger W, Moller HJ, Bondy B, Ackenheil M. 2004b. Single nucleotide polymorphism and haplotype analysis of a novel tryptophan hydroxylase isoform (TPH2) gene in suicide victims. *Biol. Psychiatry* 56:581–86

Annu. Rev. Psychol. 2006. 57:139–66
doi: 10.1146/annurev.psych.56.091103.070307
Copyright © 2006 by Annual Reviews. All rights reserved
First published online as a Review in Advance on October 3, 2005

SLEEP, MEMORY, AND PLASTICITY

Matthew P. Walker[1,2] and Robert Stickgold[2]

*Sleep and Neuroimaging Laboratory[1] and Center for Sleep and Cognition,[2] Beth Israel
Deaconess Medical Center, Boston, Massachusetts 02215, and Department of Psychiatry,
Harvard Medical School, Boston, Massachusetts 02215;
email: mwalker@hms.harvard.edu, rstickgold@hms.harvard.edu*

Key Words declarative memory, procedural memory, reconsolidation, REM
sleep, learning

■ **Abstract**   Although the functions of sleep remain largely unknown, one of the
most exciting hypotheses is that sleep contributes importantly to processes of memory
and brain plasticity. Over the past decade, a large body of work, spanning most of the
neurosciences, has provided a substantive body of evidence supporting this role of sleep
in what is becoming known as sleep-dependent memory processing. We review these
findings, focusing specifically on the role of sleep in (*a*) memory encoding, (*b*) memory
consolidation, (*c*) brain plasticity, and (*d*) memory reconsolidation; we finish with a
summary of the field and its potential future directions.

CONTENTS

INTRODUCTION

An exciting renaissance is currently under way within the biological sciences, centered on the question of why we sleep, and focusing specifically on the dependence of memory and plasticity on sleep. Although this resurgence is relatively recent in the annals of sleep research, the topic itself has a surprisingly long history. In the early nineteenth century, the British psychologist David Hartley proposed that dreaming might alter the strength of associative memory links within the brain (Hartley 1801). Yet it was not until 1924 that Jenkins and Dallenbach performed the first systematic studies of sleep and memory to test Ebbinghaus's theory of memory decay (Jenkins & Dallenbach 1924). Their findings showed that memory retention was better following a night of sleep than after an equivalent amount of time awake. However, they concluded that the memory benefit following sleep was passive and resulted from a lack of sensory interference during sleep. They did not consider the possibility that the physiological state of sleep itself could actively orchestrate these memory modifications.

It is only in the past half century, following the discovery of rapid eye movement (REM) and non-REM (NREM) sleep (Aserinsky & Kleitman 1953), that research began testing the hypothesis that sleep, or even specific stages of sleep, actively participated in the process of memory development. This review explores this relationship between what has become known as sleep-dependent memory processing and its associated brain basis, sleep-dependent plasticity.

DELINEATIONS AND DEFINITIONS

We begin our discussion of interactions between sleep and memory by clarifying the complexities that these terms encompass.

Sleep States

To begin, it is important to note that the brain does not reside in one single physiological state across the 24-hour day, but instead cycles through periods of differing neural and metabolic activity, associated with distinct biological states, most obviously divided into those of wake and sleep. Sleep itself has been broadly divided into REM and NREM sleep, which alternate across the night in humans in a 90-minute cycle (Figure 1A, see color insert). In primates and felines, NREM sleep has been further divided into substages 1 through 4, corresponding to increasingly deeper states of sleep (Rechtschaffen & Kales 1968) (Figure 1A). The deepest NREM stages, stages 3 and 4, are collectively referred to as "slow wave sleep" (SWS), based on a prevalence of low-frequency cortical oscillations in the electroencephalogram (EEG). Dramatic changes in brain electrophysiology, neurochemistry and functional anatomy accompany these sleep stages, making them biologically distinct from the waking brain, and dissociable from one another (Hobson & Pace-Schott 2002). Thus, sleep cannot be treated as a homogeneous state, which either does or does not affect memory. Instead, each sleep stage possesses a set of physiological and neurochemical mechanisms that may contribute uniquely to memory consolidation.

Memory Categories

In the same way that sleep cannot be considered homogeneous, the spectrum of memory categories believed to exist in the human brain, and the processes that create and sustain memory, appear equally diverse. Although often used as a unitary term, "memory" is not a single entity. Human memory has been subject to several different classification schemes, the most popular based on the distinction between declarative and nondeclarative memory (Schacter & Tulving 1994, Squire & Zola 1996) (Figure 1*B*). Declarative memory can be considered as the consciously accessible memories of fact-based information (i.e., knowing "what"). Several subcategories of the declarative system exist, including episodic memory (autobiographical memory for events of one's past) and semantic memory (memory for general knowledge, not tied to specific events) (Tulving 1985). Current neural models of declarative memory formation emphasize the critical importance of structures in the medial temporal lobe, especially the hippocampus (Eichenbaum 2000), a structure that is thought to form a temporally ordered retrieval code for neocortically stored information, and to bind together disparate perceptual elements of a single event. In contrast, nondeclarative memory is regarded as nonconscious, and includes procedural memory (i.e., knowing "how"), such as the learning of actions, habits, and skills, as well as implicit learning, and appears to be less dependent on medial temporal lobe structures.

Although these categories offer convenient and distinct separations, they rarely operate in isolation in real life. For example, language learning requires a combination of memory sources, ranging from nondeclarative memory for procedural motor programs to articulate speech, to memory of grammatical rules and structure, and through to aspects of declarative memory for the source of word selection. This too must be kept in mind as we consider the role of sleep in learning and memory.

Memory Stages

Just as memory cannot be considered monolithic, there similarly does not appear to be one sole event that creates or develops it. Instead, memory appears to develop in several unique stages over time (Figure 1*C*). For example, memories can be initially formed or "encoded" by engaging with an object or performing an action, leading to the formation of a representation of the object or action within the brain. Following encoding, the memory representation can undergo several subsequent stages of development, the most commonly recognized of which is consolidation. The term "memory consolidation" classically refers to a process whereby a memory, through the simple passage of time, becomes increasingly resistant to interference from competing or disrupting factors in the absence of further practice (McGaugh 2000). That is to say, the memory becomes more stable. It should be noted, however, that although most forms of memory appear to require subsequent consolidation following encoding, not all tasks appear to be resistant to competitive interference almost immediately, and hence do not demonstrate this characteristic of time-dependent consolidation (Goedert & Willingham 2002).

Recent findings have begun to extend the definition of consolidation. For example, consolidation can be thought of as not only stabilizing memories, but also as enhancing them—two processes that may be mechanistically distinct (Walker 2005). The stabilization phase of consolidation appears to occur largely during wake cycles (Brashers-Krug et al. 1996, Muellbacher et al. 2002, Walker et al. 2003a). The enhancement stage appears to occur primarily, if not exclusively, during sleep, either restoring previously lost memories (Fenn et al. 2003) or producing additional learning (Fischer et al. 2002; Gais et al. 2000; Karni et al. 1994; Korman et al. 2003; Stickgold et al. 2000a,b; Walker et al. 2002a,b), both without the need for further practice. From this perspective, the enhancement phase of memory consolidation causes either the active restoration of a memory that had shown behavioral deterioration, or the enhancement of a memory over its simple maintenance. Thus, consolidation can be expanded to include more than one phase of postencoding memory processing, with each phase occurring in specific brain states such as wake or sleep, or even in specific stages of sleep (Brashers-Krug et al. 1996; Karni et al. 1994; Muellbacher et al. 2002; Smith & MacNeill 1994; Stickgold et al. 2000b; Walker 2005; Walker et al. 2002a, 2003a,b).

Following its initial stabilization, a memory can be retained for days to years, during which time it can be recalled. But the act of memory recall itself is now believed to destabilize the memory representation, making it again labile and subject to potential degradation. Reconsolidation therefore has been proposed to transform the now destabilized memory into a restabilized form (Nader 2003). When a destabilized memory is not reconsolidated, it can degrade relatively quickly.

Although this chapter focuses primarily on the effects of sleep on encoding, stabilization, enhancement, and reconsolidation, it is important to note that additional postencoding stages of memory processing should also be appreciated. These include the integration of recently acquired information with past experiences and knowledge (a process of memory association), the anatomical reorganization of memory representations (memory translocation), and even the active erasure of memory representations, all of which appear to occur outside of awareness and without additional training or exposure to the original stimuli (Stickgold & Walker 2005), and may also be considered stages of memory consolidation. It is interesting to note that sleep has already been implicated in all of these steps (Crick & Mitchison 1983, Stickgold 2002, Stickgold et al. 1999, Walker et al. 2003a).

SLEEP AND MEMORY ENCODING

Some of the first studies to investigate the relationship between sleep and human memory examined the influence of sleep on posttraining consolidation (see sections below) rather than its influence on initial encoding. However, more recent data have described the detrimental consequence of inadequate pretraining sleep on successful memory encoding. The section below offers an overview of this evidence that spans a range of phylogeny and is supported across a variety of descriptive levels, from molecules to behavior.

Sleep and Memory Encoding—Human Studies

One of the earliest studies to report the effects of sleep deprivation on declarative memory encoding in humans was by Morris et al. (1960), who found that "temporal memory" (memory for when events occur) was significantly disrupted by a night of pretraining deprivation. These findings have been revisited in a more rigorous study by Harrison & Horne (2000), again using the temporal memory paradigm. The task comprised photographs of unknown faces, with the temporal memory component involving recency discrimination, together with a confidence judgment. Significant impairments of temporal memory were evident in a group deprived of sleep for 36 hours, which scored significantly lower than did controls; significant impairment was evident even in a subgroup that received caffeine to overcome nonspecific effects of lower arousal. Furthermore, the sleep-deprived subjects displayed significantly worse insight into their memory-encoding performance.

Based on data from studies indicating that memory encoding (as measured by the success of later recall) relies on the integrity of the prefrontal cortex (PFC) (e.g., Brewer et al. 1998, Canli et al. 2000, Henson et al. 1999, Wagner et al. 1998), and that baseline PFC reductions in cerebral metabolic rate are evident following one night of deprivation, the authors hypothesized that sleep deprivation impaired prefrontal function critical for effective memory encoding.

In similar studies, Drummond et al. (2000) directly examined this hypothesis by using functional magnetic resonance imaging (fMRI) to investigate the effects of 35-hour total sleep deprivation on encoding of a verbal memory task. As in previous studies, total sleep deprivation resulted in significantly worse acquisition of verbal learning. Surprisingly, however, subjects showed more PFC activation during encoding when sleep deprived than when not sleep deprived. In contrast, regions of the medial temporal lobe were significantly less activated during encoding when sleep deprived. Perhaps most interesting, the parietal lobes, which were not activated during encoding following normal sleep, were significantly activated after sleep deprivation. These findings confirm that sleep deprivation induces a significant behavioral impairment in verbal memory encoding, and suggest that these impairments are mediated by a dynamic set of bidirectional changes—overcompensation by prefrontal regions combined with a failure of the medial temporal lobe to engage normally, leading to compensatory activation in the parietal lobes (Drummond & Brown 2001).

We recently investigated the impact of sleep deprivation on declarative memory encoding of both emotional and nonemotional material (M.P. Walker, unpublished results). Subjects were either sleep deprived for 36 hours or allowed to sleep normally prior to an incidental memory encoding session composed of sets of emotionally negative, positive, and neutral words. Following two subsequent nights of sleep, subjects returned for an unexpected recognition task. Overall, subjects in the sleep-deprived condition exhibited a 40% reduction in memory retention

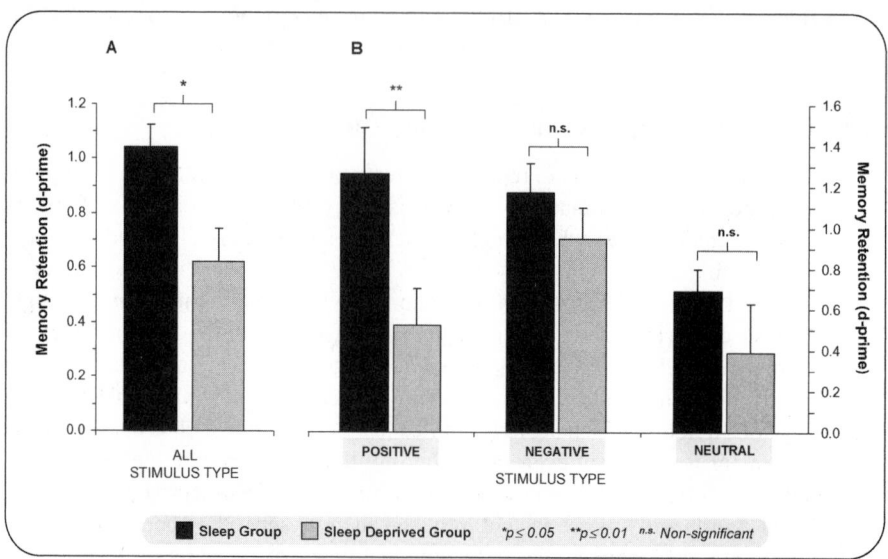

Figure 2   Sleep deprivation and encoding of emotional and nonemotional declarative memory. (*A*) Effects of 36 hours of total sleep deprivation on encoding of human declarative memory when combined across all emotional and nonemotional categories. (*B*) Effects when separated into emotional (positive and negative valence) and nonemotional (neutral valance) categories.

relative to subjects who had slept normally prior to encoding (Figure 2*A*); these results represent a striking impairment of declarative memory formation under conditions of sleep deprivation. When these data were separated into the three emotional categories (positive, negative, or neutral), the encoding deficit remained, although the magnitude of effect differed across the emotion categories (Figure 2*B*). Within the sleep control group, both positive and negative stimuli were associated with superior retention levels relative the neutral condition, consonant with the notion that emotion facilitates memory encoding (Phelps 2004). However, there was severe disruption of encoding and hence later memory retention deficit for neutral and especially positive emotional memory in the sleep-deprived group, which exhibited a significant 59% retention deficit relative to the control condition for positive emotional words. Most interesting, however, was the resistance of negative emotional memory to sleep deprivation, showing a markedly smaller (19%) and nonsignificant impairment.

These data indicate that sleep deprivation severely impairs the encoding of declarative memories, resulting in significantly worse retention two days later. Although the effects of sleep deprivation are directionally consistent across subcategories, the most profound impact is on the encoding of positive emotional stimuli, and to a lesser degree, emotionally neutral stimuli, while the encoding of negative stimuli appears more resistant to the effects of prior sleep deprivation.

Sleep and Memory Encoding—Animal Studies

In animals, pretraining sleep deprivation has been demonstrated to impair the encoding of numerous memory tasks (Smith 1985, Stern 1971). For example, using the Morris water maze in a configuration that is hippocampally dependent (nonvisible platform), Guan et al. (2004) demonstrated that 6 hours of total sleep deprivation prior to training results in a severe disruption of encoding, as assessed by retention 24 hours later. In contrast, learning of the nonspatial task version (visible platform; hippocampally independent) was more resistant to prior sleep deprivation, suggesting first that the impairments for spatial memory were not a consequence of gross alternations in attention or stress, and second that sleep deprivation may selectively disrupt hippocampal-based encoding. Beaulieu & Godbout (2000) subsequently demonstrated that even selective deprivation of REM sleep for eight hours prior to training is sufficient to impair encoding on this task. Furthermore, in a more complex configuration of the task that requires increased frontal cortex involvement (continual switching of the platform location), prior REM sleep deprivation induced even greater retest deficits, which suggests that both basic hippocampal spatial memory and more complex spatial learning requiring additional frontal involvement are susceptible to a lack of prior REM.

REM sleep deprivation also has detrimental effects on the encoding of other hippocampally mediated tasks, including one-way and two-way avoidance learning, taste aversion, and passive avoidance tasks (see McGrath & Cohen 1978, Smith 1985). Even short (five-hour) bouts of pretraining REM sleep deprivation significantly impair encoding of two-way avoidance learning in rats, producing deficits that cannot be overcome by additional practice during training (Gruart-Masso et al. 1995).

An interesting dissociation of sleep deprivation effects is seen using a fear-conditioning task. The contextual versus cued memory paradigm in animals offers the ability to distinguish memory processing mediated primarily by the hippocampus (context) from that mediated primarily by the amygdala (cue). Using this task, Ruskin et al. (2004) demonstrated that pretraining sleep deprivation (predominantly REM) profoundly impaired contextual memory encoding (>50%) measured 24 hours later, whereas cued learning was largely unaffected. These data suggest that pretraining sleep deprivation may affect memory encoding by neuroanatomically distinct systems, impairing hippocampal encoding processes while having only minor effects on encoding mediated by the amygdala (McDermott et al. 2003). These findings, which are strikingly similar to those described above in humans, suggest that encoding of both neutral and positive memory events are most severely impaired by sleep deprivation, while encoding of more negative stimuli, presumably in concert with the amygdala, exhibit greater immunity.

Building on these behavioral findings, a number of animal studies have gone on to explore the potential cellular and molecular underpinnings of sleep deprivation–induced encoding deficits; many of these studies have focused on the hippocampus. At the cellular level, REM sleep deprivation (ranging from of 24 to 72 hours) not only reduces the basic excitability of hippocampal neurons, but also significantly impairs the formation of long-term potentiation [LTP; a foundational mechanism of memory formation (Kandel 2001)] within those neurons (Davis et al. 2003, McDermott et al. 2003). Furthermore, the LTP that does develop decays within 90 minutes, a finding that suggests that even in the event of successful LTP induction, hippocampal neurons are still unable to maintain these plastic changes after REM deprivation (Davis et al. 2003).

At the molecular level, nerve growth factor is significantly reduced in the hippocampus following six hours of REM sleep deprivation, and brain-derived neurotrophic factor is significantly decreased in the brain stem and cerebellum (Sei et al. 2000). This anatomically differentiated pattern of molecular disruption suggests a selective elimination of hippocampal nerve growth factor secretion, normally a key event in the regulation of neuronal plasticity (Kandel 2001). Finally, Guan et al. (2004) have explored the impact of prior sleep deprivation on levels of extracellular signal–regulated kinase (ERK)—a protein intimately linked to LTP formation and learning (Kelleher et al. 2004). When rats were trained on the hippocampally dependent Morris water maze following three or six hours of total sleep deprivation, behavioral encoding impairments were accompanied by significantly reduced levels of hippocampal ERK in the six-hour group (Figure 3), and to a lesser extent, in the three-hour group. Interestingly, when rats were allowed a short (two-hour) period of recovery sleep after the sleep deprivation, subsequent memory encoding and hippocampal ERK returned to normal levels (Figure 3).

SLEEP AND MEMORY CONSOLIDATION

In addition to the impact of prior sleep deprivation on memory encoding, a plethora of work also demonstrates the impact of sleep deprivation after learning on later memory consolidation. Through the use of a variety of behavioral paradigms, evidence of sleep-dependent memory consolidation has now been found in numerous species, including human and nonhuman primates, cats, rats, mice, and zebra finch.

Human Studies—Declarative Memory

Much of the early work investigating sleep and memory in humans focused on declarative learning tasks. These studies offered mixed conclusions, some in favor of sleep-dependent memory processing, and others against it. For example, De Koninck et al. (1989) demonstrated significant increases in posttraining REM sleep after intensive foreign language learning, with the degree of successful learning correlating with the extent of REM sleep increase. Such findings suggest that REM sleep plays an active role in memory consolidation, and that posttraining increases reflect a homeostatic response to the increased demands for such consolidation. However, Meienberg (1977) found no evidence of altered posttraining sleep architecture following learning of a verbal memory task. Similar inconsistencies have

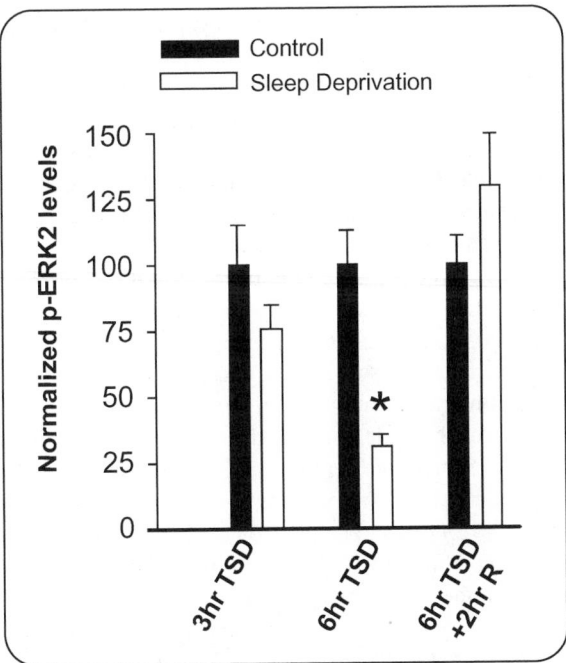

Figure 3   Phospho-extracellular signal-regulated kinase 2 (pERK2) in the rat hippocampus. pERK2 levels were significantly reduced after six hours total sleep deprivation (6 hr TSD), but returned to above control levels after two hours recovery (2 hr R) sleep following six hours sleep deprivation. Asterisk indicates significant difference between the control and sleep-deprived rats.

been reported both for the degree to which encoding of declarative memories alters subsequent sleep-stage properties and for the degree of learning impairment that follows selective sleep deprivation (e.g., Chernik 1972; Empson & Clarke 1970; Lewin & Glaubman 1975; Meienberg 1977; Plihal & Born 1997; Zimmerman et al. 1970, 1978). Recently, several studies by Born and his colleagues have shown actual improvement on a word-pair associates task after SWS-rich early night sleep (Gais & Born 2004), as well as modification of this posttraining sleep (Gais et al. 2002). These findings are striking in the face of earlier studies that showed no effect. However, the discrepancy may reflect the nature of the word pairs used. Whereas older studies used unrelated word pairs, such as dog–leaf, Born used related word pairs, such as dog–bone (Gais & Born 2004). The nature of the learning task thus shifts from forming and retaining completely novel associations (dog–leaf) to the strengthening or tagging of well-formed associations (dog–bone) for subsequent recall.

Thus, as with memory encoding, the role of sleep in declarative memory consolidation, rather than being absolute, might depend on more subtle aspects of the information being learned. Indeed, several studies suggest that factors such as task difficulty (Empson & Clarke 1970, Tilley & Empson 1978) and emotional salience (Wagner et al. 2001) can strongly influence the degree of sleep dependency. Furthermore, a thorough examination of different declarative memory categories, including episodic and semantic forms, has not been completed (Cipolli & Salzarulo 1980), and such an investigation may further clarify the apparent contradictions regarding the roles of both SWS and REM sleep in declarative memory consolidation (Smith 2001).

Such studies have only begun to test sleep-related memory processes. Indeed, all of these studies have used tasks of recall and recognition as outcome measures, thereby focusing exclusively on processes of memory enhancement and resistance to normal decay, and no study has looked at such processes as memory stabilization, association, translocation, and reconsolidation, discussed above. More recent studies, however, have demonstrated that the strengths of associative memories are altered in a state-dependent manner. Two reports have shown that REM sleep provides a brain state in which access to weak associations is selectively facilitated (Stickgold et al. 1999), and flexible, creative processing of new information is enhanced (Walker et al. 2002b). It has also been demonstrated that, following initial practice on a numeric-sequence problem-solving task, a night of sleep can trigger insight into a hidden rule that can enhance performance strategy the following morning (Wagner et al. 2004).

Taken as a whole, these studies suggest a rich and multifaceted role for sleep in the processing of human declarative memories. Although contradictory evidence is found for a role in the processing of simple, emotion-free declarative memories, such as the learning of unrelated word pairs, a substantial body of evidence indicates that both SWS and REM sleep contribute to the consolidation of complex, emotionally salient declarative memories, embedded in networks of previously existing associative memories. In light of this evidence, pronouncements of a lack of relationship between REM sleep and "memory" (e.g., Siegel 2001, Vertes & Eastman 2000) appear to be unfortunate overgeneralizations that disregard evidence that specific sleep stages play distinct roles in different stages of memory processing in separate memory systems.

Human Studies—Procedural Memory

The reliance of procedural, nondeclarative memory on sleep is now a robust and persistent finding. These data span a wide variety of functional domains, including both perceptual (visual and auditory) and motor skills.

MOTOR LEARNING   Motor skills have been broadly classified into two forms—motor adaptation (e.g., learning to use a computer mouse) and motor sequence learning (e.g., learning a piano scale) (Doyon et al. 2003). Beginning with motor sequence learning, a night of sleep can trigger significant improvements in speed and accuracy on a sequential finger-tapping task, while equivalent periods of wake

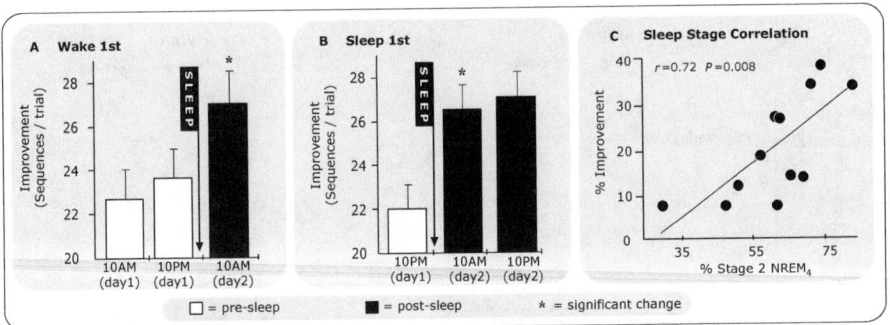

Figure 4 Sleep-dependent motor skill learning. (*A*) Wake first: After morning training (10 AM, *unfilled bar*), subjects showed no significant change in performance when tested after 12 hours of wake time (10 PM, *unfilled bar*). However, when tested again following a night of sleep (10 AM, *filled bar*), performance had improved significantly. (*B*) Sleep first: After evening training (10 PM, *unfilled bar*), subjects displayed significant performance improvements just 12 hours after training following a night of sleep (10 AM, *filled bar*), yet expressed no further significant change in performance following an additional 12 hours of wake time (10 PM, *filled bar*). (*C*) The amount of overnight improvement on the motor skill task correlated with the percentage of stage 2 non-rapid eye movement (NREM) sleep in the last (fourth) quarter of the night (stage 2 $NREM_4$). Asterisks indicate significant improvement relative to training, and error bars indicate standard error of the mean.

provide no significant benefit (Walker et al. 2002a). These sleep-dependent benefits appear to be specific to both the motor sequence learned and hand used to perform the task (Fischer et al. 2002, Korman et al. 2003). Furthermore, overnight learning gains correlate with the amount of stage 2 NREM sleep, particularly late in the night (Figure 4*A–C*) (Walker et al. 2002a). This sleep window corresponds to a time when sleep spindles—a defining electrophysiological characteristic of stage 2 NREM— reach peak density (De Gennaro et al. 2000). Spindles have been proposed to trigger intracellular mechanisms required for synaptic plasticity (Sejnowski & Destexhe 2000), and they increase following training on a motor task (Fogel et al. 2001). Thus, sleep spindles produced in late-night sleep may trigger key cellular events that in turn initiate mechanisms for neural plasticity.

At the behavioral level, the motor sequence task described above has been dissected to determine where in the motor program this sleep-dependent improvement occurs (Kuriyama et al. 2004). More specifically, differences in transition speeds between each of the separate key-press movements, before and after sleep, were analyzed. For example, in the sequence 4-1-3-2-4, there are four unique key-press transitions: (*a*) from 4 to 1, (*b*) from 1 to 3, (*c*) from 3 to 2, and (*d*) from 2 to 4. When individual subjects' transition-speed profiles were analyzed before sleep, the speed of individual key-press transitions within the sequence were not equal (Figure 5*A*, unfilled circles), with some transitions seemingly easy (fast) and others problematic (slow), as if the entire sequence was being parsed into smaller

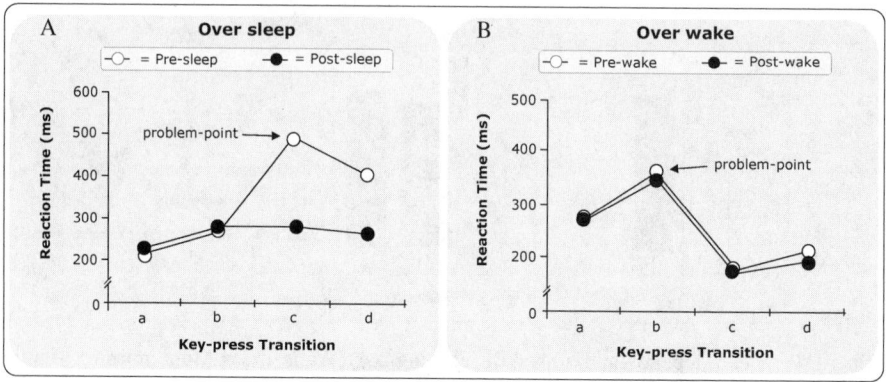

Figure 5 Single-subject examples of changes in transition speeds. Within a five-element motor sequence (e.g., 4-1-3-2-4), there are four unique key press transitions: (*a*) from 4 to 1, (*b*) from 1 to 3, (*c*) from 3 to 2, and (*d*) from 2 to 4. (*A*) The transition profile at the end of training before sleep (*unfilled circles*) demonstrated considerable variability, with certain transitions being particularly slow (most difficult; "problem points"), whereas other transitions appear to be relatively rapid (easy). Following a night of sleep (*filled circles*), there was a specific reduction (improvement) in the time required for the slowest problem point transition. (*B*) Similarly, at the end of training before a waking interval, transition profiles were uneven (*unfilled circles*), with some particularly slow transitions (problem points) and other relatively fast transitions (easy). However, in contrast to postsleep changes, no change in transition profile was observed following eight hours of wake (*filled circles*).

subsequences during initial learning [a phenomena termed "chunking" (Sakai et al. 2003)]. Surprisingly, after a night of sleep, the problematic slow transitions ("problem points") were preferentially improved, whereas transitions that had already been effectively mastered prior to sleep did not change (Figure 5*A*, filled circles). Most remarkable, however, in subjects who were trained and retested after an eight hour waking interval across the day, no such improvement was seen in the profile of key-press transitions at any location within the sequence (Figure 5*B*).

These findings suggest that the sleep-dependent consolidation process involves the unification of smaller motor memory units into one single memory element by selectively improving problem regions of the sequence. This overnight process would therefore offer a greater degree of performance automation, effectively optimizing speed across the motor program, and would explain the sleep-dependent improvements in speed and accuracy previously reported. But more importantly, it again suggests that the role of sleep is more subtle and complex than to simply increase the strength of existing memory representations.

Using a different sequential finger-tapping task (finger-to-thumb movements rather than keyboard typing), Fisher et al. (2002) have shown that sleep during the first day or night following training is critical for the delayed performance improvements. In their case, however, they described a correlation between overnight improvement and amounts of REM sleep rather than stage 2 NREM. This discrepancy remains to be resolved, but it is possible that the more novel finger-to-thumb task requires REM sleep, whereas the keyboard typing version, a simple variant of a well-learned skill (i.e., typing), is consolidated during stage 2 NREM. A similarly subtle distinction has been reported by Robertson et al. (2004), who recently demonstrated sleep-dependent enhancement of performance on a perceptual-motor sequence task when there was explicit awareness of the presence of a repeating sequence, but not when awareness was only gained implicitly. In this study, delayed overnight learning with explicit awareness correlated with amounts of NREM sleep.

Moving from motor sequence learning to motor adaptation learning, Smith & MacNeill (1994) have shown that selective sleep deprivation impairs retention of a visuomotor adaptation task. All subjects were trained and tested on the task and were retested one week later. However, some subjects were either completely or selectively deprived of different sleep stages across the first night following memory acquisition. At later retest, subjects deprived of stage 2 NREM sleep showed the most pronounced deficits in motor performance, which again suggests that stage 2 NREM is a crucial determinant of successful motor memory enhancement.

Huber et al. (2004) have similarly demonstrated that following initial memory acquisition of a motor reaching-adaptation task, delayed learning was observed exclusively across a night of sleep, and not across equivalent periods of wake. Furthermore, through the use of high-density EEG, they were able to show that daytime motor skill practice was accompanied by a discrete increase in the subsequent amount of NREM slow-wave EEG activity over the parietal cortex at the start of the night, and that this increase in slow-wave activity was proportional to the amount of delayed learning that developed overnight; subjects showing the greatest increase in slow-wave activity in the parietal cortex that night produced the largest motor skill enhancement the next day.

Taken together, these reports build a convincing argument in support of sleep-dependent learning across several forms of motor skill memory. All these studies indicate that a night of sleep triggers delayed learning, without the need for further training. In addition, overnight motor skill improvements consistently display a strong relationship to NREM sleep, and, in some cases, to specific NREM sleep-stage windows at specific times in the night.

VISUAL PERCEPTUAL LEARNING   Learning of a visual texture discrimination task, which does not benefit from 4–12 hours of wake following training (Stickgold et al. 2000b), improves significantly following a night of sleep (Karni et al. 1994) and appears to require both SWS and REM sleep. Selective disruption of REM sleep resulted in a loss of overnight improvement (Karni et al. 1994). Similarly, selective deprivation of either early sleep (normally dominated by SWS) or late-night sleep (normally dominated by REM and stage 2 NREM) impair overnight consolidation, a finding that suggests that consolidation is initiated by SWS-related processes, but that subsequent REM sleep then promotes additional enhancement (Gais et al.

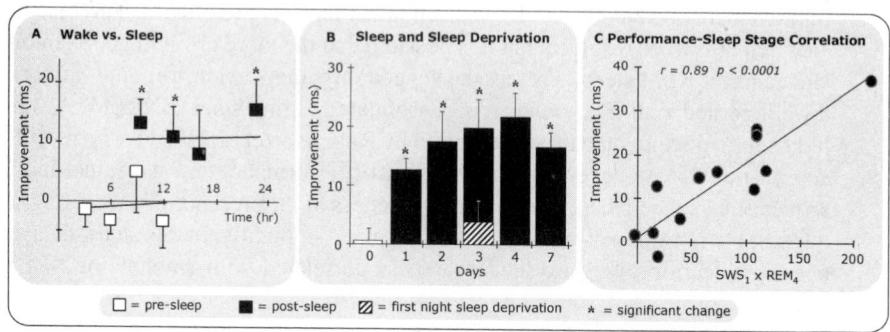

Figure 6   Sleep-dependent visual skill learning. Subjects were trained (during which time, baseline performance was measured) and then retested at a later time; improvement [ms (milliseconds)] in performance is illustrated across time. Each subject was retested only once, and each point represents a separate group of subjects. (*A*) Wake versus sleep: Subjects who were trained and then retested on the same day, after either 3, 6, 9, or 12 hours of subsequent wake (*unfilled squares*) showed no significant improvement as a consequence of the passage of waking time across at any of the four time points. In contrast, subjects who were trained and then retested 8, 12, 15, or 23 hours after one night of sleep (*filled squares*) showed a significant improvement occurring as a consequence of sleep. In total, $n = 57$, with $n = 7$ to 9 for individual points. (*B*) Sleep and sleep deprivation. Subjects ($n = 89$) who were trained and retested 1–7 days later (*filled bars*) continued to improve after the first night, without additional practice. Subjects ($n = 11$) sleep deprived the first night after training showed no improvement (*crosshatched bar*), even after two nights of recovery sleep. (*C*) Overnight improvement was correlated with the percent of slow-wave sleep (SWS) in the first quarter of the night (SWS$_1$) and rapid eye movement (REM) sleep in the last quarter of the night (REM$_4$). *$p < 0.05$; error bars indicate standard error of the mean.

2000). Overnight improvement is specifically sleep dependent, not time dependent (Figure 6*A*) (Stickgold et al. 2000b), and correlates positively with the amount of both early-night SWS and late-night REM sleep. Indeed, the product of these two sleep parameters explains more than 80% of intersubject variance (Figure 6*C*). In addition, these delayed performance benefits are absolutely dependent on the first night of sleep following acquisition (Figure 6*B*) (Stickgold et al. 2000a).

AUDITORY LEARNING   Evidence of sleep-dependent auditory skill learning has also been reported. Using a pitch memory task, Gaab et al. (2004) have shown that delayed performance improvements develop only across a night of sleep and not across similar wake periods. Atienza and colleagues have also described evidence of both time- and sleep-dependent auditory memory consolidations, including sleep-dependent changes in brain-evoked response potentials (ERPs) (Atienza et al. 2002, 2004). Although posttraining sleep deprivation did not prevent continued behavioral improvements, ERP changes normally associated with the automatic shift of attention to relevant stimuli failed to develop following a posttraining night

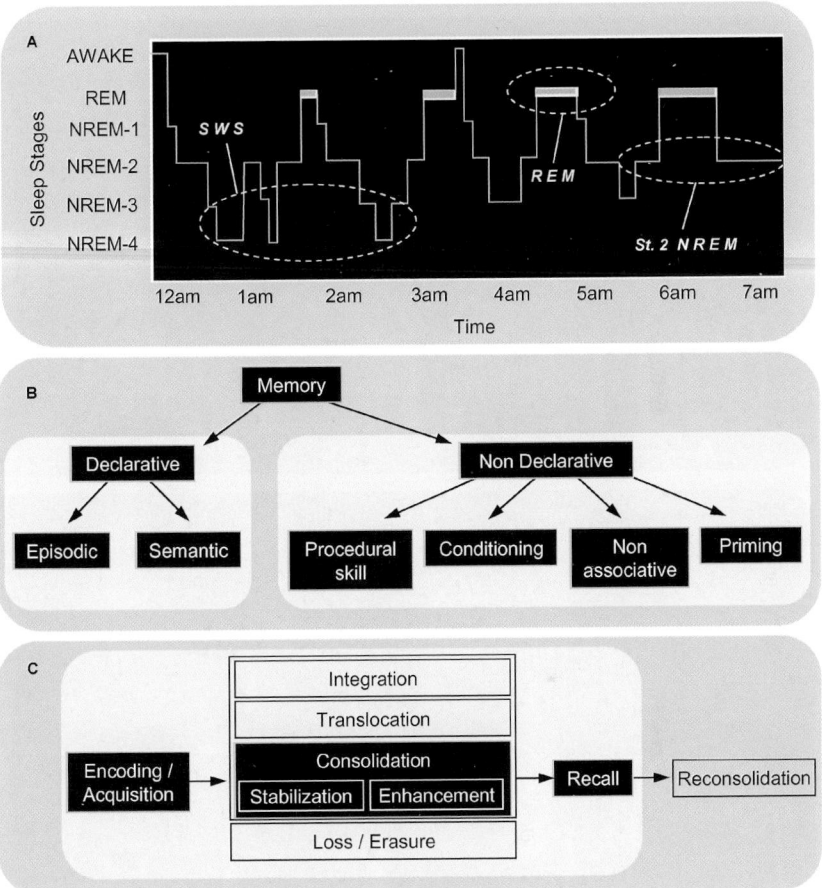

Figure 1 The sleep cycle, memory systems, and memory stages. (*A*) The human sleep cycle. Across the night, rapid eye movement (REM) and non-REM (NREM) sleep cycle every 90 minutes in an ultradian manner, while the ratio of NREM to REM sleep shifts. During the first half of the night, NREM stages 3 and 4 slow wave sleep (SWS) dominate, whereas stage 2 NREM and REM sleep prevail in the latter half of the night. Electroencephalogram patterns also differ significantly between sleep stages, with electrical oscillations such as K-complexes and sleep spindles occurring during stage 2 NREM, slow (0.5–4 Hz) delta waves developing in SWS, and theta waves seen during REM. (*B*) Memory systems. Human memory is most commonly divided into declarative forms, including episodic and semantic memory, and nondeclarative forms, including an array of different types including procedural skill memory. (*C*) Developing stages of memory. Following initial encoding of a memory, several ensuing stages are proposed, beginning with consolidation and including integration of the memory representation and translocation of the representation or erasure of the memory. Also, following later recall, the memory representation is believed to become unstable once again, requiring periods of reconsolidation.

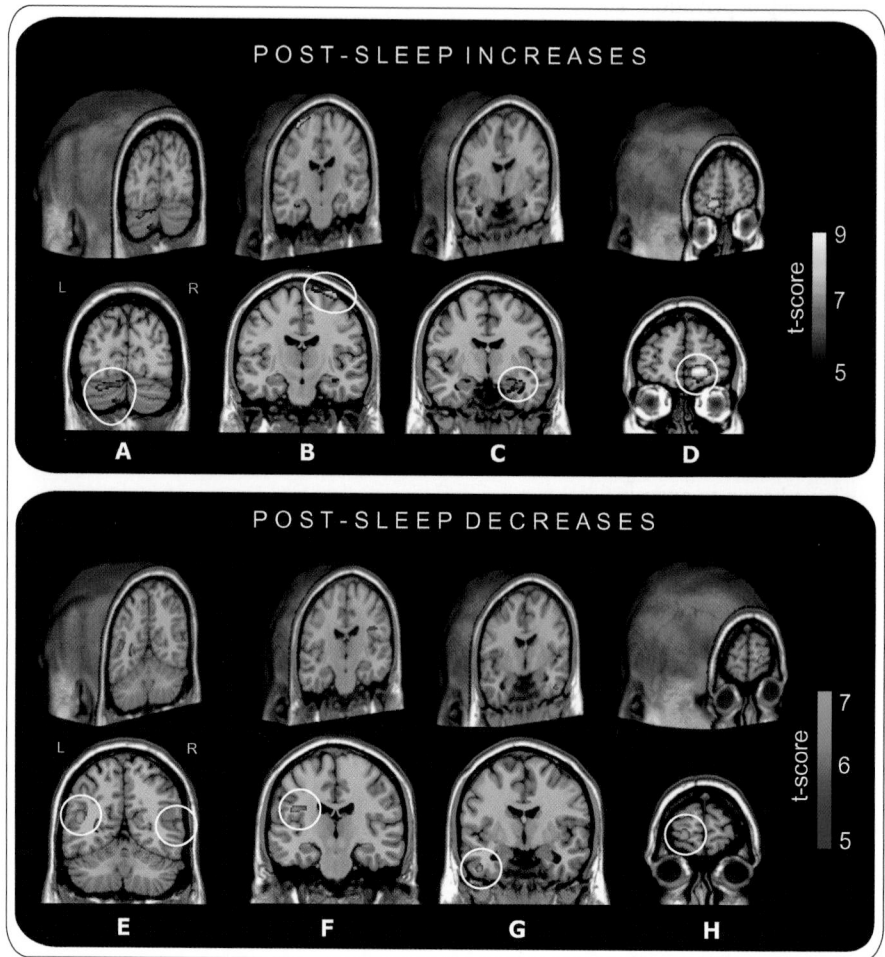

Figure 8   Sleep-dependent motor memory reorganization in the human brain. Subjects were trained on a sleep-dependent motor skill task and then tested 12 hours later, either following a night of sleep or following intervening wake, during a functional magnetic resonance imaging (fMRI) brain-scanning session. Scans after sleep and wake were compared (subtracted), resulting in regions showing increased fMRI activity postsleep (in red/yellow; *A–D*) or decreased signal activity (in blue; *E–H*) postsleep, relative to postwake. Activation patterns are displayed on three-dimensional rendered brains (*top panel* of each graphic), together with corresponding coronal sections (*bottom panel* of each graphic). Following sleep, regions of increased activation were identified in the right primary motor cortex (*A*), the left cerebellum (*B*), the right hippocampus (*C*), and the right medial prefrontal cortex (*D*). Regions of decreased activity postsleep were expressed bilaterally in the parietal lobes (*E*), together with the left insula cortex (*F*), left temporal pole (*G*), and left frontopolar area (*H*), all regions of the extended limbic system. All data are displayed at a corrected threshold of p < 0.05.

of sleep deprivation. These findings make clear the danger of presuming that a lack of behavioral improvement is equivalent to an absence of beneficial plastic changes within the brain, and they highlight the importance of using combined behavioral and physiological analyses. Finally, Fenn et al. (2003) have shown periods of wake following training on a synthetic speech-recognition task result in a degradation of task performance that a subsequent night of sleep can restore, which suggests a process of sleep-dependent consolidation capable of reestablishing previously learned complex auditory skill memory.

It therefore appears that, as with motor skills, learning of perceptual skills, both visual and auditory, depends on sleep for the development of delayed learning, and several different sleep stages may be involved in producing this form of overnight consolidation.

PROCEDURAL MEMORY AND DAYTIME NAPS   Although the majority of sleep-dependent studies have investigated learning across a night of sleep, several reports have begun to examine the benefits of daytime naps on perceptual and motor skill tasks. Based on evidence that motor learning continues to develop overnight, the influence of daytime naps on the sequential finger-tapping task has been explored (Walker & Stickgold 2005). Two groups of subjects were trained on the task in the morning. One group subsequently obtained a 60- to 90-minute midday nap while the other group remained awake. When retested later that same day, those subjects who napped displayed a significant 16% learning enhancement, whereas those who did not nap showed no significant improvement (Figure 7). This nap-mediated improvement is, however, at the expense of subsequent overnight learning. Thus, although the control subjects showed 24% improvement overnight, the nap subjects showed only an additional 7%, for a total of 23%—essentially identical to that seen in the control group.

As with motor skill learning, daytime naps also appear to benefit visual skill learning, although the characteristics of these effects are subtly different. Mednick and colleagues have shown that if a visual skill task is repeatedly administered across the day, performance deteriorates rather than remaining stable or improving (Mednick et al. 2002). This may reflect a selective fatigue of brain regions recruited during task performance, a characteristic not observed in the motor system. However, if a 30- to 60-minute daytime nap is introduced among these repeated tests, the performance deterioration is ameliorated. If a longer nap period is introduced, ranging from 60 to 90 minutes and containing both SWS and REM sleep, performance not only returns to baseline, but also is enhanced (Mednick et al. 2003). Furthermore, these benefits did not prevent additional significant improvements across the following night of sleep, in contrast to findings for motor skill task performance.

Together these studies build a cohesive argument that daytime naps confer a robust learning benefit to both visual and motor skills and, in the case of visual skill learning, are capable of restoring performance deterioration caused by repeated practice across the day.

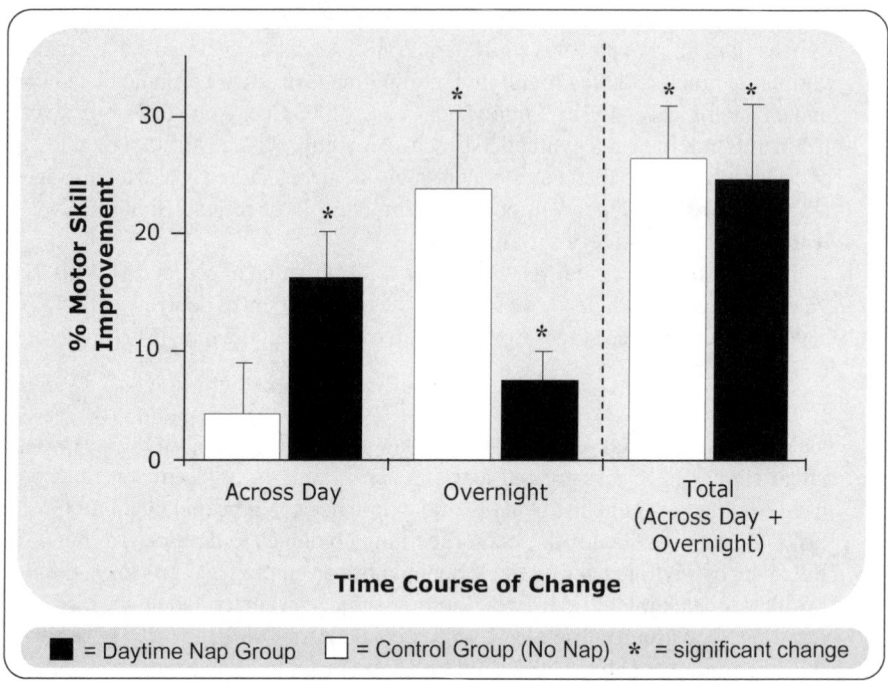

Figure 7 Daytime naps and motor skill learning. Subjects practiced the motor skill task in the morning, and either obtained a 60- to 90-minute midday nap or remained awake across the first day. When retested later that same day, subjects who experienced a 60- to 90-minute nap (*filled bar*, Across Day) displayed significant performance speed improvements of 16%, whereas subjects who did not nap showed no significant enhancements (*unfilled bar*, Across Day). When retested a second time after a full night of sleep, subjects in the nap group showed only an additional 7% increase in speed overnight (*filled bar*, Overnight), whereas subjects in the control group expressed a significant 24% overnight improvement following sleep (*unfilled bar*, Overnight). Therefore, 24 hours later, the groups averaged nearly the same total amount of delayed learning (*filled* and *unfilled bars*, Total). Asterisks indicate significant improvement and error bars indicate standard error of the mean.

SLEEP AND BRAIN PLASTICITY

Memory formation depends on brain plasticity—lasting structural and/or functional neural changes in response to stimuli (such as experiences). If sleep is to be considered a critical mediator of memory consolidation, then evidence of sleep-dependent plasticity would greatly strengthen this claim. In this section, we consider a mounting wealth of data describing sleep-dependent brain plasticity; our focus is on neuroimaging studies in humans (see Walker & Stickgold 2004 for a detailed discussion of cellular and molecular data).

Modification of Posttraining Sleep and Brain Activation

Several studies have investigated whether daytime training is capable of modifying functional brain activation during subsequent sleep. Based on animal studies, neuroimaging experiments have explored whether the signature pattern of brain activity elicited while practicing a memory task actually reemerges, i.e., is "replayed," during subsequent sleep. Using brain imaging, Maquet and colleagues have shown that patterns of brain activity expressed during training on a serial reaction time motor task reappear during subsequent REM sleep, whereas no such change in REM sleep brain activity occurs in subjects who received no daytime training (Maquet et al. 2000). Furthermore, the extent of learning during daytime practice exhibits a positive relationship to the amount of reactivation during REM sleep (Peigneux et al. 2003). As with previously described animal studies (Datta 2000), these findings suggest that it is not simply experiencing the task that modifies subsequent sleep physiology, but the process of learning itself. Similar findings have been reported using a virtual maze task. Daytime task learning is initially associated with hippocampal activity. Then, during posttraining sleep, there was a reemergence of hippocampal activation, this time specifically during SWS. The most compelling finding, however, is that the amount of SWS reactivation in the hippocampus is proportional to the amount of next-day task improvement, which suggests that this reactivation leads to off-line memory improvement (Peigneux et al. 2004). Such sleep-dependent replay may potentially modify synaptic connections established within specific brain networks during practice, strengthening some synaptic circuits while potentially weakening others in the endeavor of refining the memory.

Overnight Reorganization of Memory Representations

A second approach, which more directly examines sleep-dependent plasticity, compares patterns of brain activation before and after a night of sleep. In contrast to approaches that measure changes in functional activity *during* sleep, this technique aims to determine whether improved performance results from an overnight, sleep-dependent *restructuring* of the neural representation of the memory. Using the sleep-dependent motor skill task, differences between patterns of brain activation before and after sleep have recently been investigated using fMRI (Walker et al. 2005a). Following a night of sleep, and relative to an equivalent intervening period awake, increased activation was identified in motor control structures of the right primary motor cortex (Figure 8A, see color insert) and left cerebellum (Figure 8B)—changes that allow more precise motor output (Ohyama et al. 2003) and faster mapping of intention to key-press (Ungerleider et al. 2002). There were also regions of increased activation in the medial prefrontal lobe and hippocampus (Figure 8C,D), structures recently identified as supporting improved sequencing of motor movements (Koechlin et al. 2000, 2002; Poldrack & Rodriguez 2003; Schendan et al. 2003). In contrast, decreased activity postsleep was identified bilaterally in the parietal cortices (Figure 8E), possibly reflecting a reduced need for conscious spatial monitoring (Muller et al. 2002,

Seitz et al. 1990, Toni et al. 1998) as a result of improved task automation (Kuriyama et al. 2004), together with regions of signal decrease throughout the limbic system (Figure 8*F–H*), which suggests a decreased emotional task burden. In total, these results suggest that sleep-dependent motor learning is associated with a large-scale plastic reorganization of memory throughout several brain regions, allowing skilled motor movements to be executed more quickly, more accurately, and more automatically following sleep. These findings hold important implications for understanding the brain basis of perfecting real-life skills and may signify a potential role for sleep in clinical rehabilitation following brain damage.

fMRI has also been used to investigate whether overnight reorganization similarly occurs in sensory-perceptual systems using the sleep-dependent visual texture discrimination task described earlier (Walker et al. 2005b). Subjects were trained with or without intervening sleep. Relative to the condition without sleep, retest following sleep was associated with significantly greater activation in an area of primary visual cortex corresponding to the visual target location. However, there were also several other regions of increased postsleep activity, throughout both the ventral object recognition (inferior parietal and occipital-temporal junction) and dorsal object location (superior parietal lobe) pathways (Ungerleider & Haxby 1994), together with corresponding decreases in the right temporal pole, a region involved in emotional visual processing. Thus, a night of sleep appears to reorganize the representation not only of procedural motor but also of visual skill memories, with greater activation throughout the visual processing streams offering improved identification of both the stimulus form and its location in space, and with signal decreases in the temporal pole reflecting a reduced emotional task burden resulting from the overnight learning benefits.

Maquet et al. (2003) have investigated the detrimental effects of sleep deprivation on underlying brain activity using a visuomotor adaptation task—the only such study to date. Subjects were trained on the task, tested, and retested three days later, with half the subjects deprived of sleep the first night. At retest, subjects performed both the previously learned motor task and a new, related task. Controls, who slept all three nights, showed both enhanced behavioral performance at retest and a selective increase in activation in the superior temporal sulcus (a region involved in the evaluation of complex motion patterns) relative to subjects deprived of sleep the first night. In contrast, no such enhancement of either performance or brain activity was observed in these subjects, indicating that sleep deprivation had interfered with a latent process of plasticity and consolidation. This study indicates that sleep deprivation disrupts not only consolidation, but also the underlying neural mechanisms that support it.

SLEEP AND MEMORY RECONSOLIDATION

Reconsolidation

Recent studies (Nader 2003) suggest that upon recall of previously consolidated information, the memory returns to an unstable state, once more requiring consolidation, or "reconsolidation." But we know much less about memory reconsolidation than we do about memory consolidation. Although originally reported in the 1960s (Misanin et al. 1968, Schneider & Sherman 1968), the details of memory reconsolidation have only recently come under intensive investigation (Nader 2003), and most of these more recent studies have focused on the degree to which the process of reconsolidation is the same as or different from the initial processes of encoding and stabilization (Alberini 2005). But additional questions have not been as widely addressed. Conceptually, a consolidated memory can undergo at least four processes: (*a*) reactivation, which leads to (*b*) destabilization, which in turn leads to either (*c*) degradation or (*d*) reconsolidation. Yet the temporal evolution of these individual steps, the mechanisms and brain states that produce them, and even their biological functions, remain unclear.

Time Course of Reconsolidation

Determining the time course over which destabilization develops is difficult since neither cellular-molecular nor behavioral correlates have been identified. But its duration has been studied extensively because, by definition, the destabilized state ends when reconsolidation is completed. For example, when reconsolidation of learning on a radial maze task was blocked with propanalol either 5 minutes, 2 hours, or 5 hours after reexposure to the maze (and, presumably, reactivation of the memory), error rates, measured 24 hours after reactivation, increased sixfold, threefold, or not at all, respectively (Przybyslawski et al. 1999), which suggests a half-life for the destabilized state of about 2 hours. Inhibition of reconsolidation for conditioned taste aversion showed a similar half-life for the destabilized state, on the order of 1 hour, with reconsolidation again apparently complete by 6 hours (Gruest et al. 2004). Similarly, protein synthesis inhibitors injected 6 hours after reexposure had no effect on destabilized fear-conditioned memories (Nader et al. 2000). Thus, reconsolidation would appear to be complete (and hence, destabilization ended) 6 hours after reexposure, at which time the memory trace is again resistant to interference.

Once destabilized, and in the absence of subsequent reconsolidation, degradation of a memory has generally been considered a passive process, perhaps based on molecular turnover. Alternatively, it may be that the memory is not degraded at all, but its recall blocked. The nature of this degradation currently remains unclear, and degradation is defined behaviorally as diminished performance of the learned task.

Little data is available on the time course over which degradation occurs. Following reactivation and blockade of reconsolidation, previously learned behaviors are still intact 2 hours (Suzuki et al. 2004) and 4 hours (Debiec et al. 2002, Duvarci & Nader 2004, Nader et al. 2000) later, with no sign that degradation has begun. This makes sense because reconsolidation appears to take at least this long and it would be counterproductive for memories to begin to degrade before reconsolidation normally has completed. At the other end of the process, any degradation of the memory appears to be complete 24 hours after reactivation (Boccia et al. 2004, Debiec & Ledoux 2004, Duvarci & Nader 2004; see also Myers & Davis 2002).

Hints of the complex mechanisms governing reconsolidation as well as its possible function come from studies showing that inhibitors of cholinergic (Boccia et al. 2004) and noradrenergic (Przybyslawski et al. 1999) neuromodulation can also block reconsolidation. In addition, N-methyl-D-aspartate antagonists reportedly can block the destabilization normally associated with reactivation (Nader et al. 2004). Thus, the reconsolidation process appears to be controlled by a number of neuromodulators and plasticity-related neurotransmitters. But perhaps the most direct evidence of a functional role for modulation of reconsolidation comes from human studies of sleep-dependent memory processing.

Sleep and Reconsolidation

As was described above for memory consolidation, it generally has been assumed that reconsolidation processes progress over a fixed time, independent of brain state. Yet as more and more phases of consolidation are found to be influenced by, and in some cases dependent on, sleep, it is important to ask what role sleep might play in reconsolidation and its associated processes. Although few data pertain directly to this question, we offer the hypothesis that both degradation and reconsolidation processes can, and in some circumstances must, occur during sleep. Indeed, most rodent studies of reconsolidation have been carried out during the light (sleep) phase of the circadian cycle, and it is likely that animals in these studies slept between reactivation and subsequent measurements of reconsolidation.

Evidence suggesting a role for sleep comes again from the human motor sequence task discussed above (Walker et al. 2003a). When retested 24 hours after training (on day 2), subjects showed overnight sleep-dependent enhancements of both speed and accuracy (Figure 9A, none). However, if subjects trained on a second, competing sequence 10 minutes after the first sequence on day 1, interference effects on sleep-dependent consolidation were observed the next day (Figure 9A, 10′); the normal delayed overnight improvement in accuracy was completely blocked (Walker et al. 2002a). When the time between learning the two sequences was increased from 10 minutes to either 6 hours or 24 hours, no significant interference was observed (Figure 9A, 6 hr and 24 hr). Thus, stabilization of the memory occurred over a period between 10 minutes and 6 hours, affording the original memory immunity from the interfering effects of a second competing memory, immunity that was still present 24 hours later, following sleep.

In contrast, when the original memory was reactivated at 24 hours (through 90 seconds of rehearsal), just prior to interference training on day 2, a 57% decrease in accuracy was seen across the subsequent night of sleep (Figure 9B, 48 hr), returning subjects' accuracy to slightly below the level seen at the end of the original training session. Thus, reactivation led to destabilization of the sleep-enhanced memory. Presumably, under normal conditions, in the absence of competing interference training, the memory would become restabilized over the next 6 hours, becoming once again resistant to interference, although such reconsolidation was not explicitly measured.

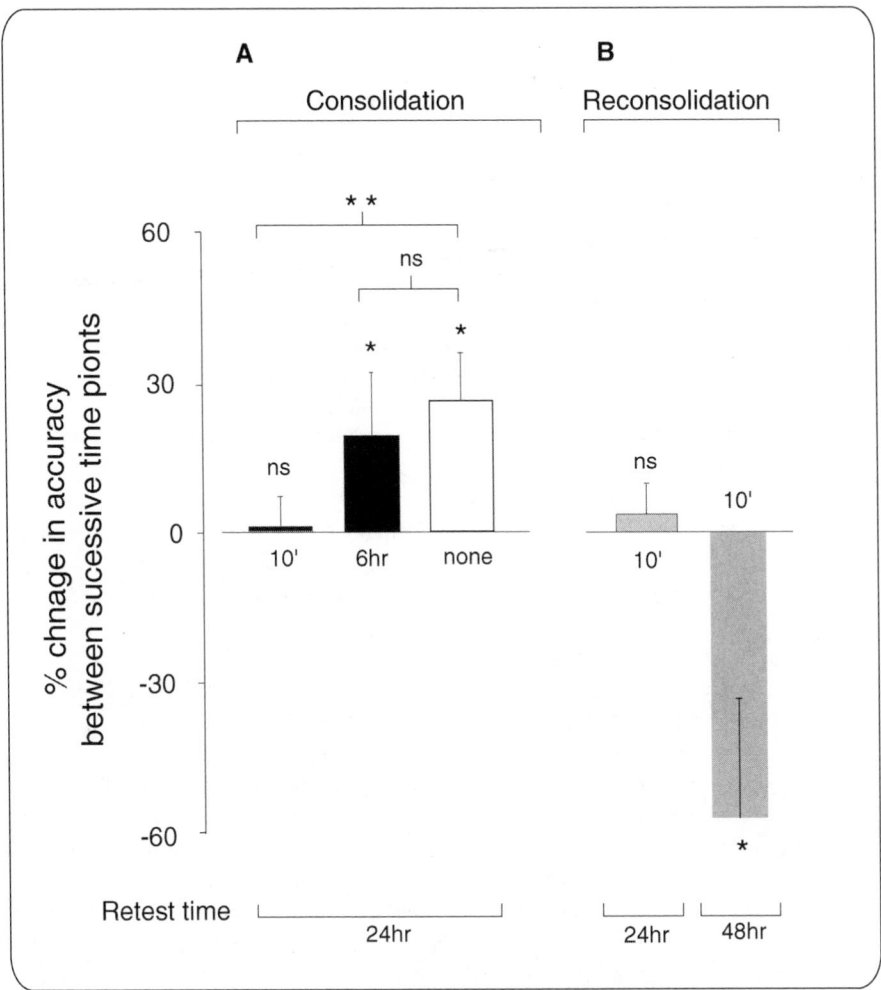

Figure 9   Reconsolidation of sleep-dependent learning. (*A*) Consolidation: Overnight improvement in accuracy was blocked by interference training (a second competing motor sequence, *filled bars*) at 10′, but not at 6 hours posttraining relative to controls without interference (none, *unfilled bar*). (*B*) Reconsolidation: Interference training 10′ after reactivation (retest time 24 hours, *gray bar*) did not cause an immediate deterioration in the overnight improvement, but 24 hours after reactivation and interference training, the initial overnight improvement was abolished (retest time 48 hours, *gray bar*). Asterisks indicate significant improvement; error bars indicate standard error of the mean; values are calculated as the percentage difference in accuracy between successive test-retest intervals.

These results lead to two conclusions. First, reconsolidation can be blocked by ecologically relevant stimuli, such as a competing learning experience, and without resorting to extreme electrical or chemical interventions (Walker et al. 2003a) previously used to prevent reconsolidation. Second, the deterioration in performance might be limited to a reversal of earlier sleep-dependent consolidation.

SUMMARY

Over the past 25 years, the field of sleep and memory has grown exponentially, with the number of publications per year doubling between the years 2000 and 2004. These reports, ranging from cellular and molecular studies in animals to behavioral studies in humans, have provided a wealth of converging evidence that sleep-dependent mechanisms of neural plasticity lead to the consolidation of learning and memory across a range of animal species.

At the molecular level, inadequate pretraining sleep appears to compromise hippocampally dependent modulation of molecules critically involved in memory formation, resulting in impaired memory encoding. Significant numbers of genes also appear to be up-regulated specifically in brain tissue during posttraining sleep, and at least one immediate early gene related to synaptic plasticity, *zif-286*, is up-regulated during REM sleep expressly in response to environmental or direct electrical stimulation of the hippocampus (for a review, see Walker & Stickgold 2004).

At the electrophysiological level, studies in rats have shown that retention of learning of a shuttle-box avoidance task increases subsequent P-wave density, and is strongly correlated with this increase, while in humans, spindle density increases following training on a declarative memory task and, again, this increase correlates with subsequent improvement on the task. In rats, patterns of neuronal activation expressed during waking exploration reappear during subsequent sleep; in humans, patterns of regional brain activation seen during daytime task training are repeated during subsequent REM sleep.

At the behavioral level, animal studies have found robust increases in REM sleep following task training, and decrements in performance after REM deprivation, even when retesting is delayed until one week after the period of deprivation. In contrast, several animal studies have failed to find evidence of either increased REM sleep or deterioration following deprivation. Most likely this reflects a combination of methodological problems and conditions under which consolidation is, in fact, not sleep dependent. Similarly, human studies have provided examples where increases in REM sleep are seen following training, where REM or stage 2 NREM deprivation diminishes subsequent performance, and where overnight improvement correlates with REM, SWS, or stage 2 NREM sleep. Furthermore, these overnight learning benefits are associated with a system-level reorganization of memory throughout the brain.

It is now clear that sleep mediates learning and memory processing, but the way in which it does so remains largely unknown. The future of the field is truly exciting, and the challenge to neuroscience will be to uncover the mechanisms of brain plasticity that underlie sleep-dependent memory processing and to expand our understanding of sleep's role beyond encoding, consolidation, and reconsolidation, into the constellation of additional processes that are critical for efficient memory development. Work across the neurosciences will be necessary to answer these questions, but with the current rate of growth of research in the field, the next decade should provide important advances in our understanding of this critical function of sleep. By way of this multidisciplinary approach, and with a measured appreciation of the fundamental role that sleep plays in consolidating and reforming memories, we can look forward to new advances in understanding memory and treating its disorder.

ACKNOWLEDGMENTS

This work was supported by grants from the National Institutes of Health (MH48, 832; MH65,292; MH06,9935; and MH67,754) and the National Science Foundation (BCS-0121953).

The *Annual Review of Psychology* is online at http://psych.annualreviews.org

LITERATURE CITED

Alberini CM. 2005. Mechanisms of memory stabilization: Are consolidation and reconsolidation similar or distinct processes? *Trends Neurosci.* 28:51–56

Aserinsky E, Kleitman N. 1953. Regularly occurring periods of eye motility and concurrent phenomena during sleep. *Science* 118:273–74

Atienza M, Cantero JL, Dominguez-Marin E. 2002. The time course of neural changes underlying auditory perceptual learning. *Learn. Mem.* 9:138–50

Atienza M, Cantero JL, Stickgold R. 2004. Posttraining sleep enhances automaticity in perceptual discrimination. *J. Cogn. Neurosci.* 16:53–64

Beaulieu I, Godbout R. 2000. Spatial learning on the Morris Water Maze Test after a short-term paradoxical sleep deprivation in the rat. *Brain Cogn.* 43:27–31

Boccia MM, Acosta GB, Blake MG, Baratti CM. 2004. Memory consolidation and reconsolidation of an inhibitory avoidance response in mice: effects of i.c.v. injections

of hemicholinium-3. *Neuroscience* 124:735–41

Brashers-Krug T, Shadmehr R, Bizzi E. 1996. Consolidation in human motor memory. *Nature* 382:252–55

Brewer JB, Zhao Z, Desmond JE, Glover GH, Gabrieli JD. 1998. Making memories: brain activity that predicts how well visual experience will be remembered. *Science* 281:1185–87

Canli T, Zhao Z, Brewer J, Gabrieli JD, Cahill L. 2000. Event-related activation in the human amygdala associates with later memory for individual emotional experience. *J. Neurosci.* 20(RC99):1–5

Chernik DA. 1972. Effect of REM sleep deprivation on learning and recall by humans. *Percept. Mot. Skills* 34:283–94

Cipolli C, Salzarulo P. 1980. Sentence memory and sleep: a pilot study. *Sleep* 2:193–98

Crick F, Mitchison G. 1983. The function of dream sleep. *Nature* 304:111–14

Datta S. 2000. Avoidance task training potentiates phasic pontine-wave density in the rat: a mechanism for sleep-dependent plasticity. *J. Neurosci.* 20:8607–13

Davis CJ, Harding JW, Wright JW. 2003. REM sleep deprivation–induced deficits in the latency-to-peak induction and maintenance of long-term potentiation within the CA1 region of the hippocampus. *Brain Res.* 973:293–97

Debiec J, LeDoux JE. 2004. Disruption of reconsolidation but not consolidation of auditory fear conditioning by noradrenergic blockade in the amygdala. *Neuroscience* 129: 267–72

Debiec J, LeDoux JE, Nader K. 2002. Cellular and systems reconsolidation in the hippocampus. *Neuron* 36:527–38

De Gennaro L, Ferrara M, Bertini M. 2000. Topographical distribution of spindles: variations between and within NREM sleep cycles. *Sleep Res. Online* 3:155–60

De Koninck J, Lorrain D, Christ G, Proulx G, Coulombe D. 1989. Intensive language learning and increases in rapid eye movement sleep: evidence of a performance factor. *Int. J. Psychophysiol.* 8:43–47

Doyon J, Penhune V, Ungerleider LG. 2003. Distinct contribution of the cortico-striatal and cortico-cerebellar systems to motor skill learning. *Neuropsychologia* 41:252–62

Drummond SP, Brown GG. 2001. The effects of total sleep deprivation on cerebral responses to cognitive performance. *Neuropsychopharmacology* 25:S68–73

Drummond SP, Brown GG, Gillin JC, Stricker JL, Wong EC, Buxton RB. 2000. Altered brain response to verbal learning following sleep deprivation. *Nature* 403:655–57

Duvarci S, Nader K. 2004. Characterization of fear memory reconsolidation. *J. Neurosci.* 24:9269–75

Eichenbaum H. 2000. A cortical-hippocampal system for declarative memory. *Nat. Rev. Neurosci.* 1:41–50

Empson JA, Clarke PR. 1970. Rapid eye movements and remembering. *Nature* 227:287–88

Fenn KM, Nusbaum HC, Margoliash D. 2003. Consolidation during sleep of perceptual learning of spoken language. *Nature* 425:614–16

Fischer S, Hallschmid M, Elsner AL, Born J. 2002. Sleep forms memory for finger skills. *Proc. Natl. Acad. Sci. USA* 99:11987–91

Fogel S, Jacob J, Smith C. 2001. *Increased sleep spindle activity following simple motor procedural learning in humans.* Presented at Congr. Physiol. Basis Sleep Med., Uruguay

Gaab N, Paetzold M, Becker M, Walker MP, Schlaug G. 2004. The influence of sleep on auditory learning—a behavioral study. *Neuroreport* 15:731–34

Gais S, Born J. 2004. Low acetylcholine during slow-wave sleep is critical for declarative memory consolidation. *Proc. Natl. Acad. Sci. USA* 101:2140–44

Gais S, Molle M, Helms K, Born J. 2002. Learning-dependent increases in sleep spindle density. *J. Neurosci.* 22:6830–34

Gais S, Plihal W, Wagner U, Born J. 2000. Early sleep triggers memory for early visual discrimination skills. *Nat. Neurosci.* 3:1335–39

Goedert KM, Willingham DB. 2002. Patterns of interference in sequence learning and prism adaptation inconsistent with the consolidation hypothesis. *Learn. Mem.* 9:279–92

Gruart-Masso A, Nadal-Alemany R, Coll-Andreu M, Portell-Cortes I, Marti-Nicolovius M. 1995. Effects of pretraining paradoxical sleep deprivation upon two-way active avoidance. *Behav. Brain Res.* 72:181–83

Gruest N, Richer P, Hars B. 2004. Memory consolidation and reconsolidation in the rat pup require protein synthesis. *J. Neurosci.* 24:10488–92

Guan Z, Peng X, Fang J. 2004. Sleep deprivation impairs spatial memory and decreases extracellular signal-regulated kinase phosphorylation in the hippocampus. *Brain Res.* 1018:38–47

Harrison Y, Horne JA. 2000. Sleep loss and temporal memory. *Q. J. Exp. Psychol.* 53: 271–79

Hartley D. 1801. *Observations on Man, His Frame, His Deity, and His Expectations (1749/1966).* Gainesville, FL: Scholars Facsimile Reprint

Henson RN, Rugg MD, Shallice T, Josephs O, Dolan RJ. 1999. Recollection and familiarity in recognition memory: an event-related functional magnetic resonance imaging study. *J. Neurosci.* 19:3962–72

Hobson JA, Pace-Schott EF. 2002. The cognitive neuroscience of sleep: neuronal systems, consciousness and learning. *Nat. Rev. Neurosci.* 3:679–93

Huber R, Ghilardi MF, Massimini M, Tononi G. 2004. Local sleep and learning. *Nature* 430:78–81

Jenkins JG, Dallenbach KM. 1924. Obliviscence during sleep and waking. *Am. J. Psychol.* 35:605–12

Kandel ER. 2001. The molecular biology of memory storage: a dialogue between genes and synapses. *Science* 294:1030–38

Karni A, Tanne D, Rubenstein BS, Askenasy JJ, Sagi D. 1994. Dependence on REM sleep of overnight improvement of a perceptual skill. *Science* 265:679–82

Kelleher RJ 3rd, Govindarajan A, Tonegawa S. 2004. Translational regulatory mechanisms in persistent forms of synaptic plasticity. *Neuron* 44:59–73

Koechlin E, Corrado G, Pietrini P, Grafman J. 2000. Dissociating the role of the medial and lateral anterior prefrontal cortex in human planning. *Proc. Natl. Acad. Sci. USA* 97:7651–56

Koechlin E, Danek A, Burnod Y, Grafman J. 2002. Medial prefrontal and subcortical mechanisms underlying the acquisition of motor and cognitive action sequences in humans. *Neuron* 35:371–81

Korman M, Raz N, Flash T, Karni A. 2003. Multiple shifts in the representation of a motor sequence during the acquisition of skilled performance. *Proc. Natl. Acad. Sci. USA* 100:12492–97

Kuriyama K, Stickgold R, Walker MP. 2004. Sleep-dependent learning and motor skill complexity. *Learn. Mem.* 11:705–13

Lewin I, Glaubman H. 1975. The effect of REM deprivation: Is it detrimental, beneficial, or neutral? *Psychophysiology* 12:349–53

Maquet P, Laureys S, Peigneux P, Fuchs S, Petiau C, et al. 2000. Experience-dependent changes in cerebral activation during human REM sleep. *Nat. Neurosci.* 3:831–36

Maquet P, Schwartz S, Passingham R, Frith C. 2003. Sleep-related consolidation of a visuomotor skill: brain mechanisms as assessed by functional magnetic resonance imaging. *J. Neurosci.* 23:1432–40

McDermott CM, LaHoste GJ, Chen C, Musto A, Bazan NG, Magee JC. 2003. Sleep deprivation causes behavioral, synaptic, and membrane excitability alterations in hippocampal neurons. *J. Neurosci.* 23:9687–95

McGaugh JL. 2000. Memory—a century of consolidation. *Science* 287:248–51

McGrath MJ, Cohen DB. 1978. REM sleep facilitation of adaptive waking behavior: a review of the literature. *Psychol. Bull.* 85:24–57

Mednick SC, Nakayama K, Cantero JL, Atienza M, Levin AA, et al. 2002. The restorative effect of naps on perceptual deterioration. *Nat. Neurosci.* 28:677–81

Mednick SC, Nakayama K, Stickgold R. 2003. Sleep-dependent learning: a nap is as good as a night. *Nat. Neurosci.* 6:697–98

Meienberg P. 1977. The tonic aspects of human REM sleep during long-term intensive verbal learning. *Physiol. Psychol.* 5:250–56

Misanin JR, Miller RR, Lewis DJ. 1968. Retrograde amnesia produced by electroconvulsive shock after reactivation of a consolidated memory trace. *Science* 160:554–55

Morris GO, Williams HL, Lubin A. 1960. Misperception and disorientation during sleep. *Arch. Gen. Psychiatry* 2:247–54

Muellbacher W, Ziemann U, Wissel J, Dang N, Kofler M, et al. 2002. Early consolidation in human primary motor cortex. *Nature* 415:640–44

Muller RA, Kleinhans N, Pierce K, Kemmotsu N, Courchesne E. 2002. Functional MRI of motor sequence acquisition: effects of learning stage and performance. *Brain Res. Cogn. Brain Res.* 14:277–93

Myers KM, Davis M. 2002. Systems-level

reconsolidation: reengagement of the hippocampus with memory reactivation. *Neuron* 36:340–43

Nader K. 2003. Memory traces unbound. *Trends Neurosci.* 26:65–72

Nader K, Ben Mamou C, Komorowski B. 2004. *Double dissociation of the mechanisms mediating the induction of reconsolidation from those mediating the expression of a conditioned response.* Presented at Soc. Neurosci., Washington, DC

Nader K, Schafe GE, LeDoux JE. 2000. Fear memories require protein synthesis in the amygdala for reconsolidation after retrieval. *Nature* 406:722–26

Ohyama T, Nores WL, Murphy M, Mauk MD. 2003. What the cerebellum computes. *Trends Neurosci.* 26:222–27

Peigneux P, Laureys S, Fuchs S, Collette F, Perrin F, et al. 2004. Are spatial memories strengthened in the human hippocampus during slow wave sleep? *Neuron* 44:535–45

Peigneux P, Laureys S, Fuchs S, Destrebecqz A, Collette F, et al. 2003. Learned material content and acquisition level modulate cerebral reactivation during posttraining rapid-eye-movements sleep. *Neuroimage* 20:125–34

Phelps EA. 2004. Human emotion and memory: interactions of the amygdala and hippocampal complex. *Curr. Opin. Neurobiol.* 14:198–202

Plihal W, Born J. 1997. Effects of early and late nocturnal sleep on declarative and procedural memory. *J. Cogn. Neurosci.* 9:534–47

Poldrack RA, Rodriguez P. 2003. Sequence learning: What's the hippocampus to do? *Neuron* 37:891–93

Przybyslawski J, Roullet P, Sara SJ. 1999. Attenuation of emotional and nonemotional memories after their reactivation: role of beta adrenergic receptors. *J. Neurosci.* 19:6623–28

Rechtschaffen A, Kales A. 1968. *A Manual Standardized Terminology, Techniques and Scoring System for Sleep Stages of Human Subjects.* Bethesda, MD: U.S. Dep. Health

Robertson EM, Pascual-Leone A, Press DZ. 2004. Awareness modifies the skill-learning benefits of sleep. *Curr. Biol.* 14:208–12

Ruskin DN, Liu C, Dunn KE, Bazan NG, La-Hoste GJ. 2004. Sleep deprivation impairs hippocampus-mediated contextual learning but not amygdala-mediated cued learning in rats. *Eur. J. Neurosci.* 19:3121–24

Sakai K, Kitaguchi K, Hikosaka O. 2003. Chunking during human visuomotor sequence learning. *Exp. Brain Res.* 152:229–42

Schacter D, Tulving E. 1994. What are the memory systems of 1994? In *Memory Systems 1994*, ed. D Schacter, E Tulving, pp. 1–38. Cambridge: MIT Press

Schendan HE, Searl MM, Melrose RJ, Stern CE. 2003. An fMRI study of the role of the medial temporal lobe in implicit and explicit sequence learning. *Neuron* 37:1013–25

Schneider AM, Sherman W. 1968. Amnesia: a function of the temporal relation of footshock to electroconvulsive shock. *Science* 159:219–21

Sei H, Saitoh D, Yamamoto K, Morita K, Morita Y. 2000. Differential effect of short-term REM sleep deprivation on NGF and BDNF protein levels in the rat brain. *Brain Res.* 877:387–90

Seitz RJ, Roland E, Bohm C, Greitz T, Stone-Elander S. 1990. Motor learning in man: a positron emission tomographic study. *Neuroreport* 1:57–60

Sejnowski TJ, Destexhe A. 2000. Why do we sleep? *Brain Res.* 886:208–23

Siegel JM. 2001. The REM sleep-memory consolidation hypothesis. *Science* 294:1058–63

Smith C. 1985. Sleep states and learning: a review of the animal literature. *Neurosci. Biobehav. Rev.* 9:157–68

Smith C. 2001. Sleep states and memory processes in humans: procedural versus declarative memory systems. *Sleep Med. Rev.* 5:491–506

Smith C, MacNeill C. 1994. Impaired motor memory for a pursuit rotor task following

Stage 2 sleep loss in college students. *J. Sleep Res.* 3:206–13

Squire LR, Zola SM. 1996. Structure and function of declarative and nondeclarative memory systems. *Proc. Natl. Acad. Sci. USA* 93:13515–22

Stern WC. 1971. Acquisition impairments following rapid eye movement sleep deprivation in rats. *Physiol. Behav.* 7:345–52

Stickgold R. 2002. EMDR: a putative neurobiological mechanism of action. *J. Clin. Psychol.* 58:61–75

Stickgold R, James L, Hobson JA. 2000a. Visual discrimination learning requires posttraining sleep. *Nat. Neurosci.* 2:1237–38

Stickgold R, Scott L, Rittenhouse C, Hobson JA. 1999. Sleep-induced changes in associative memory. *J. Cogn. Neurosci.* 11:182–93

Stickgold R, Walker MP. 2005. Memory consolidation and reconsolidation: What is the role of sleep? *Trends Neurosci.* 28:408–15

Stickgold R, Whidbee D, Schirmer B, Patel V, Hobson JA. 2000b. Visual discrimination task improvement: a multi-step process occurring during sleep. *J. Cogn. Neurosci.* 12:246–54

Suzuki A, Josselyn SA, Frankland PW, Masushige S, Silva AJ, Kida S. 2004. Memory reconsolidation and extinction have distinct temporal and biochemical signatures. *J. Neurosci.* 24:4787–95

Tilley AJ, Empson JA. 1978. REM sleep and memory consolidation. *Biol. Psychol.* 6:293–300

Toni I, Krams M, Turner R, Passingham RE. 1998. The time course of changes during motor sequence learning: a whole-brain fMRI study. *Neuroimage* 8:50–61

Tulving E. 1985. How many memory systems are there? *Am. Psychol.* 40:385–98

Ungerleider LG, Doyon J, Karni A. 2002. Imaging brain plasticity during motor skill learning. *Neurobiol. Learn. Mem.* 78:553–64

Ungerleider LG, Haxby JV. 1994. "What" and "where" in the human brain. *Curr. Opin. Neurobiol.* 4:157–65

Vertes RP, Eastman KE. 2000. The case against memory consolidation in REM sleep. *Behav. Brain Sci.* 23:867–76; discussion 904–1121

Wagner AD, Schacter DL, Rotte M, Koutstaal W, Maril A, et al. 1998. Building memories: remembering and forgetting of verbal experiences as predicted by brain activity. *Science* 281:1188–91

Wagner U, Gais S, Born J. 2001. Emotional memory formation is enhanced across sleep intervals with high amounts of rapid eye movement sleep. *Learn. Mem.* 8:112–19

Wagner U, Gais S, Haider H, Verleger R, Born J. 2004. Sleep inspires insight. *Nature* 427:352–55

Walker MP. 2005. A refined model of sleep and the time course of memory formation. *Behav. Brain Sci.* 28:51–64; discussion 64–104

Walker MP, Brakefield T, Hobson JA, Stickgold R. 2003a. Dissociable stages of human memory consolidation and reconsolidation. *Nature* 425:616–20

Walker MP, Brakefield T, Morgan A, Hobson JA, Stickgold R. 2002a. Practice with sleep makes perfect: sleep-dependent motor skill learning. *Neuron* 35:205–11

Walker MP, Brakefield T, Seidman J, Morgan A, Hobson JA, Stickgold R. 2003b. Sleep and the time course of motor skill learning. *Learn. Mem.* 10:275–84

Walker MP, Liston C, Hobson JA, Stickgold R. 2002b. Cognitive flexibility across the sleep-wake cycle: REM-sleep enhancement of anagram problem solving. *Brain Res. Cogn. Brain Res.* 14:317–24

Walker MP, Stickgold R. 2004. Sleep-dependent learning and memory consolidation. *Neuron* 44:121–33

Walker MP, Stickgold R. 2005. It's practice, with sleep, that makes perfect: implications of sleep-dependent learning and plasticity for skill performance. *Clin. Sports Med.* 24:301–17

Walker MP, Stickgold R, Alsop D, Gaab N, Schlaug G. 2005a. Sleep-dependent motor memory plasticity in the human brain. *Neuroscience* 133:911–17

Walker MP, Stickgold R, Jolesz FA, Yoo

S-S. 2005b. The functional anatomy of sleep-dependent visual skill learning. *Cereb. Cortex* (first publ. Feb. 9, 2005; doi: 10.1093/cercor/bhi043)

Zimmerman JT, Stoyva JM, Metcalf D. 1970. Distorted visual feedback and augmented REM sleep. *Psychophysiology* 7:298–303

Zimmerman JT, Stoyva JM, Reite ML. 1978. Spatially rearranged vision and REM sleep: a lack of effect. *Biol. Psychiatry* 13:301–16

Annu. Rev. Psychol. 2006. 57:167–97
doi: 10.1146/annurev.psych.56.091103.070324
Copyright © 2006 by Annual Reviews. All rights reserved
First published online as a Review in Advance on September 16, 2005

NEUROECOLOGY

David F. Sherry

*Department of Psychology, Program in Neuroscience, University of Western Ontario,
London, Ontario, Canada N6A 5C2; email: sherry@uwo.ca*

Key Words brain, cognition, evolution, behavior, comparative method

■ **Abstract** Neuroecology is the study of adaptive variation in cognition and the
brain. The origin of neuroecology dates from the 1980s, when researchers in behavioral
ecology began to apply the methods of comparative evolutionary biology to cognitive
processes and the underlying neural mechanisms of cognition. The comparative approach, however, is much older. It was a mainstay of ethology, it has been part of the
study of neuroanatomy since the seventeenth century, and it was used by Darwin to
marshal evidence for the theory of natural selection. Neuroecology examines the relations between ecological selection pressures and species or sex differences in cognition
and the brain. The goal of neuroecology is to understand how natural selection acts on
cognition and its neural mechanisms. This chapter describes the general approach of
neuroecology, phylogenetic comparative methods used in the field, and new findings
on the cognitive mechanisms and brain structures involved in mating systems, social
organization, communication, and foraging. The contribution of neuroecology to psychology and the neurosciences is the information it provides on the selective pressures
that have influenced the evolution of cognition and brain structure.

CONTENTS

0066-4308/06/0110-0167$20.00

INTRODUCTION

Neuroecology is the study of adaptive variation in cognition and the brain. It uses experimental and comparative methods to understand the evolution of animal cognition—specifically the effects of natural and sexual selection on cognition—and identifies correlations among ecological selection pressures, cognition, and brain structure. Although neuroecology focuses on behavior that animals exhibit in nature, it uses experimental laboratory methods to investigate cognition and comparative anatomical methods to examine the neural correlates of cognition.

Comparative neuroanatomy and the comparative study of behavior have long histories (Darwin 1872, Kruger 2004, Nieuwenhuys 1998, Striedter 2005, Tinbergen 1963). The origins of neuroecology are more recent, however, and are found in the rapid growth of behavioral ecology (Krebs & Davies 1978, 1997). Behavioral ecology examines the function and adaptive significance of animal behavior, especially animal social behavior, using mathematical models to develop theory and empirical field and laboratory research to test predictions derived from theory. Behavioral ecology was initially concerned almost exclusively with the function and evolution of behavior but later began to address causal questions about behavior, particularly questions about the role of learning, memory, and cognition in adaptive behavior. Neuroecology grew out of this interest in causal mechanisms. It examines the cognitive processes and neural structures that underlie adaptive behavior.

Neuroecological research has examined the relations between cognition and the brain in the context of mating systems, social organization, communication, and foraging. This article begins by describing an example of neuroecological research on the relation between mating system, spatial ability, and the mammalian hippocampus. This is followed by a discussion of comparative methods used in neuroecology and a review of recent research on several current topics including food storing and the avian hippocampus, sex differences in the hippocampus, the neural control of birdsong, behavioral innovation and the forebrain, and social and nonsocial influences on the evolution of the primate brain.

Mating System, Spatial Ability, and the Hippocampus: A Case Study in Neuroecology

Meadow voles (*Microtus pennsylvanicus*), like most mammals, are polygynous. Males compete for mates in a scramble competition in which a large home range and superior spatial ability provide a competitive advantage (Spritzer et al. 2005a,b). Male home ranges are larger than are those of females, and encompass the territories of multiple females (Gaulin & FitzGerald 1986, 1989). Males perform better than females on controlled laboratory tests of spatial ability (Gaulin & FitzGerald 1989). Males with better spatial ability, assessed in the Morris water maze, have larger home ranges, visit the nests of more females, and revisit their most preferred females more often than do males with poorer spatial ability (Spritzer et al. 2005b). Males that visit the most females produce more offspring. Spritzer et al. (2005b) found, however, that although males with better spatial ability produced more offspring than did males with poorer spatial ability (4.85 $\pm$ 1.41 versus 4.00 $\pm$ 1.37 pups) this difference was not significant. They concluded that the relatively high density of female nests in the seminatural outdoor enclosures used in their studies might have reduced the advantage that males with better spatial ability would experience under more natural conditions.

Remarkably, female meadow voles that are offered a choice of mate in the laboratory prefer to mate with males with better spatial ability (Spritzer et al. 2005a). It is not clear by what mechanism female mate choice favors males with better spatial ability, but testosterone levels affect male spatial ability (Galea et al. 1999), and females are known to distinguish olfactorily among males with different testosterone levels (Ferkin et al. 1994, Leonard et al. 2001).

Pine voles (*Microtus pinetorum*) and prairie voles (*Microtus ochrogaster*), unlike most species of vole, are monogamous. Males of these species associate with females during reproduction, provide paternal care, and have home ranges equal in size to those of females (FitzGerald & Madison 1983; Gaulin & FitzGerald 1986, 1989).

While polygynous male meadow voles perform better than females on standardized tests of spatial ability, there is no sex difference in spatial ability between monogamous male and female pine voles (Gaulin & FitzGerald 1986) or prairie voles (Gaulin & FitzGerald 1989). Experiments show that activity levels and spatial experience cannot account for these species-specific sex differences (Gaulin et al. 1990, Gaulin & Wartell 1990).

Not only do male and female meadow voles differ in home range size and spatial ability, but males also have a larger hippocampus than females, a sex difference not found in monogamous prairie voles (Jacobs et al. 1990).

The relations discovered between vole mating system, home range size, spatial ability, and size of the hippocampus illustrate the major features of research in neuroecology: a focus on naturally occurring behavior and the coupling of comparative analysis of cognition with comparative analysis of the brain. The general conclusion drawn from this work is that different mating systems in *Microtus* have subjected males and females to different selective pressures. Intrasexual competition among male meadow voles for mating opportunities has resulted in sexual selection for increased home range size in males, accompanied by selection for spatial competence required to navigate a larger home range. Female meadow voles are unaffected by this selective pressure, although their preference to mate with males with better spatial ability may result in additional intersexual, or epigamic, sexual selection for spatial ability in males. Selection for spatial ability has produced evolutionary change in one of the neural structures that serves spatial ability, the hippocampus. Among monogamous voles, males do not compete for mates by increasing their home range size and so sex-specific selective pressures on spatial ability and the hippocampus are absent. This association between mating system, cognition, and the brain has led to further questions about the causes of sex differences in spatial ability and to new findings about neuroendocrine effects on hippocampal neurogenesis and spatial ability (Omerod & Galea 2003, Omerod et al. 2004). Sex-specific correlations between home range size and brain structure have been found in prefrontal and parietal cortex of meadow voles (Kavaliers et al. 1998) and in the hippocampus of polygynous rodents in other taxa (Jacobs & Spencer 1994, Sherry et al. 1996).

THE COMPARATIVE METHOD

Neuroecology makes extensive use of the comparative method. The comparative method was a staple tool in Darwin's arguments for the efficacy of natural selection in producing evolutionary change (Darwin 1859) and has been used ever since to analyze adaptation. Ethologist Esther Cullen used the comparative method to understand differences in breeding behavior between ground-nesting gulls and cliff-nesting kittiwakes (Cullen 1957). Comparison of these two species showed that many of the differences in their behavior could be interpreted as adaptive modification of kittiwake parental care and ontogeny to nesting on narrow cliff ledges, with the attendant risk of falling into the sea. This comparison examined two closely related species that shared most of their evolutionary history and concluded that differences between them were the result of specific selective pressures acting on kittiwakes.

In psychology, research on animals is often described as "comparative" even in the absence of comparisons among different species because of the implicit comparison to humans. Some explicitly comparative research has examined the behavior of different species chosen because they represented what were thought to be higher and lower levels of complexity of a psychological process such as learning (Bitterman 1975). Comparative research of this kind foundered on the realization that the *scala naturae* was a poor model of evolutionary change (Hodos & Campbell 1969) and the realization that differences between species in a psychological process such as learning could only with great difficulty be disentangled from differences between species in perception, behavior, and responses to the conditions under which behavior was observed.

Most recent comparative research on behavior and the brain, including research in neuroecology, compares species selected with greater attention to phylogeny, the evolutionary genealogy of species. These comparisons can involve a small number of closely related species that differ in some important aspect of their ecology or behavior such that differences discovered can be attributed to specific evolutionary selection pressures acting within an evolutionary history that is largely shared. Cullen's (1957) study of kittiwakes is an example of this approach, as is the research on voles described above. Other comparative research examines species that share a common feature of their ecology or behavior but are not closely related phylogenetically. In analyses of this kind, similarities between species, given their differing evolutionary histories, are attributed to the shared feature of ecology or behavior. Unrelated species of food-storing birds, for example, share some properties of memory and brain organization and are an example of this kind of comparative analysis (see Food-Storing Birds and the Avian Hippocampus, below). Phylogenetic comparative methods provide general statistical procedures for comparing species of any degree of relatedness and have become the standard in neuroecology.

Phylogenetic Comparative Methods

Phylogenetic comparative methods test for associations among traits using phylogeny—the evolutionary relations among species—to control for features shared by descent from a common ancestor. These methods, developed largely within biology in the 1980s, are statistically much more sophisticated than were earlier comparative techniques. This sophistication developed because statistical tests on data obtained on different species require a way of dealing with the nonindependence of these data caused by the evolutionary relations among the species examined.

The goal of comparative analysis is to determine whether there is a consistent association between characters of interest, such as size of the song repertoire and size of the song control nuclei of the avian brain, or between a character such as song and a feature of the environment. A character is any recognizable trait, attribute, feature, or property of an organism that can be used as the basis of comparison (Lincoln et al. 2001, Ridley 1996). Characters can be discontinuous, like the presence or absence of antlers, or continuous, like the size of a brain structure. Physical traits, behavior, social system, geographic distribution, population size, or any other attribute can be treated as a character in comparative analyses. If statistical tests show that an association among characters occurs more often than expected by chance, then it also shows that the characters tend to evolve together. If a character is consistently found in association with some feature of the environment, it is therefore likely that the character is an adaptation to that feature of the environment. The statistical advances in phylogenetic comparative methods deal with the fact that characters can also be associated with each other, or with a feature of the environment, not because of evolutionary adaptation but because of shared ancestry.

Closely related animals are similar to each other, a phenomenon called phylogenetic inertia. This observation is so obvious that we rarely ask why closely related animals are similar. Phylogenetic inertia, however, has at least three causes (Harvey & Purvis 1991). The first is that the time elapsed since two species diverged may not have allowed for much change in the characters of interest. The second is that closely related animals tend to occur in the same ecological niche—fast-flowing streams or muskeg bogs, for example—and this environment exerts the same selective pressures on both species. The third cause of phylogenetic inertia is that responses to selection are affected by phenotype. The range of adaptive responses that closely related animals can make to changing selection pressures is very similar. For these reasons, many characters are similar in closely related animals. How can adaptive responses among characters, or between characters and features of the environment, be distinguished from characters that are shared as a consequence of phylogenetic inertia?

Independent Contrasts

Species are not drawn randomly from a common distribution in the way the null hypothesis of most statistical tests assumes samples of data are drawn from a common population. Species are instead points at the terminals of a hierarchically branching evolutionary tree (Figure 1), and this introduces the problem of statistical nonindependence (Felsenstein 1985, Harvey & Mace 1982). Similar nonindependence due to history, known as Galton's problem, occurs in comparative analyses of culture and language (Mace & Holden 2005). A number of solutions have been proposed, but the most widely accepted in current practice are variations on Felsenstein's method of independent contrasts (Felsenstein 1985). The method of independent contrasts requires that the true phylogeny of the species compared is known. The method of independent contrasts consists of taking contrasts, or difference measures, on pairs of points in the phylogenetic tree (Figure 2). Statistical tests can then be performed to determine whether the magnitude of contrasts in one variable is related to the magnitude of contrasts in another. Contrasts, unlike data for the species themselves, are independent because a contrast between Species A and Species B does not influence the contrast between Species C and Species D. Furthermore, these contrasts are independent of contrasts taken at higher branching points in the tree, such as the contrast between the mean value for Species A and B and the mean for Species C and D. The logic is similar to that of orthogonal comparisons in conventional statistical analysis. In a phylogenetic comparative analysis, a data set of n species will yield $n - 1$ independent contrasts.

The method of independent contrasts requires an accurate phylogeny for the group of animals under study, and Felsenstein saw this as the principal limitation of his method (Felsenstein 1985), but as more phylogenies become available through the use of molecular techniques, the method of independent contrasts has become the preferred statistical procedure in comparative analyses of behavior and the brain (MacDougall-Shackleton & Ball 1999, Madden 2001, Nicolakakis & Lefebvre 2000, Reader & Laland 2002). As Harvey & Purvis (1991) point out, obtaining a satisfactory phylogeny is not always straightforward, and any phylogeny has built into it implicit or explicit assumptions about how evolution works. Different assumptions can lead to different phylogenetic trees, and these different trees can

Poecile

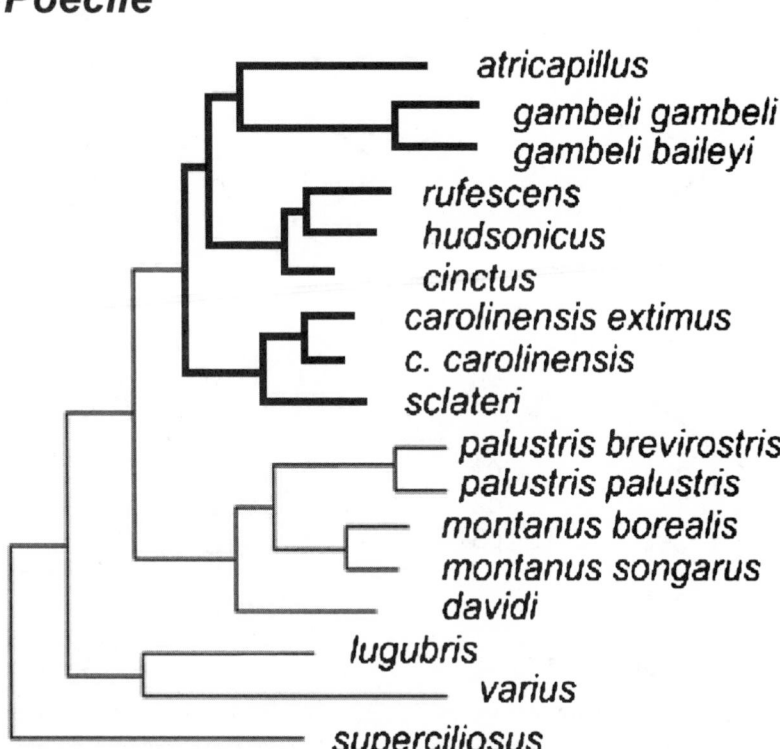

Figure 1 Phylogeny of the genus Poecile, part of a larger phylogeny proposed by Gill et al. (2005) for the family Paridae, the chickadees and tits. Associations among characters in this genus will be strongly influenced by the many North American members of the group (heavy lines). These species are closely related and are likely to share characters as a consequence of common descent, making data obtained on them nonindependent. Redrawn with permission from Gill et al. (2005).

sometimes lead to different conclusions about adaptive relations among characters or the relation of characters to a feature of the environment (Iwaniuk 2004). A solution to the problem of imperfectly resolved phylogenies that Harvey & Purvis (1991) describe is sensitivity analysis, essentially performing the comparative analysis using each plausible phylogenetic tree and then determining to what extent the conclusions depend on phylogeny.

Phylogenetic Signal

Two further aspects of phylogenetic comparative methods have generated a good deal of discussion. The first is that natural selection may sometimes have a stabilizing effect, in which case the result of intense selection is no discernable change

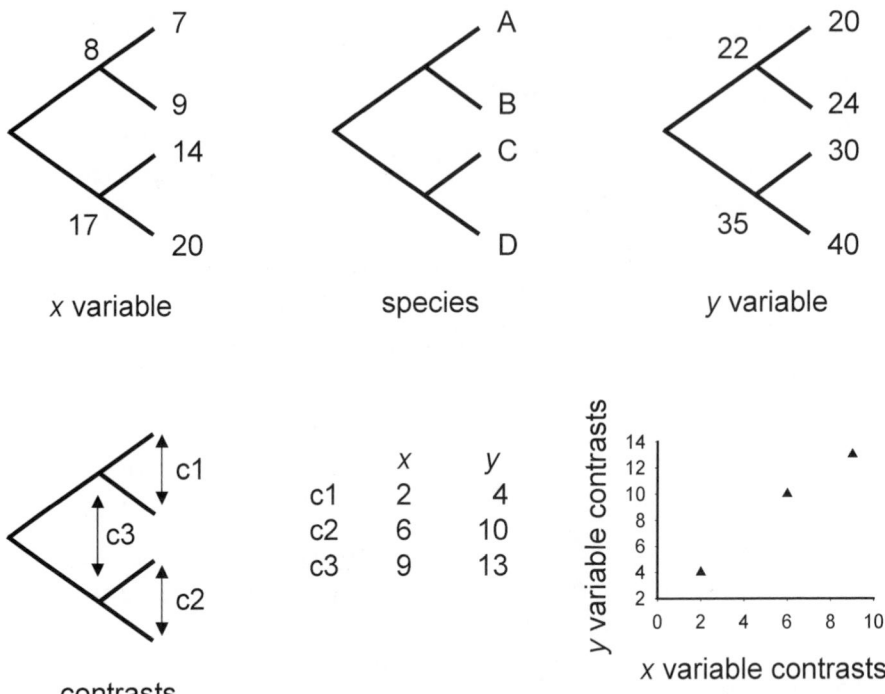

Figure 2 The method of independent contrasts. Two variables, x and y, are measured on four species, A, B, C and D. The phylogenetic tree for these species, and the values of variables x and y for each species, are shown in the upper row of the figure. Values shown at branching nodes are mean values for species at the terminal branches of the node. Contrasts, or differences, can be calculated for each variable between species A and B, C and D, and the branching nodes, as shown. The calculated contrasts are independent of each other, unlike values for the species themselves. Contrasts can then plotted against each other, as shown in the bottom right of the figure. This plot shows that the contrasts are correlated, that is, the magnitude of a change in character x between species is associated with the magnitude of a change in character y. Redrawn with permission from Purvis & Rambaut (1995).

in a character (Martins 2000). This effect of selection will not be detected by the method of independent contrasts because the method is designed to detect change in a character, not the effects of stabilizing selection. The second is that for characters that change rapidly between speciation events, the phylogenetic comparative method may be inappropriate and introduce problems of nonindependence where none existed (Rheindt et al. 2004). Characters such as birdsong, for example, may change rapidly within a species. When this is the case, the character may show little trace of its phylogenetic history. Rheindt et al. (2004) looked at the relation between the acoustic structure of birdsong and the habitat in which the song is broadcast. Previous studies have shown that the properties of song are correlated with the physical properties of the habitat in which the song is sung (Brown & Handford 2000, Morton 1975). This is because different habitats cause different kinds of degradation in sound, making the song difficult to recognize or detect at a distance. The hard surfaces of forest trees introduce echo while the movement of air in open grassland causes "dropouts," or inaudible segments within a song. The structure of birdsong may be adapted to the acoustic environment, much as Haydn and Mozart adapted their music for performance in a sound-absorbing room, a resonant concert hall, or out-of-doors (Forsyth 1985).

However, Rheindt et al. (2004) found that the physical properties of a bird's song are not correlated with its phylogenetic history. The rates of evolution of birdsong, they concluded, are much more rapid than speciation events, with the result that the properties of song they measured—highest frequency, lowest frequency, and dominant frequency—retain no trace of their phylogenetic origin. Correcting for phylogenetic inertia when none is present can influence the outcome of comparative analyses. Rheindt et al. (2004) therefore recommend testing for "phylogenetic signal"—statistical indication that phylogeny does introduce nonindependence—before using methods like independent contrasts that remove the effects of phylogeny. There is not yet enough information to tell whether brain structure and cognition exhibit the kind of rapid evolutionary change described by Rheindt et al. (2004), but their recommendation seems a sensible one and is not difficult to apply in neuroecological analyses.

Control Variables

The constituent parts of large animals are also large, and this applies to the brain as it does to other structures. Allometric relations between brain and body size and among parts of the brain have been extensively described (Harvey & Krebs 1990). The metrics used to estimate the size of the brain and its component parts can make a great deal of difference to the conclusions drawn from comparative analyses. De Winter & Oxnard (2001) and Finlay & Darlington (1995) came to radically different conclusions about major patterns in the evolution of the mammalian brain largely as a result of using different methods to control for total brain size. Finlay & Darlington (1995) concluded that for major brain regions, relative size was essentially the same across mammals, whereas de Winter & Oxnard (2001) found that the relative size of major brain areas varied independently in primates, insectivores, and bats in ways that reflected the perceptual and motor specializations of these animals.

The methods used to control for allometric effects are sometimes justified by empirical observations, sometimes justified only by convention. Corrections for body weight, brain weight, brain volume, or size of a brain structure such as the forebrain or the brainstem are commonly used. In general, measurements on the brain make better control variables than do body weight measurements because body weight can vary within individuals depending on nutrition, season, reproductive condition, and migratory state. In large-scale studies, data on brain size and body size often come from different sources, and differences in body size can occur between individuals of the same species due to sex, age, and the population from which the sample was drawn.

Byrne & Corp (2004) make the further point that using body size as an allometric control for size of a brain region assumes a particular model of brain function, namely that large bodies require more brain to control them. According to this model, if two animals both have brains that are 10% larger than expected for their body weight, then they both have the same additional capacity beyond that required for control functions. This clearly is not the case, however, for a mouse and an elephant that are both found to have brains 10% larger than expected. The greater-than-expected brain size of the elephant provides more information processing capacity, in terms of neurons and synaptic connections, than that of the mouse. For this reason, Byrne and Corp argue, the proportion of total brain size taken up by a particular neural structure is a more realistic measure of resources devoted to that structure and the functions it performs.

There is a variety of ways of using control variables, including taking ratios of the size of the structure of interest to the control variable, calculating residuals from a regression between the structure of interest and the control variable, and including control variables in multiple regression or general linear models. Ratios are widely used, but multivariate methods like regression or the general linear model have the advantage that they make the most use of the relations among measured variables in the data set (Darlington & Smulders 2001).

With the logic of the comparative method in mind, we move on to areas of current research in neuroecology.

FOOD-STORING BIRDS AND THE AVIAN HIPPOCAMPUS

Birds in three passerine families store food: the Paridae, chickadees and tits; the Corvidae, jays and crows; and the Sittidae, nuthatches. Birds in all three groups store food in widely scattered distributions within their home range. For chickadees and tits, this is an area of several hectares, whereas for birds like Clark's nutcracker, cache sites may be distributed over many square kilometers. The birds place either a single food item or a small number of items in each cache. Having scattered their stored food over a wide area, probably to protect it from other animals that pilfer caches, food-storing birds face the problem of retrieving this food. Early research showed that food-storing birds retrieve their caches by remembering where they placed them (Cowie et al. 1981, Sherry et al. 1981, Shettleworth & Krebs 1982, Tomback 1980, Vander Wall 1982), and a large body of experimental results has since confirmed this basic finding and added a great deal of new information on how memory for cache sites works (Balda et al. 1997, Shettleworth 2003, Smulders & DeVoogd 2000a). Birds remember the locations of caches with respect to landmarks near cache sites, remember the geometric relations among cache sites and landmarks, and use sun compass information to orient to cache sites (Balda & Wiltschko 1991, Duff et al. 1998, Wiltschko & Balda 1989). Memory for cache sites can be very long lasting (Balda & Kamil 1992, Hitchcock & Sherry 1990), and retrieval behavior indicates the birds remember what kind of food was stored at a particular site (Clayton & Dickinson 1998, Sherry 1984). Clayton & Dickinson (1998) found that birds integrate the spatial location of a food cache with the kind of food placed in the cache and the time this was done. Although subsequent work has questioned Clayton and Dickinson's claim that memory for cache sites resembles human episodic memory (Hampton et al. 2005, Hampton & Schwartz 2004, Roberts 2002), it seems likely that food-storing birds retain in some form information of different kinds about cache sites, including the risk of cache loss (Hampton & Sherry 1994) and whether or not the bird has retrieved the stored food itself (Sherry 1984).

Lesions of the hippocampus disrupt the ability of food-storing birds to retrieve their caches (Krushinskaya 1966, Sherry & Vaccarino 1989) and produce a selective deficit in memory for spatial locations (Broadbent & Colombo 2000; Hampton & Shettleworth 1996a,b; Shiflett et al. 2003). Lesions of the hippocampus have similar selective effects on components of orientation in homing pigeons (Bingman et al. 1995).

Comparisons between food-storing and non-food-storing birds have shown some interesting relations between behavior and the relative size of the hippocampus. Comparisons at the taxonomic level of families and subfamilies showed that food-storing birds have, on average, a larger hippocampus than do non-food-storing birds (Krebs et al. 1989, Sherry et al. 1989). Within families of food-storing birds, there is also evidence that species that store more have a larger hippocampus than do species that store less (Hampton et al. 1995, Healy & Krebs 1992). This relation between the intensity of food storing and hippocampal size was recently questioned in a reanalysis of existing data by Brodin & Lundborg (2003), who found no consistent relation between behavior and hippocampal size in either Parids or Corvids. In subsequent work, however, Brodin and his colleagues found that their initial analysis was confounded, remarkably, by differences in hippocampal size between North American and European birds. This continental difference in hippocampal size, with Eurasian species having larger hippocampuses than those of North American species, occurs among non-food-storing birds as well as food-storing birds (Garamszegi & Lucas 2005). Reanalysis confirmed that food-storing birds have consistently larger hippocampuses than do non-food-storing species when continental differences are taken into account (Lucas et al. 2004). In a similar large-scale study using phylogenetic contrasts, Garamszegi & Eens (2004) found a positive relation between food-hoarding behavior and relative size of the hippocampus.

Seasonal Change in the Hippocampus

Food storing is seasonal in birds. Chickadees and tits begin storing food in fall and continue through the winter and early spring (Haftorn 1956, Ludescher 1980,

Nakamura & Wako 1988, Odum 1942). Food storing in these birds is a short-term strategy. Much of the food they store is retrieved within a few days at most (Cowie et al. 1981, Stevens & Krebs 1986). Storing probably serves to reduce within-day variability in food availability and to guarantee a supply of food at night-fall, before beginning the overnight fast (Lucas & Walter 1991, McNamara et al. 1990). In some food-storing tits, however, stored food is recovered months after it was first cached (Brodin & Ekman 1994). In corvids such as Clark's nutcracker, there is also pronounced seasonality in food storing. These birds harvest and store pine seeds when they are produced in abundance in fall, move to lower eleva-tions during the winter, and return in spring to breed and collect their caches (Tomback 1980).

Smulders et al. (1995, 2000) found the relative size of the hippocampus changed seasonally in black-capped chickadees, reaching a maximum in October at about the time food storing begins. Subsequent attempts to uncover the factors controlling seasonal change in hippocampal size, however, have not been successful (Krebs et al. 1995, MacDougall-Shackleton et al. 2003). A number of experiments have shown that whereas changes in day length, from a summer to a fall photoperiod or from a winter to a spring photoperiod, have the expected effect on food-storing behavior, they have no effect on the relative size of the hippocampus (Krebs et al. 1995, MacDougall-Shackleton et al. 2003). It is possible that these studies, con-ducted in captivity, could not duplicate the high level of food storing with attendant demands on the hippocampus that chickadees experience in the wild and for this reason showed no effect of photoperiod on hippocampal size. Research with brood parasitic cowbirds, in which sex differences in hippocampal size are associated with the mode of brood parasitic behavior, has reported seasonal change in hip-pocampal size (Clayton et al. 1997), as have studies of rodents that are sexually dimorphic in hippocampal size (Yaskin 1984), so it is possible that seasonal change in the size of the hippocampus occurs in food-storing birds in the wild but is not easily observed in captivity.

Hippocampal Neurogenesis

Whether or not the avian hippocampus undergoes seasonal change in overall size, it is clear that it does undergo seasonal change in its neuron population. Barnea & Nottebohm (1994, 1996) gave black-capped chickadees the cell birth–maker triti-ated thymidine, which is incorporated into the nuclei of dividing cells at the DNA synthesis phase of cell division. Birds were released into the wild and recaptured six weeks later. There was a peak in the incorporation of new neurons—called neu-ronal recruitment by Barnea and Nottebohm—into the hippocampus in October. The production of new hippocampal neurons does not vary seasonally (Hoshoo-ley & Sherry 2004), indicating that the observed pattern in neuronal recruitment is due to seasonal change in survival and incorporation of new neurons into the hippocampus.

Woodpeckers, Storm-petrels, and Bowerbirds

Food storing is known to occur in other birds, including shrikes, New Zealand robins, hawks, owls, and woodpeckers. There is very little information about memory for cache sites or the relative size of the hippocampus in these birds, with the exception of a study by Volman et al. (1997) of woodpeckers. Two species in the genus *Melanerpes* store food in quite different ways. The red-bellied woodpecker *Melanerpes carolinus* creates scattered caches of food, rather like food-storing chickadees and jays. The red-headed woodpecker *Melanerpes erythrocephalus* stores food concentrated in a "larder" that it defends against other animals. Scatter-hoarding red-bellied woodpeckers must move through their home range to retrieve their caches and it is likely, though not proven, that they make demands on memory that the larder-hoarding red-headed woodpecker, with its concentrated supply of stored food, does not. The hippocampus is larger, relative to the size of the rest of the brain in red-bellied woodpeckers, than in red-headed woodpeckers (Volman et al. 1997). Volman and her colleagues also looked at two other species, the hairy woodpecker *Picoides villosus* and the downy woodpecker *Picoides pubescens*. The relative size of the hippocampus in these birds was comparable to that of the scatter-hoarding red-bellied woodpecker, even though neither *Picoides* species is thought to store food extensively. This result is not what one would predict from an association between food hoarding and hippocampal size. The lack of correlation between food hoarding and hippocampal size in *Picoides* woodpeckers may show that there is, in general, no consistent relation between food storing and hippocampal size (Bolhuis & Macphail 2001), but the pattern observed in passerine food-storers and *Melanerpes* woodpeckers suggests otherwise. It may be that other selective pressures, for example for spatial ability appropriate to the large home ranges of hairy and downy woodpeckers, have acted to increase hippocampal size in these birds (Volman et al. 1997). It is also possible that *Picoides* woodpeckers store food more than is generally realized (Burchsted 1987, Volman et al. 1997). In any case, data for two species of *Melanerpes* woodpeckers conform to the pattern observed in passerine food storers, whereas data for two species of *Picoides* woodpeckers do not.

Leach's storm-petrels nest in dense colonies in burrows in the ground. They forage at night and return to their burrows in darkness. Abbot et al. (1999) compared the size of the hippocampus in two populations of storm-petrels with different nest site preferences: forest, where reproductive success was higher but burrows appeared difficult for the birds to relocate, and open meadows, where reproductive success was lower but burrows appeared easier to find. The relative size of the hippocampus was greater in forest-nesting storm-petrels than in meadow-nesting birds (Abbott et al. 1999). This difference in hippocampal size between forest-nesting and meadow-nesting birds could come about in a number of ways. Birds that differ in hippocampal size may prefer different nesting habitats, experience with a nesting habitat may affect hippocampal size, or the storm-petrels nesting in the two habitats may be different subpopulations exposed to different selection pressures on hippocampal size. Whatever the reasons for the observed difference in hippocampal size, the results show a relation between hippocampal size and the difficulty of relocating the home burrow.

Male bowerbirds build complex bowers, sometimes decorated with colorful objects that are attractive to females. Madden (2001) determined endocranial volume from X rays of museum specimens for nine species of bowerbirds, one related non-bower-building species, and four unrelated but ecologically similar Australo-Papuan species. Because a number of these species are endangered, brain tissue was not collected and instead endocranial volume was treated as a measure of total brain size. Bowerbirds had significantly larger brains than did either related or non-related nonbower builders. Within bowerbirds, bower complexity was positively correlated with brain size for both major groups of bowerbirds, the avenue-building and the maypole-building species. The method of independent contrasts showed a strong overall relationship between brain size and bower complexity (Madden 2001). Bower building is known to improve with experience and probably makes demands on learning, memory, and other cognitive capacities, including memory for the sources of colorful objects. As Madden points out, it would be informative to determine which brain regions contribute to the overall differences in brain size that were found, but data of this kind are unlikely to become available. As it stands, the results of this research indicate that sexual selection, in the form of female preference for bower complexity, has affected both bower building behavior and total brain size.

SEX DIFFERENCES IN THE HIPPOCAMPUS

Research on vole mating systems, described above, showed that the relative size of the hippocampus differed between the sexes in the presence of sex-specific selection for spatial ability. Males of a polygynous species had a larger hippocampus than did females, whereas no sex difference occurred in monogamous species. Most mammals are polygynous, and a larger hippocampus is found in males in many species (Galea et al. 1999, Jacobs & Spencer 1994, Sherry et al. 1996).

Sex differences in a cognitive or neuroanatomical character are particularly strong evidence for the action of natural or sexual selection because alleles favored by selection in one sex are passed on to both sexes, unlike genes favored by selection in one species but not another. For sex differences in the effects of autosomal genes to occur, not only must there be selection for particular alleles but there must also be selection for modifiers that restrict the effects of these alleles to only one sex (Lande 1980).

It is possible that greater hippocampal size in males has little to do with sex differences in cognition or behavior but is instead a consequence of sexual differentiation. Greater male hippocampal size may be a pleiotropic effect of genes selected for other functions, a side effect of maleness rather than a character associated with spatial ability, home range size, and polygyny. Evidence against this interpretation comes from research on hippocampal size in brood parasitic birds in which selection on female spatial ability has produced a larger hippocampus in females than in males.

Brood Parasites

Brown-headed cowbird (*Molothrus ater*) females lay their eggs in the nests of other species, where the cowbird eggs are incubated and the young cowbirds are raised by their host parents. Female cowbirds lay at or before dawn and therefore search little if at all for host nests at this time (Rothstein et al. 1984). They spend the rest of the morning in host nest habitat, where field studies describe them walking on the forest floor while scanning the canopy, watching the nest-building activity of other birds, and flying into understory vegetation and flushing incubating birds from their nests (Clotfelter 1998, Norman & Robertson 1975, Scott 1991). It is likely that they are searching for potential nests in which to lay eggs on subsequent days. There is evidence that females are selective about the stage of completion of host nests and avoid laying eggs in nests that are unfinished, contain no other eggs, or have a complete host clutch (Nolan 1978). This latter preference may prevent placing a cowbird egg among host eggs that are about to hatch. Males do not assist females in their search for host nests (Rothstein et al. 1987). About midday, females join males and feed in grain fields and livestock yards, often at a considerable distance from forest habitats where host nests are found.

The hippocampus of female cowbirds is larger, relative to the size of the rest of the brain, than the hippocampus of males (Sherry et al. 1993). No sex difference is found in closely related nonparasitic members of the Icterid blackbird family to which cowbirds belong (Sherry et al. 1993).

Cowbirds are a diverse group, most species of which are found in South and Central America. The screaming cowbird (*Molothrus rufoaxillaris*) is a specialist brood parasite, laying eggs in the nests of only one host species. Male and female screaming cowbirds search together for nests of their host. The host is a cowbird, the nonparasitic bay-winged cowbird (*M. badius*). Bay-winged cowbirds usurp the nests of other birds but incubate their own eggs and care for their own young themselves. A third species, the shiny cowbird (*M. bonariensis*), is a generalist parasite. Like the North American brown-headed cowbird, it parasitizes hundreds of host species, and females search for host nests unassisted by males.

Female shiny cowbirds have a larger hippocampus, relative to the size of the rest of the brain, than that of males (Reboreda et al. 1996). No sex difference in the size of the hippocampus occurs in either the specialist screaming cowbird (in which both males and females search for host nests) or the nonparasitic bay-winged cowbird (Reboreda et al. 1996). As with food-storing birds and small mammals, there is some evidence for seasonal change in the size of the hippocampus in female shiny cowbirds (Clayton et al. 1997). Sex differences in nest-searching behavior in the wild, coupled with sex differences in the size of the hippocampus, would predict a sex difference in favor of females in spatial ability, but the only experimental data on sex differences in cognition in cowbirds show an unexpected pattern of female superiority when visual cues indicate the presence of food but not when spatial cues indicate the presence of food (Astié et al. 1998). It is possible that searching for food in the task used by Astié et al. (1998) does not tap the cognitive abilities used by female shiny cowbirds to find host nests, but it is also possible that sex differences in cognition in cowbirds, if they exist, are not what one might predict from results with food-storing birds and polygynous voles.

THE SONG CONTROL NUCLEI

Research on birdsong and the neural circuitry controlling the production of bird-song is probably the prototype for neuroecological research. Male songbirds learn the songs that they sing, and this phenomenon has become a model system for the study of learning and the neural basis of behavior. Research on birdsong has had a profound influence on our understanding of communication, learning, neural plasticity, neurogenesis, and sex differences in brain and behavior. Zeigler & Marler (2004) provide an extensive survey of recent research. Given the wealth of research findings in this area, I narrow the focus to phylogenetic comparative analyses of birdsong. Surprisingly, there are relatively few phylogenetic comparative studies of the neural control of song. Recent reviews, in fact, have urged greater use of phylogenetic comparative methods to dispel current misconceptions about birdsong due to reliance on a few model species in the laboratory (Beecher & Brenowitz 2005, Brenowitz & Beecher 2005).

Two circuits in the avian brain control the learning and production of song. Area HVC—HVC being the preferred name of the area, rather than an acronym (Reiner et al. 2004)—is part of both the anterior circuit that is primarily involved in song learning and the posterior circuit that is primarily a motor control circuit responsible for song production. Area HVC undergoes dramatic seasonal variation in size in many passerines. One hypothesis is that this increase in size is related to the learning of new songs (Nottebohm 1981), but HVC varies seasonally not only in species that learn new songs each season but also in species that sing the same song from year to year (Tramontin & Brenowitz 2000). Because variation in HVC size is not always associated with learning new songs, it has been proposed that its increase in size, and the recruitment of new neurons into HVC, provides more precise motor control of song, which becomes highly stereotyped during the spring breeding season, when song production is at its highest level (Tramontin & Brenowitz 2000).

In most species of passerine birds, males have much more varied songs and a much higher level of song output than do females. Indeed, in most temperate-zone species, females do not sing at all. The principal functions of song are territory defense and mate attraction, and it is therefore not surprising that males sing more than do females. Dramatic differences between males and females in the size of the song control nuclei HVC and RA (robust nucleus of the arcopallium), another nucleus in the posterior song control circuit, have been described in many species, and these sex differences in the brain are often associated with sex differences in song complexity or song production. MacDougall-Shackleton & Ball (1999) performed a phylogenetic comparative analysis of 20 species of songbirds and found a clear association between sex differences in song and sex differences in the relative size of HVC. Earlier claims of no association between sex differences in song and sex differences in the brain (Gahr 1998) were not supported.

In a comparative phylogenetic study of 45 species of songbirds, DeVoogd et al. (1993) found a clear association between song repertoire size and size of area HVC, but not area X, a nucleus in the anterior song circuit. The number of syllables per song was not associated with the size of either structure. Despite the lack of any association between area X and the song variables measured, the size of area HVC and area X were positively associated. Because area X is part of the anterior song circuit, it is usually assigned a greater role in song acquisition than in song production. It appears that evolution of a larger song repertoire exerts a greater selective pressure on the size of HVC, part of the motor control circuit for song output, than on the size of area X, part of the song-acquisition circuit. As might be expected, this study found no association between relative size of the hippocampus and song repertoire size (DeVoogd et al. 1993).

Further phylogenetic comparative analyses examined the relation between song complexity and the size of song control nuclei within a more restricted group, the European warblers in the family Sylviidae (Székely et al. 1996). The advantages of restricting analysis to a smaller group is that measures of song complexity, in this case song repertoire size, are more likely to be comparable than in comparisons within large taxonomic groups, where songs may vary in complexity along many dimensions. In addition, it was possible to standardize histological and volumetric methods for this smaller group of species. The results showed a clear positive relation between contrasts in repertoire size and contrasts in HVC volume among the eight species examined. No relations between repertoire size and size of the song nuclei RA, area X, or LMAN (lateral magnocellular nucleus of the anterior nidopallium) were found (Székely et al. 1996). European warblers were not included in the large-scale phylogenetic study of DeVoogd et al. (1993), described above, so the present study, in addition to providing greater precision in measures of repertoire size and song nucleus volume, also provides an independent test of the relation between song complexity and the brain. As shown in research on the hippocampus, augmentation of specific behavioral and cognitive functions is associated with evolutionary change in specific structures in the brain.

INNOVATION AND THE AVIAN FOREBRAIN

In neuroecological studies of cognition, there are limits to the number of species for which it is possible to obtain behavioral data. In their study of song repertoire size, Székely et al. (1996) felt that restricting analysis to a small number of species allowed greater precision in the measurement of behavior. There are also purely practical limitations to collecting data on a large number of species. The number of species of food-storing birds far exceeds the number of species for which there are controlled laboratory studies of memory and spatial ability. In addition, it is necessary that data be collected under the same conditions, using the same control procedures and protocols if results are to be truly comparable, and it is not always possible to ensure that different species are actually being observed under comparable conditions. One hour of food deprivation may be effective in motivating one species to respond for food, but ineffective for another. Because the animals are different, and that is the purpose of comparative studies, differences in their reactions to laboratory manipulations are to be expected. As the number of species increases, obtaining comparable data on cognitive ability quickly becomes a formidable task.

Lefebvre and his colleagues have found an ingenious way around this problem by using archival sources of data on the behavior of a very large number of bird species (Lefebvre et al. 1998, 1997; Nicolakakis & Lefebvre 2000; Nicolakakis et al. 2003; Sol & Lefebvre 2000; Sol et al. 2002; Timmermans et al. 2000). Scientific journals of ornithology often contain, in addition to research papers, a section of short notes. The contents of these notes range from brief reports of empirical research to more informal observations on distribution, breeding, migration, and other behavior. A traditional feature of these notes is observations on unusual behavior noted by professional or amateur ornithologists. Lefebvre and his colleagues systematically searched the short notes sections of ornithological journals published in North America, Britain and Europe, Australia, New Zealand, and Asia for reports of unusual feeding behavior, which they termed "feeding innovation." Behavior had to meet at least one of two criteria to be included in the innovation data set. The food or foraging technique had to be highly unusual for the species, or the author or editors had to state explicitly that this was the first known published report of the behavior. Innovations included such behavior as American robins capturing and eating salmon smolts (Bayer 1980) and house sparrows searching car radiator grilles for insects (Simmons 1984).

The frequency of these reports, tabulated by taxonomic order, could then be compared to expected frequencies of innovation, calculated using the total number of innovations observed for all species and the proportion of species in each taxonomic order. From the observed and expected values, Lefebvre and colleagues calculated a relative index of innovation (Lefebvre et al. 1997). The correlation between mean forebrain size, obtained from Portmann (1947), and the index of innovation could then be calculated.

Several notable results emerge from this analysis. There is considerable variation in innovation rate among avian orders. The highest rates of innovative feeding behavior are shown by one group of Passeriformes, the Corvids (crows and jays), and by the Ciconiiformes (storks, herons, and ibises) and the Falconiformes (eagles, hawks, and falcons). The lowest rates of innovation occur among the Anseriformes (ducks and geese), the Galliformes (pheasants and quail), and the Columbiformes (pigeons and doves). There is a strong correlation between innovation rates calculated separately for different geographic areas, for example between Great Britain and North America. The major result of these studies, however, is a strong correlation between innovation rate and relative forebrain size in birds (Lefebvre et al. 1997, 1998; Nicolakakis & Lefebvre 2000; Nicolakakis et al. 2003; Sol & Lefebvre 2000; Sol et al. 2002; Timmermans et al. 2000).

The use of such an archival source of information on feeding innovation has both advantages and disadvantages. In its favor, it is not affected by motivational variables, reactions of animals to captivity, laboratory artifacts, or the use of particular experimental paradigms to assess animal cognition. This latter advantage may be particularly crucial for avoiding assumptions about the nature of animal cognition that are implicit in any experimental paradigm. The innovation index is, at least potentially, vulnerable to a number of biases, however, and Lefebvre and his colleagues have performed extensive statistical tests for the presence of such biases (Nicolakakis & Lefebvre 2000). The purpose of these statistical refinements was to test whether the relation between forebrain size and innovative feeding behavior was due to the behavior of the birds or the behavior of human observers of birds.

The most obvious bias is that some orders of birds may be more *speciose*, that is, richer in species, than are others. Studies of innovation control for this by comparing the frequency of innovation records for each order to the frequency expected given the number of species of birds in that order. Another potential bias is that some species may be more abundant than others, or more readily seen by the casual observer. If either is the case, then these species would contribute more records of innovative feeding behavior not because they show greater behavioral innovation but simply because they are more often encountered by human observers. Nicolakakis & Lefebvre (2000) tested for such biases by examining an additional category of behavior, reports of unusual nesting behavior, chosen because nesting in birds is generally viewed as less flexible and less open to change by the effects of experience. If biases and confounding variables are responsible for the relation between unusual feeding behavior and forebrain size, then a relation should also be observed between unusual nesting behavior and forebrain size. If, however, behavioral flexibility and innovation is related to forebrain size, then the relation should be observed for feeding alone. They found a significant relation between forebrain size and feeding innovation but not between forebrain size and nesting innovation.

In addition, Nicolakakis & Lefebvre (2000) calculated interrater reliabilities in the scoring of short notes and controlled for mode of juvenile development, population size, reporting bias, and research effort devoted to each species by adding each of these variables to their analysis of the relation between innovation rate and forebrain size. Finally, the method of independent contrasts was used to include phylogeny in the analysis and was compared to a nonphylogenetic analysis that used multiple regression.

As in earlier studies, the number of species per taxonomic group had a major effect on reports of innovation, but this could be controlled for by calculating expected innovation rates. Population size, reporting bias, and research effort accounted for no significant variation in reported innovation rate for either feeding or nesting, and interrater reliabilities were high. Analysis of the data using independent contrasts produced the same result as multiple regression, a significant effect of forebrain size on feeding innovation but not on nesting innovation.

An analysis of Australasian records yields essentially the same relation between innovation rate and forebrain size found in Europe and North America (Lefebvre et al. 1998) along with some additional information that could be extracted from the Australasian records. One of the journals from which observations of innovative feeding methods were taken changed editorial policy in the middle of the period surveyed, yielding two 28-year periods: 1940–1968, when short notes were contributed primarily by amateur ornithologists, and 1969–1997, when they were contributed primarily by professionals with institutional affiliations. Reported innovation frequencies were highly correlated for the two periods.

Components of the Forebrain

The avian forebrain is made up of many regions serving different sensory systems and integrative functions. Comparative analysis of the kind described above has shown that some forebrain areas are more strongly correlated with innovation rate than are others (Timmermans et al. 2000). Avian brain forebrain nomenclature was recently revised by Reiner et al. (2004), and the following discussion uses the revised terminology with the original designation by Timmermans et al. (2000) in parentheses. The forebrain area most strongly correlated with innovation rate is the mesopallium (hyperstriatum ventrale). Other brain regions, such as the nidopallium (neostriatum), lateral striatum and globus pallidus (striatopallidal complex), and Wulst (Wulst) are positively correlated with innovation frequency but make only nonsignificant contributions when entered in a multiple regression model that includes the mesopallium. The size of many of these areas is correlated. Mesopallium and nidopallium are highly correlated in size, and the size of the mesopallium + nidopallium is highly correlated with total forebrain size. Nevertheless, the results of Timmermans et al. (2000) show that the primary contribution to the relations found between forebrain size and innovation rate is made by the mesopallium, a complex area of the avian brain serving many cognitive functions also served by the mammalian neocortex.

THE PRIMATE BRAIN

Comparative research on the primate brain has a long history, motivated in large part by attempts to trace the evolutionary history of humans and identify the selective pressures that produced the human brain and the unique repertoire of human cognitive capacities. Recent neuroecological research on the evolution of the primate brain has focused on hypothesized selective factors that may have influenced evolution of the primate brain, including social learning, innovative feeding and foraging, tool use, and social manipulation. A recurring theme in recent research has been the relative importance of social versus nonsocial influences on evolution of the primate brain. Neocortex size has been found to correlate with group size, and much current discussion of primate cognition focuses on the evolutionary importance of social manipulation and deception (Byrne & Whiten 1988, Whiten & Byrne 1997). Two studies illustrate recent neuroecological research on the primate brain.

Reader & Laland (2002) used the approach of Lefebvre and his colleagues, described above, to examine the relation between social learning, innovation, and tool use. They collected reports of these three behaviors from journals of primatology, relying on the original authors' descriptions of social learning, tool use, and behavior to adjudicate whether or not the behavior was novel (Reader & Laland 2001). Most of the records of innovation pertained to foraging. They then correlated frequency of social learning, tool use, and innovation with size of the neocortex plus striatum, a set of structures they called the "executive brain." Brainstem size was used as a control variable, and phylogeny was controlled using independent contrasts. Control for research effort devoted to different species consisted of determining the frequency of articles devoted to each species in the journals examined and taking residual values from a plot of the frequency of observed behavior against research effort. This procedure essentially determines whether there is a higher or lower frequency of reports of the behavior of interest given the amount of research effort devoted to that species. Interrater reliability tests were also conducted along with statistical controls for field versus laboratory studies, possible effects of experimental manipulation, food provisioning, and human influences on the primates observed in the corpus of studies examined. They found strong positive associations between two of their three measures of executive brain size and the frequencies of innovation, social learning, and tool use. The same pattern emerged with and without phylogenetic correction. Significant associations were found for both uncorrected measures of neocortex plus striatum and for the ratio of this measure to brainstem size.

Interestingly, Reader & Laland's (2001, 2002) results also show strong correlations between their behavioral measures, that is, between innovation and social learning, innovation and tool use, and social learning and tool use. There are a number of possible interpretations for this pattern of results. It may be that all three are manifestations of a single underlying cognitive capacity. It is also possible that each results from a different underlying cognitive capacity but all three evolved together. The possibility that can be rejected by these data is that there have been tradeoffs, as is sometimes proposed, between social learning and the more asocial innovative acquisition of skills and novel behavior.

Byrne & Corp (2004) performed a similar analysis using frequencies of deception in primate social groups obtained from a survey of researchers conducting long-term field studies of primates. They found significant associations between the frequency of reports of deception (corrected for research effort) and neocortex size. Interestingly, these associations were independent of group size. The authors take these results as support for the idea that social manipulation and tactical deception have played a role in the evolution of large primate brains.

THE NEUROECOLOGICAL APPROACH

A Critique of Neuroecology

The term neuroecology came into general use, ironically, following its use in a critique that took researchers in the field to task on many fronts (Bolhuis & Macphail 2001, Macphail & Bolhuis 2001). Neuroecologists, according to Bolhuis and Macphail, confused the causes and functions of animal behavior, drew unwarranted conclusions from data, and invoked a notion of modularity that differs from Fodor's (1983). A number of their arguments reiterate earlier assertions that memory is a central system with no domain specificity, rather than multiple systems with functional specialization, and that there is no evidence for differences in cognition among species of animals or for associations between brain structure size and cognition (Macphail 1982). Many of the specific points of the critique, especially those regarding interpretation of data, have been rebutted in a series of replies and commentaries (Dwyer & Clayton 2002, Flombaum et al. 2002, Hampton et al. 2002, Healy et al. 2005, MacDougall-Shackleton & Ball 2002, Shettleworth 1998). The consensus that has emerged from the ensuing discussion is that Bolhuis and Macphail misunderstood a number of fundamental ideas in neuroecology and found fault with their own versions of these ideas [though this is not the view of Bolhuis (2005)]. They asserted, for example, that neuroecological research on song learning predicts that male songbirds should be better than females at auditory learning (Bolhuis & Macphail 2001). Bolhuis & Macphail (2001) then describe research showing that this is not so. As MacDougall-Shackleton & Ball (2002) point out, however, there is no reason to expect that male songbirds are better than females in general at auditory learning. Both males and females learn the songs of their local population and learn to recognize and discriminate among songs. The correct prediction is that males are better than females at learning to sing, and the preponderance of empirical evidence shows this. In the exceptional cases in which females do learn to sing, they, too, have song control nuclei of the kind usually found only in males (MacDougall-Shackleton & Ball 1999), which supports the neuroecological prediction of an association between song learning and the song control nuclei (MacDougall-Shackleton & Ball 2002).

Bolhuis and Macphail may also have had expectations for a simpler and more consistent pattern of results in neuroecology than do most researchers in this field. Complicating factors, data that do not fit expectations, and predictions that are disconfirmed are well known to neuroecological researchers and are the norm in any area of the life sciences. To return to the example presented at the very beginning of this chapter, polygynous male meadow voles have larger home ranges than do females, better spatial ability, and a larger hippocampus. These males compete for mates by expanding their home ranges, and males with better spatial ability have an advantage in this competition. Males with larger ranges and better spatial ability should therefore mate with more females and have more offspring. They do mate with more females, but they do not have more offspring (Spritzer et al. 2005b). Males that mate more frequently should produce more offspring, almost of logical necessity, but results of Spritzer et al.'s (2005b) study show that they do not. Researchers must therefore choose between discarding all that has gone before— correlations among behavior, home range size, spatial ability, the hippocampus, and mating frequency—as being in error, or instead conclude that there is still something about the relation between spatial ability and reproductive success that is not understood. Perhaps, as Spritzer et al. (2005b) suppose, the close spacing of female nests in the seminatural enclosures that made it possible to collect data on competition by male meadow voles for mating opportunities eliminated any advantage that males with better spatial ability would normally possess. Perhaps it did not. In any case, unanswered questions are surely the origin of all scientific inquiry (MacDougall-Shackleton & Ball 2002).

A number of points raised by Bolhuis and Macphail are clearly correct, however, and had been addressed earlier within the field of neuroecology. One of these points is that there is a limit to the kinds of questions that can be answered by examining the relative size of parts of the brain. The same criticism could be made, and has been made, of electrophysiological recording, lesion studies, brain imaging, and immediate early gene expression. The point is nevertheless correct. Any one method can only provide certain kinds of information, and answering the most general questions about cognition and the brain requires converging evidence of many kinds. For this reason, neuroecology is increasingly turning to methods that provide different information than can be obtained by examining structure size or changes in structure size. Current research on the hippocampus of food-storing birds, for example, examines patterns of neurogenesis (Barnea & Nottebohm 1994, 1996; Hoshooley & Sherry 2004; Smulders et al. 2000), immediate early gene expression (Smulders & DeVoogd 2000b), NMDA (N-methyl-d-aspartate) receptor activity (Shiflett et al. 2004), and glucocorticoid (Pravosudov 2003) and social influences (Pravosudov & Omanska 2005) on hippocampal anatomy and function.

Future Directions

The central idea of neuroecology is that there are relations between brain structure and cognition that can be predicted from selection pressures that animals are exposed to in the wild. There are at least two ways this could come about. Natural selection, acting on behavioral outcomes, may select from among the naturally occurring variation in neural traits those that more effectively serve the function in question, for example, remembering the spatial location of scattered food caches or producing a large song repertoire. One of the many outcomes of such selection is differences between species in the relative size of different brain areas and correlations between brain structure and specific cognitive abilities. An alternative account of relations between brain structure and cognitive functions is that the brain is not modified by selection for these functions but instead by other selective or nonselective processes in evolution, and the outcome is structural features of the brain that permit certain cognitive functions. The human brain permits reading, for example, but natural selection for reading ability, if there is any, is probably too recent to have had much effect on brain structure. As Lefebvre et al. (1997) note, the correlational approach used in comparative studies cannot distinguish between these two alternatives, which need not be mutually exclusive. If, however, the correlations that have been described between behavior, cognition, and the brain are not the result of selection for specific cognitive functions and neural mechanisms, the challenge is to identify and describe the nonselective or nonspecific processes that have produced these correlations. Finlay & Darlington (1995) proposed changes in the timing of neural development and changes in overall brain size to account for the broad patterns they observed in the size in mammalian brain structures. Their analysis also found few differences among major taxonomic groups, whereas alternative analyses detected significant adaptive modification of components of the mammalian brain (de Winter & Oxnard 2001). Although the nonspecific processes proposed by Finlay & Darlington (1995) may indeed play a role in evolutionary change in the brain, they do not account for the correlations between behavior, cognition, and the brain identified in neuroecological research.

Neuroecology seems at times preoccupied with the size of brain structures, whether the hippocampus, song control nuclei, or other structures. In part, this is mere convenience. Structural size differences are conspicuous, technically easy to measure, and available for many species, whereas more fine-scale measures such as dendritic arborization, patterns of immediate early gene expression, distributions of receptor types, or rates of neurogenesis—that probably do reveal more about how the brain works—are obtained more slowly and are available on far fewer species. In fact, given the many ways brain function could be modified, it is surprising that gross size differences crop up so often in comparisons between species or between the sexes. As noted above, neuroecology is increasingly moving toward more fine-scale analyses of brain structure and function. Several questions remain, however. Central among them is the question of why differences in behavior are so often associated with differences in brain structure size. What does an increase in size provide, in functional terms? Jerison (1973) articulated the "law of proper mass," which states that the relative proportion of the brain devoted to a structure reflects the relative importance in the life of the animal of the function or functions performed by that structure, but this is really a statement of the question.

One way of viewing the problem is in terms of costs of maintaining a brain structure of any size. A large hippocampus may provide increased processing capacity for many hippocampus-dependent cognitive operations, but at a cost. Neural tissue is energetically costly to operate (Laughlin 2001). Systems that act to maintain a neural structure and regulate its activity, such as the neuroendocrine system, may also be costly (MacDougall-Shackleton & Ball 1999). These costs of maintaining an increased structure size limit the resources that can be used in other ways, may force tradeoffs, and result in differences between species, differences between the sexes, and seasonal differences within individuals in brain structure size.

CONCLUSIONS

Neuroecology developed from an increased appreciation of the importance of cognitive processes and their neural correlates within the field of behavioral ecology. It uses phylogenetic comparative methods to identify cognitive processes and neural structures that are associated with specific selective pressures that animals are exposed to in nature. Neuroecological research on species and sex differences in cognition is usually conducted in controlled laboratory settings, and neuroanatomical methods are used to identify species or sex differences in brain regions that play a role in specific cognitive processes. The size of candidate brain structures is often the neuroanatomical correlate examined, but more fine-scale measures of neural structure and activity are increasingly used in neuroecology. This approach has identified a variety of associations between apparent selective pressures that animals are exposed to in the wild and cognitive processes and neural structures. Species and sex differences in the hippocampus of birds and mammals, in the song control nuclei of birds, in the avian forebrain, and in regions of the primate brain have been found that are associated with selective pressures imposed by foraging, mating system, communication, and social organization. The phylogenetic comparative methods used in many of these studies have identified a number of these selective pressures and indicate that natural selection and sexual selection have modified cognitive processes and brain structures across a broad range of animals.

ACKNOWLEDGMENTS

I thank Kevin Laland, Louis Lefebvre, Jeff Lucas, Scott MacDougall-Shackleton, and Bill Roberts for their many helpful comments on the manuscript. Preparation of this paper was supported by the Natural Sciences and Engineering Research Council of Canada.

The *Annual Review of Psychology* is online at http://psych.annualreviews.org

LITERATURE CITED

Abbott ML, Walsh CJ, Storey AE, Stenhouse IJ, Harley CW. 1999. Hippocampal volume is related to complexity of nesting habitat in Leach's storm-petrel, a nocturnal Procellariiform seabird. *Brain Behav. Evol.* 53:271–76

Astié AA, Kacelnik A, Reboreda JC. 1998. Sexual differences in memory in shiny cowbirds. *Anim. Cogn.* 1:77–82

Balda RP, Kamil AC. 1992. Long-term spatial memory in Clark's nutcracker, *Nucifraga columbiana. Anim. Behav.* 44:761–69

Balda RP, Kamil AC, Bednekoff PA. 1997. Predicting cognitive capacities from natural history. *Curr. Ornithol.* 13:333–66

Balda RP, Wiltschko W. 1991. Caching and recovery in scrub jays: transfer of sun-compass directions from shaded to sunny areas. *Condor* 93:1020–23

Barnea A, Nottebohm F. 1994. Seasonal recruitment of hippocampal neurons in adult free-ranging black-capped chickadees. *Proc. Natl. Acad. Sci. USA* 91:11217–21

Barnea A, Nottebohm F. 1996. Recruitment and replacement of hippocampal neurons in young and adult chickadees: an addition to the theory of hippocampal learning. *Proc. Natl. Acad. Sci. USA* 93:714–18

Bayer RD. 1980. Novel use of an unusual food: American robins eating parts of fish. *J. Field Ornithol.* 51:74–75

Beecher MD, Brenowitz EA. 2005. Functional aspects of song learning in songbirds. *Trends Ecol. Evol.* 20:144–49

Bingman VP, Jones T-J, Strasser R, Gagliardo A, Ioalé P. 1995. Homing pigeons, hippocampus and spatial cognition. In *Behavioural Brain Research in Naturalistic and Semi-Naturalistic Settings* (Proceedings of the NATO Advanced Study Institute, Acquafredda di Maratea, Italy, Sept. 10–20, 1994), ed. E Alleva, A Fasolo, H-P Lipp, L Nadel, L Ricceri, pp. 207–23. Dordrecht, The Netherlands: Kluwer Acad.

Bitterman ME. 1975. The comparative analysis of learning. *Science* 188:699–709

Bolhuis JJ. 2005. Function and mechanism in neuroecology: looking for clues. *Anim. Biol.* In press

Bolhuis JJ, Macphail EM. 2001. A critique of the neuroecology of learning and memory. *Trends Cogn. Sci.* 5:426–33

Brenowitz EA, Beecher MD. 2005. Song learning in birds: diversity and plasticity, opportunities and challenges. *Trends Neurosci.* 28:127–32

Broadbent NJ, Colombo M. 2000. Visual and spatial discrimination behavior following hippocampal lesions in pigeons. *Psychobiology* 28:463–75

Brodin A, Ekman J. 1994. Benefits of food hoarding. *Nature* 372:510

Brodin A, Lundborg K. 2003. Is hippocampus volume affected by specialization for food hoarding in birds? *Proc. R. Soc. Lond. B Biol. Sci.* 270:1555–63

Brown TJ, Handford P. 2000. Sound design for vocalizations: quality in the woods, consistency in the fields. *Condor* 102:81–92

Burchsted AE. 1987. Downy woodpecker caches food. *Wilson Bull.* 99:136–37

Byrne RW, Corp N. 2004. Neocortex size predicts deception rate in primates. *Proc. R. Soc. Lond. B Biol. Sci.* 271:1693–99

Byrne RW, Whiten A, eds. 1988. *Machiavellian Intelligence: Social Expertise and the Evolution of Intellect in Monkeys, Apes, and Humans.* Oxford, UK: Clarendon

Clayton NS, Dickinson A. 1998. Episodic-like memory during cache recovery by scrub jays. *Nature* 395:272–74

Clayton NS, Reboreda JC, Kacelnik A. 1997. Seasonal changes of hippocampus volume in parasitic cowbirds. *Behav. Process.* 41:237–43

Clotfelter ED. 1998. What cues do brown-headed cowbirds use to locate red-winged blackbird host nests? *Anim. Behav.* 55:1181–89

Cowie RJ, Krebs JR, Sherry DF. 1981. Food storing by marsh tits. *Anim. Behav.* 29:1252–59

Cullen E. 1957. Adaptations in the kittiwake to cliff-nesting. *Ibis* 99:275–302

Darlington RB, Smulders TV. 2001. Problems with residual analysis. *Anim. Behav.* 62:599–602

Darwin C. 1859. *On the Origin of Species by Means of Natural Selection.* London: John Murray

Darwin C. 1872. *The Expression of the Emotions in Man and Animals.* London: John Murray

DeVoogd TJ, Krebs JR, Healy SD, Purvis A. 1993. Relations between song repertoire size and the volume of brain nuclei related to song: comparative evolutionary analyses amongst oscine birds. *Proc. R. Soc. Lond. B Biol. Sci.* 254:75–82

de Winter W, Oxnard CE. 2001. Evolutionary radiations and convergences in the structural organization of mammalian brains. *Nature* 409:710–14

Duff SJ, Brownlie LA, Sherry DF, Sangster M. 1998. Sun compass orientation and landmark orientation by black-capped chickadees (*Parus atricapillus*). *J. Exp. Psychol. Anim. Behav. Process.* 24:243–53

Dwyer DM, Clayton NS. 2002. A reply to defenders of the faith. *Trends Cogn. Sci.* 6:109–11

Felsenstein J. 1985. Phylogenies and the comparative method. *Am. Nat.* 125:1–15

Ferkin MH, Sorokin ES, Renfroe MW, Johnston RE. 1994. Attractiveness of male odors to females varies directly with plasma testosterone concentration in meadow voles. *Physiol. Behav.* 55:347–53

Finlay BL, Darlington RB. 1995. Linked regularities in the development and evolution of mammalian brains. *Science* 268:1578–84

FitzGerald RW, Madison DM. 1983. Social organization of a free-ranging population of pine voles, *Microtus pinetorum*. *Behav. Ecol. Soc.* 13:183–87

Flombaum JI, Santos LR, Hauser MD. 2002. Neuroecology and psychological modularity. *Trends Cogn. Sci.* 6:106–8

Fodor JA. 1983. *The Modularity of Mind: An Essay on Faculty Psychology.* Cambridge, MA: MIT Press

Forsyth M. 1985. *Buildings for Music.* Cambridge, MA: MIT Press

Gahr M, Sonnenschein E, Wickler W. 1998. Sex difference in the size of the neural song control regions in a dueting songbird with similar song repertoire size of males and females. *J. Neurosci.* 18:1124–31

Galea LAM, Perrot-Sinal TS, Kavaliers M, Ossenkopp K-P. 1999. Relations of hippocampal volume and dentate gyrus width to gonadal hormone levels in male and female meadow voles. *Brain Res.* 821:383–91

Garamszegi LZ, Eens M. 2004. The evolution of hippocampus volume and brain size in relation to food hoarding in birds. *Ecol. Lett.* 7:1216–24

Garamszegi LZ, Lucas JR. 2005. Continental variation in relative hippocampal volume in birds: the phylogenetic extent of the effect and the potential role of winter temperatures. *Biol. Lett.* 1:330–33

Gaulin SJC, FitzGerald RW. 1986. Sex differences in spatial ability: an evolutionary hypothesis and test. *Am. Natur.* 127:74–88

Gaulin SJC, FitzGerald RW. 1989. Sexual selection for spatial-learning ability. *Anim. Behav.* 37:322–31

Gaulin SJC, FitzGerald RW, Wartell MS. 1990. Sex differences in spatial ability and activity in two vole species (*Microtus ochrogaster* and *M. pennsylvanicus*). *J. Comp. Psychol.* 104:88–93

Gaulin SJC, Wartell MS. 1990. Effects of experience and motivation on symmetrical-maze performance in the prairie vole (*Microtus ochrogaster*). *J. Comp. Psychol.* 104:183–89

Gill FB, Slikas B, Sheldon FH. 2005. Phylogeny of titmice (Paridae): II. Species relationships based on sequences of the mitochondrial cytochrome-B gene. *Auk* 122:121–43

Haftorn S. 1956. Contribution to the food biology of tits especially about storing of surplus food. Part IV. A comparative analysis of *Parus atricapillus* L, *P. cristatus*, and *P. ater* L. *K. Norske Vidensk. Selsk. Skr.* 1956:1–54

Hampton RR, Hampstead BM, Murray EA. 2005. Rhesus monkeys (*Macaca mulatta*) demonstrate robust memory for what and where, but not when, in an open-field test of memory. *Learn. Motiv.* 36:245–59

Hampton RR, Healy SD, Shettleworth SJ, Kamil AC. 2002. "Neuroecologists" are not made of straw. *Trends Cogn. Sci.* 6:6–7

Hampton RR, Schwartz BL. 2004. Episodic memory in nonhumans: What, and where, is when? *Curr. Opin. Neurobiol.* 14:192–97

Hampton RR, Sherry DF. 1994. The effects of cache loss on choice of cache sites in black-capped chickadees. *Behav. Ecol.* 5:44–50

Hampton RR, Sherry DF, Shettleworth SJ, Khurgel M, Ivy G. 1995. Hippocampal volume and food-storing behavior are related in parids. *Brain Behav. Evol.* 45:54–61

Hampton RR, Shettleworth SJ. 1996a. Hippocampal lesions impair memory for location but not color in passerine birds. *Behav. Neurosci.* 110:831–35

Hampton RR, Shettleworth SJ. 1996b. Hippocampus and memory in a food-storing and in a nonstoring bird species. *Behav. Neurosci.* 110:946–64

Harvey PH, Krebs JR. 1990. Comparing brains. *Science* 249:140–46

Harvey PH, Mace GM. 1982. Comparisons between taxa and adaptive trends: problems of methodology. In *Current Problems in Sociobiology*, ed. King's Coll. Sociobiol. Group, pp. 343–61. London: Cambridge Univ. Press

Harvey PH, Purvis A. 1991. Comparative methods for explaining adaptation. *Nature* 351:619–24

Healy SD, de Kort SR, Clayton NS. 2005. The hippocampus, spatial memory and food hoarding: a puzzle revisited. *Trends Ecol. Evol.* 20:17–22

Healy SD, Krebs JR. 1992. Food storing and the hippocampus in corvids: Amount and volume are correlated. *Proc. R. Soc. Lond. B Biol. Sci.* 248:241–45

Hitchcock CL, Sherry DF. 1990. Long-term memory for cache sites in the black-capped chickadee. *Anim. Behav.* 40:701–12

Hodos W, Campbell CBG. 1969. Scala naturae: why there is no theory in comparative psychology. *Psychol. Rev.* 76:337–50

Hoshooley JS, Sherry DF. 2004. Neuron production, neuron number, and structure size are seasonally stable in the hippocampus of the food-storing black-capped chickadee (*Poecile atricapillus*). *Behav. Neurosci.* 118:345–55

Iwaniuk AN. 2004. Brood parasitism and brain size in cuckoos: a cautionary tale on the use of modern comparative methods. *Int. J. Comp. Psychol.* 17:17–33

Jacobs LF, Gaulin SJC, Sherry DF, Hoffman GE. 1990. Evolution of spatial cognition: Sex-specific patterns of spatial behavior predict hippocampal size. *Proc. Natl. Acad. Sci. USA* 87:6349–52

Jacobs LF, Spencer WD. 1994. Natural space-use patterns and hippocampal size in kangaroo rats. *Brain Behav. Evol.* 44:125–32

Jerison HJ. 1973. *The Evolution of Brain and Intelligence in Vertebrates.* New York: Academic

Kavaliers M, Ossenkopp K-P, Galea LAM, Kolb B. 1998. Sex differences in spatial learning and prefrontal and parietal cortical dendritic morphology in the meadow vole, *Microtus pennsylvanicus*. *Brain Res.* 810:41–47

Krebs JR, Clayton NS, Hampton RR, Shettleworth SJ. 1995. Effects of photoperiod on food-storing and the hippocampus in birds. *Neuroreport* 6:1701–4

Krebs JR, Davies NB, eds. 1978. *Behavioural Ecology: An Evolutionary Approach.* Oxford, UK: Blackwell Sci.

Krebs JR, Davies NB, eds. 1997. *Behavioural Ecology: An Evolutionary Approach.* Oxford, UK: Blackwell Sci. 4th ed.

Krebs JR, Sherry DF, Healy SD, Perry VH, Vaccarino AL. 1989. Hippocampal specialization of food-storing birds. *Proc. Natl. Acad. Sci. USA* 86:1388–92

Kruger L. 2004. An early illustrated comparative neuroanatomy of the brain: Samuel Collins' *A Systeme of Anatomy* (1685) and the emergence of comparative neurology in 17th century England. *J. Hist. Neurosci.* 13:195–217

Krushinskaya NL. 1966. Some complex forms of feeding behaviour of nut-cracker *Nucifraga caryocatactes*, after removal of old cortex. *Z. Evoluz. Biochim. Fisiol.* II:563–68

Lande R. 1980. Sexual dimorphism, sexual selection, and adaptation in polygenic characters. *Evolution* 34:292–305

Laughlin SB. 2001. Energy as a constraint on the coding and processing of sensory information. *Curr. Opin. Neurobiol.* 11:475–80

Lefebvre L, Gaxiola A, Dawson S, Timmermans S, Rozsa L, Kabai P. 1998. Feeding innovations and forebrain size in Australasian birds. *Behaviour* 135:1077–97

Lefebvre L, Whittle P, Lascaris E, Finkelstein A. 1997. Feeding innovations and forebrain size in birds. *Anim. Behav.* 53:549–60

Leonard ST, Ferkin MH, Johnson MM. 2001. The response of meadow voles to an over-mark in which the two donors differ in gonadal hormone status. *Anim. Behav.* 62:1172–77

Lincoln R, Boxshall G, Clark P. 2001. *A Dictionary of Ecology, Evolution and Systematics.* London: Cambridge Univ. Press

Lucas JR, Brodin AdK SR, Clayton NS. 2004. Does hippocampal size correlate with the degree of caching specialization? *Proc. R. Soc. Lond. B Biol. Sci.* 271:2423–29

Lucas JR, Walter LR. 1991. When should chickadees hoard? Theory and experimental results. *Anim. Behav.* 41:579–601

Ludescher F-B. 1980. Fressen und Verstecken von Sämereien be der Weidenmeise Parus montanus im Jahresverlauf unter konstanten Ernährungsbedingungen. *Ökologie der Vögel* 2:135–44

MacDougall-Shackleton SA, Ball GF. 1999. Comparative studies of sex differences in the song-control system of songbirds. *Trends Neurosci.* 22:432–36

MacDougall-Shackleton SA, Ball GF. 2002. Revising hypotheses does not indicate a flawed approach. *Trends Cogn. Sci.* 6:68–69

MacDougall-Shackleton SA, Sherry DF, Clark AP, Pinkus R, Hernandez AM. 2003. Photoperiodic regulation of food-storing and hippocampus volume in black-capped chickadees *Poecile atricapilla. Anim. Behav.* 65:805–12

Mace R, Holden CJ. 2005. A phylogenetic approach to cultural evolution. *Trends Ecol. Evol.* 20:116–21

Macphail EM. 1982. *Brain and Intelligence in Vertebrates.* Oxford, UK: Clarendon

Macphail EM, Bolhuis JJ. 2001. The evolution of intelligence: adaptive specializations versus general process. *Biol. Rev.* 76:341–64

Madden J. 2001. Sex, bowers and brains. *Proc. R. Soc. Lond. B Biol. Sci.* 268:833–38

Martins EP. 2000. Adaptation and the comparative method. *Trends Ecol. Evol.* 15:296–99

McNamara JM, Houston AI, Krebs JR. 1990. Why hoard? The economics of food storing in tits, *Parus* spp. *Behav. Ecol.* 1:12–23

Morton ES. 1975. Ecological sources of selection on avian sounds. *Am. Natur.* 109:17–34

Nakamura H, Wako Y. 1988. Food storing behaviour of willow tit *Parus montanus. J. Yamashina Inst. Ornithol.* 20:1–20

Nicolakakis N, Lefebvre L. 2000. Forebrain size and innovation rate in European birds: feeding, nesting and confounding variables. *Behaviour* 137:1415–29

Nicolakakis N, Sol D, Lefebvre L. 2003. Behavioural flexibility predicts species richness in birds, but not extinction rate. *Anim. Behav.* 65:445–52

Nieuwenhuys R. 1998. Comparative neuroanatomy: place, principles and programme. In *The Central Nervous System of Vertebrates,* ed. R Nieuwenhuys, HJ ten Donkelaar, C Nicholson, pp. 273–326. Berlin: Springer-Verlag

Nolan V Jr. 1978. The ecology and behavior of the prairie warbler *Dendroica discolor. Ornithol. Monogr.* 26:1–595

Norman RF, Robertson RJ. 1975. Nest-searching behavior in the brown-headed cowbird. *Auk* 92:610–11

Nottebohm F. 1981. A brain for all seasons: cyclical anatomical changes in song control nuclei of the canary brain. *Science* 214:1368–70

Odum EP. 1942. Annual cycle of the black-capped chickadee—3. *Auk* 59:499–531

Omerod BK, Galea LAM. 2003. Reproductive status influences the survival of new cells in the dentate gyrus of adult male meadow voles. *Neurosci. Lett.* 346:25–28

Omerod BK, Lee TT-Y, Galea LAM. 2004. Estradiol enhances neurogenesis in the dentate gyri of adult male meadow voles by increasing the survival of young granule neurons. *Neuroscience* 128:645–54

Portmann A. 1947. Etudes sur la cérébralisation des oiseaux. II. Les indices intra-cérébraux. *Alauda* 15:1–15

Pravosudov VV. 2003. Long-term moderate elevation of corticosterone facilitates avian food-caching behaviour and enhances spatial memory. *Proc. R. Soc. Lond. B Biol. Sci.* 270:2599–604

Pravosudov VV, Omanska A. 2005. Dominance-related changes in spatial memory are associated with changes in hippocampal cell proliferation rates in mountain chickadees. *J. Neurobiol.* 62:31–41

Purvis A, Rambaut A. 1995. Comparative analysis by independent contrasts (CAIC): an Apple Macintosh application for analysing comparative data. *Comput. Appl. Biosci.* 11: 247–51

Reader SM, Laland KN. 2001. Primate innovation: sex, age and social rank. *Int. J. Primatol.* 22:787–805

Reader SM, Laland KN. 2002. Social intelligence, innovation, and enhanced brain size in primates. *Proc. Natl. Acad. Sci. USA* 99: 4436–41

Reboreda JC, Clayton NS, Kacelnik A. 1996. Species and sex differences in hippocampus size in parasitic and non-parasitic cowbirds. *Neuroreport* 7:505–8

Reiner A, Perkel DJ, Bruce LL, Butler AB, Csillag A, et al. 2004. Revised nomenclature for avian telencephalon and some related brainstem nuclei. *J. Comp. Neurol.* 473:377–414

Rheindt FE, Grafe TU, Abouheif E. 2004. Rapidly evolving traits and the comparative method: How important is testing for phylogenetic signal? *Evol. Ecol. Res.* 6:377–96

Ridley M. 1996. *Evolution*. Cambridge, MA: Blackwell Sci.

Roberts WA. 2002. Are animals stuck in time? *Psychol. Bull.* 128:473–89

Rothstein SI, Verner J, Stevens E. 1984. Radiotracking confirms a unique diurnal pattern of spatial occurrence in the parasitic brown-headed cowbird. *Ecology* 65:77–88

Rothstein SI, Yokel DA, Fleischer RC. 1987. Social dominance, mating and spacing systems, female fecundity, and vocal dialects in captive and free-ranging brown-headed cowbirds. In *Current Ornithology*, ed. RF Johnston, pp. 127–85. New York: Plenum

Scott DM. 1991. The time of day of egg laying by the brown-headed cowbird and other icterines. *Can. J. Zool.* 69:2093–99

Sherry DF. 1984. Food storage by black-capped chickadees: memory for the location and contents of caches. *Anim. Behav.* 32:451–64

Sherry DF, Forbes MRL, Khurgel M, Ivy GO. 1993. Females have a larger hippocampus than males in the brood-parasitic brown-headed cowbird. *Proc. Natl. Acad. Sci. USA* 90:7839–43

Sherry DF, Galef BGG Jr, Clark MM. 1996. Sex and intrauterine position influence the size of the gerbil hippocampus. *Physiol. Behav.* 60:1491–94

Sherry DF, Krebs JR, Cowie RJ. 1981. Memory for the location of stored food in marsh tits. *Anim. Behav.* 29:1260–66

Sherry DF, Vaccarino AL. 1989. Hippocampus and memory for food caches in black-capped chickadees. *Behav. Neurosci.* 103:308–18

Sherry DF, Vaccarino AL, Buckenham K, Herz RS. 1989. The hippocampal complex of food-storing birds. *Brain Behav. Evol.* 34: 308–17

Shettleworth SJ. 1998. *Cognition, Evolution, and Behavior*. New York: Oxford Univ. Press

Shettleworth SJ. 2003. Memory and hippocampal specialization in food-storing birds: challenges for research on comparative cognition. *Brain Behav. Evol.* 62:108–16

Shettleworth SJ, Krebs JR. 1982. How marsh tits find their hoards: the roles of site preference and spatial memory. *J. Exp. Psychol. Anim. Behav. Proc.* 8:354–75

Shiflett MW, Smulders TV, Benedict L, DeVoogd TJ. 2003. Reversible inactivation of the hippocampal formation in food-storing black-capped chickadees (*Poecile atricapillus*). *Hippocampus* 13:437–44

Shiflett MW, Tomaszycki ML, Rankin AZ, DeVoogd TJ. 2004. Long-term memory for spatial locations in a food-storing bird (*Poecile atricapilla*) requires activation of NMDA receptors in the hippocampal formation during learning. *Behav. Neurosci.* 118:121–30

Simmons KEL. 1984. House sparrows collecting insects from cars. *Br. Birds* 77:121

Smulders TV, DeVoogd TJ. 2000a. The avian hippocampal formation and memory for hoarded food: spatial learning out in the real world. In *Brain, Perception, Memory*, ed. JJ Bolhuis, pp. 127–48. London: Oxford Univ. Press

Smulders TV, DeVoogd TJ. 2000b. Expression of immediate early genes in the hippocampal formation of the black-capped chickadee (*Poecile atricapillus*) during a food-hoarding task. *Behav. Brain Res.* 114:39–49

Smulders TV, Sasson AD, DeVoogd TJ. 1995. Seasonal variation in hippocampal volume in a food-storing bird, the black-capped chickadee. *J. Neurobiol.* 27:15–25

Smulders TV, Shiflett MW, Sperling AJ, DeVoogd TJ. 2000. Seasonal change in neuron number in the hippocampal formation of a food-hoarding bird: the black-capped chickadee. *J. Neurobiol.* 44:414–22

Sol D, Lefebvre L. 2000. Behavioural flexibility predicts invasion success in birds introduced to New Zealand. *Oikos* 90:599–605

Sol D, Timmermans S, Lefebvre L. 2002. Behavioural flexibility and invasion success in birds. *Anim. Behav.* 63:495–502

Spritzer MD, Meikle DB, Solomon NG. 2005a. Female choice based on male spatial ability and aggressiveness among meadow voles. *Anim. Behav.* 69:1121–30

Spritzer MD, Solomon NG, Meikle DB. 2005b. Influence of scramble competition for mates upon the spatial ability of male meadow voles. *Anim. Behav.* 69:375–86

Stevens TA, Krebs JR. 1986. Retrieval of stored seeds by marsh tits *Parus palustris* in the field. *Ibis* 128:513–25

Striedter GF. 2005. *Principles of Brain Evolution*. Sunderland, MA: Sinauer Assoc.

Székely T, Catchpole CK, DeVoogd A, Marchl Z, DeVoogd TJ. 1996. Evolutionary changes in a song control area of the brain (HVC) are associated with evolutionary changes in song repertoire among European warblers (*Sylviidae*). *Proc. R. Soc. Lond. B Biol. Sci.* 263:607–10

Timmermans S, Lefebvre L, Boire D, Basu P. 2000. Relative size of the hyperstriatum ventrale is the best predictor of feeding innovation rate in birds. *Brain Behav. Evol.* 56:196–203

Tinbergen N. 1963. On aims and methods of ethology. *Zeitschr. Tierpsychol.* 20:410–33

Tomback DF. 1980. How nutcrackers find their seed stores. *Condor* 82:10–19

Tramontin AD, Brenowitz EA. 2000. Seasonal plasticity in the adult brain. *Trends Neurosci.* 23:251–58

Vander Wall SB. 1982. An experimental analysis of cache recovery in Clark's nutcracker. *Anim. Behav.* 30:84–94

Volman SF, Grubb TCJ, Schuett KC. 1997. Relative hippocampal volume in relation to food-storing behavior in four species of woodpeckers. *Brain Behav. Evol.* 49:110–20

Whiten A, Byrne RW, eds. 1997. *Machiavellian Intelligence II: Extensions and Evaluations*. Cambridge, UK: Cambridge Univ. Press

Wiltschko W, Balda RP. 1989. Sun compass orientation in seed-caching scrub jays (*Aphelocoma coerulescens*). *J. Comp. Physiol. A* 164:717–21

Yaskin VA. 1984. Seasonal changes in brain morphology in small mammals. In *Winter Ecology of Small Mammals*, ed. JF Merritt, pp. 183–91. Pittsburgh, PA: Carnegie Mellon Univ. Press

Zeigler HP, Marler P, eds. 2004. *Behavioral Neurobiology of Birdsong*. Vol. 1016. New York: Ann. NY Acad. Sci. 788 pp.

Annu. Rev. Psychol. 2006. 57:199–226
doi: 10.1146/annurev.psych.57.102904.190208
First published online as a Review in Advance on August 11, 2005

THE EVOLUTIONARY PSYCHOLOGY OF FACIAL BEAUTY

Gillian Rhodes

*School of Psychology, University of Western Australia, Crawley, Perth, WA 6009,
Australia; email: gill@psy.uwa.edu.au*

Key Words   facial attractiveness, face perception, evolutionary psychology,
mate choice, adaptation

■ **Abstract**   What makes a face attractive and why do we have the preferences
we do? Emergence of preferences early in development and cross-cultural agreement on attractiveness challenge a long-held view that our preferences reflect arbitrary standards of beauty set by cultures. Averageness, symmetry, and sexual dimorphism are good candidates for biologically based standards of beauty. A critical
review and meta-analyses indicate that all three are attractive in both male and female faces and across cultures. Theorists have proposed that face preferences may be
adaptations for mate choice because attractive traits signal important aspects of mate
quality, such as health. Others have argued that they may simply be by-products of
the way brains process information. Although often presented as alternatives, I argue that both kinds of selection pressures may have shaped our perceptions of facial
beauty.

CONTENTS

0066-4308/06/0110-0199$20.00   **199**

INTRODUCTION

> ... [O]ur inner faculties are *adapted* in advance to the features of the world in which we dwell .... [O]ur various ways of feeling and thinking have grown to be what they are because of their utility in shaping our *reactions* on the outer world.

> (James 1892/1984, p. 11)

There are few more pleasurable sights than a beautiful face. Attractive faces activate reward centers in the brain (Aharon et al. 2001, O'Doherty et al. 2003), they motivate sexual behavior and the development of same-sex alliances (Berscheid & Reis 1998, Berscheid & Walster 1974, Feingold 1990, Rhodes et al. 2005c, Thornhill & Gangestad 1999), and they elicit positive personality attributions (the "what is beautiful is good" stereotype—Dion et al. 1972, Eagly et al. 1991, Langlois et al. 2000) and positive treatment in a variety of settings (Hosoda et al. 2003, Langlois et al. 2000). It is not surprising, therefore, that philosophers, scientists, and ordinary people have long puzzled over what makes a face attractive and why we have the preferences we do (Etcoff 1999).

A long-held view in the social sciences is that standards of beauty are arbitrary cultural conventions (Berry 2000, Etcoff 1999). Even Darwin favored this view after observing large cultural differences in beautification practices (Darwin 1998/1874). However, two observations suggest that some preferences may be part of our biological, rather than our cultural, heritage. First, people in different cultures generally agree on which faces are attractive (Cunningham et al. 1995; Langlois et al. 2000; Perrett et al. 1994, 1998; Rhodes et al. 2001b, 2002; but see Jones & Hill 1993 for weaker agreement). Second, preferences emerge early in development, before cultural standards of beauty are likely to be assimilated (Geldart et al. 1999; Langlois et al. 1987, 1991; Rubenstein et al. 1999, 2002; Samuels et al. 1994; Samuels & Ewy 1985; Slater et al. 1998, 2000).

Because preferences affect mate choice (e.g., Rhodes et al. 2005c), they may have evolved through sexual selection, whereby traits (including preferences) enhance reproductive success. Three candidates have been proposed for sexually selected preferences. The first is a preference for averageness, i.e., proximity to a spatially average face for a population. The second is a preference for bilateral symmetry. The third is a preference for sexual dimorphism, i.e., for feminine traits in female faces and masculine traits in male faces.

These traits have been proposed to signal mate quality so that preferences for them may be adaptations for finding good mates (Gangestad & Thornhill 1997; Penton-Voak & Perrett 2000a; Rhodes & Zebrowitz 2002; Thornhill & Gangestad 1993, 1999; Symons 1979). However, it is also possible that these preferences are by-products of the way brains process information, with no link between preferred traits and mate quality (e.g., Enquist & Arak 1994, Jansson et al. 2002, Johnstone 1994).

The first aim of this review is to assess the appeal of the three candidates for biologically based preferences: for averageness, symmetry, and sexual dimorphism.

The second aim is to understand what evolutionary mechanisms may have shaped these preferences and to try to resolve the debate about whether or not attractive traits signal mate quality.

WHAT MAKES A FACE ATTRACTIVE?

In his excellent book on beauty, Armstrong (2004) argues that beauty cannot be explained by a single principle, such as Hogarth's serpentine line, mathematically harmonious proportions, or a match of form to function. Similarly, there is no gold standard for facial beauty. Components of attractiveness may include averageness, symmetry, sexual dimorphism, a pleasant expression, good grooming, youthfulness (Berry 2000, Cunningham 1986, Etcoff 1999, Rhodes & Zebrowitz 2002, Thornhill & Gangestad 1999), and, for known faces, can reflect nonphysical characteristics, such as how much one likes the person (Kniffin & Wilson 2004).

There may also be different kinds of attractiveness (e.g., sexual attractiveness, attractiveness as a potential ally, cuteness) with different affective and motivational consequences (e.g., sexual arousal, competitiveness, caregiving). However, most studies have simply asked people to judge "attractiveness," which assumes some common aesthetic/affective judgment for faces of both sexes. These judgments appear to reflect sexual attractiveness for opposite-sex faces, with responses correlating almost perfectly with ratings of desirability to date (0.97) or marry (0.93) (Cunningham et al. 1990). They may also elicit judgments of sexual attractiveness (to the opposite sex) for same-sex faces, because men and women generally agree on attractiveness (Langlois et al. 2000). This agreement could reflect the assessment of sexual attractiveness in same-sex faces, to assess their danger as potential rivals for mates, or it could reflect some more generic aesthetic or affective response that is made to all faces. Agreement about which faces are attractive not only occurs between men and women, but also between people from different cultures (e.g., Langlois et al. 2000). Therefore, contrary to the popular maxim that beauty is in the eye of the beholder, preferences are not highly idiosyncratic and we can sensibly ask, what makes a face attractive?

Here I focus on averageness, symmetry, and sexual dimorphism, the three candidates for biologically based preferences. There is now a critical mass of studies, making a meta-analytic, as well as conceptual, review useful. Meta-analyses combine data across studies, giving estimates of the strength of the association (effect size) between attractiveness and given traits. They will also allow us to examine whether preferences generalize across sex and race of faces, and to assess formally the effects of potentially important methodological variables.

Separate meta-analyses were conducted for averageness, symmetry, and sexual dimorphism. The results are summarized in Table 1 (for details, see the Supplemental Material link for Electronic Appendices 1–3 in the online version of this chapter at http://www.annualreviews.org/). Effect size R's are reported, but analyses used Zr's. An initial sexual dimorphism meta-analysis showed a large effect of face sex, $F(1,38) = 26.16$, $p < 0.0001$ (0.64 ± 0.39, $N = 18$, female faces;

TABLE 1   Summary of effect size (R) statistics for the attractiveness of averageness, symmetry, and sexual dimorphism. All calculations were conducted on Zr's

	Attractiveness and averageness	Attractiveness and symmetry	Attractiveness and femininity	Attractiveness and masculinity
All faces				
Mean effect size (ES)	0.52	0.25	0.64	−0.12
Standard deviation	0.41	0.34	0.39	0.55
95% Confidence interval	0.42–0.61	0.16–0.33	0.51–0.74	−0.35–0.14
Number of studies	20	23	10	15
Number of face samples	45	63	18	22
Mean weighted ES (by N faces)	0.54	0.23	0.61	0.16
Normal faces only				
Mean ES	0.40	0.23	0.64	0.35
Standard deviation	0.33	0.23	0.45	0.20
95% Confidence interval	0.29–0.51	0.17–0.30	0.41–79	0.23–0.45
Number of distinct face samples	27	42	9	10
Mean weighted ES (by N faces)	0.40	0.24	0.58	0.27

-0.12 ± 0.55, $N = 22$, male faces), so separate meta-analyses were conducted for female and male faces (see Supplemental Material link for Electronic Appendix 3 in the online version of this chapter at http://www.annualreviews.org/). Effects sizes are interpreted following Cohen (1977), with 0.10, 0.30, and 0.50 considered small, medium, and large, respectively.

Averageness

An average face has mathematically average trait values for a population (Figure 1). Faces that are high in averageness are low in distinctiveness. Averageness would be a good candidate for a biologically based preference, if it signals mate quality.

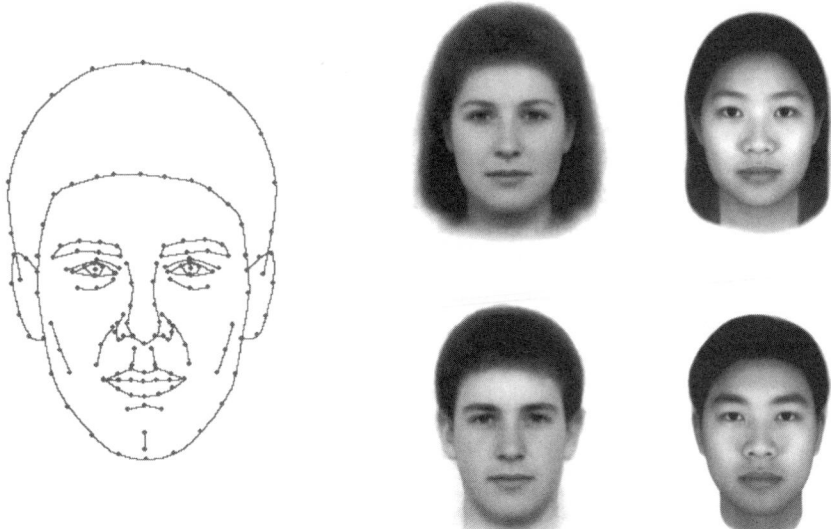

Figure 1 Landmark points used to create averaged composites. Lines have been added to illustrate how points capture the layout of internal features and the face outline, but only the points are actually used. Averaged composites of Caucasian and Chinese female (*top*) and male (*bottom*) faces. Each composite is created from 24 faces.

Several theorists have proposed that average traits reflect developmental stability, i.e., the ability to withstand stress during development (e.g., Møller & Swaddle 1997, Thornhill & Møller 1997) and heterozygosity, which may increase disease resistance (Gangestad & Buss 1993, Thornhill & Gangestad 1993). Average traits may also be functionally optimal (e.g., average nose optimal for breathing), which should improve condition (Koeslag 1990, Symons 1979). Therefore, averageness could signal aspects of mate quality, such as good condition and/or heritable resistance to disease. The proposed link between averageness and mate quality is examined below. Here I consider whether average faces are indeed attractive.

In an influential paper, Langlois and her colleagues (1990) demonstrated the appeal of computer-generated averaged composites of faces. These were generally more attractive than the component faces, and as faces were added (up to about 16), the composites became more attractive.

These counterintuitive results were met with skepticism. Surely beauty is extraordinary and cannot be explained by averageness, which is ordinary. Critics suggested that perhaps the composites were not really average (Alley & Cunningham 1991, Benson & Perrett 1992, Pittenger 1991), and they were right. The composites had nonaverage features (large eyes and lips) because feature outlines were not aligned prior to blending, and they had smooth complexions and a soft-focus look, which are attractive but not average (Benson & Perrett 1992, Little & Hancock 2002). However, composites remained attractive when features were aligned (O'Toole et al. 1999, Rhodes et al. 1999b, Rhodes & Tremewan 1996) and when same (or no) complexion appeared on all the images (Little & Hancock 2002, O'Toole et al. 1999, Rhodes et al. 1999b, Rhodes & Tremewan 1996). Therefore, the appeal of average composites is not due to enlarged features or smooth complexions.

Critics also suggested that reduction of (randomly distributed) facial asymmetries by averaging might explain the appeal of composites (Alley & Cunningham 1991). However, averageness remains attractive when the effects of symmetry are statistically controlled (Rhodes et al. 1999b) and when profiles are used, so that symmetry is unaffected (Valentine et al. 2004). Nor is the appeal of averaged composites due to their youthful appearance or pleasant expressions. These are attractive traits (Cunningham et al. 1995, Zebrowitz et al. 1993), but average faces remain attractive when these effects are statistically controlled (O'Toole et al. 1999, Rhodes et al. 1999b). Finally, the appeal of average faces is unlikely to be an artifact of combining idiosyncratic preferences across participants, because inter-rater agreement on attractiveness is high (Langlois et al. 2000). Therefore, although composites can have some nonaverage features, these do not fully explain their appeal.

Converging evidence for the appeal of average faces comes from studies using normal, unmanipulated faces. Typical faces, which are closer to the population average, are consistently rated as more attractive than distinctive faces (e.g., Light et al. 1981; Morris & Wickham 2001; O'Toole et al. 1994; Rhodes & Tremewan 1996; Rhodes et al. 1999b, 2005c; Vokey & Read 1992). Furthermore, the attractiveness of individual faces can be increased (or reduced) by moving their configurations toward (or away from) an average configuration for that sex (O'Toole et al. 1999, Rhodes et al. 1999b, Rhodes & Tremewan 1996).

The meta-analysis showed a large effect of averageness on attractiveness (0.52 ± 0.41, M $\pm$ SD; 95% CI $= 0.42$–0.61, $N = 45$) (Table 1). The effect size was larger for manipulated images (0.67 ± 0.43, $N = 18$) than for real faces (0.40 ± 0.33, $N = 27$), t(43) $= 3.20$, $p < 0.003$, consistent with the idea that some (nonaverage) features of composites may contribute to their appeal. However, the appeal of averageness was still moderate (0.40) for real faces. Examination of the funnel plot (see Supplemental Material link for Electronic Appendix 1 in the online version of this chapter at http://www.annualreviews.org/) suggested little publication bias. Funnel plots show effect size as a function of sample size. Variability is expected to decrease with increasing sample size, and effect sizes should be distributed symmetrically around the large sample mean. An asymmetric distribution indicates likely publication bias.

Although most studies use ratings of averageness, a few have attempted to measure it. Effect sizes were smaller for measurements (0.09 ± 0.36, $N = 5$) than for ratings (0.47 ± 0.28, $N = 22$), t(25) $= 2.76$, $p < 0.02$. Current measurement methods are poor, capturing only a limited part of a face's structure and nothing of its fattiness or skin quality (see Rhodes et al. 2005c for discussion), and ratings may be the more valid measure. They covary with physical manipulations of averageness (e.g., Rhodes & Tremewan 1996) and draw on a perceptual system that is highly sensitive to subtle facial variations. Whatever indices are used, they should be independent (e.g., rated by different participants) because effect sizes are inflated when they are not (0.73 ± 0.42, $N = 8$, nonindependent; 0.47 ± 0.38, $N = 37$, independent), t(43) = 2.66, $p < 0.02$. A medium effect size is obtained when independent indices are used with real faces (0.37 ± 0.33, 95% CI = 0.24 –0.49, $N = 23$). This is the best estimate of the effect size.

The appeal of averageness did not differ significantly for male (0.57 ± 0.56, $N = 12$) and female (0.41 ± 0.20, $N = 15$) faces, t(25) = 1.24, $p = 0.225$. Most studies have combined male and female ratings because men and women agree on attractiveness (Langlois et al. 2000). However, effect sizes are lower for opposite-sex ratings (0.30 ± 0.33, $N = 13$) than when same-sex ratings are included (0.71 ± 0.51, $N = 2$, same-sex; 0.61 ± 0.40, $N = 28$, combined), F(2,40) = 4.99, $p < 0.02$ (opposite versus combined differ on Scheffé S, $p < 0.02$). Therefore, it may be wise to keep opposite-sex and same-sex ratings distinct in future studies.

Most studies have used Western faces and participants. However, average faces may also be attractive in non-Western cultures (to own-race raters) because there was no significant effect of face-race, t(27) = 0.03, $p = 0.98$ (0.59 ± 0.41, $N = 20$, Western; 0.59 ± 0.39, $N = 9$, non-Western). These results are consistent with a perceptual mechanism that favors average faces, although what is average will certainly vary between populations. Perceptual adaptation results suggest that mental representations of what is average (for a given sex and race) are constantly updated by experience (Rhodes et al. 2003b).

Clearly, average faces are attractive. However, there are some important caveats. These results don't mean that *all* attractive faces are average (contra Langlois & Roggman 1990) or that average faces are *optimally* attractive (see below). Nevertheless, average facial configurations are more attractive than most faces, and this preference must be explained.

Symmetry

Over the past decade, research on the attractiveness of facial symmetry has been prolific, motivated by the idea that symmetry advertises mate quality (e.g., Gangestad & Thornhill 1997, Gangestad et al. 1994, Palmer & Strobeck 1986, Parsons 1990, Polak 2003, Thornhill & Gangestad 1999, Thornhill & Møller 1997, Watson & Thornhill 1994). Fluctuating asymmetries (FAs) are nondirectional (random) deviations from perfect symmetry in bilaterally paired traits. In nonhuman animals, FA in body traits reflects developmental instability (inability to withstand stress during development), increasing with inbreeding, homozygosity, parasite load, poor nutrition, and pollution (Møller & Swaddle 1997, Parsons 1990, Polak 2003). In humans, body FA increases with inbreeding, premature birth, psychosis, and mental retardation (Livshits & Kobylianski 1991). If similar relationships exist for facial FA, then it could signal mate quality.

Symmetric bodies are attractive to many animals, including humans (Brooks & Pomiankowski 1994, Concar 1995, Gangestad & Simpson 2000, Thornhill &

Gangestad 1994, Watson & Thornhill 1994). But are symmetric faces attractive? Early studies suggested that they were not, with normal (slightly asymmetric) faces preferred to perfectly symmetric versions (Kowner 1996, Langlois et al. 1994, Samuels et al. 1994, Swaddle & Cuthill 1995). However, more recent studies found that perfectly symmetric faces were more attractive than the original, slightly asymmetric, faces (e.g., Perrett et al. 1999; Rhodes et al. 1998, 1999a,b) and that their appeal could not be explained by any associated increase in averageness (Rhodes et al. 1999b) or change in skin texture (Perrett et al. 1999, Rhodes et al. 1999a).

The discrepancy seems to reflect differences in how the perfectly symmetric faces were made (Rhodes et al. 1999b). In the early studies, symmetric faces were made by reflecting each hemiface about the vertical midline to create two symmetric chimeras (Kowner 1996, Samuels et al. 1994). However, these chimeras typically display structural abnormalities in aspect ratios and the sizes of midline features. For example, if the nose bends sideways, then the nose will be abnormally wide in one chimera and abnormally narrow in the other. Slight deviations from front-on views in the original photographs result in abnormally wide or narrow chimeras and abnormal eye spacing. Attractiveness decreases with deviations from average facial configurations, so these abnormalities will offset any preference for symmetry per se. When perfectly symmetric faces are made by blending normal and mirror-reversed images (Figure 2), they are more attractive than the original, slightly asymmetric, faces (e.g., Perrett et al. 1999; Rhodes et al. 1998, 1999a,b). The only exception is a study by Swaddle & Cuthill (1995), but failure to control expression and remove blemishes before morphing could have contributed to failure to find a symmetry preference in this study. The meta-analysis confirmed that symmetry is attractive when blends are used ($0.43 \pm 0.32, N = 16$) but not when chimeras are used ($-0.62 \pm 0.30, N = 3$), $t(17) = 5.71, p < 0.0001$.

Converging evidence for the appeal of facial symmetry comes from studies with normal faces. Natural variations in symmetry covary with attractiveness (Jones & Hill 1993, for some ethnic groups; Grammer & Thornhill 1994; Mealey et al. 1999; Rikowski & Grammer 1999; Rhodes et al. 1998, 1999a,b; Scheib et al. 1999; Zebrowitz et al. 1996). Symmetry remains attractive when the effects of averageness are statistically controlled, which suggests that the two contribute independently to attractiveness (Rhodes et al. 1999b). The meta-analysis showed a medium effect size for normal faces ($0.23 \pm 0.23, N = 42$). All but one of these studies used independent indices of symmetry and attractiveness. The funnel plot showed no evidence of publication bias for normal faces, but a possible bias (to publish large effects) for blends (see Supplemental Material link for Electronic Appendix 2 in the online version of this chapter at http://www.annualreviews.org/).

The meta-analysis revealed no significant effects of sex of face, $F(2,60) = 1.79$, $p = 0.18 (0.17 \pm 0.36, N = 26$, female; $0.26 \pm 0.20, N = 27$, male; 0.40 ± 0.50, $N = 10$, combined); sex of rater, $F(2,57) = 0.40, p = 0.67 (0.31 \pm 0.20, N = 28$, opposite-sex; $0.13 \pm 0.01, N = 2$, same-sex; $0.28 \pm 0.35, N = 30$, combined); or race of face, $F(2,34) = 2.28, p = 0.12 (0.32 \pm 0.25, N = 20$, Western;

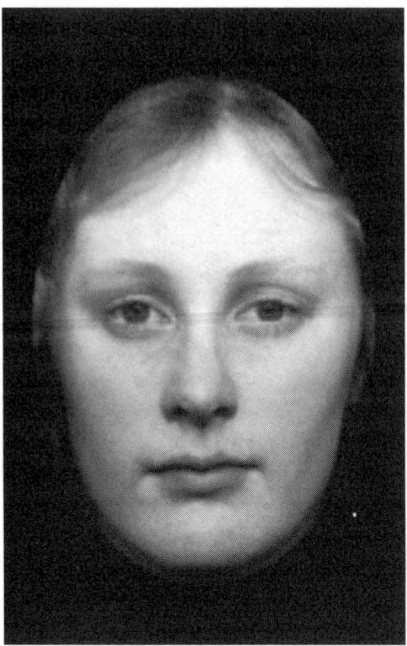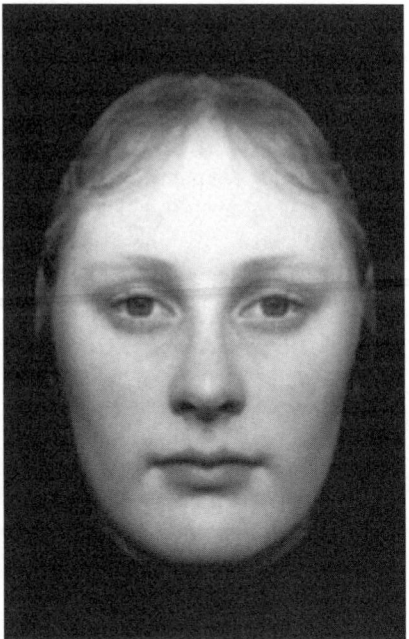

Figure 2   Original face (*left*) and symmetric blend (*right*).

0.11 ± 0.34, $N = 9$, non-Western; 0.26 ± 0.19, $N = 8$, both). In all cases, the effect sizes were small to medium.

Although motivated by the idea that symmetry might signal mate quality, few studies have isolated FA, which is the theoretically relevant construct. This is important because directional asymmetries (DAs), which are consistent across a population and do not signal mate quality, also occur in faces (Simmons et al. 2004). Jones & Hill (1993) attempted to measure FA but measured only six traits. They also failed to demonstrate repeatability, which is important because FA is distributed as measurement error and needs to be distinguished from it (Simmons et al. 2004). Other studies claim to measure FA, but do not. For example, asymmetry is often measured by summing the offsets (from a vertical midline) of the midpoints of a few bilaterally paired landmarks (see, e.g., Grammer & Thornhill 1994). In a perfectly symmetric face, the sum would be zero. Although referred to as facial FA, this measure includes DA. Interestingly, symmetry ratings seem to reflect FA, but not DA, and may be a valid proxy for FA (Simmons et al. 2004). People apparently adapt to DA, which is consistent across a population, and notice deviations from it. Ratings change systematically when facial symmetry is manipulated, confirming their validity (see, e.g., Rhodes et al. 1999b), and are probably sensitive to more subtle facial asymmetries than are current measurement methods. Therefore, on theoretical grounds, ratings may be preferable to measurements.

The meta-analysis, however, showed no significant effect of whether symmetry was rated (0.30 ± 0.24, $N = 14$) or measured (0.19 ± 0.22, $N = 28$), $F(1,40) = 2.38$, $p = 0.13$.

Scheib and colleagues (1999) have argued that the apparent appeal of symmetry is not driven by perceptions of symmetry. They found an association between symmetry (of the whole face) and attractiveness when only a hemiface was shown (Scheib et al. 1999). They argued that the appeal of symmetry must therefore be mediated by the appeal of some other correlated trait because symmetry is not present in hemifaces. However, there certainly are cues to symmetry in hemifaces. For example, if more than half of the nose or mouth is visible then the face cannot be symmetric. Therefore, these results may not challenge the appeal of symmetry.

Sexual Dimorphism

Male and female faces diverge at puberty (Farkas 1988). In males, testosterone stimulates the growth of the jaw, cheekbones, brow ridges, center of the face (from brow to bottom of nose), and facial hair. In females, growth of these traits is inhibited by estrogen, which may also increase lip size (see Thornhill & Møller 1997 for a review). Because sexual dimorphism increases at puberty, sexually dimorphic traits signal sexual maturity and reproductive potential (Johnston & Franklin 1993; Symons 1979, 1992, 1995; Thornhill & Gangestad 1996).

Sexual dimorphism may also signal differences in mate quality between sexually mature individuals. In animals, large sexual ornaments can signal low parasite loadings (Hamilton & Zuk 1982, Møller 1990, Wedekind 1992), although they do not always do so (Getty 2000, Møller et al. 1999). They can also signal immunocompetence, possibly because testosterone stresses the immune system, so that only healthy males can afford large male traits (Folstad & Karter 1992, Møller et al. 1999, Peters 2000). Perhaps masculine facial traits could also signal health and immunocompetence (Thornhill & Gangestad 1993, 1999). So too could feminine traits, if high levels of female hormones also stress the immune system (see Rhodes et al. 2003a for discussion). Masculine traits may also honestly signal dominance and status, which enhance mate value (Buss 1989, Mueller & Mazur 1996).

For these reasons, a preference for masculinity in male faces (and perhaps also femininity in female faces) is a good candidate for a biologically based preference. Many animals, including humans, find extreme sexually dimorphic body traits attractive (Andersson 1994). But is sexual dimorphism attractive in faces?

FEMININITY   Femininity is clearly attractive in female faces. Whether feminine traits are measured (Cunningham 1986, Cunningham et al. 1995, Johnston & Franklin 1993, Jones & Hill 1993, Koehler et al. 2004), rated (Bruce et al. 1994, Dunkle & Francis 1990, Koehler et al. 2004, O'Toole et al. 1998, Rhodes et al. 2003a), or manipulated (Johnston et al. 2001, Perrett et al. 1998, Rhodes et al. 2000), they are attractive. Furthermore, composites of very attractive female faces have more feminine features (a smaller chin and higher cheekbones) and are preferred to more average composites (Perrett et al. 1994). Exaggeration of feminine features further increases attractiveness (Johnston & Franklin 1993; Perrett et al. 1994, 1998; Rhodes et al. 2000; Russell 2003). Finally, when people generate beautiful female faces on a computer, they produce faces with more feminine traits (smaller chins, smaller lower face area, fuller lips) than average (Johnston & Franklin 1993).

Overall, femininity is strongly attractive (0.64 ± 0.39, 95% CI = 0.51–0.74, $N = 18$), with large effect sizes whether normal (0.64 ± 0.46, $N = 9$) or manipulated (0.64 ± 0.34, $N = 9$) images are used. Most studies combined data from male and female raters, so the effect of rater sex could not be examined. The preference generalizes across face race, at least for Caucasian, Asian, and Jamaican faces (Penton-Voak et al. 2004, Perrett et al. 1998, Rhodes et al. 2000), with no significant effect of face race, $F(2,8) = 0.87$, $p = 0.45$ (0.73 ± 0.34, $N = 6$, Western; 0.57 ± 0.39, $N = 4$, non-Western; 0.53 ± 0, $N = 1$, both). O'Toole et al. (1998) have suggested that female attractiveness may be virtually synonymous with femininity because attractiveness predicts time taken to classify the sex of a female face almost as well as its femininity.

Most studies used independent measures of attractiveness and femininity. Those that did not use independent measures yielded marginally larger effect sizes (0.82 ± 0.21, $N = 3$) than those that did (0.58 ± 0.38, $N = 15$), $F(1,16) = 4.29$, $p < 0.06$, supporting the need for independent measures, although the effect remained large when independent indices were used. Too few studies were available to assess possible publication bias in the funnel plot (see Supplemental Material link for Electronic Appendix 3 in the online version of this chapter at http://www.annualreviews.org/).

MASCULINITY   The appeal of masculine traits is less clear. An early study using schematic faces indicated that masculinized male faces (thick brows, thin lips, square chins, and small eyes) were preferred to feminized ones (Keating 1985), but more recent studies using photographic sex continua generally show a preference for feminized male faces (Penton-Voak et al. 2004, Perrett et al. 1998, Rhodes et al. 2000; but see Johnston et al. 2001). The meta-analysis confirmed that masculinity is unattractive when these manipulated faces are used (-0.47 ± 0.51, $N = 12$). Perrett and colleagues (1998) suggest that this preference may reflect the perception of more positive personality traits (less dominant, warmer, more honest and cooperative, and more likely to be a good parent) in less masculine faces.

In these studies, masculinity was manipulated by varying the differences of an averaged male composite from an averaged female composite. But averaged male composites do not capture masculine traits well (for related concerns, see Johnston et al. 2001, Meyer & Quong 1999, Swaddle & Reierson 2002). Male traits like coarse skin textures and square jaws are generally lost in the averaging process, making male composites look less masculine than individual male faces (Little & Hancock 2002). Sex continua made using these composites may therefore tell us little about the optimal level of masculinity. They may also bias responses against the masculinized shapes that are inconsistent with the feminine skin textures displayed. When testosterone-related traits are manipulated in individual male faces, no preference for feminization (or masculinization) was observed (Swaddle & Reierson 2002).

Studies with normal faces present quite a different picture. Ratings of masculinity correlate positively with attractiveness, although the associations are weaker than for femininity (Cunningham et al. 1990, Gillen 1981, Koehler et al. 2004, Neave et al. 2003, O'Toole et al. 1998, Rhodes et al. 2003a, Scheib et al. 1999). Measurement studies also suggest that masculine traits, such as large chins, can be attractive in male faces (Cunningham et al. 1990, Grammer & Thornhill 1994, Penton-Voak et al. 2001, Scheib et al. 1999), although there are limitations to these studies. Few traits may be measured, and even then results may be inconsistent across traits (e.g., Cunningham et al. 1990), and sexual dimorphism of the chosen traits is rarely validated (for exceptions, see Koehler et al. 2004, Penton-Voak et al. 2001). The meta-analysis confirmed that masculinity is attractive for normal male faces ($0.35 \pm 0.20, N = 10$), but not for faces from sex continua (-0.47 ± 0.51, $N = 12$), $F(1,20) = 4.12, p < 0.0002$. There was no significant effect of whether or not independent indices were used for normal faces, $F(1,8) = 0.09, p = 0.77$ ($0.36 \pm 0.27, N = 5$, independent; $0.32 \pm 0.13, N = 5$, nonindependent). The funnel plot indicated a possible publication bias against small effects for normal faces (see Supplemental Material link for Electronic Appendix 3 in the online version of this chapter at http://www.annualreviews.org/).

Both average and masculine traits contribute (independently) to male attractiveness (Little & Hancock 2002, O'Toole et al. 1998). There may also be curvilinear components to the relationship between masculinity and attractiveness, indicating a preference for moderate rather than extreme levels of masculinity (Cunningham et al. 1990). There are insufficient data to determine whether masculinity is attractive to both males and females, and in non-Western faces.

MENSTRUAL CYCLE EFFECTS   Women's preferences shift toward relatively masculine faces during the fertile phase of the menstrual cycle (for women not on oral contraceptives) (Frost 1994, Johnston et al. 2001, Penton-Voak et al. 1999, Penton-Voak & Perrett 2000b). Women in the fertile phase find darker (more masculine) complexions more attractive in male (but not female) Caucasian faces (although lighter complexions were always optimal) (Frost 1994). More masculine images on male-female shape continua are preferred in the fertile phase of the cycle, although the preferred image varies from feminized (Penton-Voak et al. 1999) to average (Penton-Voak & Perrett 2000b) to masculinized (Johnston et al. 2001). Although these continua do not represent masculinity veridically (see above), they do capture *relative* masculinity. Rated masculinity and dominance (Perrett et al. 1998), and the size of some male traits (chin length and eyebrow thickness) (Rhodes et al. 2000), all increase with increasing "masculinization" of the images. Therefore, relatively more masculine traits are preferred when conception is likely. This cyclic shift has been interpreted as evidence for adaptive preferences that are tuned to good genes when conception is likely (especially for short-term mates or extrapair partners) (Perrett et al. 1998). This interpretation requires that masculine traits are honest signals of mate quality, an assumption that is examined below.

Summary

Averageness and symmetry are both attractive in male and female faces, with medium to large effect sizes in all cases. Sexual dimorphism is also attractive. Femininity is attractive in female faces and is preferred to averageness. Masculinity is also attractive in male faces, although the effect is smaller than for female faces, and average traits also contribute (independently) to male attractiveness. Reported preferences for feminized male faces appear to be an artifact of using sex continua that do not adequately capture sexual dimorphism. Preferences for averageness, symmetry, and femininity generalize across race of face. It remains to be seen whether the masculinity preference generalizes across race. Finally, note that if averaged composites of male faces fail to display typical levels of masculinity, as suggested above, then the conclusion that averageness is attractive in male faces must rest primarily on the data from real faces.

THE EVOLUTION OF PREFERENCES

What selection pressures might have shaped the evolution of these preferences? To the extent that preferences influence mate choice (see, e.g., Rhodes et al. 2005c), they could be sexually selected. In sexual selection, preferences evolve because they enhance reproductive success (Andersson 1994, Barrett et al. 2002). Sexual selection can also arise from competition between same-sex individuals (displays and fights), but that component is not considered here. There are several models of sexual selection, and a central distinction is whether attractive traits signal mate quality (for reviews, see Andersson 1994, Andersson & Iwasa 1996, Cronin 1991).

Preferences could evolve in the absence of any link between attractive traits and mate quality if attractive individuals have offspring who are preferred as mates (Fisher 1915). This Fisherian runaway selection can in principle drive the evolution of extreme sexual ornaments like the peacock's tail, although it cannot explain how preferences for arbitrary traits arise initially. The model requires that both preferences and attractive traits are heritable and evolve together. Nothing is known about whether face preferences or attractive facial traits are heritable.

Alternatively, attractive traits could signal mate quality so that preferences increase offspring viability (see, e.g., Hamilton & Zuk 1982, Zahavi 1975). Attractive mates would provide direct benefits, such as resources, parental care, or reduced risk of contagion, and/or indirect genetic benefits, such as heritable resistance to disease. Evidence for genetic benefits has been found in several species (see, e.g., Møller & Alatalo 1999). The success of this "good genes" model has motivated much of the work on human face preferences and fueled suggestions that face preferences are adaptations for mate choice (Etcoff 1999; Fink & Penton-Voak 2002; Grammer et al. 2003; Johnston & Franklin 1993; Symons 1979; Thornhill et al. 2003; Thornhill & Gangestad 1993, 1999; Thornhill & Møller 1997).

However, preferences can also result as "by-products" of the way brains process information (Endler & Basolo 1998, Ryan & Rand 1993). In these models, attractive traits elicit strong responses from perceptual systems. Such models may explain why preferences emerge for some traits rather than others, and they can even explain intriguing cases of preferences for traits that don't occur in conspecifics (e.g., Basolo 1990). Although initially developed to account for the evolutionary origin of preferences (e.g., Ryan & Rand 1993), they have sometimes been presented as alternatives to mate quality accounts of the origin and maintenance of preferences (e.g., Enquist et al. 2002).

In the following two sections, I consider how face preferences might have evolved. Are preferences adaptations for mate choice, with attractive traits signaling mate quality? Or are they by-products of the way brains process information? Of course, multiple selection pressures can shape preferences (see, e.g., Weary et al. 1993), and both mate quality and by-product models may be needed to understand the evolution of these preferences.

Preferences as Adaptations for Mate Choice

Adaptations are specialized mechanisms that evolved to solve a specific problem (Williams 1966). On the mate quality account, face preferences are adaptations for mate choice. In this view, the psychological mechanisms used to assess attractiveness should show evidence of design for identifying good mates (Thornhill & Gangestad 1999). For example, faces that look healthy should be perceived as attractive, and they are (Grammer & Thornhill 1994, Henderson & Anglin 2003, Jones et al. 2001, Kalick et al. 1998). However, such results could reflect a powerful attractiveness halo effect, whereby positive traits like health are indiscriminately attributed to attractive individuals. One study has attempted to rule out a halo account by showing that symmetry looks healthy when attractiveness is statistically controlled, but it's not clear how this association reflects mechanisms for assessing attractiveness (Jones et al. 2001).

Many researchers have attempted to test the mate quality hypothesis by examining whether attractive traits currently reflect mate quality. This approach has been challenged because good nutrition and modern medicine could have broken any links with health (just as modern contraception breaks links with reproductive success) (Daly & Wilson 1999; Thornhill & Gangestad 1996, 1999). Nevertheless, it is informative about the selection pressures that maintain preferences, and to the extent that the past resembles the present, it may be informative about past selection pressures.

Quality has many components—health, intelligence, fertility, parental care potential—but most research has focused on whether attractive facial traits signal health. The anatomical complexity of faces would make them susceptible to stressors during development, and our expertise as face perceivers would make us sensitive to any resulting variation (Peterson & Rhodes 2003). So it is plausible that faces might signal health and that we would be sensitive to any such signals. We saw above that attractive faces are perceived as healthy, but is this honest advertising?

ATTRACTIVENESS AND HEALTH   Meta-analyses suggest a weak association of attractiveness with mental health and a moderate association with physical health (Feingold 1992, Langlois et al. 2000). However, the latter result was based on only five studies, some of which used dubious health measures (e.g., self-reported symptoms over brief periods). More recently, Hume & Montgomerie (2001) reported a moderate association of attractiveness with physical health for women but not for men, using self-reported lifetime incidence and severity of diseases.

The study with the best lifetime health data comes from Kalick and colleagues (1998). They studied a large sample for which records of the incidence and severity of infectious diseases were available from the Institute of Human Development. Furthermore, these individuals were born in the 1920s, prior to the use of antibiotics and vaccinations that may disrupt links between attractiveness and health. There was no significant relationship between attractiveness at age 17 and health (or number of offspring) either during development or later in life. However, a recent reanalysis of these data found a moderate association between attractiveness at 17 and later (adult) health for faces below the median in attractiveness (Zebrowitz & Rhodes 2004). Interestingly, attractiveness in a mate is valued more in societies with high parasitism rates and poorer health (Gangestad & Buss 1993).

Male facial attractiveness is also associated with heterozygosity in the major histocompatibility complex, which plays an important role in immune function (Roberts et al. 2005), indicating a possible link with immunocompetence. Attractiveness is moderately associated with longevity (Henderson & Anglin 2003), weakly associated with physical fitness, independent of current exercise levels (Honekopp et al. 2004), and moderately to strongly associated with indices of sperm quality (Soler et al. 2003).

Taken together, these studies suggest links between facial attractiveness and health, at least when the organism is sufficiently challenged. However, the evidence is far from strong. Several studies need replication and many are methodologically weak, with poor health measures (e.g., Shackelford & Larsen 1999) or small samples (Henderson & Anglin 2003). Of course, not all components of attractiveness are expected to signal health (e.g., pleasant expressions). Below, I consider those that are.

AVERAGENESS AND HEALTH   Marked deviations from facial averageness occur in some chromosomal disorders (Hoyme 1994, Thornhill & Møller 1997). In the Institute of Human Development sample, first studied by Kalick and colleagues

(1998), facial averageness at 17 years was moderately associated with childhood health for males and weakly associated with current annual health for females (Rhodes et al. 2001c). These associations were driven by faces below median averageness (Zebrowitz & Rhodes 2004). These results indicate a link between facial averageness and health in both clinical and nonclinical samples. However, this conclusion rests on a single nonclinical sample. Clearly, replication is needed.

SYMMETRY AND HEALTH   There is little evidence that human facial symmetry signals health. The best evidence is that facial asymmetries are associated with some chromosomal disorders (Hoyme 1994, Thornhill & Møller 1997). However, without evidence that similar asymmetries do not occur in healthy individuals, we cannot be sure that facial asymmetry is a valid signal of ill health.

Furthermore, despite numerous attempts, no studies have found a convincing link between facial symmetry and health in nonclinical samples. Neither rated nor measured facial symmetry was associated with health at any point during development in the Institute of Human Development sample (Rhodes et al. 2001c). Weak associations have been reported between measured facial asymmetry and a few self-reported health symptoms over a brief period in a student sample, but the results failed to replicate in a second sample (Shackelford & Larsen 1997). Moreover, more than 1000 correlations were examined, raising the probability of type I statistical errors. Hume & Montgomerie (2001) found weak, nonsignificant associations between asymmetry (combined body and face) and self-reported lifetime health problems. No clear associations have been found between facial asymmetry and self-reported health symptoms or physiological fitness (Honekopp et al. 2004, Tomkinson & Olds 2000).

Could it be that a preference for facial symmetry evolved because of a past link with health that has been broken by modern medicine? Evidence for a link between symmetry and health in populations from harsher environments would support such a hypothesis. However, in the absence of such evidence, and the fact that links between health and averageness have not been broken, the broken link hypothesis is unconvincing.

Could these largely negative results reflect failure to isolate FA, which is the theoretically relevant variable? Perhaps yes, but symmetry ratings, which may be a good proxy for FA (Simmons et al. 2004), also showed little association with health (Rhodes et al. 2001c). Interestingly, meta-analyses have cast doubt on links between FA and health (condition) in nonhuman animals (Polak 2003, Tomkins & Simmons 2003).

SEXUAL DIMORPHISM AND HEALTH   Many studies indicate a link between secondary sexual traits and health in male animals (e.g., Møller et al. 1999). Limited human data suggest a link between sexually dimorphic traits and health in male faces. In the Institute of Human Development sample, facial masculinity was weakly, but significantly, associated with adolescent health in males (Rhodes et al.

2003a). Again, this link was restricted to faces that were below the median in masculinity, suggesting that low levels of masculinity signal poor health (Zebrowitz & Rhodes 2004). Curiously, although femininity is more attractive than masculinity, no link was found with health for female faces (Rhodes et al. 2003a).

SUMMARY AND IMPLICATIONS   Facial attractiveness and some of its components may have modest associations with health, although the evidence is far from overwhelming. The link may be strongest when stress is greatest, with unattractive deviations from averageness and symmetry associated with some chromosomal disorders and associations in nonclinical samples often limited to faces below the median in attractiveness. In nonclinical samples, links with health have been found for averageness and masculinity (male faces) but not for symmetry or femininity (female faces).

Before interpreting these results, we should consider their limitations. Health generally has not been measured well. Subjective and unvalidated self-report measures of illnesses or symptoms often are used. These are vulnerable to memory failures and biases whereby unattractive individuals, who may be unhappy because of poorer treatment (see, e.g., Langlois et al. 2000), recall more negative experiences (see, e.g., Teasdale & Russell 1983) than do more attractive individuals. Self-reports of recent symptoms are less susceptible to memory biases but provide limited information about health. Only the Institute for Human Development sample has health scores based on detailed, lifetime medical records. Overall, the number of studies is small, and relatively few unpublished data sets with no association between appearance and health could change the picture. More studies are needed that use samples for which objective, detailed health information is available. Samples from traditional societies, where modern medical interventions are limited, would also be informative if good health information was available.

Notwithstanding these caveats, the reported associations of health with attractiveness and some of its components suggest that preferences are not arbitrary, but instead may be adaptations for mate choice. In some cases, the associations were restricted to faces below the median in attractiveness, possibly reflecting stronger selection pressure to avoid low-quality mates than to make distinctions among higher-quality individuals.

Little is known about whether attractive individuals provide indirect genetic benefits, such as heritable resistance to disease, or direct benefits, such as reduced risk of contagion or better parental care, or both. The better treatment and outcomes afforded attractive individuals could contribute to any direct benefits. Any preference for genetically heterozygous individuals would presumably evolve via direct benefits because heterozygosity is not heritable. The same would be true for the preference for averageness, if its health benefits result from heterozygosity (Gangestad & Buss 1993, Thornhill & Gangestad 1993). However, some heritable benefits seem likely, given the heritability of health (Bouchard et al. 1990, Flint & Goodwin 1999, Reed & Dick 2003, Winkelman et al. 2000).

Femininity is the strongest component of female attractiveness, but it showed no association with health (although only one study has looked for this). Femininity may signal fertility rather than health per se (Johnston 2000, Johnston & Franklin 1993, Symons 1979). The reasoning is that high estrogen/androgen ratios are associated with both feminine characteristics (e.g., small jaw, full lips) and fertility. A preference for feminine faces, therefore, would target sexually mature females. Facial femininity could also signal individual differences in fertility in adult females, to the extent that femininity declines with age.

The hallmark of an adaptation is specialized design (Williams 1966). The shift to prefer more masculine male faces at the fertile phase of the menstrual cycle could be a specialization for obtaining indirect genetic benefits when conception is likely, given that masculinity signals health (Rhodes et al. 2003a). However, it remains to be seen whether the health benefits are heritable. An increased preference for healthy-looking faces in the luteal (postfertile) phase of the menstrual cycle has been interpreted as a specialization for obtaining direct benefits, such as reduced risk of contagion, after conception (Jones et al. 2004). Interestingly, no cyclic change has been found in the preference for facial symmetry (Koehler et al. 2002), which appears to be a poorer indicator of health.

Another possible specialization is a preference for mixed-race faces, which look healthier than single-race faces (Rhodes et al. 2005b). If parents from different races are more likely to have different locally adapted gene complexes than are parents from the same race, then a preference for mixed-race faces could be a specialization for obtaining heterozygous mates with enhanced disease resistance. Alternatively, a preference for mixed-race faces could be an inbreeding avoidance mechanism.

Restriction of preferences to opposite-sex faces could indicate specialized design for mate choice. However, there is no evidence for such restriction (see meta-analyses). Nor does a restriction of preference seem likely, given the similarity of male and female faces; its absence is certainly not evidence against preferences being adaptations for mate choice.

Preferences as By-Products of How Brains Process Information

By-product accounts attribute preferences to general information processing mechanisms that evolved through natural selection, in the absence of any link with mate quality. However, there does seem to be a link between attractive traits and health, so where does this leave by-product accounts? One possibility is that multiple selection pressures have shaped preferences (Weary et al. 1993). For example, attractive traits may arise as by-products of information processing systems but subsequently may evolve into honest indicators of mate quality (Garcia & Ramirez 2005). Alternatively, information-processing mechanisms may determine which of many honest indicators of mate quality come to be preferred.

A variety of information-processing mechanisms has been proposed to contribute to the evolution of preferences. Symmetry and averageness preferences have both been attributed to generalization effects in recognition (Enquist & Arak 1994, Jansson et al. 2002, Johnstone 1994). When trained to treat slightly asymmetric patterns as members of the same category, generalization produces strong responses to the symmetric category prototype or average. Preferences for extreme sexual dimorphism have been attributed to learning mechanisms that produce "peak shift," whereby extreme exemplars generate stronger responses than do the training exemplars in discrimination learning (Enquist & Arak 1994, Enquist et al. 2002, Guilford & Dawkins 1991, Weary et al. 1993).

Support for these accounts initially came from neural network simulations, in which preferences emerged from a variety of training situations in the absence of any link between the preferred traits and mate quality. These simulations may not behave like real biological recognition systems (Dawkins & Guilford 1995), but studies with animals and humans yield similar results (Ghirlanda et al. 2002, Jansson et al. 2002, Rhodes 1996). It remains an open question, however, whether the natural environment provides the kind of "training" needed to induce the face preferences that we have, although attempts have been made to address this question for animal preferences (Weary et al. 1993). Nor is it obvious that strong responses in recognition tasks are the same as preferences, which have affective and motivational components.

A preference for average (and symmetric) faces could also be a by-product of their subjective familiarity and a preference for familiar stimuli (Bornstein 1989, Halberstadt et al. 2003, Langlois & Roggman 1990, Langlois et al. 1994, Light et al. 1981, Rhodes et al. 2001a, Zajonc 1968). It is currently unclear just how familiarity and associated perceptual fluency (Reber et al. 2004) contribute to these preferences (Corneille et al. 2005, Langlois et al. 1994, Monin 2003), although the appeal of average faces does not seem to be a generalized mere exposure effect (Halberstadt et al. 2003; Rhodes et al. 2001a, 2005a).

If preferences are by-products of the way that brains process information, then they should not be restricted to potential mates but should occur widely for familiar stimuli. And they do. Average exemplars are attractive in every category examined (Halberstadt & Rhodes 2000, 2003; Halberstadt et al. 2003), and symmetry is attractive for many stimuli (Corballis & Beale 1976, Kubovy 2000). The generality of these preferences suggests that general information-processing mechanisms contribute to them. An interesting exception may be inverted faces, for which a symmetry preference is not found (Little & Jones 2003). However, this result is not inconsistent with recognition by-product accounts that require experience with a class of objects for preferences to emerge because inverted faces are rarely seen (see, e.g., Enquist et al. 2002).

The original goal of by-product accounts of preferences was to explain the ultimate (evolutionary) causes of preferences. However, they are also informative about their proximate causes, i.e., the psychological mechanisms that currently generate preferences. The studies reviewed above suggest that a variety of information-processing mechanisms contribute to our preferences. These include mechanisms that abstract category prototypes and generalize responses from exemplars to prototypes and learning mechanisms that respond strongly to extreme exemplars.

CONCLUSIONS AND FUTURE DIRECTIONS

An evolutionary perspective in psychology is not new, as the William James quote at the outset of this chapter indicates. However, the past decade has seen evolutionary psychology emerge as a distinct field within psychology (Barkow et al. 1992, Barrett et al. 2002, Pinker 1997). In this chapter, we have seen how an evolutionary perspective has shaped research on facial attractiveness. We have seen that averageness, symmetry, and sexual dimorphism are attractive in both male and female faces (contrary to recent claims that feminine male faces are attractive). We have seen some evidence that attractive traits may signal health, which is an important aspect of mate quality, although the evidence is far from compelling. And we have seen that the way our brains process information also shapes our preferences.

There are many exciting directions for future research. More studies are needed on whether facial attractiveness and its components signal health and other aspects of mate quality. Recently, male facial attractiveness has been linked to genetic heterozygosity at sites involved in immune function. Future studies should determine which components of male attractiveness (masculinity, averageness, symmetry) mediate this link, and whether female attractiveness is also linked to heterozygosity at these sites. A more direct test of a link between attractiveness and immunocompetence could also be done by challenging the immune system.

We know little about whether preferences generate heritable genetic benefits as proposed by the good genes model. We know little about the heritability of attractive facial traits and face preferences, as required by both Fisherian and good genes models. We know little about how facial attractiveness interacts with body attractiveness to determine overall attractiveness. We know that newborn infants prefer to look at faces that adults find attractive but know little about what traits they prefer. We know little about whether preferences change during development (e.g., at puberty). We know little about individual differences in face preferences, and whether they reflect different optimal strategies for individuals of differing mate value (Little et al. 2001, Penton-Voak et al. 2003) or self-similarity preferences (Buston & Emlen 2003, De Bruine 2004). We know that experience affects what we find attractive (Perrett et al. 2002, 2003; Rhodes et al. 2003b), but we know little about the temporal dynamics of these effects, including whether there are sensitive periods in which experience has stronger effects and whether sexual imprinting occurs in humans (Little & Perrett 2002). Clearly, the evolutionary psychology of facial attractiveness is just beginning!

ACKNOWLEDGMENTS

This work was supported by the Australian Research Council. I thank Leigh Simmons, Leslie Zebrowitz, Jamin Halberstadt, Marianne Peters, Dave Perrett, and Daphne Maurer for stimulating discussions about these issues. I also thank Leigh Simmons, Daphne Maurer, Hugh Wilson, Fran Wilkinson, Linda Jeffery, and members of the Facelab for comments on an earlier version of the manuscript. I thank Chris Winkler for assistance with the literature searches and Louise Ewing for assistance with literature searches and manuscript preparation.

The *Annual Review of Psychology* is online at http://psych.annualreviews.org

LITERATURE CITED

Aharon I, Etcoff NL, Ariely D, Chabris CF, O'Connor E, Breiter HC. 2001. Beautiful faces have variable reward value: fMRI and behavioral evidence. *Neuron* 32:537–51

Alley TR, Cunningham MR. 1991. Averaged faces are attractive, but very attractive faces are not average. *Psychol. Sci.* 2:123–25

Andersson M. 1994. *Sexual Selection.* Princeton, NJ: Princeton Univ. Press

Andersson M, Iwasa Y. 1996. Sexual selection. *Trends Ecol. Evol.* 11:53–58

Armstrong J. 2004. *The Secret Power of Beauty: Why Happiness is in the Eye of the Beholder.* London: Allen Lane

Barkow JH, Cosmides L, Tooby J, eds. 1992. *The Adapted Mind.* New York: Oxford Univ. Press

Barrett L, Dunbar R, Lycett J. 2002. *Human Evolutionary Psychology.* Princeton, NJ: Princeton Univ. Press

Basolo AL. 1990. Female preference predates the evolution of the sword in sword-tail fish. *Science* 250:808–10

Benson P, Perrett D. 1992. Face to face with the perfect image. *New Sci.* 1809:32–35

Berry DS. 2000. Attractiveness, attraction, and sexual selection: evolutionary perspectives on the form and function of physical attractiveness. In *Advances in Experimental Social Psychology*, ed. MP Zanna, 32: 273–342. San Diego, CA: Academic

Berscheid E, Reis HT. 1998. Attraction and close relationships. In *The Handbook of Social Psychology*, ed. DT Gilbert, ST Fiske,

G Lindzey, pp. 193–281. New York/London: Oxford Univ. Press. 4th ed.

Berscheid E, Walster E. 1974. Physical attractiveness. *Adv. Exp. Soc. Psychol.* 7:157–15

Bornstein RF. 1989. Exposure and affect: overview and meta-analysis of research, 1968–1987. *Psychol. Bull.* 106:265–89

Bouchard TJ, Lykken DT, McGue M, Segal NL, Tellegen A. 1990. Sources of human psychological differences: the Minnesota study of twins reared apart. *Science* 250:223–50

Brooks M, Pomiankowski A. 1994. Symmetry is in the eye of the beholder. *Trends Ecol. Evol.* 9:201–2

Bruce V, Burton A, Dench N. 1994. What's distinctive about a distinctive face? *Q. J. Exp. Psychol.* 47A:119–41

Buss DM. 1989. Sex differences in human mate preferences: evolutionary hypotheses tested in 37 cultures. *Behav. Brain Sci.* 12:1–49

Buston PM, Emlen ST. 2003. Cognitive processes underlying mate choice: the relationship between self perception and mate preference in Western society. *Proc. Natl. Acad. Sci. USA* 100:8805–10

Cohen J. 1977. *Statistical Power Analysis for the Behavioural Sciences.* New York: Academic. Rev. ed.

Concar D. 1995. Sex and the symmetrical body. *New Sci.* 146:40–44

Corballis MC, Beale IL. 1976. *The Psychology of Left and Right.* Hillsdale, NJ: Erlbaum

Corneille O, Monin B, Pleyers G. 2005. Is positivity a cue or a response option? Warm-glow vs. evaluative-matching in the familiarity for attractive and not-so-attractive faces. *J. Exp. Soc. Psychol.* 41(4):431–37

Cronin H. 1991. *The Ant and the Peacock: Altruism and Sexual Selection from Darwin to Today.* Cambridge: Cambridge Univ. Press

Cunningham MR. 1986. Measuring the physical in physical attractiveness: quasi-experiments on the sociobiology of female facial beauty. *J. Personal. Soc. Psychol.* 50: 925–35

Cunningham MR, Barbee AP, Pike CL. 1990. What do women want? Facialmetric assessment of multiple motives in the perception of male facial physical attractiveness. *J. Personal. Soc. Psychol.* 59:61–72

Cunningham MR, Roberts AR, Barbee AP, Druen PB, Wu C-H. 1995. "Their ideas of beauty are, on the whole, the same as ours": consistency and variability in the cross-cultural perception of female physical attractiveness. *J. Personal. Soc. Psychol.* 68:261–79

Daly M, Wilson MI. 1999. Human evolutionary psychology and animal behaviour. *Anim. Behav.* 57:509–19

Darwin C. 1998/1874. *The Descent of Man.* Amherst, NY: Prometheus

Dawkins MS, Guilford T. 1995. What are conventional signals? *Anim. Behav.* 49:1689–95

De Bruine L. 2004. Facial resemblance increases the attractiveness of same-sex faces more than other-sex faces. *Proc. R. Soc. Lond. Ser. B Biol. Sci.* 271:2085–90

Dion K, Berscheid E, Walster E. 1972. What is beautiful is good. *J. Personal. Soc. Psychol.* 24:285–90

Dunkle JH, Francis PL. 1990. The role of facial masculinity/femininity in the attribution of homosexuality. *Sex Roles* 23:157–67

Eagly AH, Ashmore RD, Makhijani MG, Longo LC. 1991. What is beautiful is good: a meta-analytic review of research on the physical attractiveness stereotype. *Psychol. Bull.* 110:109–28

Endler JA, Basolo AL. 1998. Sensory ecology, receiver biases and sexual selection. *Trends Ecol. Evol.* 13:415–20

Enquist M, Arak A. 1994. Symmetry, beauty and evolution. *Nature* 372:169–72

Enquist M, Ghirlanda S, Lundquist D, Wachtmeister CA. 2002. An ethological theory of attractiveness. See Rhodes & Zebrowitz 2002, pp. 127–51

Etcoff N. 1999. *Survival of the Prettiest: The Science of Beauty.* New York: Anchor/Doubleday. 325 pp.

Farkas LG. 1988. Age- and sex-related changes in facial proportions. In *Anthropometric Proportions in Medicine*, ed. LG Farkas, IR Munro, pp. 29–56. Springfield, IL: Thomas

Feingold A. 1990. Gender differences in effects of physical attractiveness on romantic attraction: comparison across five research domains. *J. Personal. Soc. Psychol.* 59:981–93

Feingold A. 1992. Good-looking people are not what we think. *Psychol. Bull.* 111:304–41

Fink B, Penton-Voak I. 2002. Evolutionary psychology of facial attractiveness. *Curr. Dir. Psychol. Sci.* 11:154–58

Fisher RA. 1915. The evolution of sexual preference. *Eugen. Rev.* 7:184–92

Flint J, Goodwin G. 1999. Psychiatric genetics: a genetic basis for health? *Curr. Biol.* 9: R326–28

Folstad I, Karter AJ. 1992. Parasites, bright males, and the immunocompetence handicap. *Am. Nat.* 139:603–22

Frost P. 1994. Preference for darker faces in photographs at different phases on the menstrual cycle: preliminary assessment of evidence for a hormonal relationship. *Percept. Mot. Skills* 79:507–14

Gangestad SW, Buss DM. 1993. Pathogen prevalence and human mate preferences. *Ethol. Sociobiol.* 14:89–96

Gangestad SW, Simpson JA. 2000. The evolution of human mating: tradeoffs and strategic pluralism. *Behav. Brain Sci.* 23:573–87

Gangestad SW, Thornhill R. 1997. Human sexual selection and developmental stability. In *Evolutionary Social Psychology*, ed. JA Simpson, DT Kenrick, pp. 169–96. Hillsdale, NJ: Erlbaum

Gangestad SW, Thornhill R. 2003. Facial

masculinity and fluctuating asymmetry. *Evol. Hum. Behav.* 24:231–41

Gangestad SW, Thornhill R, Yeo RA. 1994. Facial attractiveness, developmental stability, and fluctuating asymmetry. *Ethol. Sociobiol.* 15:73–85

Garcia CM, Ramirez E. 2005. Evidence that sensory traps can evolve into honest signals. *Nature* 434:501–5

Geldart S, Maurer D, Carney K. 1999. Effects of eye size on adults' aesthetic ratings of faces and 5-month-olds' looking times. *Perception* 28:361–74

Getty T. 2000. Signalling health versus parasites. *Am. Nat.* 159:363–71

Ghirlanda S, Jansson L, Enquist M. 2002. Chickens prefer beautiful humans. *Hum. Nat.* 13:383–89

Gillen B. 1981. Physical attractiveness: a determinant of two types of goodness. *Personal. Soc. Psychol. Bull.* 7:384–87

Grammer K, Fink B, Moller AP, Thornhill R. 2003. Darwinian aesthetics: sexual selection and the biology of beauty. *Biol. Rev.* 78:385–407

Grammer K, Thornhill R. 1994. Human (*Homo sapiens*) facial attractiveness and sexual selection: the role of symmetry and averageness. *J. Comp. Psychol.* 108:233–42

Guilford T, Dawkins MS. 1991. Receiver psychology and the evolution of animal signals. *Anim. Behav.* 42:1–14

Halberstadt J, Rhodes G. 2000. The attractiveness of nonface averages: implications for an evolutionary explanation of the attractiveness of average faces. *Psychol. Sci.* 11:285–89

Halberstadt J, Rhodes G. 2003. It's not just average faces that are attractive: computer-manipulated averageness makes birds, fish, and automobiles attractive. *Psychon. Bull. Rev.* 10:149–56

Halberstadt J, Rhodes G, Catty S. 2003. Subjective and objective familiarity as explanations for the attraction to average faces. In *Advances in Psychology Research*, ed. SP Shovov, 22:35–49. New York: Nova Sci.

Hamilton WD, Zuk M. 1982. Heritable true fitness and bright birds: a role for parasites? *Science* 218:384–87

Henderson JJA, Anglin JM. 2003. Facial attractiveness predicts longevity. *Evol. Hum. Behav.* 24:351–56

Honekopp J, Bartholome T, Jansen G. 2004. Facial attractiveness, symmetry and physical fitness in young women. *Hum. Nat.* 15:147–67

Hosoda M, Stone-Romero EF, Coats G. 2003. The effects of physical attractiveness on job-related outcomes: a meta-analysis of experimental studies. *Pers. Psychol.* 56:431–62

Hoyme HE. 1994. Minor anomalies: diagnostic clues to aberrant human morphogenesis. In *Developmental Instability: Its Origins and Evolutionary Implications*, ed. TA Markow, pp. 309–17. Dordrecht, The Netherlands: Kluwer Acad.

Hume DK, Montgomerie R. 2001. Facial attractiveness signals different aspects of "quality" in women and men. *Evol. Hum. Behav.* 22:93–112

James W. 1892/1984. *Psychology, Briefer Course*. Cambridge, MA: Harvard Univ. Press

Jansson L, Forkman B, Enquist M. 2002. Experimental evidence of receiver bias for symmetry. *Anim. Behav.* 63:617–21

Johnston VS. 2000. Female facial beauty: the fertility hypothesis. *Pragmatics Cogn.* 8:107–22

Johnston VS, Franklin M. 1993. Is beauty in the eye of the beholder? *Ethol. Sociobiol.* 14:183–99

Johnston VS, Hagel R, Franklin M, Fink B, Grammer K. 2001. Male facial attractiveness: evidence for hormone-mediated adaptive design. *Evol. Hum. Behav.* 22:251–67

Johnstone RA. 1994. Female preference for symmetrical males as a by-product of selection for mate recognition. *Nature* 372:172–75

Jones BC, Little AC, Burt D, Perrett DI. 2004. When facial attractiveness is only skin deep. *Perception* 33:569–76

Jones BC, Little AC, Penton-Voak IS, Tiddeman BP, Burt DM, Perrett DI. 2001. Facial symmetry and judgements of apparent health: support for a "good genes" explanation of the attractiveness-symmetry relationship. *Evol. Hum. Behav.* 22:417–29

Jones D, Hill K. 1993. Criteria of facial attractiveness in five populations. *Hum. Nat.* 4: 271–96

Kalick S, Zebrowitz LA, Langlois JH, Johnson RM. 1998. Does human facial attractiveness honestly advertise health? Longitudinal data on an evolutionary question. *Psychol. Sci.* 9:8–13

Keating CF. 1985. Gender and the physiognomy of dominance and attractiveness. *Soc. Psychol. Q.* 48:61–70

Kniffin K, Wilson DS. 2004. The effect of nonphysical traits on the perception of physical attractiveness: three naturalistic studies. *Evol. Hum. Behav.* 25:88–101

Koehler N, Rhodes G, Simmons LW. 2002. Are human female preferences for symmetrical male faces enhanced when conception is likely? *Anim. Behav.* 64:233–38

Koehler N, Simmons LW, Rhodes G, Peters M. 2004. The relationship between sexual dimorphism in human faces and fluctuating asymmetry. *Proc. R. Soc. Lond. Ser. B Biol. Sci.* 271:S233–36

Koeslag JH. 1990. Koinophilia groups sexual creatures into species, promotes stasis, and stabilizes sexual behavior. *J. Theor. Biol.* 144:15–35

Kowner R. 1996. Facial asymmetry and attractiveness judgment in developmental perspective. *J. Exp. Psychol. Hum. Percept. Perform.* 22:662–75

Kubovy M. 2000. Visual and design arts. In *Encyclopedia of Psychology*, ed. AE Kazdin, pp. 188–93. London: Oxford Univ. Press

Langlois JH, Kalakanis L, Rubenstein AJ, Larson A, Hallam M, Smoot M. 2000. Maxims or myths of beauty? A meta-analytic and theoretical review. *Psychol. Bull.* 126:390–423

Langlois JH, Ritter JM, Roggman LA, Vaughn LS. 1991. Facial diversity and infant preferences for attractive faces. *Dev. Psychol.* 27: 79–84

Langlois JH, Roggman LA. 1990. Attractive faces are only average. *Psychol. Sci.* 1:115–21

Langlois JH, Roggman LA, Casey RJ, Ritter JM, Reiser-Danner LA, Jenkins VY. 1987. Infant preferences for attractive faces: rudiments of a stereotype? *Dev. Psychol.* 23:363–69

Langlois JH, Roggman LA, Musselman L. 1994. What is average and what is not average about attractive faces? *Psychol. Sci.* 5:214–20

Langlois JH, Roggman LA, Reiser-Danner LA. 1990. Infants' differential responses to attractive and unattractive faces. *Dev. Psychol.* 26:153–59

Light LL, Hollander S, Kayra-Stuart F. 1981. Why attractive people are harder to remember. *Personal. Soc. Psychol. Bull.* 7:269–76

Little AC, Burt DM, Penton-Voak IS, Perrett DI. 2001. Self-perceived attractiveness influences human female preferences for sexual dimorphism and symmetry in male faces. *Proc. R. Soc. Lond. Ser. B Biol. Sci.* 268:39–44

Little AC, Hancock PJB. 2002. The role of masculinity and distinctiveness in judgments of human male facial attractiveness. *Br. J. Psychol.* 93:451–64

Little AC, Jones B. 2003. Evidence against perceptual bias views for symmetry preferences in human faces. *Proc. R. Soc. Lond. Ser. B Biol. Sci.* 270:1759–63

Little AC, Perrett DI. 2002. Putting beauty back in the eye of the beholder. *Psychologist* 15:28–32

Livshits G, Kobyliansky E. 1991. Fluctuating asymmetry as a possible measure of developmental homeostasis in humans: a review. *Hum. Biol.* 63:441–66

Mealey L, Bridgstock R, Townsend GC. 1999. Symmetry and perceived facial attractiveness: a monozygotic co-twin comparison. *J. Personal. Soc. Psychol.* 76:151–58

Meyer DA, Quong MW. 1999. The bio-logic of facial geometry. *Nature* 397:661–62

Møller AP. 1990. Effects of a haematophagus mite on the barn swallow (*Hirundo rustics*):

a test of the Hamilton and Zuk hypothesis. *Evolution* 44:771–84

Møller AP, Alatalo RV. 1999. Good genes effects in sexual selection. *Proc. R. Soc. Lond. Ser. B Biol. Sci.* 266:85–91

Møller AP, Christe P, Lux E. 1999. Parasitism, host immune function, and sexual selection. *Q. Rev. Biol.* 74:3–74

Møller AP, Swaddle JP. 1997. *Asymmetry, Developmental Stability and Evolution.* New York: Oxford Univ. Press

Monin B. 2003. The warm glow heuristic: when liking leads to familiarity. *J. Personal. Soc. Psychol.* 85:1035–48

Morris PE, Wickham LHV. 2001. Typicality and face recognition: a critical re-evaluation of the two factor theory. *Q. J. Exp. Psychol. A* 54:863–77

Mueller U, Mazur A. 1996. Facial dominance of West Point cadets as a predictor of later military rank. *Soc. Forces* 74:823–50

Neave N, Laing S, Fink B, Manning JT. 2003. Second to fourth digit ratio, testosterone and perceived male dominance. *Proc. R. Soc. Lond. Ser. B Biol. Sci.* 270:2167–72

O'Doherty J, Winston J, Critchley H, Perrett D, Burt DM, Dolan RJ. 2003. Beauty in a smile: the role of medial orbitofrontal cortex in facial attractiveness. *Neuropsychologia* 41:147–55

O'Toole AJ, Deffenbacher KA, Valentin D, Abdi H. 1994. Structural aspects of face recognition and the other-race effect. *Mem. Cogn.* 22:208–24

O'Toole AJ, Deffenbacher KA, Valentin D, McKee K, Huff D, Abdi H. 1998. The perception of face gender: the role of stimulus structure in recognition and classification. *Mem. Cogn.* 26:146–60

O'Toole AJ, Price T, Vetter T, Bartlett JC, Blanz V. 1999. 3D shape and 2D surface textures of human faces: the role of "averages" in attractiveness and age. *Image Vis. Comput.* 18:9–19

Palmer AC, Strobeck C. 1986. Fluctuating asymmetry: measurement, analysis, pattern. *Annu. Rev. Ecol. Syst.* 17:391–421

Parsons PA. 1990. Fluctuating asymmetry: an epigenetic measure of stress. *Biol. Rev.* 65:131–45

Penton-Voak IS, Jacobson A, Trivers R. 2004. Populational differences in attractiveness judgments of male and female faces: comparing British and Jamaican samples. *Evol. Hum. Behav.* 25:355–70

Penton-Voak IS, Jones BC, Little AC, Baker S, Tiddeman BP, et al. 2001. Symmetry, sexual dimorphism in facial proportions and male facial attractiveness. *Proc. R. Soc. Lond. Ser. B Biol. Sci.* 268:1617–23

Penton-Voak IS, Little AC, Jones BC, Burt DM, Tiddeman BP, Perrett DI. 2003. Female condition influences preferences for sexual dimorphism in faces of male humans (*Homo sapiens*). *J. Comp. Psychol.* 117:264–71

Penton-Voak IS, Perrett DI. 2000a. Consistency and individual differences in facial attractiveness judgements: an evolutionary perspective. *Soc. Res.* 67:219–44

Penton-Voak IS, Perrett DI. 2000b. Female preference for male faces changes cyclically: further evidence. *Evol. Hum. Behav.* 21:39–48

Penton-Voak IS, Perrett DI. 2001. Male facial attractiveness: perceived personality and shifting preferences for male traits across the menstrual cycle. *Adv. Stud. Behav.* 30:219–59

Penton-Voak IS, Perrett DI, Castles DL, Kobayashi T, Burt DM, et al. 1999. Menstrual cycle alters face preference. *Nature* 399:741–42

Perrett DI, Burt DM, Penton-Voak IS, Lee KJ, Rowland DA, Edwards R. 1999. Symmetry and human facial attractiveness. *Evol. Hum. Behav.* 20:295–307

Perrett DI, Burt DM, Penton-Voak I, Little AC. 2003. Investigating an imprinting-like phenomenon in humans: partners and opposite-sex parents have similar hair and eye colour. *Evol. Hum. Behav.* 24:43–51

Perrett DI, Lee KJ, Penton-Voak I, Rowland D, Yoshikawa S, et al. 1998. Effects of sexual dimorphism on facial attractiveness. *Nature* 394:884–87

Perrett DI, May KA, Yoshikawa S. 1994. Facial

shape and judgments of female attractiveness. *Nature* 368:239–42

Perrett DI, Penton-Voak I, Little AC, Tiddeman B, Burt DM, et al. 2002. Facial attractiveness judgments reflect learning of parental age characteristics. *Proc. R. Soc. Lond. Ser. B Biol. Sci.* 269:873–80

Peters A. 2000. Testosterone treatment is immunosuppressant in superb fairy wrens, yet free-living males with high testosterone are more immunocompetent. *Proc. R. Soc. Lond. Ser. B Biol. Sci.* 267:883–89

Peterson MA, Rhodes G, eds. 2003. *Perception of Faces, Objects, and Scenes: Analytic and Holistic Processes.* New York: Oxford Univ. Press. 393 pp.

Pinker S. 1997. *How the Mind Works.* New York: Norton

Pittenger JB. 1991. On the difficulty of averaging faces: comments on Langlois and Roggman. *Psychol. Sci.* 2:351–53

Polak M. 2003. *Developmental Instability: Causes and Consequences.* New York: Oxford Univ. Press

Reber R, Schwarz N, Winkielman P. 2004. Processing fluency and aesthetic pleasure: is beauty in the perceiver's processing experience? *Personal. Soc. Psychol. Rev.* 8:364–82

Reed T, Dick DM. 2003. Heritability and validity of healthy physical aging (wellness) in elderly male twins. *Twin Res.* 6:22–234

Rhodes G. 1996. *Superportraits: Caricatures and Recognition.* Hove, UK: Psychol. Press

Rhodes G, Chan J, Zebrowitz LA, Simmons LW. 2003a. Does sexual dimorphism in human faces signal health? *Proc. R. Soc. Lond. Ser. B Biol. Sci.* 270:S93–95

Rhodes G, Halberstadt J, Brajkovich G. 2001a. Generalization of mere exposure effects to averaged composite faces. *Soc. Cogn.* 19:57–70

Rhodes G, Halberstadt J, Jeffery L, Palermo R. 2005a. The attractiveness of average faces is not a generalised mere exposure effect. *Soc. Cogn.* 23:205–17

Rhodes G, Harwood K, Yoshikawa S, Nishitani M, McLean I. 2002. The attractiveness of average faces: cross-cultural evidence and possible biological basis. In *Facial Attractiveness: Evolutionary, Cognitive and Social Perspectives*, ed. G Rhodes, LA Zebrowitz, pp. 35–58. Westport, CT: Ablex

Rhodes G, Hickford C, Jeffery L. 2000. Sex-typicality and attractiveness: Are supermale and superfemale faces super-attractive? *Br. J. Psychol.* 91:125–40

Rhodes G, Jeffery L, Watson TL, Clifford CWG, Nakayama K. 2003b. Fitting the mind to the world: face adaptation and attractiveness aftereffects. *Psychol. Sci.* 14:558–66

Rhodes G, Lee K, Palermo R, Weiss M, Yoshikawa M, McLean I. 2005b. Attractiveness of own-race, other-race and mixed-race faces. *Perception* 34:319–40

Rhodes G, Proffitt F, Grady JM, Sumich A. 1998. Facial symmetry and the perception of beauty. *Psychon. Bull. Rev.* 5:659–69

Rhodes G, Roberts J, Simmons L. 1999a. Reflections on symmetry and attractiveness. *Psychol. Evol. Gend.* 1:279–95

Rhodes G, Simmons L, Peters M. 2005c. Attractiveness and sexual behaviour: Does attractiveness enhance mating success? *Evol. Hum. Behav.* 26:186–201

Rhodes G, Sumich A, Byatt G. 1999b. Are average facial configurations attractive only because of their symmetry? *Psychol. Sci.* 10:52–58

Rhodes G, Tremewan T. 1996. Averageness, exaggeration, and facial attractiveness. *Psychol. Sci.* 7:105–10

Rhodes G, Yoshikawa S, Clark A, Lee K, McKay R, Akamatsu S. 2001b. Attractiveness of facial averageness and symmetry in non-Western cultures: in search of biologically based standards of beauty. *Perception* 30:611–25

Rhodes G, Zebrowitz LA. 2002. *Facial Attractiveness: Evolutionary, Cognitive, and Social Perspectives.* Westport, CT: Ablex. 311 pp.

Rhodes G, Zebrowitz LA, Clark A, Kalick S, Hightower A, McKay R. 2001c. Do facial averageness and symmetry signal health? *Evol. Hum. Behav.* 22:31–46

Rikowski A, Grammer K. 1999. Human body

odour, symmetry and attractiveness. *Biol. Sci.* 266:869–74

Roberts SC, Little AC, Gosling LM, Perrett D, Carter V, et al. 2005. MHC-heterozygosity and human facial attractiveness. *Evol. Hum. Behav.* 26:213–26

Rubenstein AJ, Kalakanis L, Langlois JH. 1999. Infant preferences for attractive faces: a cognitive explanation. *Dev. Psychol.* 35:848–55

Rubenstein AJ, Langlois JH, Roggman LA. 2002. What makes a face attractive and why: the role of averageness in defining facial beauty. See Rhodes & Zebrowiz 2002, pp. 1–33

Russell R. 2003. Sex, beauty, and the relative luminance of facial features. *Perception* 32:1093–107

Ryan MJ, Rand AS. 1993. Sexual selection and signal evolution: the ghost of biases past. *Philos. Trans. R. Soc. Lond.* 340:187–95

Samuels CA, Butterworth G, Roberts T, Graupner L, Hole G. 1994. Facial aesthetics—babies prefer attractiveness to symmetry. *Perception* 23:823–31

Samuels CA, Ewy R. 1985. Aesthetic perception of faces during infancy. *Br. J. Dev. Psychol.* 3:221–28

Scheib JE, Gangestad SW, Thornhill R. 1999. Facial attractiveness, symmetry and cues of good genes. *Proc. R. Soc. Lond. Ser. B Biol. Sci.* 266:1913–17

Shackelford TK, Larsen RJ. 1997. Facial asymmetry as an indicator of psychological, emotional, and physiological distress. *J. Personal. Soc. Psychol.* 72:456–66

Shackelford TK, Larsen RJ. 1999. Facial attractiveness and physical health. *Evol. Hum. Behav.* 20:71–76

Simmons LW, Rhodes G, Peters M, Koehler N. 2004. Are human preferences for facial symmetry focused on signals of developmental instability? *Behav. Ecol.* 15:864–71

Slater A, Quinn PC, Hayes R, Brown E. 2000. The role of facial orientation in newborn infants' preference for attractive faces. *Dev. Sci.* 3:181–85

Slater A, Van der Schulenberg C, Brown E, Badenoch M, Butterworth G, et al. 1998. Newborn infants prefer attractive faces. *Infant Behav. Dev.* 21:345–54

Soler C, Nunez M, Gutierrez R, Nunez J, Medina P, et al. 2003. Facial attractiveness in men provides clues to semen quality. *Evol. Hum. Behav.* 24:199–207

Swaddle JP, Cuthill IC. 1995. Asymmetry and human facial attractiveness—symmetry may not always be beautiful. *Proc. R. Soc. Lond. Ser. B Biol. Sci.* 261:111–16

Swaddle JP, Reierson GW. 2002. Testosterone increases perceived dominance but not attractiveness in human males. *Proc. R. Soc. Lond. Ser. B Biol. Sci.* 269:2285–89

Symons D. 1979. *The Evolution of Human Sexuality.* London: Oxford Univ. Press

Symons D. 1992. On the use and misuse of Darwinism in the study of human behaviour. In *The Adapted Mind*, ed. JH Barkow, L Cosmides, pp. 137–59. London: Oxford Univ. Press

Symons D. 1995. Beauty is in the adaptations of the beholder: the evolutionary psychology of human female sexual attractiveness. In *Sexual Nature, Sexual Culture: Chicago Series on Sexuality, History, and Society*, ed. PR Abramson, SD Pinkerton, pp. 80–119. Chicago: Univ. Chicago Press

Teasdale JD, Russell ML. 1983. Differential effects of induced mood on the recall of positive, negative and neutral words. *Br. J. Clin. Psychol.* 22:163–71

Thornhill R, Gangestad SW. 1993. Human facial beauty—averageness, symmetry, and parasite resistance. *Hum. Nat. Interdiscip. Biosoc. Perspect.* 4:237–69

Thornhill R, Gangestad SW. 1994. Human fluctuating asymmetry and sexual behavior. *Psychol. Sci.* 5:297–302

Thornhill R, Gangestad SW. 1996. The evolution of human sexuality. *Trends Ecol. Evol.* 11:98–102

Thornhill R, Gangestad SW. 1999. Facial attractiveness. *Trends Cogn. Sci.* 3:452–60

Thornhill R, Gangestad SW, Miller R, Scheyd G, McCollough JK, Franklin M. 2003. Major histocompatibility complex genes, symmetry, and body scent attractiveness in men and women. *Behav. Ecol.* 14:668–78

Thornhill R, Moller AP. 1997. Developmental stability, disease and medicine. *Biol. Rev. Camb. Philos. Soc.* 72:497–548

Tomkins JL, Simmons LW. 2003. Fluctuating asymmetry and sexual selection: paradigm shifts, publication bias and observer expectation. In *Developmental Instability: Causes and Consequences*, ed. M Polak, pp. 231–61. New York: Oxford Univ. Press

Tomkinson GR, Olds TS. 2000. Physiological correlates of bilateral symmetry in humans. *Int. J. Sports Med.* 21:545–50

Valentine T, Darling S, Donnelly M. 2004. Why are average faces attractive? The effect of view and averageness on the attractiveness of female faces. *Psychon. Bull. Rev.* 11:482–87

Vokey JR, Read J. 1992. Familiarity, memorability, and the effect of typicality on the recognition of faces. *Mem. Cogn.* 20:291–302

Watson PM, Thornhill R. 1994. Fluctuating asymmetry and sexual selection. *Trends Ecol. Evol.* 9:21–25

Weary DM, Guilford TC, Weisman RG. 1993. A product of discriminative learning may lead to female preferences for elaborate males. *Evolution* 47:333–36

Wedekind C. 1992. Detailed information about parasites revealed by sexual ornamentation. *Proc. R. Soc. Lond. Ser. B Biol. Sci.* 247:169–74

Williams GC. 1966. *Adaptation and Natural Selection: A Critique of Some Current Evolutionary Thought*. Princeton, NJ: Princeton Univ. Press

Winkelman BR, Hagar J, Kraus WE, Merlini P, Keavney B, et al. 2000. Genetics of coronary heart disease: current knowledge and research principles. *Am. Heart J.* 140:S11–26

Zahavi A. 1975. Mate selection—a selection for handicap. *J. Theor. Biol.* 53:205–14

Zajonc RB. 1968. Attitudinal effects of mere exposure. *J. Personal. Soc. Psychol. Monogr. Suppl.* 9:1–27

Zebrowitz LA, Olson K, Hoffman K. 1993. Stability of babyfacedness and attractiveness across the life span. *J. Personal. Soc. Psychol.* 64:453–66

Zebrowitz LA, Rhodes G. 2004. Sensitivity to "bad genes" and the anomalous face overgeneralization effect: cue validity, cue utilization, and accuracy in judging intelligence and health. *J. Nonverbal Behav.* 28:167–85

Zebrowitz LA, Voinescu L, Collins MA. 1996. "Wide-eyed" and "crooked-faced": determinants of perceived and real honesty across the life span. *Personal. Soc. Psychol. Bull.* 22:1258–69

Annu. Rev. Psychol. 2006. 57:227–54
doi: 10.1146/annurev.psych.57.102904.190100
Copyright © 2006 by Annual Reviews. All rights reserved
First published online as a Review in Advance on August 9, 2005

EXPLANATION AND UNDERSTANDING

Frank C. Keil

*Department of Psychology, Yale University, New Haven, Connecticut 06520-8205;
email: frank.keil@yale.edu*

Key Words   concepts, causality, cognition, cognitive development, illusions of
knowing, domain specificity, stances

■ **Abstract**   The study of explanation, while related to intuitive theories, concepts,
and mental models, offers important new perspectives on high-level thought. Explanations sort themselves into several distinct types corresponding to patterns of causation, content domains, and explanatory stances, all of which have cognitive consequences. Although explanations are necessarily incomplete—often dramatically so in
laypeople—those gaps are difficult to discern. Despite such gaps and the failure to
recognize them fully, people do have skeletal explanatory senses, often implicit, of the
causal structure of the world. They further leverage those skeletal understandings by
knowing how to access additional explanatory knowledge in other minds and by being
particularly adept at using situational support to build explanations on the fly in real
time. Across development and cultures, there are differences in preferred explanatory
schemes, but rarely are any kinds of schemes completely unavailable to a group.

CONTENTS

INTRODUCTION

Humans are driven to acquire and provide explanations. Within months of uttering their first words, children ask "why." Preverbal infants explore phenomena that puzzle them in an attempt to uncover an explanation of why an effect occurred. As adults, we must frequently choose between explanations of why politicians lost, why the economy is failing, or why a war is not winnable. Moreover, explanations are not merely the work of experts. Our friends explain why they have failed to honor a commitment or why a loved one is behaving oddly. Our enemies may offer unflattering explanations of our successes. Explanations are therefore ubiquitous and diverse in nature. This review considers the varieties of explanations, their components and structure, and their uses.

WHAT EXPLANATIONS AND EXPLANATORY UNDERSTANDINGS ARE

Explanations were once thought to be "deductive-nomological" in nature (Hempel & Oppenheim 1948). In this view, explanations are like proofs in logic. A set of basic laws (the nomological part) are stated as axioms and then the deductive consequences of those laws are explored like a logical proof. The complex of laws and the deductive sequence constitute the explanation. Thus, an explanation of the periodicity of pendulums might assume certain laws of classical mechanics and the deductive consequences of those laws when considered in conjunction with additional initial statements about pendulums. This model of explanation has not fared well in the philosophy of science (Salmon 1989). Scientists do not normally proceed in that manner as individuals, and even disciplines as a whole rarely follow so neatly the progression of a proof. Moreover, as one considers explanations in sciences other than physics, even superficial similarities to deductive chains start to disappear (Salmon 1989). For laypeople as compared with scientists, the deductive-nomological model seems even less plausible.

Everyday explanations depart radically from the image of people methodically considering a set of axioms and running through a deductive chain. For example, people frequently prefer one explanation to another without explicitly being able to say why. They often seem to draw on implicit explanatory understandings that are not easy to put in explicit terms (Kozhevnikov & Hegarty 2001). Even without strictly adhering to the deductive-nomological model of explanations, some explanations in domains such as biology hardly invoke laws at all (Bechtel & Abrahamsen 2005). In many cases, we think of explanations as providing some sense of mechanism (Bechtel & Abrahamsen 2005, Chater & Oaksford 2005, Glennan 2002). Indeed, when explanations of psychological phenomena are stated in law-like ways without mechanism (e.g., if X, then Y), they often instead are called "effects," which suggests that they are not really explanations (Cummins 2000).

People often recruit causal mechanisms on the basis of one-trial learning (Chater & Oaksford 2005) and not on the basis of a long-term gradual accumulation of statistical data in a manner specified by Hume and since explored in psychology (e.g., Cheng 1997, Dickinson 2001). Although statistical reasoning can certainly guide the formation of causal explanations, in many everyday cases, one or two trial exposures seem to activate a pre-existing schema of a mechanism.

Although the ability to provide verbally explicit explanations may be too strict a criterion to count as having explanatory understanding, not all forms of implicit knowledge that enable prediction will count. One purpose of this review is to convey a better sense of implicit explanatory understanding. More broadly, not only the processes of creating and discovering explanations but also the processes of providing and receiving them are considered, as all these activities are intuitively part of what is meant by "explanatory understanding."

EXPLANATIONS, THEORIES, AND MENTAL MODELS

Explanations are related to theories; but a focus on explanations brings different issues and bodies of research to the foreground (e.g., Brem & Rips 2000). One difference concerns the transactional nature of explanations. Explanations are often between individuals and reflect an attempt to communicate an understanding. Even within one mind, explanations occur in a manner different from intuitive theories. One can attempt to explain an event to oneself, as sometimes is revealed when people are heard saying to themselves out loud how something works. Even young children playing alone can be observed to explain things to themselves as a verbal strategy to help solve a task (Berk 1994). Explanations create trajectories. Recipients of explanations, if the explanations are at all successful, are expanding their understanding in real time. The transactive process also frequently implies conceptual change. Theories can undergo conceptual change (see, e.g., Carey 1985), but they do not need to and can be highly stable over extended periods, especially when very successful.

Explanations may highlight incompleteness. An explainer will often encounter gaps in understanding that may remain largely invisible when in the form of intuitive theories. Thus, the process of trying to explain explicitly a system to another, or even to oneself, often brings the incompleteness of one's understanding into much harsher relief (Keil et al. 2004).

Explanations contrast with mental models as well, which can range from formal representations of logical patterns (Johnson-Laird 1983) to image-like representations of the workings of a system (Gentner & Stevens 1983). Mental models are readouts of relations from a mental array and often are understood in spatial terms. Explanations normally are not seen as mental blueprints or plans that are then read off. They include the interpretations of such plans or blueprints.

Explanations therefore contrast with both intuitive theories and models because of their transactional component, their role in expanding knowledge, and their interpretative role. They are also different from simple, procedural knowledge. Knowing how to operate an automated teller machine or make an international phone call might not entail having any understanding of how either system works. Even a seemingly simple act such as exchanging money at an airport may carry with it no explanatory understanding of how relative currency values are determined. The study of explanations offers insights not obvious from other points of view. Explanations view people less as autodidacts and more as social, interacting agents (Harris 2002).

ARE THERE DIFFERENT KINDS OF EXPLANATIONS?

Explanations occur in different ways (Keil & Wilson 2000a). One can explain why Aunt Edna insulted Uncle Billy at the family holiday dinner, why giraffes have long necks, why salt melts ice, or why seat belts prevent traffic fatalities. There are explanations of individual histories, and of why one thing is functionally "meant" for another. Do all these kinds of explanations work similarly or do they have different properties and perhaps even different developmental trajectories? We can contrast explanations in terms of the causal patterns they employ, the explanatory stances they invoke, the domains of phenomena being explained, and whether they are value or emotion laden.

Causal Patterns

Explanations often refer to causal relations, but in at least four distinct ways: common cause, common effect, linear causal chains, and causal homeostasis. In common-cause explanations, a single cause is seen as having a branching set of consequences (Sober 1984). For example, a virus infects a person and then has a cascade of effects that creates a downward-branching hierarchy differentiating over time. Common-cause explanations are frequently found in diagnoses of problems, such as medical disease, equipment malfunction (e.g., auto repair), or software bugs.

Common-effect explanations involve cases where causes converge to create an event. These sorts of explanations are common in history, where a major event might be attributed to the confluence of several factors. Thus, the defeat of the Spanish Armada in 1588 might be attributed to the converging causes of the Netherlands Revolt, severe weather at sea, personal problems of Phillip II of Spain, and the brilliant marine tactics of Lord Charles Howard.

Explanations as simple linear chains are a special degenerate case of common cause and common effect explanations; namely, there is one unique serial chain from a single initial cause through a series of steps to a single effect. One fanciful case is the child's verse of how a missing horseshoe nail led to the loss of a kingdom. Simple linear explanations may be quite rare in real life, however. Even if things start with a single chain of effects and causes, at some point those effects start to have multiple effects of their own and the structure starts to branch. Moreover, other causes enter in and influence the reasoning process downstream, thus violating the notion of a single cause.

Causal homeostatic explanations are fundamental to explanatory discourse about natural kinds (Boyd 1999). These explanations seek to account for why sets of things seem to endure as stable sets of properties. A causal homeostatic explanation does not seek to explain how a cause progresses over time to create some effect or effects, but rather how an interlocking set of causes and effects results in a set of properties enduring together as a stable set over time that then exists as a natural kind. Thus, it seeks to explain why feathers, hollow bones, nest building, flight, and a high metabolic rate might all reinforce the presence of each other in birds (Boyd 1999, Keil 1989).

Several psychological issues arise in the context of these four broad patterns: First, people do seem to find some patterns more natural to think about than other patterns (Ahn et al. 2000, Rehder & Hastie 2004). Second, these differences in naturalness may in turn lead to cognitive biases and distortions in explanations and explanatory understandings. Finally, people may view certain patterns as domain biased, such as seeing causal homeostasis as especially apt for living kinds (Ahn 1998, Keil 1989).

Explanatory Stances

A different way of contrasting types of explanations involves "stances" (Dennett 1987) or "modes of construal" (Keil 1995). People may adopt a stance or mode of construal that frames an explanation. These stances are not in themselves theories; they are far too vague and nonpredictive. However, they do posit certain kinds of relations and properties, and even arguments, as central. Dennett (1987), for example, focused on the mechanical stance, the design stance, and the intentional stance. The mechanical stance considers simple physical objects and their interactions. The design stance considers entities as having purposes and functions that occur above and beyond mechanical interactions (Lombrozo 2004). Some have argued that functional, teleological interpretations come all too readily to mind in evolutionary "storytelling" that infers functional explanations for cases that don't need them (Gould & Lewontin 1979). Similarly, some see young children as "promiscuously teleological" (Kelemen 1999), whereas still others see them as more selective in their use of functional explanations (Greif et al. 2005, Keil 1992). There are also debates as to whether a design stance or teleological mode of construal requires a notion of an intentional designer (e.g., Bloom 1996, Keil 1995, Kelemen & Carey 2005). Related issues concern the proper scope of teleological arguments in the sciences (Allen et al. 1998). Finally, the intentional stance considers entities as having beliefs, desires, and other mental contents that govern their behavior. Entities are assumed to be governed by a belief-desire calculus and to have mental representations that have causal consequences. Adopting an intentional stance, however, may not require having a full-fledged folk psychology (Bloom & German 2000, Gergely et al. 1995).

The same event often can be characterized by each of the distinct stances and thereby yield quite different insights and explanations. For example, a diver going into a tuck position might be explained in terms of the physics of rotating objects (a mechanical stance), in terms of the purpose of pulling in the limbs close to the body (design stance), and in terms of the beliefs the diver has about her actions and the motivations that drive them (the intentional stance). Each of these ways of framing the action will afford different insights and, potentially, different distortions. Similarly, atypical stances sometimes are adopted to shed additional insight into a system or for pedagogical reasons. One can discuss students in a crowded high school hallway between classes as billiard balls careening about, and one can describe magnets as liking certain metals or materials as having memories. There, too, distorted understandings can result (Gentner & Gentner 1983).

Is there a developmental progression of a mechanical stance, a design stance, and an intentional stance? Or does a design stance depend on an earlier emerging intentional stance? Or do they all appear in parallel early in development as foundational core ways of explaining? These questions are some of the most actively investigated in the field today (German & Johnson 2002, Keil et al. 2005, Kelemen 1999, Lombrozo & Carey 2005).

Explanatory Domains

Explanations also can be contrasted in terms of domains roughly corresponding to academic disciplines. Are there distinct explanatory types in intuitive biology, physics, chemistry, psychology, economics, and sociology? Are the ways we explain phenomena pertaining to reproduction of organisms profoundly different from how we explain trajectories of projectiles and the stratifications of social groups? In the philosophy of science, there has been a sea change of opinion in which older reductionist/eliminativist views have been replaced by pluralistic views (Salmon 1989). Thus, biologists, especially evolutionary biologists, might well invoke functional arguments (even as they also caution against reverse causality) far more than physicists or chemists. Psychologists might not consider monotonic relations between inputs and outputs to be as pervasive as are those in the physical sciences, and may expect probabilistic relations usually to obtain between causes and effects (Lehman et al. 1988). A more systematic taxonomy of explanatory domains awaits a more complete formal way of describing the structure of explanations.

Social- and Emotion-Laden Explanations

Explanation may have a different character when it is socially or morally laden. In social attributions, for example, motivational factors seem to color how we construct and accept explanations. Moreover, the presence of explanations can influence how we emotionally experience events (see, e.g., Wilson et al. 2005). The literature is far too vast to consider here in detail (see, e.g., Macrae & Bodenhausen 2000, Malle 2004), but the following point merits mention. Even if motivational factors heavily influence social explanations, such influences in themselves may not change the explanations' structure. The same kinds of causal patterns may still be favored, the same sorts of probabilistic distributions preferred, and the same domains of regularities considered as relevant. Emotions and motivation may simply shift a threshold for acceptance of evidence, or strength of causation. Moral explanations are another special case. A difference may exist between moral thoughts that have the form of explanations and those that defy explanations in phenomena known as "moral dumbfounding" (Greene & Haidt 2002, Haidt 2001). People sometimes explain their moral judgments by reference to a set of principles, rules, or laws; but other times, often with cases of such taboos as incest, sacrilege, and torture, people have "gut" responses more akin to disgust or perception without apparent explanation. The kind of person sought out to provide a moral explanation might also be conceived differently from other kinds of experts (Danovitch & Keil 2005).

WHAT EXPLANATIONS ARE FOR

There are several reasons why we engage in explanations and seek them out. The most commonly offered reason is to be able to predict similar events in the future (Heider 1958). We explain, for example, why a stretch of road is particularly slippery in cold, wet weather so that, on future occasions of similar weather, we might anticipate those conditions more effectively.

Explanations are also used in diagnosis. One might ask why a system failed and then repair a part to bring it back to its normal function (Graesser & Olde 2003). There is little sense of making a prediction in such cases. One is not concerned with predicting but rather with restoring operation of a system. In "broken" mechanical, biological, and social systems, we often seek explanations to "fix" them. Other times, we develop explanations of the causal efficacy or inefficacy of a new action or tool. We might try several different ways of getting a car out of the mud, and when we finally succeed, we try to come up with an explanation for the method that succeeded so that we can reproduce that method in the future. Again, there is less the feeling of prediction here and more the sense of identifying a causally critical component that one wants to reproduce.

We also often seek explanations for one-time events in which predictions for the future seem completely implausible. The press might search endlessly for explanations of why the car carrying Princess Diana ended up in a fatal crash, but nowhere in that search for explanations is there any motive to predict future crashes. The constellation of factors leading up to that crash was clearly so unusual and unique that looking for an explanation in service of a prediction makes little sense. Why then, do people search for explanations in such cases? The notion of learning from one's mistakes does carry with it the idea of predictive value, but often the motive is more one of affixing blame. One may seek an explanation simply to determine the guilty party that needs to pay for damages or be punished.

In the study of history, the search for explanations of events, such as the fall of a dynasty or the start of a war, is often accompanied with severe warning about not using those explanations to predict future events. Thus, there is a great deal of controversy over whether it is appropriate to use counterfactuals in historical analysis (Ferguson 1999).

Other times we engage in explanations to justify or rationalize an action. We explain that we punished a child for his own good, or that we didn't bother voting in an election because our vote would not have mattered anyway, or that we were sickeningly sweet to an enemy because of the strategic value of being nice on that occasion. Our explanations are attempts to represent our actions to others as sensible, well intentioned, pragmatic, or appropriate. Such acts of persuasion can often be self-directed. Thus, it is not uncommon to explain to oneself why one has engaged in a certain act as a way of making sense of one's own actions. I might be surprised at my burst of anger at a meeting and later explain it in terms of situational as opposed to dispositional factors. I might do much worse on a test than expected and explain it in terms of lack of studying, and, in doing so, shift the reason from one of ability to that of effort.

Finally, explanations can be in the service of aesthetic pleasure. One can explain a work of art, a mystery of cosmology, or the intricacies of a poem with the sole goal of increasing appreciation in another, providing that person with a better polished lens through which to view the explanandum. Explanations in their own right can be immensely rewarding things and may be sought out as such, even by the youngest of children (Gopnik 1998). When a young child asks "why," she often simply wants to appreciate more the nature of something that she has observed, with no further agenda.

In short, explanations are used in many different ways beyond mere prediction. It is not yet clear how their content might vary as a function of their use. For example, are self-directed explanations largely ones about ability and individual differences in a social comparison context? Are justifications of actions usually explanations offered in a moral context or are they simply part of a much larger set of ways of describing why we did what we did, just as an accountant might explain an audit procedure? Are explanations of systems fundamentally different from those of individual histories? For example, contrast an explanation of why a particular couple got married with why couples in general get married.

Perhaps explanations have only limited use in day-to-day life because it would take too long to construct an explanation every time one was needed (Fodor 1998). But explanations don't have to work in real time. Instead, they may frequently serve to help people know how to weight information or how to allocate attention when approaching a situation. It used to be doctrine that explanation-based processing of information was slow and later in tasks, whereas early processing was more associative and fast; more recent findings illustrate that in many cases, presumably where some sort of precompiling takes place, explanation-based effects can occur in the earliest steps of processing (Keil et al. 1998; Luhmann et al. 2002).

INTRINSIC LIMITS OF EXPLANATIONS

Explanations are ubiquitous, come in a variety of forms and formats, and are used for a variety of purposes. Yet, one of the most striking features about most explanations is their limitations. For most natural phenomena and many artificial ones, the full set of relations to be explained is enormous, often indefinitely large and far beyond the grasp of any one individual (Wilson & Keil 1998).

The problem of overwhelming complexity may seem to be unrealistic given how often we seem to be successful with our explanations in everyday life, but that is precisely the point. Somehow, people manage to get by with highly incomplete or partial explanations of how the world around them works. Are there systematic ways in which we extract a gist of the causal structure of the world? The problem is analogous to that confronted by the realistic artist who must attempt to convey, in a two-dimensional plane, the vastly larger amount of information that is embodied in a three-dimensional array (Cavanaugh 1999). Artists use a number of conventions and exploit interpretive "tricks" of the perceptual system. It seems likely that our explanations make similar moves, although we have yet to understand the nature of such compressions of information. To use a different analogy, in categorization, for at least some classes of objects in the artifacts realm, there is a "basic" or optimal level at which to encode information about categories (Murphy 2002, Rosch et al. 1976). Are there comparable optimal levels of causal description in various domains of the physical world? (For a related discussion of the "compression problem" and "global insight," see Fauconnier & Turner 2002.) As discussed below, the problem of the intrinsic limits of explanation is exacerbated by a tendency to overestimate the depth of our own understandings. It is bad enough that explanations have indefinite depth; it is much worse if we realize too late when we are out of our explanatory depth.

THE CENTRAL ROLE OF CAUSALITY

Not all explanations are about causal relations. One can explain how a mathematical result is achieved, why a design is symmetrical in a subtle manner, how a jazz improvisation resolves itself, or why China is bordered by 14 different countries. Yet, the vast majority of our everyday explanations invoke notions of cause and effect. Moreover, when an explanation contains both causal and noncausal elements, the causal ones tend to occupy center stage and dominate patterns of judgment (Murphy & Medin 1985). Similarly, causal understanding shifts perceptions of the normalcy of properties (Ahn et al. 2003). Causality seems to have a privileged role in most explanations.

Philosophers of science have classically turned to the notion of cause to illustrate why some things explain others and not the opposite. Thus, although the presence of a shadow is lawfully related to a flagpole and the time of day, the flagpole and the sun explain the shadow (Bromberger 1966). The shadow cannot explain the flagpole or the sun. Lawful relations and tight correlations do not have the sense of an explanation when the causal relations are absent or inappropriate (Cartwright 2004).

Counterfactual thought also illustrates the central importance of cause in explanations (Lewis 1973). We sense the meaning of a causal relation by stating that, ceteris paribus, a particular event B would not have occurred if event A had not occurred first. This "would have" relationship is meant to highlight causation as opposed to mere correlation. Although the ways in which counterfactuals illuminate the nature of causation are philosophically complex (Collins et al. 2001), at a psychological level we often turn to counterfactuals to explore causal relations or make them more salient (Roese 1997). Counterfactual thought is often triggered by other features, such as the atypicality of an event (Kahneman & Miller 1986), which may then in turn trigger more causal thought. It can also serve to set up a simulation heuristic, in which an event is considered with minor perturbations as a way of better understanding its causal structure (Kahneman & Tversky 1982). The ways in which counterfactual thinking highlight, or perhaps sometimes distort, causal relations are complex and remain an active area of exploration (Spellman & Mandel 1999). One mechanism may involve shifting perceptions of baseline probabilities of the actual event as opposed to alternative events, thereby making a potential cause seem either more or less inevitable (Spellman & Mandel 1999).

Although older views often saw the world as governed by one unified set of laws, i.e., physics, those views do not seem to capture actual science. One alternative argues for a "dappled world" in which there are local causal regularities and fragments, and not a global unified explanation of everything (Cartwright 1999). Even at the same level of reduction, such as the interactions of bounded objects, there might be different domains of regularities. Thus, the movements of a falling leaf may have little in common with those of a falling apple, as the leaf brings in relations of fluid dynamics and the apple those of more classical Newtonian mechanics. If the world is a heterogeneous collection of different causal patterns, it is reasonable to ask if those patterns result in different explanatory styles. Indeed, evolutionary psychologists have argued that there might be a selective advantage to develop different explanatory schemes to resonate with these different kinds of causal regularities (Cosmides & Tooby 1987). Just as organisms have developed different sense organs to handle the heterogeneous forms of information carried in sound, light, and chemicals, they may also have developed mental organs to grasp different kinds of causal regularities that have stably existed in the world for millions of years.

Probabilistic and deterministic causation are also importantly different. Evolutionary theory, economics, and much of psychology are deeply dependent on notions of probabilistic causation. Yet, in the simple mechanics of macroscopic bounded objects, we often think of discrete causes of events. The philosophy of science has long recognized that both types of causation have explanatory value in the different sciences (Humphreys 1989, Salmon 1980). Higher levels of education in some areas of the social sciences may foster a sensitivity to certain kinds of probabilistic causal reasoning (see, e.g., Lehman et al. 1988), which suggests we tend to weigh an interpretative causal schema more or less strongly as a function of the perceived domain.

Adults and children therefore tend to associate particular kinds of causal schemata with specific domains. Beyond such domain differences, however, there are also consistent biases towards specific causal patterns. Features that are earlier in causal chains are often deemed more important in category learning (Ahn et al. 2000), and features that are more causally interdependent on others are similarly more critical in category learning and induction (Sloman et al. 1998). Thus, people prefer explanations in which the most emphasized features and properties either are early in a causal chain or are the most causally interdependent on others.

In some studies, common-cause, common-effect, and simple cause-chain schemas facilitated induction to the same extent for biological kinds, artifacts, and nonliving natural kinds (Rehder & Hastie 2004). Similarly, a preference for the first element in a causal chain, the causal status effect, has been found to be influential in both artifact and biological domains (Ahn 1998). Yet, even children as young as three, when spontaneously asking questions about novel artifacts and novel animals, seem to seek out different kinds of causal relations, asking about the functions of artifacts as a whole but not of animals. With animals, children focus more on the locations in which they are found (Greif et al. 2005). Thus, although a wide array of causal patterns can be applied to each kind, there are different preference orderings across domains.

A related influence of causal structure can be found in a "causal diversity effect" (Kim & Keil 2003). Single causes usually have downwardly branching sets of effects and causes. Thus, a bacterial infection might initially cause a white blood cell elevation and fever. Those effects in turn might cause anemia and headache, which in turn can cause other effects. The further apart two final effects are in the branching tree of causes the more they are judged good evidence for the initial cause. Explanations are more appealing when they use diverse forms of evidence for initial causes. Indeed, in 1847, William Whewell, the first philosopher of science, argued for the notion of "consilience," in which the most appealing scientific explanations were ones for which evidence of effects came from maximally diverse sources (Whewell 1847).

Causality has figured prominently in explanatory thinking in recent years in the context of Bayesian learning and related paradigms. Causal patterns may be discerned from merely correlational ones by construction of "causal Bayes nets" (Glymour 2001), which track patterns of nested contingencies in a manner that strongly rules out noncausal relations. For example, if one screens off a particular variable X and the effect Y no longer occurs, evidence accumulates for a causal relationship between X and Y. Not only adults but also young children use such strategies to infer causal relations (Gopnik & Glymour 2004, Sobel et al. 2004). More recently, Bayesian techniques have explored how particular causal and relational patterns might be learned and linked to domains in a manner that guides explanatory interpretation. For example, in one study, a learning system that was fed data about biological systems constructed a taxonomic interpretative structure and then used that structure to guide future learning (Kemp et al. 2004). The system was quickly able to detect the taxonomic relations and then use them to constrain further learning. In a different domain, such as political party preferences, a different relational structure would be learned. The most relevant case involves a learning system that learned to distinguish relational patterns quite similar to those of causal chains, causal hierarchies, and causal homeostasis (Kemp et al. 2004). Not all causal knowledge may arise from Bayesian learning; indeed, prior causal explanatory schemes may distort Bayesian learning in systematic ways (Krynski & Tennebaum 2003). In short, there is a recent convergence between behavioral studies, which show sensitivity at all ages to a wide range of causal and relational structures, and newer techniques of modeling learning, which show the detection of such structures in specific domains and then the use of them to further constrain learning in those domains. Those simulation accounts are also revealing how prior beliefs about certain causal relational patterns can constrain further Bayesian learning in a domain and, therefore, generation of explanations.

Analogies often are critical to successful causal explanations, especially those of systems as opposed to singular event sequences. Analogies have been used in scientific explanations ever since the first attempts at understanding nature have been recorded (Holyoak & Thagard 1995). Analogies can be used both in the process of scientific discovery and in the process of giving an explanation, but they may work in different ways. In day-to-day discovery in the actual laboratory, analogies may be plentiful but may be relatively mundane as they make linkages between closely related areas. In a molecular biology laboratory, scientists might use analogies from one gene of the HIV virus to another gene of the same virus (Dunbar 1995, Dunbar & Blanchette 2001). In contrast, when scientists explain systems to outsiders or teach students, the analogies may draw on much more distant domains, such as the familiar solar-system-as-atom case (Gentner 1983) or electricity as a flowing liquid (Home 1981). Thus, when people are seeking an explanatory understanding in an area, they might use close analogies; but when they are actually trying to formulate explanations to others, analogies between more distant domains may become more common. Different facets of explanation therefore seem to draw on different forms of analogies enabling access to different levels of causal analysis. Because analogies draw on intrinsically relational patterns and because relational patterns may be at the core of many explanations, analogies also help both adults and children to go beyond surface patterns to see the causal patterns that lie beneath (Gentner et al. 1995).

RECOGNIZING BAD EXPLANATIONS AND CHOOSING THE BEST EXPLANATION

Three important dimensions guide our evaluations of explanations: circularity, relevance, and coherence. These criteria can be surprisingly elusive in real-world contexts. For example, although some cases of circularity are blatantly empty, e.g., "This diet pill works because it helps people lose weight," more complex and lengthy circularities can be much harder to detect (Rips 2002). People tend to confuse pragmatic factors, such as repetition of facts, with true circularities in evaluating the reasonableness of explanations. They recognize circularity in its simplest and most straightforward forms, but can be easily sidetracked in more complex bodies of discourse. Thus, our ability to detect faulty explanations, even ones that are logically circular, is not fail-safe.

Relevance would also seem to be straightforward. Yet, levels of abstraction, analogies, and surprising connections to other domains can complicate the assessment of relevance. In one view, an input is relevant to the extent that, at any time, the cognitive effects of processing that input are positive (Wilson & Sperber 2004). Explanations are good if they are high on this dimension of relevance. Relevance can also be understood as a principle of speech act theory: Speakers should be informative (Grice 1975). Explanations therefore suffer if presented at the wrong level of detail. Thus, if asked why John got on the train from New Haven to New York, a good explanation might be that he had tickets for a Broadway show. An accurate but poor explanation at too low a level might say that he got on the train because he moved his right foot from the platform to the train and then followed with his left foot. An accurate but poor explanation at too high a level might say that he got on the train because he believed that the train would take him to New York from New Haven. Finding the appropriate level of analysis has long been a problem in analyses of event structures (e.g., Schank & Abelson 1977), so it should be no surprise that it is an important factor in judging the appropriateness of an explanation.

Explanations can also go awry for another speech act–related reason concerning egocentrism. Although originally discovered by Piaget (1926) in children and later expanded on a variety of communication tasks (e.g., Kraus & Glucksberg 1969), egocentrism is a common problem for people of all ages (Keysar et al. 1998, Nickerson 2001). An explanation of how something works will fail either if it provides too much detail or if it presupposes too much and skips over essential details. One version of this deficit sees adults and children alike as laboring under a "curse of knowledge," in which having knowledge biases one to think that others have the same knowledge (Birch & Bloom 2003). More broadly, we may try to understand what others know by looking at our own knowledge and using that as a model to project what others know (Nickerson 2001). We adjust our explanation to take into account the other, but by using our own knowledge as a point of departure, we may egocentrically distort it. This process influences explanations by making us miscalculate the informational common ground between explainer and explainee (Clark 1996). Although speakers attempt to negotiate a common ground (Clark 1996), the egocentrism bias intrudes.

Explanations can also be seen as bad if they fail to cohere, or "hang together." The different elements of an explanation must work in concert to achieve an internally consistent package. The doctrine of coherentism is seen as an important alternative to foundationalist views of scientific explanations that attempt to reduce all phenomena to the bedrock of physics (Amini 2003). Coherentism argues that a set of statements at a particular level of explanation, such as the psychological, can cohere as a tightly organized and interrelated unit that offers insights and explanations in its own right, without having to depend on lower levels of explanation (Amini 2003).

Coherence has been defined in terms of constraint satisfaction (Thagard 2000, Thagard & Verbeurgt 1998). A set of elements is coherent to the extent that each element in a set positively constrains other ones, often causally. Elements can also be negatively constraining, that is, they contradict or causally block other elements. One can quantitatively derive coherence values from sets of elements and implement those analyses in computational systems such as neural networks (see, e.g., Thagard 2000, Thagard & Verbeurgt 1998). These formal analyses are difficult to apply to everyday explanations, but the degree to which elements hang together seems to be an important intuitive component in evaluating the quality of explanations. Coherence is also related to a notion of systematicity, the extent to which elements form a tightly interconnected, mutually supporting relational structure. For example, Gentner & Toupin (1986) suggest that a focus on relational predicates can reveal cases in which elements are tightly linked as opposed to merely being properties associated with a category.

There are, however, both conceptual and empirical problems with the idea that people are highly sensitive to coherence. Conceptually, there is the problem of "holism" (Fodor 1998): Virtually all elements eventually are causally connected to all others. Thus, if one were trying to explain how a multispeed bicycle works, much of the coherence would seem to rest in how the mechanical elements of a bicycle interact with each other. Yet, those metal mechanical elements are also constrained by elements having to do with human anatomy, physiology, and goals. Similarly, they are constrained by riding surfaces, economics of construction, and so on in an ever-widening set of relations. This holism problem may be surmountable by heuristics that prune out links to other elements that are below a certain level of density; but such heuristics are difficult to implement in practice and are highly sensitive to context.

Empirically, a full commitment to coherence seems to evaporate when people are probed concerning their actual beliefs about how the world works. They seem to violate coherence in two ways. First, they often seem to know only fragments of a full system. Those fragments may consist of so few elements that they hardly qualify as cohering. In the extreme, people may have little more than a set of phenomenological primitives, or p-prims, that are very small pieces of understanding with few relations of consistency or coherence to other elements (Di Sessa 1993, Di Sessa et al. 2004). Second, people often seem to have sets of beliefs that directly contradict each other (Chin & Brewer 1993, Winer et al. 2002). The conflicts may be ignored until they are made explicit; and even then, any changes in beliefs may be resisted. Coherence may be most powerful when all relevant elements are explicitly considered at the same time. However, given the limits of working memory, the number of such elements actually considered is likely to be quite small. In short, coherence and systematicity influence our sense of the quality of explanations, but they also are limited in ways that are not yet fully understood.

We frequently have to choose between competing explanations. Sometimes both explanations might be possible as converging sources of influence, but other times they may directly conflict such that only one can be correct. Explanation choice between reasonable explanations may be quite distinct from rejecting truly inappropriate explanations. One bias governing explanation choice may involve the order in which we receive explanations. Thus, if we are presented with parts of one causal explanation of how a system works, we may then discount subsequently presented fragments from an alternative explanation, often on the basis of a single trial of learning. Causal discounting may not require an explicit evaluation and comparison of two explanations, and it often may occur in a more automatic manner outside of awareness (Oppenheimer 2005).

Choices between explanations have been described as operating through a process known as inference to the best explanation (IBE) (Harman 1965). In IBE, an individual generates alternative hypotheses and then considers, as a result of those hypotheses, tradeoffs between external verification of the hypotheses and some metric of internal parsimony. Thus, if an explanation seems to predict and account for a huge array of natural phenomena but is a large set of seemingly unrelated ad hoc elements, it might be preferred less than one with a bit less predictive power but with a much simpler internal structure. IBE approaches, however, require clarifications of notions of parsimony, inference, and empirical success. Simplicity and complexity are notoriously slippery notions (e.g., Chater & Vitanyi 2003, Sober 1975), and as noted earlier, logical inference as a deductive chain rarely characterizes real life cognition either in scientists or in laypeople.

We may also choose between explanations by asking which of two mechanisms seems more plausible, or how well a mechanism conforms to early emerging causal schemata. Plausibility can also be driven by familiarity with similar classes of mechanisms. Explanation choice may also be guided by the extent to which a visual animation of mechanism easily comes to mind (Barsalou 1999, Hegarty 1992). Appeals to mechanism, however, have been criticized for relying on preexisting causal schemata that ultimately may have to be stipulated as innate (Glymour 2001). In summary, we use a wide array of heuristics to evaluate explanations and may use additional ones when choosing between two reasonable alternatives.

ILLUSIONS OF EXPLANATORY UNDERSTANDING

The pursuit of explanations and the desire to offer them are driven by our intuitions concerning the quality of explanations we already have. In trying to gain an explanatory understanding of a system, one stops upon reaching a "working understanding." People often claim to have rushes of insight or flashes of understanding, yet these intuitions often may not be accurate. People do have strong senses of making cognitive advances in understanding, ranging from a visceral "rush" of understanding (Gopnik 1998) to being in a cognitive "flow" (Cziksentmihalyi 1990). The "aha" sense has been discussed ever since Archimedes was described as euphorically shouting, "Eureka!" To some extent, these intuitions must be tracking real progress in understanding; but recent evidence also suggests that these intuitions are only crude indicators that can mislead, sometimes quite dramatically.

People of all ages tend to be miscalibrated with respect to their explanatory understandings; that is, they think they understand in far more detail than they really do how some aspect of the world works or why some pattern in the world exists. This bias, the "illusion of explanatory depth" or IOED (Rozenblit & Keil 2002), can be demonstrated by asking people to rate how well they understand devices such as helicopters, cylinder locks, and zippers. Having given those ratings, they are asked to describe in detail everything they know about how some of the devices work. They are then asked to re-rate their understanding (*a*) in light of having given an explanation, (*b*) having attempted to answer a critical diagnostic question (e.g., How do you pick a lock?), and finally, (*c*) having been given a concise expert explanation of how the device works. (The last measure helps assess whether they had a more implicit understanding they couldn't verbalize in the earlier trials but that fosters a surge of recognition when the expert explanation is presented.)

There is a consistent strong IOED, with later ratings being substantially lower than earlier ones (Rozenblit & Keil 2002). This drop in ratings, however, does not occur for self-assessments of other kinds of knowledge such as facts (e.g., capitals of countries), procedures (e.g., how to make an international phone call), or narratives (e.g., plots of familiar movies). The IOED is therefore not merely another case of a general overconfidence effect (e.g., Krueger & Dunning 1999, Yates et al. 1997). There is something about partial explanatory understanding that provides particularly compelling senses of knowing more than one really does. The same specificity is found in quite young children as well (Mills & Keil 2004).

Why should explanatory understanding mislead us into thinking we know more than we really do, whereas other forms of knowledge are much more accurately assessed? Several distinctive properties of explanations, many of them described above, seem to be involved (Keil et al. 2004). Explanations are especially vulnerable to function-for-mechanism confusions because of their hierarchical structure. Explanations also have relatively unclear end states, making it more difficult to assess success. Moreover, explanations rarely are offered or heard in much detail, which makes it difficult to have much practice in assessing one's own explanatory understanding. Finally, we may confuse our ability to represent or to know fully an explanation in our heads with the ability to fuse more fragmentary understandings with situational cues that fill out critical explanatory detail when an object is directly in front of us in real time and is available for inspection (Clark 1997). These factors are not as dominant for procedures, facts, or narratives.

Consider in a bit more detail the function-for-mechanism confusions. Many complex systems both in nature and in the manufactured world can be understood as hierarchically organized sets of relatively autonomous units or "stable subassemblies" (Simon 1996, 2000). With most artifacts and with many systems in biology, there are salient functional relations between the highest levels of these systems. Thus, a computer mouse controls the movement of a cursor on a screen, a carburetor mixes fuel and air, and a kidney filters blood. When we learn one of these causal-functional relations, we get an appropriate surge of insight into an explanatory relation that we did not have before. The problem occurs when we attach that surge of insight to an inappropriately low level of analysis. That is, we might assume that we have gained some insight into the workings of the mouse, the ways in which fuel and air are mixed, or how the kidney actually processes blood. Moreover, if we have achieved some success at deciphering a set of mechanistic relations for a system in real time when it is in front of us, we may mistake that success and the genuine understanding we have at higher functional levels with having a stored mental representation of lower level, more mechanistic relations.

People also seem to use misleading heuristics to assess how well they understand a system. Most notably, if they can see or easily visualize several components of a system, they are more convinced they know how it works. Thus, the more easily visible are parts in a system, relative to hidden ones, the stronger the IOED (Rozenblit & Keil 2002). Visual influences of this sort may be related to the appeal of visual "mental animations" in constructing and evaluating explanations of devices (Hegarty 1992).

HOW DO WE DEAL WITH GAPS IN EXPLANATORY UNDERSTANDING?

Even though we often think we understand a system in far more detail than we really do, we rarely think we have a fully exhaustive understanding of any complex system (Keil 2003a,b). How, then, do we deal with recognized gaps in explanatory understanding? Sometimes we suppress our ignorance through a memory distortion of the explanatory failure or by a reconstruction of the event itself into a more explanatorily tractable form (see, e.g., Schacter et al. 1995). We might also attempt to fill in the gap by acquiring new details of function and/or mechanism. Finally, we may recognize the gap and decide to "outsource" it to another mind, believing that the outsourced area of understanding supports our own explanations in a safe and reliable manner.

This third way of dealing with gaps is relatively unexplored in psychology, yet may represent the dominant way in which we handle incomplete understandings. We are not isolated learners each on our own desert island of intellectual exploration. We rely heavily on expertise in other minds. The study of distributed cognition has long recognized this fact (e.g., Crowley et al. 2001, Hutchins 1995), but largely has involved demonstrations of how people in groups share cognitive burdens and achieve results not possible as individual problem solvers (Cole & Engestrom 1993, Crowley et al. 2001, Hutchins 1995). With incomplete explanations, however, we often are not in direct interaction with others. Instead, we rely on others who are removed from us in both space and time.

To use others as sources of information, we have to know if they are speaking from an area of expertise or are posturing, bluffing, or otherwise unreliable. Sources can be deficient on several distinct grounds: motivational states, general competence, or competence in the area that is being explained. Motivational states matter when we believe that explainers have conflicts of interest (Walster et al. 1966). The drug company spokesperson who touts the scientific reasons for taking the company's new drug seems less credible than the independent scientists or consumer advocates making the same claims, but who are normally critical of the drug companies. People do discount explanations when such conflicts of interest are made salient (Miller 1999). Moreover, such discounting occurs early in a child's development (Mills & Keil 2005). We also discount the quality of a person's explanation if we feel that the person is incompetent as revealed by being intoxicated, uneducated, or excessively emotional. Finally, it may be important to know when people do not care if what they are saying is true or false and are simply attempting to make another person think that they know what they are talking about (Frankfurt 2005).

Even when sources are not contaminated by self-interest or obvious global incompetence, we may discount them as outside their area of expertise. Such intuitions arise from an ability to track not only the divisions of labor noted by Smith and Durkheim (e.g., Durkheim 1893, Smith 1776), but also the corresponding divisions of cognitive and linguistic labor (Kitcher 2001, Putnam 1975). To surmount gaps in our own knowledge, we need to know what groups of experts are relevant.

Adults and surprisingly young children can often use their coarse, fragmentary explanatory understandings to leverage access to much deeper explanations when needed (Danovitch & Keil 2004, Keil 2005, Lutz & Keil 2002). Thus, if a person has a better-than-average understanding of one phenomenon, we can guess about what else they are likely to know on the basis of our own more limited knowledge of how causal regularities in the world cluster. For example, if a person knows a lot about how spinning tops stay up, adults and children alike will infer that the same person is likely to know more about why basketballs bounce than why animals have to breathe (Keil 2005). They assume that there is a pattern of causal regularities concerning bounded objects in motion such that an expert on one phenomenon arising from those regularities is likely to understand other phenomena arising from the same regularities. One may not know much about those regularities, but instead may have just a shallow impression of distinctive causal patterns corresponding roughly to physical mechanics. In this way, great gaps in understanding can rest on firmer ground. A related line of work examines how adults and children evaluate testimony, and suggests a similar early emerging sense of how to decide what messages are more reliable than others (Clément et al. 2004, Harris 2002).

HOW DO EXPLANATORY SKILLS DEVELOP?

Explanatory skills develop along several dimensions. Most obvious are the explanations offered by children. A second dimension concerns children's understanding of what makes a good explanation. Finally, there are the developing abilities to evaluate one's own explanatory understanding and the epistemological status of explanations.

Signs of explanatory ability may first be seen when children ask questions about the workings of the world around them. Although some "why" questions can simply be attempts to get parents to change their minds (e.g., "Why can't I have dessert before dinner?"), in many other cases young children ask questions that try to uncover mechanisms or explain inconsistencies. Young preschoolers will ask "why" questions about the causal structure of the world, questions that are shaped by the causal explanations they receive from parents and others (Hickling & Wellman 2001). In their answers, parents tend to focus more on prior causal factors than on consequences, and such answers are indeed the ones being sought (Callanan & Oakes 1992). Children often give off information about their level of understanding in their gestures when they ask questions, information that is not always fully utilized by parents. Thus, when parents are taught how to attend to children's gestures in asking questions, adult explanations will show an improvement in quality and effectiveness (Kelly et al. 2002). The subtlety of children's questions can be quite striking, e.g., preschoolers ask about the functions of artifacts as wholes but only about the parts of animals (Greif et al. 2005).

Almost as early as the first "why" questions are the first attempts at explanations. Although certainly the explanations of three-year-olds differ in complexity and clarity from those of an older child or adult, they will offer causal accounts that seem to be roughly appropriate for the domain involved. Psychological phenomena are explained with psychological relations, physical events with physical causal relations, and biological patterns with biological mechanisms (Gelman 2002, Hickling & Wellman 2001, Inagaki & Hatano 2002, Wellman & Schult 1997). Thus, within a year of having any facility with language, children map causal patterns in the world with kinds of explanations roughly corresponding to those patterns. They do so systematically and consistently for at least the domains of biology, psychology, and physical mechanics and social conventions (Gelman & Kremer 1991, Hickling & Wellman 2001). In one pioneering set of studies in this area, preschoolers reliably chose different kinds of explanatory schemas to account for departures from physical, social conventional, and moral regularities (invoking magic, defective mental states, and ill will, respectively) (Lockhart 1981).

The ability to explain events after the fact may emerge earlier than the ability to predict those events. For example, in explaining the mental behaviors of others, preschoolers sometimes find it easier to explain why a person was deceived or mistaken than that they will be mistaken in the same task (Bartsch 1998, Wimmer & Mayringer 1998). This pattern may be related to the hindsight bias in adults in which people who are given an explanation of an outcome falsely assume they could have predicted that outcome.

In many cases, implicit explanatory understanding seems to precede explicit versions in development, often by several years. This progression can sometimes be uncovered by eye-tracking studies in which children anticipate with their eyes more advanced explanations while explicitly offering more primitive ones (e.g., Clements et al. 2000). Similarly, gestures can reveal an explanatory understanding that hasn't yet appeared in explicit terms (Garber & Goldin-Meadow 2002). What sort of implicit knowledge, however, should count as explanatory understanding as opposed to a simpler tracking of some causal or relational pattern? Implicit precursors of explicit forms are better candidates than are patterns of causal tracking buried in cognitively impenetrable modules.

As described earlier, children's explanations do suffer, sometimes dramatically, from an inability to gauge correctly the level of understanding in another. Not until quite late in development do children have a mature sense of the "epistemology" of explanations (Kuhn & Franklin 2005). A mature epistemology of explanations sees explanations as falsifiable, recognizes evidence as the usual means for falsification, and realizes that theory and evidence are different and play complementary roles (Kuhn & Franklin 2005). During adolescence, teenagers shift from viewing explanations as absolutist to viewing knowledge as more pluralistic or relativistic (Hofer & Pintrich 2002, Kuhn & Franklin 2005). Younger children assume that there must be one correct explanation and that science or other areas of inquiry proceed by adding more true facts and principles to that explanation. Only later do they appreciate that two different communities of equally reputable scientists and scholars might disagree on which of two competing explanations is correct. Moreover, the transition out of absolutist ways of understanding occurs in a domain-specific manner, for example, occurring earlier for aesthetic judgments than for more fact-based reasoning (Kuhn et al. 2000).

EXPLANATION ACROSS CULTURES

Although cultures may differ in their dominant explanatory styles, they rarely, if ever, have a particular explanatory style completely unavailable to them. That more dated view of cultural differences, often aided and abetted by implicit assumptions of western cultures as being more scientific, analytic, and abstract in explanatory styles, no longer seems plausible (see, e.g., Cole & Means 1981, Sperber & Hirschfeld 1999). Instead, cultural differences are now more commonly thought of as different default hierarchies. A particular explanatory style may be the first option in one culture and a less-prominent option in another, but rarely is one form of explanation completely unavailable. One well-known example of explanatory differences occurs in cultures that are considered collectivist or concerned more with the rights of the group relative to those of the individual, versus cultures that are individualist and that have the opposite emphasis (Triandis 1995). Collectivist cultures tend to provide more situational explanations about behaviors, whereas individualist cultures tend to provide more dispositional explanations. Extending beyond the social realm, even inanimate objects, such as the movement of a stick in a stream, may be explained in more situational terms in a collectivist culture and more dispositionally in an individualist culture (Nisbett 2003). Do these different orderings of explanatory styles hold across all domains, e.g., a situational bias for phenomena ranging from physical mechanics to social interactions, or do the orderings themselves differ across domains and cultures in a more complex interactional pattern? Based on analogous results for moral reasoning (e.g., Turiel 1998), the more complex interactional result seems likely.

Different explanatory styles may also emerge as a function of the predominant practices of a culture. Cultures using forms of agriculture that are sensitive to soil conservation might adopt more ecologically oriented forms of biological explanation that see more commonalities in explanations for both plants and animals than other groups using slash and burn agriculture. Similarly, people may reason about the same groups of fish in goal-centered versus ecological ways because of different cultural lenses (Medin & Atran 2004, Medin et al. 2005). More subtly, some groups in a domain may make inductions based on reference to ideals in a category, while others may make similar inductions based on category-central prototypes (Lynch et al. 2000).

A different pattern of cultural variation in explanatory form happens when a core explanatory idea is shared, but it becomes elaborated on in different ways across cultures. Consider, for example, vitalism, the tendency to assume that living things have vital forces inside them that are responsible for growth and, in animals, for activity (Inagaki & Hatano 2002). Many cultures may share this explanatory framework but will fill it out differently. One may intentionalize agents within living things, whereas another might use a notion of fluid energy (Inagaki & Hatano 2002, 2004). In a related vein, it appears that all cultures adopt a kind of Cartesian dualism in explanations about minds and bodies, but they fill out the details in very different ways (Bloom 2004). Many turn to religious notions of the soul, others invoke animistic spirits, while still others may rely on a shared being in several bodies at once. These examples illustrate a differentiation model in which a core explanatory schema is shared by all cultures but can become manifested in quite different concrete ways.

The influence of culture, context, and even social class on explanatory styles is clearly a growth area for research. Already, however, it seems likely that the predominant pattern will be one in which no culture is completely blocked from certain forms of explanatory styles or schemes. Instead, it seems more plausible that cultures will vary in the ordering preferences of such explanatory forms in each domain and in terms of how they fill out the more mechanistic details of each scheme.

CONCLUSIONS

The processes of constructing and understanding explanations are intrinsic to our mental lives from an early age, with some sense of explanatory insight present before children are even able to speak. A focus on explanation and understanding brings to the fore issues and perspectives that are not as prominent in discussions of related topics such as intuitive theories and mental models. Explanations are sought after and provided not only in interpersonal interactions but also within the mind of a single individual. There is considerable diversity in kinds of explanations in terms of the causal patterns they invoke, the broad stances they employ, and the more local domains in which they occur. Qualitatively different patterns of explanation seem to be used in talking about domains such as physical mechanics, biological function, and social interactions. A major challenge remains in specifying in more detail the structures of these explanatory types and demarcating the sorts of domains that are responsible for such structural differences. Explanatory types may also vary as a function of the different uses of explanations beyond those of prediction, such as for justification and rationalization, culpability determination, and aesthetic insight.

The causal and relational complexity inherent in much of the world makes many explanations necessarily incomplete or flawed. We therefore must rely on coarser gists that provide effective explanatory frameworks while nonetheless missing many details. We are adept at supplementing these gists by "outsourcing" knowledge to other minds and relying on the divisions of cognitive labor that occur in all cultures. People also use a wide variety of heuristics to recognize bad explanations and additional ones to choose among competing explanations that may be reasonable. These skills, however, do not prevent us from frequently overestimating the depth of our explanatory understanding, often dramatically, in ways that are systematically related to the entity or system being explained. All of us throughout the world may share the same drive for explanation, the same assortment of explanatory styles and strategies for dealing with gaps, and similar developmental patterns. Our differences may lie in which explanatory styles come to mind first in specific contexts, not in terms of fundamental explanatory abilities.

ACKNOWLEDGMENTS

Preparation of this review and some of the research described herein were supported by NIH grant R-37-HD023922 to Frank Keil. Thanks to Esther Schlegel for help in manuscript preparation.

The *Annual Review of Psychology* is online at http://psych.annualreviews.org

LITERATURE CITED

Ahn W. 1998. Why are different features central for natural kinds and artifacts? The role of causal status in determining feature centrality. *Cognition* 69:135–78

Ahn W, Kalish CW. 2000. The role of mechanism beliefs in causal reasoning. See Keil & Wilson 2000b, pp. 199–226

Ahn W, Kim NS, Lassaline ME, Dennis MJ. 2000. Causal status as a determinant of feature centrality. *Cogn. Psychol.* 41:361–416

Ahn W, Novick L, Kim NS. 2003. "Understanding it makes it more normal": Causal explanations influence person perception. *Psychon. Bull. Rev.* 10:746–52

Allen C, Bekoff M, Lauder G, eds. 1998. *Nature's Purposes: Analyses of Function and Design in Biology*. Cambridge, MA: MIT Press

Amini M. 2003. Has foundationalism failed? A critical review of *Coherence in Thought and Action* by Paul Thagard. *Hum. Nat. Rev.* 3:119–23

Barsalou L. 1999. Perceptual symbol systems. *Behav. Brain Sci.* 22:577–609

Bartsch K. 1998. False belief prediction and explanation: which develops first and why it matters. *Int. J. Behav. Dev.* 22(2):423–28

Bechtel W. 1994. Levels of description and explanation in cognitive science. *Minds Mach.* 4:1–25

Bechtel W, Abrahamsen A. 2005. Explanation: a mechanistic alternative. *Stud. Hist. Philos. Sci. C Stud. Hist. Philos. Biol. Biomed. Sci.* 36:421–41

Berk LE. 1994. Why children talk to themselves. *Sci. Am.* 271(5):78–83

Birch SA, Bloom P. 2003. Children are cursed: an asymmetric bias in mental state attribution. *Psychol. Sci.* 14:283–86

Bloom P. 1996. Intention, history, and artifact concepts. *Cognition* 60:1–29

Bloom P. 2004. *Descartes' Baby: How the Science of Child Development Explains What Makes Us Human.* New York: Basic Books

Bloom P, German T. 2000. Two reasons to abandon the false belief task as a test of theory of mind. *Cognition* 77:B25–31

Boyd R. 1999. Homeostasis, species, and higher taxa. In *Species: New Interdisciplinary Studies*, ed. R Wilson, pp. 141–85. Cambridge, MA: MIT Press

Brem SK, Rips LJ. 2000. Explanation and evidence in informal argument. *Cogn. Sci.* 24: 573–604

Bromberger S. 1966. Why-questions. In *Readings in the Philosophy of Science*, ed. BA Brody, pp. 66–84. Englewood Cliffs, NJ: Prentice Hall

Callanan M, Oakes L. 1992. Preschoolers' questions and parents' explanations: causal thinking in everyday activity. *Cogn. Dev.* 7: 213–33

Carey S. 1985. *Conceptual Change in Childhood.* Cambridge, MA: Bradford Books/MIT Press

Cartwright N. 1999. *The Dappled World: A Study of the Boundaries of Science.* London: Cambridge Univ. Press

Cartwright N. 2004. From causation to explanation and back. In *The Future for Philosophy*, ed. B Leiter, pp. 230–45. London: Oxford Univ. Press

Cavanaugh P. 1999. Pictorial art and vision. In *MIT Encyclopedia of Cognitive Sciences*, ed. RA Wilson, FC Keil, pp. 648–51. Cambridge, MA: MIT Press

Chater N, Oaksford M. 2005. Mental mechanisms: speculations on human causal learning and reasoning. In *Information Sampling and Adaptive Cognition,* ed. K Fiedler, P Juslin. London: Cambridge Univ. Press. In press

Chater N, Vitanyi P. 2003. Simplicity: a unifying principle in cognitive science? *Trends Cogn. Sci.* 7(1):19–22

Cheng PW. 1997. From covariation to causation: a causal power theory. *Psychol. Rev.* 104:367–405

Chinn CA, Brewer WF. 1993. The role of anomalous data in knowledge acquisition: a theoretical framework and implications for science instruction. *Rev. Educ. Res.* 63:1–49

Church RB, Goldin-Meadow S. 1986. The mismatch between gesture and speech as an index of transitional knowledge. *Cognition* 23:43–71

Clark A. 1997. *Being There: Putting Brain, Body and World Together Again.* Cambridge, MA: MIT Press

Clark HH. 1996. *Using Language.* London: Cambridge Univ. Press

Clément F, Koenig M, Harris PL. 2004. The ontogenesis of trust. *Mind Lang.* 19:360–79

Clements W, Rustin CL, McCallum S. 2000. Promoting the transition from implicit to explicit understanding: a training study of false belief. *Dev. Sci.* 3(1):81–92

Cole M, Engestrom Y. 1993. A cultural approach to distributed cognition. In *Distributed Cognitions: Psychological and Educational Considerations*, ed. G Salomon, pp. 1–46. New York: Cambridge Univ. Press

Cole M, Means B. 1981. *Comparative Studies of How People Think: An Introduction.* Cambridge, MA: Harvard Univ. Press

Collins J, Hall E, Paul L. 2001. *Causation and Counterfactuals.* Cambridge, MA: MIT Press

Cosmides L, Tooby J. 1987. From evolution to behavior: evolutionary psychology as the missing link. In *The Latest on the Best: Essays on Evolution and Optimality*, ed. J Dupre, pp. 277–306. Cambridge, MA: MIT Press

Crowley K, Callanan MA, Jipson J, Galco J, Topping K, Shrager J. 2001. Shared scientific thinking in everyday parent-child activity. *Sci. Educ.* 85:712–32

Cummins R. 2000. "How does it work?" versus "What are the laws?" Two conceptions of psychological explanation. See Keil & Wilson 2000b, pp. 117–45

Cziksentmihalyi M. 1990. *Flow: The Psychology of Optimal Experience*. New York: HarperCollins

Danovitch JH, Keil FC. 2004. Should you ask a fisherman or a biologist? Developmental shifts in ways of clustering knowledge. *Child Dev.* 5:918–31

Danovitch JH, Keil FC. 2005. *Scientists or saints: the emergence of an understanding of the mental characteristics needed to solve moral or scientific problems*. Poster presented at 2005 Meet. Soc. Child Dev., Atlanta, GA

Dennett D. 1987. *The Intentional Stance*. Cambridge, MA: MIT Press

Dickinson A. 2001. Causal learning: an associative analysis. *Q. J. Exp. Psychol.* 54B:3–25

di Sessa A. 1993. Towards an epistemology of physics. *Cogn. Instruct.* 10:105–225

di Sessa A, Gillespie NM, Esterly JB. 2004. Coherence versus fragmentation in the development of the concept of force. *Cogn. Sci.* 28:843–900

Dunbar K. 1995. How scientists really reason: scientific reasoning in real-world laboratories. In *The Nature of Insight*, ed. R Sternberg, J Davidson, pp. 365–96. Cambridge, MA: MIT Press

Dunbar K, Blanchette I. 2001. The in vivo/in vitro approach to cognition: the case of analogy. *Trends Cogn. Sci.* 5:334–39

Durkheim E. 1893/1997. *The Division of Labor in Society*. Transl. G Simpson. New York: Free Press (From French)

Fauconnier G, Turner M. 2002. *The Way We Think: Conceptual Blending and the Mind's Hidden Complexities*. New York: Basic Books

Ferguson N, ed. 1999. *Virtual History: Alternatives and Counterfactuals*. New York: Basic Books. First publ. 1997 by Picador, London

Fodor JA. 1975. *The Language of Thought*. New York: Thomas Crowell

Fodor JA. 1998. *Concepts: Where Cognitive Science Went Wrong*. New York: Oxford Univ. Press

Frankfurt H. 2005. *On Bullshit*. Princeton, NJ: Princeton Univ. Press

Garber P, Goldin-Meadow S. 2002. Gesture offers insight into problem-solving in adults and children. *Cogn. Sci.* 26:817–31

Gelman R. 2002. Cognitive development. In *Stevens' Handbook of Experimental Psychology*, ed. H Pashler, DL Medin, R Gallistel, J Wixted, 3:396–443. New York: Wiley. 3rd ed.

Gelman SA. 2003. *The Essential Child*. New York: Oxford Univ. Press

Gelman SA, Kremer KA. 1991. Understanding natural cause: children's explanations of how objects and their properties originate. *Child Dev.* 62(2):396–414

Gentner D. 1983. Structure-mapping: a theoretical framework for analogy. *Cogn. Sci.* 7(2):155–70

Gentner D, Gentner D. 1983. Flowing waters or teeming crowds: mental models of electricity. In *Mental Models*, ed. D Gentner, AL Stevens, pp. 99–129. Hillsdale, NJ: Erlbaum

Gentner D, Rattermann MJ, Markman AB, Kotovsky L. 1995. Two forces in the development of relational structure. In *Developing Cognitive Competence: New Approaches to Process Modeling*, ed. T Simon, G Halford, pp. 263–313. Hillsdale, NJ: Erlbaum

Gentner D, Stevens A. 1983. *Mental Models*. Hillsdale, NJ: Erlbaum

Gentner D, Toupin C. 1986. Systematicity and surface similarity in the development of analogy. *Cogn. Sci.* 10:277–300

Gergely G, Nadasdy Z, Csibra G, Biro S. 1995. Taking the intentional stance at 12 months of age. *Cognition* 56(2):165–93

German TP, Johnson SA. 2002. Function and the origins of the design stance. *J. Cogn. Dev.* 3:279–300

Glennan S. 2002. Rethinking mechanistic explanation. *Philos. Sci.* 69:S342–53

Glymour C. 1998. Learning causes: psychological explanations of causal explanations. *Minds Machines* 8(1):39–60

Glymour C. 2001. *The Mind's Arrows: Bayes Nets and Graphical Causal Models in Psychology.* Cambridge, MA: MIT Press

Gopnik A. 1998. Explanation as orgasm. *Minds Machines* 8(1):101–18

Gopnik A, Glymour C, Sobel D. 2004. Causal maps and Bayes nets: a theory of causal inference in young children. *Psychol. Rev.* 111(1):1–30

Gould SJ, Lewontin RC. 1979. The spandrels of San Marco and the Panglossion paradigm: a critique of the adaptationist programme. *Proc. R. Soc. Lond. B* 205:581–98

Graesser AC, Olde BA. 2003. How does one know whether a person understands a device? The quality of the questions the person asks when the device breaks down. *J. Educ. Psychol.* 95:524–36

Greene J, Haidt J. 2002. How (and where) does moral judgment work? *Trends Cogn. Sci.* 6(12):517–23

Greif M, Guitterez F, Keil F, Kemler-Nelson D. 2005. *What do children want to know about animals and artifacts? Domain-specific requests for information.* Poster presented at 2005 Meet. Soc. Child Dev., Atlanta, GA

Grice HP. 1975. Logic and conversation. In *Syntax and Semantics*, ed. P Cole, J Morgan, pp. 41–58. New York: Academic

Griffiths TL, Baraff ER, Tenenbaum JB. 2004. Using physical theories to infer hidden causal structure. *Proc. 26th Annu. Conf. Cogn. Sci. Soc., Chicago*, pp. 446–51. Mahwah, NJ: Erlbaum

Haidt J. 2001. The emotional dog and its rational tail. *Psychol. Rev.* 108:814–34

Harman G. 1965. The inference to the best explanation. *Philos. Rev.* 74:88–95

Harris PL. 2002. What do children learn from testimony? In *The Cognitive Basis of Science*, ed. P Carruthers, SP Stich, M Siegal, pp. 316–34. London: Cambridge Univ. Press

Hegarty M. 1992. Mental animation: inferring motion from static displays of mechanical systems. *J. Exp. Psychol. Learn. Mem. Cogn.* 18:1084–102

Heider F. 1958. *The Psychology of Interpersonal Relations.* New York: Wiley

Hempel CG. 1965. *Aspects of Scientific Explanation.* New York: Free Press

Hempel CG, Oppenheim P. 1948. Studies in the logic of explanation. *Philos. Sci.* 15:135–75

Hickling AK, Wellman HM. 2001. The emergence of children's causal explanations and theories: evidence from everyday conversation. *Dev. Psychol.* 37:668–83

Hofer B, Pintrich P. 2002. *Epistemology: The Psychology of Beliefs About Knowledge and Knowing.* Mahwah, NJ: Erlbaum

Holyoak KJ, Thagard P. 1995. *Mental Leaps: Analogy in Creative Thought.* Cambridge, MA: MIT Press

Home RW. 1981. *The Effluvial Theory of Electricity.* New York: Arno

Humphreys P. 1989. *The Chances of Explanation: Causal Explanations in the Social, Medical, and Physical Sciences.* Princeton, NJ: Princeton Univ. Press

Hutchins E. 1995. *Cognition in the Wild.* Cambridge, MA: MIT Press

Inagaki K, Hatano G. 2002. *Young Children's Naïve Thinking About the Biological World.* New York: Psychol. Press

Inagaki K, Hatano G. 2004. Vitalistic causality in young children's naive biology. *Trends Cogn. Sci.* 8:356–62

Johnson-Laird PN. 1983. *Mental Models.* Cambridge, MA: Harvard Univ. Press

Kahneman D, Miller DT. 1986. Norm theory: comparing reality to its alternatives. *Psychol. Rev.* 93:136–53

Kahneman D, Tversky A. 1982. The simulation heuristic. In *Judgment Under Uncertainty: Heuristics and Biases*, ed. D Kahneman, P Slovic, A Tversky, pp. 201–8. New York: Cambridge Univ. Press

Kayoko I, Giyoo H. 2004. Vitalistic causality in

young children's naive biology. *Trends Cogn. Sci.* 8(8):356–62

Keil FC. 1989. *Concepts, Kinds and Cognitive Development.* Cambridge, MA: MIT Press

Keil FC. 1992. The emergence of an autonomous biology. In *Modularity and Constraints in Language and Cognition: The Minnesota Symposia,* ed. M Gunnar, M Maratsos, pp.103–38. Hillsdale, NJ: Erlbaum

Keil FC. 1995. The growth of causal understandings of natural kinds: modes of construal and the emergence of biological thought. In *Causal Cognition,* ed. A Premack, D Sperber, pp. 234–62. New York: Oxford Univ. Press

Keil FC. 2003a. Categorization, causation and the limits of understanding. *Lang. Cogn. Process.* 18:663–92

Keil FC. 2003b. Folkscience: coarse interpretations of a complex reality. *Trends Cogn. Sci.* 7:368–73

Keil FC. 2003c. That's life: coming to understand biology. *Hum. Dev.* 46:369–77

Keil FC. 2005. Doubt, deference and deliberation. *Oxf. Stud. Epistemol.* In press

Keil FC, Greif M, Kerner R. 2005. A world apart: artifacts. In *Creations of the Mind: Essays on Artifacts and Their Representation,* ed. E Margolis. Oxford Univ. Press. In press

Keil FC, Rozenblit LR, Mills C. 2004. What lies beneath? Understanding the limits of understanding. In *Thinking and Seeing: Visual Metacognition in Adults and Children,* ed. DT Levin, pp. 227–49. Cambridge, MA: MIT Press

Keil FC, Smith C, Simons DJ, Levin DT. 1998. Two dogmas of conceptual empiricism: implications for hybrid models of the structure of knowledge. *Cognition* 65:103–35

Keil FC, Wilson RA. 2000a. Explaining explanation. See Keil & Wilson 2000b, pp. 1–18

Keil FC, Wilson RA. 2000b. *Explanation and Cognition.* Cambridge, MA: MIT Press

Kelemen D. 1999. Function, goals, and intention: children's teleological reasoning about objects. *Trends Cogn. Sci.* 3:461–68

Kelemen D, Carey S. 2005. The essence of artifacts: developing the design stance. In *Creation of the Mind: Essays on Artifacts and Their Representation,* ed. E Margolis, S Lawrence. New York: Oxford Univ. Press. In press

Kelly SD, Singer M, Hicks J, Goldin-Meadow S. 2002. A helping hand in assessing children's knowledge: instructing adults to attend to gesture. *Cogn. Instruct.* 20(1):1–26

Kemp CS, Perfors A, Tenenbaum JB. 2004. Learning domain structures. *Proc. 26th Annu. Conf. Cogn. Sci. Soc., Chicago,* pp. 663–68. Mahwah, NJ: Erlbaum

Keysar B, Barr DJ, Horton WS. 1998. The egocentric basis of language use: insights from a processing approach. *Curr. Dir. Psychol. Sci.* 7:46–50

Kim NS, Keil FC. 2003. From symptoms to causes: diversity effects in diagnostic reasoning. *Mem. Cogn.* 31:155–65

Kitcher P. 2001. *Science, Truth and Democracy.* London: Oxford Univ. Press

Kozhevnikov M, Hegarty M. 2001. Impetus beliefs as default heuristics: dissociation between explicit and implicit knowledge about motion. *Psychon. Bull. Rev.* 8(3):439–53

Krauss RM, Glucksberg S. 1969. The development of communication: competence as a function of age. *Child Dev.* 40:255–66

Krueger J, Dunning D. 1999. Unskilled and unaware of it: how difficulties in recognizing one's own incompetence lead to inflated self-assessments. *J. Personal. Soc. Psychol.* 77:1121–34

Krynski TR, Tenenbaum JB. 2003. The role of causal models in reasoning under uncertainty. *Proc. 25th Annu. Conf. Cogn. Sci. Soc.,* pp. 692–97. London: LEA

Kuhn D, Black J, Keselman A, Kaplan D. 2000. The development of cognitive skills to support inquiry learning. *Cogn. Instruct.* 18:495–523

Kuhn D, Franklin S. 2005. The second decade: What develops (and how)? In *Handbook of Child Psychology,* series ed. W Damon, R Lerner, vol. ed. D Kuhn, RS Siegler, Vol. 2. 6th ed. In press

Lehman DR, Lempert RO, Nisbett RE. 1988.

The effects of graduate training on reasoning: formal discipline and thinking about everyday life events. *Am. Psychol.* 43:431–43

Lewis D. 1973. *Counterfactuals*. Cambridge, MA: Harvard Univ. Press

Lockhart KL. 1981. The development of knowledge about uniformities in the environment: a comparative analysis of the child's understanding of social, moral, and physical rules. *Dissert. Abstr. Int.* 41:2793

Lombrozo T. 2004. *Teleological explanation*: *causal constraints and regularities*. Paper presented at 1st joint meet. Soc. Philos. Psychol. Eur. Soc. Philos. Psychol., Barcelona, Spain

Lombrozo T, Carey S. 2005. Functional explanation and the function of explanation. *Cognition*. In press

Luhmann CC, Ahn WK, Palmeri TJ. 2002. Theories and similarity: categorization under speeded conditions. *Proc. 24th Annu. Conf. Cogn. Sci. Soc.*, pp. 590–95. Mahwah, NJ: Erlbaum

Lutz DR, Keil FC. 2002. Early understanding of the division of cognitive labor. *Child Dev.* 73:1073–84

Lynch EB, Coley JD, Medin DL. 2000. Tall is typical: central tendency, ideal dimensions and graded category structure among tree experts and novices. *Mem. Cogn.* 28(1):41–50

Machamer P, Darden L, Craver C. 2000. Thinking about mechanisms. *Philos. Sci.* 67:1–25

Macrae CN, Bodenhausen GV. 2000. Social cognition: thinking categorically about others. *Annu. Rev. Psychol.* 51:93–120

Malle BF. 2004. *How the Mind Explains Behavior: Folk Explanations, Meaning, and Social Interaction*. Cambridge, MA: MIT Press

Markman EM. 1977. Realizing that you don't understand: a preliminary investigation. *Child Dev.* 48(3):986–92

Medin DL, Atran S. 2004. The native mind: biological categorization, reasoning and decision making in development across cultures. *Psychol. Rev.* 111:960–83

Medin DL, Ross N, Atran S, Cox D, Wakaua HJ, et al. 2005. The role of culture in the folkbiology of freshwater fish. *Cogn. Psychol.* In press

Miller DT. 1999. The norm of self-interest. *Am. Psychol.* 54:1053–60

Mills C, Keil FC. 2004. Knowing the limits of one's understanding: the development of an awareness of an illusion of explanatory depth. *J. Exp. Child Psychol.* 87:1–32

Mills C, Keil FC. 2005. The development of cynicism. *Psychol. Sci.* 16:385–90

Murphy GL. 2002. *The Big Book of Concepts*. Cambridge: MIT Press

Murphy GL, Medin DL. 1985. The role of theories in conceptual coherence. *Psychol. Rev.* 92:289–316

Nickerson RS. 2001. The projective way of knowing. *Curr. Dir. Psychol. Sci.* 10:168–72

Nisbett R. 2003. *The Geography of Thought*. New York: Free Press

Oppenheimer DM. 2004. Spontaneous discounting of availability in frequency judgment tasks. *Psychol. Sci.* 15:100–5

Piaget J. 1926. *The Language and Thought of the Child*. New York: Routledge & Kegan Paul

Putnam H. 1975. The meaning of meaning. In *Language, Mind and Knowledge*, ed. K Gunderson, pp. 131–93. Minneapolis: Univ. Minn. Press

Rehder B, Hastie R. 2004. Category coherence and category-based property induction. *Cognition* 91:113–53

Rips LJ. 2002. Circular reasoning. *Cogn. Sci.* 26:767–95

Roese NJ. 1997. Counterfactual thinking. *Psychol. Bull.* 121:133–48

Rosch E, Mervis C, Gray W, Johnson D, Boyes-Braem P. 1976. Basic objects in natural categories. *Cogn. Psychol.* 8:382–439

Rozenblit LR, Keil FC. 2002. The misunderstood limits of folk science: an illusion of explanatory depth. *Cogn. Sci.* 26:521–62

Salmon W. 1980. Probabilistic causality. *Pacific Philos. Q.* 61:50–74

Salmon W. 1984. *Scientific Explanation and the Causal Structure of the World*. Princeton, NJ: Princeton Univ. Press

Salmon W. 1989. Four decades of scientific explanation. In *Scientific Explanation*, ed. P Kitcher, W Salmon, pp. 3–219. Minneapolis: Univ. Minn. Press

Schacter DL, Coyle JT, Fischbach GD, Mesulam MM, Sullivan LE, eds. 1995. *Memory Distortion: How Minds, Brains, and Societies Reconstruct the Past*. Cambridge, MA: Harvard Univ. Press

Schank RC, Abelson RP. 1977. *Scripts, Plans, Goals and Understanding*. Hillsdale, NJ: Erlbaum

Simon HA. 1996. *Science of the Artificial*. Cambridge, MA: MIT Press. 3rd ed.

Simon HA. 2000. Discovering explanations. In *Cognition and Explanation*, ed. R Wilson, F Keil, pp. 21–59. Cambridge, MA: MIT Press

Sloman SA, Love BC, Ahn W. 1998. Feature centrality and conceptual coherence. *Cogn. Sci.* 22:189–228

Smith A. 1776/1904. *An Inquiry into the Nature and Causes of the Wealth of Nations*. London: Methuen

Sobel D, Tenenbaum JB, Gopnik A. 2004. Children's causal inferences from indirect evidence: backwards blocking and Bayesian reasoning in preschoolers. *Cogn. Sci.* 28:303–33

Sober E. 1975. *Simplicity*. Oxford, UK: Clarendon

Sober E. 1984. Common cause explanation. *Philos. Sci.* 51:212–41

Spellman BA, Mandel DR. 1999. When possibility informs reality: counterfactual thinking as a cue to causality. *Curr. Dir. Psychol. Sci.* 8:120–23

Sperber D, Hirschfeld LR. 1999. Culture, cognition and evolution. In *MIT Encyclopedia of the Cognitive Sciences*, ed. R Wilson, F Keil, pp. cxi–cxxxii. Cambridge, MA: MIT Press

Thagard P. 2000. *Coherence in Thought and Action*. Cambridge, MA: MIT Press

Thagard P, Verbeurgt K. 1998. Coherence as constraint satisfaction. *Cogn. Sci.* 22:1–24

Triandis HC. 1995. *Individualism and Collectivism*. Boulder, CO: Westview

Turiel E. 1998. Moral development. In *Handbook of Child Psychology*, 3:863–932. New York: Wiley. 5th ed.

Walster E, Aronson E, Abrahams D. 1966. On increasing the persuasiveness of a low-prestige communicator. *J. Exp. Soc. Psychol.* 2:325–42

Wellman HM, Schult CA. 1997. Explaining human movements and actions: children's understanding of the limits of psychological explanation. *Cognition* 62:291–324

Whewell W. 1847. *The Philosophy of the Inductive Sciences*. London: Cass

Wilson D, Sperber D. 2004. Relevance theory. In *Handbook of Pragmatics*, ed. G Ward, L Horn, pp. 607–32. Oxford, UK: Blackwell Sci.

Wilson RA, Keil FC. 1998. The shadows and shallows of explanation. *Minds Machines* 8:137–59

Wilson TD, Centerbar DB, Kermer DA, Gilbert DT. 2005. The pleasures of uncertainty: prolonging positive moods in ways people do not anticipate. *J. Personal. Soc. Psychol.* 88:5–21

Wimmer H, Mayringer H. 1998. False belief understanding in young children: Explanations do not develop before predictions. *Int. J. Behav. Dev.* 22:403–22

Winer GA, Cottrell JE, Gregg V, Fournier JS, Bica LA. 2002. Fundamentally misunderstanding visual perception: adults' beliefs in visual emissions. *Am. Psychol.* 57:417–24

Yates JF, Lee JW, Bush JG. 1997. General knowledge overconfidence: cross-national variations, response style, and "reality." *Organ. Behav. Hum. Decis. Process.* 70(2):87–94

Annu. Rev. Psychol. 2006. 57:255–84
doi: 10.1146/annurev.psych.57.102904.190124
First published online as a Review in Advance on August 31, 2005

ADOLESCENT DEVELOPMENT IN INTERPERSONAL AND SOCIETAL CONTEXTS

Judith G. Smetana, Nicole Campione-Barr, and Aaron Metzger

Department of Clinical & Social Sciences in Psychology, University of Rochester, Rochester, New York 14627; email: Smetana@psych.rochester.edu, campione@psych.rochester.edu, metzger@psych.rochester.edu

Key Words   adolescence, parenting, siblings, peers, romantic relationships

■ **Abstract**   In this chapter we review theoretical and empirical advances in research on adolescent development in interpersonal and societal contexts. First, we identify several trends in current research, including the current emphasis on ecological models and the focus on diversity in and relational models of adolescent development. Next, we discuss recent research on interpersonal relationships, with an eye toward identifying major research themes and findings. Research on adolescents' relationships with parents, siblings, other relatives, peers, and romantic partners, and adolescents' involvement in community and society is reviewed. Future directions in research on adolescent development are discussed.

CONTENTS

INTRODUCTION AND OVERVIEW

Since the publication of the last comprehensive review of research on adolescence in this series (Steinberg & Morris 2001), which followed a 13-year lag from the previous review (Petersen 1988), the psychological study of adolescence has come

0066-4308/06/0110-0255$20.00

of age. The number of papers pertaining to adolescent development published in the major developmental sciences journals such as *Child Development* and *Developmental Psychology* has been increasing steadily, while developmental science journals focusing specifically on adolescence continue to thrive. The Society for Research in Adolescence, the professional society that provides a multidisciplinary and international home for researchers interested in adolescent development, recently celebrated its twenty-first birthday. Moreover, two major handbooks of adolescence (Adams & Berzonsky 2003, Lerner & Steinberg 2004) and several major reviews (Collins & Steinberg 2005, Steinberg & Silk 2002) have been published recently. Although there are many reasons for the increased attention to development during adolescence (Steinberg & Morris 2001), the dramatic physical growth and physiological changes that characterize adolescence, combined with the many individual, cognitive, social, and contextual transitions that occur during this period, conspire to make adolescence an ideal period of the lifespan to study the interaction of different developmental systems (Collins et al. 2000).

Several trends characterize recent research on adolescent development. In terms of meta-theoretical and theoretical considerations, ecological approaches to human development (Bronfenbrenner 1979, Bronfenbrenner & Morris 1998), which gained in prominence in the 1980s and 1990s, continue to dominate the field (Lerner & Steinberg 2004, Steinberg & Morris 2001). Ecological approaches, which focus on understanding interactions among developing persons, the contexts of development, and the processes that account for development (Bronfenbrenner & Morris 1998), have increased our understanding of adolescent development beyond the proximal influences of the family and have yielded important new insights into contextual variations in adolescent development. Moreover, during the past decade, there has been an increased emphasis on (and greater methodological sophistication in) studies that examine the multiple interactions among different contexts, such as family, schools, and neighborhoods (e.g., Cook et al. 2002). Other approaches have gained significant footholds as well. For instance, recent research informed by family systems theory (Minuchin 2002) has led to a greater awareness of the relationships and mutual influences among different subsystems in the family. The interest in extending attachment theory beyond infancy has led to research examining adolescents' representations of relationships with parents, peers, and romantic partners, and several longitudinal studies have become available to test the crucial prediction that relationships during infancy influence the course of social relationships in adolescence and young adulthood.

Another notable trend in recent research on adolescence is the greater attention to studying diverse populations of youth. During the 1990s this research focused most heavily on studies of African American adolescents (Steinberg & Morris 2001), but as we move into the twenty-first century, several shifts are evident. First, reflecting the changing demographic landscape of the United States, research is slowly becoming more inclusive, focusing more broadly on the development of Asian, Hispanic, and occasionally, Eastern European youth (but unfortunately, almost never on Native American youth). Along with the increased inclusivity, there is increasing recognition of the significant heterogeneity among adolescents treated as part of a single racial or ethnic group (Chao & Tseng 2002, Harwood et al. 2002, Parke & Buriel 1998). More specifically, researchers are becoming more careful about specifying the national origins or background of adolescent participants, rather than treating their racial or ethnic background in global ways (e.g., "Asian" or "Latino"). Reflecting the demographic trends, immigration has emerged as an important new topic for research, and there has been more systematic consideration of the interacting effects of ethnicity, immigration, and social class (Chao & Tseng 2002, Fuligni 1998b). In addition, research is gradually moving beyond social address models of ethnicity or race to examine the processes that account for the influence of race and ethnicity on adolescents' values, beliefs, and behavior, including the influence of family obligations (Fuligni et al. 1999, 2002) and family interdependence (Phinney et al. 2000, 2005). Several scholars have called attention to the need to consider the adaptive (and maladaptive) strategies that ethnic minority adolescents use to cope with their status and have provided elegant integrative models for conceptualizing the potentially stressful effects of exposure to prejudice and discrimination (Garcia Coll et al. 1996, Spencer & Dupree 1996). Though still relatively scarce, empirical research employing such models is increasing (e.g., DuBois et al. 2002). There are ongoing debates about the optimal designs for studying minority youth, but changes in research emphasis have been accompanied by some shifts in research designs from comparative approaches that document group differences to within-group analyses that examine the processes that account for development and adjustment among adolescents of a single ethnic group or cultural background (Phinney & Landin 1998).

In their review, Steinberg & Morris (2001) noted that "parents, problems, and hormones" (p. 85) were among the most popular topics of recent research on adolescence. In the new millennium, research has continued to emphasize parenting and parent-adolescent relationships, although increasingly these relationships have been considered in the context of, or as linked with, other relationships, contexts (for instance, parent influences on peer relationships or the interactions among parents, peers, and neighborhoods), or biological or hereditary influences (see Collins et al. 2000 for an elaboration of current integrative models and research designs that address these issues). The problematic outcomes of adolescence also have continued to dominate research, although this emphasis has been accompanied by a dramatic increase in interest in positive youth development (Larson 2000, Lerner et al. 2000). The impact of the biological changes of puberty has been a longstanding and enduring topic for research, but interest in this topic has waned in the past few years, although attention to the biological changes of adolescence has not. Technical and methodological advances, particularly in the use of neural imaging techniques such as functional magnetic resonance imaging, as well as the increased prominence of the developmental neurosciences, have led to increased interest in and understanding of structural and functional changes in the adolescent brain. While discussion of this research is beyond the scope of this chapter, the research indicates that changes in the prefrontal cortex (increases in myelination and synaptic pruning) and the limbic system continue well into the twenties and appear to be related to cognitive functioning and self-regulation (Keating 2004, Spear 2000).

Another robust trend is that the study of adolescence has become more relational. This is evident in the greater focus on adolescents' relationships beyond the family, in the tendency to view other social relationships as complementary to rather than supplanting relationships with parents, and in the reconceptualization of major developmental processes of adolescence such as autonomy in more relational terms (Collins & Steinberg 2005). Consistent with this emphasis, we focus our review on adolescents' interpersonal relationships, broadly construed. We review progress and trends in several areas of ongoing and recent interest, including family relationships (relationships with parents, siblings, and other relatives), extrafamilial relationships (peer and romantic relationships), and adolescents' relationships to their communities and broader society, as conceptualized within the emerging area of civic engagement. We cannot hope to review all the available literature here. Rather, this chapter builds on previous reviews and focuses on trends, new findings, and potential avenues for further research. Furthermore, our focus here is primarily on adolescence as it is experienced in contemporary U.S. society. Future trends in research on adolescence, including topics or issues in need of further attention, are noted at the conclusion of the chapter.

Definitions of Adolescence

Most researchers have parsed adolescence into three developmental periods, entailing early adolescence (typically ages 10–13), middle adolescence (ages 14–17), and late adolescence (18 until the early twenties). It is commonly said that adolescence begins in biology and ends in culture, because the transition into adolescence is marked by the dramatic biological changes of puberty, while the transition to adulthood is less clearly marked. Transitions to adulthood have been defined sociologically in terms of marriage and family formation, completion of education, and entrance into the labor force. As these transitions are occurring at later ages in contemporary society, Arnett (2000, 2004) has proposed that the period between ages 18 and 25 should be treated as a separate developmental period, which he labels emerging adulthood. Arnett's claim rests on the significant demographic diversity (and instability) of this period, as well as the increases in identity exploration that typically occur at this time. Until recently, however, most of the research on adolescent development has focused on early and middle adolescence, with less research focusing on transitions out of adolescence. Thus, the utility of distinguishing between late adolescence and emerging adulthood remains to be empirically determined. The research on adolescent brain development, which shows that brain maturation is not complete, and new research demonstrating that mature decision making does not emerge until the middle twenties (Cauffman & Steinberg 2000), also has the potential to reshape our definitions of adolescence and the transitions to young adulthood.

FAMILY RELATIONSHIPS

Parent-Adolescent Relationships

The nature and quality of adolescents' relationships with parents continues to be one of the most heavily researched topics on adolescence. Despite decades of psychological research to the contrary, the persistent perception in the popular culture is that adolescence is a difficult period entailing significant moodiness, storm and stress, and willful disobedience toward parents. Yet, overwhelming evidence from the past 30 years indicates that extreme alienation from parents, active rejection of adult values and authority, and youthful rebellion are the exception, not the norm, that only a small proportion of adolescents (from 5%–15%, depending on the sample) experience emotional turmoil and extremely conflicted relations with parents, and that extreme difficulties typically have their origins prior to adolescence (Collins & Laursen 2004, Steinberg 1990).

Nevertheless, adolescent-parent relationships do go through significant transformations during adolescence, and parents perceive adolescence as the most challenging and difficult stage of childrearing (Buchanan et al. 1990). During adolescence, European American and European youth spend progressively less time with parents and family and more time with peers (Larson et al. 1996), although decreases in shared time depend to some extent on the type of activity considered (Dubas & Gerris 2002). Longitudinal research using the experience sampling method to examine adolescents' daily moods indicates that adolescents' negative emotional states increase as they transition into and move through adolescence, although the downward trend stops (but does not reverse) in late adolescence (Larson et al. 2002). Family relationships are transformed from more hierarchical relationships at the outset of adolescence to more egalitarian relationships by late adolescence (Youniss & Smollar 1985).

CONFLICT, DISTANCING, AND SEPARATION   Bickering, squabbling, and disagreements over everyday issues characterize parent-adolescent relationships, particularly during early adolescence (Collins & Laursen 2004, Holmbeck 1996, Smetana 1996). Although high levels of conflict during adolescence are deleterious for adolescent development, relationships, and future adjustment (Laursen & Collins 1994), researchers now agree that conflict in early adolescence is a normative and temporary perturbation that is functional in transforming family relationships. Moreover, moderate conflict with parents is associated with better adjustment than either no conflict or frequent conflict (Adams & Laursen 2001) and does not influence the subsequent quality of parent-adolescent relationships (as assessed longitudinally), although closeness and support are highly stable over time (Smetana et al. 2004b). A longstanding assumption was that conflict with parents follows a U-shaped trajectory across adolescence, with conflict peaking in middle adolescence and then declining. A recent meta-analysis (Laursen et al. 1998) has demonstrated, however, that the trajectory depends on how conflict is assessed. The rate (number of conflicts and their frequency of occurrence) peaks in early adolescence and then declines, while conflict intensity increases from early to middle adolescence, with mother-daughter dyads experiencing more conflicts than other parent-child configurations.

Reflecting the available research, Laursen et al's (1998) meta-analysis included studies of primarily white, middle-class families. Since then, research has emphasized ethnic, racial, and cultural variations in conflict expression and resolution and has been guided by the cultural psychology assumption that conflict in interpersonal relationships is more characteristic of individualistic cultures than cultures (or ethnic groups) that espouse more interdependent, familistic, or collectivist values (Markus et al. 1997, Rothbaum et al. 2000). Yet, age-related increases in parent-adolescent disagreements consistently have been found in studies examining American families of varying cultural and ethnic backgrounds (Fuligni 1998a, Phinney et al. 2005, Smetana & Gaines 1999) and among adolescents in Asian cultures (Yau & Smetana 1996, 2003), although perhaps at a lower frequency than among European American youth (Fuligni 1998a). Increases in conflict in early adolescence have been explained within evolutionary (Steinberg 1989), psychoanalytic (Holmbeck 1996), social-psychological (Laursen 1995), and social-cognitive (Collins 1990; Smetana 1988, 2002) frameworks, but whether the theoretical lens focuses on the biological changes of puberty or advances in adolescent social cognition, all of these approaches have in common the notion that parent-adolescent conflict leads to adolescents' greater independence from parents. Moreover, developmental issues also are salient for parents; conflict with adolescents among parents who are facing midlife issues contributes to psychological symptoms and life dissatisfaction, particularly for mothers (Silverberg & Steinberg 1990).

Most conflicts with parents during adolescence are resolved by disengaging (e.g., walking away) or giving in to parents (Montemayor 1983, Smetana et al. 1991b), but European American adolescents are less compliant with parents' wishes than are adolescents of other ethnicities, and the more acculturated adolescents become, the more they resemble European American youth (Phinney et al. 2005). Conflict resolution has been claimed to provide adolescents with developmentally appropriate opportunities to learn negotiation skills (Grotevant & Cooper 1985), but surprisingly little research has examined this proposition.

Structural changes in the family, like divorce and remarriage, have been found to lead to a temporary disruption of adolescent-parent relationships, including increased conflict, particularly in the first two years following a divorce and with the new stepparent (Hetherington & Kelly 2002). However, some evidence suggests that adolescent-parent conflict is less frequent in stably divorced, mother-headed households than in two-parent households, perhaps because mother-adolescent relationships in stably divorced families tend to be less hierarchical (Smetana et al. 1991a). Likewise, economic strain, both chronic (Gutman & Eccles 1999, McLoyd 1998) and more sudden (for instance, among Midwestern farming families who experienced economic decline; Conger et al. 1992, 1993), is associated with more negative parent-adolescent relationships, including greater parent-adolescent conflict and more negative emotions, as well as more harsh, punitive parenting. Indeed, a recent meta-analysis has shown that socioeconomic disadvantage is strongly and consistently related to harsh, unresponsive parenting (Grant et al. 2003).

CLOSENESS AND WARMTH   A well-established finding is that both adolescents' feelings of support, closeness, and intimacy and objectively observed assessments of warmth and cohesion in adolescent-parent relationships decline during adolescence (Buhrmester & Furman 1987; Conger & Ge 1999; Furman & Buhrmester 1985, 1992), although evidence from several studies suggests that relationships improve once adolescents leave home (Dubas & Petersen 1996). Similar developmental trajectories in warmth and closeness have been found in ethnic minority youth, with some variations in the timing of when closeness declines (Fuligni 1998a), and closer, more secure attachment to parents during adolescence is associated with greater social competence and better psychosocial adjustment (Allen et al. 1998).

Relationships with mothers and fathers have been found to differ in both quality and substance. Studies consistently show that across ages, adolescents are closer (Buhrmester & Furman 1987) and spend more time in direct interaction (Larson & Richards 1994) with mothers than with fathers. Adolescents also talk more about private matters like dating and sexual attitudes and information with mothers than with fathers (Larson & Richards 1994, Noller & Callan 1990). They are equally likely to talk about more impersonal issues, such as schoolwork, future plans, and social issues with either parent. Steinberg & Silk (2002) attribute this difference to the perception that fathers provide informational and material support while mothers provide more emotional support. Given the consistent finding that adolescents' relationships with mothers and fathers differ, surprisingly little empirical research includes fathers or examines the differential influence of mothers and fathers on adolescent development.

PARENTING STYLES   Along with adolescent-parent relationships, the effects of parenting on adolescent development continue to be very heavily researched, although there have been significant shifts in approach over the past decade. Baumrind's (1991) tripartite parenting typology, which has been refined to classify parenting into four categories derived from two orthogonal dimensions of demandingness and responsiveness (Maccoby & Martin 1983), continues to be the most popular approach. A well-established finding, supported by vast numbers of studies, is that adolescents raised in authoritative homes (where parents are both demanding and responsive) are more psychosocially competent as assessed on a wide array of outcomes than are adolescents raised in authoritarian, permissive, or rejecting-neglecting homes (Steinberg 2001). Furthermore, the benefits of authoritativeness trump the benefits of consistency in parenting; adolescents reared in homes where only one parent is authoritative have been shown to be more academically competent than adolescents reared in homes where parents are consistent but not authoritative in their parenting (Fletcher et al. 1999).

Authoritative parenting is more prevalent among European American than among ethnic minority parents and among middle- than among lower-socioeconomic-status families. Steinberg (2001) has concluded that authoritative parenting benefits youth of all ethnicities and socioeconomic statuses. Some have argued, however, that parenting should be assessed in terms of indigenous, culturally salient values. For instance, Chao (1994, 2001) has claimed that the strictness that characterizes Chinese parenting reflects a Confucian, child-centered emphasis on the importance of training (guan) rather than the more punitive, adult-centered attitudes that are reflected in authoritarian parenting. Moreover, there is some evidence that the positive effects of authoritative parenting, at least for immigrant Chinese youth, reflect the influence of greater exposure to American society (Chao 2001). Darling & Steinberg (1993) have conceptualized parenting styles as an emotional context that changes the meaning of different parenting practices. This model recasts parenting styles as part of a reciprocal, bidirectional process between parents and adolescents (Kuczynski 2003) and highlights the importance of parenting styles as influencing adolescents' willingness to be socialized by parents (Grusec & Goodnow 1994).

DIMENSIONAL APPROACHES   During the past decade, there has been a shift toward more dimensional approaches to studying parenting during adolescence and particularly toward greater specificity in defining those dimensions. For instance, rather than viewing parental control as a single dimension that ranges from high to low, distinctions have been made between overly intrusive parental control (referred to as psychological control) that attempts to control adolescents' thoughts and feelings and undermine adolescents' psychological development (Barber 1996, 2002) and behavioral control, or parental rules, regulations, supervision, monitoring, and management of adolescents' activities. Proactive parenting and parents' use of harsh discipline in early childhood (Pettit et al. 2001), as well as perceptions of parental overcontrol over issues that adolescents believe should be under personal jurisdiction (Smetana & Daddis 2002), have been found to lead to adolescents' feelings of psychological control. In turn, high levels of psychological control have been associated with both internalizing and externalizing problems (Barber 1996, 2002; Conger et al. 1997; Pettit et al. 2001).

Parental monitoring as a form of behavioral control is increasingly important in adolescence because it allows parents to keep track of their adolescents' activities, peer associations, and whereabouts while permitting greater autonomy. Numerous studies indicate that inadequate parental monitoring is associated with externalizing problems such as drug use, truancy, and antisocial behavior (see Steinberg & Silk 2002), while greater parental monitoring is associated with higher academic achievement and better adolescent adjustment (Lamborn et al. 1996, Pettit et al. 2001). Although it has been assumed that low socioeconomic status is associated with poor monitoring and supervision, associations have been inconsistent

(Hoff et al. 2002). Interestingly, though, recent research indicates that adolescents growing up in highly affluent communities are at increased risk for substance use, anxiety, and depression due to a lack of parental monitoring and supervision as well as pressures to achieve and lack of emotional closeness with parents (Luthar 2003, Luthar & Becker 2002).

Recently, Kerr & Stattin (2000, Stattin & Kerr 2000) observed that parental monitoring and surveillance typically have been operationalized in terms of parents' knowledge of their adolescents' activities and whereabouts, rather than parents' actual tracking and surveillance. In a large longitudinal study of Swedish 14-year-olds, Kerr & Stattin (2000) demonstrated that only adolescents' willingness to disclose to parents, and not parents' attempts to obtain information or actively control their teens' behavior, influenced adolescents' associations with deviant peers and problem behaviors. Furthermore, they controlled for closeness in the parent-adolescent relationship, ruling out the alternate explanation that child disclosure is a proxy for good parent-adolescent relationships. Parents appear more likely to solicit information when their adolescents are already more involved in problem behavior (Kerr & Stattin 2000, Tilton-Weaver & Galambos 2003).

Kerr & Stattin's (2000, Stattin & Kerr 2000) findings are provocative, because they challenge the well-established conclusion that parental monitoring and control are essential for successful adolescent development; their results highlight adolescents' agency in their own development. Although current theoretical perspectives emphasize the reciprocal interplay between parents and adolescents and the importance of adolescents' willingness to be socialized (e.g., Darling & Steinberg 1993, Grusec & Goodnow 1994, Kuczynski 2003), the strong presumption in much research on parenting is that the direction of effects is from parents to adolescents. Thus, it is not surprising that Kerr & Stattin's (2000) findings have been challenged. In reanalyses of longitudinal data from a large sample of youth in California and Wisconsin, Fletcher et al. (2004) found that parental control contributed significantly to both parental knowledge and reductions in juvenile delinquency. The debate about how to define parental monitoring is not yet fully resolved, but it highlights the need to better understand adolescents' strategies for information management (Darling et al. 2000, Marshall et al. 2005) and the implications of disclosure and secrecy for parenting and adolescent development (Finkenauer et al. 2002, Smetana et al. 2005). The findings also suggest the need for greater attention to how parents acquire knowledge of adolescents' activities and act on that knowledge (Crouter & Head 2002).

Observational studies of family interactions provide further evidence for the reciprocal nature of interactions between parents and adolescents. In both cross-sectional and longitudinal analyses, family interactions that allow adolescents the opportunity to express independent thoughts and feelings while maintaining closeness and connection to parents facilitate higher self-esteem, better psychosocial competence, less depression, greater ego and identity development, and more mature moral reasoning (Allen et al. 1994a,b; Grotevant & Cooper 1985; Hauser et al. 1991; Walker & Taylor 1991). The context of risk moderates these effects, however.

In low-risk families, undermining autonomy is associated with poorer quality adolescent-parent relationships, but in high-risk families, undermining autonomy is associated with better quality adolescent-parent relationships (McElhaney & Allen 2001). Several large-scale cross-sectional and longitudinal studies of family decision making in ethnically diverse samples likewise have shown that joint decision making between parents and adolescents is associated with better adjustment and less deviance (Dornbusch et al. 1990, Dowdy & Kliewer 1998, Fuligni & Eccles 1993, Lamborn et al. 1996, Smetana et al. 2004a), although the findings are moderated by ethnicity, community context (Lamborn et al. 1996), domain of the decision, and age (Smetana et al. 2004a). That is, while parental involvement in decision making is advantageous in early and middle adolescence, adolescents' increased decision-making autonomy between middle and late adolescence leads to better adjustment in late adolescence (Smetana et al. 2004a).

A final note is that much of the progress in understanding parenting and parent-adolescent relationships during the past decade has come from studies utilizing adolescent informants, but agreement between parents' and adolescents' views of parenting or relationships typically is low to moderate. Adolescents' and parents' moods and emotions (Larson & Richards 1994), perceptions of relationship quality (Callan & Noller 1986), beliefs about parental authority, and reasoning about conflicts (Smetana 1988, 1989; Smetana & Gaines 1999) all increasingly diverge with age. These discrepancies may be potentially meaningful and developmentally salient because they point to areas of tension and disagreement in family life.

Sibling Relationships

Although most of the research on adolescents' family relationships has focused on relationships with parents, interest in adolescents' relationships with their brothers and sisters and the influence of these relationships on adolescent development has increased substantially over the past decade, due in part to the increased prominence of family systems theory (Minuchin 2002), with its focus on different subsystems of the family, and to the interest in behavioral genetics. Studying siblings offers an ideal opportunity to examine the aspects of the environment that family members share in common (e.g., shared environmental influences) and the aspects that are not shared (e.g., nonshared environmental influences). Moreover, sibling relationships are highly salient to adolescents; early adolescents have more conflicts with siblings than with anyone else (e.g., fathers, grandparents, friends, or teachers; Furman & Buhrmester 1985) except maybe mothers (Collins & Laursen 1994), but relationships with brothers and sisters are also important sources of companionship, affection, and intimacy (Buhrmester & Furman 1990, Lempers & Clark-Lempers 1992). The quality of the relationship has been found to vary by birth order. Older siblings are perceived as more domineering and more nurturing than are later-born siblings, while later-born siblings admire and feel closer to their older brothers and sisters than their brothers or sisters feel toward them (Furman & Buhrmester 1992). Like relationships with parents, relationships with siblings are transformed during adolescence to become more egalitarian, less asymmetrical, less conflictive, and less close, most likely because siblings spend less time together as they get older (Raffaelli & Larson 1987).

The research has shown that better relationships with brothers and sisters lead to better adjustment during adolescence (Stocker et al. 2002). Even after controlling for level of parental and peer support, greater support from brothers and sisters has been associated longitudinally with lower levels of internalizing problems for both younger and older adolescents and with less externalizing behavior, particularly when girls perceive more support from an older brother (Branje et al. 2004). At the other extreme, however, sibling similarity in problem behavior, early sexual activity, and drug use suggests that older siblings' involvement in these behaviors is a risk factor for younger siblings (Ardelt & Day 2002, East & Jacobson 2001, Slomkowski et al. 2001).

Much attention has focused on parents' differential treatment of their offspring as an example of nonshared environmental influences. Both parents and siblings perceive parents as treating siblings differently (Daniels et al. 1985), although Kowal & Kramer (1997) found that the majority of early adolescents in their sample perceived their parents' differential treatment as fair and justified on the basis of age, personality, and need. Nevertheless, parents' differential treatment has been found to affect siblings' development (Daniels et al. 1985) and adjustment (Feinberg & Hetherington 2001). The effects of parents' differential treatment persist even after controlling for the effects of parenting, particularly when parenting is low in warmth or high in negativity (Feinberg & Hetherington 2001). Parents' (and particularly fathers') differential treatment has been associated with higher levels of negative behavior between siblings (Brody et al. 1992, Feinberg & Hetherington 2001).

Similarities and differences in siblings' behavior and relationships with parents also have been of interest and have been explained within two competing theoretical frameworks. According to social learning theory, older siblings may serve as models for younger siblings; the research indicates that older siblings are seen as more effective models only if younger siblings perceive their older siblings as likable and nurturing, so that the younger sibling wants to be around and learn from them (Whiteman & Buchanan 2002). In contrast, sibling deidentification theory posits that adolescents respond to parents' differential treatment by defining themselves as different from each other, pursuing different domains of competence and interest to avoid comparison and rivalry (Schachter 1985). Research indicates that sibling deidentification is more frequent and intense among siblings who are more similar in gender, age, and birth order (Schachter & Stone 1987) and may be especially salient during adolescence because of the developmental salience of identity development (Updegraff et al. 2000).

In addition, siblings may establish different relationships with their parents as a way to improve the quality of their relationships with each other and, perhaps, reduce sibling conflict and rivalry. Increasing differentiation in siblings' relationships with parents during adolescence has been associated longitudinally with increased warmth (between both siblings) and decreased conflict and competition among first- but not second-born adolescents (Feinberg et al. 2003). These effects also vary developmentally. Shanahan et al. (2005) found that regardless of birth order, maternal warmth declined when children reached early and middle adolescence, and conflict increased for both siblings when the first-born transitioned into adolescence.

Most research has focused on the effects of parent-adolescent relationships on sibling relationships, but recent research has begun to focus on sibling influences on parent-adolescent relationships. This research has demonstrated that parents' prior childrearing experience with their first-born siblings influences their expectations, behavior, and relationships with later-born offspring when they reach adolescence. For instance, parents' experiences with their first-born children influences their expectations for their younger child's adolescence, even with the effects of temperament controlled (Whiteman & Buchanan 2002). Furthermore, parents have less conflict with and greater knowledge of daily activities for later-born than first-born adolescents (Whiteman et al. 2003). Longitudinal designs that examine changes in siblings' relationships with each other and with parents at the same chronological age or developmental transition hold particular promise for unconfounding developmental and sibling effects.

Grandparents and Other Relatives

There has been surprisingly little research on adolescents' relationships with relatives other than parents or siblings. In their primarily European American middle-class sample, Furman & Buhrmester (1992) found that relationships with grandparents become more distant (both less supportive and less conflictive) as adolescents grow older, but few studies have followed up this finding with more detailed analyses. Furthermore, the available evidence suggests that relationships with grandparents and other relatives may vary in ethnic minority families. Multigenerational families are more common among African American than among European American families (Parke & Buriel 1998), but significant increases in the number of African American children orphaned or abandoned due to parental AIDS/HIV, incarceration, and drug use has led to increasing numbers of African American grandparents assuming primary childrearing responsibilities for their grandchildren (McAdoo 2002). The implications of "off-time" parenting for grandparents have been studied (McAdoo 2002), but the implications of being raised by grandparents for adolescent development have not. Furthermore, as divorce and remarriage become increasingly normative in American society, adolescents' relationships with multiple sets of grandparents and stepgrandparents warrant attention.

More generally, the available research indicates that ethnic minorities, especially African American and Latino families in the United States, have social networks that are more cohesive and include a larger proportion of extended family members than do European American families, and that these kin networks are important sources of emotional and instrumental support (Harwood et al.

2002, Hatchett & Jackson 1993, Taylor & Roberts 1995). Despite variability in the importance, extensiveness, fluidity, and amount of contact with kin networks, family influences on adolescent development have been limited primarily to studies of nuclear rather than extended families. More research on the distinct relationships adolescents have with different relatives and their influence on adolescent development is warranted.

EXTRAFAMILY INFLUENCES

Peer Relationships

The view that framed early research was that peer culture provides a negative and divergent source of influence from parents (Coleman 1961). An updated but similar view of peer influence has captured recent attention (Harris 1998), although the research evidence does not support this view. Rather, parents and peers have been found to be influential in different arenas of adolescents' lives. Parents remain important sources of influence regarding long-term issues (like career choices and moral issues and values), whereas peers influence orientations to adolescent culture such as matters of taste, style, and appearances, although antisocial conformity to peers peaks around ninth grade. Moreover, Brown (2004) has pointed out that peer influence may range from direct peer pressure to much more indirect sources of influence. Ongoing concerns about the negative influence of peers have led to research examining parental influence on peer relations. Parents often serve as managers and consultants for adolescents' peer relationships, and parental guidance (rather than direct prohibition) can effectively influence and change adolescents' selection of friends (Mounts 2001, 2004).

Three levels of adolescents' peer relations have been described (Brown 2004). The dyadic level includes adolescents' friendships, which remain the most actively studied area of adolescents' peer relations (Brown & Klute 2003), and romantic relationships (discussed in the following section). Adolescents also congregate in small groups of peers (generally 6 to 12), known as cliques, which are based on friendship and shared activities and provide contexts for interaction. Despite the popular image of adolescents as "cliquish," research indicates that less than half of adolescents are members of cliques and that clique membership is somewhat fluid, although girls are more likely to be clique members than are boys (Ennett & Bauman 1996). Clique members are likely to be of the same age, race, socioeconomic background, and during early adolescence, the same sex. The third level of peer interaction consists of crowds, which generally emerge during early to middle adolescence. Crowds are based on shared reputations or stereotyped images (e.g., jocks, brains, nerds or geeks, stoners) among youth who may not necessarily spend much time together (Brown 2004). Crowds help to locate adolescents in the social hierarchy and channel adolescents into interactions with others who share the same reputation; therefore, they provide a context for developing identity. At each of these levels of organization, research has proceeded in a number of different directions.

Research on the quality of adolescent friendships has progressed considerably in recent years (Brown & Klute 2003). Much research has focused on changes in the positive qualities of friendship over the course of adolescence; adolescents' friendships become closer, more intimate, more disclosing, and more supportive with age (Furman & Buhrmester 1992). Close friendships provide adolescents with developmentally salient opportunities to improve their social skills and social competence (Collins & Steinberg 2005). Adolescents' friends are highly similar in background, values, orientations to school and peer culture, and antisocial behavior (Hartup 1996), and one of the persistent questions about adolescent friendships is whether this similarity is due to selection (choosing friends who are similar) or influence (mutual socialization), although most agree that both processes are at work (Brown 2004). Furthermore, because friendships are nested within larger peer networks, the influence of friendships may be overestimated when larger peer influences are at work (Brown 2004). Research also has looked beyond influence and selection to assess the processes of parallel events and assortative pairing on similarity.

During the past few years, some intriguing new topics focusing on the "dark side" of adolescent friendships and peer groups have emerged. At the dyadic level, research on corumination (Rose 2002) has shown that early adolescents (typically girls) may extensively discuss issues, revisit problems, and focus on negative feelings within relatively healthy and intimate relationships. Corumination may provide the link between the incongruent finding that girls have more intimate friendships but also more internalizing symptoms than do boys. Research also has explored the influence of jealousy in early adolescent friendships (Parker et al. 2005, Roth & Parker 2001), which may occur when same-sex (again, typically girls') friends begin to develop romantic interests. Jealousy, as perceived by others, is associated with greater loneliness, aggression, and maladjustment in social relationships. Research also has examined adolescents' reasoning about peer group exclusion based on gender and racial stereotypes (Killen et al. 2002) and as a function of adolescents' peer group identification (e.g., cheerleaders, jocks, or preppies versus dirties, druggies, and Gothics; Horn 2003); adolescents who belong to high-status crowds have been found to view exclusion as less wrong and less unfair than do adolescents who either do not belong to a group or who belong to low-status groups. But the picture is not all negative; Horn (2003) also found that overall, adolescents have a high level of respect for peers from all backgrounds, and Killen et al. (2002) found that intergroup contact increased adolescents' thinking about fairness and equality when considering racial exclusion.

The characteristics of popular and unpopular adolescents have been an enduring topic of research (Rubin et al. 1998, Steinberg & Morris 2001). Sociometric studies have indicated that there are different subtypes of unpopular adolescents, including adolescents who are rejected and withdrawn and adolescents who are rejected and aggressive, and that these different forms of peer rejection have different correlates and developmental trajectories. Adolescents who are withdrawn tend to be lonely, suffer low self-esteem, and be at risk for internalizing disorders, whereas youth who are rejected and aggressive are at risk for externalizing problems (Rubin et al. 1995).

Popular adolescents are well known, attractive, athletic, and accepted by other popular youth (Adler & Adler 1998), but differentiations also have been made among popular youth. Recent research indicates that popularity is associated with both prosocial and antisocial behavior (LaFontana & Cillessen 2002, Rodkin et al. 2000), although popular-aggressive adolescents may be seen as socially skilled and socially prominent but disliked by peers (Farmer et al. 2003). "Mean girls" have been a trendy topic, both in popular culture and adolescent developmental research (Underwood 2003). Consistent with the popular image, more popular early adolescent girls have been found to be more relationally aggressive, which leads to increased popularity over time (Rose et al. 2004). Relationally aggressive behaviors (like excluding, ignoring, and spreading rumors) may allow young girls to control their peers in ways that lead them to be seen as high in status and popular. Finally, popularity is associated with better social adaptation and adjustment, but it also leads to significant increases over time in peer-sanctioned, minor deviant behavior, including drug and alcohol use and minor delinquency (Allen et al. 2005).

Perhaps in response to high-profile events such as the 1999 Columbine shootings by two teenagers at a Colorado high school, there has been a striking increase in research on antipathies in adolescent peer relations, including bullying, victimization, and harassment (Juvonen & Graham 2001, Nishina & Juvonen 2005). Research on bullies and their victims has shown that up to three-quarters of young adolescents experience some type of bullying and that up to one-third of them experience more extreme forms of coercion (Juvonen et al. 2000). Bullying, which refers to repeated aggressive behavior that occurs within particular interpersonal relationships that are characterized by a power imbalance (Olweus 1999), peaks in early adolescence and then decreases in frequency (Borg 1999). Direct bullying (e.g., physical or verbal attacks) is more frequent among males, whereas indirect (e.g., relational) bullying is more frequent among females, and white and Latino adolescents are bullied more than black adolescents (Borg 1999). Research has shown that there are distinct characteristics of youth singled out as victims; they are perceived to be physically weaker and have fewer friends than nonvictims (Olweus 1993a,b; Pellegrini 1994; Perry et al. 1988). The consequences of victimization include lower self-esteem in middle adolescence and depressive symptoms in early adulthood (Olweus 1993a,b), as well as increased school-related difficulties (i.e., lower grades, disliking school, and absenteeism; Eisenberg et al. 2003). Due to the pervasiveness of bullying and its damaging effects on adolescent adjustment, school-based bullying prevention and intervention programs are on the rise (Olweus 1999, Smith et al. 2003).

Romantic Relationships

Although adolescents' romantic relationships would seem like an obvious and important area of study for developmental scientists interested in adolescents' psychological development, until recently the topic has languished, for both pernicious and benign reasons (Collins 2003). Currently, however, research on adolescents' dating and romantic relationships is burgeoning. Dating and romantic relationships are a significant part of adolescents' social world (Bouchey & Furman 2003, Brown 2004); current research has corrected the misperception that these relationships are fleeting and transitory, as had been presumed (Collins 2003). Instead, the research has shown that romantic relationships are normative during middle adolescence, that they are relatively stable after early adolescence, and that they influence both current functioning and later psychosocial development. By tenth grade, interactions with romantic partners are more frequent than interactions with parents, siblings, or friends (Laursen & Williams 1997) and provide as much support as relationships with mothers (Furman & Burhmester 1992). Moreover, high school students spend a great deal of time thinking about these relationships (Richards et al. 1998). By the end of high school, nearly three-fourths of all U.S. adolescents report having had a romantic relationship in the last 18 months (Bouchey & Furman 2003).

Research on dating and romantic relationships during adolescence has proceeded in several directions. One direction has been to chart normative changes in the features of romantic relationships. In very early research, Dunphy (1963) proposed that adolescents progress through a five-stage sequence of structural changes in peer relationships that entails transitions from small unisexual cliques to associations between male and female cliques, to the formation of a larger heterosexual crowd, which provides a context for dating (first among clique leaders and then later more broadly among all members), and finally, crowd dissolution in favor of a loose association of heterosexual couples. Although this account stood unexamined for nearly half a century, recent research has provided evidence for its validity among contemporary youth (although the sequence may unfold over a longer time span, as the average age of marriage moves upward to the mid-twenties). Studies have shown that early adolescents spend a great deal of time thinking about (but not actually interacting with) the opposite sex (Richards et al. 1998) and that initial interactions with the opposite sex typically occur first in mixed-sex contexts. More experience with mixed-gender friendship groups facilitates adolescents' involvement in romantic relationships (Connolly et al. 2000, 2004).

The social context, including relationships with friends and parents, has been examined as sources of influence on the quality and progression of romantic relationships. Thus far, researchers have focused on either peer influence or parental influence or their additive effects (Collins & Steinberg 2005), but more complex models of the interactive influences of parents, friends, and peers on adolescents' romantic relationships have been lacking. Peer relationships may influence the development of romantic relationships by providing a context for establishing romantic relationships, by influencing the nature of those relationships and the choice of romantic partners, and by influencing relationship processes (Bouchey & Furman 2003). The quality of adolescents' friendships has been shown to be closely associated with the quality of romantic relationships (Connolly & Johnson 1996, Furman 1999).

Likewise, researchers have examined continuity between earlier parent-child relationships and adolescents' romantic experience and relationships. According to attachment theory, representations of attachment to caregivers formed early in life influence later romantic relationships through expectancies about closeness and intimacy (Furman et al. 2002, Furman & Wehner 1997), but some evidence suggests that attachment representations of friendships mediate the relationship between adolescents' working models of their relationships with parents and their views of romantic relationships (Furman et al. 2002). Parental socialization practices, such as effective parental monitoring or a history of parental responsiveness and autonomy support, also may influence the development of romantic relationships, either directly or through their effect on social competence, self-esteem, and self-worth (Collins & Sroufe 1999, Gray & Steinberg 1999).

Relatively little research to date has examined the meaning of romantic inter-actions and relationships to adolescents, but some evidence indicates that early adolescents' notions of romance are very idealized and stereotypic and primarily meet needs for status attainment, sexual experimentation, and recreation. Over time, as adolescents gain experience interacting with the opposite sex, romantic relationships begin to fulfill needs for support or caregiving (Connolly et al. 2000, Feiring 1999, Furman & Wehner 1997).

Another line of research has examined individual differences in dating, with the focus primarily on the consequences of early dating. Research has consistently shown that for both boys and girls early dating is associated with poorer psychosocial adjustment, including poorer self-esteem, lower academic achievement, more alcohol and substance abuse, and earlier involvement in sexual activity (Bouchey & Furman 2003, Collins & Steinberg 2005). The causal relationships are not clearly established, however, and youth who are involved in these activities may begin their involvement in dating earlier than other teens. Moreover, the desired timetable for dating, pacing of sexual intimacy, and tolerance for diversity may vary by friendship group and reputational crowds (Brown 2004), as well as by ethnicity, cultural background, and gender. Furthermore, individual differences in dating among older adolescents need further study.

Despite the rapid progress made in recent years in understanding the development, features, and significance of adolescents' romantic relationships, research in this area has been largely focused on middle-class, European American, heterosexual youth (Bouchey & Furman 2003). More research on the normative development of romantic relationships in ethnic minority and sexual minority (e.g., gay, lesbian, or bisexual) youth is needed (but see Diamond & Savin-Williams 2003 for progress in this area). Furthermore, to date, research has focused primarily on individual self-reports rather than considering the dyad as a unit of analysis; future research should examine the perceptions and experiences of both romantic partners as well as the influence of discrepancies in their perspectives for adolescent development and adjustment.

ENGAGEMENT IN COMMUNITY AND SOCIETY

Adolescents' involvement in their communities and society has become a topic of intense interest in the past few years. Although civic involvement has been studied in the past as an aspect of adolescents' political socialization, there has been a dramatic resurgence of interest in the topic (Flanagan 2004b, Sherrod et al. 2002), due in part to the more general interest in positive psychology (Seligman & Csikszentmihalyi 2000) and the more specific interest in positive youth development (Larson 2000, Lerner et al. 2000). In addition, research has been generated in response to claims from social commentators that American youth have become too self-centered and individualistic and not sufficiently concerned with community and social responsibility (Bellah et al. 1985, Putnam 2000). Finally, the interest in youth civic engagement is based on the assumption, supported by some research, that involvement in extracurricular activities at school and community-based youth organizations facilitates adolescent development in ways that will lead to greater community and civic involvement in adulthood.

The evidence suggests that involvement in community organizations and service influences the development of greater compassion and interdependence (Yates & Youniss 1996), engagement in community service (Hart & Atkins 2002), feelings of affection and attachment to the larger social order (Flanagan 2004b, Flanagan & Faison 2002), a greater understanding of democracy (Flanagan et al. 2005a), and civic or moral identity (Hart & Fegley 1995, Youniss et al. 1997, Youniss & Yates 1999), particularly when adolescents have an opportunity to reflect on their involvement (Youniss et al. 1999). Thus, civic engagement in adolescence is seen as an important pathway in training youth for future citizenship, although the evidence to date is largely correlational or based on treatment studies that do not include random assignment. Evidence for the links between adolescent involvement and adult participation is based primarily on retrospective accounts, but several short-term longitudinal studies have shown that service learning in high school does lead to a greater sense of social responsibility (Flanagan 2004b) and changes in students' priorities (Johnson et al. 1998).

Initially, the studies in this area focused on the demographic and family factors associated with greater civic involvement and volunteer community service in adolescence. The evidence suggests that higher socioeconomic status, college attendance and higher educational aspirations, greater religiosity, greater parental involvement in civic organizations or political issues, and higher academic self-esteem are all associated with greater civic involvement and volunteering in adolescence (Johnson et al. 1998; Youniss et al. 1997, 1999; Youniss & Yates 1999). Adolescents who volunteer also tend to be more mature, more altruistic, and are more likely to be female (Eisenberg & Morris 2004). Some studies have examined ethnic disparities in civic engagement, but the available evidence suggests that socioeconomic status rather than race or ethnicity is a better predictor of civic and political participation (Flanagan 2004b).

Service learning has become normative for American youth. The results of several large-scale studies attempting to document the benefits of service learning have found inconsistent results and mostly transient positive gains (Melchior 1998). This has led researchers to investigate how specific characteristics of youth civic involvement, for instance between required school-based and voluntary community-based youth programs, influence positive developmental outcomes (Flanagan 2004a,b; Metz & Youniss 2003). Required school-based service positively impacts students' intentions to be involved in the future, even when adolescents were less inclined to participate prior to the required service (Metz & Youniss 2005).

Recent research has examined the optimal organization or structure of organizations to facilitate engagement. A systematic review of programs indicates that organizations that allow adolescents the freedom to make real decisions and take leadership roles while adults still provide some structure help to promote positive youth outcomes (Eccles & Gootman 2002). In addition, organizations that are centered on a specific philosophy, cause, or ideology appear to infuse adolescent participation with meaning (Flanagan 2004a, Youniss et al. 1999). The informal, less hierarchically organized environment of community youth organizations fosters adolescents' affective ties to their community (Flanagan 2004a, Flanagan & Van Horn 2003) and provides an environment where at-risk youth may feel efficacious and respected by adults (Kahne et al. 2001). This is particularly important given the disparity in civic identity and development between adolescents from affluent versus poor urban environments (Atkins & Hart 2003). Community organizations also may provide adolescents with the opportunity to interact with a heterogeneous group of individuals, which has been linked to adolescents' social trust, tolerance, and reduction of stereotypes (Flanagan et al. 2005b). Social trust is proposed to be crucial to democratic societies because it leads to an investment in the social order and commitment to community involvement; it is also associated with a more positive belief in people and a more hopeful outlook on society (Flanagan et al. 2005b).

Much of the research in this area has been guided by applied and social policy concerns, and integrative frameworks for understanding civic engagement remain to be developed. Furthermore, and although rarely made explicit, most of the research thus far appears to be guided by the social learning assumption that adolescents' civic beliefs and behaviors are molded by their involvement with parents, schools, or the characteristics of youth organizations, and more dynamic models of civic engagement are needed. Other research has shown, for instance, that among U.S. adolescents as well as adolescents in other cultures, basic understandings of concepts of rights, civil liberties, and democratic decision making develop in middle childhood, but that the ability to view these issues as overriding when they conflict with other concerns in complex situations increases with age (Helwig 1995, Helwig et al. 2003, Neff & Helwig 2002). Although the seeds of civic involvement are no doubt sown in childhood, very little longitudinal research has examined the mutual interactions among individual, family, and community in childhood and early adolescence that facilitate civic participation and involvement in late adolescence and young adulthood.

CONCLUSIONS AND FUTURE DIRECTIONS

As we move into the twenty-first century, significant progress has been made in understanding adolescent development in different interpersonal and community contexts. Research on enduring topics like adolescent-parent and peer relationships has expanded to become more contextual and more inclusive, but ethnic, racial, and cultural variations are vastly understudied in newer areas of emphasis, such as sibling and romantic relationships. In general, ethnic minority adolescents remain overrepresented in studies of risk and underrepresented in research on normative development (Hagen et al. 2004).

The newly emerging research on civic engagement is part of a broader trend toward considering developmental assets and positive youth development, and this new focus is giving increased prominence to topics that have been ignored or even shunned in the past, such as adolescent well-being, religiosity and spirituality, and compassion and altruism. Likewise, new technological advances in communication, including Internet use and access to the World Wide Web, Internet chat rooms, instant messaging, and text messaging, are changing the way adolescents communicate with peers and are raising concerns about differential access among youth of different socioeconomic statuses, leading to a new "digital divide" (Pew Internet Am. Life Proj. 2004). The influence of these emerging technologies on adolescent development remains to be determined. The challenge in these emerging areas of research is to bring strong integrative, conceptual, and developmental frameworks to bear and to incorporate the findings into our existing knowledge base on adolescent development.

Another noteworthy trend has been the increased emphasis on collaboration among researchers, practitioners, and policy makers. Recent shifts in research and funding priorities challenge researchers to focus more on research that is amenable to translation into applied and policy arenas. A notable example is recent research on adolescents' decision-making competencies and developmental maturity in the context of the legal system (Cauffman & Steinberg 2000; Steinberg 2000, 2004; Steinberg & Scott 2003). Finally, in the last review of adolescent research appearing in this series, Steinberg & Morris (2001) concluded that research on cognitive development during adolescence "has been moribund for some time" (p. 101), but new developments noted previously in the developmental neurosciences and in brain imaging along with a reinvigorated study of adolescent meta-cognition, reasoning, and consciousness (Keating 2004), as well as moral and social cognition (Smetana 2006), hold much promise for an integrative view of transformations in cognitive functioning during adolescence.

More generally, the ascendance of ecological models, which has been aided by recent innovations in statistical methods, including developments in multilevel and growth-curve modeling, has led to a greater understanding of how contexts constrain, shape, and influence adolescent development. Despite significant gains, these advances also have led to a field that has become markedly less developmental. Over the past 30 years, the pendulum has swung from largely decontextual research focusing on intraindividual processes of development to research that is highly contextual but has little to say about intraindividual processes (Steinberg & Morris 2001). Topics such as identity, intimacy, self-understanding, and ego and moral development that formed the cornerstone of the developmental study of adolescence in earlier decades have been replaced with a focus on individual differences in adjustment. Moreover, adolescents construct, interpret, and make meaning of the social contexts they inhabit, and although it is surely the case that their active agency influences their developmental trajectory, the constructive nature of adolescent development is not readily apparent in current theorizing or empirical research. Our understanding of adolescent development would be enhanced by a renewed interest in studying longitudinal changes in intraindividual processes of development as adolescents assert choices, make decisions, and develop within different contexts and cultures.

The *Annual Review of Psychology* is online at http://psych.annualreviews.org

LITERATURE CITED

Adams GR, Berzonsky MD, eds. 2003. *Blackwell Handbook of Adolescence*. Oxford: Blackwell Sci.

Adams R, Laursen B. 2001. The organization and dynamics of adolescent conflict with parents and friends. *J. Marriage Fam.* 63:97–110

Adler PA, Adler P. 1998. *Peer Power: Preadolescent Culture and Identity*. New Brunswick, NJ: Rutgers Univ. Press

Allen JP, Hauser ST, Bell KL, O'Connor TG. 1994a. Longitudinal assessment of autonomy and relatedness in adolescent-family interactions as predictors of adolescent ego development and self-esteem. *Child Dev.* 65:179–94

Allen JP, Hauser ST, Eickholt C, Bell KL, O'Connor TG. 1994b. Autonomy and relatedness in family interactions as predictors of expressions of negative adolescent affect. *J. Res. Adolesc.* 4:535–52

Allen JP, Moore CM, Kuperminc GP, Bell KL. 1998. Attachment and adolescent psychosocial functioning. *Child Dev.* 69:1406–19

Allen JP, Porter MR, Marsh P, McFarland FC, McElhaney KB. 2005. Two faces of adolescents' success with peers; adolescent popularity, social adaptation, and deviant behavior. *Child Dev.* 76:747–60

Ardelt M, Day L. 2002. Parents, siblings, and peers: close social relationships and adolescent deviance. *J. Early Adolesc.* 22:310–49

Arnett JJ. 2000. Emerging adulthood: a theory of development from the late teens through the twenties. *Am. Psychol.* 55:469–80

Arnett JJ. 2004. *Emerging Adulthood: The Winding Road from the Late Teens Through the Twenties*. New York: Oxford Univ. Press

Atkins R, Hart D. 2003. Neighborhoods, adults, and the development of civic identity in urban youth. *Appl. Dev. Sci.* 3:156–64

Barber BK. 1996. Parental psychological control: revisiting a neglected construct. *Child Dev.* 67:3296–3319

Barber BK, ed. 2002. *Parental Psychological Control of Children and Adolescents*. Washington, DC: Am. Psychol. Assoc.

Baumrind D. 1991. Effective parenting during

the early adolescent transition. In *Advances in Family Research,* ed. PA Cowan, EM Hetherington, 2:111–63. Hillsdale, NJ: Erlbaum

Bellah RN, Madsen R, Sullivan WM, Swidler A, Tipton SM. 1985. *Habits of the Heart: Individualism and Commitment in American Life.* New York: Harper & Row

Borg MG. 1999. The extent and nature of bullying among primary and secondary school children. *Educ. Res.* 42:137–53

Bornstein MH, ed. 2002. *Handbook of Parenting,* Vols. 1–4. Mahwah, NJ: Erlbaum. 2nd ed.

Bouchey HA, Furman W. 2003. Dating and romantic experience during adolescence. See Adams & Berzonsky 2003, pp. 313–29

Branje SJT, van Lieshout CFM, van Aken MAG, Haselager GJT. 2004. Perceived support in sibling relationships and adolescent adjustment. *J. Child Psychol. Psychiatry* 45: 1385–96

Brody G, Stoneman Z, McCoy JK. 1992. Associations of maternal and paternal direct and differential behavior with sibling relationships: contemporaneous and longitudinal analyses. *Child Dev.* 63:82–92

Bronfenbrenner U. 1979. *The Ecology of Human Development: Experiments by Nature.* Cambridge, MA: Harvard Univ. Press

Bronfenbrenner U, Morris PA. 1998. The ecology of developmental process. In *Handbook of Child Psychology, Theoretical Models of Human Development,* ed. W Damon, RM Lerner, 1:993–1028. New York: Wiley. 5th ed.

Brown BB. 2004. Adolescents' relationships with peers. See Lerner & Steinberg 2004, pp. 363–94. New York: Wiley. 2nd ed.

Brown BB, Klute C. 2003. Friendships, cliques, and crowds. See Adams & Berzonsky 2003, pp. 330–48

Buchanan CM, Eccles JS, Flanagan C, Midgley C, Feldlaufer H, Harold RD. 1990. Parents' and teachers' beliefs about adolescents: effects of sex and experience. *J. Youth Adolesc.* 19:363–94

Buhrmester D, Furman W. 1987. The develop-

ment of companionship and intimacy. *Child Dev.* 58:1101–13

Buhrmester D, Furman W. 1990. Perceptions of sibling relationships during middle childhood and adolescence. *Child Dev.* 61:1387–96

Callan VJ, Noller P. 1986. Perceptions of communicative relationships in families with adolescents. *J. Marriage Fam.* 48:813–20

Cauffman E, Steinberg L. 2000. (Im)maturity of judgment in adolescence: why adolescents may be less culpable than adults. *Behav. Sci. Law* 18:741–60

Chao RK. 1994. Beyond parenting control and authoritarian parenting style: understanding Chinese parenting through the cultural notion of training. *Child Dev.* 65:1111–19

Chao RK. 2001. Exploring research on the consequences of parenting style for Chinese Americans and European Americans. *Child Dev.* 72:1832–43

Chao RK, Tseng V. 2002. Parenting of Asians. See Bornstein 2002, 4:59–93

Coleman JS. 1961. *The Adolescent Society.* New York: Free Press

Collins WA. 1990. Parent-child relationships in the transition to adolescence: continuity and change in interaction, affect, and cognition. In *From Childhood to Adolescence: A Transitional Period?* ed. R Montemayor, GR Adams, TP Gulotta, pp. 85–106. Newbury Park, CA: Sage

Collins WA. 2003. More than a myth: the developmental significance of romantic relationships during adolescence. *J. Res. Adolesc.* 13: 1–24

Collins WA, Laursen B. 2004. Parent-adolescent relationships and influences. See Lerner & Steinberg 2004, pp. 331–61

Collins WA, Maccoby E, Steinberg L, Hetherington EM, Bornstein M. 2000. Contemporary research on parenting: the case for nature and nurture. *Am. Psychol.* 55:218–32

Collins WA, Sroufe LA. 1999. Capacity for intimate relationships: a developmental construction. In *Contemporary Perspectives on Adolescent Relationships,* ed. W Furman,

BB Brown, C Feiring, pp. 125–47. New York: Cambridge Univ. Press

Collins WA, Steinberg L. 2005. Adolescent development in interpersonal context. In *Handbook of Child Psychology*, ed. N. Eisenberg. In press

Conger RD, Conger K, Elder G, Lorenz F, Simons R, Whitbeck L. 1992. A family process model of economic hardship and adjustment of early adolescent boys. *Child Dev.* 63:526–41

Conger RD, Conger K, Elder G, Lorenz F, Simons R, Whitbeck L. 1993. Family economic stress and adjustment of early adolescent girls. *Dev. Psychol.* 29:206–19

Conger K, Conger RD, Scaramella LV. 1997. Parents, siblings, psychological control, and adolescent adjustment. *J. Adolesc. Res.* 12:113–38

Conger RD, Ge X. 1999. Conflict and cohesion in parent-adolescent relations: changes in emotional expression from early to mid-adolescence. In *Conflict and Cohesion in Families: Causes and Consequences*, ed. MJ Cox, J Brooks-Gunn, pp. 185–206. Mahwah, NJ: Erlbaum

Connolly J, Craig W, Goldberg A, Pepler D. 2004. Mixed-gender groups, dating, and romantic relationships in early adolescence. *J. Res. Adolesc.* 14:185–207

Connolly J, Furman W, Konarksi R. 2000. The role of peers in the emergence of heterosexual romantic relationships in adolescence. *Child Dev.* 71:1395–408

Connolly J, Johnson AM. 1996. Adolescents' romantic relationships and the structure and quality of their close interpersonal ties. *Pers. Relat.* 3:185–95

Cook TD, Herman MR, Phillips M, Settersten RA. 2002. Some ways in which neighborhoods, nuclear families, friendship groups, and schools jointly affect changes in early adolescent development. *Child Dev.* 73:1283–309

Crouter AC, Head MR. 2002. Parental monitoring and knowledge of children. See Bornstein 2002, 3:461–83

Daniels D, Dunn, J, Furstenberg FF, Plomin R. 1985. Environmental differences within the family and adjustment differences within pairs of adolescent siblings. *Child Dev.* 56:764–74

Darling N, Steinberg L. 1993. Parenting style as context: an integrative model. *Psychol. Bull.* 113:486–96

Darling N, Hames K, Cumsille P. 2000. *When Parents and Adolescents Disagree*: *Disclosure Strategies and Motivations*. Presented at Soc. Res. Child Dev. Biennial Meet., Chicago, IL

Diamond LM, Savin-Williams RC. 2003. The intimate relationships of sexual-minority youth. See Adams & Berzonsky 2003, pp. 393–412

Dornbusch SM, Ritter PL, Mont-Reynaud R, Chen Z. 1990. Family decision-making and academic performance in a diverse high school population. *J. Adolesc. Res.* 5:143–60

Dowdy BB, Kliewer W. 1998. Dating, parent-adolescent conflict, and behavioral autonomy. *J. Youth Adolesc.* 27:473–92

Dubas JS, Gerris JRM. 2002. Longitudinal changes in the time parents spend in activities with their adolescent children as a function of child age, pubertal status, and gender. *J. Fam. Psychol.* 16:415–27

Dubas JS, Petersen AC. 1996. Geographical distance from parents and adjustment during adolescence and young adulthood. In *Leaving Home: Understanding the Transition to Adulthood. New Directions for Child Development*, ed. JA Graber, JS Dubas, 71:3–19. San Francisco, CA: Jossey-Bass

DuBois DL, Burk-Braxton C, Swenson LP, Tevendale HD, Hardesty JL. 2002. Race and gender influences on adjustment in early adolescence: investigation of an integrative model. *Child Dev.* 73:1573–92

Dunphy DC. 1963. The social structure of urban adolescent peer groups. *Sociometry* 26:230–46

East PL, Jacobson LJ. 2001. The younger siblings of teenage mothers: a follow-up of their pregnancy risk. *Dev. Psychol.* 37:254–64

Eccles JS, Gootman JA, eds. 2002. *Community*

Programs to Promote Youth Development. Washington, DC: Natl. Acad. Press

Eisenberg ME, Neumark-Sztainer D, Perry C. 2003. Peer harassment, school connectedness and school success. *J. Sch. Health* 73: 311–16

Eisenberg N, Damon W, eds. 1998. *Handbook of Child Psychology, Volume 3, Social, Emotional, and Personality Development.* New York: Wiley. 5th ed.

Eisenberg N, Morris AS. 2004. Moral cognitions and prosocial responding in adolescence. See Lerner & Steinberg 2004, pp. 155–88

Ennett ST, Bauman KE. 1996. Adolescent social networks: school, demographic, and longitudinal considerations. *J. Adolesc. Res.* 11: 194–215

Farmer TW, Estell DB, Bishop JL, O'Neal KK, Cairns BD. 2003. Rejected bullies or popular leaders? The social relations of aggressive subtypes of rural African American early adolescents. *Dev. Psychol.* 9:992–1004

Feinberg M, Hetherington EM. 2001. Differential parenting as a within-family variable. *J. Fam. Psychol.* 15:22–37

Feinberg ME, McHale SM, Crouter AC, Cumsille P. 2003. Sibling differentiation: sibling and parent relationship trajectories in adolescence. *Child Dev.* 74:1261–74

Feiring C. 1999. Gender identity and the development of romantic relationships in adolescence. In *Contemporary Perspectives on Adolescent Relationships*, ed. W Furman, BB Brown, C Feiring, pp. 211–32. New York: Cambridge Univ. Press

Finkenauer C, Engels RC, Meeus W. 2002. Keeping secrets from parents: advantages and disadvantages of secrecy in adolescence. *J. Youth Adolesc.* 2:123–36

Flanagan C, Faison N. 2001. Youth civic development: implications of research for social policy and programs. In *Social Policy Report: A Publication for the Society for Research in Child Development*, ed. L Sherrod, pp. 3–14. Ann Arbor, MI: Soc. Res. Child Dev.

Flanagan CA. 2004a. Institutional support for morality: community-based and neighborhood organizations. In *Nurturing Morality. Issues in Children's and Families' Lives*, ed. TA Thorkildsen, HJ Walberg, pp. 173–83. New York: Kluwer Acad.

Flanagan CA. 2004b. Volunteerism, leadership, political socialization, and civic engagement. See Lerner & Steinberg 2004, pp. 721–45

Flanagan CA, Gallay LS, Gill S, Gallay E, Nti N. 2005a. What does democracy mean? Correlates of adolescents' views. *J. Adolesc. Res.* 20:193–218

Flanagan CA, Gill S, Gallay LS. 2005b. Social participation and social trust in adolescence: the importance of heterogeneous encounters. In *Processes of Community Change and Social Action. The Claremont Symposium on Applied Social Psychology*, ed. AM Omoto, pp. 149–66. Mahwah, NJ: Erlbaum

Flanagan CA, Van Horn B. 2003. Youth civic development: a logical next step in community youth development. In *Community Youth Development: Practice, Policy, and Research*, ed. FA Villarruel, DF Perkins, LM Borden, JG Keith. pp. 273–97. Thousand Oaks, CA: Sage

Fletcher AC, Steinberg L, Sellers EB. 1999. Adolescents' well-being as a function of perceived interparental consistency. *J. Marriage Fam.* 61:599–610

Fletcher AC, Steinberg L, Williams M. 2004. Parental influences on adolescent problem behavior: revisiting Stattin and Kerr. *Child Dev.* 75:781–96

Fuligni AJ. 1998a. Authority, autonomy, and parent-adolescent conflict and cohesion: a study of adolescents from Mexican, Chinese, Filipino, and European backgrounds. *Dev. Psychol.* 34:782–92

Fuligni AJ. 1998b. The adjustment of children from immigrant families. *Curr. Dir. Psychol. Sci.* 7:99–103

Fuligni AJ, Eccles J. 1993. Perceived parent-child relationships and early adolescents' orientations toward peers. *Dev. Psychol.* 29: 622–32

Fuligni AJ, Tseng V, Lam M. 1999. Attitudes toward family obligations among American adolescents from Asian, Latin American, and European backgrounds. *Child Dev.* 70:1030–44

Fuligni AJ, Yip T, Tseng V. 2002. The impact of family obligation on the daily behavior and psychological well being of Chinese American adolescents. *Child Dev.* 73:306–18

Furman W. 1999. Friends and lovers: the role of peer relationships in adolescent heterosexual romantic relationships. In *Relationships as Developmental Contexts: Minnesota Symposia on Child Development*, ed. WA Collins, B Laursen, 30:133–54. Hillsdale, NJ: Erlbaum

Furman W, Buhrmester D. 1985. Children's perceptions of the personal relationships in their social networks. *Dev. Psychol.* 21:1016–24

Furman W, Buhrmester D. 1992. Age and sex in perceptions of networks of personal relationships. *Child Dev.* 63:103–15

Furman W, Simon VA, Shaffer L, Bouchey HA. 2002. Adolescents' working models and styles for relationships with parents, friends, and romantic partners. *Child Dev.* 73:241–55

Furman W, Wehner EA. 1997. Adolescent romantic relationships: a developmental perspective. In *Romantic Relationships in Adolescence: Developmental Perspectives*, ed. S Shulman, WA Collins, pp. 21–36. San Francisco, CA: Jossey-Bass

Garcia Coll CG, Lamberty G, Jenkins R, McAdoo HP, Crnic K, et al. 1996. An integrative model for the study of developmental competencies in minority children. *Child Dev.* 67:1891–14

Grant KE, Compas BE, Stuhlmacher A, Thurm A, McMahon S, Halpert J. 2003. Stressors and child and adolescent psychopathology: moving from markers to mechanisms of risk. *Psychol. Bull.* 129:447–66

Gray RB, Steinberg L. 1999. Adolescent romance and the parent-child relationship: a contextual perspective. In *Contemporary Perspectives on Adolescent Relationship*, ed. W Furman, BB Brown, C Feiring, pp. 235–65. New York: Cambridge Univ. Press

Grotevant HD, Cooper CR. 1985. Patterns of interaction in family relationships and the development of identity exploration in adolescence. *Child Dev.* 56:415–28

Grusec JE, Goodnow JJ. 1994. The impact of parental discipline methods on the child's internalization of values: a reconceptualization of current points of view. *Dev. Psychol.* 30:4–19

Gutman LM, Eccles JS. 1999. Financial strain, parenting behaviors, and adolescent achievement: testing model equivalence between African American and European American single- and two-parent families. *Child Dev.* 70:1464–76

Hagen JW, Nelson MJ, Velissaris N. 2004. *Comparison of Research in Two Major Journals on Adolescence.* Presented at Biennial Meet. Soc. Res. Adolesc., Baltimore, MD

Harris JR. 1998. *The Nurture Assumption.* New York: Free Press

Hart D, Atkins R. 2002. Civic competence in urban youth. *Appl. Dev. Sci.* 6:227–36

Hart D, Fegley S. 1995. Prosocial behavior and caring in adolescence: relations to self-understanding and social judgment. *Child Dev.* 66:1346–59

Hartup WW. 1996. The company they keep: friendships and their developmental significance. *Child Dev.* 67:1–13

Harwood R, Leyendecker B, Carlson V, Asencio M, Miller A. 2002. Parenting among Latino families in the U.S. See Bornstein 2002, 4:21–46

Hatchett SJ, Jackson JS. 1993. African American extended kin systems. In *Family Ethnicity: Strength in Diversity*, ed. HP McAdoo, pp. 90–108. Newbury Park, CA: Sage

Hauser ST, Powers SI, Noam GG. 1991. *Adolescents and Their Families: Paths of Ego Development.* New York: Free Press

Helwig CC. 1995. Adolescents' and young adults' conceptions of civil liberties: freedom of speech and religion. *Child Dev.* 66:152–66

Helwig CC, Arnold ML, Tan D, Boyd D. 2003. Chinese adolescents' reasoning about democratic and authority-based decision making in peer, family, and school contexts. *Child Dev.* 74:783–800

Hetherington EM, Kelly J. 2002. *For Better or Worse: Divorce Reconsidered.* New York: Norton

Hoff E, Laursen B, Tardif T. 2002. Socioeconomic status and parenting. See Bornstein 2002, 2:231–52

Holmbeck GN. 1996. A model of family relational transformations during the transition to adolescence: parent-adolescent conflict and adaptation. In *Transitions Through Adolescence: Interpersonal Domains and Context,* ed. JA Graber, J Brooks-Gunn, AC Petersen, pp. 167–99. Mahwah, NJ: Erlbaum

Horn SS. 2003. Adolescents' reasoning about exclusion from social groups. *Dev. Psychol.* 39:71–84

Johnson MK, Beebe T, Mortimer JT, Snyder M. 1998. Volunteerism in adolescence: a process perspective. *J. Res. Adolesc.* 8:309–32

Juvonen J, Graham S, eds. 2001. *Peer Harassment in School: The Plight of the Vulnerable and Victimized.* New York: Guilford

Juvonen J, Nishina A, Graham S. 2000. Peer harassment, psychological adjustment, and school functioning in early adolescence. *J. Educ. Psychol.* 92:349–59

Kahne J, Nagaoka J, Brown A, O'Brien J, Quinn T, Thiede K. 2001. Assessing after-school programs as settings for youth development. *Youth Soc.* 32:421–46

Keating D. 2004. Cognitive and brain development. See Lerner & Steinberg 2004, pp. 45–84

Kerr M, Stattin H. 2000. What parents know, how they know it, and several forms of adolescent adjustment: further support for a reinterpretation of monitoring. *Dev. Psychol.* 36:366–80

Killen M, Lee-Kim J, McGlothlin H, Stangor C. 2002. How children and adolescents evaluate gender and racial exclusion. *Monogr. Soc. Res. Child Dev.* Ser. No. 271, Vol. 67(4), pp. 1–180

Kowal A, Kramer L. 1997. Children's understanding of parental differential treatment. *Child Dev.* 68:113–26

Kuczynski L, ed. 2003. *Handbook of Dynamics in Parent-Child Relations.* Thousand Oaks, CA: Sage

LaFontana KM, Cillessen AH. 2002. Children's perceptions of popular and unpopular peers: a multimethod assessment. *Dev. Psychol.* 38:635–47

Lamborn S, Dornbusch S, Steinberg L. 1996. Ethnicity and community context as moderators of the relation between family decision-making and adolescent adjustment. *Child Dev.* 66:283–301

Larson RW. 2000. Toward a psychology of positive youth development. *Am. Psychol.* 55:170–83

Larson RW, Moneta G, Richards MH, Wilson S. 2002. Continuity, stability, and change in daily emotional experience across adolescence. *Child Dev.* 73:1151–65

Larson RW, Richards MH. 1994. *Divergent Realities: The Emotional Lives of Mothers, Fathers, and Adolescents.* New York: Basic Books

Larson RW, Richards MH, Moneta G, Holmbeck G, Duckett E. 1996. Changes in adolescents' daily interactions with their families from ages 10–18: disengagement and transformation. *Dev. Psychol.* 32:744–54

Laursen B. 1995. Conflict and social interaction in adolescent relationships. *J. Res. Adolesc.* 5:55–70

Laursen B, Collins WA. 1994. Interpersonal conflict during adolescence. *Psychol. Bull.* 115:197–209

Laursen B, Coy K, Collins WA. 1998. Reconsidering changes in parent-child conflict across adolescence: a meta-analysis. *Child Dev.* 69:817–32

Laursen B, Williams VA. 1997. Perceptions of interdependence and closeness in family and peer relationships among adolescents with and without romantic partners. In *Romantic Relationships in Adolescence: New Directions for Child Development,* ed. S Shulman, WA Collins, 78:3–20. San Francisco, CA: Jossey-Bass

Lempers JD, Clark-Lempers DS. 1992. Young, middle, and late adolescents' comparisons of the functional importance of five significant relationships. *J. Youth Adolesc.* 21:53–96

Lerner RM, Fisher CB, Weinberg RA. 2000. Toward a science for and of the people: promoting civil society through the application of developmental science. *Child Dev.* 71:11–20

Lerner RM, Steinberg L, eds. 2004. *Handbook of Adolescent Psychology.* Hoboken, NJ: Wiley. 2nd ed.

Luthar SS. 2003. The culture of affluence: psychological costs of material wealth. *Child Dev.* 74:1581–93

Luthar SS, Becker BE. 2002. Privileged but pressured? A study of affluent youth. *Child Dev.* 73:1593–10

Maccoby EE, Martin J. 1983. Socialization in the context of the family: parent-child interaction. In *Handbook of Child Psychology: Socialization, Personality, and Social Development,* ed. EM Hetherington, 4:1–101. New York: Wiley

Markus HR, Mullally PR, Kitayama S. 1997. Diversity in modes of cultural participation. In *The Conceptual Self in Context: Culture, Experience, Self-Understanding,* ed. U Neisser, D Jopling, pp. 13–61. London: Cambridge Univ. Press

Marshall SK, Tilton-Weaver LC, Bosdet L. 2005. Information management: considering adolescents' regulation of parental knowledge. *J. Adolesc.* In press

McAdoo H. 2002. African American parenting. See Bornstein 2002, 4:47–58

McElhaney KB, Allen JP. 2001. Autonomy and adolescent social functioning: the moderating effect of risk. *Child Dev.* 72:220–35

McLoyd V. 1998. Socioeconomic disadvantage and child development. *Am. Psychol.* 53: 185–204

Melchior A. 1998. *Final Report: National Evaluation of Learn and Serve America and Community-Based Programs.* Waltham, MA: Brandeis Univ. Cent. Hum. Resour.

Metz E, Youniss J. 2003. September 11 and service: a longitudinal study of high school students' views and responses. *Appl. Dev. Sci.* 7:148–55

Metz E, Youniss J. 2005. Longitudinal gains in civic development through school-based required service. *Polit. Psychol.* 26:413–37

Minuchin P. 2002. Looking toward the horizon: present and future in the study of family systems. In *Retrospect and Prospect in the Psychological Study of Families,* ed. S McHale, W Grolnick. Mahwah, NJ: Erlbaum

Montemayor R. 1983. Parents and adolescents in conflict: all families some of the time and some families most of the time. *J. Early Adolesc.* 3:83–103

Mounts NS. 2001. Young adolescents' perceptions of parental management of peer relationships. *J. Early Adolesc.* 21:91–122

Mounts NS. 2004. Adolescents' perceptions of parental management of peer relationships in an ethnically diverse sample. *J. Adolesc. Res.* 19:446–67

Neff KD, Helwig CC. 2002. A constructivist approach to understanding the development of reasoning about rights and authority within cultural contexts. *Cogn. Dev.* 17:1429–50

Nishina A, Juvonen J. 2005. Daily reports of witnessing and experiencing peer harassment in middle school. *Child Dev.* 76:435–50

Noller P, Callan VJ. 1986. Adolescent and parent perceptions of family cohesion and adaptability. *J. Adolesc.* 9:97–106

Noller P, Callan VJ. 1990. Adolescents' perceptions of the nature of their communication with parents. *J. Youth Adolesc.* 19:349–62

Olweus D. 1993a. *Bullying at School: What We Know and What We Can Do.* Oxford: Blackwell Sci.

Olweus D. 1993b. Victimization by peers: antecedents and long-term outcomes. In *Social Withdrawal, Inhibition and Shyness in Children,* ed. KH Rubin, JB Asendorf, pp. 315–41. Hillsdale, NJ: Erlbaum

Olweus D. 1999. Sweden. In *The Nature of School Bullying: A Cross-National Perspective,* ed. PK Smith, Y Morita, J Junger-Tas, D Olweus, R Catalano, P Slee, pp. 7–27. New York: Routledge

Parke RD, Buriel R. 1998. Socialization in the family: ethnic and ecological perspectives. See Eisenberg & Damon 1998, pp. 463–552

Parker JG, Low CM, Walker AR, Gamm BK. 2005. Friendship jealousy in young adolescents: individual differences and links to sex, self-esteem, aggression, and social adjustment. *Dev. Psychol.* 41:235–50

Pellegrini AD. 1994. The rough play of adolescent boys of differing sociometric status. *Int. J. Behav. Dev.* 17:525–40

Perry DG, Kusel SJ, Perry LC. 1988. Victims of peer aggression. *Dev. Psychol.* 24:807–14

Petersen AC. 1988. Adolescent development. *Annu. Rev. Psychol.* 39:583–607

Pettit GS, Laird RD, Bates JE, Dodge KA, Criss MM. 2001. Antecedents and behavior-problem outcomes of parental monitoring and psychological control in early adolescence. *Child Dev.* 72:583–98

Pew Internet Am. Life Proj. 2004. *Internet Survey, Latest Trends.* http://www.pewinternet.org/trends.asp

Phinney JS, Kim-Jo T, Osorio S, Vilhjalmsdottir P. 2005. Autonomy-relatedness in adolescent-parent disagreements: ethnic and developmental factors. *J. Adolesc. Res.* 20:8–39

Phinney JS, Landin J. 1998. Research paradigms for studying ethnic minority families within and across groups. In *Studying Minority Adolescents: Conceptual, Methodological, and Theoretical Issues*, ed. V McLoyd, L Steinberg, pp. 89–109. Mahwah, NJ: Erlbaum

Phinney JS, Ong A, Madden T. 2000. Cultural values and intergenerational value discrepancies in immigrant and non-immigrant families. *Child Dev.* 71:528–39

Putnam RD. 2000. *Bowling Alone. The Collapse and Revival of American Community.* New York: Simon & Schuster

Raffaelli M, Larson RW. 1987. *Sibling Interactions in Late Childhood and Early Adolescence.* Presented at Biennial Meet. Soc. Res. Child Dev., Baltimore, MD

Richards MH, Crowe PA, Larson R, Swarr A. 1998. Developmental patterns and gender differences in the experience of peer companionship during adolescence. *Child Dev.* 69:154–63

Rodkin PC, Farmer TW, Pearl R, Van Acker R. 2000. Heterogeneity of popular boys: antisocial and prosocial configurations. *Dev. Psychol.* 36:14–24

Rose AJ. 2002. Co-rumination in the friendships of girls and boys. *Child Dev.* 73:1830–43

Rose AJ, Swenson LP, Waller EM. 2004. Overt and relational aggression and perceived popularity: developmental differences in concurrent and prospective relations. *Dev. Psychol.* 40:378–87

Roth MA, Parker JG. 2001. Affective and behavioral responses to friends who neglect their friends for dating partners: influences of gender, jealousy, and perspective. *J. Adolesc.* 24:281–96

Rothbaum F, Pott M, Azuma H, Miyake K, Weisz J. 2000. The development of close relationships in Japan and the United States: paths of symbiotic harmony and generative tension. *Child Dev.* 71:1121–42

Rubin K, Bukowski W, Parker JG. 1998. Peer interactions, relationships, and groups. See Eisenberg & Damon 1998, pp. 619–700

Rubin K, Chen X, McDougall P, Bowker A, McKinnon J. 1995. The Waterloo Longitudinal Project: predicting internalizing and externalizing problems in adolescence. *Dev. Psychopathol.* 7:751–64

Schachter FF. 1985. Sibling deidentification in the clinic: devil vs. angel. *Fam. Process.* 24:415–27

Schachter FF, Stone RK. 1987. Comparing and contrasting siblings: defining the self. *J. Child. Contemp. Soc.* 19:55–75

Seligman MEP, Csikszentmihalyi M. 2000. Positive psychology: an introduction. *Am. Psychol.* 55:5–14

Shanahan L, McHale SM, Osgood DW, Crouter AC. 2005. *Development of Differential Parental Warmth Toward Siblings from Middle Childhood to Late Adolescence.* Presented at Biennial Meet. Soc. Res. Child Dev., Atlanta, GA

Sherrod L, Flanagan C, Youniss J. 2002. Dimensions of citizenship and opportunities for youth development: the what, why, when, where, and who of citizenship development. *Appl. Dev. Sci.* 6:264–72

Silverberg S, Steinberg L. 1990. Psychological well-being of parents at midlife: the impact of early adolescent children. *Dev. Psychol.* 26:658–66

Slomkowski C, Rende R, Conger KJ, Simons RL, Conger RD. 2001. Sisters, brothers, and delinquency: social influence during early and middle adolescence. *Child Dev.* 72:271–83

Smetana JG. 1988. Concepts of self and social convention: adolescents' and parents' reasoning about hypothetical and actual family conflicts. In *21st Minnesota Symposium on Child Psychology: Development During the Transition to Adolescence*, ed. MR Gunnar, WA Collins, pp. 77–122. Hillsdale, NJ: Erlbaum

Smetana JG. 1989. Adolescents' and parents' reasoning about actual family conflict. *Child Dev.* 60:1052–67

Smetana JG. 1996. Adolescent-parent conflict: implications for adaptive and maladaptive development. In *Rochester Symposium on Developmental Psychopathology. Adolescence: Opportunities and Challenges*, ed. D Cicchetti, SL Toth, 7:1–46. Rochester, NY: Univ. Rochester Press

Smetana JG. 2002. Culture, autonomy, and personal jurisdiction in adolescent-parent relationships. In *Advances in Child Development and Behavior*, ed. HW Reese, R Kail, 29:51–87. New York: Academic

Smetana JG. 2006. Social domain theory: consistencies and variations in children's moral and social judgments. In *Handbook of Moral Development*, ed. M Killen, JG Smetana, pp. 119–54. Mahwah, NJ: Erlbaum

Smetana JG, Campione-Barr N, Daddis C. 2004a. Developmental and longitudinal antecedents of family decision-making: defining healthy behavioral autonomy for African American adolescents. *Child Dev.* 75:1418–34

Smetana JG, Daddis C. 2002. Domain-specific antecedents of psychological control and parental monitoring: the role of parenting

beliefs and practices. *Child Dev.* 73:563–80

Smetana JG, Gaines C. 1999. Adolescent-parent conflict in middle-class African American families. *Child Dev.* 70:1447–63

Smetana JG, Metzger A, Campione-Barr N. 2004b. African American adolescents' relationships with parents: developmental transitions and longitudinal patterns. *Child Dev.* 75:932–47

Smetana JG, Metzger A, Gettman DC, Campione-Barr N. 2005. Disclosure and secrecy in adolescent-parent relationships. *Child Dev.* In press

Smetana JG, Yau J, Hanson S. 1991b. Conflict resolution in families with adolescents. *J. Res. Adolesc.* 1:189–206

Smetana JG, Yau J, Restrepo A, Braeges J. 1991a. Adolescent-parent conflict in married and divorced families. *Dev. Psychol.* 27:1000–10

Smith PK, Ananiadou K, Cowie H. 2003. Interventions to reduce school bullying. *Can. J. Psychiatry* 48:591–99

Spear P. 2000. The adolescent brain and age-related behavioral manifestations. *Neurosci. Biobehav. Rev.* 24:417–63

Spencer M, Dupree D. 1996. African American youths' ecocultural challenges and psychosocial opportunities: an alternative analysis of problem behavior outcomes. In *Adolescence: Opportunities and Challenges*, ed. D Cicchetti, SL Toth, pp. 259–82. Rochester, NY: Univ. Rochester Press

Stattin H, Kerr M. 2000. Parental monitoring: a reinterpretation. *Child Dev.* 71:1072–85

Steinberg L. 1989. Pubertal maturation and parent-adolescent distance: an evolutionary perspective. In *Advances in Adolescent Development*, ed. GR Adams, R Montemayor, T Gullotta, 1:71–97. Beverly Hills, CA: Sage

Steinberg L. 1990. Interdependency in the family: autonomy, conflict, and harmony in the parent-adolescent relationship. In *At the Threshold: The Developing Adolescent*, ed. SS Feldman, GR Elliot, pp. 255–76. Cambridge, MA: Harvard Univ. Press

Steinberg L. 2000. Should juvenile offenders be tried as adults? *Poverty Res.* 4:3–4

Steinberg L. 2001. We know some things: adolescent-parent relationships in retrospect and prospect. *J. Res. Adolesc.* 11:1–19

Steinberg L. 2004. Risk-taking in adolescence: what changes, and why? *Ann. NY Acad. Sci.* 1021:51–58

Steinberg L, Morris AS. 2001. Adolescent development. *Annu. Rev. Psychol.* 52:83–110

Steinberg L, Scott E. 2003. Less guilty by reason of adolescence: developmental immaturity, diminished responsibility, and the juvenile death penalty. *Am. Psychol.* 58:1009–18

Steinberg L, Silk J. 2002. Parenting adolescents. See Bornstein 2002, 1:103–33

Stocker C, Burwell RA, Briggs ML. 2002. Sibling conflict in middle childhood predicts children's adjustment in early adolescence. *J. Fam. Psychol.* 16:50–57

Taylor RD, Roberts D. 1995. Kinship support and maternal and adolescent well-being in economically disadvantaged African-American families. *Child Dev.* 66:1585–97

Tilton-Weaver LC, Galambos NL. 2003. Adolescents' characteristics and parents' beliefs as predictors of parents' peer management behaviors. *J. Res. Adolesc.* 13:269–300

Underwood MK. 2003. *Ice and Fire: Anger and Aggression Among Girls.* New York: Guilford

Updegraff KA, McHale SM, Crouter AC. 2000. Adolescents' sex-typed friendship experiences: Does having a sister versus a brother matter? *Child Dev.* 71:1597–10

Walker L, Taylor JH. 1991. Family interactions and the development of moral reasoning. *Child Dev.* 62:264–83

Whiteman SD, Buchanan CM. 2002. Mothers' and children's expectations for adolescence: the impact of perceptions of an older sibling's experience. *J. Fam. Psychol.* 16:157–71

Whiteman SD, McHale SM, Crouter AC. 2003. What parents learn from experience: the first child as a first draft? *J. Marriage Fam.* 65:608–21

Yates M, Youniss J. 1996. Community service and political-moral identity in adolescents. *J. Res. Adolesc.* 54:248–61

Yau J, Smetana JG. 1996. Adolescent-parent conflict among Chinese adolescents in Hong Kong. *Child Dev.* 67:1262–75

Yau J, Smetana JG. 2003. Adolescent-parent conflict in Hong Kong and Mainland China: a comparison of youth in two cultural contexts. *Int. J. Behav. Dev.* 27:201–11

Youniss J, McLellan JA, Yates M. 1997. What we know about engendering civic identity. *Am. Behav. Sci.* 40:620–31

Youniss J, McLellan JA, Yates M. 1999. Religion, community service, and identity in American youth. *J. Adolesc.* 22:243–53

Youniss J, Smollar JM. 1985. *Adolescents' Relations with Mothers, Fathers, and Friends.* Chicago: Univ. Chicago Press

Youniss J, Yates M. 1999. Youth service and moral-civic identity: a case for everyday morality. *Educ. Psychol. Rev.* 14:361–76

Annu. Rev. Psychol. 2006. 57:285–315
doi: 10.1146/annurev.psych.57.102904.190044
First published online as a Review in Advance on August 25, 2005

ENDURING EFFECTS FOR COGNITIVE BEHAVIOR THERAPY IN THE TREATMENT OF DEPRESSION AND ANXIETY

Steven D. Hollon, Michael O. Stewart, and Daniel Strunk

*Department of Psychology, Vanderbilt University, Nashville, Tennessee 37203;
email: steven.d.hollon@vanderbilt.edu, michael.o.stewart@vanderbilt.edu,
dan.strunk@vanderbilt.edu*

Key Words   enduring effects, prevention, relapse, recurrence, psychotherapy

■ **Abstract**   Recent studies suggest that cognitive and behavioral interventions have enduring effects that reduce risk for subsequent symptom return following treatment termination. These enduring effects have been most clearly demonstrated with respect to depression and the anxiety disorders. It remains unclear whether these effects are a consequence of the amelioration of the causal processes that generate risk or the introduction of compensatory strategies that offset them and whether these effects reflect the mobilization of cognitive or other mechanisms. No such enduring effects have been observed for the psychoactive medications, which appear to be largely palliative in nature. Other psychosocial interventions remain largely untested, although claims that they produce lasting change have long been made. Whether such enduring effects extend to other disorders remains to be seen, but the capacity to reduce risk following treatment termination is one of the major benefits provided by the cognitive and behavioral interventions with respect to the treatment of depression and the anxiety disorders.

CONTENTS

0066-4308/06/0110-0285$20.00

ENDURING EFFECTS FOR COGNITIVE BEHAVIOR THERAPY IN THE TREATMENT OF DEPRESSION AND ANXIETY

Psychosocial interventions have long been touted as providing enduring change. Not only are they said to reduce existing distress or improve functioning, they are believed to do so in a manner that produces lasting change over time. The question is whether this is true: Do psychosocial interventions truly produce enduring effects, and, if so, how do they compare with other major interventions like psychoactive medications?

Our primary focus is on enduring effects: Do the benefits of treatment last over time, beyond the termination of the intervention? We also address the nature of the underlying mechanisms. Enduring effects could be a consequence of the resolution of causal processes that contribute to risk or they could reflect the acquisition of compensatory factors that offset the pernicious effects of those causal processes (Barber & DeRubeis 1989). However, in most instances, we will be lucky if we can establish whether intervention effects endure, much less how those enduring effects are achieved.

Enduring effects can be of at least two kinds. *Treatment* effects reduce existing problems that would not have gone away on their own; they can be said to be enduring to the extent that the problem does not come back. In such instances, all that is required to document that a treatment has an enduring effect is that the changes produced be stable over time. If problems do return, then a treatment still can be said to have an enduring effect if problems return at a lesser rate or intensity than would have been the case if the treatment had not been provided. *Preventive* effects reduce risk for future problems. Such effects may not be immediately apparent in terms of the outcomes of interest; rather, their beneficial effects may become apparent only over time. Nonetheless, to have an enduring effect, an intervention must set in motion causal processes that interrupt the sequence of events leading to the onset or return of the disorder. That means that even delayed effects must reflect ongoing causal processes that may be subject to detection.

If psychosocial interventions do have enduring effects, how would they be detected? For an effect to be said to endure, its benefits must extend beyond the end of the period of intervention. When enduring effects are absolute (when symptoms do not return or expected onsets do not occur), then no comparison is required other than the lack of change from the end of treatment over time. When enduring effects are probabilistic (when symptoms do return to some extent or onsets do occur for some), then gains must be maintained or deterioration forestalled relative to some type of comparison condition. With respect to treatment, evidence for enduring effects is most compelling when subsequent symptom return is reduced relative to some other equally efficacious intervention and the relative value of those effects is best established by comparison to the most efficacious continuing interventions.

Enduring effects may also affect the rate at which symptoms appear; a treatment can be said to have an enduring effect if it slows the progression of a disorder even if it does not prevent its ultimate onset or return. For this reason, it may be important to chart the rate at which symptoms are manifest over time. The situation is further complicated when symptom onset or return leads patients to seek additional treatment, since efficacious subsequent treatment can reduce the very symptoms that led patients to seek this additional treatment. Cross-sectional assessments at fixed time points that do not take into account differential rates of onset and return or intercurrent treatment are less than wholly adequate, and most investigators now prefer to use some type of survival analysis (Greenhouse et al. 1989, Willett & Singer 1993) or model individual trajectories over time in a manner that allows for the consideration of multiple causal influences (Gibbons et al. 1993, Willett et al. 1991).

Efficacious treatments can fall into at least three categories, depending on their mechanisms of action and the nature of the underlying disorder. Some may be purely *palliative*; that is, they suppress the expression of symptoms so long as they are applied but do nothing to address the processes that drive the underlying disorder. Other interventions may be *curative* in the sense that they eliminate or reverse the underlying process that would otherwise lead to the continuation of the disorder. Still other interventions can be said to be *prophylactic*. These interventions eliminate or offset processes that contribute to risk for future onsets. Both curative and prophylactic interventions can be said to have enduring effects, with the former keeping symptoms from coming back (relapse) and the latter preventing wholly new onsets (recurrence).

Existing interventions can be classified with respect to this typology. As effective as medications are for many psychiatric disorders, there is no evidence that they are anything more than palliative; that is, they suppress symptoms so long as they are taken, but often do little to alter the course of the underlying disorder or to reduce subsequent risk once their use is discontinued. The cognitive and behavioral interventions, on the other hand, actually may be curative and possibly even prophylactic; that is, there is evidence that they produce lasting change or even reduce future risk. To the extent that this is true, it means that patients need not stay in treatment forever or that disorders can actually be prevented and possibly never even expressed (Hollon et al. 1992b). Dynamic-interpersonal and humanistic-experiential interventions typically have not been tested in a way that would allow for the detection of enduring effects.

In this article, we highlight the evidence for the statements above. The bulk of the evidence to date comes from the literature on depression and the anxiety disorders and involves the cognitive and behavior therapies (collectively referred to throughout the review as CBT). Typically, this takes the form of comparisons between patients treated to remission with CBT versus medication, then followed over time following treatment termination. The review is illustrative rather than exhaustive, and not all relevant studies are described, although we have made a special effort to discuss studies that could have shown enduring effects for other kinds of treatments or that failed to show enduring effects for CBT.

TREATMENT AND PREVENTION OF DEPRESSION

Depression is one of the most prevalent of the psychiatric disorders and a leading cause of disability worldwide. Although most patients remit from any given episode, symptoms often come back at some later time, and depression is now considered to be a largely recurrent disorder (when it is not chronic). Several different types of interventions have been shown to be efficacious in its treatment (see Hollon et al. 2002 for a review). Antidepressant medication (ADM) has been shown to be superior to placebo controls in literally thousands of trials and tends to suppress symptoms for as long as it is continued or maintained, but there is no evidence that it does anything to reduce underlying risk once its use is terminated. Both interpersonal psychotherapy (IPT) and CBT appear to be about as efficacious as ADM with respect to the reduction of acute distress; moreover, IPT appears to have a greater breadth of effect with respect to enhancing the quality of relationships, whereas CBT appears to be more enduring than ADM. More purely behavioral interventions have not been tested often, but have performed well in recent trials. Family-focused therapy shows promise in preventing relapse or recurrence in bipolar disorder, but has been little tested in unipolar depression. More traditional dynamic psychotherapy has fared poorly in direct comparisons with other interventions (although questions can be raised about the adequacy with which it has been implemented), and humanistic-experiential therapies have not been often tested.

Cognitive Therapy and the Prevention of Relapse

Among the various efficacious interventions, cognitive therapy (CT) has produced the most consistent evidence of enduring effects. In this variant of CBT, patients are trained to collect information in a systematic fashion to offset the influence of maladaptive information-processing strategies and to conduct behavioral experiments to test the accuracy of their negative beliefs (Beck et al. 1979). Patients also are encouraged to examine the accuracy of their beliefs using a series of logical tools (cognitive restructuring), and a premium is placed on teaching the patient to do the therapy for him- or herself, in recognition of the chronic recurrent nature of depression. Preparation for termination is addressed from the beginning of therapy (serving to justify the extensive use of homework) and explicit practice is provided in relapse prevention throughout.

Patients treated to remission in CT appear to be about half as likely to relapse following treatment termination as are patients treated to remission with medications.

A recent trial conducted by our group is illustrative. In that study, patients with moderate to severe depression were found to be more likely to respond to 8 weeks of treatment with either CT or ADM than with pill-placebo (a demonstrable treatment effect); by 16 weeks, response rates to the two active interventions were virtually identical (just under 60%) (DeRubeis et al. 2005). At that point, patients who had responded to medications were randomly assigned to continuation ADM or withdrawn onto pill-placebo and followed over the ensuing year. Patients who responded to CT terminated treatment and were allowed no more than three booster sessions (not more than one per month) over that same interval. As shown on the left in Figure 1, patients withdrawn onto pill-placebo were considerably more likely to relapse over the ensuing 12-month interval than were patients continued on medication (adjusted relapse rates of 76.2% versus 47.2%, 23.8% versus 52.8% survival); patients with a history of prior exposure to CT (30.8% relapse or 69.2% survival) did as least as well as patients continued on ADM (Hollon et al. 2005). With a hazard ratio of 0.30, prior exposure to CT reduced risk for relapse by about 70% relative to medication withdrawal. By way of contrast, continuation medication

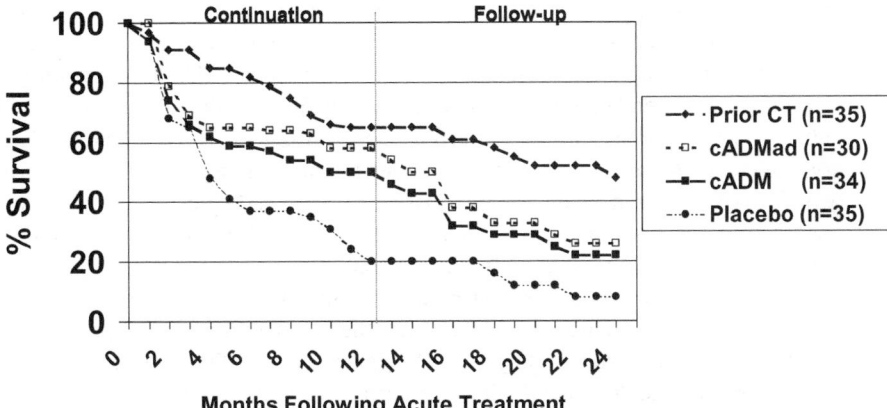

Figure 1 Cumulative proportion of depressed treatment responders who survived without relapse during continuation (first 12 months) and cumulative proportion of recovered patients who survived without recurrence during subsequent follow-up (months 13–24). Prior cognitive therapy allowed only three booster sessions following acute response (first 12 months) and no sessions following recovery (months 13–24); continuation antidepressant medication (cADM) patients continued on active medications following acute response (first 12 months), then withdrawn from all pills following recovery (months 13–24); cADMad patients represent that subset of cADM patients who adhered to prescribed medication during continuation phase (first 12 months); placebo patients withdrawn from active medications onto pill-placebo following acute response (first 12 months), then withdrawn from all pills following recovery (months 13–24). Adapted from Hollon et al. (2005), copyright 2005 by the American Medical Association. Reprinted by permission.

reduced risk by half relative to medication withdrawal (with a hazard ratio of 0.50). Even when nonadherence was taken into account (*dashed line* in Figure 1), prior CT did as well as continuation medication. This suggests that prior CT has an enduring effect that is at least as large in magnitude as keeping patients on medications, a purely palliative intervention that is the current standard of treatment for recurrent depression (Am. Psychiatric Assoc. 2000).

This is one of the most robust findings with respect to enduring effects in the literature. In several earlier trials, patients treated to remission in cognitive therapy were only about half as likely to relapse as were patients treated to remission with medications alone following treatment termination (Blackburn et al. 1986, Kovacs et al. 1981, Simons et al. 1986), and no more likely to relapse than were patients continued on medications (Evans et al. 1992). Only two studies have failed to find enduring effects for prior CT (Perlis et al. 2002, Shea et al. 1992); one involved the use of a medication (fluoxetine) with a particularly long half-life, and questions have been raised about the adequacy of the therapy provided in the other (Jacobson & Hollon 1996).

Although promising, these findings do not speak directly to the prevention of recurrence, defined as the onset of wholly new episodes (Frank et al. 1991). Depressed patients appear to be at elevated risk for symptom return (relapse) for the first six to nine months following initial response to medications when it is likely that the underlying episode has yet to run its course (Hollon et al. 1990). No good pharmacotherapist would withdraw patients from medications so soon after initial response, and it has become standard practice to continue patients on medications for at least six months after initial remission. Clearly, the early withdrawal practiced in the studies just described was done for research purposes only and does not reflect standard clinical practice. Nonetheless, studies of this kind do establish that CBT has an enduring effect that lasts beyond the end of treatment. Current medical practice is moving in the direction of maintaining patients with a history of recurrence (the vast majority of all depressed patients) on medication indefinitely (Am. Psychiatric Assoc. 2000). In that context, it would be important to know if CBT's enduring effects extend to the prevention of recurrence.

There are reasons to think that the effects might prevent recurrence. In the Hollon et al. 2005 study, we continued to follow patients who survived without relapse for another year (months 13–24 following the end of acute treatment). Patients who survived the full year of continuation treatment without relapse were withdrawn from medications at that time and compared to patients with a history of prior exposure to CT. Given that all of these patients had gone a full 12 months without relapse following initial remission, they were assumed to be fully recovered from the treated episode and any subsequent return of symptoms was considered to represent the onset of a wholly new episode (recurrence). As suggested by the slopes of the curves in the right half of Figure 1 (months 13–24), recovered patients withdrawn from medications were more likely to experience a recurrence over that second year of follow-up than were patients with a history of prior exposure to CT (Hollon et al. 2005). Only 5 of 20 recovered patients with a history of prior exposure to CT experienced a recurrence during that second year of naturalistic follow-up relative to 7 of 14 patients treated to recovery with medications alone. Taking attrition into account, the adjusted recurrence rates were 17.5% for prior CT versus 53.6% for prior continuation ADM, with a hazard ratio of 0.15 (meaning that prior CT reduced risk for recurrence relative to medication withdrawal by about 85%). Although larger studies are needed, these findings suggest that CT's enduring effect may extend beyond relapse to the prevention of recurrence. To the extent that this is true, it would mean that CT is not only curative (by virtue of bringing the treated episode to an end), but also possibly prophylactic (in the sense of forestalling the onset of wholly new episodes).

One important caveat must be mentioned. Such studies of enduring effects typically have relied on naturalistic follow-ups of acute treatment trials. Although patients in those trials initially were randomized to the different treatment conditions, subsequent attrition and nonresponse could have served to unbalance the groups with respect to preexistent patient characteristics. Differences in such characteristics (if they exist) could in turn be related to subsequent risk for relapse or recurrence. Thus, initial treatment could act as a "differential sieve" that systematically unbalances the groups with respect to underlying risk (Klein 1996). In the Hollon et al. 2005 study, only about 60% of the patients assigned to either condition both completed and responded to treatment and were therefore eligible to take part in the continuation phase. Losing nearly half the sample provides ample opportunities for differential retention to unbalance the groups; it is quite possible that patients who responded to CT were simply at lower risk for relapse for reasons unrelated to treatment than were patients who responded to medication treatment. There is little existing evidence that CT's enduring effect is an artifact of differential retention (responders to the different treatments rarely differ in meaningful ways), but there is nothing in the logic of the typical follow-up design that precludes the possibility.

The best way to reduce this risk to internal validity is to minimize the proportion of patients who fail to enter the period of risk. Attrition and nonresponse are inherent in any study, but there are design decisions that can be made to reduce their magnitude. For example, patients could be treated to criteria (remission or recovery) rather than for a fixed time prior to treatment termination. Similarly, the study design could be set to minimize the differences between conditions other than those directly relevant to the question of interest. For example, all patients might be medicated and psychotherapy provided for half on a random basis (rather than comparing the two single modalities directly) to minimize differences resulting solely from the provision of medications.

Such a strategy depends on the absence of interactions between drugs and psychotherapy. Two studies found that CBT's enduring effect was robust whether it is provided alone or in combination with medications (Blackburn et al. 1986, Evans et al. 1992), but a third found that relapse rates were higher when CT was provided in combination with medication relative to CT alone or CT plus placebo (Simons et al. 1986). Moreover, the existing combinatorial trials were all conducted with the older tricyclic medications; it remains to be seen if newer medications with less problematic side effects and broader profiles of action will undermine CT's enduring effects. In a subsequent section, we discuss indications that such medications may sometimes interfere with the enduring effects of CBT in the treatment of anxiety.

There also are indications that CBT or related interventions may have enduring effects when provided after medications have been used to reduce acute distress. For example, Paykel and colleagues found that adding CT to medication treatment for partial responders not only helped resolve residual symptoms but also reduced risk for subsequent relapse after the end of the psychosocial treatment (Paykel et al. 1999). Even more interestingly, Fava and colleagues found that adding an enhanced version of CT, called "well-being therapy," to medications for remitted patients in continuation treatment reduced risk for recurrence following medication withdrawal (Fava et al. 1998). Finally, an innovative integration of acceptance and meditation called "mindfulness-based cognitive therapy" has been shown to reduce risk for relapse and recurrence following treatment termination in patients first treated to remission with medications (Teasdale et al. 2000).

There are even indications that CBT may have a preventive effect when provided to children and adolescents at risk (Gillham et al. 2000). Clarke and colleagues have conducted a pair of studies in adolescents at risk by virtue of having a parent with a history of depression; in both trials, training in skills designed to facilitate affective regulation reduced risk for subsequent diagnosable disorder (Clarke et al. 1995, 2001). Similarly, evidence has been found of preventive effects in nondepressed subjects selected on the basis of problematic cognitive style both in children (Jaycox et al. 1994) and college students (Seligman et al. 1999). By definition, preventive effects are enduring effects, since the benefits are obtained long after the intervention is over.

Other types of interventions simply have not been adequately tested. Dynamic psychotherapy has rarely been found to be efficacious with respect to acute treatment; although it is possible to have an enduring effect in the absence of any immediate effect, it is unlikely that such an effect would be detected. IPT has been shown to prevent relapse or recurrence when continued (Klerman et al. 1974) or maintained (Frank et al. 1990), but there is little evidence of any enduring effect once its use is terminated (Hollon et al. 2002). IPT was included in the National Institute of Mental Health Treatment of Depression Collaborative Research Program along with CT and medications, but medication treatment was extended for the first several months of the posttreatment follow-up (Shea et al. 1992). As described above, the program was one of only two studies to date not to find an enduring effect for CT, and it is not clear whether any such effect could have been detected given the methods used. The follow-up phase of an earlier acute treatment trial found no indication that prior IPT had any enduring effect relative to medication withdrawal, but that design relied on a single cross-sectional assessment that would likely have failed to detect the presence of enduring effects (Weissman et al. 1981). There are indications that more purely behavioral interventions also might have enduring effects, a point to which we return in a subsequent section.

In a disorder such as depression, patients who experience a relapse or recurrence following medication withdrawal are likely to seek additional treatment; if symptom return is not monitored in an ongoing fashion, the outcome of interest will likely be missed because subsequent treatment will reduce the distress before the next assessment. That is why we prefer to monitor symptom status in a continuous (albeit retrospective) fashion. Given that patients withdrawn from medications typically experience more symptom return, they are more likely to require additional treatment. Periodic assessments focused solely on current symptom levels typically fail to detect such differences because the effects of subsequent treatment tend to offset the very symptom return that led patients to get back on medications in the first place (Evans et al. 1992).

Mechanisms Underlying Enduring Change

How do cognitive and behavior therapies produce their enduring effects? Cognitive theory suggests that change in what people believe and the way they process information is the primary mechanism of change in CT (Beck 1991). Several studies have shown that thinking does change over the course of therapy; however, the kinds of "surface-level" automatic negative thoughts found in the stream of consciousness typically change as much in pharmacotherapy or other successful interventions as they do in CT (Imber et al. 1990, Simons et al. 1984). What does appear to change in a more specific fashion are the underlying beliefs and information-processing propensities often found in depression, such as core beliefs about the self or the way an individual explains the causes of negative life events. Such core beliefs and information-processing styles tend to lie dormant until activated by negative affect or external stress and serve as the stable cognitive predispositions in a larger diathesis-stress model of depression (Hollon et al. 1992b).

For example, in an earlier trial, we found that CT and medication treatment produced comparable rapid change in depression, with 90% of the symptom change occurring in the first six weeks treatment (Hollon et al. 1992a), but that patients treated to remission with CT were only half as likely to relapse following treatment termination as were patients treated to remission with medications (Evans et al. 1992). Change in "surface-level" automatic negative thoughts such as a sense of hopelessness was nonspecific with respect to treatment modality and mirrored the rapid rate of change shown by depressive symptoms, although it did predict subsequent change in depression to a greater extent in CT than in medication treatment (DeRubeis et al. 1990). At the same time, patients treated to remission with CT showed considerably greater change in underlying attribution style (the way they explained negative life events), and the bulk of that differential change occurred in the second half of treatment, well after the bulk of change in depression (Hollon et al. 1990). Moreover, this differential change in attribution style predicted the greater rate of relapse in the patients treated with medications alone relative to CT following treatment termination. Change in these more stable information-processing proclivities mediated the enduring effects of CBT in a sample of at-risk young adults provided with a preventive intervention (Seligman et al. 1999). Taken together, these findings suggest that change in cognition mediates the enduring effect found for CBT, but it is change in stable cognitive predispositions and underlying information-processing proclivities that is key to prevention.

We do not yet have a good sense as to whether these changes reflect true accommodation in underlying cognitive predispositions or the acquisition of compensatory mechanisms, since existing measures are susceptible to either process (Barber & DeRubeis 1989). Anecdotal reports from patients suggest that it is more the latter, at least at first, as they describe needing to remind themselves to engage in formal cognitive restructuring techniques when they start to interpret negative life events in a problematic manner. Nonetheless, these same patients describe these capacities as becoming more automatic over time, such that they are less likely to jump to negative conclusions, a process more in keeping with the notion of accommodation. This area merits further investigation.

Teasdale and colleagues also reported that change in underlying information-processing proclivities mediated differential relapse, although in their trial it was becoming less extreme that was beneficial, not simply becoming less negative (Teasdale et al. 2001). That is, patients who became unrealistically positive were also at greater risk, a pattern that we have replicated in findings in our most recent trial (Hollon et al. 2005). Some patients appear to become unduly positive in CT, overshooting even normal controls, something we do not see in ADM. This unrealistic optimism appears to leave patients at elevated risk and produces a curvilinear relation between cognitive change and subsequent relapse that is quite distinct from the linear relation observed for ADM. It is unclear why some patients become unduly optimistic, although we suspect it reflects a triumph of wishful thinking over the more tedious process of reality testing. Whatever its source, it is clearly specific to CT, but it is not something that we have observed in earlier studies. This is something that needs to be addressed in future studies.

Finally, Tang & DeRubeis (1999) have observed that many patients treated with CT show "sudden gains" following a single session that account for the bulk of the change they show across the course of treatment. These sudden gains occur at different times for different patients, but tend to be preceded by cognitive change and followed by improved ratings of the therapeutic alliance. In effect, it is as if the patient suddenly "understands" that their thinking is unduly negative, rather than their personalities that are flawed or even their life situations that are to blame. Once they come to this realization, they seem to do a better job of managing their own affect and behavior. Patients who show sudden gains tend to get better faster and to stay better longer than do patients who show a more gradual pattern of response. At the same time, process studies indicate that attention to specific concrete beliefs and behaviors early in treatment leads to greater subsequent change in depression and higher ratings of the quality of the therapeutic relationship (DeRubeis & Feeley 1990, Feeley et al. 1999). Taken in aggregate, these findings suggest that patients are most likely to show enduring change when their therapists focus on specific behavioral and cognitive strategies in a structured manner, but that this change is likely to emerge in a rapid and unpredictably idiosyncratic fashion across patients.

Enduring Effects in Behavior Therapy

Recent studies suggest that more purely behavioral interventions may also produce enduring effects. In a component analysis, Jacobson and colleagues found that the behavioral strategies used in the early stages of CT produced as much change as the complete treatment package when extended over the full course of therapy (Jacobson et al. 1996). Most critically for the current discussion, there was no evidence of differential risk for relapse following treatment termination (Gortner et al. 1998). This led to the articulation of a more fully realized contextual intervention, called "behavioral activation" (BA), that emphasizes the functional connection between behaviors and outcomes and eschews attention to the content of cognitions (Jacobson et al. 2001, Martell et al. 2001). In a recent trial, BA was found to be as efficacious as ADM with respect to acute treatment (Dimidjian et al. 2005) and as enduring as CT with respect to the prevention of subsequent relapse and recurrence (KS Dobson, SD Hollon, S Dimidjian, KB Schmaling, RJ Kohlenberg, R Gallop, S Rizvi, JK Gollan, DL Dunner, NS Jacobson, manuscript in preparation). Given that therapists pay little attention to thought content in BA (other than noting the role of rumination in maintaining behavioral avoidance), it is clear that direct efforts to address beliefs and information-processing proclivities may not be required to produce enduring change. However, it remains possible that these largely behavioral strategies work through underlying cognitive mechanisms to produce their enduring effects (Bandura 1977). Additional research will be required to resolve this issue. For now, the best that we can do is to note that there is good evidence for enduring effects in CT for depression (quite possibly mediated by changes in underlying cognitive predispositions) and promising indications that these enduring effects may also extend to more behavioral interventions through mechanisms yet unknown.

Prevention of Bipolar Disorder

Patients with bipolar disorder are at risk for episodes of mania or hypomania as well as depression. Genetic factors play a greater role in bipolar disorder than in unipolar depression, and the course is marked by frequent relapse and recurrence. Medication forms the core of treatment and most patients are maintained indefinitely on lithium or mood stabilizers to forestall symptom onset (especially mania), with antidepressants often added to deal with depressive symptoms (Am. Psychiatric Assoc. 2002).

Psychosocial interventions typically are used in an adjunctive fashion and it has only been in recent years that empirical studies have demonstrated their value. Teaching patients to detect prodromal signs and seek prompt medical help has been shown to reduce the frequency of onset of full manic episodes (Perry et al. 1999), and interpersonal and social rhythm therapy has been found to reduce the frequency of depressive relapse (Malkoff-Schwartz et al. 1998). Family-focused treatment, designed to reduce stress and improve communication, has been found to reduce the frequency of mania and depression both during and after the end of treatment (Miklowitz et al. 2003). This represents one of the few instances in which enduring effects have been documented for any psychosocial intervention other than CBT.

Lam and colleagues found that adding CT to medication management over a six-month period reduced risk for subsequent relapse relative to medications alone for the rest of the year in bipolar patients not currently in episode (Lam et al. 2003). A subsequent follow-up found that this advantage was maintained over the next year and a half, but largely reflected differences that emerged during and shortly after treatment (Lam et al. 2005). Thus, although CT had a beneficial effect (in that patients did better during treatment when CT was added to medications), it is not clear that it had an enduring effect such that patients previously treated with CT were at any lower risk of relapse once its use was terminated than were patients receiving medication only (a direct comparison of the conditional probabilities of relapse for each specific interval following the termination of the psychosocial treatment would have been of interest).

However, survival analyses based on time to first relapse are not the best way to detect enduring effects when differences emerge during treatment, since high-risk patients are more likely to be retained (and thus remain at risk) by the more efficacious treatment (Hollon et al. 2002). Thus, it is possible that documented success of CT in preventing relapse during its initial application led to the differential retention of more high-risk patients going into the later months of the follow-up, thereby obscuring possible enduring effects. In this regard, it is of interest that patients previously treated with CT spent fewer months in episode during the extended follow-up than did patients treated with medication management alone, an index that would not be biased by differential retention. This suggests that CT with bipolar patients may have the same kind of enduring effect that has been found so often in unipolar depression.

PANIC AND THE ANXIETY DISORDERS

Is there evidence for enduring effects in other disorders? Such evidence does exist, especially with respect to panic and the anxiety disorders, although it is not as well documented as for depression and is largely limited to CBT (Hollon & Beck 2004). In this section, we review panic and the anxiety disorders.

Catastrophic Cognitions in Panic and Agoraphobia

As for depression, different theoretical models exist and each posits different interventions for panic disorder and agoraphobia. Biological models view panic as the consequence of the spontaneous discharge of neural centers deep in the brain stem or limbic system and treat the symptoms with medications (Lydiard et al. 1996). Behavioral models regard panic attacks to be a conditioned response to internal or external cues that need to be extinguished via exposure; agoraphobia is regarded as reinforced avoidance behavior that needs to be suppressed through response prevention (Barlow & Lehman 1996). Cognitive models emphasize the role of catastrophic misinterpretations of benign bodily sensations and encourage patients to test the accuracy of their beliefs via inducing the physiological sensations that they most fear (Beck & Emery 1985, Clark 1986). Interventions based on all three models have been shown to be both specific and efficacious in the treatment of panic disorder (DeRubeis & Crits-Christoph 1998).

There are consistent indications that treatment effects achieved with the psychosocial interventions are more likely to endure following treatment termination than are those obtained with medications (Roth & Fonagy 2005). For example, Sharp and colleagues (1996) found that patients treated with CBT (alone or in combination with medication) were more likely to maintain gains at a six-month posttreatment follow-up than were patients treated with fluvoxamine alone. Loerch and colleagues (1999) found that adding CBT enhanced response relative to either moclobemide or placebo alone and that those patients in the latter two conditions were far more likely to seek additional treatment across a naturalistic follow-up. In perhaps the best of the early trials, Clark and colleagues (1994) found CT superior to either imipramine (an older tricyclic ADM) pharmacotherapy or applied relaxation in a sample of patients with panic disorder (and each superior to a wait-list control); across a subsequent six-month follow-up, only 5% of the CT patients relapsed following treatment termination, compared with 40% of the patients withdrawn from medications. Moreover, as specified by theory, CT produced a reduction in catastrophic cognitions that was greater than that of either of the other two active treatments, and the frequency of such beliefs at the end of treatment predicted subsequent risk for relapse following treatment termination.

Barlow and colleagues (2000) also found an enduring effect for prior CBT, as well as a cautionary note with regard to its combination with medication. In a multisite study, patients with panic disorder (with or without mild agoraphobia) were randomly assigned to three months of weekly acute treatment followed by six months of monthly maintenance treatment with either CBT or imipramine, each alone and in combination, or pill-placebo, again alone and in combination with CBT. Each single modality was superior to pill-placebo, with combined treatment somewhat better still by the end of maintenance treatment. Imipramine produced higher quality response among treatment completers, but CBT was more enduring. As shown in Figure 2, adjusted relapse rates were 8% for patients who responded to CBT alone (92% survival) versus 25% for responders to imipramine alone (75% survival). Curiously, adding active medication appeared to undermine the enduring effects of CBT, as 36% of the patients in the combined condition relapsed (64% survival). It is unlikely that purely psychological processes mediated this effect (such as misattributing treatment gains solely to medications), since only 4% of the patients treated with the combination of CBT plus pill-placebo relapsed

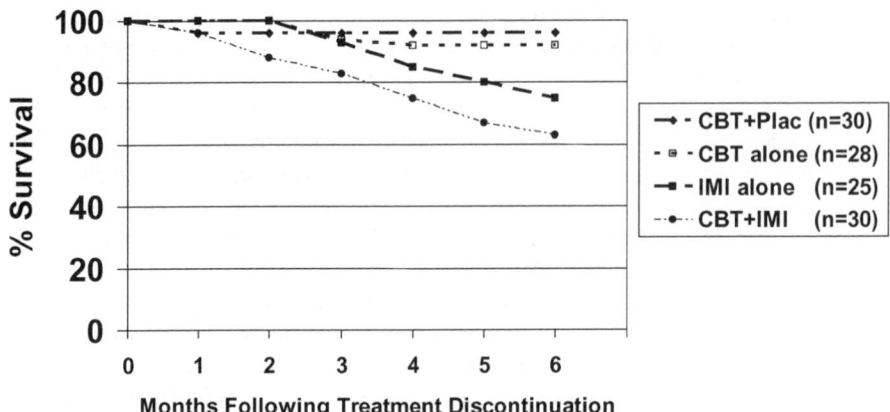

Figure 2 Proportion of panic patients meeting criteria for relapse following termination as a function of prior treatment condition. CBT + Plac patients received cognitive behavior therapy plus pill-placebo; CBT-alone patients received cognitive behavior therapy only; IMI-alone patients received imipramine pharmacotherapy only; CBT + IMI patients received cognitive behavior therapy plus imipramine pharmacotherapy. Adapted from Barlow et al. (2000).

(96% survival). It also is unlikely that this effect was an artifact of differential retention, since response rates were as high when CBT was combined with pill-placebo as with active medication.

This pattern of findings suggests that if adding medication suppresses CBT's enduring effect, it does so through largely pharmacological mechanisms. For example, it is possible that the presence of active medication acts to retard learning, either by suppressing interioceptive cues in a manner that slows the process of habituation (behavioral) or by reducing the opportunity for disconfirmation of catastrophic expectations (cognitive). That is, medication may operate through biological mechanisms that suppress the occurrence of panic for so long as it is taken, but that interfere with other learning-based mechanisms that would have produced more lasting change.

This is not the first time that the addition of medications has undermined the enduring effect of a psychosocial intervention. In an earlier trial, Marks and colleagues combined either exposure or relaxation with alprazolam (a high-potency benzodiazapine) or placebo in a factorial design. Agoraphobic patients treated with the combination of exposure plus alprazolam showed a higher rate of relapse than did patients treated with the combination of exposure plus placebo (Marks et al. 1993). It would appear that medication is more likely to interfere with the enduring effects of CBT for panic and agoraphobia than has been the case to date in the treatment of depression.

The precise nature of the mechanisms involved remains unclear, but it is possible that they will vary as a function of the nature of the disorder and the specific medication. Disorders such as panic with rapid symptom onset may be more sus-ceptible to interference effects than are disorders with greater temporal stability, such as depression. At the same time, patients are particularly likely to attribute change to fast-acting medications such as alprazolam, and any medication that produces rapid and transitory change in affective states is particularly likely to induce state-dependent learning. Moreover, medications with short half-lives are particularly likely to produce discontinuation effects, making them harder to with-draw and increasing the risk of relapse following termination. In fact, the sequen-tial application of CBT has been used to facilitate withdrawal from high-potency benzodiazapines such as alprazolam, which can provoke rebound panic attacks fol-lowing discontinuation (Bruce et al. 1999, Otto et al. 1993). It remains to be seen whether such a sequential strategy will prove useful in helping patients withdraw from newer antidepressants with short half-lives, such as venlafaxine or paroxe-tine, and whether those medications will interfere with CBT's enduring effect if provided in combination during active treatment.

There are few indications that either dynamic-eclectic or humanistic-experiential interventions are efficacious in the treatment of panic disorder, much less have en-during effects. More purely behavioral interventions tend to produce gains that endure (Arntz & Van den Hout 1996, Öst & Westling 1995), although enduring effects have not been clearly documented. Presence of agoraphobic avoidance pre-dicts poorer overall response, and tests of enduring effects have been few (Bouchard et al. 1996). Nonetheless, it is clear that CBT has an enduring effect in the treat-ment of panic disorder. As in the treatment of depression, this effect is most evident in comparisons to drugs and represents one of the main advantages of CBT over medications.

Hypochondriasis and Concerns about Physical Illness

Patients with hypochondriasis believe they have a physical illness and take lit-tle comfort from medical reassurance. Although common in medical settings, the disorder has rarely been studied empirically and has long been thought to be impervious to treatment. Cognitive theory suggests that hypochondriasis is a con-sequence of an enduring tendency to misinterpret innocuous physical sensations as symptoms of a serious illness, much as in panic disorder, with the key difference being the perceived imminence of the medical catastrophe (Warwick & Salkovskis 1990). Patients in CT are encouraged to examine the evidence for their beliefs and to conduct behavioral experiments in which they induce symptoms by focusing attention on their body. Reassurance seeking and "body checking" are discouraged to reduce the operation of safety behaviors, and patients are encouraged to keep a daily record of negative thoughts and rational responses.

Recent studies suggest the efficacy of this approach. Warwick and colleagues (1996) found CT superior to a wait-list control after four months of treatment, with gains essentially maintained at a three-month follow-up. Clark and colleagues (1998) found CT superior to a wait-list control on all measures and better than behavioral stress management on symptoms of hypochondriasis, with gains essentially maintained over a subsequent 12-month follow-up. Barsky & Ahern (2004) found that six sessions of CBT (similar but not identical to the approach described above) produced greater change in symptoms of hypochondriasis compared with usual medical care across a 12-month posttreatment follow-up.

Given that hypochondriasis has long been thought to be refractory to treatment, these findings are most promising; this is especially the case for indications that gains endure over time following treatment termination. Evidence for enduring effects would be even more compelling if prior CBT were to prove more stable over time than some alternative intervention of equal initial efficacy; however, with the possible exception of behavioral stress management, no other treatment (including medications) has yet been found to be efficacious in the treatment of hypochondriasis.

Generalized Anxiety Disorder and the Primacy of Worry

In recent years, cognitive symptoms like pervasive apprehension and worry have come to be seen as the core symptoms of generalized anxiety disorder (GAD) (Brown et al. 1994). CBT involving the combination of relaxation training and cognitive restructuring has been found to be both efficacious and specific in a number of comparisons to other interventions and control conditions, and applied relaxation has shown promise in a smaller number of trials (DeRubeis & Crits-Christoph 1998). More purely behavioral interventions based on exposure are difficult to implement, since there is often no clear external referent to target. Medication treatment is often problematic; minor tranquilizers can induce dependence and tend to lose potency with prolonged use, and antidepressants do nothing to reduce future risk (Nathan & Gorman 1998). More traditional forms of psychotherapy have long been touted, but rarely tested.

Treatment gains for CBT are generally well maintained over time, both in adults (Borkovec & Ruscio 2001) and in geriatric populations (Stanley et al. 2003). Differences favoring cognitive strategies sometimes have emerged following treatment termination relative to more purely behavioral interventions (Borkovec & Costello 1993), and Durham and colleagues (2003) recently reported that patients in CBT exhibited lower overall symptom severity and less interim treatment in the 8–14 years following treatment termination than did patients receiving either dynamic or pharmacological treatment.

Nonetheless, there is a general sense that more can be done with the treatment of GAD. For example, Borkovec and colleagues (2002) found that interpersonal difficulties remaining after treatment with CBT predicted poorer status across follow-up, and they called for the inclusion of strategies that targeted these problems. Similarly, Fava and colleagues (2005) found that adding strategies designed to promote a sense of well-being enhanced the efficacy of CBT, with gains maintained across a one-year follow-up. Finally, Ladouceur and colleagues (1999) have dropped relaxation training entirely to focus on more purely cognitive targets such as intolerance of uncertainty and cognitive avoidance. A recent controlled trial found this more purely cognitive intervention superior to a delayed treatment control; 77% of all participants treated with CBT no longer met criteria for GAD following treatment (Ladouceur et al. 2000). In a subsequent trial, participants provided with group CBT did better than a wait-list control and continued to improve across a 24-month follow-up (Dugas et al. 2003). It remains to be seen how this approach will compare to more conventional renditions of CBT that incorporate more explicitly behavioral components, but treatment effects for each appear to be well maintained over time.

Interpersonal Anxiety and Social Phobia

Social phobia (also known as social anxiety disorder) tends to begin early in life and often follows a chronic course (Davidson et al. 1993). Social phobia involves an undue fear of evaluation by others and the accompanying desire to avoid situations in which scrutiny is anticipated. A number of pharmacological agents have been found to reduce distress, including the monoamine oxidase inhibitors and, more recently, the selective serotonin reuptake inhibitors (SSRIs) (Hidalgo et al. 2001). Behavioral approaches based on exposure to social situations (often supplemented with training in social skills) generally have been efficacious, although gains have not always been well maintained over time (DeRubeis & Crits-Christoph 1998). Cognitive approaches target beliefs regarding personal defects that could lead to ridicule or censure by others in social situations (Beck & Emery 1985), and a recent extension focuses on the elimination of safety behaviors that retard the disconfirmation of those beliefs (Wells et al. 1995).

Although the effects produced by exposure alone have not always been stable over time, they do appear to be more enduring than are those produced by medications. Blomhoff and colleagues (2001) found that sertraline (an SSRI) was superior to exposure therapy in a primary-care sample, but that patients treated with the psychosocial intervention continued to improve across a subsequent year-long follow-up, whereas those treated with sertraline (alone or in combination) tended to deteriorate after treatment termination (Haug et al. 2003). Similarly, a naturalistic study of long-term treatment outcomes in social phobia found that concomitant use of benzodiazepines during active treatment was associated with greater risk of relapse in patients treated with exposure (Fava et al. 2001). These reports are reminiscent of the findings in panic and agoraphobia that adding medication may undermine the enduring effects of CBT (Barlow et al. 2000, Marks et al. 1993). There are also indications that the addition of cognitive restructuring facilitates the maintenance of gains produced by exposure to social situations (e.g., Butler et al. 1984, Heimberg et al. 1993).

Perhaps the best evidence for the enduring effects of CBT in social phobia comes from a two-site comparison to medications that did a particularly nice job of controlling for allegiance across sites and conditions (Heimberg et al. 1998). In that trial, patients with social phobia were randomly assigned to cognitive behavioral group therapy (CBGT) alone, phenelzine (a monoamine oxidase inhibitor) alone, pill-placebo, or educational-supportive group therapy. Both active treatments were superior to the two control conditions; phenelzine produced somewhat faster response than did CBGT, but rates of response were comparable by the end of acute treatment (12 weeks). Responders to the two active treatments were provided with six months of additional maintenance treatment and then tracked across a subsequent six-month interval following treatment termination. As shown in Figure 3, there was clear evidence for an enduring effect for the psychosocial intervention; none of the patients previously treated with CBGT relapsed following treatment termination versus 33% of the patients previously treated with phenelzine (100% versus 67% survival) (Liebowitz et al. 1999).

Clark and colleagues have suggested that patients with social phobia focus undue attention on their image of themselves in social situations and engage in safety behaviors (strategies designed to protect them from feared consequences) that make them appear less socially skilled and prevent them from learning that they can handle the feared encounters (Wells et al. 1995). Patients are videotaped engaging in various social situations, both with and without safety behaviors, and are then invited to watch both tapes and rate themselves on various characteristics. Patients typically find that they appear more relaxed and socially skilled when they drop their safety behaviors and that their internal images of themselves are more negative and self-derogatory than they actually appear. Moreover, patients show greater change in beliefs and greater reductions in anxiety when they drop their safety behaviors in exposure situations.

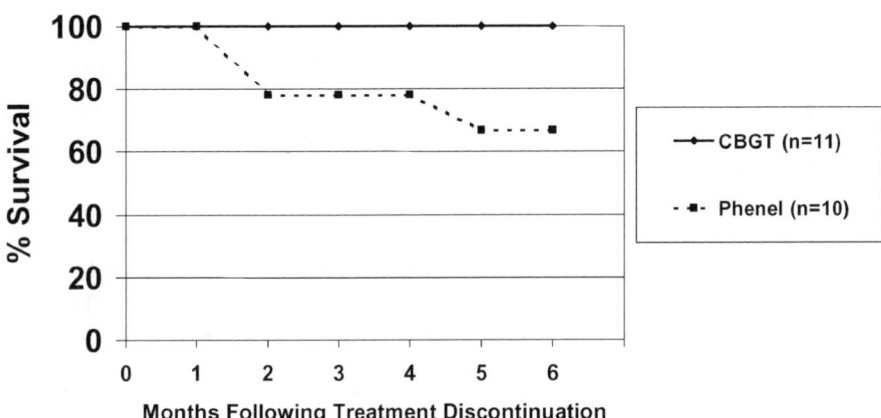

Figure 3 Relapse following successful treatment among patients with social phobia treated with cognitive behavioral group therapy (CBGT) or medications. CBGT patients were previously treated with cognitive behavioral group therapy; phenelzine patients previously treated with the monoamine oxidase inhibitor phenelzine. Adapted from Liebowitz et al. (1999).

Clark and colleagues have argued that targeting self-focused attention and encouraging patients to drop their safety behaviors during exposure can facilitate their capacity to learn from experience and hasten their response to treatment. A recent comparison suggests that this newer individual approach may be superior to more conventional CBGT, which had been done in groups to take advantage of the opportunities afforded for exposure to social situations (Stangier et al. 2003). In another recent comparison, Clark and colleagues found that patients with social phobia who were treated with individual CBT in the manner described above showed greater reductions in measures of social phobia across 16 weeks of active treatment than did patients treated with either fluoxetine or placebo. Moreover, the advantage observed for CBT relative to medication was essentially maintained across three months of booster treatment and was still evident at a 12-month follow-up following treatment termination (Clark et al. 2003). These findings, combined with those obtained by Liebowitz and colleagues (1999) with CBGT, suggest that CBT for social phobia has an enduring effect not found with medication.

Specific Phobias and the Perception of Danger

Specific phobias involve an intense fear of certain objects or situations and a corresponding desire to avoid being in their presence. Behavior theory suggests that phobias are established via traumatic conditioning and maintained by avoidance behaviors that prevent their extinction (Mowrer 1948). Behavioral interventions such as systematic desensitization and exposure plus response prevention are clearly efficacious and represent the current standard of treatment (DeRubeis & Crits-Christoph 1998). Gains typically are well maintained, although return of fear (spontaneous recovery) sometimes does occur, especially when contextual cues favor the retrieval of memories associated with fear acquisition rather than extinction (Bouton 1993). Being on a psychoactive substance during exposure appears to alter those cues (Mystkowski et al. 2003), and treatment has been shown to be more enduring when provided in the absence of medications (Marks et al. 1972).

Cognitive theory posits that individuals with specific phobias perceive greater danger or risk in the feared situation than do other people and suggests that such beliefs often are activated only in the presence of the feared object (Beck & Emery 1985). Öst and colleagues have had great success with single-session cures by adjusting the nature of the exposure to test the idiosyncratic beliefs expressed by patients as they approach the object of their fears (Hellström et al. 1996, Hellström & Öst 1995, Öst et al. 1997). Other groups have obtained similar results (Thom et al. 2000, Thorpe & Salkovskis 1997). Whether this approach will enhance the stability of change relative to more purely behavioral interventions remains to be seen, but it does appear to facilitate the rapidity of change.

Obsessive-Compulsive Disorder and Personal Responsibility

Obsessive-compulsive disorder (OCD) is characterized by obsessive thoughts and images that evoke anxiety and compulsive behaviors or ritualistic mental acts that serve to reduce distress. OCD tends to be a chronic recurrent disorder. Naturalistic data suggest that full remission is rare and relapse is common after partial remission (Eisen et al. 1999); nearly half of all patients will show a chronic course (Skoog & Skoog 1999). Comparison across studies indicates that patients with OCD show a lower rate of placebo response than do patients with other types of anxiety disorders (Huppert et al. 2004).

Exposure plus response prevention (ERP) is both efficacious and specific in the treatment of OCD (DeRubeis & Crits-Christoph 1998). Although it need not be the case, ERP for this disorder typically is presented as a test of the consequences of choosing not to act to undo the obsessions, making it a largely cognitive behavioral intervention. Pharmacotherapy with the serotonin reuptake inhibitor (SRI) clomipramine and the other selective SSRIs has also been shown to be efficacious (Eddy et al. 2004). Treatment response is often quite substantial for both approaches, with up to two-thirds of all patients showing clear improvement and about one-third of all patients showing full recovery. Nonetheless, symptoms tend to persist at moderate levels for most patients, and few controlled comparisons have tracked the maintenance of gains over extended periods.

Foa & Kozak (1996) reviewed studies that examined the long-term outcome of OCD patients treated with ERP and found that more than three-quarters of all patients had maintained response up to two-and-a-half years after treatment termination. By way of contrast, the available double-blind discontinuation medication trials show a different picture (Romano et al. 2001); relapse rates often are high and typically exceed those for continuation medication (Koran et al. 2002, Pato et al. 1988, Ravizza et al. 1996). Hembree and colleagues (2003) conducted a naturalistic follow-up of patients treated with ERP, serotonergic medications, or their combination. Although differences were not evident across the whole sample, patients previously treated with ERP had less severe symptoms than did patients who were not among those not currently on medications.

Foa and colleagues (2005) provided the first direct comparison of ERP versus medications in the treatment of OCD in a study that afforded an opportunity to evaluate the stability of response following treatment termination. In that trial, adult patients with OCD of at least one-year duration were randomly assigned to ERP or clomipramine pharmacotherapy, each alone and in combination, or a pill-placebo control. Acute treatment lasted for 12 weeks and was quite intense; exposure sessions were conducted daily for the first three weeks and dosage levels were pushed aggressively (as appropriate) to a maximum of 250 mg/day. At the end of treatment, all three active treatments were superior to pill-placebo, ERP was superior to medications alone, and adding medication did little to enhance response to ERP. Response rates among all assigned were 62% for ERP, 70% for combined treatment, 42% for clomipramine alone, and 8% for placebo.

Treatment responders were then monitored over a subsequent 12-week period following the end of active treatment. ERP was discontinued and patients who responded to clomipramine (alone or in combination) were tapered off medications over a four-week period. Relapse was defined as a return to pretreatment levels of severity or a clinical state that warranted resumption of treatment. As shown in Figure 4, responders to medications alone were more likely to relapse following treatment termination than were patients previously treated with ERP alone or in combination (Simpson et al. 2004). Among treatment responders, 45% of the medication-alone patients relapsed (55% survival) relative to 12% of the patients treated with ERP (88% survival). As for depression (but unlike panic disorder), there was no indication that adding medications during acute treatment did anything to undermine the enduring effect of CBT; the rate of survival without relapse following ERP alone was 89% versus 87% for the combination.

It is unlikely that differential retention could have accounted for these findings, since clomipramine alone produced a lower rate of response than ERP alone and did little to enhance response when provided in combination. For acute treatment to act like a "differential sieve," medication treatment would have had to enhance response selectively among high-risk patients, and there is just no indication that that was the case in this trial. Response to ERP was more complete than to medication alone, meaning that patients treated with clomipramine alone required less symptom return to meet criteria for relapse. Yet, this does not undermine the validity of

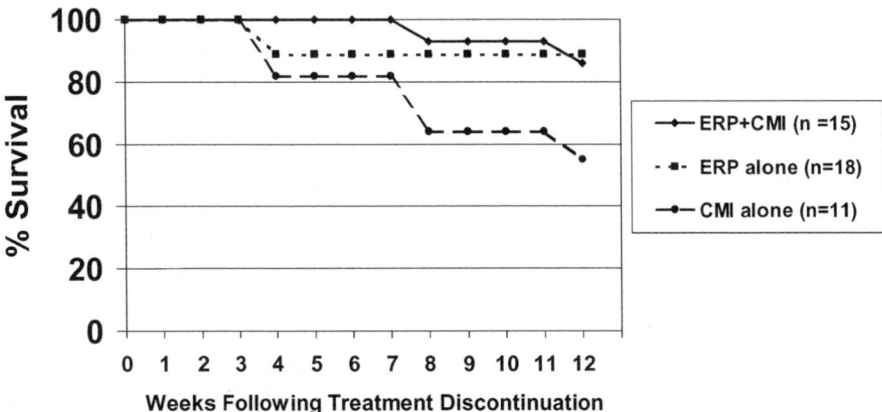

Figure 4   Time to relapse following successful treatment for obsessive-compulsive disorder with exposure plus response prevention (ERP) or clomipramine (CMI) pharmacotherapy (alone or in combination). ERP + CMI patients were previously treated with exposure plus response prevention plus clomipramine; ERP-alone patients were previously treated with exposure plus response prevention alone; CMI patients were previously treated with clomipramine alone. Adapted from Simpson et al. (2004), copyright 2004 by Wiley-Liss, Inc. Reprinted by permission.

the enduring effect (ERP may produce more complete remission than medications). Symptom severity at the end of treatment did predict subsequent risk differentially within the respective conditions; among the patients treated with ERP, relapse was largely confined to patients with more residual symptoms, whereas among the patients treated with medication alone even patients with fewer residual symptoms were at risk for relapse. This would be expected if medications suppressed symptom expression independent of individual differences in underlying risk.

The literature is mixed with respect to the relative benefits of ERP versus more purely cognitive approaches (Van Oppen et al. 1995, McLean et al. 2001, Vogel et al. 2004). Salkovskis (1999) suggests that people who are prone to OCD have exaggerated beliefs about personal responsibility and argues that making that a focus of treatment during exposure can enhance response and contribute to the stability of gains. The only trial to date to explore that approach found good maintenance of gains over a six-month follow-up, but did not provide comparisons to either more conventional ERP or medication treatment (Freeston et al. 1997). More studies are clearly needed comparing such different versions of CBT (and each to medication maintenance), but results to date suggest that CBT for OCD has an enduring effect not found for medications.

Posttraumatic Stress Disorder

Posttraumatic stress disorder (PTSD) involves the occurrence of a distinctive set of symptoms in response to traumatic events; symptoms include increased arousal, persistent avoidance, flashbacks and intrusive recollections, affective constriction, and a sense of interpersonal detachment. The nature of the trauma can be diverse, including sexual and other assaults, motor vehicle and other accidents, and combat trauma, with the last the most refractory to treatment (Bradley et al. 2005). Not everyone who experiences trauma develops PTSD, but for those who do, it often becomes chronic. Simple debriefing strategies applied in an unselective fashion immediately after trauma may actually increase the risk for developing PTSD (Mayou et al. 2000), but preventive interventions applied in a more selective fashion to targeted populations appear to reduce subsequent risk (Bryant et al. 1998, Foa et al. 1995).

Although PTSD tends to be a chronic condition that does not remit spontaneously once it is established, treatment with several different types of interventions appears to lead to large initial gains that are often well maintained over time (Bradley et al. 2005). Prolonged exposure (flooding), stress-inoculation training (combining relaxation training and controlled breathing with some limited cognitive restructuring), and cognitive reprocessing of the trauma have all been shown to be efficacious in the treatment of PTSD. Some studies suggest that prolonged exposure may have a more sustained effect than does stress-inoculation training (Foa et al. 1991), and that adding stress-inoculation training to prolonged exposure may undermine the enduring effects of the latter (Foa et al. 1999), but those indications are neither robust across trials nor consistent across research groups (Marks et al.

1998, Resick et al. 2002, Tarrier et al. 1999). Eye-movement desensitization and reprocessing continues to be controversial; although typically superior to control conditions (Marcus et al. 1997; Wilson et al. 1995, 1997), there is little evidence of specific efficacy and it sometimes is outperformed by other active interventions (Devilly & Spence 1999, Ironson et al. 2002, Taylor et al. 2003). ADM (especially the SSRIs) has been shown to be efficacious and is less likely to induce dependence than are minor tranquilizers or alcohol, but does nothing to reduce risk once its use is discontinued (Ballenger et al. 2004).

Resick and colleagues developed an approach called cognitive processing therapy that targets specific maladaptive beliefs related to safety, trust, and self-esteem (Resick & Schnicke 1992). In this approach, patients are encouraged to write detailed descriptions of the traumatic event and read them back to the therapist as a form of exposure, and the implications are then discussed. In a recent trial, cognitive processing therapy was found to be at least as efficacious and enduring as prolonged exposure and superior to a minimal treatment control; patients in the control condition showed comparable gains when provided subsequent active treatment (Resick et al. 2002).

Ehlers & Clark (2000) have argued that PTSD becomes persistent when individuals process trauma in a way that leads to a continued sense of current threat. As they describe, the paradox of PTSD from a cognitive perspective is that memories for prior events create a current state of anxiety, which usually implies a sense of impending threat. This sense of current threat is seen as a consequence of the combination of excessively negative appraisals of the implications of the prior trauma and a disturbance of autobiographical memory characterized by poor elaboration and perceptual priming. This model differs from earlier cognitive formulations by specifying more fully the processes contributing to the maintenance of distress and addressing the idiosyncratic nature of the appraisals made by different individuals. As such, it represents an evolution in theory that may well guide the development of the next generation of cognitive interventions.

In a recent trial, Ehlers and colleagues (2003) applied this approach to the treatment of a sample of motor vehicle accident survivors who met criteria for persistent PTSD. Potential participants were first asked to self-monitor symptoms for a three-week period, and those who fell below criteria for subsequent risk were excluded (about 12%). Those who did not recover with self-monitoring alone were then randomly assigned to treatment with this newly elaborated version of CT, a self-help booklet based on those same principles, or repeated assessments only. Treatment lasted for three months, with subsequent assessments at six and nine months following the start of treatment. Participants treated with CT were less likely to meet criteria for PTSD at the end of treatment than were participants provided with either self-help or assessment only (21% versus 79% and 72%, respectively). Although the sample as a whole continued to improve over time, CT retained its relative advantage over the other conditions; only 11% of the participants who received CT met criteria for PTSD at the nine-month follow-up relative to 61% of the self-help participants and 55% of the assessment-only controls.

These studies provide support for the notion that the effects of CBT endure in the treatment of PTSD. The absence of comparisons to efficacious medication treatments such as the SSRIs makes it hard to demonstrate this effect as persuasively as can be done for other disorders, but it is clear that the effects of treatment do not erode over time. Thus, the preponderance of evidence appears to suggest that CBT has an enduring effect in the treatment of PTSD.

CONCLUSIONS

CBT appears to have an enduring effect in the treatment of depression and the anxiety disorders that reduces risk for subsequent symptom return. This enduring effect is most evident in comparison to medication treatment, which appears to be largely palliative in nature, and represents one of the major advantages for CBT. Clear documentation exists relative to medication treatment with respect to depression, panic, social phobia, and OCD. Despite the absence of comparisons to prior medication treatment, there is also evidence of stability of gains for several of the other anxiety disorders (tests for enduring effects are largely lacking in other disorders). There are indications that adding medications may undermine the enduring effects of CBT in some instances; such interference could be a consequence of either pharmacological or psychological mechanisms and may vary as a function of medication and disorder. With the exception of family-focused treatment for bipolar disorder, there are few indications that other psychosocial interventions have enduring effects, although this possibility has rarely been explored. The nature of the underlying mechanisms remains to be determined, but CBT appears to have an enduring effect in the treatment of depression and the anxiety disorders that may preclude the need for extended medication treatment.

The *Annual Review of Psychology* is online at http://psych.annualreviews.org

LITERATURE CITED

Am. Psychiatric Assoc. 2000. Practice guideline for the treatment of patients with major depressive disorder (revision). *Am. J. Psychiatry* 157(Suppl. 4):1–45

Am. Psychiatric Assoc. 2002. Practice guideline for the treatment of patients with bipolar disorder (revised). *Am. J. Psychiatry* 159(Suppl. 4):1–50

Arntz A, Van den Hout M. 1996. Psychological treatments of panic disorder without agoraphobia: cognitive therapy versus applied relaxation. *Behav. Res. Ther.* 34:113–21

Ballenger JC, Davidson JR, Lecrubier Y, Nutt

DJ, Marshall RD, et al. 2004. Consensus statement update on posttraumatic stress disorder from the International Consensus Group on Depression and Anxiety. *J. Clin. Psychiatry* 65(Suppl. 1):55–62

Bandura A. 1977. Self-efficacy: toward a unifying theory of behavioral change. *Psychol. Rev.* 84:181–215

Barber JP, DeRubeis RJ. 1989. On second thought: where the action is in cognitive therapy for depression. *Cogn. Ther. Res.* 13:441–57

Barlow DH, Gorman JM, Shear MK, Woods

SW. 2000. Cognitive-behavioral therapy, imipramine, or their combination for panic disorder: a randomized controlled trial. *JAMA* 283:2529–36

Barlow DH, Lehman CL. 1996. Advances in the psychosocial treatment of anxiety disorders. *Arch. Gen. Psychiatry* 53:727–35

Barsky AJ, Ahern DK. 2004. Cognitive behavior therapy for hypochondriasis: a randomized controlled trial. *JAMA* 291:1464–70

Beck AT. 1991. Cognitive therapy: a 30-year retrospective. *Am. Psychol.* 46:368–75

Beck AT, Emery G. 1985. *Anxiety Disorders and Phobias: A Cognitive Perspective.* New York: Basic Books

Beck AT, Rush AJ, Shaw BF, Emery G. 1979. *Cognitive Therapy of Depression.* New York: Guilford

Blackburn IM, Eunson KM, Bishop S. 1986. A two-year naturalistic follow-up of depressed patients treated with cognitive therapy, pharmacotherapy and a combination of both. *J. Affect. Disord.* 10:67–75

Blomhoff S, Haug TT, Hellström K, Holme I, Humble M, et al. 2001. Randomised controlled general practice trial of sertraline, exposure therapy and combined treatment in generalized social phobia. *Br. J. Psychiatry* 179:23–30

Borkovec TD, Costello E. 1993. Efficacy of applied relaxation and cognitive behavioral therapy in the treatment of generalized anxiety disorder. *J. Consult. Clin. Psychol.* 61:611–19

Borkovec TD, Newman MG, Pincus AL, Lytle R. 2002. A component analysis of cognitive-behavioral therapy for generalized anxiety disorder and the role of interpersonal problems. *J. Consult. Clin. Psychol.* 70:288–98

Borkovec TD, Ruscio AM. 2001. Psychotherapy for generalized anxiety disorder. *J. Clin. Psychiatry* 62(Suppl. 11):37–42

Bouchard S, Gauthier J, LaBerge B, French D, Pelletier MH, Godbout C. 1996. Exposure versus cognitive restructuring in the treatment of panic disorder with agoraphobia. *Behav. Res. Ther.* 34:213–24

Bouton ME. 1993. Context, time, and memory retrieval in the interference paradigms of Pavlovian learning. *Psychol. Bull.* 114:80–99

Bradley R, Greene J, Russ E, Dutra L, Westen D. 2005. A multidimensional meta-analysis of psychotherapy for PTSD. *Am. J. Psychiatry* 162:214–27

Brown TA, Barlow DH, Liebowitz MR. 1994. The empirical basis of generalized anxiety disorder. *Am. J. Psychiatry* 151:1272–80

Bruce TJ, Spiegel DA, Hegel MT. 1999. Cognitive-behavioral therapy helps prevent relapse and recurrence of panic disorder following alprazolam discontinuation: a long-term follow-up of the Peoria and Dartmouth studies. *J. Consult. Clin. Psychol.* 67:151–56

Bryant RA, Harvey AG, Dang ST, Sackville T, Basten C. 1998. Treatment of acute stress disorder: a comparison of cognitive-behavioral therapy and supportive counseling. *J. Consult. Clin. Psychol.* 66:862–66

Butler G, Cullington A, Munby M, Amies P, Gelder M. 1984. Exposure and anxiety management in the treatment of social phobia. *J. Consult. Clin. Psychol.* 52:642–50

Clark DM. 1986. A cognitive approach to panic. *Behav. Res. Ther.* 24:461–70

Clark DM, Ehlers A, McManus F, Hackmann A, Fennell M, et al. 2003. Cognitive therapy versus fluoxetine in generalized social phobia: a randomized placebo-controlled trial. *J. Consult. Clin. Psychol.* 71:1058–67

Clark DM, Salkovskis PM, Hackmann A, Middleton H, Anastasiades P, Gelder M. 1994. A comparison of cognitive therapy, applied relaxation and imipramine in the treatment of panic disorder. *Br. J. Psychiatry* 164:759–69

Clark DM, Salkovskis PM, Hackmann A, Wells A, Fennell M, et al. 1998. Two psychological treatments for hypochondrias: a randomised controlled trial. *Br. J. Psychiatry* 173:218–25

Clarke GN, Hawkins W, Murphy M, Sheeber LB, Lewinsohn PM, Seeley JR. 1995. Targeted prevention of unipolar depressive disorder in an at-risk sample of high school adolescents: a randomized trial of a group cognitive intervention. *J. Am. Acad. Child Adolesc. Psychiatry* 34:312–21

Clarke GN, Hornbrook MC, Lynch F, Polen M, Gale J, et al. 2001. Offspring of depressed parents in a HMO: a randomized trial of a group cognitive intervention for preventing adolescent depressive disorder. *Arch. Gen. Psychiatry* 58:1127–34

Davidson JRT, Hughes DL, George LK, Blazer DG. 1993. The epidemiology of social phobia: findings from the Duke Epidemiological Catchment Area Study. *Psychol. Med.* 23:709–18

DeRubeis RJ, Crits-Christoph P. 1998. Empirically supported individual and group psychological treatments for adult mental disorders. *J. Consult. Clin. Psychol.* 66:37–52

DeRubeis RJ, Evans MD, Hollon SD, Garvey MJ, Grove WM, Tuason VB. 1990. How does cognitive therapy work? Cognitive change and symptom change in cognitive therapy and pharmacotherapy for depression. *J. Consult. Clin. Psychol.* 58:862–69

DeRubeis RJ, Feeley M. 1990. Determinants of change in cognitive therapy for depression. *Cogn. Ther. Res.* 14:469–82

DeRubeis RJ, Hollon SD, Amsterdam JD, Shelton RC, Young PR, et al. 2005. Cognitive therapy vs. medications in the treatment of moderate to severe depression. *Arch. Gen. Psychiatry* 62:409–16

Devilly GJ, Spence SH. 1999. The relative efficacy and treatment distress of EMDR and a cognitive-behavior trauma protocol in the amelioration of posttraumatic stress disorder. *J. Anxiety Disord.* 13:131–57

Dimidjian S, Hollon SD, Dobson KS, Schmaling KB, Kohlenberg RJ. 2005. Behavioral activation, cognitive therapy, and antidepressant medication in the acute treatment of major depression. *J. Consult. Clin. Psychol.* In press

Dugas MJ, Ladouceur R, Léger E, Freeston MH, Langlois F, et al. 2003. Group cognitive-behavioral therapy for generalized anxiety disorder: treatment outcome and long-term follow-up. *J. Consult. Clin. Psychol.* 71:821–25

Durham RC, Chambers JA, MacDonald RR, Power KG, Major K. 2003. Does cognitive-behaviour therapy influence the long-term outcome of generalized anxiety disorder? An 8–14-year follow-up of two clinical trials. *Psychol. Med.* 33:499–509

Eddy KT, Dutra L, Bradley R, Westen D. 2004. A multidimensional meta-analysis of psychotherapy and pharmacotherapy for obsessive-compulsive disorder. *Clin. Psychol. Rev.* 24:1011–30

Ehlers A, Clark DM. 2000. A cognitive model of posttraumatic stress disorder. *Behav. Res. Ther.* 38:319–45

Ehlers A, Clark DM, Hackmann A, McManus F, Fennell M, et al. 2003. A randomized controlled trial of cognitive therapy, a self-help booklet, and repeated assessments as early interventions for posttraumatic stress disorder. *Arch. Gen. Psychiatry* 60:1024–32

Eisen JL, Goodman WK, Keller MB, Warshaw MG, DeMarco LM, et al. 1999. Patterns of remission and relapse in obsessive-compulsive disorder: a 2-year prospective study. *J. Clin. Psychiatry* 60:346–51

Evans MD, Hollon SD, DeRubeis RJ, Piasecki JM, Grove WM, et al. 1992. Differential relapse following cognitive therapy and pharmacotherapy for depression. *Arch. Gen. Psychiatry* 49:802–8

Fava GA, Grandi S, Rafanelli C, Ruini C, Conti S, Belluardo P. 2001. Long-term outcome of social phobia treated by exposure. *Psychol. Med.* 31:899–905

Fava GA, Rafanelli C, Grandi S, Conti S, Belluardo P. 1998. Prevention of recurrent depression with cognitive behavioral therapy. *Arch. Gen. Psychiatry* 55:816–20

Fava GA, Ruini C, Rafanelli C, Finos L, Salmaso L, et al. 2005. Well-being therapy of generalized anxiety disorder. *Psychother. Psychosom.* 74:26–30

Feeley M, DeRubeis RJ, Gelfand LA. 1999. The temporal relation of adherence and alliance to symptom change in cognitive therapy for depression. *J. Consult. Clin. Psychol.* 67:578–82

Foa EB, Dancu CV, Hembree EA, Jaycox LH, Meadows EA, Street GP. 1999. Comparison of exposure therapy, stress inoculation training, and their combination for reducing posttraumatic stress disorder in female assault victims. *J. Consult. Clin. Psychol.* 67:194–200

Foa EB, Hearst-Ikeda D, Perry KJ. 1995. Evaluation of a brief cognitive-behavioral program for the prevention of chronic PTSD in recent assault victims. *J. Consult. Clin. Psychol.* 63:948–55

Foa EB, Kozak MJ. 1996. Psychological treatment for obsessive-compulsive disorder. In *Long-Term Treatments of Anxiety Disorders*, ed. MR Mavissakalian, RF Prien, pp. 285–309. Washington, DC: Am. Psychiatric Press

Foa EB, Liebowitz MR, Kozak MJ, Davies S, Campeas R, et al. 2005. Randomized, placebo-controlled trial of exposure and ritual prevention, clomipramine, and their combination in the treatment of obsessive-compulsive disorder. *Am. J. Psychiatry* 162: 151–61

Foa EB, Rothbaum BO, Riggs DS, Murdock TB. 1991. Treatment of posttraumatic stress disorder in rape victims: a comparison between cognitive-behavioral procedures and counseling. *J. Consult. Clin. Psychol.* 59:715–23

Frank E, Kupfer DJ, Perel JM, Cornes C, Jarrett DB, et al. 1990. Three-year outcomes for maintenance therapies in recurrent depression. *Arch. Gen. Psychiatry* 47:1093–99

Frank E, Prien RF, Jarrett RB, Keller MB, Kupfer DJ, et al. 1991. Conceptualization and rationale for consensus definitions of terms in major depressive disorder: remission, recovery, relapse, and recurrence. *Arch. Gen. Psychiatry* 48:851–55

Freeston MH, Ladouceur R, Gagnon F, Thibodeau N, Rheaume J, et al. 1997. Cognitive-behavioral treatment of obsessive thoughts: a controlled study. *J. Consult. Clin. Psychol.* 65:405–13

Gibbons RD, Hedeker D, Elkin I, Waternaux C, Kraemer HC, et al. 1993. Some conceptual and statistical issues in analysis of longitudinal psychiatric data: application to the NIMH Treatment of Depression Collabora-

tive Research Program dataset. *Arch. Gen. Psychiatry* 50:739–50

Gillham JE, Shatte AJ, Freres DR. 2000. Preventing depression: a review of cognitive-behavioral and family interventions. *Appl. Prevent. Psychol.* 9:63–88

Gortner ET, Gollan JK, Dobson KS, Jacobson NS. 1998. Cognitive-behavioral treatment for depression: relapse prevention. *J. Consult. Clin. Psychol.* 66:377–84

Greenhouse JB, Stangl D, Bromberg J. 1989. An introduction to survival analysis: statistical methods for analysis of clinical trial data. *J. Consult. Clin. Psychol.* 57:536–44

Haug TT, Blomhoff S, Helstrøm IH, Holme I, Humble M, et al. 2003. Exposure therapy and sertraline in social phobia: 1-year follow-up of a randomised controlled trial. *Br. J. Psychiatry* 182:312–18

Heimberg RG, Liebowitz MR, Hope DA, Schneier FR, Holt CS, et al. 1998. Cognitive behavioral group therapy vs. phenelzine therapy for social phobia: 12-week outcome. *Arch. Gen. Psychiatry* 55:1133–41

Heimberg RG, Salzman DG, Holt CS, Blendell KA. 1993. Cognitive-behavioral group treatment for social phobia: effectiveness at five-year follow-up. *Cogn. Ther. Res.* 17:325–39

Hellström K, Fellenius J, Öst LG. 1996. One versus five sessions of applied tension in the treatment of blood phobia. *Behav. Res. Ther.* 34:101–12

Hellström K, Öst LG. 1995. One-session directed exposure vs. two forms of manual directed self-exposure in the treatment of spider phobia. *Behav. Res. Ther.* 33:959–65

Hembree EA, Riggs DS, Kozak MJ, Franklin ME, Foa EB. 2003. Long-term efficacy of exposure and ritual prevention therapy and serotonergic medications for obsessive-compulsive disorder. *CNS Spectr.* 8:363–71

Hidalgo RB, Barnett SD, Davidson JRT. 2001. Social anxiety disorder in review: two decades of progress. *Int. J. Neuropsychopharmacol.* 4:279–98

Hollon SD, Beck AT. 2004. Cognitive and cognitive-behavioral therapies. In *Garfield and Bergin's Handbook of Psychotherapy and Behavior Change: An Empirical Analysis*, ed. MJ Lambert, pp. 447–92. New York: Wiley. 5th ed.

Hollon SD, DeRubeis RJ, Evans MD, Wiemer MJ, Garvey MJ, et al. 1992a. Cognitive therapy and pharmacotherapy for depression: singly and in combination. *Arch. Gen. Psychiatry* 49:774–81

Hollon SD, DeRubeis RJ, Seligman MEP. 1992b. Cognitive therapy and the prevention of depression. *Appl. Prevent. Psychol.* 1:89–95

Hollon SD, DeRubeis RJ, Shelton RC, Amsterdam JD, Salomon RM, et al. 2005. Prevention of relapse following cognitive therapy versus medications in moderate to severe depression. *Arch. Gen. Psychiatry* 62:417–22

Hollon SD, Evans MD, DeRubeis RJ. 1990. Cognitive mediation of relapse prevention following treatment for depression: implications of differential risk. In *Psychological Aspects of Depression*, ed. RE Ingram, pp. 117–36. New York: Plenum

Hollon SD, Thase ME, Markowitz JC. 2002. Treatment and prevention of depression. *Psychol. Sci. Public Interest* 3:39–77

Huppert JD, Schultz LT, Foa EB, Barlow DH, Davidson JRT, et al. 2004. Differential response to placebo among patients with social phobia, panic disorder, and obsessive-compulsive disorder. *Am. J. Psychiatry* 161: 1485–87

Imber SD, Pilkonis PA, Sotsky SM, Elkin I, Watkins JT, et al. 1990. Mode-specific effects among three treatments for depression. *J. Consult. Clin. Psychol.* 58:352–59

Ironson G, Freund B, Strauss JL, Williams J. 2002. Comparison of two treatments for traumatic stress: a community-based study of EMDR and prolonged exposure. *J. Clin. Psychol.* 58:113–28

Jacobson NS, Dobson KS, Truax PA, Addis ME, Koerner K, et al. 1996. A component analysis of cognitive-behavioral treatment for depression. *J. Consult. Clin. Psychol.* 64:295–304

Jacobson NS, Hollon SD. 1996. Prospects for future comparisons between drugs and psychotherapy: lessons from the CBT-versus-pharmacotherapy exchange. *J. Consult. Clin. Psychol.* 64:104–8

Jacobson NS, Martell CR, Dimidjian S. 2001. Behavioral activation treatment for depression: returning to contextual roots. *Clin. Psychol. Sci. Pract.* 8:255–70

Jaycox LH, Reivich KJ, Gillham J, Seligman MEP. 1994. Prevention of depressive symptoms in school children. *Behav. Res. Ther.* 32:801–16

Klein DF. 1996. Preventing hung juries about therapy studies. *J. Consult. Clin. Psychol.* 64:74–80

Klerman GL, DiMascio A, Weissman M, Prusoff B, Paykel ES. 1974. Treatment of depression by drugs and psychotherapy. *Am. J. Psychiatry* 131:186–91

Klerman GL, Weissman M, Rounsaville BJ, Chevron ES. 1984. *Interpersonal Psychotherapy of Depression*. New York: Basic Books

Koran LM, Hackett F, Rubin A, Wolkow R, Robinson D. 2002. Efficacy of sertraline in the long-term treatment of obsessive-compulsive disorder. *Am. J. Psychiatry* 159: 88–95

Kovacs M, Rush AT, Beck AT, Hollon SD. 1981. Depressed outpatients treated with cognitive therapy or pharmacotherapy: a one-year follow-up. *Arch. Gen. Psychiatry* 38: 33–39

Ladouceur R, Dugas MJ, Freeston MH, Leger E, Gagnon F, Thibodeau N. 2000. Efficacy of a cognitive-behavioral treatment for generalized anxiety disorder: evaluation in a controlled clinical trial. *J. Consult. Clin. Psychol.* 68:957–64

Ladouceur R, Dugas MJ, Freeston MH, Rheaume J, Blais F, et al. 1999. Specificity of generalized anxiety disorder symptoms and processes. *Behav. Ther.* 30:191–207

Lam DH, Hayward P, Watkins ER, Wright K, Sham P. 2005. Relapse prevention in patients with bipolar disorder: cognitive therapy outcome after 2 years. *Am. J. Psychiatry* 162:324–29

Lam DH, Watkins ER, Hayward P, Bright J, Wright K, et al. 2003. A randomized controlled study of cognitive therapy for relapse prevention for bipolar affective disorder: outcome of the first year. *Arch. Gen. Psychiatry* 60:145–52

Liebowitz MR, Heimberg RG, Schneier FR, Hope DA, Davies S, et al. 1999. Cognitive-behavioral group therapy versus phenelzine in social phobia: long-term outcome. *Depress. Anxiety* 10:89–98

Loerch B, Graf-Morgenstern M, Hautzinger M, Schlegel S, Hain C, et al. 1999. Randomized placebo-controlled trial of moclobemide, cognitive-behavioural therapy and their combination in panic disorder with agoraphobia. *Br. J. Psychiatry* 174:205–12

Lydiard RB, Brawman-Mintzer O, Ballenger JC. 1996. Recent development in the psychopharmacology of anxiety disorders. *J. Consult. Clin. Psychol.* 64:660–68

Malkoff-Schwartz S, Frank E, Anderson B, Sherrill JT, Siegel L, et al. 1998. Stressful life events and social rhythm disruption in the onset of manic and depressive bipolar episodes: a preliminary investigation. *Arch. Gen. Psychiatry* 55:702–7

Marcus SV, Marquis P, Sakal C. 1997. Controlled study of treatment of PTSD using EMDR in an HMO setting. *Psychotherapy* 34:307–15

Marks I, Lovell K, Noshirvani H, Livanou M, Thrasher S. 1998. Treatment of posttraumatic stress disorder by exposure and/or cognitive restructuring: a controlled study. *Arch. Gen. Psychiatry* 55:317–25

Marks IM, Swinson RP, Basoglu M, Kuch K, Noshirvani H, O'Sullivan G. 1993. Alprazolam and exposure alone and combined in panic disorder with agoraphobia: a controlled study in London and Toronto. *Br. J. Psychiatry* 162:776–87

Marks IM, Viswanathan R, Lipsedge MS, Gardner R. 1972. Enhanced relief of phobias following flooding during waning diazepam. *Br. J. Psychiatry* 121:493–505

Martell CR, Addis ME, Jacobson NS. 2001. *Depression in Context: Strategies for Guided Action.* New York: Norton

Mayou RA, Ehlers A, Hobbs M. 2000. Psychological debriefing for road traffic accident victims. *Br. J. Psychiatry* 176:589–93

McLean PD, Whittal ML, Thordarson DS, Taylor S, Sochting I, et al. 2001. Cognitive versus behavior therapy in the group treatment of obsessive-compulsive disorder. *J. Consult. Clin. Psychol.* 69:205–14

Miklowitz DJ, George EL, Richards JA, Simoneau TL, Suddarth RL. 2003. A randomized study of family-focused psychoeducation and pharmacotherapy in the outpatient management of bipolar disorder. *Arch. Gen. Psychiatry* 60:904–12

Mowrer OH. 1948. Learning theory and the neurotic paradox. *Am. J. Orthopsychiatry* 18:571–610

Mystkowski JL, Mineka S, Vernon LL, Zinbarg RE. 2003. Changes in caffeine states enhance return of fear in spider phobia. *J. Consult. Clin. Psychol.* 71:243–50

Nathan PE, Gorman JM, eds. 1998. *A Guide to Treatments That Work.* New York: Oxford Univ. Press

Öst LG, Ferebee I, Furmark T. 1997. One-session group therapy of spider phobia: direct versus indirect treatments. *Behav. Res. Ther.* 35:721–32

Öst LG, Westling BE. 1995. Applied relaxation vs. cognitive behavior therapy in the treatment of panic disorder. *Behav. Res. Ther.* 33:145–58

Otto MW, Pollack MH, Sachs GS, Reiter SR, Meltzer-Brody S, Rosenbaum JF. 1993. Discontinuation of benzodiazepine treatment: efficacy of cognitive-behavioral therapy for patients with panic disorder. *Am. J. Psychiatry* 150:1485–90

Pato MT, Zohar-Kadouch R, Zohar J, Murphy DL. 1988. Return of symptoms after discontinuation of clomipramine in patients with obsessive-compulsive disorder. *Am. J. Psychiatry* 145:1521–25

Paykel ES, Scott J, Teasdale JD, Johnson AL, Garland A, et al. 1999. Prevention of relapse in residual depression by cognitive therapy. *Arch. Gen. Psychiatry* 56:829–35

Perlis RH, Nierenberg AA, Alpert JE, Pava J, Matthews JD. 2002. Effects of adding cognitive therapy to fluoxetine dose increase on risk of relapse and residual depressive symptoms in continuation treatment of major depressive disorder. *J. Clin. Psychopharmacol* 22:474–80

Perry A, Tarrier N, Morriss R, McCarthy E, Limb K. 1999. Randomised controlled trial of efficacy of teaching patients with bipolar disorder to identify early symptoms of relapse and obtain treatment. *Br. Med. J.* 318:149–53

Ravizza L, Barzega G, Bellino S, Bogetto F, Maina G. 1996. Drug treatment of obsessive-compulsive disorder (OCD): long-term trial with clomipramine and selective serotonin reuptake inhibitors (SSRIs). *Psychopharmacol. Bull.* 32:167–73

Resick PA, Nishith P, Weaver TL, Astin MC, Feuer CA. 2002. A comparison of cognitive-processing therapy with prolonged exposure and a waiting condition for the treatment of chronic posttraumatic stress disorder in female rape victims. *J. Consult. Clin. Psychol.* 70:867–79

Resick PA, Schnicke MK. 1992. Cognitive processing therapy for sexual assault victims. *J. Consult. Clin. Psychol.* 60:748–56

Romano S, Goodman W, Tamura R, Gonzales J. 2001. Long-term treatment of obsessive-compulsive disorder after an acute response: a comparison of fluoxetine versus placebo. *J. Clin. Psychopharmacol.* 21:46–52

Roth A, Fonagy P. 2005. *What Works for Whom? A Critical Review of Psychotherapy Research.* New York: Guilford. 2nd ed.

Salkovskis PM. 1999. Understanding and treating obsessive-compulsive disorder. *Behav. Res. Ther.* 37(Suppl. 1):S29–52

Seligman MEP, Schulman P, DeRubeis RJ, Hollon SD. 1999. December 21. The prevention of depression and anxiety. *Prevent. Treat.* 2:Article 8. Retrieved July 4, 2002, from http://journals.apa.org/prevention/volume2/pre0020008a.html

Sharp DM, Power KG, Simpson RJ, Swanson V, Moodie E, et al. 1996. Fluvoxamine, placebo and cognitive behavior therapy used alone and in combination in the treatment of panic disorder and agoraphobia. *J. Anxiety Disord.* 10:219–42

Shea MT, Elkin I, Imber SD, Sotsky SM, Watkins JT, et al. 1992. Course of depressive symptoms over follow-up: findings from the National Institute of Mental Health Treatment of Depression Collaborative Research Program. *Arch. Gen. Psychiatry* 49:782–87

Simons AD, Garfield SL, Murphy GE. 1984. The process of change in cognitive therapy and pharmacotherapy for depression. *Arch. Gen. Psychiatry* 41:45–51

Simons AD, Murphy GE, Levine JL, Wetzel RD. 1986. Cognitive therapy and pharmacotherapy for depression: sustained improvement over one year. *Arch. Gen. Psychiatry* 43:43–48

Simpson HB, Liebowitz MR, Foa EB, Kozak MJ, Schmidt AB, et al. 2004. Posttreatment effects of exposure therapy and clomipramine in obsessive-compulsive disorder. *Depress. Anxiety* 19:225–33

Skoog G, Skoog I. 1999. A 40-year follow-up of patients with obsessive-compulsive disorder. *Arch. Gen. Psychiatry* 56:121–27

Stangier U, Heidenreich T, Peitz M, Lauterbach W, Clark DM. 2003. Cognitive therapy for social phobia: individual versus group treatment. *Behav. Res. Ther.* 41:991–1007

Stanley MA, Beck JG, Novy DM, Averill PM, Swann AC, et al. 2003. Cognitive-behavioral treatment of late-life generalized anxiety disorder. *J. Consult. Clin. Psychol.* 71:309–19

Tang TZ, DeRubeis RJ. 1999. Sudden gains and critical sessions in cognitive-behavioral therapy for depression. *J. Consult. Clin. Psychol.* 67:894–904

Tarrier N, Pilgrim H, Sommerfield C, Faragher B, Reynolds M, et al. 1999. A randomized trial of cognitive therapy and imaginal exposure in the treatment of chronic posttraumatic stress disorder. *J. Consult. Clin. Psychol.* 67:13–18

Taylor S, Thordarson DS, Maxfield L, Fedoroff IC, Lovell K, Ogrodniczuk J. 2003. Comparative efficacy, speed, and adverse effects of three PTSD treatments: exposure therapy, EMDR, and relaxation therapy. *J. Consult. Clin. Psychol.* 71:330–38

Teasdale JD, Scott J, Moore RG, Hayhurst H, Pope M, Paykel ES. 2001. How does cognitive therapy prevent relapse in residual depression: evidence from a controlled trial. *J. Consult. Clin. Psychol.* 69:347–57

Teasdale JD, Segal Z, Williams JMG, Ridgeway VA, Soulsby JM, Lau MA. 2000. Prevention of relapse/recurrence in major depression by mindfulness-based cognitive therapy. *J. Consult. Clin. Psychol.* 68:615–23

Thom A, Sartory G, Hohren P. 2000. Comparison between one-session psychological treatment and benzodiazepine in dental phobia. *J. Consult. Clin. Psychol.* 68:378–87

Thorpe SJ, Salkovskis PM. 1997. The effect of one-session treatment for spider phobia on attentional bias and beliefs. *Br. J. Clin. Psychol.* 36:225–41

Van Oppen P, de Haan E, van Balkom A, Spinhoven P, Hoogduin K, van Dyck R. 1995. Cognitive therapy and exposure in vivo in the treatment of obsessive-compulsive disorder. *Behav. Res. Ther.* 33:379–90

Vogel PA, Stiles TC, Götestam KG. 2004. Adding cognitive therapy elements to exposure therapy for obsessive-compulsive disorder: a controlled study. *Behav. Cogn. Psychother.* 32:275–90

Warwick HMC, Clark DM, Cobb AM, Salkovskis PM. 1996. A controlled trial of cognit-ive-behavioural treatment of hypochondriasis. *Br. J. Psychiatry* 169:189–95

Warwick HMC, Salkovskis PM. 1990. Hypochondriasis. *Behav. Res. Ther.* 28:105–17

Weissman MM, Klerman GL, Prusoff B, Sholomskas D, Padian N. 1981. Depressed outpatients: results one year after treatment with drugs and/or interpersonal therapy. *Arch. Gen. Psychiatry* 38:51–55

Wells A, Clark DM, Salkovskis P, Ludgate J, Hackmann A, Gelder M. 1995. Social phobia: the role of in-situation safety behaviours in maintaining anxiety and negative beliefs. *Behav. Ther.* 26:153–61

Willett JB, Ayoub CC, Robinson D. 1991. Using growth modeling to examine systematic differences in growth: an example of change in functioning of families at risk of maladaptive parenting, child abuse, or neglect. *J. Consult. Clin. Psychol.* 59:38–47

Willett JB, Singer JD. 1993. Investigating onset, cessation, relapse, and recovery: Why you should, and how you can, use discrete-time survival analysis to examine event occurrence. *J. Consult. Clin. Psychol.* 61:952–65

Wilson SA, Becker LA, Tinker RH. 1995. Eye movement desensitization and reprocessing (EMDR) treatment for psychologically traumatized individuals. *J. Consult. Clin. Psychol.* 63:928–37

Wilson SA, Becker LA, Tinker RH. 1997. Fifteen-month follow-up of eye movement desensitization and reprocessing (EMDR) treatment for posttraumatic stress disorder and psychological trauma. *J. Consult. Clin. Psychol.* 65:1047–56

Annu. Rev. Psychol. 2006. 57:317–44
doi: 10.1146/annurev.psych.56.091103.070154
First published online as a Review in Advance on July 8, 2005

CURRENT STATUS AND FUTURE DIRECTIONS IN COUPLE THERAPY

Douglas K. Snyder and Angela M. Castellani

Department of Psychology, Texas A&M University, College Station, Texas 77843-4235;
email: d-snyder@tamu.edu, angela_castellani@hotmail.com

Mark A. Whisman

Department of Psychology, University of Colorado, Boulder, Colorado 80309-0345;
email: whisman@colorado.edu

Key Words marital therapy, couple therapy, couple research, couple change processes, couple treatment predictors

■ **Abstract** Couple therapy research affirms that various approaches to couple treatment produce statistically and clinically significant improvement for a substantial proportion of couples in reducing overall relationship distress. Recent studies have extended these findings in indicating the effectiveness of couple-based interventions for a broad range of coexisting emotional, behavioral, or physical health problems in one or both partners. In contrast to these encouraging results, research also indicates that a sizeable percentage of couples fail to achieve significant gains from couple therapy or show significant deterioration afterward. Research on processes of change and predictors of treatment outcome in couple therapy provides preliminary evidence regarding factors potentially contributing to variable treatment response. The chapter concludes with 12 recommendations regarding future directions in couple therapy research and clinical training.

CONTENTS

INTRODUCTION

The fundamental challenges of psychotherapy research—whether evaluating individual, couple, or family interventions—are to identify effective treatments, understand their underlying mechanisms of change, and delineate aspects of the therapist, client, or context that influence their outcome. In this chapter, we examine the effectiveness of couple-based interventions for treating general relationship distress as well as coexisting emotional, behavioral, and physical health problems. We discuss methods for evaluating processes of change in couple therapy and predictors of treatment outcome, along with empirical findings in these domains. We conclude with recommendations for future research and clinical training in couple therapy.

THE PREVALENCE AND IMPACT OF COUPLE DISTRESS

Couple therapy continues to gain in stature as a vital component of mental health services. Three factors contribute to this growing recognition: (*a*) the prevalence of couple distress in both community and clinic samples; (*b*) the impact of couple distress on both the emotional and physical well-being of adult partners and their offspring; and (*c*) increased evidence of the effectiveness of couple therapy not only in treating couple distress and related relationship problems but also as a primary or adjunct treatment for a variety of individual emotional, behavioral, or physical health disorders.

Couple distress is prevalent in both community epidemiological studies and in research involving individual treatment samples. In the United States, the most salient indicator of couple distress remains a divorce rate of approximately 50% among married couples (Kreider & Fields 2002), with about half of these occurring within the first seven years of marriage. Independent of divorce, the research literature suggests that many, if not most, marriages experience periods of significant turmoil that place them at risk for dissolution or symptom development (e.g., depression or anxiety) in one or both partners at some point in their lives. In a recent national survey, the most frequently cited causes of acute emotional distress were relationship problems including divorce, separation, and other marital strains (Swindle et al. 2000). Other recent studies indicate that maritally discordant individuals are overrepresented among individuals seeking mental health services, regardless of whether they report marital distress as their primary complaint (Lin et al. 1996). In a study of 800 employee assistance program (EAP) clients, 65% rated family problems as "considerable" or "extreme" (Shumway et al. 2004).

The linkage of relationship distress to disruption of individual emotional and physical well-being emphasizes the importance of improving and extending empirically based strategies for treating couple distress. Research indicates that couple distress covaries with individual emotional and behavioral disorders beyond general distress in other close relationships (Whisman et al. 2000). Moreover, couple distress—particularly negative communication—has direct adverse effects on cardiovascular, endocrine, immune, neurosensory, and other physiological systems that, in turn, contribute to physical health problems (Kiecolt-Glaser & Newton 2001). Nor are the effects of couple distress confined to the adult partners. Gottman (1999) cites evidence indicating that "marital distress, conflict, and disruption are associated with a wide range of deleterious effects on children, including depression, withdrawal, poor social competence, health problems, poor academic performance, a variety of conduct-related difficulties, and markedly decreased longevity" (p. 4). In brief, couple distress has a markedly high prevalence; has a strong linkage to emotional, behavioral, and health problems in the adult partners and their offspring; and is among the most frequent primary or secondary concerns reported by individuals seeking assistance from mental health professionals.

THE EFFECTIVENESS OF COUPLE THERAPY IN TREATING RELATIONSHIP DISTRESS

How effective is couple therapy? Previous reviews affirm that various versions of couple therapy produce moderate, statistically significant, and often clinically significant effects in reducing relationship distress. In this section, we examine current findings regarding the effectiveness of couple therapy for treating overall relationship distress. In the subsequent section, we review evidence regarding the effectiveness of couple therapy for co-occurring individual and relationship problems.

Since Christensen & Heavy's (1999) review of couple therapy in the *Annual Review of Psychology*, several qualitative and quantitative (meta-analytic) reviews of couple therapy have appeared. Shadish & Baldwin (2003) reviewed six previous meta-analyses of studies comparing couple therapy versus no-treatment control groups, including four published reviews (Dunn & Schwebel 1995, Hahlweg & Markman 1988, Johnson et al. 1999, Shadish et al. 1993) and two unpublished reviews (Dutcher 1999, Wilson 1986). The samples of couple therapy studies included in each of these reviews ranged from 4 [Johnson et al.'s (1999) review of emotion-focused couple therapy (EFCT)] to 163 [Shadish et al.'s (1993) review of couple and family therapy, of which 62 studies emphasizing couple therapy were reanalyzed by Wilson (1986)]. Mean effect sizes across these six meta-analyses ranged from approximately 0.50 (Wilson 1986) to 1.30 (Johnson et al. 1999). Based on their review of these studies, Shadish & Baldwin (2003) reported an overall mean effect size of 0.84 for couple therapy, indicating that the average person receiving treatment for couple distress was better off at termination than were 80% of individuals in the no-treatment control group.

Shadish & Baldwin (2003) also noted that their mean effect size for couple therapy was generally comparable to or larger than that obtained by alternative interventions ranging from individual therapy to medical interventions. They found little evidence of differential effectiveness across different theoretical orientations to couple therapy, particularly once other covariates (e.g., reactivity of measures) were controlled. Noting the small number of couple therapy approaches listed by the American Psychological Association Division 12 Task Force (Chambless & Hollon 1998) as either well established [behavioral couple therapy (BCT)] or probably efficacious [EFCT and insight-oriented couple therapy (IOCT)], Shadish & Baldwin (2003) argued that clinicians should also consider "meta-analytically supported treatments" such as cognitive-behavioral, systemic, and eclectic approaches to couple therapy as viable approaches to treating general couple distress. They also noted that numerous studies of couple therapy (particularly those emphasizing behavioral treatments) raised unanswered questions regarding their clinical representativeness in that they failed to use clients referred through usual routes and experienced therapists in actual clinic settings. Finally, among those studies reporting data from follow-up at six months or longer, treatment effects tended to be reduced but still significant.

Findings from alternative viewpoints or more recent research provide complementary perspectives to conclusions reached by Shadish & Baldwin in their 2003 summary. One such addition involves a follow-up meta-analysis of 30 randomized experiments with distressed couples contrasting BCT with a no-treatment control (Shadish & Baldwin 2005). Their more recent analysis included 13 studies (7 published in journals and 6 unpublished dissertations) not included in the Shadish et al. (1993) review. Overall, these 30 studies of BCT yielded a mean effect size of 0.59, which was smaller than the mean effect size of 0.84 for couple therapy pooled across theoretical approaches reported by Shadish & Baldwin (2003), and which indicated that the average individual receiving BCT was better off at the end of treatment than were 72% of individuals in the control condition. In accounting for the more recent, smaller effect size obtained for BCT, the authors noted the consequence of including nonpublished dissertations with smaller sample sizes and small or negative effect sizes. They also reported that of the various components comprising behavioral couple interventions (e.g., communication training, problem-solving training, contingency contracting, behavior exchange, desensitization, cognitive restructuring, and emotional expressiveness training), only communication and problem-solving training led to larger effects, whereas use of cognitive restructuring actually led to smaller effects. Shadish & Baldwin (2005) found that the effects of BCT were unrelated to "dose" (defined by number and length of sessions), reactivity of the dependent variables considered (e.g., self-report measures of affect or cognition versus observational ratings of communication behavior), or clinical representativeness.

Other than BCT, the sole approach to couple therapy evaluated in multiple trials is EFCT, which combines an experiential, intrapsychic focus on inner emotional experience with an emphasis on cyclical, self-reinforcing interactions (Johnson et al. 1999). In four randomized trials, EFCT was superior to a waiting-list control condition in reducing relationship distress, yielding recovery rates of 70%–73% and a weighted mean effect size of 1.31 (Johnson 2002).

In addition to the two couple therapy approaches evaluated in multiple clinical trials, several approaches have demonstrated positive outcomes in treating couple distress in only one trial. First, Snyder & Wills (1989) compared insight-oriented approaches to couple therapy with behavioral approaches in a controlled clinical trial involving 79 distressed couples. The insight-oriented condition emphasized the interpretation and resolution of conflictual emotional processes related to developmental issues, collusive interactions, and maladaptive relationship patterns. At termination after approximately 20 sessions, couples in both treatment modalities showed statistically and clinically significant gains in relationship satisfaction compared with a wait-list control group. Treatment effect sizes at termination for behavioral and insight-oriented conditions were 1.01 and 0.96, respectively; treatment gains were substantially maintained at six-month follow-up. However, at four years following treatment, 38% of couples in the behavioral condition had experienced divorce, in contrast to only 3% of couples treated in the insight-oriented condition (Snyder et al. 1991).

Second, Goldman & Greenberg (1992) compared integrated systemic couple therapy (ISCT) and EFCT with each other and with a wait-list control condition in a randomized clinical trial of 42 couples. ISCT sought to disrupt repetitive, self-perpetuating negative interactional cycles by changing the meaning attributed to these cycles; changes in meaning were promoted by restructuring interactions and reframing the problems using positive connotation followed by prescribing of the symptom, encouraging the couple to "go slow," and finally prescribing a relapse or reenactment of previous negative interactions. At the end of 10 one-hour weekly sessions, ISCT and EFCT were both found to be superior to the control condition and to be equally effective in alleviating marital distress, facilitating conflict resolution and goal attainment, and reducing target complaints. Moreover, couples who received ISCT showed greater maintenance of gains in marital satisfaction and goal attainment at four-month follow-up.

More recently, findings have emerged for an integrative behavioral approach to couple therapy (IBCT; Jacobson & Christensen 1996) that combines traditional behavioral techniques for promoting change (specifically, communication and behavior-exchange skills training) with strategies aimed at fostering emotional acceptance. Interventions aimed at increasing acceptance include promoting tolerance and encouraging partners to appreciate differences and to use them to enhance their marriage. In the largest randomized clinical trial of couple therapy ever conducted, Christensen and colleagues (2004) compared the expanded IBCT with traditional BCT by assigning 134 distressed couples to the two conditions, stratified into moderately and severely distressed groups. Couples in IBCT made steady improvements in satisfaction throughout the course of treatment, whereas BCT couples improved more quickly than IBCT couples early in treatment but then plateaued later in treatment. Both treatments produced similar levels of clinically significant improvement by the end of treatment (71% of IBCT couples and 59% of BCT couples were reliably improved or recovered, based on self-reports of overall relationship satisfaction).

Although various specific approaches to couple therapy have now demonstrated effectiveness in reducing relationship distress in controlled trials, a substantial percentage of individuals fail to show significant improvement from these treatments and an even greater percentage of individuals show deterioration in gains at follow-up. Specifically, previous research has shown that about one third of couples fail to achieve significant gains from treatment, and in only half of treated couples do both partners show significant improvement in marital satisfaction at termination. Moreover, assessment at two years or longer after termination indicates significant deterioration among 30%–60% of treated couples (Cookerly 1980, Jacobson et al. 1987, Snyder et al. 1991). Such findings have fostered two alternative lines of attack for treating couple distress: (*a*) distillation and emphasis of common factors hypothesized to contribute to beneficial effects across "singular" treatment approaches, and (*b*) pluralistic models incorporating multiple components of diverse treatment approaches.

Adopting the former strategy, Sprenkle & Blow (2004) argued that common mechanisms of change cutting across the diverse couple therapies account for the absence of significant differences in their overall effectiveness. They cited five types or classes of common factors characterizing psychotherapy in general, and three factors specific to couple or family therapy. Common factors viewed as generic to psychotherapy include (*a*) client characteristics (e.g., learning style, perseverance, and compliance with instructions or assignments), (*b*) therapist characteristics (e.g., abilities to foster a therapeutic alliance and to match activity level to clients' expectations or preferences), (*c*) characteristics of the therapeutic relationship (e.g., emotional connectedness and congruence between the therapist's and client's specific expectations or goals), (*d*) expectancy or placebo effects, and (*e*) nonspecific interventions promoting emotional experiencing, cognitive mastery, and behavioral regulation. Those common factors viewed by Sprenkle & Blow (2004) as specific to couple or family therapies include (*a*) emphasis on the interpersonal context in which specific problems occur, (*b*) inclusion of multiple members of the extended family system in direct treatment, and (*c*) fostering an expanded therapeutic alliance across partners or multiple members of the family as a whole. To date, there has been little research documenting specific treatment effects attributable to proposed common factors—and no efforts in designing couple treatment approaches explicitly intended to maximize the therapeutic impact of common factors (Sexton et al. 2004).

An alternative to the common factors approach involves efforts to incorporate active, specific treatment components from diverse approaches into multicomponent interventions in a systematic manner. Such approaches have variously been described as "integrative" (e.g., Gurman 1981, 2002) or "pluralistic" (Snyder 1999), and are distinguished from eclecticism by their systematic selection or synthesis within a conceptually coherent model. Gurman (2002) described a "depth-behavioral" integrative approach to couple therapy that emphasizes the critical interrelation of intrapsychic and interpersonal factors in couples' interactions and defines the goal of couple therapy as the loosening and broadening of each spouse's implicit matrix of assumptions, expectations, and requirements of intimate interpersonal contact. This is accomplished through interpretation, cognitive restructuring, and creation of therapeutic tasks to promote each spouse's exposure to those aspects of him- or herself and his or her partner that are blocked from awareness. Snyder (1999) proposed a hierarchical approach to couple therapy incorporating structural, behavioral, and cognitive techniques earlier in the therapeutic sequence and drawing on insight-oriented techniques termed "affective reconstruction" later in treatment primarily if relationship problems prove resistant to the earlier interventions. In affective reconstruction, previous relationships, their affective components, and strategies for emotional gratification and anxiety containment are reconstructed, with a focus on identifying for each partner recurring maladaptive patterns in their interpersonal conflicts and coping styles across relationships. In addition, interventions examine ways in which previous coping strategies vital to prior relationships represent distortions or inappropriate solutions for emotional intimacy and satisfaction in the current relationship. Neither the integrative depth-behavioral approach proposed by Gurman (2002) nor the pluralistic approach advocated by Snyder (1999) has been subjected to empirical evaluation, although both approaches build on couple treatment approaches previously supported in randomized clinical trials.

THE EFFECTIVENESS OF COUPLE THERAPY IN TREATING COMORBID DISORDERS

The co-occurrence between overall couple distress and specific relationship problems, as well as individual emotional or behavioral disorders, has been well established in the research literature over the past decade. Based on these findings, new couple-based treatments have emerged for treating distressed couples for whom one or both partners have coexisting emotional, behavioral, or physical health problems (Snyder & Whisman 2003). Snyder & Whisman (2004a) examined the covariation between general relationship distress and problems in specific areas of the couple's relationship in a sample of 1020 community couples and 50 couples in therapy, based on partners' scores on the Marital Satisfaction Inventory—Revised (Snyder 1997). Results indicated that individuals reporting moderate or higher global relationship distress were five to six times more likely than nondistressed persons to report specific relationship problems in the areas of physical aggression, the sexual relationship, finances, and child rearing. Whisman (1999; Whisman & Uebelacker 2005) evaluated the association between marital distress and 12-month prevalence rates of 13 psychiatric disorders in 2538 married persons comprising the National Comorbidity Survey. Results indicated that maritally distressed persons were two to three times more likely than were nondistressed persons to experience disorders involving mood, anxiety, or substance abuse.

The co-occurrence between overall couple distress and specific individual or relationship problems has led to three couple-based treatment strategies for addressing these comorbid difficulties (Baucom et al. 1998). The first uses general couple therapy to reduce overall relationship distress based on the premise that marital conflict serves as a broad stressor that contributes to the development, exacerbation, or maintenance of specific individual or relationship problems. The second strategy involves developing disorder-specific couple interventions that focus on particular partner interactions presumed to directly influence either the co-occurring problems or their treatment. The third couple-based strategy involves partner-assisted interventions in which one partner serves as a "surrogate therapist" or coach in assisting the other partner with individual problems.

Couple-Based Treatment of Specific Relationship Problems

Couple-based interventions have been well established as effective in treating two specific components of relationship functioning: difficulties in the sexual relationship and problems of physical aggression. Recent findings also suggest the effectiveness of couple therapy in treating couples dealing with issues of infidelity.

SEXUAL DIFFICULTIES   Epidemiological data indicate that 43% of women and 31% of men will experience sexual dysfunction during their lifetime (Laumann et al. 1999). A recent review of couple-based treatments for sexual dysfunctions (Regev et al. 2003) concluded that (*a*) sex therapy, primarily consisting of sensate focus, is comparable to communication therapy in primary and secondary anorgasmic women; (*b*) couples receiving couple therapy in addition to sex therapy demonstrate more pronounced and comprehensive treatment gains, including significantly more intense experiences of sex and sexual desire; and (*c*) sex therapy positively influences both sexual and marital problems, whereas general couple therapy appears to facilitate resolution of marital problems only. Baucom et al. (1998) identified several couple-based interventions with documented effectiveness in treating female sexual dysfunctions related to lifelong or situational orgasmic disorders or hypoactive sexual desire. In partner-assisted treatment of orgasmic disorders, male partners participate with their female partner in techniques of sensate focus; toward the end of treatment, women are coached in sharing effective techniques of masturbation with their partners. Couple-based interventions also assist couples in discussing and resolving specific difficulties they experience in their sexual interactions. Findings have affirmed the efficacy of couple interventions in treating women with primary or secondary orgasmic disorders, with improvement rates ranging from 65% to 90%. Additional evidence supports combining general behaviorally oriented couple therapy with orgasm-consistency training in the treatment of women reporting hypoactive sexual desire (Hurlbert et al. 1993). Baucom et al. (1998) noted that few studies of couple-based interventions have targeted male sexual disorders despite evidence that sexual and marital problems are more closely linked in men than in women and despite reports of recent increases in male complaints of low sexual desire.

PHYSICAL AGGRESSION   Mild to moderate physical aggression (e.g., pushing, grabbing, shoving, or slapping) occurs in more than half of couples seeking couple therapy (Holtzworth-Munroe et al. 2003). Among couple therapy samples, as much as 85% of partner aggression is reciprocal, with both partners engaging in primarily low levels of aggression. Moreover, psychological aggression (e.g., verbal abuse or threats of violence) predicts physical abuse a year later (Murphy & O'Leary 1989). Although most therapists agree that couple therapy is inappropriate for couples characterized by severe physical aggression (primarily violence by male partners resulting in female partners' injuries), couple-based interventions have been effective in treating mild to moderate levels of aggression. Such interventions emphasize anger management (e.g., recognition of anger, time-outs, and self-regulation techniques) and communication skills (e.g., emotional expressiveness and problem solving). In their review of randomized trials comparing conjoint treatment to gender-specific treatment, Holtzworth-Munroe et al. (2003) concluded that conjoint couple therapy that has a direct and specific focus on eliminating violence "may be as effective as the more widely utilized gender specific treatments" (p. 227). A more recent study compared the outcomes of a domestic violence-focused treatment for 51 couples randomly assigned to either individual couple therapy, a multicouple group treatment, or a no-treatment comparison group (Stith et al. 2004). Male partner rates of physical aggression at six-month follow-up were highest in the comparison group (66%) and lower in the multicouple group (25%) than in the individual-couple therapy group (43%). Moreover, both marital aggression and acceptance of physical aggression decreased significantly among participants in the multicouple group therapy but not among participants in either the individual-couple therapy or no-treatment comparison conditions, a finding that suggests the multicouple group format has an incremental impact in changing underlying attitudes toward relationship aggression.

EXTRAMARITAL AFFAIRS   Research suggests that, on average, between 1.5% and 4% of married individuals will engage in extramarital sex in any given year (Allen et al. 2005), and approximately one in three men aged 60–69 and one in five women aged 40–49 report engaging in extramarital sex at some point in their lives (Wiederman 1997). Although couples report extramarital affairs as a leading cause of divorce and couple therapists describe infidelity as among the most difficult problems to treat (Whisman et al. 1997), until recently there has been almost no empirical study of interventions for couples dealing with affairs. Atkins and colleagues (2005b) examined treatment outcomes for 19 couples reporting an affair by one of the partners participating in the randomized trial of IBCT versus BCT by Christensen and colleagues (2004). Results showed that couples who reported infidelity were more distressed when they began treatment than were couples who did not report infidelity, but couples for whom there had been an affair also improved at a greater rate during the course of therapy than did couples not dealing with infidelity. Gordon et al. (2004) reported findings from a replicated case study of an integrative approach designed specifically to assist couples recovering from an extramarital affair. The six-month intervention comprised three phases that targeted (*a*) coping with initial emotional and behavioral disruption of individual and relationship functioning following discovery or disclosure of the affair; (*b*) exploring individual, relationship, and outside contextual factors contributing to the initial onset or maintenance of the affair; and (*c*) reaching an informed decision about how to move on, either individually or as a couple. At termination, the majority of participants in the study reported less emotional and marital distress, and individuals whose partner had participated in the affair reported greater forgiveness toward their partner.

Couple-Based Treatment of Mental and Physical Health Problems

Research has documented the effectiveness of couple-based interventions for a broad range of emotional and behavioral dysfunctions, including alcohol and related substance-use disorders, mood and anxiety disorders, and chronic pain and related health problems. Promising couple-based interventions have also recently emerged for a variety of other difficulties; interventions that have received at least preliminary empirical evidence of their effectiveness are described here.

SUBSTANCE-USE DISORDERS   Alcohol- and drug-use disorders comprise the most common psychiatric disorders in the general population, with lifetime prevalence rates of 23.5% and 11.9%, respectively (Kessler et al. 1994). BCT for alcoholism and drug abuse aims to alter couple and family interaction patterns to promote a family environment more conducive to abstinence and sobriety (e.g., by reducing the partner's recurring complaints about past drinking and promoting attention to positive aspects of current sober behavior), as well as to improve communication and positive activities (Fals-Stewart et al. 2003). BCT for alcohol and drug abuse typically involves 15–20 outpatient couple sessions over five to six months. In their review of the literature regarding BCT, O'Farrell & Fals-Stewart (2000) concluded:

> First, BCT for both alcoholism and drug abuse produces more abstinences and fewer substance-related problems, happier relationships, fewer couple separations and lower risk for divorce than does individual-based treatment. Second, domestic violence is substantially reduced after BCT for both alcoholism

and drug abuse. Third, cost outcomes after BCT are very favorable for both alcoholism and drug abuse, and are superior to individual-based treatment for drug abuse (p. 51).

Recently, Fals-Stewart and colleagues (2005a) examined the clinical efficacy and cost-effectiveness of a shortened version of BCT with 100 alcoholic male patients and their partners. In the shortened version, couples participated in only 6 rather than 12 conjoint sessions; alcoholic clients participated in an additional 12 weekly individual sessions. Results indicated that those assigned to the brief version had posttreatment and 12-month outcomes equivalent to clients receiving standard BCT, thereby supporting the cost-effectiveness of this shortened intervention.

MOOD DISORDERS   Lifetime prevalence rates for major depressive episode and dysthymia are estimated at 17.1% and 6.4%, respectively (Kessler et al. 1994). Three clinical trials have shown that behavioral couple interventions for depression emphasizing behavior exchange, communication and problem-solving skills, and cognitive interventions (e.g., cognitive reframing and directing attention to positive change) are effective in relieving depression when provided to maritally distressed couples with a depressed partner (Gupta et al. 2003). Furthermore, compared with individual-based therapies, BCT has the incremental benefit of improving overall relationship satisfaction. Clinical guidelines for providing BCT for depressed individuals are provided by Beach & Gupta (2003). Similarly, conjoint couple therapy incorporating components of interpersonal psychotherapy for depression aimed at helping depressed individuals better understand and negotiate their interpersonal relationships has been shown to be effective in treating depression (Foley et al. 1989). More recently, Leff et al. (2000) reported promising results for systemic couple therapy, using interventions designed to reduce problematic patterns of interacting, for depressed married individuals with a critical spouse. Finally, Dessaulles et al. (2003) compared 14 sessions of EFCT with pharmacotherapy in treating wives' major depression in 18 couples randomly assigned to treatment condition. Both interventions were equally effective in reducing depressive symptoms, although there was some evidence that women receiving EFCT made greater improvement following termination than those receiving pharmacotherapy.

ANXIETY DISORDERS   Excessive anxiety is one of the most frequent mental health problems in the United States, with a lifetime prevalence rate of developing any anxiety disorder at 24.9% (Kessler et al. 1994). In their review of couple-based interventions for anxiety disorders, Baucom et al. (2003) noted that anxiety disorders may negatively impact couple functioning by disrupting interaction patterns, increasing tension and arguments, restricting relationship activities, or decreasing attention to the needs of the nonanxious partner. Baucom et al. (2003) described ways in which efficacious treatments for anxiety disorders (e.g., exposure and response prevention, cognitive restructuring, and relaxation training) can be incorporated into either (*a*) partner-assisted interventions using the partner to assist with exposure exercises and provide support or (*b*) couple-based interventions focusing on ways in which couple functioning maintains anxiety symptoms, as well as ways in which the anxiety influences couple functioning. In their review of specific couple-based interventions for various anxiety disorders, Baucom et al. (1998) concluded that partner-assisted exposure treatment of obsessive-compulsive disorder is at least as effective as treating the patient without such assistance; they also determined that exposure interventions for agoraphobia may show enhanced benefit from involving the partner even when there is no overt relationship distress, a conclusion affirmed in a recent review by Byrne et al. (2004).

PAIN AND PHYSICAL ILLNESS   Over the past 15 years, psychosocial pain researchers have become increasingly interested in the role that partners play in how patients adjust to pain and in involving partners in psychosocial pain-management efforts (Keefe et al. 2006). For example, partners can encourage patients in acquiring more effective pain-control strategies, and can be discouraged themselves from criticizing appropriate coping skills, enforcing the patient's rest, or insisting that pain medication is the only way to manage pain. Moreover, couple-based interventions for chronic pain—and for physical illness more generally—can help partners to cope with their own emotional struggles with caretaking, promote more effective communication around pain and emotional distress, and facilitate couple processes for providing emotional and tangible support, dealing with conflict, and expressing affection and intimacy (Keefe et al. 2006).

Keefe and colleagues (1996) randomly assigned 88 patients with osteoarthritic knee pain to spouse-assisted coping skills training, a conventional coping skills training condition alone, or an arthritis education and partner-support control condition. Patients in the spouse-assisted coping skills training condition received training in a variety of cognitive and behavioral pain-coping skills (e.g., relaxation, imagery, distraction techniques, activity pacing, goal setting, and cognitive restructuring) and they and their partners received training in various couples skills (e.g., joint practice, communication skills, behavioral rehearsal, problem solving, and maintenance training). Patients in the partner-assisted coping skills training had the best outcomes across multiple criteria, whereas those in the arthritis education–social support control condition had the worst outcomes. Moreover, patients in the partner-assisted coping skills training who showed increases in marital adjustment were more likely to show lower levels of psychological disability, physical disability, and pain behavior at 12-month follow-up.

Couple-based interventions for patients dealing with cancer have resulted in similar findings. Specifically, Keefe and colleagues (2005) recently completed a study that tested the effects of a partner-guided pain management intervention for 78 patients with end-of-life cancer pain. The intervention, delivered by a nurse, integrated information about cancer pain with training in three pain-coping skills and emphasized the role these skills could play in controlling patient and partner emotional responses and relational exchanges. Results indicated that patients receiving this intervention tended to report reduced levels of pain, and that their spouses improved in their sense of efficacy for helping the patient control pain and tended to report reduced levels of caregiver strain.

Finally, a recent study examined the impact of an eight-session couple therapy for nine couples in which one partner was diagnosed with a terminal illness (Mohr et al. 2003). Conjoint sessions emphasized (*a*) helping patients and their partners to find meaning together through examining beliefs, goals, and values; (*b*) increasing intimacy, emotional support, and reciprocity; and (*c*) facilitating conversations about death and dying. Results indicated improvements in couples' relationship quality and significant decreases in patients' distress about dying and the frequency of partners' worry about their partner dying.

Given the direct adverse impact of couple distress on cardiovascular and immunological functioning (Kiecolt-Glaser & Newton 2001)—and the indirect negative effects on health through couple influences on nutrition, substance use, and exercise—it is not surprising that couple-based interventions have been developed for a range of health-related concerns including obesity and nicotine use as well as alcohol- and drug-use disorders as described above. Common to such treatments are specific interventions aimed at changing patients' interpersonal environments linked to health-risk behaviors, encouraging healthy alternatives through partners' use of social reinforcement, and generally decreasing relationship stress (see also Schmaling & Sher 2000). Although evidence for some of these treatments emerged almost 25 years ago (e.g., spouse involvement in the behavioral treatment of overweight women; Pearce et al. 1981), other promising developments (e.g., couple-based interventions for patients diagnosed with coronary artery disease; Sher et al. 2002) await further empirical evaluation.

EMERGING TREATMENTS FOR OTHER DISORDERS   Couple-based treatments continue to be developed at an increasing pace for a broad spectrum of individual emotional, behavioral, and health-related difficulties. Although evidence for these treatments' effectiveness remains primarily anecdotal, several noteworthy exceptions exist. Monson et al. (2004) described recent findings from cognitive-behavioral couple treatment of posttraumatic stress disorder (PTSD) in a pilot study of seven couples in which the husband was diagnosed with PTSD secondary to Vietnam combat experiences. The treatment emphasized three components involving psychoeducation about PTSD and relationship problems, communication skills training, and interventions targeting cognitions contributing to the association between PTSD and relationship problems. Following the 15-session treatment, clinicians' and partners' ratings of the veterans' PTSD symptoms showed significant improvement, with effect sizes exceeding 1.00; the veterans' self-reported reductions in PTSD symptoms were not statistically significant (in part due to the small sample), but still yielded a moderate effect size of 0.64. Wives' own ratings of anxiety also improved with this couple-based intervention, and both partners reported improved social functioning in the household.

Finally, two couple-based treatments have been developed for couples in which one partner has been diagnosed with borderline personality disorder (BPD). The first (Fruzzetti & Iverson 2006) builds on dialectical behavior therapy (DBT) for individuals with BPD. In a sample of 22 couples participating in a six-session couples group, decreases in invalidating behaviors (e.g., dismissive, minimizing, or rejecting statements) and increases in validating responses (e.g., acceptance and understanding) pre- to posttreatment predicted decreased levels of individual and relationship distress in a moderately distressed sample (Lillis & Fruzzetti 2004). More recently, Kirby & Baucom (2004) reported results of a couple-based group intervention combining elements of DBT with cognitive behavioral couple therapy (CBCT) for 10 couples in which one partner had been diagnosed with BPD and had already received individual DBT. Following 16 two-hour sessions (with five couples per group), the women partners showed less depression and related negative affect, increases in positive affect, and improved ability to regulate their own emotions; effect sizes ranged from 0.72 to 1.00.

PROCESSES OF CHANGE IN COUPLE THERAPY

How does couple therapy work? Although each of the empirically supported approaches to couple therapy posits specific processes or mechanisms of change, there has been little research explicitly indicating these proposed mechanisms as responsible for observed therapeutic effects. In this section, we briefly describe three approaches to examining change processes in couple therapy. We then summarize the few available empirical findings related to change mechanisms in the context of theoretical formulations underlying the major approaches to couple therapy.

Methods of Investigating Change Processes

REGRESSION ANALYSIS OF MEDIATION   Probably the best-known and most widely used approach for examining change processes in therapy involves use of regression analysis, following procedures outlined by Baron & Kenny (1986), for establishing mediation effects. Using these guidelines, a proposed mediating variable (e.g., communication processes) is shown to account (either entirely or partially) for the relation between some predictor variable (e.g., treatment condition status) and some outcome variable (e.g., relationship satisfaction) when the following four conditions are met: (*a*) The predictor affects the criterion (e.g., treatment leads to increased relationship satisfaction); (*b*) the predictor affects the mediator (e.g., treatment leads to gains in communication skills); (*c*) the mediator affects the criterion (e.g., gains in communication skills lead to increased relationship satisfaction), controlling for the predictor; and (*d*) the relation between the predictor and the criterion is reduced (partial mediation) or eliminated (complete mediation) after controlling for the relation between the mediator and the criterion. In "moderated mediation" (see Whisman & Snyder 1997), the mediating or change mechanisms are demonstrated to have a stronger effect for one group than for another (e.g., mediating effects of therapeutic alliance for couples receiving BCT versus EFCT, or effects of behavior-exchange skills training for younger couples relative to older ones).

HIERARCHICAL LINEAR MODELING ANALYSIS OF CHANGE PROCESSES   More recently, couple researchers (e.g., Doss et al. 2005) have examined the relation between proposed mechanisms of change and outcome variables through the use of hierarchical linear modeling (HLM; Raudenbush & Bryk 2001), also known as growth curve analysis. This approach to identifying change mechanisms involves two steps. First, multiple assessments of some criterion variable are used to estimate a trajectory, or growth curve, which allows investigators to describe the nature of change for a given criterion or outcome within a sample. In the second step of growth curve analysis, the parameters summarizing change of each person are treated as new dependent variables that are then predicted from other within- or between-subject variables proposed as mechanisms of change.

TASK ANALYSIS OF CHANGE PROCESSES   A third approach to investigating change processes involves task analysis of proximal outcomes that occur within or between sessions by focusing on specific therapeutic events (Heatherington et al. 2005, Rice & Greenberg 1984). Such task analysis involves disassembling the therapeutic process into smaller, measurable in-session units or events to capture the actual sequence of therapist-client interactions and then delineating the linkage of these events to proximal or "mini" outcomes that presumably build on each other and contribute to molar, more distal outcomes (e.g., relationship satisfaction at termination). For example, an investigator examining presumed mechanisms of change in EFCT might examine events delimited by therapist clarification of underlying primary attachment-related fears and the client's owning and expressing those fears in a "softened" manner, and the linkage of this sequence to the other partner's likelihood of shifting from antagonistic or defensive responses to empathic or nurturing ones.

Empirical Findings Regarding Change Processes

Previous reviews (e.g., Gottman 1998, Lebow 2000) have generally concurred in their conclusion that little empirical evidence exists regarding presumed mechanisms of change in couple therapy. Such conclusions rest in part from disappointing findings from mediation analyses adopting the traditional regression approach. For example, whereas BCT emphasizes the importance of improving communication skills as a means of reducing relationship distress—and although such skills do typically increase among couples receiving BCT—several studies have failed to find an association between the magnitude of changes in communication behaviors and gains in relationship satisfaction. Similarly, although CBCT has been shown to produce positive change in targeted cognitions (e.g., expectancies and attributions), changes in these cognitions have not been linked to couples' gains in satisfaction following CBCT (see Whisman & Snyder 1997 for a summary of relevant studies).

However, recent findings drawing on HLM and task analysis offer encouragement regarding significant developments in identifying change mechanisms in couple therapy. For example, Doss et al. (2005) used hierarchical growth curve analysis to examine mechanisms of change in 134 couples randomly assigned to either traditional BCT or ICBT. Both therapies were effective in increasing emotional acceptance and improving communication behaviors across the course of therapy; however, these changes differed by treatment modality in a manner consistent with their respective presumed change mechanisms. Specifically, acceptance increased significantly more for couples in IBCT than for couples in BCT, whereas couples in BCT showed larger gains in positive communication. Moreover, examination of change separately in the first and second halves of therapy indicated that change in targeted behaviors was a powerful mechanism of change early in therapy, whereas in the second half of therapy, emotional acceptance was more strongly related to changes in relationship satisfaction.

Task analysis has been used successfully to examine change processes in both IBCT and EFCT. In a pilot study with 12 distressed couples randomly assigned to either IBCT or traditional BCT (Cordova et al. 1998), couples in IBCT showed relatively more constructive detachment (i.e., talking about problems without blaming or being compelled to solve them—both indicators of acceptance) over the course of therapy and more "soft expressions" of emotion in late sessions relative to earlier ones. Changes in husbands' and wives' constructive detachment from early to late sessions predicted couples' gains in relationship satisfaction.

The most compelling findings regarding specific change processes in couple therapy have emerged using a task-analysis approach to investigating change in EFCT. An early study by Johnson & Greenberg (1988) comparing partner exchanges in "best" sessions of three successfully treated couples versus those for three couples with poor outcome showed that high-change couples exhibited more frequent "softening" events in which a previously critical partner expressed vulnerability and asked for comfort and connection from his or her spouse. A second report regarding three task analytic studies of EFCT (Greenberg et al. 1993) showed that (a) couples receiving EFCT demonstrated more shifts from hostility to affiliative behaviors than did wait-list couples; (b) best sessions as identified by couples were characterized by more depth of experiencing and affiliative and autonomous statements than were sessions identified as poor; and (c) intimate, emotionally laden self-disclosure by one partner was more likely to lead to affiliative statements by the other partner than were other randomly selected responses. Finally, a recent task analysis of four EFCT sessions by Bradley & Furrow (2004) found that emotional experiencing and the disclosure of attachment-related affect and fears were the key client features of successful softening events; consistent with proposed mechanisms of change in EFCT, specific therapist interventions linked to softening events involved intensifying a couple's emotional experience and promoting intrapsychic awareness and interpersonal shifts in attachment-related interactions.

PREDICTORS OF COUPLE THERAPY OUTCOME

For whom does couple therapy work? As documented in the preceding sections, there is considerable variability in individuals' response to couple therapy. Hence, investigators have been interested in predicting outcome to treatment. In this section, we briefly describe methods for identifying predictors of treatment response, distinguishing between methods emphasizing prognostic versus prescriptive indicators. We then review empirical findings regarding predictors of couple therapy outcome.

Methods of Identifying Predictors of Treatment Outcome

IDENTIFYING PROGNOSTIC INDICATORS FROM ANALYSES OF MAIN EFFECTS   In evaluating predictors of treatment outcome, investigators have made a distinction between prognostic indicators, which predict response to a particular treatment (or response across treatments, irrespective of specific approach), and prescriptive indicators, which predict response to one versus another treatment (Hollon & Najavits 1988). Identifying a prognostic indicator requires only evaluating the association between the predictor variable and some outcome measure. This can be done by regressing posttreatment outcome scores on the predictor, controlling for pretreatment scores on the outcome variable; similar analyses can be done with dichotomous outcomes (e.g., clinical significance outcomes) using logistic regression analyses. The overwhelming preponderance of research on predictors of response to couple therapy has emphasized the delineation of these more general prognostic indicators.

IDENTIFYING PRESCRIPTIVE INDICATORS FROM ANALYSES OF INTERACTIONS   Evaluating whether some variable predicts outcome to one specific treatment versus another treatment—that is, identifying prescriptive indicators—requires testing for an interaction or moderator effect. Prescriptive indicators are examined using the aptitude-treatment interaction (ATI) paradigm (Cronbach & Snow 1977, Dance & Neufeld 1988). In using regression to identify prescriptive indicators, one tests for a significant treatment $\times$ predictor interaction indicating that the association between the predictor and treatment outcome varies as a function of the type of treatment (i.e., that the type of treatment moderates the association between the predictor and outcome). Alternative approaches for identifying prescriptive indicators exist when using analysis of individual growth curves (Rogosa 1991).

Research design requirements for identifying prescriptive indicators are more rigorous than those for identifying more general prognostic indicators, particularly as these relate to adequate power for detecting effects (Whisman & McClelland 2005). For example, using Cohen's (1987) power tables, an investigator would need to obtain minimum sample sizes of 26, 55, or 392 participants in order to have adequate power (i.e., power of .80, at $\alpha = .05$) for detecting large, medium, or small effect sizes, respectively. However, prescriptive indicators generally offer far greater usefulness for clinicians than do prognostic indicators in that the former go beyond the question of who responds well to therapy to address issues of treatment selection in evaluating who responds well to which kinds of intervention.

Empirical Findings Regarding Predictors of Couple Therapy Outcome

PROGNOSTIC INDICATORS OF TREATMENT RESPONSE   Over the past several decades, a substantial body of research has identified general prognostic indicators of response to couple therapy including demographic, relationship, and individual characteristics. Most of these findings have been derived from controlled clinical trials of BCT and are reviewed in greater detail by Whisman et al. (2005); exceptions are noted where applicable.

Several studies have found that younger couples respond more favorably to BCT (Baucom 1984, Hahlweg et al. 1984, O'Leary & Turkewitz 1981), whereas others have found no association between age and treatment outcome (Crowe 1978, Jacobson et al. 1986). In addition, Crowe (1978) found that less-educated couples had better response to BCT than those with higher education. A prediction study collapsing across behavioral and insight-oriented treatment conditions (Snyder et al. 1993) found that initial status of being unemployed or employed in a position of unskilled labor predicted poor treatment outcome four years after termination. In a controlled trial of IBCT versus traditional BCT, couples who were married longer showed greater treatment gains, regardless of condition (Atkins 2005a).

Results from various studies indicate that couples having the greatest difficulties in their relationship are less likely to benefit from treatment, with initial levels of relationship distress accounting for up to 46% of the variance in treatment outcome (Johnson 2002). Lack of commitment and behavioral steps taken toward divorce have been associated with poor treatment outcome to BCT in two studies (Beach & Broderick 1983, Hahlweg et al. 1984) but not in another (Jacobson et al. 1986). Hahlweg et al. (1984) found that BCT outcome was predicted by negative communication behavior. Snyder et al. (1993) found that poorer outcome to couple therapy was predicted by lower relationship quality, greater negative relationship affect and disengagement, and greater desired change in the relationship. By contrast, initial levels of relationship distress were not significantly related to treatment outcome in a study of EFCT (Johnson & Talitman 1997), although partners' therapeutic alliance accounted for 22% of the variance in response to treatment.

Whisman & Jacobson (1990) operationalized inequality of partners' power in their marriage in terms of asymmetry in the relative frequencies of verbal communication content patterns, and found that power inequality prior to therapy predicted positive treatment outcome at posttest and at six-month follow-up. Gray-Little et al. (1996) operationalized power in terms of which partner had more influence in a problem-solving interaction, and found that wife-dominant couples improved the most in response to couple therapy in terms of increased satisfaction and improved communication. In a study of EFCT, Johnson & Talitman (1997) found that the best predictor of outcome was the wife's belief that her partner still cared for her.

Greater interpersonal sensitivity and emotional expressiveness—as determined by measures of "femininity"—have been found to predict better outcome at termination (Baucom & Aiken 1984) and long-term follow-up (Snyder et al. 1993) but were not predictive in a third study (Jacobson et al. 1986). Couples in which partners exhibit a higher degree of traditionality (i.e., higher affiliation needs in the wife and higher independence needs in the husband) have been shown to have poorer response to BCT (Jacobson et al. 1986). Partners' higher levels of depressed affect have been linked to poorer outcome in one study (Snyder et al. 1993) but not in another (Jacobson et al. 1986).

Although findings regarding prognostic indicators of couple treatment response are mixed and the predictive utility of any single predictor appears modest, incremental prediction from multiple indicators pooled across predictor domains can be substantial. For example, in the study comparing BCT with IOCT (Snyder et al. 1991), the unconditional probability (base rate) of divorce or relationship distress four years after completing couple therapy was .35. In their analyses pooling replicated predictors across partners and across demographic, individual, and relationship domains, Snyder et al. (1993) were able to double the accuracy in predicting four-year follow-up status from prognostic indicators obtained either at intake or termination (with conditional probabilities of .71 and .86, respectively).

PRESCRIPTIVE INDICATORS OF TREATMENT RESPONSE   In contrast to findings regarding general prognostic indicators of response to couple therapy, research identifying prescriptive indicators of couple treatment response has been rare. An early study by O'Leary & Turkewitz (1981) suggested that younger couples responded better to behavioral interventions emphasizing behavior-exchange skills, whereas older couples showed more favorable response to general communication skills training. More recently, research comparing IBCT with traditional BCT suggests that severely distressed couples may respond more favorably to BCT than to IBCT during the initial stages of treatment, although both treatments produce equivalent gains at outcome and preliminary findings indicate that IBCT may produce more enduring gains at extended follow-up (Atkins & Christensen 2004). Moreover, exploratory analyses from this clinical trial reported by Atkins et al. (2005a) suggested that sexually dissatisfied couples showed slower initial response but more consistent gains overall in IBCT versus BCT.

DIRECTIONS FOR FUTURE RESEARCH AND TRAINING

Previous reviews of couple therapy have identified a variety of directions for further research and training in couple-based treatments. Based on these reviews and our own evaluation of the literature, we have extracted 12 essential directions for future research and training.

Directions for Research

Couple therapy outcome research will benefit from smaller-level studies such as single- or replicated-case designs, analysis of treatment components, and open clinical trials. We adopt this conclusion without alteration from a review of methodological issues in couple research by Christensen et al. (2005). Christensen and colleagues noted limitations in funding for large clinical trials of couple therapy, and emphasized that "working with a smaller number of couples in a more detailed manner often can provide the understanding and insight needed before launching a more time-consuming and expensive randomized clinical trial" (Christensen et al. 2005, p. 13). Such smaller-scale investigations also promote outcome research in community agency and private practice settings potentially addressing issues of representativeness remaining from studies conducted exclusively within the university research context.

Couple therapy research needs to extend beyond initial treatment impact to identify individual, relationship, and treatment factors contributing to deterioration or relapse and effective means of reducing or eliminating these effects. Among those individuals who initially respond favorably to couple therapy, approximately 30%–60% subsequently evidence significant deterioration. Numerous reviews (e.g., Johnson 2002, Lebow & Gurman 1995) have noted the need to develop specific interventions targeting relapse as well as guidelines regarding their delivery (e.g., timing and format of their delivery as well as criteria for targeting couples at greatest risk) to reduce deterioration effects.

Research on couple therapy needs to move beyond existing therapies to examine integrative approaches—including indicators for selecting, sequencing, and pacing specific treatment components, alternative integrative models, and moderators of therapeutic effectiveness. This conclusion was asserted by Snyder & Whisman (2003, 2004b) specifically as it relates to treating couples with coexisting mental and physical disorders, but has also been voiced by others (e.g., Lebow & Gurman 1995) as it applies to couple therapy more generally. Efforts to decompose couple-based interventions into their smallest transportable components should lead to research on the most effective ways of reassembling these in a manner uniquely tailored to couples' variation in individual and relationship functioning (Snyder et al. 2003). Each intervention incorporated into an integrative approach needs to be considered with respect to its necessity, sufficiency, and interactive effects.

Couple-based interventions for specific individual and relationship problems need to be developed and examined for both their intermediate and long-term effectiveness. Significant progress in this regard has been achieved over the past decade; however, much of the literature espousing couple-based interventions for emotional and behavioral disorders relies on qualitative analyses or anecdotal evidence. Evaluations of existing or new couple therapies for specific disorders need to be complemented by studies examining the adaptation of existing approaches to couple distress when specific dysfunctions (e.g., personality disorders)—although not an explicit target of treatment—moderate both treatment process and outcome.

Greater attention needs to be focused on the generalizability of research findings across such potential moderators as age, family life stage, gender, culture and ethnicity (including interethnic couples), family structure (including composition of stepfamily and extended family systems), and nontraditional relationships (including cohabiting and same-gender couples). Virtually every recent review of couple therapy research has decried the lack of findings regarding the generalizability of treatment outcome and processes across these or similar potential moderators. Among the clinical trials of couple therapy reviewed in the preceding sections, only the comparison of IBCT with traditional BCT (Christensen et al. 2004) included significant representation (22%) from ethnically diverse groups. Cross-cultural comparisons of couple therapy—particularly couple-based treatments of individual emotional or health problems—are rare, despite documented differences in how couples of diverse cultural backgrounds contend with mental and physical illness (Osterman et al. 2003). Research on couple therapy for specific disorders tends to focus on one gender to the exclusion of the other—e.g., sampling men with substance use disorders or women with affective disorders. Empirical studies of couple therapy with same-gender couples are virtually nonexistent.

Because of the growing concerns about spiraling health care costs, research needs to assess the costs, benefits, cost-benefit ratio, and cost-effectiveness of couple-based interventions. We embrace this conclusion verbatim as asserted by Fals-Stewart et al. (2005b) in a recent article defining various components of cost analysis and methods for calculating these indices. Fals-Stewart and colleagues determined that the few evaluations of cost-benefit and cost-effectiveness of couple- and family-based interventions completed to date have yielded favorable results; nevertheless, they noted that evaluations of this sort for couple and family therapies have lagged behind those for other psychosocial interventions.

Studies of couple therapy outcome need to be complemented by research on change processes. Again, this recommendation regarding future research has been articulated in virtually every review of couple therapy appearing in the past decade. Further bolstering the appeal for research on mechanisms of change are encouraging findings from recent studies drawing on HLM and especially those using an events-based or task analysis approach. In their recent review of change process research in couple and family therapy, Heatherington et al. (2005) identify five critical foci toward which future process research should be oriented: (*a*) midrange theories about systemic change processes; (*b*) client change processes (e.g., partner behaviors facilitating proximal outcomes); (*c*) intrapersonal processes (e.g., emotion and cognition); (*d*) strategies for analyzing data from multiple participants;

and (*e*) consistent with a recommendation noted above, investigation of the degree to which various change processes generalize across diverse populations.

Research regarding mediators and moderators of treatment outcome requires attention to critical design issues to ensure the potential for identifying relevant effects. Recent papers have emphasized methodological issues in examining change processes in psychotherapy generally (e.g., Doss 2004) and moderators in couple and family research specifically (Whisman & McClelland 2005). For example, the power to detect small or moderate effects may be enhanced not only by increasing sample size but also by using more reliable and accurate measures and by increasing variance of the predictor or moderator variable. The latter point is particularly important because inclusion and exclusion criteria for clinical trials often result in restricted range of predictor variables. For example, one is prohibited from examining the effects of individual psychopathology on couple therapy process or outcome if individuals with emotional or behavioral disorders are excluded from the clinical trial.

Couple-based interventions likely will be enhanced by incorporating basic research on emotion regulation processes. There has been growing interest over the past decade in the role of emotion regulation processes in couples and families (Snyder et al. 2006). Individuals' ability to regulate their emotions effectively— especially in interpersonal contexts that involve potentially caustic exchanges— plays a pivotal role in keeping individuals and their significant relationships functioning well. Poor or inadequate emotion regulation at either the intrapersonal or the interpersonal levels may be a major contributing factor in relationship dissatisfaction and dissolution. Moreover, research on emotion regulation may facilitate better understanding of the role of individual psychopathology on couple therapy processes and outcomes.

Directions for Clinical Training

Couple therapists should be trained in common factors and mechanisms of change that potentially undergird most forms of successful treatment. We concur with this conclusion as asserted by Sprenkle & Blow (2004) while also recognizing caveats noted by Sexton et al. (2004) that the common factors perspective may "overlook the multilevel nature of practice, the diversity of clients and settings, and the complexity of therapeutic change" (p. 131). Recognizing the therapeutic effects of nonspecific (common) treatment components does not obviate attending to the critical role of specific treatment counterparts (Snyder et al. 1988). For example, fundamental but nonspecific interventions facilitating the therapeutic alliance may be necessary but insufficient for treating relationship distress unless followed by specific interventions such as challenging dysfunctional attributions, emphasizing and heightening primary emotions, or interpreting recurring maladaptive relationship patterns.

Couple therapists need to be trained to conceptualize and practice integratively across diverse theoretical orientations. The complexity of individual, interpersonal, and situational factors contributing to the development, exacerbation, or maintenance of couple distress often requires selecting, sequencing, and pacing multiple interventions falling outside of any one theoretical approach (Snyder et al. 2003). Therapists are often vulnerable to viewing presenting complaints through the filtering lens of their own preferred theoretical or treatment modality. Treating difficult couples with coexisting mental or physical health problems, in particular, may be hindered if interventions are restricted to one particular theoretical tradition. Even when practicing within a given treatment approach, couple therapists need to be trained in how to "make their next move" (Sprenkle 2002a) in terms of selecting among either specific or nonspecific interventions consistent with that approach.

Couple therapists need to be competent in recognizing and treating the recursive influences of individual and relationship difficulties. Given robust findings regarding the comorbidity of relationship distress with individual emotional and behavioral problems in both community and clinical samples, couple therapists must be schooled in psychopathology and principles of individual assessment and treatment, including familiarity with biological interventions for relationship difficulties rooted at least in part in physical or mental illness of one or both partners. Similarly, couple therapists need to be familiar with both existing and emerging couple-based interventions for individual emotional and physical health problems, as well as adaptations of existing treatments made necessary by such difficulties. As evidence of the disconnection between research findings and clinical practice, Fals-Stewart & Birchler (2001) surveyed program administrators from 398 community-based outpatient substance abuse treatment programs in the United States regarding use of different family- and couple-based therapies in their programs. Whereas 27% of the programs provided some type of couple-based treatment, less than 5% of the agencies used behaviorally oriented couple therapy and none used BCT specifically. Consequently, greater efforts are needed to identify possible barriers impeding the transfer of couple-based interventions from research to practice settings and to develop strategies aimed at reducing or eliminating these barriers.

CONCLUSIONS

Couple therapy comprises an essential component of mental health services. Research demonstrates its effectiveness in treating generalized relationship distress as well as comorbid relationship problems and individual emotional and behavioral difficulties. Systematic investigations delineating processes of change and prescriptive indicators of treatment response will be critical to narrow the oft-cited gap between clinical research and practice. Recent findings offer considerable encouragement for translating the results of couple therapy research into improved training of couple therapists and more effective interventions in community agency and practice settings.

The *Annual Review of Psychology* is online at http://psych.annualreviews.org

LITERATURE CITED

Allen ES, Atkins DC, Baucom DH, Snyder DK, Gordon KC, et al. 2005. Intrapersonal, interpersonal, and contextual factors in engaging in and responding to extramarital involvement. *Clin. Psychol. Sci. Pract.* 12:101–30

Atkins DC, Berns SB, George W, Doss B, Gattis K, et al. 2005a. Predicting success in a randomized clinical trial of marital therapy. *J. Consult. Clin. Psychol.* In press

Atkins DC, Christensen A. 2004. *Marital Satisfaction and Stability for Two Years Post-Treatment: Comparing the Trajectories of TBCT and IBCT.* Presented at Assoc. Adv. Behav. Ther., New Orleans, LA

Atkins DC, Eldridge KE, Baucom DH, Christensen A. 2005b. Behavioral marital therapy and infidelity: optimism in the face of betrayal. *J. Consult. Clin. Psychol.* 73:144–50

Baron RM, Kenny DA. 1986. The moderator-mediator variable distinction in social psychological research: conceptual, strategic, and statistical considerations. *J. Personal. Soc. Psychol.* 51:1173–82

Baucom DH. 1984. The active ingredients of behavioral marital therapy: the effectiveness of problem-solving/communication training, contingency contracting, and their combination. See Hahlweg & Jacobson 1984, pp. 73–88

Baucom DH, Aiken PA. 1984. Sex role identity, marital satisfaction, and response to behavioral marital therapy. *J. Consult. Clin. Psychol.* 52:438–44

Baucom DH, Shoham V, Mueser KT, Daiuto AD, Stickle TR. 1998. Empirically supported couple and family interventions for marital distress and adult mental health problems. *J. Consult. Clin. Psychol.* 66:53–88

Baucom DH, Stanton S, Epstein NB. 2003. Anxiety disorders. See Snyder & Whisman 2003, pp. 57–87

Beach SRH, Broderick JE. 1983. Commitment: a variable in women's response to marital therapy. *Am. J. Fam. Ther.* 11:16–24

Beach SRH, Gupta M. 2003. Depression. See Snyder & Whisman 2003, pp. 88–113

Bradley B, Furrow JL. 2004. Toward a mini-theory of the blamer softening event: tracking the moment-by-moment process. *J. Marital Fam. Ther.* 30:1–12

Byrne M, Carr A, Clark M. 2004. The efficacy of couples-based interventions for panic disorder with agoraphobia. *J. Fam. Ther.* 26: 105–25

Chambless DL, Hollon SD. 1998. Defining empirically supported therapies. *J. Consult. Clin. Psychol.* 66:7–18

Christensen A, Atkins DC, Berns S, Wheeler J, Baucom DH, et al. 2004. Traditional versus integrative behavioral couple therapy for significantly and chronically distressed married couples. *J. Consult. Clin. Psychol.* 72:176–91

Christensen A, Baucom DH, Vu CA, Stanton S. 2005. Methodologically sound, cost-effective research on the outcome of couple therapy. *J. Fam. Psychol.* 19:6–17

Christensen A, Heavy CL. 1999. Interventions for couples. *Annu. Rev. Psychol.* 50:165–90

Cohen J. 1987. *Statistical Power Analysis for the Behavioral Sciences.* Hillsdale, NJ: Erlbaum. 474 pp. 2nd ed.

Cookerly JR. 1980. Does marital therapy do any lasting good? *J. Marital Fam. Ther.* 6:393–97

Cordova JV, Jacobson NS, Christensen A. 1998. Acceptance versus change interventions in behavioral couple therapy: impact on couples' in-session communication. *J. Marital Fam. Ther.* 24:437–55

Cronbach LJ, Snow RE. 1977. *Aptitudes and Instructional Methods: A Handbook for Research on Interactions.* Oxford, UK: Irvington. 574 pp.

Crowe MJ. 1978. Conjoint marital therapy: a controlled outcome study. *Psychol. Med.* 8:623–36

Dance KA, Neufeld RWJ. 1988. Aptitude-treatment interaction research in the clinical setting: a review of attempts to dispel the "patient uniformity" myth. *Psychol. Bull.* 104:192–213

Dessaulles A, Johnson SM, Denton WH. 2003. Emotion-focused therapy for couples in the treatment of depression: a pilot study. *Am. J. Fam. Ther.* 31:345–53

Doss BD. 2004. Changing the way we study change in psychotherapy. *Clin. Psychol. Sci. Pract.* 11:368–86

Doss BD, Thum YM, Sevier M, Atkins DC, Christensen A. 2005. Improving relationships: mechanisms of change in couple therapy. *J. Consult. Clin. Psychol.* In press

Dunn RL, Schwebel AI. 1995. Meta-analytic review of marital therapy outcome research. *J. Fam. Psychol.* 9:58–68

Dutcher TD. 1999. *A meta-analytic study of marital therapy modalities and clients' presenting problems*. PhD thesis. Union Inst. 73 pp.

Fals-Stewart W, Birchler GR. 2001. A national survey of the use of couples therapy in substance abuse treatment. *J. Subst. Abuse Treat.* 20:277–83

Fals-Stewart W, Birchler GR, O'Farrell TJ. 2003. Alcohol and other substance abuse. See Snyder & Whisman 2003, pp. 159–80

Fals-Stewart W, Klostermann K, Yates BT, O'Farrell TJ, Birchler GR. 2005a. Brief relationship therapy for alcoholism: a randomized clinical trial examining clinical efficacy and cost-effectiveness. *Psychol. Addict. Behav.* In press

Fals-Stewart W, Yates BT, Klostermann K. 2005b. Assessing the costs, benefits, cost-benefit ratio, and cost-effectiveness of marital and family treatments: why we should and how we can. *J. Fam. Psychol.* 19:28–39

Foley SH, Rounsaville BJ, Weissman MM, Sholomaskas D, Chevron E. 1989. Individual versus conjoint interpersonal psychotherapy for depressed patients with marital disputes. *Int. J. Fam. Psychiatry* 10:29–42

Fruzzetti AE, Iverson KM. 2006. Intervening with couples and families to treat emotion dysregulation and psychopathology. See Snyder et al. 2006. In press

Goldman A, Greenberg L. 1992. Comparison of integrated systemic and emotionally focused approaches to couples therapy. *J. Consult. Clin. Psychol.* 60:962–69

Gordon KC, Baucom DH, Snyder DK. 2004. An integrative intervention for promoting recovery from extramarital affairs. *J. Marital Fam. Ther.* 30:213–31

Gottman JM. 1998. Psychology and the study of marital processes. *Annu. Rev. Psychol.* 49: 169–97

Gottman JM. 1999. *The Marriage Clinic: A Scientifically Based Marital Therapy*. New York: Norton. 456 pp.

Gray-Little B, Baucom DH, Hamby SL. 1996. Marital power, marital adjustment and therapy outcome. *J. Fam. Psychol.* 10:292–303

Greenberg LS, Ford CL, Alden L, Johnson SM. 1993. In-session change in emotionally focused therapy. *J. Consult. Clin. Psychol.* 61: 78–84

Gupta M, Coyne JC, Beach SRH. 2003. Couples treatment for major depression: critique of the literature and suggestions for some different directions. *J. Fam. Ther.* 25:317–46

Gurman AS. 1981. Integrative marital therapy: toward the development of an interpersonal approach. In *Forms of Brief Therapy*, ed. SH Budman, pp. 415–57. New York: Guilford. 482 pp.

Gurman AS. 2002. Brief integrative marital therapy: a depth-behavioral approach. In *Clinical Handbook of Couple Therapy*, ed. AS Gurman, NS Jacobson, pp. 180–220. New York: Guilford. 731 pp. 3rd ed.

Hahlweg K, Jacobson NS, ed. 1984. *Marital Interaction: Analysis and Modification*. New York: Guilford. 450 pp.

Hahlweg K, Markman HJ. 1988. Effectiveness of behavioral marital therapy: empirical status of behavioral techniques in preventing and alleviating marital distress. *J. Consult. Clin. Psychol.* 56:440–47

Hahlweg K, Schindler L, Revenstorf D, Brengelmann JC. 1984. The Munich marital therapy study. See Hahlweg & Jacobson 1984, pp. 3–26

Heatherington L, Friedlander ML, Greenberg L. 2005. Change process research in couple and family therapy: methodological challenges and opportunities. *J. Fam. Psychol.* 19:18–27

Hollon SD, Najavits L. 1988. Review of empirical studies on cognitive therapy. In *American Psychiatric Press Review of Psychiatry*, ed. AJ Frances, RE Hales, 7:643–66. Washington, DC: Am. Psychiatr. Press. 720 pp.

Holtzworth-Munroe A, Marshall AD, Meehan JC, Rehman U. 2003. Physical aggression. See Snyder & Whisman 2003, pp. 201–30

Hurlbert DF, White LC, Powell RD, Apt C. 1993. Orgasm consistency training in the treatment of women reporting hypoactive sexual desire: an outcome comparison of women-only groups and couples-only groups. *J. Behav. Ther. Exp. Psychiatry.* 24: 3–13

Jacobson NS, Christensen A. 1996. *Integrative Couple Therapy: Promoting Acceptance and Change.* New York: Norton. 283 pp.

Jacobson NS, Follette WC, Pagel M. 1986. Predicting who will benefit from behavioral marital therapy. *J. Consult. Clin. Psychol.* 54: 518–22

Jacobson NS, Schmaling KB, Holtzworth-Munroe A. 1987. Component analysis of behavioral marital therapy: 2-year follow-up and prediction of relapse. *J. Marital Fam. Ther.* 13:187–95

Johnson SM. 2002. Marital problems. See Sprenkle 2002b, pp. 163–90

Johnson SM, Greenberg LS. 1988. Relating process to outcome in marital therapy. *J. Marital Fam. Ther.* 14:175–83

Johnson SM, Hunsley J, Greenberg L, Schindler D. 1999. Emotionally focused couples therapy: status and challenges. *Clin. Psychol. Sci. Pract.* 6:67–79

Johnson SM, Talitman E. 1997. Predictors of success in emotionally focused marital therapy. *J. Marital Fam. Ther.* 23:135–52

Keefe FJ, Ahles TA, Sutton L, Dalton J, Baucom DH, et al. 2005. Partner-guided cancer pain management at end of life: a preliminary study. *J. Pain Symptom Manage.* 29:263–72

Keefe FJ, Caldwell DS, Baucom DH, Salley A, Robinson E, et al. 1996. Spouse-assisted coping skills training in the management of osteoarthritis knee pain. *Arthritis Care Res.* 9:279–91

Keefe FJ, Porter LS, Labban J. 2006. Emotion regulation processes in disease-related pain: a couples-based perspective. See Snyder et al. 2006. In press

Kessler RC, McGonagle KA, Zhao S, Nelson CB, Hughes M, et al. 1994. Lifetime and 12-month prevalence of DSM-III-R psychiatric disorders in the United States: results from the National Comorbidity Survey. *Arch. Gen. Psychiatry* 51:8–19

Kiecolt-Glaser JK, Newton TL. 2001. Marriage and health: his and hers. *Psychol. Bull.* 127:472–503

Kirby JS, Baucom DH. 2004. *Treating Emotional Dysregulation in a Couples Context: A Pilot Study of a Couples Skills Group Intervention.* Presented at Assoc. Adv. Behav. Ther., New Orleans, LA

Kreider RM, Fields JM. 2002. Number, timing, and duration of marriages and divorces: 1996. *Current Pop. Rep. P70–80.* Washington, DC: US Census Bur.

Laumann EO, Paik A, Rosen RC. 1999. Sexual dysfunction in the United States: prevalence and predictors. *J. Am. Med. Assoc.* 281:537–44

Lebow JL. 2000. What does the research tell us about couple and family therapies? *J. Clin. Psychol.* 56:1083–94

Lebow JL, Gurman AS. 1995. Research assessing couple and family therapy. *Annu. Rev. Psychol.* 46:27–57

Leff J, Vearnals S, Brewin CR, Wolff G, Alexander B, et al. 2000. The London Depression Intervention Trial: randomised controlled trial of antidepressants v. couple therapy in the treatment and maintenance of people with depression living with a partner: clinical outcome and costs. *Br. J. Psychiatry* 177:95–100

Lillis EA, Fruzzetti AE. 2004. *DBT for Couples: A Brief Intervention for the Treatment of Couple and Individual Distress.* Presented at Assoc. Adv. Behav. Ther., New Orleans, LA

Lin E, Goering P, Offord DR, Campbell D, Boyle MH. 1996. The use of mental health services in Ontario: epidemiologic findings. *Can. J. Psychiatry* 41:572–77

Mohr DC, Moran PJ, Kohn C, Hart S, Armstrong K, et al. 2003. Couple therapy at the end of life. *Psychooncology* 12:620–27

Monson CM, Stevens SP, Schnur PP. 2004. Cognitive-behavioral couple's treatment for posttraumatic stress disorder. In *Focus on Posttraumatic Stress Disorder Research*, ed. TA Corales. pp. 251–80. Hauppauge, NY: Nova Sci. 290 pp.

Murphy CM, O'Leary KD. 1989. Psychological aggression predicts physical aggression in early marriage. *J. Consult. Clin. Psychol.* 57:579–82

O'Farrell TJ, Fals-Stewart W. 2000. Behavioral couples therapy for alcoholism and drug abuse. *J. Subst. Abuse Treat.* 18:51–54

O'Leary KD, Turkewitz H. 1981. A comparative outcome study of behavioral marital therapy and communication therapy. *J. Marital Fam. Ther.* 7:159–69

Osterman GP, Sher TG, Hales G, Canar WJ, Singla R, et al. 2003. Physical illness. See Snyder & Whisman 2003, pp. 350–69

Pearce JW, LeBow MD, Orchard J. 1981. Role of spouse involvement in the behavioral treatment of overweight women. *J. Consult. Clin. Psychol.* 49:236–44

Raudenbush SW, Bryk AS. 2001. *Hierarchical Linear Models: Applications and Data Analysis Methods.* Newbury Park, CA: Sage. 485 pp. 2nd ed.

Regev LG, O'Donohue W, Avina C. 2003. Sexual dysfunction. See Snyder & Whisman 2003, pp. 181–200

Rice LN, Greenberg LS. 1984. *Patterns of Change: Intensive Analysis of Psychotherapy Process.* New York: Guilford. 308 pp.

Rogosa D. 1991. A longitudinal approach to ATI research: models for individual growth and models for individual differences in response to intervention. In *Improving Inquiry in Social Science: A Volume in Honor of Lee J. Cronbach*, ed. RE Snow, DE Wiley, pp. 221–48. Hillsdale, NJ: Erlbaum. 423 pp.

Schmaling KB, Sher TG, ed. 2000. *The Psychology of Couples and Illness: Theory, Research, and Practice.* Washington, DC: Am. Psychol. Assoc. 407 pp.

Sexton TL, Ridley CR, Kleiner AJ. 2004. Beyond common factors: multilevel-process models of therapeutic change in marriage and family therapy. *J. Marital Fam. Ther.* 30:131–49

Shadish WR, Baldwin SA. 2003. Meta-analysis of MFT interventions. *J. Marital Fam. Ther.* 29:547–70

Shadish WR, Baldwin SA. 2005. Effects of behavioral marital therapy: a meta-analysis of randomized controlled trials. *J. Consult. Clin. Psychol.* 73:6–14

Shadish WR, Montgomery LM, Wilson P, Wilson MR, Bright I, et al. 1993. Effects of family and marital psychotherapies: a meta-analysis. *J. Consult. Clin. Psychol.* 61:992–1002

Sher TG, Bellg AJ, Braun L, Domas A, Rosenson R, et al. 2002. Partners for life: a theoretical approach to developing an intervention for cardiac risk reduction. *Health Educ. Res.* 17:597–605

Shumway ST, Wampler RS, Dersch C, Arredondo R. 2004. A place for marriage and family services in employee assistance programs (EAPs): a survey of EAP client problems and needs. *J. Marital Fam. Ther.* 30:71–79

Snyder DK. 1997. *Manual for the Marital Satisfaction Inventory—Revised.* Los Angeles: West. Psychol. Serv. 126 pp.

Snyder DK. 1999. Affective reconstruction in the context of a pluralistic approach to couples therapy. *Clin. Psychol. Sci. Pract.* 6:348–65

Snyder DK, Mangrum LF, Wills RM. 1993. Predicting couples' response to marital therapy: a comparison of short- and long-term predictors. *J. Consult. Clin. Psychol.* 61:61–69

Snyder DK, Schneider WJ, Castellani AM. 2003. Tailoring couple therapy to individual differences: a conceptual approach. See Snyder & Whisman 2003, pp. 27–51

Snyder DK, Simpson JA, Hughes JN, eds. 2006. *Emotion Regulation in Families: Pathways to Dysfunction and Health.* Washington, DC: Am. Psychol. Assoc. In press

Snyder DK, Whisman MA, eds. 2003. *Treating Difficult Couples: Helping Clients with Coexisting Mental and Relationship Disorders.* New York: Guilford. 448 pp.

Snyder DK, Whisman MA. 2004a. *Comorbid Relationship and Individual Distress: Challenges for Intervention and Research.* Presented at Assoc. Adv. Behav. Ther., New Orleans, LA

Snyder DK, Whisman MA. 2004b. Treating distressed couples with coexisting mental and physical disorders: directions for clinical training and practice. *J. Marital Fam. Ther.* 30:1–12

Snyder DK, Wills RM. 1989. Behavioral versus insight-oriented marital therapy: effects on individual and interspousal functioning. *J. Consult. Clin. Psychol.* 57:39–46

Snyder DK, Wills RM, Faitler SL. 1988. Distinguishing specific from nonspecific interventions in comparative outcome studies: reply to Collins and Thompson. *J. Consult. Clin. Psychol.* 56:934–35

Snyder DK, Wills RM, Grady-Fletcher A. 1991. Long-term effectiveness of behavioral versus insight-oriented marital therapy: a four-year follow-up study. *J. Consult. Clin. Psychol.* 59:138–41

Sprenkle DH. 2002a. Editor's introduction. See Sprenkle 2002b, pp. 9–25

Sprenkle DH, ed. 2002b. *Effectiveness Research in Marriage and Family Therapy.* Alexandria VA: Am. Assoc. Marriage Fam. Ther. 370 pp.

Sprenkle DH, Blow AJ. 2004. Common factors and our sacred models. *J. Marital Fam. Ther.* 30:113–29

Stith SM, Rosen KH, McCollum EE, Thomsen CJ. 2004. Treating intimate partner violence within intact couple relationships: outcomes of multi-couple versus individual couple therapy. *J. Marital Fam. Ther.* 30:305–18

Swindle R, Heller K, Pescosolido B, Kikuzawa S. 2000. Responses to nervous breakdowns in America over a 40-year period: mental health policy implications. *Am. Psychol.* 55:740–49

Whisman MA. 1999. Marital dissatisfaction and psychiatric disorders: results from the National Comorbidity Survey. *J. Abnorm. Psychol.* 108:701–6

Whisman MA, Dixon AE, Johnson B. 1997. Therapists' perspectives of couple problems and treatment issues in couple therapy. *J. Fam. Psychol.* 11:361–66

Whisman MA, Jacobson NS. 1990. Power, marital satisfaction, and response to marital therapy. *J. Fam. Psychol.* 4:202–12

Whisman MA, McClelland GH. 2005. Designing, testing, and interpreting interactions and moderator effects in family research. *J. Fam. Psychol.* 19:111–20

Whisman MA, McKelvie ML, Chatav Y. 2005. Couple distress. In *Improving Outcomes and Preventing Relapse in Cognitive Behavioral Therapy,* ed. MM Anthony, DR Ledley, RG Heimberg. New York: Guilford. In press

Whisman MA, Sheldon CT, Goering P. 2000. Psychiatric disorders and dissatisfaction with social relationships: Does type of relationship matter? *J. Abnorm. Psychol.* 109:803–8

Whisman MA, Snyder DK. 1997. Evaluating and improving the efficacy of conjoint couple therapy. In *Clinical Handbook of Marriage and Couples Interventions,* ed. WK Halford, HJ Markman, pp. 679–93. New York: Wiley. 720 pp.

Whisman MA, Uebelacker LA. 2005. Distress and impairment associated with relationship discord in a national sample of married or cohabiting adults. *J. Fam. Psychol.* In press

Wiederman MW. 1997. Extramarital sex: prevalence and correlates in a national survey. *J. Sex Res.* 34:167–74

Wilson GL. 1986. The comparative efficacy of alternative treatments in the resolution of marital dysfunction. PhD thesis. Univ. Montana. 108 pp.

Annu. Rev. Psychol. 2006. 57:345–74
doi: 10.1146/annurev.psych.57.102904.190034
Copyright © 2006 by Annual Reviews. All rights reserved
First published online as a Review in Advance on August 23, 2005

ATTITUDES AND PERSUASION

William D. Crano

Department of Psychology, Claremont Graduate University, Claremont,
California 91711; email: William.crano@cgu.edu

Radmila Prislin

Department of Psychology, San Diego State University, San Diego, California 92182;
email: rprislin@sunstroke.sdsu.edu

Key Words   attitude formation, attitude change, majority and minority influence, attitude strength, affect, attitude-behavior consistency

■ **Abstract**   Study of attitudes and persuasion remains a defining characteristic of contemporary social psychology. This review outlines recent advances, with emphasis on the relevance of today's work for perennial issues. We reiterate the distinction between attitude formation and change, and show its relevance for persuasion. Single- and dual-process models are discussed, as are current views on dissonance theory. Majority and minority influence are scrutinized, with special emphasis on integrative theoretical innovations. Attitude strength is considered, and its relevance to ambivalence and resistance documented. Affect, mood, and emotion effects are reviewed, especially as they pertain to fear arousal and (un)certainty. Finally, we discuss attitude-behavior consistency, perhaps the reason for our interest in attitudes in the first place, with emphasis on self-interest and the theory of planned behavior. Our review reflects the dynamism and the reach of the area, and suggests a sure and sometimes rapid accumulation of knowledge and understanding.

CONTENTS

INTRODUCTION

The study of attitudes and persuasion remains a vital feature of contemporary social psychology. Allport's (1935, p. 784) dictum that attitudes are our "most distinctive and indispensable concept" remains as true today as it was 70 years ago. It also is true that recent advances have incited even more activity than usual in this dynamic realm. Technological developments, including a growing appreciation for computer-mediated persuasion (McKenna & Bargh 2000, Postmes et al. 2001, Sassenberg & Boos 2003) and the use of virtual reality as a medium for study (Blascovich et al. 2002), have added heat to an already boiling pot.

Recent reviews (Ajzen 2001, Albarracín et al. 2005, Haddock & Zanna 1999, Olson & Maio 2003, Perloff 2003, Wood 2000) provide useful snapshots of the field, and distinctive subareas have attracted considerable attention. These subareas include the study of attitude functions (Maio & Olson 2000), attribute importance (van der Pligt et al. 2000), group norms (Terry & Hogg 2000), consensus and social influence (Prislin & Wood 2005), attitude representations (Lord & Lepper 1999), dual-process theories (Chaiken & Trope 1999), applied social influence (Butera & Mugny 2001b), media and persuasion (Bryant & Zillman 2002, Crano & Burgoon 2002), measurement and interpretation of implicit attitudes (Bassili & Brown 2005, Fazio & Olson 2003, Greenwald et al. 2002, Greenwald & Nosek 2001), and a long-overdue reconsideration of resistance (Knowles & Linn 2004). Special pleasures are provided readers of the proceedings of a Festschrift (Jost et al. 2004) held in honor of William J. McGuire (1966, 1969, 1985), author of arguably the finest reviews of attitudes and opinions to have graced the social psychological literature, and a retrospective of some of Robert B. Zajonc's studies, noteworthy both for their wondrous creativity and their impact (Bargh & Apsley 2001). With his Sydney symposium, Forgas and colleagues continue to contribute to our understanding of attitudes and related constructs (Forgas & Williams 2000, Forgas et al. 2003).

In this review, we focus primarily on the literature published between 1999 and 2004. We opt for these boundaries to complement and update related reviews by Ajzen (2001), who covered the period up to 1999, by Fazio & Olson (2003), who were concerned with the use of implicit measures in social cognition, and by Wood (2000), whose focus was the interface between social influence and persuasion, with a strong emphasis on minority influence. Our focus, which is somewhat at variance with these earlier offerings, is on attitude formation; evaluative conditioning and mere exposure; attitude change; majority and minority influence; attitude strength; affect, mood, and emotion; and attitude-behavior consistency. Given the evident intensity of research, it is impossible even to note all of the important work in this area. We instead offer an integrative analysis that calls attention to emergent approaches to issues of long-standing concern.

ATTITUDE FORMATION

A prime factor that must be considered when reflecting on persuasion concerns the fundamental construct of attitude. Defining attitude has been ongoing at least since Thurstone's (1928) time. Today, most accept the view that an attitude represents an evaluative integration of cognitions and affects experienced in relation to an object. Attitudes are the evaluative judgments that integrate and summarize these cognitive/affective reactions. These evaluative abstractions vary in strength, which in turn has implications for persistence, resistance, and attitude-behavior consistency (Holland et al. 2002a, Petty et al. 2004).

EVALUATIVE CONDITIONING AND MERE EXPOSURE

Although sometimes confused, processes of attitude formation and change are not identical, nor are their outcomes. Attitude formation can occur in many ways, the principal distinction among them being the extent to which individuals consciously embrace or reject an attitude object. At the less aware end of the spectrum are the conditioning models. Olson & Fazio's (2001, 2002) implicit learning paradigm proposes that preferences can be learned below conscious awareness. Considerable research has backed this position (Hammerl 2000, Walther & Trasselli 2003; but see Field 2000, Priluck & Till 2004). Walther (2002) showed that the association of a valenced and a nonvalenced attitude object affects the evaluation of the latter, and this effect spreads to targets related to the initially nonvalenced object. Evaluative conditioning of this type is not dependent on strong temporal reinforcement contingencies, and so is unlikely to trigger awareness. Walther's spreading attitude effect suggests that evaluative conditioning is more than acquiescence to experimental demand (De Houwer et al. 2001, Dijksterhuis 2004).

Mere exposure to a stimulus also can influence attitude formation at below-conscious levels (Bargh 2001, Lee 2001), possibly because exposure frequency is experienced as affectively positive (Winkielman & Cacioppo 2004). It must be emphasized that mere exposure and conditioning are concerned with attitude formation, not change. Indeed, considerable evidence indicates that these "below conscious awareness" processes are unlikely to produce change (Cacioppo et al. 1992, Courbet 2003, Till & Priluck 2000, Walther 2002). This observation suggests that social marketing campaigns that associate positive role models with desirable behaviors (e.g., avoiding drugs or alcohol) might prove useful for those who hold neutral to positive initial attitudes toward the recommended actions, but they are unlikely to move the sinners to the inside of the church.

ATTITUDE CHANGE

Single- and Dual-Process Models

Factors that do affect attitude change have been a staple of social psychology from its earliest days. The standard models of change, which continue to garner considerable attention, take a number of different forms, but their basic understandings of the cause-effect patterns of attitude change are limited. In the classical models, messages are presented, processed, and if successful, move recipients' attitudes toward the advocated position. The revised attitude, in turn, may influence subsequent behavior under appropriate conditions. The elaboration likelihood model (ELM) and the heuristic/systematic model (HSM) are exemplars of dual-process models that embody this general process of message reception, attitude change, (and perhaps) behavior change (Chen & Chaiken 1999, Petty & Wegener 1999, Wegener & Carlston 2005). Dual-process models hold that if receivers are able and properly motivated, they will elaborate, or systematically analyze, persuasive messages. If the message is well reasoned, data based, and logical (i.e., strong), it will persuade; if it is not, it will fail. Auxiliary features of the context will have little influence on these outcomes. However, if message targets are unmotivated (or unable) to process a message, they will use auxiliary features, called "peripheral cues" (e.g., an attractive source), or heuristics (e.g., "Dad's usually right") to short-circuit the more effortful elaboration process in forming an attitudinal response. Such attitudes are less resistant to counterpressures, less stable, and less likely to impel behavior than are those formed as a result of thorough processing.

Without question, the dual-process models remain today's most influential persuasion paradigms, as they have been since their inception. In these models, source and message may play distinct roles that, in concert with motivation and ability to process information, determine the outcomes of persuasive interactions. Kruglanski and colleagues (Kruglanski & Thompson 1999a,b; Thompson et al. 2000) have challenged the dual-process view in their unimodel, which accepts the importance of motivation and ability in persuasion, but describes a single cognitive process that accounts for the effects of source and message in persuasion.

This position provoked a fascinating exchange of views in *Psychological Inquiry* [1999, Vol. 10(2)].

The cognition in persuasion model (Albarracín 2002, Albarracín & Wyer 2001) also takes a single-process perspective, but postulates a series of processing stages that occur in response to persuasive messages. The cognition in persuasion model has not amassed the comprehensive database of the dual-process models, but its interesting treatment of distraction, mood, and initial attitude variations suggests it may supply useful insights into fundamental persuasion processes.

Source

The bustle of research focused on persuasion processes has refocused attention on many unresolved issues. Nearly 20 years have passed since the initial ELM publications, but attempts still are underway to specify a theory-based model of message strength (Areni 2003, Hosman et al. 2002). Another old chestnut, the sleeper effect, also has come under renewed scrutiny. Consistent with ELM/HSM-based expectations, discounting before or after a message is elaborated, as a consequence of source status or other instructional manipulations, moderates the sleeper effect (Kumkale & Albarracín 2004).

Source effects also have received considerable attention over the past two decades in minority influence research, the study of the ways in which a minority faction can persuade the majority to accept its (counterattitudinal) position. Majority sources typically produce immediate change related to the focus of their persuasive messages. Such change, however, often is transitory. Minority sources, on the other hand, often produce change on issues related to, but not identical to, the topic of their persuasive message (indirect change). When minorities do effect focal change, it usually occurs after a temporal delay (Crano 2001b). Minority influence findings pose problems for dual-process theories, as source status ordinarily is considered a peripheral (heuristic) cue, and thus long-term changes in response to minority sources are theoretically incomprehensible. Attempts at integrating these anomalous findings (Crano 2000, 2001b) have drawn on social identity theory to illustrate how apparently peripheral cues can motivate systematic processing.

Message

Message effects have come under increased scrutiny owing to recent research on the unimodel. Kruglanski and colleagues have proposed that a need for closure might result in primacy effects in persuasion (Pierro et al. 2004), as might the cognitive load of the persuasion context (Kruglanski & Stroebe 2005). In addition, the unexpectedness of a source/message pairing has been found to amplify a message's persuasive muscle (Erb et al. 2002). Apparently, source/message inconsistencies increase message scrutiny, resulting in greater effects—assuming high message quality (Petty et al. 2001b).

Dissonance

An alternative to the "attitudes cause behavior" paradigm posits that attitudes may be a consequence as well as a cause of behavior. One of the most long-lived expressions of this approach is dissonance theory, advanced by Festinger (1957), who undoubtedly would be astonished to find controversy still attending his classic study with Carlsmith (Festinger & Carlsmith 1959, Harmon-Jones 2000b), and active research on free choice (Kitayama et al. 2004), postdecision regret (Brownstein et al. 2004), and even selective exposure to (in)consistent data (Jonas et al. 2001). Joule & Azdia (2003) have supported their "radical model," which argues for a return to the original version of dissonance theory, and rejects the many alternatives that have developed over the years (also see Beauvois & Joule 1999). Harmon-Jones et al.'s (2003) action-oriented model, which posits that cognitive discrepancies generate dissonance because they interfere with efficient belief-consistent actions, also is compatible with the fundamental premises of dissonance, as is recent research that demonstrates vicarious dissonance arousal (Monin et al. 2004, Norton et al. 2003). In a useful integration, Stone & Cooper's (2001, 2003) self-standards model posits that inconsistent dissonance results might be attributed to dissimilar standards people had set for themselves, and the consequences of variations in self-esteem for discrepancies between these standards and actions (Cesario et al. 2004, Olson & Stone 2005). Discrepancies could cause disparities in dissonance arousal as a consequence of varying self-standards.

Matz & Wood (2005) showed that disagreement with group members mediates the effects of dissonance arousal mechanisms, and McKimmie et al. (2003) suggest that group support attenuates dissonance, consistent with social identity–based expectations. Spillover from research on implicit attitude measures (Fazio & Olson 2003) is evident in Gawronski & Strack's (2004) finding that a standard dissonance manipulation affected explicitly measured, but not implicitly measured, attitudes. Their explicit measure produced clear dissonance effects, but their implicit measure did not. The authors suggest that dissonance will occur on judgments that involve explicit propositional syllogistic reasoning, but not on affective, association-based (implicit) beliefs. This analysis suggests a dual-process approach in which associative versus propositional processes respond differently to persuasion pressures.

MINORITY AND MAJORITY INFLUENCE

Attitude change induced by a minority source represents a special case in persuasion. Minority influence researchers focus on intraindividual processes that are activated in response to opinion-based minority advocacy. These processes include cognitive reactions or thoughts recipients generate to minority appeals (Wood 2000). A hallmark of the prevailing information-processing approach is the examination of cognitive responses, either in their own right or as mediators of change. Responses generated to minority and majority advocacy are compared, and social conditions, usually represented by group membership, are treated as part of the information to be processed (El-Alayli et al. 2002, Prislin & Wood 2005).

Social Consensus

An emerging focus in the information-processing approach concerns the role of social consensus (Erb & Bohner 2001). Because level of consensus is the defining feature of majority and minority status, it presumably is crucial to understanding social influence. Some hold that mere consensus has evaluative implications, i.e., positions are valued proportional to the level of support they receive. These valenced inferences bias the processing of attitude-relevant information, which in turn determines ultimately the positions that are adopted. In a test of this idea, Erb & Bohner (2001) documented that consensus did bias information processing; it did not operate merely as a peripheral cue that fostered heuristic adoption of a position (Martin et al. 2002). This view resonates with Mackie's (1987) objective consensus approach to social influence, which postulates systematic processing of consensually advocated positions because of their presumed validity, greater likelihood of adoption, and positive identity implications. Disagreements with consensually advocated positions violate expectations, and thus motivate systematic processing to facilitate understanding. The important role of consensus also was recognized in a recently proposed attributional model of persuasion (Ziegler et al. 2004), which posits that minority and majority messages, which reflect different levels of consensus, are elaborated under different conditions. Ziegler et al. showed that a nonconsensual (minority) message was elaborated when it was consistently advocated and highly distinctive; a consensual (majority) message was elaborated when it was inconsistently advocated and not distinctive.

Minority Effects on Attitude Formation/Change

It appears that incongruence with consensus-implied expectations activates message processing to the extent that consistent advocacy of a nonconsensual (minority) position, and inconsistent advocacy of a consensual (majority) position, violates expectations. This proposition seems most likely in contexts involving attitude formation (versus attitude change). The formation versus change distinction has received increased attention in minority influence research (Crano 2001a, Crano & Alvaro 1998, Crano & Hannula-Bral 1994) and may prove useful in disentangling earlier inconsistencies.

Further evidence that degree of attitude formation may moderate processing was supplied by Erb et al. (2002), who found greater elaboration of minority (versus majority) messages when they challenged well-formed attitudes, but more elaboration of majority messages when they targeted ill-formed attitudes. This line of research is consistent with Moscovici's (1980) proposition that conflict is a necessary precondition for minority-induced attitude change, although the change may be indirect or delayed. Normative support based on majority consensus, conversely, which is championed by the mere (and objective) consensus approaches, may function more powerfully in attitude formation contexts. A variable that might interact with the attitude formation/change distinction concerns the perceived subjective or objective nature of the issue or decision under investigation. Models of minority and majority influence that deal comprehensively with attitude formation or change, the objective or subjective nature of the issue, focal versus indirect attitude change, and the transitory or persistent nature of this change are not common, but their development is a hopeful sign of progress (Butera & Mugny 2001a, Crano & Alvaro 1998, Crano & Hannula-Bral 1994, Gordijn et al. 2002).

Cognitive Responses

Cognitive responses to minority and majority influence need not be limited to message processing and resultant attitudinal reactions. The scope and quality of thought also may affect problem solving. Supporting Nemeth's (1995) model of convergent-divergent thought, De Dreu & West (2001) found that minority dissent stimulated innovation in organizational teams by inspiring critical, divergent problem analyses. Active discussion and participatory decision making encouraged minority dissent and processing of the minority's message (De Dreu 2001). Added benefits of minority dissent included improved integrative complexity (Antonio et al. 2004), an enlarged range of unshared information considered by group members, and superior problem solving (Brodbeck et al. 2002, Choi & Levine 2004). Authentic minority dissent proved more efficient than simulated ("devil's advocate") minority dissent in generating superior thought processes (Nemeth et al. 2001). In an extension of this orientation, De Dreu et al. (1999) demonstrated that minority-induced indirect attitude change was caused by divergent thought, whereas majority-induced focal change was caused by convergent thought. The causal link was established by independent manipulations of consensual support and processing mode.

Leniency

Arguing that consensual support derives its meaning from group membership, a thriving line of research highlights the link between size of support for attitudinal positions and social identification (Crano 2000, David & Turner 1999, Falomir et al. 2000, Gordijn et al. 2001, Mackie & Hunter 1999, Phillips 2003). Integrating insights of social identification and the information-processing approaches, Crano's (2001b) leniency contract postulates that in-group minorities exert influence because of the lenient, open-minded evaluation afforded members of the same social category. The counterattitudinal nature of minority advocacy precludes its direct acceptance by the majority. Although not directly accepted, minority advocacy is nevertheless elaborated by the majority as they attempt to understand the unexpected position held by their in-group members. Shared in-group membership allows for relatively open-minded elaboration, which ultimately creates pressure for change on related attitudes. If sufficiently great, such change puts pressure on the focal issue, which consequently is modified to restore cognitive consistency. Empirical tests have supported the model and documented that changes on related attitudes persist long enough to trigger changes on the focal issues to reestablish balance within the attitudinal system (Crano & Chen 1998). Together with findings that attitudes changed in response to minority advocacy are resistant to subsequent persuasive attacks (Martin et al. 2003), these results suggest that minority-inspired attitudes may be especially strong.

Shared group membership may affect reactions to social influence not only through motivated reasoning about in-group (minority) members but also through social cognition processes (Mackie & Hunter 1999). In-group status may contribute to an individuated representation of minority arguments, whereby each minority member is perceived as an independent information source. Perceived independence of judgment, considered a prerequisite for the validity of advocacy (Asch 1952), may enhance the persuasive power of in-group minorities. These minorities may capitalize on the effects of individuated representation of arguments by employing communication strategies that emphasize an active (Kerr 2002), consistent advocacy (Myers et al. 2000), while appealing to a shared superordinate belief system within the group (Smith et al. 2000).

Dynamics

The dynamic nature of social influence is evident not only in cognitive adjustments within an individual but also in structural adjustments within a group (Latané & Bourgeois 2001; Prislin et al. 2000, 2002; Vallacher et al. 2002b). According to Prislin and colleagues' dynamic gain-loss asymmetry model of change in minority and majority positions, movement from valued majority to devalued minority is experienced as loss; the opposite movement is experienced as gain. These movements have implications for influence because losses generally are experienced more intensely than gains. Empirical support for this postulated asymmetry was obtained in a series of studies that documented new minorities' dramatically negative reactions toward their groups, which were not offset by new majorities' mildly positive reactions toward theirs (Prislin et al. 2000, 2002). In the attitudinal domain, new minorities tended to agree with the newly emerging consensus (Prislin et al. 2000) and to interpret attitudinal differences among group members as diversity rather than deviance (Prislin et al. 2002). In contrast, new majorities strengthen their attitudes by enhancing attitudinal importance, broadening the latitudes of positions they find unacceptable, and expressing less tolerance of opposing views. These complementary attitudinal and group-reaction results suggest that the likely response of new majorities to new minorities is hostility or antagonism.

Dynamic changes in minority size also can affect influence, as expanding minorities become more influential as they gain converts (Clark 1999, 2001). Empirical investigations of the processes underlying this effect reveal that the increased power of expanding minorities stems from targets' increased elaboration of their appeals, as they try to understand what drew others to the minority. Interestingly, expanding majorities seem to lose their capacity to influence. Their expansion apparently triggers reactance in targets who struggle to preserve freedom of thought (Gordijn et al. 2002).

Dynamic models of social influence have begun to capture the complexity of influence processes exchanged between real-life minorities and majorities. Pioneering attempts to examine these processes in organizational (De Dreu 2001), political (Levine & Kaarbo 2001, Smith & Diven 2002), cross-cultural (Ng & Van Dyne 2001), self-evaluative (Vallacher et al. 2002a), economic and other settings (Butera & Mugny 2001b) promise to enrich theory and to foster innovative methodological approaches. Particularly relevant theoretically is the issue of the motives that drive influence exchanges between minorities and majorities, and temporal changes in information processing strategies that mediate social influence (Prislin & Wood 2005). These issues likely will mark the next generation of social influence research.

ATTITUDE STRENGTH

Dimensionality

Attitudes changed in response to minority influence generally are stronger than those that evolve in response to majority pressure (Martin et al. 2003). The study of attitude strength suggests why this might be so. Recent research on attitude strength has addressed the issue of latent structure, which involves the interconnectedness of various strength-related features and the processes that underlie their development. Factor-analytic studies documented the multidimensional structure of attitude strength, but findings regarding dimensionality have proved inconsistent (Bassili 1996, Krosnick et al. 1993, Prislin 1996). Recent studies have relied on experimental methods to examine dimensionality by focusing on the antecedents and consequences of various strength-related features. The logic guiding these studies is that to the extent that strength-related features signify the same latent dimension, they should have the same antecedents and produce the same consequences, but should not cause each other (Bizer & Krosnick 2001, Visser et al. 2003). Research based on this reasoning has demonstrated that attitude importance, though related to attitude accessibility and commitment, is a distinct construct. It was differentially affected by various aspects of subjective experience with the attitude object (Bizer & Krosnick 2001, Holland et al. 2003), and had distinct effects on information processing and behavior (Visser et al. 2003).

Processes

Findings about antecedents of strength features led to questions about the processes through which such features develop. Emerging evidence suggests a dual-process mechanism. Supporting this possibility is the finding that attitude certainty may be inferred effortlessly from ease of attitude retrieval (accessibility) (Holland et al. 2003), or through an effortful analytic process of retrieving attitude-pertinent beliefs (Haddock et al. 1999). This latter analytic process also was suggested in the development of attitude accessibility from the elaboration of attitude-relevant information (Priester & Petty 2003). Future research would benefit from a unifying framework for addressing the issues of dimensionality and the development of attitude strength.

A related, emerging, theme concerns the social foundations of attitude strength. Indicating that not only attitudes but also meta-attitudinal characteristics (e.g., strength) are sensitive to social support, research demonstrates that attitudes are judged as more important (Prislin et al. 2000) and are expressed more quickly (Bassili 2003) when they are socially shared. Attitude certainty increases through projections of similarity with in-group and dissimilarity with out-group members (Holtz 2003, 2004). Increased attitude certainty and decreased ambivalence as a consequence of social support render attitudes resistant to persuasion (Visser & Mirabile 2004). Thus, attitude strength originates, at least in part, from the social context in which attitudes are held.

Resistance

Likely growing out of interest in features that make attitudes strong, research on resistance to persuasion is reviving an old and long-dormant interest (McGuire 1964). This revival has created an outburst of efforts to conceptualize resistance and understand its underlying processes (Knowles & Linn 2004). Numerous conceptualizations have been offered, with most defining resistance in terms of the outcome of a persuasive attempt (versus a process or motivation) (Jacks & O'Brian 2004, Quinn & Wood 2004, Tormala & Petty 2002). Resistance to persuasion can originate in cognitive and affective reactions to the appeal (Fuegen & Brehm 2004, Jacks & Devine 2000, Pfau et al. 2001). Negative cognitive and affective reactions can be combined in a number of specific resistance strategies, whose likelihood of use appears to vary with their social desirability. Apparently, socially desirable strategies that attack the appeal are more likely to be used than are those that derogate the appeal's source (Jacks & Cameron 2003). The impact of different strategies in resisting persuasion may vary over time. A rare longitudinal study of resistance revealed a relatively persistent effect of counterarguing over time, but only a delayed impact of strengthening of the existing attitude (Pfau et al. 2004).

Highlighting the role of metacognitive factors (people's perceptions and thoughts about their own cognitive states and processes) in resistance to persuasion, Tormala and collaborators argue that resistance does not necessarily leave initial attitudes intact (Tormala & Petty 2002). Rather, resistance strengthens initial attitudes to the extent that it is perceived as succeeding even in the face of strong messages (Tormala & Petty 2004a) emanating from expert sources (Tormala

& Petty 2004b). When resistance is perceived as effortful, or achieved through creation of mediocre counterarguments, initial attitudes, though preserved, may weaken (Petty et al. 2004). Activation of the resistance process depends on motives created by the persuasive context (Wood & Quinn 2004), thus allowing for interventions that may instigate defensive motivation to resist deceptive and potentially harmful persuasion (Sagarin et al. 2002).

Ambivalence

A related line of research experiencing a renaissance is concerned with attitudinal ambivalence (Conner & Sparks 2002, Jones et al. 2000). The current popularity of the construct first introduced almost four decades ago (Scott 1966) likely reflects its innovative conceptualization of attitudes. Allowing attitudes simultaneously to include both positive and negative evaluations opens the question of the operative (structural) or experiential (phenomenological) status of ambivalence. Newby-Clark et al. (2002) argue that structural coexistence of mutually opposite evaluations generates the experience of ambivalence if the evaluations are simultaneously accessible.

The theoretical value of the ambivalence construct lies in its novel definition of attitudes as two separate dimensions rather than a single bipolar dimension. In the empirical literature, however, ambivalence has been treated mostly as a distinct aspect of attitude strength (Armitage & Conner 2000, Maio et al. 2000a,b, van der Pligt et al. 2000), as is evident in research on the moderating role of ambivalence on information processing, attitude change, and attitude-behavior consistency. Not only is information processing more effortful at high levels of ambivalence (van Harreveld
et al. 2004, van der Pligt et al. 2000), it is qualitatively different (Broemer 2002). The well-documented moderator effects of ambivalence on attitude-behavior consistency (Armitage 2003, Armitage & Conner 2000, Conner et al. 2002, Costarelli & Colloca 2004, Sparks et al. 2004), attitude pliability (Armitage & Conner 2000), and decision making (Hänze 2001) provide additional evidence of strength properties. Higher levels of ambivalence are associated with weaker attitude-behavior relationships, greater attitudinal pliability, and elaboration-oriented versus action-oriented approaches to decision making.

In line with the emerging emphasis on the social foundations of attitudes, there is growing evidence about the importance of social factors in generating and alleviating ambivalence. Priester & Petty (2001), extending research on antecedents of ambivalence from typically examined intrapersonal to interpersonal factors, demonstrated that perceptions of interpersonal attitudinal discrepancy contributed to subjective ambivalence beyond personal influence factors. The experience of ambivalence motivates the search for corrective information, making those with ambivalent attitudes especially susceptible to consensus influence (Hodson et al. 2001).

Ambivalence toward social targets appears especially important because of its role in forming social perceptions (Bell & Esses 2002, Maio et al. 2001) and regulating social relations. At the group level, perhaps the strongest argument for the link between attitudinal ambivalence and social relations has been proposed in the theory of ambivalent sexism (Glick & Fiske 2001, Glick et al. 2004), which posits that simultaneously held hostile and benevolent attitudes toward men and women not only reflect, but support, gender inequality. Feather's (2004) alternative explanation sees the origin of ambivalent attitudes in contradictory values. Uniting these and other approaches to ambivalent attitudes toward social groups is the motivational position, within which ambivalence is understood as a compromise strategy of satisfying opposing social motives (Mucchi-Faina et al. 2002). Elucidating motivational conflicts underlying attitudinal ambivalence remains an important challenge.

AFFECT, MOOD, AND EMOTION

The study of affect or emotion in attitudes continues to generate research on attitude structure, wherein affect is examined as part of the holy affect-cognition-behavior trinity of attitude organization, as well as research on attitude change, where affect is examined as a determinant of the judgmental processes underlying reactions to persuasive messages. Affect as a distinct component of attitude structure is assumed to have primacy in responses to attitude objects (Cervellon & Dubé 2002, Huskinson & Haddock 2004). According to the affective primacy hypothesis, emotional associations to an attitude object are activated more rapidly than are nonemotional (cognitive) associations. However, Giner-Sorolla (2001, 2004) suggests the primacy of affective (over cognitive) reactions only at high levels of extremity, and for affectively based (versus cognitively based) evaluations. Consistent with prevailing dual-process models, Giner-Sorolla (1999) theorizes that the affect associated with an attitude object varies along a continuum ranging from immediate to deliberate. Immediate affect is evident in evaluative bipolar feelings and emotions that are activated rapidly and effortlessly, whereas deliberate affect is evident in discrete, qualitatively different emotions that are activated gradually, over time. This distinction resonates with Ito & Cacioppo's (2001) evaluative space model, which postulates a multiplicity of evaluative mechanisms. The presumed independence of evaluative mechanisms allows for the lower level structures automatically to process attitude objects in terms of affective significance while higher level mechanisms direct attention to other features of the object. Evaluative processing at different levels ultimately may result in dual attitudes whose implicit (automatic, immediate) and explicit (deliberate, delayed) expressions are evaluatively unharmonious.

The distinction between affect and cognition in attitude structure has implications for attitude change. According to the matching hypothesis, persuasive appeals are effective to the extent they match the structural (affective-cognitive) makeup of the targeted attitude (Edwards 1990). Revisiting this hypothesis, Fabrigar & Petty (1999) resolved methodological difficulties of previous research and found that affective persuasion was more effective in changing attitudes based on affect than attitudes derived from cognitions, but the obverse, that cognitive persuasion was more effective in changing attitudes derived from cognitions, was not supported.

Fear

Affect has been examined not only as a distinct component of attitude structure but also as a contextual variable with implications for persuasion (Petty et al. 2001a). The contextual conceptualization is concerned with two types of feelings and emotions: those activated by the persuasive message, and general feelings and emotions unrelated to the persuasive appeal. The former, often operationalized as message-activated fear and studied in persuasive campaigns aimed at health-related attitudes, has produced conflicting results (Petty et al. 2003). Relying on dual-process models of persuasion, Das et al. (2003) examined information processing as well as attitude change in response to fear appeals. They found that fear appeals generated favorable cognitive responses and consequent attitude change if participants felt vulnerable to threat. Thus, vulnerability operated as a motivator that fostered positive evaluation of the arguments in the fear-arousing message and resultant attitude change.

Information and Processing

Associated research has investigated the manner in which affect that is unrelated to a persuasive appeal shapes reactions to the appeal and the processes through which such influence occurs. Conceptualizing extraneous, appeal-unrelated affect as information whose impact is best understood within the dual-process models of persuasion, Albarracín and colleagues (Albarracín 2002, Albarracín & Kumkale 2003, Albarracín & Wyer 2001) found that reliance on affect as information was determined by ability and motivation to process the persuasive appeal. Affect served as information in persuasion at moderate levels of processing, where it was identified as a potential criterion for judgment. At low levels of processing, affect was not identified, and at high processing levels, it was recognized as irrelevant for judgments about persuasive appeals. Thus, ability and motivation to process have a curvilinear impact on the influence of extraneous, appeal-unrelated affect (Albarracín & Kumkale 2003).

Attempts to understand how affect influences processing have focused on the disparate effects of valenced affective states on elaboration. Previous research strongly suggested supremacy of negative states in promoting argument elaboration. Recent research paints a more complex picture. Bohner & Weinerth (2001) observed the facilitative effects of negative affect on processing only when the persuasive appeal was considered legitimate. Negative affect triggered by a legitimate appeal presumably signaled potential threat and motivated careful scrutiny. In contrast, negative affect associated with an appeal judged illegitimate was interpreted as a reaction to the illegitimacy, which lowered motivation for careful message scrutiny.

In a demonstration of the opposite effect, Raghunatan & Trope (2002) showed that positive mood may serve as a resource when processing self-relevant appeals. According to the mood-as-resource hypothesis, positive moods serve as buffers, enabling a person to process potentially threatening but useful information about self-relevant issues. Supporting the hypothesis, the authors found that under conditions of high self-relevance, positive mood fostered careful scrutiny of negative information, which in turn led to attitude change. In contrast, under the conditions of low self-relevance, negative mood, which apparently served as information, led to more elaborate processing.

Certainty and Carryover

In addition to hedonic tone, affective states are characterized by a number of features stemming from the appraisal process. Much like meta-attitudinal characteristics of attitude strength (Bassili 1996), these meta-cognitive characteristics of affective states represent impressions of one's feelings and emotions (control, responsibility, certainty). Of these, the certainty associated with an emotion appears especially consequential for processing persuasive appeals. Tiedens & Linton (2001), drawing on previously documented congruency along appraisal dimensions between incidental emotional states and subsequent judgments (Lerner & Keltner 2000), reasoned that certainty associated with an emotion could spill over to subsequent judgments and ultimately determine processing intensity. In support, they found that both positive and negative emotions characterized by certainty fostered heuristic processing, whereas positive and negative emotions characterized by uncertainty promoted systematic processing. Moreover, the same emotion had different effects on processing, fostering elaboration when associated with uncertainty, but attenuating processing when associated with certainty. Thus, certainty associated with an emotion carries over to determine certainty about subsequent persuasive situations and resultant processing.

The carryover effect of emotional states is evident in research on emotion-induced biases in likelihood estimates (DeSteno et al. 2002). Using emotional states as information, people arrive at biased estimates of the likelihood of events, over-estimating emotion-congruent events and underestimating emotion-incongruent ones (DeSteno et al. 2000). These emotion-induced biases in likelihood estimates imply that the persuasive impact of messages may depend on the match between emotions and the emotional framing of messages. In support of this hypothesis, DeSteno et al. (2004) found that participants reacted favorably to persuasive appeals to the extent that the emotional consequences mentioned in the appeal matched the emotions they experienced while receiving the appeal.

Contemporary research demonstrates that there is more to the affect-persuasion relationship than the mere valence of emotional states. Specific emotional states and their associated appraisal-related characteristics determine reactions to persuasive appeals through a matching process, which appears to be highly specific. In this process, emotional states function as signals that inform targets of persuasive appeals about their environments. The biasing effect of emotional states, however, has been demonstrated under a restricted range of conditions. Moreover, it is reasonable to assume a multiplicity of mechanisms responsible for emotional states' effects. Future research should establish the boundary conditions of such effects and identify the mechanisms implicated in their operation.

ATTITUDE-BEHAVIOR CONSISTENCY

Because attitudes predict behavior, they are considered the crown jewel of social psychology. Sparked by LaPierre's (1934) pioneering study, research on the predictive power of attitudes and the moderation of attitude-behavior bonds remains vital, vigorous, and continuous. Moderators of attitude-behavior consistency (ABC) fall into three categories: meta-attitudinal, self-interest, and assessment-related. Cook & Sheeran's (2004) meta-analysis of 44 studies that examined meta-attitudinal characteristics indicative of attitude strength (accessibility, involvement, certainty, ambivalence, affective-cognitive consistency, and temporal stability) revealed that all the characteristics except involvement moderated ABC, with temporal stability being the strongest. Extending these findings, Holland et al. (2002b) demonstrated that strong (versus weak) attitudes not only were more predictive of behavior, but also were less sensitive to behavioral feedback. Strong attitudes remained stable irrespective of the behavior exhibited between two attitude assessments, whereas weak attitudes were significantly affected by behavior.

Self-Interest

However strong, attitudes may not be manifested behaviorally if the manifestation violates the norm of self-interest. Ratner & Miller (2001) showed that the fear of publicly supporting favored causes in which one had no stake prevented nonvested individuals from acting on their attitudes. Self-interest moderates ABC, as shown in research on the effect of vested interest across a range of policy-relevant decisions (Lehman & Crano 2002). In general, the more closely attitudes are tied to the self, the more likely they are to serve as a basis for attitude-consistent actions. Their potency in determining behavior likely stems from their stability, as self-defining attitudes are less sensitive to context (Sparks 2000).

Assessment

In a demonstration of the moderating roles of the mode of assessment, Neumann et al. (2004) showed that explicit measures of attitudes assessing deliberate, reflective evaluations (e.g., questionnaires) were better predictors of self-reported, deliberative behavioral intentions. In contrast, implicit measures assessing automatic, impulsive evaluations (e.g., Implicit Association Test; Greenwald et al. 1998) were better predictors of automatic avoidance/approach tendencies in reactions toward people with AIDS. Taken together, these studies suggest that underlying, latent characteristics of evaluations reflected in different measures of attitudes may be largely unrelated functionally. As such, they may activate different processes that make unique contributions to behavior (Gawronski & Strack 2004, Vargas et al. 2004).

Theory of Planned Behavior

The MODE model (motivation and opportunity as determinants of spontaneous versus thoughtful information processing; Fazio & Towles-Schwen 1999) proposes that attitudes guide behavior either through deliberate or spontaneous (automatic) processes. The former are activated by strong motivation and the opportunity to engage in conscious deliberation; activation of the latter depends on accessibility. The most prominent of the deliberative processes models is the theory of planned behavior (TPB) (Ajzen 2001; Ajzen & Fishbein 2000, 2005), which postulates that behavior follows from intentions and perceived control over behavior. Intentions are derived from considerations of attitudes, subjective norms, and perceived behavioral control. A voluminous TPB-inspired literature testifies to the model's heuristic value. A meta-analysis of 185 studies revealed that the constitutive elements of the theory explained significant variance in intentions (18%) and subsequent behaviors (13%); subjective norms emerged as the weakest predictor (Armitage & Conner 2001).

Terry et al. (2000a) criticized the conceptualization of the normative component of the TPB and offered an alternative more in line with a social influence perspective. Drawing on social identity and social categorization theories, they argued that only attitudes supported by in-group norms would predict behavior. Support for this reasoning was found in a series of studies demonstrating stronger ABC in participants exposed to attitude-congruent (versus incongruent) in-group norms (Terry et al. 2000b, White et al. 2002), especially when participants strongly identified with the group (Smith & Terry 2003).

Behavioral intentions, the most immediate predictor of behavior in the TPB, represent plans to act toward desired goals. The impressive volume of research on the predictive validity of intentions allowed for several meta-analytical reviews, which recently were included as entries in an overarching synthesis. Sheeran's (2002) meta-analysis of 10 meta-analyses revealed that on average, intentions explained 28% of variance in subsequent behavior. Quite a sizeable portion of unexplained variance is problematic, regardless of whether intentions are conceptualized as causes of actions, as is the case in the TPB, or as focal constitutive conditions of actions (Greve 2001). Reasoning by analogy to attitude strength, Sheeran & Abraham (2003) argued that strong, but not weak, intentions predict behavior. Empirical evidence for this argument was found in studies showing that behavior was closely related to strong intentions indicated by high certainty, attitudinal rather than normative control, greater experience, self-relevance, and anticipated regret for inaction (Abraham & Sheeran 2003, Sheeran & Orbell 2000). These properties made intentions stable over time (see also Conner et al. 2000), rendering them reliable predictors of behavior.

Alternatively, predictive validity of intentions may be improved by correcting for the hypothetical bias (Ajzen et al. 2004). This bias, evident in activation of unduly favorable beliefs and attitudes in the context of a hypothetical behavior (intention), was found responsible for inconsistency between intentions to make monetary donations and actual donations to a scholarship fund. When warned of the bias, participants corrected their overly optimistic intentions, making them better predictors of their later actual behavior (Ajzen et al. 2004).

In addition to interventions aimed at making intentions more realistic or strong, consistency between intentions and behavior may be increased by developing a plan for engaging in an intended behavior (Gollwizer 1999). Implementation intentions involve making decisions in advance about crucial aspects of behavior initiation and maintenance. The environmental cues contained in implementation intentions are thought to activate behavior automatically. The association between context and behavior should cue enactment of behavior upon every encounter with relevant contextual factors. In support of the hypothesis that implementation intentions promote performance of an intended behavior, Sheeran & Orbell (1999, 2000) found that individuals who specified in advance how, when, and where they would perform a behavior were more likely than those who did not make such plans to adhere to their intentions to regularly take vitamin C and to attend cervical cancer screening (also see Fishbein 2000, Fishbein et al. 2002).

Whereas implementation intentions establish conscious strategies for attaining desired goals, self-regulatory volitional efficiency contributes to goal attainment through conscious and nonconscious mechanisms that address operationally how behavior is achieved (Kuhl 2000). Orbell (2004) found that volitional efficiency, assessed as concentration on a goal and self-determination, moderated the effects of behavioral intentions on actual behavior; participants high on volitional efficiency were more likely than those low on volitional efficiency to act on their intentions. Moreover, volitional efficiency mediated the effect of perceived behavior control on behavior, supporting Ajzen's (2002) claim that a direct effect of controllability on behavior is as much attributable to internal, self-regulatory capacity as it is to external behavioral influences.

Habit

An aspect of the TPB that has generated lively exchanges among researchers is the role of habits or frequently performed past behaviors (Ouellette & Wood 1998) in predicting future behavior. In contrast to the TPB postulate that effects of any distal variable, including past behavior, are mediated by intentions, Verplanken & Aarts (1999) argue that intentions may lose their predictive power once strong habits are formed. In such cases, a reasoned process of deliberation presumably is replaced by a spontaneous mode of operation, which is automatically activated upon encountering relevant cues. Criticizing the construct of habit on conceptual and operational grounds, Ajzen (2002) argues that residual effects of past behavior cannot be attributed to habit. Rather, he calls for further explorations of factors responsible for translations of beliefs into actions. Far from being settled, this debate on habits will likely generate new insight into automaticity versus reasoning in human action. James (1890), Tolman (1932), and Hull (1943) might be amused to discover that the focal issue of their times is still hotly debated in the twenty-first century.

CONCLUDING REMARKS

This review has pointed to some likely foci of attention and, hopefully, progress in the years to come. We expect that considerable efforts will continue to be made to understand the nature of attitudes that are measured via explicit versus implicit methods. Theories that make sense of overlaps and discontinuities in the constructs defined by standard and implicit measurement techniques are beginning to develop within specific subfields (e.g., dissonance, affect and persuasion), and more encompassing models may be anticipated. Hand in glove with this progression is a revitalized interest in attitude formation (versus change), which will help integrate basic social-psychophysical concerns with the less exotic pursuits of persuasion practitioners. Study of the effects of minority sources in influence, which helped rejuvenate persuasion research, likely will continue to feature prominently. Recent models that integrate dual process conceptions of attitude change with social identity approaches promise to contribute to a deeper understanding of the fundamental persuasion process in the social context. We anticipate that deliberative processes of change will be differentiated more precisely from more automatic processes, and this development should further advance understanding, as will study of the effects of incongruous pairings of source with message. Internal and external pressures will likely orient persuasion research more strongly toward applications; even fundamental theory-building research may be grounded more firmly in the problems of the real world. This progression is not to be shunned, as we may infer from the recommendations Campbell (1988) advanced so many years ago in his "Experimenting Society" homily. The requirements, indeed, demands, placed on persuasion researchers have never been greater, nor have been the opportunities to contribute meaningfully to science and society. It will be fascinating to see how, not whether, the field responds.

ACKNOWLEDGMENTS

Preparation of this chapter was facilitated by a grant from the National Institute on Drug Abuse (R01-DA015957–02).

The *Annual Review of Psychology* is online at http://psych.annualreviews.org

LITERATURE CITED

Abraham C, Sheeran P. 2003. Acting on intentions: the role of anticipated regret. *Br. J. Soc. Psychol.* 42:495–511

Ajzen I. 2001. Nature and operation of attitudes. *Annu. Rev. Psychol.* 52:27–58

Ajzen I. 2002. Residual effects of past on late behavior: habituation and reasoned action perspectives. *Personal. Soc. Psychol. Rev.* 6: 107–22

Ajzen I, Brown TC, Carvajal F. 2004. Explaining the discrepancy between intentions and actions: the case of hypothetical bias in contingent valuation. *Personal. Soc. Psychol. Bull.* 30:1108–21

Ajzen I, Fishbein M. 2000. Attitudes and the attitude-behavior relation: reasoned and automatic processes. In *European Review of Social Psychology*, ed. W Stroebe, M Hewstone, pp. 1–33. Chichester, UK: Wiley

Ajzen I, Fishbein M. 2005. The influence of attitudes on behavior. See Albarracín et al. 2005, pp. 173–221

Albarracín D. 2002. Cognition in persuasion: an analysis of information processing in response to persuasive communications. In *Advances in Experimental Social Psychology*, ed. MP Zanna, 34:61–130. San Diego, CA: Academic

Albarracín D, Johnson BT, Zanna MP, eds. 2005. *The Handbook of Attitudes*. Hillsdale, NJ: Erlbaum

Albarracín D, Kumkale GT. 2003. Affect as information in persuasion: a model of affect identification and discounting. *J. Personal. Soc. Psychol.* 84:453–69

Albarracín D, Wyer RS. 2001. Elaborative and nonelaborative processing of a behavior-related communication. *Personal. Soc. Psychol. Bull.* 27:691–705

Allport GW. 1935. Attitudes. In *Handbook of Social Psychology*, ed. C Murchison, pp. 798–884. Worcester, MA: Clark Univ. Press

Antonio AL, Change JJ, Hakuta K, Kenny DA, Levin S, Milem JF. 2004. Effects of racial diversity on complex thinking in college students. *Psychol. Sci.* 15:507–10

Areni CS. 2003. The effects of structural and grammatical variables on persuasion: an elaboration likelihood model perspective. *Psychol. Market.* 20:349–75

Armitage CJ. 2003. Beyond attitudinal ambivalence: effects of belief homogeneity on attitude-intention-behavior relations. *Eur. J. Soc. Psychol.* 33:551–63

Armitage CJ, Conner M. 2000. Attitudinal ambivalence: a test of three key hypotheses. *Personal. Soc. Psychol. Bull.* 26:1421–32

Armitage CJ, Conner M. 2001. Efficacy of the theory of planned behavior: a meta-analytic review. *Br. J. Soc. Psychol.* 40:471–99

Asch SE. 1952. *Social Psychology.* Englewood Cliffs, NJ: Prentice-Hall

Baker WE. 1999. When can affective conditioning and mere exposure directly influence brand choice? *J. Advert.* 28:31–46

Bargh JA. 2001. The psychology of the mere. See Bargh & Apsley 2001, pp. 25–37

Bargh JA, Apsley DK, eds. 2001. *Unraveling the Complexities of Social Life: A Festschrift in Honor of Robert B. Zajonc*. Washington, DC: Am. Psychol. Assoc.

Bassili JN. 1996. Meta-judgmental vs. operative indexes of psychological attributes: the case of measures of attitude strength. *J. Personal. Soc. Psychol.* 71:637–53

Bassili JN. 2003. The minority slowness effect: subtle inhibitions in the expression of views not shared by others. *J. Personal. Soc. Psychol.* 84:261–76

Bassili JN, Brown RD. 2005. Implicit and explicit attitudes: research, challenges, and theory. See Albarracín et al. 2005, pp. 543–74

Beauvois JL, Joule RV. 1999. A radical point of view on dissonance theory. In *Cognitive Dissonance: Progress on A Pivotal Theory of Social Psychology*, ed. E Harmon-Jones, J Mills, pp. 43–70. Washington, DC: Am. Psychol. Assoc.

Bell DW, Esses VM. 2002. Ambivalence and response amplification: a motivational perspective. *Personal. Soc. Psychol. Bull.* 28: 1143–52

Bizer GY, Krosnick J. 2001. Exploring the structure of strength-related attitude features: the relation between attitude importance and attitude accessibility. *J. Personal. Soc. Psychol.* 81:566–86

Blascovich J, Loomis J, Beall A, Swinth K, Hoyt C, Bailenson J. 2002. Immersive virtual environment technology as a research tool for social psychology. *Psychol. Inq.* 13:103–25

Bohner G, Weinerth T. 2001. Negative affect can increase or decrease message scrutiny: the affect interpretation hypothesis. *Personal. Soc. Psychol. Bull.* 27:1417–28

Brodbeck FC, Kerschreiter R, Mojzisch A, Frey D, Schulz-Hardt S. 2002. The dissemination of critical, unshared information in decision-making groups: the effects of pre-discussion dissent. *Eur. J. Soc. Psychol.* 32:35–56

Broemer P. 2002. Relative effectiveness of differently framed health messages: the influence of ambivalence. *Eur. J. Soc. Psychol.* 32:685–703

Brownstein A, Read SJ, Simon D. 2004. Bias at the racetrack: effects of individual expertise and task importance on predecision reevaluation of alternatives. *Personal. Soc. Psychol. Bull.* 30:891–904

Bryant J, Zillmann D. 2002. *Media Effects: Advances in Theory and Research.* Mahwah, NJ: Erlbaum

Butera F, Mugny G. 2001a. Conflicts and social influences in hypothesis testing. See De Dreu & De Vries 2001, pp. 160–82

Butera F, Mugny G. 2001b. *Social Influence in Social Reality: Promoting Individual and Social Change.* Ashland, OH: Hogrefe & Huber

Cacioppo JT, Marshall-Goodell BS, Tassinary L, Petty R. 1992. Rudimentary determinants of attitudes: classical condition is more effective when prior knowledge about the attitude stimulus is low than high. *J. Exp. Soc. Psychol.* 28:207–33

Campbell DT. 1988. The experimenting society. In *Methodology and Epistemology for Social Science: Selected Papers,* ed. S Overman, pp. 290–314. Chicago, IL: Univ. Chicago Press

Cervellon M-C, Dubé L. 2002. Assessing the cross-cultural applicability of affective and cognitive components of attitude. *J. Cross-Cult. Psychol.* 33:346–57

Cesario J, Grant H, Higgins E. 2004. Regulatory fit and persuasion: transfer from "feeling right." *J. Personal. Soc. Psychol.* 86:388–404

Chaiken S, Trope Y. 1999. *Dual Process Theories in Social Psychology.* New York: Guilford

Chen S, Chaiken S. 1999. The heuristic-systematic model in its broader context. See Chaiken & Trope 1999, pp. 73–96

Choi HS, Levine JM. 2004. Minority influence in work teams: the impact of newcomers. *J. Exp. Soc. Psychol.* 40:273–80

Clark RD III. 1999. Effects of number of majority defectors on minority influence. *Group Dyn.* 3:303–12

Clark RD III. 2001. Effects of majority defection and multiple minority sources on minority influence. *Group Dyn.* 5:57–62

Conner M, Sheeran P, Norman P, Armitage CJ. 2000. Temporal stability as a moderator of relationships in the theory of planned behavior. *Br. J. Soc. Psychol.* 39:449–93

Conner M, Sparks P. 2002. Ambivalence and attitudes. *Eur. Rev. Soc. Psychol.* 12:37–70

Conner M, Sparks P, Povey R, Shepherd JR, Armitage CJ. 2002. Moderator effects of attitudinal ambivalence on attitude-behavior relations. *Eur. J. Soc. Psychol.* 32:705–18

Cooke R, Sheeran P. 2004. Moderation of cognition-intention and cognition-behavior relations: a meta-analysis of properties of variables from the theory of planned behavior. *Br. J. Soc. Psychol.* 43:159–86

Costarelli S, Colloca P. 2004. The effects of attitude ambivalence on pro-environmental behavioral intentions. *J. Environ. Psychol.* 23:279–88

Courbet D. 2003. L'influence publicitaire en l'absence de souvenir des messages: les effets implicites de la simple exposition aux marques. *Cah. Int. Psychol. Soc.* 57:39–51

Crano WD. 1997. Vested interest, symbolic politics, and attitude-behavior consistency. *J. Personal. Soc. Psychol.* 72:485–91

Crano WD. 2000. Milestones in the psychological analysis of social influence. *Group Dynam.* 4:68–80

Crano WD. 2001a. Directed social influence. In *The Social Mind: Cognitive and Motivational Aspects of Interpersonal Behavior*, ed. JP Forgas, KD Williams, pp. 389–405. New York: Cambridge Univ. Press

Crano WD. 2001b. Social influence, social identity, and ingroup leniency. In *Group Consensus and Minority Influence: Implications for Innovation*, ed. CKW De Dreu, NK De-Vries, pp. 122–43. Oxford, UK: Blackwell

Crano WD, Alvaro EM. 1998. The context/comparison model of social influence: mechanisms, structure, and linkages that underlie indirect attitude change. In *European Review of Social Psychology*, ed. W Stroebe, M Hewstone, 8:175–202. Chichester, UK: Wiley

Crano WD, Burgoon M, eds. 2002. *Mass Media and Drug Prevention: Classic and Contemporary Theories and Research*. Mahwah, NJ: Erlbaum

Crano WD, Chen X. 1998. The leniency contract and persistence of majority and minority influence. *J. Personal. Soc. Psychol.* 74:1437–50

Crano WD, Hannula-Bral KA. 1994. Context/categorization model of social influence: minority and majority influence in the formation of a novel response norm. *J. Exp. Soc. Psychol.* 30:247–76

Das EHH, de Wit JBF, Stroebe W. 2003. Fear appeals motivate acceptance of action recommendations: evidence for a positive bias in the processing of persuasive messages. *Personal. Soc. Psychol. Bull.* 29:650–64

David B, Turner JC. 1999. Studies in self-categorization and minority conversion: the in-group minority in intragroup and intergroup contexts. *Br. J. Soc. Psychol.* 38:115–34

De Dreu CKW. 2001. Team innovation and team effectiveness: the importance of minor-

ity dissent and reflexivity. *Eur. J. Work Organ. Psychol.* 11:285–98

De Dreu CKW, De Vries NK, eds. 2001. Group concensus and minority influence: implications for innovation. Oxford, UK: Blackwell

De Dreu CKW, De Vries NK, Gordijn EH, Schuurman MS. 1999. Convergent and divergent processing of majority and minority arguments: effects of focal and related attitudes. *Eur. J. Soc. Psychol.* 29:329–48

De Dreu CKW, West M. 2001. Minority dissent and team innovation: the importance of participation in decision making. *J. Appl. Psychol.* 86:1191–201

De Houwer J, Thomas S, Baeyens F. 2001. Associative learning of likes and dislikes: a review of 25 years of research on human evaluative conditioning. *Psychol. Bull.* 127:853–69

DeSteno D, Petty RE, Rucker DD, Wegener DT, Braveman J. 2004. Discrete emotions and persuasion: the role of emotion-induced expectancies. *J. Personal. Soc. Psychol.* 86:43–56

DeSteno D, Petty RE, Wegener DT, Rucker DD. 2000. Beyond valence in the perception of likelihood: the role of emotion specificity. *J. Personal. Soc. Psychol.* 78:397–416

DeSteno D, Petty RE, Wegener DT, Rucker DD. 2002. Emotion and persuasion: thoughts on the role of emotional intelligence. In *The Wisdom of Feeling: Psychological Processes in Emotional Intelligence*, ed. L Feldman Barrett, P Salovey, pp. 292–310. New York: Guilford

Dijksterhuis A. 2004. I like myself but I don't know why: enhancing implicit self-esteem by subliminal evaluative conditioning. *J. Personal. Soc. Psychol.* 86:345–55

Edwards K. 1990. The interplay of affect and cognition in attitude formation and change. *J. Personal. Soc. Psychol.* 59:202–16

El-Alayli A, Park ES, Messé LA, Kerr NL. 2002. Having to take a stand: the interactive effects of task framing and source status. *Group Process. Intergroup Relat.* 5:233–48

Erb H-P, Bohner G. 2001. Mere consensus effects in minority and majority influence. In

Group Consensus and Minority Influence: Implications for Innovation, ed. CKW De Dreu, NK DeVries, pp. 40–59. Malden, MA: Blackwell

Erb H-P, Bohner G, Rank S, Einwiller S. 2002. Processing minority and majority communications: the role of conflict and prior attitudes. *Personal. Soc. Psychol. Bull.* 28:1172–82

Fabrigar LR, Petty RE. 1999. The role of affective and cognitive bases of attitudes in susceptibility to affectively and cognitively based persuasion. *Personal. Soc. Psychol. Bull.* 25:363–81

Falomir JM, Mugny G, Pérez JA. 2000. Social influence and identity conflict. See Terry & Hogg 2000, pp. 245–64

Fazio RH, Olson MA. 2003. Implicit measures in social cognition research: their meaning and use. *Annu. Rev. Psychol.* 54:297–327

Fazio RH, Towles-Schwen T. 1999. The MODE model of attitude-behavior processes. See Chaiken & Trope 1999, pp. 97–116

Feather NT. 2004. Value correlates of ambivalent attitudes toward gender relations. *Personal. Soc. Psychol. Bull.* 30:3–12

Festinger L. 1957. *A Theory of Cognitive Dissonance*. Evanston, IL: Row Peterson

Festinger L, Carlsmith JM. 1959. Cognitive consequences of forced compliance. *J. Abnorm. Soc. Psychol.* 58:203–10

Field AP. 2000. "I like it, but I'm not sure why:" Can evaluative conditioning occur without conscious awareness? *Conscious. Cogn.* 9:13–36

Fishbein M. 2000. The role of theory in HIV prevention. *AIDS Care* 12:273–78

Fishbein M, Cappella J, Hornik R, Sayeed S, Yzer M, Ahern RK. 2002. The role of theory in developing effective anti-drug public service announcements. See Crano & Burgoon 2002, pp. 89–117

Forgas JP, Williams KD. 2000. *Social Influence: Direct and Indirect Processes*. Philadelphia, PA: Psychol. Press

Forgas JP, Williams KD, von Hippel W, eds. 2003. *Social Judgments: Implicit and Explicit Processes*. New York: Cambridge Univ. Press

Fuegen K, Brehm J. 2004. The intensity of affect and resistance to social influence. See Knowles & Linn 2004, pp. 39–64

Fuller LK, ed. 2003. *Media-Mediated AIDS*. Cresskill, NJ: Hampton

Gawronski B, Strack F. 2004. On the propositional nature of cognitive consistency: dissonance changes explicit, but not implicit attitudes. *J. Exp. Soc. Psychol.* 40:535–42

Giner-Sorolla R. 1999. Affect in attitude: immediate and deliberative perspectives. See Chaiken & Trope 1999, pp. 441–56

Giner-Sorolla R. 2001. Affective attitudes are not always faster: the moderating level of extremity. *Personal. Soc. Psychol. Bull.* 27:666–77

Giner-Sorolla R. 2004. Is affective material in attitudes more accessible than cognitive material? The moderating role of attitude basis. *Eur. J. Soc. Psychol.* 34:761–80

Glick P, Fiske ST. 2001. Ambivalent sexism. In *Advances in Experimental Social Psychology*, ed. MP Zanna, 33:115–88. San Diego, CA: Academic

Glick P, Lameiras M, Fiske ST, Eckes T, Masser B, et al. 2004. Bad but bold: ambivalent attitudes toward men predict gender inequality in 16 nations. *J. Personal. Soc. Psychol.* 86:713–28

Gollwizer PM. 1999. Implementation intentions: strong effects of simple plans. *Am. Psychol.* 54:493–503

Gordijn EH, De Vries NK, De Dreu CKW. 2002. Minority influence on focal and related attitudes: change in size, attributions, and information processing. *Personal. Soc. Psychol. Bull.* 28:1315–26

Gordijn EH, Postmes T, De Vries NK. 2001. Devil's advocate or advocate of oneself: effects of numerical support on pro- and counterattitudinal self-persuasion. *Personal. Soc. Psychol. Bull.* 27:395–407

Greenwald AG, Banaji MR, Rudman LA, Farnham SD, Nosek BA, Mellott DS. 2002. A unified theory of implicit attitudes, stereotypes, self-esteem, and self-concept. *Psychol. Rev.* 109:3–25

Greenwald AG, McGhee DE, Schwartz JL. 1998. Measuring individual differences in implicit cognition: the implicit association test. *J. Personal. Soc. Psychol.* 73:1464–80

Greenwald AG, Nosek BA. 2001. Health of the implicit association test at age 3. *Z. Exp. Psychol.* 48:85–93

Greve W. 2001. Traps and gaps in action explanation: theoretical problems of psychology of human action. *Psychol. Rev.* 108:435–57

Haddock G, Rotheman AJ, Reber R, Schwartz N. 1999. Forming judgments of attitude certainty, intensity, and importance: the role of subjective experience. *Personal. Soc. Psychol. Bull.* 25:771–82

Haddock G, Zanna MP. 1999. Affect, cognition, and social attitudes. In *European Review of Social Psychology*, ed. W Stroebe, M Hewstone, pp. 75–100. Chichester, UK: Wiley

Hammerl M. 2000. I like it, but only when I'm not sure why: evaluative conditioning and the awareness issue. *Conscious. Cogn.* 9:37–40

Hänze M. 2001. Ambivalence, conflict, and decision-making: attitudes and feelings in Germany toward NATO's intervention in the Kosovo war. *Eur. J. Soc. Psychol.* 31:693–706

Harmon-Jones E. 2000a. Cognitive dissonance and experienced negative affect: evidence that dissonance increased experienced negative affect even in the absence of aversive consequences. *Personal. Soc. Psychol. Bull.* 26:1490–501

Harmon-Jones E. 2000b. Reconsidering Festinger and Carlsmith's 1959 classic experiment testing cognitive dissonance theory. *Rev. Int. Psychol. Soc.* 13:193–201

Harmon-Jones E, Peterson H, Vaughn K. 2003. The dissonance-inducing effects of an inconsistency between experienced empathy and knowledge of past failures to help: support for the action-based model of dissonance. *Basic Appl. Soc. Psychol.* 25:69–78

Hodson G, Maio GR, Esses VM. 2001. The role of attitudinal ambivalence in suscepti-

bility to consensus. *Basic Appl. Soc. Psychol.* 23:197–205

Holland RW, Meertens RM, Van Vugt M. 2002a. Dissonance on the road: self esteem as a moderator of internal and external self-justification strategies. *Personal. Soc. Psychol. Bull.* 28:1713–24

Holland RW, Verplanken B, van Knippenberg A. 2002b. On the nature of attitude-behavior relations: the strong guide, the weak follow. *Eur. J. Soc. Psychol.* 32:869–76

Holland RW, Verplanken B, van Knippenberg A. 2003. From repetition to conviction: attitude accessibility as a determinant of attitude certainty. *J. Exp. Soc. Psychol.* 39:594–601

Holtz R. 2003. Intragroup or intergroup attitude projection can increase opinion certainty: Is there classism at college? *J. Appl. Soc. Psychol.* 33:1922–44

Holtz R. 2004. Group cohesion, attitude projection, and opinion certainty: beyond interaction. *Group Dynam.* 8:112–25

Hosman LA, Huebner TM, Siltanen SA. 2002. The impact of power-of-speech style, arguments, and need for cognition on impression formation, cognitive responses, and persuasion. *J. Lang. Soc. Psychol.* 21:361–79

Hull CL. 1943. *Principles of Behavior: An Introduction to Behavior Theory.* New York: Appleton-Century

Huskinson TLH, Haddock G. 2004. Individual differences in attitude structure: variance in the chronic reliance on affective and cognitive information. *J. Exp. Soc. Psychol.* 40:82–90

Ito TA, Cacioppo JT. 2001. Affect and attitudes: a social neuroscience approach. In *Affect and Social Cognition*, ed. JP Forgas, pp. 50–74. Mahwah, NJ: Erlbaum

Jacks ZJ, Cameron KA. 2003. Strategies for resisting persuasion. *Basic Appl. Soc. Psychol.* 25:145–61

Jacks ZJ, Devine P. 2000. Attitude importance, forewarning of message content, and resistance to persuasion. *Basic Appl. Soc. Psychol.* 22:19–29

Jacks ZJ, O'Brian ME. 2004. Decreasing

resistance by affirming the self. See Knowles & Linn 2004, pp. 235–58

James W. 1890. *The Principles of Psychology.* London: Macmillan

Jonas E, Schulz-Hardt S, Frey D, Thelen N. 2001. Confirmation bias in sequential information search after preliminary decisions: an expansion of dissonance theoretical research on selective exposure information. *J. Personal. Soc. Psychol.* 80:557–71

Jones K, Broemer P, Diehl M. 2000. Attitudinal ambivalence. *Eur. Rev. Soc. Psychol.* 11:35–74

Jost JT, Banaji MR, Prentice DA, eds. 2004. *Perspectivism in Social Psychology: The Yin and Yang of Scientific Progress.* Washington, DC: Am. Psychol. Assoc.

Joule R-V, Azdia T. 2003. Cognitive dissonance, double forced compliance, and commitment. *Eur. J. Soc. Psychol.* 33:565–71

Kerr NL. 2002. When is a minority a minority? Active versus passive minority advocacy and social influence. *Eur. J. Soc. Psychol.* 32: 471–83

Kitayama S, Snibbe AC, Markus HR, Suzuki T. 2004. Is there any "free" choice? Self and dissonance in two cultures. *Psychol. Sci.* 15:527–33

Knowles ES, Linn JA, eds. 2004. *Resistance and Persuasion.* Mahwah, NJ: Erlbaum

Krosnick J, Boninger DS, Chuan YC, Berent MK, Carnot CG. 1993. Attitude strength: one construct or many related constructs? *J. Personal. Soc. Psychol.* 65:1132–51

Kruglanski AW, Stroebe W. 2005. The influence of beliefs and goals on attitudes: issues of structure, function, and dynamics. See Albarracín et al. 2005, pp. 323–68

Kruglanski AW, Thompson EP. 1999a. The illusory second mode or, the cue is the message. *Psychol. Inq.* 10:182–93

Kruglanski AW, Thompson EP. 1999b. Persuasion by a single route: a view from the unimodel. *Psychol. Inq.* 10:83–109

Kruglanski AW, Thompson EP, Spiegel S. 1999. Separate or equal? Bimodal notions of persuasion and a single-process "unimodel." See Chaiken & Trope 1999, pp. 293–313

Kuhl J. 2000. A functional-design approach to motivation and self-regulation: the dynamics of personality systems interactions. In *Self-Regulation: Directions and Challenges for Future Research*, ed. M Boekaerts, PR Pintrich, M Zeidner, pp. 111–69. New York: Academic

Kumkale GT, Albarracín D. 2004. The sleeper effect in persuasion: a meta-analytic review. *Psychol. Bull.* 130:143–72

LaPierre RT. 1934. Attitudes vs. actions. *Soc. Forces* 13:230–37

Latané B, Bourgeois MJ. 2001. Successfully simulating dynamic social impact: three levels of prediction. In *Social Influence: Direct and Indirect Processes. The Sydney Symposium of Social Psychology*, ed. JP Forgas, KD Williams, pp. 61–76. Philadelphia, PA: Psychol. Press

Lee AY. 2001. The mere exposure effect: an uncertainty reduction explanation revisited. *Personal. Soc. Psychol. Bull.* 27:1255–66

Lehman BJ, Crano WD. 2002. The pervasive effects of vested interest on attitude-criterion consistency in political judgment. *J. Exp. Soc. Psychol.* 38:101–12

Lerner JS, Keltner D. 2000. Beyond valence: toward a model of emotion-specific influences on judgment and choice. *Cogn. Emot.* 81:146–59

Levine JM, Kaarbo J. 2001. Minority influence in political decision-making. In *Group Consensus and Minority Influence: Implications for Innovation*, ed. CKW De Dreu, NK DeVries, pp. 229–57. Oxford, UK: Blackwell

Lord CG, Lepper MR. 1999. Attitude representation theory. In *Advances in Experimental Social Psychology*, ed. MP Zanna, 31:265–343. San Diego, CA: Academic

Mackie DM. 1987. Systematic and nonsystematic processing of majority and minority persuasive communications. *J. Personal. Soc. Psychol.* 43:41–52

Mackie DM, Hunter SB. 1999. Majority and minority influence: the interaction of social identity and cognition mediators. In *Social Identity and Social Cognition*, ed. D Abrams,

M Hogg, pp. 332–53. Malden, MA: Blackwell

Maio GR, Esses V, Bell DW. 2000a. Examining conflict between components of attitudes: ambivalence and inconsistency are distinct construct. *Can. J. Behav. Sci.* 30:58–70

Maio GR, Fincham FD, Lycett EJ. 2000b. Attitudinal ambivalence toward parents and attachment style. *Personal. Soc. Psychol. Bull.* 26:1457–64

Maio GR, Greenwald K, Bernard M, Esses VM. 2001. Effects of intergroup ambivalence on information processing: the role of physiological arousal. *Group Process. Intergroup Relat.* 4:355–78

Maio GR, Olson J. 2000. *Why We Evaluate: Functions of Attitudes.* Mahwah, NJ: Erlbaum

Martin R, Gardikiotis A, Hewstone M. 2002. Levels of consensus and majority and minority influence. *Eur. J. Soc. Psychol.* 32:645–65

Martin R, Hewstone M, Martin PY. 2003. Resistance to persuasive messages as a function of majority and minority influence. *J. Exp. Soc. Psychol.* 39:585–93

Matz DC, Wood W. 2005. Cognitive dissonance in groups: the consequences of disagreement. *J. Personal. Soc. Psychol.* 88:22–37

McGuire WJ. 1964. Inducing resistance to persuasion: some contemporary approaches. In *Advances in Experimental Social Psychology*, ed. L Berkowitz, 1:191–229. New York: Academic

McGuire WJ. 1966. Attitudes and opinions. *Annu. Rev. Psychol.* 17:475–514

McGuire WJ. 1969. The nature of attitudes and attitude change. In *The Handbook of Social Psychology*, ed. G Lindzey, E Aronson, pp. 136–314. Reading, MA: Addison-Wesley

McGuire WJ. 1985. Attitudes and attitude change. In *The Handbook of Social Psychology*, ed. G Lindzey, E Aronson, pp. 233–346. New York: Random House

McKenna K, Bargh JA. 2000. Plan 9 from cyberspace: the implications of the Internet for personality and social psychology. *Personal. Soc. Psychol. Rev.* 4:57–75

McKimmie BM, Terry DJ, Hogg MA,

Manstead A. 2003. I'm a hypocrite, but so is everyone else: group support and the reduction of cognitive dissonance. *Group Dynam.* 71:214–24

Miller DT, Benôit M, Prentice DA. 2000. Pluralistic ignorance and inconsistency between private attitudes and public behaviors. See Terry & Hogg 2000, pp. 95–113

Monin B, Norton MI, Cooper J, Hogg MA. 2004. Reacting to an assumed situation vs. conforming to an assumed reaction: the role of perceived speaker attitude in vicarious dissonance. *Group Process. Intergroup Relat.* 7: 207–20

Moscovici S. 1980. Toward a theory of conversion behavior. In *Advances in Experimental Social Psychology*, ed. L Berkowitz, 13:209–39. San Diego, CA: Academic

Mucchi-Faina A, Costarelli S, Romoli C. 2002. The effects of intergroup context of evaluation on ambivalence toward the ingroup and the outgroup. *Eur. J. Soc. Psychol.* 32:247–59

Myers RA, Brashers DA, Hanner J. 2000. Majority-minority influence: identifying argumentative patterns and predicting argument-outcome links. *J. Commun.* 50:3–30

Nemeth CJ. 1995. Dissent as driving cognitions, attitudes, and judgments. *Soc. Cogn.* 13:273–91

Nemeth CJ, Brown KS, Rogers JD. 2001. Devil's advocate versus dissent: stimulating quantity and quality. *Eur. J. Soc. Psychol.* 31: 707–20

Neumann R, Hülsenbeck K, Seibt B. 2004. Attitude toward people with AIDS and avoidance behavior: automatic and reflexive bases of behavior. *J. Exp. Soc. Psychol.* 40:543–50

Newby-Clark IR, McGregor I, Zanna MP. 2002. Thinking and caring about cognitive inconsistency: When and from whom does attitudinal ambivalence feel uncomfortable? *J. Personal. Soc. Psychol.* 82:157–66

Ng KY, Van Dyne L. 2001. Individualism-collectivism as a boundary condition for effectiveness of minority influence in decision making. *Organ. Behav. Hum. Dec.* 84:198–225

Norton MI, Monin B, Cooper J, Hogg MA. 2003. Vicarious dissonance: attitude change from the inconsistency of others. *J. Personal. Soc. Psychol.* 85:47–62

Olson JM, Stone J. 2005. The influence of behavior on attitudes. See Albarracín et al. 2005, pp. 223–71

Olson MA, Fazio RH. 2001. Implicit attitude formation through classical conditioning. *Psychol. Sci.* 12:413–17

Olson MA, Fazio RH. 2002. Implicit acquisition and manifestation of classically conditioned attitudes. *Soc. Cogn.* 20:89–104

Olson MA, Maio G. 2003. Attitudes in social behavior. In *Handbook of Psychology: Personality and Social Psychology*, ed. T Millon, MJ Lerner, 5:299–325. New York: Wiley

Orbell S. 2004. Personality systems interactions theory and the theory of planned behavior: evidence that self-regulatory volition components enhance enactment of studying behavior. *Br. J. Soc. Psychol.* 42:95–112

Ouellette JA, Wood W. 1998. Habit and intention in everyday life: the multiple processes by which past behavior predicts future behavior. *Psychol. Bull.* 124:54–74

Perloff RM. 2003. *The Dynamics of Persuasion: Communication and Attitudes in the 21st Century*. Mahwah, NJ: Erlbaum. 2nd ed.

Petty RE, Krosnick J, eds. 1995. *Attitude Strength: Antecedents and Consequences.* Hillsdale, NJ: Erlbaum

Petty RE, DeSteno D, Rucker DD. 2001a. The role of affect in attitude change. In *Affect and Social Cognition*, ed. JP Forgas, pp. 212–33. Mahwah, NJ: Erlbaum

Petty RE, Fabrigar LR, Wegener D. 2003. Emotion factors in attitudes and persuasion. In *Handbook of Affective Sciences*, ed. RJ Davidson, KR Scherer, HH Goldsmith, pp. 752–72 . Oxford, UK: Oxford Univ. Press

Petty RE, Fleming MA, Priester JR, Feinstein AH. 2001b. Individual versus group interest violation: surprise as a determinant of argument scrutiny and persuasion. *Soc. Cogn.* 19: 418–42

Petty RE, Tormala ZL, Rucker DD. 2004. Resisting persuasion by counterarguing: an attitude strength perspective. See Jost et al. 2004, pp. 37–51

Petty RE, Wegener DT. 1999. The elaboration likelihood model: current status and controversies. See Chaiken & Trope 1999, pp. 37–72

Pfau M, Compton JA, Parker KA, Wittenberg EM, Ferguson M, et al. 2004. The traditional explanation for resistance versus attitude accessibility: Do they trigger distinct or overlapping processes of resistance? *Hum. Comm. Res.* 30:329–60

Pfau M, Roskos-Ewoldes D, Wood M, Yin S, Cho J, et al. 2003. Attitude accessibility as an alternative explanation for how inoculation confers resistance. *Commun. Monogr.* 70:39–51

Pfau M, Szabo EA, Anderson J, Morrill J, Zubric J, Wan H-H. 2001. The role and impact of affect in the process of resistance to persuasion. *Hum. Comm. Res.* 27:216–52

Phillips KW. 2003. The effects of categorically based expectation on minority influence: the importance of congruence. *Personal. Soc. Psychol. Bull.* 29:3–13

Pierro A, Mannetti L, Kruglanski AW, Sleeth-Keppler D. 2004. On the reduced impact of "cues" under high-motivation conditions of persuasion studies. *J. Personal. Soc. Psychol.* 86:251–64

Postmes T, Spears R, Sakhel K, de Groot D. 2001. Social influence in computer-mediated groups: the effects of anonymity on group behavior. *Personal. Soc. Psychol. Bull.* 27:1243–54

Priester JR, Petty RE. 2001. Extending the bases of subjective attitudinal ambivalence: interpersonal and intrapersonal antecedents of evaluative tension. *J. Personal. Soc. Psychol.* 80:19–34

Priester JR, Petty RE. 2003. The influence of spokesperson trustworthiness on message elaboration, attitude strength, and advertising effectiveness. *J. Consum. Psychol.* 13:408–21

Priluck RL, Till BD. 2004. The role of contingency awareness, involvement, and need for cognition on attitude formation. *J. Acad. Market. Sci.* 32:329–44

Prislin R. 1996. Attitude stability and attitude strength: One is enough to make it stable. *Eur. J. Soc. Psychol.* 26:447–77

Prislin R, Brewer M, Wilson DJ. 2002. Changing majority and minority positions within a group versus an aggregate. *Personal. Soc. Psychol. Bull.* 28:504–11

Prislin R, Limbert W, Bauer E. 2000. From majority to minority and vice versa: the asymmetrical effects of gaining and losing majority position within a group. *J. Personal. Soc. Psychol.* 79:385–95

Prislin R, Wood W. 2005. Social influence: the role of social consensus in attitude and attitude change. See Albarracín et al. 2005, pp. 671–706

Quinn JM, Wood W. 2004. Forewarnings of influence appeals: inducing resistance and acceptance. See Knowles & Linn 2004, pp. 193–213

Raghunatan R, Trope Y. 2002. Walking the tightrope between feeling good and being accurate: mood as a resource in processing persuasive messages. *J. Personal. Soc. Psychol.* 83:510–25

Ratner RK, Miller DT. 2001. The norm of self-interest and its effects on social action. *J. Personal. Soc. Psychol.* 81:5–16

Sagarin BJ, Cialdini RB, Rice WE, Serna SB. 2002. Dispelling the illusion of invulnerability: the motivations and mechanisms of resistance to persuasion. *J. Personal. Soc. Psychol.* 83:526–41

Sassenberg K, Boos M. 2003. Attitude change in computer-mediated communication: effects of anonymity and category norms. *Group Process. Intergroup Relat.* 6:405–22

Scott WA. 1966. Measures of cognitive structure. *Multivar. Behav. Res.* 1:391–95

Sheeran P. 2002. Intention-behavior relations: a conceptual and empirical review. *Eur. Rev. Soc. Psychol.* 12:1–36

Sheeran P, Abraham C. 2003. Mediator of moderators: temporal stability of intention and the intention-behavior relation. *Persoanl. Soc. Psychol. Bull.* 29:205–15

Sheeran P, Orbell S. 1999. Implementation intentions and repeated behavior: augmenting the predictive validity of the theory of planned behavior. *Eur. J. Soc. Psychol.* 29: 349–69

Sheeran P, Orbell S. 2000. Using implementation intentions to increase attendance for cervical cancer screening. *Health Psychol.* 19: 283–89

Smith CM, Diven PJ. 2002. Minority influence and political interest groups. In *The Social Psychology of Politics*, ed. V Ottati, R Tindale, J Edwards, F Bryant, L Heath, DC O'Connell, Y Suarez-Balcazar, E Posavac, pp. 175–92. New York: Kluwer Acad./Plenum

Smith CM, Dykema-Engblade A, Walker A, Niven T, McGough T. 2000. Asymmetrical social influence in freely interacting groups discussing death penalty: a shared representation interpretation. *Group Process. Intergroup Relat.* 3:387–401

Smith JR, Terry DJ. 2003. Attitude-behavior consistency: the role of group norms, attitude accessibility, and mode of behavioral decision-making. *Eur. J. Soc. Psychol.* 33: 591–608

Sparks P. 2000. Subjective expected utility-based attitude-behavior models: the utility of self-identity. See Terry & Hogg 2000, pp. 31–46

Sparks P, Harris PR, Lockwood N. 2004. Predictors and predictive effects of ambivalence. *Br. J. Soc. Psychol.* 43:371–83

Stone J. 2003. Self-consistency for low self-esteem in dissonance processes: the role of self-standards. *Personal. Soc. Psychol. Bull.* 29:846–58

Stone J, Cooper J. 2001. A self-standards model of cognitive dissonance. *J. Exp. Soc. Psychol.* 37:228–43

Stone J, Cooper J. 2003. The effect of self-attribute relevance on how self-esteem moderates attitude change in dissonance processes. *J. Exp. Soc. Psychol.* 39:508–15

Terry DJ, Hogg MA, eds. 2000. *Attitudes, Behavior, and Social Context: The Role of*

Norms and Group Membership. Mahwah, NJ: Erlbaum

Terry DJ, Hogg MA, McKimmie BM. 2000a. Attitude-behavior relations: the role of ingroup norms and mode of behavioral decision-making. *Br. J. Soc. Psychol.* 39:337–61

Terry DJ, Hogg MA, White KM. 2000b. Attitude-behavior relations: social identity and group membership. See Terry & Hogg 2000, pp. 67–93

Thompson EP, Kruglanski AW, Spiegel S. 2000. Attitudes as knowledge structures and persuasion as a specific case of subjective knowledge acquisition. See Maio & Olson 2000, pp. 59–95

Thurstone LL. 1928. Attitudes can be measured. *Am. J. Sociol.* 33:529–54

Tiedens LZ, Linton S. 2001. Judgment under emotional certainty and uncertainty: the effects of specific emotions on information processing. *J. Personal. Soc. Psychol.* 81:973–88

Till BD, Priluck RL. 2000. Stimulus generalization in classical conditioning: an initial investigation and extension. *Psychol. Market.* 17:55–72

Tolman EC. 1932. *Purposive Behavior in Animals and Men.* New York: Appleton

Tormala ZL, Petty R. 2002. What does not kill me makes me stronger: the effects of resisting persuasion on attitude certainty. *J. Personal. Soc. Psychol.* 83:1298–313

Tormala ZL, Petty R. 2004a. Resistance to persuasion and attitude certainty: the moderating role of elaboration. *Personal. Soc. Psychol. Bull.* 30:1446–57

Tormala ZL, Petty R. 2004b. Source credibility and attitude certainty: a metacognitive analysis of resistance to persuasion. *J. Consum. Psychol.* 14:427–42

Vallacher RR, Nowak A, Froehlich M, Rockloff M. 2002a. The dynamics of self-evaluation. *Personal. Soc. Psychol. Rev.* 6:370–79

Vallacher RR, Read SJ, Nowak A. 2002b. The dynamical perspective in personality and social psychology. *Personal. Soc. Psychol. Rev.* 6:264–73

van der Pligt J, De Vries NK, Manstead A, van Harreveld F. 2000. The importance of being selective: weighing the role of attribute importance in attitudinal judgment. In *Advances in Experimental Social Psychology*, ed. MP Zanna, 32:135–200. San Diego, CA: Academic

van Harreveld F, van der Pligt J, de Vries NK, Wenneker C, Verhue D. 2004. Attitudinal ambivalence and information integration in attitudinal judgment. *Br. J. Soc. Psychol.* 43:431–47

Vargas PT, von Hippel W, Petty RE. 2004. Using partially structured attitude measures to enhance the attitude-behavior relationship. *Personal. Soc. Psychol. Bull.* 30:197–211

Verplanken B, Aarts H. 1999. Habit, attitude, and planned behavior: Is habit an empty construct or an interesting case of goal-directed automaticity? *Eur. J. Soc. Psychol.* 10:101–34

Visser PS, Krosnick JA, Simmons JP. 2003. Distinguishing the cognitive and behavioral consequences of attitude importance and certainty: a new approach to testing the common-factor model. *J. Exp. Soc. Psychol.* 39:118–41

Visser PS, Mirabile RR. 2004. Attitudes in the social context: the impact of social network composition on individual-level attitudes strength. *J. Personal. Soc. Psychol.* 87:779–95

Walther E. 2002. Guilty by mere association: evaluative conditioning and the spreading attitude effect. *J. Personal. Soc. Psychol.* 82:919–34

Walther E, Trasselli C. 2003. I like her, because I like myself: self-evaluation as a source of interpersonal attitudes. *Exp. Psychol.* 50:239–46

Wegener DT, Carlston DE. 2005. Cognitive processes in attitude formation and change. See Albarracín et al. 2005, pp. 493–542

White KM, Hogg MA, Terry DJ. 2002. Improving attitude-behavior correspondence through exposure to normative support from a salient group. *Basic Appl. Soc. Psychol.* 24:91–103

Winkielman P, Cacioppo JT. 2004. Mind at ease

puts a smile on the face: psychophysiological evidence that processing facilitation elicits positive affect. *J. Personal. Soc. Psychol.* 81:989–1000

Wood W. 2000. Attitude change: persuasion and social influence. *Annu. Rev. Psychol.* 51: 539–70

Wood W, Quinn JM. 2004. Forewarned and forearmed? Two meta-analytic syntheses of forewarning of influence appeals. *Psychol. Bull.* 129:119–38

Wood W, Rhodes N, Biek M. 1995. Working knowledge and attitude strength: an information processing analysis. In *Attitude Strength: Antecedents and Consequences,* ed. R Petty, J Krosnick, pp. 283–313. Hillsdale, NJ: Erlbaum

Ziegler R, Diehl M, Zigon R, Fett T. 2004. Source consistency distinctiveness and consensus: the three dimensions of the Kelley ANOVA model of persuasion. *Personal. Soc. Psychol. Bull.* 30:352–64

Annu. Rev. Psychol. 2006. 57:375–400
doi: 10.1146/annurev.psych.57.102904.190038
First published online as a Review in Advance on July 8, 2005

PSYCHOLOGICAL PERSPECTIVES ON LEGITIMACY AND LEGITIMATION

Tom R. Tyler

*Department of Psychology, New York University, New York, New York 10003;
email: tom.tyler@nyu.edu*

Key Words authority, leadership, procedural justice, intergroup relations, stereotyping

■ **Abstract** Legitimacy is a psychological property of an authority, institution, or social arrangement that leads those connected to it to believe that it is appropriate, proper, and just. Because of legitimacy, people feel that they ought to defer to decisions and rules, following them voluntarily out of obligation rather than out of fear of punishment or anticipation of reward. Being legitimate is important to the success of authorities, institutions, and institutional arrangements since it is difficult to exert influence over others based solely upon the possession and use of power. Being able to gain voluntary acquiescence from most people, most of the time, due to their sense of obligation increases effectiveness during periods of scarcity, crisis, and conflict. The concept of legitimacy has a long history within social thought and social psychology, and it has emerged as increasingly important within recent research on the dynamics of political, legal, and social systems.

CONTENTS

0066-4308/06/0110-0375$20.00

PSYCHOLOGICAL PERSPECTIVES ON LEGITIMACY AND LEGITIMATION

This review focuses on legitimacy—the belief that authorities, institutions, and social arrangements are appropriate, proper, and just. This quality is important because when it exists in the thinking of people within groups, organizations, or societies, it leads them to feel personally obligated to defer to those authorities, institutions, and social arrangements. Legitimation refers to the characteristic of being legitimized by being placed within a framework through which something is viewed as right and proper. So, for example, a set of beliefs can explain or make sense of a social system in ways that provide a rationale for the appropriateness or reasonableness of differences in authority, power, status, or wealth. This has the consequence of encouraging people to accept those differences. Irrespective of whether the focus is on an individual authority or an institution, legitimacy is a property that, when it is possessed, leads people to defer voluntarily to decisions, rules, and social arrangements.

The focus of this chapter is a new one for the *Annual Review of Psychology*. However, the themes of this chapter are related to those touched upon in prior volumes, including intergroup relations (Hewstone et al. 2002), the psychology of stereotyping (Major & O'Brien 2005), social identity (Ellemers et al. 2002), social influence (Cialdini & Goldstein 2004), and justice (Miller 2001).

Legitimacy

Throughout the history of social thought, it has been recognized that people can exercise influence over others by possessing power. Power is the ability to shape the gains and losses of others either by threatening or using coercion to deter undesired behavior or by promising rewards to promote desired behavior. A core aspect of social dynamics, therefore, is that power provides a means to shape behavior with the consequence that, as an early social theorist noted, "The strong do what they will, the weak endure what they must" (Thucydides 1982, p. 351), or as a recent political leader, Mao Tse-Tung, opined, "Political power grows out of the barrel of a gun." The argument that behavior in social settings is linked to the ability to reward and punish is not only central to psychological theories, but is also influential in political science, sociology, and economics as well as in law, public policy, and management.

While accepting the realities of power in social life, early social theorists—including Aristotle and Plato—also recognized that seeking to gain influence over others based solely on the possession of power is costly and inefficient. The use of power, particularly coercive power, requires a large expenditure of resources to obtain modest and limited amounts of influence over others. It is therefore important that under some circumstances people are also influenced by others because they believe that the decisions made and rules enacted by others are in some way right or proper and ought to be followed (Zelditch 2001). In other words, subordinates also "relate to the powerful as moral agents as well as self-interested actors; they are cooperative and obedient on grounds of legitimacy as well as reasons of prudence and advantage" (Beetham 1991, p. 27).

The classic argument of political and social theorists has been that for authorities to perform effectively, those in power must convince everyone else that they "deserve" to rule and make decisions that influence the quality of everyone's lives. In other words, "Every authority system tries to cultivate a belief in its legitimacy" (Zelditch & Walker 2003, p. 217). Central to the idea of legitimacy is the belief that some decision made or rule created by these authorities is valid in the sense that it is entitled to be obeyed by virtue of who made the decision or how it was made. While some argue that it is impossible to rule using only power, and others suggest that it is possible but more difficult, it is widely agreed that authorities benefit from having legitimacy and find governance easier and more effective when a feeling that they are entitled to rule is widespread within the population.

Recent social science–based expositions on legitimacy have evoked the same underlying concept to define legitimacy. Psychologists French & Raven (1959) refer to legitimacy as social influence induced by feelings of "should," "ought to," or "has a right to," i.e., by appeals to an "internalized norm or value." Suchman (1995) argues that "Legitimacy is a generalized perception or assumption that the actions of an entity are desirable, proper, or appropriate within some socially constructed system of norms, values, beliefs and definitions" (p. 574). Referring to legitimacy as "authorization," Kelman & Hamilton (1989) argue that when an authority is legitimate, "the duty to obey superior orders" replaces personal morality, with people allowing legitimate authorities to define the boundaries of appropriate behavior in a given situation (p. 16). Or, more simply, legitimacy is the perception that one "ought to obey" another (Hurd 1999). Hence, legitimacy is an additional form of power that enables authorities to shape the behavior of others distinct from their control over incentives or sanctions (Ford & Johnson 1998, French & Raven 1959).

Why is legitimacy important? As noted, seeking to govern a society or manage an organization based upon the possession of power alone first requires enormous expenditures of resources to create a credible system of surveillance through which to monitor public behavior to punish rule violators. In addition, resources must be available to provide incentives for desired behavior, rewarding people for acting in ways that benefit the group. Studies show that these strategies of governance can be successful. For example, recent research suggests that deterrence strategies do shape crime-related behavior (Nagin 1998). However, the same research shows that such instrumental influences are small and come at a high material cost. This leaves societies vulnerable because disruptions in the control of resources brought on by periods of scarcity or conflict quickly lead to the collapse of effective social order. When the public views government as legitimate, it has an alternative basis for support during difficult times. Further, when government can call upon the values of the population to encourage desired behavior, society has more flexibility about how it deploys its resources. In particular, the government is better able to use collective resources to benefit the long-term interests of the group because the resources are not required for the immediate need to ensure public order.

The roots of the modern approach to legitimacy lie in the writing of Weber (1968). Like Freud and Durkheim, Weber argues that social norms and values become a part of people's internal motivational systems and guide their behavior separately from the impact of incentives and sanctions. As a result, "control by others is replaced by self-control, as social norms and values are internalized and become part of the individual's own desires concerning how to behave" (Hoffman 1977, p. 85). People who internalize social norms and values become self-regulating, taking on the obligations and responsibilities associated with those norms and values as aspects of their own motivation. One aspect of values—obligation—is a key element in the concept of legitimacy. It leads to voluntary deference to the directives of legitimate authorities and rules. Hence, unlike influence based upon the influencer's possession of power or resources, the influence motivated by legitimacy develops from within the person who is being influenced (King & Lenox 2000; Tyler & Huo 2002, ch. 7).

A legitimating ideology is a set of justifications or "legitimizing myths" (Major 1994, Sidanius & Pratto 1999) that lead a political or social system and its authorities and institutions to be viewed as normatively or morally appropriate by the people within the system. A wide variety of forms of legitimation are found through history and across societies and cultures. A classic typology of legitimating ideologies is found in the work of Weber (1968), who distinguishes between legitimacy based upon deference to customs and values (traditional authority), legitimacy based upon devotion to the actions or character of an authority (charismatic authority), and legitimacy linked to the process of rule creation and interpretation (rational bureaucratic authority). Weber's work makes clear that the legitimation of authority and institutions through "the rule of law," while widespread in modern societies, is only one of many ways in which social arrangements might potentially be justified.

Legitimacy in Psychology

The idea of legitimacy underlies many of the important contributions of American social psychology. The work of Lewin and associates on the dynamics of authority both demonstrates the influence of the legitimacy acquired by leadership style on the willingness to accept the recommendation of authorities and argues for the important role that democratic governance has in the creation and maintenance of legitimacy (Gold 1999, Lewin 1951, Lewin et al. 1939). Similarly, both Milgram's and Kelman's research on deference to authority demonstrates the powerful influence of directives from a legitimate authority on behavior (Kelman & Hamilton 1989, Milgram 1975). In addition, research by Thibaut and colleagues shows that decision acceptance is linked to the fairness of the procedures by which authorities make decisions (Thibaut & Walker 1975). Underlying all of these findings is the implicit impact of the legitimacy of an authority, however derived, on its ability to influence others.

Despite the importance of these implicit studies of legitimacy, the concept of legitimacy itself has not played a central role in social psychology since the era of the group dynamics movement (French & Raven 1959). However, recently there has been a resurgence of attention to issues of legitimacy and legitimation within both social psychology and the social sciences more generally. Although some of this work mirrors earlier research in focusing on the legitimacy of authorities in individual or small group settings, much of recent attention has been directed toward legitimacy as a factor in large organizations and in societies.

Legitimacy and the Dynamics of Authority

The most concrete influence of legitimacy occurs when people make decisions or create rules designed to shape the behavior of others. The question of whether others will accept those decisions and rules is always a key one in social settings, particularly when decision-makers are not backed up with either credible coercive potential or the promise of rewards. As a result, the ability to secure compliance is often viewed as the litmus test of effective leadership. Consistent with the longstanding arguments of legitimacy theories, recent studies suggest that having legitimacy facilitates the ability to gain decision acceptance and to promote rule-following.

In the legal arena, research on people's personal interactions with police officers and judges indicates that people who view those authorities as legitimate are more likely to accept their decisions, an effect that is distinct from the general finding that people are more likely to accept decisions that are more favorable and/or fairer (Tyler & Huo 2002, ch. 7). Similarly, studies in organizational settings indicate that legitimacy facilitates the personal exercise of authority. Porter et al. (2003) show that, in work teams, the legitimacy of the request for backup behavior from others shapes the degree to which other team members provide backup. In addition, Smith et al. (2003) show that when people are given reasons for injustice within a group (i.e., in this case told that inequality is more legitimate), they identify more strongly with their group and cooperate more fully with it in resolving social dilemmas. In each of these cases, authorities who are viewed as more legitimate have their decisions more easily deferred to by others.

WHY ARE AUTHORITIES LEGITIMATE? During the past several decades, a large literature on procedural justice has developed within social psychology (DeCremer & Tyler 2005; Tyler 2000, 2004b; Tyler & Blader 2003; Tyler & Lind 1992; Tyler & Smith 1998). A core finding of that literature is that authorities and institutions are viewed as more legitimate and, therefore, their decisions and rules are more willingly accepted when they exercise their authority through procedures that people experience as being fair (Tyler 2001). This procedural effect is widespread (for recent reviews, see Cohen-Charash & Spector 2001, 2002; Colquitt et al. 2001, 2005).

In legal settings, people are found to be more willing to defer to the decisions of formal and informal legal authorities when those decisions are made fairly

(Hoffman 2005, Paternoster et al. 1997, Shestowsky 2004, Tyler & Huo 2002). One important recent development is the widespread use and study of restorative justice conferences in lieu of trials. These conferences, which are experienced by those involved as procedurally fairer than trials, lead to greater cooperation with the law (Nugent et al. 2003, Poulson 2003, Roberts & Stalans 2004). This finding mirrors the earlier finding that mediation, which is viewed as procedurally fairer, leads to greater decision acceptance by disputants (Shestowsky 2004).

Similarly, studies in work organizations support the argument that those author- ities who exercise their authority fairly are more likely to be viewed as legitimate and to have their decisions accepted (Ambrose 2002; Cohen-Charash & Spector 2001, 2002; Colquitt et al. 2001; Konovsky 2000). Further, these studies demon- strate that experiencing fair procedures when dealing with authorities generally encourages people to become committed to organizations, leading to a variety of forms of cooperation, including rule-following and making extra-role efforts to help the organization be effective and successful (Tyler & Blader 2000). In other words, legitimacy both helps within particular situations and encourages more general actions on behalf of the group.

Legitimacy as a System-Level Attribute

Legitimacy is also an issue on the group, organizational, or system level, where the legitimacy of authorities and institutions is part of the overall climate or culture of a group. Discussions of the stability of social and political systems have long emphasized the importance to effective governance of having widespread consent from those within the system. Such widespread consent enables the more effective exercise of social and political authority, since authorities can appeal to members based upon their shared sense of values. As Kelman (1969) argues, "It is essential to the effective functioning of the nation-state that the basic tenets of its ideology be widely accepted within the population" (p. 278). Hence, effective democratic governance depends upon the legitimacy of the state.

Recent discussions of the dynamics of organizations focus on legitimacy in work organizations (Elsbach 2001, Elsbach & Sutton 1992, Haslam 2004, Kostova & Zaheer 1999, Suchman 1995). Like earlier work on political legitimacy, these discussions stress that organizational viability is enhanced when members view organizational rules and authorities as legitimate and entitled to be obeyed. Studies within work-based organizational settings show that, as predicted by legitimacy theory, employees are more willing to follow organizational rules and authorities when they believe that they are legitimate (Tyler & Blader 2005).

Studies suggest that legitimacy has an important role in securing support for work organizations. Bansal & Clelland (2004) show, for example, that firms viewed as legitimate are more highly insulated from unsystematic variations in their stock prices; Pollock & Rindova (2003) demonstrate that the legitimacy that companies acquire through media presentations of their initial public offerings shapes investor behavior; and research suggests that firms with legitimacy are generally more likely to survive (Baum & Oliver 1991, Human & Provan 2000, Rao 1994, Zimmerman & Zeitz 2002).

Across all types of organizations, the core argument of legitimacy theory is that legitimacy provides a "reservoir of support" for institutions and authorities, something besides immediate self-interest, which shapes reactions to their policies (Weatherford 1992). Such a reservoir is of particular value during times of crisis or decline, when it is difficult to influence people by appealing to their immediate self-interest, and when there are risks concerning whether they will receive the long-term gains usually associated with continued loyalty to the group. Recent research supports this "reservoir of support" argument.

Studies of the 2000 U.S. Supreme Court decision in *Bush v. Gore* suggest that in gaining deference for a controversial decision, the Court benefited from the widespread public view that the Court is a legitimate political institution (Gibson et al. 2003). The many recent changes in the government within various societies around the world, including South Africa and the former Soviet republics, have provided additional field settings within which the underlying assumptions of legitimacy theory have been tested. These changes in government have also rekindled interest in understanding how to create and maintain institutional legitimacy, since issues of social disintegration and internal conflict become salient when governments collapse and new forms of social order must be created. This reemphasis on understanding how to legitimate new governments is consistent with the earlier "major preoccupation of political scientists and sociologists [with legitimacy] in the post-colonial, nation-building era after the Second World War" (Sears 2003, p. 323). That preoccupation with establishing legitimacy was fueled by the fear that, without legitimate authorities and institutions, societies would descend into anarchy and chaos.

The political perspective is that when a new government comes into being, a key factor shaping its success is the degree to which it can establish legitimacy among the general populace. As Gibson suggests, "In a new political system few resources are more coveted than political legitimacy. Legitimacy is an endorphin of the democratic body politic; it is the substance that oils the machinery of democracy, reducing the friction that inevitably arises when people are not able to get everything they want from politics. Legitimacy is loyalty; it is a reservoir of goodwill that allows the institutions of government to go against what people may want at the moment without suffering debilitating consequences" (Gibson 2004, p. 289). For this reason, those seeking to solidify their exercise of authority create institutions that they hope will receive public support (Trochev 2004).

Research on emerging governments supports the argument that political institutions, including courts, can legitimate and gain acceptance for unpopular decisions and policies (Gibson et al. 1998, Machura 2003). On the other hand, studies also raise questions about the breadth of such legitimation effects. Gibson & Caldiera (2003), for example, find that the Constitutional Court in South Africa has little power to legitimate unpopular decisions, as reflected in self-reported willingness to acquiesce to unpopular Court decisions.

Although the positive consequences of legitimacy are important, it is important to note that legitimacy can serve as the basis for justifying oppression and harm to others. The potential risks of legitimacy are treated at length by Kelman & Hamilton (1989) and by Kelman (2001). In particular, because people authorize another to make judgments for them about what is appropriate conduct, they no longer feel that their own moral values are relevant to their conduct. Consequently, when directed by that legitimate authority to engage in immoral actions, people are found to be strikingly willing to do so (Kelman 2001, Milgram 1975).

WHAT LEGITIMATES AUTHORITIES AND INSTITUTIONS?   Recent research suggests that the key aspect of authorities and institutions that shapes their legitimacy and, through it, the willingness of people to defer to the decisions of authorities and to the rules created by institutions is the fairness of the procedures through which institutions and authorities exercise authority. This procedural justice effect on legitimacy is found to be widespread and robust and occurs in legal, political, and managerial settings (Tyler 2000, 2001; Tyler & Smith 1998).

In the legal arena, people are found to believe authorities are more legitimate when they view their actions as consistent with fair procedures (Sunshine & Tyler 2003; Tyler & Huo 2002, ch. 4). As a result, when the authorities engage in unfair procedures such as racial profiling (Tyler & Wakslak 2004) or the use of unnecessary force (Seron et al. 2004), they lose public support, whereas acting fairly increases deference (Cohn et al. 2000, Gibson 2002).

Similarly, political authorities and institutions lose legitimacy when they do not adhere to procedural fairness norms (Clawson et al. 2001, Farnsworth 2003, Gangl 2003, Hibbing & Theiss-Morse 2002, Kershaw & Alexander 2003, Murphy 2004). Recent research on political institutions and authorities in new democracies supports the argument that procedural issues underlie the legitimacy of political authorities and institutions. A study of Eastern European countries by Kluegel & Mason (2004) suggests that both procedural and distributive justice judgments about the economic system shape political support, and other studies show that evidence of procedural injustice, in the form of corruption, undermines political support (Seligson 2002).

Finally, the legitimacy of the leaders of work organizations, ranging from supervisors to CEOs, is linked to the fairness of the procedures they use to make decisions in work settings (Tyler & Blader 2000, 2005). This research indicates that four aspects of procedures make independent contributions to procedural justice judgments: organization-level decision-making, organization-level interpersonal treatment, supervisor-level decision-making, and supervisor-level interpersonal treatment (Blader & Tyler 2003).

The procedural base of legitimacy has widespread implication for the legitimation of authority in organizational settings. In political processes, the widespread effort to create deliberative political procedures is motivated, in part, by the demonstration that public participation in such procedures enhances political legitimacy (Carpini et al. 2004). The efforts of the legal system to create more informal legal procedures such as mediation reflect a similar recognition that the public experiences these procedures as fairer, and their use enhances the legitimacy of legal authority (Landsman 2003, Shestowsky 2004). And, in work settings, the use of open and participatory styles of leadership has been linked to the desire to build legitimacy and gain cooperation from employees (DeCremer & van Knippenberg 2002, Keyes et al. 2000, Tyler 2002). Studies in work settings are particularly important because they demonstrate that the use of fair procedures not only encourages deference to authorities, but also motivates a variety of types of voluntary positive efforts on behalf of one's organization.

Hegtvedt et al. (2003) argue that rather than viewing procedural justice and legitimacy as being in a causal relationship, the two can be thought of as joint inputs into the interpretation of outcomes. Their model suggests that both procedural justice and collective legitimacy shape the attributions that people make for the decisions of an allocator. First, people are influenced by how the allocator acts. If the allocator uses fair procedures, people are less likely to make internal attributions for unfair outcomes, and more likely to attribute the unfair outcomes to external contingencies. Separately, people are influenced by what they are told others think about the allocator. If the allocator is supported by either peers or authorities, the allocator is more legitimate (Zelditch & Walker 2000). If people view the allocator as legitimate, they are less likely to make internal attributions and more likely to make external attributions when that allocator makes an unfair distribution.

Hegtvedt et al. (2003) further argue for an interaction between procedural justice and legitimacy and unfair outcomes. They suggest that, when people receive unfair outcomes, they are less likely to react cognitively or behaviorally to that experience of distributive injustice if there is procedural justice or if the authority is legitimate. Hence, the presence of either procedural justice or legitimacy leads unfair outcomes to have less impact upon the individual because they are less likely to be interpreted as being unfair.

Finally, Hegtvedt & Johnson (2000) suggest that legitimacy may have the effect of shaping assessments of the fairness of allocation procedures. They suggest that "subordinates are more likely to tolerate certain levels of procedural injustice by strongly endorsed or authorized allocators" (p. 306). In particular, they argue that when experiencing unfair allocation outcomes from a legitimate authority, people are less likely to interpret the allocation procedures leading to those outcomes as being unfair. Since procedural unfairness leads to losses of legitimacy, this suggests that prior legitimacy may create a cushion of support against the loss of legitimacy in response to receiving an unfair outcome.

Mueller & Landsman (2004) find support for this argument in a study of child welfare social workers who completed questionnaires about their work organization. Consistent with expectations, those respondents who viewed authorities as legitimate were both more likely to evaluate the promotion procedures they used as being fair and to evaluate the outcomes of those procedures as being fair. In research conducted in the legal arena, Tyler & Huo (2002) similarly find that those people who evaluate legal authorities as generally more legitimate evaluate the fairness of the procedures used by those authorities, as well as the outcomes that those procedures produce, as being fairer. Hence, legitimacy may provide a framework through which actions are evaluated and judged to be just or unjust.

Finally, it is important to recognize that procedural justice is not the only basis upon which authority can be legitimated. Law, as an example, has also been legitimated by reference to its substance, as when legal authorities incorporate scientific and technical experience into a "rationality" that legitimates law (Stryker 1994, 2000). And, more generally, quantification and the ability to compare outcomes on commensurable dimensions legitimates decisions (Espeland & Stevens 1998). So, for example, the use of indices such as the Social Sciences Citation Index to establish reputation and make decisions about promotion and compensation appears rational and, therefore, legitimate.

Rationality is related to ideas of procedural justice because it reflects neutrality and factuality in decision-making. But the type of rationality outlined is also directly connected to the argument that decisions accurately reflect the merits of a case. Hence, while much of procedural justice research has focused on producing "justice," this aspect of procedures is related to their ability to produce "truth" (Thibaut & Walker 1978). In a trial, for example, the "true" innocence of the defendant is typically unknown, so the legitimacy of the verdict is established by the fairness of the trial procedures. However, the legitimacy of the verdict can also be established by evidence that compellingly reveals the truth, as when DNA tests have recently been used to exonerate those wrongly accused or convicted of crimes.

Legitimacy and Societal Mechanisms of Resource Allocation

In addition to recognizing that the decisions and rules enacted by authorities or institutions are judged against criteria of legitimacy, people also judge the legitimacy of social arrangements such as economic markets and/or the social or economic standing of people or groups. Whenever there are differences in social or economic standing between people or between groups, issues are raised about the legitimacy of those differences and of the processes through which they arise. As an example, the differences in the economic and social status of white and minority group members in the United States raise questions about the legitimacy of our economic and social system. In other words, legitimation and the acceptance or rejection of legitimizing myths occurs more broadly than just with decisions and rules promulgated by authorities and institutions. One important example of such a broader institution is the economic system—the primary system for the allocation of social benefits and burdens. Within the American economic system, the primary allocation system for economic outcomes is the market (Dye 1990).

People are found to accept a variety of types of legitimating myths about markets. They uncritically accept meritocratic explanations for economic inequality (Jost et al. 2003), they focus blame for failure on individuals, not the system (Kluegel & Smith 1986), and perceived societal status predicts judgments of competence (Fiske et al. 2002). As suggested by theories of legitimation, people do not simply accept economic markets as efficient and effective systems of allocation.

They further believe that the market system is a normatively appropriate and fair system for resource allocation (Jost et al. 2003). Consequently, they believe that people deserve the outcomes they receive from markets and they resist governmental interventions in the economic sphere through policies such as affirmative action (Tyler 2004).

THE PROCEDURAL LEGITIMATION OF MARKETS   As was true with authorities and institutions, recent evidence suggests that societal allocations are legitimated through the procedures that produce them (Jost et al. 2003, Tyler & McGraw 1986). That is, people defer to individual and group-based inequities because they believe that the use of markets to make economic allocations is a fair, and therefore legitimate, procedure for determining who receives what in society. People are found to focus first on the fairness of market procedures and to use these procedural judgments to determine whether they support government controls over markets or government corrections for market outcomes via procedures such as affirmative action (Tyler 2004). If people view market procedures as fair, they give little weight to evidence of potential distributive unfairness in the form of individual or group-based outcome differences.

Legitimacy and Intergroup Relations

Zelditch (2001) points out that the range of what might potentially be legitimated is broad, and includes authorities, institutions, polities, status hierarchies, and inequalities of wealth or status. An example of system-level legitimation that has received considerable attention in recent research is support for or opposition to the previously noted group differences in economic or social status, i.e., for inequalities. Large and persistent group-based differences in social and economic status are found in societies throughout the world. In the United States, these differences are found to be linked to ethnic group membership, with minority group members being less well off in terms of both economic and social status.

American legitimating myths justify these differences through reference to stereotypes about the characteristics of the members of groups. For example, minority group members are argued to deserve subordinate economic status because they are "lazy" or "not intelligent," and holding higher status is associated with possessing more favorable traits, such as competence (Fiske et al. 2002). These legitimizing myths often reflect basic cultural beliefs about what is "natural." For example, Mahalingam (2003) demonstrates that core beliefs about the "essential" features of the members of different castes support existing social inequalities in India by suggesting that different lifestyles best fit the essential characteristics of the people within different castes. Similarly, evaluative judgments about cultural practices are used to legitimate the power of doctors in hospitals (Latimer 2004).

Central to recent discussions of intergroup relations is the argument that the reactions of the members of groups are influenced by their views about whether group status is legitimate or illegitimate (Tajfel 1974). Ellemers et al. (1993) support this by demonstrating that low-status group members view their low status as more acceptable and identify more strongly with the low-status group when they judge status to be the result of a legitimate procedure for allocating people into groups. Additionally, when the assignment of low status to a group is illegitimate, people within the low-status group are dissatisfied with the position of their group and show competitive behavior toward the other group.

Other studies suggest that high-status group members may also be influenced by perceived legitimacy, with those who view their high status as illegitimate being less likely to engage in discrimination toward low-status group members (Turner 1999). Recent experimental research confirms that illegitimacy judgments increase people's tendency to express bias toward the members of other groups (Hornsey et al. 2003). And Levin et al. (2002) show that among low-status group members, ideologies justifying inequality are linked to favoring the high-status group only when status differences are viewed as legitimate.

In the context of American intergroup relations, Major (1994) argues that the degree to which people view existing social arrangements as legitimate is central to their reaction to those arrangements. If race-based discrepancies in outcomes are viewed as legitimate, people do not take action. If they are not, they lead to anger and to various forms of social action. Major (1994) further argues that people "tend to legitimate the status quo, even when it is disadvantageous to the self" (p. 309). They do so through the manner in which they structure their attributions for the causes of success and failure. For example, people locate cause in people, rather than in social systems; view themselves as having exaggerated control over their own outcomes; and believe that the world is a just place in which people get the outcomes they deserve. Major refers to these beliefs as legitimizing myths because they legitimate the existing social system.

In more recent research, it has been shown that legitimacy of group status leads differences in ability among groups to be less threatening. Schmader et al. (2001) examine the tendency of people to devalue a domain in response to information that their group is worse in that domain than another, higher-status, group. They found that when group status is legitimate, those in a low-status group do not devalue a domain because a legitimately higher-status group is better at it than their group is. When group status is illegitimate, they do. Similarly, when differences in group status are legitimate, people are less likely to interpret the negative outcomes they receive from high-status group members as reflecting discrimination (Major et al. 2002). Hence, when the high-status group holds its status legitimately, its attributions and actions are less threatening to low-status group members. Similar findings emerge in a study of nation-based soccer teams in Europe (Leach et al. 2003).

Major & Schmader (2001) also argue that legitimacy shapes the motivations that are engaged when people are involved in understanding the social world. When the system is legitimate, people are motivated to interpret their experiences in ways that justify existing conditions, finding reasons for the appropriateness of existing social arrangements. Hence, they do not attribute responsibility to factors such as discrimination that undermine the perception that the system is just. When the system is not legitimate, on the other hand, people are motivated by ego-defensive attributions, i.e., they seek to protect their sense of self and their feelings of self-worth, and they are more likely to engage in system-based attributions such as discrimination. Hence, the existence of legitimacy leads to event interpretations that provide further support for the status quo, whereas an illegitimate system encourages patterns of attribution that further undermine legitimacy.

Recent studies provide insights into the origin of perceptions of the legitimacy of group status. Weber et al. (2002) use both laboratory and field studies to demonstrate that groups that view their status as linked to holding distinct prototypical attributes are more likely to view group differences as legitimate, and to feel less guilt about their advantages. For example, the members of the dominant group may be viewed as prototypically hard working. In contrast, those lacking in such legitimacy for their status show more guilt about their advantages, as well as displaying more negative intergroup attitudes. These findings suggest that increasing the perceived prototypicality of subgroup norms is one approach to improving the legitimacy of subgroups.

A meta-analysis of the influence of membership in high-status groups finds that reactions to high-status group membership consistently are shaped by assessments of the legitimacy or illegitimacy of that status (Bettencourt et al. 2001). High-status group members identify more with their in-group than do low-status group members when group status is legitimate, but not when it is illegitimate. Further, on relevant dimensions, favorable in-group bias and unfavorable out-group bias is stronger among high-status groups when group differences are legitimate. In other words, people in high-status groups are more likely to think in self-serving ways when their high status is legitimate.

The psychological dynamics of high- and low-status groups are further developed in social dominance theory (Sidanius & Pratto 1999). According to social dominance theory, the struggle for status among groups is played out through competition to gain acceptance for ideologies that support or undermine the legitimacy of the status of dominant and subordinate groups. Dominant groups encourage the acceptance of hierarchy-enhancing ideologies that legitimate their dominant status, whereas subordinate groups support hierarchy-attenuating ideologies, which endorse greater equality among groups. In addition, because dominant groups control existing social institutions, those institutions act in ways that support and maintain existing group-based inequality, such as advocating hierarchy-enhancing policies (Sidanius et al. 2001, 2004; Sidanius & Pratto 1999, ch. 5–8). Not all institutions support the status quo. Some institutions, for example, universities, are hierarchy attenuating, i.e., they act in ways that undermine existing group-based inequalities.

A key empirical argument developing from social dominance theory is that those people who are more highly motivated to accept group-based dominance will be more accepting of ideologies that legitimate existing group-based inequality. The desire to accept group-based dominance is indexed by social dominance orientation.

Further, the social roles to which individuals are drawn will be shaped by their social dominance orientation. Those high in social dominance orientation will be more accepting of legitimating myths and more likely to be found in institutional roles that involve supporting the status quo—for example, the role of a police officer (Dambrun et al. 2002, Pratto et al. 1997, Sidanius et al. 1994). Opposition to social dominance leads to support for antisystem roles, such as radical, terrorist, and college professor (Levin et al. 2003). Recent research suggests that this occurs both because people self-select into roles consistent with their ideologies (Sidanius et al. 2003) and because people are socialized by the institutions that they join (Sinclair et al. 1998).

Two additional mechanisms are also proposed. One is institutional selection, with people whose ideologies match their institution's objectives receiving higher institutional rewards (Pratto et al. 1997). The other is differential attrition, with those whose values conflict with institutional objectives hypothesized to be more likely to drop out of the institution (van Laar et al. 1999).

Using data collected in the National Election Study, Federico & Sidanius (2002) explore the influence of political sophistication on the relationship between prejudice and attitudes toward affirmative action. The authors argue that the desire of whites to maintain group-based advantages by acting on legitimating stereotypes that support the dominance of their group (i.e., prejudice) conflicts with the American ideal that racial equality is a key element of the American creed. They explore whether respondents who are more sophisticated and more aware of this conflict are less able to maintain legitimating myths supporting their group's interests, and therefore show a weaker influence of legitimating stereotypes (prejudice) on their policy views about affirmative action. Their findings suggest that sophistication does not change the relationship between prejudice and policy support, with whites at all levels of political sophistication showing a similarly strong influence of their legitimating stereotypes on their policy positions (also see Sidanius et al. 1996).

The suggestion that people are motivated to justify the current social system is also a key hypothesis of system justification theory. System justification theory focuses directly on the argument that stereotyping is a form of system justification through which existing social arrangements are legitimated by reference to the characteristics of different groups (Jost & Banaji 1994). For example, the members of dominant groups are viewed as intelligent and hard working, which justifies their possession of economic wealth and social status, whereas the portrayal of subordinate group members as lazy and weak seems to justify their lack of possession of wealth and status. More generally, the theory focuses on "system-justification [as] the psychological process by which existing social arrangements are legitimized, even at the expense of personal and group interest" (Jost & Banaji 1994, p. 2), and the authors note that "stereotypes serve for their adherents the function of preserving the status quo" (p. 10).

Studies support this argument by showing that if people are primed with social status information, they develop stereotypes to justify that social ordering (Jost

2001, Jost & Burgess 2000, Jost et al. 2001). Most recently, studies of implicit attitudes suggest that both the members of disadvantaged and advantaged groups show evidence of such justifications. The members of disadvantaged groups are found to exhibit favoritism toward other groups (i.e., the advantaged), especially on implicit measures that minimize self-presentational issues. Members of advantaged groups, in contrast, are found to exhibit favoritism toward their own group (the advantaged) on implicit measures. Hence, both the advantaged and the disadvantaged support stereotypes justifying the position of the advantaged in studies using measurement strategies designed to minimize social desirability in responding (Jost et al. 2004).

Recent research argues for a more nuanced view of stereotypes by suggesting that both the advantaged and the disadvantaged will be stereotyped in ways that are favorable in some respects, but that also support existing social arrangements (Kay & Jost 2003). For example, the disadvantaged are presented as poor but happy, whereas the advantaged are depicted as rich but miserable. Similarly, men are viewed as agentic but not communal, whereas women are viewed as communal, but not agentic (Jost & Kay 2005). These complementary stereotypes "psychologically offset the one-sided advantage of any single group and contribute to an image of society in which everyone benefits through a balanced dispersion of benefits" (Jost & Kay 2005, p. 498; also see Kay et al. 2005). This argument is also made by Glick & Fiske (2001), who suggest the importance of "ambivalent" stereotypes that combine both positive and negative characteristics when describing out-groups.

Other types of research also support the basic argument that people are motivated to justify or legitimate the status quo. For example, Robinson & Kray (2001) show that those defending the status quo make little cognitive effort to understand the arguments of those urging changes, leading to frequent misinterpretations of their arguments. In addition, when people make arguments that challenge a person's representations of the status quo, they are more likely to be perceived to be acting out of personal self-interest (O'Brien & Crandall 2005). Finally, people are found to be motivated to believe that (1) existing social arrangements are just; (2) they have not personally suffered from discrimination; and (3) harboring emotions such as resentment is socially inappropriate (Olson & Hafer 2001). These cognitive and motivational factors generally encourage deference to existing social conditions.

WHY ARE PEOPLE MOTIVATED TO ENGAGE IN SYSTEM JUSTIFICATION?   Studies suggest that system-justifying ideologies decrease anxiety, uncertainty, guilt, frustration, and dissonance, and increase satisfaction with one's situation in life (Jost & Hunyady 2002). Interestingly, this is true for both the disadvantaged and the advantaged (Chen & Tyler 2001). Although research has focused upon the reactions of the disadvantaged to their plight, theories of justice suggest that those who have "too much" also have a psychological problem to resolve. Studies of the advantaged suggest that they are also motivated to create "legitimizing myths" to make their advantaged status seem appropriate (Chen & Tyler 2001). For example, those who attain their positions through family connections often create periods of "internship" that allow them to legitimize their subsequent rapid advance to the top of family firms, whereas those who gain admission to elite colleges through legacy admissions try to cloak such procedures in a merit-based framework. This idea is captured very well in the comment that "Some people are born on third base and go through life thinking they hit a triple" (Switzer 2005).

These findings suggest that the motivation to justify is a general one, with justifications of one's position serving palliative psychological functions for both the advantaged and the disadvantaged. Among the advantaged, one consequence of such justifications is diminished support for both social change and assistance to the disadvantaged. If, after all, the advantaged believe that they made it on their own, then they might reasonably expect others to do the same.

Distinguishing Legitimacy from Morality

Legitimacy is an internal value that is linked to personal feelings of obligation and responsibility to others. In these ways, it is similar to the moral values that are also an internal motivational guide to behavior. The influence of moral values upon behavior is like the influence of legitimacy in that both are internalized values that are taken on by individuals as a personal responsibility—i.e., to obey legitimate authorities and to act in ways consistent with personal moral values.

Although legitimacy and morality are similar in many ways, they are also clearly differentiable. Legitimacy is a perceived obligation to societal authorities or to existing social arrangements. Moral values are personal standards to which people attempt to align their behavior. Often moral values and legitimacy work together. For example, with most everyday laws, people obey the law because they feel that they ought to obey legitimate authorities and because they believe that the conduct prohibited by law is morally wrong (Tyler 1990, 2003). However, they do not always work in concert. In his work on obedience to authority, Kelman argues that morality operates as a check against following immoral orders given by legitimate authorities (Kelman & Hamilton 1989). He finds that when people deal with legitimate authorities, they authorize those authorities to make decisions about what is right and wrong. Hence, they suspend their normal motivation to keep their behavior in line with their moral values. In settings of this type, only legitimacy shapes behavior.

Recent studies suggest that people's moral values also shape their reactions to rules (Darley et al. 2003) and to public authorities such as the police (Sunshine & Tyler 2003a). Past studies show that people follow rules when they think those rules accord with their moral values (Robinson & Darley 1995). Recent studies indicate that people's views about appropriate sentencing decisions in criminal cases are driven by their morally based desire to give wrongdoers the punishment they deserve, and not by the instrumental goal of preventing future criminal activity either by the criminals themselves or by others whose actions might be shaped by the punishment the criminal receives. People punish based upon the moral wrong reflected by the level and type of crime committed (Carlsmith et al. 2002, Darley et al. 2000).

The Normative Status of Legitimacy

Past social psychological research has focused on legitimacy as a form of influence and has explored when legitimacy shapes people's thoughts, feelings, and behavior. However, the recent emphasis of legitimacy research on societal-level institutions highlights the importance of social theories in shaping the normative perspective that is taken on legitimacy as a topic of study. That perspective, of necessity, must be rooted in political and sociological theories about the social nature of societies (Parkin 1972).

The views of the classic social theorists already noted are linked to the underlying assumptions of "consensus" views of society (Dahl 1956, Easton 1965, Lipset 1959, Parsons 1967, Sears 2003). Those views argue that all members of society benefit from the social and political stability that is facilitated by widespread beliefs that existing authorities and institutions are legitimate. Hence, there is no fundamental societal conflict underlying the study of legitimacy. Legitimacy is a valuable attribute for an institution if it promotes acceptance of its decisions and the rules it promulgates, and stability and institutional effectiveness are virtues that benefit all members of society.

The primary question of concern from a consensus perspective has been when and to what degree legitimacy actually shapes behavior—i.e., does legitimacy work as an influence strategy? The focus of rational actor models on the influence of rewards and punishment on behavior has led an emphasis in recent years on those instrumental factors rather than upon the development and maintenance of values such as legitimacy as part of an overall model of governance linked to political culture (Green & Shapiro 1994). Writers in an earlier era argued that the key to a stable society was the widespread development of such supportive values (Easton 1965), leading to a focus in earlier research on the socialization of values such as legitimacy and support for legal and political authority (Easton & Dennis 1969, Hess & Torney 1967, Hyman 1959, Sears 1975).

An alternative view of the society develops from conflict theories of society, models rooted in Marxism (Parkin 1972), but equally consistent with both realistic group conflict theory (Taylor & Moghaddam 1994) and social identity theory (Hogg & Abrams 1988). These models argue that groups within society are in conflict over valued resources and favored identities. Each group seeks to gain dominance over others, with the result that institutional arrangements and legitimizing ideologies favoring one group are often not beneficial to those within other groups.

This view of society leads to the argument that the process of legitimation favors the dominant group over others. It is not in the interest of subordinate groups to defer to the authorities and institutions that dominant groups have created to serve their interests. Hence, from this perspective, widespread deference to legitimate authorities is beneficial only to those in the dominant group who seek to perpetuate their privileges by using their hegemonic control over culture to create ideologies, myths, and rituals that legitimate their favored position. Subordinate groups would be better off rejecting existing authorities and institutions and challenging the status quo by seeking social change (Tyler & McGraw 1986).

Such conflict-based models of society underlie many of the contributions to a recent volume on the psychology of legitimacy (Jost & Major 2001). In a review of this work, Sears argues that "The idealistic hope behind much of [the work in this volume] is that subordinate groups will see through the illusory legitimizing myths fostered by dominant groups to a 'true' consciousness more in harmony with their own real interests, and will then mobilize collectively to pursue them" (Sears 2003, p. 320).

As the literature reviewed suggests, there is substantial evidence that legitimacy encourages a wide variety of forms of public cooperation in many, but clearly not all, social settings. In particular, those who support authorities and institutions defer to their decisions and to the policies and rules they create (Elsbach 2001, Tyler 2001, Tyler & Huo 2002). Hence, the central empirical premise of legitimacy is well supported—legitimacy is an effective influence strategy—and those who view system stability as a valuable attribute can and do benefit when they are able to create and maintain this supportive value. Therefore, the question of how to view these findings is a socially important one. Consensus theorists regard them as positive, conflict theorists as disturbing.

One approach to reconciling these different approaches to legitimacy lies in understanding how legitimacy is created and maintained. The findings reviewed consistently suggest that the legitimacy of authorities and institutions is linked to the fairness of the procedures by which they exercise their authority. Hence, the pursuit of public support requires institutions and authorities to adhere to lay principles of procedural justice. The effort to create and maintain legitimacy, in other words, leads institutions to have a focus upon those who are being led, and their conceptions of justice and fairness. Widespread legitimacy will exist only when the perspectives of everyday members are enshrined in institutions and in the actions of authorities. This suggests that a focus on legitimacy empowers the members of organizations and societies.

The risk, pointed to by conflict theorists, is that justice judgments themselves will be the result of "false consciousness," with the members of subordinate groups adopting the legitimating myths put forward by the dominant class (Fox 1999, Haney 1991). An example of this type of myth acceptance has been noted already in research on economic markets. Belief in the procedural justice of markets is widespread within American society, even among those who benefit the least from their operation (Jost et al. 2003). Further, this belief generally is not influenced by evidence that the market operates in ways that lead to wide group-based differences in economic outcomes (Tyler 2004). These results are consistent with the argument that in at least some instances the justice judgments shaping assessments of legitimacy may reflect the perspective of a particular social group. The extent to which this is the case awaits future research.

Overview

The idea of legitimacy has a long history within social thought and is important across the social sciences. The research reviewed shows the breadth of recent research on legitimacy and the depth of support for the basic argument of legitimacy theory. The concept of legitimacy is an ancient one, and the contribution of recent research is to test empirically its utility in a variety of social settings.

Consistent with the arguments of legitimacy theory, research shows that people are not influenced simply by the possession and use of power. Those authorities who seek to lead groups through incentives and/or coercion find it difficult to shape behavior effectively through these mechanisms, and they have difficulty creating and maintaining their influence over others. Therefore, those leading groups, organizations, and societies benefit when they have legitimacy among the members of their groups. Leaders have legitimacy when people view their authority as being appropriate and proper, with the consequence that they feel obligated to defer to the decisions made by leaders with legitimacy and the policies and rules they create.

What are the implications of the empirical findings outlined in this chapter? Dominant models of social control currently focus upon two ways that authorities can gain cooperation from the public. One way is via the threat of punishment, which promotes rule following. The other is via demonstrating competence in managing community problems, which encourages the public to help authorities. However, research findings are not consistent with these models. For example, the police have made dramatic improvements in the objective quality of their performance in recent decades, but that has not led to increases in public support for the police (National Research Council 2004, Skogan & Meares 2004). Why not? Because research suggests the public primarily views the police as legitimate, and cooperates with the police, when they experience the police as exercising their authority fairly. Hence, changes in the objective performance of the police in the control of crime and disorder do not strongly connect with public cooperation. For the police to gain cooperation, they need to focus on the fairness of police procedures, since fairer procedures would increase police legitimacy (Tyler 2004a). Similar arguments apply to the courts (Tyler 2001).

This review of recent research further suggests that legitimacy is important far beyond the prototypical case in which people defer to particular decisions made by authorities or rules created by institutions. The development of legitimizing myths that legitimate social arrangements is ubiquitous through society and is found with the justification of mechanisms for allocating economic and social status as well as with group-based differences in economic and social status. A number of studies in recent years document the pervasiveness and importance of the human desire to make sense of existing social arrangement by endowing those arrangements with the assessment that they are appropriate and reasonable. This motivation is found among those who benefit from and, more paradoxically, those who are disadvantaged by those arrangements.

Finally, research also suggests what creates and sustains legitimacy. Authorities and institutions are legitimated by the manner in which they make decisions and exercise authority. Unlike a more instrumental perspective, which suggests that authorities gain influence over others when they can either deliver desired outcomes or credibly threaten others with harm, recent research demonstrates that people's deference to others is also based upon factors other than the ability to deliver rewards or punishments. To at least some extent, legitimacy derives from judgments about how those others exercise authority, judgments not based upon the favorability or even the fairness of the decisions the authorities make, but upon beliefs about what are fair or ethical procedures for exercising authority. Hence, the exercise of authority via fair procedures legitimates that authority, and encourages voluntary deference.

ACKNOWLEDGMENTS

I thank Naomi Ellemers, Susan Fiske, John Jost, Brenda Major, and Jim Sidanius for comments on a draft of this chapter.

The *Annual Review of Psychology* is online at http://psych.annualreviews.org

LITERATURE CITED

Ambrose ML. 2002. Contemporary justice research. *Organ. Behav. Hum. Decis. Process.* 89:803–12

Bansal P, Clelland I. 2004. Talking trash: legitimacy, impression management, and unsystematic risk in the context of the natural environment. *Acad. Manage. J.* 47:93–103

Baum J, Oliver C. 1991. Institutional linkages and organizational mortality. *Admin. Sci. Q.* 36:187–218

Beetham D. 1991. *The Legitimation of Power.* Atlantic Highlands, NJ: Humanities

Bettencourt BA, Dorr N, Charlton K, Hume DL. 2001. Status differences and in-group bias. *Psychol. Bull.* 127:520–42

Blader S, Tyler TR. 2003. A four-component model of procedural justice: defining the meaning of a "fair" process. *Personal. Soc. Psychol. Bull.* 29:747–58

Carlsmith KM, Darley JM, Robinson PH. 2002.

Why do we punish? *J. Personal. Soc. Psychol.* 83:284–99

Carpini MXD, Cook FL, Jacobs LR. 2004. Public deliberation, discursive participation, and citizen engagement. *Annu. Rev. Polit. Sci.* 7:315–44

Chen E, Tyler TR. 2001. Cloaking power: legitimizing myths and the psychology of the advantaged. In *The Use and Abuse of Power*, ed. JA Bargh, AY Lee-Chai, pp. 241–61. Philadelphia: Psychol. Press

Cialdini RB, Goldstein NJ. 2004. Social influence: compliance and conformity. *Annu. Rev. Psychol.* 55:591–621

Clawson RA, Kegler ER, Waltenberg EN. 2001. The legitimacy-conferring authority of the U.S. Supreme Court. *Am. Polit. Res.* 29:566–51

Cohen Charash Y, Spector PE. 2001. The role of justice in organizations. *Organ. Behav. Hum. Decis. Process.* 86:278–321

Cohen Charash Y, Spector PE. 2002. Erratum to the role of justice in organizations. *Organ. Behav. Hum. Decis. Process.* 89:1215

Cohn ES, White SO, Sanders J. 2000. Distributive and procedural justice in seven nations. *Law Hum. Behav.* 24:553–79

Colquitt JA, Conlon D, Wesson M, Porter COL, Ng KL. 2001. Justice at the millennium: a meta-analytic review of 25 years of organizational justice. *J. Appl. Psychol.* 86:425–45

Colquitt JA, Greenberg J, Zapata-Phelan CP. 2005. What is organizational justice? A historical overview. In *Handbook of Organizational Justice*, ed. J Greenberg, JA Colquitt, pp. 3–58. Mahwah, NJ: Erlbaum

Dahl R. 1956. *A Preface to Democratic Theory.* Chicago: Univ. Chicago Press

Dambrun M, Guimond S, Duarte S. 2002. The impact of hierarchy-enhancing vs. hierarchy-attenuating academic majors on stereotyping. *Curr. Res. Soc. Psychol.* 7:114–36

Darley JM, Carlsmith KM, Robinson PH. 2000. Incapacitation and just deserts as motives for punishment. *Law Hum. Behav.* 24:659–83

Darley JM, Tyler TR, Bilz K. 2003. Enacting justice: the interplay of individual and institutional perspectives. In *The Sage Handbook of Social Psychology*, ed. MA Hogg, J Cooper, pp. 458–76. London: Sage

DeCremer D, Tyler TR. 2005. Managing group behavior: the interplay between procedural justice, sense of self, and cooperation. In *Advances in Experimental Social Psychology*, ed. M Zanna, pp. 151–218. New York: Academic

DeCremer D, van Knippenberg D. 2002. How do leaders promote cooperation? The effects of charisma and procedural fairness. *J. Appl. Psychol.* 87: 858–66

Dye T. 1990. *The Political Legitimacy of Markets and Governments.* Greenwich, CT: JAI

Easton D. 1965. *A Systems Analysis of Political Life.* Chicago: Univ. Chicago Press

Easton D, Dennis J. 1969. *Children in the Political System.* Chicago: Univ. Chicago Press

Ellemers N, Spears R, Doosje B. 2002. Self and social identity. *Annu. Rev. Psychol.* 53:161–86

Ellemers N, Wilke H, van Knippenberg A. 1993. Effects of the legitimacy of low group or individual status on individual and collective status-enhancement strategies. *J. Personal. Soc. Psychol.* 64:766–78

Elsbach KD. 2001. The architecture of legitimacy: constructing accounts of organizational controversies. See Jost & Major 2001, pp. 391–415

Elsbach KD, Sutton RI. 1992. Acquiring organizational legitimacy through illegitimate actions. *Acad. Manage. J.* 35:699–738

Espeland WN, Stevens ML. 1998. Commensuration as a social process. *Annu. Rev. Sociol.* 24:313–43

Farnsworth SJ. 2003. Congress and citizen discontent: public evaluations of the membership and one's own representative. *Am. Polit. Res.* 21:66–80

Federico C, Sidanius J. 2002. Sophistication and the antecedents of whites' racial policy attitudes. *Public Opinion Q.* 66:145–76

Fiske ST, Cuddy AJC, Glick P, Xu J. 2002. A model of (often mixed) stereotype content: competence and warmth respectively follow from perceived status and competition. *J. Personal. Soc. Psychol.* 82:878–902

Ford R, Johnson C. 1998. The perception of power: dependence and legitimacy in conflict. *Soc. Psychol. Q.* 61:16–32

Fox DR. 1999. Psycholegal scholarship's contribution to false consciousness about injustice. *Law Hum. Behav.* 23:9–30

French JRP Jr, Raven BH. 1959. The bases of social power. In *Studies in Social Power*, ed. D Cartwright, pp. 150–67. Ann Arbor: Univ. Mich. Inst. Soc. Res.

Gangl A. 2003. Procedural justice theory and evaluations of the lawmaking process. *Polit. Behav.* 25:119–49

Gibson JL. 2002. Truth, justice, and reconciliation: judging the fairness of amnesty in South Africa. *Am. J. Polit. Sci.* 46:540–56

Gibson JL. 2004. *Overcoming Apartheid: Can Truth Reconcile a Divided Nation?* New York: Russell Sage Found.

Gibson JL, Caldiera GA. 2003. Defenders of democracy? Legitimacy, popular acceptance, and the South African Constitutional Court. *J. Polit.* 65:1–30

Gibson JL, Caldiera GA, Baird VA. 1998. On the legitimacy of national high courts. *Am. Polit. Sci. Rev.* 92:343–58

Gibson JL, Caldiera GA, Spence LK. 2003. The Supreme Court and the US Presidential election of 2000: wounds, self-inflicted or otherwise? *Br. J. Polit. Sci.* 33:535–56

Gibson JL, Caldiera GA, Spence LK. 2005. Why do people accept public policies they oppose? Testing legitimacy theory with a survey-based experiment. *Polit. Res. Q.* In press

Glick P, Fiske ST. 2001. Ambivalent stereotypes as legitimizing ideologies. See Jost & Major 2001, pp. 278–306

Gold M. 1999. *The Complete Social Scientist: A Kurt Lewin Reader.* Washington, DC: Am. Psychol. Assoc. Press

Green DP, Shapiro I. 1994. *Pathologies of Rational Choice Theory.* New Haven, CT: Yale Univ. Press

Haney C. 1991. The 14th amendment and symbolic legality: Let them eat due process. *Law Hum. Behav.* 15:183–204

Haslam SA. 2004. *Psychology in Organizations.* Thousand Oaks: Sage. 2nd ed.

Hegtvedt KA, Clay-Warner J, Johnson C. 2003. The social context of responses to injustice: considering the indirect and direct effects of group-level factors. *Soc. Justice Res.* 16:343–66

Hegtvedt KA, Johnson C. 2000. Justice beyond the individual: a future with legitimation. *Soc. Psychol. Q.* 63:298–311

Hess RD, Torney JV. 1967. *The Development of Political Attitudes in Children.* Chicago, IL: Aldine

Hewstone M, Rubin M, Wills H. 2002. Intergroup bias. *Annu. Rev. Psychol.* 53:575–604

Hibbing JR, Theiss-Morse E. 2002. *Stealth Democracy: Americans' Beliefs About How Government Should Work.* New York: Cambridge Univ. Press

Hoffman EA. 2005. Dispute resolution in a worker cooperative: formal procedures and procedural justice. *Law Soc. Rev.* 39:51–82

Hoffman M. 1977. Moral internalization. *Adv. Exp. Soc. Psychol.* 10:85–133

Hogg MA, Abrams D. 1988. *Social Identifications: A Social Psychology of Intergroup Relations and Group Processes.* New York: Routledge

Hornsey MJ, Spears R, Cremers I, Hogg MA. 2003. Relations between high and low power groups: the importance of legitimacy. *Personal. Soc. Psychol. Bull.* 29:216–27

Human SE, Provan KG. 2000. Legitimacy building in the evolution of small firm multilateral networks: a comparative study of success and demise. *Admin. Sci. Q.* 45:327–65

Hurd I. 1999. Legitimacy and authority in international politics. *Int. Organ.* 53:379–408

Hyman H. 1959. *Political Socialization: A Study of the Psychology of Political Behavior.* New York: Free Press

Jost JT. 2001. Outgroup favoritism and the theory of system justification. In *Cognitive Social Psychology*, ed. G Moskowitz, pp. 89–102. Mahwah, NJ: Erlbaum

Jost JT, Banaji MR. 1994. The role of stereotyping in system-justification and the production of false consciousness. *Br. J. Soc. Psychol.* 33:1–27

Jost JT, Banaji MR, Nosek BA. 2004. A decade of system justification theory. *Polit. Psychol.* 25:881–919

Jost JT, Blount S, Pfeffer J, Hunyady G. 2003. Fair market ideology: its cognitive-motivational underpinnings. *Res. Organ. Behav.* 25:53–91

Jost JT, Burgess D. 2000. Attitudinal ambivalence and the conflict between group and system justification motives in low-status groups. *Personal. Soc. Psychol. Bull.* 26:293–305

Jost JT, Burgess D, Mosso CO. 2001. Conflicts of legitimation among self, group, and system: the integrative potential of system justification theory. In *The Psychology of Legitimacy: Emerging Perspectives on Ideology, Justice, and Intergroup Relations*, ed. JT Jost, B Major, pp. 363–90. Cambridge: Cambridge Univ. Press

Jost JT, Hunyady O. 2002. The psychology of

system justification and the palliative function of ideology. *Eur. Rev. Soc. Psychol.* 13:111–53

Jost JT, Kay AC. 2005. Exposure to benevolent sexism and complementary gender stereotypes. *J. Personal. Soc. Psychol.* 88:498–509

Jost JT, Major B. 2001. *The Psychology of Legitimacy: Emerging Perspectives on Ideology, Justice, and Intergroup Relations.* Cambridge: Cambridge Univ. Press

Jost JT, Pelham BW, Sheldon O, Sullivan BN. 2003. Social inequality and the reduction of ideological dissonance on behalf of the system. *Eur. J. Soc. Psychol.* 33:13–36

Kay AC, Jost JT. 2003. Complementary justice: effects of "poor but happy" and "poor but honest" stereotype exemplars on system justification and implicit activation of the justice motive. *J. Personal. Soc. Psychol.* 85:823–37

Kay AC, Jost JT, Young S. 2005. Victim derogation and victim enhancement as alternative routes to system justification. *Psychol. Sci.* 16:240–46

Kershaw TS, Alexander S. 2003. Procedural fairness, blame attributions, and Presidential leadership. *Soc. Justice Res.* 16:79–93

Keyes CL, Hysom SJ, Lupo KL. 2000. The positive organization: leadership legitimacy, employee well-being, and the bottom line. *Psychol. Manage. J.* 4:143–53

Kelman HC. 1969. Patterns of personal involvement in the national system: a sociopsychological analysis of political legitimacy. In *International Politics and Foreign Policy*, ed. J. Rosenau, pp. 276–88. New York: Free Press. Rev. ed.

Kelman HC. 2001. Reflections on social and psychological processes of legitimization and delegitimization. See Jost & Major 2001, pp. 54–76

Kelman HC, Hamilton VL. 1989. *Crimes of Obedience.* New Haven, CT: Yale Univ. Press

King A, Lenox M. 2000. Industry self-regulation without sanctions. *Acad. Manage. J.* 43:698–716

Kluegel JR, Mason DS. 2004. Fairness matters: social justice and political legitimacy in post-

communist Europe. *Eur. Asia Stud.* 56:813–34

Kluegel JR, Smith ER. 1986. *Beliefs About Inequality.* Hawthorne, NY: Aldine de Gruyter

Konovsky MA. 2000. Understanding procedural justice and its impact on business organizations. *J. Manag.* 26:489–511

Kostova T, Zaheer S. 1999. Organizational legitimacy under conditions of complexity. *Acad. Manage. Rev.* 24:64–81

Landsman S. 2003. Lay participation in legal processes and the development of democracy. *Law Polit.* 25:173–78

Latimer J. 2004. Commanding materials: (re)legitimating authority in the context of multi-disciplinary work. *Sociology* 38:757–75

Leach CW, Spears R, Branscombe NR, Doosje B. 2003. Malicious pleasure: schadenfreude at the suffering of another group. *J. Personal. Soc. Psychol.* 84:932–43

Levin S, Federico CM, Sidanius J, Rabinowitz JL. 2002. Social dominance orientation and intergroup bias. *Personal. Soc. Psychol. Bull.* 28:144–57

Levin S, Henry PJ, Pratto F, Sidanius J. 2003. Social dominance and social identity in Lebanon. *Group Process. Intergroup Behav.* 6:353–68

Lewin K. 1951. *Field Theory in Social Science.* New York: Harper

Lewin K, Lippitt R, White RK. 1939. Patterns of aggressive behavior in experimentally created social climates. *J. Soc. Psychol.* 10:271–99

Lipset SM. 1959. Some social requisites of democracy. *Am. Polit. Sci. Rev.* 53:69–105

Machura S. 2003. Fairness, justice, and legitimacy: experiences of people's judges in South Russia. *Law Polit.* 25:123–50

Mahalingam R. 2003. Essentialism, culture, and power: representations of social class. *J. Soc. Issues* 59:733–49

Major B. 1994. From social inequality to personal entitlement. *Adv. Exp. Soc. Psychol.* 26:293–356

Major B, Gramzow RH, McCoy SK, Levin S, Schmader T, Sidanius J. 2002. Perceiving personal discrimination: the role of group status and legitimizing ideology. *J. Personal. Soc. Psychol.* 82:269–82

Major BN, O'Brien LT. 2005. The social psychology of stigma. *Annu. Rev. Psychol.* 56: 393–421

Major B, Schmader T. 2001. Legitimacy and the construal of social disadvantage. See Jost & Major 2001, pp. 176–204

Milgram S. 1975. *Obedience to Authority*. New York: Harper Colophon

Miller DT. 2001. Disrespect and the experience of injustice. *Annu. Rev. Psychol.* 52:527–54

Mueller CW, Landman MJ. 2004. Legitimacy and justice perceptions. *Soc. Psychol. Q.* 67: 189–202

Murphy K. 2004. The role of trust in nurturing compliance: a study of accused tax avoiders. *Law Hum. Behav.* 28:187–209

Nagin D. 1998. Criminal deterrence research at the outset of the twenty-first century. *Crime Justice* 23:1–42

Natl. Res. Counc. 2004. *Fairness and Effectiveness in Policing: The Evidence.* Committee to Review Research on Police Policy and Practices, ed. W Skogan, K. Frydl, Comm. Law Justice, Div. Behav. Soc. Sci. Educ. Washington, DC: Natl. Acad. Press

Nugent WR, Williams M, Umbreit, 2003. Participation in victim-offender mediation and the prevalence and severity of subsequent delinquent behavior. *Utah Law Rev.* 2003:137–66

O'Brien LT, Crandall CS. 2005. Perceiving self-interest: power, ideology, and maintenance of the status quo. *Soc. Justice Res.* 18: 1–24

Olson JM, Hafer CL. 2001. Tolerance of personal deprivation. See Jost & Major 2001, pp. 157–75

Parkin F. 1972. *Class Inequality and Political Order*. New York: Praeger

Parsons T. 1967. Some reflections on the place of force in social process. In *Sociological Theory and Modern Society*, ed. T. Parsons, pp. 264–96. New York: Free Press

Paternoster R, Brame R, Bachman R, Sherman

L. 1997. Do fair procedures matter? *Law Soc. Rev.* 31:163–204

Pollock TG, Rindova VP. 2003. Media legitimation effects in the market for initial public offerings. *Acad. Manage. J.* 46:631–42

Porter COLH, Hollenbeck JR, Ilgen DR, Ellis APJ, West JW, Moon H. 2003. Backing up behaviors in teams: the role of personality and legitimacy of need. *J. Appl. Psychol.* 88:391–403

Poulson B. 2003. A third wave: a review of empirical research on the psychological outcomes of restorative justice. *Utah Law Rev.* 2003:167–204

Pratto F, Stallworth L, Sidanius J, Siers B. 1997. The gender gap in occupational role attainment. *J. Personal. Soc. Psychol.* 72:37–53

Rao H. 1994. The social construction of reputation: certification contests, legitimation, and the survival of organizations in the American automobile industry: 1985–1912. *Strateg. Manage. J.* 15:29–44

Roberts JV, Stalans L. 2004. Restorative sentencing: exploring the views of the public. *Soc. Justice Res.* 17:315–34

Robinson P, Darley J. 1995. *Justice, Liability, and Blame: Community Views and the Criminal Law.* Boulder, CO: Westview

Robinson RJ, Kray L. 2001. Status versus quo: naïve realism and the search for social change and perceived legitimacy. See Jost & Major 2001, pp. 135–56

Schmader T, Major B, Eccleston C, McCoy SK. 2001. Devaluing domains in response to threatening intergroup comparisons. *J. Personal. Soc. Psychol.* 80:782–96

Sears DO. 1975. Political socialization. In *Handbook of Political Science*, ed. FI Greenstein, NW Polsby, 2: 93–153. Reading, MA: Addison-Wesley

Sears DO. 2003. The psychology of legitimacy. *Polit. Psychol.* 25:318–23

Seligson MA. 2002. The impact of corruption on regime legitimacy. *J. Polit.* 64:408–33

Seron C, Pereira J, Kovath J. 2004. Judging police misconduct. *Law Soc. Rev.* 38:665–710

Shestowsky D. 2004. Procedural preferences in alternative dispute resolution. *Psychol. Public Policy Law* 10:211–49

Sidanius J, Levin S, Federico CM, Pratto F. 2001. Legitimizing ideologies: the social dominance approach. See Jost & Major 2001, pp. 307–31

Sidanius J, Liu J, Pratto F, Shaw J. 1994. Social dominance orientation, hierarchy-attenuators and hierarchy-enhancers. *J. Appl. Soc. Psychol.* 24:338–66

Sidanius J, Pratto F. 1999. *Social Dominance.* New York: Cambridge Univ. Press

Sidanius J, Pratto F, Bobo L. 1996. Racism, conservatism, affirmative action, and intellectual sophistication: a matter of principled conservatism or group dominance? *J. Personal. Soc. Psychol.* 70:476–90

Sidanius J, Pratto F, van Laar C, Levin S. 2004. Social dominance theory: its agenda and method. *Polit. Psychol.* 25:845–80

Sidanius J, van Laar C, Levin S, Sinclair S. 2003. Social hierarchy maintenance and assortment into social roles. *Group Process. Intergroup Relat.* 6:333–52

Sinclair S, Sidanius J, Levin S. 1998. The interface between ethnic and social system attachment. *J. Soc. Issues* 54:741–57

Skogan WG, Meares TL. 2004. Lawful policing. *Ann. Am. Acad. Polit. Soc. Sci.* 593:66–83

Smith ER, Jackson JW, Sparks CW. 2003. Effects of inequality and reasons for inequality on group identification and cooperation in social dilemmas. *Group Process. Intergroup Relat.* 6:201–20

Stryker R. 1994. Rules, resources, and legitimacy processes. *Am. J. Sociol.* 99:847–910

Stryker R. 2000. Legitimacy processes as institutional politics. *Res. Sociol. Organ.* 17:179–224

Suchman MC. 1995. Managing legitimacy: strategic and institutional approaches. *Acad. Manage. Rev.* 20:571–610

Sunshine J, Tyler TR. 2003. The role of procedural justice and legitimacy in shaping public support for policing. *Law Soc. Rev.* 37:513–48

Sunshine J, Tyler TR. 2003a. Moral solidarity, identification with the community, and the importance of procedural justice: the police as prototypical representatives of a group's moral values. *Soc. Psychol. Q.* 66:153–65

Switzer B. 2005. Quotation #23536 from Michael Moncur's (Cynical) Quotations. http://www.quotationspage.com/quote/

Tajfel H. 1974. Social identity and intergroup behavior. *Soc. Sci. Inf.* 13:65–93

Taylor DM, Moghaddam FM. 1994. *Theories of Intergroup Relations.* Westport, CT: Praeger

Thibaut J, Walker L. 1975. *Procedural Justice.* Hillsdale, NJ: Erlbaum

Thibaut J, Walker L. 1978. A theory of procedure. *Calif. Law Rev.* 66:541–66

Thucydides. 1982. *The Peloponnesian War (Book 5).* Transl. TE Wick, R Crawley. New York: Modern Library (From Greek)

Trochev A. 2004. Less democracy, more courts: a puzzle of judicial review in Russia. *Law Soc. Rev.* 38:513–48

Turner JC. 1999. Some current issues in research on social identity and self-categorization theories. In *Social Identity*, ed. N Ellemers, R Spears, B Doosje, pp. 6–34. Oxford: Blackwell Sci.

Tyler TR. 1990. *Why People Obey the Law.* New Haven, CT: Yale Univ. Press

Tyler TR. 2001. A psychological perspective on the legitimacy of authorities and institutions. See Jost & Major 2001, pp. 416–36

Tyler TR. 2000. Social justice: outcome and procedure. *Int. J. Psychol.* 35:117–25

Tyler TR. 2001. Public trust and confidence in legal authorities: What do majority and minority group members want from the law and legal authorities? *Behav. Sci. Law* 19:215–35

Tyler TR. 2002. Leadership and cooperation in groups. *Am. Behav. Sci.* 45:769–82

Tyler TR. 2003. Procedural justice, legitimacy, and the effective rule of law. *Crime Justice* 30:431–505

Tyler TR. 2004. Affirmative action in an institutional context. *Soc. Justice Res.* 17:5–24

Tyler TR. 2004a. Enhancing police legitimacy. *Ann. Am. Acad. Polit. Soc. Sci.* 593:84–99

Tyler TR, Blader S. 2000. *Cooperation in Groups*. Philadelphia, PA: Psychol. Press

Tyler TR, Blader S. 2003. Procedural justice, social identity, and cooperative behavior. *Personal. Soc. Psychol. Rev.* 7:349–61

Tyler TR, Blader S. 2005. Can businesses effectively regulate employee conduct? The antecedents of rule following in work settings. *Acad. Manage. J.* In press

Tyler TR, Huo YJ. 2002. *Trust in the Law*. New York: Russell Sage Found.

Tyler TR, Lind EA. 1992. A relational model of authority in groups. *Adv. Exp. Soc. Psychol.* 25:115–91

Tyler TR, McGraw K. 1986. Ideology and the interpretation of personal experience: procedural justice and political quiescence. *J. Soc. Issues* 42:115–28

Tyler TR, Smith H. 1998. Social justice and social movements. In *Handbook of Social Psychology*, ed. D Gilbert, S Fiske, G Lindzey, 2:595–629. New York: McGraw-Hill. 4th ed.

Tyler TR, Wakslak C. 2004. Profiling and the legitimacy of the police. *Criminology* 42:13–42

Van Laar C, Sidanius J, Rabinowitz JL, Sinclair S. 1999. The three Rs of academic achievement: reading, 'riting, and racism. *Personal. Soc. Psychol. Bull.* 25:139–51

Weatherford MS. 1992. Measuring political legitimacy. *Am. Polit. Sci. Rev.* 86:149–66

Weber M. 1968. *Economy and Society*, ed. G Roth, C Wittich. Berkeley: Univ. Calif. Press

Weber U, Mummendey A, Waldzus S. 2002. Perceived legitimacy of intergroup status differences: its prediction by relative ingroup prototypicality. *Eur. J. Soc. Psychol.* 32:449–70

Zelditch M Jr. 2001. Theories of legitimacy. See Jost & Major 2001, pp. 33–53

Zelditch M Jr. 2001. Processes of legitimation: recent developments and new directions. *Soc. Psychol. Q.* 64:4–17

Zelditch M Jr, Walker HA. 2000. The normative regulation of power. *Adv. Group Processes* 17:155–78

Zelditch M Jr, Walker HA. 2003. The legitimacy of regimes. *Adv. Group Processes* 20:217–49

Zimmerman MA, Zeitz GJ. 2002. Beyond survival: achieving new venture growth by building legitimacy. *Acad. Manage. Rev.* 27:414–31

Annu. Rev. Psychol. 2006. 57:401–21
doi: 10.1146/annurev.psych.57.102904.190127
Copyright © 2006 by Annual Reviews. All rights reserved
First published online as a Review in Advance on August 11, 2005

PERSONALITY AND THE PREDICTION OF CONSEQUENTIAL OUTCOMES

Daniel J. Ozer and Verónica Benet-Martínez

*Department of Psychology, University of California, Riverside, California 92521;
email: daniel.ozer@ucr.edu, veronbm@mail.ucr.edu*

Key Words individual differences, traits, life outcomes, consequences

■ **Abstract** Personality has consequences. Measures of personality have contemporaneous and predictive relations to a variety of important outcomes. Using the Big Five factors as heuristics for organizing the research literature, numerous consequential relations are identified. Personality dispositions are associated with happiness, physical and psychological health, spirituality, and identity at an individual level; associated with the quality of relationships with peers, family, and romantic others at an interpersonal level; and associated with occupational choice, satisfaction, and performance, as well as community involvement, criminal activity, and political ideology at a social institutional level.

CONTENTS

INTRODUCTION

What makes a personality characteristic important? While theory may direct attention to some variables, and factor analytic analyses of trait terms and measures might suggest other variables, the ultimate test of any individual difference personality characteristic is its implicative meaning. Does the construct help us understand what people want, say, do, feel, or believe? Although personality characteristics have the capacity to predict individual differences in behavior within circumscribed laboratory contexts, such results are largely of theoretical interest unless the specific situation is one of compelling importance. But certain life outcomes and events are widely recognized as important—important for individuals and important for the society in which they live. Successful prediction of such consequential outcomes is a demonstration of the practical importance of personality that demands attention, and any successful theory of personality must account for those personality differences that have consequential implications.

Recent emphases in personality research have included personality structure, personality process, and personality stability and change (see, for example Caspi et al. 2005, Cervone 2005). Each of these topics has been a core concern of personality psychology throughout its history. But these topics do not directly address what we understand to be the source of abiding interest in individual differences in character and temperament since antiquity. Personality matters, not just in ways that interest the differential psychologist or those attached to a "romantic" conception of human nature (Hofstee & Ten Berge 2004), but also in ways that matter to most people and policy makers.

There is not and probably never will be some final list of important life outcomes. There will always be disagreement about what makes an outcome consequential or important, and such disagreement will not be resolved by new data or advances in theory. Beliefs about what are important life outcomes are not simply value-laden, but are constitutive of values. So we make no claim that all of the outcomes we examine will be regarded as universally important, or that we have included all of the important outcomes that might be nominated. Rather, we suggest that most of our readers will find most of the outcomes we discuss to be of consequence in their own lives. We assert, without providing evidence, that most people care about their own health and well being, care about their marital relationships, and care about success and satisfaction in their career. These may not be outcomes understood as universally important across time and culture, but neither are they concerns unique to our own venue of southern California at the start of the twenty-first century.

What personality characteristics might be used to forecast consequential life outcomes, and what characteristics might best serve to enable a useful summary of the current literature? Personality psychology is now in the fortunate position to offer the same answer to both questions: The broad superordinate dimensions (extraversion, agreeableness, conscientiousness, neuroticism, and openness or intellect) of the Five Factor Model of Personality (John & Srivastava 1999) are now widely used in the personality and prediction literature, and studies that utilize different dimensions often reference these dimensions of the Big Five model. Of the many different kinds of units used in personality psychology (Hooker & McAdams 2003), trait dimensions, by virtue of their context independence and noncontingent nature, should be most useful for predicting the multiply determined outcomes that arise from the natural aggregation of acts and events as they occur through time and across situations. More contingent and context-specific units may well be required to understand the mechanisms by which traits and outcomes are related; but that is not the present task. Alternatively, there is much to be said for the use of narrow traits and more focused predictor variables (Paunonen et al. 2003). From the perspective of maximizing accuracy in prediction, using multiple, narrow trait measures is likely to be more effective than using fewer broader measures. But there is no consensus about what might constitute even the beginning of a comprehensive list of narrow traits. Ideally, prediction would utilize a consistent set of broad superordinate dimensions (like the Big Five) plus whatever narrow predictors provided incremental validity for specific outcomes. Identifying narrow predictors for specific outcomes with incremental validity above the Big Five as a criterion is a research endeavor only now really getting underway. There is yet another reason to focus on the prediction of outcomes from the Big Five: Further refinement of these factors might best be pursued by attending to the structure of the external correlates of the factors (as Gangestad & Snyder 2000 show for the case of self-monitoring) rather than solely on the structure of the factor indicators.

In our review of the literature, we characterize three different types of outcomes: Individual, interpersonal, and social/institutional. By individual outcomes, we mean those outcomes that can be manifested by an individual outside of a social context, in contrast to interpersonal outcomes that inherently involve other individuals. Moreover, this involvement is personal in a sense: It generally matters who the other is. By social/institutional outcomes, we mean more impersonal, organizational, and sometimes, societal-level processes involving interactions with more generalized others. These distinctions are as much a convenience for organizing a vast literature as they are a claim about the structure of consequential life outcomes.

INDIVIDUAL OUTCOMES

By individual outcomes, we mean those that do not inherently depend upon a social process in order to define or give meaning to the outcome variable. Physical health and psychopathology are routinely understood as individual outcomes, while the inclusion here of happiness, spirituality, and virtue reflects the growing influence of positive psychology. Although these variables might be understood as features of personality rather than outcomes influenced by personality, we would argue that conscientiousness (to choose the most difficult trait for our view) as a virtue and conscientiousness as a trait are not quite the same things, though they clearly are related. Someone might be conscientious (in the trait sense) for purely instrumental purposes, and this would not constitute a virtue under at least some conceptions of that term.

Identity and self-concept, understood as outcomes, provide the greatest challenge to this kind of organizational scheme. The role of the individual, important others, and the larger social environment most certainly play a part in the development of self and identity; but ultimately, we believe that individuals experience aspects of their identity as a part of themselves, and so we include identity as an individual outcome.

Happiness and Subjective Well-Being

Few topics have attracted as much recent attention in personality psychology as the study of subjective well-being (SWB), persons' evaluations of their own lives (Diener et al. 1999). SWB includes both a cognitive component, such as a judgment of one's life satisfaction (Diener et al. 1985), and an affective component that includes the experience of positive and absence of negative emotions (Larsen 2000). Two robust conclusions from studies in this area are that personality dispositions are strong predictors of most components of SWB (see Diener & Lucas 1999 for a review), and demographic and contextual factors, including age, sex, marital status, employment, social class, and culture, are only weakly to moderately related to SWB (Diener et al. 1999, Ryan & Deci 2001).

Studies trying to unpack the link between personality dispositions and SWB mainly point to the relations between certain largely genetic, affective/cognitive traits related to neuroticism and extraversion (e.g., positive and negative affect, optimism, self-esteem) and the way individuals appraise and react to environmental rewards and punishments (DeNeve & Cooper 1998). Specifically, individuals high in extraversion and low in neuroticism tend to see events and situations in a more positive light, are less responsive to negative feedback, and tend to discount opportunities that are not available to them. Individual differences in conscientiousness, agreeableness, and openness to experience are less strongly and consistently associated with SWB, mostly because these traits sources reside in "rewards in the environment" (Diener & Lucas 1999). In summary, SWB is strongly predicted by personality traits that are largely a function of temperament (i.e., extraversion and neuroticism) and moderately predicted by personality dispositions significantly driven by environmental influences (conscientiousness, agreeableness, and openness to experience).

Recent cross-cultural studies of SWB (Benet-Martínez & Karakitapoglu-Aygün 2003, Kwan et al. 1997, Schimmack et al. 2002) shed light on some possible moderator and mediator variables in the relation between personality factors and SWB. First, the links between both extraversion and neuroticism and SWB are moderated by culture. In individualist societies like the United States, where pleasure and positive mood are highly emphasized and valued, hedonic balance (i.e., the ratio of positive to negative affect) is a particularly strong predictor of SWB (Schimmack et al. 2002). Secondly, across cultures, the links between the Big Five and SWB are largely mediated by intra- and interpersonal esteem evaluations. Specifically, self-esteem appears to be a powerful mediator of the influence of extraversion, neuroticism, and conscientiousness on SWB, whereas relational esteem (i.e., satisfaction with relationships with family and friends) mediates the influence of agreeableness and extraversion on SWB (Benet-Martínez & Karakitapoglu-Aygün 2003, Kwan et al. 1997). Although the relative weights of self-esteem and relationship harmony in predicting SWB vary across cultures (e.g., self-esteem is a uniquely important predictor in Western cultures), the weights of each of the Big Five dimensions on self-esteem and relationship harmony seem to be cross-culturally equivalent (Benet-Martínez & Karakitapoglu-Aygün 2003, Kwan et al. 1997).

Spirituality and Virtues

There is very little research directly investigating the relation between personality dispositions and variables referring to religious or spiritual concerns. This lack of attention to spiritual matters in personality psychology is puzzling for two reasons, as described by Emmons (1999): First, personality psychologists such as Allport and Murphy were among the first to study religion and spirituality from a psychological perspective. Despite this early interest in spirituality, the topic fell out of favor in the 1960s and 1970s, as various controversies flourished. Second, personality psychology's neglect of spirituality has occurred in the context of a discipline centrally concerned with understanding the whole person, a concern that undoubtedly involves understanding what is meaningful to the person and how this meaning is experienced as bringing growth and transcendence to one's life. Emmons (1999) argues that spiritual and religious goals and practices are not only a distinctive element of a person's beliefs and behaviors; for many, religious beliefs and practices may be a central theme of their identity.

Piedmont (1999, 2004) developed a measure of spiritual transcendence, with universality, connectedness, and prayer fulfillment subscales, that is unrelated to the traits of the Five Factor Model and has incremental validity in predicting post-treatment symptoms and coping resources in an outpatient substance abuse sample. MacDonald (2000) also explored the links between basic personality traits and spiritual concerns and behaviors. Five distinct components are identified and described by MacDonald: cognitive orientation (perceptions and attitudes regarding spirituality), experiential/phenomenological (mystical, transcendental, and transpersonal experiences), existential well-being (a sense of meaning, purpose, and resilience regarding one's existence), paranormal beliefs (including ESP and other paranormal phenomena), and religiousness (religious practices). These five components are differentially related to the Big Five personality constructs but are not subsumed by them. In particular, the religiousness and cognitive orientation components were most notably predicted by agreeableness and conscientiousness. Not surprisingly, the experiential/phenomenological and paranormal components were predicted by openness, while existential well-being was strongly predicted by extraversion and low neuroticism.

Recent theoretical work on the classification and delineation of core character strengths and virtues—which can be grouped in terms of their relevance to wisdom, courage, humanity, justice, temperance, and transcendence (Peterson & Seligman 2002)—convincingly relates most of these attributes to different sets of personality dispositions. Clearly, certain traits facilitate or impede the development of specific strengths and virtues (e.g., agreeableness facilitates compassion, conscientiousness facilitates perseverance, openness fosters creativity), while at the same time the cultivation of these virtues consolidates the very same personality dispositions from which these virtues sprang. Although most of the aforementioned personality-virtue links have yet to be examined empirically, the following virtues have been shown to have clear associations with personality: gratitude (extraversion and agreeableness; McCullough et al. 2002), forgiveness (agreeableness and openness; Thompson et al. 2005), inspiration (extraversion and openness; Thrash & Elliot 2004), and humor (low neuroticism and agreeableness; Cann & Calhoun 2001).

Physical Health and Longevity

Personality traits have a stable and cumulative effect on both the health and length of individuals' lives (Caspi et al. 2005). With regard to longevity, studies show that positive emotionality (extraversion) and conscientiousness predict longer lives (Danner et al. 2001, Friedman et al. 1995), and hostility (low agreeableness) predicts poorer physical health (e.g., cardiovascular illness) and earlier mortality (Miller et al. 1996). The relation between neuroticism and health and longevity is more complex, given that some studies support an association between neuroticism and increased risk of actual disease, whereas others show links with illness behavior only (Smith & Spiro 2002). The link between personality and health may reflect three different though overlapping processes (Contrada et al. 1999). First, personality traits are associated with factors that cause disease. The hostility component of low agreeableness (i.e., anger, cynicism, and mistrust) is associated with sympathetic nervous system activation that is in turn associated with coronary artery disease (Smith & Spiro 2002). Whether personality has a causal role or whether the association is spurious remains unclear (Caspi et al. 2005). Second, personality may lead to behaviors that protect or diminish health. Extraversion is associated with more numerous social relationships and greater social support, both of which are positively correlated with health outcomes (Berkman et al. 2000). Various unhealthy habits and behaviors including smoking, improper diet, and lack of exercise are negatively correlated to conscientiousness (Bogg & Roberts 2004, Hampson et al. 2000). Last, personality traits are related to the successful implementation of health-related coping behaviors (David & Suls 1999, Scheier & Carver 1993) and adherence to treatment regimens (Kenford et al. 2002). The increasing evidence for these three personality-health processes is clarifying the particular health outcomes associated with particular traits (Caspi et al. 2005): Agreeableness (e.g., hostility) seems to be most directly associated with the disease processes, conscientiousness (e.g., low impulse control) is clearly implicated in health-risk behaviors, and neuroticism (e.g., vulnerability and rumination) seems to contribute to disease by shaping reactions to illness.

Finally, in contrast with the more traditional medical approach to personality and health, which tends to focus on "negative" traits such as anxiety, hostility, and impulsivity, positive psychology research informs us about personality traits that define resiliency (e.g., optimism, self-esteem, creativity), predict health, and represent important resources for the individual and society (Seligman & Csikszentmihalyi 2000). There is growing evidence that the positive emotions and dispositions subsumed by the extraversion dimension lead to improved coping and the development of psychological skills and resources (Fredrickson & Joiner 2002).

Psychopathology

The previously described links between personality and SWB are not sufficient for understanding the relation between personality and psychopathology (e.g., personality disorders, clinical depression, and schizophrenia). This is so because SWB is not synonymous with mental or psychological health (Diener et al. 1999). Some delusional individuals may feel happy and satisfied with their lives, and yet we would not say that they possess mental health.

Recent research demonstrates strong links between the personality dispositions and both Axis I and II psychological disorders. Specifically, substance abuse disorders are largely predicted by higher openness and lower conscientiousness (Trull & Sher 1994). Anxiety disorders are primarily predicted by higher neuroticism, and depression is mostly linked to neuroticism and low extraversion (Trull & Sher 1994). Associations between personality traits and Axis II disorders are even more evident given the growing prevalence of dimensional conceptualizations of personality disorders. Dimensional models of personality disorders suggest that they may be understood as extreme expressions of personality traits (Trull & Durrett 2005). It is apparent that personality disorders have substantial associations with the five factors; neuroticism has the strongest relationship with personality disorders, whereas openness to experience has only a modest relationship.

Self-Concept and Identity

While many psychologists would understand self-concept and identity to be an integral part of personality, how one characterizes oneself, the groups one belongs to, and the goals and values one possesses may be understood as outcomes as well. The structure of social and personal identifications, goals, and priorities that constitute self and identity (Marcia 1980) may be understood not only as a function of life experience and cultural context, but also as a domain where personality dispositions play a part. How do personality traits influence self-concept and identity? Work in this area shows that personality traits affect the formation of identity, while at the same time identity both directs and becomes a part of personality through exploration and commitment processes in identity development (Helson & Srivastava 2001). Clancy & Dollinger (1993) have shown robust relations between personality traits and Marcia's (1980) four categories of identity development (achieved, moratorium, diffuse, and foreclosed). Specifically, foreclosure is predicted by low levels of openness to experience; identity achievement is predicted by low neuroticism, conscientiousness, and extraversion. Both moratorium and diffusion stages involve neuroticism. Additionally, diffusion is inversely related to agreeableness. Openness to experience may be the most important personality trait in terms of impact on identity development (Duriez et al. 2004, Helson & Srivastava 2001).

Furthering this typological approach to identity, recent longitudinal studies have explored the interactive roles of personality and identity over the life span, while focusing on more complex identity constructs such as identity consolidation (development of a coherent, grounded, and positive identity; Pals 1999) and identity integration (Helson & Srivastava 2001). This work shows that identity consolidation is predicted by an early configuration of personality traits related to openness to experience (desire for exploration and stimulation), low neuroticism (low rumination), and conscientiousness (ambition). This pattern of personality traits leads to an organized and committed yet flexible exploration of identity, which in turn predicts well-being. These identity choices lead to particular personal and professional choices that consolidate earlier personality traits (Helson & Srivastava 2001, Pals 1999). The influence of personality traits is seen both at the level of narrower, cognitive, identity-relevant processes such as identity language (Pennebaker & King 1999), autobiographical memories (Thorne & Klohnen 1993), and self-concept clarity (Campbell et al. 1996), as well as at the broad level of life story narratives (McAdams 2001).

Personality dispositions also influence more contextualized types of identities, such as cultural identity. For example, among immigrants, ethnic cultural identity is mainly predicted by conscientiousness and agreeableness (i.e., warmth and commitment towards one's culture of origin), whereas identification with the dominant host culture is largely predicted by openness and extraversion (Benet-Martínez & Haritatos 2005, Ryder et al. 2000). Further, supporting other studies on identity consolidation, openness to experience and low neuroticism predict the degree to which an individual's ethnic and mainstream identities are well integrated within a coherent sense of self (Benet-Martínez & Haritatos 2005).

INTERPERSONAL OUTCOMES

One of the most important tasks faced by individuals is the establishment and maintenance of successful relationships with friends and peers, family members, and romantic partners. Relationships do have emergent properties, but the nature and quality of the relationship nonetheless is partially shaped by the dispositions and skills of the individuals involved. The length and quality of most relationships is predicted by socioemotional competence (or socioemotional intelligence), a broad cognitive, affective, and behavioral construct typically operationalized in terms of social skills (e.g., ability to engage and effectively maintain social interaction), emotional skills (expression, empathy, regulation), popularity, and relationship satisfaction (Bost et al. 1998, Cantor & Kilstrom 1987).

Although socioemotional competence involves personality characteristics related to all the Big Five domains (Sjöberg 2001, van der Zee et al. 2002, Vollrath et al. 2004), the strongest personality links are shown for the components of empathy, which seems to be primarily a combination of extraversion and agreeableness, and emotional regulation, which is best predicted by low neuroticism. The above personality–social behavior links are robust and interesting but too broad for an adequate understanding of the role played by personality in more specific types of relationships, including family, peer, and romantic relationships, as we describe below.

Peer and Family Relationships

Much of the research examining personality and its role in friendships and peer relations has been conducted with children and adolescents. Given how much time children spend at school and playing with friends, understanding how children and adolescents successfully establish and maintain friendships is important for its own sake (i.e., to predict personal and school adjustment) and also because social adjustment in childhood has been shown to be a very strong predictor of the quality of relationships in adulthood (Parker & Asher 1987).

Of all of the Big Five dimensions, agreeableness and extraversion are the best predictors of processes and outcomes related to peer relations in children, such as peer acceptance and friendship (Jensen-Campbell et al. 2002). Specifically, low agreeableness (hostility) and low extraversion (being withdrawn) are associated with rejected peer status (Newcomb et al. 1993). These findings are not surprising given that both agreeableness and extraversion are related to motives and skills necessary to build and maintain satisfying relations with peers. Longitudinal studies of peer relations in children show that the benefits of agreeableness accumulate over time by protecting children from victimization (Jensen-Campbell et al. 2002).

Personality also affects the quality of the relationship young adults have with their parents. These intergenerational relationships are negatively affected by young adults' neuroticism, low conscientiousness, and low extraversion (Belsky et al. 2003). These findings support the notion that the very same life events and experiences that affect intergenerational relationships in young adulthood (e.g., timing of parenthood, when the young adult leaves home, or length of unemployment) could be a function of earlier and concurrent personality traits (Caspi et al. 2005).

Surprisingly few studies have examined the personality predictors of popularity, status, and peer acceptance in adulthood. This is unfortunate since these social outcomes (i.e., amount of respect, influence, and prominence a person enjoys in the eyes of others) presumably influence professional and personal social networks and support. Most of the available evidence points to extraversion (but not agreeableness) as the most important predictor of popularity and status among adults. Paunonen (2003), for instance, finds evidence that extraversion is related to popularity, dating variety, and self-reported attractiveness. The Anderson et al. (2001) study of the links between personality and status also supports extraversion as the main predictor of social acceptance, concurrently and over time, and for both sexes. This study is also informative regarding the role (or lack thereof) played by the other Big Five dimensions in adult peer relations: Neuroticism appears to be a (negative) predictor of status among men only, supporting the traditional gender role expectation that men who feel anxious and vulnerable are less deserving of status and respect (Anderson et al. 2001). Agreeableness does not predict status for either women or men, which supports the socioanalytic notion that status (or "getting ahead") may be inimical to "getting along" (Hogan 1983). Status is unrelated to either conscientiousness or openness in informal groups; however, as noted by Anderson et al. (2001), conscientiousness may play a role in more formal organizations and professional groups, where task performance and achievement play a central role.

Romantic Relationships

Some of the richest evidence for the consequentiality of personality dispositions with regard to interpersonal relations stems from longitudinal studies exploring the links between adult personality and romantic relationships. Attaining and maintaining a satisfying romantic relationship is a central feature of most adult lives, and such relationships play a key role in fostering emotional well-being and physical health (Berscheid 1999). Do personality dispositions explain why some individuals are involved in satisfying romantic relationships, whereas others are involved in less satisfying and more distressed relationships?

Neuroticism and low agreeableness consistently emerge as predictors of negative relationship outcomes such as relationship dissatisfaction, conflict, abuse, and ultimately dissolution (Karney & Bradbury 1995). Naturally, the predisposition to easily experience anger and frustration, distress, and anxiety is potentially destructive for relationships (although see Gottman 1994 for a discussion of how interpersonal conflict may not always be detrimental in intimate relationships). Relationship quality is directly affected by neuroticism (Donnellan et al. 2005); this relation between neuroticism and relationship dissatisfaction involves a reciprocal process such that negative emotions increase relationship distress, which in turn accentuates negative emotionality (Robins et al. 2002). These effects seem to be consistent across relationships, as neuroticism and low agreeableness predict dissatisfaction across relationships with different partners (Robins et al. 2002). Longitudinal evidence shows that personality traits predict not only concurrent relationship outcomes, but also future ones (Donnellan et al. 2005).

Recent multimethod research with dyads shows that the link between personality and relationship status and quality is more than an artifact of shared method variance arising from self-report measurement procedures (Donnellan et al. 2004, Watson et al. 2000). Watson et al. (2000) used both self-ratings and partner ratings of personality in both dating and married samples. Positive and negative affect were related to relationship satisfaction in the predicted direction in both samples. Conscientiousness and agreeableness predicted satisfaction in dating couples, whereas extraversion predicted satisfaction in the married couples.

In general, there appears to be modest to moderate assortative marriage across a wide range of psychological characteristics (e.g., intellectual abilities, values, political attitudes, and religious beliefs) and sociodemographic variables (e.g., age, education). But recent studies of personality and assortment indicate low levels of partner similarity in personality (Gattis et al. 2004, Luo & Klohnen 2005, Watson et al. 2004). It is not clear whether spouse similarity and relationship satisfaction are related, with some studies suggesting a positive relation (e.g., Luo & Klohnen 2005), whereas others (Gattis et al. 2004) report that personality similarity does not independently predict relationship satisfaction.

Finally, it is important to note that personality dispositions, besides predicting romantic relationship outcomes such as quality, satisfaction, and length, also influence relationship-relevant cognitive-motivational mechanisms such as attitudes, goals, and emotional scripts that people bring to their romantic relationships. Traits from all the Big Five domains have been related to attachment styles (Shaver & Brennan 1992), dating attitudes and behavior (Schmitt 2002), and love styles (Heaven et al. 2004).

SOCIAL/INSTITUTIONAL OUTCOMES

In this section, we examine three outcomes in the world of work and occupation: vocational interests, work satisfaction, and job performance. These three outcomes subsume the basic components of work of interest to psychology: What kind of work is preferred, how well is it performed, and how much satisfaction is attained? There has been a surge of recent interest in the relation between personality and political attitudes and ideology, giving proof to the longevity and fruitfulness of the construct of authoritarianism. Criminality and community involvement are also discussed below, representing the extremes of antisocial and prosocial societal outcomes.

Occupational Choice and Performance

Organizations and institutions require individuals to fill specific roles that require different skills and bestow different rewards. Individuals seek, to varying degrees, roles that provide personal satisfaction and reward. This is most clearly true in the context of individuals' work, occupation, and relation with an employer, but is also true in their relations with their community, though here arrangements may be much less formal.

Two recently completed meta-analyses (Barrick et al. 2003, Larson et al. 2002) examining the relation between personality traits and occupational types concurred in finding that extraversion was related to social and enterprising occupational interests, agreeableness to social interests, and openness to investigative and artistic interests. Neuroticism was not related to any occupational interest. Barrick et al. (2003) (but not Larson et al. 2002) reported conscientiousness to be related to conventional interests. Personality traits appear to broadly influence occupational interests and choices.

The meta-analytic finding that conscientiousness predicts job performance reported by Barrick & Mount (1991) was broadly influential. Research examining job and occupational variables began to include personality and especially Big Five measures, and personality researchers began to examine the consequential meaning of the five factors. Barrick et al. (2001) performed a meta-analysis of the meta-analytic studies of the relation between job performance and Big Five personality traits. Conscientiousness predicts performance, assessed in various ways, in all included occupations. Smaller, though nearly as broad, effects were found for extraversion and emotional stability—which seem important for some, though not all, occupational groups—while only weak and narrow effects for agreeableness and openness were identified. So, for example, agreeableness relates to job performance when a teamwork criterion is used. Perhaps the most well known occupation-specific measure of job performance is grade point average for students, and it can hardly be a surprise to find a positive relation between GPA and conscientiousness (Paunonen 2003). Another educational outcome, the number of years of education, is related to intellect, or openness (Goldberg et al. 1998).

Although job performance is inarguably an important outcome from the standpoint of the employer, the employees may be more concerned with their feelings about work and their perceptions of the workplace. The meta-analysis of Thoresen et al. (2003) examined work attitudes and job perceptions and their relation to positive and negative affect. For present purposes, equating these affect variables with extraversion and neuroticism is straightforward because (*a*) studies using measures of extraversion and neuroticism included in the meta-analysis were so coded, and (*b*) a trait-state moderator variable had little effect. The results of Thoresen et al. (2003) show that extraversion and emotional stability are associated with job satisfaction and organizational commitment, and are negatively related to a wish to change jobs and with outcomes associated with burnout. Conscientiousness may best predict how well one does at work, but extraversion and emotional stability are more important for understanding how one feels about work.

Career success may be understood as having both extrinsic (e.g., salary and authority) and intrinsic (satisfaction) components. In longitudinal data, both extrinsic and intrinsic career success were predicted by childhood conscientiousness, openness, and emotional stability. When controlling for other personality variables, agreeableness was negatively related to extrinsic success (Judge et al. 1999).

Roberts et al. (2003) report that personality assessed in late adolescence affects various workplace experiences and outcomes in early adulthood. Emotional stability (negative emotionality) is most strongly related to financial security; agreeableness (positive emotionality-communion) is related to occupational attainment. Resource power and work involvement are predicted by extraversion (positive emotionality-agency).

Political Attitudes and Values

Although political attitudes may be most frequently understood as predictor rather than outcome variables, the political attitudes and beliefs of individuals in a democratic society may affect social policies in diverse and consequential ways. Certainly, candidates for public office and those who financially support these candidates appear to believe that political attitudes are important. Since the publication of *The Authoritarian Personality* (Adorno et al. 1950), linkages between personality and political beliefs have been of considerable interest. Saucier's (2000) analysis of the broad domain of social and political attitudes ("isms") suggests that openness is related to the content of social attitudes, with political conservativism and right-wing authoritarianism being negatively related to this personality characteristic. Heaven & Bucci (2001) also report this negative association between openness and right-wing authoritarianism. Van Hiel et al. (2004) report this same negative correlation between openness and conservative political beliefs, as well as smaller relations between these same beliefs and low agreeableness and conscientiousness.

Jost et al. (2003a) integrate personality characteristics within a motivated social cognition approach to understanding political conservativism, and their meta-analysis suggests that death anxiety, dogmatism–intolerance of ambiguity, and the needs for order, structure, and closure are positive correlates of conservativism, whereas negative correlates include openness to experience, uncertainty tolerance, and integrative complexity. These traits, individually and as a set, suggest a susceptibility to a fear of uncertainty that may be assuaged by political conservativism. Greenberg & Jonas (2003) object to the Jost et al. (2003a) claims, posing an alternative conception of conservativism and suggesting that other political points of view may also serve the same psychological function. In their view, the rigidity or fixedness of one's political point of view is independent of the left-versus-right content of political belief. Jost et al. (2003b) respond both by considering the temporal context of political movements and by directly pitting a "rigidity-of-the-right" hypothesis against the alternative "ideological extremity" hypothesis. The evidence reviewed by Jost et al. (2003a,b) is more consistent with associating conservativism rather than extremity of belief with psychological rigidity, though some studies do suggest that both processes may be involved. One of the next challenges would appear to be to examine extreme liberalism to determine when rigidity does, and does not, come into play.

One might also ask whether specific substantive features of conservative ideology are associated with particular person attributes. Van Hiel & Mervielde (2004) found political conservativism to be negatively related to openness, and their data suggest that this relationship is apparently more a function of cultural than of economic conservative beliefs.

When it comes to candidates and elections, Caprara & Zimbardo (2004) describe a model of the political process that depends directly and considerably on the personalities of voters and their perceptions of candidates' personalities. They report that those supporting more liberal candidates describe themselves and the candidates they prefer as higher on openness and agreeableness, whereas those who support more conservative candidates describe themselves and the candidates they support as more extraverted and conscientious. This congruency involving the perceived personality of the politician, the personality of the voter, and the ideological preferences of the politician and the voter suggests a deep involvement of personality in the political process.

Volunteerism and Community Involvement

Among the more socially important kinds of outcomes that might be imagined are prosocial behavior and volunteerism. Clearly, there are important differences among people in their willingness to get involved in helping others, both in formal contexts of volunteering and social service as well as in less planned, everyday acts of helping. Penner et al. (1995) have developed a measure of prosocial behavior that includes an other-oriented empathy scale that correlates strongly with agreeableness. Helpfulness, a second factor on Penner's measure, appears more related to extraversion. These interpersonal traits are related to a wide variety of prosocial behaviors and volunteerism (Penner 2002). The link between volunteerism and the interpersonal traits of extraversion and agreeableness was also found in a large college student sample (Carlo et al. 2005), where there is some evidence that the trait-behavior link was mediated by prosocial motivation.

Extraversion and agreeableness not only predict community involvement, but these same traits also seem to predict who assumes a leadership role. The interpersonal traits of extraversion and agreeableness are positively associated with a transformational leadership style among community leaders (Judge & Bono 2000).

Criminality

Criminal activity lies at the opposite end of the spectrum of community involvement, but it is not simply the opposite or lack of altruism. Krueger et al. (2001) found that antisocial behavior and altruism are distinct, with different origins and correlates. In contrast to the involvement of extraversion in prosocial behavior, antisocial behavior was associated with low constraint and negative emotionality (low conscientiousness and neuroticism).

Low conscientiousness seems to be consistently associated with various aspects of criminal and antisocial actions: It is related to behavior problems in adolescent boys (Ge & Conger 1999), antisocial behavior (Shiner et al. 2002), deviance and suicide attempts (Verona et al. 2001), and along with low agreeableness, low conscientiousness is associated with substance abuse (Walton & Roberts 2004). Wiebe (2004) reports that low agreeableness and low conscientiousness predict criminal acts in college student and in prison samples. But Wiebe (2004) also warns that self-deception and/or other deception may importantly attenuate the ability to predict criminal acts from self-reported personality traits.

TABLE 1 Summary of the relation between personality traits and consequential outcomes*

	Individual outcomes	Interpersonal outcomes	Social institutional outcomes
Extraversion	Happiness: subjective well-being Spirituality & virtues: existential well-being, gratitude, inspiration Health: longevity, coping, resilience Psychopathology: (−) depression, (−/+) personality disorders Identity: majority culture identification (for minorities)	Peer & family relations: peers' acceptance and friendship (children and adults); dating variety, attractiveness, status (adults) Romantic relations: satisfaction	Occupational choice & performance: social and enterprising interests, satisfaction, commitment, involvement Community involvement: volunteerism, leadership
Agreeableness	Spirituality & virtues: religious beliefs and behavior, gratitude, forgiveness, humor Health: longevity; (−) heart disease Psychopathology: (−/+) personality disorders Identity: ethnic culture identification (for minorities)	Peer & family relations: peers' acceptance and friendship (children) Romantic relations: satisfaction (dating couples only)	Occupational choice & performance: social interests, job attainment, (−) extrinsic success Community involvement: volunteerism, leadership Criminality: (−) criminal behavior
Conscientiousness	Spirituality & virtues: religious beliefs and behavior Health: longevity, (−) risky behavior Psychopathology: (−) substance abuse, (−/+) personality disorders Identity: achievement, ethnic culture identification (for minorities)	Peer & family relations: family satisfaction Romantic relations: satisfaction (dating couples only)	Occupational choice & performance: performance, success Political attitudes & values: conservativism Criminality: (−) antisocial and criminal behavior
Neuroticism	Happiness: (−) subjective well-being Spirituality & virtues: (−) existential well-being, (−) humor Health: (−) coping Psychopathology: anxiety, depression, (+/−) personality disorders Identity: (−) identity integration/consolidation	Peer & family relations: (−) family satisfaction, (−) status (males only) Romantic relations: dissatisfaction, conflict, abuse, dissolution	Occupational choice & performance: (−) satisfaction, (−) commitment, (−) financial security, (−) success Criminality: antisocial behavior
Openness	Spirituality & virtues: existential/phenomenological concerns, forgiveness, inspiration Psychopathology: substance abuse Identity: (−) foreclosure, identity integration/consolidation, majority culture identification (for minorities)		Occupational choice & performance: investigative and artistic interests, success Political attitudes & values: (−) right-wing authoritarianism, liberalism

*Note: (−) indicates a negative relation between the trait and outcome.

CONCLUSION

In discussing the relation between personality characteristics and consequential outcomes, we have not attempted to evaluate effect size. The various meta-analyses cited here provide such estimates, and in not noting the specific results, we do not wish to suggest that such quantitative indicators are unimportant. However, making fine distinctions about the relative sizes of particular effects may be largely premature, and we wish to emphasize a rather different consideration. Any nonzero effect of a personality characteristic on most of the outcome measures we describe would be a large effect in practical terms. In parallel to the argument of Abelson (1985), it should be clear that even if the relation between agreeableness and volunteerism is small, then even a small change in mean agreeableness scores might increase by thousands the number of volunteers serving community needs in AIDS clinics and elsewhere. Our claim is not that personality effects are "large" at a completely disaggregated level of analysis (i.e., the prediction of what one person will do on a particular occasion), but rather that personality effects are ubiquitous, influencing each of us all the time, and when aggregated to the population level such effects are routinely consequential.

Our account of specific outcomes associated with personality factors is summarized in Table 1. At first glance, it is apparent from the table that each of the five superordinate traits is broadly implicative. It would be impossible, simply from the summary of the evidence as presented in Table 1, to claim that any of the five traits has a narrow and circumscribed set of correlates. There is, in fact, but one empty cell in the table: Openness as yet has no well-documented effects in the interpersonal domain that we were able to locate. Any nominee for a sixth factor should possess the same kind of breadth in its external correlates as shown by the present five. This is not to say that additional variables outside of the five-factor structure are not useful in prediction. But the expectation, at present, is that such a variable will have a narrower band of consequential outcomes. Nor should Table 1 be taken as an endorsement of the claim that the five superordinate traits are those that should be used in applied prediction contexts. As noted earlier, there is both good reason and some evidence to expect that larger effects would be obtained by using multiple narrow predictor variables (Paunonen et al. 2003). Although such an approach would maximize predictive accuracy, it would do so at the price of cumulative knowledge of the kind depicted in Table 1. When the mechanism that relates personality process to consequential outcome is identified, then the time to utilize specific measures of that process will have arrived.

Arguments about whether personality is consistent over time and context, arguments about the proper units of personality, and arguments about the utility of different types of measures have all had one common and unfortunate effect: They have obscured the reasons why proponents of different positions cared about personality in the first place, and first and foremost among these reasons is that personality matters.

The *Annual Review of Psychology* is online at http://psych.annualreviews.org

LITERATURE CITED

Abelson R. 1985. A variance explanation paradox: when a little is a lot. *Psychol. Bull.* 97:129–33

Adorno TW, Frenkel-Brunswik E, Levinson DJ, Sanford RN. 1950. *The Authoritarian Personality.* New York: Harper

Anderson C, John OP, Keltner D, Kring AM. 2001. Who attains social status? Effects of personality and physical attractiveness in social groups. *J. Personal. Soc. Psychol.* 81: 116–32

Barrick MR, Mount MK. 1991. The Big Five personality dimensions and job performance: a meta analysis. *Personal. Psychol.* 44:1–26

Barrick MR, Mount MK, Gupta R. 2003. Meta-analysis of the relationship between the Five Factor model of personality and Holland's occupational types. *Personal. Psychol.* 56:45–74

Barrick MR, Mount MK, Judge TA. 2001. Personality and performance at the beginning of the new millennium: What do we know and where do we go next? *Int. J. Sel. Assess.* 9:9–30

Belsky J, Jaffee SR, Caspi A, Moffitt T, Silva PA. 2003. Intergenerational relationships in young adulthood and their life course, mental health, and personality correlates. *J. Fam. Psychol.* 17:460–71

Benet-Martínez V, Haritatos J. 2005. Bicultural Identity Integration (BII): components and socio-personality antecedents. *J. Personal.* 73:1015–50

Benet-Martínez V, Karakitapoglu-Aygün Z. 2003. The interplay of cultural values and personality in predicting life-satisfaction: comparing Asian- and European-Americans. *J. Cross-Cult. Psychol.* 34:38–61

Berkman LF, Glass T, Brissette I, Seeman TE. 2000. From social integration to health. *Soc. Sci. Med.* 51:843–57

Berscheid E. 1999. The greening of relationship science. *Am. Psychol.* 54:260–66

Bogg T, Roberts BW. 2004. Conscientiousness and health behaviors: a meta-analysis. *Psychol. Bull.* 130:887–919

Bost KK, Vaughn BE, Washington WN, Cielinski KL, Bradbard MR. 1998. Social competence, social support, and attachment: demarcation of construct domains, measurement, and paths of influence for preschool children attending Head Start. *Child Dev.* 69:192–218

Campbell JD, Trapnell PD, Heine SJ, Katz IM, Lavallee LF, Lehman DR. 1996. Self-concept clarity: measurement, personality orrelates, and cultural boundaries. *J. Personal. Soc. Psychol.* 70:141–56

Cann A, Calhoun LG. 2001. Perceived personality associations with differences in sense of humor: stereotypes of hypothetical others with high or low senses of humor. *Humor: Int. J. Humor Res.* 14:117–30

Cantor N, Kihlstrom JF. 1987. *Personality and Social Intelligence.* Englewood Cliffs, NJ: Prentice Hall

Caprara GV, Zimbardo PG. 2004. Personalizing politics: a congruency model of political preference. *Am. Psychol.* 59:581–94

Carlo G, Okun MA, Knight GP, de Guzman MRT. 2005. The interplay of traits and motives on volunteering: agreeableness, extraversion, and prosocial value motivation. *Personal. Individ. Differ.* 38:1293–305

Caspi A, Roberts BW, Shiner RL. 2005. Personality development: stability and change. *Annu. Rev. Psychol.* 56:453–84

Cervone D. 2005. Personality architecture: within-person structures and processes. *Annu. Rev. Psychol.* 56:423–52

Clancy SM, Dollinger SJ. 1993. Identity, self, and personality: I. Identity status and the Five Factor model of personality. *J. Res. Adolesc.* 3:227–45

Contrada RJ, Cather C, O'Leary A. 1999. Personality and health: dispositions and processes in disease susceptibility and adaptation to illness. In *Handbook of Personality,* ed. LA Pervin, OP John, pp. 576–604. New York: Guilford

Danner DD, Snowdon DA, Friesen WV. 2001. Positive emotions in early life and longevity: findings from the nun study. *J. Personal. Soc. Psychol.* 80:804–13

David J, Suls J. 1999. Coping efforts in daily life: role of Big Five traits and problem appraisal. *J. Personal.* 67:119–40

DeNeve KM, Cooper H. 1998. The happy personality: a meta-analysis of 137 personality traits and subjective well-being. *Psychol. Bull.* 124:197–229

Diener E, Emmons RA, Larsen RJ, Griffin S. 1985. The Satisfaction with Life Scale. *J. Personal. Assess.* 49:71–75

Diener E, Lucas RE. 1999. Personality and subjective well-being. In *Well-Being: The Foundations of Hedonic Psychology*, ed. D Kahneman, E Diener, N Schwarz, pp. 213–29. New York: Russell Sage Found.

Diener E, Suh EM, Lucas RE, Smith HL. 1999. Subjective well-being: three decades of progress. *Psychol. Bull.* 125:276–302

Donnellan MB, Conger RD, Bryant CM. 2004. The Big Five and enduring marriages. *J. Res. Personal.* 38:481–504

Donnellan MB, Larsen-Rife D, Conger RD. 2005. Personality, family history, and competence in early adult romantic relationships. *J. Personal. Soc. Psychol.* 88:562–76

Duriez B, Soenens B, Beyers W. 2004. Personality, identity styles, and religiosity: an integrative study among late adolescents in Flanders (Belgium). *J. Personal.* 72:877–908

Emmons RA. 1999. Religion in the psychology of personality: an introduction. *J. Personal.* 67:873–88

Fredrickson BL, Joiner T. 2002. Positive emotions trigger upward spirals toward emotional well-being. *Psychol. Sci.* 13:172–75

Friedman HS, Tucker JS, Schwartz JE, Tomlinson-Keasey C, Martin LR, et al. 1995. Psychosocial and behavioral predictors of longevity. *Am. Psychol.* 50:69–78

Gangestad SW, Snyder M. 2000. Self-monitoring: appraisal and reappraisal. *Psychol. Bull.* 126:530–55

Gattis KS, Berns S, Simpson LE, Christensen A. 2004. Birds of a feather or strange birds? Ties among personality dimensions, similarity, and marital quality. *J. Fam. Psychol.* 8:564–74

Ge X, Conger RD. 1999. Adjustment problems and emerging personality characteristics from early to late adolescence. *Am. J. Community Psychol.* 27:429–59

Goldberg LR, Sweeney D, Merenda PF, Hughes JE. 1998. Demographic variables and personality: the effects of gender, age, education, and ethnic/racial status on self-descriptions of personality attributes. *Personal. Individ. Differ.* 24:393–403

Gottman JM. 1994. *What Predicts Divorce? The Relationship Between Marital Processes and Marital Outcomes*. Hillsdale, NJ: Erlbaum

Greenberg J, Jonas E. 2003. Psychological motives and political orientation–the left, the right, and the rigid: comment on Jost et al. 2003. *Psychol. Bull.* 129:376–82

Hampson SE, Andrews JA, Barckley M, Lichtenstein E, Lee ME. 2000. Conscientiousness, perceived risk, and risk-reduction behaviors: a preliminary study. *Health Psychol.* 19:247–52

Heaven PC, Bucci S. 2001. Right-wing authoritarianism, social dominance orientation and personality: an analysis using the IPIP measure. *Eur. J. Personal.* 15:49–56

Heaven PC, DaSilva T, Carey C, Holen J. 2004. Loving styles: relationships with personality and attachment atyles. *Eur. J. Personal.* 18:103–13

Helson R, Srivastava S. 2001. Three paths of adult development: conservers, seekers, and achievers. *J. Personal. Soc. Psychol.* 80:995–1010

Hofstee WKB, Ten Berge JMF. 2004. Personality in proportion: a bipolar proportional scale for personality assessments and its consequences for trait structure. *J. Personal. Assess.* 83:120–27

Hogan R 1983. A socioanalytic theory of

personality. In: MM Page ed. *Nebraska Symposium on Motivation 1982*, Lincoln: Univ. Nebraska Press, pp. 55–89

Hooker K, McAdams DP. 2003. Personality reconsidered: a new agenda for aging research. *J. Gerontol. B Psychol. Sci. Soc. Sci.* 58:296–304

Jensen-Campbell LA, Adams R, Perry DG, Workman KA, Furdella JQ, Egan SK. 2002. Agreeableness, extraversion, and peer relations in early adolescence: winning friends and deflecting aggression. *J. Res. Personal.* 36:224–51

John OP, Srivastava S. 1999. The Big Five Trait taxonomy: history, measurement, and theoretical perspectives. In *Handbook of Personality: Theory and Research* ed. LA Pervin, OP John, pp. 102–38. New York: Guilford

Jost JT, Glaser J, Kruglanski AW, Sulloway FJ. 2003a. Political conservatism as motivated social cognition. *Psychol. Bull.* 129:339–75

Jost JT, Glaser J, Kruglanski AW, Sulloway FJ. 2003b. Exceptions that prove the rule—using a theory of motivated social cognition to account for ideological incongruities and political anomalies: reply to Greenberg and Jonas 2003. *Psychol. Bull.* 129:383–93

Judge TA, Bono JE. 2000. Five Factor model of personality and transformational leadership. *J. Appl. Psychol.* 85:751–65

Judge TA, Higgins CA, Thoresen CJ, Barrick MR. 1999. The Big Five personality traits, general mental ability, and career success across the lifespan. *Personnel Psychol.* 52:621–52

Karney BR, Bradbury TN. 1995. The longitudinal course of marital quality and stability: a review of theory, method, and research. *Psychol. Bull.* 118:3–34

Kenford SL, Smith SS, Wetter DW, Jorenby DE, Fiore MC, Baker TB. 2002. Predicting relapse back to smoking: contrasting affective and physical models of dependence. *J. Consult. Clin. Psychol.* 70:216–27

Krueger RF, Hicks BM, McGue M. 2001. Altruism and antisocial behavior: independent tendencies, unique personality correlates, distinct etiologies. *Psychol. Sci.* 12:397–402

Kwan VS, Bond MH, Singelis TM. 1997. Pancultural explanations for life-satisfaction: adding relationship harmony to self-esteem. *J. Personal. Soc. Psychol.* 73:1038–51

Larsen RJ. 2000. Toward a science of mood regulation. *Psychol. Inq.* 11:129–41

Larson LM, Rottinghaus PJ, Borgen FH. 2002. Meta-analyses of Big Six interests and Big Five personality factors. *J. Voc. Behav.* 61:217–39

Luo S, Klohnen EC. 2005. Assortative mating and marital quality in newlyweds: a couple-centered approach. *J. Personal. Soc. Psychol.* 88:304–26

MacDonald DA. 2000. Spirituality: description, measurement, and relation to the Five Factor model of personality. *J. Personal.* 68:153–97

Marcia JE. 1980. Identity in adolescence. In *Handbook of Adolescent Psychology*, ed. J Adelson. New York: Wiley, pp. 159–87

McAdams DP. 2001. The psychology of life stories. *Rev. Gen. Psychol.* 5:100–22

McCullough ME, Emmons RA, Tsang J. 2002. The grateful disposition: a conceptual and empirical topography. *J. Personal. Soc. Psychol.* 82:112–27

Miller TQ, Smith TW, Turner CW, Guijarro ML, Hallet AJ. 1996. A meta-analytic review of research on hostility and physical health. *Psychol. Bull.* 119:322–48

Newcomb AF, Bukowski WM, Pattee L. 1993. Children's peer relations: a meta-analytic review of popular, rejected, neglected, controversial, and average sociometric status. *Psychol. Bull.* 113:99–128

Pals J. 1999. Identity consolidation in early adulthood: relations with ego-resiliency, the context of marriage, and personality change. *J. Personal. Soc. Psychol.* 67:295–329

Parker JG, Asher SR. 1987. Peer relations and later personal adjustment: Are low-accepted children at risk? *Psychol. Bull.* 102:357–89

Paunonen SV. 2003. Big Five factors of personality and replicated predictions of behavior. *J. Personal. Soc. Psychol.* 84:411–22

Paunonen SV, Haddock G, Forsterling F, Keinonen M. 2003. Broad versus narrow personality measures and the prediction of behaviour across cultures. *Eur. J. Personal.* 17:413–33

Pennebaker JW, King LA. 1999. Linguistic styles: language use as an individual difference. *J. Personal. Soc. Psychol.* 77:1296–312

Penner LA. 2002. Dispositional and organizational influences on sustained volunteerism: an interactionist perspective. *J. Soc. Issues* 58:447–67

Penner LA, Fritzsche BA, Craiger JP, Freifeld TR. 1995. Measuring the prosocial personality. In *Advances in Personality Assessment*, ed. J Butcher, CD Spielberger, 10:147–63. Hillsdale, NJ: Erlbaum

Peterson C, Seligman M. 2002. *The VIA Taxonomy of Human Strengths and Virtues*. Washington, DC: Am. Psychol. Assoc.

Piedmont RL. 1999. Does spirituality represent the sixth factor of personality? Spiritual transcendence and the Five Factor Model. *J. Personal.* 67:985–1013

Piedmont RL. 2004. Spiritual transcendence as a predictor of psychosocial outcome from an outpatient substance abuse program. *Psychol. Addict. Behav.* 18:213–22

Roberts BW, Caspi A, Moffitt TE. 2003. Work experiences and personality development in young adulthood. *J. Personal. Soc. Psychol.* 84:582–93

Robins RW, Caspi A, Moffitt TE. 2002. It's not just who you're with, it's who you are: personality and relationship experiences across multiple relationships. *J. Personal.* 70:925–64

Ryan RM, Deci EL. 2001. On happiness and human potentials: a review of research on hedonic and eudaimonic well-being. *Annu. Rev. Psychol.* 52:141–66

Ryder AG, Alden LE, Paulhus DL. 2000. Is acculturation unidimensional or bidimensional? A head-to-head comparison in the prediction of personality, self-identity, and adjustment. *J. Personal. Soc. Psychol.* 79:49–65

Saucier G. 2000. Isms and the structure of social attitudes. *J. Personal. Soc. Psychol.* 78:366–85

Scheier MF, Carver CS. 1993. On the power of positive thinking. *Curr. Dir. Psychol. Sci.* 2:26–30

Schimmack U, Radhakrishnan P, Oishi S, Dzokoto V, Ahadi S. 2002. Culture, personality, and subjective well-being: integrating process models of life-satisfaction. *J. Personal. Soc. Psychol.* 82:582–93

Schmitt D. 2002. Personality, attachment, and sexuality related to dating relationship outcomes: contrasting three perspectives on personal attribute interaction. *Br. J. Soc. Psychol.* 41:589–610

Seligman M, Csikszentmihalyi M. 2000. Positive psychology: an introduction. *Am. Psychol.* 55:5–14

Shaver PR, Brennan K. 1992. Attachment styles and the "Big Five" personality traits: their connections with each other and with romantic relationship outcomes. *Personal. Soc. Psychol. Bull.* 18:536–45

Shiner R, Masten AS, Tellegen A. 2002. A developmental perspective on personality in emerging adulthood: childhood antecedents and concurrent adaptation. *J. Personal. Soc. Psychol.* 83:1165–77

Sjöberg L. 2001. Emotional intelligence: a psychometric analysis. *Eur. Psychol.* 6:79–95

Smith TW, Spiro A. 2002. Personality, health, and aging: prolegomenon for the next generation. *J. Res. Personal.* 36:363–94

Thompson L, Snyder CR, Hoffman L, Michael ST, Rasmussen HN, et al. 2005. Dispositional forgiveness of self, others, and situations. *J. Personal.* 73:313–59

Thoresen CJ, Kaplan SA, Barsky AP, Warren CR, de Chermont K. 2003. The affective underpinnings of job perceptions and attitudes: a meta-analytic review and integration. *Psychol. Bull.* 129:914–45

Thorne A, Klohnen E. 1993. Interpersonal memories as maps for personality consistency. In *Studying Lives Through Time: Personality and Development*, ed. DC Funder, RD Parke, C Tomlinson-Keasey, K Widaman, pp. 223–54. Washington, DC: Am. Psychol. Assoc.

Thrash TM, Elliot AJ. 2004. Inspiration: core

characteristics, component processes, antecedents, and function? *J. Personal. Soc. Psychol.* 87:957–73

Trull TJ, Durrett CA. 2005. Categorical and dimensional models of personality disorder. *Annu. Rev. Clin. Psychol.* 1:355–80

Trull TJ, Sher KJ. 1994. Relationship between the Five Factor model of personality and Axis I disorders in a nonclinical sample. *J. Abnorm. Psychol.* 103:350–60

van der Zee K, Thijs M, Schakel L. 2002. The relationship of emotional intelligence with academic intelligence and the Big Five. *Eur. J. Personal.* 16:103–25

Van Hiel A, Mervielde I. 2004. Openness to experience and boundaries in the mind: relationships with cultural and economic conservative beliefs. *J. Personal.* 72:659–86

Van Hiel A, Mervielde I, DeFruyt F. 2004. The relationship between maladaptive personality and right wing ideology. *Personal. Individ. Differ.* 36:405–17

Verona E, Patrick CJ, Joiner TE. 2001. Psychopathy, antisocial personality, and suicide risk. *J. Abnorm. Psychol.* 110:462–70

Vollrath M, Krahé B, Hampson S. 2004. Editorial: personality and social relations. *Eur. J. Personal.* 18:239

Walton KE, Roberts BW. 2004. On the relationship between substance use and personality traits: abstainers are not maladjusted. *J. Res. Personal.* 38:515–35

Watson D, Hubbard B, Wiese D. 2000. General traits of personality and affectivity as predictors of satisfaction in intimate relationships. evidence from self- and partner-ratings. *J. Personal.* 68:413–49

Watson D, Klohnen EC, Casillas A, Nus Simms E, Haig J, Berry DS. 2004. Match makers and deal breakers: analyses of assortative mating in newlywed couples. *J. Personal.* 72:1029–68

Wiebe RP. 2004. Delinquent behavior and the Five Factor model: hiding in the adaptive landscape? *Individ. Differ. Res.* 2:38–62

Annu. Rev. Psychol. 2006. 57:423–51
doi: 10.1146/annurev.psych.57.102904.190057
Copyright © 2006 by Annual Reviews. All rights reserved
First published online as a Review in Advance on September 13, 2005

CHILD DEVELOPMENT AND THE PHYSICAL ENVIRONMENT

Gary W. Evans

Departments of Design and Environmental Analysis and of Human Development, Cornell University, Ithaca, New York 14853-4401; email: gwe1@cornell.edu

Key Words environmental psychology, toxins, noise, crowding, housing, neighborhood, schools

■ **Abstract** Characteristics of the physical environment that influence child development are discussed. Topics include behavioral toxicology, noise, crowding, housing and neighborhood quality, natural settings, schools, and day care settings. Socioemotional, cognitive, motivation, and psychophysiological outcomes in children and youths are reviewed. Necessary methodological and conceptual advances are introduced as well.

CONTENTS

CHILD DEVELOPMENT AND THE PHYSICAL ENVIRONMENT

Thinking about the ecological context in which human development unfolds has focused on the psychosocial characteristics of children's environments (Bronfenbrenner 1979, 2005), largely ignoring the physical context of human development even though many of the underlying processes that connect context to development are similar for physical and psychosocial environmental factors (Wachs 2000, 2003; Wohlwill & Heft 1987). This article summarizes the role of the physical environment in child development. *Children, Youth and Environment* (http://www.colorado.edu/journals/cye/index.htm) is a primary journal on this topic. Children's physical health is not covered in this chapter because of space limitations (see Wigle 2003 for a recent overview on this topic).

0066-4308/06/0110-0423$20.00

Behavioral Toxicology

LEAD   Heavy metals, inorganic solvents, and pesticides commonly found in the ambient environment affect child development. Lead, mercury, and polychlorinated biphenyls (PCBs) are the most studied behavioral toxins, with more limited data available on other heavy metals, solvents, and pesticide exposure. Needleman (1979) showed that accumulated body lead burden was associated with IQ deficits in grade school children. The results of this study have been widely replicated with statistical controls for socioeconomic status (SES), prospective designs, and dose-response functions (Dietrich 2001, Hubbs-Tait et al. 2005, Koger et al. 2005, Wigle 2003). Lead exposure early in life reduces IQ on the order of three points per 10 μg/dl of blood. In a follow-up study of the same children, Needleman et al. (1990) demonstrated greater reading deficits, lower class ranks, and more high school dropouts as a function of early childhood lead exposure. Lead levels below current "safe" thresholds produce IQ deficits in three- to five-year-olds (Canfield et al. 2003) as well as in elementary school–aged children (Bellinger & Needleman 2003, Chiodo et al. 2004). The Chiodo study also uncovered deficits in reaction time, visual-motor integration, and attention. Teachers also reported more inattention and social withdrawal as a function of lead exposure. In a national sample of 6- to 16-year-olds, an inverse relation was uncovered between lead levels lower than 5 μg per deciliter and reading and math (Lanphear et al. 2000).

Toxins can also influence socioemotional development. Child lead poisoning survivors subsequently manifest increased hyperactivity, impulsivity, and aggression following their recovery. Moreover, these adverse outcomes often persist throughout adulthood (Bellinger & Adams 2001, Dietrich et al. 2001, Hubbs-Tait et al. 2005). In Needleman's 1979 study, teacher ratings of students' externalizing behaviors were also related to body lead burden. Preschool children with body lead burdens above 15 μg/dl, independent of SES and maternal mental health status, had elevated behavioral problems (Sciarillo et al. 1992). One- to three-year-olds with higher lead body burdens evidenced greater hyperactivity, distractibility, and lower frustration tolerance with SES controls (Mendelsohn et al. 1998). Furthermore, in the 11-year follow-up by Needleman et al. (1990), juvenile delinquency was associated with lead levels assessed in elementary school. In a different cohort, Needleman and colleagues uncovered a significant association between skeletal lead concentration and both teacher and parent ratings of externalizing symptomology among 11-year-olds (Needleman et al. 1996). Prenatal blood lead levels are also associated (independent of SES) with self-reported and parent-reported delinquency in adolescence (Dietrich et al. 2001).

MERCURY   Methyl mercury has well-documented influences on cognitive development among children. Male but not female infants manifested sensory-motor difficulties in relation to maternal mercury body burden (McKeown-Eyssen et al. 1983), and 6-year-olds had diminished IQ scores and language development in relation to maternal mercury exposure (Kjellstrom et al. 1989).

In utero, low-level methyl mercury exposure was unrelated to a series of sensory motor and mental status tests from birth through preschool age (Davidson et al. 1998). A second study of low-level, in utero mercury exposure also uncovered no adverse cognitive development sequelae in one-year-olds, but negative outcomes (hand-eye coordination, motor speed, visual attention, memory, language development, and multiple measures of intelligence) began to emerge by age 7 (Grandjean et al. 1997).

PCBs   A series of studies of children prenatally exposed to PCBs from maternal ingestion of Lake Michigan fish has also indicated adverse cognitive developmental impacts (Jacobson & Jacobson 2000). Newborns showed hyporesponsiveness to visual and auditory stimulation. These relations were replicated in a study of lower level, background PCB exposure in North Carolina (Rogan et al. 1986). Among the children in the Jacobson & Jacobson study, deficits in visual recognition memory in 7-month-olds, independent of SES, was linearly related to PCB exposure levels in utero and persisted at a follow-up examination among 4-year-olds. By age 11, these children manifested poorer attention regulation, lower IQ, and reading deficits. In the North Carolina sample, higher prenatal PCB exposure was also related to psychomotor performance at ages 12, 18, and 24 months, but no mental deficiencies were noted (Gladen et al. 1988). This study, however, did not find any linkages between PCB exposure and cognitive development among early-elementary school children (Gladen & Rogan 1991). Work in the Netherlands with 3- to 4-year-olds also revealed cognitive deficits related to PCB exposure (Patandin et al. 1999), and a recent study employing more advanced PCB analytic techniques has largely replicated the Lake Michigan findings in a population on Lake Ontario (Darvill et al. 2000, Stewart et al. 2003).

One additional developmental impact of environmental toxins warrants mention. In a series of studies of families discovering they had been exposed to hazardous wastes in their communities, multiple indices of psychological distress, some lasting years, were revealed (Edelstein 1988, 2002). Symptoms included fear and panic, sleep disturbance, feelings of loss of control and helplessness, fatalism, and elevated family conflict.

With the exception of age at exposure, behavioral toxicology research has not paid sufficient attention to possible moderators of adverse impacts (Hubbs-Tait et al. 2005, Koger et al. 2005). Prenatal low-level lead ($<10 \ \mu g/dl$) effects are milder among higher SES infants, whereas at higher lead levels, SES offers no apparent protective effect (Bellinger 2000, Hubbs-Tait et al. 2005). Prenatal exposure to environmental tobacco smoke in 2-year-olds produces deficits in cognitive development that are accentuated by socioeconomic disadvantage (Rauh et al. 2004). Jacobson & Jacobson (2002) reasoned that social class might protect young children from neurotoxicity because of enhanced parental stimulation. Maternal intellectual stimulation during the early postnatal period partially mediated some of the adverse impacts of PCB exposure on young children's cognitive deficiencies.

Noise

READING   The primary sources of noise exposure among children are transportation, music, and other people. Noise is typically measured as sound level with decibels, a logarithmic scale. A change in 10 decibels is perceived as approximately twice as loud. Children exposed to transportation noise (principally aircraft) manifest significant delays in reading. Most of the evidence is cross-sectional, comparing airport noise-impacted and nearby, quiet schools, typically with statistical controls for SES (Evans & Hygge 2005, Evans & Lepore 1993). Reading effects occur at sound levels far below those sufficient to produce hearing damage. Several investigators have also prescreened children for normal hearing. Haines et al. (2002), however, found no relation between airport noise and reading. Cross-sectional findings on noise and reading have been supplemented by prospective longitudinal data (Hygge et al. 2002), intervention studies with sound attenuation (Bronzaft 1981, Cohen et al. 1986, Fed. Interagency Comm. Aviation Noise 2004, Maxwell & Evans 2000), and linear dose-response functions between noise exposure and reading deficits (Green et al. 1982, Lukas et al. 1981, Stansfeld 2005).

Children in higher grades are more adversely impacted by ambient noise exposure (Bronzaft 1981, Bronzaft & McCarthy 1975, FICAN 2004, Green et al. 1982, Lukas et al. 1981, Maser et al. 1978). Children with greater exposure duration, independent of grade levels (Cohen et al. 1973, 1986; FICAN 2004; Lukas et al. 1981) and pre-existing reading deficiencies (Maser et al. 1978), and those exposed to noise both at home and at school, suffer greater adverse reading impacts (Cohen et al. 1986, Lukas et al. 1981). In addition, Wachs (1978) found that male but not female 12- to 14-month-olds in noisier homes had deficits in intellectual functioning. Older male infants (15–23 months of age) were not affected by noise levels in the home.

COGNITIVE PROCESSES   Long-term memory, particularly for complex verbal materials, is adversely affected by chronic noise exposure (Evans et al. 1995, Haines et al. 2001a, Hiramatsu et al. 2004, Hygge et al. 2002, Matsui et al. 2004, Stansfeld et al. 2005) as well as acute noise exposure (Hygge 2003, Hygge et al. 2003). Several laboratory studies also show that recall is more sensitive to noise interference than is recognition. Meis and colleagues (1998), comparing simulated and actual aircraft noise exposure in the lab and in the field, found parallel adverse impacts on more complex materials. Haines et al. (2001b), however, found no impacts of chronic noise exposure on prose materials varying in difficulty. Children's incidental memory appears fragile to noise exposure (Heft 1979, Lercher et al. 2003). Short-term memory does not appear sensitive to chronic noise unless it is sufficiently loud as to mask encoding of stimuli (Evans & Hygge 2005). Most noise and cognition studies use visually presented stimuli or employ stimuli not loud enough to mask perception of verbal materials. The effects of noise on children's cognition is likely related to more central information processes. One candidate is allocation of attention. Individuals appear to focus their attention on the more critical, important stimuli during noise exposure, but at the cost of attention to more peripheral information (Hockey 1979, Smith & Jones 1992). Several studies with children have uncovered relations between chronic noise exposure and poorer attention as measured by visual search tasks (e.g., finding a target symbol in a visual array) (Heft 1979, Karsdorf & Klappach 1968, Moch-Sibony 1984, Muller et al. 1998) and an auditory search task in relation to school airport noise exposure (Haines et al. 2001c). Failure to replicate effects of noise on visual search (Evans et al. 1995, Hambrick-Dixon 1986, Matsui et al. 2004) could be explained by temporal parameters. Cohen et al. (1986) found that exposure to airport noise for more than two years led to poorer visual search performance, whereas shorter periods of noise exposure had the opposite effect.

There may be a connection between attention reallocation under noise and adverse effects on reading. Children appear to adapt to chronic noise exposure by ignoring or tuning out auditory stimuli. An unintended consequence of this coping strategy, however, is indiscriminate filtering of auditory stimuli in general, including speech, a fundamental building block of reading. Children with no discernable hearing loss who live under chronic noise are less adept at tasks dependent upon speech perception (Cohen et al. 1973, 1986; Evans et al. 1995; Evans & Maxwell 1997; Hygge et al. 2002; Moch-Sibony 1984). The cognitive impacts of noise may begin early. Six-month-old infants with more difficult temperament revealed cognitive deficits to noise, although easygoing babies did not (Wachs & Gandour 1983).

Noise affects adults who in turn may influence children's cognitive development. Teachers in noisy schools report greater fatigue, annoyance, and less patience than do well-matched counterparts teaching in quieter schools (Evans & Hygge 2005, Kryter 1994). Teaching time is lost as instructors pause during noise bursts, and teaching styles may be altered in noisy settings (Evans & Hygge 2005). Parents in noisier and more chaotic homes are less responsive to their children (Corapci & Wachs 2005, Matheny et al. 1995, Wachs 1989, Wachs & Camli 1991).

PSYCHOPHYSIOLOGY   Studies have revealed that chronic exposure to loud noise, typically from airports, elevates blood pressure levels in children (Cohen et al. 1986; Evans et al. 1995, 1998, 2001; Ising et al. 1990a,b; Karagodina et al. 1969; Karsdorf & Klappach 1968; Regecova & Kellcrova 1995; Schmeck & Poustka 1993; Wu et al. 1993). Chronic noise exposure also elevates neuroendocrine stress hormones in children (Evans et al. 1995, 1998, 2001; Ising & Braun 2000; Ising & Ising 2002; Ising et al. 2004; Maschke et al. 1995).

MENTAL HEALTH   Community noise exposure is a well-established irritant, producing annoyance and interference with some outdoor activities among adults (Job 1988). Noise reliably suppresses altruistic behavior and can accentuate aggression among adults already primed by violent stimuli and/or provocation (Cohen & Sapacapan 1984). Neither affective responses to noise nor interpersonal behaviors have received much attention in children. A few studies on children and psychological distress have yielded mixed results. One team of investigators found prospective evidence for adverse impacts of chronic airport noise on elementary school children's self-reported psychological well-being (Bullinger et al. 1999). Moreover, the longer children had been exposed to noise after the opening of the new airport, the greater the adverse impacts. Lercher et al. (2002) demonstrated a linear dose-response function between self-reported and teacher ratings of psychological distress and community noise levels, independent of SES. Haines et al. were unable to replicate these findings (2001a,c) but did find a link to elevated hyperactivity (2001b). More recently, a large study (Stansfeld et al. 2004) found the same pattern of no impacts on overall psychological symptoms with the exception of elevated hyperactivity.

MOTIVATION   In the first human studies of learned helplessness, adults performed a task under escapable or inescapable loud noise or under quiet conditions. Participants who worked under inescapable noise were less likely to perform successfully a subsequent task to avoid noise than those who had previously worked in escapable noise or quiet (Hiroto 1974, Krantz et al. 1974). Adults are also less persistent on challenging tasks following uncontrollable versus controllable noise exposure or quiet conditions (Glass & Singer 1972). Both types of motivational indices among adults are robust, replicated in many laboratory and field studies (Cohen 1980, Evans & Stecker 2004). Fourth-graders exposed to uncontrollable acute noise (Glass 1977) and children as young as four react similarly to chronic noise (Bullinger et al. 1999; Cohen et al. 1986; Evans et al. 1995, 2001; Maxwell & Evans 2000; Moch-Sibony 1984). Wachs (1987) also demonstrated that one-year-old males but not females in noisier homes exhibited less mastery orientation in a toy play task.

METHODOLOGICAL ISSUES   Exposure to poor-quality physical conditions is linked to psychosocial conditions, especially poverty. Moreover, some people may drift into poorer living conditions or be less able to escape from them because of prior physical and/or mental health liabilities. These facts raise questions about the causal role of the physical environment in children's well-being. Most studies of environmental conditions and child development are cross-sectional and thus vulnerable to selection bias plus other unaccounted-for variables. On the other hand, nearly all cross-sectional investigations of the physical environment and child development have incorporated statistical controls for sociodemographic characteristics. Furthermore, several of the associations shown in field studies have been replicated in the laboratory. In addition, a few of the ambient environmental effects on children have been shown in prospective, longitudinal studies and in intervention studies. In a few cases, dose-response curves have been generated between physical conditions and child development. Moreover, for many of the behavioral sequelae of environmental exposure reviewed herein, plausible underlying mechanisms have been theorized and in some instances tested.

Some methodological aspects of environment and child development research can lead to underestimation rather than overestimation of effects. Crude estimates of environmental exposure lead to underestimation of environmental effects. Children's exposures to physical conditions often are not well estimated. Children move in and out of settings daily and over their life course. Most studies of children and the physical environment use residential or school location as the marker for ambient exposure. For some physical conditions (e.g., noise), children are protected by building interiors, whereas for others (e.g., crowding), effects are amplified by buildings. Furthermore, range restriction in environmental exposures can truncate estimates of covariance with developmental outcomes. Studies of residential crowding in North America, for instance, have very little range in household densities, effectively underestimating potential impact on children's development. The practice of statistically controlling for social class in studies of children and the physical environment raises important challenges given the high colinearity between poverty and environmental quality, along with exposure to a host of psychosocial risk factors among children (Evans 2004). Furthermore, duration of exposure to environmental conditions may be as important as intensity, yet few studies incorporate temporal parameters into their designs. Another methodological issue that may cause underestimation of environmental effects is reliance upon insensitive developmental outcomes. Simple cognitive tasks or psychiatric illness are two common examples.

Crowding

INTERPERSONAL BEHAVIORS   The number of people per room, rather than areal markers of density (e.g., people per acre), is the critical index of crowding related to human well-being (Baum & Paulus 1987, Evans 2001). A number of studies converge on elevated levels of social withdrawal among preschool children when interacting under more crowded conditions. Several of these studies randomly exposed children to different levels of density. Liddell & Kruger, Loo, and McGrew observed the same child under variable density conditions (Hutt & Vaizy 1966; Liddell & Kruger 1987, 1989; Loo 1972; McGrew 1970; Preiser 1972). Liddell & Kruger (1989) found that home density was positively associated with social withdrawal among children at nursery school. Hutt & Vaizy (1966) noted that withdrawal was more marked among autistic children relative to typical 3- to 8-year-olds. The links between density and withdrawal occur among 10- to 12-year-olds living at home (Evans et al. 1998) and among male 14- to 18-year-olds in prison (Ray et al. 1982).

Parents are less responsive to young children in more crowded homes, irrespective of social class, and these relations begin before 12 months of age (Bradley & Caldwell 1984, Bradley et al. 1994, Evans et al. 1999, Wachs 1989, Wachs & Camli 1991). Reduced parental monitoring of children also occurs in higher density homes (Gove & Hughes 1983, Hassan 1977, Mitchell 1971). Social withdrawal may reflect coping with too much unwanted social interaction.

Controlling for SES, both children and their parents report more strained, negative familial interactions in high-density homes (Baldassare 1981, Bartlett 1998,

Booth 1976, Chombart de Lauwe 1961, Fuller et al. 1993, Gasparini 1973, Gove & Hughes 1983, Light 1973, Loo & Ong 1984, Saegert 1982, Youssef et al. 1998). Greater child maltreatment among low-income children was uncovered in more crowded homes (Martin & Walters 1982, Wolock & Horowitz 1979). Punitive parenting mediated relations between residential density and psychological distress in low-income 8- to 10-year-olds (Evans & Saegert 2000). Interpersonal strains between parents and children in crowded homes also accounted in part for negative socioemotional and physiological stress outcomes in 10- to 12-year-olds, irrespective of SES (Evans et al. 1998). Residential crowding also erodes social support among adults over time, which in turn leads to greater psychological distress (Lepore et al. 1991).

Elevated aggression and conflict as well as diminished cooperation occurs among more crowded preschoolers (Bates 1970, Rohe & Nuffer 1977, Rohe & Patterson 1974, Ruopp et al. 1979), elementary school children (Ginsburg & Pollman 1975, Murray 1974, Shapiro 1975), and adolescents (Aiello et al. 1979). Some studies have not found links between density and aggression among young children (Fagot 1977, Smith & Connolly 1977). Liddell & Kruger (1987) found diminished cooperation but no changes in conflict among more crowded nursery school children. Loo's (1972) contradictory results may be because of density levels. In subsequent work with higher density levels, male but not female 5-year-olds in more crowded conditions acted more aggressively (Loo & Kennelly 1978). Another factor in crowding and aggression among children is the number of play resources such as toys or play equipment. Although Smith & Connolly (1977) uncovered no links between density in the nursery school and aggressive behavior, resource availability had a strong impact. Rohe & Patterson (1974) showed that when density was high and resources adequate, little impact was seen on aggression in preschoolers. However, if high density was combined with low resources, aggression increased. Higher ratios of preschoolers to activity areas led to more off-task behavior and marginally less constructive play (Kantrowitz & Evans 2004).

Personal characteristics may buffer the impacts of crowding on aggression. Loo & Kennelly (1978) found that boys but not girls responded negatively to crowded conditions. The same interaction was uncovered in 9- to 17-year-olds (Aiello et al. 1979). Loo (1978a) showed that 5-year-olds reacted with greater aggression than did 10-year-olds to similar density conditions, whereas Aiello found no developmental differences among 9- to 17-year-olds. Typical and brain-damaged children between 3 and 8 years of age reacted with more aggression to crowded conditions, whereas autistic children manifested extreme withdrawal (Hutt & Vaizey 1966).

MENTAL HEALTH   Elementary school children who live in more crowded homes, independent of social class, reveal higher levels of neuroticism (Murray 1974), psychological distress (Evans et al. 2001, 2002; Evans & Saegert 2000; Rutter et al. 1974), poorer behavioral adjustment at school (Booth & Johnson 1975; Evans et al.

1998, 2002; Saegert 1982), and lower social and cognitive competency (Shaw & Emery 1988). Goduka et al. (1992), however, found no relations between household crowding and self-concept among 5- to 6-year-olds. Daily problem behaviors among adolescents in a crisis shelter fluctuated in response to the census—as the shelter became more populated, behavioral problems increased (Teare et al. 1995). Several adult studies show associations between residential crowding and psychological distress net of SES, including a prospective, longitudinal study (Lepore et al. 1991).

A few findings indicate moderation of density effects on mental health among children. Evans et al. (2002) found that the adverse effect of crowded housing on both self- and teacher ratings of psychological distress among third- and fourth-graders was exacerbated by residence in larger, multifamily structures. Preschoolers in crowded day care centers had greater behavioral disturbances if they also lived in more crowded homes (Maxwell 1996). Bradley et al. (1994) demonstrated that low-density housing contributed to resilience among socioemotional and cognitive development in low-birth-weight babies at age 3. Consistent with these findings, the elevated psychological distress of 8- to 10-year-olds in more crowded homes is exacerbated by family turmoil (Evans & Saegert 2000). Malnutrition early in life is frequently associated with babies who are more apathetic and less responsive. Rahmanifar and colleagues (1993) found that such effects were accentuated in more crowded homes. Finally, the adverse impact of laboratory crowding on behavioral disturbances among 5-year-olds was exacerbated by pre-existing hyperactivity or anxiety (Loo 1978b).

MOTIVATION   Laboratory crowding in seventh- and eighth-graders increased vulnerability to helplessness induction from unsolvable word problems (Rodin 1976) and produced less task persistence among high school students (Sherrod 1974). Sherrod found that when adolescents had perceived control over crowding, the motivational deficits were eliminated. Chronic crowding, net of SES, has been linked to lower motivation in task performance paradigms in children ranging from 6 to 12 years of age (Evans et al. 1998, 2001; Rodin 1976). The Rodin (1976) as well as Evans et al. (2001) studies also uncovered dose-response relations between residential density and helplessness. One study with 10- to 12-year-olds found the crowding-helplessness link among girls only (Evans et al. 1998).

COGNITIVE PROCESSES   Given the potential for crowding to disrupt ongoing activities such as studying as well as its potential to interfere with exploration and play activities (Heft 1985), several researchers have scrutinized connections between crowding and cognition. Nearly all of these studies statistically control for SES. Psychomotor development (Widmayer et al. 1990) but not mental development (Gottfried & Gottfried 1984) is related to residential density among 12-month-olds. With maturation, however, mental development becomes negatively related to crowding at 18 and 24 months of age (Gottfried & Gottfried 1984). These same investigators also showed negative relations between residential density and

30-, 36-, and 42-month indices of verbal, perceptual, and quantitative performance, and at 39 months with language development. The IQ scores of children 30 months of age were also negatively associated with residential crowding (Wachs 1978). Preschool-age children living in more crowded homes suffer cognitive deficits in verbal and math ability (Goduka et al. 1992). Using a different achievement index, Maxwell (1996) found no association among preschoolers. Elementary school–aged children from more crowded homes do more poorly on standardized reading tests (Evans et al. 1998, Rutter et al. 1970, Saegert 1982, Wedge & Petzing 1970) and perceive themselves as lower in scholastic competency (Evans & Saegert 2000). Essen et al. (1978) showed these relations in both 7- and 16-year-olds and replicated the effect prospectively with the 16-year-olds. In addition, school performance through high school is negatively associated with residential crowding (Booth 1976, Hassan 1977, Ray et al. 1982), as is educational attainment at age 25 (Conley 2001). Older (18 and 24 months) but not younger (7 to 15 months) infants, especially males (Wachs 1979), living in more crowded homes suffer deficits in object spatial relations and understanding of cause and effect (Wachs 1976, Wachs et al. 1971). Toddlers also show impaired semantic memory in more crowded homes (Gottfried & Gottfried 1984). Kindergarten children from higher density homes perform more poorly on visual search (Heft 1979).

Many school districts in the United States are experiencing severe overcrowding (Campaign Fiscal Equality 1999). Crowding in day care centers was associated with attentional deficits (Maxwell 1996). When kindergarten classrooms were more crowded, children were off task more than when classroom density was reduced. Density was manipulated by altering available classroom space over time with class size held constant (Krantz 1974). Poor nutrition may exacerbate some of the harmful impacts of classroom crowding on young children's behaviors (Grantham-McGregor et al. 1998). Although investigators have not conceptualized class size as a manipulation of density, smaller class sizes in the earlier grades enhance concurrent and subsequent standardized test scores for children, particularly for disadvantaged children (Greenwald et al. 1996, Ehrenberg et al. 2001). In addition, teachers spend less time disciplining children in smaller classes (Ehrenberg et al. 2001).

Studies disentangling family size from density typically find that density, not family size, is the critical variable (Booth 1976, Conley 2001, Evans et al. 1999, Gottfried & Gottfried 1984, Gove & Hughes 1983, Loo & Ong 1984, Saegert 1982, Wachs 1979). Similar conclusions emanate from crowding effects in childcare centers (Legendre 2003) and adolescent crisis shelters (Teare et al. 1995). Laboratory studies holding group size constant and manipulating area also indicate that density is salient. Some of the links between crowding and cognitive development might be caused by changes in parent-child interactions. For example, parents in more crowded homes talk less to their infants (Wachs 1979, Wachs & Camli 1991) and use less sophisticated speech from infancy to two and a half years of age (Evans et al. 1999). Children in crowded homes lack a place to study and find it more difficult to get away from their family to be alone (Gove & Hughes

1983). Children with a place to study in crowded homes suffer fewer cognitive consequences (Michelson 1968, Wachs 1979).

PSYCHOPHYSIOLOGICAL   Unfortunately, just a handful of studies have examined physiological stress concomitants of crowding among children. Legendre (2003) found cortisol rise over the morning period in day-care children was greater among children in more crowded conditions. Aiello et al. (1979), in a laboratory study, showed that male but not female skin conductance levels were higher under crowded conditions, and the longer the exposure, the greater the elevation. Evans et al. (1998) found the same gender-by-density interaction for blood pressure among 10- to 12-year-olds in terms of residential crowding. Evans & Saegert (2000), in a study of 8- to 10-year-olds, found that both male and female children in higher density apartments had elevated overnight epinephrine and norepinephrine, especially when there was greater family turmoil in the household. Ray and colleagues (1982) found no adverse impacts of prison crowding on adolescent males, but unreliable blood pressure monitoring procedures were used.

Housing and Neighborhood Quality

HOUSING TYPE   Housing type, housing quality, structure and predictability of daily routines, and residential mobility have been investigated in relation to child development. Juveniles in census tracts with larger proportions of multiple-dwelling units, controlling for SES, have greater rates of juvenile delinquency (Gillis 1974), and younger children in high-rise compared with low-rise buildings evidence more behavioral problems (Ineichen & Hooper 1974, Richman 1977, Saegert 1982) and weaker academic performance (Michelson 1968). However, Richman (1974) and Homel & Burns (1989) did not replicate these effects, and Saegert (1982) found they held only for boys. The impact of living on higher floor levels may be stronger for preschoolers than for children in primary school (Oda et al. 1989). This may be explained by greater restrictions on outdoor play behavior and the resulting tension and isolation that occur, particularly for younger mothers home with their children (Churchman & Ginsberg 1984, Gittus 1976, Littlewood & Sale 1972, Ranson 1991, Stewart 1970).

HOUSING QUALITY   Several studies indicate potential adverse impacts of housing quality on children's socioemotional development (Blackman et al. 1989, Davie et al. 1972, Evans et al. 2001, Hunt 1990, LeClair & Innes 1997, Tracy et al. 1993). Most of these studies incorporate statistical controls for SES. The results hold for adolescents as well (LeClair & Innes 1997, Obasanjo 1998). Gifford & Lacombe (2004) showed that both teacher and parent ratings of elementary school children's levels of psychological distress were influenced by housing quality, independent of SES. Some studies, however, have uncovered no relation between housing quality and young children's psychological well-being (Greenberg et al. 1999, Kasl et al. 1982). Cognitive development also suffers in relation to housing quality. Teacher ratings of first-graders' (Greenberg et al. 1999) and third-graders' (Michelson 1968) social and academic competency along with standardized test scores are significantly linked to housing quality, controlling for SES. Wilner et al. (1962) found that, among a sample of slum dwellers, families who moved into better housing witnessed significant improvements in elementary school performance compared with well-matched families who remained. A nationally representative cohort of British children living in substandard housing had lower standardized test scores in eighth and eleventh grade (Douglas 1964), with SES controls. Furthermore, the longer the children were exposed to substandard housing, the stronger the association. Adolescents in poor-quality housing in two different samples with good controls for SES manifested more absentmindedness and forgetting (Obasanjo 1998).

MEDIATING PROCESSES   An interesting question raised by these findings is, What proximal processes are disrupted by inadequate housing? One candidate is strained, interpersonal relationships. Residents of multifamily compared with single-family homes, controlling for SES, report greater marital and parent-child conflict (Edwards et al. 1982, Moore 1975), and high-rise housing is associated with less socially supportive relationships with neighbors (Evans et al. 2003). Adolescents in poorer quality housing perceive less social support from family members as well as from friends (Obasanjo 1998). Children in poor quality housing get sick more often (primarily upper respiratory infections and physical injuries), which translates into more school absenteeism (Shaw 2004). Some aspects of inadequate housing quality may reflect parental organization and efficiency (e.g., clutter and cleanliness). Dunifon and colleagues (2004) showed that links between residential cleanliness and children's educational attainment in adulthood held net of time devoted to housework by parents.

CHAOS   With controls for SES, the regularity of events in the home (e.g., homework and bedtime schedule) (Fiese et al. 2002) as well as levels of unpredictability and confusion in the home (Wachs & Corapci 2005) are related to socioemotional functioning. Children ages 6 to 9 in households with more structure and routines have better academic achievement and fewer behavioral adjustment problems (Brody & Flor 1997). Chaotic home environments are associated with multimethodological indicators of psychological distress among middle school children (Evans et al. 2005). Fisher & Feldman (1998) showed that high school students in households with less cohesion, orderliness, and clarity of rules and roles were more emotionally distressed six years later. Children ages 3 to 4 in more chaotic homes reveal cross-sectional and longitudinal deficits in cognitive development as well (Petrill et al. 2004). Elementary school children in a national study of divorce adjusted better emotionally and performed better at school and on achievement tests if their household had more routine and structure (Guidubaldi et al. 1986). Adolescents in remarried families were more satisfied with family life in households with more regular routines (Henry & Lovelace 1995). Temperament may moderate the relation between family routines and adjustment. Sprunger et al. (1985) found that babies with more regular biological cycles (eat, sleep, cry) benefited more from a structured, predictable household routine.

Explanations for the adverse impacts of chaotic early childhood settings have focused primarily on parent-child relationships and on self-regulatory ability. Families in households with more routines are more cohesive, happier, and have less conflict (Jensen et al. 1983). Parents of infants in more chaotic homes, net of SES, are less responsive and offer fewer learning stimulation opportunities (Corapci & Wachs 2005). Six- to nine-year-olds in more chaotic households, independent of income, have more difficulty self-regulating, which in turn accounts for most of the shared variance between chaos and both academic achievement and socioemotional adjustment (Brody & Flor 1997). Moreover, children in more chaotic preschools are less compliant (Wachs et al. 2004). Adolescents from less cohesive, unstructured homes also engaged in riskier health behaviors as young adults (Fisher & Feldman 1998). One final aspect of housing quality, residential stability, is worth mentioning. Numerous studies reveal that children exposed to more frequent residential relocations, independent of SES, experience worse psychological adjustment (for reviews, see Adam 2004, Humke & Schaefer 1995).

NEIGHBORHOOD   Housing is embedded in neighborhoods that also have potential developmental consequences. Several adverse child outcomes are related to residence in economically impoverished neighborhoods with individual-level SES statistical controls (Leventhal & Brooks-Gunn 2000), but the role of physical neighborhood characteristics is unclear. Among the potential developmentally salient physical characteristics of neighborhoods are residential instability, housing quality, noise, crowding, toxic exposure, quality of municipal services, retail services (e.g., bars, liquor stores, nutritional foods), recreational opportunities, including natural settings, street traffic, accessibility of transportation, and the physical quality of both educational and health care facilities (Evans 2004, Macintyre et al. 1993, Wandersman & Nation 1998).

Nine- to eleven-year-olds had greater psychological distress in poorer physical-quality neighborhoods, independent of familial SES (Homel & Burns 1989). Similar neighborhood physical quality and mental health trends, controlling for individual SES levels, have been uncovered among adults in cross-sectional (Steptoe & Feldman 2001) and longitudinal (Dalgard & Tambs 1997) studies. Close proximity to street traffic, in addition to raising the risk of pediatric injuries (Macpherson et al. 1998), is correlated with restrictions in outdoor play among 5-year-olds, smaller social networks for these children, and diminished social and motor skills (Huttenmoser 1995). Households on streets with higher traffic volume interact less with their neighbors relative to those residing on less congested streets (Appleyard & Lintell 1972).

NATURAL SETTINGS   Children prefer outdoor settings, particularly those predominated by nature, when queried or observed in naturalistic play activities (Chawla

2002, Hart 1978, Korpela 2002, Moore & Schneekloth 1989). One reason for this may be the wider array of motoric and social play opportunities and greater independent mobility afforded by such spaces (Heft 1988; Kytta 2002, 2004). Children and adults also find natural settings more restorative, reducing cognitive fatigue, and enhancing positive affect (Kaplan & Kaplan 1989, Kaplan & Talbot 1983). A meta-analysis of outdoor learning experiences (e.g., Outward Bound) revealed an effect size of 0.34. Moreover, the longer the outdoor experience, the stronger the benefits (Hattie et al. 1997). Access to nearby nature may be beneficial as well. Girls but not boys residing in public housing more proximate to natural outdoor spaces (i.e., trees, grass) evidenced better attentional and emotional self-regulation ability (Faber Taylor et al. 2002). These same male and female children played more and engaged in more complex play (e.g., creative play) in outdoor spaces containing more nature as compared with spaces that were barren (Faber Taylor et al. 1998). Elementary school children play in more complex ways in natural versus built play spaces (Kirkby 1989). Preschool children engaged in more physically demanding play and developed better motor skills when they played in more natural areas compared with traditional playgrounds (Fjortoft 2004). Play in natural areas also benefits children with attention deficit-hyperactivity disorder (Faber Taylor et al. 2001, Kuo & Faber Taylor 2004). Nearby nature may also enhance attention (Wells 2000) and buffer some of the ill effects of chronic stressor exposure among typical children (Wells & Evans 2003).

Schools and Day Care

SCHOOL SIZE   In addition to classroom size (see Crowding section above), school size, the quality of school buildings, the degree of openness in classrooms, and various ambient qualities (e.g., temperature, lighting) have been examined in relation to child outcomes (Lackney 2005). Numerous investigators have uncovered evidence on the benefits of smaller schools. Larger schools have worse standardized test scores (typically with statistical controls for population SES) (for reviews, see Cotton 1996, Greenwald et al. 1996, Howley et al. 2000, Lackney 2004, Schneider 2002). The median effect size for school size on standardized tests is $\beta = 0.035$ (Greenwald et al. 1996). The benefits of smaller schools on achievement may be even greater for low-income students (Cotton 1996, Howley et al. 2000). Smaller schools are also consistently related to more positive student attitudes, better attendance, fewer behavioral problems, greater extracurricular involvement, stronger feelings of connectedness (Cotton 1996), and greater parental involvement in school activities (Schneider 2002).

BUILDING QUALITY   In 1995, nearly one third of American children attended public schools in disrepair (Gen. Account. Off. 1995), and 3.5 million children attended schools so dilapidated they were labeled nonoperational (Natl. Cent. Educ. Stat. 1999). Both students and teachers find such conditions demoralizing

(Fine et al. 2004, Schneider 2002). There is a burgeoning literature on school facility quality and student achievement. The largest program of research is by Earthman and colleagues (Al-Enezi 2002, Earthman 1998), and it shows modest but consistent negative correlations between facility quality and standardized test scores, with schoolwide SES controls. Staff ratings of structural (e.g., heating and ventilation, wall and floor conditions) and cosmetic (e.g., painting, maintenance) conditions are related to standardized test scores in high schools and elementary schools. Similar results have been uncovered in other sites (O'Neill & Oates 2001, Schneider 2002). More readily discernable conditions (i.e., cosmetic) appear more salient in relation to test scores. Potential validity concerns from reliance upon staff ratings of building quality are mollified to some extent by equivalent findings in other studies relying upon expert ratings of school buildings (Berner 1993, Branham 2004a, Buckley et al. 2004, Lewis 2000). Branham (2004b) also uncovered an inverse association between building quality and attendance and dropout rates in secondary schools. Comparisons between older and improved elementary school facilities across the state of Georgia (McGuffey & Brown 1978), within the same school district (Bowers & Burkett 1988), using a cohort design before and after moving to a new facility (Phillips 1997), and a before/after comparison of test scores for the same building following renovation (Berry 2002), all reveal improved test scores plus better attendance for the latter study.

OPEN-PLAN DESIGN   Open schools with few floor-to-ceiling walls have been compared in studies with traditional, enclosed classrooms. The data on achievement converge on little or no impacts of open- versus traditional-plan facilities (Ahrentzen et al. 1982, Gifford 2002, Gump 1987, Weinstein 1979), with parallel results for indices of self-concept (Giaconia & Hedges 1982). Open-plan schools and day care manifest problems with distraction and off-task time (Cotterell 1984, Gump & Good 1976, Moore 1986, Neill 1982). Noise levels are higher in open-plan schools (Kyzar 1977), and teacher complaints about noise in open-plan schools are common (Bennett et al. 1980, Weinstein 1979). Proximity to unshielded circulation systems also contributes to distraction in both preschools (Greenman 1988, Olds 2001) and elementary schools (Evans & Lovell 1979, Lackney 2004). Systematic modifications of open-plan spaces providing greater demarcation and clearer boundaries between learning areas reduced off-task time and interruptions (Evans & Lovell 1979, Weinstein 1977).

Another common difficulty noted in open school designs is uneven use of space, with large areas of unused space often accompanied by space on the periphery where users are cramped together (Propst 1972, Rivlin & Rothenberg 1976). Clustering of activity areas with clear boundaries appears to relieve this problem and fosters comfort in day-care settings (Greenman 1988, Moore & Lackney 1993, Olds 2001, Sanoff 1995, Weinstein 1987). Fourth-graders showed increased but short-lived use of privacy booths when introduced into their classrooms (Weinstein 1982). Preschoolers frequently used secluded spaces, particularly in more crowded classrooms (Lowry 1993), and elementary school children prefer more enclosed spaces (Ahrentzen & Evans 1984, Gramza 1970, Lowry 1993). Small niches and enclosures plus other design elements (lighting, comfortable/soft furniture, flooring materials) appear to support a more homey, less institutional setting for young children (Ahrentzen et al. 1982, Greenman 1988, Lackney 2004, Moore & Lackney 1993, Olds 2001, Sanoff 1995, Weinstein 1987).

Both teaching style and student personal characteristics can moderate the impacts of school architecture on children. Elementary school children with lower task persistence (Reiss & Dydhalo 1975), lower IQ (Grapko 1972), lower academic achievement orientation, greater external locus of control (Solomon & Kendal 1976), and English as a second language (Traub & Weiss 1974) perform more poorly in open-plan schools. Children in open-plan schools with more traditionally oriented teachers fare worse than those with teachers attuned to open education (Gump 1987).

LIGHTING AND INDOOR CLIMATE   Illumination in American schools is sufficiently bright that variations in intensity are unlikely to influence performance. Some work suggests potential benefits of exposure to natural light in schools (Heschong Mahone 1999, Nicklas & Bailey 1997). These studies suffer from methodological flaws. More rigorous work comparing Swedish elementary school children in windowless classrooms with children in classrooms with windows in the winter reveals disturbances in diurnal cortisol rhythms along with concomitant shifts in concentration (Kuller & Linsten 1992).

In addition to light, climatic conditions may influence student comfort and performance in school. Well-controlled laboratory studies with children indicate performance decrements that increase over time and with more demanding task requirements among elementary school children exposed to increased levels of heat (Johansson 1975, Schoer & Shaffran 1973, Wyon et al. 1979). Air-conditioning enhances school performance during the warm season but not during cooler periods (Pepler 1971). Teachers in primary schools rate their pupils as more lethargic and less diligent on hot compared with cooler days (Humphreys 1974).

Environmental contaminants in school buildings, such as mold, allergens, and various chemicals found in cleaning products, combustion byproducts, and building materials, are known respiratory irritants and asthma triggers and have been associated with absenteeism levels among school children (EPA 2003). The impacts of these substances are exacerbated by poorly maintained heating, ventilation, and air-conditioning systems and low ventilation rates. Changes in ventilation rates that affected carbon monoxide levels were associated with both objective (Myhrvold et al. 1996) and subjective (Smedje et al. 1996) indices of attention among school children. Implementation of air cleaning technology in two day care centers reduced particulates, which was accompanied by drops in absenteeism (Rosen & Richardson 1999).

SUMMARY AND CONCLUSIONS

The physical environment can influence child development directly and via adult caregivers. In addition to studies with stronger research designs examining the role of environmental qualities in child development, more work is needed on underlying mechanisms to account for developmental impacts of the physical environment. Prime candidates include parent-child interaction and other interpersonal processes, self-regulation, physiological adaptations, and control beliefs. This work should investigate how the intensity—but also the predictability and continuity of such mechanisms—is altered by the physical environment. In addition to examining the role of age, other moderators warranting attention are gender, temperament, nutrition, intelligence, and prematurity.

We also know little about the role of cumulative exposure to multiple environmental conditions upon children. Childhood exposure to environmental conditions is not random. Low-income children are disproportionately exposed to multiple suboptimal physical and social environmental conditions (Evans 2004) that portend adverse developmental impacts (Repetti et al. 2002, Taylor et al. 1997). Multiple rather than singular risk exposure may be a particularly critical aspect of the adverse developmental effects of childhood poverty.

ACKNOWLEDGMENTS

I thank Jim Dunn, Staffan Hygge, Lorraine Maxwell, Susan Saegert, Nicole Simon, Ted Wachs, and Nancy Wells for critical feedback on earlier drafts of this article. Preparation of this article was partially supported by the W.T. Grant Foundation and the John D. and Catherine T. MacArthur Foundation.

The *Annual Review of Psychology* is online at http://psych.annualreviews.org

LITERATURE CITED

Adam EK. 2004. Beyond quality: parental and residential stability and children's adjustment. *Curr. Dir. Psychol. Sci.* 13:210–13

Ahrentzen S, Evans GW. 1984. Distraction, privacy, and classroom design. *Environ. Behav.* 16:437–54

Ahrentzen S, Jue G, Skorpanich MA, Evans GW. 1982. School environments and stress. In *Environmental Stress*, ed. GW Evans, pp. 224–55. New York: Cambridge Univ. Press

Aiello JR, Nicosia G, Thompson DE. 1979. Physiological, social, and behavioral consequences of crowding on children and adolescents. *Child Dev.* 50:195–202

Al-Enezi M. 2002. *The study of the relationship between school building conditions and academic achievement of 12th grade students in Kuwaiti public schools.* Unpubl. doctoral dissert. Virginia Polytech. Univ., Blacksburg

Appleyard D, Lintell M. 1972. The environmental quality of city streets. *J. Am. Inst. Plan.* 38:84–101

Baldassare M. 1981. The effects of household density on sub groups. *Am. Sociol. Rev.* 46: 110–18

Bartlett S. 1998. Does inadequate housing perpetuate children's poverty? *Childhood* 5: 403–20

Bates B. 1970. *Effects of social density on the behavior of nursery school children.*

Unpubl. doctoral dissert. Univ. Oregon, Eugene

Baum A, Paulus PB. 1987. Crowding. In *Handbook of Environmental Psychology*, ed. D Stokols, I Atlman, pp. 533–70. New York: Wiley

Bellinger DC. 2000. Effect modification in epidemiologic studies of low-level neurotoxicant exposures and health outcomes. *Neurotoxicol. Teratol.* 22:133–40

Bellinger DC, Adams HF. 2001. *Environmental Pollutant Exposures and Children's Cognitive Abilities*. Mahwah, NJ: Erlbaum

Bellinger DC, Needleman HL. 2003. Intellectual impairment and blood lead levels. *N. Engl. J. Med.* 349:500–2

Bennett N, Andrae J, Hegarty P, Wade B. 1980. *Open Plan Schools*. Atlantic Highlands, NJ: Humanities

Berner MM. 1993. Building conditions, parental involvement, and student achievement in the District of Columbia public school system. *Urban Educ.* 28:6–29

Berry MA. 2002. *The contribution of restoration and effective operation and maintenance programs on indoor environmental quality and educational performance in schools*. Presented at Indoor Air 2002, Monterey, CA

Blackman T, Evason E, Melaughs M, Woods R. 1989. Housing and health: a case study of two areas in West Belfast. *J. Soc. Policy* 18: 18–27

Booth A. 1976. *Urban Crowding and Its Consequences*. New York: Praeger

Booth A, Edwards JN. 1976. Crowding and family relations. *Am. Sociol. Rev.* 41:308–21

Booth A, Johnson DR. 1975. The effect of crowding on child health and development. *Am. Behav. Sci.* 18:736–49

Bowers JH, Burkett CW. 1988. Physical environment influences related to student achievement, health, attendance and behavior. *CEFP J.* 26:33–34

Bradley RH, Caldwell B. 1984. The home inventory and family demographics. *Dev. Psychol.* 20:315–20

Bradley RH, Whiteside L, Mundfrom DJ, Casey PH, Kelleher K, et al. 1994. Early indications of resilience and their relation to experiences in the home environments of low birthweight, premature children living in poverty. *Child Dev.* 65:346–60

Branham D. 2004a. The wise man builds his house upon the rock: the effects of inadequate school building infrastructure on student attendance. *Soc. Sci. Q.* 85:1112–28

Branham D. 2004b. The wise man builds his house upon the rock: the effects of inadequate school infrastructure on student performance. http://www.uh.edu/cpp/school.pdf

Brody GH, Flor DL. 1997. Maternal psychological functioning, family processes, and child adjustment in rural, single-parent, African American families. *Dev. Psychol.* 33:1000–11

Bronfenbrenner U. 1979. *The Ecology of Human Development*. Cambridge, MA: Harvard Univ. Press

Bronfenbrenner U, ed. 2005. *Making Human Beings Human*. Los Angeles: Sage

Bronfenbrenner U, Evans GW. 2000. Developmental science in the 21st century: emerging theoretical models, research designs, and empirical findings. *Soc. Dev.* 9:115–25

Bronzaft A, McCarthy D. 1975. The effect of elevated train noise on reading ability. *Environ. Behav.* 7:517–27

Bronzaft AL. 1981. The effect of a noise abatement program on reading ability. *J. Environ. Psychol.* 1:215–22

Buckley J, Schneider M, Shang Y. 2004. LAUSD school facilities and academic performance. http://www.edfacilities.org/PUBS /LAUSD%20REPORT.PDF

Bullinger M, Hygge S, Evans GW, von Meis M. 1999. The psychological costs of aircraft noise among children. *Zentralblatt Hygeine Umweltmed.* 202:127–38

Campaign Fiscal Equal. 1999. *Facilities: Conditions in New York*. New York: Campaign Fiscal Equal.

Canfield RL, Henderson CR, Cory-Slechta DA, Cox C, Jusko TA, Lanphear BP. 2003. Intellectual impairment in children with blood lead concentrations below 10 μg per deciliter. *N. Engl. J. Med.* 348:1517–26

Chawla L, ed. 2002. *Growing Up in an Urbanized World*. London: Earthscan

Chiodo LM, Jacobson SW, Jacobson JL. 2004. Neurodevelopmental effects of postnatal lead exposure at very low levels. *Neurotoxicol. Teratol.* 26:359–71

Chombart de Lauwe PH. 1961. The sociology of housing methods and prospects of research. *Int. J. Comp. Sociol.* 2:23–41

Churchman A, Ginsberg Y. 1984. The image and experience of high-rise housing in Israel. *J. Environ. Psychol.* 4:27–41

Cohen S. 1980. Aftereffects of stress on human performance and social behavior: a review of research and theory. *Psychol. Bull.* 88:82–108

Cohen S, Evans GW, Stokols D, Krantz DS. 1986. *Behavior, Health, and Environmental Stress*. New York: Plenum

Cohen S, Glass DC, Singer JE. 1973. Apartment noise, auditory discrimination, and reading ability in children. *J. Exper. Soc. Psychol.* 9:407–22

Cohen S, Spacapan S. 1984. The social psychology of noise. In *Noise and Society*, ed. DM Jones, AJ Chapman, pp. 221–45. New York: Wiley

Conley D. 2001. A room with a view or a room of one's own? Housing and social stratification. *Sociol. Forum* 16:263–80

Corapci F, Wachs TD. 2005. Does parental mood or efficacy mediate the influence of environmental chaos upon parenting behavior? *Merrill-Palmer Q.* In press

Cotterell JL. 1984. Effects of school architectural design on student and teacher anxiety. *Environ. Behav.* 16:455–79

Cotton K. 1996. School size, school climate, and student performance. http://www.nwrel.org/scpd/sirs/10/c020.html

Dalgard OS, Tambs K. 1997. Urban environment and mental health. A longitudinal study. *Br. J. Psychiatry* 171:530–36

Darvill T, Lonky E, Reihman J, Stewart P, Pagano J. 2000. Prenatal exposure to PCBs and infant performance on the Fagan Test of Infant Intelligence. *Neurotoxicology* 21:1029–38

Davidson PW, Myers GJ, Cox C, Axtell C, Shamlaye C, et al. 1998. Effects of prenatal and postnatal methylmercury exposure from fish consumption on neurodevelopment. *J. Am. Med. Assoc.* 280:701–7

Davie R, Butler N, Goldstein H. 1972. *From Birth to Seven: The Second Report of the National Child Development Study*. London: Natl. Child. Bur.

Dietrich K, Ris MD, Succop P, Berger O, Bornschein R. 2001. Early exposure to lead and juvenile delinquency. *Neurotoxicol. Teratol.* 23:511–18

Douglas JW. 1964. *The Home and the School*. London: MacGibbon & Kee

Dunifon R, Duncan GJ, Brooks-Gunn J. 2004. The long-term impact of parental organization and efficiency. In *Family Investments in Children: Resources and Behaviors that Promote Success*, ed. A Kalil, T De Liere, pp. 85–118. Mahwah, NJ: Erlbaum

Earthman GI. 1998. *The quality of school buildings, student achievement, and student behavior*. Presented at Int. Conf. Quality School Facilities Maint., Vienna, Austria

Edelstein MR. 1988. *Contaminated Communities: The Social and Psychological Impacts of Residential Toxic Exposure*. Boulder, CO: Westview

Edelstein MR. 2002. Contamination: the invisible built environment. In *Handbook of Environmental Psychology*, ed. RB Bechtel, A Churchman, pp. 559–88. New York: Wiley

Edwards JN, Booth A, Edwards PK. 1982. Housing type, stress, and family relations. *Soc. Forces* 61:241–57

Ehrenberg RG, Brewer DJ, Gamoran A, Willms JD. 2001. Class size and student achievement. *Psychol. Sci. Public Int.* 2:1–30

Environ. Prot. Agency. 2003. Indoor air quality and student performance. http://www.epa.gov/iaq/schools/images/iaq_and_student_performance.pdf

Essen J, Fogelman K, Head J. 1978. Children's housing and their health and physical development. *Child Care Health Dev.* 4:357–69

Evans GW. 2001. Environmental stress and

health. In *Handbook of Health Psychology*, ed. ABT Revenson, pp. 365–85. Hillsdale, NJ: Erlbaum

Evans GW. 2003. A multimethodological analysis of cumulative risk and allostatic load among rural children. *Dev. Psychol.* 39:924–33

Evans GW. 2004. The environment of childhood poverty. *Am. Psychol.* 59:77–92

Evans GW, Bullinger M, Hygge S. 1998. Chronic noise exposure and physiological response: a prospective, longitudinal study of children under environmental stress. *Psychol. Sci.* 9:75–77

Evans GW, Gonnella C, Marcynyszyn LA, Gentile L, Salpekar N. 2005. The role of chaos in poverty and children's socioemotional adjustment. *Psychol. Sci.* In press

Evans GW, Hygge S. 2005. Noise and performance in children and adults. In *Noise and Its Effects*, ed. L Luxon, D Prasher. London: Whurr. In press

Evans GW, Hygge S, Bullinger M. 1995. Chronic noise and psychological stress. *Psychol. Sci.* 6:333–38

Evans GW, Lepore S, Shejwal BR, Palsane MN. 1998. Chronic residential crowding and children's well being: an ecological perspective. *Child Dev.* 69:1514–23

Evans GW, Lepore SJ. 1993. Nonauditory effects of noise on children: a critical review. *Child. Environ.* 10:31–51

Evans GW, Lercher P, Kofler WW. 2002. Crowding and children's mental health: the role of house type. *J. Environ. Psychol.* 22:221–31

Evans GW, Lercher P, Meis M, Ising H, Kofler W. 2001. Community noise exposure and stress in children. *J. Acoust. Soc. Am.* 109:1023–27

Evans GW, Lovell B. 1979. Design modification in an open-plan school. *J. Educ. Psychol.* 71:41–49

Evans GW, Maxwell L. 1997. Chronic noise exposure and reading deficits: the mediating effects of language acquisition. *Environ. Behav.* 29:710–28

Evans GW, Maxwell L, Hart B. 1999. Parental

language and verbal responsiveness to children in crowded homes. *Dev. Psychol.* 35:1020–23

Evans GW, Saegert S. 2000. Residential crowding in the context of inner city poverty. In *Theoretical Perspectives in Environment-Behavior Research*, ed. SE Wapner, JE Demick, TE Yamamoto, HE Minami, pp. 247–68. New York: Plenum

Evans GW, Stecker R. 2004. The motivational consequences of environmental stress. *J. Environ. Psychol.* 24:143–65

Evans GW, Wells NM, Chan E, Saltzman H. 2000. Housing and mental health. *J. Consult. Clin. Psychol.* 68:526–30

Evans GW, Wells NM, Moch A. 2003. Housing and mental health: a review of the evidence and a methodological and conceptual critique. *J. Soc. Issues* 59:475–500

Faber Taylor A, Kuo FE, Sullivan WC. 2001. Coping with ADD: the surprising connects to green play settings. *Environ. Behav.* 33:54–77

Faber Taylor A, Kuo FE, Sullivan WC. 2002. Views of nature and self-discipline: evidence from inner city children. *J. Environ. Psychol.* 22:49–63

Faber Taylor A, Wiley A, Kuo FE, Sullivan WC. 1998. Growing up in the inner city: green spaces as places to grow. *Environ. Behav.* 30:3–27

Fagot BI. 1977. Variations in density: effect on task and social behaviors of preschool children. *Dev. Psychol.* 13:166–67

Fed. Interagency Comm. Aviation Noise. 2004. *Relation Between Aircraft Noise Reduction in Schools and Standardized Test Scores.* Washington, DC: FICAN

Fiese BH, Tomcho TJ, Douglas M, Josephs K, Poltrock S, Baker T. 2002. A review of 50 years of research on naturally occurring family routines and rituals: cause for celebration? *J. Fam. Psychol.* 16:381–90

Fine M, Burns A, Payne YA, Torre ME. 2004. Civics lessons: the color and class of betrayal. *Teach. Coll. Rec.* 106:2193–223

Fisher L, Feldman SS. 1998. Familial antecedents of young adult health risk behavior:

a longitudinal study. *J. Fam. Psychol.* 12:66–80

Fjortoft I. 2004. Landscape as playscape. *Child. Youth Environ.* 14:21–44

Fuller TD, Edwards JN, Vorakitphokatorn S, Sermsri S. 1993. Household crowding and family relations in Bangkok. *Soc. Probl.* 40:410–30

Gasparini A. 1973. Influence of the dwelling on family life: a sociological survey in Modena, Italy. *Ekistics* 216:344–48

Gen. Account. Off. 1995. *School Facilities: Conditions of America's Schools.* Washington, DC: U.S. Gen. Account. Off.

Giaconia RM, Hedges LV. 1982. Identifying features of effective open education. *Rev. Educ. Res.* 52:579–602

Gifford R. 2002. *Environmental Psychology.* Victoria, Can.: Optimal

Gifford R, Lacombe C. 2004. *Housing quality and children's socioemotional health.* Presented at Eur. Netw. Housing Res., Cambridge, UK

Gillis AR. 1974. Population density and social pathology: the case of building type, social allowance and juvenile delinquency. *Soc. Forces* 53:306–14

Ginsburg HJ, Pollman V. 1975. *Variation of aggressive interaction among male elementary school children as a function of changes in spatial density.* Presented at meet. Soc. Res. Child Dev., Denver, Colo.

Gittus E. 1976. *Flats, Families and the Under-Fives.* London: Routledge & Kegan Paul

Gladen BC, Rogan WJ. 1991. Effects of perinatal polychlorinated biphenyls and dichlorodiphenyl dichloroethene on later development. *J. Pediatr.* 119:58–63

Gladen BC, Rogan WJ, Hardy P, Thullen J, Tingelstad J, Tully M. 1988. Development after exposure to polychlorinated biphenyls and dichlorodiphenyl dichloroethene transplacentally and through human milk. *J. Pediatr.* 113:991–95

Glass DC. 1977. *Behavior Patterns, Stress, and Coronary Disease.* Hillsdale, NJ: Erlbaum

Glass DC, Singer JE. 1972. *Urban Stress: Experience On Noise and Social Stressors.* New York: Academic

Glenn LE, Nerbonne GP, Tolhurst GC. 1978. Environmental noise in a residential institution for mentally retarded persons. *Am. J. Ment. Defic.* 82:594–97

Goduka IN, Poole DA, Aotaki-Phenice L. 1992. A comparative study of black South African children from three different contexts. *Child Dev.* 63:509–25

Gottfried AW, Gottfried AE. 1984. Home environment and cognitive development in young children of middle-socioeconomic-status families. In *Home Environment and Cognitive Development*, ed. AW Gottfried, pp. 57–115. New York: Academic

Gove WR, Hughes M. 1983. *Overcrowding in the Household.* New York: Academic

Gramza AF. 1970. Children's preferences for enterable play boxes. *Percept. Mot. Skills* 31:177–78

Grandjean P, Weihe P, White RF, Debes F, Araki S, et al. 1997. Cognitive deficit in 7-year-old children with prenatal exposure to methylmercury. *Neurotoxicol. Teratol.* 19:417–28

Grantham-McGregor S, Chang S, Walker S, Powell C. 1998. School feeding studies in Jamaica. In *Nutrition, Health, and Child Development*, pp. 104–18. Washington, DC: Pan Am. Health Org.

Grapko MG. 1972. A comparison of open space and traditional classroom structures according to independence measures in children, teachers' awareness of children's personality variables, and children's academic progress. *Ontario Dept. Educ. Rep.*, Toronto, Can.

Green KB, Pasternack BS, Shore RE. 1982. Effects of aircraft noise on reading ability of school-age children. *Arch. Environ. Health* 37:24–31

Greenberg MT, Lengua LJ, Coie JD, Pinderhughes EE. 1999. Predicting developmental outcomes at school entry using a multiple-risk model: four American communities. *Dev. Psychol.* 35:403–17

Greenman J. 1988. *Caring Spaces, Learning Spaces.* Redmond, WA: Exchange

Greenwald R, Hedges LV, Laine RD. 1996. The effect of school resources on student achievement. *Rev. Educ. Res.* 66:361–96

Guidubaldi J, Cleminshaw HK, Perry JD, Nastasi BK, Lightel J. 1986. The role of selected family environment factors in children's post-divorce adjustment. *Fam. Relat.* 35:141–51

Gump PV. 1987. School and classroom environments. In *Handbook of Environmental Psychology*, ed. D Stokols, I Altman, pp. 691–732. New York: Wiley

Gump PV, Good LR. 1976. Environments operating in open space and traditionally designed schools. *J. Archit. Res.* 5:20–27

Haines MM, Stansfeld SA, Brentnall S, Head J, Berry B, et al. 2001b. The West London study: the effects of chronic aircraft noise on child health. *Psychol. Med.* 31:1385–96

Haines MM, Stansfeld SA, Head J, Job RFS. 2002. Multi-level modeling of aircraft noise on performance tests in schools around Heathrow London airport. *Int. J. Epidemiol. Commun. Health* 56:139–44

Haines MM, Stansfeld SA, Job RFS, Berglund B, Head J. 2001a. Chronic aircraft noise exposure, stress responses, mental health and cognitive performance in school children. *Psychol. Med.* 31:265–77

Haines MM, Stansfeld SA, Job RFS, Berglund B, Head J. 2001c. A follow-up study of effects of chronic aircraft noise exposure on child stress responses and cognition. *Int. J. Epidemiol.* 30:839–45

Hambrick-Dixon PJ. 1986. Effects of experimentally imposed noise on task performance of black children attending day care centers near elevated subway trains. *Dev. Psychol.* 22:259–64

Hart R. 1978. *Children's Experience of Place.* New York: Irvington

Hassan R. 1977. Social and psychological implications of high population density. *Civilisations* 27:230–26

Hattie J, Marsh HW, Neill J, Richards G. 1997. Adventure education and outward bound. *Rev. Educ. Res.* 67:43–87

Heft H. 1979. Background and focal environmental conditions of the home and attention in young children. *J. Appl. Soc. Psychol.* 9:47–69

Heft H. 1985. High residential density and perceptual-cognitive development: an examination of the effects of crowding and noise in the home. In *Habitats for Children*, ed. JF Wohlwill, W van Vliet, pp. 36–76. Hillsdale, NJ: Erlbaum

Heft H. 1988. Affordances of children's environments. *Child. Environ.* 5:29–37

Henry CS, Lovelace SG. 1995. Family resources and adolescent family life satisfaction in remarried family households. *J. Fam. Issues* 16:765–86

Heschong Mahone Group. 1999. Daylight in schools: an investigation into the relationship between daylighting and human performance. *Calif. Bd. Energy Effic. Rep.*, Fair Oaks, Calif.

Hiramatsu K, Tokuyama T, Matsui T, Miyakita T, Osada Y, Yamamoto T. 2004. The Okinawa Study: effect of chronic aircraft noise exposure on memory of school children. *Proc. Noise Public Health Probl. Int. Congr., 8th*, pp. 179–180. Schiadam, The Netherlands

Hiroto D. 1974. Locus of control and learned helplessness. *J. Exp. Psychol.* 102:187–93

Hockey G. 1979. Stress and cognitive components of skilled performance. In *Human Stress and Cognition*, ed. V Hamilton, DM Warburton, pp. 141–77. New York: Wiley

Homel R, Burns A. 1989. Environmental quality and the wellbeing of children. *Soc. Indic. Res.* 21:133–58

Howley C, Strange M, Bickel R. 2000. Research about school size and school performance in impoverished communities. http://www.ael.org/eric/page.cfm?&scopre=ssrid=243

Hubbs-Tait L, Nation J, Krebs N, Bellinger DC. 2005. Neurotoxicants, micronutrients, and social environments. *Psychol. Sci. Public Interest.* In press

Humke C, Schaefer C. 1995. Relocation: a review of the effects of residential mobility on children and adolescents. *Psychol. J. Hum. Behav.* 32:16–24

Humphreys MA. 1974. Relating wind, rain and temperature to teachers' reports of young children's behaviour. In *Psychology and the Built Environment*, ed. D Canter, T Lee, pp. 19–28. Chichester, UK: Wiley

Hunt S. 1990. Emotional distress and bad housing. *Health Hyg.* 11:72–79

Hutt C, Vaizey MJ. 1966. Differential effects of group density on social behaviour. *Nature* 209:1371–72

Huttenmoser M. 1995. Children and their living surroundings: empirical investigations into the significance of living surroundings for the everyday life and development of children. *Child. Environ.* 12:403–13

Hygge S. 2003. Classroom experiments on the effects of different noise sources and sound levels on long-term recall and recognition in children. *Appl. Cogn. Psychol.* 17:895–914

Hygge S, Boman E, Enmarker I. 2003. The effects of road traffic noise and meaningful irrelevant speech on different memory systems. *Scand. J. Psychol.* 44:13–21

Hygge S, Evans GW, Bullinger M. 2002. A prospective study of some effects of aircraft noise on cognitive performance in school children. *Psychol. Sci.* 13:469–74

Ineichen B, Hooper D. 1974. Wives' mental health and children's behaviour problems in contrasting residential areas. *Soc. Sci. Med.* 8:369–74

Ising H, Braun C. 2000. Acute and chronic endocrine effects of noise: review of the research conducted at the Institute for Water, Soil and Air Hygiene. *Noise Health* 2:7–24

Ising H, Ising M. 2002. Chronic noise increases cortisol in the first half of the night caused by road traffic noise. *Noise Health* 4:13–21

Ising H, Lange-Asschenfeldt H, Moriske HJ, Born J, Eilts M. 2004. Low-frequency noise and stress: bronchitis and cortisol in children exposed chronically to traffic noise and exhaust fumes. *Noise Health* 6:21–28

Ising H, Rebentisch E, Babisch W, Curio I, Sharp D, Baumgartner H. 1990a. Medically relevant effects of noise from low-altitude flights—results of an interdisciplinary pilot study. *Environ. Int.* 16:411–23

Ising H, Rebentisch E, Poustka F, Curio I. 1990b. Annoyance and health risk caused by military low-altitude flight noise. *Int. Arch. Occup. Environ. Health* 62:357–63

Jacobson JL, Jacobson SW. 2002. Breastfeeding and gender as moderators of teratogenic effects on cognitive development. *Neurotoxicol. Teratol.* 24:349–58

Jacobson SW, Jacobson JL. 2000. *Teratogenic Insult and Neurobehavioral Function in Infancy and Childhood.* Mahwah, NJ: Erlbaum

Jensen EW, James SA, Boyce WT, Hartnett SA. 1983. The family routines inventory: development and validation. *Soc. Sci. Med.* 17:201–11

Job RFS. 1988. Community response to noise: a review of factors influencing the relationship between noise exposure and reaction. *J. Acoust. Soc. Am.* 83:991–1001

Johansson CK. 1975. Mental and perceptual performance in heat. *Rep. Doc. 4.* Stockholm: Swed. Inst. Build. Res.

Johansson CR. 1983. Effects of low intensity, continuous and intermittent noise on mental performance and writing pressure of children with different intelligence and personality characteristics. *Ergonomics* 26:275–88

Kantrowitz EJ, Evans GW. 2004. The relation between the ratio of children per actual area and off-task behavior and type of play in day care centers. *Environ. Behav.* 36:541–57

Kaplan R, Kaplan S. 1989. *The Experience of Nature.* New York: Cambridge Univ. Press

Kaplan S, Talbot JF. 1983. Psychological benefits of wilderness experience. In *Behavior and the Natural Environment*, ed. JF Wohlwill, I Altman, pp. 163–203. New York: Plenum

Karagodina IL, Soldatkina SA, Vinokur IL, Klimukhin AA. 1969. Effect of aircraft noise on the population near airports. *Hyg. Sanit.* 34:182–227

Karsdorf G, Klappach H. 1968. The influence of traffic noise in the health and performance of secondary school students in a large city. *Zeitschriftfurdie gesamte Hyg.* 14:52–54

Kasl SW, Will J, White M, Marcuse P. 1982. Quality of the residential environment and mental health. In *Advances in Environmental Psychology*, ed. A Baum, JE Singer, pp. 1–30. Hillsdale, NJ: Erlbaum

Kirkby M. 1989. Nature as refuge in children's environments. *Child. Environ. Q.* 6:1–12

Kjellstrom T, Kennedy P, Wallis S, Stewart A, Friberg L, et al. 1989. Physical and mental development of children with prenatal exposure to mercury from fish. *Rep. 3642*, Natl. Swed. Environ. Prot. Board

Koger SM, Schettler T, Weiss B. 2005. Environmental toxins and developmental disabilities. *Am. Psychol.* 60:243–55

Korpela K. 2002. Children's environment. In *Environmental Psychology*, ed. RB Bechtel, A Churchman, pp. 363–73. New York: Wiley

Krantz DS, Glass DC, Snyder M. 1974. Helplessness, stress level, and coronary-prone behavior pattern. *J. Exper. Soc. Psychol.* 10: 284–300

Krantz PJ. 1974. *Ecological arrangements in the classroom*. Unpubl. doctoral dissert. Lawrence: Univ. Kansas

Kryter K. 1994. *The Handbook of Hearing and the Effects of Noise*. New York: Academic Press

Kuller R, Lindsten C. 1992. Health and behavior of children in classrooms with and without windows. *J. Environ. Psychol.* 12:305–17

Kuo F, Faber Taylor A. 2004. A potential natural treatment for attention-deficit/hyperactivity disorder. *Am. J. Public Health* 94: 1580–86

Kytta M. 2002. Affordances of children's environments. *J. Environ. Psychol.* 22:109–23

Kytta M. 2004. The extent of children's independent mobility and the number of actualized affordances as criteria for child-friendly environments. *J. Environ. Psychol.* 24:179–98

Kyzar K. 1977. Noise pollution and schools. *Counc. Educ. Facil. Plan. J.* 4:10–11

Lackney JA. 2004. Thirty three principles of educational design. http:/schoolstudio.engr.wisc.edu/33principles.html

Lackney JA. 2005. New approaches for school design. In *The SAGE Handbook of Educational Administration*, ed. FW English, pp. 506–37. Los Angeles: Sage

Lanphear BP, Dietrich K, Auinger P, Cox C. 2000. Cognitive deficits associated with blood lead concentrations <10 μg/dL in US children and adolescents. *Public Health Rep.* 115:521–29

LeClair J, Innes F. 1997. Urban ecological structure and perceived child and adolescent psychological disorder. *Soc. Sci. Med.* 44:1649–59

Legendre A. 2003. Environmental features influencing toddlers' bioemotional reactions in day care centers. *Environ. Behav.* 35:523–49

Lepore S, Evans GW, Schneider M. 1991. The dynamic role of social support in the link between chronic stress and psychological distress. *J. Personal. Soc. Psychol.* 61:899–909

Lercher P, Evans GW, Meis M. 2003. Ambient noise and cognitive processes among primary school children. *Environ. Behav.* 35:725–35

Lercher P, Evans GW, Meis M, Kofler WW. 2002. Ambient neighbourhood noise and children's mental health. *Occup. Environ. Med.* 59:380–86

Leventhal T, Brooks-Gunn J. 2000. The neighborhoods they live in: the effects of neighborhood residence on child and adolescent outcomes. *Psychol. Bull.* 126:309–37

Lewis M. 2000. Where children learn: facility conditions and student test performance in the Milwaukee public schools. http://www.cefpi.org/pdf/issue12.pdf

Liddell C, Kruger P. 1987. Activity and social behavior in a South African township nursery: some effects of crowding. *Merrill-Palmer Q.* 33:195–211

Liddell C, Kruger P. 1989. Activity and social behavior in a crowded South African township nursery: a follow-up study on the effects of crowding at home. *Merrill-Palmer Q.* 35:209–26

Light R. 1973. Abused and neglected children in America: a study of alternative policies. *Harvard Educ. Rev.* 43:556–98

Littlewood J, Sale R. 1972. *Children at Play: A Look at Where They Play and What They Do on Housing Estates*. London: Dep. Environ.

Loo C, Ong P. 1984. Crowding perceptions, attitudes, and consequences among the Chinese. *Environ. Behav.* 16:55–87

Loo CM. 1972. The effects of spatial density on the social behavior of children. *J. Appl. Soc. Psychol.* 2:372–81

Loo CM. 1978a. Issues of crowding research: vulnerable participants, assessing perceptions and developmental differences. *J. Popul.* 1:336–48

Loo CM. 1978b. Behavior problem indices: the differential effects of spatial density on low and high scorers. *Environ. Behav.* 10:489–510

Loo CM, Kennelly D. 1978. Social density. *Environ. Psychol. Nonverbal Behav.* 2:226–49

Lowry P. 1993. Privacy in the preschool environment: gender differences in reaction to crowding. *Child. Environ.* 10:130–39

Lukas JS, DuPree RB, Swing JW. 1981. *Report of a Study on the Effects of Freeway Noise on Academic Achievement of Elementary School Children and a Recommendation for a Criterion Level for School Noise Abatement Programs.* Sacramento: Calif. Dep. Health Serv.

Macintyre S, Maciver S, Soomans A. 1993. Area, class and health: Should we be focusing on places or people? *J. Soc. Policy* 22:213–34

Macpherson A, Roberts I, Pless IB. 1998. Children's exposure to traffic and pedestrian injuries. *J. Public Health* 88:1840–43

Martin MJ, Walters J. 1982. Familial correlates of selected types of child abuse and neglect. *J. Marriage Fam.* 44:267–76

Maschke C, Ising H, Arndt D. 1995. Nachtlicher verkehrslarm und gesundheit: ergebnisse von labor- und- feldstudien (night-time traffic noise exposure and health: results from laboratory and field studies). *Bundesgesundheitsblatt* 38:130–36

Maser AL, Sorensen PH, Kryter KD, Lukas JS. 1978. *Effects of intrusive sound on classroom behavior: data from a successful lawsuit.* Presented at West. Psychol. Assoc., San Francisco

Matheny A, Wachs TD, Ludwig J, Phillips K. 1995. Bringing order out of chaos: psychometric characteristics of the confusion, hubbub, and order scale. *J. Appl. Dev. Psychol.* 16:429–44

Matsui T, Stansfeld SA, Haines MM, Head J. 2004. Children's cognition and aircraft noise exposure at home—The West London Schools Study. *Noise Health* 7:49–58

Maxwell L. 1996. Multiple effects of home and day care crowding. *Environ. Behav.* 28:494–511

Maxwell L, Evans GW. 2000. The effects of noise on preschool children's prereading skills. *J. Environ. Psychol.* 20:91–97

McGrew PL. 1970. Social and spatial density effects on spacing behaviour in preschool children. *J. Child Psychol. Psychiatry* 11:197–205

McGuffey CW, Brown CL. 1978. The impact of school building age on school achievement in Georgia. *Counc. Educ. Facil. Plan. J.* 16:6–14

McKeown-Eyssen G, Ruedy J, Neims A. 1983. Methylmercury exposure in northern Quebec: II. Neurologic findings in children. *Am. J. Epidemiol.* 118:470–79

Meis M, Hygge S, Evans GW, Bullinger M. 1998. Effects of traffic noise on implicit and explicit memory: results from field and laboratory studies. *Proc. Int. Congr. Noise Public Health Probl., 7th.* Sydney: Noise Effects 98 Ltd.

Mendelsohn AL, Dreyer B, Fierman A, Rosen C, Legano L, et al. 1998. Low level lead exposure and behavior in early childhood. *Pediatrics* 101:10–17

Michelson W. 1968. Ecological thought and its application to school functioning. *Proc. Annu. East. Res. Inst. Assoc. Supervis. Curric. Dev., 14th.* Washington, DC

Mitchell RE. 1971. Some social implications of high-density housing. *Am. Sociol. Rev.* 36:18–29

Moch-Sibony A. 1984. Study of the effects of noise on the personality and certain intellectual and psychomotor aspects of children. Comparison between a soundproofed and a non-soundproofed school. *Le Travail Humain* 44:170–78

Moore GT. 1986. Effects of the spatial definition of behavior settings on children's behavior: a quasi-experimental field study. *J. Environ. Psychol.* 6:205–31

Moore GT, Lackney JA. 1993. School design: crisis, educational performance, and design applications. *Child. Environ.* 10:99–112

Moore NC. 1975. Social aspects of flat dwelling. *Public Health Lond.* 89:109–15

Moore R, Schneekloth L. 1989. Children and vegetation [special issue]. *Child. Environ. Q.* 6:Entire issue

Muller F, Pfeiffer E, Jilg M, Paulsen R, Ranft U. 1998. Effects of acute and chronic traffic noise on attention and concentration of primary school children. *Proc. Int. Congr. Noise Public Health Probl., 7th,* Sydney

Murray R. 1974. The influence of crowding on children's behavior. In *Psychology and the Built Environment*, ed. D Canter, T Lee, pp. 112–17. London: Wiley

Myhrvold AN, Olsen E, Lauridsen O. 1996. Indoor environment in schools—pupils' health and performance in regard to CO2 concentrations. *Presented at Indoor Air '96. Seventh Int. Conf. Indoor Air Qual. Climate*, Nagoya, Jap.

Nat. Cent. Educ. Statist. 1999. How old are America's public schools? Washington, DC: U.S. Dep. Educ.

Nat. Cent. Educ. Statist. 2000. Conditions of America's public school facilities. Washington, DC: U.S. Dep. Educ.

Needleman HL, Gunnoe C, Leviton A, Reed R, Peresie H, et al. 1979. Deficits in psychologic and classroom performance of children with elevated dentine lead levels. *N. Engl. J. Med.* 300:689–95

Needleman HL, Riess JA, Tobin MJ, Biesecker GE, Greenhouse JB. 1996. Bone lead levels and delinquent behavior. *JAMA* 275:363–69

Needleman HL, Schell A, Bellinger D, Leviton A, Allred EN. 1990. The long-term effects of exposure to low doses of lead in childhood. *N. Engl. J. Med.* 322:83–88

Neill SRSJ. 1982. Preschool design and child behaviour. *J. Child Psychol. Psychiatry* 23:309–18

Nicklas MH, Bailey GB. 1997. Analysis of the performance of students in daylit schools. http://www.deptplanetearth.com

Obasanjo OO. 1998. *The impact of the physical environment on adolescents in the inner city*. Unpubl. doctoral dissert., Ann Arbor: Univ. Mich.

Oda M, Taniguchi K, Wen M-L, Higurashi M. 1989. Effects of high-rise living on physical and mental development of children. *J. Hum. Ergol.* 18:231–35

Olds AR. 2001. *Childcare Design Guide*. New York: McGraw-Hill

O'Neill DJ, Oates AD. 2001. The impact of school facilities on student achievement, behavior, attendance, and teacher turnover rate in central Texas middle schools. *CEFPI's Educ. Facil. Plan.* 36:14–22

Patandin S, Lanting CI, Mulder PGH, Boersma ER, Sauer PJJ, Weisglas-Kuperus N. 1999. Effects of environmental exposure to polychlorinated biphenyls and dioxins on cognitive abilities in Dutch children at 42 months of age. *J. Pediatr.* 134:33–41

Pepler RD. 1971. Variation in students' test performances and in classroom temperatures in climate-controlled and non-climate-controlled schools. *Am. Soc. Heat. Refrig. Air Cond. Eng. Trans.* 77:35–42

Petrill SA, Pike A, Price T, Plomin R. 2004. Chaos in the home and socioeconomic status are associated with cognitive development in early childhood: environmental mediators identified in a genetic design. *Intelligence* 32:445–60

Phillips RW. 1997. *Educational facility age and the academic achievement and attendance of upper elementary school students*. Unpubl. doctoral thesis. Athens: Univ. Georgia

Preiser WFE. 1972. Work in progress: behavior of nursery school children under different spatial densities. *Man-Environ. Syst.* 2:247–50

Propst R. 1972. Making open space work. *AIA J.* 9:22–26

Rahmanifar A, Kirksey A, Wachs TD, McCabe GP, Bishry Z, et al. 1993. Diet during lactation associated with infant behavior and caregiver-infant interaction in a semirural Egyptian village. *J. Nutr.* 123:164–75

Ranson R. 1991. *Healthy Being.* London: E & FN Spon

Rauh VA, Whyatt RM, Garfinkel R, Andrews H, Hoepner L, et al. 2004. Developmental effects of exposure to environmental tobacco smoke and material hardship among inner-city children. *Neurotoxicol. Teratol.* 26: 373–85

Ray DW, Wandersman A, Ellisor J, Huntington DE. 1982. The effects of high density in a juvenile correctional institution. *Basic Appl. Soc. Psychol.* 3:95–108

Regecova V, Kellcrova E. 1995. Effects of urban noise pollution on blood pressure and heart rate in school children. *J. Hypertens.* 13:405–12

Reiss S, Dyhdalo N. 1975. Persistance, achievement, and open-space environments. *J. Educ. Psychol.* 67:506–13

Repetti RL, Taylor SE, Seeman TE. 2002. Risky families: family social environments and the mental and physical health of offspring. *Psychol. Bull.* 128:330–66

Richman N. 1974. The effects of housing on pre-school children and their mothers. *Dev. Med. Child Neurol.* 16:53–58

Richman N. 1977. Behaviour problems in pre-school children: family and social factors. *Br. J. Psychiatry* 131:523–27

Rivlin LG, Rothenberg M. 1976. The use of space in open classrooms. In *Environmental Psychology*, ed. HME Proshansky, WHE Ittelson, LGE Rivlin, pp. 479–89. New York: Holt, Rinehart & Winston

Rodin J. 1976. Density, perceived choice and response to controllable and uncontrollable outcomes. *J. Exper. Soc. Psychol.* 12:564–78

Rogan WJ, Gladen BC, McKinney JD, Carreras N, Hardy P, et al. 1986. Neonatal effects of transplacental exposure to PCBs and DDE. *J. Pediatr.* 109:335–41

Rohe WM, Nuffer E. 1977. *The effects of density and partitioning on children's behavior.* Presented at Meet. Am. Psychol. Assoc., Washington, DC

Rohe WM, Patterson AH. 1974. *The effects of varied levels of resources and density on behavior in a day care center.* Presented at Annu. Conf. Environ. Design Res. Assoc., Milwaukee, Wisc.

Rosen KG, Richardson G. 1999. Would removing indoor air particulates in children's environments reduce rate of absenteeism? A hypothesis. *Sci. Total Environ.* 234:87–93

Ruopp R, Travers J, Glantz F, Coelen C. 1979. *Children at the Center.* Cambridge, MA: ABT

Rutter M, Tizard J, Whitmore K. 1970. *Education, Health, and Behaviour.* London: Longman

Rutter M, Yule B, Quinton D, Rowlands O, Yule W, Berger M. 1974. Attainment and adjustment in two geographical areas: III. Some factors accounting for area differences. *Br. J. Psychiatry* 125:520–33

Saegert S. 1982. Environment and children's mental health: residential density and low-income children. In *Handbook of Psychology and Health*, ed. A Baum, JE Singer, pp. 247–71. Hillsdale, NJ: Erlbaum

Sanoff H. 1995. *Creating Environments for Young Children.* Mansfield, OH: Book Masters

Schmeck K, Poustka F. 1993. Psychiatric and psychophysiological disorders in children living in a military jetfighter training area. In *Proc. 6th Int. Congr. Noise Public Health Probl.*, ed. M Vallet, Nice, France

Schneider M. 2002. Publi. school facilities and teaching: Washington, DC and Chicago. http://www.ncbg.org/documents/NCBG%20Final%20Teachers%20Report.doc

Schoer L, Shaffran F. 1973. A combined evaluation of three separate research projects on the effects of thermal environment on learning and performance. *Am. Soc. Heat. Refrig. Air Cond. Eng. Trans.* 79:97–108

Sciarillo WG, Alexander G, Farrell KP. 1992. Lead exposure and child behavior. *Am. J. Public Health* 82:1356–60

Shapiro S. 1975. Some classroom ABC's. *Elem. School J.* 75:437–41

Shaw DS, Emery RE. 1988. Chronic family adversity and school-age children's adjustment. *J. Am. Acad. Child Adolesc. Psychiatry* 27:200–6

Shaw M. 2004. Housing and public health. *Annu. Rev. Public Health* 25:397–418

Sherrod D. 1974. Crowding, perceived control, and behavioral aftereffects. *J. Appl. Soc. Psychol.* 4:171–86

Smedje G, Norback D, Edling C. 1996. Mental performance by secondary school pupils in relation to the quality of indoor air. In *Proc. Int. Conf. Indoor Air Qual. Climate, 7th*, Nagoya, Japan

Smith AP, Jones DM. 1992. Noise and performance. In *Handbook of Human Performance*, ed. AP Smith, DM Jones, pp. 1–28. London: Academic

Smith PK, Connolly KJ. 1977. Social and aggressive behaviour in preschool children as a function of crowding. *Soc. Sci. Inform.* 16:601–20

Solomon D, Kendall AJ. 1976. Individual characteristics and children's performance in "open" and "traditional" classroom settings. *J. Educ. Psychol.* 68:613–25

Sprunger LW, Boyce WT, Gaines JA. 1985. Family-infant congruence: routines and rhythmicity in family adaptations to a young infant. *Child Dev.* 56: 564–72

Stansfeld SA, Berglund B, Clark C, Lopez-Barrio I, Fischer P, et al. 2005. Aircraft and road traffic noise and children's cognition and health: a cross-national study. *Lancet* 365:1942–49

Steptoe A, Feldman PJ. 2001. Neighborhood problems as sources of chronic stress: development of a measure of neighborhood problems, and associations with socioeconomic status and health. *Ann. Behav. Med.* 23:177–85

Stewart PW, Reihman J, Lonky EI, Darvill TJ, Pagano J. 2003. Cognitive development in preschool children prenatally exposed to PCBs and MeHg. *Neurotoxicol. Teratol.* 25:11–22

Stewart W. 1970. *Children in Flats: A Family Study*. London: Nat. Soc. Prev. Cruelty Child.

Taylor SE, Repetti R, Seeman SE. 1997. What is an unhealthy environment and how does it get under the skin? *Annu. Rev. Psychol.* 48:411–47

Teare JF, Smith GL, Osgood DW, Peterson RW, Authier K, Daly DL. 1995. Ecological influences in youth crisis shelters: effects of social density and length of stay on youth problem behaviors. *J. Child Family Stud.* 4:89–101

Tracy EM, Green RK, Bremseth MD. 1993. Meeting the environmental needs of abused and neglected children: implications from a statewide survey of supportive services. *Soc. Work Res. Abstr.* 29:21–26

Traub RE, Weiss J. 1974. Studying openness in education. *J. Res. Dev. Educ.* 8:47–59

Wachs TD. 1976. Utilization of a Piagetian approach in the investigation of early experience effects: a research strategy and some illustrative data. *Merrill-Palmer Q.* 22:11–30

Wachs TD. 1978. The relationship of infants' physical environment to their binet performance at 2 1/2 years. *Int. J. Behav. Dev.* 1:51–65

Wachs TD. 1979. Proximal experience and early cognitive-intellectual development: the physical environment. *Merrill-Palmer Q.* 25:3–41

Wachs TD. 1987. Specificity of environmental action as manifest in environmental correlates of infant's mastery motivation. *Dev. Psychol.* 23:782–90

Wachs TD. 1989. The nature of the physical microenvironment: An expanded classification system. *Merrill-Palmer Q.* 35:399–419

Wachs TD. 2000. *Necessary But Not Sufficient: The Respective Roles of Single and Multiple Influences on Individual Development.* Washington, DC: Am. Psychol. Assoc.

Wachs TD. 2003. Expanding our view of context: the bio-ecological environment and development. *Adv. Child Dev.* 31:363–409

Wachs TD, Camli O. 1991. Do ecological or individual characteristics mediate the influence of the physical environment on maternal behavior? *J. Environ. Psychol.* 11:249–64

Wachs TD, Corapci F. 2005. Environmental chaos, development and parenting across cultures. In *Social and Cognitive Development in the Context of Individual, Social, and Cultural Processes*, ed. C Raeff, J Benson. New York: Routledge. In press

Wachs TD, Gandour MJ. 1983. Temperament, environment, and six-month cognitive-intellectual development: a test of the organismic specificity hypothesis. *Int. J. Behav. Dev.* 6:135–52

Wachs TD, Gurkas P, Kontos S. 2004. Predictors of preschool children's compliance behavior in early childhood classroom settings. *J. Appl. Dev. Psychol.* 25(4):439–57

Wachs TD, Uzgiris IC, Hunt JM. 1971. Cognitive development in infants of different age levels and from different environmental backgrounds: an explanatory investigation. *Merrill-Palmer Q.* 17:283–317

Wandersman A, Nation M. 1998. Urban neighborhoods and mental health: psychological contributions to understanding toxicity, resilience, and interventions. *Am. Psychol.* 53: 647–56

Wedge P, Petzing J. 1970. Housing for children. *Housing Rev.* 19:165–66

Weinstein CS. 1977. Modifying student behavior in an open classroom through changes in the physical design. *Am. Educ. Res. J.* 14: 249–62

Weinstein CS. 1979. The physical environment of the school: a review of the research. *Rev. Educ. Res.* 49: 577–610

Weinstein CS. 1982. Privacy-seeking behavior in an elementary school classroom. *J. Environ. Psychol.* 2:23–35

Weinstein CS. 1987. Designing preschool classrooms to support development. In *Spac-*

es for Children, ed. CS Weinstein, TG David, pp. 159–86. New York: Plenum

Wells NM. 2000. At home with nature. *Environ. Behav.* 32:775–95

Wells NM, Evans GW. 2003. Nearby nature: a buffer of life stress among rural children. *Environ. Behav.* 35:311–30

Widmayer SM, Peterson LM, Lamer M, Carnahan S, Calderon A, et al. 1990. Predictors of Haitian-American infant development at twelve months. *Child Dev.* 61:410–15

Wigle DT. 2003. *Child Health and the Environment*. New York: Oxford Univ. Press

Wilner DM, Walkley R, Pinkerton T, Tayback M. 1962. *The Housing Environment and Family Life*. Baltimore: Johns Hopkins Univ. Press

Wohlwill JF, Heft H. 1987. The physical environment and the development of the child. In *Handbook of Environmental Psychology*, ed. D Stokols, I Altman, pp. 281–328. New York: Wiley

Wolock I, Horowitz B. 1979. Child maltreatment and material deprivation among AFDC-recipient families. *Soc. Serv. Rev.* 53:175–94

Wu T-N, Chiang H-C, Huang J-T, Chang P-Y. 1993. Comparison of blood pressure in deaf-mute children and children with normal hearing: association between noise and blood pressure. *Int. Arch. Occup. Environ. Health* 65:119–23

Wyon DP, Andersen I, Lundqvist GR. 1979. The effects of moderate heat stress on mental performance. *Scand. J. Work Environ. Health* 5:352–61

Youssef RM, Attia MS-E-D, Kamel MI. 1998. Children experiencing violence: I. Parental use of corporal punishment. *Child Abuse Negl.* 22:959–73

Annu. Rev. Psychol. 2006. 57:453–85
doi: 10.1146/annurev.psych.57.102904.190136

CONSUMER PSYCHOLOGY: Categorization, Inferences, Affect, and Persuasion

Barbara Loken

Department of Marketing, University of Minnesota, Carlson School of Management, Minneapolis, Minnesota 55455; email: bloken@csom.umn.edu

Key Words   information processing, attitudes, judgments, literature review

■ **Abstract**   This chapter reviews research on consumer psychology with emphasis on the topics of categorization, inferences, affect, and persuasion. The chapter reviews theory-based empirical research during the period 1994–2004. Research on categorization includes empirical research on brand categories, goals as organizing frameworks and motivational bases for judgments, and self-based processing. Research on inferences includes numerous types of inferences that are cognitively and/or experienced based. Research on affect includes the effects of mood on processing and cognitive and noncognitive bases for attitudes and intentions. Research on persuasion focuses heavily on the moderating role of elaboration and dual-process models, and includes research on attitude strength responses, advertising responses, and negative versus positive evaluative dimensions.

CONTENTS

INTRODUCTION

A recent *Annual Review of Psychology* chapter (Simonson et al. 2001) describes the consumer behavior literature as divided into three major subgroups: (*a*) the consumer information processing segment, (*b*) the behavioral decision theory (BDT) segment, and (*c*) the postmodernist, postpositivist, interpretive segment, the first two of which have psychological foundations. The first subgroup, consumer information processing, includes consumer cognition and affect, and is the focus of the present review. Consumer information processing has as its theory base social and cognitive psychology (e.g., research by Bargh 2002, Barsalou 1999, Chaiken 1980, Fishbein & Ajzen 1975, Fiske & Neuberg 1990, Higgins 2002, Markus & Kunda 1986, Petty & Cacioppo 1986, and Wyer & Srull 1989, to name just a few). The BDT literature, which includes topics such as choice models, economic psychology, and consumer search strategies, draws from a somewhat different psychological literature (see Simonson et al. 2001) and is covered in this review only to the extent that it overlaps with topics addressed. Individual differences research (personality, individual difference measures, and expertise) and domain-specific findings such as price perceptions, ethics and socially responsible business practices, social marketing, survey research, Internet marketing, and others, are not reviewed here unless applicable to the theoretical issues addressed. Included in this review is theoretically based, empirical research in consumer psychology published primarily in four journals: *Journal of Consumer Research, Journal of Consumer Psychology, Journal of Marketing Research*, and *Journal of Marketing*.

From 1982 to 1998, *Annual Review of Psychology* articles reviewed the consumer psychology literature every four years (Kassarjian 1982, Bettman 1986, Cohen & Chakravarti 1990, Tybout & Artz 1994, Jacoby et al. 1998). In 2001, Simonson et al. broke with tradition and wrote a historical perspective on consumer research and a more general discussion of philosophical debates in the discipline. With the expansive nature of the field, it has become increasingly difficult to evaluate all consumer psychology literature in a single review.

The present chapter returns to a more traditional review of consumer research, but differs from prior reviews in that it is both narrower in topic focus (consumer categorization, inferences, affect, and persuasion) and covers a broader range of years, 1994–2004, with primary emphasis on research in the years 1997–2004.

Research in the years 1994–1996 was reviewed previously (Jacoby et al. 1998), and is included to the extent that it helps frame and clarify research on the topics addressed. Research published outside the designated years or in publications outside of the four journals noted is included selectively.

CONSUMER CATEGORIZATION

During the review period, research on brand categories (e.g., Healthy Choice products) and goal-derived categories (e.g., things to eat in my car on the way to work) has increased relative to more traditional research on product categories (e.g., automobiles, shampoos). Research on brand categories has focused on the manner in which perception of new category members (brand extensions) are influenced by category beliefs and affect and also on how information about new category members reciprocally influence beliefs and attitudes about the category. Research on goal-derived categories focuses on the flexibility of category representations, and the effects of goals on cognition and affect. Research on the self, as a category and as a basis for processing information, has continued and is increasingly directed toward the study of self-construals and multicultural views of the self.

Similarity-Based Category Inferences to New Category Members

Consumers regularly use category information in making judgments about a new category member. For example, test-driving a Lexus hybrid automobile may lead consumers to infer that it shares similarities with a traditional Lexus (e.g., high performance, prestige, leather seats). Similarity-based inferences such as these have been the focus of research on brand categories. A brand category, such as Lexus, can be viewed as both a set of attributes (e.g., high performance, prestige) and a set of exemplar products (e.g., Lexus sedans, Lexus SUVs), and in any given context, information about either attributes or products may be accessible (Loken et al. 2002, Meyvis & Janiszewski 2004). Similarly, accessible information about the extension (e.g., Lexus hybrid) may pertain to its product category (hybrids), its individuating attributes (e.g., its front panel display), or its connection to the parent brand (Lexus). To the extent that accessible information about the brand category and accessible information about the brand extension increase consumers' perceptions of similarity between the parent brand and extension, category inferences should be more likely to occur. This well-established finding continues in the review period; greater perceived similarity (or perceived "fit") between the parent brand and the new brand extension increases acceptance of the brand extension, whether due to product category similarity or brand-specific associations (Barone et al. 2000, Bottomley & Holden 2001, Klink & Smith 2001). Similarity (between the parent brand and new extension) has also been viewed as a heuristic in decision making. Similarity is more often used in evaluating brand extensions when the product category information of either the parent brand (Meyvis & Janiszewski 2004) or the extension (Klink & Smith 2001) is the only information accessible or available, and is less often used when the extension's individuating attribute information is available (Klink & Smith 2001). To the extent that both product category similarity and brand attribute similarity reflect a common goal, they will both predict extension acceptance; if goals are incongruent, other factors (e.g., only product category similarity or only brand attribute similarity) may determine extension acceptance (Martin & Stewart 2001).

In addition to research on brand extensions, other consumer research replicates earlier findings of a positive relationship between a category member's typicality (or similarity to other category members) and the category member's evaluation. In general, more typical category members are better liked (Carpenter & Nakamoto 1996; Folkes & Patrick 2003, study 3; Simonin & Ruth 1998; Veryzer & Hutchinson 1998; Zhang & Sood 2002).

Another type of similarity-based comparison involves the alignability of attributes of the new category stimulus and the existing category (e.g., Gentner & Markman 1997, Gregan-Paxton 2001, Gregan-Paxton & John 1997, Moreau & Markman 2001, Roehm & Sternthal 2001). Alignable differences (versus differences that are not alignable) are more memorable (Zhang & Markman 1998), comparative ads are more effective than noncomparative ads when brands can be compared along the same (versus different) attributes (Zhang et al. 2002; see also Lurie 2004 for research on structural properties of attributes), and brand evaluations are more prone to revision when counterattitudinal information can be compared along the same attributes as accessible brand information (Pham & Muthukrishnan 2002).

A different perspective argues that resolving a moderate disparity produces positive affect, which is applied to the object evaluated (Peracchio & Meyers-Levy 1994). Per this view, an object that is moderately dissimilar from a category will be better liked than either a similar or extremely dissimilar object. This moderate incongruity effect was found for people with low prior knowledge about the category, who required more effort to resolve the incongruity (Peracchio & Tybout 1996), and disappeared when people had low motivation to process information (e.g., under high risk conditions, Campbell & Goodstein 2001).

Assimilation and Contrast

Theories of assimilation/contrast argue that if, during encoding, an object is perceived as similar to a category, it will be assimilated to the category and take on its features and affect; a contrast response occurs when responses to the object are adjusted away from the comparison standard, if an object is perceived as dissimilar to a comparison standard, and usually occurs at the time of judgment. Contrast effects occur when situational cues include dissimilarities information (Hafner 2004, Wanke et al. 1998) or individuating information highlights dissimilarities (Cooke et al. 2002), when sufficient cognitive resources are available for processing contextual information or when people are high in need for cognition (Meyers-Levy & Tybout 1997), and when remembered information is recounted analytically rather than episodically (Bickart & Schwarz 2001). Others argue that contrast effects are not due to more cognitive effort, but rather depend on whether the accessible context information (the standard of comparison) is well defined (Levin & Levin 2000) and is both distinctive and relevant (Stapel et al. 1998). Finally, although assimilation responses are generally the default response, in some situations contrast effects can be the default (Raghunathan & Irwin 2001).

The Influence of New Category Members on the Category

Information about new category members can also influence existing category beliefs. For example, brand extensions (new category members) can have effects on beliefs and attitudes about the parent brand category that are either negative (dilution of the brand) or positive (enhancement). Beliefs about a well-known brand were influenced negatively when information about a brand extension (John et al. 1998) or information about a brand context (Buchanan et al. 1999) was incongruent with beliefs about the brand (see also Milberg et al. 1997). People processed the incongruent information thoughtfully and analytically (Buchanan et al. 1999). Negative dilution, as well as positive enhancement, effects were replicated under conditions of high motivation (Gurhan-Canli & Maheswaran 1998) and when extension information was high in accessibility (Ahluwalia & Gurhan-Canli 2000). Under low motivation, people used nonanalytic processing; more (versus less) prototypical extensions modified parent brand evaluations (Gurhan-Canli & Maheswaran 1998). That is, extremely atypical category members had less impact on category beliefs than did moderately atypical category members. When extension information was low in accessibility, diagnostic cues were used; negative information (producing dilution effects) was more diagnostic for brand evaluations when extensions were in similar, but not dissimilar, categories to the parent brand, and positive information (producing enhancement effects) was more diagnostic when extensions belonged to dissimilar, rather than similar, categories (Ahluwalia & Gurhan-Canli 2000).

Negative brand extension information can also affect existing individual products of the parent brand if these products are not already strongly established in the minds of consumers (John et al. 1998). Outside a laboratory setting, too, people were found to update their perceptions of the parent brand and individual products of the brand based on their experiences with brand extensions (Erdem 1998).

Finally, priming a new brand extension can increase the accessibility of the parent brand category, particularly when the parent brand category is not already chronically accessible (Morrin 1999). Researchers have examined primes in a variety of other contexts, too, including prosmoker and antismoker stereotypes (Pechmann & Knight 2002), exemplars in television viewing (Shrum et al. 1998), and product expensiveness judgments (Adaval & Monroe 2002).

Goals as Organizing Frameworks

Goals can serve as organizing frameworks for product or purchase information (Huffman 1996, Martin & Stewart 2001), and multiple goals can coexist within a given individual (Sengupta & Johar 2002). Activating a goal can influence members of a consideration set (Chakravarti & Janiszewski 2003, Ratneshwar et al. 1996), increase similarity perceptions of objects that do not visually resemble each other (Ratneshwar et al. 2001), and increase the attractiveness of objects related to those goals (Martin & Stewart 2001, Ratneshwar et al. 2000); objects not related to the goal are devalued (Brendl et al. 2003). Goal-derived categories have flexible boundaries; similarities between category members were found to vary depending on whether a personal or situational goal was salient (Ratneshwar et al. 2001). When goals conflict (i.e., a single product cannot meet all salient goals) or when there is goal ambiguity (i.e., a lack of salient goals), consumers are more likely to consider alternatives from different product categories (Ratneshwar et al. 1996). When people violated their goals, they showed decreased performance on a subsequent task, as compared to people with no goals (Soman & Cheema 2004).

Motivational and self-regulatory approaches to assessing goals have increased in interest (e.g., Ariely & Levav 2000, Bagozzi & Dholakia 1999, Baumeister 2002, Higgins 2002, Krishnan & Shapiro 1999). Researchers have compared consumers who were promotion-focused and prevention-focused using a variety of operationalizations (e.g., independent versus interdependent self-views, Aaker & Lee 2001; ideals versus "oughts," Pham & Avnet 2004). Consumers who were promotion-focused (versus prevention-focused) were persuaded more by positive (versus negative) outcomes (Aaker & Lee 2001), subjective affective responses to an ad (versus message substance, Pham & Avnet 2004), hedonic, attractive, performance-related attributes (versus utilitarian, unattractive, reliability-related attributes, Chernov 2004a), and actions that departed from (versus preserved) the status quo (Chernov 2004b).

Factors That Influence Category Expansion and Flexibility

Consumers need to have stable representations of objects and events in memory that can be used for interpreting and evaluating objects and events in their environment. Category stability was demonstrated by Viswanathan & Childers (1999) in their reanalysis of Loken & Ward's (1990) study of prototypicality measures. Using the same attributes, with minor modifications, to measure attribute-based indices of prototypicality yielded—almost a decade later—significant relationships between these attribute-based measures and a global typicality measure. A new, fuzzy set–based measure also predicted global typicality.

Category representations also require flexibility and the ability to adapt to changes in the environment. In addition to the flexibility of goal-derived categories, noted earlier, research finds that category boundaries become broader or narrower, and more or less flexible, depending on motivational, ability, and contextual factors. A positive mood state may increase motivation to engage in relational elaboration, as demonstrated by greater clustering of brands recalled by product category membership and greater recall of brand names when they were in the same product categories as stimulus brands (Lee & Sternthal 1999). When people were in a more (versus less) positive mood (Barone & Miniard 2002, Barone et al. 2000) and received information about a new brand category member (brand extension) that was moderately dissimilar to the parent brand category, they were more likely to perceive the brand extension as similar to the parent brand category and evaluate it favorably. However, mood did not enhance evaluations of extensions of unfavorable parent brands (Barone & Miniard 2002).

When consumers were exposed five times (versus once) to information about a brand category's positive link to an incongruent brand extension, their perceptions of extension consistency increased and they evaluated the extension more favorably (Lane 2000). When a brand's benefits were accessible, which occurred more for brand categories with more (versus less) diverse members, new incongruent category extensions were rated more positively (Meyvis & Janiszewski 2004). Innovative consumers, who tend to be less risk averse, were more accepting of incongruent category members (Klink & Smith 2001).

Ability and knowledge factors also increase flexibility. Experts (relative to novices) were more likely to organize information by product subcategories, retrieve different brands for different usage occasions (Cowley & Mitchell 2003), and store information about alternatives in a way that increased flexibility in evaluating the same product across different usage occasions (Mitchell & Dacin 1996). Older children, relative to younger children, define categories more by complex functional (versus perceptual) cues (John 1999; see also Achenreiner & John 2003). Owners (versus nonowners) of a brand (Kirmani et al. 1999) have broader, more flexible categories when making judgments. Strategies taught to consumers to break down frequency estimates into subcategories (e.g., unbundling credit card expenses) can reduce errors and processing effort (Menon 1997, Srivastava & Raghubir 2002).

Self as a Category

The self category has been described as flexible or malleable (Aaker 1999). The same individual may retrieve and use different self-views, depending upon the chronic and temporal accessibility of these inputs, in the form of cultural views (Aaker & Lee 2001, Briley & Wyer 2002, Brumbaugh 2002, Forehand & Deshpande 2001, Lau-Gesk 2003, Mandel 2003), social identities (Bolton & Reed 2004, Reed 2004), or personality traits (Aaker 1999). A social identity that is salient, important to the self, and evaluatively diagnostic (versus one that is not) is more likely to influence attitudes (Reed 2004), and thinking dominated by a strong salient identity is more resistant to corrective procedures (Bolton & Reed 2004). Self-appraisals regarding performance or reflections of what others might think influenced more global self-definitions (Laverie et al. 2002). In comparison with an independent self-view, priming an interdependent self-view has been associated with more financial risk-taking and less social risk-taking (Mandel 2003), and with prevention goals (Aaker & Lee 2001). Priming cultural identity (whether Chinese or American) produced a group mind-set that increased prevention goals (Briley & Wyer 2002).

Research continues to find that information processing with respect to the self increases elaborative thought and persuasion, such as when generating self stories (West et al. 2004) or when processing strong message arguments relative to the self (Burnkrant & Unnava 1995). But these positive effects of self-referencing on attitudes were found to be eliminated when consumers were not motivated to process the ad information (Meyers-Levy & Peracchio 1996), or when elaboration was excessive and created tedium or critical thinking (Burnkrant & Unnava 1995, Meyers-Levy & Peracchio 1996). The type of self-referencing used by consumers is also important. Self-referencing that is retrospective (with reference to autobiographical experiences from one's past) includes more thoughts with contextual detail than does self-referencing that is anticipatory (imagining experiences in one's future). If an ad provides detailed contextual information, this information interferes with retrospective thinking (which has its own detailed representations) but facilitates anticipatory thinking (Krishnamurthy & Sujan 1999).

CONSUMER INFERENCES

Inferences Based on Omitted Conclusions

Consumers make inferences beyond what they read or see in the text of a message, and these inferences can have an impact on judgments (Kardes et al. 2001, 2004b). When ads omitted (versus included) a key element, recall was improved along dimensions related to the element (Sengupta & Gorn 2002). When a comparative ad stated a specific (versus vague) cost savings amount (relative to a named comparison brand) for one service provided by the brand, consumers inferred that the brand was also superior on other, missing, service price data, contributing to suboptimal choices (Pechmann 1996). Greater motivation and ability increase the likelihood that consumers will engage in spontaneous inferences. Consumers were more likely to complete ambiguously cropped objects in ads under high than under low motivation conditions (Peracchio & Meyers-Levy 1994) and to later falsely recall the object as intact, although completing these objects did not necessarily improve evaluations of the product in the ads. With regard to deceptive inferences, highly motivated consumers were more likely to make invalid inferences from one type of deceptive ad claim (incomplete comparison claims); however, they were less likely to be deceived by ads that required detailed processing for nondeception to occur (inconspicuous qualification claims, Johar 1995). When cognitive capacity was high, consumers were also more likely to use product disclosures to correct or update their judgments about the product (Johar & Simmons 2000).

Singular Brand Versus Multiple Brand Inferences

Research examines contexts in which a single brand is evaluated relative to contexts in which a brand is compared with alternative brands. Consumers are not always motivated to consider and compare alternative brands (Mantel & Kardes 1999), even when information about multiple brands is presented (Wang & Wyer 2002). When consumers do compare brands, generally under high motivation conditions, they rate a favorable focal brand less positively (relative to focusing on a single brand; Posavac et al. 2004; Hsee & Leclerc 1998), disregard features that are common across brands, leading to biased evaluations (Wang & Wyer 2002), and show greater direction-of-comparison effects (Mantel & Kardes 1999). Consumers also show correction effects when they are made aware that relevant information is missing (when the format is changed from a noncomparative to a comparative format, or vice versa; Muthukrishnan & Ramaswami 1999).

Inferences Based on Irrelevant Attributes

Irrelevant attributes (e.g., silk in shampoo) can have an impact on brand preferences (Carpenter et al. 1994), and these initial preferences can be self-perpetuating because of selective interpretation of subsequent experience data (Muthukrishnan & Kardes 2001). Adding irrelevant information to supportive product benefit information reduced people's beliefs about the product benefit, even when people acknowledged the irrelevance of the information and when the irrelevant information increased the product's similarity to a liked typical product (Meyvis & Janiszewski 2002). Others find that, while the effects of irrelevant information are persistent, when the true irrelevancy is clarified to consumers, the effects are reduced (Carpenter et al. 1994, study 2), and when future brand extensions continue to use irrelevant attributes, a brand's equity may suffer (Broniarczyk & Gershoff 2003). Brown & Carpenter (2000) find that trivial attributes may have either positive or negative value depending on whether such valuation helps consumers accomplish a goal.

Inferences Based on Experiential and Sensory Data

Experiential data are engaging (Hoch 2002), accessible (Park et al. 1994), and viewed as nonpartisan and unambiguous (see Hoch 2002 for a review). Experience information tends to be more influential than advertising information (Kempf & Smith 1998), and even imagined experience can be convincing to consumers (Hoch 2002).

But product experiences are not always unambiguous (Wooten & Reed 1998), and consumers believe they learn from experience even when those experiences are largely uninformative (Muthukrishnan & Kardes 2001). Other people's opinions influenced evaluation of a product if those opinions were considered before the consumer had had a chance to consider the evaluative implications of their own product experience (Wooten & Reed 1998). Even memory for a product experience has been found to change in the direction of advertised information (presented after the product experience) that provides a different interpretation of the experience (Braun 1999), although only when product familiarity is low (Cowley & Janis 2004). Advertising was more likely to frame the interpretation of product experiences for older than for younger children (Moore & Lutz 2000). Research shows other fallibilities associated with experience data (Alba & Hutchinson 2000, Hoch 2002).

Although people like experience data, experience attribute claims (claims based on attributes that the consumer can verify only through direct experience) are generally regarded as less credible than search attributes, which are verifiable without consumption (Jain et al. 2000), but will be used by consumers when these attributes are the only data available and are accompanied by a high (versus low) credibility source (Jain & Posavac 2001).

Sensory experience data aside from traditional product usage also have an impact on judgment, and research on them has increased in emphasis during the review period. When consumers experienced sound quality, and were provided criteria with which to evaluate it (i.e., reducing its ambiguity and increasing its diagnosticity), their memory of the information improved, they placed more weight on it, and made better choices (Shapiro & Spence 2002). Other inferences based on auditory systems include those based on the consumer's formal writing system (phonetic versus logographic; Tavassoli & Han 2001, Tavassoli & Lee 2003, Zhang & Schmitt 2004), the speed and pitch of an announcer's voice (Chattopadhyay et al. 2003), and the phonetic structure of brand names (Yorkston & Menon 2004). When experiencing a product by touch, consumers' confidence in judgments increased if they were high (versus low) along a need-for-touch dimension (Peck & Childers 2003). Ambient scent improved memory for familiar and unfamiliar brands (Morrin & Ratneshwar 2003).

Visual elements, such as pictures (McQuarrie & Mick 2003), color as a backdrop on Internet Web sites (Gorn et al. 2004, Mandel & Johnson 2002), product shape (Folkes & Matta 2004, Raghubir & Krishna 1999, Wansink & Van Ittersum 2003), aesthetic design and unity (Veryzer & Hutchinson 1998), angle of vision, cutting rate, camera motion (Larsen et al. 2004), typeface (Childers & Jass 2002, Henderson et al. 2004), and numerical information (Viswanathan & Childers 1996), have been found to convey meaning and influence processes such as information search, elaborative processing, attitudes, and consumption. Visual elements can also cause interference effects if ads for two different brands have similar pictures (Kumar 2000, Kumar & Krishnan 2004).

A more direct link between perceptual (sensory-motor) data and cognition has emerged. Features of an ad compete for available cognitive resources if they require processing two elements simultaneously from the same (versus different) sensory modality (Olsen 1997, Tavassoli & Lee 2003, Unnava et al. 1996). Features of an ad can also be complementary and increase advertising effectiveness when perceptual and other features (e.g., celebrity endorser, picture, brand name, scent, plot of accompanying television show) are congruent with product attribute information (Luna & Peracchio 2001, Mitchell et al. 1995, Russell 2002).

Conditional Inferences, Correlations, and Causal Reasoning

Research on conditional inferences found that when a belief in a conclusion was supported by a set of arguments that independently led to the same conclusion, it was more resistant to persuasion attempts than when a belief was supported by a set of arguments that only when considered together led to the same conclusion (Kardes et al. 2001). Areni (2002) proposes a model of belief probabilities for precise predictions of argument effectiveness.

Baumgartner (1995) found that people engaged in an active, theory-guided appraisal of the empirical data they received; when a theory was not available, the resulting judgment was suboptimal. Consumers were more sensitive to inter-attribute correlational data when information load was low or when consumers were motivated to elaborate (Kardes et al. 2004a), but were less prone to spillover effects of negative information when they were highly committed to the brand (Ahluwalia et al. 2001). While associative network theory continues to be a prominent paradigm for examining belief interconnections and consumer learning (Morrin 1999), others (van Osselaer & Janiszewski 2001) argue for a more dynamic adaptive network theory in which association strengths are not learned independently on the basis of the co-occurrence of two cues, but instead are updated and evolve as cues interact. Attribution theory (Weiner 2000) and dialectical thinking processes (Kahle et al. 2000) are useful for understanding the causal reasoning strategies of consumers, and causal reasoning has been found to be shared across cultural subgroups, which in turn influence the causal reasoning of individuals (Sirsi et al. 1996).

Metacognitive Experiences and Knowledge

Judgments are based not only on what information comes to mind, but also on how it comes to mind (Lee 2004). In a dialogue published recently in the *Journal of Consumer Psychology* on consumers' metacognitive experiences, Schwarz (2004) argues that content-based theories of judgment formation cannot account for the subjective experiences that accompany thought processes that often give rise to counterintuitive findings. Processing fluency (e.g., the ease with which information is recalled) and other subjective experiences can be informational inputs used in judgments. Researchers discussed whether these metacognitive experiences (particularly with regard to processing fluency) were more likely to influence judgments under low motivation (Schwarz 2004) or under both low- and high-motivation (Lee 2004) conditions, the extent to which discrepancies from expectations (and the direction of those discrepancies) increase the use of naïve theories, how judgment and choice contexts differ (Huber 2004), and the importance of both affective and cognitive metacognitive experiences as signals in judgments (Pham 2004).

Researchers also have demonstrated that consumers form metacognitive beliefs about persuasion tactics and marketers' motives (e.g., Boush et al. 1994, Campbell & Keller 2003, Friestad & Wright 1995). The use of these beliefs depends on whether, like other beliefs, they are easily accessible (Brown & Krishna 2004, Campbell & Kirmani 2000, Shiv et al. 1997) or an ulterior motive by the marketer is made salient (Warlop & Alba 2004).

Brand Name Inferences

Some brand names carry meanings that are more transferable than are others to new product extensions (Wanke et al. 1998). Keller et al. (1998) found that a brand name that implied superiority on a specific attribute (e.g., PicturePerfect televisions) rather than a nonsuggestive name (e.g., Emporium) led to better memory for related product attributes but inhibited recall of unrelated product attributes. A general superiority name is often preferred to a category-specific name when extending to new product categories (Sen 1999), and focusing on a specific brand attribute rather than the brand name can sometimes reduce consumers' evaluations of brand extensions (van Osselaer & Alba 2003).

When two brand names are combined (e.g., Slim Fast chocolate cake mix by Godiva) the composite benefits more when the header brand (Slim Fast) is combined with a complementary brand (Godiva) than when presented alone or combined with a noncomplementary brand (e.g., Haagen-Dazs; Park et al. 1996). In brand alliances, both brands are affected, but familiar (versus unfamiliar) brands contribute more to brand evaluations (Siminon & Ruth 1998; see also Levin & Levin 2000). When the ingredient in a brand extension is branded (e.g., Tide with Irish Spring scent), more initial acceptance is found, but, unless the branded ingredient represents a dissimilar attribute, using a new ingredient name (e.g., Tide with EverFresh scent) improves long-range expansion of the brand to new categories (Desai & Keller 2002).

Accessibility-Diagnosticity Model

A number of psychological theories incorporate the constructs of accessibility (salience) and diagnosticity (relevance). In consumer research, the framework of Feldman & Lynch (1988), which argues that judgments are a function of the accessibility and the diagnosticity of information inputs relative to the accessibility and diagnosticity of alternative inputs, has been used for understanding judgment revision (Pham & Muthukrishnan 2002), behavioral frequency judgments (Menon et al. 1995), car repurchase decisions (Fitzsimons & Morwitz 1996), the effects of previously formed attitudes on choice (Baker 2001), cultural differences in the use of cues (Aaker 2000), and brand extension information effects on family brand evaluations (Ahluwalia & Gurhan-Canli 2000). A variant of the accessibility-diagnosticity model, the mere-accessibility model, has been proposed to account for conditions under which accessibility alone is sufficient to determine judgments, for example when ease-of-retrieval occurs at a low awareness level and functions as an heuristic in decision making, when the cognitive demands of the task are too high, or when extra cognitive effort is unwarranted (Menon & Raghubir 2003).

Biases and Motivated Reasoning

Among the types of biases that have been examined in the review period are the truth effect (Law et al. 1998), the inclusion effect (Joiner & Loken 1998), predecisional distortion (Russo et al. 1998), anchor-and-adjustment (Wansink et al. 1998), frequency heuristics (Alba et al. 1999), false consensus (West 1996), self-positivity (Lin et al. 2003, Menon et al. 2002, Raghubir & Menon 1998), negativity (Ahluwalia 2002), forward and backward telescoping (Morwitz 1997), and metacognitive biases (Alba & Hutchinson 2000).

Although most of the research on biases in consumer research has assumed cognitive bases for errors or deficits, research increasingly has examined bias as motivated reasoning. Researchers argue, for example, that inconsistent information (Jain & Maheswaran 2000) and impression and defensive goals (Ahluwalia 2002) increase consumers' selectively processing information in a biased manner. Other research finds that biases were reduced when consumers had sufficient motivation and ability to counter the bias, i.e., when accuracy in judgments was rewarded (West 1996), when the evidence against the bias was strong, when the bias was based on events not controllable, and when the judgments did not pertain to or protect the view of self (Kamins et al. 1997, Lin et al. 2003, Menon & Johar 1997).

CONSUMER AFFECT, MOOD, FEELINGS, AND ATTITUDES

The importance of the role of affect has increased during the review period, and emotional states increasingly are being added to traditional models of consumer behavior (e.g., satisfaction/dissatisfaction, Phillips & Baumgartner 2002; decision choice models, Luce et al. 1999). Most research during the review period on affect and attitudes falls into two general categories: (*a*) research on the types of processes by which moods and feelings influence judgments, and (*b*) more traditional research on the cognitive (versus noncognitive) bases for attitudes and the role of cognition and attitudes in predicting intentions and behavior.

The Effects of Mood on Judgments and Processing

Mood affects judgments; being in a positive mood can increase consumers' preferences for products. Mood can spread to others, too, who in turn will like the product (Howard & Gengler 2001). Predominant theoretical rationales for mood effects are mood-congruency theories, which argue that moods increase the accessibility of mood-congruent thoughts (e.g., Isen et al. 1992), and affect-as-information theories, which argue that moods are used (often mistakenly) as a source of information in evaluations of a target (e.g., Schwarz 1997). The information value of a mood may derive from its arousal dimension, its valence dimension, or both (Gorn et al. 2001). Mood valence has more effect on product judgments when mood information is a relevant basis for the judgments, for example, for consumers using consummatory or hedonic (versus instrumental) criteria (Adaval 2001, Pham 1998, Yeung & Wyer 2004) or when the affective tone of a target ad is ambiguous (Gorn et al. 2001). Adaval (2003) found that moods influenced judgments through their effects on the extremity of evaluative implications of cognitions about the target rather than increased importance weights attached to the information. Yeung & Wyer (2004), however, found that when people have already formed an impression of a product based on a picture that elicits affect, subsequent mood and other information that becomes available has less impact on product judgments.

Research has also examined the regulatory processes in which consumers engage. Feelings convey both contextual appraisal information as well as motivational (goal-relevant) information (see Pham 2004). Some mood research suggests that consumers were willing to make decision errors in order to maintain a positive mood (Meloy 2000). But other research suggests that when the stakes are high (e.g., life threatening), consumers will forego short-term mood maintenance for longer-term gains (Keller et al. 2003), or will even maintain a negative mood if it will improve task performance; that is, people will guide affect regulation in a functional manner (Cohen & Andrade 2004).

Moods also affect type of processing. Some research supports the idea that people in a positive mood engage in nonanalytic, top-down, creative processing styles, and people in a negative mood engage in analytic, effortful processing (Keller et al. 2002, Murry & Dacin 1996). Shiv & Fedorikhin (1999) find that people will choose based on utilitarian considerations (e.g., fruit salad over cake) unless their processing load is high, in which case they will choose based on hedonic considerations (cake over fruit salad). Other findings suggest that people in a positive mood are *not* less motivated to process information (Adaval 2003, Pham et al. 2001), but instead rely more on strategic thinking (Lee & Sternthal 1999) or diagnostic inputs (Pham 1996), especially when the risks of not being informed are very high (Keller et al. 2003).

Aside from testing these theories of affect, consumer research finds that emotions are predictable and can be measured reliably. Consumers tend to provide reliable measures of emotion (Richins 1997) and have a shared knowledge of emotion categories (Ruth 2001), and negative emotions (which people prefer to avoid) cause predictable shifts in choice patterns (Luce et al. 1999). Baumgartner et al. (1997) showed how moment-to-moment emotional responses to an ad could be integrated into an overall evaluation of the ad.

Cognitive Versus Noncognitive Bases for Attitudes

Many of the existing theories of mood and affect are consistent with traditional attitude research that assumes cognitions underlie attitudes and that feelings are used in reasoning processes (cf. Adaval 2003, Pham et al. 2001). Nevertheless, a debate published in the *Journal of Consumer Psychology* (1995, 1997) raises issues about whether attitudes are primarily belief based (driven by cognition) or nonbelief based (driven by affect or other factors). Central to the debate is whether automaticity effects, degree of effort in processing, or mood and bodily reactions reflect degree of cognitive or belief-based processing (e.g., Fishbein & Middlestadt 1995, 1997; Haugtvedt & OSU Consumer Psychology Seminar 1997; Herr 1995; Miniard & Barone 1997; Priester & Fleming 1997; Schwarz 1997). Fishbein and Middlestadt argue that regardless of whether processing of information is more or less effortful (with respect to attention, counterarguing, or elaboration), such processing activity is cognitive and has impact effects on other cognitions that are more proximal determinants of attitude. These proximal determinants (i.e., salient beliefs and the evaluative implications of those beliefs) would need to be ruled out empirically in order to conclude that attitudes are not belief based. Using these criteria, some research (Fishbein & Middlestadt 1995) finds that attitude toward an ad influenced attitude toward a behavior indirectly through cognitive structure, whereas other research (Bodur et al. 2000) finds that the connection between affect and attitude was direct and not mediated by cognitive structure.

Most cognitive psychologists would agree that cognition includes an array of conscious and unconscious processes and representations (cf. Barsalou 1999). A growing number of consumer studies examine implicit brand attitudes, attitudes that may be activated automatically and outside conscious awareness (Bargh 2002, Maison et al. 2004, Shapiro 1999). Increased emphasis is being placed on development of appropriate measurement techniques to assess automaticity and nonconscious processing (see Krishnan & Chakravarti 1999), such as the Implicit Association Test (Brunel et al. 2004).

Cognition, Affect, and Behavioral Intentions

A first avenue of research on intentions has examined factors that affect the relationship between behavioral intentions and behavior. The process of measuring a purchase intention (called the "mere measurement" effect) has been found to increase subsequent purchase in the product category, probably because it increases the accessibility of cognitions about the product category and cognitions of accessible brands in the category (Morwitz & Fitzsimon 2004). The effect was found to decay after three months (Chandon et al. 2004) and was attenuated when consumers viewed the intention question as a persuasion attempt and had sufficient cognitive capacity for correction (Williams et al. 2004). Asking people to predict whether they will perform a behavior also increases the probability of their performing the behavior (Spangenberg & Greenwald 1999).

A second avenue of research examines models of determinants of behavioral intentions. Tests of the theory of reasoned action (Fishbein & Ajzen 1975) and a variant found support across four countries, although, in general, components explained more variance in Western (United States, Italy) than in Eastern (China, Japan) cultures (Bagozzi et al. 2000). The models also explained differences in cultural orientation (independent versus interdependent). In a related model of social behavior, Lee (2000) found that the normative factor was a stronger determinant of behavioral intention among collectivists, whereas the attitude factor was a stronger determinant among individualists.

A meta-analysis (Notani 1998) of the theory of planned behavior (Ajzen 1991), which is an extension of the theory of reasoned action, found that the construct of perceived behavioral control (PBC) predicted behavior more when it reflected control over factors primarily internal (versus external) to the individual, when it was operationalized as a global measure (rather than as a set of beliefs), when the behaviors were familiar (versus unfamiliar), and when the sample included nonstudent (versus student) samples. The meta-analysis also found attitude toward performing a behavior was a more consistent predictor than PBC of behavioral intention, and intention was a stronger predictor than PBC of behavior, supporting the original theory of reasoned action.

MODELS OF PERSUASION

Elaboration

The moderating role of elaborative thought on persuasion has been a key research issue in the past decade. Amount of elaborative thought (high versus low) and valence of thought (favorable or unfavorable) have been examined extensively. Type of thought has also been studied, such as analysis of item-specific versus relational thoughts (e.g., Malaviya et al. 1996), thoughts that vary as a function of specific goals (e.g., Escales & Luce 2004, Sengupta & Johar 2000), thoughts about the self (Meyers-Levy & Peracchio 1996), and metacognitive thoughts and experiences (e.g., Schwarz 2004). More commonly, elaborative thought has been examined as a function of how information is framed by goals or contextual factors. Research on the amount of elaborative thought predicted by dual process models, in particular, has been plentiful.

DUAL-PROCESS MODELS OF PERSUASION   Consumer research on the elaboration likelihood model (Petty & Cacioppo 1986), the heuristic-systematic model (Chaiken 1980), and other dual-process models (e.g., Fiske & Neuberg 1990) has continued to stack up evidence in favor of two levels of processing (sometimes regarded as two ends of a continuum), one in which the level of consumer motivation and elaborative thought is high and relies on detailed, systematic, or central-route processing, and a second, more heuristic or peripheral route that is generally associated with lower levels of motivation and elaborative thought. Research finds that highly motivated consumers, who engaged in more elaborative processing, were more influenced by negative (versus positive) frames and message claims (Block & Keller 1995, Shiv et al. 2004), had more persistent attitudes (Haugtvedt et al. 1994, Sengupta et al. 1997), were more influenced by argument strength (versus number of arguments) in a collectivist culture (Aaker & Maheshwaran 1997), placed less emphasis on country of origin as a processing cue (Gurhan-Canli & Maheswaran 2000), and engaged more in adaptive learning of feature-benefit associations (van Osselaer & Janiszewski 2001). Consumers also processed information more systematically when message arguments were preceded by counterfactual ("if only") thinking (Krishnamurthy & Sivaraman 2002) and when the message arguments were compatible with self-regulatory focus (Aaker & Lee 2001).

Incongruity of persuasive elements also increased elaboration. Information was processed more systematically when comparative ads featured dissimilar (versus similar) brands, especially when individuals were low in need for cognition (Priester et al. 2004), when information was inconsistent with prior preferences (Jain & Maheshwaran 2000), when brand extensions were incongruent with expectations regarding the parent brand (Gurhan-Canli & Maheswaran 1998), and when message items were inconsistent with expectations, particularly for elderly adults (Yoon 1997). Consumers elaborated more on messages from endorsers who were untrustworthy (e.g., from endorsing too many products) than from endorsers who were trustworthy (Priester & Petty 2003).

Consumers showed more heuristic processing when information was in a narrative versus an unorganized list form, presumably because the narrative form is structurally similar to daily life experiences (Adaval & Wyer 1998). Heuristic processing was also found more for elderly (than for younger) adults (Yoon 1997), who show reduced ability over time to remember detailed information.

Under low motivation conditions, people may also rely more on their subjective accessibility experiences rather than content (Schwarz 2004). Children (versus adults) focused more on surface than on deep cues (Zhang & Sood 2002; cf. John 1999), and younger children engaged in less elaboration than did older children (Moore & Lutz 2000).

Cues that have been traditionally regarded as peripheral or heuristic (e.g., brand names and endorser attractiveness) led to more attitude persistence (Sengupta et al. 1997) and were processed more centrally or systematically (and elaborated upon more) when the cue was perceived to have relevance to the message arguments (e.g., endorser attractiveness, Shavitt et al. 1994; source effects, Kirmani & Shiv 1998) or was perceived as diagnostic (e.g., Aaker & Maheswaran 1997). Other variables, too, have been found to take on multiple roles in a persuasive message, such as rhetorical questions (Ahluwalia & Burnkrant 2004), message framing (Meyers-Levy & Maheswaran 2004), and color (Meyers-Levy & Peracchio 1995). Also, both types of thought (heuristic and systematic) can occur concurrently (Meyers-Levy & Maheswaran 2004).

Finally, even though high arousal is generally believed to reduce cognitive capacity, Pham (1996) found that when consumers were highly aroused, they selected informative diagnostic cues over a peripheral cue (endorser status). People also seemed to use different routes to persuasion because different types of information were perceived as diagnostic under different routes rather than because they had different desired levels of accuracy (Pham & Avnet 2004).

PROBLEM-SOLVING AND ELABORATIVE THOUGHT   Problem-solving thinking that increases cognitive elaboration can increase the persuasiveness of a message. Two-sided advertisements in which the positive and negative attributes were logically related increased favorable inferences, especially when people had sufficient processing time to elaborate upon them (Bohner et al. 2003). Time (and presumably effort) can also reduce logical inconsistencies in beliefs (Kardes et al. 2001). Analogies require substantial cognitive resources, so they are more effective if used by experts who devote substantial resources to the processing task. They can even be effective for novices if substantial resources are allocated to the task and the novices are trained in how to map structural relations between a base and a target (Roehm & Sternthal 2001).

NEGATIVE EFFECTS OF ELABORATION ON PERSUASION   Elaboration can have a neutral or negative effect on attitudes if consumers are elaborating upon irrelevant, nondiagnostic, or negative information (e.g., Grewal et al. 1997, Priester et al. 2004, Schlosser & Shavitt 2002). Asking a hypothetical question that contained negative information about a political candidate contaminated voting choices; increased contamination occurred as elaboration increased and the questions focused on aspects relevant to the choice (Fitzsimons & Shiv 2001). Too much cognitive elaboration can be viewed as cognitive effort, which people view as costly and tend to avoid (Fiske & Taylor 1984); when cognitive effort was expended without resolution or other benefits, negative affect and behavior resulted (Garbarino & Edell 1997).

When reasons against (as compared with reasons for) choosing a BMW over a Mercedes were easy to retrieve, or consumers imagined that they were easy to retrieve, consumers decreased (versus increased) their evaluations of the BMW relative to the Mercedes (Wanke et al. 1997), although results were attributed to fluency of retrieval rather than to negative thought content. A reasons analysis was also found to lower attitude stability (Sengupta & Fitzsimons 2004), increase attitude ambivalence (Sengupta & Johar 2002), increase culture-bound thoughts (Briley et al. 2000), and was disruptive of the link between attitude and behavior when attitudes at delay were reconstructed from contextual cues and there was a mismatch between original and delayed attitudes (Sengupta & Fitzsimons 2000).

Resource-matching theory (Peracchio & Meyers-Levy 1997) argues that processing is most efficient when the level of cognitive resources required for a task match the consumer's level of available cognitive resources. It's the dose that makes the poison (Paracelsus); too much elaboration can lead to irrelevant thoughts or counterarguments (Keller & Block 1997); having too few resources relative to those required can lead to heuristic processing (Peracchio & Meyers-Levy 1997). Both high and low levels of fear appeals have been persuasive, as long as available and required resources matched (Keller & Block 1996). Mantel & Kellaris (2003) found that perceptions of time were estimated to be longer when the available and required resources were matched, because information linked to the time period was more easily reconstructed.

Attitude Strength, Resistance, and Confidence

Some research has examined the longer-term effects of previously formed attitudes on subsequent processing and evaluations. Haugtvedt et al. (1994) found that even when people showed similar levels of attitude persistence, extremity, and confidence, they were more resistant to attack if the basis for their attitude included more substantive product information. Priester & Petty (2003), too, show that equally extreme attitudes can vary in their cognitive bases, their strength, and their effectiveness. Priester et al. (2004) found that strong brand attitudes influenced choice because they increased the brand's inclusion in the consumer's consideration set.

Attitude certainty and thought confidence have been viewed as metacognitive responses to ads. When people counterargued a message, it increased their attitude certainty and their attitude-intention link, but only if the message was from an expert source (Tormala & Petty 2004). Just as strong attitudes are more likely than weaker attitudes to guide behavior, stronger beliefs (confidence in one's thoughts) are more likely to guide attitudes; increased confidence in positive thoughts increased the effectiveness of ads, and increased confidence in negative thoughts decreased their effectiveness (Brinol et al. 2004).

Ad Repetition, Ad Spacing, Incidental Ad Exposure, and Fluency

With increased ad repetition, consumers' attention decreases (based on detection of eye movements), but the order in which visual elements of the ad are scanned remains the same (Pieters et al. 1999). Ad repetition increases attitude persistence, and when ads are substantively varied, repetition increases attitude resistance (Haugtvedt et al. 1994). Changing the ad executions and the modality of the advertising (e.g., between target and competitive advertising) also reduces competitive interference effects (Unnava & Sirdeshmukh 1994).

Incidental ad exposure may occur when consumers are focusing on a primary task (e.g., reading a magazine article) and nevertheless process advertising information that is not the focus (e.g., a print ad on the same or adjoining page). Incidental ad exposure is found to increase perceptual fluency, the perception of ad or brand familiarity (Shapiro et al. 1997), inclusion of the brand in the consumer's consideration set (Shapiro 1999, Shapiro et al. 1997), and perhaps conceptual fluency as well (Janiszewski & Meyvis 2001, Shapiro 1999).

Background music interfered with processing when the time interval between ad presentations was short under incidental learning, but it did not change the effect of time interval on recall under more effortful processing conditions (Olsen 1997). Based on a meta-analysis (Janiszewski et al. 2003) of the spacing effect (i.e., the time interval between presentations of ad material), the most effective schedule may be one in which ads alternate between encouraging intentional processing (e.g., using media such as television ads) and promoting incidental processing (e.g., using media such as billboards).

Differences in Negative and Positive Evaluative Dimensions

Evaluations (positive/negative responses) are pervasive and dominant human responses (Jarvis & Petty 1996) that sometimes are performed automatically, unintentionally, and/or without awareness (Bargh 2002). Consumer research finds that negations (versus affirmations), whether they involve reporting a questionnaire response (e.g., disliking versus liking judgments; Herr & Page 2004) or processing message information (e.g., not difficult to use versus difficult to use; Grant et al. 2004), require more elaboration and are less spontaneously generated, suggesting a two-step process required for processing negations. When persuasive stimulus information that contained negative (versus positive) information or that was framed in a negative (versus positive) way required and/or motivated greater elaboration (as reported earlier; see also Cox & Cox 2001), it was often more persuasive (Block & Keller 1995, Homer & Batra 1994, Meyers-Levy & Maheswaren 2004, Shiv et al. 2004), especially when consumers were accuracy-motivated (Ahluwalia 2002) or perceived the negative tactic used as fair (Shiv et al. 1997). On the other hand, consumers who processed narratives and imagined scenarios were more resistant to incorporating negative (Adaval & Wyer 1998) and corrective information (Bolton 2003), their inferences about a firm's service providers were more resistant to negative than positive information (Folkes & Patrick 2003), and the greater influence of negative (versus positive) information was attenuated when consumers were impression-motivated but reversed when consumers were defense-motivated (Ahluwalia 2002).

Exposure to both positive and negative information weakens attitudes if reconciliation of evaluative items is not a salient goal or if issue elaboration is prevented. Attitudes also weaken when people feel inconsistencies in preexisting beliefs and attitudes or when they feel ambivalent, experiencing both positive and negative affect toward an attitude object (Sengupta & Johar 2002). Conflicting affective or emotional responses (Mick & Fournier 1998), that is, mixed emotions, may be difficult to manage (Williams & Aaker 2002), but in some cases, conflict in emotions may be a naturally occurring phenomenon. Ambivalent "weakened" attitudes may not always reflect weakness; older (versus younger) and Asian (versus Anglo) Americans have been found to be more adaptable in accepting mixed emotions (Williams & Aaker 2002).

CONCLUSIONS

In the review period, general conclusions about psychological phenomena (e.g., dual processes of persuasion, relationship between category similarity and affect) have been followed up through studies that examine (*a*) the effects in more diverse and numerous domains and contexts than found previously (demonstrating the effects' generalizability and importance), and (*b*) contingencies and exceptions to these effects. The difficult task of determining the size and nature of the contingencies for many of these topic domains has not yet been accomplished.

However, the moderating roles of elaboration, accessibility, and diagnosticity have been successfully used to understand the patterns associated with contingent effects in a variety of consumer domains.

Amount of elaborative thought and valence of thought is an important moderating variable studied extensively in the review period. Not surprisingly, thoughtfulness or increased elaboration has been found to positively influence persuasion or problem solving in most cases because the information elaborated upon was, by and large, positive, relevant message information. When the information elaborated upon was irrelevant or negative, its effect on persuasion was reduced. When the information elaborated upon was biased, change occurred in a manner consistent with the bias or stereotypic thinking. To the extent that the effort of elaboration led to positive outcomes (such as reduced uncertainty or feelings of successful resolution of inconsistencies), these positive outcomes, in some cases, became associated with the attitude object. Most of the research on elaboration in the review period examined positive (or negative) thoughts about the message rather than positive (or negative) thoughts about the processes of elaboration (resolution or effort).

Interesting new research directions have emerged in the review period that pattern after some of the effects of social and cognitive psychology. Consumer research has placed increased emphasis on consumers' flexibility or malleability in retrieving different and multiple cognitive representations that, depending on the context, reflect different individual goals, cultural orientations, views of self, naïve theories or beliefs about the way the world works, and even differences in affective states and experiences. Research on retrieval and use of these multiple and different representations highlights the dynamic role of information accessibility in cognitive and affective judgments.

Research has also increasingly examined how consumers are motivated to control, manage, or self-regulate their cognitions and affect. People demonstrate control over affective processes and goals, sometimes undertake corrective processes to adjust for errors in accuracy or unwanted influences, and have knowledge of persuasion strategies. The role of context is important in determining when these control and corrective processes are used and in determining the nature of the cognitive or affective representations used in judgments. But research is also increasing on the role of implicit cognitions and affect and nonconscious ways in which cognition and sensory experiences influence affect and judgment. Finally, the relationship between sensory-motor, perceptual, and experiential information on the one hand, and cognition on the other, has emerged as an important research topic.

ACKNOWLEDGMENTS

The author gratefully acknowledges the perspective and comments of Joan Meyers-Levy, Deborah Roedder John, Durairaj Maheswaran, Frank Kardes, Rohini Ahluwalia, Bob Wyer, and Curt Haugtvedt on an earlier draft of this article. Preparation for this article was supported in part by a McKnight-BER research grant from the Carlson School of Management, University of Minnesota.

The *Annual Review of Psychology* is online at http://psych.annualreviews.org

LITERATURE CITED

Aaker JL. 1999. The malleable self: the role of self-expression in persuasion. *J. Market. Res.* 36(1):45–58

Aaker JL. 2000. Accessibility or diagnosticity? Disentangling the influence of culture on persuasion processes and attitudes. *J. Consum. Res.* 26(4):340–57

Aaker JL, Lee AY. 2001. "I" seek pleasures and "we" avoid pains: the role of self-regulatory goals in information processing and persuasion. *J. Consum. Res.* 28(1):33–49

Aaker JL, Maheswaran D. 1997. The effect of cultural orientation on persuasion. *J. Consum. Res.* 24(3):315–28

Achenreiner GB, John DR. 2003. The meaning of brand names to children: a developmental investigation. *J. Consum. Psychol.* 13(3):220–29

Adaval R. 2001. Sometimes it just feels right: the differential weighting of affect-consistent and affect-inconsistent product information. *J. Consum. Res.* 28(1):1–17

Adaval R. 2003. How good gets better and bad gets worse: understanding the impact of affect on evaluations of known brands. *J. Consum. Res.* 30(3):352–67

Adaval R, Monroe KB. 2002. Automatic construction and use of contextual information for product and price evaluations. *J. Consum. Res.* 28(4):572–88

Adaval R, Wyer RS. 1998. The role of narratives in consumer information processing. *J. Consum. Psychol.* 7(3):207–45

Ahluwalia R. 2002. How prevalent is the negativity effect in consumer environments? *J. Consum. Res.* 29(2):270–79

Ahluwalia R, Burnkrant RE. 2004. Answering questions about questions: a persuasion knowledge perspective for understanding the effects of rhetorical questions. *J. Consum. Res.* 31(1):26–42

Ahluwalia R, Gurhan-Canli Z. 2000. The effects of extensions on the family brand name:

an accessibility-diagnosticity perspective. *J. Consum. Res.* 27(3):371–81

Ahluwalia R, Unnava HR, Burnkrant RE. 2001. The moderating role of commitment on the spillover effect of marketing communications. *J. Market. Res.* 38(4):458–70

Ajzen I. 1991. Attitudinal versus normative messages: an investigation of the differential effects of persuasive communications on behavior. *Sociometry* 34:263–80

Alba JW, Hutchinson JW. 2000. Knowledge calibration: what consumers know and what they think they know. *J. Consum. Res.* 27(2):123–56

Alba JW, Mela CF, Shimp TA, Urbany JE. 1999. The effect of discount frequency and depth on consumer price judgments. *J. Consum. Res.* 26(2):99–114

Areni CS. 2002. The proposition-probability model of argument structure and message acceptance. *J. Consum. Res.* 29(2):168–87

Ariely D, Levav J. 2000. Sequential choice in group settings: taking the road less traveled and less enjoyed. *J. Consum. Res.* 27(3):279–90

Bagozzi RP, Dholakia UM. 1999. Goal-setting and goal-striving in consumer behavior. *J. Market.* 63:19–32

Bagozzi RP, Wong N, Abe S, Bergami M. 2000. Cultural and situational contingencies and the theory of reasoned action: application to fast food restaurant consumption. *J. Consum. Psychol.* 9(2):97–106

Baker WE. 2001. The diagnosticity of advertising generated brand attitudes in brand choice contexts. *J. Consum. Psychol.* 11(2):129–39

Bargh JA. 2002. Losing consciousness: automatic influences on consumer judgment, behavior, and motivation. *J. Consum. Res.* 29(2):280–85

Barone MJ, Miniard PW. 2002. Mood and brand extension judgments: asymmetric effects for desirable versus undesirable brands. *J. Consum. Psychol.* 12(4):283–90

Barone MJ, Miniard PW, Romeo J. 2000. The influence of positive mood on brand extension evaluations. *J. Consum. Res.* 26(4):386–400

Barsalou LW. 1999. Perceptual symbol systems. *Behav. Brain Sci.* 22:577–660

Baumgartner H. 1995. On the utility of consumers' theories in judgments of covariation. *J. Consum. Res.* 21(4):634–43

Baumgartner H. 2002. Toward a personology of the consumer. *J. Consum. Res.* 29(2):286–92

Baumgartner H, Sujan M, Padgett D. 1997. Patterns of affective reactions to advertisements: the integration of moment-to-moment responses into overall judgments. *J. Market. Res.* 34(2):219–32

Baumeister RF. 2002. Yielding to temptation: self-control failure; impulsive purchasing, and consumer behavior. *J. Consum. Res.* 28(4):670–76

Bettman JB. 1986. Consumer psychology. *Annu. Rev. Psychol.* 37:257–90

Bickart B, Schwarz N. 2001. Service experiences and satisfaction judgments: the use of affect and beliefs in judgment formation. *J. Consum. Psychol.* 11(1):29–41

Block LG, Keller PA. 1995. When to accentuate the negative: the effects of perceived efficacy and message framing on intentions to perform a health-related behavior. *J. Market. Res.* 32(2):192–203

Bodur HO, Brinberg D, Coupey E. 2000. Belief, affect and attitude: alternative models of the determinants of attitude. *J. Consum. Psychol.* 9(1):17–28

Bohner G, Einwiller S, Erb H, Siebler F. 2003. When small means comfortable: relations between product attributes in two-sided advertising. *J. Consum. Psychol.* 13(4):454–63

Bolton LE. 2003. Stickier priors: the effects of nonanalytic and analytic thinking in new product forecasting. *J. Market. Res.* 40:65–79

Bolton LE, Reed A II. 2004. Sticky priors: the perseverance of identity effects on judgments. *J. Market. Res.* 41(4):397–411

Bottomley PA, Holden SJS. 2001. Do we really know how consumers evaluate brand extensions? Empirical generalizations based on secondary analysis of eight studies. *J. Market. Res.* 38(4):494–500

Boush DM, Friestad M, Rose GM. 1994. Adolescent skepticism toward TV advertising and knowledge of advertiser tactics. *J. Consum. Res.* 21(1):165–75

Braun KA. 1999. Postexperience advertising effects on consumer memory. *J. Consum. Res.* 25(4):319–34

Brendl CM, Markman AB, Messner C. 2003. The devaluation effect: activating a need devalues unrelated objects. *J. Consum. Res.* 29(4):463–73

Briley DA, Morris MW, Simonson I. 2000. Reasons as carriers of culture: dynamic versus dispositional models of cultural influence on decision making. *J. Consum. Res.* 27(2):157–78

Briley DA, Wyer RA. 2002. The effect of group membership salience on the avoidance of negative outcomes: implications for social and consumer decisions. *J. Consum. Res.* 29(3):400–15

Brinol P, Petty RE, Tormala ZL. 2004. Self-validation of cognitive responses to advertisements. *J. Consum. Res.* 30(4):559–73

Broniarczyk SM, Gershoff AD. 2003. The reciprocal effects of brand equity and trivial attributes. *J. Market. Res.* 40(2):161–75

Brown CL, Carpenter GS. 2000. Why is the trivial important: A reasons-based account for the effects of trivial attributes in choice. *J. Consum. Res.* 26(4):372–85

Brown CL, Krishna A. 2004. The skeptical shopper: a metacognitive account for the effects of default options on choice. *J. Consum. Res.* 31(3):529–39

Brumbaugh AM. 2002. Source and nonsource cues in advertising and their effects on the activation of cultural and subcultural knowledge on the route to persuasion. *J. Consum. Res.* 29(2):258–69

Brunel FF, Tietje BC, Greenwald AG. 2004. Is the implicit association test a valid and valuable measure of implicit consumer social cognition? *J. Consum. Psychol.* 14(4):385–415

Buchanan L, Simmons CJ, Bickart BA. 1999. Brand equity dilution: retailer display and context brand effects. *J. Market. Res.* 36(3):345–55

Burnkrant RE, Unnava HR. 1995. Effects of self-referencing on persuasion. *J. Consum. Res.* 22(1):17–26

Campbell MC, Goodstein RC. 2001. The moderating effect of perceived risk on consumers' evaluations of product incongruity: preference for the norm. *J. Consum. Res.* 28(3):439–49

Campbell MC, Keller KL. 2003. Brand familiarity and advertising repetition effects. *J. Consum. Res.* 30(2):292–304

Campbell MC, Kirmani A. 2000. Consumer's use of persuasion knowledge: the effects of accessibility and cognitive capacity on perceptions of an influence agent. *J. Consum. Res.* 27(1):69–83

Carpenter GS, Glazer R, Nakamoto K. 1994. Meaningful brands from meaningless differentiation: the dependence on irrelevant attributes. *J. Market. Res.* 31(3):339–50

Carpenter GS, Nakamoto K. 1996. Impact of consumer preference formation on marketing objectives and second mover strategies. *J. Consum. Psychol.* 5(4):325–58

Chaiken S. 1980. Heuristic versus systematic information processing and the use of source versus message cues in persuasion. *J. Personal. Soc. Psychol.* 39:752–66

Chakravarti A, Janiszewski C. 2003. The influence of macro-level motives on consideration set composition in novel purchase situations. *J. Consum. Res.* 30(2):244–58

Chandon P, Morwitz VG, Reinartz WJ. 2004. The short- and long-term effects of measuring intent to repurchase. *J. Consum. Res.* 31(3):566–72

Chattopadhyay A, Dahl DW, Ritchie RJB, Shahin KN. 2003. Hearing voices: the impact of announcer speech characteristics on consumer response to broadcast advertising. *J. Consum. Psychol.* 13(3):198–204

Chernov A. 2004a. Goal-attribute compatibility in consumer choice. *J. Consum. Psychol.* 13(1,2):141–50

Chernov A. 2004b. Goal orientation and consumer preference for the status quo. *J. Consum. Res.* 31(3):557–65

Childers TL, Jass J. 2002. All dressed up with something to say: effects of typeface semantic associations on brand perceptions and consumer memory. *J. Consum. Psychol.* 12(2):93–106

Cohen JB, Andrade EB. 2004. Affective intuition and task-contingent affect regulation. *J. Consum. Res.* 31(2):358–67

Cohen JB, Chakravarti D. 1990. Consumer psychology. *Annu. Rev. Psychol.* 41:243–88

Cooke ADJ, Sujan H, Sujan M, Weitz BA. 2002. Marketing the unfamiliar: the role of context and item-specific information in electronic agent recommendations. *J. Market. Res.* 39(4):488–98

Cowley E, Janis E. 2004. Not necessarily better, but certainly different: a limit to the advertising misinformation effect on memory. *J. Consum. Res.* 31(1):229–35

Cowley E, Mitchell AA. 2003. The moderating effect of product knowledge on the learning and organization of product information. *J. Consum. Res.* 30(3):443–54

Cox D, Cox AD. 2001. Communicating the consequences of early detection: the role of evidence and framing. *J. Market.* 65(3):91–103

Desai KK, Keller KL. 2002. The effects of ingredient branding strategies on host brand extendibility. *J. Market.* 66(1):73–93

Erdem T. 1998. An empirical analysis of umbrella branding. *J. Market. Res.* 35(3):339–51

Escales JE, Luce MF. 2004. Understanding the effects of process-focused versus outcome-focused thought in response to advertising. *J. Consum. Res.* 31(2):274–85

Feldman JM, Lynch JG. 1998. Self-generated validity and other effects of measuring belief, attitude, intention, and behavior. *J. Appl. Psychol.* 73(3):421–35

Fishbein M, Ajzen I. 1975. *Belief, Attitude, Intention, and Behavior: An Introduction to Theory and Research.* Reading, MA: Addison-Wesley

Fishbein M, Middlestadt SB. 1995. Noncognitive effects on attitude formation and change: fact or artifact? *J. Consum. Psychol.* 4(2):181–202

Fishbein M, Middlestadt SB. 1997. A striking lack of evidence for nonbelief-based attitude formation and change: a response to five commentaries. *J. Consum. Psychol.* 6(1):107–15

Fiske ST, Neuberg SL. 1990. A continuum of impression formation, from category-based to individuating processes: influences of information and motivation on attention and interpretation. In *Advances in Experimental Social Psychology*, ed. MP Zanna, 23:1–74. New York: Academic

Fiske ST, Taylor SE. 1984. *Social Cognition.* New York: Random House

Fitzsimons GJ, Morwitz VG. 1996. The effect of measuring intent on brand-level purchase behavior. *J. Consum. Res.* 23(1):1–11

Fitzsimons GJ, Shiv B. 2001. Nonconscious and contaminative effects of hypothetical questions on subsequent decision making. *J. Consum. Res.* 28(2):224–38

Folkes V, Matta S. 2004. The effect of package shape on consumers' judgments of product volume: Attention as a mental contaminant. *J. Consum. Res.* 31(2):390–401

Folkes VS, Patrick VM. 2003. The positivity effect in perceptions of services: seen one, seen them all? *J. Consum. Res.* 30(1):125–37

Forehand MR, Deshpande R. 2001. What we see makes us who we are: priming ethnic self-awareness and advertising response. *J. Market. Res.* 38(3):336–49

Friestad M, Wright P. 1995. Persuasion knowledge: lay people's and researchers' beliefs about the psychology of advertising. *J. Consum. Res.* 22(1):62–74

Garbarino EC, Edell JA. 1997. Cognitive effort, affect, and choice. *J. Consum. Res.* 24(2):147–58

Gentner D, Markman AB. 1997. Structural alignment in analogy and similarity. *Am. Psychol.* 52(1):45–56

Gorn GJ, Chattopadhyay A, Sengupta J, Tripathi S. 2004. Waiting for the web: how screen color affects time perception. *J. Market. Res.* 41(2):215–25

Gorn GJ, Pham MT, Sin LY. 2001. When arousal influences ad evaluation and valence does not (and vice versa). *J. Consum. Psychol.* 11(1):43–55

Grant SJ, Malaviya P, Sternthal B. 2004. The influence of negation on product evaluations. *J. Consum. Res.* 31(3):583–91

Gregan-Paxton J. 2001. The role of abstract and specific knowledge in the formation of product judgments: an analogical learning perspective. *J. Consum. Psychol.* 11(3):141–48

Gregan-Paxton J, John DR. 1997. Consumer learning by analogy: a model of internal knowledge transfer. *J. Consum. Res.* 24(3):266–84

Grewal D, Kavanoor S, Fern EF, Costley M, Barnes JH. 1997. Comparative advertising: a meta-analysis of the empirical evidence. *J. Market.* 61(4):1–15

Gurhan-Canli Z, Maheswaran D. 1998. The effects of extensions on brand name dilution and enhancement. *J. Market. Res.* 35(4):464–73

Gurhan-Canli Z, Maheswaran D. 2000. Determinants of country-of-origin evaluations. *J. Consum. Res.* 27(1):96–108

Hafner M. 2004. How dissimilar others may still resemble the self: assimilation and contrast after social comparison. *J. Consum. Psychol.* 14(1,2):187–95

Haugtvedt CP, Ohio State Univ. Consum. Psychol. Semin. 1997. Beyond fact or artifact: an assessment of Fishbein and Middlestadt's perspectives on attitude change processes. *J. Consum. Psychol.* 6(1):99–106

Haugtvedt CP, Schumann DW, Schneier WL, Warren WL. 1994. Advertising repetition and variation strategies: implications for understanding attitude strength. *J. Consum. Res.* 21(1):176–89

Henderson PW, Giese JL, Cote JA. 2004. Impression management using typeface design. *J. Market.* 68(4):60–72

Herr PM. 1995. Whither fact, artifact, and attitude: reflections on the theory of reasoned action. *J. Consum. Psychol.* 4(4):371–80

Herr PM, Page CM. 2004. Asymmetric association of liking and disliking judgments: So what's not to like? *J. Consum. Res.* 30(4):588–601

Higgins ET. 2002. How self-regulation creates distinct values: the case of promotion and prevention decision making. *J. Consum. Psychol.* 12(3):177–91

Hoch SJ. 2002. Product experience is seductive. *J. Consum. Res.* 29(3):448–54

Homer PM, Batra R. 1994. Attitudinal effects of character-based versus competence-based negative political communication. *J. Consum. Psychol.* 3(2):163–85

Howard DJ, Gengler C. 2001. Emotional contagion effects on product attitudes. *J. Consum. Res.* 28(2):189–201

Hsee CK, Leclerc F. 1998. Will products look more attractive when presented separately or together? *J. Consum. Res.* 25(2):175–86

Huber J. 2004. A comment on metacognitive experiences and consumer choice. *J. Consum. Psychol.* 14(4):356–59

Huffman C. 1996. Goal change, information acquisition, and transfer. *J. Consum. Psychol.* 5(1):1–15

Isen AM, Niedenthal P, Cantor N. 1992. The influence of positive affect on social categorization. *Motiv. Emot.* 16:65–78

Jacoby J, Johar GV, Morrin M. 1998. Consumer behavior: a quadrennium. *Annu. Rev. Psychol.* 49:319–44

Jain SP, Buchanan B, Maheswaran D. 2000. Comparative and noncomparative advertising: the moderating impact of pre-purchase verifiability. *J. Consum. Psychol.* 9(4):201–12

Jain SP, Posavac SS. 2001. Prepurchase attribute verifiability, source credibility, and persuasion. *J. Consum. Psychol.* 11(3):169–80

Jain SP, Maheswaran D. 2000. Motivated reasoning: a depth-of-processing perspective. *J. Consum. Res.* 26(4):358–71

Janiszewski C, Meyvis T. 2001. Effects of brand logo complexity, repetition, and spacing on processing fluency and judgment. *J. Consum. Res.* 28(1):18–32

Janiszewski C, Noel H, Sawyer AG. 2003. A meta-analysis of the spacing effect in verbal learning: implications for research on advertising repetition and consumer memory. *J. Consum. Res.* 30(1):138–49

Jarvis WB, Petty RE. 1996. The need to evaluate. *J. Personal. Soc. Psychol.* 70:172–94

Johar GV. 1995. Consumer involvement and deception from implied advertising claims. *J. Market. Res.* 32(3):267–79

Johar GV, Simmons CJ. 2000. The use of concurrent disclosures to correct invalid inferences. *J. Consum. Res.* 26(4):307–22

John DR. 1999. Consumer socialization of children: a retrospective look at twenty-five years of research. *J. Consum. Res.* 26(3):183–213

John DR, Loken B, Joiner C. 1998. The negative impact of extensions: Can flagship products be diluted? *J. Market.* 62(1):19–32

Joiner C, Loken B. 1998. The inclusion effect and category-based induction: theory and application to brand categories. *J. Consum. Psychol.* 7(2):101–29

Kahle LR, Liu RR, Rose GM, Kim W. 2000. Dialectical thinking in consumer decision making. *J. Consum. Psychol.* 9(1):53–58

Kamins MA, Folkes VS, Perner L. 1997. Consumer responses to rumors: good news, bad news. *J. Consum. Psychol.* 6(2):165–87

Kardes FR, Cronley ML, Kellaris JJ, Posavac SS. 2004a. The role of selective information processing in price-quality inferences. *J. Consum. Res.* 31(2):368–74

Kardes FR, Cronley ML, Pontes MC, Houghton DC. 2001. Down the garden path: the role of conditional inference processes in self-persuasion. *J. Consum. Psychol.* 11(3):159–68

Kardes FR, Posavac SS, Cronley ML. 2004b. Consumer inference: a review of processes, bases, and judgment contexts. *J. Consum. Psychol.* 14(3):230–56

Kassarjian HH. 1982. Consumer psychology. *Annu. Rev. Psychol.* 33:619–49

Keller KL, Heckler SE, Houston MJ. 1998. The effects of brand name suggestiveness on advertising recall. *J. Market.* 62(1):48–57

Keller PA, Block LG. 1996. Increasing the persuasiveness of fear appeals: the effect of arousal and elaboration. *J. Consum. Res.* 22(4):448–59

Keller PA, Block LG. 1997. Vividness effects: a resource-matching perspective. *J. Consum. Res.* 24(3):295–304

Keller PA, Lipkus IM, Rimer BK. 2002. Depressive realism and health risk accuracy: the negative consequences of positive mood. *J. Consum. Res.* 29(1):57–69

Keller PA, Lipkus IM, Rimer BK. 2003. Affect, framing, and persuasion. *J. Market. Res.* 40(1):54–65

Kempf DAS, Smith RE. 1998. Consumer processing of product trial and the effects of prior advertising: a structural modeling approach. *J. Market. Res.* 35(3):325–38

Kirmani A, Shiv B. 1998. Effects of source congruity on brand attitudes and beliefs: the moderating role of issue-relevant elaboration. *J. Consum. Psychol.* 7(1):25–47

Kirmani A, Sood S, Bridges S. 1999. The ownership effect in consumer responses to brand line stretches. *J. Market.* 63(1):88–101

Klink RR, Smith DC. 2001. Threats to the external validity of brand extension research. *J. Market. Res.* 38(3):326–426

Krishnamurthy P, Sivaraman A. 2002. Counterfactual thinking and advertising responses. *J. Consum. Res.* 28(4):650–58

Krishnamurthy P, Sujan M. 1999. Retrospection versus anticipation: the role of the ad under retrospective and anticipatory self-referencing. *J. Consum. Res.* 26(1):55–69

Krishnan HS, Chakravarti D. 1999. Memory measures for pretesting advertisements: an integrative conceptual framework and a diagnostic template. *J. Consum. Psychol.* 8(1):1–37

Krishnan HS, Shapiro S. 1999. Prospective and retrospective memory for intentions: a two-component approach. *J. Consum. Psychol.* 8(2):141–66

Kumar A. 2000. Interference effects of contextual cues in advertisements on memory for ad content. *J. Consum. Psychol.* 9(3):155–66

Kumar A, Krishnan S. 2004. Memory interference in advertising: a replication and extension. *J. Consum. Res.* 30(4):602–11

Lane VR. 2000. The impact of ad repetition and ad content on consumer perceptions of incongruent extensions. *J. Market.* 64(2):80–91

Larsen V, Luna D, Peracchio LA. 2004. Point of view and pieces of time: a taxonomy of image attributes. *J. Consum. Res.* 31(1):102–11

Lau-Gesk LG. 2003. Activating culture through persuasion appeals: an examination of the bicultural consumer. *J. Consum. Psychol.* 13(3):301–15

Laverie DA, Kleine RE III, Kleine SS. 2002. Reexamination and extension of Kleine, Kleine, and Kernan's social identity model of mundane consumption: the mediating role of the appraisal process. *J. Consum. Res.* 28(4):659–69

Law S, Hawkins SA, Craik FIM. 1998. Repetition-induced belief in the elderly: rehabilitation age-related memory deficits. *J. Consum. Res.* 25(2):91–107

Lee AY. 2004. The prevalence of metacognitive routes to judgments. *J. Consum. Psychol.* 14(4):349–55

Lee AY, Sternthal B. 1999. The effects of positive mood on memory. *J. Consum. Res.* 26(2):115–27

Lee JA. 2000. Adapting Triandis's model of subjective culture and social behavior relations to consumer behavior. *J. Consum. Psychol.* 9(2):117–26

Levin IP, Levin AM. 2000. Modeling the role of brand alliances in the assimilation of product evaluations. *J. Consum. Psychol.* 9(1):43–52

Lin Y, Lin C, Raghubir P. 2003. Avoiding anxiety, being in denial, or simply stroking self-esteem: Why self-positivity? *J. Consum. Psychol.* 13(4):464–77

Loken B, Joiner C, Peck J. 2002. Category attitude measures: exemplars as inputs. *J. Consum. Psychol.* 12(2):149–62

Loken B, Ward J. 1990. Alternative approaches to understanding the determinants of typicality. *J. Consum. Res.* 17:111–26

Luce MF, Payne JW, Bettman JR. 1999. Emotional trade-off difficulty and choice. *J. Market. Res.* 36(2):143–59

Luna D, Peracchio LA. 2001. Moderators of language effects in advertising to bilinguals: a psycholinguistic approach. *J. Consum. Res.* 28(2):284–95

Lurie NH. 2004. Decision making in information rich environments: the role of information structure. *J. Consum. Res.* 30(4):473–86

Maison D, Greenwald AG, Bruin RH. 2004. Predictive validity of the implicit association test in studies of brands, consumer attitudes, and behavior. *J. Consum. Psychol.* 14(4):427–42

Malaviya P, Kisielius J, Sternthal B. 1996. The effect of type of elaboration on advertising process and judgment. *J. Market. Res.* 33:410–21

Mandel N. 2003. Shifting selves and decision making: the effects of self-construal priming on consumer risk taking. *J. Consum. Res.* 30(1):30–40

Mandel N, Johnson EJ. 2002. When Web pages influence choice: effects of visual primes on experts and novices. *J. Consum. Res.* 29(2):235–45

Mantel SP, Kardes FR. 1999. The role of direction of comparison, attribute-based processing, and attitude-based processing in consumer preference. *J. Consum. Res.* 25(4):335–52

Mantel SP, Kellaris JJ. 2003. Cognitive determinants of consumers' time perceptions: the impact of resources required and available. *J. Consum. Res.* 29(4):531–38

Markus H, Kunda Z. 1986. Stability and malleability in the self-concept in the perception of others. *J. Personal. Soc. Psychol.* 51(4):858–66

Martin IM, Stewart DW. 2001. The differential impact of goal congruency on attitudes, intentions, and the transfer of brand equity. *J. Market. Res.* 38(4):471–93

McQuarrie EF, Mick DG. 2003. Visual and verbal rhetorical figures under directed processing versus incidental exposure to advertising. *J. Consum. Res.* 29(4):579–87

Meloy MG. 2000. Mood-driven distortion of product information. *J. Consum. Res.* 27(3):345–59

Menon G. 1997. Are the parts better than the whole? The effects of decompositional questions on judgments of frequent behaviors. *J. Market. Res.* 32:335–46

Menon G, Block LG, Ramanathan S. 2002. We're at as much risk as we are led to believe: effects of message cues on judgments of health risk. *J. Consum. Res.* 28(4):533–49

Menon G, Johar GV. 1997. Antecedents of positivity effects in social versus nonsocial judgments. *J. Consum. Psychol.* 6(4):313–37

Menon G, Raghubir P. 2003. Ease-of-retrieval as an automatic input in judgments: a mere-accessibility framework? *J. Consum. Res.* 30(2):230–43

Menon G, Raghubir P, Schwarz N. 1995. Behavioral frequency judgments: an accessibility-diagnosticity framework. *J. Consum. Res.* 22(2):212–28

Meyers-Levy J, Maheswaran D. 2004. Exploring message framing outcomes when systematic, heuristic, or both types of processing occur. *J. Consum. Psychol.* 14(1,2):159–67

Meyers-Levy J, Peracchio LA. 1995. Understanding the effects of color: how the correspondence between available and required resources affects attitudes. *J. Consum. Res.* 22(2):121–38

Meyers-Levy J, Peracchio LA. 1996. Moderators of the impact of self-reference on persuasion. *J. Consum. Res.* 22(4):408–23

Meyers-Levy J, Tybout AM. 1997. Context effects at encoding and judgment in consumption settings: the role of cognitive resources. *J. Consum. Res.* 24(1):1–14

Meyvis T, Janiszewski C. 2002. Consumers' beliefs about product benefits: the effect of obviously irrelevant product information. *J. Consum. Res.* 28(4):618–35

Meyvis T, Janiszewski C. 2004. When are broader brands stronger brands? An accessibility perspective on the success of brand extensions. *J. Consum. Res.* 31(2):346–57

Mick DG, Fournier S. 1998. Paradoxes of technology: consumer cognizance, emotions, and coping strategies. *J. Consum. Res.* 25(2):123–43

Milberg S, Park CW, McCarthy M. 1997. Managing negative feedback effects associated with brand extension: the impact of alternative branding strategies. *J. Consum. Psychol.* 6(2):119–40

Miniard PW, Barone MJ. 1997. The case for noncognitive determinants of attitude: a critique of Fishbein and Middlestadt. *J. Consum. Psychol.* 6(1):77–93

Mitchell A, Dacin PA. 1996. The assessment of alternative measures of consumer expertise. *J. Consum. Res.* 23(3):219–39

Mitchell DJ, Kahn BE, Knasko SC. 1995. There's something in the air: effects of congruent or incongruent ambient odor on consumer decision making. *J. Consum. Res.* 22(2):229–38

Moore ES, Lutz RJ. 2000. Children, advertising, and product experiences: a multimethod inquiry. *J. Consum. Res.* 27(1):31–48

Moreau CP, Lehmann DR, Markman AB. 2001. Entrenched knowledge structures and consumer response to new products. *J. Market. Res.* 38(1):14–29

Morrin M. 1999. The impact of brand extensions on parent brand memory structures and retrieval processes. *J. Market. Res.* 36(4):517–25

Morrin M, Ratneshwar S. 2003. Does it make sense to use scents to enhance brand memory? *J. Market. Res.* 40(1):10–26

Morwitz VG. 1997. It seems like only yesterday: the nature and consequences of telescoping errors in marketing research. *J. Consum. Psychol.* 6(1):1–29

Morwitz VG, Fitzsimons GJ. 2004. The mere-measurement effects: Why does measuring intentions change actual behavior? *J. Consum. Psychol.* 14(1,2):64–74

Murry JP, Dacin PA. 1996. Cognitive moderators of negative-emotion effects: implications for understanding media context. *J. Consum. Res.* 22(4):439–47

Muthukrishnan AV, Kardes F. 2001. Persistent preferences for product attributes: the effects of the initial choice context and uninforma-tive experience. *J. Consum. Res.* 28(1):89–104

Muthukrishnan AV, Ramaswami S. 1999. Contextual effects on the revision of evaluative judgments: an extension of the omission-detection framework. *J. Consum. Res.* 26(1):70–84

Notani AS. 1998. Moderators of perceived behavioral control's predictiveness in the theory of planned behavior: a meta-analysis. *J. Consum. Psychol.* 7(3):247–71

Olsen DG. 1997. The impact of interstimulus interval and background silence on recall. *J. Consum. Res.* 23(4):295–311

Park CW, Jun SY, Shocker AD. 1996. Composite branding alliances: an investigation of extensions and feedback effects. *J. Market. Res.* 33:453–66

Park CW, Mothersbaugh DL, Feick L. 1994. Consumer knowledge assessment. *J. Consum. Res.* 21(1):71–82

Pechmann C. 1996. Do consumers overgeneralize one-sided comparative price claims, and are more stringent regulations needed? *J. Market. Res.* 33(2):150–62

Pechmann C, Knight SJ. 2002. An experimental investigation of the joint effects of advertising and peers on adolescents' beliefs and intentions about cigarette consumption. *J. Consum. Res.* 29(1):5–19

Peck J, Childers TL. 2003. Individual differences in haptic information processing: the "need for touch" scale. *J. Consum. Res.* 30(3):430–42

Peracchio LA, Meyers-Levy J. 1994. How ambiguous cropped objects in ad photos can affect product evaluations. *J. Consum. Res.* 21(1):190–214

Peracchio LA, Meyers-Levy J. 1997. Evaluating persuasion-enhancing techniques from a resource-matching perspective. *J. Consum. Res.* 24(2):178–92

Peracchio LA, Tybout AM. 1996. The moderating role of prior knowledge in schema-based product evaluation. *J. Consum. Res.* 23(3):177–92

Petty RE, Cacioppo JT. 1986. *Communication and Persuasion: Central and Peripheral*

Routes to Attitude Change. New York: Springer-Verlag

Pham MT. 1996. Cue representation and selection effects of arousal on persuasion. *J. Consum. Res.* 22(4):373–87

Pham MT. 1998. Representatives, relevance, and the use of feelings in decision making. *J. Consum. Res.* 25(2):144–57

Pham MT. 2004. The logic of feeling. *J. Consum. Psychol.* 14(4):360–9

Pham MT, Avnet T. 2004. Ideals and oughts and the reliance on affect versus substance in persuasion. *J. Consum. Res.* 30(4):503–18

Pham MT, Cohen JB, Pracejus JW, Hughes GD. 2001. Affect monitoring and the primacy of feelings in judgment. *J. Consum. Res.* 28(2):167–88

Pham MT, Muthukrishnan AV. 2002. Search and alignment in judgment revision: implications for brand positioning. *J. Market. Res.* 39(1):18–30

Phillips DM, Baumgartner H. 2002. The role of consumption emotions in the satisfaction response. *J. Consum. Psychol.* 12(3):243–52

Pieters R, Rosbergen E, Wedel M. 1999. Visual attention to repeated print advertising: a test of scanpath theory. *J. Market. Res.* 36(4):424–38

Posavac SS, Sanbonmatsu DM, Kardes FR, Fitzsimons GJ. 2004. The brand positivity effect: when evaluation confers preference. *J. Consum. Res.* 31(3):643–51

Priester JR, Dholakia UM, Fleming MA. 2004. When and why the background contrast effect emerges: thought engenders meaning by influencing the perception of applicability. *J. Consum. Res.* 31(3):491–501

Priester JR, Godek J, Nayakankuppum DJ, Park K. 2004. Brand congruity and comparative advertising: When and why comparative advertisements lead to greater elaboration. *J. Consum. Psychol.* 14(1,2):115–23

Priester JR, Fleming MA. 1997. Artifact or meaningful theoretical constructs? Examining evidence for nonbelief- and belief-based attitude change processes. *J. Consum. Psychol.* 6(1):67–76

Priester JR, Nayakankuppam D, Fleming MA, Godek J. 2004. The A^2SC^2 model: the influence of attitudes and attitude strength on consideration and choice. *J. Consum. Res.* 30(4):574–87

Priester JR, Petty RE. 2003. The influence of spokesperson trustworthiness on message elaboration, attitude strength, and advertising effectiveness. *J. Consum. Psychol.* 13:408–21

Raghubir P, Krishna A. 1999. Vital dimensions in volume perception: Can the eye fool the stomach? *J. Market. Res.* 36(3):313–26

Raghubir P, Menon G. 1998. AIDS and me, never the twain shall meet: the effects of information accessibility on judgments of risk and advertising effectiveness. *J. Consum. Res.* 25(1):52–63

Raghunathan R, Irwin JR. 2001. Walking the hedonic product treadmill: default contrast and mood-based assimilation in judgments of predicted happiness with a target product. *J. Consum. Res.* 28(3):355–68

Ratneshwar S, Barsalou LW, Pechmann C, Moore M. 2001. Goal-derived categories: the role of personal and situational goals in category representations. *J. Consum. Psychol.* 10(3):147–57

Ratneshwar S, Mick DG, Huffman C, eds. 2000. *The Why of Consumption: Contemporary Perspectives on Consumer Motives, Goals and Desires.* London/New York: Routledge

Ratneshwar S, Pechmann C, Shocker AD. 1996. Goal-derived categories and the antecedents of across-category consideration. *J. Consum. Res.* 23(3):240–50

Reed A II. 2004. Activating the self-importance of consumer selves: exploring identity salience effects on judgments. *J. Consum. Res.* 31(2):286–95

Richins ML. 1997. Measuring emotions in the consumption experience. *J. Consum. Res.* 24(2):127–46

Roehm ML, Sternthal B. 2001. The moderating effect of knowledge and resources on the persuasive impact of analogies. *J. Consum. Res.* 28(2):257–72

Russell CA. 2002. Investigating the effectiveness of product placements in television shows: the role of modality and plot connection congruence on brand memory and attitude. *J. Consum. Res.* 29(3):306–18

Russo JE, Meloy MG, Medvec VH. 1998. Predecisional distortion of product information. *J. Market. Res.* 35(4):438–52

Ruth JA. 2001. Promoting a brand's emotion benefits: the influence of emotion categorization processes on consumer evaluations. *J. Consum. Psychol.* 11(2):99–113

Schlosser AE, Shavitt S. 2002. Anticipating discussion about a product: Rehearsing what to say can affect your judgments. *J. Consum. Res.* 29(1):101–15

Schwarz N. 1997. Moods and attitude judgments: a comment on Fishbein and Middlestadt. *J. Consum. Psychol.* 6(1):93–98

Schwarz N. 2004. Metacognitive experiences in consumer judgment and decision making. *J. Consum. Psychol.* 14(4):332–48

Sen S. 1999. The effects of brand name suggestiveness and decision goal on the development of brand knowledge. *J. Consum. Psychol.* 8(4):431–55

Sengupta J, Fitzsimons GJ. 2000. The effects of analyzing reasons for brand preferences: disruption or reinforcement. *J. Market. Res.* 37(3):318–30

Sengupta J, Fitzsimons GJ. 2004. The effect of analyzing reasons on the stability of brand attitudes: a reconciliation of opposing predictions. *J. Consum. Res.* 31(3):705–11

Sengupta J, Goodstein RC, Boninger DS. 1997. All cues are not created equal: obtaining attitude persistence under low-involvement conditions. *J. Consum. Res.* 23(4):351–61

Sengupta J, Gorn GJ. 2002. Absence makes the mind grow sharper: effects of element omission on subsequent recall. *J. Market. Res.* 39(2):186–202

Sengupta J, Johar GV. 2002. Effects of inconsistent attribute information on the predictive value of product attitudes: toward a resolution of opposing perspectives. *J. Consum. Res.* 29(1):39–56

Shapiro S. 1999. When an ad's influence is beyond our conscious control: perceptual and conceptual fluency effects caused by incidental ad exposure. *J. Consum. Res.* 26(1):16–36

Shapiro S, MacInnis DJ, Heckler SE. 1997. The effects of incidental ad exposure on the formation of consideration sets. *J. Consum. Res.* 24(1):94–104

Shapiro S, Spence MT. 2002. Factors affecting encoding, retrieval, and alignment of sensory attributes in a memory-based brand choice task. *J. Consum. Res.* 28(4):603–17

Shavitt S, Swan S, Lowrey TM, Wanke M. 1994. The interaction of endorser attractiveness and involvement in persuasion depends on the goal that guides message processing. *J. Consum. Psychol.* 3(2):137–62

Shiv B, Britton JAE, Payne JW. 2004. Does elaboration increase or decrease the effectiveness of negatively versus positively framed messages? *J. Consum. Res.* 31(1):199–208

Shiv B, Edell JA, Payne JW. 1997. Factors affecting the impact of negatively and positively framed ad messages. *J. Consum. Res.* 24(3):285–94

Shiv B, Fedorikhin A. 1999. Heart and mind in conflict: the interplay of affect and cognition in consumer decision making. *J. Consum. Res.* 26(3):278–92

Shrum LJ, Wyer RS, O'Guinn TC. 1998. The effects of television consumption on social perceptions: the use of priming procedures to investigate psychological processes. *J. Consum. Res.* 24(4):447–58

Siminon BL, Ruth JA. 1998. Is a company known by the company it keeps? Assessing the spillover effects of brand alliances on consumer brand attitudes. *J. Market. Res.* 35(1):30–42

Simonson I, Carmon Z, Dhar R, Drolet A, Nowles S. 2001. Consumer research: in search of identity. *Annu. Rev. Psychol.* 52:249–75

Sirsi AK, Ward JC, Reingen PH. 1996. Microcultural analysis of variation in sharing of causal reasoning about behavior. *J. Consum. Res.* 22(4):345–72

Soman D, Cheema A. 2004. When goals are counterproductive: the effects of violation of a behavioral goal on subsequent performance. *J. Consum. Res.* 31(1):52–62

Spangenberg ER, Greenwald AG. 1999. Social influence by requesting self-prophecy. *J. Consum. Psychol.* 8(1):61–89

Srivastava J, Raghubir P. 2002. Debiasing using decomposition: the case of memory-based credit card expense estimates. *J. Consum. Psychol.* 12(3):253–64

Stapel DA, Koomen W, Velthuijsen AS. 1998. Assimilation or contrast? Comparison relevance, distinctness, and the impact of accessible information on consumer judgments. *J. Consum. Psychol.* 7(1):1–14

Tavassoli NT, Han JK. 2001. Scripted thought: processing Korean Hancha and Hangul in a multimedia context. *J. Consum. Res.* 28(3):482–93

Tavassoli NT, Lee YH. 2003. The differential interaction of auditory and visual advertising elements with Chinese and English. *J. Market. Res.* 40(4):468–81

Tormala ZL, Petty RE. 2004. Source credibility and attitude certainty: a metacognitive analysis of resistance to persuasion. *J. Consum. Psychol.* 14(4):427–42

Tybout AM, Artz N. 1994. Consumer psychology. *Annu. Rev. Psychol.* 45:131–69

Unnava HR, Agarwal S, Haugtvedt CP. 1996. Interactive effects of presentation modality and message-generated imagery on recall of advertising information. *J. Consum. Res.* 23(1):81–8

Unnava HR, Sirdeshmukh D. 1994. Reducing competitive ad interference. *J. Market. Res.* 31(3):403–11

Van Osselaer SMJ, Alba JW. 2003. Locus of equity and brand extension. *J. Consum. Res.* 29(4):539–50

Van Osselaer SMJ, Janiszewski C. 2001. Two ways of learning brand associations. *J. Consum. Res.* 28(2):202–23

Veryzer RW, Hutchinson JW. 1998. The influence of unity and prototypicality on aesthetic responses to new product designs. *J. Consum. Res.* 24(4):374–94

Viswanathan M, Childers TL. 1996. Processing of numerical and verbal product information. *J. Consum. Psychol.* 5(4):359–85

Viswanathan M, Childers TL. 1999. Understanding how product attributes influence product categorization: development and validation of fuzzy set-based measures of gradedness in product categories. *J. Market. Res.* 36(1):75–94

Wang J, Wyer RS. 2002. Comparative judgment processes: the effects of task objectives and time delay on product evaluations. *J. Consum. Psychol.* 12(4):327–40

Wanke M, Bless H, Schwarz S. 1998. Context effects in product line extensions. *J. Consum. Psychol.* 7(4):299–322

Wanke M, Bohner G, Jukowitsch A. 1997. There are many reasons to drive a BMW: Does imagined ease of argument generation influence attitudes? *J. Consum. Res.* 24(2):170–77

Wansink B, Kent RJ, Hoch SJ. 1998. An anchoring and adjustment model of purchase quantity decisions. *J. Market. Res.* 35(1):71–81

Wansink B, Van Ittersum K. 2003. Bottoms up! Peripheral cues and consumption volume. *J. Consum. Res.* 30(3):455–63

Warlop L, Alba JW. 2004. Sincere flattery: trade-dress imitation and consumer choice. *J. Consum. Psychol.* 14(1,2):21–27

Weiner B. 2000. Attributional thoughts about consumer behavior. *J. Consum. Res.* 27(3):382–87

West PM. 1996. Predicting preferences: an examination of agent learning. *J. Consum. Res.* 23(1):68–80

West PM, Huber J, Min KS. 2004. Altering experienced utility: the impact of story writing and self-referencing on preferences. *J. Consum. Res.* 31(3):623–30

Williams P, Aaker JL. 2002. Can mixed emotions peacefully coexist? *J. Consum. Res.* 28(4):636–49

Williams P, Fitzsimons GJ, Block LG. 2004. When consumers do not recognize "benign" intention questions as persuasion attempts. *J. Consum. Res.* 31(3):540–50

Wooten DB, Reed A II. 1998. Informational influence and the ambiguity of product experience: order effects on the weighting of evidence. *J. Consum. Psychol.* 7(1):79–99

Wyer RS, Srull TJ. 1989. *Memory and Cognition in Its Social Context*. Hillsdale, NJ: Erlbaum

Yeung CWM, Wyer RS. 2004. Affect, appraisal, and consumer judgment. *J. Consum. Res.* 31(2):412–24

Yoon C. 1997. Age differences in consumers' processing strategies: an investigation of moderating influences. *J. Consum. Res.* 24(3):329–42

Yorkston E, Menon G. 2004. A sound idea: pho-netic effects of brand names on consumer judgments. *J. Consum. Res.* 31(1):43–51

Zhang S, Kardes FR, Cronley ML. 2002. Comparative advertising: effects of structural alignability on target brand evaluations. *J. Consum. Psychol.* 12(4):303–11

Zhang S, Markman AB. 1998. Overcoming the early entrant advantage: the role of alignable and nonalignable differences. *J. Market. Res.* 35(4):413–26

Zhang S, Schmitt BH. 2004. Activating sound and meaning: the role of language proficiency in bilingual consumer environments. *J. Consum. Res.* 31(1):220–28

Zhang S, Sood S. 2002. "Deep" and "surface" cues: brand extension evaluations by children and adults. *J. Consum. Res.* 29(1):129–41

Annu. Rev. Psychol. 2006. 57:487–503
doi: 10.1146/annurev.psych.56.091103.070258
Copyright © 2006 by Annual Reviews. All rights reserved
First published online as a Review in Advance on August 9, 2005

CLASSROOM GOAL STRUCTURE, STUDENT MOTIVATION, AND ACADEMIC ACHIEVEMENT

Judith L. Meece

School of Education, University of North Carolina, Chapel Hill, North Carolina
27599-3500; email: Meece@email.unc.edu

Eric M. Anderman

College of Education, University of Kentucky, Lexington, Kentucky 40506-0017;
email: Eande1@pop.uky.edu,

Lynley H. Anderman

College of Education, University of Kentucky, Lexington, Kentucky 40506-0001;
email: Lande2@pop.uky.edu

Key Words   motivational orientations, classroom environment, cognitive engagement

■ **Abstract**   Over the past 25 years, achievement goal theory has emerged as one of the most prominent theories of achievement motivation. This chapter uses an achievement goal framework to examine the influence of classroom and school environments on students' academic motivation and achievement. Considerable evidence suggests that elementary and secondary students show the most positive motivation and learning patterns when their school settings emphasize mastery, understanding, and improving skills and knowledge. Whereas school environments that are focused on demonstrating high ability and competing for grades can increase the academic performance of some students, research suggests that many young people experience diminished motivation under these conditions. The implications of achievement goal theory for examining the impact of school reform are discussed.

CONTENTS

INTRODUCTION

The American classroom has changed significantly over the past 25 years. Computers and interactive software are common in most classrooms today, and rows of student desks have been replaced with moveable tables and chairs that promote collaborative learning among two or more students. Many states and school districts have reduced class size to increase learning opportunities, especially for young or high-risk students. Reform at the middle school level has introduced block scheduling, advisory teams, schools-within-schools, and other structural changes to meet the developmental needs of young adolescents. Additionally, major professional organizations such as the National Council of Teachers of Mathematics have called for paradigm shifts in how teachers think about learning and teaching. Rather than focusing on rote learning and memorization, curriculum standards that began to emerge in the early 1990s emphasized the importance of individual inquiry, problem solving, collaborative learning, and mastery of key concepts. As these reforms were beginning to take hold, new federal legislation, the *Leave No Child Left Behind Act of 2001*, was enacted to increase accountability and performance standards for public schools. It is anticipated that this new legislation will close achievement gaps and ensure that all students, regardless of any existing disadvantage, will make significant achievement gains in school.

With the exception of research on class size, little evidence is available to evaluate the effects of various reform efforts of the past 25 years on student learning and motivation. Even fewer studies have examined how these different reform efforts influence important aspects of the classroom or school environment that young people experience. Child development research suggests that schools, along with the family and peer group, are one of the most influential social contexts for children's development (Eccles 2004). In this chapter, we adopt an achievement goal framework for examining the influence of different classroom and school environments on children's development as learners. We emphasize the influence of classroom environments not only on students' academic engagement and achievement, but also on their motivation and their self-perceptions. Schools, in our view, play a critical role in all aspects of children's development.

The chapter begins with a brief discussion of achievement goal theory in relation to other prominent achievement motivation theories. Subsequent sections describe the types of achievement goals students adopt in classroom settings, the measures that are used to assess achievement goals, and the influence of different achievement goals on various developmental outcomes, including measures of motivation to learn, classroom engagement and adjustment, and academic achievement. The chapter also includes research on the ways instructional practices, such as grading and evaluation practices, can create different goal structures in the classroom and influence student outcome measures. We next discuss efforts to change the goal structures of classrooms and schools. Finally, in our conclusion, we discuss the implications of achievement goal theory for understanding the impact of reform efforts on students and suggest some directions for future research.

ACHIEVEMENT GOAL THEORY AND CLASSROOM ENVIRONMENTS

Overview of Achievement Goal Theory

Motivational theories focus on the processes that explain goal-directed activity (Pintrich & Schunk 2002, p. 5). Generally, motivation theorists are interested in explaining physical activity such as task engagement and persistence, as well cognitive activities such as problem solving and decision making. In educational research, motivation theories are most often used to explain students' activity choice, engagement, persistence, help seeking, and performance in school. Motivation is also used as a measure of school adjustment (Roeser & Eccles 1998). Students who are alienated or disaffected generally lack motivation to attend school and to engage in learning.

Motivation research has a long history, beginning with the philosophy of William James and extending to achievement goal theories of the 1980s. Many early theories explained motivated behavior in terms of drives, instincts, motives, and other internal traits (Weiner 1990). Motivation has also been explained in terms of behavioral associations involving reward contingencies (Pintrich & Schunk 2002). More contemporary theories focus on social-cognitive processes as sources of motivation. This view is represented in attribution theories of motivation, which link achievement striving to how individuals interpret their success and failures in achievement situations (Weiner 1979). Another social-cognitive approach to motivation, expectancy-value theory, links achievement-related behavior to individual expectancy and value perceptions (Atkinson 1964; Eccles 1983; Wigfield & Eccles 1992, 2000). Individuals are more likely to engage in a particular achievement task when they expect to do well and when the task has some value to them. Similarly, self-efficacy theories of achievement motivation emphasize the importance of individual judgments of capability (Bandura 1986, Schunk 1991).

Achievement goal theory is situated in this social-cognitive view of motivation. Within the past 25 years, it has emerged as one of the most prominent theories of motivation (Anderman & Wolters 2005, Pintrich 2000). It has also served as an important lens for analyzing the influence of different classroom structures and school environments on student motivation and learning. Rather than focusing on ability perceptions and causal attributions, goal theories of motivation focus on the types of goals individuals pursue in achievement situations. Goal theorists view behavior as purposeful, intentional, and directed toward the attainment of certain goals (Pintrich & Schunk 2002). Achievement goal theorists focus specifically on goals involving the development or demonstration of competence (Maehr & Nicholls 1980, Nicholls 1984). According to Nicholls (1984, p. 328), "the distinguishing feature of achievement behavior is its goal of competence or perception of competence," and ability can be defined in several different ways. Thus, the criteria or standards of excellence people use to judge their competence are key to achievement goal theory. This point is critical because classrooms and school environments differ with regard to the evaluation standards used to assess students' academic progress and achievement (Ames 1992a,b; Ames & Archer 1988; Eccles & Midgley 1989; Nicholls 1989).

Defining Achievement Goals

Achievement goal theorists focus on students' intentions or reasons for engaging, choosing, and persisting at different learning activities. Early research on achievement goals focused on two contrasting forms of approach motivation and have been labeled learning versus performance (Dweck & Elliot 1983), task involved versus ego involved (Nicholls 1984), mastery versus ability focused (Ames 1992a, Ames & Archer 1988), and task focused versus ability focused (Maehr & Midgley 1991). Although there has been some debate as to whether these goal pairs represent similar constructs (Thorkildsen & Nicholls 1998), most researchers today view these goal sets as having sufficient overlap to be treated as conceptually similar constructs (Pintrich & Schunk 2002). For the purposes of this chapter, we use "mastery" and "performance" to describe these different goal orientations.

A mastery goal orientation is defined in terms of a focus on developing one's abilities, mastering a new skill, trying to accomplish something challenging, and trying to understand learning materials. Success is evaluated in terms of self-improvement, and students derive satisfaction from the inherent qualities of the task, such as its interest and challenge. By contrast, a performance goal orientation represents a focus on demonstrating high ability relative to others, striving to be better than others, and using social comparison standards to make judgments of ability and performance. A sense of accomplishment is derived from doing better than others and surpassing normative performance standards.

In recent years, researchers have distinguished between two types of performance goals. Performance-approach goals focus on the attainment of favorable judgments of competence; whereas performance-avoidance goals focus on avoiding unfavorable judgments of ability (Elliot & Church 1997, Elliot & Harackiewicz 1996). Similarly, Pintrich (2000) argued that mastery goals should be broken down into master-approach goals and mastery-avoid goals. When students are focused on mastery-approach variables, they want to learn, master, and truly understand the task at hand. In contrast, when students are focused on mastery-avoid goals, they want to avoid misunderstanding or not being able to learn from a specific task. Thus far, mastery-approach and mastery-avoid goals have not been widely studied.

Relations of Individual Achievement Goals to Achievement-Related Behavior

Research has identified a number of achievement-related patterns that are "set in motion" by different motivational goals (Elliot & Dweck 1988, p. 11). Much of this research indicates that students show the most positive achievement patterns when they are focused on mastery goals. With this goal focus, students persist at difficult tasks (Elliot & Dweck 1988, Stipek & Kowalski 1989), report high levels of task involvement (Harackiewicz et al. 2000), report high levels of effort and persistence (Grant & Dweck 2003, Miller et al. 1996, Wolters 2004), and use learning strategies that enhance conceptual understanding and recall of information (Ames & Archer 1988; Elliot & McGregor 2001; Grant & Dweck 2003; Green & Miller 1996; Meece et al. 1988; Meece & Miller 2001; Nolen 1988, 2001; Nolen & Haladyna 1990; Wolters 2004). Mastery goals are also associated with positive perceptions of academic ability and self-efficacy (Meece et al. 1988, Midgley et al. 1998, Roeser et al. 1996, Wolters 2004). The positive relations of mastery goals to both achievement behaviors and ability perceptions are found across grade levels and subject areas. One significant limitation of this research is that few researchers have demonstrated positive links between mastery goals and academic performance. For the most part the expected positive relation between mastery goals and academic performance has not been consistently found (Barron & Harackiewicz 2001, Elliot & Church 1997, Harackiewicz et al. 2000, Herman et al. 2005, Miller et al. 1996, Pintrich 2000, Skaalvik 1997), although Wolters and his colleagues (1996) reported a positive relation for a sample of junior high school students.

Performance goals also show some interesting relations to achievement-related behaviors across studies. A good deal of evidence suggests that performance goals are associated with surface-level learning strategies (memorizing and rehearsing information), which do not necessarily promote conceptual understanding (Elliot & Harackiewicz 1996, Graham & Golan 1991, Kaplan et al. 2002b, Meece et al. 1988, Nolen 1988). Performance goals are also associated with self-handicapping strategies (e.g., goofing off, procrastinating, etc.) for late elementary school–aged children (Urdan et al. 1998), with academic cheating behaviors among middle school students (Anderman et al. 1998), and with lower grades for college students (Elliot & Church 1997, Elliot & McGregor 2001, Skaalvik 1997). However, these patterns are not consistent across studies, and researchers have emphasized the need to distinguish between approach and avoidance forms of performance goals (Harackiewicz et al. 2002). Some evidence suggests that performance-approach goals (demonstrating ability and outperforming others) are positively associated with persistence and achievement outcomes, especially for college students (Elliot et al. 1999, Harackiewicz et al. 2002).

Although performance and mastery goals are most commonly examined as separate goal orientations, evidence suggests that students hold multiple goals in classroom situations (Bouffard et al. 1995, Harackiewicz et al. 1998, Meece & Holt 1993, Pintrich 2000, Wentzel 1992). Research has further suggested that multiple combinations of goals (e.g., high mastery and high performance) may have different motivation and achievement outcomes. Current studies emphasize the need to acknowledge that learners may simultaneously adopt multiple goals that are relatively more or less adaptive for learning. However, it is still not clear what combination of goals is most adaptive for which group of students, achievement tasks, and learning contexts (Midgley et al. 2001).

It is also important to point out that the findings described above were based on assessments of personal goal orientations. These goal orientations may be shaped, in part, by critical dimensions of the classroom and school environment where the assessments take place. The section below describes how the goal structures of classrooms are assessed, and their relation to personal goals and learning outcomes.

CLASSROOM GOAL STRUCTURES

Along with providing a framework for studying individual differences in student motivation, achievement goal theory is also useful for analyzing the influence of classroom environments on students' motivation and learning patterns. Research focused on the classroom has examined how teachers may create different goal structures in the classrooms through their use of various instructional, evaluation, and grouping strategies (Kaplan et al. 2002b). For example, some teachers are known to differ in their use of ability grouping or competitive grading practices, which can increase the salience of performance goals. Other teachers focus on skill development, mastery, and improvement, which can lead students to adopt a mastery orientation. As described below, a variety of measures have been used to assess the goal structures of classrooms, including student questionnaires, teacher reports, and observations.

The TARGET System

Ames & Archer (1988) first designed and used a student-report measure to assess the salience of mastery and performance goals in the classroom. On the basis of existing research and theory, they identified a set of classroom dimensions differentially related to the adoption of each goal orientation. For example, to assess a mastery goal structure, students were asked to rate their agreement with items related to the importance of understanding their work, learning from their mistakes, and working hard to learn in their classrooms. Building on this research,

TABLE 1   Dimensions of the TARGET system*

Task dimension
  Variety, challenge, organization, and interest level of learning activities

Authority dimension
  Opportunities to take responsibility for learning, to make decisions, and to assume
  leadership role

Recognition dimension
  Incentives and rewards focused on individual effort, improvement, and accomplishments

Grouping dimension
  Heterogeneous grouping structures that promote peer collaboration and cooperation

Evaluation dimension
  Evaluation systems that are varied, private, and assess individual progress, improvement,
  and mastery

Timing dimension
  Opportunities to plan schedules and complete assignments at appropriate and optimal
  rates

*From Ames (1992a,b).

Ames (1992a,b) developed the TARGET system for identifying key instructional practices associated with a mastery or performance orientation in the classroom. The TARGET system focuses on instructional strategies related to task assignments (T), authority relations (A), recognition systems (R), grouping procedures (G), evaluation practices (E), and use of time (T). Examples of instructional practices that would potentially emphasize a mastery goal structure are shown in Table 1. Researchers have recently used the TARGET system to create survey instruments to assess students' perceptions of the goal structure of high school (Greene et al. 2004) and college (Church et al. 2001) classes.

Patterns of Adaptive Learning Survey (PALS)

Midgley and her colleagues (2002) have developed a variety of methods to assess the salience of different goal structures in the classroom. The Patterns of Adaptive Learning Survey (PALS) has been widely used to assess students' perceptions of the classroom goal structures, as well as personal goal orientations. Building on the research of Ames (1992a), the PALS goal structure measures focus on classroom- or school-level practices that reflect either mastery- or performance-oriented instructional practices. Sample items from the PALS for assessing classroom goal structures are presented in Table 2. These scales demonstrate high internal consistency (Midgley 2002). In addition, confirmatory factor analyses procedures indicate that classroom goal structures are distinct from personal goal orientations (Wolters 2004). However, as described below, students' perceptions of classroom goal structures are predictive of the types of personal goals students adopt in the classroom.

TABLE 2   Sample items to assess classroom goal structures: Patterns of Adaptive Learning Survey*

Mastery goal structure

    My teacher thinks mistakes are okay as long as we are learning.

    My teacher wants us to understand our work, not just memorize it.

    My teacher really wants us to enjoy learning new things.

    My teacher recognizes us for trying hard.

    My teacher gives us time to really explore and understand new ideas.

Performance goal structure

    My teacher points out those students who get good grades as an example to all of us.

    My teacher lets us know who gets the highest scores on a test.

    My teacher makes it obvious when certain students are not doing well on their work.

    My teacher tells us how we compare with other students.

    Only a few students do really well in my class.

    My teacher calls on smart students more than on other students.

---

*From Anderman & Midgley (2002), Midgley et al. (1997).

PALS researchers have also collected information from teachers about their goal-related approaches to instruction (Urdan et al. 1998). From a list of statements, teachers were asked to identify instructional strategies they used in their classroom. Items assessed teachers' emphasis on mastery goals ("In my classroom, I stress to my students that I want them to understand their work, not memorize it") and performance goals ("In my classroom, I point out those students who do well academically, as a model for other students"). Students of these teachers were also asked to provide reports of the classroom goal structure. Results indicate low positive correlations between teacher and student reports of the same goal emphasis. Additionally, these two sources of data each contributed uniquely to the prediction of student outcomes (Urdan et al. 1998).

Observational and Multimethod Studies of Classroom Goal Structures

Meece (1991) combined survey and observational data to study differences in the goal structures of 10 elementary science classrooms. Using classroom means on student mastery goal ratings, classes were characterized as low or high mastery. Observational records were then analyzed to identify differences in teaching approaches. The results revealed that teachers of low- and high-mastery-oriented students differed in the degree to which they (a) promoted meaningful learning and understanding, (b) adapted instruction to the developmental levels and personal interests of their students, (c) established learning structures supportive of student autonomy and peer collaboration, and (d) emphasized the intrinsic value of learning. In a similar study, Patrick et al. (2001) used the PALS measures of classroom goal structures to identify 4 fifth-grade classrooms that were perceived by students as emphasizing either (a) high mastery and low performance, (b) high performance and low mastery, (*c*) both high mastery and performance, and (*d*) both low mastery and performance. Observational data were then used to compare the instructional practices of those teachers. Overall, there were a number of differences in practices between the high- and low-mastery-oriented classrooms and many fewer differences between the high- and low-performance classes. Two themes that distinguished the high- and low-mastery-oriented teachers were (*a*) differences in teachers' apparent implicit theories of how students learn, and (*b*) the interface between the social and affective climate of the classrooms with the academic dimension (see Anderman et al. 2002).

In another study, Turner and her colleagues (2002) used multiple methods to examine instructional variables related to students' use of avoidance strategies in mathematics. In this study, qualitative analyses of classroom discourse suggested that high-mastery/low-avoidance classrooms were characterized by instructional practices such as affording students the opportunity to demonstrate new abilities, providing motivational support for learning, and helping students to understand complex topics. When combined with data on student outcomes, findings indicated that perceptions of a mastery goal structure were related to less frequent use of avoidance strategies.

CLASSROOM GOAL STRUCTURES, PERSONAL GOALS, AND ACHIEVEMENT BEHAVIOR

We discussed above how students' personal achievement goals shape their behavior and learning in educational settings. How might classroom goal structures play a role in these processes? Classroom goal structures are generally viewed as precursors of students' personal goal orientations, which are thought to have a more proximal influence on motivation and achievement patterns (Church et al. 2001, Greene et al. 2004, Nolen 2001, Nolen & Haladyna 1990, Roeser et al. 1996, Urdan 2004). Additionally, student characteristics such as gender, ability level, or existing goal orientations are believed to influence the ways students perceive the classroom environment (Roeser et al. 1996). For the most part, studies using path analysis methods support these claims. Students' personal goal orientations correspond with their perceptions of the classroom goal structure (Anderman & Midgley 1997, Roeser et al. 1996, Urdan 2004), and these relations are found even when differences in student characteristics are controlled. When students perceive their classrooms or schools as emphasizing effort and understanding, they are more likely to adopt mastery-oriented goals. Conversely, students are more likely to adopt performance-oriented goals when they perceive their school environment as focused on competition for grades and social comparisons of ability. Consistent with earlier research, students' personal goals in turn are related in the expected manner to various motivation, strategy use, and performance measures. Thus, several studies indicate that classroom goal structures influence student behavior and learning by shaping the type of personal goals that students adopt.

There is also some evidence to suggest that perceptions of the classroom goal structure may exert a direct effect on outcome measures as well. The use of multi-level data analysis procedures enables researchers to test the predictive influence of classroom goal structures at both the individual and classroom levels (Kaplan et al. 2002b, Turner et al. 2002, Urdan et al. 1998, Wolters 2004). In this research, learning environments may be characterized as having either a greater mastery or performance focus (or a simultaneous focus on both mastery and performance) when students' perceptions of the goal structure are aggregated to the classroom or school level.

Evidence to date indicates that approximately 5% to 35% of the variation in students' goal structure perceptions is related to classroom differences. When added to the analyses, mean perceptions of the classroom goal structure explain variance in some outcome measures not explained by individual perceptions of classroom goal structures, personal achievement goals, or student background characteristics. For example, Turner and her colleagues (2002) reported that aggregated perceptions of the classroom emphasis on mastery emerged as a significant negative predictor of avoidance behaviors in a large sample of sixth-grade students. Similarly, Kaplan and colleagues (2002b) found that ninth-grade students reported less disruptive behavior in classes perceived on the average as emphasizing a mastery goal structure. In another study of junior high school students, Wolters (2004) found that mean perceptions of performance-approach goal structures explained variance in students' self-efficacy ratings, over and above students' personal achievement goals and background characteristics. Studies using multilevel data analysis procedures also reveal that teachers' reports of their instructional practices can also explain classroom differences in some student outcome measures (Anderman et al. 2001, Anderman & Young 1994, Kaplan et al. 2002b), but these relations generally are not as strong as individual or group-level perceptions of the learning environment. Therefore, it is the students' subjective perceptions that are most critical for understanding achievement-related patterns in the classroom (Ames 1992a, Meece et al. 2003, Ryan & Grolnick 1986).

APPLICATIONS OF GOAL THEORY TO SCHOOL TRANSITIONS AND REFORM

School Transitions and Goal Structures

Research generally indicates negative effects of the transition from elementary school to middle school on student motivation (e.g., Eccles & Midgley 1989, Wigfield et al. 1991). Eccles & Midgley (1989) argued that the contexts of most middle schools focus less on intrinsic involvement with tasks, and more on grades and comparisons, than do elementary schools. Whereas Eccles & Midgley's arguments were not based in goal theory, they strongly echoed the sentiments of goal theorists. More recently, empirical research has demonstrated that Eccles and Midgley's observations are supported when examined via the lens of goal theory.

For example, in one study, Midgley et al. (1995) examined the self-reported instructional practices of elementary and middle school teachers. Results indicated that elementary school teachers reported using instructional practices that emphasized mastery goals more than did middle school teachers. In a related study, Anderman & Midgley (1997) conducted longitudinal research examining changes in perceived goal structures across the transition from elementary to middle school. Results indicated that students perceived a greater emphasis on mastery goals during instruction prior to the middle school transition than after the transition. In addition, students reported more of an emphasis on performance goals after the transition to middle school than before. In another longitudinal study, Anderman & Anderman (1999) found that personal mastery goals decreased and personal performance goals increased as students made the transition from elementary to middle school.

Goal orientation also is related to other changes in motivation across the middle school transition. Anderman (1999) examined changes in students' reported levels of affect before and after the transition to middle school. Results indicated that perceptions of a performance goal structure in classrooms predicted a decline in positive affect across the transition. The Anderman & Anderman (1999) study also found that increases in performance goals across the transition were negatively associated with perceptions of school belonging, whereas increases in mastery orientation across the transition were associated positively with a perceived sense of school belonging.

Applications of Goal Theory to School Reform

Achievement goal research has focused on examining student outcomes in laboratory or classroom settings. However, a few researchers have used goal orientation theory to help guide school reform. Most prominently, Midgley & Maehr (1999) engaged in several projects aimed at the reform of school-wide and classroom-specific instructional practices, based on achievement goal theory. Briefly summarized, these researchers worked with teachers, parents, and administrators at both the elementary and middle school level to examine and reform instructional practices in line with achievement goal–orientation theory. Working groups met for several years to critically examine school policies and practices in light of mastery and performance goals. Instructional staff members were continuously asked to examine the potential effects of their schools' policies on a variety of outcomes. More specifically, staff members considered whether individual policies fostered mastery or performance goals.

Using a quasi-experimental design, Maehr & Midgley (1999) demonstrated that the schools were able to change their policies and practices in order to foster the development of personal mastery goals in students. Teachers consciously chose to emphasize mastery goals over performance goals, and the various changes in practice and policy that were implemented had positive effects on a number of outcomes (e.g., Anderman et al. 1999, Maehr & Midgley 1996, Midgley & Maehr 1999). For example, in the middle school study, longitudinal analyses indicated that students who made the transition from elementary school to the middle school that had used goal theory to guide reform exhibited fewer shifts toward performance and extrinsic goals over time than did students who transitioned into a more performance-oriented comparison school (Anderman et al. 1999).

Goal Structures and Current Reforms in Education

This chapter began with a discussion of current school reform efforts. Of the reforms currently underway in America's schools, the *No Child Left Behind Act of 2001* (NCLB) is expected to have the most widespread impact on students, teachers, and schools. This legislation requires school personnel to assess annually students' progress in reading and mathematics from grade 3 to 8, to increase teacher quality, to use scientifically validated teaching practices, and to provide alternatives for parents when schools are low performing. The implementation and enforcement of NCLB have sparked a good deal of controversy. For motivation researchers, the major concern is the impact of testing and accountability on teacher and students on the motivational climate on classrooms and schools. Although public scrutiny of test scores may motivate teachers and students to work harder (Roderick & Engel 2001), research on classrooms goal structures suggests that a focus on testing and evaluation can lead to a performance orientation in classrooms and schools. For older and high-ability students, a performance goal structure may enhance motivation and achievement. However, studies of elementary and middle school students, who will be most affected by NCLB, show a different pattern. For these students, performance goals are negatively related to intrinsic motivation, to adaptive forms of coping in the presence of challenge and failure, and to deeper processing of course material. Performance goal structures are also correlated with greater self-reported cheating and disruptive behaviors in the classroom, which can reduce learning opportunities for all students. A careful examination of the effects of NCLB on student achievement, motivation, and emotional well-being is needed to address current controversies in the field.

SUMMARY

In the past 25 years, goal theories of achievement have emerged as an important framework for analyzing the influence of learning environments on a range of developmental and learning outcomes. Much of this research indicates that young people adopt the most positive and adaptive approach to learning when the school environment emphasizes learning, understanding, and improving skills and knowledge. Although classroom environments that are focused on demonstrating ability and competing for grades can increase the self-efficacy beliefs and academic performance of some students, evidence suggests that many young people experience diminished motivation under these conditions. Students also report more disruptive behaviors (teasing, talking out of turn, etc.) as well as increases in school truancy and academic cheating under performance goal structures (Anderman & Midgley 2002, Kaplan et al. 2002a, Roeser & Eccles 1998).

Results across studies also emphasize the important role of students' perceptions of their learning environments (Schunk & Meece 1992). We have known for some time that young people interpret and respond differently to their schooling experiences. To some degree, students' perceptions may resemble teachers' or observers' reports. However, the "functional significance" of students' classroom and school experiences is most important in studies of children's development in school settings (Ryan & Grolnick 1986, p. 550). It is important therefore to examine the school environment from the learners' perspective (McCombs 2003, Meece et al. 2003).

One intriguing anomaly in achievement goal research is the lack of strong relations between mastery goals and student achievement. Students who are master oriented report a desire to learn and to improve their abilities, yet this personal and classroom goal focus is generally unrelated to measures of academic performance, such as grades and test scores, when prior ability is controlled (Anderman & Midgley 1997, Elliot & Church 1997, Elliot et al. 1999, Harackiewicz et al. 2000, Herman et al. 2005, Roeser et al. 1996, Skaalvik 1997, Wolters 2004). In part, this missing link may be due to how academic performance is measured. Most measures of achievement are not designed to assess a student's deep understanding of a concept or content area. Grant & Dweck (2003) recently reported that mastery goals show stronger positive relations to performance measures when a high degree of challenge is present, when processing of complex or difficult material is needed, or when the learning task itself is personally valued. Additionally, there is evidence to suggest that the influence of mastery goals on learning outcomes may be mediated through self-efficacy beliefs (Roeser et al. 1996) or deep processing strategies (Grant & Dweck 2003). Accordingly, as originally conceived, learning or mastery goals set in motion various affective or cognitive processes that have a more immediate impact on academic performance. The processes by which mastery goals affect academic performance needs further examination (Grant & Dweck 2003, Herman et al. 2005). Moreover, most studies of classroom goal structures pay little attention to the quality of instruction students receive (Meece et al. 2003). A mastery goal focus is likely to have a greater impact on student achievement, especially for students who lack prerequisite knowledge and skills, when teaching practices facilitate mastery of concepts and content. Additional studies are needed to examine the quality of instruction students receive in mastery-focused classrooms.

The *Annual Review of Psychology* is online at http://psych.annualreviews.org

LITERATURE CITED

Ames C. 1992a. Classrooms: goals, structures, and student motivation. *J. Educ. Psychol.* 84:261–71

Ames C. 1992b. Achievement goals and the classroom climate. In *Student Perceptions in the Classroom*, ed. DH Schunk, JL Meece, pp. 327–48. Hillsdale, NJ: Erlbaum

Ames C, Archer J. 1988. Achievement goals in the classroom: student learning strategies and motivation processes. *J. Educ. Psychol.* 80:260–67

Anderman EM, Anderman EM. 1999. Social predictors of changes in students' achievement goal orientations. *Contemp. Educ. Psychol.* 25:21–37

Anderman EM, Eccles JS, Yoon KS, Roeser R, Wigfield A, Blumenfeld P. 2001. Learning to value mathematics and reading: relations to mastery and performance-oriented instructional practices. *Contemp. Educ. Psychol.* 26(1):76–95

Anderman EM, Griesinger T, Westerfield G. 1998. Motivation and cheating during early adolescence. *J. Educ. Psychol.* 90:84–93

Anderman EM, Maehr ML, Midgley C. 1999. Declining motivation after the transition to middle school: schools can make a difference. *J. Res. Dev. Educ.* 32:131–47

Anderman EM, Midgley C. 1997. Changes in personal achievement goals and the perceived goal structures across the transition to middle schools. *Contemp. Educ. Psychol.* 22:269–98

Anderman EM, Midgley C. 2002. Methods for studying goals, goal structures, and patterns of adaptive learning. In *Goals, Goal Structures, and Patterns of Adaptive Learning*, ed. C Midgley, pp. 1–53. Mahwah, NJ: Erlbaum

Anderman EM, Young AJ. 1994. Motivation and strategy use in science: individual differences and classroom effects. *J. Res. Sci. Teach.* 31(8):811–31

Anderman EM, Wolters C. 2006. Goals, values, and affects: influences on student motivation. In *Handbook of Educational Psychology*, ed. P Alexander, P Winne. New York: Simon & Schuster/Macmillan. 2nd ed. In press

Anderman L. 1999. Classroom goal orientation, school belonging, and social goals as predictors of students' positive and negative affect following the transition to middle school. *J. Res. Dev. Educ.* 32:89–103

Anderman L, Anderman E. 1999. Social predictors of change in students' achievement goal orientations. *Contemp. Educ. Psychol.* 25:21–37

Anderman LH, Patrick H, Hruda LZ, Linnenbrink E. 2002. Observing classroom goal structures to clarify and expand goal theory. In *Goals, Goal Structures, and Patterns of Adaptive Learning*, ed. C Midgley, pp. 243–78. Mahwah, NJ: Erlbaum

Atkinson JW. 1964. *An Introduction to Motivation.* Princeton, NJ: Van Nostrand

Bandura A. 1986. *Social Foundations of Thought and Action: A Social Cognitive Theory.* Englewood Cliffs, NJ: Prentice Hall

Barron K, Harackiewicz J. 2001. Achievement goals and optimal motivation: testing multiple goal models. *J. Personal. Soc. Psychol.* 80:706–22

Bouffard T, Boisvert T, Vezeau C, Larouche C. 1995. The impact of goal orientation on self-regulation and performance among college students. *Br. J. Educ. Psychol.* 65:317–29

Church MA, Elliot A, Gable S. 2001. Perceptions of classroom environment, achievement goals, and achievement outcomes. *J. Educ. Psychol.* 93:43–54

Dweck CS, Elliot ES. 1983. Achievement motivation. In *Handbook of Child Psychology. Socialization, Personality, and Social Development*, ed. EM Hetherington, pp. 643–91. New York: Wiley

Eccles JS. 1983. Expectancies, values, and academic behaviors. In *Achievement and Achievement Motives*, ed. JT Spence, pp. 75–176. San Francisco: Freeman

Eccles JS. 2004. Schools, academic motivation, and stage-environment fit. In *Handbook of Adolescent Psychology*, ed. RM Lerner, L Steinberg, pp.125–53. Hoboken, NJ: Wiley. 2nd ed.

Eccles JS, Midgley CM. 1989. Stage-environment fit: developmentally appropriate classrooms for young adolescents. In *Research on Motivation in Education*, ed. C Ames, R Ames, pp. 139–86. San Diego, CA: Academic

Elliot AJ, Church MA. 1997. A hierarchical model of approach and avoidance achievement motivation. *J. Personal. Soc. Psychol.* 72(1):218–32

Elliot AJ, Harackiewicz JM. 1996. Approach and avoidance achievement goals and intrinsic motivation: a mediational analysis. *J. Personal. Soc. Psychol.* 70(3):461–75

Elliot AJ, McGregor H. 2001. A 2 × 2 achievement goal framework. *J. Personal. Soc. Psychol.* 80:501–19

Elliot AJ, McGregor H, Gable S. 1999. Achievement goals, study strategies, and exam performance: a mediational analysis. *J. Educ. Psychol.* 91:549–63

Elliot E, Dweck C. 1988. Goals: an approach to motivation and achievement. *J. Personal. Soc. Psychol.* 54:5–12

Graham S, Golan S. 1991. Motivational influences on cognition: task involvement, ego involvement, and depth of information processing. *J. Educ. Psychol.* 83:187–96

Grant H, Dweck C. 2003. Clarifying achievement goals and their impact. *J. Personal. Soc. Psychol.* 85:541–53

Greene BA, Miller RB. 1996. Influences on achievement: goals, perceived ability, and cognitive engagement. *Contemp. Educ. Psychol.* 21:181–92

Greene BA, Miller RB, Crowson M, Duke B, Akey K. 2004. Predicting high school students' cognitive engagement and achievement: contributions of classroom perceptions and motivation. *Contemp. Educ. Psychol.* 29: 499–517

Harackiewicz JM, Barron KE, Elliot AJ. 1998. Rethinking achievement goals: when are they adaptive for college students and why? *Educ. Psychol.* 33:1–21

Harackiewicz JM, Barron KE, Pintrich PR, Elliot AJ, Thrash T. 2002. Revision of achievement goal theory: necessary and illuminating. *J. Educ. Psychol.* 94:638–45

Harackiewicz JM, Barron KE, Tauer J, Carter S, Elliot AJ. 2000. Short-term and long-term consequences of achievement goals: predicting interest and performance over time. *J. Educ. Psychol.* 92:316–30

Herman P, Gomez L, Tester K. 2005. *Mastery goals in middle grades science classrooms: Are they really related to achievement?* Poster presented at Annu. Meet. Am. Educ. Res. Assoc., Montreal

Kaplan A, Gheen M, Midgley C. 2002a. Classroom goal structure and student disruptive behaviour. *Br. J. Educ. Psychol.* 72:191–212

Kaplan A, Middleton MJ, Urdan T, Midgley C. 2002b. Achievement goals and goal structures. In *Goals, Goal Structures, and Patterns of Adaptive Learning*, ed. C Midgley, pp. 21–55. Hillsdale, NJ: Erlbaum

Maehr M, Midgley C. 1991. Enhancing student motivation: a schoolwide approach. *Educ. Psychol.* 26:399–427

Maehr M, Midgley C. 1996. *Transforming School Cultures*. Boulder, CO: Westview

Maehr M, Nicholls JG. 1980. Culture and achievement motivation: a second look. In *Studies in Cross-Cultural Psychology*, ed. N Warren, pp. 221–67. New York: Academic

McCombs B. 2003. Applying educational psychology knowledge base in educational reform: from research to application to policy. In *Comprehensive Handbook of Psychology*, ed. WM Reynolds, GE Miller, Vol. 7, pp. 583–607. New York: Wiley

Meece JL. 1991. The classroom context and children's motivational goals. In *Advances in Achievement Motivation Research*, ed. M Maehr, P Pintrich, pp. 261–85. New York: Academic

Meece JL, Blumenfeld PC, Hoyle R. 1988. Students' goal orientations and cognitive engagement in classroom activities. *J. Educ. Psychol.* 80:514–23

Meece JL, Herman P, McCombs B. 2003. Relations of learner-centered teaching practices to adolescents' achievement goals. *Int. J. Educ. Res.* 39:457–75

Meece JL, Holt K. 1993. Variations in students' achievement goal patterns. *J. Educ. Psychol.* 85:582–90

Meece JL, Miller SD. 2001. A longitudinal analysis of elementary school students' achievement goals in literacy activities. *Contemp. Educ. Psychol.* 26:454–80

Midgley C. 2002. *Goals, Goal Structures, and Patterns of Adaptive Learning.* Hillsdale, NJ: Erlbaum

Midgley C, Anderman EM, Hicks L. 1995. Differences between elementary and middle school teachers and students: a goal theory approach. *J. Early Adolesc.* 15(1):90–113

Midgley C, Kaplan A, Middleton M. 2001. Performance-approach goals: good for what, for whom, under what circumstances, and at what cost? *J. Educ. Psychol.* 93:77–86

Midgley C, Kaplan A, Middleton M, Maehr ML, Urdan T, et al. 1998. The development and validation of scales assessing students' achievement goal orientations. *Contemp. Educ. Psychol.* 23:113–31

Midgley C, Maehr M. 1999. Using motivation theory to guide school reform. In *Promoting Positive Outcomes: Issues in Children's and Families' Lives*, ed. AJ Reynolds, HJ Walberg, RP Weissberg, pp. 129–59. Washington, DC: Child Welfare League Am.

Midgley C, Maehr M, Hicks L, Roeser R, Urdan T, et al. 1997. *Patterns of Adaptive Learning Survey (PALS).* Ann Arbor: Univ. Mich. Press

Miller R, Greene B, Montalvo G, Ravindran B, Nichols J. 1996. Engagement in academic work: the role of learning goals, future consequences, pleasing others, and perceived ability. *Contemp. Educ. Psychol.* 21:388–422

Nicholls JG. 1984. Achievement motivation: conception of ability, subjective experience, task choice, and performance. *Psychol. Rev.* 91:328–46

Nicholls JG. 1989. *The Competitive Ethos and Democratic Education.* Cambridge, MA: Harvard Univ. Press

Nolen SB. 1988. Reasons for studying: motivational orientations and study strategies. *Cogn. Instruct.* 5:269–87

Nolen SB. 2001. Learning environment, motivation, and achievement in high school science. *J. Res. Sci. Teach.* 40:347–68

Nolen SB, Haladyna TM. 1990. Personal and environmental influences on students' beliefs about effective study strategies. *Contemp. Educ. Psychol.* 15:116–30

Patrick H, Anderman LH, Ryan AM, Edelin K, Midgley C. 2001. Teachers' communication of goal orientations in four fifth-grade classrooms. *Elem. School J.* 102:35–58

Pintrich P. 2000. Multiple goals, multiple pathways: the role of goal orientation in learning and achievement. *J. Educ. Psychol.* 92:544–55

Pintrich P, Schunk D. 2002. *Motivation in Education. Theory, Research, and Applications.* Upper Saddle River, NJ: Merrill/Prentice Hall. 2nd ed.

Roderick M, Engel M. 2001. The grasshopper and the ant: motivational responses of low-achieving students to high stakes testing. *Educ. Eval. Policy Anal.* 23:197–227

Roeser RW, Eccles JS. 1998. Adolescents' perceptions of middle school: relation to longitudinal changes in academic and psychological adjustment. *J. Res. Adolesc.* 8:123–58

Roeser RW, Midgley C, Urdan TC. 1996. Perceptions of the school psychological environment and early adolescents' psychological and behavioral functioning in school: the mediating role of goals and belonging. *J. Educ. Psychol.* 88:408–22

Ryan R, Grolnick W. 1986. Origins and pawns in the classroom. Self-reports and projective assessments of individual differences in children's perceptions. *J. Personal. Soc. Psychol.* 50:550–58

Schunk DH. 1991. Self-efficacy and academic motivation. *Educ. Psychol.* 26:207–31

Schunk DH, Meece JL, eds. 1992. *Student Perceptions in the Classroom: Causes and Consequences*, pp. 287–306. Hillsdale, NJ: Erlbaum

Skaalvik EM. 1997. Self-enhancing and self-defeating ego orientation: relation with task and avoidance orientation, achievement, self-perceptions, and anxiety. *J. Educ. Psychol.* 89:71–81

Stipek DJ, Kowalski P. 1989. Learned helplessness in task-orienting versus performance-orienting testing conditions. *J. Educ. Psychol.* 81:384–91

Thorkildsen TA, Nicholls JG. 1998. Fifth-graders achievement orientations and beliefs: individual and classroom differences. *J. Educ. Psychol.* 90:179–201

Turner JC, Midgley C, Meyer DK, Gheen MQ, Anderman E, et al. 2002. The classroom environment and students' reports of avoidance strategies in mathematics: a multi-method study. *J. Educ. Psychol.* 94:88–106

Urdan T. 2004. Predictors of academic self-handicapping and achievement: examining achievement goals, classroom goal structures, and culture. *J. Educ. Psychol.* 96:251–64

Urdan T, Midgley C, Anderman EM. 1998. The role of classroom goal structure in students' use of self-handicapping strategies. *Am. Educ. Res. J.* 35:101–35

Weiner B. 1979. A theory of motivation for some classroom experiences. *J. Educ. Psychol.* 71:3–25

Weiner B. 1990. History of motivational research in education. *J. Educ. Psychol.* 82:616–22

Wentzel KR. 1992. Motivation and achievement in adolescence: a multiple goals perspective. In *Student Perceptions in the Classroom: Causes and Consequences*, ed. DH Schunk, J Meece, pp. 287–306. Hillsdale, NJ: Erlbaum

Wigfield A, Eccles JS. 1992. The development of achievement task values: a theoretical analysis. *Dev. Rev.* 2:265–310

Wigfield A, Eccles JS. 2000. Expectancy-value theory of achievement motivation. *Contemp. Educ. Psychol.* 25:68–81

Wigfield A, Eccles JS, MacIver D, Reuman D, Midgley C. 1991. Transitions at adolescence: changes in children's domain-specific self-perceptions and general self-esteem across the transition to junior high school. *Dev. Psychol.* 27:552–65

Wolters C. 2004. Advancing achievement goal theory: using goal structures and goal orientations to predict students' motivation, cognition, and achievement. *J. Educ. Psychol.* 96:236–50

Wolters C, Yu S, Pintrich P. 1996. The relation between goal orientation and students' motivational beliefs and self-regulated learning. *Learn. Individ. Differ.* 8:211–38

Annu. Rev. Psychol. 2006. 57:505–28
doi: 10.1146/annurev.psych.57.102904.190146
Copyright © 2006 by Annual Reviews. All rights reserved
First published online as a Review in Advance on September 7, 2005

ANALYSIS OF LONGITUDINAL DATA:
The Integration of Theoretical Model, Temporal Design, and Statistical Model

Linda M. Collins

*The Methodology Center and Department of Human Development and Family Studies,
Pennsylvania State University, University Park, Pennsylvania 16802-6504;
email: lmc8@psu.edu*

Key Words intensive longitudinal, longitudinal panel, growth models, latent transition analysis

■ **Abstract** This article argues that ideal longitudinal research is characterized by the seamless integration of three elements: (*a*) a well-articulated theoretical model of change observed using (*b*) a temporal design that affords a clear and detailed view of the process, with the resulting data analyzed by means of (*c*) a statistical model that is an operationalization of the theoretical model. Two general varieties of theoretical models are considered: models in which the time-related change of primary interest is continuous, and those in which it is characterized by movement between discrete states. In addition, two general types of temporal designs are considered: the longitudinal panel design and the intensive longitudinal design. For each general category of theoretical models, some of the analytic possibilities available for longitudinal panel designs and for intensive longitudinal designs are discussed. The article concludes with brief discussions of two issues particularly relevant to longitudinal research—missing data and measurement—and a few words about exploratory research.

CONTENTS

INTRODUCTION AND OVERVIEW

This is an exciting time in analysis of longitudinal data. Interest in this topic has grown steadily since the watershed Harris volume (1963) and has been reflected in other books such as Collins & Horn (1991), Collins & Sayer (2001), Gottman (1995), Nagin (2005), Nesselroade & Baltes (1979), Singer & Willett (2003a), and von Eye (1990a,b), as well as in countless journal articles. Computing resources are becoming increasingly powerful, and readily available specialized software enables scientists to apply new and highly sophisticated statistical analyses in their work. Some rich longitudinal data sets have been archived and are available to the scientific public for statistical analysis. Further, creative use of new technology, such as handheld computers and other devices, is making collection of longitudinal data characterized by more frequent and intense measurement increasingly feasible (e.g., Shiffman & Stone 2006, Walls & Schafer 2006).

As more longitudinal studies have been undertaken, and the length and intensity of longitudinal studies have increased, a fundamental tension has emerged between what Molenaar (2004) has termed "attention to interindividual variation," that is, variation between individuals, and "attention to intraindividual variation," that is, variation within individuals. Approaches focusing on interindividual variation emphasize establishment of general developmental principles that apply to all individuals. In contrast, approaches focusing on intraindividual variation emphasize understanding change within the individual, with establishment of general principles a secondary goal. This article takes the perspective that growth is a phenomenon that occurs within the individual, and therefore intraindividual variability is a primary interest in statistical modeling of longitudinal data. The importance of modeling intraindividual variability has emerged forcefully in longitudinal research (e.g., Nesselroade 1991, Rogosa et al. 1982, Rogosa & Willett 1985) and has been the impetus behind the development of many of the statistical procedures discussed here. At the same time, in science we are always engaged in inductive reasoning and so attempting to abstract general principles about interindividual variability in intraindividual change is the ultimate goal (Curran & Wirth 2004).

The main purpose of this article is not to provide an exhaustive review of analytic approaches for longitudinal data; such a review could take up this entire volume! This article also will not cover the important topic of causal inference in longitudinal data, which was discussed at length in Raudenbush (2000). Instead, the aim is to suggest a conceptual framework for longitudinal research methods, and to give the reader a flavor for some of the analytic possibilities that are now available to behavioral scientists who are interested in addressing research questions about change in empirical longitudinal data.

A CONCEPTUAL FRAMEWORK FOR LONGITUDINAL RESEARCH

Suppose a social or behavioral scientist conducts statistical analysis of longitudinal data with the objective of addressing a scientific question that involves the test of a theory. This endeavor is successful if the scientific question is correctly and unambiguously answered. Of course, in empirical settings it cannot be known whether the correct answer has been identified, so it is impossible to know whether success has been achieved in any particular instance. Most likely, the best that can be accomplished is an incomplete or partially correct answer. Nevertheless, "correct and unambiguous" is a useful ideal that behavioral scientists would like to approach as closely as they can. It is possible to identify a conceptual framework for evaluating whether longitudinal research is likely to approach the ideal of providing correct and unambiguous answers to research questions.

Longitudinal research is most likely to approach the ideal described above when it is characterized by the seamless integration of three elements: (*a*) a well-articulated theoretical model of change observed using (*b*) a temporal design that affords a clear and detailed view of the process, with the resulting data analyzed by means of (*c*) a statistical model that is an operationalization of the theoretical model. (The integration of these three elements is necessary to ideal longitudinal research but not sufficient.) Let us consider each of these three elements in turn.

Element 1: The Theoretical Model of Change

The theoretical model is a clear and comprehensive statement about the nature of the change phenomenon that is to be observed. There are many aspects of change to be considered; a helpful list is contained in McGrath & Tschan (2004). Below are listed a few aspects of change that serve as examples, and are of particular interest in the present article:

- The general or characteristic shape of change, e.g., linear, quadratic, or an irregular series of ups and downs.
- Whether there is periodicity or a cyclical nature to the change.
- Whether change is primarily a function of calendar time, a function of some other variable that is related to time (e.g., pubertal status), or in some sense is self-regulating or self-exciting.

- What time-invariant and time-varying covariates may predict change.
- Whether the relation between a covariate and the change phenomenon may itself be time varying.
- Whether the process is more or less continuous, characterized by change in level or amount; discrete, characterized by occurrence of events; or contains elements of both kinds of change.
- Whether there is meaningful interindividual variability in change.

Element 2: The Temporal Design Used to Observe the Change Phenomenon

In the natural sciences, the investigator may choose an instrument, such as a microscope, to provide a view of the phenomenon of interest. In the social and behavioral sciences, research design is a similarly important instrument that provides a view of the change phenomenon of interest. As discussed in Shadish et al. (2002), design choices must be made with great care, because some designs will result in a detailed and unobstructed view of the change phenomenon, whereas others will provide an unsatisfying or even misleading view.

An often-overlooked aspect of design that can have a substantial impact on the scientist's view of a change phenomenon is the temporal design (Collins & Graham 2002), consisting of the timing, frequency, and spacing of observations in a longitudinal study. Boker & Nesselroade (2002), Cohen (1991), Collins & Graham (1991, 2002), Gollob & Reichardt (1987, 1991), Hertzog & Nesselroade (2003), Kelly & McGrath (1988), McGrath & Tschan (2004), Singer & Willett (2003), and Windle & Davies (1999) all have argued that the most appropriate temporal design is one chosen not primarily on the basis of logistics, but instead on the basis of correspondence with the theoretical model of change. Change that occurs between observations, before a study is begun, or after a study is concluded, is not observed and therefore can at best only be inferred. Thus, for example, if the theoretical model suggests that change is rapid, or characterized by many ups and downs, then more frequent observation may be called for. If periodicity is anticipated, then the exact timing of observation may be an important consideration. If there is a particular period of time during which some important event is anticipated, then more intensive observation may be advisable at that time. (The term "time" as used here is not necessarily intended to mean literal clock time. Important outcomes may be a function of time-related variables such as pubertal development, grade in school, cognitive decline, and so on. In this case, it may make sense to express the temporal design in these terms rather than in terms of calendar time.)

Many investigators planning longitudinal studies consider only temporal designs calling for (*a*) evenly spaced observations (*b*) occurring at the same time for all study participants. However, virtually no contemporary statistical approaches to analysis of longitudinal data make the former requirement and the number that make the latter is dwindling thanks to increases in flexibility and sophistication in statistical modeling. There is little reason to fear that a temporal design informed by the theoretical model of change will complicate later data analysis, and every reason to expect that such a design is likely to provide satisfying answers to important scientific questions.

Collins & Graham (2002) explored the impact of the mismatch of theoretical model of change and temporal design on inferences about characteristics of change and relations between variables over time, and found that under many circumstances the impact can be considerable, resulting, for example, in failure to detect stages in a stage-sequential process, and incorrect conclusions about mediation. Given their findings and the pleas of the above-listed authors, it is surprising to the present author that the behavioral science community appears to give relatively little serious consideration to the impact that temporal design may have on the conclusions drawn in longitudinal research. For example, few peer-review journals routinely request that the choice of temporal design be justified scientifically or that empirical results be considered in the light of temporal design choices. This would appear to be a necessary step for understanding unexpected findings and for explaining the failure of results to replicate across studies with different temporal designs.

Element 3: The Statistical Model of Change

One critical aspect of testing theories about change in human behavior is fitting a model of the change process to empirical data. As is discussed in detail in this article, every approach to statistical analysis of longitudinal data implicitly or explicitly provides an operationalization of some model of the change process. In successful longitudinal research, the operationalization provided by the statistical model corresponds to the theoretical model of change. A mismatch of theoretical and statistical model will result in the addressing of irrelevant or even meaningless scientific questions. On the other hand, a close correspondence between theoretical and statistical model can provide an elegant test of a scientific hypothesis and a penetrating look at longitudinal data. With an unprecedented array of statistical models from which to choose, today's behavioral scientist has an excellent chance of identifying and applying a statistical model well suited to the theoretical model of interest.

Integration of the Three Elements

The seamless integration of theoretical model, temporal design, and statistical model is an ideal that rarely, if ever, is met in social and behavioral research. For some theoretical models of change, particularly those that are very sophisticated, a tailor-made statistical model may not yet be available, forcing the investigator to use a statistical model that is not completely appropriate. In many empirical settings, the degree of correspondence between the statistical model and the theoretical model is limited by the temporal design. To take a simple illustration, if a theoretical model of growth in a continuous outcome is highly complex, involving many peaks and valleys, and the temporal design provides data collected at only two points in time, the only choice of statistical model available to the investigator is linear growth, which clearly does not correspond to the theoretical model. Resource limitations, logistical considerations, and concerns such as the prospect of overburdening study participants frequently may mean that the best temporal design scientists reasonably can use will allow statistical modeling to provide only a rough approximation to a complex and nuanced theoretical model of human development. Nevertheless, this conceptual framework is useful in interpreting the results of longitudinal research. Consideration of the ways in which a particular study approaches or fails to approach the ideal of integration of theoretical model, temporal design, and statistical model may help to identify the strengths and limitations of the study, the generalizability and likely replicability of the conclusions, and directions for future research.

THE PRESENT ARTICLE

To help provide a framework for the present article, two general types of temporal designs are defined for further consideration. These definitions are to an extent arbitrary, and were chosen to allow comparison and contrast of analytic approaches. One is the longitudinal panel design, defined here as a design where there are relatively few occasions of measurement, say eight or fewer, and the observations are separated by at least six months. The second is the intensive longitudinal design, defined here as involving at least 20 occasions of measurement, spaced closely enough in time to provide a detailed look at change in the quantity being observed. The definitions leave a gray area between longitudinal panel and intensive longitudinal designs, in which, depending on the situation, a design may be considered in either category.

In the remainder of this article, two general varieties of theoretical models are considered: models in which the time-related change of primary interest is continuous, and those in which it is characterized by movement between discrete states (e.g., employment and unemployment). For each general category of theoretical models, some of the analytic possibilities available for longitudinal panel designs and for intensive longitudinal designs are discussed. The article concludes with brief discussions of two issues particularly relevant to longitudinal research, namely missing data and measurement, and a few words about exploratory research.

CHANGE IN CONTINUOUS VARIABLES

Overview

The most commonly used approach to modeling change in continuous variables is growth curve models. Growth curve models, such as hierarchical linear models

(Raudenbush 2000), fit growth trajectories for individuals and relate characteristics of these individual growth trajectories (e.g., slope) to covariates. The individual growth trajectory can be expressed as

$$Y_{ti} = \beta_{0i} + \beta_{1i} x_{ti} + e_{ti}$$

for a linear model of growth. Y_{ti} represents individual i's outcome score at time t, where $t = 1, \ldots T$; x_{ti} represents the measure of time for individual i; and β_{0i} and β_{1i} represent the intercept and slope, respectively, of linear growth for individual i. This is often referred to as the level-1 equation. The intercept and slope parameters are random effects; in other words, they may vary across individuals, as reflected in the need for the i subscript denoting individual. This leads directly to the level-2 equations:

$$\beta_{0i} = \gamma_{00} + u_{0i}$$

$$\beta_{1i} = \gamma_{10} + u_{1i}.$$

Consider a growth trajectory for individual A with intercept β_{0A} and slope β_{1A}. The level-2 equations state that individual A's intercept β_{0A} can be decomposed into two components: the grand mean of all the β_{0i}'s for all individuals, γ_{00}, and β_{0A}'s deviation from this grand mean, u_{0A}. Likewise, individual A's slope β_{1A} can be decomposed into two components: the grand mean of all the β_{1i}'s for all individuals, γ_{10}, and β_{1A}'s deviation from this grand mean, u_{1A}. Interindividual variability in intercepts is expressed in the variance of the u_{0i}'s, and interindividual variability in slope is expressed in the variance of the u_{1i}'s. It is possible to include predictors in addition to time (or even instead of time; Curran & Willoughby 2003) in the level-1 equation, and to include time-invariant predictors in the level-2 equation. As Curran (2003) showed, the hierarchical approach to growth modeling is in most cases identical to the structural equation model, or latent growth curve, approach developed by authors such as McArdle & Epstein (1987), Meredith & Tisak (1990), Muthén & Shedden (1999) and Willett & Sayer (1994).

Hierarchical linear models have proven to be a very useful general framework for fitting theoretical models of growth curves in continuous variables. In the following sections, growth curve approaches to analysis of data from both longitudinal panel designs and intensive longitudinal designs are discussed. This framework opens up the possibility of fitting some new varieties of theoretical models of change in intensive longitudinal data.

Longitudinal Panel Designs

Much longitudinal research is at the intersection of a theoretical model concerning change in continuous variables and a temporal design that is some version of a longitudinal panel design. Under these circumstances, the theoretical model that is fit in data will usually need to be limited to fairly simple polynomial models of growth. Even with this limitation, such models can be very sophisticated, particularly if several measurement occasions are available. Raudenbush (2000) and McArdle & Nesselroade (2003) provide excellent overviews of growth modeling for longitudinal panel designs. Below are listed a few brief examples of the many kinds of theoretical models that can be fit this way and the corresponding statistical models. For a more thorough treatment of the correspondence between theoretical and statistical growth curve models for continuous change, see Curran & Willoughby (2003).

DISCONTINUITY IN CONTINUOUS CHANGE: PIECEWISE GROWTH MODELS   Some theoretical models postulate that there is a discontinuity in continuous change; in other words, there is a distinct change point at which growth accelerates, decelerates, or levels off. This may simply be a change in acceleration, or it may represent a qualitative shift in some underlying process, so that different covariates are expected to predict different phases of the process. In piecewise growth models, the growth curve is divided into segments that are fit simultaneously with separate growth parameters. Cumsille et al. (2000) and Li et al. (2001) demonstrated how to fit piecewise growth curve models in which the change point is known and is the same for all subjects. Cudeck & Klebe (2002) presented an approach to piecewise growth models in which the change point may be unknown and estimated as a random effect. Even when discontinuity in continuous change is not expected, the piecewise approach may offer a straightforward and intuitively appealing alternative for fitting nonlinear models of growth.

STABILITY AND GROWTH: AUTOREGRESSIVE AND HYBRID MODELS   The autoregressive model figured prominently in early analyses of longitudinal data (Joreskog 1979). Rather than modeling change within individuals, this approach models stability by using a variable measured at one time to predict itself or another variable at a later time. Bollen & Curran (2004, Curran & Bollen 2001) and McArdle & Hamagami (2001) showed how to incorporate features of both the growth modeling and autoregressive approaches into a single hybrid model. This hybrid model can be used to examine stability and change simultaneously.

PATTERNS OF GROWTH: GROWTH MIXTURE MODELS   There are times when the investigator poses the question, what distinct patterns of growth characterize this sample? In other words, are there subgroups of individuals undergoing similar growth? Growth mixture models (Muthén 2001; Muthén & Muthén 2000; Muthén & Shedden 1999; Nagin 1999, 2005; Nagin & Tremblay 2001) identify subgroups corresponding to distinct patterns of growth in longitudinal data and can be used to estimate the prevalence of the patterns and to relate the patterns to covariates. For example, Nagin (1999) identified four prototypical trajectories of physical aggression in a sample of boys across ages 6 to 15. Using the group that never displayed any aggression as a baseline, Nagin found that having low-educated parents and a low IQ increased the risk of being in the groups characterized by chronic aggression and high levels of aggression followed by desistance, but did not increase the risk of being in the low-level aggression group. However, having a teen-aged mother increased the risk of membership in all the aggression groups.

Questions about the existence of distinctive growth patterns in data may arise simply due to a desire to obtain a descriptive sense of the "natural history" of growth in a data set. Other times questions may arise because it appears that relatively little of the variance in growth parameters can be accounted for by covariates. This suggests that there may be important covariates that have not been measured, or that there may be a complex system of interactions among the measured covariates. Under these circumstances, identifying meaningful patterns of growth and relating these patterns to covariates can be very illuminating. If there is a complex system of interactions among covariates, different covariates may predict growth parameters in different subgroups. Such effects are difficult to discern without identifying the subgroups, especially given that the overall effect of a covariate on a combined sample can be null even if it is a strong predictor in one or more subgroups.

A Variation on Longitudinal Panel Designs: Accelerated Longitudinal Designs

Some interesting developmental research questions involve continuous change unfolding across a period of time that may be years in duration. One alternative to a temporal design that involves observing the process over the entire period of development in a single cohort is an accelerated longitudinal design (Bell 1953, McArdle & Hamagami 2001). In an accelerated longitudinal design, multiple cohorts of different ages are observed longitudinally for a shorter period of time. The cohorts must be overlapping, so that for each cohort, there is at least one age at which at least one of the other cohorts is also observed. Then a statistical approach is used to combine the cohorts and estimate a single growth trajectory, extending from the youngest age observed to the oldest. The accelerated longitudinal design can save a significant amount of time, but it makes the assumption that there is no age-by-cohort interaction affecting development; in other words, it assumes that a single growth trajectory can reasonably represent all the cohorts. Duncan et al. (1996) combined data from four different overlapping age cohorts, each of which was measured at one-year intervals over a three-year period. This enabled them to estimate a growth trajectory for adolescent alcohol use extending from age 12 to age 17. They compared this growth trajectory with one based on a smaller single-cohort sample over the same age range, and found them to be essentially similar, suggesting that the assumption of no age-by-cohort interaction was met. Miyazaki & Raudenbush (2000) showed how to test this assumption empirically and presented a general framework for analysis of data from accelerated longitudinal designs.

Intensive Longitudinal Designs

Standard growth models extend directly to intensive longitudinal data, and are currently one of the most frequently chosen statistical models in this context. One very common implementation of intensive longitudinal designs in psychology is in controlled laboratory studies involving animals. In these studies, it is typical to have a nearly continuous record of important outcome behaviors, such as lever presses to obtain rewards, over several days or weeks. Donny et al. (2004) and Lanza et al. (2004) illustrated how to fit growth models to individual animal data and how to use a growth curve framework to address experimental hypotheses like the ones typically motivating laboratory studies. Growth models also can fit theoretical models of increased complexity. For example, in both animal and human data, intensive longitudinal designs may reveal periodic effects due to time of day, day of the week, weekday versus weekend, and so on. Walls et al. (2006) have provided a detailed exposition of modeling periodicity using a standard growth modeling approach.

FUNCTIONAL DATA ANALYSIS   The complexity of the theoretical models that motivate collecting intensive longitudinal data often goes beyond periodicity. Change over time may not be easily characterized by a polynomial. Instead, change may have many irregular ups and downs. There may be time-varying covariates, and some of these time-varying covariates may even have time-varying effects. A time-varying effect occurs when the strength and/or direction of a covariate changes as a function of time. It is even possible for an intervention to operate on an effect. For example, a drug abuse prevention program aimed at adolescents could reduce the influence of peer substance use on adolescent substance use; a therapy intervention aimed at depression could reduce the relation between everyday stressful events and anxiety. Functional data analysis (Fan & Gijbels 1996, Fok & Ramsay 2006, Li et al. 2006) provides a statistical model that is well suited both to these kinds of theoretical models and to intensive longitudinal data. Fok & Ramsay (2006) and Li et al. (2006) have illustrated how to apply functional data analysis in intensive longitudinal data using a growth modeling approach. Li et al. analyzed intensive longitudinal data on affect and urge to smoke collected in a sample of smokers enrolled in a cessation program. They found that urge to smoke was associated with negative affect, and that this relation grew stronger immediately after quitting smoking.

DYNAMICAL SYSTEMS   Inspired by the way change and relations between changing variables are represented in engineering, authors such as Boker (Boker & Graham 1998, Boker & Laurenceau 2006, Boker & Nesselroade 2002), who draws on dynamical systems theory, and Ramsay (2006), who draws on process control theory, have offered social and behavioral scientists new ways of thinking about growth. For example, dynamical systems theory includes the idea of intrinsic dynamics, which are features of a system that regulate change in order to maintain equilibrium. Boker & Laurenceau (2006) showed that the familiar autoregressive model can be considered a type of dynamical system that self-regulates. The dynamics of self-regulating systems can be coupled in order to examine how each system can affect regulation of the other, and the effect of external variables on the dynamical system can be examined. Using growth modeling, Boker & Laurenceau (2006) illustrated how to take a dynamical systems approach to model intimacy and disclosure in marriage. They considered each married couple a self-contained dynamical system, and examined how the systems might be coupled. They found that there was symmetric coupling between husband and wife intimacy; in other words, within a marriage, the husband's feelings of intimacy affected his wife's feelings of intimacy, and also the wife's feelings of intimacy affected her husband's. In contrast, they found that disclosure was better represented by asymmetric coupling. This means that the coupling relation went only one way; within a marriage, the husband's disclosure affected his wife's disclosure, but the wife's disclosure did not appear to affect her husband's.

CHANGE CHARACTERIZED BY MOVEMENT BETWEEN DISCRETE STATES

Overview

This section considers theoretical models of change characterized by movement between discrete states. The movement may be, for example, between healthy state to onset of a disease; employment to retirement; passing in and out of various patterns of substance use; and so on. Models involving discrete change have an important place in testing psychological theories based on stage development, which include classic theories in areas such as cognitive (Piaget 1973), moral (Kohlberg 1966), and ego (Erikson 1950) development. A more contemporary example of a stage model is the Gateway Hypothesis of drug use onset (Kandel 2002). Three related statistical models of transitions between discrete states are discussed in this section. For longitudinal panel designs, discrete-time survival analysis and latent transition analysis (LTA) are discussed. For intensive longitudinal designs, point-process models are considered. Each of these is suited to a slightly different, or differently worded, question about movement between states.

Longitudinal Panel Designs

DISCRETE-TIME SURVIVAL ANALYSIS   As discussed above, the standard longitudinal panel design involves relatively long intervals, often months or years, between occasions of measurement. Data collected using this kind of temporal design may reveal during which interval a transition, often called an event, occurred, but beyond this cannot be used to determine when the event took place. For example, consider a standard longitudinal panel study in which adolescents are measured once per year. At each time, the adolescents are asked if they have ever tried smoking. Such data may indicate that an adolescent tried smoking for the first time between the previous observation and the current one, but exactly when in that interval the encounter with tobacco occurred is unknown. Often a research question such as the following is of interest: Given that at time interval t an individual has never tried smoking, what is the probability that the individual will try smoking during a particular subsequent time interval? This question and related questions can be addressed by means of discrete-time survival analysis (e.g., Cox 1972). As the name suggests, survival analysis was originally developed in the biostatistics literature to model time until the occurrence of death and other medical events such as relapse of disease. Today its application in psychology and other areas in the behavioral sciences is growing (Singer & Willett 2003a,b).

Fundamental to survival analysis are two closely related functions, the hazard function and the survival function. Singer & Willett (2003a) presented a survival analysis of data collected yearly on a cohort of special education teachers newly hired in the Michigan public schools. The target event was leaving teaching. Let T_i represent the time interval j when individual i experienced the event; in this case, left teaching. Then the hazard for a particular time interval is

$$h(t_{ij}) = P[T_i = j | T_i \geq j],$$

or in words, the probability that individual i will experience the event during time interval j, given that individual i has not experienced the event during a previous time interval. There is a hazard associated with each time interval. For example, Singer & Willett (2003a) found that given that an individual did not leave during the first year of teaching, the probability was about 11% of leaving during the second year; given that an individual remained for at least six years, the probability was about 6% of leaving during the seventh year.

Closely related is the survival function

$$S(t_{ij}) = P[T_i > j],$$

which is the probability that individual i will not experience the event (will "survive"), conditional on not already having experienced the event in a previous time interval. Often of particular interest is the median lifetime, which is time interval during which the survival function reaches 0.5; in other words, the time interval by which half of the sample has experienced the event. Singer & Willett (2003a) found that sometime during year seven of teaching, 50% of the teachers in their sample had left.

It is possible to introduce time-invariant and time-varying covariates into a survival analysis, in order to address research questions such as whether the hazard function differs across groups or whether elevation in the hazard function corresponds to an elevation or decrease in another variable. For example, if it is of interest to examine whether more experienced teachers are more likely to remain in teaching longer, a covariate representing years of prior experience before beginning the current teaching position can be included. If it is suspected that feelings of burnout may be associated with an increased hazard of quitting, a yearly measure of burnout can be included as a covariate.

CENSORING AND SURVIVAL ANALYSIS   As discussed above, the temporal design of a study has an impact on the conclusions that can be drawn from data. This is very evident in censoring, a topic that is of great concern in survival analysis. Suppose a study is evaluating a new approach to psychotherapy for depressed inpatients. It is expected that patients receiving the new psychotherapy will go longer before experiencing a recurrence of depression. In this case, the event of interest is recurrence of depression. Suppose the new therapy is delivered, and then the patients are followed for two years. For each patient, it is recorded when the individual has a first recurrence of depression. Of course, at the end of two years not every patient will have had a recurrence of depression. At the conclusion of the two-year period, all that is known is that some patients have not had a recurrence; it is not known whether these patients will have a recurrence in the future. This is called right-censoring. Right-censoring is present in most survival analyses because rarely is it practical to conduct a study long enough for the event in question to occur for all subjects—and in some cases it is expected that some subjects will not experience a reoccurrence of the event. Somewhat less common, and more problematic, is left-censoring. Left-censoring is present when for some individuals the event in question occurred at some indeterminate time before the start of the study. Censoring is a sort of partially missing data problem. Censored individuals provide some information about the timing of the event, but not the complete information desired. In a sense, they inform about when the event did not occur, but not about exactly when it occurred. Another way to think of this is that if you are interested in modeling how long until an event occurs, it is best to time data collection so that you have a chance to observe the event. Thus, ideally censoring should be kept to a minimum. Survival and hazard models can deal with censoring, and do make use of the partial information censored data provide, but it is wise to give careful consideration to the implications of censoring in the interpretation of any results. For a careful treatment of censoring as well as many other issues related to survival analysis, see Singer & Willet (2003a,b).

LATENT TRANSITION ANALYSIS   Another approach for modeling transitions between states in data from longitudinal panel and similar designs is LTA (Langeheine 1994; Lanza et al. 2003, 2005), a version of latent class analysis (LCA). LTA addresses questions concerning prevalence of discrete states and incidence of transitions between states. LTA is suited to situations where there are numerous states, individuals can transition relatively freely among the states, and the states are measured with multiple fallible indicators.

Research questions about discrete change among an array of states are often expressed in terms of transition probabilities. A transition probability is the probability of being in state y at Time 2, conditional on membership in state x at Time 1. Inference about an individual's transitions between states is based upon the individual's state membership as assessed at each observation. When a single variable can reliably indicate state membership and the theoretical model is uncomplicated, it may be possible to model transitions between states using an ordinary contingency table approach. However, more sophistication and flexibility can be found in LTA (Goodman 1974, Langeheine 1994, Lanza et al. 2003).

LCA is a latent variable model conceptually similar to factor analysis (McDonald 1985). Generally, factor analysis is based on a covariance matrix; LCA is based on a contingency table. Whereas in factor analysis the latent variable has a continuous distribution, in LCA the distribution of the latent variable is discrete, so that each individual belongs to one and only one latent class. Extensions of latent class theory to LTA (Lanza et al. 2003, 2005) and latent Markov models (Langeheine 1994) provide a way of statistically modeling movement between latent states, including estimating the prevalence of each discrete state and the incidence of transitions between states, adjusted for measurement error. For example, Lanza & Collins (2002) used LTA to model a contingency table that included adolescent girls' self-reports, taken in grade 7 and again in grade 8, of whether they had ever tried several substances. Each latent state in the model represented which substances had been tried at a particular time, e.g., alcohol only, alcohol and cigarettes, etc. Let y designate a cell in the contingency table. Then such an LTA model can be expressed as follows:

$$P(Y = y) = \sum_{a=1}^{S} \sum_{b=1}^{S} \delta_a \tau_{b|a} \rho_{i|a} \rho_{j|a} \rho_{k|a} \rho_{l|a} \rho_{i'|b} \rho_{j'|b} \rho_{k'|b} \rho_{l'|b},$$

where S represents the number of latent states in the model; a and b represent latent state at the first and second occasion, respectively; and i, j, k, and l are observed values of variables (e.g., a response of "no" to the question about ever having tried alcohol). The δ's, τ's, and ρ's are all model parameters to be estimated. δ_a is a parameter representing the probability of membership in latent state a at the first occasion (e.g., probability of membership in the alcohol-only latent state); $\tau_{b|a}$ represents the probability of being in latent state b at the second occasion, conditional on membership in latent state a at the first occasion (e.g., probability of being in the alcohol-and-cigarettes latent state at the second occasion, conditional on membership in the alcohol-only latent state at the first occasion); and the ρ's represent the probability of observed values of variables conditional on latent state (e.g., the probability of a response of "yes" to the question about ever having tried alcohol conditional on membership in the alcohol-plus-cigarettes latent state). The ρ parameters are the conceptual equivalent of factor loadings, in that they express the relation between the observed (self-reports of substance use) and latent (substance-use state) variables.

In order to compare transitions between latent substance-use states for girls who were early pubertal developers with transitions for girls who were on-time or late developers, Lanza & Collins (2002) included indicators of pubertal status in the model described above [to do so requires estimation of some additional parameters; such models are described in detail in Lanza et al. (2003) and in Lanza et al. (2005)]. They found that the earlier developers were much more likely to be in relatively advanced substance-use states in grade 7 and to transition to more advanced substance-use states between grades 7 and 8.

The latent class approach to modeling transitions between discrete states provides several advantages as compared to an ordinary contingency table approach. First, it is straightforward to fit models that specify a kind of change, such as only forward-moving change, or that specify that any particular transition probability is fixed to zero (or any other legitimate parameter value) and to compare the fit of these different models of change in empirical data. Second, this approach provides a way of modeling measurement error, thereby producing a more accurate estimate of the transition probability matrix and other model parameters. Importantly, because this approach models measurement error, it deals in a principled way with observations that do not appear to map directly onto hypothesized states, such as individuals who report having tried cigarettes at one time and then at a later time report never having tried cigarettes. In other words, there is no need to remove such individuals from the sample or to "correct" the data to make it internally consistent (ad hoc practices with no statistical basis that are never recommended but, regrettably, are sometimes used in practice). Third, this approach provides a way of making scientific sense of large, complex contingency tables such as those formed by crosstabulating several discrete variables that have been measured repeatedly. Such contingency tables can easily have hundreds or even thousands of cells; for example, the contingency table analyzed by Lanza & Collins (2002) had 4096 cells.

RECENT DEVELOPMENTS IN LATENT CLASS MODELS FOR LONGITUDINAL DATA   The latent class approach to modeling change has been extended in some interesting directions. It is now possible to include continuous covariates in latent class models of longitudinal data (Chung et al. 2005, Dayton & Macready 1988, Humphreys & Janson 2000). For example, Chung et al. (2005) extended the analyses reported in Lanza & Collins (2002) by including a wider range of ages in the sample, and by incorporating not only pubertal development but also age and the interaction of age and pubertal development as covariates. They found that older girls whose puberty was in progress were at particularly increased risk of advancing in their substance use. Another area of extension has been in making use of observed variables at a level of measurement other than nominal. Kim & Böckenholt (2000) developed a latent class model for longitudinal data that can incorporate ordered categorical responses. Dolan et al. (2004) used a normal finite mixture approach to model stage-sequential Piagetian development in children based on a covariance matrix of continuous variables rather than a contingency table of discrete variables.

IMPACT OF TEMPORAL DESIGN ON LTA AND SIMILAR APPROACHES   The considerations about censoring discussed above apply here as well. In addition, exactly when the observations in a panel design are collected and how much time is allowed to elapse between observations can have an effect on the results obtained using the statistical analysis methods described above. For example, when the change process is rapid, or when certain states within a process are of short duration, individuals may pass into and out of one or more states between observations. In that case the prevalence of certain states may be underestimated, or the presence of some states may be overlooked altogether (Collins & Graham 2002).

Intensive Longitudinal Designs: Point-Process Models

As compared to longitudinal panel designs, intensive longitudinal designs provide information that can be used to place events in time more precisely. For example, experience sampling methods (Csikszentmihalyi & Larson 1987, Shiffman et al. 2002) involve much smaller intervals between measures than those of longitudinal panel designs. Another approach involves less frequent measurement, but includes carefully and methodically elicited recall of occurrence and dates of important past events occurring since the last measurement occasion, or sometimes even over the individual's lifetime (e.g., Kandel et al. 1997). When the timing of events of interest can be determined with a high degree of precision, a continuous-time approach may be used. A well-known example is continuous-time survival analysis (Singer & Willett 2003a). Like discrete-time survival analysis, continuous-time survival analysis is used to estimate survival and hazard functions. However, unlike discrete-time survival analysis, the continuous-time approach assumes a nearly continuous record of when the events take place. Most continuous-time survival analysis approaches can be considered a special case of the more general point-process model.

The point-process model (Cox & Lewis 1966, Cressie 1991, Diggle 1983, Lewis 1972, Rathbun et al. 2006) can be used to address questions about the frequency and timing of a single discrete event or a series of discrete events. Originally developed for use in fields such as biostatistics, ecology, and geography, point-process models are just beginning to find their way into the social and behavioral sciences. The input data for a point-process analysis is a record of each time a particular discrete event occurred over some period. Thus, point-process analyses work best with intensive longitudinal and similar temporal designs involving frequent and closely spaced measurement. For example, Rathbun et al. (2006) described a series of point-process analyses aimed at modeling smoking behavior. Data on smoking and related variables, such as emotional state at the time each cigarette was smoked, were collected nearly in continuous time, using immediate self-reports entered in handheld computers (Shiffman et al. 2002).

Fundamental to point-process models is the intensity function

$$\lambda(t) = \lim_{\delta \to 0} \frac{E\{N[t, t + \delta]\}}{\delta}.$$

In this equation, $[t, t + \delta]$ represents a time interval beginning at time t and enduring for length δ. The numerator of the right-hand side of this equation is the expected (mean) number of events N occurring during this time interval. As the length of the interval δ approaches zero, the intensity function $\lambda(t)$ becomes the instantaneous rate of event occurrence at time t. In other words, a high intensity means more occurrences of the event, on average, per unit time. Note the close similarity between the intensity function and the hazard function. In fact, the hazard function for continuous-time survival models is a special case of the intensity function for point-process models.

Point-process models can readily be used to study periodicity, such as effects attributable to month of the year, day of the week, hour of the day, etc. Rathbun et al. (2006) illustrated this by investigating how time of day and day of the week affect rates of cigarette smoking. The results yield a detailed picture of the natural history of smoking behavior. For example, they showed that during the week, peak smoking rates occurred shortly after 5 PM and again around 8:30 PM, whereas on the weekends there were no discernable peaks at those times. Point-process models can incorporate random (in other words, individual subject–level) effects, and also time-varying covariates. By adding random effects and time-varying covariates to their model, Rathbun et al. were able to show that although negative affect did not appear to be related to smoking, there was a strong relation between restlessness and smoking.

As Rathbun et al. (2006) demonstrated, point-process models open up some interesting possibilities for modeling change. A multivariate approach can be taken to examine the relations between two or more types of point processes, such as cigarette smoking and alcohol consumption. Self-exciting processes, in which the occurrence of an event itself increases the probability of another occurrence of the same event, can be modeled. Chain-smoking may be a self-exciting process if having one cigarette itself increases the probability of having another one. Another possible model of change is called a stress-release point process, in which the event becomes more likely to occur when another variable reaches a certain threshold level. For example, when nicotine in the blood falls below a certain level, the probability that cigarette smoking will occur increases. Once the event occurs, blood nicotine increases above the threshold for a time, and then gradually drops to a level low enough to trigger the next episode of cigarette smoking.

MISSING DATA

Unplanned missing data in longitudinal research can occur because a participant fails to respond to one or more questions in a questionnaire or interview, or because a participant is unavailable to the research study at one or more occasions of measurement. Scientists engaged in longitudinal research deal with unplanned missing data constantly; in fact, it is difficult to imagine a longitudinal study without at least some unplanned missing data. For this reason, how to handle missing data is an important question facing anyone who wishes to analyze longitudinal data.

For years investigators have used ad hoc procedures for dealing with missing data, such as eliminating individuals with missing data from analysis ("casewise deletion") or substituting the sample mean for missing observations ("mean substitution"). Such procedures may be convenient, but they have no basis in statistical theory. There are two potential consequences of using ad hoc procedures to deal with unplanned missingness. One is a greater-than-necessary loss of statistical power, particularly in association with casewise deletion, which involves discarding data for any subject whose data are incomplete. The other consequence is bias in results, which can occur if the cause of missingness is related to variables of scientific interest.

A much better option is to use modern missing data procedures (Schafer 1997, Schafer & Graham 2002), such as multiple imputation and maximum likelihood, which are based in statistical theory. When the assumptions underlying these procedures are met, they restore much statistical power and eliminate bias due to missing data; even when the underlying assumptions are not met, modern missing data procedures are an improvement over ad hoc methods (Collins et al. 2001). This is particularly so if variables that are highly correlated with those subject to missingness are included in the analysis. Frequently in longitudinal studies, previous or later measures of a variable may serve this role well. Collins et al. (2001) and Graham (2003) discuss why and how to implement this missing data strategy.

Most longitudinal research projects set aside resources to devote to tracking down individuals who are absent for a data-collection session. Assuming that these resources are finite and are insufficient to obtain data from all the dropouts, one can imagine two different ways of spending them: on obtaining data from as many of the dropouts as possible, or on obtaining a smaller, but representative, sample of dropouts. Graham & Donaldson (1993) showed that the latter is the better approach, and demonstrated how such a sample can be tremendously useful for making the most of modern missing data procedures in longitudinal research.

In the previous paragraphs, the term "unplanned" missing data was used to refer to data loss that is out of the investigator's control. Missing data may also be planned when an investigator chooses to collect partial data using a carefully controlled missing data design. Reasons for choosing to use a planned missing data design include economy and a desire to reduce the response burden on study participants. For more about planned missing data designs in longitudinal research, see Graham et al. (2001).

MEASUREMENT CONSIDERATIONS IN LONGITUDINAL RESEARCH

Psychology has a long tradition of measurement theory, with early roots in intelligence testing, employment testing, and factor analysis (Lord & Novick 1968). Most traditional measurement theories, such as classical test theory, are aimed primarily at developing measures sensitive to interindividual variability, and essentially ignore intraindividual variability. For example, the traditional definition of reliability, the proportion of observed score variance that is made up of true score variance, is defined entirely in terms of interindividual variability. It follows that measurement instruments evaluated by methods that focus on interindividual variability may or may not be adequate measures of intraindividual change.

A few measurement approaches have been aimed at variables measured longitudinally. Willett (1989) demonstrated how to use growth curve models to assess the longitudinal reliability of an instrument. He showed convincingly that obtaining additional observations in time can greatly improve the reliability with which a growth curve is measured. Collins & Cliff (1990) extended the Guttman scale to longitudinal data, and showed that it could be used as a basis for developing and evaluating measures for certain kinds of intraindividual change processes. Embretson (1991) showed how to use latent trait theory to develop measures of intraindividual change. An exciting feature of this approach is that it addresses a knotty problem in lifespan research, namely how to develop and equate different measures of the same construct for administration at different points across the life course.

Open questions remain in the theory and practice of measurement of intraindividual change. Coombs (1964, p. 5) wrote, "a measurement or scaling model is a theory of behavior, admittedly on a miniature level, but nevertheless theory . . . ." This suggests that any measurement theory aimed at intraindividual growth processes must start with a theoretical model of change. It follows that it is unlikely that a single approach to measurement can be adequate for development of instruments across the entire panoply of growth processes. As statistical models are invented for fitting theoretical models that specify increasingly complex change, corresponding measurement methods are needed. Such models are critical for reliable and valid measurement of growth processes, and ultimately for testing important hypotheses about intraindividual change.

A FEW WORDS ABOUT EXPLORATORY RESEARCH

This article has emphasized situations where there is a clear theoretical model guiding research. But many studies, of necessity, are not guided by theory. Some studies are breaking new ground in areas where theory is incomplete or even nonexistent. Sometimes the original theory guiding a study has been soundly refuted by the empirical data collected to test it, leaving the investigators to conduct secondary analyses with the hope of beginning to build a new theory. Where theory cannot inform choice of temporal design and statistical model, these choices must be made in a more exploratory manner.

Where there is little theory to guide choices, it may be wise for investigators to do their best to keep options open. For example, consider the choice of number and spacing of observations in a temporal design. If there are too many occasions of measurement spaced too close together, it is always possible to base analyses on a subset of measurement occasions or to aggregate (e.g., sum) occasions that are close together. However, if there are too few occasions or they are spaced too far apart, there may be little the investigator can do to recover information about what happened between observations. Thus, erring on the side of more, and more frequent, observation may be prudent.

In cases where secondary analyses are being performed on existing data in order to build a theory, it may be helpful to interpret the results in the light of the temporal design used to collect the data. This interpretation could involve considering what kinds of change processes the temporal design might reasonably have been able to reveal and what kinds the temporal design would tend to hide from view. For example, consider a secondary analysis based on a three-wave longitudinal panel study, with yearly data collection. A linear model of growth might simultaneously be an excellent representation of the empirical data and a poor representation of the underlying growth process. There may be considerable curvilinearity, even repeated peaks and valleys, in the growth process, but the temporal design obscures these features of growth, preventing them from being observed.

Exploratory studies and secondary data analyses will always have a place in social and behavioral research. The argument here is not that such studies and analyses should be avoided. Rather, the argument is that even when theory is absent, the impact of the relation between temporal design and statistical model is an important consideration in longitudinal research. Careful thought about these matters can be tremendously helpful in interpreting empirical results and building theories to be tested in future studies.

SUMMARY AND CONCLUSIONS

This article has argued that ideal longitudinal research is characterized by the seamless integration of a well-articulated theoretical model of change, an appropriate temporal design, and a statistical model that is an operationalization of the theoretical model. Although no research study is perfect, it is useful to articulate an ideal as a standard for evaluation. Using the ideal as a conceptual framework, this article has surveyed a number of familiar and less familiar approaches to analyzing longitudinal data.

Of the three elements discussed here, the theoretical model is perhaps under the most direct control of the investigator. A clear and detailed theoretical model is a necessary foundation for all longitudinal research. This model then provides the basis for choosing a temporal design. In many cases, the temporal design is not completely under the control of the investigator, due to resource limitations and other considerations. Nevertheless, an articulation of the ideal temporal design will provide a useful perspective when difficult tradeoffs have to be made and compromises reached with respect to the design that is chosen for implementation. The most appropriate statistical model is as close to a direct operationalization of the theoretical model as possible, subject to the limitations imposed by the temporal design. Even when the ideal of seamless integration of the three elements is met, unplanned missing data and measurement reliability and validity are important issues that can have a major impact.

We are entering a new era of longitudinal data analysis. Increasingly elegant statistical models and new technology supporting more intensive longitudinal data collection are enabling data analysis and design to catch up with sophisticated and nuanced psychological theories of human development and change. It will be interesting to see what the next decade brings!

ACKNOWLEDGMENTS

The preparation of this article was supported by grants P50 DA10075 and K05 DA018206 from the National Institute on Drug Abuse. The author is grateful to Amanda Gottschall for help in the preparation of this article, and to Brian Flaherty, John Graham, Stephanie Lanza, Mildred Maldonado-Molina, Joseph Schafer, Theodore Walls, and many colleagues at The Methodology Center for helpful comments.

The *Annual Review of Psychology* is online at http://psych.annualreviews.org

LITERATURE CITED

Bell RQ. 1953. Convergence: an accelerated longitudinal approach. *Child Dev.* 24:145–52

Boker SM, Graham J. 1998. A dynamical systems analysis of adolescent substance abuse. *Multivar. Behav. Res.* 33:479–507

Boker SM, Laurenceau J-P. 2006. Dynamical systems modeling: an application to the regulation of intimacy and disclosure in marriage. See Walls & Schafer 2006, pp. 195–218

Boker SM, Nesselroade JR. 2002. A method for modeling the intrinsic dynamics of intraindividual variability: recovering the parameters of simulated oscillators in multi-wave panel data. *Multivar. Behav. Res.* 37:127–60

Bollen KA, Curran PJ. 2004. Autoregressive Latent Trajectory (ALT) models: a synthesis of two traditions. *Sociol. Methods Res.* 32:336–83

Chung H, Park Y, Lanza ST. 2005. Latent transition analysis with covariates: pubertal timing and substance use behaviors in adolescent females. *Stat. Med.* 24:2895–910

Cohen P. 1991. A source of bias in longitudinal investigations of change. See Collins & Horn 1991, pp. 18–25

Collins LM, Cliff N. 1990. Using the Longitudinal Guttman Simplex as a basis for measuring growth. *Psychol. Bull.* 108:128–34

Collins LM, Graham JW. 1991. Comment on "A source of bias in longitudinal investigations of change: a problem posed to attenders at the 'Best Methods for the Analysis of Change' conference." See Collins & Horn 1991, pp. 26–30

Collins LM, Graham JW. 2002. The effect of the timing and temporal spacing of observations in longitudinal studies of tobacco and other drug use: temporal design considerations. *Drug Alcohol Depend.* 68:S85–96

Collins LM, Horn JL, eds. 1991. *Best Methods for the Analysis of Change: Recent Advances, Unanswered Questions, Future Directions.* Washington, DC: Am. Psychol. Assoc.

Collins LM, Sayer AG, eds. 2001. *New Methods for the Analysis of Change.* Washington, DC: Am. Psychol. Assoc.

Collins LM, Schafer JL, Kam CK. 2001. A comparison of inclusive and restrictive strategies in modern missing-data procedures. *Psychol. Methods* 6:330–51

Coombs CH. 1964. *A Theory of Data.* Ann Arbor, MI: Mathesis

Cox DR. 1972. Regression models and life tables. *J. Roy. Stat. Soc. Ser. B* 34:187–202

Cox DR, Lewis PAW. 1966. *The Statistical Analysis of Series of Events*. London: Chapman & Hall

Cressie N. 1991. *Statistics for Spatial Data*. New York: Wiley

Csikszentmihalyi M, Larson R. 1987. Validity and reliability of the experience-sampling method. *J. Nerv. Ment. Disord.* 175:526–36

Cudeck R, Klebe KJ. 2002. Multiphase mixed-effects models for repeated measures data. *Psychol. Methods* 7:41–63

Cumsille PE, Sayer AG, Graham JW. 2000. Perceived exposure to peer and adult drinking as predictors of growth in positive alcohol expectancies during adolescence. *J. Consult. Clin. Psychol.* 68:531–36

Curran PJ. 2003. Have multilevel models been structural equation models all along? *Multivar. Behav. Res.* 38:529–69

Curran PJ, Bollen KA. 2001. The best of both worlds: combining autoregressive and latent curve models. See Collins & Sayer 2001, pp. 105–35

Curran PJ, Willoughby MT. 2003. Implications of latent trajectory models for the study of developmental psychopathology. *Dev. Psychopathol.* 15:581–612

Curran PJ, Wirth RJ. 2004. Interindividual differences in intraindividual variation: balancing internal and external validity. *Meas. Interdisc. Res. Perspect.* 2:219–47

Dayton CM, Macready GB. 1988. Concomitant-variable latent class models. *J. Am. Stat. Assoc.* 83:173–78

Diggle PJ. 1983. *Statistical Analysis of Spatial Point Patterns*. New York: Academic

Dolan CV, Jansen BRJ, van der Maas JLJ. 2004. Constrained and unconstrained multivariate normal finite mixture modeling of Piagetian data. *Multivar. Behav. Res.* 39:69–98

Donny EC, Lanza ST, Balster RL, Collins LM, Caggiula A, Rowell P. 2004. Using growth models to relate acquisition of nicotine self-administration to break point and nicotinic receptor binding. *Drug Alcohol Depend.* 75:23–35

Duncan SC, Duncan TE, Hops H. 1996. Analysis of longitudinal data within accelerated longitudinal designs. *Psychol. Methods* 1:236–48

Embretson SE. 1991. Implications of a multi-dimensional latent trait model for measuring change. See Collins & Horn 1991, pp. 184–97

Erikson EH. 1950. *Childhood and Society*. New York: Norton

Fan J, Gijbels I. 1996. *Local Polynomical Modelling and Its Applications*. London: Chapman & Hall

Fok CCT, Ramsay JO. 2006. Periodic trends, non-periodic trends and their interactions in longitudinal or functional data. See Walls & Schafer 2006, pp. 109–23

Gollob HF, Reichardt CS. 1987. Taking account of time lags in causal models. *Child Dev.* 58:80–92

Gollob HF, Reichardt CS. 1991. Interpreting and estimating indirect effects assuming time lags really matter. See Collins & Horn 1991, pp. 243–49

Goodman LA. 1974. Exploratory latent structure analysis using both identifiable and unidentifiable models. *Biometrika* 61:215–31

Gottman JM, ed. 1995. *The Analysis of Change*. Mahwah, NJ: Erlbaum

Graham JW. 2003. Adding missing-data-relevant variables to FIML-based structural equation models. *Struct. Equation Model.* 10:80–100

Graham JW, Donaldson SI. 1993. Evaluating interventions with differential attrition: the importance of nonresponse mechanisms and use of follow-up data. *J. Appl. Psychol.* 78:119–28

Graham JW, Taylor BJ, Cumsille PE. 2001. Planned missing-data designs in analysis of change. See Collins & Sayer 2001, pp. 333–53

Harris CW, ed. 1963. *Problems in Measuring Change*. Madison: Univ. Wisc. Press

Hertzog C, Nesselroade JR. 2003. Assessing psychological change in adulthood: an overview of methodological issues. *Psychol. Aging* 18:639–57

Humphreys K, Janson H. 2000. Latent transition analysis with covariates, nonresponse, summary statistics and diagnostics: modelling children's drawing development. *Multivar. Behav. Res.* 35:89–118

Joreskog KG. 1979. Statistical estimation of structural models in longitudinal developmental investigations. In *Longitudinal Research in the Study of Behavior and Development*, ed. JR Nesselroade, PB Baltes, pp. 303–52. New York: Academic

Kandel DB. 2002. *Stages and Pathways of Drug Involvement: Examining the Gateway Hypothesis*. London: Cambridge Univ. Press

Kandel DB, Chen K, Warner L, Kessler R, Grant B. 1997. Prevalence and demographic correlates of symptoms of dependence on cigarettes, alcohol, marijuana, and cocaine in the U.S. population. *Drug Alcohol Depend.* 44:11–29

Kelly JR, McGrath JE. 1988. *On Time and Method*. Newbury Park, CA: Sage

Kim JS, Böckenholt U. 2000. Modeling stage-sequential change in ordered categorical responses. *Psychol. Methods* 5:380–400

Kohlberg L. 1966. Cognitive stages and preschool education. *Hum. Dev.* 9:5–17

Langeheine R. 1994. Latent variable Markov models. In *Latent Variables Analysis: Applications for Developmental Research*, ed. A von Eye, CC Clogg, pp. 373–95. Thousand Oaks, CA: Sage

Lanza ST, Collins LM. 2002. Pubertal timing and the stages of substance use in females during early adolescence. *Prev. Sci.* 3:69–82

Lanza ST, Collins LM, Schafer JL, Flaherty BP. 2005. Using data augmentation to obtain standard errors and conduct hypothesis tests in latent class and latent transition analysis. *Psychol. Methods* 10:84–100

Lanza ST, Donny EC, Collins LM, Balster RL. 2004. Analyzing the acquisition of drug self-administration using growth curve models. *Drug Alcohol Depend.* 75:11–21

Lanza ST, Flaherty BP, Collins LM. 2003. Latent class and latent transition analysis. See Velicer & Schinka 2003, pp. 663–85

Lewis PAW, ed. 1972. *Stochastic Point Processes*. New York: Wiley

Li F, Duncan TE, Duncan SC, Hops H. 2001. Piecewise growth mixture modeling of adolescent alcohol use data. *Struct. Equation Model.* 8:175–204

Li R, Root TL, Shiffman S. 2006. A local linear estimation procedure for functional multilevel modeling. See Walls & Schafer 2006, pp. 63–83

Lord FW, Novick MR. 1968. *Statistical Theories of Mental Test Scores*. Reading, MA: Addison-Wesley

McArdle JJ, Epstein DB. 1987. Latent growth curves within developmental structural equation models. *Child Dev.* 58:110–33

McArdle JJ, Hamagami F. 2001. Latent difference score structural models for linear dynamic analyses with incomplete longitudinal data. See Collins & Sayer 2001, pp. 137–75

McArdle JJ, Nesselroade JR. 2003. Growth curve analysis in contemporary psychological research. See Velicer & Schinka 2003, pp. 447–80

McDonald RP. 1985. *Factor Analysis and Related Methods*. Hillsdale, NJ: Erlbaum

McGrath JE, Tschan F. 2004. *Temporal Matters in Social Psychology: Examining the Role of Time in the Lives of Groups and Individuals*. Washington, DC: Am. Psychol. Assoc.

Meredith W, Tisak J. 1990. Latent curve analysis. *Psychometrika* 55:107–22

Miyazaki Y, Raudenbush SW. 2000. Tests for linkage of multiple cohorts in an accelerated longitudinal design. *Psychol. Methods* 5:44–63

Molenaar PCM. 2004. A manifesto on psychology as idiographic science: bringing the person back into scientific psychology, this time forever. *Meas. Interdisc. Res. Perspect.* 2:201–18

Muthén B. 2001. Second-generation structural equation modeling with a combination of categorical and continuous latent variables: new opportunities for latent class-latent growth modeling. See Collins & Sayer 2001, pp. 289–322

Muthén B, Muthén LK. 2000. Integrating

person-centered and variable-centered analyses: growth mixture modeling with latent trajectory classes. *Alcohol. Clin. Exp. Res.* 24:882–91

Muthén B, Shedden K. 1999. Finite mixture modeling with mixture outcomes using the EM algorithm. *Biometrics* 55:463–69

Nagin DS. 1999. Analyzing developmental trajectories: a semiparametric, group-based approach. *Psychol. Methods* 4:139–57

Nagin DS. 2005. *Group-Based Modeling of Development.* Cambridge, MA: Harvard Univ. Press

Nagin DS, Tremblay RE. 2001. Analyzing developmental trajectories of distinct but related behaviors: a group-based method. *Psychol. Methods* 6:18–34

Nesselroade JR. 1991. Interindividual differences in intraindividual change. See Collins & Horn 1991, pp. 92–105

Nesselroade JR, Baltes PB, eds. 1979. *Longitudinal Research in the Study of Behavior and Development.* New York: Academic

Piaget J. 1973. *The Child and Reality.* New York: Grossman

Ramsay JO. 2006. The control of behavioral input/output systems. See Walls & Schafer 2006, pp. 176–94

Rathbun SL, Shiffman S, Gwaltney CJ. 2006. Point process models for event history data: applications in behavioral science. See Walls & Schafer 2006, pp. 219–53

Raudenbush SW. 2000. Comparing personal trajectories and drawing causal inferences from longitudinal data. *Annu. Rev. Psychol.* 52:501–25

Rogosa DR, Brandt D, Zimowski M. 1982. A growth curve approach to the measurement of change. *Psychol. Bull.* 90:726–48

Rogosa DR, Willett JB. 1985. Understanding correlates of change by modeling individual differences in growth. *Psychometrika* 50:203–28

Schafer JL. 1997. *Analysis of Incomplete Multivariate Data.* London: Chapman & Hall

Schafer JL, Graham JW. 2002. Missing data: our view of the state of the art. *Psychol. Methods* 7:147–77

Shadish WR, Cook TD, Campbell DT. 2002. *Experimental and Quasi-Experimental Designs for Generalized Causal Inference.* Boston, MA: Houghton Mifflin

Shiffman S, Gwaltney CJ, Baladanis MH, Liu KS, Paty JA, et al. 2002. Immediate antecedents of cigarette smoking: an analysis from ecological momentary assessment. *J. Abnorm. Psychol.* 111:531–45

Shiffman S, Stone AA, eds. 2006. *The Science and Theory of Real-Time Data Capture.* New York: Oxford Univ. Press. In press

Singer JD, Willett JB. 2003a. *Applied Longitudinal Data Analysis: Modeling Change and Event Occurrence.* New York: Oxford Univ. Press

Singer JD, Willett JB. 2003b. Survival analysis. See Velicer & Schinka 2003, pp. 555–80

Velicer WF, Schinka JA, eds. 2003. *Handbook of Psychology: Research Methods in Psychology.* New York: Wiley. 711 pp.

von Eye A, ed. 1990a. *Statistical Methods in Longitudinal Research, Volume 2: Time Series and Categorical Longitudinal Data.* Boston, MA: Academic

von Eye A, ed. 1990b. *Statistical Methods in Longitudinal Research, Volume 1: Principles and Structuring Change.* Boston, MA: Academic

Walls TA, Jung H, Schwartz JE. 2006. Multilevel models for intensive longitudinal data. See Walls & Schafer 2006, pp. 3–37

Walls TA, Schafer JL. 2006. *Models for Intensive Longitudinal Data.* New York: Oxford Univ. Press

Willett JB. 1989. Some results on reliability for the longitudinal measurement of change: implications for the design of studies of individual growth. *Educ. Psychol. Meas.* 49:587–602

Willett JB, Sayer AG. 1994. Using covariance structure analysis to detect correlates and predictors of individual change over time. *Psychol. Bull.* 116:363–81

Windle M, Davies PT. 1999. Developmental research and theory. In *Psychological Theories of Drinking and Alcoholism*, ed. KE Leonard, HT Blane, pp. 164–202. New York: Guilford. 2nd ed.

Annu. Rev. Psychol. 2006. 57:529–55
doi: 10.1146/annurev.psych.57.102904.190048
Copyright © 2006 by Annual Reviews. All rights reserved
First published online as a Review in Advance on August 11, 2005

THE INTERNET AS PSYCHOLOGICAL LABORATORY

Linda J. Skitka and Edward G. Sargis

Department of Psychology, University of Illinois at Chicago, Chicago, Illinois
60607-7137; email: lskitka@uic.edu, esargis@uic.edu

Key Words   Internet, methods

■ **Abstract**   This chapter reviews studies published in American Psychological Association (APA) journals from 2003–2004 and additional studies (received in response to listserv requests) that used the Internet to collect data (N = 121 total studies). Specific examples of three kinds of Web-based research are reviewed: (*a*) translational (established methods and research questions are adapted to the Web), (*b*) phenomenological (behavior on the Web is the focus of study), and (*c*) novel (methodological innovations unique to Web-based research). Among other findings, our review indicated that 21% of APA journals published at least one article that reported on Web-based research, most Web-based psychological research uses experimental methods, a surprising number use college student samples, and deception in Web-based research is not uncommon. Strengths and weaknesses of Web-based psychological research in general, and our sample of studies in particular, are reviewed with special attention to possible concerns about sampling and the use of deception.

CONTENTS

INTRODUCTION

Just as the Internet has facilitated surprising new developments in political organizing, making money, discovering lost relatives, receiving medical advice, and
finding the perfect recipe for anything from a pie to a bomb, the Internet has also
opened new horizons to traditional data collection methods in psychology. Suddenly collecting data is as easy as posting a form, and samples of overt racists,
pet owners, depressives, or members of any other demographic, social, or psychological category are as easy to reach and use in one's research as are members of
college student subject pools.

Previous *Annual Review of Psychology* chapters devoted to the Internet have reviewed (*a*) the nuts and bolts of how to collect data using the Internet, such as getting
started with HyperText Markup Language (HTML) forms, client and server side
programming, and how to handle issues such as subject recruitment and multiple
submissions (Birnbaum 2004), and (*b*) the psychological impact of the Internet on
people's well-being and social relationships (Bargh & McKenna 2004). Other excellent resources have recently become available that provide additional guidance
on getting started doing psychological research using the World Wide Web, such
as a number of books that provide excellent how-to introductions (e.g., Birnbaum
2000, Fraley 2003). Research on best practices and methods in Web research is
also booming, leading to the development of Web archives devoted to facilitating
access to up-to-date information on Web survey methodology (WebSM). WebSM
has archived study reports of mode comparisons, meta-analyses of response rates
associated with different methods of participant recruitment, the effectiveness of
different incentives, the reliability of slider as compared to click-button scales,
and much more (see http://www.websm.org). The Pew Internet and American
Life Project provides continuously updated reports that explore the impact of the
Internet on families, communities, work and home, daily life, education, and health
care, as well as civic and political life. It releases 15–30 research reports a year and

has emerged as the authoritative voice on how the Internet is affecting any given aspect of people's lives. In addition, it tracks the degree to which Internet access is reaching across different aspects of society (see http://www.pewinternet.org/).

In short, there are already significant resources available that summarize how to use the Internet in psychological research, best research practices for Web-based research, and the impact of the Internet on many aspects of psychological and social life. Therefore, our goal in this chapter is to take a different tack. Specifically, now that more psychological researchers know how to use the Web to collect data and appear to be doing so, it may be useful to review existing psychological research that is using the Web. What kinds of substantive questions are being addressed and what kinds of methods are being employed when psychological researchers turn to the Web to collect data? To form the foundation of our review, we collected a broad sample of articles from the mainstream psychological literature that reported on original empirical research and that used the Internet as the source of their data.

METHOD

We examined all published articles in American Psychological Association (APA) journals for the years 2003–2004 for original empirical research that used the Internet as a data source to build an appropriate sample. In addition to allowing us to explore questions about what kind of psychological research is being done on the Internet, this sample of studies allowed us to infer the degree to which Internet-based research methods are penetrating research reported in the discipline's top journals.

To broaden our sample, we also posted requests for reprints and preprints of articles that reported on Internet-based psychological research on listservs associated with each of the major divisions of APA. Although these combined sampling strategies led us to identify probably only a fraction of the total number of psychological studies that have used Web-based methods, this approach nonetheless provided a basis for making descriptive estimates of how psychologists are using the Web in their research. As can be seen in Table 1, we identified a total sample of 84 articles that reported on 112 studies that were appropriate for our review.

TABLE 1   Number of Internet-based studies identified through review of American Psychological Association (APA) journals and listserv solicitations

Sampling strategy	Number of articles identified	Number of studies reported
Review of APA journals (2003–2004)	22	31
Listserv solicitation	62	81
Total number in the sample used in this review	84	112

HOW PREVALENT IS WEB-BASED RESEARCH
IN APA JOURNALS?

One-fifth (21%) of all APA journals during 2003–2004 published at least one article that collected data using the Web. That said, the overall incidence of articles using Web-based research was relatively low. Out of 1401 articles published in APA journals in 2003 and 2004, 22 (1.6%) were articles that reported on Web-based research. Moreover, as can be seen in Table 2, the overall number of articles that reported on Web-based research published in any given APA journal did not exceed 3% in 2003–2004. In summary, although there is a clear presence of Web-based research in APA journals, the overall incidence in any given journal was relatively low.

TABLE 2   American Psychological Association journals that published articles reporting on research conducted on the Web, total articles published during 2003–2004, and penetration of Web-based research

Journal	Number of articles that reported Internet research 2003–2004	Total number of articles published in 2003–2004	Penetration (% of articles that reported on Internet research)
Dreaming	1	47	2%
Emotion	1	64	1%
Health Psychology	1	137	1%
Journal of Applied Psychology	6	178	3%
Journal of Consulting and Clinical Psychology	2	208	1%
Journal of Counseling Psychology	3	87	3%
Journal of Experimental Psychology: Learning, Memory and Cognition	2	213	1%
Journal of Personality and Social Psychology	4	298	1%
Psychology of Addictive Behaviors	1	93	1%
Psychotherapy: Theory, Research, Practice, and Training	1	76	1%
Total	22	1401	2%

WHAT KINDS OF RESEARCH QUESTIONS ARE PSYCHOLOGISTS ASKING IN WEB-BASED RESEARCH?

A wide range of substantive questions is being addressed with Web-based research methods in psychology. As can be seen in Table 2, more articles of this kind appeared on a percentage basis in the *Journal of Applied Psychology* and the *Journal of Counseling Psychology* than in other APA journals. In terms of raw counts, an equal number of papers appeared in the *Journal of Personality and Social Psychology.* That said, our more extensive sample that included submissions from listservs also included articles across a broader array of inquiry, including clinical, cognitive, and sports psychology. Overall, it appears that no one area of psychology has led the charge in turning to the Web for data collection.

We classified studies into one of three types based on their approach to using the Web in research: translational, phenomenological, or novel. Below we define these three types of Web-based psychological research and provide examples of how they are used in psychological research.

Translational

The largest percentage of studies (59%) in our sample took a translational approach to using the Web in research. Translational research involves adapting materials and methods originally developed for offline use for use on the Internet. For example, Srivastava and colleagues (2003) used the Internet to test nature versus nurture models of personality development. The biological model predicts that personality should become relatively stable by adulthood (i.e., age 20 and over), whereas the contextualist model predicts that people's personality is affected by changes in their life circumstances over time. The latter perspective therefore predicts that one will see considerable variability in personality types across different age cohorts.

Srivastava et al. (2003) translated the typical paper-and-pencil version of the Big Five personality inventory to a Web-based form to test competing predictions from biological and contextualist accounts of personality. In total, 132,515 people who ranged in age from 21 to 60 found and completed the inventory. The results of this cross-sectional study found that there was considerable variability in the distributions of Big Five types across different age cohorts, including those well past the age of 30, results that were better explained by contextualist than by biological theories of personality development. Other personality researchers have adapted a variety of other personality inventories for online studies as well (e.g., Foster et al. 2003; Gosling & Bonnenburg 1998; Robins et al. 2001, 2002; Wei et al. 2004).

Other translational research adapted Milgram's (1977) "lost letter" technique for studying attitudes online by sending presumably "lost" e-mail messages to unwitting study participants (e.g., Castelli et al. 2001; Stern & Faber 1997; Vaes et al. 2003, Study 1). For example, Vaes et al. (2003) explored whether people would be more likely to respond to lost e-mail messages as a function of whether the sender was an in- or out-group member, and whether the sender's message expressed a primary or secondary emotion. Participants (400 professors at a Belgian university) "erroneously" received an e-mail from the researchers. The first line of the e-mail was an expression of primary (i.e., "I'm beside myself with rage") or secondary (i.e., "I'm filled with indignation") emotion. To manipulate group membership, the message sender was identified either as a researcher at a different university or at the same university as the recipient. In addition to exploring whether the e-mail was forwarded to the intended recipient, the researchers coded the brief explanatory note that generally accompanied the forwarded message. A solidarity index was calculated by subtracting the number of formal from informal pronouns used in the explanatory note (therefore, negative values on this index reflected greater solidarity, and positive numbers reflected greater distance from the presumed original sender of the e-mail message). Although there were no differences as a function of emotion or group membership on overall forwarding rates of the lost e-mails, forwarded messages expressed higher levels of solidarity with the original writer when it came from an in-group member who expressed a secondary emotion.

Skitka & Mullen (2002) studied reactions of a nationally representative Web-enabled sample (see description of Knowledge Networks below) to assess people's reactions to the case of Elián González (a 6-year-old Cuban boy rescued at sea in November 1999 and brought to the United States) as it unfolded over time. Participants were sent e-mail messages with embedded URLs that directed them to the survey Web site at three critical junctures in this case—several weeks prior to the raid in which U.S. government officials took the boy from relatives and reunited him with his father, two days after the raid, and then the day Elián returned to Cuba. They found that people's postresolution judgments of procedural fairness, outcome fairness, and decision acceptance were predicted solely by preraid assessments of the strength of moral conviction that people associated with the value of political freedom or parental rights. The ability to quickly field a study in response to real-world events, and to instantly contact large samples of people to participate in a survey, are each rather unique advantages of Web-based research (see also Skitka et al. 2004 and Silver et al. 2002 for examples of similar Web-based longitudinal panel designs in response to the events of September 11, 2001).

Health and sports psychologists are also turning to the Web to do research. For example, Langenbucher et al. (2004) used the Web to find 500 anabolic steroid users for their research. Links to the survey were placed on five moderated anabolic steroid discussion boards. The survey assessed the steroid users' training regimen, history of steroid use, and several other measures regarding the effects of steroid use. Results indicated that 60% of participants would use drugs that shortened their lives by an average of five years if it enabled them to enhance their physical performance. In addition, despite the risk of side effects, some of which could pose serious health risks, 54% would continue using steroids for the next 10 years and 34% expected to use anabolic steroids for the rest of their lives. In addition to being an example of translational research, the Langenbucher et al. (2005) study is also an excellent example of how the Web can facilitate access to specialized populations. In addition, the relative anonymity of the Internet probably led to higher response rates to this study than would be likely to be observed with other participant recruitment strategies, given that anabolic steroid use tends to be an intensely solitary practice, hidden even from other users (Langenbucher et al. 2004).

Cognitive researchers have also taken a translational approach to Web-based research. For example, Steyvers & Malmberg (2003) studied context effects on word recognition with both on- and offline samples of college students. Participants were presented with words that systematically varied in their context variability, that is, words that appeared in only one or several different written settings, as well as in their frequency in the English language. Participants then were asked to recall whether they had been exposed to the word in a subsequent word recognition test. Words higher in context variability were recalled less frequently than words low in context variability, regardless of whether participants completed the experiment with traditional paper-and-pencil exposure and test materials or with online exposure and test materials. Other researchers have similarly replicated numerous cognitive effects using online, rather than paper-and-pencil or en vivo presentation of stimulus materials. For example, researchers have examined the interpretation of conditional (if-then) statements (Oberauer & Wilhelm 2003) and the effects of preactivation of content categories on memory (Eichstaedt 2002) using Web-based data collection.

These are but a few examples of areas in which researchers have begun to translate their methods and approaches for use on the Web. Other researchers have successfully adapted their methods to allow them to study these psychological phenomena with online samples and have been able to use this medium to effectively extend research and theorizing in areas of persuasion (e.g., Guadagno & Cialdini 2002; Guégen & Jacob 2001, 2002; Sagarin et al. 2004), implicit attitudes (e.g., Nosek et al. 2002), decoding of nonverbal cues (Hortsman 2003), group dynamics and interaction (Postmes et al. 1999, 2001), relationship formation (McKenna et al. 2002), consumption habits (e.g., Iacobucci 2003), adult attachment (e.g., Wei et al. 2004), job satisfaction (e.g., Judge & Ilies 2004), organizational behavior (e.g., Eaton & Struthers 2002), coping with psychological trauma (Silver et al. 2002), and medical decision making (e.g., Waters et al. 2005).

In sum, increasingly diverse researchers have found that it is both useful and possible to translate traditional measures and methods of psychological research for use on the Web. In fact, the majority of the studies in our sample were straightforward translations of traditional psychological measures and methods for use on the Web. These studies were designed to ask the same kinds of questions and to employ methods that one typically uses in the psychological laboratory. The focus of translational research tends to be less on the Web per se than it is on using the Web as a tool that facilitates ease of reaching participants and ease of data collection. In short, using the Web in translational research is a means to an end, not an interesting end in itself for most of these researchers. Other researchers, however, have been more interested in the unique psychological experiences that might be associated with Web-based interaction.

Phenomenological

Phenomenological research was the next largest category of Web-based psychological research in our sample (36%). Unlike translational research that focuses on general psychological processes and can describe both on- and offline behavior, phenomenological studies are focused more on the specific nature of how Internet use and Internet-based interaction influence people's thoughts, feelings, and behavior (Skitka & Sargis 2005). Researchers have noted that there are at least four novel and important aspects of the online environment that in turn could have novel psychological consequences for those who engage in online behavior (McKenna & Bargh 2000). First, the Internet is a more anonymous interaction setting than most other social environments. Usually, one's physical appearance is one of the most salient features of an interpersonal encounter: People infer a great deal about each other based on characteristics such as gender, race, attractiveness, age, and so forth. Online, people can control what others learn about them—one's gender, etc., can be concealed, revealed, or even changed at will. Second, physical distance is no barrier for interacting with others. Third, people have greater control over the time and place of interaction than is typical of other modalities, such as the telephone or in-person encounters. For example, one can choose whether to respond to an e-mail message immediately or several days later. Fourth, Internet communication is for the most part without visual or auditory cues, such as tone of voice or body posture. Each of these four features of Internet communication in isolation or in combination can lead to online interaction and behavior different from that observed in communication modalities that do not share these relatively unique combinations of features.

McKenna and colleagues' program of research is designed to explore the capacity of the Web to allow people to try out new or less well-accepted aspects of their identities (McKenna & Bargh 1998, 2000; see also Bargh & McKenna 2004 for a review). Interaction on the Web provides a nonthreatening forum for people to explore aspects of themselves that others in their social circle might find unacceptable or offensive. People can and do use the Internet as a relatively safe way to connect with like-minded others and to explore aspects of themselves that they otherwise might have difficulty expressing in their everyday lives. To study the consequences of exploring alternative identities on the Web, McKenna & Bargh (1998) contacted samples of people who frequently posted comments on forums for those with stigmatized sexual identities (e.g., alt.homosexual, alt.bondage; Study 2) or political ideologies (e.g., alt.skinheads, misc.activism.militia, Study 3). These researchers also made a special effort to recruit lurkers to participate by posting invitations for participation in the study on these same forums. The researchers found support for the notion that participation in these online communities had important psychological and interpersonal consequences for those involved. Specifically, people who explored alternative identities in Web-based communities perceived their marginal identity as increasingly important, and this sense of importance led to higher levels of self-acceptance and to disclosing the marginalized identity to friends and family.

Other research has focused on the Web phenomena of blogging, that is, interactive Web pages that are frequently (often daily) updated by their authors. Blog content can vary from being focused on a single topic, such as cooking or politics, or can be an online journal with the author's observations on whatever comes to mind. Readers are often encouraged to post responses or reactions to blogs.

For example, Blanchard (2004) studied the sense of community among those who participated in or followed the Julie/Julia blog. Julie, a Web blogger, worked her way through every recipe in Julia Child's *Mastering the Art of French Cooking* book over the course of a year, and documented her progress and reactions to the experience online. The blog received thousands of daily hits, and provided a forum where readers could comment and the author or others could respond. Julie agreed to let Blanchard post a link on the blog that directed readers and participants to a survey Web site that assessed participants' reactions to following this particular blog. Results of the survey indicated that reading blogs does create a modest sense of community, and active participation (e.g., more frequent posting of comments) led to even stronger senses of community with other blog participants.

An excellent example of the phenomenological approach is research conducted by Kraut and colleagues on the relationship between Internet use and psychological well-being (Kraut et al. 1998, 2002; see also Bargh & McKenna 2004 for a broad review of related research). Kraut and colleagues tested two competing hypotheses about how time spent online would affect people's psychological well-being. Specifically, one could argue that because the Web facilitates social involvement with others through e-mail, instant messaging, and so on, the time spent online facilitates social connections, and for that reason, will facilitate psychological well-being. However, it is also easy to make the opposite prediction. As time online increases, it seems reasonable to assume that time available for in-person social interaction will decrease, and will lead to stronger feelings of social isolation and therefore lower levels of well-being.

To test these competing hypotheses, Kraut et al. (1998) tracked the Internet-use habits of 93 households that were provided Internet access as part of the study. Levels of Internet use, based on server logs of hours spent online, e-mail volume, and number of Web sites visited per week, were tracked. Results indicated that as time spent online increased, real-world social involvement decreased. Participants who spent more time online also reported higher levels of loneliness and depression relative to before they first obtained home access to the Web.

Kraut et al. (2002) reported on a follow-up study of the same participants approximately two years later. The results of this study found that the dismal picture that emerged when people first gained access to the Internet had disappeared once they adapted over a longer period to having home access to the Web. Results revealed that there was no effect of hours spent online on reported loneliness, and that depression was actually lower among heavier than light Web users. These results suggest that even though there may be short-term deleterious consequences with Web use, once people have Web access for a while, increased use is associated with greater social support and higher levels of well-being over time. Related research has explored whether Internet use has similar consequences across different age groups, and has found that although overall time online did not have negative effects on dispositional or daily well-being in a sample of early adolescents, instant messaging activity among close peers was a unique contributor to increased daily social anxiety and loneliness in school (Gross et al. 2002).

Other phenomenological approaches have explored the implications of online sexual role-play and interaction. Some believe that sexual role play and interaction on the Web can facilitate adjustment by providing people with needed validation or sexual education, whereas others are concerned that this kind of online activity has the possibility of interfering with people's offline personal, occupational, and social lives. Cooper et al. (2004) investigated the consequences of online sexual behavior by sending an e-mail invitation to participate in a survey dealing with online sexual behavior to every thousandth visitor to MSNBC's Web site over a one-month period. From an initial pool of 7019 respondents, 403 participants who indicated that their online sexual activities had been a problem for them, and the time they reported spending on online sexual activities seemed out of control, were classified as having online sexual problems. Of these 403 participants, only 19 were women. Consequently, the researchers confined their analyses to the 384 men for whom online use of the Internet for sexual activities appeared to be problematic. The majority of this subsample reported that they engaged in online sexual behavior to alleviate stress; moreover, most reported that they received complaints from their real-life sexual partners about their online activities. Men who turned to sexual role play and behavior online for other reasons, such as sexual education, meeting partners for offline sex, or simply to socialize, were less likely to receive complaints and were more likely to report enhanced sex lives with their partners as a consequence of their online activities than were men motivated by alleviating stress.

The above is a small sample of phenomenological psychological research conducted on the Internet. Other examples of phenomenological research on the Web include studies of cyber-ostracism (i.e., social ostracism in online situations; see, e.g., Williams et al. 2000, 2002), effectiveness of online therapies (e.g., Lange et al. 2003, Ritterband et al. 2003, Strom et al. 2004), e-mail messages as a tool for improving smoking cessation interventions (e.g., Lenert et al. 2004), and the effectiveness of emotional support in online breast cancer support groups (e.g., Lieberman et al. 2004).

Novel

Finally, a small but distinctive portion of the studies we reviewed was best categorized as novel methodological use of the Internet (5%), rather than translational or phenomenological methodological approaches. These studies used methods that to our knowledge did not mirror those typically used in non-Internet based research, that were not focused on studying how people used the Internet or the consequences of their Internet use, and that stood out for their comparative creativity in their approach. These studies are worth bringing into a separate spotlight to illustrate the truly new and innovative ways that one can use the Internet to facilitate psychological inquiry.

For example, Rentfrow & Gosling (2003, Study 4) made creative use of information freely available on the Internet to test hypotheses on the psychology of music preferences. They accessed a random sample of 500 individuals' online music libraries (selecting 10 from each state in the United States) on Web sites that were designed for sharing and downloading of music (e.g., Audiogalaxy.com, Morpheus.com, Napster.com). Music preferences were classified as a function of music genre. Of interest was whether the underlying pattern of dimensionality in music preferences revealed in these libraries paralleled those found when people were asked to report directly their music preferences (Rentfrow & Gosling 2003, Study 2). Results revealed considerable convergence across these very different methods of testing dimensionality of music preferences.

Another study tested a model of social perception by studying the accuracy of personality inferences people derived from personal Web sites (Vazire & Gosling 2004). The researchers sent e-mail messages to people who had posted personal Web pages listed in a Yahoo! directory and asked them to (*a*) complete an online personality inventory (a version of the Big Five personality inventory), and (*b*) supply the name and e-mail address of at least two people who knew them. Experimenters contacted these people and asked them to complete an online personality inventory about the Web page author. Of the 385 Web site authors contacted, 89 completed the consent form for the study and 79 completed the online survey about themselves. The experimenters received two informant responses for 70 of the page authors and at least one informant survey for 81 of the authors.

Self- and close-other ratings were compared with ratings made by third-party judges whose only information about the targets was their personal Web page. Results indicated that there was high convergence of ratings across judges, and that judges were most accurate in predicting openness, followed by conscientiousness, extraversion, and emotional stability. Although significant, judges' predictions of agreeableness were weaker than their predictions for other facets of personality on the Big Five based on knowledge of only targets' Web pages.

Other examples of novel use of the Web in psychological research include a study that staged an online auction to examine ethnic discrimination on a German online auction site. This study involved planting sellers of similar products and varying the ethnicity of their surnames. Sellers with Turkish names (a minority group in Germany) took longer to receive winning bids than did those with German names (Shobat & Musch 2003). Another novel approach involved posting different "problems" on hate-group discussion boards to examine factors that lead to advocating violence against racial minorities (Glaser et al. 2002). Other research has examined rumor transition in a naturalistic setting by studying posts in reaction to a rumor on an electronic bulletin board (Bordia & Rosnow 1998).

METHODOLOGICAL CHARACTERISTICS OF WEB-BASED PSYCHOLOGICAL RESEARCH

In addition to exploring the kinds of questions being investigated in Web-based psychological research, we coded the studies in our sample for whether researchers took correlational, experimental, qualitative, or descriptive approaches in their Web-based research, the kinds of sampling techniques they used, and whether they used informed consent, debriefed participants, and involved deception. A summary of the sample characteristics on these dimensions is presented in Table 3.

TABLE 3   Methodological characteristics of Web-based research in psychological research (using combined American Psychological Association journal and listserv samples)

Method	Percentage
Correlational	39%
Experimental	54%
Qualitative	4%
Descriptive	3%
Sample characteristics[a]	
College students	25%
Targeted sample	36%
Self-selected sample	35%
Random sample	1%
Not reported	1%
Informed consent process	
Clearly obtained	62.5%
Not obtained	12.5%
Unclear	25%
Debriefing	
Participants clearly debriefed	41%
Participants not debriefed	14%
Unclear	45%
Deception	
Yes	18%
No	82%

[a]Two of the reported studies recruited participants both via the Internet and from college student samples.

Methods

As can be seen in Table 3, the majority of studies in our sample reported on experimental research, that is, research that explicitly involved experimental manipulation of a variable or variables (54%). Many of these studies took advantage of HTML code that makes it easy to assign participants randomly to different forms when they access a Web site. Thirty-nine percent of the studies in our sample took correlational approaches and the remaining 7% were either qualitative or descriptive in approach.

Samples

We were also interested in exploring the kinds of samples researchers were attempting to obtain in Web-based research. Clearly, one of the major advantages of turning to the Web to obtain research participants is the ability to either gain access to more representative samples than one typically finds in college student subject pools or to be able to identify participants from specialized populations that are likely to be of low incidence in either the college subject pool or in the population at large. That said, a surprisingly high number of the studies in our sample appeared to be motivated to use the Web and Web-based forms in their research for other reasons, because 25% of them used the Web to collect data from college student samples. Thirty-six targeted specific groups of participants (e.g., random selections of music libraries or Web pages on Yahoo!). Thirty-five percent used what we called "opt-in" samples, that is, samples of people who find the study themselves because they are searching the Web using terms such as "personality tests."

One percent of our sample of studies used true random samples of participants (a total of 9 studies). Studies that took this approach subcontracted their research to be conducted by a company that has created a nationally representative panel of Web-enabled households, about 50% of whom did not have prior home access to the Internet before joining the survey panel (Knowledge Networks; see http://www.knowledgenetworks.com/ganp for more details).[1] A final 1% (9 studies) did not provide information about how they obtained their participants.

---

[1] Knowledge Networks recruits households to join their panel by using random-digit-dialing telephone solicitation, which ensures that there is an equal probability of households with a phone being contacted and invited to participate on the panel. Prospective panelists are offered a free device to connect to the Web and paid Internet access if they join the panel. In exchange, household members above the age of 13 are asked to complete occasional Web surveys. Panelists receive password-protected e-mail accounts, and receive e-mail messages with embedded links to surveys about three times a month. Panel characteristics closely match those of the United States census. A number of other companies also offer access to Web-based panels of people who have agreed to complete surveys, and can offer quota samples that are matched to census characteristics, or sample data weighted by propensity scores to better match census proportions of different demographic groups in the population. However, members of these panels do not include people without prior independent access to the Web. None of the studies in our sample used these alternative sources of data.

Informed Consent

Norms about how to conduct ethical research on the Web are still emerging, including whether it is necessary to collect informed consent to use materials posted on Web sites (e.g., King 1996, Eysenbach & Till 2001). Therefore, it was interesting to explore the degree to which psychological researchers are reporting whether they have obtained informed consent in Web-based research. As can be seen in Table 3, the majority of studies we reviewed explicitly mentioned that they obtained informed consent from their research participants (62.5%). No mention of whether informed consent was obtained was mentioned in 25% of the studies we reviewed, and it was clear that informed consent was not obtained in 12.5% of the studies we reviewed.

Debriefing

We also coded studies in our review for whether they debriefed their research participants. Forty-one percent of the studies we reviewed made explicit mention that research participants were debriefed, 45% were not clear about whether participants were or were not debriefed, and for 14% of the studies, it was clear that participants were not debriefed.

Deception

Finally, we also coded studies for whether they involved deception. As can be seen in Table 3, 17% of the studies in our sample involved deception of research participants. Of those studies that used deception, fewer than half indicated that they debriefed study participants. Although in some cases the deception seemed to be relatively benign, the seemingly high (to these reviewers' minds) level of deception in Web-based research deserves further discussion.

In summary, the Internet is being used primarily for experimental and correlational research. The samples researchers access vary considerably, with a surprisingly high percentage (25%) of researchers still relying on college students even when they turn to the Web to collect data. Therefore, it appears that at least some psychologists are adapting studies to be conducted on the computer using HTML forms in an effort to save the time and effort of manual data entry, and are not turning to the Web because it provides them access to either broader or more specialized samples. Although the majority of researchers who turn to the Web obtain informed consent from their research participants, not as many appear to be debriefed. Finally, 17% of the studies in our Web sample used deception, and only about half of these appeared to debrief their participants.

We discuss below what we perceived as the strengths of the studies we reviewed, as well as the potential advantages of turning to the Internet for psychological research. We then summarize what we perceive as the weaknesses of the studies we reviewed, as well as the potential disadvantages of Web-based psychological research.

THE PROMISE AND ADVANTAGES OF CURRENT WEB-BASED RESEARCH IN PSYCHOLOGY

Web-based psychological research seems to have a number of methodological virtues. Relative to other approaches to collecting data for psychological research, the virtues of Internet-based research generally include (*a*) license for greater measurement and methodological creativity, (*b*) increased efficiency, (*c*) increased access to people with special characteristics, and (*d*) potential for increased data quality.

Creative License

Whenever researchers adopt new technology, there seems to be considerable new license and experimentation in both method and measurement. The sample of studies we reviewed for this chapter often showed remarkable creativity in how researchers operationalized variables and the methods they used to test hypotheses. Sampling online music libraries, studying Web pages, manipulating posts to chat rooms to test for reactions, using graphical displays of people's personality profiles as feedback for completing a personality inventory, and much more were evident in the articles we reviewed. Many of the Web sites that were designed for data collection are also now educational Web sites that teach people about the phenomena researchers are studying (e.g., Nosek et al. 2002). In short, one advantage of turning to the Internet for data collection is that it prompts one to think outside of the traditional box and leads to creative methods and measurement. There also seems to be little research on the Web that asks people to respond to hypothetical scenarios, or to role-play; to a considerable degree, the emphasis is on behavioral indices and measures instead.

Efficiency

Internet research has a number of features that can save time and money (see Skitka & Sargis 2005). With only a little training, one can easily learn some basic programming skills in HTML and can post an interactive form to allow for data collection on the Web. With some additional investment in learning server-side programming, one can also set it up so that data are stored in spreadsheets, ready for analysis (see Birnbaum 2000, 2001; Fraley 2003). Web-based research also avoids the waste and costs associated with paper measures. Moreover, mail-merge programs potentially allow one to field a survey to thousands of prospective participants with no more than a keystroke; alternatively, one can simply post a form and wait for the participants to arrive without ever having to schedule an experimental session. Participants are not typically run through experiments either one at a time or in small groups; therefore, one also has the advantage that the time required for data collection is often independent of sample size. What might take months in the lab to accomplish can be accomplished in a matter of days or weeks on the Web.

Access to Underrepresented or Low-Incidence Samples

Another distinct advantage of Web-based research is the relative ease with which one can find members of groups that one might be particularly interested in studying. For example, many psychological disorders or characteristics that researchers would like to study may be of relatively low incidence in the population in general or in available convenience samples in particular. Searching the Web for special interest or support groups can solve the problem of both finding and accessing these kinds of specialized samples. For example, psychologists have long been interested in trying to account for the psychological factors that are likely to lead to actions of violence toward out-groups (see, e.g., Newman & Erber 2002, Staub 1989). Infiltrating real-world hate groups for the purposes of psychological research is likely to be difficult if not dangerous. Moreover, it is difficult to imagine that many college student subject pools would have sufficient numbers of members who are, or who would admit to being, members of hate groups to allow one to identify appropriate numbers of research participants. Even if one could find members of hate groups, one would not expect them to advocate violence in a laboratory session or in a telephone interview, even if it is something they otherwise would do (cf. Evans et al. 2003). Turning to the Web to test hypotheses about the factors that lead people, and especially hate group members, to advocate violence provides a solution to the usual problem of finding appropriate participants as well as the reactivity of placing these people in a situation that they know is being evaluated.

One group of researchers took advantage of the fact that there are now many hate group–sponsored chat rooms, archives, and Web sites on the Internet, and that these groups provided a novel opportunity to try to test hypotheses about factors that lead these groups to promote intergroup violence. The researchers, who posed as newcomers to a white supremacist online group, posted a problem such as "My sister is talking about getting married to a black man," or "I found out this black couple is moving next door to me" (prompts varied as a function of threat and threat type in a 3 X 3 factorial design; Glaser et al. 2002). Results indicated that hate group members were more likely to advocate violence in response to threats to their group identity (e.g., whites) than to material or economic interests.

Other researchers have similarly used the Internet to obtain access to difficult-to-reach and empirically underrepresented populations such as the anabolic steroid users mentioned above (Langenbucher et al. 2004), gays, lesbians, and bisexuals (see, e.g., Mathy et al. 2002), people with hearing loss (Cummings et al. 2002), and pet owners of a wide range of different animals (Gosling & Bonnenburg 1998). Given the huge number of special interest, news, support, and chat groups that have emerged online, any number of heretofore difficult-to-find populations have become more accessible to researchers.

Data Quality

Recent research indicates that collecting data on the Web avoids some of the data quality problems one sometimes sees when using other collection methods. As also reviewed in Skitka & Sargis (2005), Web-based surveys are lower in measurement error, survey satisficing, and social desirability bias than are surveys conducted over the phone or via intercom (Chang & Krosnick 2002a,b). Other research reveals that computerized data presentation and measurement yields similarly high-quality data as paper questionnaires or face-to-face interviews, and higher quality data than telephone surveys (Richman et al. 1999).

People might also be more likely to persist rather than abandon participation in studies that involve a lot of if-then branching conducted on the Web than in studies conducted via paper questionnaires, because branching can be programmed to occur entirely outside of the awareness of research participants. Moreover, participants are generally volunteers, so data quality may be improved because their motivation and involvement may be higher than that of college students who participate not out of any real interest, but to fulfill course requirements or to earn pocket change. Finally, people might also respond more naturally when they serve as research participants in familiar contexts (e.g., their homes) than in the unfamiliar context of a psychology laboratory.

POTENTIAL LIMITATIONS OR CAUTIONS ASSOCIATED WITH CURRENT WEB-BASED RESEARCH IN PSYCHOLOGY

Although using the Internet for research has a number of potential advantages, our review revealed that it also has a number of limitations (see also Birnbaum 2004, Skitka & Sargis 2005). Potential limitations of current Web-based psychological research include that (*a*) Web users differ from nonusers in a number of ways that may be important, (*b*) response rates to Internet surveys tend to be low, and therefore nonresponse error is quite high, (*c*) a number of technical limitations preclude what kind of research is likely to be suitable for the Web, (*d*) the high anonymity and low accountability of the Web relative to other methods of data collection may introduce a number of problems in some research contexts, (*e*) increased error may occur because of uncontrolled features of participants' context, and finally, (*f*) the potential exists for experimenter deception to "poison the pond" for future psychological research.

Nonrepresentative Samples

One potential limitation of Internet data collection, at least for researchers who take either a novel or translational rather than phenomenological approach to using the Web for research, is sample representativeness (Skitka & Sargis 2005). Although Internet samples would seem to represent a leap forward over the heavy reliance of psychologists on college student samples, psychologists may be simply replacing one flawed sampling approach with another when they turn to convenience samples of Web users. People who use the Internet are not representative of the general population, nor are online special interest groups representative of their specific groups (e.g., disabled people who are online differ in important ways from disabled people who are not online; Lenhart et al. 2003).

Based on national representative telephone surveys that explored differences between Web users and nonusers, Web users are younger, wealthier, and higher in education than are nonusers (Lenhart et al. 2003). In comparison with nonusers, Web users are also higher in trust of others, have broader social networks, and generally believe that people are more fair (Lenhart et al. 2003). Opt-in samples of Web users are also more politically knowledgeable and engaged than are random samples of the population (Chang & Krosnick 2002a,b). Although some differences between Web users and nonusers disappear when disparities in education, income, and age are controlled, other differences persist (e.g., Flemming & Sonner 1999, Taylor 2000). Taken together, these results suggest that a number of important differences exist between people who have Web access versus those who do not, and that these differences limit the generalizability of results obtained from convenience samples of Web users.

One could easily argue that the problem of noncoverage is likely to be one that will eventually take care of itself. However, it is not at all clear that penetration of Internet use is likely to continue to increase. Considerable evidence indicates that the rate of newcomers to the Web has flattened out (Lenhart et al. 2003). In addition, there is some evidence that there are high numbers of people who never intend to have online access in the home, and potentially more problematic, there are large numbers of Internet dropouts, persons who have had home access to the Internet but for a variety of reasons have abandoned it (Lenhart et al. 2003). The tendency to opt out of Internet participation is one that is entirely inconsistent with the patterns of adoption observed with other forms of information or communication technology, such as radio, telephone, or television. In short, noncoverage error contributes to sampling bias unless one uses strategies to include non-Web users in one's sample.

Nonresponse

Noncoverage error refers to the sampling error introduced because not everyone has access to the Web; nonresponse error refers to the fact that not everyone recruited to participate in a given study will choose to do so. Nonresponse can be difficult to calculate for Web studies that post an open invitation for participation because the number of people who could potentially participate but choose not to is unknown. Estimates of response rates of Web users to e-mail solicitation is about 10%, and response rates to specifically targeted banner ads are between 20% and 25%, not anywhere near acceptable response-rate levels to allow for generalization, according to survey research standards (see Couper 2000 for a review). In short, response rates appear to be quite low if the recruitment strategy is either by e-mail or by posting invitations on the Web.

Recent research into the effects of nonresponse error on data quality, however, has found that there is little evidence that recent higher levels of nonresponse in telephone surveys or exit polls has a major effect on the validity of research findings. For example, one study (Keeter et al. 2000) did a side-by-side comparison of telephone surveys that used identical methods with the exception of whether they took extra steps to garner higher response rates (e.g., whether the researchers used call-backs and other attempts to convert nonrespondents into respondents). The survey that made no particular effort to convert nonrespondents had a response rate of 36%, whereas the more rigorous survey had a response rate of almost 61%. Although there were modest differences in the demographic makeup of the samples obtained, the substantive conclusions were essentially identical across the two surveys (Keeter et al. 2000; see also Curtin et al. 2000, Merkle & Edelman 2002 for similar conclusions). However, none of the existing comparisons have explored whether surveys with nonresponse rates of 80% to 90% or more—common in Web-based research—yield conclusions similar to those with better response rates. Therefore, nonresponse bias remains a potentially serious concern for studies that use Web sampling strategies including e-mail solicitations and banner ads, or that simply wait for people to opt in to their studies.

Technical Constraints

Although the Internet affords greater flexibility in presentation of stimuli than, for example, paper questionnaires or telephone surveys, there nonetheless are a number of limitations. One cannot deliver via the Web stimuli that can be touched, tasted, or smelled (see also Birnbaum 2004). Similarly, one cannot send or receive audio or visual responses from research participants without investing in special equipment.

There are also potential concerns about both precision and control as one turns to the Web for research. People's ability to load Web pages, and how quickly they are able to do so, vary dramatically as a function of (a) whether they access the Internet via modem, cable, or a wireless connection; (b) the browser they use; (c) features of the device used to connect to the Web (e.g., RAM, processor speed); and (d) monitor refresh rates. That said, previously established laboratory effects, and in particular effects related to cognitive or visual processing, generally replicate on the Web. For example, McGraw & Wong (1992) replicated the lab finding of a right-visual-field advantage on the Web in a sample of college students. Other researchers have also had very good success in replicating a number of cognitive effects, such as Stroop task interference (Krantz & Dalal 2000, McGraw et al. 2000, Musch & Reips 2000). However, because monitor refresh rates are often slower or similar in speed to the response latencies researchers are trying to detect, the Internet may not be optimal for research that is dependent on detecting reactions to small differences in exposure or small differences in response time.

Context

In addition to error variance introduced through software and hardware variation across respondents, the experimental context is also free to vary in most Internet research, whereas it is kept more constant in laboratory studies. Some people may participate in a given Web study in the presence of others, whereas others will participate while alone; some participants may be highly distracted by other features of the environment that compete for their attention, whereas others will have little in the way of distraction, and so on. How big of a problem this might be probably depends on the phenomena being studied.

Anonymity

A related issue is that social interaction and communication on the Web are often highly if not completely anonymous: People can and do take on alternative identities and can take a number of steps to protect their real identities. People can and do set up multiple e-mail accounts, and researchers have little ability to check the veracity of any given identity. For example, Mathy et al.'s (2002) attempt to study lesbian online behavior was hampered to some degree because it is not unusual for males to pose as lesbians in chat rooms for gay and bisexual women. Although phenomenological researchers are likely to see this kind of posing as an interesting feature of Web-based communication and one worthy of study, the tendency to take on false identities on the Web poses a problem for those whose research depends on successfully identifying specific personal characteristics of research participants.

In addition to possible concerns about research participants who are "posers" of one kind or another, there are other reasons to be concerned about the anonymous nature of the Web. Higher levels of anonymity are well known to be associated with lower levels of self-awareness and individuality (i.e., deindividuation) that in turn can lead to reduced self-regulation and subsequent antisocial behavior (e.g., Deiner 1980, Zimbardo 1970). Perhaps not surprisingly, researchers have found that people are more likely to respond with hostile and aggressive responses in computer-mediated than in face-to-face interactions (Culnan & Markus 1987, Dubrovsky et al. 1991, Kiesler et al. 1984, Siegal et al. 1986, Williams et al. 2002).

In addition, the social identity model of deindividuation (Spears & Lea 1994) predicts that people conform more to group expectations in more deindividuated as compared to more individuated contexts. Therefore, one might expect people to be more likely to conform to group norms in Internet-based communication than in face-to-face interaction settings. Recent research has supported this hypothesis: People show more attitude change in the direction of a group norm in computer-mediated than in non-computer-mediated communications (Sassenberg & Boos 2003).

Increased anonymity is also associated with lower levels of accountability (see Lerner & Tetlock 1999 for a review) that in turn have a number of implications for how people think and behave online. Considerable research has found that people exhibit more bias when they are low rather than high in social accountability for their judgments, decisions, or behaviors. Low levels of accountability are associated with stronger primacy effects in impression formation (Tetlock 1983), an increased tendency to make the fundamental attribution error (Tetlock 1985), and stronger overconfidence effects (Tetlock & Kim 1987), as well as greater persistence due to "sunk costs" (Simonson & Nye 1992). The high anonymity and low accountability of Web-based communication distinguishes it from other communication modalities, a difference that may limit its generalizability.

Ethical Constraints

It seems that most Institutional Review Boards are concluding that online postings represent the public domain and that researchers do not need to obtain informed consent to use this material. There nonetheless is some debate about whether researchers should get informed consent before using Web postings for research (see Frankel & Siang 1999 for a review). Although the public domain argument is a persuasive one to researchers, the public nonetheless may see exploiting online material for research purposes as a violation of their privacy. Consistent with this idea, a number of researchers have discovered that chat room and discussion-group members felt that an implicit social contract had been violated when they discovered that researchers had observed their behavior without their consent (e.g., Finn & Lavitt 1994, King 1996). However, even when researchers do attempt to obtain informed consent, the anonymity of Internet communication can make it difficult to implement the informed consent process. Researchers cannot verify age and mental competency, and the lack of direct contact between researchers and participants makes it difficult for researchers to assess participants' comprehension of risks that may be involved in a given project.

The use of deception in psychological research on the Web is especially problematic, as mentioned above. Deception is considered by many to be ethical if the risks to participants are small, if the hypothesis cannot be tested in nondeceptive ways, and if participants can be effectively debriefed (Smith & Richardson 1983). Debriefing, however, is a difficult thing to accomplish online. With one mouse click, people can close their participation in a chat room, never to return, or similarly may leave an online experiment before reaching the debriefing. Even if participants make it to an online debriefing, or if the researchers e-mail a debriefing to them later, there is no way to be sure that the debriefing has been read (Azar 2000).

Moreover, there has been considerable concern that deception may spoil the pond in research conducted with college student subject pools, specifically, that deceptive research practices may lead students to become more distrustful and change their behavior and attitudes about research (Kelman 1967). The potential risk of deceptive research practices spoiling the online pond and creating widespread public distrust of psychological research and those who do it seems to be even more significant in potential scale and impact than potentially spoiling the pool of college student subjects. At a minimum, researchers have a responsibility to consider the potential vulnerability of the populations they study online, the level of intrusiveness of their research, how best to protect the confidentiality of those they study, and whether public awareness of a given deception has the potential to harm the public's perception of the scientific integrity of the field (Skitka & Sargis 2005).

CONCLUSIONS

Psychologists have already found many useful ways to employ the Internet to facilitate research, and studies that have used the Internet have begun to appear in the field's major journals. Many lab-based methods can be easily translated for use on the Web, and the Internet provides opportunities for considerable methodological creativity and novelty. Moreover, because the Internet is a relatively unique forum for interpersonal behavior, it is becoming the focus of psychological study in and of itself.

Our review suggests that the Internet has some potential major methodological benefits for psychological research, for example, ease in reaching either large or more specialized samples for research than one can typically find in the college student subject pool. However, our review also reveals that there are reasons to be concerned about the responsible use and interpretation of Internet-based research. For example, 17% of the studies we reviewed involved deception of people on the Internet; of these studies, slightly fewer than half reported that they fully debriefed their participants. The ethicality of using deceptive research practices in Web-based research seems to us to be especially problematic. Deceptive research practices have the potential to undermine public trust in psychological research and those who conduct it, in addition to undermining some of the benefits of the Web for those who use it as a safe way to seek out social support and connections with others.

One of the major benefits of turning to the Web for research also reveals one of its major limitations. Although Web-based samples are no doubt more diverse and representative than are college student subject pools of the populations psychologists want to study, not everyone has access to the Web, and there is some evidence that those who do have access are different in a number of important ways from those who do not. Turning to the Web for data collection therefore brings into focus the need for psychologists to think more seriously about sampling and related methodological concerns. Although cost has traditionally been a major barrier to working with more representative samples, it is not an insurmountable one. One can fund research with more representative samples with grants from private or public agencies. In addition, a recent program has emerged to provide researchers with greater access to representative samples without having to apply for an independent grant. The National Science Foundation has funded the Time-sharing Experiments for the Social Sciences program (see http://www.experimentcentral.org/tess for more information), through which researchers may apply for free access to conduct experiments with Knowledge Networks' nationally representative panel or with a nationally representative telephone sample. Although breaking free of the college student subject pool by turning to convenience samples of Web users is one step toward doing research that is more likely to generalize to the populations we wish to understand, it is an imperfect one. Psychological researchers could take further steps and aim to do more research with truly representative samples.

In summary, the Internet provides considerable opportunities to expand the ways that we conduct psychological research. As information and communication technologies continue to advance, so too will the opportunities for collecting data in new and novel ways. Our challenge will be to use each of these advances in ways that also improve the rigor and quality of psychological research.

ACKNOWLEDGMENTS

The authors thank Christopher Bauman and William McCready for reading and providing comments on earlier versions of this chapter, and Jennifer Meyer, Monica Pinedas, Jennifer Thompson, and Ashley Webb for their assistance in identifying articles that used Web-based data collection published in APA journals during 2003–2004 and for their assistance coding the study characteristics of the articles included in this review.

The *Annual Review of Psychology* is online at http://psych.annualreviews.org

LITERATURE CITED

Azar B. 2000. Online experiments: ethically fair or foul? *Monogr. Psychol.* 31:42–47

Bargh JA, McKenna KYA. 2004. The Internet and social life. *Annu. Rev. Psychol.* 55:573–90

Birnbaum MH. 2000. Surveywiz and Factorwiz: JavaScript Web pages that make HTML forms for research on the Internet. *Behav. Res. Methods Instrum. Comput.* 32:339–46

Birnbaum MH. 2001. *Introduction to Behavioral Research on the Internet.* Upper Saddle River, NJ: Prentice Hall

Birnbaum MH. 2004. Human research and data collection via the Internet. *Annu. Rev. Psychol.* 55:803–32

Blanchard AL. 2004. Virtual behavior settings: an application of behavior settings theories to virtual communities. *J. Comput-Mediat. Comm.* 9(2). http://jcmc.indiana.edu/vol9/issue2/blanchard.html

Bordia P, Rosnow RL. 1998. Rumor rest stops on the information highway: a naturalistic study of transmission patterns in a computer-mediated rumor chain. *Hum. Commun. Res.* 25:163–79

Castelli L, Zogmaister C, Arcuir L. 2001. Exemplar activation and interpersonal behavior. *Curr. Res. Psychol.* 6:33–44

Chang L, Krosnick JA. 2002a. *Comparing self-administered computer surveys and auditory*

interviews: an experiment. Paper presented at Am. Assoc. Public Opinion Res. Annu. Meet., St. Petersburg, FL

Chang L, Krosnick JA. 2002b. *RDD telephone vs. Internet survey methodology for studying American presidential elections: comparing sample representativeness and response quality.* Paper presented at Am. Polit. Sci. Assoc. Annu. Meet., Boston, MA

Cooper A, Galbreath N, Becker MA. 2004. Sex on the Internet: furthering our understanding of men with online sexual problems. *Psychol. Addict. Behav.* 18:223–30

Couper MP. 2000. Web surveys: a review of issues and approaches. *Public Opin. Q.* 64:464–94

Culnan MJ, Markus ML. 1987. Information technologies. In *Handbook of Organizational Communication*, ed. F Jablin, LL Putnam, K Roberts, L Porter, pp. 420–43. Newbury Park, CA: Sage

Cummings JN, Sproull L, Kiesler SB. 2002. Beyond hearing: where real-world and online support meet. *Group Dyn.* 6:78–88

Curtin R, Presser S, Singer E. 2000. The effects of response rate changes on the index of consumer sentiment. *Public Opin. Q.* 64:413–28

Deiner E. 1980. De-individuation: the absence of self-awareness and self-regulation in group members. In *The Psychology of Group*

Influence, ed. P Paulus, pp. 1160–71. Hillsdale, NJ: Erlbaum

Dubrovsky VJ, Kielser SB, Sethna BN. 1991. The equalization phenomenon: status effects in computer-mediated and face-to-face decision-making groups. *Hum.-Comput. Interact.* 6:119–46

Eaton J, Struthers CW. 2002. Using the Internet for organizational research: a study of cynicism in the workplace. *CyberPsychol. Behav.* 5:305–13

Eichstaedt J. 2002. Measuring differences in preactivation on the Internet: the content category superiority effect. *J. Exp. Psychol.* 49:283–91

Evans DC, Garcia DJ, Garcia DM, Baron RS. 2003. In the privacy of their own homes: using the Internet to assess racial bias. *Personal. Soc. Psychol. Bull.* 29:273–84

Eysenbach G, Till E. 2001. Ethical issues in qualitative research on Internet communities. *Br. Med. J.* 323:1103–5

Finn J, Lavitt M. 1994. Computer-based self-help groups for sexual abuse survivors. *Soc. Work Groups* 17:21–46

Flemming G, Sonner M. 1999. *Can Internet polling work? Strategies for conducting public opinion surveys on-line.* Presented at Annu. Meet. Am. Assoc. Public Opin. Res., St. Petersburg Beach, FL

Foster JD, Campbell W, Twenge JM. 2003. Individual differences in narcissism: inflated self-views across the lifespan and around the world. *J. Res. Personal.* 37:469–86

Fraley RC. 2003. *How to Conduct Psychological Research over the Internet: A Beginner's Guide to HTML and CGI/Perl.* New York: Guilford

Frankel MS, Siang S. 1999. *Ethical and legal aspects of human subjects research on the Internet: a report of a workshop June 10–11, 1999.* http://www.aaas.org/spp/dspp/sfrl/projects/intres/report.pdf

Glaser J, Dixit J, Green DP. 2002. Studying hate crime with the Internet: What makes racists advocate racial violence? *J. Soc. Issues* 58:177–93

Gosling SD, Bonnenburg AV. 1998. An integrative approach to personality research in anthrozoology: ratings of six species of pets and their owners. *Anthrozoös* 11:148–56

Gross EF, Juvonen J, Gable SL. 2002. Internet use and well-being in adolescence. *J. Soc. Issues* 58:75–90

Guadagno RE, Cialdini RB. 2002. Online persuasion: an examination of gender differences in computer-mediated interpersonal influence. *Group Dyn.* 6:38–51

Guégen N, Jacob C. 2001. Fund-raising on the Web: the effect of an electronic foot-in-the-door on donation. *CyberPsychol. Behav.* 4:705–9

Guégen N, Jacob C. 2002. Social presence reinforcement and computer-mediated communication: the effect of the solicitor's photography on compliance to a survey request made by e-mail. *CyberPsychol. Behav.* 5:139–42

Hortsman G. 2003. What do facial expressions convey: feeling states, behavioral intentions, or action requests? *Emotion* 3:150–66

Iacobucci D, ed. 2003. Consumers in cyberspace [special issue]. *J. Consum. Psychol.* 13:Entire issue

Judge TA, Ilies R. 2004. Affect and job satisfaction: a study of their relationship at work and at home. *J. Appl. Psychol.* 89:661–73

Keeter S, Miller C, Kohut A, Groves RM, Presser S. 2000. Consequences of reducing nonresponse in a national telephone survey. *Public Opin. Q.* 64:125–48

Kelman HC. 1967. Human use of human subjects: the problem of deception in social psychological experiments. *Psychol. Bull.* 67:1–10

Kiesler S, Siegal J, McGuire T. 1984. Social psychological aspects of computer-mediated communication. *Am. Psychol.* 39:1123–34

King SA. 1996. Researching Internet communities: proposed ethical guidelines for the reporting of results. *Inform. Soc.* 12:119–27

Krantz JH, Dalal R. 2000. Validity of Web-based psychological research. In *Psychological Experiments on the Internet*, ed. NM Birnbaum, pp. 35–60. Orlando, FL: Academic

Kraut R, Kiesler S, Boneva B, Cummings J, Helgeson V, Crawford A. 2002. The Internet paradox revisited. *J. Soc. Issues* 58:49–74

Kraut R, Patterson M, Lundmark V, Kiesler S, Mukopadhyay T, Scherlis W. 1998. Internet paradox: a social technology that reduces social involvement and psychological well-being? *Am. Psychol.* 53:1017–31

Lange A, Rietdijk D, Hudcovicova M, van de Ven JP, Schrieken B, Emmelkamp PMG. 2003. Intertherapy: a controlled randomized trial of the standardized treatment of post-traumatic stress through the Internet. *J. Consult. Clin. Psychol.* 71:901–9

Langenbucher J, Hildebrandt T, Carr S, Sanjuan P, Roth S, Parker S. 2004. *Patterns of anabolic steroid use among 500 male weightlifters.* Paper presented at Conf. Coll. Probl. Drug Depend., San Juan, Puerto Rico

Lenert L, Munoz RF, Perez JE, Bansod A. 2004. Automated e-mail messaging as a tool for improving quit rates in an Internet smoking cessation intervention. *J. Am. Med. Inform. Assoc.* 11:16–20

Lenhart A, Horrigan J, Rainie L, Allen K, Boyce A, et al. 2003. *The Ever-Shifting Internet Population: A New Look at Internet Access and the Digital Divide.* Washington, DC: Pew Internet Am. Life Proj.

Lerner JS, Tetlock PE. 1999. Accounting for the effects of accountability. *Psychol. Bull.* 125:255–75

Lieberman MA, Golant M, Winzelberg A, McTavish F, Gustafson DH. 2004. Comparisons: professionally directed and self-directed Internet groups for women with breast cancer. *Int. J. Self-Help Self-Care* 2:219–35

Mathy RM, Schillace M, Coleman SM, Berquist BE. 2002. Methodological rigor with Internet samples: new ways to reach underrepresented populations. *Cyberpsychol. Behav.* 5:253–66

McGraw KO, Tew MD, Williams JE. 2000. The integrity of Web-delivered experiments: Can you trust the data? *Psychol. Sci.* 11:502–6

McGraw KO, Wong SP. 1992. A common language effect size statistic. *Psychol. Bull.* 111:361–65

McKenna KYA, Bargh JA. 1998. Coming out in the age of the Internet: identity "demarginalization" through virtual group participation. *J. Personal. Soc. Psychol.* 75:681–94

McKenna KYA, Bargh JA. 2000. Plan 9 from cyberspace: the implications of the Internet for personality and social psychology. *Personal. Soc. Psychol. Rev.* 4(1):57–75

McKenna KYA, Green AS, Glason MEJ. 2002. Relationship formation and the Internet: What's the big attraction? *J. Soc. Issues* 58:9–32

Merkle D, Edelman M. 2002. Non-response in exit polls: a comprehensive analysis. In *Survey Non-response*, eds. RM Groves, DA Dillman, JL Eltinge, RJA Little, pp. 243–58. New York: Wiley

Milgram S. 1977. *The Individual in the Social World.* New York: McGraw Hill

Musch J, Reips U. 2000. A brief history of Web experimenting. In *Psychological Experiments on the Internet*, ed. M Birnbaum, pp. 61–87. Orlando, FL: Academic

Newman L, Erber R. 2002. *Understanding Genocide: The Social Psychology of the Holocaust.* New York: Oxford Univ. Press

Nosek BA, Banaji MR, Greenwald AG. 2002. Harvesting implicit group attitudes and beliefs from a demonstration Website. *Group Dyn.* 6:101–15

Oberauer K, Wilhelm O. 2003. The meaning(s) of conditionals: conditional probabilities, mental models, and personal utilities. *J. Exp. Psychol. Learn.* 29:680–93

Postmes T, Spears R, Lea M. 1999. Social identity, normative content, and "deindividuation" in computer-mediated groups. In *Social Identity: Context, Commitment, and Content*, ed. N Ellmers, R Spears, D Doosje, pp. 164–83. Oxford: Blackwell

Postmes T, Spears R, Sakhel K, de Groot D. 2001. Social influence in computer-mediated communication: the effects of anonymity on group behavior. *Personal. Soc. Psychol. Bull.* 27:1243–54

Rentfrow PJ, Gosling SD. 2003. The do re

mi's of everyday life: examining the structure and personality correlates of music preferences. *J. Personal. Soc. Psychol.* 84:1236–56

Richman W, Kiesler S, Weisband S, Drasgow F. 1999. A meta-analytic study of social desirability distortion in computer-administered questionnaires, traditional questionnaires, and interviews. *J. Appl. Psychol.* 84:754–75

Ritterband LM, Cox DJ, Walker LS, Kovatchev B, McKnight L, Patel K. 2003. An Internet intervention as adjunctive therapy for pediatric encopresis. *J. Consult. Clin. Psychol.* 71:910–17

Robins RW, Tracy JL, Trzesniewski KH, Potter J, Gosling SD. 2001. Personality correlates of self-esteem. *J. Res. Personal.* 35:463–82

Robins RW, Trzesniewski KH, Tracy JL, Gosling SD, Potter J. 2002. Global self-esteem across the lifespan. *Psychol. Aging* 17:423–34

Sagarin BJ, Britt MA, Heider J, Wood SE, Lynch J. 2004. *The distraction and persuasion effects of on-line advertisements.* Presented at Midwest. Psychol. Assoc. Annu. Meet., Chicago, IL

Sassenberg K, Boos M. 2003. Attitude change in computer-mediated communication: effects of anonymity and category norms. *Group Process. Intergroup Relat.* 6:405–22

Sears DO. 1986. College sophomores in the lab: influences of a narrow data base on social psychology's view of human nature. *J. Personal. Soc. Psychol.* 51:515–30

Shobat M, Musch J. 2003. Online auctions as a research tool: a field experiment on ethnic discrimination. *Swiss J. Soc. Psychol.* 62:139–45

Siegal J, Dubrovsky V, Kiesler S, McGuire TW. 1986. Group processes in computer-mediated communication. *Organ. Behav. Hum. Dec.* 37:157–87

Silver RC, Holman EA, McIntosh DN, Poulin M, Gil-Rivas V. 2002. Nationwide longitudinal study of psychological responses to September 11. *J. Am. Med. Assoc.* 288:1235–44

Simonson I, Nye P. 1992. The effect of account-ability on susceptibility to decision errors. *Organ. Behav. Hum. Dec.* 51:416–46

Skitka LJ, Bauman CW, Mullen E. 2004. Political tolerance and coming to psychological closure following September 11, 2001: a model comparison approach. *Personal. Soc. Psychol. Bull.* 30:743–56

Skitka LJ, Mullen E. 2002. Understanding judgments of fairness in a real-world political context: a test of the value protection model of justice reasoning. *Personal. Soc. Psychol. Bull.* 28:1419–29

Skitka LJ, Sargis EG. 2005. Social psychological research and the Internet: the promise and peril of a new methodological frontier. In *The Social Net: The Social Psychology of the Internet*, ed. Y Amichai-Hamburger, pp. 1–25. New York: Cambridge Univ. Press

Smith S, Richardson D. 1983. Amelioration of deception and harm in psychological research: the important role of debriefing. *J. Personal. Soc. Psychol.* 44:1075–82

Spears R, Lea M. 1994. Panacea or panopticon? The hidden power in computer-mediated communication. *Commun. Res.* 21:427–59

Srivastava S, John OP, Gosling SD, Potter J. 2003. Development of personality in adulthood: set like plaster or persistent change? *J. Personal. Soc. Psychol.* 84:1041–53

Staub E. 1989. *The Roots of Evil: The Psychological and Cultural Origins of Genocide.* New York: Cambridge Univ. Press

Stern SE, Faber JE. 1997. The lost e-mail method: Milgram's lost letter technique in the age of the Internet. *Behav. Res. Methods Instrum. Comput.* 29:260–63

Steyvers M, Malmberg KJ. 2003. The effect of normative context variability on recognition memory. *J. Exp. Psychol. Learn.* 29:760–66

Strom L, Pettersson R, Andersson G. 2004. Internet-based treatment for insomnia: a controlled evaluation. *J. Consult. Clin. Psychol.* 72:113–20

Taylor H. 2000. Does Internet research work? Comparing online survey results with telephone survey. *Int. J. Market Res.* 42:51–63

Tetlock PE. 1983. Accountability and perseverance of first impressions. *Soc. Psychol. Q.* 46:285–92

Tetlock PE. 1985. Accountability: a social check on the fundamental attribution error. *Soc. Psychol. Q.* 48:227–36

Tetlock PE, Kim JI. 1987. Accountability and judgment processes in a personality prediction task. *J. Personal. Soc. Psychol.* 52:700–9

Vaes J, Paladino MP, Castelli L, Leyens JP. 2003. On the behavioral consequences of infrahumanization: the implicit role of uniquely human emotion in intergroup relations. *J. Personal. Soc. Psychol.* 85:1016–34

Vazire S, Gosling SD. 2004. e-Perceptions: impressions based on personal Websites. *J. Personal. Soc. Psychol.* 87:123–32

Waters EA, Weinstein ND, Colditz GA, Emmons K. 2005. Formats for improving risk communications in medical tradeoff decisions. *J. Health Com.* In press

Wei M, Russel DW, Mallinckrodt B, Zakalik RA. 2004. Cultural equivalence of adult attachment across four ethnic groups: factor structure, structured means, and associations with negative mood. *J. Couns. Psychol.* 51:408–71

Williams KD, Cheung CKT, Choi W. 2000. CyberOstracism: effects of being ignored over the Internet. *J. Personal. Soc. Psychol.* 79:748–62

Williams KD, Govan CL, Croker V, Tynan D, Cruickshank M, Lam A. 2002. Investigations into differences between social and cyber ostracism. *Group Dyn.* 6:65–77

Zimbardo P. 1970. The human choice: individuation, reason, and order versus deindividuation, impulse, and chaos. In *Nebraska Symposium on Motivation*, ed. WJ Arnold, D Levine, 17:237–307. Lincoln: Univ. Nebraska Press

Annu. Rev. Psychol. 2006. 57:557–83
doi: 10.1146/annurev.psych.57.102904.190110
First published online as a Review in Advance on August 31, 2005

FAMILY VIOLENCE

Patrick Tolan, Deborah Gorman-Smith, and David Henry

*Institute for Juvenile Research, University of Illinois at Chicago, Chicago, Illinois 60608;
email: Tolan@uic.edu, debgs@uic.edu, DHenry@uicvm.cc.uic.edu*

Key Words domestic violence, spouse abuse, child abuse, maltreatment, elder abuse

■ **Abstract** Family violence occurs in many forms; the most prominent are domestic violence, child abuse, and elder abuse. Family violence affects many persons at some point in their life and constitutes the majority of violent acts in our society. Although there has been considerable study of the patterns, risk factors, and interventions for each form of family violence, great controversy still exists within each area. There is growing recognition of an overlap in the patterns, causes, and effective interventions across types of family violence. There is also an increasing awareness of the value of greater integration of theory and research across areas into a family violence approach through an ecological perspective. This review focuses on current knowledge related to these problems and suggests integrative steps to advance knowledge.

CONTENTS

INTRODUCTION

In the past ten years, family violence has come to be recognized as a major public health issue with important psychological components and ramifications (Am. Psychol. Assoc. 1996, Chalk & King 1998). In part, this recognition is the result of efforts to track prevalence patterns, to evaluate potential risk and protective factors, and to execute well-designed evaluations of interventions (Tolan & Gorman-Smith 2002). But much of the recognition is from advocacy about policy related to each of the major component problems: domestic violence, child abuse, and elder abuse[1] (Loseke et al. 2005, Graham-Bermann & Edleson 2001). Although science and social pressure both contribute to bringing needed interest in this problem, the difference in motivations for these two types of efforts has impeded advancement of scientific study that could lead to integration of knowledge and policy about family violence. Because there has been passionate and sophisticated advocacy on questions of how key constructs should be composed, what research is relevant, and how results should be interpreted, at times, much of the research has substantial limitations in resolving major contentions.

The field is also marked by segregated understanding and policy direction for each of the major forms of family violence (O'Leary 1993). Theory and research tend to be focused on domestic violence, child abuse, or elder abuse, with little crossover in investigators or in how issues are framed. There has been preoccupation with controversies about conceptualization, definition, and measurement within each area, rather than focus on the relation between areas and an overall understanding of violence in families (Loseke et al. 2005). Because research has been cast within area-specific perspectives, many studies are not able to address alternative explanations. Similarly, advocacy efforts to promote policy change in one area have usually focused on a single problem or perspective about family violence and in doing so have oversimplified or ignored other forms of family violence or complex issues in affecting change in violence rates (Am. Psychol. Assoc. 1996). For example, advocates for policies to affect child abuse by requiring removal of the offending parent may overlook that important ties of the nonoffending parent to the abusing parent could undermine compliance with reporting abuse.

Thus, a survey of the work of the past decade reveals disparate sets of studies, each with its own scientific and policy discussions. Also, within areas the relation of policy advocacy to research has been limited. However, there is an emerging recognition of considerable overlap in the occurrence of these problems: They share many risk factors, and effective interventions for each share many features. In addition, it is being recognized that such broader consideration helps relate

---

[1]For efficiency and consistency in referencing, we refer to the three general types of family violence with terms that are commonly used: domestic violence, child abuse, and elder abuse. This is not meant to ignore the complex issues under debate about terminology, nor is it an indication of a particular perspective on this issue.

how work to affect families with one type of violence can help affect and even prevent other forms (Chalk & King 1998). There is also growing recognition of the importance of understanding why so much violence is family based and how focusing on family may have benefits for each type (Jouriles et al. 2001). Recognition of the need for greater integration is accompanied by an appreciation that family violence is a complex problem marked by a challenging set of scientific and practical issues that need to be managed to reduce this public health threat (Graham-Bermann & Edleson 2001).

This review examines the recent research on patterns of occurrence, risk factors, and promising interventions across three major areas of family violence (domestic violence, child abuse, and elder abuse). With an orientation toward integration into a family violence perspective, this summary then serves as the basis for recommendations for conceptualizing the problem, for conducting needed research, and for proposing how such research might inform policy. Because conceptual issues remain controversial, we first address why a focus on family violence in particular is valuable and then discuss some of the issues related to controversies about defining family violence and its forms.

FOCUSING ON FAMILIES AND VIOLENCE

There are several reasons why family violence merits an integrative focus while being distinguished from other forms of violence. First, in contrast to other forms of violence, such as gang violence, violent crime, or war, family violence presupposes a relationship between those involved. Violence that occurs among family members presents a paradox in that harm is purposely inflicted by those who are supposed to care for or depend on one another (Jouriles et al. 2001). Family violence is antithetical to the widely and firmly held value of the family as a dependable, safe, and critical positive developmental influence (Am. Psychol. Assoc. 1996). The violence seems inextricably bound up in multifaceted important relationships, and addressing family relationships is essential for understanding and addressing the problem (O'Leary 1993).

Second, family violence is the most prevalent form of violence in this country (Am. Psychol. Assoc. 1996, Tolan & Gorman-Smith 2002). Regardless of age, violence between family members is more common than violence between acquaintances or strangers. Affecting violence rates depends much on understanding how violence within families occurs and can be prevented.

Third, unlike other forms of violence, relationships usually exist between family violence victims and perpetrators prior to, during, and after violent incidents or periods. Also, throughout the life cycle of the family, members can be both perpetrators and victims. Risk assessment and intervention will be enhanced if these complexities, which differentiate family violence from other forms of violence, are considered (Cordova et al. 1993, O'Leary 1993).

A fourth reason to differentiate family violence is that in most societies, violence among family members has a legal meaning that is different from other forms of violence. Some forms of violence may be viewed by many as helpful or necessary (e.g., physical punishment of children) or typical or normative (e.g., violence between siblings) and therefore not criminal or a social problem. Milder versions of most forms of family violence are common and occur at some point in many marital, child rearing, or elder care relationships (Shafer et al. 1998). Linkages of milder forms of family violence to harmful effects are inconsistent and usually modest (Magdol et al. 1997, Margolin & Gordis 2000). Because many forms of family violence are sanctioned, accepted, or considered only a minor threat, study and interventions may require more complex approaches than would occur for other types of violence. Moreover, there is a need to facilitate an understanding of the substantial harm to children who are abused, couples that injure each other, women who are battered, and elders who are harmed by those caring for them (Shafer et al. 1998). Family violence results in physical injuries and deaths, psychological impact, and detrimental functioning as well as great costs related to health care, criminal justice, and decreased productivity, particularly when it is chronic, causes serious injury, and is accompanied by other harmful and dysfunctional relationship characteristics (Am. Psychol. Assoc. 1996).

These multiple distinguishing features provide ample reason to focus on family violence. Although not wholly independent of other forms of violence, family violence presents unique conceptual, scientific, and policy challenges. A focus on family violence can also serve to relate the emerging pieces of scientific evidence and the important conceptual and policy contentions that are vexing each area. Such integration should advance understanding and effective response to this major health and social problem.

DEFINING FAMILY VIOLENCE

Much controversy exists about how to define family violence and its components. As noted by Jouriles et al. (2001), these are more than semantic disputes; they represent major differences in views about the important features of the problem.

A central controversy is the degree to which the term "family violence" should be synonymous with abuse or substantial mistreatment of family members (Jouriles et al. 2001). Should the definition encompass all acts of violence, or only serious or ongoing patterns of violence? One argument is that family violence should be limited to problems and patterns that clearly are harmful and for which there is consensus that they are not to be tolerated. Restricting the definition in this manner would assure that these serious problems are not underemphasized as the result of the inclusion of minor and more accepted acts, and would prevent a muddying of the meaning of empirical findings and policy discussions. In contrast, it has been argued that focusing only on physical violence that clearly causes serious harm is too narrow a conception because it does not include some behaviors and relationship characteristics of families that do not involve physical violence or its threat, particularly coercive control, neglect, and psychological and verbal abuse, which may occur along with, and be as threatening as, physical violence (Heise

1998). Another argument is that actual physical violence is part of a set of behaviors that define abuse, and to separate them is to neglect important contributors to the abusive impact (Jouriles et al. 2001).

The behaviors included in the definition of family violence can affect the rates, meanings, and implications drawn about family violence. The current prevailing view seems to be to equate family violence to abuse, including nonviolent abuse, because this type of abuse is most relevant in forming policy. However, while the conceptual interest may be on serious violence, it may make up only a small portion of the measure of violence. For example, studies of child abuse often include not only abused children but also children who have been neglected in regard to care for their basic needs (Jouriles et al. 2001). Because the prevalence of neglect is about three times that of physical abuse, many samples in studies of child abuse are predominately made up of children who have been neglected. If results are rendered without consideration of the sample makeup, the implications for family violence may be misunderstood (Cicchetti et al. 2000) and the different as well as overlapping effects of neglect and violence may be overlooked (Edleson 2001).

Another controversial issue is how to incorporate into the definition of family violence the gender inequities and dependency differences related to power within family relationships. A central tenet of much of the initial work bringing attention to domestic violence was that male-to-female violence differed from female-to-male violence, even when the specific acts were the same, because of social differences in gender-accorded power in male-female relationships (Am. Psychol. Assoc. 1996, Heise 1998). Others argue that failure to equate violence perpetrated by females with that perpetrated by males may lead to inappropriate characterization of violence that may harm both genders. This view is predicated on the idea that violent acts should be measured along with the circumstances of their occurrence, and then meaning should be attached to the acts to formulate understanding. To date, empirical tests do not support the contention that all violence of spouses or other couples occurs within the context of such a power differential (Johnson 1995). Similarly, emerging data that include more broadly based samples and both genders as sources suggest that much of the violence between couples is similar in frequency, seriousness, and initiation, and that it may be better explained from a relationship perspective than as the imposition of power of one person over another (Magdol et al. 1997). Other studies provide evidence of patterns of serious, quite dangerous violence primarily by men toward women, which calls into question the extent to which the survey data are sensitive to this type of domestic violence (Hines & Malley-Morrison 2004).

A fourth issue in defining family violence is the extent to which common or socially sanctioned violent behavior in family relationships should be considered problematic (Hines & Malley-Morrison 2004). If some violence is not unusual in dating, marital, and other similar intimate relationships, and if both males and females use it with no clear pattern of initiation or seriousness, how should it be considered when formulating definitions of family violence (Magdol et al. 1997)? Should the definition be limited to violence that is unusual, lasting, or that causes serious harmful effects, so that family violence can be understood as a major health threat? A similar issue arises in consideration of corporal punishment, which is a common practice in the United States. Although researchers find inconsistent results regarding negative effects of corporal punishment, parenting experts and mental health professionals are consistently negative regarding its value for disciplining children (Benjet & Kazdin 2003). A third example of this issue is the often overlooked but perhaps most prevalent form of family violence, violence between siblings (Straus & Gelles 1990). Those arguing from a human rights perspective have noted that these forms of violence would carry legal sanction if they occurred between persons in any relationship other than that of a parent and child or siblings (Hines & Malley-Morrison 2004). Others argue that equating disciplinary spanking of a child to abusive violence undercuts the credibility of findings and may distract attention from more serious violence toward children.

Each of these controversies contains disputed elements about the political ramifications of terminology, the value of studying violence apart from presumption of effects or implications, and the extent to which violent acts are seen as part of a broader set of problematic behaviors and relationship characteristics. Also, each arises from an emphasis on one part of the ecological picture of family violence, often within a specific type of family violence. Because work has been segregated within areas, and much of that work has been developed with the intent to validate a given view rather than to resolve key controversies, the field has the formidable challenge of attempting to forge conceptual consensus about how to define components of family violence while simultaneously trying to relate these areas of study. As the literature develops and reviews accumulate, it has become evident that this is a complex problem with multiple influences, and many aspects must be considered when weighing potential solutions (Daro et al. 2004, Margolin & Gordis 2000).

Numerous reviews have attempted to address this issue and to suggest why one aspect is more primary or important than another, why one view should prevail over others, and/or to suggest operational definitions that promote one connotation (see Am. Psychol. Assoc. 1996, Chalk & King 1998, Natl. Res. Counc. 1993 for examples). However, there is also increasing interest in relating these components and views in order to understand the ecology of family violence (Daro et al. 2004, Jouriles et al. 2001). Consensus is forming to consider threatening verbal behavior and intimidation as components of family violence, especially when measuring impact and characterizing patterns of such violence (Chalk & King 1998, Jouriles et al. 2001). Also, there is shared recognition that violence in family relationships may have different meanings because of dependency among family members, and that variation exists in the role that violence may play in family relationships (Johnson 1995). Growing evidence also indicates that there are multiple influences on family violence, ranging from individual, to relationship, to setting or context characteristics.

The building of further consensus would require studies that measure violent acts specifically but separately, while also measuring psychological aggression and coercive and intimidating aspects of relationships along with related components such as felt fear, intention of violent acts, relation to other relationship qualities, and developmental and functional outcomes. Such studies would permit work that could address competing hypotheses about the nature and heterogeneity of family violence forms as well as permit better understanding of the interrelations among forms of family violence and the relation of violent behavior to abuse. Accurate characterization of these features would clarify which contentions about defining family violence are most supported and how different concepts might be ordered and related—information that is critical for real advancement in risk and intervention research.

THE PREVALENCE OF FAMILY VIOLENCE

The many controversies and disagreements in the conceptualization, definition, and measurement of family violence make it difficult to ascertain the prevalence rates and patterns of its different forms (Loseke et al. 2005). For example, in domestic violence research, opinions differ on whether prevalence—in particular, gender rates—should be determined from community samples that use surveys listing aggressive acts or from clinical samples of victims or perpetrators of domestic violence (Archer 2000, Johnson 1995). Although the survey sampling method may capture the basic differences in rates, it has been argued it may relegate to low importance differences in felt fear, injury, or patterns of threatening and controlling use of violence. Population-based surveys may overlook the serious problem of women being battered and terrorized by men because such patterns are relatively rare in the general population and because such surveys do not tap psychological aspects of the violent act (Johnson 1995). These contentions also extend to the samples of interest. Much of the early work to measure domestic violence relied on reports of female victims, particularly those residing at shelters for abused women (Loseke et al. 2005). Although it served to identify the seriousness of domestic violence, this sampling approach is biased when it is used to generalize about rates or patterns of domestic violence. Johnson (1995) argued that these strategies can be complimentary and may focus on nonoverlapping populations. For example, studies of partner violence that use community samples find high rates of "common couple violence"—the "occasional lapses of control by either partner" (Archer 2000, p. 651). In contrast, studies that use clinical samples or samples selected because of their involvement as victims or perpetrators of violence tend to suggest high rates of battering by men toward women. Both approaches accurately describe patterns among their samples, but do not account well for the focus of the other. Moreover, what the studies describe in juxtaposition are two important aspects of domestic violence: (*a*) There are relatively high rates of violence among couples, with perpetration rates similar for both genders, and (*b*) male battering of females is a rare but very serious pattern within those overall rates.

Domestic Violence Prevalence

Without exception, community and representative samples report similar high rates of violent domestic or partner acts for men and women (Straus & Gelles 1990).

For example, in the National Family Violence Survey, the overall rates of assaults by women were 124 per 1000 couples, as compared with 122 per 1000 for assaults by men. The rate of minor assaults by women was 78 per 1000 couples; the rate by men was 72 per 1000. The severe assault rate by women was 46 per 1000 couples; the rate by men was 50 per 1000. None of these differences was statistically significant. Estimates were based on reports by women regarding their own and their partner's behavior, to account for the possibility that men may underreport their own assaults. Evidence suggests that among younger age groups, rates for perpetration are somewhat higher for women (Archer 2000, Magdol et al. 1997, Straus & Gelles 1990). Moffitt & Caspi (1999) used the findings of three studies with large community-based samples to compares rates of physical aggression toward partners in late adolescence and young adulthood. Perpetration rates ranged from approximately 36% to 50% for women and 25% to 40% for men. The same patterns have been found in studies using observational measures (Capaldi & Gorman-Smith 2003).

In addition to comparable rates of violence perpetration, data from national surveys and longitudinal studies indicate that violence between partners is often bidirectional, meaning that it occurs by women to men as well as by men to women (Capaldi & Clark 1998). Rates of bidirectional aggression among couples with any history of violence range from 59% to 71% (Capaldi & Clark 1998, Henton et al. 1983). In every study that has examined the issue, rates of initiation by women are as high as rates of initiation by men (Straus 2005). That is, women do not use violence only in self-defense. Couples report similar frequency and severity of violence perpetration, victimization, and levels of responsibility for initiating the violence (Henton et al. 1983, Moffitt & Caspi 1999). Contrary to what might be expected, in comparison with bidirectional violent couples, couples with unidirectional violence report fewer acts and forms of violence, and the acts are less likely to lead to more violence and injuries. Individuals participating in bidirectional aggression are also more likely to be involved in physical aggression across relationships (Capaldi & Clark 1998, Moffitt & Caspi 1999).

These survey findings suggest that few gender differences exist in overall perpetration of violence with partners. Existing findings also do not support the view that unidirectional violence is more persistent across relationships or is more serious or injurious. The strength of the sampling and measurement in these studies suggest results are valid. However, although these surveys are capable of addressing overall patterns, they are less able to characterize rarer and perhaps more harmful patterns of violence. A recent meta-analysis (Archer 2002) of sex differences in aggression between male-female partners suggests some directions for extending understanding of gender patterns and for relating overall findings to more specific patterns. In a meta-analysis of 522 articles, Archer (2002) found a higher prevalence of aggression for females than for males among younger couples (14–22 years of age), and a higher prevalence of aggression for males than for females among older couples (23–49 years of age). Injury rates among younger couples were almost equal for males and females, but rates were higher by males in samples of older couples.

Also, although this gender difference emerged, a significant proportion of injuries were sustained by males from female partners. These findings suggest that in addition to characterizing relative rates of violent acts, researchers should attempt to understand how such rates may change as a function of age, duration, status of relationship, and the relation of gender identity to these characteristics (Jouriles et al. 2001). These data do suggest value in increasing the focus on relationship factors to understand risk and develop interventions, even while proper interventions and policies contribute to efforts to address more unidirectional male-to-female violence.

Attempts have rarely been made to use more general samples to identify and adequately characterize the rate of battering of women by men. Because the base rates of this type of violence are likely to be low in community-representative samples, very large samples would be needed. Also, it has been contended that perpetrators and victims of serious battering may be less likely to report such behaviors for a variety of legal, social norm, and safety reasons (Loseke & Kurz 2005). These issues call for methods that build on trust and extended involvement, which are difficult to achieve with large sample studies. Some have argued that arrests for domestic violence can be useful in identifying such patterns, as these arrests are more likely to occur with the type of violence that characterizes battering (Loseke & Kurz 2005). Although such studies find an arrest rate for partner violence that is seven times higher for men than for women, these rates are much lower than rates found in surveys for similar behaviors. This discrepancy raises questions about whether these gender rate differences reflect actual differences in seriousness and frequency of behavior, or whether they result from a differential relation of behavior to reporting violence to police and in police reaction depending on the gender of the victim.

Child Abuse Prevalence

As with the other forms of violence, rates of family violence toward children are difficult to ascertain due to controversies and related variations in definition, measurement, methods, sampling, and reporting across studies and surveys. As noted above, many studies that attempt to measure the problem focus on child abuse, including neglect and other maltreatment of children, rather than on violence specifically. For example, the World Health Organization (2002) offers the following definition: "Child abuse or maltreatment constitutes all forms of physical and/or emotional ill-treatment, sexual abuse, or neglect or negligent treatment or commercial or other exploitation, resulting in actual or potential harm to the child's health, survival, development or dignity in the context of a relationship of responsibility, trust or power" (p. 38). Although this definition is inclusive and perhaps is helpful in serving policy discussions, it leaves unanswered the question of whether a given act would be considered abuse. Moreover, there is no explicit emphasis on differences in the relationship of the child to the perpetrator. Even when more specific criteria are used, definitions vary substantially regarding which forms of violence are included. For example, sexual violence often is not included in measures of violence toward children, nor is it studied as a separate problem. In part, this is because of the more general issue that any report of abuse toward a child can create a legal liability for the reporter, could lead to a loss of custody or other parental rights, and may otherwise be perceived as dangerous. Moreover, protections for human subjects appropriately emphasize the well-being of the child over the confidentiality of the reporter or the scientific integrity of the study. These features make it difficult to obtain valid and full reporting, even if the definition of abuse were clear and consistently applied.

Because of these reporting hindrances, child abuse prevalence estimates are most often based on official records of legal and social service agencies. These data have the same limitations as other official records about crime: Many influences determine which acts are recorded, which calls into question the usefulness of official data in measuring actual prevalence. Moreover, because child welfare budgets are major components of most state budgets, these rates can have serious political importance. In combination, these features should lead to researchers to use great caution in relying on estimates of child abuse as currently assessed and defined, and that caution should be heightened when the interest is in family violence.

With those cautions, the best available data suggest that child abuse is a prevalent problem. The most recent data from the National Clearinghouse on Child Abuse and Neglect Information (2004) are based on official reports collected from child protective services and professionals in schools, hospitals, and other agencies. These data indicate that approximately 906,000 children were victims of child abuse or neglect in 2003, which is a rate of 12.4 victims per 1000 children in the national population. More than 60% of victims experienced neglect, 19% were physically abused, 10% were sexually abused, and 5% were emotionally abused. In addition, 17% were associated with other types of abuse. Children under age 3 had the highest rates of victimization (16.4 per 1000), and girls were slightly more likely to be victims than were boys. Rates also differed by ethnic group. In 2003, an estimated 1500 children died as the result of abuse or neglect. Approximately 80% of the perpetrators were parents. Other relatives accounted for 6% of the deaths, and unmarried partners of parents accounted for 4% of perpetrators. Of those killed, 79% were younger than 4 years. As expected, community surveys suggest much higher rates of all forms of child abuse and maltreatment. For example, Straus and colleagues (1997) reported prevalence rates for physical abuse of 49 per 1000 children. Survey estimates of the prevalence of sexual abuse also show higher rates than official those reflected by records. However, the rates across surveys vary greatly (e.g., 3% to 36%), depending on the definition used, the way data are recorded, the age group surveyed, the period of exposure considered, and the extent to which the survey relies on recall of distant past events (Finkelhor et al. 1997). Unlike other forms of abuse, females are much more likely to be victims of sexual abuse than are males (approximately four times as likely).

Elder Abuse Prevalence

Similar to other areas of family violence, definition issues affect the understanding of findings about elder abuse. However, there appears to be more consistency in what definition is used. The definition most widely used and adopted is by the International Network for the Prevention of Elder Abuse, which states: "Elder abuse is a single or repeated act or lack of appropriate action, occurring within any relationship where there is an expectation of trust which causes harm or distress to an older person" (World Health Org. 2002, p. 126). Such abuse is usually divided into the following categories: (*a*) physical abuse, (*b*) psychological or emotional abuse, (*c*) financial or material abuse, (*d*) sexual abuse, and (*e*) neglect. Because elder abuse has only relatively recently been recognized as a problem, there are few studies of prevalence or incidence. Surveys using this inclusive definition indicate an overall rate of elder abuse between 4% and 6% of the population (Pillemer 2005, World Health Org. 2002). The National Center on Elder Abuse (1998) survey found that approximately 450,000 persons aged 60 and older were abused and/or neglected in the United States during a single year. Official reports that were substantiated were filed for only 16% of the victims. Rates were significantly higher for those over 80 years of age and females; 80% of victims were white.

RISK FACTORS AND EXPLANATORY MODELS

Reviewing the risk factor research for any one type of family violence could easily occupy all of the space allocated for this chapter. In-depth reviews have been published periodically and can be consulted by interested readers (e.g., Chalk & King 1998, Graham-Bermann & Edleson 2001, Margolin & Gordis 2000). Instead, we apply an ecological approach to summarize understanding of three aspects of risk explanation for each type of family violence: individual factors, relationship factors, and contextual/situational factors.

Domestic Violence Risk Factors

INDIVIDUAL CHARACTERISTICS   Research to identify risk factors for violence has largely focused on perpetration, particularly on male perpetrators. Across studies, the strongest predictors of domestic violence perpetration are a history of prior aggression and a history of violence victimization (Capaldi & Gorman-Smith 2003, Magdol et al. 1997). Low impulse control and low self-esteem have also been related to domestic violence perpetration (Kantor & Jasinski 1998). Psychopathology other than aggression also predicts domestic violence perpetration, with one study showing a rate 13 times greater among those with a diagnosable disorder than among those without (Moffitt & Caspi 1999). The forms of mental illness varied and included anxiety disorders, depression, antisocial personality disorder, and alcohol and drug dependence. Individuals who grew up in families characterized by unskilled parenting and poor family functioning also have higher rates of domestic violence (Capaldi & Clark 1998, Widom 2000).

RELATIONSHIP FACTORS   Because of the emphasis on men as perpetrators and women as victims, and related sensitivity about "blaming the victim," there has been limited attention to relationships factors in explaining domestic violence. Studies of such factors indicate that qualities of the relationship provide independent explanation even when individual characteristics are considered (Capaldi & Clark 1998). Across studies, the levels of conflict and relationship discord are most related (Chalk & King 1998). Also, while expected to relate inversely and strongly, there are negative but modest relations found for violence and positive qualities such as communication quality, felt support, and relationship satisfaction (Cordova et al. 1993, Margolin et al. 1988). Level of violence does not always correlate with levels of support and intimacy.

Evidence also indicates that partner violence, more so than other forms of violence, is related to low relationship skills or difficulty in maintaining quality relationships (Capaldi & Gorman-Smith 2003). Similarly, men who were violent in their marriage reported more felt stress during marital interactions than did nonviolent men (Margolin et al. 1988). Some have interpreted these findings as supporting the role of assortative partnering in the extent to which relationship factors affect risk for domestic violence. That is, domestic violence is at least partly dependent on constraints and similar shared histories that lead to partnering with individuals with greater aggressive tendencies (Moffitt & Caspi 1999). For example, a history of aggression and antisocial behavior in each individual in the couple relationship is likely to increase the probability of domestic violence. Conversely, partnering with a person without this history will decrease the probability of domestic violence. The question of whether the decrease is due to more relationship skills, less acceptance of violence, or less use of violence in the relationship remains to be answered. Assortative partnering by antisocial behavior has been demonstrated with several samples (Krueger et al. 1998).

These findings suggest that relationship factors can be an important component in explaining and addressing domestic violence, particularly in light of findings that suggest much bidirectional violence among couples. The data suggest that helpful findings might result from concurrent consideration of views about violence in relationships, multiple dimensions of the relationship qualities, and partner selection factors, in addition to increased assessment of these qualities.

CONTEXTUAL/SITUATIONAL FACTORS   Although partner violence exists across all socioeconomic levels, those living in poverty are disproportionately affected (Benson et al. 2004). However, beyond this basic correlation, there has been some valuable study of why this may occur. For example, women living in disadvantaged neighborhoods were more than twice as likely to be the victims of domestic violence as were women residing elsewhere; within these neighborhoods, women struggling with money in their own relationships had the greatest risk (Benson et al. 2004). Others have suggested that poverty may contribute to other processes, such as greater stress, hopelessness, or financial constraints, that mitigate against leaving the relationship (Heise 1998).

Contextual factors such as stress level have been related to domestic violence as well (O'Leary 1993). In addition, situational factors can play a role. Alcohol use by either partner is related to increased levels of domestic violence, with likelihood elevated further when both partners use alcohol (Flanzer 1993). In this case, alcohol use may act as a situational factor, increasing the likelihood of violence by reducing inhibitions and impairing an individual's ability to interpret cues.

Child Abuse Risk Factors

An ecological model emphasizing multiple influences has largely guided research on risk factors for child abuse and maltreatment (Cicchetti et al. 2000). In comparison with studies that emphasize a single aspect of this ecology, this conceptual framework has produced continuity in understanding the relation among studies and has resulted in greater theoretical progress.

INDIVIDUAL CHARACTERISTICS   Few studies have focused on child characteristics that might differentiate risk for abuse. Risk is greatest for males, younger children, and those with medical complications and disabilities (Dubowitz & Black 2001). Perpetration is related to several individual characteristics. Contrary to commonly held beliefs, physical abuse is not related to marital status or parental education (Chaffin et al. 1996), although a relation does exist for sexual abuse probability (Finkelhor et al. 1997). Age of parent has inconsistently related to physical abuse (Chaffin et al. 1996, Straus 2005). Abusers are more likely to have low self-esteem, low empathy toward the child, unrealistic expectations about child capabilities, poor impulse control, mental health problems, and a history of antisocial behavior (Natl. Res. Counc. 1993, World Health Org. 2002).

RELATIONSHIP FACTORS   Several of the individual characteristics noted above relate to parenting orientation and expectations. Thus, many of these have been studied within a relationship focus, with the assumption being that these individual differences translate to poorer parenting and other relationship factors. Studies of the relation between family functioning and parenting practices and abuse provide relatively strong evidence that abusive families tend to have poorer functioning and parent-child relationship quality than do nonabusive families (Chalk & King 1998). In addition, growing evidence indicates that domestic violence increases the likelihood of violence toward children, and even without such violence, has deleterious effects on children (Cicchetti et al. 2000, Jouriles et al. 2001). Thus, these results suggest that relationship factors are important risk contributors for child abuse, regardless of whether the factors pertain to unskilled parenting, co-occurrence of marital discord and domestic violence, or dysfunctional child-parent interactions.

CONTEXTUAL/SITUATIONAL FACTORS   Numerous studies link poverty and associated neighborhood characteristics to increased risk for child abuse (see Chalk & King 1998 for summary). However, as with domestic violence, this increase may merely indicate some more informative relations. For example, some studies found slightly higher rates of severe physical abuse among lower socioeconomic parents but did not detect socioeconomic differences for minor physical abuse (Wolfner & Gelles 1993). Also, most studies have interpreted poverty effects as reflecting stress and resource issues, similar to those found to relate to domestic violence. A recent multilevel analysis of data found, in models testing only individual and neighborhood factors, that crime and concentrated poverty were positively related to physical abuse of children, as was expected from previous research. However, when family factors were added and interactions with individual and neighborhood factors were considered, neither crime level nor concentrated poverty independently predicted abuse (Molnar et al. 2003). In communities with a large concentration of immigrants and with larger social networks among residents, abuse was lower. This suggests that the poverty relation to abuse may reflect limited resources and support (Tolan et al. 2003).

Contextual and situational factors have been considered important in explaining abuse propensity. Stress on the family, lack of adequate social supports, and residing in neighborhoods with high crime rates and limited resources have all been associated with abuse (Chalk & King 1998, Williamson et al. 1991). For example, Murphy et al. (1985) found that a family stress checklist administered before the birth of children strongly predicted whether the children would be abused, neglected, or fail to thrive 2 to 2.5 years later. Research on social support suggests a complex role in affecting risk for abuse. In some cases, the results suggest adequate social support protects against risk, whereas in other cases, the absence of needed support elevates risk (Williamson et al. 1991). In addition, the impact may depend on the type of support available. For example, Coohey & Braun (1997) found that abusing mothers evidence less emotional support but no difference in instrumental or tangible support compared with nonabusing mothers. However, Corse et al. (1990) found that tangible support was important in differentiating risk. They also reported that the support network size was smaller for abusing mothers.

ELDER ABUSE   The classes of risk factors involved in elder abuse appear to be similar to those seen in other forms of family violence, although research is much less extensive. Empirically linked individual risk factors for victimization include advanced age, illness or disability, and other types of vulnerability (Natl. Cent. Elder Abuse 1998). Individual factors linked for elder abuse perpetration are history of aggression and violence and current substance abuse (Pillemer 2005). The relationship predicting elder abuse is not the dependence of the elder on the caregiver, but rather is the dependence of the caregiver on the elder financially; mental illness or substance use problems also contribute to elder abuse (Natl. Cent. Elder Abuse 1998). Social setting and contextual factors are also important predictors, but in a more complex manner than was initially presumed. Social isolation of the elder and caregiver is associated with increased risk for elder abuse, but residing with one another also relates to risk in comparison with residing separately (Natl. Cent. Elder Abuse 1998, World Health Org. 2002). It appears that although isolation can increase risk, residing with a caregiver alone also increases risk.

Integrating Risk Explanation Within and Across Forms of Family Violence

SIMILARITY IN RISK FACTORS   Risk factors for the three major forms of violence tend to overlap substantially, and there is growing interest in how these risk factors might suggest family-focused approaches to reduce multiple forms of family violence. All three forms have substantial empirical linkages to relationship and community/situational factors as well as to individual characteristics, which suggests the value of ecological models that consider multiple influences and the interrelation of these influences in explaining risk (Tolan & Gorman-Smith 2002). However, form-specific factors emerge not only because there may be different contributors to each form of violence, but also because the relationship between perpetrator and victim differs. Thus, the relationship risk factors of natural interest for understanding domestic violence may be quite different from those of interest for child abuse. For example, in considering child abuse, at least three people are of interest: the perpetrator, the nonoffending or other parent, and the child. Careful study of multiple ecological factors, with adequate consideration of relationship factors, is important to gain a more complete understanding of the various forms that arise and how they interrelate.

RELATION OF OCCURRENCE OF FORMS OF FAMILY VIOLENCE   There is increasing recognition that the presence of one form of family violence is a risk factor for the presence of another form (Graham-Bermann & Edleson 2001). Across the life span, involvement in a given form can be a risk factor for or an outcome of the other forms. An examination of more than 30 studies of the link shows a 41% median co-occurrence of child maltreatment and domestic violence in families studied (Appel & Holden 1998). As noted earlier, childhood abuse is one of the best predictors of domestic violence (Widom 2000). Children who have witnessed violence between their parents are at increased risk for abuse themselves and for later domestic violence (Margolin & Gordis 2000). Moreover, elder abuse is related to a prior history of aggression within that relationship.

Intergenerational continuity or transmission explanations have guided much of this work, with social learning explanations of aggression as the most commonly theorized mechanism, emphasizing the ways in which exposure to domestic violence might lead to later partner violence, for example. Violence between parents may be observed and directly modeled in later relationships with partners (Widom 2000). This violence between parents legitimizes later violence against intimate partners (Heise 1998). Second, physical abuse toward a child may teach that child that aggression is a tactic to use in family relationships. Parents with a history of abuse and neglect are more likely to abuse their own children (Finkelhor et al. 1997, Widom 2000). Although there is considerable support for a role of these processes, recent efforts have started to test mediators of this transmission, such as partner choice, relationship skills, and overall aggression level (Capaldi & Gorman-Smith 2003).

UNDERSTANDING VARIATIONS IN RISK PATTERNS   While it is important to link the risk factors shared by forms of family violence and to identify how continuity of occurrence may be affected, it is also important to recognize the discontinuity of family violence. In addition, among the overall prevalence rates, several patterns of involvement probably exist (Natl. Res. Counc. 1993, Tolan & Gorman-Smith 2002). Most families with one or more of the risk factors for family violence will not exhibit family violence, and most families that have experienced one form of family violence do not exhibit other forms. Thus, it is important that ensuing studies recognize the ways in which incidents of violence and discontinuity of involvement occur and might be important in understanding risk models.

FAMILY VIOLENCE INTERVENTIONS

Many approaches to intervention have been applied for family violence (Chalk & King 1998, Natl. Res. Counc. 1993). These include legal policies and sanctions applied to the perpetrator; protective efforts, advocacy, and case management for victims; educational efforts to increase awareness and identification; group and individual programs to stop perpetration and treat effects on victims; and family interventions to address family relationship and management issues that might mitigate violence. These interventions range from universal prevention programs meant to lessen social acceptance and overall prevalence of family violence to intensive programs for treating and managing chronic offenders (Chalk & King 1998). Most programs seem to aim to prevent further exhibition of the abusive behavior when applied to perpetrators and to prevent further victimization or stem the harmful psychological and functional impacts of prior violence among victims (Tolan & Gorman-Smith 2002).

As occurs for understanding patterns and risk influences, interventions usually are focused on a specific form of family violence and few consider shared risk factors or overlap among the forms of family violence. Almost none consider that perpetrators are also often victims of some form of family violence. Also, interventions usually are developed from a particular perspective about the reasons for that form of violence. Many programs are ideologically driven or policy determined, and they are not grounded in risk-factor research (Austin & Dankwort 1999). Few efforts have been adequately evaluated. Most have not had any evaluation, and of those that have been evaluated, many did not have an adequate design to permit valid determination of efficacy. When adequate outcome designs were applied, methodological issues such as failure to achieve randomization, inadequate power, inappropriate statistical models, and serious attrition rates often occurred. When these challenges were managed, the evaluation often limited the assessment of effects to variables associated with family violence, but did not actually test effect on family violence. Thus, despite extensive intervention efforts at multiple levels, representing many perspectives, there is scarce literature with adequate empirical qualities available to guide intervention efforts (Chalk & King, 1998).

This state of affairs means that the evaluation efforts with adequate design features clearly are not representative of the broad set of approaches being applied in practice. However, the use of basic design criteria does provide some direction about promising efforts. We review here studies with adequate designs (strong quasi-experimental or experimental designs with random assignment) and complete evaluations. We also concentrate on interventions that measured outcomes directly related to violence itself wherever possible; we relied on correlates or theorized mediators when such data were not available. Because individual studies tend to focus on single forms of family violence, we summarize this knowledge within each area.

Interventions for Domestic Violence

SHELTERS FOR VICTIMS   Separation of perpetrator and victim through arrest or the use of shelters is often the first intervention for marital or partner violence. It is also among the most common interventions, comprising approximately two-thirds of the programs for this problem (Plichta 1995). While the specific approach and circumstances of shelter programs vary, most are intended to help female victims of male battering to leave the home and relationship and to develop skills, resources, and support for safe, independent living. A major challenge for evaluating such programs is the limited acceptance for experimental manipulation involving those whose safety is under imminent threat and who are in dire need of shelter. We could locate only a single study with even minimal methodology quality. The study suggests that for a portion of those coming to shelters, incidents of violence decreased after a shelter visit (Berk et al. 1986). Also, some studies suggest that provision of advocacy services as a part of separation or after exit from shelters may relate to a more effective use of resources and social support, but there is not evidence that this also reduces subsequent violence (Sullivan & Davidson 1991, Tan et al. 1995).

MANDATORY PROSECUTION OF PERPETRATORS   Based on the recognition that domestic violence is often repetitive and that domestic violence is often regarded as not serious by police, advocates argue that predictable and substantial legal consequences for domestic violence should make victims safer and deter or remove perpetrators. This led to several changes in law, including mandatory reporting by health professionals, wider use of protective orders, and required prosecution of offenders. A substantial set of studies have evaluated the effects of compulsory arrest in contrast to arrest at officer discretion (Sherman 1992, Sherman & Berk

1984) and to other interventions such as mediation or separation (Ford & Regoli 1993). Others have tested the impact of arrest when coupled with other sanctions compared with arrest alone (Steinman 1990) and arrest earlier in the cycle of violence (Ford & Regoli 1993, Hirschel & Hutchinson 1992). The results of these studies have suggested some modest but inconsistent positive effects. In part, these studies face some of the same ethical issues regarding random assignment as studies of shelters. Although place-based random assignment of policies has been used to overcome this limitation, many of those studies have site variations in effects and other methodological limitations, including limited implementation and inadequate power to detect effects (Tolan & Gorman-Smith 2002). Also, practical issues such as the fact that perpetrators in domestic violence incidents often flee by the time police arrive make it unclear whether these studies validly estimate impact.

OTHER LEGAL SANCTION APPROACHES   Popular approaches such as training court personnel and specialized courts have not been evaluated adequately to date. However, when arrest is under a warrant and victims are given the opportunity to press charges, they are more likely to be safe from subsequent violence than when arrest is done without a warrant or a misdemeanor citation is issued to the perpetrator (Hirschel & Hutchinson 1992). Evaluations have found no evidence that alternatives to traditional sentencing are related to greater safety for victims (Ford & Regoli 1993).

TREATMENT OF PERPETRATORS   Several randomized and quasi-experimental studies have evaluated psychosocial treatment of perpetrators, primarily the use of cognitive behavioral methods. The evidence from these studies is mixed, with stronger studies finding no effects. For example, Dunford (2000) conducted a four-group randomized controlled trial with more than 800 Navy personnel. Men who had assaulted their wives were randomly assigned to one of four conditions: (a) single cognitive behavioral therapy, (b) conjoint cognitive behavioral therapy with their wives, (c) rigorous monitoring consisting of individual counseling and reporting of subsequent incidents to commanding officers, and (d) a control condition in which wives received assistance in stabilization and safety planning. Results showed no evidence of significant effects for the cognitive approach or any other treatment condition based on the reports of the men or their wives. As these are among the most popular approaches, these findings are troublesome. In contrast, there is evidence that alcohol abuse treatment may help reduce domestic violence (O'Farrell et al. 2004, Stuart et al. 2003).

COUPLES OR MARITAL COUNSELING/THERAPY   Another frequently promoted approach for addressing domestic violence, particularly for less serious or more infrequent forms of domestic violence, is marital therapy that emphasizes communication, relationship skills, and conflict resolution. In another program, no significant difference was observed in a comparison of marital therapy and separate groups for the male perpetrator and the wife victim, although both methods resulted in significant drops in violence levels (O'Leary et al. 1994). The best evidence is for this approach is from a preventive effort. The Prevention and Relationship Enhancement Program (Markman et al. 1993) is a five-session program designed to modify communication, problem-solving skills, and coping with negative affect. Matched pairs of couples were randomly assigned to intervention; approximately half of the couples who were assigned to intervention declined to participate. However, decliners were retained for evaluation assessments that extended to five years post intervention. At that point, those who received the intervention had significantly lower levels of self-reported marital violence than did controls and, although not significantly different, also had lower levels of violence than did the couples who had declined.

DATING VIOLENCE AND DOMESTIC VIOLENCE PREVENTION   Dating violence, while not family violence, is often a precursor to family violence. Interventions to reduce dating violence are seen as preventive for later domestic violence. Randomized trials of two different programs found preventive effects on subsequent reports of dating violence (Foshee et al. 2004, Wolfe et al. 2003). The Youth Relationship Project (Wolfe et al. 2003), a group-based health promotion approach to dating violence, provided 18 sessions of education on abuse and power dynamics, skills training, and social action. The Safe Dates Program (Foshee et al. 2004) consisted of a 10-session classroom-based curriculum taught by health professionals, combined with a theater production by students in the program. Results from these trials suggest that such preventive efforts may be among the most valuable approaches to reducing domestic violence rates overall.

Child Abuse Interventions

COURT-MANDATED TREATMENT FOR OFFENDERS   Court-mandated treatment is one of the most common approaches in cases of child abuse. Only two studies with adequate designs have addressed this approach, and these did not focus on abuse as an outcome. They did find positive effects on parenting skills and amenability to treatment (Irueste-Montes & Montes 1988, Wolfe et al. 1988).

PARENTING PRACTICES AND FAMILY INTERVENTIONS   One of the most studied areas in child abuse is interventions to aid parenting practices and family functioning (Brunk et al. 1987). These include programs that educate, engage families in therapeutic activity, including modeling and practice to improve parenting, and attempt to engage family support services. Substantial evidence indicates that parenting practices and family functioning interventions can have positive effects on parental discipline methods (including use of nonviolent approaches), level of familial conflict, and management of stress affecting the family (see Dishion & McMahon 1998 for a review). Because these are key potential mediators of child abuse, such an approach seems promising. However, few studies tested effects of such interventions on parental abuse, and for those that did, results have not been strong (Kolko 1996, Lutzker et al. 1984).

FAMILY PRESERVATION   Another favored approach is family preservation intervention, which involves intensive social casework, family therapy, parent training, and other support services (such as day care and homemaker or nutrition services). The intent of family preservation is to provide comprehensive, wrap-around services to help high-risk families avoid the need for removal of the child for protection (Barton 1994). The preponderance of strong tests shows that these interventions reduce the length and frequency of out-of-home placements and improve parenting and family functioning. However, when subsequent rates of abuse were measured, effects were not found, except in one study that tailored services to each family's needs (Jones 1985).

HOME VISITATION FOR AT-RISK MOTHERS   The most well-evaluated approach for reducing child abuse and neglect by improving parenting is home visitation through the Nurse-Family Partnership for low-income women (Olds et al. 1997). Pre- and postnatal visits to high-risk first-time mothers by nurses or trained paraprofessionals, for up to two years after birth, are intended to improve pregnancy outcomes, child health and development, the mother's parenting skills and well-being, and the family's economic stability. Trials have consistently shown that Nurse-Family Partnerships result in significantly fewer child injuries, behavioral problems, emergency room visits, and reports of abuse. The effects may depend on the profession of the home visitor: Larger effect sizes on child abuse were obtained with nurse visitors than with paraprofessionals (Olds et al. 2004).

COGNITIVE SERVICES TO ABUSERS   Kolko (1996) compared cognitive behavioral training for the offending parent and the child with family therapy. In this well-controlled study, with one-year follow-up, both groups showed significant decreases in child abuse, but those in cognitive behavioral training evidenced lower levels of parental anger and a decreased use of physical discipline in comparison with those in family therapy. In a meta-analysis, Skowron & Reinemann (2005) summarized 21 studies of a variety of psychological interventions for child abuse. Methodological quality was high for most of the studies. Half of these studies involved random assignment, and one fourth provided longer-term follow-up data. Studies were categorized as behavioral, cognitive/behavioral, or other. Positive effects were found for all three groups, but effects were primarily found for parents' self-report about their behavior. Effects were not as great when independent assessments were used. Stronger and more consistent effects were found for non-behavioral, as compared with behavioral and cognitive/behavioral, interventions. The few studies with longer-term follow-up data showed evidence of positive effects up to several years after the interventions.

CRITICAL ASPECTS OF EFFECTIVE CHILD ABUSE INTERVENTIONS   In addition to these evaluations of specific programs, a recent meta-analysis provides some understanding of what might be critical aspects of effective child abuse interventions. In a meta-analysis, MacLeod & Nelson (2000) examined 47 studies testing interventions to affect child abuse and classified studies as either proactive or reactive. Studies of sexual abuse prevention were excluded. The proactive interventions included home visitation, multicomponent treatment (educational + community development + social services), social support interventions, and media campaigns. The reactive interventions included family preservation, multicomponent treatment (e.g., home visitation + parent training + homemaker services), social support/mutual aid, and parent training. Among the proactive programs, home visitation and the multicomponent programs had positive effects, but there was substantial heterogeneity in effects among these. Among the reactive interventions, the multicomponent and parent-training interventions had positive effects, and these findings were consistent across studies.

Elder Abuse Interventions

It is not surprising that there are fewer studies of interventions for elder abuse than for the other forms of family violence. Few studies have actually measured subsequent abuse as an outcome. The preponderance of studies have focused on reducing stress and providing respite to the caregiver; others have attempted to reduce depression, economic hardship, and anger (Beigel & Schulz 1999, Cook et al. 1999, Mittelman et al. 1995). For example, in a test of an intervention providing education and anger management training for persons who abused elders, Reay & Browne (2002) found significant reductions in caregiver strain, depression, anxiety, and negative interpersonal conflict tactics for abusers. Using a different approach, Filinson (1993) found positive effects for advocacy services on elders' goal-setting skills and use of resources, but did not report effects on subsequent incidents of abuse. These recent studies have stronger designs and suggest more positive effects than earlier efforts (Knight et al. 1993). As noted in a review by Bourgoise et al. (1996), although more comprehensive, multicomponent interventions seem to have more effects, many interventions are remarkably brief. These findings suggest that elder abuse interventions that provide respite, support, and address dependency of the caregiver on the elder are most promising.

Summary of Intervention Findings

Across the forms of family violence, there are several examples of efficacious interventions. Preventive efforts and those focused on relationship skills and family management are supported by more evidence than are other approaches. However, there is also evidence that work to manage impulse, anger, and other behavior related to abuse has promise. Also, the effective interventions are similar across forms of family violence. Even more striking is the extent to which favored and widely used interventions either have not been evaluated or, if evaluated, show no efficacy. Further, there has been little examination of how interventions work, so research is minimally informative about major contentions concerning intervention foci.

ADVANCING UNDERSTANDING OF AND IMPACT ON FAMILY VIOLENCE

Family violence research has provided important information that has only started to shed light on the patterns, prevalence, risk, and consequences of this major threat to development and well-being. This area of study has emerged out of advocacy as much as from scientific interest. The result is that the literature and "evidence" have advanced along relatively segregated lines of inquiry within particular perspectives. Because of the serious threats to safety of some children, women, and elders, there has been heightened tension about how family violence is conceptualized and studied and how research is interpreted. Although earlier work provided the important increase in attention to these problems and recognition of the extent of public health threat and costs attributable to these forms of violence, there has been more difficulty in linking such work to more recent, methodologically stronger, and more complex studies and results.

The emerging patterns across studies of prevalence, risk factors, and interventions suggest that it is not likely that family violence will be adequately explained or addressed by continuous focus on one form (e.g., domestic violence, child abuse, or elder abuse) or by the rejection of research challenging strongly held beliefs. Reconciling disparities and relating various forms seems likely to advance scientific knowledge and to direct practice and policy more reliably. Recognition seems to be emerging that while family violence is too prevalent and imposes serious harm on many, there is substantial heterogeneity in patterns of family violence, of how it occurs, and what interventions are most promising. Within these trends, there is increasing clarity that there is considerable overlap as to who is involved in various forms of family violence, and participation in each type of family violence relates to increased risk for participation in the other types. There is also growing recognition that while individuals need to be held responsible for harmful behavior. Much of family violence has multiple determinants: Beyond the individual, characteristics of the relationship and social context have consistently been found to contribute to risk, thus explaining why interventions that take these factors into account have more consistent positive effects. While there are great challenges to studying family violence, in any form, let alone in relating forms, the field is in need of integrative study that considers the ecology of contributors to family violence.

As others have argued, this means emphasizing a multifactor, multilevel understanding of violence that can (*a*) help explain the high prevalence as well as the rare but distinctly endangering patterns, (*b*) examine population patterns but also account for individual differences among any population, and (*c*) suggest both predisposing and precipitating factors (Cicchetti et al. 2000, Daro et al. 2004). These ecological models integrate and relate multiple influences to explain variations in rate and reasons for violence across populations and settings. They also have a goal of identifying meaningful patterns that have direct relevance to interventions and policy. It is likely then that sets of interventions will be identified that are effective for different populations and different aspects of family violence. Perhaps most fundamentally, such an ecological perspective can advance the research and related policy discussion beyond disputes about which part of the problem or part of the explanation is most important to a discussion that relates what seem like diverging findings. Although such a model may be challenging to articulate, refine, and test, it seems preferable to continuation of contentious agendas that constrain what can be learned, what might be considered, and most importantly, the pace of development and application of effective interventions, programs, and policies to lessen family violence (Daro et al. 2004).

The *Annual Review of Psychology* is online at http://psych.annualreviews.org

LITERATURE CITED

Am. Psychol. Assoc. Presid. Task Force Violence Family. 1996. *Violence and the Family: Report of the American Psychological Association Presidential Task Force on Violence and the Family.* Washington, DC: Am. Psychol. Assoc.

Appel AE, Holden GW. 1998. The co-occurrence of spouse and physical child abuse: a review and appraisal. *J. Fam. Psychol.* 12:578–99

Archer J. 2000. Sex differences in aggression between heterosexual partners: a meta-analytic review. *Psychol. Bull.* 126:651–80

Austin JB, Dankwort J. 1999. Standards for batterer programs. *J. Interpers. Violence* 14:152–68

Barton K. 1994. Healing at home can be cost effective. *Calif. Agric.* 48:36–38

Beigel D, Schulz R. 1999. Caregiving and a interventions in aging and mental illness. *Fam. Relat.* 48:345–54

Benjet C, Kazdin AE. 2003. Spanking children: the controversies, findings, and new directions. *Clin. Psychol. Rev.* 23:197–224

Benson ML, Litton A, Fox G. 2004. *When Violence Hits Home: How Economics and Neighborhood Play A Role. Rep. NCJ*

205004. Washington, DC: U.S. Dept. Justice, Off. Justice Programs

Berk RA, Newton PJ, Berk SF. 1986. What a difference a day makes: an empirical study of the impact of shelters for battered women. *J. Marriage Fam.* 48:431–90

Bourgoise MS, Schulz R, Burgio L. 1996. Interventions for caregivers of patients with Alzheimer's disease: a review and analysis of content. *Int. J. Aging Hum. Dev.* 43:35–92

Brayden RM, Altemeier WA, Dietrich MS, Tucker DD, Christensen MJ, et al. 1993. A prospective study of secondary prevention of child maltreatment. *J. Pediatr.* 122:511–16

Brunk M, Henggeler S, Whelan JP. 1987. Comparison of multisystemic therapy and parent training in the brief treatment of child abuse and neglect. *J. Consult. Clin. Psychol.* 55:171–78

Capaldi DM, Clark S. 1998. Prospective family predictors of aggression toward female partners for at-risk young men. *Dev. Psychol.* 34:1175–88

Capaldi DM, Gorman-Smith D. 2003. The development of aggression in young male/

female couples. In *Adolescent Romantic Relations and Sexual Behavior: Theory, Research, and Practical Implications*, ed. P Florsheim, pp. 243–78. Mahwah, NJ: Erlbaum

Chaffin M, Kelleher K, Hollenberg J. 1996. Onset of physical abuse and neglect: psychiatric, substance abuse, and social risk factors from prospective community data. *Child Abuse Negl.* 20:191–203

Chalk R, King PA. 1998. *Violence in Families: Assessing Prevention and Treatment Programs*. Washington, DC: Natl. Acad. Press

Cicchetti D, Toth SL, Maughan A. 2000. An ecological-transactional model of child maltreatment. In *Handbook of Developmental Psychopathology*, ed. AJ Sameroff, M Lewis, pp. 689–722. New York: Kluwer Acad./Plenum

Coohey C, Braun N. 1997. Toward an integrated framework for understanding child physical abuse. *Child Abuse Negl.* 21:1081–94

Cook JA, Heller T, Pickett-Schenk SA. 1999. The effect of support group participation on caregiver burden among parents of adult offspring with severe mental illness. *Fam. Relat.* 48:405–10

Cordova JV, Jacobson NS, Gottman JM, Rushe R, Cox G. 1993. Negative reciprocity and communication in couples with a violent husband. *J. Abnorm. Psychol.* 104:559–64

Corse SJ, Schmid K, Trickett PK. 1990. Social network characteristics of mothers in abusing and nonabusing families and their relationships to parenting beliefs. *J. Community Psychol.* 18:44–59

Daro D, Edleson JL, Pinderhughes H. 2004. Finding common ground in the study of child maltreatment, youth violence, and adult domestic violence. *J. Interpers. Violence* 19:282–98

Dishion TJ, McMahon RJ. 1998. Parental monitoring and the prevention of child and adolescent problem behavior: a conceptual and empirical formulation. *Clin. Child Fam. Psychol. Rev.* 1:61–75

Dubowitz H, Black MB. 2001. Child neglect. In *Child Abuse: Medical Diagnosis and Management*, ed. RM Reece, S Ludwig, pp. 339–62. Philadelphia, PA: Lippincott

Dunford FW. 2000. The San Diego Navy experiment: an assessment of interventions for men who assault their wives. *J. Consult. Clin. Psychol.* 68:468–76

Edleson JL. 2001. Studying the co-occurrence of child maltreatment and woman battering in families. In *Domestic Violence in the Lives of Children: The Future of Research, Intervention and Social Policy*, ed. SA Graham-Bermann, JL Edleson, pp. 91–110. Washington, DC: Am. Psychol. Assoc.

Filinson R. 1993. An evaluation of a program of volunteer advocates for elder abuse victims. *J. Elder Abuse Negl.* 5:77–93

Finkelhor D, Moore D, Hamby SL, Straus MA. 1997. Sexually abused children in a national survey of parents: methodological issues. *Child Abuse Negl.* 21:1–9

Flanzer JP. 1993. Alcohol and other drugs are key causal agents of violence. In *Current Controversies on Family Violence*, ed. RJ Gelles, DR Loseke, pp. 171–81. Thousand Oaks, CA: Sage

Ford DA, Regoli MJ. 1993. *The Indianapolis Domestic Violence Prosecution Experiment. Final Report, Grant 86-IJ-CX-0012 to the National Institute of Justice*. Indianapolis: Indiana Univ. Press

Foshee VA, Bauman KE, Ennett ST, Linder GF, Benefield T, Suchindran C. 2004. Assessing the long-term effects of the Safe Dates program and a booster in preventing and reducing adolescent dating violence victimization and perpetration. *Am. J. Public Health* 94:619–24

Graham-Bermann SA, Edleson JL. 2001. *Domestic Violence in the Lives of Children*. Washington, DC: Am. Psychol. Assoc.

Hamberger LK, Hastings JE. 1988. Skills training for treatment of spouse abusers: an outcome study. *J. Fam. Violence* 3:121–30

Heise L. 1998. Violence against women: an integrated ecological framework. *Violence Against Women* 4:262–90

Henton J, Gate R, Koval J, Lloyd S, Christopher S. 1983. Romance and violence in dating relationships. *J. Fam. Issues* 4:467–82

Hines D, Malley-Morrison K. 2004. *Family Violence in the United States.* Thousand Oaks, CA: Sage

Hirschel JD, Hutchinson IW. 1992. Female spouse abuse and the police response: the Charlotte, North Carolina experiment. *J. Law Crimonol.* 83:73–119

Irueste-Montes AM, Montes F. 1988. Court-ordered versus voluntary treatment of abusive and neglectful parents. *J. Child Abuse Negl.* 12:33–39

Johnson MP. 1995. Patriarchal terrorism and common couple violence: two forms of violence against women. *J. Marriage Fam.* 57:283–94

Jones MA. 1985. *A Second Chance for Families. Five Years Later. Follow-up of a Program to Prevent Foster Care.* New York: Child Welfare League Am.

Jouriles EN, McDonald R, Norwood WD, Ezell E. 2001. Issues and controversies in documenting the prevalence of children's exposure to domestic violence. In *Domestic Violence in the Lives of Children: The Future of Research, Intervention, and Social Policy,* ed. SA Graham-Bermann, JL Edleson, pp. 12–34. Washington, DC: Am. Psychol. Assoc.

Kantor GK, Jasinski JL. 1998. Dynamics and risk factors in partner violence. In *Partner Violence: A Comprehensive Review of 20 Years of Research,* ed. JL Jasinski, LM Williams, pp. 3–31. Thousand Oaks, CA: Sage

Knight BG, Lutzky SM, Macofsky-Urban D. 1993. A meta-analytic review of interventions for caregiver distress: recommendations for future research. *Gerontologist* 33:240–48

Kolko DJ. 1996. Clinical monitoring of treatment course in child physical abuse: psychometric characteristics and treatment comparisons. *Child Abuse Negl.* 20:23–43

Krueger RF, Moffitt TE, Capsi A, Bleske A, Silva PA. 1998. Assortative mating for antisocial behavior: developmental and methodological implications. *Behav. Genet.* 28:173–86

Kurz D. 1993. Physical assaults by husbands: a major social problem. In *Current Controversies on Family Violence,* ed. RJ Gelles, DR Loseke, pp. 88–103. Thousand Oaks, CA: Sage

Lackey C, Williams KR. 1995. Social bonding and the cessation of partner violence across generations. *J. Marriage Fam.* 57:295–305

Loseke DR, Gelles RJ, Cavanaugh MM. 2005. *Current Controversies on Family Violence.* Thousand Oaks, CA: Sage

Loseke DR, Kurz D. 2005. Men's violence toward women is the serious social problem. In *Current Controversies on Family Violence,* ed. DR Loseke, R Gelles, MM Cavanaugh, pp. 79–95. Thousand Oaks, CA: Sage

Lutzker JR, Campbell RV, Watson-Perczel M. 1984. Using the case study method to treat several problems in a family indicated for child neglect. *Educ. Treat. Child.* 7:315–33

MacLeod J, Nelson G. 2000. Programs for the promotion of family wellness and the prevention of child maltreatment: a meta-analytic review. *Child Abuse Negl.* 24:1127–49

Magdol L, Moffitt TE, Caspi A, Newman DL, Fagan J, Silva PA. 1997. Gender differences in partner violence in a birth cohort of 21-year-olds: bridging the gap between clinical and epidemiological approaches. *J. Consult. Clin. Psychol.* 65:68–78

Margolin G, Gordis EB. 2000. The effect of family and community violence on children. *Annu. Rev. Psychol.* 51:445–79

Margolin G, John RS, Gleberman L. 1988. Affective responses to conflictual discussions in violent and nonviolent couples. *J. Consult. Clin. Psychol.* 56:24–33

Markman HJ, Renick MJ, Floyd FJ, Stanley SM, Clements M. 1993. Preventing marital distress through communication and conflict management training: a 4- and 5-year follow-up. *J. Consult. Clin. Psychol.* 61:70–77

Mittelman M, Ferris S, Shulman E, Steinberg G, Ambinder A, et al. 1995. A comprehensive support program: effect on depression in spouse-caregivers of AD patients. *Gerontologist* 35:792–802

Moffitt TE, Caspi A. 1999. *Findings About Partner Violence from Dunedin Multidisciplinary Health and Development Study. Rep. NCJ 170018.* Washington, DC: U.S. Dep. Justice, Off. Justice Programs, Natl. Inst. Justice

Molnar BE, Buka SL, Brennan RT, Holton JK, Earls F. 2003. A multilevel study of neighborhoods and parent-to-child physical aggression: results from the Project on Human Development in Chicago neighborhoods. *Child Maltreat.* 8:84–97

Murphy S, Orkow B, Nicola RM. 1985. Prenatal prediction of child abuse and neglect: a prospective study. *Child Abuse Negl.* 9:225–35

Natl. Res. Counc. 1993. *Understanding Child Abuse and Neglect.* Washington, DC: Natl. Acad. Sci. Press

Natl. Clearinghouse Child Abuse Negl. Inform. 2004. *Child abuse and neglect fatalities: statistics and interventions.* http://nccanch.acf.hhs.gov/pubs/factsheets/fatality.cfm. Accessed June 2005

Natl. Cent. Elder Abuse. 1998. *National Elder Abuse Incidence Study. Final Report.* Washington, DC: Am. Public Hum. Serv. Assoc.

O'Farrell TJ, Murphy CM, Stephan SH, Fals-Stewart W, Murphy M. 2004. Partner violence before and after couples-based alcoholism treatment for male alcoholic patients: the role of treatment involvement and abstinence. *J. Consult. Clin. Psychol.* 72:202–17

O'Leary KD. 1993. Through a psychological lens: personality traits, personality disorders and levels of violence. In *Current Controversies on Family Violence,* ed. RJ Gelles, DR Loseke, pp. 7–30. London: Sage

O'Leary KD, Malone J, Tyree A. 1994. Physical aggression in early marriage: prerelationship and relation effects. *J. Consult. Clin. Psychol.* 62:594–602

Olds DL, Eckenrode J, Henderson CRJ, Kitzman H, Powers H, et al. 1997. Long-term effects of home visitation on maternal life course and child abuse and neglect. *J. Am. Med. Assoc.* 278:637–43

Olds DL, Robinson J, Pettitt L, Luckey DW, Holmberg J, et al. 2004. Effects of home visits by paraprofessionals and by nurses: age 4 follow-up results of a randomized trial. *Pediatrics* 114:1560–68

Pillemer K. 2005. Elder abuse is caused by the deviance and dependence of abusive caregivers. In *Current Controversies on Family Violence,* ed. DR Loseke, R Gelles, MM Cavanaugh, pp. 207–19. Thousand Oaks, CA: Sage

Plichta SB. 1995. Building paths for women to travel to freedom and safety. In *The Commonwealth Fund Symposium on Domestic Violence and Women's Health: Broadening the Conversation.* New York: Coll. Health Sci., Old Dominion Univ.

Reay AC, Browne KD. 2002. The effectiveness of psychological interventions with individuals who physically abuse or neglect their elderly dependents. *J. Interpers. Violence* 17:416–31

Shafer J, Caetano R, Clark C. 1998. Rates of intimate partner violence in the United States. *Am. J. Public Health* 88:1702–4

Sherman LW. 1992. *Policing Domestic Violence.* New York: Free Press

Sherman LW, Berk RA. 1984. The specific deterrent effects of arrest for domestic assault. *Am. Sociol. Rev.* 49:261–72

Skowron E, Reinemann DHS. 2005. Effectiveness of psychological interventions for child maltreatment: a meta-analysis. *Psychother. Theory Res. Prac.* 42:52–71

Steinman M. 1990. Lowering recidivism among men who batter women. *J. Police Sci. Admin.* 17:124–32

Straus MA. 2005. Women's violence toward men is a serious social problem. In *Current Controversies on Family Violence,* ed. DR Loseke, R Gelles, MM Cavanaugh, pp. 55–77. Thousand Oaks, CA: Sage

Straus MA, Gelles RJ. 1990. *Physical Violence in American Families: Risk Factors and Adaptations to Violence in 8,145 Families.* New Brunswick, NJ: Transaction Books

Straus MA, Sugarman D, Giles-Sims J. 1997. Spanking by parents and subsequent antisocial behavior of children. *Arch. Pediatr. Adolesc. Med.* 151:761–67

Stuart GL, Ramsey SE, Moore TM, Kahler CM, Farrell LE, et al. 2003. Reductions in marital violence following treatment for alcohol dependence. *J. Interpers. Violence* 18:1113–31

Sullivan CM, Davidson W. 1991. The provision of advocacy services to women leaving abusive partners: an examination of short-term effects. *Am. J. Community Psychol.* 19:953–60

Tan C, Basta J, Sullivan CM, Davidson WS. 1995. The role of social support in the lives of women exiting domestic violence shelters: an experimental study. *J. Interpers. Violence* 10:437–51

Tolan P, Gorman-Smith D. 2002. What violence prevention research can tell us about developmental psychopathology. *Dev. Psychopathol.* 14:713–29

Tolan P, Gorman-Smith D, Henry DB. 2003. The developmental ecology of urban males' youth violence. *Dev. Psychol.* 39:274–91

Widom CS. 2000. *Childhood victimization: early adversity, later psychopathology.* www.ncjrs.org/pdffiles1/jr000242b.pdf. Accessed June 2005

Williamson J, Bourdin C, Howe B. 1991. The ecology of adolescent maltreatment: a multilevel examination of adolescent physical abuse, sexual abuse, and neglect. *J. Consult. Clin. Psychol.* 159:449–57

Wolfe DA, Edwards B, Manion I, Koverola C. 1988. Early interventions for parents at risk of child abuse and neglect: a preliminary investigation. *J. Consult. Clin. Psychol.* 56:40–47

Wolfe DA, Wekerle C, Scott K, Straatman A, Grasley C, Reitzel-Jaffe D. 2003. Dating violence prevention with at-risk youth: a controlled outcome evaluation. *J. Consult. Clin. Psychol.* 71:279–91

Wolfner G, Gelles RJ. 1993. A profile of violence toward children: a national study. *Child Abuse Negl.* 17:197–212

World Health Org. 2002. *World Report on Violence and Health.* Geneva: World Health Org.

Annu. Rev. Psychol. 2006. 57:585–611
doi: 10.1146/annurev.psych.57.102904.190029

UNDERSTANDING AFFIRMATIVE ACTION

Faye J. Crosby

*Department of Psychology, University of California, Santa Cruz,
California 95064; email: fjcrosby@ucsc.edu*

Aarti Iyer

*School of Psychology, University of Exeter, Exeter EX4 4QG,
United Kingdom; email: a.iyer@exeter.ac.uk*

Sirinda Sincharoen

*Department of Psychology, University of California, Santa Cruz,
California 95064; email: sirinda@qc2.com*

Key Words   fairness, diversity, race, gender, justice

■ **Abstract**   Affirmative action is a controversial and often poorly understood policy. It is also a policy that has been widely studied by social scientists. In this review, we outline how affirmative action operates in employment and education settings and consider the major points of controversy. In addition, we detail the contributions of psychologists and other social scientists in helping to demonstrate why affirmative action is needed; how it can have unintended negative consequences; and how affirmative action programs can be most successful. We also review how psychologists have examined variations in people's attitudes toward affirmative action, in part as a means for testing different theories of social behavior.

CONTENTS

0066-4308/06/0110-0585$20.00

INTRODUCTION

Affirmative action means many things to many people. Over the past 40 years, the policy has been challenged in courts as well as in the organizations and university campuses where it has been implemented. The latest moment of contention came in 2003, when the U.S. Supreme Court decided the landmark cases involving the University of Michigan. Due in part to the importance of the Michigan cases, the past few years have witnessed an outpouring of research and writing on the topic of affirmative action, a fair portion of which has been produced by psychologists. The aim of our review is to introduce readers to the issues surrounding the policy and practice of affirmative action. In so doing, we highlight the major ways that legal scholars and social scientists, especially psychologists, have conducted research in this area.

Scope of this Review

The affirmative action literature that we review has three characteristics worthy of initial comment. First, publications on affirmative action are increasingly empirical. Anecdotes, autobiographies, and armchair philosophizing about affirmative action predominated until the mid-1980s, but since the 1990s, this approach has largely given way to empiricism. Second, the work has become truly interdisciplinary, stretching across the fields of education, law, sociology, and economics (e.g., Bergmann 1996, Cordes 2004, Cunningham et al. 2002, Hochschild 1999, Leonard 1996, Munro 1995, Reskin 1998), as well as psychology. Third, a significant portion of the psychological research is of an applied nature, by which we mean it applies basic theories and concepts to topics concerning affirmative action. From time to time, researchers (e.g., DeBono & Snyder 1995, Mellema & Bassili 1995) use the issue of affirmative action simply as a convenient way to test theories that have nothing to do with the specifics of affirmative action per se. Often, however, social scientists seek to make contributions to both the basic understanding of human behavior and the issues involved in creating and implementing social policies.

Although we seek to be comprehensive in the topics we cover, we do not claim to be exhaustive in our citations. The explosion of studies in recent years is great, and our space is limited. More references can be found in any of the recent major reviews of the vast literature on affirmative action (Crosby 2004, Crosby et al. 2003, Kravitz et al. 1997, Pincus 2003, Taylor-Carter et al. 1995).

We begin with a brief section on definitions, as research shows that people continue to be misinformed about what affirmative action is (Arriola & Cole 2001, Kravitz et al. 2000, Kravitz & Platania 1993, Schwindt et al. 1998, Zamboanga et al. 2002), and we know that one's understanding of affirmative action colors one's reactions to it (Golden et al. 2001). In the second section, we review the ways that social scientists have contributed to the national debates on affirmative action. The third section of our review addresses attitudes toward affirmative action.

We consider the factors that predict people's attitudes toward affirmative action, noting the implications of this research for larger theoretical questions concerning societal inequality.

What is Affirmative Action?

Affirmative action occurs whenever an organization devotes resources (including time and money) to making sure that people are not discriminated against on the basis of their gender or their ethnic group. Affirmative action has the same goal as equal opportunity, but differs from equal opportunity in being proactive (Burstein 1994). Equal opportunity is a passive policy that seeks to ensure that discrimination will not be tolerated once it is detected. In contrast, with affirmative action, organizations use established practices not only to subvert, but also to avert, discrimination (Crosby & Cordova 1996). One traditional form of affirmative action has involved reserving federal procurement dollars for minority-owned and women-owned businesses. Although set-asides no longer operate in the same fashion as in the past (Holt 2003), extensive econometric research has generally, but not unequivocally (Myers & Chan 1996), verified the effectiveness of the federal, state, and local procurement programs in enabling minority- and women-owned businesses to gain economic footholds (Bendick & Egan 1999).

Also effective is the type of affirmative action that is mandated by Executive Order (EO) 11246. Signed by President Johnson in 1965, EO 11246 stipulates that federal agencies must have affirmative action plans, as must any firm that is above a certain size and does more than minimal business with the federal government. Affirmative action plans allow organizations to monitor their own performance and devise corrections if they find themselves to be guilty of de facto discrimination (Button & Rienzo 2003). To determine whether it is guilty of discrimination, an organization performs prescribed sets of calculations by which, in essence, it examines whether or not it employs women and people of color in proportion to their availability in the qualified labor pool. Only when utilization falls short of the available pools of talent must the organization devise corrective steps.

Affirmative action in education operates in much the same way as in employment. Although the use of explicit quotas or set-asides has been outlawed since 1978, colleges and universities have continued to treat characteristics such as race as "plus factors" when making selections among qualified candidates for admission or for scholarships (Crosby et al. 2003, Lehman 2004).

Race-sensitive admissions practices in higher education have been challenged recently in the Michigan cases known as *Gratz v. Bollinger* and *Grutter v. Bollinger* (Stohr 2004). In October 1997, Jennifer Gratz, a white woman, sued the undergraduate college of the University of Michigan because she was denied admission while black students with lower test scores and grade point averages were admitted. Six weeks after Gratz filed her case, Barbara Grutter, another white woman, sued the University of Michigan Law School on similar grounds. Having heard both cases in tandem, the Supreme Court held on June 23, 2003, that race-sensitive admissions policies were constitutionally permissible because the state has a compelling interest in assuring diversity among the student bodies of state-sponsored schools. The Court also ruled that the undergraduate admissions policy was not narrowly enough tailored to withstand strict scrutiny, whereas the law school's more individualized policy was sufficiently narrowly tailored. Subsequent to the ruling, the University of Michigan changed the practices for admission to the College of Literature, Science, and the Arts to individualize the process.

CONTRIBUTIONS OF SOCIAL SCIENTISTS

Why is Affirmative Action Needed?

Many psychologists have proposed that affirmative action is needed in order to assure the diversity of student bodies and workforces (Miller 1997), an argument that was central to the Michigan cases. Another argument for affirmative action is that it helps insure that selection procedures and decisions are fair. This argument has special relevance to public debates (e.g., Crosby & Clayton 2004, Crosby et al. 2003) and was also part of the amicus brief submitted by the American Psychological Association in the Michigan cases (Am. Psychol. Assoc. 2003).

DIVERSITY   Commentators have long claimed that affirmative action is needed to help bring diversity to American schools and businesses (Tierney 1997). Until recently, the evidence for affirmative action as a facilitator of ethnic minority access to higher education involved tracking enrollment figures over time and thus was, at best, circumstantial (Allen et al. 2003, Crosby & Clayton 2004). In 1998, however, William Bowen and Derek Bok, former presidents of Princeton and Harvard Universities, respectively, published the landmark *The Shape of the River* (Bowen & Bok 1998). Their book provided the first large-scale quantitative examination of the consequences of affirmative action.

Ways to increase diversity   Many note that race-sensitive admissions policies and other forms of affirmative action enhance diversity. To examine this issue, Bowen & Bok (1998) presented detailed analyses of data from more than 80,000 students who had matriculated at 28 elite colleges and universities in 1951, 1976, and 1989. One key finding was that race-sensitive admissions policies significantly increased the numbers of African Americans who were admitted to, and who attended, the schools in the study. Contrary to the assumption—made by commentators such as Shelby Steele (1991)—that there would be a high attrition rate among ethnic minority students, those admitted as a result of race-sensitive policies graduated at the same rate as white students. Additional analyses have shown that colleges and universities cannot achieve ethnic diversity through programs that aim to expand the social classes represented in the student bodies (Kane 2003). As Bowen & Rudenstine (2003) argue, furthermore, it would be intellectually dishonest to see ethnicity or race as equal in historical importance to other dimensions of diversity such as social class.

Although Bowen & Bok (1998) were the first to provide quantitative data about the effects of race-sensitive admissions, they were not the last. In 2000, Lempert et al. (2000a) published their study of minority students who had graduated from the University of Michigan Law School between 1970 (the first year that the Law School graduating class included at least 10 students from underrepresented groups) and 1996. During the 27 years covered by the study, the Law School admissions procedures took into account race or ethnicity in a number of different ways, with the result that the proportion of minority students increased over time.

At variance with the assessment that affirmative action helps increase diversity is a recent analysis of data for some 27,000 students who were admitted to accredited law schools in 1991 and were tracked through law school and beyond (Sander 2004). The data showed that African Americans attended higher-tier law schools than did whites with comparable credentials and that African Americans were much less likely than whites to complete law school or to pass the bar. Initial credentials were highly predictive of class standing, which in turn helped predict graduation and likelihood of passing the bar. While acknowledging the historical impact of race-sensitive admissions policies (e.g., a sevenfold increase in the percentage of lawyers who are African American), Sander infers from his data that race-sensitive admissions policies currently result in fewer, rather than more, African Americans graduating from law school and passing the bar than would occur with race-neutral policies. Sander concludes that attrition would be decreased for African American law students if they were in the middle of their class at a lower-tier law school than if they were—as they presently are—at the bottom of their class in a higher-tier law school.

Sander's "mismatch" explanation has not gone unchallenged. Several scholars have indicated that his analyses rest on some illogical or indefensible assumptions about the data set and about social reality. Ayres & Brooks (2005), for example, point out that Sander assumes that the relationship between initial credentials and law school grades is the same among African Americas as among white students, and they note that his conclusions are valid only if this assumption is valid. Yet, inspection of the data set shows the assumption to be inaccurate. Other researchers warn against cavalierly generalizing from a single cohort. As Chambers et al. (2005) point out, the extent to which race-sensitive policies gave African Americans a boost is linked to the overall applicant pool and its scores. Although estimates have shown that affirmative action doubled the number of African American applicants in some years (including 1991), affirmative action has accounted for only about a 10% increase in other years (e.g., 1997). Ayers & Brooks (2005) and Chambers et al. (2005) also demonstrate that Sander pays insufficient attention to the relationship between the ranking of the school and passage of the bar, thus undermining the credibility of his central conclusion. Finally, Wilkins (2005) notes that Sander's account acknowledges neither the help given to African American graduates of lower-tier law schools by African American graduates of higher-tier law schools, nor the truth that for African Americans, simply attending law school (without passing the bar) contributes to a considerable boost in annual earnings.

Benefits of diversity   Diversity achieved through race-sensitive admissions policies has produced several positive effects. Diversity has been shown to result in positive learning outcomes and positive "democracy outcomes" for all students, including an increased ability to take the perspective of others and involvement in political affairs. Longitudinal surveys show that cross-ethnic interactions and participation in diversity courses benefit both whites and people of color (Gurin 2004; Gurin et al. 2002, 2003, 2004). The research demonstrating the salutary effects of diversity for white students as well as for students of color seems to have influenced Justice Sandra Day O'Connor, who wrote the Court's proaffirmative action opinion in the *Grutter* case (Crosby & Smith 2005). With support from the American Psychological Association (2003), Gurin (2004) was able to rebut attacks from conservative scholars, whose findings fail to support the argument that enrollment diversity improves the educational and social environment at American universities (e.g., Rothman et al. 2003).

A growing body of work from scholars outside of Michigan has substantiated the conclusions drawn by Gurin (2004) and her colleagues. Chang et al. (2004) and Whitla et al. (2003) have shown that ethnic diversity among student bodies elevates the chances that white students will have interaction with students of color. Similarly, the claims about enhanced cognition through diversity have been substantiated by research from other sources as well (Antonio et al. 2004, Tam & Bassett 2004).

The beneficial effects of diversity have been documented less extensively for work settings in comparison with classroom settings. However, studies by economists have shown that firms with vigorous affirmative action plans are as profitable as are other firms (see Crosby 2004, Ch. 3). Although increasing the diversity of workgroups incurs costs, such as increases in initial friction and turnover (see van Knippenberg et al. 2004), laboratory research has demonstrated that heterogeneous groups produce better outcomes than homogeneous groups when participants perceive that they all have something to contribute to the effort (Hewstone et al. 2002).

Bowen & Bok (1998) have articulated an additional advantage of affirmative action: the safeguarding of a well-functioning society. Ethnic minority alumni/ae in their sample made contributions to society in even greater proportion than did their white peers, in terms of professional work as well as in terms of volunteer work. In the Michigan Law School study (Lempert et al. 2000b), ethnic minority alumni/ae also report greater civic engagement than do their white peers. Similarly, studies by the American Dental Association show that significantly more African American dental students than white dental students intend to practice in inner cities (Sinkford & Valachovic 2003). Ethnic minority physicians are disproportionately likely to serve ethnic minority and poor communities (Fryer et al. 2001, Komaromy et al. 1996, Poussaint 1999). Finally, research (e.g., Wright et al. 2001) suggests that social harmony is promoted when representatives of disadvantaged groups believe that not all avenues to advancement have been closed to them (Lehman 2004). This argument in particular was critical to the thinking of the Supreme Court in the Michigan cases.

FAIRNESS   Opponents of affirmative action often characterize the policy as being unfair, claiming that it violates a cherished system of meritocracy in the United States by basing selection decisions on demographic characteristics at the expense of ability and achievement (Thernstrom & Thernstrom 1997, Zuriff 2004). Proponents take a markedly different stance. At the most basic level, proponents wonder why affirmative action is singled out for disapproval while the critics remain silent about many other common practices that disrupt meritocracy. Universities, for example, create elaborate rationalizations for why legacy children are three to four times as likely as are other candidates to be granted admission (Guerrero 1997, Rhode 1997). Further, some university athletes have benefited from special admissions criteria, even though evidence has shown that universities may not profit from athletics programs (Bowen & Levin 2003). Similarly, in employment settings, personnel decisions are often based on habit (Crosby et al. 2003) or business exigencies (Brief et al. 1997) rather than on merit.

Proponents of affirmative action generally expand their defense of the policy beyond simply pointing out that the policy is no less fair than is any other. Indeed, some view the policy as more fair than so-called equal opportunity. The fairness argument is based on two basic premises: (*a*) Sexism and racism persist in American society, and (*b*) affirmative action presents a more efficient and effective means for reducing discrimination than do the existing alternatives.

Data from multiple branches of the social sciences show that sexism and racism are still significant problems in the United States. Concerning gender, women no longer seem to be at a disadvantage in terms of educational opportunities (Crosby et al. 2003). However, women—and especially mothers—continue to be at a disadvantage relative to men in the labor force (Crosby et al. 2004, Nelson & Bridges 2001).

Concerning race, patterns of interpersonal behavior bespeak continued aversive racism on the part of whites in the United States (Saucier et al. 2005). Reliable differences on the basis of race are also found in educational opportunities, rates of pay, receipt of adequate medical care, and treatment at the hands of the judicial system (Crosby 2004, Ch. 6; Hacker 1995; Hall 2002, 2004; Laycock 2004; Pettigrew 2004; U.S. Dept. Labor 2003). For example, a 2002 study by the Institute of Medicine revealed that ethnic and racial minorities receive poorer medical care than do white people, even after statistical adjustments are made to compensate for pre-existing differences in insurance and income (Stolberg 2002). Tester studies—in which actors of different races are trained to behave in very similar ways when they go to obtain a service or make a purchase—continue to show that people of color receive worse treatment than do white people (Yinger 1993). Experiments reveal that even nominally liberal white college students give preferential treatment to other whites in campus elections, selecting white candidates over candidates of color when circumstances permit them to do so without having to confront their own prejudices (Dovidio & Gaertner 2002).

Why is affirmative action thought to be superior to other means of eliminating or reducing discrimination? The effectiveness of affirmative action derives from the fact that it is the only means of correcting injustices in the United States that does not rely on the aggrieved parties to come forward on their own behalf. Relying on victims to advocate for themselves is not a good policy, as many factors make it likely that victims will not speak up until they are so angry that potentially damaging conflicts are likely (Crosby & Ropp 2002). For instance, those who suspect that they have been discriminated against on the basis of race or gender may be reluctant to bring attention to their situation for fear of retaliation or because they feel pessimistic about winning a lawsuit (see, e.g., Sechrist et al. 2004). And, more importantly, many who are at a disadvantage on the basis of demographic characteristics do not consciously recognize that problems exist. Extensively documented is the "denial of personal discrimination," a phenomenon in which members of disadvantaged groups believe that they personally are less disadvantaged than are others in the group (Crosby et al. 2003).

Research has also reliably shown that even very liberal people (who are predisposed to acknowledge discrimination) are unable to detect any but the most blatant discrimination when they encounter gender injustices on a case-by-case basis (e.g., Cordova 1992, Rutte et al. 1994). In contrast, most affirmative action programs enable organizations to detect such biases because they require one or more individuals in an organization to monitor systematically collected data that are then viewed in aggregated displays. Once detected, problems can be corrected quietly before a situation becomes explosive.

One type of bias that has recently received much scrutiny is what sociologist Christopher Jencks (1998) calls "selective system bias." Selective system bias occurs when there are larger intergroup differences on a gating mechanism (e.g., an entrance examination) than on the behavior being predicted by the gating mechanism (e.g., college grades). Test scores are not necessarily accurate in differentiating among applicants for jobs or for school for a number of reasons (Coleman 2003, Sackett et al. 2001). Sometimes the target behavior (e.g., job performance) depends on a variety of traits so that, even if all the candidates could be ranked from best to worst on any specific trait, an overall ranking might need to combine different traits in complex ways (Taylor 1996). Sometimes the tests are simply imprecise so that applicants within a certain bandwidth of scores are indistinguishable from each other on the target behavior. A study at the University of California, for instance, discovered that differences of 200 points on the SAT II test resulted, on average, in differences of only one third of a grade in students' overall averages (Geiser & Studley 2001). Thus, students with an SAT II score of 500 might earn an average grade of B- while students with a score of 700 might earn a B average.

In sum, affirmative action can help enhance integration and fairness in education and in employment because it operates as a proactive monitoring system. Such policies may help ensure that patterns of bias—including selective system bias—are uncovered and corrected (Crosby & Smith 2005).

Does Affirmative Action have Unintended Negative Consequences?

Critics of affirmative action sometimes worry that it is a medicine that harms its patients. Even when they recognize that discrimination persists and should be addressed, critics maintain that affirmative action undermines its intended beneficiaries by promoting the stereotype that those who benefit from the policy could not succeed on their own (Sowell 2004, Zelnick 1996). Several researchers have illustrated that—under certain conditions (e.g., when the person has no other way of knowing whether or not s/he is qualified)—telling people that they have received positive outcomes simply because of, say, gender, results in self-doubt and uncertainty (e.g., Heilman & Alcott 2001, Heilman & Herlihy 1984, Heilman et al. 1990). The same scholars who document the pernicious effects of blatant privilege also document its boundary conditions: Under many conditions that are likely to exist in the real world outside the laboratory (e.g., when a person knows she is qualified to do work), the undermining effects of "affirmative action privilege" evaporate (for a summary, see Crosby 2004, pp. 146–64; see also Turner et al. 1991).

Nor is there much evidence in nonlaboratory settings of the feared assaults to self-esteem. Several surveys have shown that students of color acknowledge that white professors and students may question the abilities of ethnic minority students, and yet, simultaneously, they appreciate the opportunities afforded them by race-conscious admissions policies (Schmermund et al. 2001, Truax et al. 1997). Minority students attribute awkward situations to racial prejudices rather than to affirmative action (Elizondo & Crosby 2004). Similarly, a national probability sample found no trace of self-doubt among women and people of color who worked for organizations practicing affirmative action (Taylor 1994).

A second unintended consequence of affirmative action, according to critics, is that it functions as a form of reverse discrimination and thus increases intergroup tension (Lynch 1992). When striking down race-sensitive admissions policies at the University of Texas Law School, the Fifth Circuit Appellate Court reasoned that any categorization by ethnic or racial groups was likely to elicit animosity against the group granted preferential treatment by other ethnic groups (including whites). Indeed, one laboratory study has shown that the mere mention of affirmative action is enough to increase students' intolerance against out-group members (Maio & Esses 1998).

Although poorly conceived diversity programs may create resentment and may enlarge antiminority bias, it seems that white students who have the opportunity to interact with the beneficiaries of affirmative action tend to appreciate the contact and tend not to devalue diversity efforts (Bowen & Bok 1998; Lempert et al. 2000a,b). White people who work for affirmative action employers also seem to value race-based remedies for discrimination (Taylor 1995). Evaluations of employers, and specifically of the fairness of employment practices, are highest among whites who work for diversity-promoting firms (Parker et al. 1997).

How Can Programs be Maximally Effective?

Research suggests that having an affirmative action policy in place is not always sufficient to help organizations and universities achieve their goals of diversity and merit. Poorly constructed affirmative action programs can cause real harm. Paying attention to proper implementation is important for a number of reasons (Konrad & Linnehan 1995a,b).

Endorsement from the executive level is important to the success of many employment programs, including affirmative action (Jones 1991). The visible commitment of highly ranked officers in an administration helps legitimate affirmative action programs and brings needed resources to implement them (French 2001). In a survey of affirmative action officers, support from the top-level administrators was credited as being the single most important determinant of successful affirmative action programs (Berry 2004). CEOs of newspaper agencies who spoke in their annual reports of social responsibility, and not just of profit, tended to employ more minority reporters than did CEOs who emphasized only profitability (Ankney & Procopio 2003).

Also vital to the success of affirmative action programs is clear and persuasive communication about the goals and the mechanics of affirmative action. Effective official bulletins stress the use of a wide range of relevant and appropriate selection criteria that are considered when making employment and admissions decisions (Cascio et al. 1995, Guinier 2003). Pratkanis & Turner (1996, 1999) note that organizations benefit by making explicit the qualifying criteria for any position and making clear how well qualified all applicants are for the positions. Resistance may be lessened if the message clearly identifies prior and continuing barriers to the use of all talent and shows how aspects of the affirmative action plan dismantle the barriers. Maximally persuasive communications from the organization tend to emphasize how nonbeneficiaries benefit from the affirmative action programs (e.g., by working on the best teams possible rather than on "old boys" teams) and often invoke a sense of social responsibility (Turner & Pratkanis 1994).

Effective communication needs to go in both directions. A recent study of three Arizona police forces highlighted the importance of upward communication (Allen 2003). Successful integration of women and of ethnic minorities depended on honest involvement of those in the front ranks, and on open dialogue between such people and the policymakers. The findings of the Arizona study also underscored a point made some years ago by Hitt & Keats (1984): When new procedures are put into place, mistakes can be made. Rapid correction of the mistakes can help win allies and minimize resentment against newcomers.

One final observation about the successful implementation of affirmative action plans concerns the use of "banding" during the process of candidate evaluation. Test experts and others scholars advocate the use of a band or a range of test scores to determine eligibility rather than a single cutoff point (Kriska 1995, Sackett et al. 2001). Proponents point out that banding can allow inclusion of more diverse pools of eligible applicants while compromising little in terms of merit or productivity (Kriska 1995).

ATTITUDES TOWARD AFFIRMATIVE ACTION

Since the 1980s, social scientists have studied attitudes toward affirmative action. Some of the studies involve surveys that draw upon national probability samples (e.g., Kinder & Sanders 1996, Sidanius et al. 1992), regional or local probability samples (e.g., Kravitz et al. 2000), samples of professional people in specified organizations (e.g., Konrad & Linnehan 1995a,b), students attending a school (e.g., Chesler & Peet 2002), and samples of convenience (e.g., Sherman et al. 2003). Other studies have taken place in laboratories and have involved systematic variations in the materials presented (e.g., Clayton 1996, Kravitz & Platania 1993). Still other studies have embedded experiments within surveys (e.g., Sniderman & Carmines 1997). To date, there have been several comprehensive reviews of attitude studies (Crosby 2004, Crosby et al. 2001, Kravitz et al. 1997, Taylor et al. 1995).

What Factors Influence Attitudes Toward Affirmative Action?

Pollsters and social scientists have found attitudes toward affirmative action to vary considerably and somewhat erratically over time (Ewoh & Elliott 1997, Schuman et al. 1997, Steeh & Krysan 1996). Given the broadness of the term and confusion over its definition, fluctuations in attitudinal support are perhaps not surprising (Crosby & Cordova 1996). Apparent variability in support for affirmative action may also be a function of variations in the operationalization of attitudes. Studies have widely differed in how they measure attitudes toward affirmative action. In most studies, participants evaluate specific practices, whereas in some (e.g., Elizondo & Crosby 2004) they are asked to evaluate the generic term "affirmative action." Complicating the literature is the finding that, in any one sample, attitudes toward specific aspects of affirmative action may be determined by one set of factors such as fairness concerns, while attitudes toward other aspects or toward affirmative action in general may be determined by another set of factors such as self-interest (Kravitz 1995).

AS A FUNCTION OF THE POLICY   Attitudes toward affirmative action vary as a function of how the policy and its practice are portrayed or understood. "Soft" forms of affirmative action, such as outreach programs, are favored over "hard" forms such as programs that use race or gender as a tiebreaking factor in hiring decisions (Kravitz 1995; Kravitz & Klineberg 2000, 2004; Kravitz & Platania 1993; Nosworthy et al. 1995). People who think, or who are told, that affirmative action is a quota system or a system of racial or gender preferences tend to dislike affirmative action more than people who view it differently (Golden et al. 2001, Harris 1992, Kinder & Sanders 1996, Moore 2003, Quinn et al. 2001, Sniderman & Carmines 1997). Meanwhile, participants who have been assured that affirmative action takes merit into account support the policy more than others (Tougas et al. 1995b). Generally, the fairer a practice is perceived to be, the more highly it is rated (Bobocel et al. 1998).

Aberson (2003) found that both people of color and white people increased their support for affirmative action when justifications were provided for the policy. A few researchers have tracked the effects of different justifications or explanations on people's reactions to affirmative action (e.g., Bobocel & Farrell 1996, Murrell et al. 1994, Taylor-Carter et al. 1995). Among a sample of white citizens, Stoker (1998) found that when policies were explained or justified in terms of discrimination, endorsement declined as racial hostility increased. However, in the absence of explanations, attitudes depended on people's assumptions about the existence of racism rather than on their levels of hostility.

In the past decade, affirmative action in education has provoked more strong sentiment in the nation than has affirmative action in employment. Even though the number of Americans who are directly touched by affirmative action programs in education is only about one-quarter the number of those directly touched by affirmative action in employment, issues of equity and merit in higher education can ignite intense feelings (Downing et al. 2002).

Researchers have also systematically varied the specified target of affirmative action, finding that affirmative action is perceived to be more acceptable for some groups than for others, perhaps because of different judgments of deservingness. Most people express more enthusiasm about affirmative action programs intended to help disabled persons than about those designed to help women or minorities (Kravitz & Platania 1993). People also provide differential support for the consideration of gender compared with race. In a survey of nonstudent adults, Sniderman & Piazza (1993) found that more than 60% of participants supported the government helping women, while 20% supported the government helping blacks. Among white samples in general, support for affirmative action falls when the practice under review was said to benefit blacks (Bobo & Kluegel 1993, Moore 1995, Strolovitch 1998). Clayton (1996) found college students were most averse to categorizations based on group memberships having to do with race, as well as with religion and sexual orientation.

AS A FUNCTION OF THE PERSON   Attitudes toward affirmative action vary also as a function of characteristics of the attitude-holder. Simple demographic characteristics of attitude-holders (e.g., gender, race, education), as well as general prejudice and political ideology, turn out to be very important.

Quite a number of studies, across a variety of samples including students and workers, have compared women's and men's attitudes toward affirmative action. With some exceptions (e.g., Murrell et al. 1994), the vast majority of studies find that women endorse affirmative action much more strongly than do men (Aberson & Haag 2003, Bell et al. 1997, Golden et al. 2001, Konrad & Linnehan 1995b, Kravitz et al. 2000, Kravitz & Platania 1993, Ozawa et al. 1996, Stout & Buffum 1993, Summers 1995, Truxillo & Bauer 2000).

Similarly, endorsement of affirmative action is generally, but not always (Aberson 2003, Peterson 1994), greater among people of color than among whites (Aguirre et al. 1993, Allen 2003, Arthur et al. 1992, Bell et al. 1997, Bobo & Kluegel 1993, Bobo & Smith 1994, Citrin 1996, Clawson et al. 2003, Fine 1992, Golden et al. 2001, Klineberg & Kravitz 2003, Konrad & Linnehan 1995b, Kravitz et al. 2000, Little et al. 1998, Sigelman & Welch 1991, Stout & Buffum 1993). Compared with other groups, white men tend to be the least supportive of affirmative action (Niemann & Dovidio 1998). In some instances, the reactions of Latinos fall between those of whites and blacks (Klineberg & Kravitz 2003, Kravitz & Platania 1993). The attitudes of Asian Americans have been rarely studied, although one survey found Asian Americans tend to feel ambivalent about the policy (Inkelas 2003).

How does one's level of education factor in? Some researchers (e.g., Golden et al. 2001) have found a positive relationship between education and approval of affirmative action, whereas others (e.g., Tuch & Hughes 1996) have found no relationship. Still others have documented that levels of education mediated the relationship between prejudice and attitudes toward affirmative action such that the association was stronger for college graduates than for others (Federico & Sidanius 2002a,b).

Of special concern to researchers is the extent to which people's attitudes about affirmative action vary as a function of prejudice and political ideology. Across a substantial number of studies, researchers have found that opposition to affirmative action policies and practices is greatest among those who are the most sexist (Tougas et al. 1995a,b; Tougas & Veilleux 1990) and the most racist (Arriola & Cole 2001, Bobo 1998, Bobo & Kluegel 1993, Bobocel et al. 1998, Carmines & Layman 1998, Hayes-James et al. 2001, Hurwitz & Pefflley 1998, Lehman & Crano 2002, Little et al. 1998, Mack et al. 2002, Nosworthy et al. 1995, Sawires & Peacock 2000, Sears et al. 1997, Sidanius et al. 1996, Sniderman & Piazza 1993, Stoker 1998, Strolovitch 1998, Tuch & Hughes 1996). At least one major survey has found that modern or covert racism is an even stronger predictor of opposition to affirmative action than is old-fashioned racism (Williams et al. 1999).

Recent research has outlined some contingencies for the associations between prejudice and antiaffirmative action attitudes. Although some older studies focused on differences among groups of participants or associations among variables across an entire sample, the current practice is to look for differential associations among variables within specific subgroups. Carmines & Layman's (1998) survey of Democrats and Republicans is illustrative. Among Democrats, racial attitudes and attitudes toward activist problack policies are strongly associated; among Republicans, they are not. Other data collected by Carmines and Layman show Republicans are less likely to disparage African Americans (even poor African Americans) than to disparage poor people in general.

Other aspects of personality besides prejudice influence affirmative action attitudes. Personal experience with discrimination matters as well (Bell et al. 1997, Fried et al. 2001, Slaughter et al. 2002). In addition, personality variables that are known to vary with prejudice, like social dominance orientation, have also been found to explain significant amounts of variation in attitudes toward affirmative action (Federico & Sidanius 2000a,b). So have variables that are, arguably, unrelated to gender or racial prejudice, such as ideology (Aberson & Haag 2003, Clawson & Waltenberg 2003), identification with one's racial group (Lowery et al. 2005), conservatism (Sidanius et al. 1996), and a propensity toward individualism (Kemmelmeier 2003, Williams et al. 1999) or toward individualistic explanations (Kluegel 1990). Finally, feelings of "white guilt" about the in-group's privileges or acts of discrimination have been shown to predict support for some, but not all, constructions of affirmative action (Iyer et al. 2003, Swim & Miller 1999).

What Theories Explain Variations in Attitudes Toward Affirmative Action?

Social psychologists have proposed a number of specific theoretical frameworks to explain variations in attitudes toward affirmative action. Some researchers have directly compared these different explanations (e.g., Aberson 2003, Glaser 1994, Jacobson 1985, Lehman & Crano 2002, Strolovitch 1998). In spirited exchanges, scholars debate whether variations in support for (or opposition to) affirmative action are best explained in terms of symbolic politics, intergroup conflict, self-interest, ideologically delimited cognitions, or principled objections.

Kinder and associates (Hughes 1997, Kinder 1998, Kinder & Sanders 1996, Sears et al. 1997) argue for the symbolic politics point of view, which maintains that reactions to affirmative action are determined more by what race and race relations have come to symbolize for people, and less by what people stand to gain or lose personally from the policy. Bobo and colleagues (Bobo 1998, 2000; Bobo & Kluegel 1993; Bobo et al. 1997; Bobo & Smith 1994; Tolbert & Grummel 2003) have been the most forceful advocates of the view that battles over affirmative action reflect clashes over the interests of different social groups in America. Yet another perspective championed by Sidanius and associates (Federico & Sidanius 2000a,b; Sidanius et al. 1992, 1996) promotes the view that people's ideologies—and specifically their attachment to hierarchy (versus equality)—are the major determinants of reactions to affirmative action.

Although these three perspectives all agree that opposition to affirmative action reflects racial prejudice, they disagree about the larger framework in which to understand the dynamics of the racism. In greater contrast is the approach of Sniderman and his colleagues, who argue that a portion, although certainly not all, of the opposition to affirmative action is based in a commitment to political and economic principles, and is not simply a reflection of racism (Gilens et al. 1998; Kuklinski et al. 1997; Sniderman & Carmines 1997; Sniderman & Piazza 1993; Sniderman et al. 1991, 1993).

Examining the debates, Crosby (2004) observed that the moment may have come for accelerating the trend—visible in some of the recent contributions (e.g.,

Dawson 2000, Hughes 1997, Sidanius et al. 1992)—toward integrating the different theoretical approaches. There are several reasons why it no longer makes sense to attempt to explain attitudes toward affirmative action solely in terms of any one theory or approach. First, people may have different reasons for supporting different types of affirmative action (see Iyer et al. 2003). Second, it seems likely that many of the observed relationships among measured variables may be reconceptualized in terms of other measured or unmeasured variables. Thus, for example, one's political worldview (conceived in terms of hierarchy, political principles, or some other dimensions) may determine what one sees as being in the best interest of one's group or one's self and may determine how one judges merit. Is self or group interest then to be seen as the determinant of attitudes, or does one's assessed group interest merely symbolize one's ideology? As for principled objections to affirmative action, it is not difficult to imagine the racist who assumes that people of color are inferior to white people, and who then decries affirmative action as an abrogation of the fair principles of meritocracy for the way in which it allows "inferior" people to gain advantage (Sidanius et al. 2000).

What Are the Implications for Social Change and Social Stasis?

Close examinations of affirmative action in theory and in practice have enriched our understanding of social change and social stasis. Specifically, applied research on affirmative action has illuminated our understanding of people's behavior in systems of social inequality in three ways: (a) Even when situations contain unfairness, people prefer to see the world as just; (b) this resistance tends to be especially strong among those who benefit more from the status quo; and (c) the change in procedures brought about by affirmative action often appears to be unfair, even when the rules that are being changed are themselves arbitrary.

PERCEIVING FAIRNESS AND UNFAIRNESS   Research has shown that one basis of opposition to affirmative action is that people do not perceive the need for it, believing that race and gender discrimination are no longer widespread problems (e.g., Kluegel & Smith 1986, Son Hing et al. 2002). Surveys have shown that the poor outcomes of people in underprivileged groups are not seen as indications of racism, sexism, or any other form of prejudice. Rather, they are assumed to result from the inferior qualifications of low-status people (Moss & Tilly 2001, Stark 2004). As Jost & Banaji (1994) have pointed out, Americans are prone to finding ways to justify the status quo. Further, Americans like to see the world as a just place (Lerner 1980). A recent experiment showed that people prefer to be presented with justifications of affirmative action that referenced merit rather than an account that spoke of injustices (Elkins et al. 2003). Even people who express a strong desire to end racial and gender imbalances often give faltering support to affirmative action because of their discomfort with a policy that assumes imperfections in the status quo (Crosby 2004).

Assumptions about social structures and about people's places within the structures are not usually available to conscious thought and thus are not subject to easy correction. For example, a large-scale study of police partners and supervisors found that observers commonly looked for conformity to gender norms when making their evaluations, often without realizing it. Supervisors' evaluations of female officers thus tended to be more inaccurate than their evaluations of male officers (Gerber 2001).

Even when assumptions are brought into conscious awareness, stereotypes resist change. When people encounter members of target groups who violate their (negative) stereotypes, they often maintain the stereotype in the face of this disconfirming evidence by subtyping the group member as someone who is not prototypical of the group (Maurer et al. 1995).

Of course, people differ in their comfort with acknowledging problems with the current system (Jost et al. 2003). People who have a desire to perceive the status quo as a good and unchangeable system often exhibit a "social dominance orientation" (Sidanius & Pratto 1999), which itself is associated with greater opposition to affirmative action (e.g., Federico & Sidanius 2000a,b). Reactions to affirmative action are also conditioned by one's outlook on society (Son Hing et al. 2002). Among students who spontaneously, or through subtle manipulation, believed that discrimination was no longer a feature of society, there was a strong negative association between belief in meritocratic ideals and support for affirmative action. Among students who believed discrimination to persist, the opposite was true (Son Hing et al. 2002).

PROTECTING PRIVILEGE   Majority group members are less likely than minority group members to perceive discrimination. Studies show that white people (white men in particular) often believe that racial inequality is a thing of the past in American society in general (Wilson 2004) and in the workplace in particular (Mor Barak et al. 1998). Similarly, a survey of professional women found that black and white women were equally likely to perceive gender discrimination in the workplace, but white women were less likely than were black women to perceive race discrimination (Weber & Higginbotham 1997). In a study of faculty, white men were the group most likely to believe that meritocracy operates in academe and also most likely to think that affirmative action "perpetuates a myth of minority and female inferiority" (Witt 1990, p. 86).

One reason that high-status group members may have difficulty acknowledging group inequality is that they wish to preserve the illusion of having legitimately earned all their outcomes. White males seem to have an overdeveloped sense of entitlement, as they often do not acknowledge the structural advantages they have received as a group (Pelham & Hetts 2001). Branscombe (1998) has demonstrated that men become upset when their previously unquestioned or unobserved privilege is exposed. People who rail against "preferential treatment" afforded to ethnic minorities in college admissions plans may turn a blind eye to the preferences that continue to be handed to legacies (Bowen & Rudenstein 2003). As industrial psychologist Myrtle Bell notes, "My great-great grandmother was a slave. Anyone whose ancestors were not slaves has been given advantages that they didn't earn" (Crosby 2004, p. 231).

Another difficulty for members of high-status groups is that acknowledgment of group inequality sometimes involves a recognition that members of their own group may have participated in acts of discrimination. Admitting that one's group has committed transgressions is threatening, as it undermines people's views of their group as moral and good (Branscombe et al. 2002). Roger Wilkins (2004) illustrates this point in his recollection of a "superb" white male student who had enrolled in a course on race and culture in America. At the end of the course, the student admitted that it had been the hardest course he had taken because he "learned that [his] two heroes—[his] parents—are racists" (p. 52). In the same vein, Iyer et al. (2003, Study 2) showed that European American students were more reluctant to believe that racial discrimination was a problem when attention was drawn to their racial group's responsibility for the transgressions than when their attention was directed toward the victims. Similarly, evidence suggests that framing inequality in terms of the advantages bestowed to whites is more threatening to whites than inequality framed in terms of the disadvantages suffered by blacks (Lowery et al. 2005).

UNDERSTANDING CHANGE   One study of an organization that had implemented affirmative action to correct for known discriminatory practices uncovered an interesting phenomenon: People experience a change in procedures or rules as being unfair even when they recognized that the original rules were arbitrary or imbalanced. Follow-up experiments in the laboratory confirmed that those who benefited under one set of arbitrary rules felt sorely cheated when the rules were changed (Crosby & Franco 2003). Organizations that discover that their practices are faulty thus face a conundrum: Either they can persist with unfair practices or they can change the practices. To the extent that employees experience the change as coming "in the middle of the game," they will perceive it as a violation of procedural justice and react negatively.

IN SUM

Psychologists have joined other scholars across the social sciences, education, and the law in seeking to understand affirmative action and to determine the most beneficial ways to implement it. Research shows that many different factors influence people's reactions to affirmative action, including characteristics of the program and characteristics of the person. Research also shows that the persistence of prejudice and of discrimination is one of the major reasons why the policy is still needed today and is likely to be needed for decades to come. One can expect that the next few years will bring continued careful study of and lively debate over affirmative action and its role in promoting fairness and effectiveness across diverse settings.

ACKNOWLEDGMENTS

The authors thank Emily Farrell Keresey, Nicole Laperdon, and Kristina Schmukler for assistance with preparation of the manuscript, and Ian Ayres, Steve Bearman, David Kravitz, Richard Lempert, Brian Lowery, Dave Mayer, Jim Sidanius, Philip Tetlock, Francine Tougas, and David Wilkins for supplying information and feedback pertinent to the content.

The *Annual Review of Psychology* is online at http://psych.annualreviews.org

LITERATURE CITED

Aberson CL. 2003. Support for race-based affirmative action: self-interest and procedural justice. *J. Appl. Soc. Psychol.* 33:1212–25

Aberson CL, Haag SC. 2003. Beliefs about affirmative action and diversity and their relationship to support for hiring policies. *Anal. Soc. Iss. Public Policy* 3:121–38

Aguirre A Jr, Martinez R, Hernandez A. 1993. Majority and minority faculty perceptions in academe. *Res. Higher Educ.* 34:371–85

Allen RYW. 2003. Examining the implementation of affirmative action in law enforcement. *Public Personnel Manage.* 32:411–19

Allen RYW, Teranishi R, Dinwiddie G, Gonzalez G. 2003. Knocking at freedom's door: race, equity, and affirmative action in U.S. higher education. *J. Public Health Policy* 23:440–52

Am. Psychol. Assoc. 2003. *Barbara Grutter, Petitioner, v. Lee Bollinger, et al., Respondents, and Jennifer Gratz and Patrick Hamacher, Petitioners, v. Lee Bollinger, et al., Respondents. Brief amicus curiae of the American Psychological Association in support of respondents.* Washington, DC: Am. Psychol. Assoc.

Ankney RN, Procopio DA. 2003. Corporate culture, minority hiring, and newspaper coverage of affirmative action. *Howard J. Commun.* 14:159–76

Antonio AL, Chang MJ, Hakuta K, Kenny DA, Levin S, Milem JF. 2004. Effects of racial diversity on complex thinking in college students. *Psychol. Sci.* 15:507–10

Arriola KRJ, Cole ER. 2001. Framing the af-

firmative action debate: attitudes toward outgroup members and white identity. *J. Appl. Soc. Psychol.* 31:2462–83

Arthur W, Doverspike D, Fuentes R. 1992. Recipients' affective responses to affirmative action interventions: a cross-cultural perspective. *Behav. Sci. Law* 10:229–43

Ayres I, Brooks R. 2005. Does affirmative action reduce the number of black lawyers? *Stanford Law Rev.* In press

Bell MP, Harrison DA, McLaughlin ME. 1997. Asian American attitudes toward affirmative action in employment: implications for the model minority myth. *J. Appl. Behav. Sci.* 33:356–77

Bell MP, Harrison DA, McLaughlin ME. 2000. Forming, changing, and acting on attitude toward affirmative action programs in employment: a theory-driven approach. *J. Appl. Psychol.* 85:784–98

Bendick M Jr, Egan ML. 1999. Adding testing to the nation's portfolio of information on employment discrimination. In *A National Report Card on Discrimination in America: The Role of Testing*, ed. M Fix, MA Turner, pp. 47–68. Washington, DC: Urban Inst.

Bergmann B. 1996. *In Defense of Affirmative Action.* New York: Basic Books

Berry RM. 2004. Affirmative action in higher education: costs, benefits, and implementation. *J. Public Budget. Account. Financ. Manage.* 16:257–76

Bobo L. 1998. Race, interests, and beliefs about affirmative action: unanswered questions and new directions. *Am. Behav. Sci.* 41:985–1003

Bobo L. 2000. Race and beliefs about affirmative action: assessing the effects of interest, group threats, ideology, and racism. In *Racialized Politics: The Debate About Racism in America*, ed. DO Sears, J Sidanius, L Bobo, pp. 137–64. Chicago: Univ. Chicago Press

Bobo L, Kluegel JR. 1993. Opposition to race-targeting: self-interest, stratification ideology, or racial attitudes? *Am. Sociol. Rev.* 58:443–64

Bobo L, Kluegel JR, Smith RA. 1997. Laissez-faire racism: the crystallization of a kinder, gentler, antiblack ideology. In *Racial Attitudes in the 1990s: Continuity and Change*, ed. SA Tuch, JK Martin, pp. 15–42. Westport, CT: Praeger

Bobo L, Smith RA. 1994. Antipoverty policy, affirmative action, and racial attitudes. In *Confronting Poverty: Prescriptions for Change*, ed. SH Danziger, GD Sandefu, DH Weinberg, pp. 365–95. Cambridge, MA: Harvard Univ. Press

Bobocel DR, Farrell AC. 1996. Sex-based promotion decisions and interactional fairness: investigating the influence of managerial accounts. *J. Appl. Psychol.* 81:22–35

Bobocel DR, Son Hing LS, Davey LM, Stanley DJ, Zanna MP. 1998. Justice-based opposition to social policies: Is it genuine? *J. Personal. Soc. Psychol.* 75:653–69

Bowen WG, Bok D. 1998. *The Shape of the River: Long-Term Consequences of Considering Race in College and University Admissions*. Princeton, NJ: Princeton Univ. Press

Bowen WG, Levin SA. 2003. *Reclaiming the Game: College Sports and Educational Values*. Princeton, NJ: Princeton Univ. Press

Bowen WG, Rudenstine NL. 2003. Race-sensitive admissions: back to basics. *Chron. Higher Educ.* Feb. 7:B7–10

Branscombe NR. 1998. Thinking about one's gender group's privileges or disadvantages: consequences for well-being in women and men. *Br. J. Soc. Psychol.* 37:167–84

Branscombe NR, Doosje B, McGarty C. 2002. Antecedents and consequences of collective guilt. In *From Prejudice to Intergroup Emotions: Differentiated Reactions to Social Groups*, ed. DM Mackie, ER Smith, pp. 49–66. Philadelphia: Psychol. Press

Brief AP, Buttram RT, Riezenstein RM, Pugh SD, Callahan JD, et al. 1997. Beyond good intentions: the next steps toward racial equality in the American workplace. *Acad. Manage. Exec.* 11:59–72

Burstein P. 1994. *Equal Employment Opportunity: Labor Market Discrimination and Public Policy*. New York: de Gruyter Aldine

Button JW, Rienzo BA. 2003. The impact of affirmative action: black employment in six southern cities. *Soc. Sci. Q.* 84:1–14

Carmines EG, Layman GC. 1998. When prejudice matters: the impact of racial stereotypes on the racial policy preferences of Democrats and Republicans. In *Perceptions and Prejudice: Race and Politics in the United States*, ed. J Hurwitz, M Peffley, pp. 100–34. New Haven, CT: Yale Univ. Press

Cascio WF, Outtz J, Zedeck S, Goldstein IL. 1995. Statistical implications of six methods of test score use in personnel selection. *Hum. Perform.* 8:133–64

Chambers DL, Clydesdale TT, Kidder WC, Lempert RO. 2005. The real impact of eliminating affirmative action in American law schools: an empirical critique of Richard Sander's study. *Stanford Law Rev.* In press

Chang MJ, Astin AW, Kim D. 2004. Cross-racial interaction among undergraduates: some consequences, causes, and patterns. *Res. Higher Educ.* 45:529–53

Chesler M, Peet M. 2002. White student views of affirmative action on campus. *Divers. Factor* 10:21–29

Citrin J. 1996. Affirmative action in the people's court. *Public Int.* 122:39–48

Clawson RA, Kegler ER, Waltenburg EN. 2003. Supreme Court legitimacy and group-centric forces: black support for capital punishment and affirmative action. *Polit. Behav.* 25:289–311

Clawson RA, Waltenburg EN. 2003. Support for a Supreme Court affirmative action decision: a story in black and white. *Am. Polit. Res.* 31:251–79

Clayton S. 1996. Reactions to social categorizations: evaluating one argument against affirmative action. *J. Appl. Soc. Psychol.* 26: 1472–93

Coleman MG. 2003. African American popular wisdom versus the qualification question: Is affirmative action merit-based? *West. J. Black Stud.* 27:35–44

Cordes MW. 2004. Affirmative action after Grutter and Gratz. *North. Ill. Univ. Law Rev.* 24:691–752

Cordova DI. 1992. Cognitive limitations and affirmative action: the effects of aggregate versus sequential data in the perception of discrimination. *Soc. Justice Res.* 5:319–33

Crosby FJ. 2004. *Affirmative Action is Dead; Long Live Affirmative Action.* New Haven, CT: Yale Univ. Press

Crosby FJ, Biernat M, Williams J. 2004. The maternal wall: introduction. *J. Soc. Issues* 60:675–82

Crosby FJ, Clayton S. 2004. Affirmative action and the search for educational equity. *Anal. Soc. Iss. Public Policy* 4:243–49

Crosby FJ, Cordova D. 1996. Words worth of wisdom: toward an understanding of affirmative action. *J. Soc. Issues* 52:33–49

Crosby FJ, Ferdman BM, Wingate BR. 2001. Addressing and redressing discrimination: affirmative action in social psychological perspective. In *Blackwell Handbook of Social Psychology: Intergroup Processes*, ed. R Brown, S Gaertner, pp. 495–513. New York: Blackwell Sci.

Crosby FJ, Franco JL. 2003. Connections between the ivory tower and the multicolored world: linking abstract theories of social justice to the rough and tumble of affirmative action. *Personal. Soc. Psychol. Rev.* 7:362–73

Crosby FJ, Iyer A, Clayton S, Downing R. 2003. Affirmative action: psychological data and the policy debates. *Am. Psychol.* 58:93–115

Crosby FJ, Ropp S. 2002. Awakening to discrimination. In *The Justice Motive in Everyday Life*, ed. M Ross, DT Miller, pp. 382–96. New York: Cambridge Univ. Press

Crosby FJ, Smith AE. 2005. The University

of Michigan cases: social scientific studies of diversity and fairness. In *Legal Decision Making in Everyday Life: Controversies in Social Consciousness*, ed. RL Wiener, B Bornstein, R Schopp, S Willborn. New York: Springer-Verlag. In press

Cunningham CD, Loury GC, Skrentny JD. 2002. Passing strict scrutiny: using social science to design affirmative action programs. *Georgetown Law J.* 90:835–83

Dawson MC. 2000. Slowly coming to grips with the effects of the American racial order on American policy preferences. In *Racialized Politics: The Debate About Racism in America*, ed. DO Sears, J Sidanius, L Bobo, pp. 344–57. Chicago: Univ. Chicago Press

DeBono KG, Snyder M. 1995. Acting on one's attitudes: the role of a history in choosing situations. *Personal. Soc. Psychol. Bull.* 21:629–36

Dovidio JF, Gaertner SL. 2000. Aversive racism and selection decisions: 1989 and 1999. *Psychol. Sci.* 11:315–19

Downing R, Lubensky ME, Sincharoen S, Gurin P, Crosby FJ, et al. 2002. Affirmative action in higher education. *Divers. Factor* 10:15–20

Elizondo E, Crosby FJ. 2004. Attitudes toward affirmative action as a function of the strength of ethnic identity among Latino college students. *J. Appl. Soc. Psychol.* 34:1773–96

Elkins TJ, Bozeman DP, Phillips JS. 2003. Promotion decisions in an affirmative action environment: Can social accounts change fairness perceptions? *J. Appl. Soc. Psychol.* 33:1111–39

Ewoh AI, Elliott E. 1997. End of an era? Affirmative action and reaction in the 1990s. *Rev. Public Pers. Admin.* Fall:38–51

Federico CM, Sidanius J. 2002a. Racism, ideology, and affirmative action revisited: the antecedents and consequences of "principled objections" to affirmative action. *J. Personal. Soc. Psychol.* 82:488–502

Federico CM, Sidanius J. 2002b. Sophistication and the antecedents of whites' racial policy attitudes: racism, ideology, and affirmative action in America. *Public Opin. Q.* 66:145–76

Fine TS. 1992. The impact of issue framing on public opinion toward affirmative action programs. *Soc. Sci. J.* 29:323–34

French E. 2001. Approaches to equity management and their relationship to women in management. *Br. J. Manage.* 12:267–85

Fried Y, Levi AS, Billings SW, Browne KR. 2001. The relation between political ideology and attitudes toward affirmative action among African-Americans: the moderating effect of racial discrimination in the workplace. *Hum. Relat.* 54:561–84

Fryer GE Jr, Green LA, Vojir CP, Krugman RD, Miyoshi TJ, et al. 2001. Hispanic versus white, non-hispanic physician medical practices in Colorado. *J. Health Care Poor Underserved* 12:342–51

Geiser S, Studley R. 2001. *UC and the SAT: predictive validity and differential impact of the SAT I and SAT II at the University of California.* http://www.ucop.edu/sas/research/researchandplanning/

Gerber GL. 2001. *Women and Men Police Officers: Status, Gender, and Personality.* Westport, CT: Greenwood/Praeger

Gilens M, Sniderman PM, Kuklinski JH. 1998. Affirmative action and the politics of realignment. *Br. J. Polit. Sci.* 28:159–83

Glaser JM. 1994. Back to the Black Belt: Racial environment and white racial attitudes in the South. *J. Polit.* 56:21–41

Golden H, Hinkle S, Crosby FJ. 2001. Reactions to affirmative action: substance and semantics. *J. Appl. Soc. Psychol.* 31:73–88

Gratz v. Bollinger, 539 U.S. 244, 123 S. Ct. 2411. 2003

Grutter v. Bollinger, 529 U.S. 306, 123 S. Ct. 2325. 2003

Guerrero MAJ. 1997. Affirmative action: race, class, gender, and NOW. *Am. Behav. Sci.* 41:246–55

Guinier L. 2003. Social change and democratic values: reconceptualizing affirmative action policy. *West. J. Black Stud.* 27:45–50

Gurin PY. 2004. The educational value of diversity. In *Defending Diversity: Affirmative Action at the University of Michigan,* ed. P Gurin, JS Lehman, E Lewis, pp. 97–188. Ann Arbor, MI: Univ. Mich. Press

Gurin PY, Dey EL, Gurin G, Hurtado S. 2003. How does racial/ethnic diversity promote education? *West. J. Black Stud.* 27:20–29

Gurin PY, Dey EL, Hurtado S, Gurin G. 2002. Diversity and higher education: theory and impact on educational outcomes. *Harvard Educ. Rev.* 72:330–66

Gurin PY, Nagda BRA, Lopez GE. 2004. The benefits of diversity in education for democratic citizenship. *J. Soc. Issues* 60:17–34

Hacker A. 1995. *Two Nations: Black and White, Separate, Hostile, Unequal.* New York: Ballantine

Hall RE. 2002. A new perspective on racism: health risk to African-Americans. *Race Gend. Class* 9:100–11

Hall RE. 2004. Entitlement disorder: the colonial traditions of power as white male resistance to affirmative action. *J. Black Stud.* 34:562–79

Harris L. 1992. Unequal terms. *Columbia Journalism Rev.* 30:20

Hayes-James E, Brief AP, Dietz J, Cohen RR. 2001. Prejudice matters: understanding reactions of whites to affirmative action programs targeted to benefit blacks. *J. Appl. Psychol.* 86:1120–28

Heilman ME, Alcott VB. 2001. What I think you think of me: women's reactions to being viewed as beneficiaries of preferential selection. *J. Appl. Psychol.* 86:574–82

Heilman ME, Herlihy JM. 1984. Affirmative action, negative reaction? Some moderating conditions. *Organ. Behav. Hum. Perform.* 33:204–13

Heilman ME, Lucas JA, Kaplow SR. 1990. Self-derogating consequences of sex-based preferential selection: the moderating role of initial self-confidence. *Organ. Behav. Hum. Decis. Process.* 46:202–16

Hewstone M, Rubin M, Willis H. 2002. Intergroup bias. *Annu. Rev. Psychol.* 53:575–604

Hitt M, Keats B. 1984. Empirical identification of the criteria for effective affirmative action programs. *J. Appl. Behav. Sci.* 20:203–22

Hochschild JL. 1999. Affirmative action as culture war. In *The Cultural Territories of Race: Black and White Boundaries*, ed. M Lamont, pp. 343–68. Chicago: Univ. Chicago Press

Holt C. 2003. Strict constitutional scrutiny is not fatal in fact: Federal courts uphold affirmative action programs in public contracting. *Labor Law J.* 54:248–62

Hughes M. 1997. Symbolic racism, old-fashioned racism, and whites' opposition to affirmative action. In *Racial Attitudes in the 1990s: Continuity and Change*, ed. SA Tuch, JK Martin, pp. 45–75. Westport, CT: Praeger

Hurwitz J, Peffley M. 1998. *Perception and Prejudice: Race and Politics in the United States*. New Haven, CT: Yale Univ. Press

Inkelas KK. 2003. Caught in the middle: understanding Asian Pacific American perspectives on affirmative action through Blumer's group position theory. *J. Coll. Stud. Dev.* 44: 625–43

Iyer A, Leach CW, Crosby FJ. 2003. White guilt and racial compensation: the benefits and limits of self-focus. *Personal. Soc. Psychol. Bull.* 29:117–29

Jacobson, CK. 1985. Resistance to affirmative action: self-interest or racism? *J. Conflict Resolution* 29:306–29

Jencks, C. 1998. Racial bias in testing. In *The Black-White Test Score Gap*, ed. C Jencks, M Phillips, pp. 55–85. Washington, DC: Brookings Inst.

Jones AJ. 1991. *Affirmative Talk, Affirmative Action: A Comparative Study of the Politics of Affirmative Action*. New York: Praeger

Jost JT, Banaji M. 1994. The role of stereotyping in system justification and the production of false consciousness. *Br. J. Soc. Psychol.* 33:1–27

Jost JT, Glaser J, Kruglanski AW, Sulloway FJ. 2003. Political conservatism as motivated social cognition. *Psychol. Bull.* 129:339–75

Kane TJ. 2003. The long road to race-blindness. *Science* 302:571–73

Kemmelmeier M. 2003. Individualism and attitudes toward affirmative action: evidence from priming experiments. *Basic Appl. Soc. Psychol.* 25:111–19

Kinder DR. 1998. Attitudes and action in the realm of politics. In *The Handbook of Social Psychology*, ed. DT Gilbert, ST Fiske, G Lindzey, pp. 778–867. Boston, MA: McGraw-Hill. 4th ed.

Kinder DR, Sanders L. 1996. *Divided by Color: Racial Politics and Democratic Ideals*. Chicago: Univ. Chicago Press

Klineberg SL, Kravitz DA. 2003. Ethnic differences in predictors of support for municipal affirmative action contracting. *Soc. Sci. Q.* 84:425–40

Kluegel JR. 1990. Trends in whites' explanations of the black-white gap in socioeconomic status, 1977–1989. *Am. Sociol. Rev.* 55:512–25

Kluegel JR, Smith ER. 1986. *Beliefs about Inequality: Americans' Views of What Is and What Ought to Be*. New York: de Gruyter Aldine

Komaromy M, Grumbach K, Drake M, Vranizan K, Lurie N, et al. 1996. The role of black and hispanic physicians in providing health care for underserved populations. *N. Engl. J. Med.* 334:1305–10

Konrad AM, Linnehan F. 1995a. Formalized HRM structures: coordinating equal employment opportunity or concealing organizational practices? *Acad. Manage. J.* 38:787–820

Konrad AM, Linnehan F. 1995b. Race and sex differences in line managers' reactions to equal employment opportunity and affirmative action interventions. *Group Organ. Manage.* 20:409–39

Kravitz DA. 1995. Attitudes toward affirmative action plans directed at blacks: effects of plan and individual differences. *J. Appl. Soc. Psychol.* 25:2192–220

Kravitz DA, Harrison DA, Turner ME, Levine EL, Chaves W, et al. 1997. *Affirmative Action: A Review of Psychological and Behavioral Research*. Bowling Green, OH: Soc. Ind. Organ. Psychol.

Kravitz DA, Klineberg SL. 2000. Reactions to two versions of affirmative action among whites, blacks, and Hispanics. *J. Appl. Psychol.* 85:597–611

Kravitz DA, Klineberg SL. 2004. Predicting affirmative action attitudes: interactions of the effects of individual differences with the strength of the affirmative action plan. In *Research in the Sociology of Work: Diversity in the Work Force*, ed. N DiTomaso, C Post, pp. 107–30. Amsterdam: Elsevier

Kravitz DA, Klineberg SL, Avery DR, Nguyen AK, Lund C, Fu EJ. 2000. Attitudes toward affirmative action: correlations with demographic variables and with beliefs about targets, actions, and economic effects. *J. Appl. Soc. Psychol.* 30:1109–36

Kravitz DA, Platania J. 1993. Attitudes and beliefs about affirmative action: effects of target and of respondent sex and ethnicity. *J. Appl. Psychol.* 78:928–38

Kriska SD. 1995. Comments on banding. *Ind. Organ. Psychol.* 32:93–94

Kuklinski JH, Sniderman PM, Knight K, Piazza T, Tetlock PE, et al. 1997. Racial prejudice and attitudes toward affirmative action. *Am. J. Polit. Sci.* 41:402–19

Kunda Z, Oleson KC. 1995. Maintaining stereotypes in the face of disconfirmation: constructing grounds for subtyping deviants. *J. Personal. Soc. Psychol.* 68:565–79

Laycock D. 2004. The broader case for affirmative action: desegregation, academic excellence, and future leadership. *Tulane Law Rev.* 78:1767–843

Lehman BJ, Crano WD. 2002. The pervasive effects of vested interest on attitude-criterion consistency in political judgment. *J. Exp. Soc. Psychol.* 38:101–12

Lehman JS. 2004. The evolving language of diversity and integration in discussions of affirmative action from *Bakke* to *Grutter*. In *Defending Diversity: Affirmative Action at the University of Michigan*, ed. PY Gurin, JS Lehman, E Lewis, pp. 61–96. Ann Arbor: Univ. Mich. Press

Lempert RO, Chambers DL, Adams TK. 2000a. Michigan's minority graduates in practice: the river runs through law school. *Law Soc. Inq.* 25:395–505

Lempert RO, Chambers DL, Adams TK. 2000b.

Law school affirmative action. An empirical study of Michigan's minority graduates in practice: answers to methodological queries. *Law Soc. Inq.* 25:585–97

Leonard J. 1996. Wage disparities and affirmative action in the 1980's. *Am. Econ. Rev.* 86:285–89

Lerner MJ. 1980. *The Belief in a Just World: A Fundamental Delusion*. New York: Plenum

Little BL, Murry WD, Wimbush JC. 1998. Perceptions of workplace affirmative action plans: a psychological perspective. *Group Organ. Manage.* 23:27–47

Lowery BS, Knowles ED, Unzueta MM. 2005. *Framing inequity safely: the motivated denial of white privilege*. Unpubl. manusc., Stanford Univ., Stanford, Calif.

Lowery BS, Unzueta MM, Knowles ED. 2005. *Concern for the ingroup, apathy toward the outgroup, and opposition to affirmative action*. Unpubl. manusc., Stanford Univ., Stanford, Calif.

Lynch FR. 1992. *Invisible Victims: White Males and the Crisis of Affirmative Action*. New York: Praeger

Mack DA, Johnson CD, Green TD, Parisi AG, Thomas KM. 2002. Motivation to control prejudice as a mediator of identity and affirmative action attitudes. *J. Appl. Soc. Psychol.* 32:934–64

Maio GR, Esses VM. 1998. The social consequences of affirmative action: deleterious effects on perceptions of groups. *Personal. Soc. Psychol. Bull.* 24:65–74

Maurer KL, Park B, Rothbart M. 1995. Subtyping versus subgrouping processes in stereotype representation. *J. Personal. Soc. Psychol.* 69:812–24

Mellema A, Bassili JN. 1995. On the relationship between attitudes and values: exploring the moderating effects of self-monitoring and self-monitoring schematicity. *Personal. Soc. Psychol. Bull.* 9:885–92

Miller F. 1997. The political rhetoric of affirmative action: infusing the debate with discussions about equity and opportunity. *Am. Behav. Sci.* 41:197–204

Moore DW. 1995. Americans today are dubious

about affirmative action. *Gallup Mon. Poll* March:6–38

Moore DW. 2003. *Public: Only Merit Should Count in College Admissions.* Lincoln, NE: Gallup Organ.

Mor Barak ME, Cherin DA, Berkman S. 1998. Organizational and personal dimensions in diversity climate. *J. Appl. Behav. Sci.* 34:82–104

Moss P, Tilly C. 2001. *Stories Employers Tell: Race, Skill, and Hiring in America.* New York: Russell Sage

Munro D. 1995. The continuing evolution of affirmative action under Title VII: new directions after the Civil Rights Act of 1991. *Virginia Law Rev.* 81:565–610

Murrell AJ, Dietz-Uhler BL, Dovidio JF, Gaertner SL, Drout C. 1994. Aversive racism and resistance to affirmative action: perceptions of justice are not necessarily color blind. *Basic Appl. Soc. Psychol.* 15:71–86

Myers SL, Chan T. 1996. Who benefits from minority business set-asides? The case of New Jersey. *J. Policy Anal. Manage.* 15:202–26

Nelson RL, Bridges WP. 2001. Wage justice for women: markets, firms, and the law governing gender differences in pay. In *Handbook of Justice Research in Law*, ed. J Sanders, VL Hamilton, pp. 269–97. New York: Kluwer Acad.

Niemann YF, Dovidio JF. 1998. Tenure, race/ethnicity and attitudes toward affirmative action: a matter of self-interest. *Sociol. Perspect.* 41:783–96

Nosworthy GJ, Lea JA, Lindsay RCL. 1995. Opposition to affirmative action: racial affect and traditional value predictors across four programs. *J. Appl. Soc. Psychol.* 25:314–37

Ozawa K, Crosby M, Crosby FJ. 1996. Individualism and resistance to affirmative action: a comparison of Japanese and American samples. *J. Appl. Soc. Psychol.* 26:1138–52

Parker CP, Baltes BB, Christiansen ND. 1997. Support for affirmative action, justice perceptions, and work attitudes: a study of gender and racial-ethnic group differences. *J. Appl. Psychol.* 82:376–89

Peffley M, Hurwitz J. 1998. Whites' stereotypes of blacks: sources and political consequences. In *Perception and Prejudice: Race and Politics in the United States*, ed. J Hurwitz, M Peffley, pp. 58–99. New Haven, CT: Yale Univ. Press

Pelham BW, Hetts JJ. 2001. Underworked and overpaid: elevated entitlement in men's self-pay. *J. Exp. Soc. Psychol.* 37:93–103

Peterson RS. 1994. The role of values in predicting fairness judgments and support for affirmative action. *J. Soc. Issues* 50:95–115

Pettigrew TF. 2004. Justice deferred: a half century after Brown v. Board of Education. *Am. Psychol.* 59:521–29

Pincus FL. 2003. *Reverse Discrimination: Dismantling the Myth.* Boulder, CO: Lynne Reiner

Poussaint AF. 1999. Clinical experience and minority group students: a perspective from Harvard Medical School. *Clin. Orthop.* 362:78–84

Pratkanis AR, Turner ME. 1996. The proactive removal of discriminatory barriers: affirmative action as effective help. *J. Soc. Issues* 52:111–33

Pratkanis AR, Turner ME. 1999. The significance of affirmative action for the souls of white folk: further implications of a helping model. *J. Soc. Issues* 55:787–815

Quinn KA, Ross EA, Esses VM. 2001. Attributions of responsibility and reactions to affirmative action: affirmative action as help. *Personal. Soc. Psychol. Bull.* 27:321–31

Reskin BF. 1998. *The Realities of Affirmative Action in Employment.* Washington, DC: Am. Sociol. Assoc.

Rhode DL. 1997. Affirmative action. *Natl. Forum: Newsl. Honor Soc. Phi Kappa Phi* 77:12–17

Rothman S, Lipset SM, Nevitte N. 2003. Does enrollment diversity improve university education? *Int. J. Public Opin. Res.* 15:8–26

Rutte CG, Diekmann KA, Polzer JT, Crosby FJ, Messick DM. 1994. Organizing information and the detection of gender discrimination. *Psychol. Sci.* 5:226–31

Sackett PR, Schmitt N, Ellingson JE, Kabin

MB. 2001. High-stakes testing in employment, credentialing, and higher education: prospects in a post-affirmative action world. *Am. Psychol.* 56:302–18

Sander RH. 2004. A systemic analysis of affirmative action in American law schools. *Stanford Law Rev.* 57:367–483

Saucier DA, Miller CT, Doucet N. 2005. Differences in helping whites and blacks: a meta-analysis. *Personal. Soc. Psychol. Rev.* 9:2–16

Sawires JN, Peacock MJ. 2000. Symbolic racism and voting behavior on Proposition 209. *J. Appl. Soc. Psychol.* 30:2092–99

Schmermund A, Sellers R, Mueller B, Crosby FJ. 2001. Attitudes toward affirmative action as a function of racial identity among black college students. *Polit. Psychol.* 22:759–74

Schuman H, Steeh C, Bobo L, Krysan M. 1997. *Racial Attitudes in America: Trends and Interpretations.* Cambridge, MA: Harvard Univ. Press. Rev. ed.

Schwindt L, Hall K, Davis RH. 1998. Affirmative action in action: a case study of faculty recruitment at one major land-grant university. *NWSA J.* 10:73–100

Sears DO, Van Laar C, Carrillo M, Kosterman R. 1997. Is it really racism? The origins of white Americans' opposition to race-targeted policies. *Public Opin. Q.* 61:16–53

Sechrist GB, Swim JK, Stangor C. 2004. When do the stigmatized make attributions to discrimination occurring to the self and others? The roles of self-presentation and need for control. *J. Personal. Soc. Psychol.* 87:111–22

Sherman DK, Nelson LD, Ross LD. 2003. Naïve realism and affirmative action: adversaries are more similar than they think. *Basic Appl. Soc. Psychol.* 25:275–89

Sidanius J, Devereux E, Pratto F. 1992. A comparison of symbolic racism theory and social dominance theory as explanations for racial policy attitudes. *J. Soc. Psychol.* 132:377–95

Sidanius J, Pratto F. 1999. *Social Dominance: An Intergroup Theory of Social Hierarchy and Oppression.* New York: Cambridge Univ. Press

Sidanius J, Pratto F, Bobo L. 1996. Racism, conservatism, affirmative action, and intellectual sophistication: a matter of principled conservatism or group dominance? *J. Personal. Soc. Psychol.* 70:476–90

Sidanius J, Singh P, Hetts JJ, Federico CM. 2000. It's not affirmative action, it's the blacks: the continuing relevance of race in American politics. In *Racialized Politics: The Debate About Racism in America*, ed. DO Sears, J Sidanius, L Bobo, pp. 191–235. Chicago: Univ. Chicago Press

Sigelman L, Welch S. 1991. *Black Americans' Views of Racial Inequality: The Dream Deferred.* New York: Cambridge Univ. Press

Sinkford JC, Valachovic RW. 2003. Affirmative action: essential to achieving justice and good health for all in America. *J. Dental Educ.* 67:468–72

Slaughter JE, Sinar EF, Bachiochi PD. 2002. Black applicants' reactions to affirmative action plans: effects of plan content and previous experience with discrimination. *J. Appl. Psychol.* 87:333–44

Sniderman PM, Carmines EG. 1997. *Reaching Beyond Race.* Cambridge, MA: Harvard Univ. Press

Sniderman PM, Piazza T. 1993. *The Scar of Race.* Cambridge, MA: Harvard Univ. Press

Sniderman PM, Piazza T, Tetlock PE, Kendrick A. 1991. The new racism. *Am. J. Polit. Sci.* 35:423–47

Sniderman PM, Tetlock PE, Carmines EG, Peterson RS. 1993. The politics of the American dilemma: issue pluralism. In *Prejudice, Politics, and the American Dilemma*, ed. PM Sniderman, PE Tetlock, EG Carmines, pp. 212–36. Stanford, CA: Stanford Univ. Press

Son Hing LS, Bobocel DR, Zanna MP. 2002. Meritocracy and opposition to affirmative action: making concessions in the face of discrimination. *J. Personal. Soc. Psychol.* 83:493–509

Sowell T. 2004. *Affirmative Action Around the World: An Empirical Study.* New Haven: Yale Univ. Press

Stark S. 2004. Taking responsibility for oppression: affirmative action and racial injustice. *Public Affairs Q.* 18:205–23

Steeh C, Krysan M. 1996. The poll trends: affirmative action and the public, 1970–1995. *Public Opin. Q.* 60:128–58

Steele S. 1991. *The Content of Our Character: A New Vision of Race in America.* New York: Harper Collins

Stohr G. 2004. *A Black and White Case: How Affirmative Action Survived Its Greatest Legal Challenge.* Princeton, NJ: Bloomberg

Stoker L. 1998. Understanding whites' resistance to affirmative action: the role of principled commitments and racial prejudice. In *Perception and Prejudice: Race and Politics in the United States,* ed. J Hurwitz, M Peffley, pp. 135–70. New Haven: Yale Univ. Press

Stolberg SG. 2002. Race gap seen in health care of equally insured patients. *N.Y. Times* March 21:A1:1–2

Stout KD, Buffum WE. 1993. The commitment of social workers to affirmative action. *J. Sociol. Soc. Welfare* 20:123–35

Strolovitch DZ. 1998. Playing favorites: public attitudes toward race- and gender-targeted anti-discrimination policy. *NWSA J.* 10:27–53

Summers RJ. 1995. Attitudes toward different methods of affirmative action. *J. Appl. Soc. Psychol.* 25:1090–104

Swim JK, Miller DL. 1999. White guilt, its antecedents and consequences for attitudes toward affirmative action. *Personal. Soc. Psychol. Bull.* 25:500–14

Tam MYS, Bassett GW. 2004. Does diversity matter? Measuring the impact of high school diversity on freshman GPA. *Policy Stud. J.* 32:129–43

Taylor DA. 1996. A reconceptualization of qualified: the ultimate dilemma. *Basic Appl. Soc. Psychol.* 18:15–30

Taylor MC. 1994. Impact of affirmative action on beneficiary groups: evidence from the 1990 General Social Survey. *Basic Appl. Soc. Psychol.* 15:143–78

Taylor MC. 1995. White backlash to workplace affirmative action: peril or myth? *Soc. Forces* 73:1385–414

Taylor-Carter MA, Doverspike D, Alexander R. 1995. Message effects on the perceptions of

the fairness of gender-based affirmative action: a cognitive response theory-based analysis. *Soc. Justice Res.* 8:285–303

Taylor-Carter MA, Doverspike D, Cook K. 1995. Understanding resistance to sex and race-based affirmative action: a review of research findings. *Hum. Resour. Manage. Rev.* 5:129–57

Thernstrom SA, Thernstrom AM. 1997. *America in Black and White: One Nation Indivisible.* New York: Simon & Schuster

Tierney WG. 1997. The parameters of affirmative action: equity and excellence in the academy. *Rev. Educ. Res.* 67:165–96

Tolbert CJ, Grummel JA. 2003. Revisiting the racial threat hypothesis: white voter support for California's Proposition 209. *State Polit. Policy Q.* 3:183–202

Tougas F, Brown R, Beaton AM, Joly S. 1995a. Neosexism: Plus ça change, plus c'est pareil. *Personal. Soc. Psychol. Bull.* 21:842–49

Tougas F, Crosby FJ, Joly S, Pelchat D. 1995b. Men's attitudes toward affirmative action: justice and intergroup relations at the crossroads. *Soc. Justice Res.* 8:57–71

Tougas F, Veilleux F. 1990. The response of men to affirmative action strategies for women: the study of a predictive model. *Canadian J. Behav. Sci.* 22:424–32

Truax LR, Wood A, Wright E, Cordova DI, Crosby FJ. 1997. Undermined? Affirmative action from the targets' point of view. In *Prejudice: The Target's Perspective,* ed. JK Swim, C Stagnor, pp. 171–88. New York: Academic

Truxillo DM, Bauer TN. 2000. The roles of gender and affirmative action attitude in reactions to test score use method. *J. Appl. Soc. Psychol.* 30:1812–28

Tuch SA, Hughes M. 1996. Whites' racial policy attitudes. *Soc. Sci. Q.* 77:723–45

Turner ME, Pratkanis AR. 1994. Affirmative action: insights from social psychological and organizational research. *Basic Appl. Soc. Psychol.* 15:1–11

Turner ME, Pratkanis AR, Hardaway TJ. 1991. Sex differences in reactions to preferential selection: toward a model of preferential selection as help. *J. Soc. Behav. Personal.* 6:797–814

U.S. Department of Labor. 2003. *Unemployment Rate by Race, Age, and Sex, 2001–2003.* http://www.infoplease.com/ipa/A0104716. html

Weber L, Higginbotham E. 1997. Black and white professional-managerial women's perceptions of racism and sexism in the workplace. In *Women and Work: Exploring Race, Ethnicity, and Class*, ed. E Higginbotham, M Romero, pp. 153–75. Thousand Oaks, CA: Sage

Whitla DK, Orfield G, Silen W, Teperow C, Howard C, Reede J. 2003. Educational benefits of diversity in medical school: a survey of students. *Acad. Med.* 78:460–66

Wilkins DB. 2005. A systematic response to systemic disadvantage: a response to Sander. *Stanford Law Rev.* In press

Wilkins R. 2004. Doing the work: why we need affirmative action. *Virginia Q. Rev.* 80:41–57

Williams DR, Jackson JS, Brown TN, Torres M, Forman TA, Brown K. 1999. Traditional and contemporary prejudice and urban whites' support for affirmative action and government help. *Soc. Prob.* 46:503–27

Wilson R. 2004. Affirmative action—2003. *New Politics* 9:5–10

Witt SL. 1990. Affirmative action and job satisfaction: self-interested v. public spirited perspectives on social equity—some sobering findings from the academic workplace. *Rev. Public Pers. Admin.* 10:73–93

Wright SC, Taylor DM, Moghaddam FM. 2001. Responding to membership in a disadvantaged group: from acceptance to collective protest. In *Intergroup Relations: Essential Readings*, ed. M Hogg, D. Abrams, pp. 337–51. Philadelphia: Psychol. Press

van Knippenberg D, De Dreu CKW, Homan AC. 2004. Work group diversity and group performance: an integrative model and research agenda. *J. Appl. Psychol.* 89:1008–22

Yinger J. 1993. Access denied, access constrained: results and implications of the 1989 housing discrimination study. In *Clear and Convincing Evidence: Measurement of Discrimination in America*, ed. M Fix, RJ Struyk, pp. 69–112. Washington, DC: Urban Inst.

Zamboanga BL, Covell CN, Kepple SJ, Soto RD, Parker KD. 2002. White students' perceptions of affirmative action in graduate admission: directions for programming and college personnel development. *J. College Admiss.* 176:22–30

Zelnick B. 1996. *Backfire: A Reporter's Look at Affirmative Action*. Washington, DC: Regnery Publ.

Zuriff GE. 2004. Is affirmative action fair? *Am. Psychol.* 59:124–25

Subject Index

A

Abuse
  adolescent development in interpersonal and societal contexts, 270
  couple therapy and, 325
  family violence and, 557–79
  genetics of affective and anxiety disorders, 127
  stress and learning across lifespan, 57

Accelerated longitudinal designs
  longitudinal data analysis and, 513

Acceptance
  enduring effects for cognitive behavior therapy and, 292

Accessibility-diagnosticity model
  consumer psychology and, 464

Achievement goal theory
  classroom goal structure and, 489–92

Action-oriented model
  attitudes and persuasion, 350

Activation
  emotion and cognition, 33, 38, 45–46
  sleep, memory, and plasticity, 155

Acute stress
  stress and learning across lifespan, 56–59

Adaptive variation
  facial beauty and, 199, 212–16

  neuroecology and, 167–91

Adolescents
  child development and physical environment, 423–39
  development in interpersonal and societal contexts
    closeness, 261
    community engagement, 272–74
    conclusions, 274–75
    conflict, 259–61
    definitions of adolescence, 258
    dimensional approaches, 262–64
    distancing, 259–61
    extrafamily influences, 267–71
    family relationships, 259–67
    future research, 274–75
    grandparents, 266–67
    introduction, 255–58
    overview, 255–58
    parent-adolescent relationships, 259–64
    parenting styles, 261–62
    peer relationships, 267–70
    relatives, 266–67
    romantic relationships, 270–71
    separation, 259–61
    sibling relationships, 264–66
    societal engagement, 272–74
    warmth, 261
  genetics of affective and

    anxiety disorders, 128

Adrenalectomy
  stress and learning across lifespan, 72–74

Adrenocorticotropin
  genetics of affective and anxiety disorders, 130

Advertising
  consumer psychology and, 453, 471

Affect
  attitudes and persuasion, 345, 357–60
  consumer psychology and, 453, 465–68

Affective and anxiety disorders
  genetics of
    animal models, 121–23
    anxiety, 118–20, 124–31
    behavioral phenotypes, 123–24
    brain circuits, 124–31
    conclusions, 131–32
    critical periods, 123–26
    depression, 118–20, 129–31
    development, 123–24, 126–28
    5-HT1A receptor, 125–26
    5-HTT, 126–28
    human studies, 119–20
    hypothalamic-pituitary-adrenal axis, 129–31
    introduction, 118
    rodent studies, 120–21
    serotonin, 125–28
    tryptophan hydroxylase, 128–29

CUMULATIVE INDEXES

CONTRIBUTING AUTHORS, VOLUMES 47–57

637

CHAPTER TITLES, VOLUMES 47–57

Biological Bases of Behavior

Community Psychology

Comparative Psychology, Ethology, and Animal Behavior

Comparative Psychology, Ethology, and Evolution: Evolutionary Psychology

EVOLUTIONARY PSYCHOLOGY

Consumer Behavior

Developmental Psychology